VYAṄGYAVYĀKHYĀ
The Aesthetics of Dhvani in Theatre

VYAṄGYAVYĀKHYĀ
The Aesthetics of Dhvani in Theatre

Edited by
K.G. Paulose

Rashtriya Sanskrit Sansthan
Deemed University
Under M/o Human Resource Development
Govt. of India, New Delhi

PRINTWORLD
Publishers of Indian Traditions

Cataloging in Publication Data — DK
[Courtesy: D.K. Agencies (P) Ltd. <docinfo@dkagencies.com>]

Vyaṅgyavyākhyā : the aesthetics of dhvani in theatre /
edited by K.G. Paulose.
p. cm.
English and Sanskrit.
Includes bibliographical references (p.) and index.
ISBN 13: 9788124606995

1. Theater – India – History. 2. Theater in art. 3. Aesthetics.
4. Dhvani (Poetics). I. Paulose, K.G.

DDC 792.0954 23

ISBN 13: 978-81-246-0699-5
First published in India in 2013

Published by:
Rashtriya Sanskrit Sansthan
56-57, Institutional Area, Janakpuri, New Delhi - 110 058
Phones: (011) 2852 4993, 2852 1994, 2852 4995
e-mail: rsks@nda.vsnl.net.in
Website: www.sanskrit.nic.in

and

D.K. Printworld (P) Ltd.
Regd. Office : '*Vedaśrī*', F-395, Sudarshan Park
(Metro Station: Ramesh Nagar), New Delhi - 110 015
Phones : (011) 2545 3975; 2546 6019; Fax : (011) 2546 5926
e-mail : indology@dkprintworld.com
Web : www.dkprintworld.com

Printed by: D.K. Printworld (P) Ltd, New Delhi

For

Sarala

Preface

It had been a long cherished dream to publish *Vyaṅgyavyākhyā* (*VV*), after I came across *Naṭāṅkuśa*. It was in the late 1980s that efforts were started to bring out *Naṭāṅkuśa*, the unpublished critique of Kūṭiyāṭṭam. When I started to study the text seriously I could no more endorse the popular view that *Naṭāṅkuśa* is the result of a personal acrimony between the author and a particular actor who humiliated him. The anonymous author of *Naṭāṅkuśa*, emerged to me as a great scholar with deep knowledge in almost all branches of learning, especially in *Nāṭyaśāstra*. He has great respect for Kulaśekhara and Śaktibhadra. Above all his quarrel is not against any particular actor, but to his/her deviations from the classical stream. It came to me as a revelation that *Naṭāṅkuśa* cannot be studied in isolation. It presupposes *VV*, the work of another Nāṭyaśāstra scholar, inhcriting the same tradition.

A glimpse into the manuscripts of *VV* opened a new world before me. I could find in Kulaśekhara, a genius with great insight into the potential of theatre. When it came to his notice that the *dhvani* theory propounded in the other end of the subcontinent opened a new world of imagination to the poets, he immediately applied the same to rejuvenate the theatre. More than that, he created a band of new artistes with their disciples to carry on the mission of invigorating theatre. It is sad that as in the case of all those endowed with greatness, Kulaśekhara too was ahead of his time and his followers failed to imbibe his vision. Yet he left deep imprints in our theatrical discourses.

Inspired, I began to translate *VV* into English. The introductory parts were published in 1994 in two issues of *Pūrṇatrayī* journal. But I could not proceed further due to the heavy administrative responsibilities that fell on my shoulders. It is now that I am able to fulfil the cherished dream. Meanwhile the new enthusiasm created by the discovery of Kūṭiyāṭṭam in the later half of the last century produced many works, especially by Western scholars on different aspects of that intangible heritage. One thing that worried me was that these learned authors do not get access to the original sources of the classical theatre of Kerala – *VV* and *Naṭāṅkuśa*, the former innovative and the latter critical. I feel relieved that I could offer *Naṭāṅkuśa* to the scholarly world, in 1993, and *VV* now after a lapse of several years. Actually these could have been done in the reverse order. My hope is that access to these two mutually complimentary yet contradictory original sources will enrich our theatre studies in future by clearing many of our misconceptions.

The royal dramatist Kulaśekhara composed two dramas – *Subhadrādhanañjaya* and *Tapatīsaṃvaraṇa*. He invited an expert in *Nāṭyaśāstra* (*NŚ*) to his chamber and revealed to him that these works are pregnant with suggestive meanings and hence he would like them to be performed in an unconventional way. He himself enacted the role of each character and demonstrated his innovative notion about performance. The scholar, on the advice of the monarch, noted down the details and handed them over to the coming generations under two heads – *Dhanañjayadhvani* and *Saṃvaraṇadhvani*, both together better known as *VV* – interpreting the suggestive import. This is for the first time that a dramatist himself prescribes the acting manual. The text is in manuscripts and remains inaccessible to scholars. My attempt is to present both the performance texts of *Dhanañjayadhvani* and *Saṃvaraṇadhvani*, in a manner intelligible to modern scholarship.

• • •

The present volume has four parts. The first part introduces *VV* in all its aspects. The second part – the Prologue – gives a brief survey of Sanskrit theatre till the tenth century and prepares the ground for *VV*. The third part carries the performance texts of *Dhanañjayadhvani* and *Saṃvaraṇadhvani*. The last part – Epilogue – deals with the developments in theatre after Kulaśekhara. I have ear-marked three milestones in the long journey. The fountainhead, of course, is *NŚ* (second century BCE). *VV* (ninth century CE), an innovative improvisation from *NŚ*, is distanced from it by over a thousand years. What follows is a revolt from the adherents of Kulaśekhara on some of the practices adopted by the acting community, in the form of *Naṭāṅkuśa* (fifteenth century CE). These three texts encapsulate the history of classical theatre in Kerala. The enquiry will not be complete without reference to the contemporary theatre.

The text prepares the connoisseurs for a mature assessment of the performance, by locating the chronicles from Bharata to Bhāsa as a prerequisite for a heightened understanding of classical theatre. The first chapter in the second part presents a rosy picture of the ninth century capital city of Mahodayapuram with cool breeze, full-blown white lotuses, wandering traders proclaiming the prosperity and the passionate youth embracing the harlots. The festive atmosphere prevails everywhere. What follows is the description of the circumstances that led to the composition of *VV*. Chapter IV onwards, it introduces the hero, the clown and the heroine. The modest interlude in between the First and Second Acts is highly significant from the point of *VV*. The entry of the maid and her retrospective narration later are developed into *Naṅṅyārkūttu*. The retrospection of the Chamberlain blossomed into a full performance text. These two illustrate the concept of Kulaśekhara that the dramatic text is only a seed and that the actor, like a farmer, has to grow, a tree from that seed. A recent example of this kind of expansion is the newly-designed recapitulation of Subhadrā in the Fifth Act. These three instances of *Naṅṅyārkūttu*, *Kāñcukīyam* and recapitulation of Subhadrā are the real inheritors of the traditional Kulaśekhara mode of acting. The Second Act contains the retrospective narration of Lord Kṛṣṇa which is a rare specimen. The second part of the performance text carries *Saṃvaraṇadhvani* with notes and translations. The Epilogue, as a post-script, analyses the impact of Kulaśekhara in the evolution of the classical theatre of *Kūṭiyāṭṭam*, *Kṛṣṇanāṭṭam*, Kathakali and Mohinīyāṭṭam. The great name in the contemporary era is that of Bhāsa. An attempt has been made to look at Bhāsa, especially his *Mahābhārata* plays, from a different angle. Bhāsa resonates, in the present world, the voice of the subalterns, of those marginalized and of those who were condemned to hide in the bye-ways. The journey in search of the roots consummates in re-inventing Bharata through Kulaśekhara.

• • •

I would take this opportunity to remember the support and blessings I received for this work. The scholar who would have been most delighted by the publication of *VV* is unfortunately no more with us. The late K. Ayyappa Panikkar had fully understood the theatrical significance of *VV*. When I published the preliminary chapters in 1994, he immediately got it translated into Malayalam and published it in his journal *Keralakavitha*. In his review on *Naṭāṅkuśa* and also in the preface to my *Kūṭiyāṭṭam Theatre: The Earliest Living Tradition*, he persistently advised me to concentrate on *VV*.

Introductory studies by four eminent scholars enrich this text.

Prof. Kamaleswar Dutt Tripathi is the master of Nāṭyaśāstra of our age. Those who have listened to him know the depth of his erudition.

Radhavallabh Tripathi is one among the leading NŚ scholars of our time. Apart from his many works on *NŚ*, the journal *Nāṭya* that he edits is a resourceful treasure to the lovers of Sanskrit theatre. He has translated *Naṭāṅkuśa* into Hindi and then serialized in the journal.

N.P. Unni is the pioneer of Kulaśekhara studies. His guidance has helped me a lot. He has graciously allowed me to use his English translations of *NŚ* and other works.

Kavalam Narayana Panikkar is a maestro in theatre. He is director, playwright and lyricist in whose heart reverberates the rhythm of rural life. I identify his presentations as the powerful representations of *NŚ/VV* tradition.

Killimangalam Vasudevan Nambutiripad, lovingly called "Suprant" due to his long association with Kalamandalam as the office superintendent, is a living legend of classical theatre. The manuscript of *Naṭāṅkuśa* was preserved in his house. He is a source of constant inspiration in all my intellectual pursuits.

I owe a lot to the Kūṭiyāṭṭam fraternity of artists and enthusiasts, especially my colleagues K.P. Achyutan, M.R.S. Menon and others in the International Centre for Kūṭiyāṭṭam, Tripunithura, who have always been a source of inspiration. Two names deserve special mention in this study – Margi Madhu who produced the Kañcukīyam and Usha Nannyar who retrieved the recapitulation of Subhadrā. Both of them, along with many others, are our hope for the survival of Kūṭiyāṭṭam in future. I would refer to Venuji in this context not only as the director of *Śākuntalam*, but also as one responsible for the exposure of Kūṭiyāṭṭam to the world theatre movement. The Sangeet Natak Akademi (SNA), New Delhi, had been generous in promoting Kūṭiyāṭṭam even from the 1970s. The present chairperson Leela Samson, herself a gifted artiste, is specially fond of this art form. SNA's Kūṭiyāṭṭam Kendra at Thiruvananthapuram under K.K. Gopalakrishnan, Director, is a source of hope for the Kūṭiyāṭṭam community.

M.G.S. Narayanan stands foremost among our historians who gave us valuable information about the medieval history of Kerala. The findings of Kesavan Veluthat, Rajan Gurikkal and M.R. Raghava Varrier also helped me a lot in tracing the evolution of Kūṭiyāṭṭam in a historical setting.

Heike Moser, whom we fondly call Priya, has done rewarding research in the field of Kūṭiyāṭṭam. Her study on *Mantrāṅkam* and *Naṅṅyārkūttu* are important. Virginie Johan is an enthusiastic student of Kūṭiyāṭṭam. She has been kind to provide me with a lot of material.

Acquaintance with the vast literature on theatre either through interactions or by careful reading has enriched my knowledge and has exalted my vision presented in this volume. The host of scholars and authors include Kapila Vatsyayan, the late K.P. Narayana Pasharoti and L.S. Rajagopal, Bruce M. Sullivan, Farley P. Richmond, C. Rajendran, David Shulman, N.K. Geetha, Chandradasan, Philiph B. Zarrilli, Clifford R. Johns, Diana Daugherty, P. Venugopal, Mundoli Narayanan, Ramesh Varma, T.M. Abraham, P. Gangadharan, P.K. Narayanan Nambiar and K.V. Vasudevan. The list just goes on.

Before concluding this note I express my gratitude to all those who have enriched our knowledge on ancient theatre. I have the humble satisfaction that I could present to the world of scholars the two original sources for understanding Kūṭiyāṭṭam.

2 October 2013

K.G. Paulose

Acknowledgement

It would have almost impossible for me to compile this edition without the support of many individuals and institutions. To name all of them seems to be a hilarious task. However, few names worth a mention. My foremost acknowledgement goes to Prof. Radhavallabh Tripathi, Vice-Chancellor, Rashtriya Sankrit Sansthan, New Delhi, for taking up the publication of this work.

I express my gratitude to Dr K.G. Sreelekha, Professor and Director of Oriental Manuscript Library, University of Kerala, for giving access to the manuscripts. My thanks are also due to Shri P.L. Shaji for the help he rendered in reading the manuscripts. I am indebted to Madhassy Narayanan, Puthiyedam for typesetting the matter from raw manuscripts, and Abida and Nujum of Eggs Cochin for the layout of the book. I am thankful to them for the sleepless nights we spent together to transform the archaic material to an intelligible form.

I would also put on record my appreciation for the sincere will and co-operation of C.V. Sukumar Kottakkal, Jayan Warrier, C.K. Saneesh, Itamar, Shafeer P. Ahammed and Thulasi Kakkat for giving me the precious photographs used in this volume. It is also my pleasure to acknowledge Shri Sushil Mittal, director, D.K. Printworld, New Delhi, and his team for their dedicated and timebound efforts in bringing out this book in an elegant manner.

Key to Transliteration

Malayalam	Sanskrit	Key	Malayalam	Sanskrit	Key
അ	अ	a	ണ	ण	ṇa
ആ	आ	ā	ത	त	ta
ഇ	इ	i	ഥ	थ	tha
ഈ	ई	ī	ദ	द	da
ഉ	उ	u	ധ	ध	dha
ഊ	ऊ	ū	ന	न	na
ഋ	ऋ	ṛ	പ	प	pa
എ	-	e	ഫ	फ	pha
ഏ	ए	ē	ബ	ब	ba
ഐ	ऐ	ai	ഭ	भ	bha
ഒ	-	o	മ	म	ma
ഓ	ओ	ō	യ	य	ya
ഔ	औ	au	ര	र	ra
അം	अं	aṃ	ല	ल	la
അഃ	अः	aḥ	വ	व	va
ക	क	ka	ശ	श	śa
ഖ	ख	kha	ഷ	ष	ṣa
ഗ	ग	ga	സ	स	sa
ഘ	घ	gha	ഹ	ह	ha
ങ	ङ	ṅa	ള	ळ	ḷa
ച	च	ca	ക്ഷ	क्ष	kṣa
ഛ	छ	cha	ഴ	-	ṛa
ജ	ज	ja	റ	-	ṟa
ഝ	झ	jha	റ്റ	-	ṟṟa
ഞ	ञ	ña			
ട	ट	ṭa			
ഠ	ठ	ṭha			
ഡ	ड	ḍa			
ഢ	ढ	ḍha			

Contents

Part II
Performance Text

I. Dhanañjayadhvani

Introduction

Performative Tradition of Sanskrit Plays

Significance of "Vyaṅgyavyākhyā"

K.D. Tripathi

(Co-ordinator, Indira Gandhi National Centre for the Arts, Varanasi)

Nāṭya has been defined as the "*abhinaya* of *rasa* and *bhāva*". Etymologically the term *abhinaya* is derived from the root √*Nī* to carry, with the prefix *abhi* in the sense of towards. Hence, *abhinaya* is the theatrical action or performance communicating *bhāva*s and carrying them to the spectator. These *bhāva*s are aroused in the hearts of a responsive audience and ultimately they are ideally transformed into *rasa*s.

Śārṅgadeva, therefore, understands *nāṭya* quite in consonance with the concept of Bharata and Abhinava, primarily as *rasa* and secondarily as *abhinaya*.

According to the Upaniṣads, as interpreted by Advaitism, Ultimate Reality which is Consciousness or the Self is pure knowledge (*jñāna*). It is static and without activity (*niṣkriya*). It is also devoid of self-consciousness, as there is no duality. The "Self" does not have a "notself" to help define itself. According to the Āgamic tradition, on the contrary, consciousness (*citi* or *saṁvit*) as it is called, is knowledge (*jñāna*) and activity (*kriyā*), both in one, for the same consciousness is Śiva or the Self, who is again "Śiva and Śakti" or *jñāna* and *kriyā* or again *prakāśa* and *vimarśa* all in one. Śiva is one by denotation and it is only by connotation that he is viewed as Śiva and Śakti. Śiva or consciousness is conceived as being dynamic, and the very dynamism of "Śiva" is called "Śakti" or "Kriyā".

This dynamism of the Self is reflected at three levels: speech, body and mind. It may be further pointed out that such a process of externalization involves a journey from consciousness to activity, through desire and knowledge. Our own "becoming" is reflected at three levels: the verbal, the bodily, and the mental activities.

This is the reason that the *Nāṭyaśāstra* (*NŚ*) speaks of three intrinsic channels of *abhinaya,* namely *vācika*, *āṅgika* and *sāttvika,* and the *vṛttis* (modes) of verbal, corporeal and psychic behaviour in life and their expression in theatre. There are "Bhāratī", pertaining to speech, "Sāttvatī" pertaining to mind; and "Kaiśikī" as well as "Ārabhaṭī" pertaining to body. Kaiśikī refers to soft, graceful and beautiful feminine body of bodily activity and Ārabhaṭī to a vigorous male one. In fact, Kaiśikī has a broader connotation, signifying all graceful female activity, and Ārabhaṭī all manly and energetic actions. Sanskrit drama has always been understood in terms of performance or (*prayoga*), i.e. in terms of *kriyā*.

Thus, whatever is extrinsically *abhinaya* is intrinsically *rasa*. Hence, while expounding the following *padārthas* (subjects) dealt within the *NŚ*, namely — (1) *rasa*, (2) *bhāva*, (3) *abhinaya*, (4) *dharmī*, (5) *vṛtti*, (6) *pravṛtti*, (7) *siddhi*, (8) *svara*, (9) *ātodya*, (10) *gāna* and (11) *raṅga*. *NŚ* begins with exposition of *rasa*, after having dealt with the questions of the origin of *nāṭya*, the nature of theatrical space, dance as a part of theatre, preliminaries or (*pūrvaraṅga*) and the elaborate discussion about the nature and significance of *pūrvaraṅga* itself. Thus, *nāṭya* is ultimately *rasa*. In order to make the *sahṛdaya* experience *rasa* through *bhāva*, the performer is required to delineate *bhāva* through delineation of the *vibhāvas*, *anubhāvas* and *sañcārins*. This necessitates the exposition of *bhāvas* after *rasa*.

Bhāvas cannot be communicated without *abhinaya*. This is the reason why after the exposition of *rasa* and *bhāvas*, there is the exposition of *abhinaya* in *NŚ*.

Since *nāṭya* is primarily a visual form and needs body-language, hence *āṅgika* comes first. A very broad treatment has been given to *āṅgikābhinaya*. The *āṅgika* has several layers of contextual meaning inherent in the text. This contextual framework is an essential prerequisite for understanding the classification of the body into *aṅgas*, *upāṅgas* (the main and subsidiary limbs of the body) and their *viniyoga* ("uses", "usages", "applicability"), the sign-language, based on their varied movements and postures.

Kapila Vatsyayan's remarks are important in this regard.

> The principle of *viniyoga* allows variation and creation of a fairly free vocabulary of acting and expression in drama (*nāṭya*). An analysis of several *viniyogas* of the specific movements of a "limb" or "part" reveals that they are neither realistic imitations of human, animal and plant life nor the flourish of arms and hands as supplementary embellishments which serve as aids to songs.
>
> Many explore directional space, and others are evolved as a result of a careful observation of nature. The principle of establishing correlatives and correspondences is integral to the system at every juncture. This is the strength of *abhinaya* which today distinguishes Indian dance forms from all others.

She goes deeper into body kinetics and relates it to the cosmogonic meaning inherent in the sacrificial altars in the Vedic *yajñas*, and explains the forms in a wider cosmogonic and philosophical terminology of Indian theatre. Finally, related to the general notion of performance are *aṅga-karma* or *upāṅga-karma*, the specific acts or the ways of using major and minor limbs for expressing dramatic meaning.

We next turn to the underlying principle of the *āṅgikābhinaya* which broadly governs the very use of body language.

Sāmānyābhinaya

The *NŚ*, at the beginning of the eighth chapter, underlines the three integral elements (*vastu*) of the *āṅgika*. *Nṛtta* (pure dance), *śākhā* (lit. branch, the movements of face, thighs, arms, shanks, feet, etc. made in due order in the manner of branches of a tree) and, *aṅkura* (lit. "sprout", the generative or imaginative acting). *Nṛtta*, as an element of *nāṭya*, has been given a very elaborate treatment in numerous chapters beginning with Chapter 8 and ending with Chaptre 12, whereas *śākhā* and *aṅkura* have been defined aphoristically in the "Sāmānyābhinaya" chapter. *Śākhā* and *aṅkura*, together with *Vākya*, *sūcā*, *nivṛtyāṅkura* and *nāṭyāyita*, form the central aspect of the *āṅgika-sāmānya-abhinaya* in the performance of Sanskrit drama. *NŚ* offers a penetrating insight into the *sāmānyābhinaya* and the *citrābhinaya* in Chapters 22 and 25 respectively (Baroda edition), in their syntactical aspect.

This *abhinaya*-syntax is based on the device of employing the various elements of *vāk-karma* and *aṅga-karma* together with such emotive manifestations as the *sāttvika bhāvas*, *romāñca* (a thrill, horripilation), *vaivarṇya* (change of colour or complexion, paleness), *vepathu* (trembling), etc. and the *sāttvikālalaṃkāras*: *bhāva* (feelings), *hāva* (ordinary expressions from feeling), *helā* (graceful expressions arising from the ordinary feelings), etc. They are arranged by a very flexible logic which offers innumerable artistic ways of expressing the meaning of the theatrical text. The logic of permutation and combination is termed *miśra* by Kohala as we will discuss. The *sāmānyābhinaya* represents the very general aspect of the *abhinaya*. For instance, the emotion of love (*rati*), manifests itself in *hāva*, *bhāva*, *helā*, etc. which may be observed in the ordinary behaviour of young girls with only minor differences in the mode of expression from girl to girl. It is the same with the verbal and corporeal expressions. Although the *sāmānyābhinaya* represents the general aspect of the *abhinaya*, it may express a very specific meaning through the logic of *paurvāparya* (blending or mixing various elements of *abhinaya*) in order to express the ultimate poetic meaning embodied in the *rasa*.

The meaning of the term *sāmānyābhinaya* has been variously understood. While Manmohan Ghosh renders it as "homogeneous acting", Kapila Vatsyayan prefers to call it "basic *abhinaya*". Bharata Gupta translates it as "mixing" and takes *samānīkaraṇa* as the unification of various elements of performances.

Abhinavabhāratī offers important insights based on meanings inherent in the term. According to Abhinavagupta *sāmānyābhinaya* may be understood as a mode of *abhinaya* in which different elements or components of *abhinaya*, i.e. *āṅgika*, *vācika* and *sāttvika*, and other elements are combined harmoniously. He explains this aspect of *abhinaya* through a remarkable image where the actor is compared to a perfumer (*kirāṭa*). A perfumer, after having brought the sweet smelling substances from the merchants' stall, makes a homogeneous mixture while saying to himself, so much so of this one and that one first and so on and, thus, makes a wonderful perfume. In the same way, a performer combines his acquired skills, blending them inwardly, to give a wonderful performance. This imagery of the perfumer underlines the process in which an artist freely creates according to his own experience of "life" (*loka*), acquisition of the Śāstric tradition (Veda) and choice out of the norms laid down for communicating a particular emotion of situation (*adhyātma*). It also emphasizes the freedom of artist's own innovations and experimentations, underlying the actor's own judgement in selection of conventional techniques on one hand and creating ever fresh on the other. This may be seen as corresponding to the concept of *Manodharma*.

Abhinavagupta goes on to offer another equally important image of a "firebrand" (*alātacakra*) fastly moving in a circle. This fast movement gives an impression that it is not a torch or torches but a complete, undivided circle of fire. Such is the case with the mixing of different elements of *abhinaya*. We have already seen that a performance may be understood in terms of *kriyā*. The successive moments of action, when seen in a continuity, appear as one unified action. So *abhinaya*, although taking place in a succession, appears as one unified act. This is another side of *sāmānyābhinaya*.

This image of *alātacakra* suggests the underlying temporal aspect of cyclical rhythm as well as representation. This homogeneous and unified enactment is at the same time "unique" (*anya*, lit. different) because it is extremely pleasant. The interpretation offered above is based on the understanding of *sāmānya* as "the fact of being *sama*" (in equilibrium, i.e. harmony or unified) and *anya* (unique). The word *sāmānya* occurring in the compound *sāmānyābhinaya* may be interpreted in other ways as well. *Sāmānyābhinaya* may be interpreted in other ways as well. *Sāmānya* may, therefore, be taken to be basic or essential or universal aspect of the *abhinaya*.

The *sāmānyābhinaya* can also be divided into parts. There are emotional (*sāttvika*), corporeal (*śārīra*) and verbal (*vācika*) channels of *sāmānyābhinaya*. The *sāttvika sāmānyābhinaya* is well known as *hāva*, *bhāva*, *helā*, etc. *Sattva* means *manas* (the mind) and no *abhinaya* can attain its height unless it is *sattvaniṣṭha* (grounded in *sattva*). *Sāttvikābhinaya* cannot be done with a wavering and a restless mind. Therefore, "resting in one's own being, i.e. *sattva*" is essential for a powerful acting and the enactment of the *sāttvikābhāvas* is considered to be the touchstone or the test for the actor.

After the *sāttvika sāmānyābhinaya* the sixfold *śārīra-sāmānyābhinaya*, namely *vākya*, *sūcā*, *aṅkura*, *śākhā*, *nāṭyāyita* and *nivṛttyāṅkura* has been taught. *Vākyābhinaya* is the corporeal acting simultaneous with the verbal enactment of the Sanskrit and Prākṛta texts in verse and prose, endowed with the *rasa* and *bhāva*. *Sūcā* is the mode of *śārīra-sāmānyābhinaya* in which the inner reflection of the actor is expressed through gesture and followed by *vākyānhinaya*. Thus, it is called *sūcā* (literally "suggestive", "indicative") or *sūcī* (needle), i.e. the one which pierces through the time and enacts the text, leading to the text being corporeally uttered. Abhinavagupta points out that the object of the *sūcā* is suggesting the theme (*vastu*) being reflected upon (*vimarśa* or *abhisandhāna*) by the actor.

Aṅkura (sprout) is the mode of *abhinaya* that reveals through pure gesture the latent multilayered meaning of the poetic text, without uttering the words. It unfolds the meaning inherent in the text that is visualized by the artist according to his own genius (*pratibhā*). It can only be performed by a proficient artist (*nipuṇa-sādhya*). This *aṅkura* is essentially of the nature of *sūcā* which is deeply rooted in reflection (*vimarśa*), but differs from it in the sense that it opens the door for an endless elaboration.

NŚ underlines the fact that *aṅkura* is brought about through generation (*utpatti*), i.e. spontaneous rise of new meaning as *bhāva*s, ideas and situations expressed through transmissions, permutations and combinations. An equivalent *utpatti*, *upaja* is even now prevalent in musical terminology of north India. Śārṅgadeva and Kallinātha have clearly enunciated the distinction between *sūcā* and *aṅkura*. Although both belong to the category of "imaginative acting", *sūcā* precedes the sentence to be delivered (*bhāvi-vākya-viṣayiṇī*) and *aṅkura* elaborates the innermost meaning of the sentence already uttered (*bhūta-vākya-viṣaya*).

Śākhā is the *abhinaya* performed through the head, face, thighs, hands and legs with the predominance of *vartana* (specific treatment given to the movements of these limbs). The same term *bartāva* – i.e. *bartāva* of the *svaras*, etc. – occurs in the north Indian musical terminology.

If body is viewed as a trunk, the hands, lege, etc. may be seen as its branches (*śākhā*).

The *nāṭyāyita* is the ingenious device to express various levels of time by a play within a play. It also includes *abhinaya* of the *dhruvā*s employed by the performer (*prayoktṛ*). It is called *nāṭyāyita* because though not independently a full-fledged play or the direct play, it functions like a play. *Nāṭyāyita* means "that which resembles a *nāṭya*". When a drama within a drama takes place, drama proper is the real drama, whereas the other drama within the fold of drama, appears to be, but is not an independent drama. *Nāṭyāyita* is, therefore, a type of "simple-drama" or "pseudo-drama". Abhinavagupta compares it with a dream within a dream. This variety of *nāṭyāyita* is termed as *rūpakaniṣṭha* (based on a play).

The other kind of *nāṭyāyita* is one when the *abhinaya* takes place simultaneously with the rendering or recitation (*gāna*) of a *dhruvā* song. It occurs, for instance, when there is an entry or an exit of the character. This form of *nāṭyāyita* is employed in order to heighten the theatricality of the entries and exits, for the actor who is to appear immediately after the *dhruvā* as this particular character, first delineates the poetic and metaphoric meaning of the *dhruvā*. It is called, according to Abhinavagupta, *kāryāntaraniṣṭha*, "rooted in the initiative of someone else (who is not the poet), i.e. of the *prayoktṛ*".

It may be stated here that a *dhruvā* describes the character with a symbol. For instance, in describing the *apsarases*, friends of Urvaśī in *Vikramorvaśīya*, Kālidāsa employs the metaphor of sad geese, wandering in search of their friend, i.e. Urvaśī.

Thus, the first variety of *nāṭyāyita* is a theatrical device employed in Sanskrit drama to simultaneously express different levels of time. The second variety is meant for projecting two aspects of the theatre, the one based on the drama-text written by playwright or received from the oral tradition, and the other one sometimes given by the playwright himself as an addition to the text of drama and sometimes introduced by the *sūtradhāra* (the performer). Thus, this second variety of *nāṭyāyita* related to *dhruvā* is called as "simple" drama or "pseudo-drama" because the text is technically not written by the playwright. It is a "non-drama" which is regulating the proper drama. Therefore, "non-drama" assumes the role as if it is primary drama.

The *nivṛttyāṅkura* is the form of acting when a character does not respond through the speech, but rather reacts to dialogue or the dramatic situation through gestures. It is called *nivṛttyāṅkura* because it is a spontaneous imaginative and responsive *abhinaya* when there is the suspension (*nivṛtti*) of the character's own dialogue. It lasts as long as there is more than one actor on the stage.

Vācika-sāmānyābhinaya is the presentation of a very general aspect of the language-use. It includes conversation or talking (*ālāpa*), prattling (*pralāpa*), lamenting (*vilāpa*), repeated speaking (*anulāpa*), dialogue (*saḥlāpa*), suppressing or concealing the words by alteration of the words spoken before (*apalāpa*), message (*sandeśa*), agreement, for example, by saying "you have said what was uttered by me" (*atideśa*), specific mention (*nirdeśa*), pretext (*vyapadeśa*), instruction (*upadeśa*) and indirect communication (*apadeśa*).

From another angle, such general aspect of the use of speech may be categorized as *pratyakṣa* (direct) and *parokṣa* (indirect) or as related to the present, past and future time, or as *ātmastha* or *parastha*.

Abhinaya may be classified again as either *ābhyantara* "interior to the *NŚ*", i.e. conforming to its rules, or *bāhya* (exterior to it), when it is done freely. The *abhinaya*, which is performed by physical efforts that are not silent, hurried or complex and that rest on proper tempo (*laya*), time (*kāla*) and measurement of *kalās*, and in which words are distinctly uttered without harshness and hurry, is called *ābhyantara*. When it is of the opposite kind, observing free movements and not being combined with songs and instrumental music, it is called *bāhya*.

Thus, although it becomes clear that the Sanskrit theatre is mainly a training-oriented one, a theatre activity, which would blossom outside the sphere of regular training and flow spontaneously in life, is not ruled out. This lengthy aspect of Sanskrit theatre that are repeatedly referred to in the accounts of the play productions are found in the works of Kālidāsa, Dāmodaragupta and Kallinātha.

Citrābhinaya

Citrābhinaya is complementary to the *sāmānyābhinaya*. *Abhinavabhāratī* makes a distinction between the *sāmānya* and *citra abhinaya* on the ground that the *sāmānyābhinaya* is meant for the delineation of the *bhāvas* or the emotive states, whereas the *citrābhinaya* is employed for the portrayal of the *vibhāvas*, either *ālambanas* (stimuli) or *uddīpanas* (i.e. environment).

One may wonder in what way the *abhinaya* of the *bhāvas* differs from the *abhinaya* of natural events and objects like sunrise and sky. Although the basic semiotic of the fourfold *abhinaya* is the same, it is the actual way of employing them which differs in the two cases.

As in normal life, emotive states, stimuli and environment are intertwined, so it happens in the realm of *abhinaya*. Although the complementary nature of the *sāmānya* and *citra abhinaya* may be clearly seen in any excellent performance of the traditional *nāṭya* or *nṛtya*, the threefold *sāmānyābhinaya*, particularly the *sāttvikābhinaya*, the *sūcā*, the *aṅkura* and other kinds of *āṅgika-sāmānyābhinaya,* is predominantly employed in expressing the *bhāvas*. An illustration from Kūṭiyāṭṭam may be cited here. For delineation of *vibhāvas*, *Kailāsoddharaṇa*, in which Rāvaṇa lifts mount Kailāsa, is elaborately delineated and the objects established. The actor establishes and lifts the mountain through *āṅgikābhinaya*, and then proceeds to play with it by tossing it up in sky and catching it in hands as if playing with a ball. The imaginative representation of the *vibhāva* is preceded by the casual enactment of *bhāvas*. During the *vibhāva* representation, there is a mixture of elaborate delineation of the *sañcārins*. It ends with *bhāvābhinaya*, but predominantly it may be taken as an example of *citrābhinaya*. *Sāmānyābhinaya* may be seen in the enactment of *bhāvas* forming the main theme of the play.

NŚ and the *Abhinavabhāratī* lay emphasis on the specificity (*viśeṣa*) of the *aṅga-karma* and *upāṅga-karma* as well as on the *sāttvika* and *vācikābhinaya* in the *citrābhinaya*.

The specific *hastas* (hand postures) have been prescribed in order to express a particular object or natural event. But the basis of distinction between *sāmānya* and *citra abhinaya* is founded respectively on the distinction of *bhāva* and *vibhāva*. *Vibhāva* is the vision of the "other", i.e. *ālambana*, on whom the emotive state depends, for instance, the person one loves, and *uddīpana* is the stimulant, the favourable environment and conditions.

Thus the same *abhinaya,* which communicates and concretizes the abstract emotive states, is able to represent the most concrete objects of nature. Therefore, this denomination of *abhinaya* is taken to be *citra* (wonderful). This clear distinction paves the way for a certain order of theatre practice in the delineation of the *bhāva*, *vibhāva* and *anubāvas.*

Vākyārthābhinaya and *Padārthābhinaya*

We have already stated that *nāṭya* is essentially poetic meaning, i.e. *rasa* represented by the single unbroken sentence communicated through body language. Like a verbal sentence in all of its various parts it conveys meaning, but unable as utterance, it transmits the deeper sentiments of emotions through different gestures and expressions, which enact both the words and sentences of the source-text.

The *abhinaya* communicates the whole, undivided meaning, which is *rasa*. The level of *abhinaya* is called *vākyārthābhinaya* or *rasābhinaya*. It is reached gradually through the *abhinaya* of each meaningful word (*pada*), and even parts of the words. An *abhinaya* at this level is *padārthābhinaya*, as well as *prakṛtyārthābhinaya* (*abhinaya* of the meaning of the original base of a word which is used in the language by addition of the affixes), and *pratyayārthābhinaya* (the atomic meanings of the affixes). This level of *abhinaya* is called *bhāvābhinaya* and includes *vibhāvābhinaya*. The peak of the *abhinaya* is *rasābhinaya*, the supreme objective of traditional Indian theatre.

Continuity of Nāṭyaśāstra Tradition: Kūṭiyāṭṭam and Vyaṅgyavyākhyā

The history of the performance of Sanskrit drama has been reconstructed on the basis of references available in Sanskrit literature and its commentaries. Numerous scholars such as V. Raghavan, S.K. De and Kapila Vatsyayan have offered good summaries of the development of this art form, but an attempt to analyse the accounts given by Kālidāsa, Dāmodara Gupta and Kallinātha still awaits the attention of the scholars. These accounts also provide a continuity of the performance-tradition through centuries; and it will be interesting to view the contemporary play performance in Kūṭiyāṭṭam from this angle. Kūṭiyāṭṭam presents the unique characteristics of the traditional theatre of Kerala. It is the only surviving tradition of Sanskrit theatre, but its links with *NŚ* has been debated by the scholars. Some maintain that both Kūṭiyāṭṭam and Kathakali represent a tradition independent of *NŚ*. They state that the *anukaraṇa* in the *NŚ* tradition is a physical imitation. *Anukaraṇa* may be viewed in four ways according to them:

1. An imitation of the external appearance and behaviour of a known model. This is mime and tends mostly to evoke laughter, with the mimic looked upon as a clown or jester.
2. Where a model is not readily available, an equivalent one is identified and its form and behaviour are conceived and given meaning. This is humanistic and applicable mostly to historical chapters. In many dance forms, this imitation of form is adopted.
3. Where neither a model nor its equivalent is available, a form is given to a conceptual creation. This applies to mythological characters like the ten-headed Rāvaṇa or a pseudo-humanized bird like *haṃsa* (the swan).
4. The next, ultimate stage in *anukaraṇa* transcends the mimetic in all respects and attempts at meta-creation through imagination on the basis of the conceived form and behaviour.

After analysing *anukaraṇa* in this way, they conclude that while *NŚ* makes use of former two kinds of *anukaraṇa*, Kathakali involves the latter two.

This argument is based on a gross intepretation and understanding of *NŚ*. Nowhere in *NŚ* is the theory of *nāṭya* enunciated as *anukaraṇa* in the sense of mimesis; and *abhinaya* transcending the mimetic in all respects, is not confined only to Kathakali. Scholars characterize this type of *abhinaya* as "the meta-creation through imagination". It seems rather that it represents an elaborate creative process of performance known as *anukīrtana* of *bhāvas*, and the main instrument adopted to attain this objective is that of the *āṅgika sāmānyābhinaya* as well as *citrābhinaya* in *NŚ*.

The techniques employed by Kūṭiyāṭṭam and Kathakali are similar to the devices taught in the "Sāmānyābhinaya" chapter of *NŚ*. "Upaślokana" in Kūṭiyāṭṭam is one of these devices. So is *manodharma* found in both Kathakali and Kūṭiyāṭṭam. Similarly, the *āṅgikābhinaya* and the elaborate *netrābhinaya*, preceding the dialogue in Kūṭiyāṭṭam, as well as the elaboration of the expressive and suggested meaning of the dialogue text are nothing but *sūcā* and *aṅkura*. *Sūcābhinaya* is regarded as the very life and soul of *abhinaya*. Had there not been in Kerala the lone surviving tradition of Sanskrit theatre, which is Kūṭiyāṭṭam, the performative aspects of *sūcā* and *aṅkura* could not have been made known. Therefore, Kūṭiyāṭṭam and Kathakali do not represent a *nāṭya* tradition completely dissociated from *NŚ*. On the contrary, they reflect its continuity.

As far as the different places and modes of the *vācika*, the use of *mudrās* (hand gestures) different from those which have been enlisted in *NŚ* and the costume and the make-up used in Kathakali are concerned, all these differences may be explained by changes in a tradition over the course of time, and by diffusion and diversity arising from the assimilation of regional variations. Kūṭiyāṭṭam is purely a Sanskrit theatre tradition that preserves the very old mode of *vācika* according to the instructions laid down in *NŚ*. The device of *karṣaṇa* (elongation) of the *vācika* provides room for simultaneous *āṅgikābhinaya* which ultimately culminates into *vākyārthābhinaya* mentioned by Dāmodara Gupta, Abhinavagupta and Śārṅgadeva. The *vācika* of Kūṭiyāṭṭam cannot be taken to be the only mode of *vācika* taught in *NŚ*, rather there seem to have been innumerable modes of *vācika* spread all over India that survive in contemporary folk-theatre traditions. The *nālāvṛtti* (repeating four times the dialogue/text) in Kūṭiyāṭṭam is definitely a very old form. Dāmodara Gupta of Kashmir appears to be aware of this sort of *vācika*. This also indicates that *nālāvṛtti* as a mode of *vācika* was known in Kashmir from an early period. It may be observed that such a *vācika* style may be employed either in the minimal scripts, such as the texts of Bhāsa plays preserved in Kūṭiyāṭṭam tradition, or in other plays of Kūṭiyāṭṭam tradition, or in a drama-performance taking place, act by act, over a number of days. We can simply guess that the maximal text like those of Kālidāsa, Śūdraka, Viśākhadatta and Bhavabhūti presented continuously in one day or one night, or even in several sessions, had a different and more rapid mode of *vācika*.

The intonate aspect of *vācika* in Sanskrit drama presents another difficulty. How did the actor capture the intonation of Sanskrit and Prākṛta dialogues when Sanskrit and Prākṛta ceased to be the language of daily use.

Rājaśekhara gives some clues to help solve this problem. He observes that the people in different regions spoke and recited the text with the intonation of their mother tongue. Thus the *vācika* in Kūṭiyāṭṭam may reveal some aspects which are very old and mentioned in *NŚ*, as well as others that have their roots in the region of Kerala.

It has also been held that the Kathakali system of *abhinaya* is based on the control over *prāṇa* and *rasavāyu*. It is fundamentally different from the Nāṭyaśāstric system of *abhinaya* which maintains supremacy of *sāttvikābhinaya*, such as *vaivarṇya* (change of colour of the face, i.e. turning pale), or *romāñca* (horripilation). These cannot be expressed by the Kathakali actor, whose facial make up is so thick and whose costume is made of thick loose jacket.

But such objections also cannot be entertained. *Abhinavabhāratī* refers to the importance of life-controlling *prāṇa* (breath). This control over the vital breath is an imperative for proficiency in *sāttvikābhinaya* which is supreme in *abhinaya*. It is, therefore, central in *abhinaya* and is in quite consonance with the *NŚ* tradition. In spite of a very elaborate *āhārya*, the Kūṭiyāṭṭam and Kathakali actors very successfully show the *sāttvika* such as *vaivarṇya*. Horripilation does not necessarily need to the actual raising of the hairs, for it may be done in other ways, such as expressing thrill through facial expressions. Thus, both Kathakali and Kūṭiyāṭṭam are not entirely independent of Nāṭyaśāstric tradition. They have been developed from the same Sanskrit theatre tradition which has been essentially a poetic theatre, for Sanskrit dramatists have always been recognized as poet-playwrights.

Kūṭiyāṭṭam has preserved in an astonishing measure the *pūrvaraṅga* of Sanskrit drama, which simply shows that the theatre practice prevalent among the artists has survived, even if forgotten by some of the post-Nāṭyaśāstrakāras.

Vyaṅgyavyākhyā's publication has enabled us to understand the performative tradition of *NŚ* which has been enshrined in the illuminating review of the *chalita-prayoga* in *Mālavikāgnimitram* of Kālidāsa and in the description of *nāṭya-prayoga* referred to in *Kumārasambhavam*. The practice of the same has been hinted at in *Kuṭṭanimatam*, in Śāradātanaya's *Bhāvaprakāśa*, Śārṅgadeva's *Saṅgītaratnākara* and the commentary of Kallinātha thereon. But nowhere such vivid narrative account of the *prayoga* (performance) aspect is available, as we find in *Vyaṅgyavyākhyā*, especially when we go through the text side by side the performative tradition of "Kūṭiyāṭṭam". Once I asked great traditional scholar of *NŚ* hailing from Kerala, namely Pandita Narayana Pasharoti about the distinction between *anukaraṇa* and *bhāvānukīrtana* and came the reply — the same distinction which lies between *abhidhā* and *vyañjanā*. With the publication of *Vyaṅgyavyākhyā*, the explanation given by Pandita Pasharoti becomes more intelligible. To my mind, the performance aspect Kulaśekhara explained to the author of *Vyaṅgyavyākhyā* would not have happened without the presence of some sort of living performative tradition prior to Kulaśekhara which must have presented suggestal sense. It is an invaluable source of understanding the *prayoga* aspect of Sanskrit theatre generally based on *NŚ* and particularly evolved in Kerala along with its regional specifications.

K.G. Paulose deserves all the laudations from us for bringing the work of paramount importance into light, which will be a great source for understanding the history of the performance of Sanskrit plays through its continuity in tenth century CE and onward. When this tradition is studied in comparison with the living traditions of Indian folk theatre of north and south, it will bring remarkable conclusions.

Nāṭyaśāstra and Its Regional Manifestations

Radhavallabh Tripathi
(Vice-Chancellor, Rashtriya Sanskrit Sansthan, New Delhi)

NĀṬYAŚĀSTRA (NŚ) was compiled to set models and standards for the playwrights and performers. Being *ākaragrantha* (the sourcebook) as well as the most voluminous authentic ancient text on the art of drama, it naturally cast an everlasting impact on Indian theatric traditions including the regional traditions of performance. The philosophy and vision for theatre spelled out by *NŚ* have percolated so deeply in forms of dance and drama in India that despite all the geographical, social and anthropological differences, this single unique text of Bharatamuni has paved the way for the sustenance of and synchronization between diverse regional theatric traditions of India. The tenets of *NŚ* in some way or other are reflected in the regional theatre forms like:

- **North** — *Bhāṇḍa Pather* and *Bhāṇḍa* of Kashmir
- **North-East** — *Aṅkīya Naṭa, Lai Haroaba, Bare Chaharia Bhaona* (all from Assam), Manipuri *rāsa*, etc.
- **Northern India** — *Rāmalīlā, Rāsalīlā, Svāṅga, Nauṭaṅkī,* etc.
- **Central India** — *Māñca* (in Malwa), *Nācā* (in Chhattisgarh)
- **Rajasthan** — *Khayāl*
- **Gujarat** — *Bhavāi*
- **Andhra Pradesh and Karnataka** — *Harikathā, Yakṣagāna, Kucipuḍī,* etc.
- **Kerala and Tamil Nadu** — *Kṛṣṇāṭṭam, Rāmāṭṭam, Therukūttu, Kathakali, Vīthīnāṭakam, Kūṭiyāṭṭam, Bhāgavatamelā,* etc.

There are certain features that all regional theatres share with each other, and these characteristics have been by and large borrowed by these regional theatres directly or indirectly from *NŚ*. These features are: (i) The preliminaries or *pūrvaraṅga*; (ii) *rasa*-oriented aesthetics; (iii) non-linear concept of time and space; and (iv) philosophy and techniques of *abhinaya*, specially the *āṅgika abhinaya* (physical gesticulation) including the *karaṇas* and the *aṅgahāras*. Besides, a number of theatrical conventions like *kakṣyā-vibhāga* (division of the stage in imaginary zones) and *bhūmikā-vikalpa* (distribution of roles) required for visualizing such concepts were reflected in diverse regional traditions of performance through Bharata's vision of theatre.

Interaction between Veda and *loka*, *mārga* and *deśī*, and classic and folk has been a mark of Indian tradition. *NŚ* defines *loka* (society) as one of the three *pramāṇas* (parameters) for *nāṭya*, the other two being Veda (the Nāṭyaveda or Śāstra) and *adhyātma* (listening to the inner voice — actor's own discretion). Bharatamuni himself created a scope for an approach to the regional practices and regional forms for the performers by the way of recommending that if an actor cannot decide his course of action for the performance either through Śāstra or through his own discretion, he should approach *loka*. This apart, some of the fundamental elements of theatre that have been enumerated by him (VI.10),* are also indirectly linked to regional practices. They are *lokadharmī* (the natural mode, under *dharmī* — the *modus operandi*), *vṛtti*s (styles), *pravṛtti*s (tendencies) and *mānuṣī siddhi* (the human success) under *siddhi* (the success). *Lokadharmī* is the practice of theatre in conformity to the behaviour of people in actual life. It hardly has any connection with folk theatre as sometimes it is supposed to have, neither does it mean adaptation of the practices of regional theatres. However, the terms used by Bharata to define *lokadharmī* imbibe a consideration for regional forms of theatre.

Lokadharmī is said to be the form of theatre that is enjoined with *lokavārtā-kriyā* (the activities belonging to life of people at empirical level) and devoid of any playful display of various parts of the body of the performer, devoid of any decor that is added out of imagination by the performer. It is true that most of traditional forms of theatre as prevailing in different regions adopt the *nāṭyadharmī* (the conventional mode) in a greater degree that the *lokadharmī*, but the very inclusive nature of the latter as spelled out by Bharata has scope for introducing regional theatric practices.

The concept of *pravṛtti* is very much linked to the theory of *lokadharmī*. *Pravṛtti* means studying the actual tendencies of human behaviour as prevailing in different regions. To illustrate *pravṛtti*s, Bharata divides the Indian subcontinent into four regions, and on the basis of this division four types of *pravṛtti*s are defined. An actor is supposed to study the behavioural patterns of diverse regions of this country as well as regional theatre practices.

Bharata was aware of diverse regional theatre practices represented by the minor forms of drama which were later on termed as *uparūpaka*s. In the last chapter of *NŚ*, he informs that his sons, trained by him in Nāṭyaveda later on began to perform the *śilpaka*s of rustic nature (*grāmyadharmaka*). *Śilpaka* is one of the *uparūpaka*s. The sons of Bharata, in the *śilpaka*s performed by them, presented the life and deeds of the sages residing in the vicinity of Himalayas by the way of *viḍambana* (caricature) and *vyaṅgyakaraṇa* (satire).

The sages being laughed at in this way, got infuriated and cursed the actors to be expelled from the divine region of the Himalayas and to become śūdras. Ultimately, Bharatamuni asked them to go towards south and continue with their performances.

This episode from the *NŚ* suggests that Bharata was sympathetic to those who experimented with regional forms of theatre. He has been not only studying these forms closely, he also adopted the motifs and techniques from the regional forms of theatre in formulating his system of classical theatre. The very concept of *prayoga* or the types of the theatric performance confirms the tendency in *NŚ* for allowances to regional forms. *Prayoga* is mainly of two types — *ābhyantara* (internal) and *bāhya* (external). The *ābhyantara prayoga* is performed by trained artists and stands in total commitment to Śāstra. The performers of *bāhya prayoga* on the other hand, might be completely ignorant of the Śāstra, or might have studied Śāstra with the masters or *nāṭyācāryas*, but guided by their own intuition or skill, they can transgress the norms of the Śāstra or take liberty with its dicta due to their contact with the regional theatre forms. Bharata says that such actors should be allowed to go on with their performances (that might be following regional variations) (XXII.77-80). The *bāhya prayoga* is thus a theatre of the people. *NŚ* in this way makes room for the inclusion of regional forms and local colours in its classical mould.

Siddhi (success) is of two types — *daivī* (divine) and *mānuṣī* (human). In the former, the audience transcend their own time–space frame to reach a different level of time and space. They are in complete harmony with the sentiments projected through the performance and quite attuned to the world created there. With a perfect sense of belonging to this another level of time and space, they are not even in a position to react to the performance as an art. The trio of the actor, audience and the poetic world is merged in a harmony. In *mānuṣī siddhi,* however, the situation is quite different. The contents of the play in performance are communicated by the actor to the spectator through an interpretative method. The actor and the spectator both are aware of the process of communication and the method of interpretation that the performer employs. The later visualizes the performance remaining rooted in his own frame of time and space and is able to appreciate the performance unfolding a different level of time and space. The actor stands as an interpreter between this level and the historic present of the spectator. He is a medium leading them to the vision of the world as conceived by the dramatist or the poet. The spectator can perceive this world and at the same time he can also appreciate the quality of the performance by the actor. He remains in the state of flux — between involvement and detachment. The state of awareness is maintained throughout. The application of the *mānuṣī siddhi* would bring theatre close to the regional theatric practices. The *sūtradhāra* addresses the audience in many regional theatre forms to create an "alienation effect". The audience can enjoy the play in performance and appreciate it in various ways, they can even exhibit their appreciation for an actor by immediately showering gifts, etc. on him or her (XXVII.2-13).

In his discourse on *bhūmikā-vikalpa* (ascribing roles), Bharata has classified the *bhūmikā* or assumption of roles by the actors in three types — *anurūpā* (congruous), *virūpā* (incongruous) and *rūpānusāriṇī* (tending to become similar), depending on the aptitude of the performer, i.e. whether he or she is alike to the role, he or she is unlike to it, or he or she tends to become alike with it. Bharata would prefer the *anurūpā* type only, but at the same time, he allows the other two types also, depending on the circumstances. This brings out the multiplicity of theatric traditions that have influenced the *Nāṭyaśāstra*. Many regional forms of theatre, take recourse to *virūpā* and *rūpānusāriṇī* types of *bhūmikā*s, i.e. female characters being enacted by the male actors, the role of a young man being done by an actor quite old in age, etc.

Nāṭyāyita is one of the six types of *śārīra abhinaya* under *sāmānya abhinaya* as described in *NŚ* (chap. XXII). In *nāṭyāyita* an actor performing a character joins the song being sung about that very particular character, which he or she is rendering. Alternately, the actors form an audience to watch the play within the play on the stage. Bharata also discusses the concept of *līlā* in his treatment of *sāmānya abhinaya*. *Līlā* evinces the typical practice prevailing in various forms of folk theatres and the element of alienation in the performance. In *līlā* the heroine narrates or performs the character or deeds of her lover before her friends. She thus distances herself from her own role to assume another role. The performance of *śrīgadita*, a precursor to *līlā* theatre, is characterized by *līlā*.

Bharata has not dealt with any one of these minor forms of drama — or the regional forms of theatre, except *nāṭikā*, and *nāṭikā* in no way can be adjusted or identified as any regional form of theatre, it is created by blending and shortening of *nāṭaka* and *prakaraṇa* for the purpose of performance in a royal court.

NŚ is a text on the *mārga* (classic) tradition of our theatre and its author left the exposition of the *deśī* (the regional traditions) to his successors. He proclaims at the end of *NŚ* that whatever has been left out by me will be taken up by Kohala in his *Uttaratantra* (XXXVII.18). In the first chaper of *NŚ*, Kohala's name is mentioned in the list of 100 disciples of Bharata that were present when Bharata delivered his discourse on *NŚ* before Ātreya and other sages in reply to their five queries. Mahendra Sūri, Hemacandra's student, has referred to Kohala as a *muni* (sage) and one of the disciples of Bharatamuni. From references by Abhinavagupta, Hemcandra, Rāmacandra-Guṇacandra Sāgaranandin and a host of other authors, we gather that Kohala did compose his own *NŚ*, but this work — sometimes referred as *Kohalīyanāṭyaśāstra*, is no more extant. There are a number of later texts on *nāṭya* (theatre), *nṛtya* (dance) or *saṅgīta* (music) dealing with regional theatre forms. The text of Kohala was available to the authors of some of these texts, and also most probably to Abhinavagupta, Rāmacandra-Guṇacandra and Hemacandra.

Nṛttaratnāvalī (*NR*) of Jāyasenāpati is one of the most comprehensive texts on dance, and it provides most extensive treatment of the subject with definitions of regional varieties of various categories — *deśīnṛtta, deśīpāda, deśīcārīs, deśīkaraṇas*, etc. In fact, *NR* and Someśvara's stupendous work on arts — *Mānasollāsa* or *Abhilāṣitārthacintāmaṇi* — are two of the most authentic texts providing extensive treatment on the regional theatre forms. At the very outset of *Mānasollāsa* Someśvara says that he was enamoured seeing the folk dances of the community of śabaras (a tribe) and he wanted to adopt such dances for the presentations in his court.

Deśī as been defined as the gamut of variations resulting due to regional practices in dance, drama and music. Śārṅgadeva in his *Saṅgītaratnākara* (*SR*) defines *deśī* as the way of performance prevalent in diverse regions (*SR*, I.23). Śāradātanaya in his *Bhāvaprakāśa* (*BP*) says that *deśī* is a musical composition in regional language (*BP*, chap. 10, p. 390). Sudhākalaśa, in his *Saṅgītasāroddhāra* (I.8) rightly expands the idea of *deśī* to *gīta* (songs), *vādya* (percussions) and *nāṭya*. *Nāṭyasarvasvadīpikā* (*NSD*) attributed to Ādibharata describes the special feature of *deśī* traditions of dance, songs and music in respect of their quality of appeasement to local masses and their receptivity for change according to popular taste (*NSD*, II.2.26). Śārṅgadeva in *SR* and Mataṅga in *Bṛhaddeśī* provide extensive treatment to *deśī* traditions of music and dance. A text *Deśīnṛttasamudra* has been referred by V. Raghavan that is no longer available.

Other texts that refer to or provide definitions of minor or regional forms of drama are *Nāṭyadarpaṇa* (*ND*) of Rāmacandra and Guṇacandra, Bhoja's *Śṛṅgāraprakāśa* (*ŚP*), Hemacandra's *Kāvyānuśāsana* (*KS*), Sāgaranandin's *Nāṭakalakṣaṇaratnakośa* (*NLRK*), Amṛtānandayogin's *Alaṃkārasaṃgraha* (*AS*), Vipradāsa's *Saṅgītacandra* (*SC*), *Sāhityadarpaṇa* (*SD*) of Viśvanātha, Puṇḍarīka Viṭṭhala's *Nartananirṇaya* (*NN*), Kumbhakarṇa's *Nṛttaratnakośa* and *Saṅgītarāja* (*SR*), Śubhaṅkara's *Saṅgītaḍamodara* (*SaṅD*), Raghunātha's *Nāṭyamanoramā* (*NM*) and *Nṛttasaṃgraha* (*NṛS*) by an anonymous author.

As we are not in possession of the text of Kohala or *Kohalīyanāṭyaśāstra*, it is not possible to say what term he had used to denote the regional forms of theatre. Abhinavagupta seems to have gone through the text of Kohala and he very often cites or refers to Kohala. *Nṛttaprabandha* — the term used by Abhinavagupta for regional theatric forms or minor forms of drama may have been borrowed from Kohala. Abhinavagupta quotes the definitions of some of the *nṛttaprabandhas* attributing them to *cirantanas* (the ancients or some ancient master). In all probability, these definitions are from the text of Kohala that is now lost to us.

As the regional forms have been constantly growing, and were constantly being defined and redefined by the *ācārya*s in Bharata's tradition, several optional terms are used for these so-called *nṛttaprabandhas*. *Nṛtya*, *saṃkīrṇa rūpaka* and *anya rūpaka* are the terms that can be applied to these minor forms of drama according to Dhanañjaya and Dhanika (*Daśarūpaka*, *vṛtti* on I.8, III.33); Hemacandra uses the term *geyarūpaka* for them; Śubhaṅkara, Dattila and Sāgaranandin call them *gauṇarūpaka*s (minor plays), while authors of *ND* use the term *anya rūpaka* (other plays) for them. It is in *AS* and *SD* that these forms of drama find the nomenclature of the *uparūpaka*. They are also called *deśī rūpaka*s or *deśya prabandhas*. In fact, they are prototypes of a variety of regional forms of theatre in this vast peninsula.

There can be no limit to the number of these *deśī* forms of drama. Considering the multiplicity of traditions that these minor forms belong to, we find that the number is constantly increasing, and contrary to the limit of ten that is mostly accepted in case of the number of *rūpaka*s, any attempt to prescribe a limit of number for these regional forms could be futile. We find that the *ācārya*s had been observing the process of emergence of new forms of theatre in different regions and their growth in relation to regional variations and they were also trying to define and standardize the emerging new forms.

Abhinavagupta has quoted the definitions of the following regional forms of theatre named as *nṛttaprabandhas*, as given by some ancient *ācārya* or *ācāryas* — *rāsaka*, *ḍombī*, *prasthāna*, *bhāṇikā*, *bhāṇa*, *ṣidgaka*, *hallīsaka* and *rāmākrīḍa*. Elsewhere, he has given a detailed description of *ḍombikā* or *ḍombī*. Dhanika has enumerated *ḍombī*, *śrīgadita*, *bhāṇa*, *bhāṇī*, *prasthāna*, *rāsaka* and *kāvya* as seven varieties of *nṛtya* like *bhāṇa* (*bhāṇa* here is different from the *rūpaka* named *bhāṇa*). Amṛtānandayogin in his *AS* (IX.2-3) has defined sixteen *uparūpakas* — *nāṭikā*, *saṭṭaka*, *troṭaka*, *goṣṭhī*, *prekṣaṇaka*, *bhāṇikā*, *saṃllāpaka*, *prasthāna*, *kāvya*, *hallīsa*, *rāsaka*, *śrīgadita*, *lāsikā*, *durmallī*, *nāṭyarāsaka* and *ullāpya*. Viśvanātha adds *prakaraṇī* and *śilpaka*, in this list, and makes them eighteen (*SD* VI.5). Viśvanātha and some other authors talk of eighteen *uparūpaka*s, which are — *nāṭaikā*, *troṭaka*, *goṣṭhī*, *saṭṭaka*, *nāṭyarāsaka*, *prasthāna*, *ullāpyaka*, *kāvya*, *citrakāvya*, *preṅkhaṇa*, *rāsaka*, *saṃlāpaka*, *śrīgadita*, *śilpaka*, *vilāsikā*, *durmallikā*, *prakaraṇī*, *hallīsa* and *bhāṇikā*. *AP* and *SP* count twenty-seven and twenty-four types of *rūpaka*s and they include the regional forms also in their treatment. Śāradātanaya raises the number to thirty by adding *mallikā*, *kalpavallī* and *pārijātaka* (*BP*, chap. VIII, p. 221). Out of the thirty *rūpaka*s that he has cited, ten are *rasātmaka* and remaining twenty are *bhāvātmaka* according to him.

It is Jāyasenāpati who introduces a number of local forms of dance-drama and even dances belonging to the tribes and rural areas in south in this gamut of *uparūpaka*s or *nṛttaprabandha*s, such as — *daṇḍarāsaka*, *carcarīnāṭyam śabaranṛtyam kaivāra*, *gharghara*, *vāgaḍanṛttam preraṇīpaddhati*, *śivapriyanṛttam*, *cintunṛttam*, *kandukanṛttam*, *bhāṇḍikanṛttam*, *cāraṇanṛttam*, *dohakanṛttam*, *bahurūpanṛttam* and *kollāṭanṛttam*.

NM and *NṛS* define *jakkaḍī* — a dance form accompanied with songs in *mlechcha bhāṣā* or Persian languages. It is performed by the Yavanas. *Kavikāmadhenu,* a text quoted in *Bharatakośa* by Ramakrishna Kavi, deals with a form of drama called *deśya* (*BK* 283). It is composed in a regional language, has three *sandhi*s, and consists of descriptions of spring festivals and beauties of this earth. It also presents descriptions of war, the rogues as characters and has either *śṛṅgāra* or *vīra* as dominant *rasa*s.

The number of these so-called *uparūpaka*s went on increasing from one (in Bharata's *NŚ*) to more than forty. Many of these are dance-dramas prevailing in different regions. Some of them are mere songs or dances, they are included in the gamut of these regional theatre forms as combined with narration of an episode or presentation of a theme, they also assumed dramatic proportions.

Considering the nomenclatures and characteristics of these *nṛttaprabandha*s, *nṛtya*s, *deśīrūpaka*s, *geyarūpaka*s or *uparūpaka*s, we can identify many of them as regional forms of theatre that are still being practised today in some part or the other of this vast peninsula. For example, *prekṣaṇaka* is defined by the authors of *SP* and *ND* as a play that has many special characters and is performed in the streets, *samāja*s (social gatherings or fares) and pubs, etc. (*SP* XI.311; *ND* IV.218). *Prekṣaṇaka* has been a folk form confined to the Madhyadeśa (central part of the country) and Gujarat. The southern regions had different traditions of *prekṣaṇaka*, as *BP* and *AS* (IX.122-25) define it as a play full of robust actions and involving characters of low status (*hīnanāyaka*) to be performed without a *sūtradhāra* (the stage manager). *Nartanaka* seems to be a graceful form of *prekṣaṇaka* and is characterized by *padārthābhinaya* (*BP*, chap. IX, p. 263), *saṭṭaka* can be taken to be regional variation of *nāṭikā*. If we take into account the geographical area in which most of the *saṭṭaka*s were composed and performed, it is Madhyadeśa. In the same way, a *nāṭaka* becomes *toṭaka* or *troṭaka* when dances and songs in local languages are introduced within its texture *Vikramorvaśīyam* of Kālidāsa, the sole available specimen of *toṭaka* or *troṭaka* has become a unique specimen of folk forms or regional forms of ancient Indian theatre.

Ḍombī is feminine of *ḍomba*, *ḍombikā* is its synonym. Like *śrīgadita*, it belongs to the theatre of females. *Ḍomba* was a tribe in ancient India. The word *ḍoma* derived from it is used in languages of north India for sweepers and scavengers. The female dancer performing *ḍombī* is also called *ḍombī* or *ḍombikā*. *Ḍombī* was a form abounding in songs, music and dances. The songs accompanying its performance were also called *ḍombī*-songs and the accompanying dance was also called *ḍombī* dance (*Abh.*, pt. I, p. 181). Abhainavagupta suggests that the dancer called *ḍombī* sings the *gāthā*s and also performs on them. This singing and performance is accompanied with her narration. This feature of narration in accompaniment to dance and singing is a precursor of *Harikathā* as practised in Andhra and Karnataka, and also brings *ḍombī* very close to the minor forms like *bhāṇa* and *bhāṇikā*, so that the later theorists have even confused between *ḍombī*, *bhāṇa* and *bhāṇikā*. From the description of *ḍombikā* or *ḍombī*, provided by Abhinavagupta and Kalhaṇa, it is also clear that it was a regional form of theatre practised in the locality of Kashmir. Hemacandra thinks that it might have originated from the *deśī nṛtya*. Abhinavagupta says that *ḍombī* is full of grace and *rasa* and the poets have been composing new *ḍombī*s in *jātibhāṣā* (local dialects) (*Abh.*, pt. IV, p. 280).

Goṣṭhī, *rāsaka*, *daṇḍarāsaka*, *nāṭyarāsaka* and *hallīsaka* — all these forms are dances or dance-dramas that have been in vogue in agrarian society. They basically belonged to Kṛṣṇa-cult and introduction of secular themes in their performances might have occurred at a later stage. The definitions of *goṣṭhī* given in *BP* and *SD* establish it as a proto-type of *rāsalīlā*. Basically, it must have been a small play or dance representing the deeds of Kṛṣṇa performed by the *gopa* community (shepherds) in the vicinity of a *goṣṭha* (pan) (*SP* 11.308). *BP*, however, allows the possibility of other themes also for *goṣṭhī* by the way of prescribing the plot of *goṣṭhī* as *utpādya* (imaginary) (*BP*, chap. VIII, p. 256).

Rāsaka is a circular dance involving various items in *latā*, *bhedyaka*, *piṇḍī*, etc. by as many as sixty-four performers (*Abh.* in *NŚ* chap. IV). On the other hand, *AS* (IX.138-51), *SanD* (p. 95), *NLRK* (p. 304) and *SD* (VI.290) define *rāsaka* as a farce with a fool as a hero, given to rustic ways. *SanD* retains both alternatives — *rāsaka* as a play depicting the deeds of the boy Kṛṣṇa and *rāsaka* as a secular farce. In *nāṭyarāsaka*, some female characters re-enact the acts of Lord Kṛṣṇa. It is a play full of love and romance, set in the mood of spring season. Later *ācāryas* however give an alternate set of definitions identifying *nāṭyarāsaka* as a play with a great hero and a *pīṭhamarda* as his assistant, and a lady in love waiting for the hero (*BP*, chap. IX, p. 263; *SD* VI.285; *AS* IX.159-61). *Rāsaka* and *nāṭyarāsaka* assume the form of *daṇḍarāsaka* if the dancers are holding sticks for beating and they become *hallīsaka* if the dance movements are circular (*SP* XI.309). *BP* (chap. IX, pp. 266-67), *AS* (IX.136-38) and *SD* (VI.298) define *hallīsaka* as a play with secular themes. *Hallīsaka* has close resemblance with *carcarī* and *chalita* also (Vema, *BK*, p. 203).

As per definitions given in *SP* (XI.280-81), *BP* (chap. IX, p. 258), *SD* (VI.292-93) and *AS* (chap. IX, 51b-153a), *Śrīgadita* is similar to *nāṭyarāsaka* in respect of its theme. *Śidgaka* is a counterpart of *nāṭyarāsaka* or *śrīgadita*. A representation of the mischief of the husband by a lady becomes *śidgaka* (*Abh,* chap. IV). *Prasthāna* is a dance or a dance-drama based on the theme of departure. In the definition as quoted by Abhinava, it is a graceful form where the dance movements are based on the march of elephants and other animals. Other *ācāryas* define it as a play with amorous sentiments and based on delineating the theme of separation. *AS* prescribes that characters of low community — the *dāsa*s and *dāsī*s as its protagonists, and depiction of scenes of drinking, etc. as its theme. *SP* visualizes the use of four *apasārakas* (songs) in it (*Abh*., chap. IV; *SP* XI.283-85; *BP* chap. IX, p. 262; *AS* IX.131-33; *SD* VI.286). *Ullopyaka* and *śilpaka* are closely related. The twenty-seven components of *śilpaka* are used in *ullopyaka*, it has tableau of gods or heroes profusely adorned with bright costumes (*BP*, chap. IX, p. 266; *AS* IX.161-62; *SD* VI.287). *Sallāpaka* (*saṃlāpaka* or *sallāpa*) resembles the *rūpaka*s like *samavakāra* and *ḍima*, depicting scenes like attack and surrounding a city (*SD* VI.291; *BP,* chap. VIII, p. 256; *AS* IX.133b-136a, IX.136b-131a). *Mattallikā*, *mallikā*, *pārijāṭakam*/*pārijātalatā* and *kalpavallī* these forms are based on narration and singing of *gāthā*s. *Preṅkhaṇam*, *durmallikā*/*durmilitā*/*durmallī* and *śilpakam*-type of plays present people of low caste and characters of lower strata of society, or *viṭa*s, *pīṭhamarda*s, etc. (*SD* VI.289, VI.293; *ND,* p. 191; *SP* XI.282-83; *BP*, chap. IX, p. 267, chap. VIII, p. 257; *AS* IX.155-58). *Vilāsikā* or *lāsikā* is described only in two texts — *AS* and *SD*.

From the foregoing account of *uparūpaka*s, it is clear that they are closely related to regional theatre forms. Sometimes the *ācārya*s like Bhoja, Someśvara and others define an *uparūpaka* itself as a regional form of theatre. Some of the *uparūpaka*s can be identified with particular regional theatre forms that are still in practice with slight variations, for example, *nāṭyarāsaka* and *daṇḍarāsaka* have manifested as the *garabā* in Gujarat, and the *rāsaka* and *hallīsaka* have become *rāsalīlā* in northern parts of the country as well as *bhāgavatamelā* or *vīthīnāṭakam* in southern parts. *Ḍombī*, *bhāṇa*, *bhāṇī* or *bhāṇikā* have evolved in various forms like Paṇḍavānī in central parts of the country; *harikathā* or *kīrtaniyanāṭa* in north-east and southern regions.

The interaction between the performance traditions of the *rūpaka*s and the *uparūpaka*s paved the way for emergence of regional theatre forms. Some of the *uparūpaka*s or regional forms that were basically community dances or folk dances got enriched by drawing elements from the performance traditions of the *rūpaka*s and the *uparūpaka*s and assumed larger dramatic proportions. The enactment of particular themes or episodes in *uparūpaka*s has shaped the regional theatre forms to a great extent. The performance of the animals in *prasthāna* led to enactment of *daśāvatāra* (Viṣṇu's ten incarnations) in many regional theatre forms.

It is the way of blending *lāsyāṅgas* that gives a local habitation to many forms of drama. *Lāsyāṅgas* are used in some of the major forms of drama (*daśarūpakas*) also as per definitions in Bharata's text. They are employed in *vīthī* and *bhāṇa* (*rūpaka*). Some of the *lāsyāṅgas* assume the characteristics of regional theatres. For example, the tenth *lāsyāṅga* is *uktapratyukta*, consisiting of interesting repartees and rejoinders in the dialogues. This *uktapratyukta* and *trimūḍhaka* together with *nāndī*, *prarocanā* and *bharatavākya* are used in some form or the other in various regional forms of theatres.

The narration by *sūtradhāra* is a feature that distinguishes the two performance traditions of *rūpakas* and *uparūpakas*. *Sūtradhāra* has various names in different regional theatre forms. In Kūṭiyāṭṭam of Kerala, the *vidūṣaka* performs the functions of a *sūtradhāra*. *Sūtradhūra* in *terukūttu* or *vīthīnāṭakam* is called *kattiyakaran*, and he goes on addressing the audience and also having exchange of words with other characters. His interference on the stage when the drama is being performed is called *pottuvacanam*.

The authors in the field of Nāṭyaśāstra have always been re-adjusting various categories or enlarging them in view of the developments in the performance traditions. Sometimes such amendments come due to the impact of regional forms of theatre also, especially the multiplication in the number of *hastas*, *sthānakas*, etc. and the addition of *deśī* forms of *cārīs*, *hastas*, *pādas*, etc. must owe their origin to the regional forms of theatres. In fact, there is a growing tendency amongst the followers of Bharata to search the counterparts of various categories described by the great master in regional theatre forms.

Kerala has provided the most vibrant stage for correspondences with the Nāṭyaśāstra, and the dialogue between the classic and the regional traditions of theatre. The theatre of Kūṭiyāṭṭam thrived for centuries and continued to enthrall the audiences with its authentic exposition of Bharata's texts combined with improvizations. Kerala has also given us some of the most fascinating texts on actual performance of Sanskrit plays. K.G. Paulose, one of the most renowned specialists of the theory and practice of Sanskrit theatre amongst us, has done a yeoman's service by his critical edition and translation of *Vyaṅgyavyākhyā* — a rare and valuable text providing insights into the dramatic world of Kulaśekharavarman from the viewpoint of performance. I am confident that this work by Paulose will go a long way for establishing Indian theatre at global level.

Introducing Vyaṅgyavyākhyā

N.P. Unni

Former Vice-Chancellor, Sree Sankaracharya University, Kalady

Kerala has produced many art forms of very high antiquity. Saṅghakkali, Kūttu, Kṛṣṇanaṭṭam, Muṭiyeṭṭu, Kathakali, Tiṟa, Tuḷḷal, etc. are some of the popular forms. The most ancient and the most important among them is Kūṭiyāṭṭam.

Kūṭiyāṭṭam is perhaps the earliest known form of enacting Sanskrit drama in Kerala and it is different from other forms of dramatic representations known to have existed elsewhere. The very name is suggestive, for *kūṭi* means together and *āṭṭam* means acting and so the term yields the idea of acting together.

Kūṭiyāṭṭam has certainly contributed much towards the cultural progress of Kerala. It has given rise to some of the important movements both in the field of art and in the field of literature. For instance, Kathakali, the dance drama which has the status of being the reservoir of all arts, owes its origin to Kūṭiyāṭṭam. Dress, make-up, costumes, instruments, steps, etc. in Kathakali have been directly borrowed from this art form. In the field of literature the adoption of local language also in enacting the Sanskrit drama has raised the importance of Malayalam. Sanskrit and Malayalam blended together to produce an artificial, but lively, literary language styled Maṇipravālam which has been defined as the mixture of languages; the local dialect Malayalam and Classical Sanskrit. The verses to be recited by *vidūṣaka* in staging Kūṭiyāṭṭam have been written in this beautiful literary medium. This mixture of two languages belonging to two different language families has made a unique contribution to the growth of Malayalam language.

Sanskrit dramas are not staged as such in Kūṭiyāṭṭam. Individual acts from well-known classical dramas are selected and adapted. Each of such acts is known by a different name. In other words every act which is staged in Kūṭiyāṭṭam is rewritten according to the specifications of the Kerala stage. Hence very often original verses and lines written by the actors find a place in the adapted scenes of the classical dramas. Such verses are always written with a view to enhance the theatrical effect of a particular act. An instance may be cited from the First Act of *Subhadrādhanañjayam* (*SD*) adapted to the Kerala stage.

asti prastutatāruṇyā tatraivātyantasundarī
bhaginī vāsudevasya subhadrā nāma kanyakā

This verse is not found in the text. Dhanañjaya (Dhan) is describing Subhadrā to *vidūṣaka* (Vid) who uses the local language Malayalam to reply. He is made to deride the hero when he utters each word.

Dhan	*Asti* (There is)
Vid	Who my dear friend? Lord Kṛṣṇa?
Dhan	*Subhadrā nāma* (by name Subhadarā)
Vid	Oh! My friend I know well. Alas! You are attracted by that ageing Subhadrā.
Dhan	*Prastutatāruṇyā* (quite young)
Vid	What? A young girl? Oh! You are in love with that lame squint-eyed teeth-protruding ugly servant-maid?
Dhan	*Atyantasundarī* (very beautiful)
Vid	What? Very beautiful and young damsel? Let me think about it. Oh! I know. You are a prince of the Lunar race and the friend of Kṛṣṇa. Yet you fall in love with a servant-maid. Alas!
Dhan	*Bhaginī Vāsudevasya.* (The sister of Vasudeva.)
Vid	The sister of Vāsudeva? (laughing) How pitiable for a learned man like you to love a woman married to somebody. By this time she must have got three or four children.
Dhan	*Kanyakā* (*A maiden.*)

Now *vidūṣaka* admits his folly and appreciates the choice of his friend. For such adaptation there are two kinds of stage manuals called *Āṭṭaprakāram* and *Kramadīpikā* written by the actors. Such works are valuable as the sources for history of the growth and development of the Sanskrit theatre in Kerala. These manuals adapt classical dramas by supplying introductory portions and vernacular translations and parodies. Kulaśekhara's plays became popular as soon as they were composed. The demands made by the flourishing stage of Kerala were great. At a time when original dramas were not forthcoming from the south, his plays immediately found universal admiration. The reason for the popularity of his plays can easily be explained. The author was by no means a mere dramatist. He happened to be the emperor of the whole of Kerala. From the *Vyaṅgyavyākhyā* (*VV*) on SD it is clearly known that the author put these dramas on the public stage only after getting the approval of renowned brahmaṇa connoisseur of the period whom he invited to his palace with due respect. Only after being assured of their perfection did he put his dramas on the stage by professional actors.

Actors show a preference to the dramas of Kulaśekhara since they suited their purpose in staging a drama having a Purāṇic theme in times of festivals. In spite of their indebtedness to other classical works these plays must have been appreciated well by the audience. A Malayalam poem, "Uṇṇunīlisandeśam" (fourtenth century CE) contains a reference to the Kūṭiyāṭṭam performance of the Third act of *Tapatīsaṃvaraṇam* (*TS*) most probably staged in the Taliyil Temple. The hero of the poem recalls in a message to his forlorn wife a particular incident in their life . "We have been witnessing a Kūṭiyāṭṭam when the Naṅṅyār acting the role of Tapatī who is indignant on account of Saṃvaraṇa's love for somebody else, recited her lines in Prākṛt casting her eyes on me. And you ran away in a fit of anger never to be seen for a while." *Mantrāṅkam* has quoted a verse each from the dramas of Kulaśekhara.

Often Cākyārs stage the Kūṭiyāṭṭam of *SD* without actually putting Draupadī on the stage. Probably because she has to appear only in the last scene and even there only for a few moments. In order to present her for a short while a Naṅṅyār will have to don the costume. But the anonymous author of *Naṭāṅkuśa* is not prepared to allow any concession in staging a drama of such an eminent personality as Kulaśekhara. He is of the view that the injunctions of the dramatist should not be violated. This work contains illustrations from both of his dramas in addition to the references to several other dramas adapted for the Kerala stage. There is a popular saying in Malayalam which refers to the Sixth act of *TS* that one should bow before a Cākyār who has flown and a Naṅṅyār who has floated on water. The first part refers to the *paṟakkuṅkūttu* based on *Nāgānanda* and the second part refers to the representation of Tapatī jumping in the river Ganges and floating on the water until she is rescued by Samvaraṇa. This is known in Kūṭiyāṭṭam by the name *oṛukal*, literally meaning the act of floating. It is not easy to depict this scene in which the heroine is being drifted away by the strong currents. *Nāṭyaśāstra* has given instructions to enact such events.

It is accepted on all hands that the golden age of Sanskrit theatre of Kerala was the period of Kulaśekhara and that it was during this period that the staging of Sanskrit drama was reformed. Though the antiquity of the dance-drama tradition of the south cannot be fixed with any definite dateline, it is certain that histrionics received appreciation and sustenance as early as the second century CE; for the Kerala prince Elango Adigal has given an account of the performance of a Cākyār. Classical Sanskrit dramas might have been staged and well appreciated by the elite from very ancient period. *Mattavilāsa* of Pallava king Mahendravikrama Varman also was produced on the Kerala stage successfully. Kulaśekhara himself observed that the dramas of Kālidāsa, especially *Abhijñānaśākuntalam* have pleased the audience to such an extent that it was difficult for another poet to attract its attention. Further he referred to the well-known classical dramatists like Śūdraka and Harṣa who had won the admiration of the audience. Harṣa's *Nāgānanda* has even given rise to a performance practice called *paṟakkuṃkūttu*. All these show the well-established tradition of a flourishing Sanskrit stage in Kerala. Such performances must have been on the traditional lines, the whole drama being produced in the course of a single day.

There must have been two different, though fundamentally related, stages in Kerala, the traditional and the reformed. While the former represented the usual dramatic performances, the latter afforded an ideal medium to enlighten the caste Hindu audience with the exposition of Purāṇic themes. Thus the stage was shifted from the sparsely attended palace dance halls to the crowded precincts of the *sanctum sanctorum*.

Naṭāṅkuśa severely criticizes the Cākyārs of Kerala for taking too much liberty with the text and for contravening the principles of dramaturgy. The attack is rather one-sided; all the same it deserves attention. It does not agree with the use of the local language Malayalam in staging Sanskrit drama, for according to it if the dramatist uses Prākṛt the actor should follow it. The comic episodes enacted by the *vidūṣaka* showing vulgar tendency are to be avoided. Here brāhmaṇas are described as indulging in illicit connection with śūdra women, which is against the Dharmaśāstras. Another attack is for disobeying the instructions of the dramatists. While staging the last act of *SD*, Draupadī is not on the stage. This omission according to the critic cannot be tolerated. If the dramatist creates a character, she must be put on the stage even if it is only for a short while.

Naṭāṅkuśa refers to the royal dramatist of Kerala with great respect. It seems quite probable that if the royal dramatist himself had introduced the use of Malayalam in the Kerala stage the anonymous author would not have condemned the innovation with such vehemence. In other words, it is safe to hold that Kulaśekhara reformed the stage only on lines that are permitted or rather implied by the canons of Hindu dramaturgy.

For a clear and authentic account as to the part of the dramatist in this reformation, a close study of the commentaries is essential. There is no reason to doubt the authenticity of the *Vyaṅgyavyākhyā* commentaries styled *Saṃvaraṇadhvani* and *Dhanañjayadhvani*. A perusal of the *VV* commentaries presents one with a picture in all vividness the conception of the stage and stage craft in the days of Kulaśekhara. The commentaries are composed with the specific purpose of explaining the various sentiments, moods and ideas employed in the dramas of Kulaśekhara as well as their mode of representation for the benefit of the actor. Much importance is bestowed upon gesture language, for the suggested meaning is to be conveyed through imitative and symbolic gestures. The suggested meaning is employed in these plays specifically to cater to the taste of the elite connoisseurs.

Expansion of the scope of textual lines is another noteworthy phenomenon of the Kerala stage. The actor is free to introduce into the performance what he seems fit to the particular occasion. To facilitate the actor who may not be scholar always, stage manuals are provided. Another peculiarity is with regard to the *pūrvasambandha*. Almost every character who appears for the first time in the play is well introduced narrating the various important incidents in their life. The actor donning the particular role must inform the audience of his story up to the moment by the expressive gestures. Here he is not allowed any verbal narration. Hence only connoisseurs are able to follow the introductory part. The commentaries supply the relevant details.

It is safer to rely upon more or less authentic account of a contemporary scholar than basing one's conclusion on unfounded traditions. Hence one may be justified in concluding that the innovations contained in *VV* represent substantially the contributions of Kulaśekhara Varman to the Sanskrit stage in Kerala. It remains an undisputed fact that Kulaśekhara is perhaps the only dramatist who dictated rules and chalked out ways to present Sanskrit dramas in a new garb. It is only natural for him to do so since he himself has donned the roles of dramatic personae of his own plays. By laying more stress on the representational aspect and providing the actor with a wide facility to show his talents he has proved that even a stereotyped Sanskrit drama could serve as a popular recreation. And in this respect the art has gained its purpose that *nāṭya* is the one recreation for people of different tastes.

The text of *VV* remained in manuscripts. Many scholars put their hands on it. Even the great Ganapati Sastrikal desired to publish it. It is only now that it is made available to the scholarly world, thanks to the efforts of K.G. Paulose. Earlier he had brought to light *Naṭāṅkuśa* which was hailed a historic occasion for the theatre. This, undoubtedly, is another such occasion.

Indian Theatre: Crisis of Identity

Padmabhushan Kavalam Narayana Panikkar

Dr KG Paulose introduces the great Kerala playwright Kulaśekhara in glowing terms as follows:

> The outside world did not know that Ānandavardhana had a strong champion in the distant southern-most tip of Indian peninsula who applied the principle of *dhvani* to theatre and paved the way for the survival of *Nāṭyaśāstra*'s *prayoga-mārga*.

Evidently this has reference to the *Vyaṅgyavyākhyā*. The dominant characteristic of *Vyaṅgyavyākhyā* is that it is the chronicle of how the text reaches the domain of performance. It can be construed as the forerunner of the later contributions of the Chakyārs of Kerala towards preservation of acting manuals like *Āṭṭaprakāram* and *Kramadīpikā*. The author enacting the different roles in his own texts postulates the significant philosophy of *svayaṃ prekṣaka* which quality can be attributed to the Cosmic Dancer, Lord Śiva – the one having a dual quality of being an actor/creator as well as a creatively critical spectator. Mahendravikrama Varman, the author of *Mattavilāsaprahasaṇa,* in the opening benediction qualifies "Kapālīśvara" as *yaḥ prekṣakaśca svayam*. This rare quality is inherited only by rare poet-playwrights like Bhāsa, Śaktibhadra and Kulaśekhara. Among these, Kulaśekhara was successful in reassessing his own creative work with a critical perspective and recreating the *dhvanipāṭha* (sub-text) by supplementing the non-sound areas of the text with interpretative action. In the *prayoga* of *Nāṭyaśāstra*, *dhvani* plays a pivotal role and *Vyaṅgyavyākhyā*, no doubt, is a great contribution to the evolution of theatre traditions in India. This coupled with *rasa* provides the uniqueness of India's contributions in performing arts in comparison with those of the West.

Abhinavagupta explains the word *kāvyārtha* as *rasa*, the making of which can be attributed to none other than the actor. The main function of the actor is the creation of *arthakriyā* (refer to the dictum *arthakriyākāritvam bharatatvam* expounded by Karthika Tirunal in his *Bālarāmabhāratam*) for which *rasa* has to be expressed in a holistic manner through *bhāva* (emotion). The *vācika, sāttvika* and *āṅgika*, all work in unison for cumulative output. Also the *vibhāva* (excitant), *anubhāva* (ensuant) work on a supportive level for the sprouting of the *sthāyibhāva* into *rasa*. Proper combination is essential for this evolution. The evolution which is contemplated in the Sanskrit theatre is based on journey from *kriyā* to *rasa*, from the outer reality as discussed in the text to the deeper interior level. Kulaśekhara had written two plays pregnant with inner meaning, *Tapatīsaṃvaraṇam* and *Subhadrādhanañjayam* and substantiated his stand on the magical efficacy of *dhvani* and experienced himself how the mindscape of each character would reflect to detail the respective *bhāva* in enactment.

When we come across a play like *Subhadrādhanañjayam* we feel the basic text as the emanant point dealing with story telling or narrative with characters of mundane nature and as such it is earthy and earthily with human feelings even when they belong to mythical or epic dimension. The growth of these characters and events from narrative level to higher areas of representational advancement is made possible through the eloquence that lies latent in the non-sound areas of the text which could provide the springboard for the para-textual areas of interpretations. What is stated in the text is attractive through the story point of view; but its eloquence works as the sprouting of a seed into a full-fledged tree with branches, foliages, etc.

Vyaṅgyavyākhyā liberates the actor from the rigour of the text and allows him to illustrate the sub-text through improvised acting (*manodharma*). The *Naṭāṅkuśa* (a critique on this text also has been published by K.G. Paulose), on the other hand, tries to provide a hook on the actor and prescribes manacle on the actor's imagination. It is harsh in criticizing certain theatre practices in Kūṭiyāṭṭam on the basis that they go against the established tenets of the *Nāṭyaśāstra*. The criticism levelled against *Nirvahaṇa* (when a character is introduced, a detailed description is given about his earlier life) is legitimate to some extent on two reasons. One is that sense of propriety is prone to be lost. The other is the risk of losing the beauty of suggestion. Regarding the criticism that it is ridiculous for Hanumān in his costume to transform into the role of Sītā in Aṅgulīyāṅkam cannot be acceptable to the basic principle of transformation in *nāṭya*. The technique of transformation or Pakarnnāṭṭam can claim to have its roots in *Yoga-Sūtras* with a different connotation – *bandhakaraṇa śaidhilyāt pracarasamvedanāt ca, cittasya paraśarīraiva* (Through relaxation of the causes of bondage and the free flow of consciousness the *yogi* enters another's body at will – B.K.S. *Iyengar, Light on the Yoga-Sūtras of Patañjali*). These lines have relevance to the conscious impersonation of characters in the dynamics of theatre. This idea of transformation is an essential tool of expression even among the common people while they transact ideas with the help of language and the language assumes its spirit of representation by shift of emphasis from first person to others involved in the narration. The technique of transformation goes beyond one level, i.e. from actor to character and reaches out to multiple levels of *sañcāribhāvas*. In the *ekāhārya* (solo acting) of Hanumān crossing the ocean, he transforms into different characters whom he encounters like Mainākam, Chāyāgrahī and Surasā. Such transformation is not the creation of many levels of illusion; rather it would work as transitory emotions strengthening the *sthāyibhāva*.

From my experience in directing some major Sanskrit plays I felt that the text necessitates beyond doubt certain advanced situations which prompted the transformation of character which was to be carried on to further levels of emotional representation. One such situation from Bhāsa's *Karṇabhāram* may be pointed out in which Karṇa narrates to his charioteer Śalyar while he is in the battlefield of Kurukṣetra, how he had learned the art of archery from Paraśurāma. If it is a mere textual narration, it would never bring in the dramatic potential involved in the text. The *vyaṅgya* that lies latent in the text gave me sufficient courage to interpret forcefully, when the character Śalyar emerges from within Karṇa himself as Paraśurāma. If I had not done that the whole narrative would have remained flat and prosaic without evoking any emotions. Karṇa was narrating a story which was possibly not unknown to Śalyar or for that matter any compatriot of Karṇa. It can easily be believed that Karṇa was narrating the tale to himself rather than to Śalyar. Hearing this Śalyar used to ask *tatastataḥ*, what happened then? Śalyar was asking this question standing behind Karṇa and enacting as if he was emerging from within Karṇa. Śalyar hearing the narration worked up his imagination to get transformed into the role of Paraśurāma and extended his creative support to Karṇa's story telling. Finally when the narrative and the accompanying dual enactment were over Karṇa called out "Oh! Śalyarāja" and Śalyar occupied the space behind Karṇa and returned to his persona. A clockwise movement by the actor for tying up into the role of Paraśurāma and an anti-clock-wise movement for untying himself into the role of Śalyar were employed and the technique was easily discernible and aesthetically acceptable to the audience. Karṇa's *ekāhārya* would also have been worthy to be tried out; but then the presence of Śalyar demanded the inclusion of that character also in the production.

Is *Vyaṅgyavyākhyā* a chronicle as elaborately codified as the later production manuals like the *Āṭṭaprakāram* and *Kramadīpikā* of Cākyārs? Is it meant as a performance score of the two texts of Kulaśekhara, *Subhadrādhanañjayam* and *Tapatīsaṃvaraṇam*, treating them as the pretexts and developing into extensive visual rendering? Or is it more a literary elaboration layering on the semantic and semiotic details? On the vācika aspect the elaboration based on the *Vyaṅgyavyākhyā* essentially has to relate to the rhetoric and prosody which should go beyond the text like study of speech, sound patterns, alliterations, assonance, pitch, intonation, air thrust and the like. On the *āṅgika* the application of *cārī*s, *karaṇa*s, *mudrā*s, etc. would definitely lead the suggestions in the pre-text to artistic explorations. The concurrent function of *sāttvika* leads the *Vyaṅgyavyākhyā* towards the final evolution of *rasa*.

Paulose strongly holds the view that *Vyaṅgyavyākhyā* mode of acting of Sanskrit dramas is certainly not a break away from *Nāṭyaśāstra*. He is also emphatic on one important point that there was no Kūṭiyāṭṭam at the time of Kulaśekhara or even earlier. When he affirms that Kūṭiyāṭṭam came into existence one or two centuries after Kulaśekhara, the chronological order of our artistic events and personages gets into confusion. He strongly holds on to the view that Tola who is described as the jester friend of Kulaśekhara in a popular and oft-quoted myth is "an imaginary figure", it being "not supported by facts". Ulloor in his *Keralasāhityacaritram* (vol. 1, p. 162) extensively deals with the contributions of Tolan to the art of Kūṭiyāṭṭam. Ulloor here affirms the fact that Tolan, under the supervision of Kulaśekhara had prepared two types of theatre manuals known as *Āṭṭaprakāram* and *Kramadīpikā*, consisting of detailed stage directions on costumes, gestures, stage design, etc. as well as the stage practices to be followed by the *vidūṣaka*. Ulloor admits that he had believed earlier that Kulaśekhara was a contemporary of Ādiśaṅkara. Later he changed his view fixing Kulaśekhara to sometime between tenth and eleventh centuries CE, arguing that his time was only after the *dhvani* theory had established its sway, i.e. after ninth century CE. The historicity of these views cannot be proved beyond doubt as they remain only at the realm of myths.

The accepted belief among scholars that Śaktibhadra lived at the time of Śrīśaṅkara (CE 780–820) is refuted by Paulose who fixes him in the twelfth century CE If this is to be accepted the story that Śaktibhadra happened to meet Śrīśaṅkara will have to be treated as an unbelievable legend. But no convincing reason is forthcoming to affirm the stand to place Śaktibhadra in the twelfth century, except the fact that Kulaśekhara does not refer his name along with Mahendravikrama Varman and Bodhāyana. Substantive evidence in this regard has yet to be adduced. Legend has it that Śaktibhadra happened to meet Śaṅkarācārya and read out his *Āścaryacūḍāmaṇi* text to him. It may be pointed out in this context that *Ulloor* has categorically stated (vol. 5, chapter 9 of his work, *Sāhityacaritram*) that before Śaktibhadra's time there were only two *prahasana*s known to Kerala Bodhāyana's *Bhagavadajjukīyam* and Mahendravikrama Varman's Mattavilāsa. Let alone the confusion about the date, *Āścaryacūḍāmaṇi* remains a unique work which offers creative challenges lying hidden in it and worthy to be explored in the light of the principles involved in the concept of *Vyaṅgyavyākhyā*. Of course, *Āścaryacūḍāmaṇi* as a text had never passed through an empirical process of interpretative analysis by its author as in the case of *Subhadrādhanañjayam* and *Tapatīsaṃvaraṇam*. The Cākyārs only at a later stage had been able to prescribe an experiential methodology for its enactment with visual impact.

S.S. Barlingay (*A Modern Indian Aesthetics Theory*, p. 24) while elaborating the definition of *abhinaya* writes:

> *Abhinaya* means something which is facial or bodily. No message can be transmitted between one individual and another or from the dramatist to the actors and then to spectators unless it is encoded in bodily and sound signs.

The signals involved in *abhinaya* are essentially *āṅgika* and *vācika* with added flavour of *sāttvika* representation. Does *Vyaṅgyavyākhyā* anticipate the stage devices and theatre practices as tools for bringing out the interpretation of *dhvani*? Does it propose employing techniques of decoding the pre-text and encoding it into sub-text or only making the commentary and explaining the context and meaning of the text? It can be gathered from the *Vyaṅgyavyākhyā* that primary meaning of the text has to be presented through the fourfold acting for the benefit of the common audience. But the suggested sense has to be communicated through movements of the eyes to the spectators. It is gain saying that bringing out the meaning (*artha*) involves *arthakriyā*, transforming meaning into action also. The credit goes to the creative genius of the Cākyārs of Kerala for having discovered and introduced certain conventions and stage practices which had contributed a lot to the art of transformation in solo-acting.

In the present study, Paulose has dealt extensively, in the beginning chapter with a comparative analysis of *Nāṭyaśāstra*, *Vyaṅgyavyākhyā*, *Naṭāṅkuśa* and Kūṭiyāṭṭam. It covers a wide spectrum of Indian performing arts in their conceptual variations of *mārgī* and *deśī*. There are many common as well as uncommon features making each of the above-mentioned four topics important and relevant in its own sphere. The author rightly holds on to the profundity, clarity and social bearing of *Nāṭyaśāstra* and compares its tenets with the *deśī* practices as evinced in its different levels of application. While reading his comments we are tempted to differently view how the *mārgī* works in *deśī*, how *deśī* works in *mārgī*, how they coincide and how they seem to be variant and variegated. *Naṭāṅkuśa* strictly holds the view that Kūṭiyāṭṭam goes against the prescriptions of *Nāṭyaśāstra*. The author of the *Vyaṅgyavyākhyā* studies enumerates his views which are six in number. The view that Kūṭiyāṭṭam is an actor's theatre and it has developed imaginative acting hinted by Bharata seems to be a valid assessment. The multiple impersonation is accepted in Kūṭiyāṭṭam; but whether Bharata totally rejects this is to be examined in the light of how the enactment in *ekāhārya* (solo) acting is to be carried out in the *rūpaka* variety, *bhāṇa*. The art of transformation cannot be avoided when one actor has to present the story-telling and it is to be imagined whether such representations would develop into the stage of multiple impersonation. The observation that Kūṭiyāṭṭam through *vidūṣaka* can interact with contemporary life and voice its concerns is to be understood in relation to the practice that the Cākyār actors had inherited from their predecessors. Paravoor Kūttacākayyan, a forerunner of the Cākyārs was once enacting Kotticheytam, an excerpt from *Śilappadikāram* in the presence of Emperor Ceran Senkuttuvan and his consort Venmal. The actor is said to have made a situational reference to the emperor and queen while describing the Ardhanārīśvara. This reference throws light on the impact of the contextual reference reflected in the art of story-telling. This method of enactment had its roots in the innovative technique of elaborative acting which would make the text a point of origination providing a causative thrust to indulge in embellishment and imagination. The fact that *Vyaṅgyavyākhyā* emphasizes on the principle of liberation of the actor is supportive of this method of descriptive acting. At the same time the actor's autonomy has to be assiduously curbed when it assumes the level of privileged licence. There was the necessitation for such an acrimonious curb when the Cākyār actors transcended their legitimate domain. Paulose by selecting *Vyaṅgyavyākhyā* now and *Naṭāṅkuśam* earlier for his elaborate critique has been able to project an extremely sensitive problem related to the know-how of Indian histrionics. This especially is to be viewed as inevitable at a time when Indian theatre is facing a crisis of identity and groping in the dark to relate to its national character. Paulose's untiring efforts in creating awareness of our tradition and its immense potential deserve all encomium. His clarity of vision and liveliness in analysis are well mooted and well intentioned. I wish that his work on *Vyaṅgyavyākhyā* will be made a guide by all practitioners of performing arts especially theatre people who nurture belief in the Indianness in Indian performing arts.

Kudos to his meaningful attempt which opens up avenues towards the enrichment of Indian theatre.

Part I
Prologue

I

Nāṭyaśāstra and Vyaṅgyavyākhyā

This chapter introduces Vyaṅgyavyākhyā (*VV*) in its relation to Nāṭyaśāstra (*NŚ*). In his invocatory verse itself the author declares that he wrote the dramas observing the canons formulated by Bharata in his *NŚ*. He has built up the edifice of *VV* on the strong foundation laid down by Bharata ten hundred years prior to him. It is important, therefore, to know *NŚ* and its author sage Bharata before entering into the discussion of *VV*.

Nāṭyaśāstra is an encyclopaedic work on theatre by Bharata, *c*. 2 BCE. Bharata was a talented actor and, in all probability, the head of a dramatic group. He had with him the recorded aphorisms of his predecessors, the deep insight he gained from his own experiences and the rich knowledge he acquired by interaction with the contemporary conventions. There was also a vibrant popular theatre before him. Dramatic troupes travelled from cities to cities, villages to villages and made their performances either in streets or in make-shift temporary tents. Thousands thronged to see them. They treated the actors with cheer, applauded in loud voices and at times, rolled on ground in wild excitement. The aim of these performances was *haseti – rameti*, to make them laugh and merry.[1]

Nāṭyaśāstra

Bharata too enjoyed it; but he wanted his troupe to act differently. He prescribed a grammar for theatre emulating his predecessor Pāṇini who culled out a sophisticated language from the existing popular tongues. Bharata codified the instructions for those who composed dramas and who transformed the texts to performances.[2]

---

1 नटो रङ्गमज्जे समाजमज्जे सञ्जालीकेण जणं हासेति रमेति। (नटो रङ्गमञ्जे समाजमञ्जे सत्यालीकेन जनं हासयति रमयति।) Samyutta Nikāya IV. 2.

The actor presents an unreal world and makes the spectator to believe that it is real. Yet the spectators suspend their disbelief and enjoy his actions. The prime objective of performance in all cultures was to entertain, to amuse. The common folk did not expect anything more than that from theatre.

2 कविप्रयोक्त्रोरूपदेशपरं शास्त्रम्। Nāṭyaśāstra is intended to instruct the poets and actors. Abhinavabharatī on Ch. I *NŚ*.

1. i. Grammar for Theatre

The first thing he did was to effect a change in the space of performance. Magnificent theatre-houses were constructed. None of them did have the capacity to accommodate more than four hundred spectators. The closed door performance distanced not only the detractors, but also the enthusiastic masses from theatre. Bharata devised for his actors, in the place of acrobatic exercises prevailed in the street-plays, a strict code of stylised acting with the predominance of *satva*. By these innovations, Bharata elevated theatre to classical heights. *NŚ* thus became the fountainhead of the theatrical activities in India. There were surely instances and attempts to violate Bharata's prescribed grammar. Regional varieties with the abundance of music and dance came to be successfully performed. These performances were in course of time, incorporated to the main stream as *uparūpakas* along with the ten original *rūpakas*, though they did not follow the prescribed rigid structure.[3]

Bharata's disciples put forth five questions to him for clarification:

i. how did *nāṭya* originate?

ii. for whom?

iii. what all are its components?

iv. on what authority does it function? and lastly,

v. how can it be performed on stage?[4]

NS, though not in the same format, answers the questions raised by Bharata's disciples. Bharata did not arrange his answers systematically. But his text as a whole clarifies all the doubts. He gives a legendary account on the origin with divine intervention. Lord

---

3 'Viewed in this way, Nāṭyaśāstra symbolises the synthesis of three streams of culture – the vedic represented by Indra, the Indus civilisation represented by Śiva and the folk tradition of Śrīkṛṣṇa. – *Kūṭiyāṭṭam Theatre: The Earliest living Tradition*, 2006- P35.
Rūpaka is the general term in Sanskrit to denote dramatic performances. Bharata has described ten varieties. Uparūpaks eighteen or more are not systematic dramatic presentations. Many of them have love or comic as the sentiment and dancing and singing constitute the mode of presentation . The characters are drawn mostly from the lower strata of society. Gamblers, out castes and slaves have a free play in these forms. Language is Prākṛt in most cases.

4 त्रैलोक्यस्यास्य सर्वस्य नाट्यं भावानुकीर्तनम्। Bharata clarifies to the demons that nāṭya is not vikaraṇa (mimicry) as you take it; it is actually bhāvānukīrtana. There are three words – bhāva, anu, kīrtanam. Anu – paścat = after. Kīrtana is eulogy, glorification; not as it is, but as it aught to be. Bhāva here stands for imagination. Kālidāsa uses the word in this sense in Meghadūta. Yakṣa's wife draws the portrait of yakṣa, lean by separation through imagination. Yakṣa was handsome in her company; but became lean and pitiable in separation. This she has not seen. Then how does she draw him- *bhāvagamyam*. She imagines how he would be and draws him in that state – matsādṛśyam virahatanu vā bhāvagamyam likhanti. Bhāvānukīrtana therefore denotes the idealised representations as imagined by the actor.

Brahmā created *nāṭya* to instil lofty ideas in society. He created it as a play-thing – *Krīḍanīyaka*, but the motto is moral upliftment of the people. Bharata here proclaims that *haseti-rameti* alone cannot be the objective of a performance. Learning Vedas are confined to a few, theatre is for all. This answers the second question. *Nāṭya* has five components – *pañcāṅgaṃ nāṭyam, āṅgika – vācika – sātvika abhinayas*, music and percussion. Dance is also added later as the sixth component. To the fourth query, his answer is that *nāṭya* evolved out of the sacred Vedas and it functions on the authority of Vedas. The entire text answers the last question – the *prayogamārga*, mode of presentation.

1. ii. Concept of Imitation

Bharata reveals his concept of imitation in a highly symbolic way. The demons revolted against the first performance depicting the story of the churning of the milky ocean. Their complaint was that their portrayal was nothing less than a betrayal. Bharata pacifies them revealing the real nature of imitation as Bhāvānukīrtana. Three words are important here – *anukaraṇa, vikaraṇa and anukīrtana*. These forms and their distinct connotations are significant. *Anukaraṇa* is imitation. Imitation has two levels – *vikaraṇa* is mimicry and *anukīrtana* is idealised representation. The former evokes laughter on the spectators, but provokes those who are imitated. It cannot claim to be a piece of art. Bharata here condemns the practices followed in the popular theatre. People may throng in thousands and may laugh and become merry. Does it elevate the sensibility of the spectator? The protest of the demons deserves no better explanation. *Anukīrtana* is the imagined representation of an idealised situation. The actor has not seen Duṣyanta or Śakuntalā. How would he have expressed his love? The actor can only imagine. He has to reconstruct a Duṣyanta and imagine his reflections. There is nothing personal in it. Bharata prescribes stylisation in acting to trans-personalise the act. This concept of imitation is cardinal in *NŚ*. *Bhāva* is the keyword in *Nāṭyaśāstra*.[5] Bharata uses the word with four different connotations – The word is derived from the root *bhū* which denotes permanent existence. Eight

5 Bharata uses the word bhāva in the following meanings:

i.	bhavati iti bhāvaḥ	The eight/nine permanent mental disposition.
ii.	bhāvayati iti bhāvaḥ	The forty one (49-8) which extend the eight basic emotions to the audience for making them aesthetically relishable.
iii.	bhāvānukīrtanam	Bhāva as idealisation.
iv.	bhāvagamyaṃ likhantī	Imaginative re-construction.

Kulaśekhara adds a fifth meaning which will be discussed later.

emotions like love, anger etc., are latent in the mind. *Bhāva* denotes them. They are in an abstract state and invisible to others. They can be expressed only through their correlatives: the transient moods (33) and involuntary expressions (8). The persons described, the situation and their voluntary expressions are innumerable. The eight latent emotions are communicated thorough the transient moods (33) and involuntary expressions (8). Thus the emotional complex comprises of all the 49 *bhāvas*. *Bhāva* is used to distinguish the transient moods from permanent mental states in acting. Word by word acting is prescribed for it at a later period. The fourth meaning of *bhāva* is related to imagination. Kālidāsa uses *bhāva* in that sense in Meghadūta. The primary responsibility of the author and the actor is to portray the emotive experience of the character. The author is silent; he speaks through the actor. Actor also is silent. He transfigures himself to the character. The actor/character has only his body to interact with the audience. He transforms his body to a language. He does this transformation through movement of limbs – *āṅgika*, verbal rendering – *vācika* and facial expressions – *sātvika*. Of course, the costumes also help him. Hence *abhinaya* is the most important aspect in theatre and Bharata devotes a major part of the text for the discussion of *abhinaya* in all its minute details.[6]

1. iii. *Abhinaya*

Bharata's treatment of *abhinaya* is elaborate and exhaustive. He adopts several principles for its classification – twofold division to *nāṭyadharmī* and *lokadharmī*; fourfold to *āṅgika*, *vācika*, *sātvika* and *āhārya*; again to *sāmānya* and *citra*. Bharata discusses the details of *abhinaya* in three contexts. In *bhāvādhyāya* and *rasādhyāya* (ch. vi and vii) he gives instruction regarding the presentation of each of the mental states and their moods. For example, pathos can be enacted in this way: The sight of the murder of the dear one or the hearing of unpleasant words may generate the sentiment of pathos. This is to be represented by actions like crying aloud, being unconscious, lamenting and weeping bitterly as also by physical torture and beating one's chest (NS ch. vi 77-78) The treatment of acting here is exhaustive. Yet it deals them as separate units for each mental state and mood. In the 24th chapter he tries to co-ordinate these individual units. He calls it *sāmānyābhinaya* - generic representation. He usually gives the order from external to internal – physical, the verbal and at the end, the innermost mental. Here the order is reversed and starts with *sātvika*;

6 Abhinaya literally means to bring forward. Abhinaya brings the emotion of the character on stage to the audience. It is the medium of communication in theatre.

not only that, he declares that it is the most important one and the whole edifice of *nāṭya* is erected on its foundation.[7] This also is his justification for keeping a distance from the realistic theatre in which presentations are mostly physical. This process of homogenisation is to bring up a totality of the different units of acting, music dance and percussion. Hence instruction here is more to the director than to the actor. The effect on stage is compared to that of fire-wheel (*alātacakra*) an illusion of totality. This effect is achieved by *samānīkaraṇa*. Acting discussed earlier is of distinct units, here the process is that of homogenisation that gives moments of transcendental bliss to the audience. Kālidāsa beautifully portrays this experience while he describes the dance of Mālavikā.[8] Not content with the elaborations on *abhinaya* in the previous chapters Bharata gives further details in chapter 26. He signifies abhinaya described here as special representation – *citrābhinaya*. The advise here is to the actors as to how the characters and particular situations are to be enacted. For example; by raising both the hands and assuming the pose of *pataka* and *svastika*, one should lift up the head and look upwards employing different kinds of glances to show things like morning, sky, planets, stars and other objects of the sky... (NS. xxvi, 1-4) The sequence of Bharata's treatment of *abhinaya* is interesting – first training to the actor taking it in separate units, then instruction to combine them harmoniously to create a total effect and lastly, advice to enact special situations. The stress in *sāmānyābhinaya* chapter is on the realisation of *rasas*, but in *citrābhinaya* it is to the *vibhāvas* – creating visual images. All the three put together gives a fairly clear idea of Bharata's concept of actor-audience interaction. And this answers the fifth question of his disciples. Though Bharata concentrated on dramatists and actors, he had the audience always in his mind. He discusses their aesthetic response which is the criterion of the success of a performance in all its details in the next chapter.

Vyaṅgyavyākhyā

The most important development in the field of aesthetics after *NŚ* was the application of *rasa* to poetry through the medium of *dhvani*. Ānandavardhana propounded the theory of *dhvani* in Kashmir in the 9th c. CE. He had to face stiff resistance from his contemporaries at home. Luckily for him, *dhvani* had been accepted as pivotal in Indian aesthetic thought, since Abhinavagupta set up a strong foundation in his

7 Efforts should be more on satva (internal emotions) since nāṭya (dramatic production) is based on satva. The representation where the internal emotion is dominant is called the superior one. *NŚ* XXIV-1-2.

8 Bhāsa and Bharathā, Dr. K.D. Tripathi, *Bhāsasopānam* – 1994.

Locana. Ever since *dhvani* attained a pivotal role in Indian aesthetic thought. This is known to all. But the outside world did not know that *Ānandavardhana* had a strong champion in the distant southern most tip of Indian peninsula who applied the principle of *dhvani* to theatre and paved the way for the survival of *Nāṭyaśāstra*'s *prayogamārga*. The royal dramatist Kulaśekhara who ruled the Cera country with his capital at Mahodayapuram realised the potential of suggestion in theatre and revolutionised the performance tradition of Sanskrit dramas. His creative insights are recorded in the *Vyaṅgyavyākhyā* (*VV*). *VV* is to theatre what *Locana* is to literature. The significance of *VV* is not fully recognised as it remained in manuscripts.[9]

1. iv. Cultural Exchanges Between Kashmir and Kerala

The *Kṣitiratnamālā* an old treatise on Kerala puts on record that Perumāls had been brought from Kashmir, Avantī and Cola to rule over Kerala.[10] Whether any king from Kashmir ruled over Kerala or not, both the provinces had inter fluent current of cultural relations. *Śaṅkarācārya* travelled all the way from Kerala to establish the *mutt* at Badarinath. Kashmir poets like Śambhu Ballaṭa and Kśemendra have paid high tributes to the beauty of Kerala women which reveals their close familiarity of the land. *Nyāyaśāstra*, published in Trivandrum Sanskrit Series contains a commentary by Vāsudeva who is the son of Sūryasūri of Kashmir. *Alaṅkāraśāstra* is another work which has a *vṛtti* by Maṇkuka, a minister of Kashmir. *Kuṭṭanīmata*, the 9th century *Mahākāvya* of Dāmodaragupta, a minister of Kashmir is known well to the *cākyārs* of Kerala and they draw verses from it during their narration. No wonder, *Dhvanyāloka* caught the attention of Kulaśekhara soon after its inception in Kashmir. He is almost a contemporary of *Abhinava* though we are not sure whether he had seen his *Locana*. Anyhow, the fact remains that the manuscript of *Abhinavabhāratī* was preserved in Kerala.

1. v. Authors' Silence

Kulaśekhara was an voracious reader, good critic and enthusiastic connoisseur. He was a master of the *Mahābhārata* and composed two dramas based on the themes of these epics. At the same time he was a sceptic with regard to the customary mode of

9 MSS T. 281 of Oriental Manuscript Library, University of Kerala, Thiruvananthapuram. The present editor published with English translation the introductory part of *VV* in two instalments in the Pūrṇatrayī Journal of Government Sanskrit College, Thripunithura, Vol XIX, XX -1993.

10 A Souvenir of the Silver Jubilee celebration of the Department of publication of oriental manuscripts, Trivandrum, 1934.

presentation of Sanskrit dramas. He wanted to find out why people came to watch plays when they already know the story. The sequence of the events were well-known to them. For those who know the story nothing is there to hold on till the end. The progression is on expected lines as described in the source-text. They have no anxiety regarding the 'what' in the story. What they want to know is the 'how' of it. How this particular event is presented by this actor or his troupe? Conventional methods are not sufficient to satisfy the audience if their concern is with the 'how' of it. It was in this predicament that *Ānandavardhana* came for his help. An actor will have infinite prospects if he presents the silence hidden by great dramatists in their words. To present the explicit is not a great thing; what is great is to interpret the implicit in the words. Excited over the new revelation he called the actors and scholars around him. He told them:

> 'Wise men say that poetry endowed with suggested sense is commendable. Hence I wrote two dramas pregnant with inner meaning. I will take the role of an actor and show you how it is to be represented on stage.[11]

Kulaśekhara himself enacted the role of every character to demonstrate to them the mode of presentation. A scholar in his court wrote down these details and handed over to others and through generations to us. This, perhaps, would be the first stage-script by the dramatist himself for his own dramatic text. Author composes not only the text, but also sub-texts! This opened a new epoch in the history of Sanskrit theatre. Kulaśekhara has made two innovations in the prevailing form of performance – retrospection and suggestive acting.

1. vi. Retrospection

Texts give the following direction at the entry of every character – *tataḥ praviśati*... Enters after 'that'; after 'what'? The spectators have every right to know it. But the text is silent. Hence Kulaśekhara insists that every actor at the time of his/her first entry shall introduce the character to the audience and narrate the past events up to the present moment. In the *Subhadrādhanañjaya* (SD), for example, Dhanañjaya, when he comes first to the stage shall convey the audience that the Pāṇḍavas were

---

11 ध्वनियुक् काव्यसरणिः शस्तेति प्रोच्यते बुधैः।
एतस्माद् ध्वनियुक्ता सा रचिता नाटकद्वयी।।
द्रष्टव्या भवता सेयं नाटकलक्षणवेदिनाा।
तां पश्यन्नबधार्यैषा सदसद्वेति कथ्यताम्।।
This is the request made by the royal dramatist to the scholar.

living in the forest, Nārada had made some arrangements for the five brothers to live with Pāñcālī, he had to break it, as an act of atonement he started for the year-long pilgrimage and at the end of it he is moving to Dvārakā to meet Subhadrā being enamoured by her charm. This is *pūrvasambandha* - connecting the present to the past. Only after establishing the character in this way, can he start to enact his role prescribed in the text.

An actor has to confront with several problems here. He has not a text to depend on for narration. The acting, therefore, is devoid of verbal rendering. This makes matters more complicated. But this gives the actor an added advantage too. He is liberated from the constraints of the text. There is a challenge in it. He has to build up the castle on his own. There is another problem, perhaps, more daring. While recounting the past events the actor who has already imitated a character turns out to be a narrator. He cannot make it effective merely by reporting, he has to change to the roles of the persons and their actions to make the narration lively and dramatic. Dhanañjaya transfigures, in course of narration, to Nārada, Dharmaputra, Kuntī so on and so forth. The actor on stage, transforms himself to a stage where in all these reflected characters, pass through. This is an exhilarating trans-dramatic experience both for the actor and for the spectator. This phenomenon, is technically called *pakarnnāṭṭam* - multiple impersonation. This is contrary to the concepts of Bharata. Imitated characters are not permitted to assume in the same costume, roles of reflected characters. Moreover, dance, not drama is exempted from the specification of *āhārya*. This process of retrospective narration, enacted by a single character elevates the multi-character conventional stage to the highest level of artistry. The role of actor in a performance is also redefined. Actor enters the stage imitating a particular character, now two more functions are imposed on him – that of narrator and of interpreter. The actor in the conventional Sanskrit stage is an imitator, in the innovative stage he is a narrator and interpreter too.[12]

1. vii. Sub-texts

Great poets often speak through their silence. Hidden in every text are many sub-texts. Actor now has the added responsibility of de-coding the inner-meanings to the audience. There are different layers among the audience. Kulaśekhara classifies them into two – *prekṣaka* and *nānāloka*. The former are learned scholars, the others

12 For more details *Kūṭiyāṭṭam Theatre – The Earliest Living Tradition*, Bharatiya Book Corporation, New Delhi.

belong to the ordinary folk. The latter will be satisfied by the external meaning. The *prekṣaka* requires special treatment. After communicating the outer meaning through fourfold acting, actor shall interact with the *prekṣakas* and convey the suggested sense through the movement of eyes. He shall not use words, or even gesticulation to convey the hidden meaning. *Netrābhinaya* alone is permitted for suggested sense. This can be well illustrated by a sentence from the introductory part of SD. Vidūṣaka enters and pray for alms.

Bhagavanto maharṣayaḥ! bhikṣām datta! Give alms! oh! sages.

Vidūṣaka enacts this part pretending to be hungry. The audience, pleased, gives a big applause. The actor now concentrates on the *prekṣakas* in front of him. By subtle movements of eyes he tells them that what he wants is not food, but something else. The feminine gender in the word *bhikṣā* suggests a woman, i.e. Subhadrā. She is deeply in love with Arjuna. But her elder brother has promised her to someone else. We have come to seek her hand as alms for Arjuna. The actor can interact with the *prekṣaka* in this way until both are satisfied. *Ānandavardhana* accepted the *vyaṅgya-vyañjaka* relation in poetry. Similarly external meaning – fourfold acting correlation is conventional and accepted by all. Kulaśekhara's creative interpretation is the *vyaṅgya-vyañjaka* relation. *Subhadrāvṛttānta* is *vyaṅgya*, *vyañjaka* is the feminine gender. *Netrābhinaya* stands for *vyañjanāvyāpāra*.

Kulaśekhara's theatre visualised the immense potential of suggestion and created many sub-texts with in the dramatic text. In the post-Kulaśekhara period actors added other plays also to the repertory. The Bhagavadajjuka and Mattavilāsa were already popular here. The plays now ascribed to *Bhāsa* appeared on Kerala stage during this period, i.e. 11th-12th centuries of CE. The *Nāgānanda* and *Kalyāṇasaugandhika* were also added to the repertoire. This was a period of hectic activity. Malayalam language entered the Sanskrit theatre at this stage paving the way for the emergence of *Kūṭiyāṭṭam* as an autonomous theatre-form. The most important addition after the evolution of Sanskrit drama to *Kūṭiyāṭṭam* was, of course, Śaktibhadra's *Āścaryacūḍāmaṇī* which the present editor would like to place to the 12th century of CE. All the other classical forms of Kerala – Kṛṣṇanaṭṭam, Kathakaḷi and Mohiniyaṭṭam, were highly influenced by the acting techniques of Kūṭiyāṭṭam. The classical theatre of Kerala rests on the solid foundation laid down in *VV*.

II

Nāṭyaśāstra and Kūṭiyāṭṭam

Is the *VV* mode of acting of Sanskrit drama a break from the *NŚ* tradition of acting? Certainly not; instead, it is an improvisation of the acting techniques which Bharata had prescribed in *NŚ*.

2. i. Improvised Acting

Bharata anticipates in his treatment of sāmānya representation the process of imaginative acting. This is the most important innovative technique of Kulaśekhara. Sāmānyābhinayas of śārīra are six-fold: vākya, sūca, aṅkura, śākhā, nāṭyāyita and nivṛtyaṅkura.[1] Of these two are important for us in this study – aṅkura and nivṛtyaṅkura. The former is the expression of the inner heart deeply permeated by satva. In the first Act of Ratnāvalī where Sāgarikā is excluded from paying homage to Kāma, she hides herself behind a tree and whispers – 'I will also offer flowers to Kāma'. This gives the actress ample occasion to give expression to her suppressed feelings. She desires to love Udayana and to be loved by him. This is the sprout – aṅkura – of love in her heart. Such situations give the actress opportunity to exhibit her histrionic talents through improvisation. Nivṛtyaṅkura, in essence, is the same; the only difference is that the expression comes as a response to the words of others. In the second Act of the same play, Vidūṣaka asks the king whether Sāgarikā did please his eyes? Overhearing this, Sāgarikā eagerly awaits the king's answer. Nivṛtyaṅkura is the echo of other's words in one's heart. It sprouts when the dialogue is suspended (nivṛtta).

In both these instances the actor is liberated from the text. He can reveal his inner self through imaginative acting. This bud – aṅkura-of Bharata bloomed forth as

1 षडात्मकस्तु शारीरो वाक्यं सूचात्मकस्तथा।
शाखा नाट्यायितं चैव निवृत्यङ्कुर एव च।।
हृदयस्थो निर्वचनैरङ्गाभिनयः कृतो निपुणसाध्यः।
सूचैवैत्पत्तिकृतो विज्ञेयस्त्वङ्कुराभिनयः ।। *NŚ*, XXII

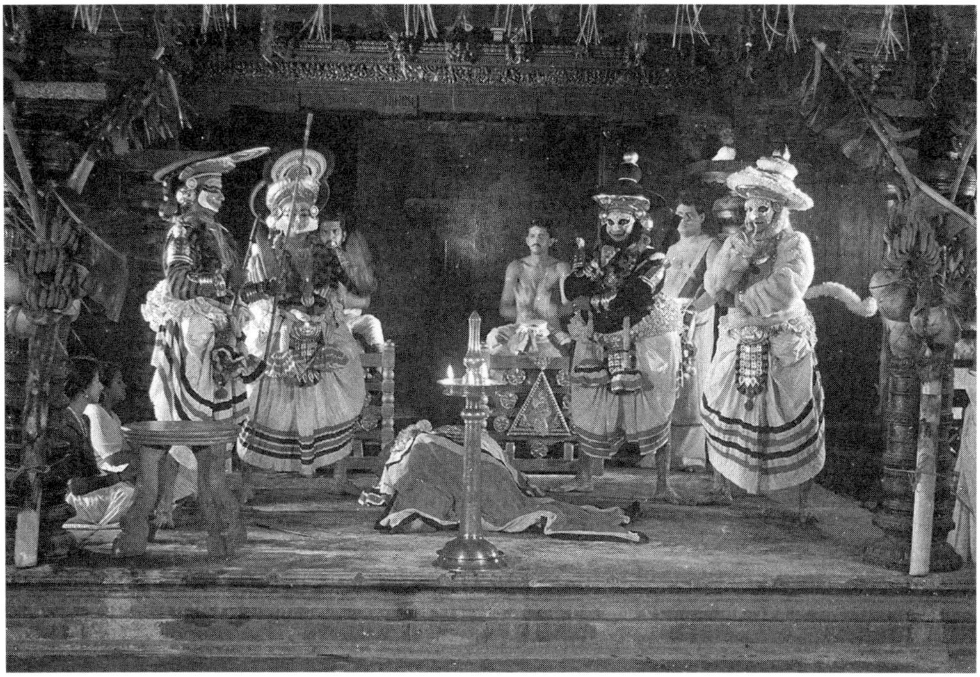

Balivadham, the first act of Abhiṣekanāṭakam of Bhāsa

manodharma in Kulaśekhara. Imaginative acting is an extension and elaboration of homogenisation in performance.

2. ii. Kuṭṭanīmatam

Theatre reached this stage of perfection after passing through several phases in its development. The Kuṭṭanīmata of Dāmodaragupta of the 8th c. CE shows a definite improvement from the *NŚ* scheme of acting. He wrote KM in the form of practical lessons imparted by a senior courtesan to a young girl for initiating her to the profession. In the course of her discussion she gives the details of the enactment of the first Act of Ratnāvalī. Three points are relevant to us in this performance.

i. Nāṭya is presented, by three young girls, in the form of a dance.
ii. The performance deviates from the text.
iii. Importance is given to sātvikābhinaya.

The prince compliments the actress for her talent to delineate the subtle difference between karuṇa and vipralambha though they share the same emotional complexity. The great Māṇi Mādhava Cākyār used to explain the difference thus –

the enactment of karuṇa ends with despair in the eyes; that of vipralambha with a ray of hope indicating reunion. The above three characteristics were developed later, in Kūṭiyāṭṭam theatre.

Kerala being the land of Advaita, Abhinava's Śaiva philosophy did not produce any impact here; but not so his aesthetics. The *Locana* gives the details of the mode of acting a verse in *Ratnāvalī*.[2]

> If I gaze at this creeper, as if viewing a lady who is overcome by love,
> queen Vāsavadattā will get angry.

This is the description of a creeper in the garden; what is suggested is his love for Sāgarikā. The instruction regarding the mode of acting of this verse is this – 'The contextual meaning (creeper) has to be communicated through elaborate padārthābhinaya, the suggested sense (beloved) shall be indicated by subtle movements of eyes and vākyārthābhinaya. It could be wrong to give no gesture at all to the second meaning.'

The prayogamārga of contextual and suggested meanings became a pet theme for Kerala actors and we can safely assume that Abhinavagupta anticipated the acting mode of Kūṭiyāṭṭam.

2. iii. Emergence of Kūṭiyāṭṭam

There is wrong notion even among the learned that Kulaśekhara introduced innovations in Kūṭiyāṭṭam. There was no Kūṭiyāṭṭam at his time or earlier. It emerged one or two centuries after him. His innovations revitalised a stagnant Sanskrit stage and paved the way for the emergence of Kūṭiyāṭṭam.[3] There were socio-cultural reasons behind it.

---

2 उद्दामौत्कलिकां विपाण्डुररुचं प्रारब्धजृम्भां क्षणा-
दायासं श्वसनोद्गमैरविरलैरातन्वतीमात्मनः।
अद्योद्यानलतामिमां समदनां नारीमिवान्यां ध्रुवं
पश्यन् कोपविपाटलद्युति मुखं देव्या करिष्याम्यहम्।।
अभिनयोऽत्र प्राकरणिके प्रतिपदम्। अप्राकरणिके तु वाक्यार्थाभिनयेनोपाङ्गादिना। सर्वथा नाभिनय इत्यलमवान्तरेण।
'The outer meaning has to be enacted word-by-word. An indication by side glance will be enough for the implied.' Abhinavagupta extends here the *vācya-vyaṅgya* paradigm of poetry to theatre – *Locana* for Udyota II, 17.

3 Kūṭiyāṭṭam has attracted the attention of scholars and theatre activists in India and abroad. Many brilliant studies have also come out during the last fifty years. Most of the studies rely on grandma-fables handed over through generation. What some of the learned expositions lack is a sense of history and a scientific approach. Over-ritualisation is a common characteristic of these studies (see Mundoli Narayanan, *Over-ritualisation of Performance, Western Discourses on Kūṭiyāṭṭam* in TDR

The post Kulaśekhara period saw drastic changes in the social life. The centralised rule of Ceras crumbled. Capital was shifted from Crangannore to Quilon. Local chieftains rose in power fighting with each other for supremacy. They needed divine legitimacy which the priestly class provided inventing new stories. The chieftains, in turn, rewarded the priests with feudatory rights. Both the administration and priesthood needed security for the survival of their newly acquired status. Theatre became a tool in their hands. Budhists had used Sanskrit theatre, earlier for the promotion of their religion. The priests emulated them. They had to fight the heterodox doctrines of the opponents of Vedic belief, ie Budhists, Jains and Lokāyatikas who had high influence in the Kerala society. This they did by incorporating discussions repudiating the views of *nāstikas* in the beautiful social satire of Bhagavadajjuka

---

So. 2 (T 190) 2006. And also *Present-day Kūṭiyāṭṭam*, Christian Du Comb in TDR: 51:3 (T 195) 2007. Some put unduly stress on a metaphor used by Kālidāsa – *Kāntam Kratum Cākṣuṣam* to argue that Kūṭiyāṭṭam is a visual sacrifice and take it to exotic levels.

We cannot blame the authors or doubt their sincerity. The fact is that original sources were not available to them. The original sources for a study of Kūṭiyāṭṭam are the Vyaṅgyavyākhyā and *Naṭāṅkuśa*. The stage manuals also are of some help. Unfortunately all the above works which are in Sanskrit were not available to the scholarly world when these studies were published.

In these circumstances we have to get a clear idea on the following points for a fruitful research on Kūṭiyāṭṭam.

i. Kūṭiyāṭṭam did not exist at the time of Kulaśekhara or earlier. He made his innovations on the presentation of Sanskrit dramas, not on Kūṭiyāṭṭam.

ii. Sanskrit theatre in Kerala and later Kūṭiyāṭṭam inherit the *NS* tradition as is clear from the introductions of *VV* and *Naṭāṅkuśa*.

iii There was no ritualisation of Kūṭiyāṭṭam at any stage of its development. When it moved to the temples the plays were restructured to suit the atmosphere. For example, Buddhist characters, lunatic etc. were eliminated. Ritualistic salutations were added at the beginning and the end. These changes did not affect the aesthetics or the secular credentials of Sanskrit theatre. Instead wit and criticism of Vidūṣaka made it more popular.

iv. *Tola* is an imaginary figure.

Association of Kulaśekhara with *Tola* in introducing local language to Sanskrit theatre is not supported by facts. Kulaśekhara did not permit any character to use languages other than that of the dramatic text. Inflation of the role of vidūṣaka is a later development in which Kulaśekhara has no hand. It may also be remembered that *Naṭāṅkuśa* which held Kulaśekhara in high esteem does not refer to *Tola*. It holds the actors responsible for the so called aberrations and distortions.

We have to believe that Kulaśekhara's innovations in the existing mode of presentation of Sanskrit drama paved the way for the emergence of Kūṭiyāṭṭam in the post-Kulaśekhara period. The pity of it is that the actors who paid lip service to the royal dramatist ignored his instructions. They did not continue the practice of even his pet theme of presentation of suggestive import. Kūṭiyāṭṭam did not preserve the mode of acting inner meaning. It is a challenge before the present generation of talented actors to revive this hoary tradition.

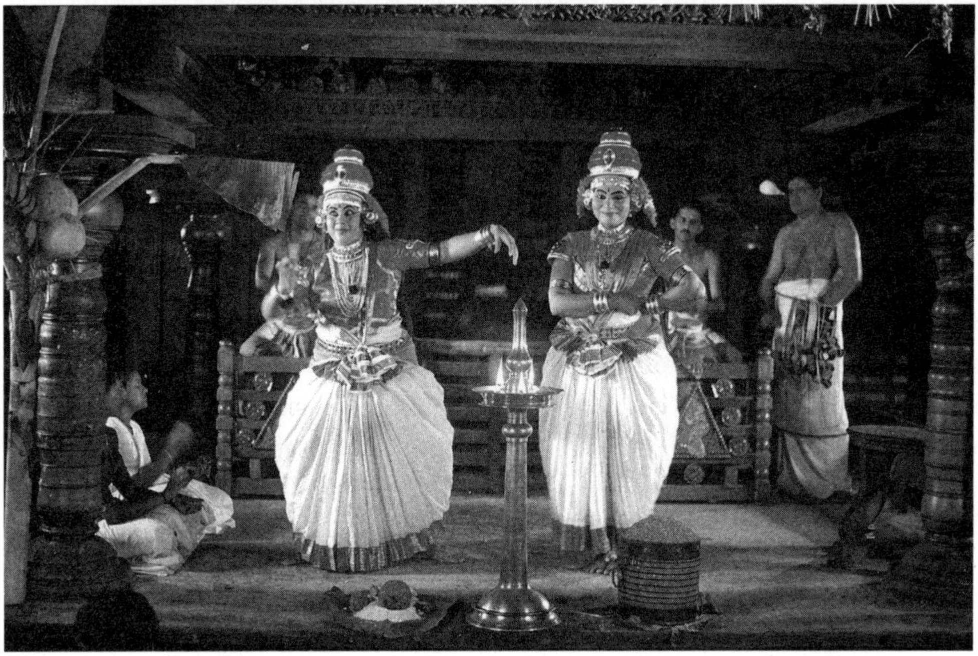

Aesthetics of Kūṭiyāṭṭam in the post-renaisance period. Choreography of Painkulam Rama Chakyar – heroine and maid in Bhagavajjukam; Kalamandalam Giriji and Kalamandalam Shylaja

consequently extending the period of its performance to 35 days.[4] The third act of Pratijñāyaugandharāyaṇa was used for instructions in polity. The performance was extended to 41 days. When Sanskrit theatre became a medium for cultural indoctrination focus was shifted, embarrassing the adherents of *NŚ,* to the nānāloka. Local language was introduced to the Sanskrit stage to please them. Śaṇḍilya the disciple started this in Bhagavadajjuka. Soon it was followed by Vasantaka, the minister of King Udayana. He did it wonderfully well by incorporating parodies, interesting stories etc. to the narrative text. His incarnation as a local story-teller symbolises the localisation of Sanskrit theatre in Kerala.

2. iv. Deviation from Nāṭyaśāstra

i. Kūṭiyāṭṭam follows the principles of *NŚ,* yet it is different from it. The most important deviation is in the mode of presentation. *Bharata's* primary concern was *nāṭya*; *Kūṭiyāṭṭam* transforms *nāṭya* to *āṭṭam* (dance). *Nāṭya* is prose;

4 KG Paulose, Bhagavadajjuka in Kūṭiyāṭṭam, New Bharatiya Book Corporation, New Delhi.

dance adds poetry to it. To illustrate this *Kulaśekhara* gives a new dimension to the concept of *bhāva*.

ii. *Bharata* conceives a stage with multiple characters stage. *Kūṭiyāṭṭam* prefers solo performance. Started as retrospective narration in Pūrvasambandha it developed as recapitulation (nirvahaṇa) in *Kūṭiyāṭṭam*. Solo acting provides the most exciting moments to the connoisseurs. This makes *Kūṭiyāṭṭam* an actor's theatre.

iii. Imaginative acting, hinted at by *Bharata*, is fully developed in *Kūṭiyāṭṭam*. Multiple impersonation which *Bharata* does not permit, is accepted in *Kūṭiyāṭṭam*. These two make the presentation an exhilarating experience.

iv. *Bharata* permits the jester to use local language. The *Vidūṣaka* in *Kūṭiyāṭṭam* made the maximum use of this provision and monopolised, so to say, the stage for days together. This enabled him to interact with contemporary life and voice its concerns in an otherwise closed society. Functioning as the fourth estate he made Sanskrit theatre lively and relevant.

v. *Bharata* prescribes a rigid structure for drama; *Kūṭiyāṭṭam* always violates it. It has a loose structure and the performance is elastic. The dramatic text or the author are more or less irrelevant as the actors follow the stage-scripts prepared by their masters.

vi. The actor in *Bharata's* scheme is an imitator. In *Kūṭiyāṭṭam*, he is an imitator, narrator and interpreter.

Bharata with his ten different types of performances envisioned a theatre providing entertainment to all. He took elements from the Vedas to make them accessible to those who were denied the benefit of it. Playfulness (krīḍanīyaka) and openness (sārvavarṇika) were his ideals. Kūṭiyāṭṭam moved away from Bharata when it ritualised and confined the drama in the four walls of temple theatre. It was only when the performances were brought to public space that it came back to *NŚ*. Bharata's theatre was secular in character.

2. v. Rasa and Dhvani

NS tradition gives stress on rasa. It is the end product of a situation. Kulaśekhara is concerned more with internalisation of emotions – the mental process leading to that situation. This mānasī avasthā, the actor presents through imaginative acting – manodharma. This leads to multiple impersonation – Pakarnnāṭṭam. Manodharma and Pakarnnāṭṭam are the two cardinal concepts that Kerala contributed to the national theatre.

In India, dṛśya and śravya passed through separate streams. Bharata expounded rasa and provided a medium for its expression – abhinaya. Poetry could not accommodate rasa, though it aspired much, in its scheme for want of an appropriate medium. Ānandavardhana provided the much awaited medium for rasa in poetry – dhvani. It was left to Kulaśekhara to apply dhvani to theatre. Theatre already had one medium – abhinaya. By making it the touchstone, Kulaśekhara made dhvani sharp and subtle too. That is the importance of netrābhinaya and the *Vyaṅgyavyākhyā* mode of performance.

Bharata's theatre has undergone several changes over the centuries. It has reached the zenith of its glory in *Kūṭiyāṭṭam*, the only living tradition of the ancient theatre. *Kūṭiyāṭṭam* makes acting sharp and subtle while unfolding, confidentially, the inner-heart of the character through ocular movements, transports acting to the trance-dramatic levels in multiple impersonation and provides challenging situations to the actor to exhibit his creative genius disregarding the constraints of text, time and space.

III
Textual Analysis

The author of the two dramas, Kulaśekhara, was a ruler of Kerala with his capital at Mahodayapuram. He was the king of the second Cera empire. Two Cera kings held the honorary title of Kulaśekhara and hence the identification of the royal dramatist is a problem. There were disputes among scholars in this matter. We are now more equipped to find out a solution on scientific terms.

3. i. The Cera Empire

Kerala was part of *Dakṣiṇāpatha*, separated from *Āryāvarta* by the Vindhya mountains. The southern territory was ruled over by several dynasties, most prominent among them being Cera, Cola and Pāṇḍya. Their geographical boundaries and administrative jurisdiction changed very often.

The Ceras ruled at two intervals – the first during Saṅgham age and the last for three centuries from 9th CE. Very little is known about the first Cera empire. Fortunately we have reliable sources – epigraphic, inscriptional and literary – to know moor about the second Cera empire. The three centuries of Cera rule brought peace, prosperity and fame to the country.

Mahodayapuram, the modern Koṭuṅṅallūr in Thrissur district, was the capital of the second Cera empire.[1] Mahodayapuram was a continuation of the ancient port known as Muziris which was the first emporium in India for the Romans. It was also a centre of Jews, Jains and Buddhists. Christians in Kerala believe that the legendary St. Thomas landed here in 52 CE. We have reliable evidences with regard to the reign of the following Cera rulers.

Sthāṇu Ravi Kulaśekhara	844-870
Rāmavarma Rājaśekhara[2]	870-883
Bhāskararavivarma	962-1021
Rāma Kulaśekhara	1089-1122

1 Dr. Kesavan Veluthat, *The Early Medieval in South India*, Oxford University Press, 2009.

2 *Kurumattūr Praśasti of Rāma Rājaśekhara*, MR Raghava Varier, Kulasekhara Theatre Festival 2013, International Centre for Kutiyattam Tripunithura, Kerala.

3. ii. Sthāṇu Ravi Kulaśekhara (844-870), the author

Sarvānanda in his *Tīkāsarvasva* commentary on Amarakosa, composed in 1159 CE, makes specific reference to the Āścaryamañjarī of Kulaśekhara. It shows that by this time the author had earned authority to be quoted in a lexicon. This is the upper limit. The author of Dhvanyaloka flourished in the court of Avantivarman who ruled Kashmir between 855 to 885 CE. So we can safely assume that the royal playwright was a contemporary of Anandavardhana. The present writer would like to identify the playwright with Sthāṇu Ravi Kulaśekhara who ruled between 844 to 870. The reasons for this placement are discussed below:

Sthāṇu Ravi was perhaps, the most renowned monarch in the line. Several inscriptions extol his benevolence. Many poets and scholars adorned his court. The famous astronomer Śaṅkaranārāyaṇa who commented on *Laghubhāskarīya* and the Yamaka poet Vāsudeva were among them. Vāsudeva's master was Parameśvara who was an illustrious expounder of *Mahābhārata* and hence reverentially called by all Bharataguru.

Kulaśekhara wrote the plays at a mature age. We can assume that the Brahmin scholar respectfully called to the palace from Parameśvaramaṅgalam can be Parameśvara ie, Bharataguru. The extra-ordinary respect the king shows to the scholar in bringing him in a specially arranged boat, dissolving of the assembly on his arrival and leading him to the secret chamber inaccessible to others indicate the greatness of the visitor. His age and scholarship deserve such a reception. If this be true there is nothing wrong in assuming that the scribe of *Vyaṅgyavyākhyā* is Parameśvara of Parameśvaramaṅgalam, Bharataguru himself. He is now at an advanced age, alone having lost his son who used to perform the customary obligations.

The monarch envisioned a new world of aesthetics in his two dramatic compositions; but was not confident as to how the connoisseurs will receive it. He sought the advice of the Paramācārya and being encouraged by him, demonstrated different roles in his presence. Bharataguru either directly or through a disciple noted down the details and prepared the first acting manual, Vyaṅgyavyākhyā. Perhaps his old age might not have permitted him to complete the second text, hence it is left unfinished. The following points strengthen the identification of Sthanu Ravi as the playwright:

i. After 985 when Rāja Rāja ascended the throne of Cola empire, Kerala began to be threatened by this eastern neighbour and the history of Kerala became filled with records of skirmishes and battles between the two powers. A peaceful atmosphere conducive for a king to indulge in literary activities was available in the Cera rule only in the pre-Rāja Rāja period.[3]

ii. The royal dramatist was a contemporary of Anandavrdhana. He had only a vague notion about the new theory of dhvani originated in the distant North. He had not learned the details of it. He comprehends vakrokti, vyapadeśokti etc. under the orbit dhvani. The author of *Vyaṅgyavyākhyā* has to be placed close to Dhvanyaloka.

iii. The socio-cultural atmosphere of the emerging bhakti cult around the temple life as revealed from inscriptions favours an early date.

iv. Dr. M.G.S. Narayanan holds that the Onam celebrations of Kerala owes its origion to Sthanu Ravi. The temple dedicated to Vamana at Trikkakkara is connected with the king. We know that the royal dramatist was specially fond of Vamana. SD and the dhvani text refer several times to the temple dedicated to Vamana where the heroine offers prayer. The king's love for Vamana, read with the Onam supports his authorship of the dramas.

The only objection to this identification is a quotation in *Vyaṅgyavyākhyā* of Bhojasūtra of a posterior period, which remains unresolved.[4]

Two objections can be raised against this placement: The reference in the introductory part of Samvaraṇadhvani to *Daśarūpaka* and to Bhoja both belonging to the 11th century. It has now been accepted that reference to *Daśarūpaka* is to the 18th chapter of *NŚ*. The author of *VV* was ignorant of Dhanañjaya's text. *VV* accepts śāntarasa on stage. Had the author heard of Dhanañjaya's objection of it in theatre, there would at least have been a mention to it. *VV*, similarly is unaware of Dhanañjaya's three-fold classification of nṛtta,nṛtya and nāṭya. Hence he followed Bharata's old classification. With regard to the reference to Bhoja, one is not sure that it is to the author of *Sarasvatīkaṇṭhābharaṇa*. None of the available works of Bhoja is in sūtra style nor does contain the sutra cited. The reference may be to some older sūtra-text lost to us. In these circumstances, it will be safe to conclude that the playwrite was a senior comtemporary of Anandavardhana of 9th c. CE.

---

3 John Sreven Sowle in his thesis *The Traditions, Training and performance of Kūṭiyāṭṭam*, p. 72

4 Dr. NP Unni has analysed all the arguments regarding the date of Kulaśekhara and concluded on the basis of the reference to Bhoja that Kulaśekhara flourished some where between the latter part of 11th century and the early part of the 12th c. AD. For details see the Introduction of *Tapatīsaṃvaraṇa*, Nag Publications, Delhi, 1987.

Kulaśekhara wrote three works – Āścaryamañjarī, a prose and two dramas – Tapatīsamvaraṇam and Subhadrādhanañjayam. The former is available only in references. Of the dramas he wrote TS first and SD next, however, without long intervals. His Guru also wrote dhvani text to TS first and took up SD later and left it incomplete. Now *VV* is available for three Acts of TS and 1½ Acts of SD.

3.iv. Stage and Performance

Kulaśekhara was an ardent admirer of Bharata. Even while introducing innovations he was careful to link them to *NŚ* tradition. He had mastered all the śāstras and was an expert in *Mahābhārata*. Among the dramatists Kālidāsa was his favourite. His dramas on several occasions betray the influence of Kālidāsa. Kulaśekhara had a splendid assembly of scholars, poets and actors in his court. He found time in the midst of his royal responsibilities to enjoy poetry and to enter on intellectual discourses. The atmosphere prevailed in the palace was a symbol of the pleasant and peaceful life in the country. Traders roamed about in the city, rice-plants bore ripe corns overhead, lustful youths embraced the harlots and festivals celebrated all around. The period marked a golden era in the history of Kerala.

Regular intellectual discourses were held in the palace. Plays were presented on festive occasions. Large number of people, both elite and folk, attended those presentations held in theatre-halls attached to the palace or in public places. Theatre used the minimum stage property. A three-wicked lamp stood at the centre in front of the stage. Actors entering on the stage moved to the lamp and fixed their eyes in contemplation for a while. Then they bowed to the audience and entered into the stance of their role in the play. There is no reference to preliminary rites and dhruva songs in *VV*. But this might have been observed as prescribed by Nāṭyaśāstra because *nāndi* and *prastāvana* are seen in the dramatic text.

Curtain is another property frequently referred to in the text. Two men hold the curtain at the entry of every character. They keep holding it until the actor is ready for appearance. Another curtain is fixed behind dividing the stage and green room. When a character enters in a hurry he holds it. This entry is technically termed apaṭīkṣepa. Curtains are also used to create different levels of acting on the Stage. In the first act of Tapatīsamvaraṇa, King and vidūṣaka are on the stage. The queen and her maid hide behind to overhear them. They are separated by a curtain. The curtains were in plain clothes. There is no indication of any kind of drawing to suggest the time/space of acting. Performance starts with the music of naṭī.

The actors were well trained. There are veiled uncomplimentary references in *VV* to actors who have not received proper training. There were families who look up acting as a livelihood. Actors were called bharatas. We have references to bharatakulas. Senior member of the family might have been the nāṭyācārya. The sūtradhāra in TS is a preceptor. The role of vidūṣaka is done by his disciple. He is anxious to see the image of himself reflected in his disciple's acting. Girls also joined the classes. The young lady referred to by the sūtradhāra in SD belongs to a family of actors. She has learned acting, music, dancing etc. Training given by the nāṭyācārya equips them to be masters of all arts needed for the performance. It is probable that this girl after becoming queen started to train female actors in the palace.

The performance of a play extended for several days. Śivarāma, the commentator of TS states at the end of the first Act that the portion to be played on a day is over (ēkadinaprayōjyasya). It means that only one Act is presented a day. Only one verse is chosen from one Act for elaborate acting. This is clear from *VV*. At that time there will be only that character on the stage. In retrospective narrations also the acting is solo. This is an important shifting from Bharata's stage. At the end of the solo acting other characters join and make the stage multi-charactered. Later this solo performance came to be known as kūttu as against Kūṭiyāṭṭam where other characters also join.

There were two distinct levels of acting. The four-fold acting for nānāloka and the specific ocular acting for the elite. The proficiency of an actor is assessed in his ability in harmonizing the two levels.

3. v. Author's Erudition

Even a cursory look at *VV* will reveal the deep knowledge of the author in various branches of study. He quotes extensively from ancient sources. His mastery over śruti, smṛti and dharmaśāstra texts, not to mention literary sources, is amazing. Kāmaśāstra, jyotiṣa, śilpaśāstra, aśvaśāstra, tantraśāstra – all come handy for the versatile scholar.[5] He quotes abundantly from lexicons to denote the different meanings for bringing out the suggested sense.

One wonders as to why he fills a performance text that too one dealing with the theme of delicate love with all these ostentatious quotations. It is doubtful whether he

5 Some of the texts / authors he quotes are given here:
Amarasimha, Paramesvara, Acharya, Pitamaha, Kamasastra, Samudrikasastra, Smriti, Anekarthah, Itihasa, Guruvachanam, Vedavyasa, Natyasastra, Guha, Brihaspati, Usanan, Manu, Surasuracharya, Acharasastra, Jayamangala, Vyjayanthi, Vasishta, Aswasastra, Bhargavamatah, Lokokti, Agastya, Silpasastra, Saravakhyasruti, Tantrasastra, Bhojasutra.

expected his actors to present all the quotes and arguments on stage. It seems that he was explaining the rationale behind the line of thought accepted for vicārābhinaya. He had to convince rationally and authoritatively the prekṣakas why he chose such a psychological progression for his characters in such a situation. This seems to be more a justification to his own self as also instruction to the actors to build up their confidence.

3. vi. Actor-spectator Interaction

Bharata as an actor was conscious of the significance of the response of the audience. It is for the spectators that a play is produced. He devotes a full chapter to analyse this relation (Ch. 27 – *Siddhivyañjakam* – indications of success). Bharata gives a true picture of the audience response to a performance.

यस्तुष्टौ तुष्टिमायाति शोके शोकमुपैति च।।
क्रुद्धः क्रोधे भये भीतः स श्रेष्ठः प्रेक्षकः स्मृतः। XXVII, 57

He alone is called a truly great spectator who feels good when others are glad, become miserable when others feel misery, gets angry when others are angry and feels frightened when others are afraid.

Bharata envisions a silent, sublime enjoyment also.

न शब्दो यत्र न क्षोभो न चोत्पातनिदर्शनम्।
सम्पूर्णता च रङ्गस्य दैवी सिद्धिस्तु सा स्मृता।। XXVII, 27

No sound, no agitation nor any calamity caused by elements like meteor is there. The theatre is full with audience. Such a position is called divine siddhi.

Bharata had in mind the process of critical appreciation when he defined the arbitrators (*Prāśnika*)

चारित्राभिजनोपेता शान्तवृत्ताः श्रुतान्विताः।
यशोधर्मरताश्चैव मध्यस्था वयसान्विताः।।
षडङ्गनाट्यकुशलाः प्रबुद्धाः शुचयः समाः।
चतुरातोद्यकुशलाः नेपथ्यज्ञाः सुधार्मिकाः।।
देशभाषाविधानज्ञाः कलाशिल्पविचक्षणाः।
चतुर्थाभिनयज्ञाश्च सूक्ष्मज्ञा रसभावयोः।।
शब्दछन्दोविधानज्ञा नानाशास्त्रविचक्षणाः।
एवंविधास्तु कर्तव्याः प्राश्निका नाट्यदर्शने।। XXVII, 46-49

In order to assess the virtues and blemishes of the dramatic performance, arbitrators should be employed possessing the following qualifications. They should have:

i. great moral strength and should belong to noble families;
ii. their nature should be quiet and should possess sound knowledge in the scientific lore;
iii. they should have zest for fame and virtue;
iv. they should be impartial and mature in age;
v. connoisseurs in dramaturgy with its six-fold auxiliaries, good learning and purity of heart;
vi. equanimity in intellectual attainments, experts in the four types of musical instruments (tata, anavaddha, suṣira and ghana)
vii. knowledgeable in the matter of dress;
viii. pious by nature, proficient in regional languages, expertise in arts and artefacts;
ix. familiar with the principles of the four types of representation (speech, emotion, gesture and dress);
x. considerable acquaintance with rasas and bhāvas (sentiments and emotions),
xi. conversant with the rules of grammar and prosody and well-versed in the different śāstras.

Kulaśekhara identifies multiple layers in the audience, the most prominent being *nānāloka* (ordinary folk) and *Prekṣaka* (elite). The former are pleased by the normal mode of four-fold acting. They rejoice over what they see and express their responses without any inhibitions. They inherit the *haseti-rameti* culture. But the *Prekṣakas* are serious. Kulaśekhara combines the divine siddhi and the ability of *Prāśnikas* of Bharata to define his *Prekṣakas* in TS.

के पुनः प्रेक्षका इति चेत् –

अष्टौ दश च विद्यास्ताः नाट्यवेदो यथाविधि।
स्मरशास्त्रं च यैर्ज्ञातं तान् विदुः प्रेक्षकान् बुधाः।।

Those who are thorough with the eighteen branches of knowledge (four Vedas, four auxiliary Vedas, six Vedic limbs, dharmaśāstra, mīmāṃsā, nyāya and purāṇa) dramaturgy and the science of love making are known as prekṣakas. The ordinary people are called nānāloka. Correspondingly two levels of acting are prescribed – the macro level four-fold acting for the ordinary people and the micro level ocular gestures for the elite. On all occasions Vyaṅgyavyākhyā distinguishes these two levels of acting. Some examples of the instruction regarding this multi-level acting are given below:

i. अभिनयेन नानालोकान्, भावेन प्रेक्षकान्।
Acting to please *nānāloka* and bhāva to please the *prekṣaka*.
Bhāva is defined later.

ii. इति ध्वनिं दृशोर्विभावयन् बाह्यार्थेन नानालोकान् सुखयेत्।
Communicate the suggested sense to the prekṣaka through eyes and give delight to the *nānāloka* by presenting the outer meaning.

Actually, *prekṣakas* are the target audience of Kulaśekhara when he unfolds the theory of interpretation of implied meaning through ocular movements.

The different levels among the viewers influence the acting process. The actor has to please the *nānāloka* by external meaning, costumes, percussions, spectacles etc. Then he has to concentrate on the elite in the front row and satisfy them by communicating the inner meaning through stylised acting through eyes.

The actor now is confronted with an unusual conflict. What will the *nānāloka* do when he concentrates on the Prekṣakas. And will not the Prekṣaka feel exhausted when the actor pleases the *nānāloka*. Kulaśekhara would reply that the efficiency of an actor lies in his ability to harmonise, keeping a balance, between the two layers. It has to be admitted that this is a difficult task. Synchronisation of the actor-Prekṣaka interaction through subtle ocular movements and actor-nānāloka responses through external means is the basics of Kulaśekhara's aesthetics of theatre. The concept of multiple levels in acting and in appreciation is unique to *VV*.

3. vii. Vicārābhinaya (विचाराभिनयः)

The author has promised at the outset to prescribe the prayogamārga of *Prāveśika* and Sthāyibhāva. The former is externalisation of the internal thought-process. Śivarāma, the commentator of *Subhadrādhanañjayam* has coined a wonderful term to denote this process – विचाराभिनयः। [6]

Every actor at the time of his first entry narrates the past incidents. There is no verbal text prescribed for it. The actor internalises the situation and finds out suitable code for its communication. Retrospection, descriptive narration etc. come under *Vicārābhinaya*. The actor sometimes interprets the situation as through the imitated character and some times through the character reflected by the imitated character. This can be done only by multiple impersonations. Imaginative acting is a prerequisite of *Vicārābhinaya* which is effectively presented through multiple impersonations. Manodharma and Pakarnnāṭṭam are two modes by which the internal thoughts are externalised.

---

6 अतो विचाराभिनयेन पूर्वत्रापि गौरवमासाद्य शिथिलयन्ती केति विधेयम्। – Śivarāma on I, 12.

Some instances of *Vicārābhinaya* in *VV* are given below:

i. The actor enters the stage, fixes his eyes on the three wicked lamp and thinks (सचिन्तं निःश्वस्य):

Dhanañjaya: (Sighing thoughtfully) Ah! Even though the year-long pilgrimage has already come to an end;

'Pitiable indeed are my deeds! I am at a loss to carry out my obligations. Brave as I am I have seen all the beautiful objects with a mind dettached, heard all that are melodious. Yet, my mind becomes fickle.

(Controls the mind and takes a long breath. He continues)

अहो ! Ah! How did this change come to my mind?

The alluring sidelong glances of Pāñcālī held me back when I was leaving Indraprastha. She prevented me from leaving her with words drenched in the nectar of love.

> Lord! most beloved! dear one! the very life and breath of me! Please don't go, don't go.

She looked longingly as though praying with her eyes-

> Don't leave me. Don't forget our enchanting mutual love when you come across other women, on your way.

When I insisted on leaving, she looked me in rancour.

> Alas! What she feared has come true.
>
> I had pledged an ascetic life during the period of pilgrimage. Yet, when I reached the Ganges, I married the daughter of the serpent king; later I enjoyed the company of the daughter of the Pāṇḍya King. Travellers who pass through different places will tell these stories among themselves and they will one day fall in the ears of Pāñcālī. She will think that what she had feared has come true. In order to avoid any suspicion, I used to narrate to my friend Kauṇḍinya, in spite of his scolding me, sweet things about Pāñcālī.
>
> Dear friend! when will I see the moon like face of Pāñcālī?
>
> How lovingly will she receive me when I enter the city at the end of the pilgrimage? (Prāveśikam of Dhanañjaya in SD) Dramatic text gives only an exclamation Ah!. The actor interprets his mental condition.

ii. अथैवं तया वीक्षमाणोऽयं धनञ्जयः सरोमविक्रियं सस्मृतमात्मगतमिति स्मरेत्।

Dhanañjaya, thus glanced by her, remembers with horripilation his internal self in this way.

iii. सस्मृतमात्मगतमिति स्मरेत्।

Remembers the internal self.

iv. आत्मगतमेवं स्मरेत्...।

Remember the internal feelings in this way

v. सलज्जं आत्मगतं स्मरति।

Bashfully remembers the inner self

vi. आत्मगतं उक्त्वा...।

Expressing the inner-self

Externalisation through vicārābhinaya is often denoted by words like स्मरेत्, आत्मानं, उक्त्वा etc.

3. viii. Multiple Impersonation (*pakarnnāṭṭam*)

Kulaśekhara has specifically demonstrated the technique of pakarnnāṭṭam at least in two instances.

i. The context is the conversation between the king and jester. Seeing the drops of sweat on the cheeks of the divine lady the king begins to see the manifestation of love in her. The practical method of acting is given below:

When the first word of the śloka *apāṅgapātaiḥ* is recited, the indication that the first mischief of Cupid's bow, horripilation and the second, sweating is indicated by the action of the eyes and hand gestures. He delights the audience by the convincing action of the eyes and by acting *as the heroine*.

The actor who has taken the role of the hero should transform himself to a female character to act out in detail the horripilation and the sweating of the heroine.[7] This is an instance of pakarnnāṭṭam.

ii. The action involved in the śloka āpātalam is described as below:[8]

Jester: These girls who are the very personifications of forest creepers are looking at you.

King: True, just as the creeper, which hugs the mango tree, beats its breasts, kisses the tender lips and gazes with the buzzing sound of the bees.

The action of this part:

7 *Tapatīsaṃvaraṇa,* Act II.

8 *Ibid.,* Act II.

Convincing the audience by means of dhvani, *actor turns himself into a creeper*, acts out the outer meaning and pleases the general audience.

Here the actor is turning himself into a creeper to convincingly demonstrate the part where the creeper embraces the mango tree.

3. ix. *Ekalocanam*

In the description of koṭṭicceṭam enacted by Paṟavūr Cākyār in Cilappatikāram half of the body belonging to Śiva moves and the other half belonging to Umā remains static. This was a dance. It is not clear how the actors performed this. Did they do both the parts simultaneously or one after the other? It must have been acted one by one and then repeated with such speed that spectators failed to notice the sequence. This kind of acting is inherited from the tradition of dance. Tradition compares the Cakravāka bird which looks at its departing lover with an eye full of sorrow and the setting sun with an eye of anger to a talented dancer.[9]

The story of the Cākyār's eyes being distorted during the performance of Śākuntala due to the quick exchange of glances between the running antelope and the carriage is well known. The acting of eye in separate roles expressing different sentiments is commonly known as ekalocanam – signification of one emotion with one eye and other emotion with another eye. The ekalocana in Kūṭiyāṭṭam and lately of Kathakaḷi is the contribution of dance to drama. Vyaṅgyavyākhyā prescribes this style of acting in drama too.

The king seeing the horripilation in the lower part of his body evokes the emotions of happiness and sadness separately by using his skilful eyes. The sadness is because of his fatigued body and happiness because the horripilation is an indication of his attainment of desire. We do not know whether the emotions of sadness were indicated in one eye and the emotion of happiness in the other eye simultaneously or whether there was an interplay of these emotions. These two features of *pakarnnāṭṭam* and *ekalocanam* are borrowed from dance.

9 एकेनाक्ष्णा प्रविततरुषा वीक्षते व्योमसंस्थं
भानोर्बिंबं, सजललुळितेनापरेणात्मकान्तम्।
अह्नच्छेदे दयितविरहाशङ्किनी चक्रवाकी
द्वौ सङ्कीर्णौ रचयति रसौ नर्तकीव प्रगद्भा।।
In the evening fearing the impending separation from her lover the cakravāki bird, like a talented dancing girl, looks the setting sun with an eye red with anger and her lover with the other eye filled with tears.

Vicārābhinaya is like the Vastudhvani in poetry. At times it remains only as a description, but on other occasions it can stimulate the emotional complex and lead to the realisation of Rasa.

3. x. *Bhāvābhinaya*

Bhāva is a word in Sanskrit, the real significance of which has not been fully understood by many. It is already used in four contexts (Ch. I – FN 5). Kulaśekhara added a fifth sense to *bhāva* – more comprehensive and significant.

The word *bhāva* generally, stands for mental condition. But here it is used in a different sense. The receptive audience has to be pleased by the presentation of bhāva.

Bhāva should be used until the receptive audience's face bloom and they shed tears of joy. This is the meaning of bhāva. Bhāva is a part of dance. There are six parts for it – the brightness of the lamp, unity of body movements, the beauty of the costumes, the cleverness or dexterity of usage, beautiful shape and music. By combining the six elements it attempts to make the receptive audience happy; to please and entertain the general audience through one's acting. Now look at these pairs:

Receptive audience	: bhāva, to please
The general public	: abhinaya, to entertain

What is meant by bhāva? Bhāva = acting through the eyes + dance. This can be illustrated by an acting sequence, ie, acting of Menakā after her entry, in TS:

> In Bharata's *Nāṭyaśāstra* dance is of two types – *tāṇḍava*, forceful and *lāsya*, graceful. The men do the *tāṇḍava*. The women decked with ornaments do the *lāsya*. Menakā should stand in front of the lamp, look into the eyes of the heroine and indicate the textual content with eyes. This is the style of acting typical of the women characters.

In the performance, prominence is given to the dancing part. Here is another instance explicating the acting style:

Rambhā comes near the heroine and enlightens her about the hero.

> How to let the girl know about the news of the hero? Is it by direct expression or through dhvani. Direct speech is not desirable. Then how is she to be enlightened? By using words with subtle meaning – *dhvani*, or by mere *bhāva* or by ultimate expression, *parambhāva*? Even so, using words pregnant with dhvani, the meaning may be illustrated by using *bhāva*.

The four possibilities of abhinaya in explicating the news of the hero to the heroine are as given below:

i. Direct speech *spaṣṭokti.* The outer meaning for the general public, four-fold acting.
ii. Suggestive word *dhvani.* Acting the suggestive sense for the receptive audience.
iii. Bhāva alone *kevalabhāva.* Netrābhinaya, through ocular movements to the elite audience.
iv. Emotional complex *parambhāva.* Performance on dancing style, for the receptive audience.

Acting of the second and third type is recommended in this particular context.

This is the difference between theatres of Bharata and of Kulaśekhara. Bharata delighted the audience using the four types of abhinaya, clear gestures and direct expressions. Kulaśekhara used dance which made the emotions powerful. He felt the former as prosaic and the latter as poetic. The aesthetic charm rests on the poetic way of acting. Bharata gave the grammar of acting, Kulaśekhara added poetry to acting.

Vyaṅgyavyākhyā defines the concept of *bhāva* succinctly. This is the essence of the acting technique of Kulaśekhara. It may be noted that this *bhāva* is different from the *bhāva* that Bharata describes.

Bhāva when used in the instrumental stands for the entire emotional complex mediating between these two levels. In other places it expresses the ordinary meaning of *sthāyibhāva*. See the comments in *VV* given below:

विवेकभाजोः दृष्ट्योः प्रेक्षकान् भावेनैव बोधयन् त्रिवर्त्युज्वलितस्य दीपस्य पुरस्तिष्ठेत्। यावत्प्रेक्षकमुखमुदश्रु विकसति तावद् भावेनैव प्रयोक्त्रा प्रयोक्तव्यः। कथं भवेनैवेति चेत् –

नृत्तस्याङ्गीह भावः स्यादङ्गान्यपि च तानि षट्।
दीपौज्ज्वल्यं लयैक्यं च भूमिकासौष्ठवं ततः।।
रागप्रयोगनैपुण्यं प्रयोक्त्राकृतिभद्रता।
गातुर्ज्ञेयानि तान्येवं प्रयोक्त्रा प्रेक्षकैरपि।।
ऐक्यमङ्गाङ्गिनो कृत्वा भावैस्तु रमयेत् स तम्।
अन्यानभिनयेनैमान् नानालोकान् विनोदयेत्।।

The six parts are external, the ordinary people enjoy them. But the soul is *bhāva. prekṣaka* alone is capable of enjoying it.

Dance (*nṛtta*): soul (अङ्गि) – *bhāva*

Components (अङ्ग) (six) – brightness of the lamp, unity of body movements beautiful costumes, dexterity of usage attractive form, music.

Kulaśekhara uses the word *nṛtta* to denote both *nṛtta* and *nṛtya*.

This inter relation of the principal and subsidiaries corresponds to the primary meaning – suggested sense in poetry expounded by Ānandavardhana in *Dhvanyāloka*.

The micro-movement of the eyes through which the actors often express complex emotions are a class by themselves.

इह तु सूचितो भावः दृष्टावेव प्रतिष्ठितः दृष्टया तु सूचितो भावः पश्चादङ्गैर्विभाव्यते।

The relation between the two equations, *prayoktṛ-prekṣaka* (actor-audience) and *dṛg-bhāva* (eye-emotion) is the most significant aspect in Kulaśekhara's dramatic theory.

3. xi. *Navarasa*

Many of the examples for *dhvani* given by Kulaśekhara in Vyaṅgyavyākhyā relates to Vastu – *Vicārābhinaya*. He had a comprehensive view of *rasa* too. He describes how Vyāsa has been successful in depicting all the nine *rasas* in *Mahābhārata*.

At the end of the war, *karuṇa* could be seen in the shrieks and cries of the women;
bībhatsa, could be seen in the scene where Aśvatthāmā slew the sleeping people;
vīra and *raudra* are evoked in the scene where Bhīma kills Duśśāsana;
bhaya can be seen amongst the enemy kings;
adbhuta in the people who see the Pāṇḍavas fighting to take back the cows;
hāsya in the scene of Pāñcālīsvayamvaraṃ where the suitors take bow and arrows;
śānta where Dharmaputra unmoved in the disrobing scene and
śṛṅgāra in Subhadrā's love towards Arjuna.

See how the dramatist identifies Dharmaputra as the embodiment of *śānta*. The scene selected to evoke laughter is also suggestive. In Prabandhakkūttu the actors present this scene humorously even now.

Conclusion

A close study of the dramatic and performance texts of the two dramas will unfold the myriad forms of an imaginative theatre. Kulaśekhara's vision set the classical Sanskrit theatre on a strong foundation in his life-time; it continues to inspire the contemporary theatre to find out a new idiom to interpret ancient texts to meet the challenges of present-day life.

Part II

Performance Text

Vyaṅgyavyākhyā

I

Dhanañjayadhvani

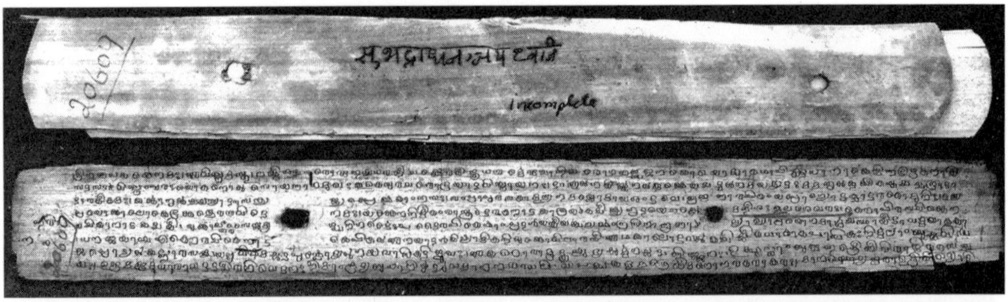

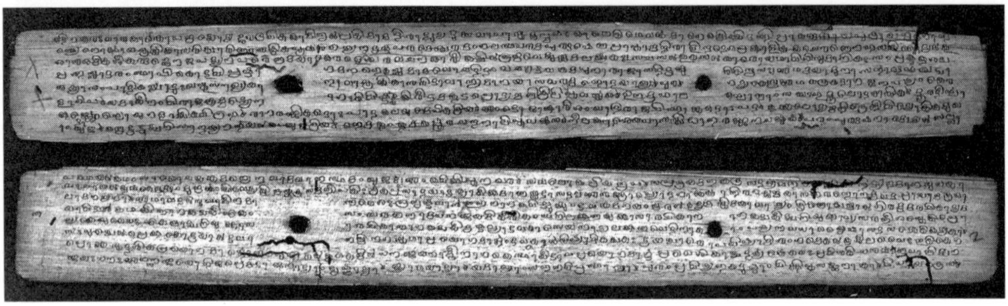

Walking in time, now we knock at the doors of the last century in the first millennium, the golden age of the Ceras. As explained, the Nāṭyaśāstra – scholar recorded the performance text for the two dramas as desired by the royal dramatist, in the order of composition, first for TS then for SD. He named them Samvaraṇadhvani and Dhanañjayadhvani respectively.

The expert composed the dhvani text for the first three acts of TS and closed it down finding no scope for dhvani thereafter. Then he took up SD and in a delightful mood gave graphic descriptions of himself, the King and the capital city of Mahodayapuram. Thereafter he explained the circumstances that led to the composition of these texts. By the 'api' in 'Dhanañjayepi' in the introductory verse he indicates that TS has already been covered. His joy, unfortunately, was short- lived. After completing the first Act he gave an exhaustive elaboration to the interlude and put his hand on the second Act. Ignoring the risk of repetition he presented Kṛṣṇa in great detail and left the rest untouched, perhaps, owing to his failing health or to death. Thus, the performance text available to us consists of the first three Acts of TS and a little over one Act of SD. Śivarāma (13c.), the celebrated commentator of Kulaśekhara's plays respectfully refers to these texts in the introduction of his vivaraṇa commentary for TS.

ग्रन्थकारसमकालभवेन व्यङ्ग्यरूप इह चारुतरोऽर्थः।
व्याकृतः सुमतिना पदवाक्ये सोपयोगमधुना स्फुटयामि।।

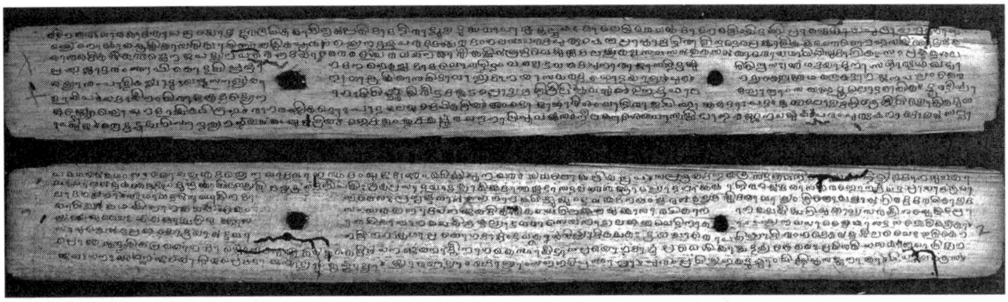

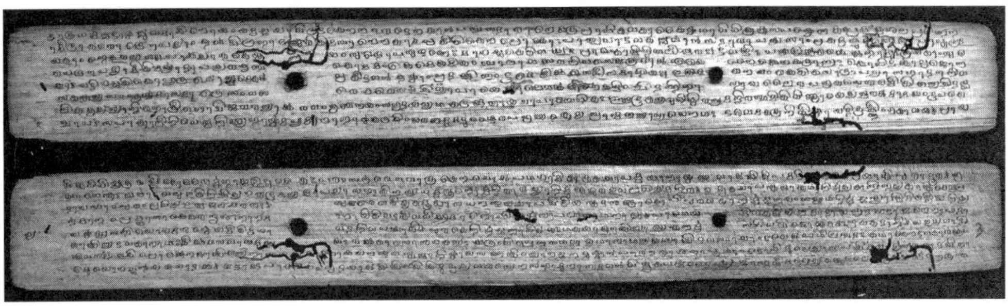

The only Ms available to us of these texts is the one owned by Kailasapurathu Govinda Pisharoti in the palace library (No. 67) in Thiruvanantapuram. This palm-leaf Ms, in early Malayalam script is very old and is worn-out in many places. Turavur Narayana Sastri, an eminent traditional scholar of the last century transcribed this in paper in Devanāgarī script for the Oriental Manuscript Library Thiruvanantapuram in 1915 CE (ME 1090). The text is in 310 pages – 1 to 124 Dhanañjayadhvani and 125 to the end Samvaraṇadhvani. The common title for the two texts in the codex is Dhanañjayasamvaraṇadhvani. The reason for reversing the sequence of composition remains to be explained.

This edition is based on the above (Mss T.281), preserved in the Oriental Manuscript Library of Kerala University.The scholar-scribe left out the worn out parts as such. I too keep them blank, leaving the challenge to our young scholars to search for other Mss to fill up the gaps. Mahāmahopādhyāya T. Ganapati Sastrikal, the renowned curator, provided a much sophisticated title to the text – Vyaṅgyavyākhyā, juxtaposing the meanings of the two enchanting epithets of Śivarāma, vyaṅgyarūpa iha cārutarorthaḥ and vyākṛtaḥ. The name soon gained acceptance in the academic circles. The name, though not supported by Mss, is retained here. The order of the performance text in the Mss is faithfully followed in this edition.

Trivandrum Palace Library – No. 1604, Cata. P 2635-37. Palm leaf size 14½"×2". Leaves 43. 8-9 line per page and 58-66 letters per line. Script Malayalam.

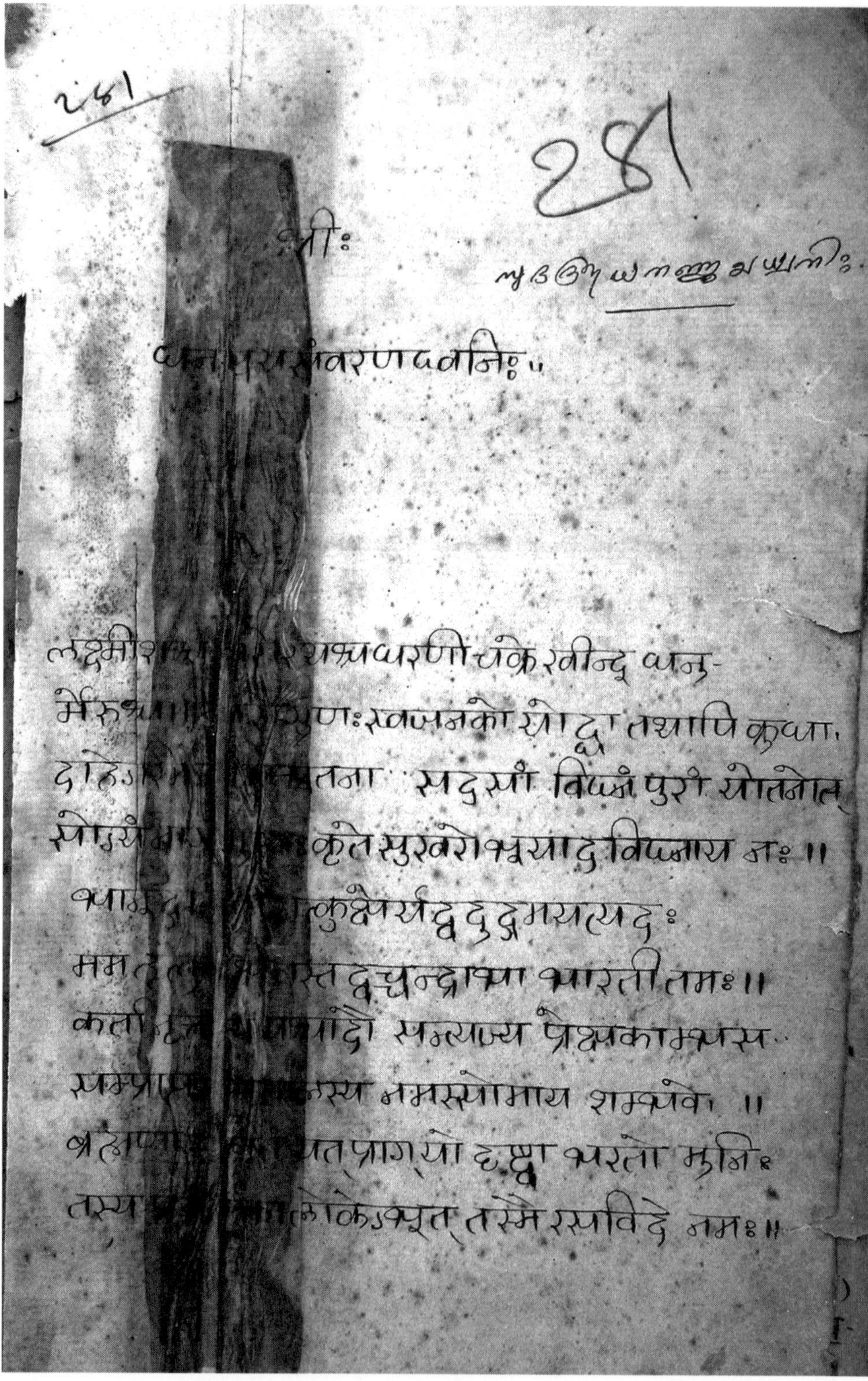

श्रीः

[illegible]वरणध्वनिः ॥

लक्ष्मीश[illegible]ग्रचरणौ चक्रे रवीन्दू चान्-
मेरुश्चा[illegible]णः स्वजनको यो दृष्टा तथापि क्रुधा ।
दोहे[illegible]तना सदृशीं विघ्नं पुरीं योऽतनोत्
सोऽयं[illegible]कृते सुखरो भूयाद् विघ्नाय नः ॥
ध्या[illegible]त्कुक्षेर्यद् दुग्धमयस्य दः
मम [illegible]स्त दुग्धचन्द्राभा भारतीतमः ॥
कली[illegible]दौ सन्त्यज्य प्रेक्षकाम्भस-
सम्प्राप्य[illegible]स्य नमस्योमाय शम्भवे ॥
ब्रह्मणा[illegible]तप्राग् यो दृष्ट्वा भरतो मुनिः
तस्य [illegible]लोकेऽभूत् तस्मै रसविदे नमः ॥

IV
The Beginning

Invocation

लक्ष्मीशश्च शरो रथश्च धरणी चक्रे रवीन्दूधनु-
मेरुश्चाहिवरो गुणः स्वजनको योद्धा तथापि क्रुधा।
दाहेऽस्मिन्नभिभूतनाकिसदसां विघ्नं पुरा योऽतनोत्
सोऽयं नागमुखः कृते सुरवरो भूयादविघ्नाय नः।।[1]

May the elephant-faced God Gaṇapati
ward off all
the obstacles that stand on our way:
the God, who in his anger did not
hesitate to throw an obstruction
even to the heavenly beings fighting
a formidable battle
in which none other than
his father was the warrior;
the very earth
with sun and moon as wheels
on both sides
turned out to be the chariot;
the mount Meru forming the bow,
the string for which was
the chief of the serpents and the arrow,
lo! the Lord Viṣṇu himself![1]

1 The author begins Vyaṅgyavyākhyā with the customary invocation. The Gods in different forms served Śiva in his fight for the destruction of the three cities (Tripura) of the demon kings. The reference to Tripuradahana in the invocative verse is important in many ways. According to *Nāṭyaśāstra* the first play presented before Śiva was the ḍima Tripuradahana. Vāsudeva, the renowned author of *Yudhiṣṭhiravijaya* who was patronised by king Kulaśekhara wrote a Kāvya on the same theme. Vidūṣaka in the drama also refers to the incident when Dhanañjaya strikes the arrows against the demon in the first Act.

४.१. नाट्याविर्भावः

भानूद्गतिर्जगत्कुक्षेर्यद्वदुद्गमयत्यदः
मम हृत्कुक्षितस्तद्वच्चन्द्राभा भारती तमः।
कर्ता नृत्तस्य यश्चादौ सन्त्यज्य प्रेक्षकाम्भसः
सम्प्राप्तरसतालस्य नमस्सोमाय शम्भवे।।
ब्रह्मणा रचितं यत्प्राग् यो दृष्ट्वा भरतो मुनिः।
तस्य प्रयोक्ता लोकेऽभूत् तस्मै रसविदे नमः।।
यत्तेन निर्मितं शास्त्रं भरतं नाटकाश्रयम्।
तद्वीक्ष्य हृदये चक्रे महीशः कुलशेखरः।।
तेनापि रसचित्तेन रचिता नाटकद्वयी।
युक्ता रसलयैस्सद्यः ध्वनिगर्भैः पदैरपि।।
तेषां प्रदर्शयन्ती यद् ध्वन्यर्थं रसिनां नृणाम्।
व्याख्या प्रयोगमार्गश्च स्थायिभावं मया कृता।।
धनञ्जयाह्वये तेन रचिते नाटकेऽपि तत्।
अनया दर्शयिष्यामि तन्नियुक्तोऽखिलं रसी।।[2]

४.२. शरत्कालवर्णना

अथ कालोऽभवत् कश्चित् शीतवातातपान्वितः।
निर्मलाम्बुच्छविस्वच्छप्रोद्यत्कल्हारसञ्चयः
विषमच्छदपुष्पोद्यद्गन्धवासितदिङ्मुखः।।
अकठोरामृदू चाप्युद्यच्छर्म गच्छद्वणिग्जनः।
उत्फुल्लाम्बुरुहश्रेणी विराजितरसश्चयः।।
उद्भ्रमद्भ्रमरारावददद्विरहिवेदनः।
हिमांशूद्यत्सुधानिर्यद्रवमाननरावलिः।।
विपक्वकलमश्रेणीमनोहरतराकरः।
मानसोद्यन्मरालश्रीविद्योदितदिगन्तरः।।
वारकान्तोपगूढोद्यच्छरद्रवितकामिहृत्।
प्रतिमामन्दिराभ्युद्यदुत्सवापास्तकल्मषः।।

2 In this introductory part, the author narrates the circumstances that led to the composition of the stage manuals. Kulasekhara wrote *TS* first and *SD* later. The scholar recorded the manuals in the same order. These introductory narration sould have been prefaced to Samvaranadhvani. Why it was done otherwise remains unexplained.

4. i. The Origin of Nāṭya

The rays of the rising sun
remove darkness from the 'recess of the universe'
May, likewise, the moon -like lusture of the Goddess of speech
dispel the darkness from my heart.
I bow to Śambhu, inseparably united to Umā,
who in the beginning created the art of dancing
bestowing in it rythm and emotion
so as to remove the darkness from the minds of the spectators.
Homage to Bharata, the enjoyer of aesthetic pleasure
who introduced in this world the art of histrionics
as he learned from Brahmā who created it.
Observing the canons formulated by the sage
King Kulaśekhara, endowed with an aesthetic mind,
composed two dramas abounding in
rhythm, sentiments and suggestive words.
I have, to felicitate a better exposure to the
connoisseurs, commented upon the two dramas
brining out fully the suggestive import, the permenent mood
and the mode of representation.
What follows is the commentary
written by me as directed by him,
for one of them Subhadrādhanañjayam,
in tune with these Principles.[2]

4. ii. The Autumn Season in Mahodayapuram

Then came the autumnal season with its
breeze cool and heat so gentle
Water as clear as crystal,
Full blown white lotuses were seen all around
The fragrance emnated from the flower of
Saptacchada perfumed all the
quarters of the sky
the climate so moderate – neither too hot nor cool;
Traders roamed about in the street proclaiming,

४.३. केरलेश्वरवचनकारिणः ब्रह्मबन्धोरागमनम्।

कालेऽथेति वर्तमाने कस्मिश्चिदह्नि प्रातरुत्थाय पुत्रापहृतगार्हस्थ्येन चूर्णिकासरिद्वारि अनुष्ठितपूर्वसन्ध्येन दृष्टपरमेश्वरमङ्गलस्थपरमपुरुषेण प्राप्तात्ममन्दिराळिन्ददेशप्रक्षालितकरचरणेन हसन्तिकोद्यत्कृशानु-शमितशीतरुग्णेन जपध्यानपरेण मया केरलेश्वरवचनकारी कश्चिद् ब्रह्मबन्धुः समलक्ष्यत।[1]

स च सत्कृतसत्कारो यथाविधि सुमानितः
सम्पृष्टकुशलप्रश्नः सादरं स्थापितो भुवि।
पृष्टागमनहेतुः स मामवोचदिदं वचः
भवन्तमधुना राजा सन्दिदृक्षुरिति स्म सः।।

अथ मयामुना सहारूढखट्वाशय्यासम्पादितस्वादुवस्तुसौख्यया नावा चूर्णिकासरिदावह्यमानया सत्वरं महोदयाख्यं पुरं गम्यते स्म।

४.४. राज्ञः कुलशेखरस्य वर्णना

अथ तत्र तथा गच्छन्नपश्यं केरलाधिपम्।
समासीनं विराजन्तं मध्ये नागारिविष्टरम्।।
किरीटमकुटप्रोद्यन्मणिश्रीलिप्तवर्णकम्।
उन्नम्रफालघोणांसबाहुमूलोदरान्वितम्।।
दूरदीर्घाक्षिदोर्जङ्घायुगलाञ्चितविग्रहम्।
रागरञ्जितदोः पादपद्मयुग्मेधितश्रियम्।।
अम्भोजाक्षारिशङ्खादिराजचिह्नात्तदोः पदम्।
कुण्डलोद्यन्मणिश्रेणीविद्योतितमुखाम्बुजम्।।
कण्ठभूध्वनिसौन्दर्यगर्हयत्कम्बुजश्रियम्।
हेमकुङ्कुमकर्पूरचन्दनालिप्तवक्षसम्।।
नीलकौशेयवासत्विडाहरज्जनचक्षुषम्।
परम्पुरुषनामोद्यत्सल्लापकथयत्कथम्।।
सङ्कोचयन्तमन्येन वामबाहुस्थमम्बुजम्।
अङ्कविक्षिप्तनखरं सर्वलोकप्रियं नृपम्।।

1 Reference to the messenger as brahmabandhu is of special interest to us. It denotes a contemptous Brahmin. Accordingly to traditional stories Cākyārs,the traditional actors are degraded Brahmins. Does it mean that the king sent an actor of his court to fetch the scholar to the palace for discussion on dramatic topics?

as though, the prosperity of the city
The row of lotus flowers, bees moving around
with the hissing sound, tormented the hearts of lovers
suffering separation from their dear ones.
The rays of moon too, dipped in nectar though,
melted the hearts of beings
Rice-plants bearing ripe corn overhead
enhanced the charm of the fields
Swans, on their way back to Mānasa lake,
moved in the sky
They gave indeed a new splendour to the horizon.
Lustful youth, their hearts melting enjoyed
the embrace of the harlots.
Festivals, depriving people of their
sins were celebrated
in the abodes where in stood the many idols.

4. iii. Arrival of a Messenger of the King

One morning, as usual, I got up early in the morning; went up to river Cūrṇi to perform the morning rites. Then I paid homage to Viṣṇu the supreme deity at the Parameśvaramaṅgalam Temple. Returning home I washed my hands and legs and warmed myself before the blazing fire. While I was in meditation, a messenger from the King of Kerala appeared before me.

I received him with due respect, offered a seat with welcoming words. Then I enquired the purpose of his visit. He informed me: 'the King wishes to see you'. Then I followed him to the city of Mahodayapuram through the river Cūrṇikā in a canoe provided with cot, bed and other comforts.

4. iv. Description of King Kulaśekhara

There I met the King seated on a throne. His natural lusture seemed to have increased owing to the radiance of rich stones adoring his crown. An elevated forehead, a prominent nose lofty shoulders, long eyes and lengthy shakes contributed much to adorn his person. The red-tinged forearms and feet betrayed the sign of a king, since they possessed auspicious marks of lotus, wheel, conchshell etc. His face glittered in the brilliance of rich stones on his earrings. His neck surpassed the conch-shell

४.५. राजा प्रयोगमार्गं प्रदर्शयति

सप्रश्रयमहं तत्र सदस्यवहितोऽगमम्।
निष्यन्दमानसुधया वाचा सत्कुरुते स्म माम्।।
मुहूर्तं स्थितवत्यस्मिन् मय्यत्र स महीपतिः।
श्रितप्रसादया दृष्ट्या वीक्षमाणः सभासदः।।
अनुज्ञाप्योदगात् तस्मान्निरगच्छन्मया सह।
रहो नर्म वदन् प्रायान्मन्त्रशालामनन्यगाम्।।
अथावदत् सुखासीनं मां नरेशः प्रहृष्टवान्।
इह नाटकविच्चुञ्चुं भवन्तमनयं स्मरन्।।
कृत्यमस्ति मया वाच्यं श्रृणोत्वस्माद्गिरं मम।
रचिताद्य मया विद्वन् कथञ्चिन्नाटकद्वयी।।
एकं संवरणं नाम धनञ्जयमितीतरम्।
ध्वनिलक्षणयुक्ता सा रचिता नाटकद्वयी।।[2]
ध्वनियुक्काव्यसरणिः शस्तेति प्रोच्यते बुधैः।
एतस्मात् ध्वनियुक्ता सा रचिता नाटकद्वयी।।
द्रष्टव्या भवता सेयं नाट्यलक्षणवेदिना।
तां पश्यन्नवधार्यैषा सदसद्वेति कथ्यताम्।।
साधुश्चेत् प्रेक्षको भूयात् भवानस्मि नटस्तथा।
प्रयोगमार्गं भवते दर्शयिष्यामि तत्वतः।
भूयश्चारोपयिष्यामि रङ्गमेतत् कुशीलवैः।।

इति तेन प्रोक्तस्तद्दर्शितप्रयोगमार्गोहमधुना तत्कृतेऽस्मिन् धनञ्जयनाम्नि नाटके स्थायिभावप्रयोग-मार्गप्रावेशिकाश्च प्रदर्श्यन्ते।

2 Refers to the Dhvani doctrine propounded by Ānandavardhana in Dhvanyāloka.

in sound and shape. His chest was anointed with gold, saffron, comphor and sandal paste. The blue silken garment worn by him attracted the attention of the onlookers. He was engaged in conversation, the topic being Viṣṇu, the supreme spirit. The lotus held in his left hand was being closed by the other with finger nail resting on his lap. He was loved and admired by one and all.

4. v. King Shows the Mode of Presentation

With modesty, I entered the assembly hall. The king received me with sweet words. Hardly had I stood there for a moment the king with a smiling look saught the permission of the assembly and retired to his private chamber along with me. Conversing humourously we entered the council hall inaccessible to others. Once I was seated comfortably the king spoke to me in a pleasing manner.

I have brought you here, Oh! Scholar since you are a master in the art of histrionics. I wish to assign a work to you. I have composed two dramas – *Samvaraṇa* and *Dhanañjaya*. Suggestive poetry has found acceptance at the hands of scholars. Hence in composing these dramas, I have often used the suggestive words. You are proficicnt in thc art of histrionics. Go through them, judge their merit and tell me whether they are good or not. If they are any good, be a spectator: I shall myself present before you each character in the proper way. Then I shall have them staged by professional actors.

Thus he showed me the mode of presentation. Following it, I am elaborating the sentiment, mode of enactment and the entry of charcters in his drama, *Subhadrādhanañjaya.*

V

Retrospective Narration

पूर्वसम्बन्धः [1]

(ततः प्रविशति धनुर्बाणपाणिः धनञ्जयः।)[2]

अथ धनञ्जयो निजप्रेमभाजनाभ्यां कृष्णाभ्यां ज्यायाभ्यां यमाभ्यां सह हरिप्रस्थाख्यां पुरीं प्रविश्य हतदुष्टां विक्षिप्तसज्जनां तां विधाय तत्र सभ्रातृवर्गस्सभार्यस्सुखमासीनोऽयम् –

५.१. नारदागमनम्[3]

यदृच्छयाविर्भूतेन नारदेन तान् पञ्च सदारानेकत्र प्रापितवता तैर्यथाविधि कृतसपर्येण तत्पृष्टकुशलप्रश्नेन अमी भ्रातरो द्रौपद्यां कुर्वद्विग्रहा मा स्युरिति मन्वानेन तां प्रतीति तेन प्रोक्ताः पाण्डवाः –

भवतः सर्वान् सदारान् पञ्च साम्प्रतं द्रष्टुमस्मीह सम्प्राप्तः। श्रूयतां हेतुरस्य। सपार्षत्या तु यूयं सुन्दोपसुन्दयोः अवस्था[4] मा गच्छतेति वक्तुं प्राप्तोऽस्मि। हि बली स्मरः।

भवद्भिः पञ्चभिस्सर्वैस्सहाद्य क्रियतां बुधैः।
द्रौपद्यामिति मर्यादा पश्यत श्रृण्वतो मम।।
एकमेकमियं बाला वत्सरं निवसेत् क्रमात्।
एकेनैकेन तत्रान्यः कोऽपि भर्ता व्रजेन्न ताम्।।
यदि गच्छति कोऽप्यत्र सोऽब्दमेकं व्रती भवेत्।
कुर्यात् प्रदक्षिणं भूमेस्तीर्थसेवी समाहितः।।

इति तेन सङ्केतितया द्रौपद्या सहादौ निवसतस्तस्य युधिष्ठिरस्यासम्पूर्णमासमात्रे संवत्सरे गते सशुचिव्यवसाये काले वर्ममाने,

५.२. धनञ्जयकृतम् मर्यादाभञ्जनम्

कस्मिंश्चिदह्नि ह हा खलैरपहृतधेनुरस्मि इति कस्यचिदस्खलितकृत्यस्याग्निहोत्रिणो द्विजवरस्यार्तस्वरं श्रृण्वन्नयं सहृदयव्यथः तद्रक्षणाय चापान्वेषी गुरुभूतस्य युधिष्ठिरस्य मन्दिरस्थमिति विज्ञायेत्यस्मरत् –

मामकं भूपतेश्चापं सपाञ्चालिनि वेश्मनि।
आहार्यमप्यनाहार्यं तत्र किं शरणं मम।।

Retrospection[1]

(Then enters Dhanañjaya with bow and arrow in his hands)[2]

Dhanañjaya came to Hariprastha, along with his beloved Draupadī, the two elder and the twin younger brothers; warded off the evil spirits and made it a dignified habitation for the righteous people. All of them spent the days happily.

5. i. Arrival of Nārada[3]

One day, quite unexpectedly, sage Nārada appeared before them. All the five, accompanied by their wife, assembled to pay homage to the sage. After the exchange of formal pleasantries, Nārada said:

---

1 The retrospection by Dhanañjaya of his past in the first act of *Subhadrādhanañjaya* is the best example for the process of internalisation of events conceived by Kulaśekhara in *Vyaṅgyavyākhyā*. He calls this Pūrvasambandha – connecting the present to the past.

2 This is the stage direction in the original drama immediately following the nāndi, prologue and viṣkambha. The act properly begins here. The omission of the preliminaries in this manual does not seem to be deliberate. The actual performance would have been in tune with the text, i.e., entry of Dhanañjaya after the prologue. The viṣkambha might perhaps have been omitted as its content is included here. The commentator did not incorporate the introductory portion in his manual as he found nothing special in it. The Pūrvasambandha is a new device introduced by Kulaśekhara for the presentation of Sanskrit dramas. The stage direction for entry of characters in Sanskrit dramas is – ततः प्रविशति – Enters after that, after what? The spectators have a right to know what preceded his entry. Kulaśekhara holds that poetic justice demands that every character at the time of his/her first appearance should narrate his/her past up to the present point thus connecting the present to the past. Only after establishing the character he can act his textual role. Later the Kūṭiyāṭṭam theatre adopted this technique and developed it. There it is called nirvahaṇa, the recapitulation.
In classical plays like *Svapnavāsavadatta* and *Śākuntala* the Vidūṣaka narrates in a humorous tone, his past experiences. Kulaśekhara might have taken the cue from them.
The story here is told in the third person, though actor is impersonated as the character. In other words, the actor here is a narrator and not an imitator. In course of his narration, at times, he turns out to be an interpreter too. This too had far reaching consequences on the Kerala stage.
No words are used for narration; everything is done by gesture. The method is that of remembering इत्यस्मरत् of the past incident. The present writer would prefer to call this Vicārābhinaya. Now it is interesting to know as to how the actor would have presented the roles of Nārada, Draupadī, Gada and the sages as recollected by Dhanañjaya. It seems that he might have transformed, as in mono acting, himself to the different characters and presented by gestures, their respective roles. This is the transformation or intermixture of roles, Pakarnnāṭṭam.

3 This part of the story is taken from the Ādiparva of *Mahābhārata*. After Pāñcālīsvayamvara, Dhṛtarāṣṭra called back the Pāṇḍavas from their exile. A city was constructed in Indraprastha (Hariprastha) and

दुष्टैरपह्रियन्तेऽद्य ब्राह्मणस्यास्य धेनवः।
भवेम तत्र निर्वीर्यो यदि तूष्णीं गता वयम्।।
प्रायश्चित्तविधिर्यत्र कल्पितो यैर्महात्मभिः।
तैः परं स न चैवात्र तेन चोत्पथगामिता।।
ततश्चापं मया हार्यं जवात् क्षितिपमन्दिरात्।
ते प्रयान्ति पुराद्दूरं हृत्वा धेनूः खलाः खलु।।

इति निश्चित्य गुरुभूतस्य द्रौपद्या सहासीनस्य धर्मसूनोर्मन्दिरात् ज्यानिर्मुक्तशर इव प्रविश्य मन्दिरं उद्धृतचापः तस्मात्तथा निर्गत्य तान्निहत्य तास्तस्मै प्रदाय स्वां पुरं प्रविश्य गुरुजनचरणाम्बुजशेखरीकृत-मूर्धा स धनञ्जयश्चापद्वितीयस्तदनुज्ञातोऽपि पुरतो निर्गच्छन्नयं सव्यथं निर्गच्छन्त्या स्तिमितस्निग्धनिष्यन्दमाणप्रेम्णा साकेकरदृशा नाथ मा गा इति वदन्तीव वीक्ष्यमाणोऽपि मार्गयापनाय पाथेयमिव तद्वीक्षणमादाय[५] हृदयभाजने गाढमाबध्य सन्नियोगोऽनुष्ठेय इति दृशा वदन्निव पाञ्चालीं पुरतो निर्गच्छन्नासीत्।

अथ तया कौण्डिन्याख्यं तन्नर्मसचिवं द्विजोत्तममाहूय तदानीं स इत्यवादि –

कौण्डिन्य भवता नाथः तीर्थसेवासमुत्सुकः।
रक्षता सोऽनुगन्तव्यः क्षेत्रं विप्रेण सर्वदा।।
यथा नाथस्य कस्यांश्चिदवस्थायां भवेत् पथि।
प्रमादः तथा तेन भवता रक्ष्य एव सः।।[६]

इति प्रोक्तेन कौण्डिन्येनानुगम्यमानोऽयं धनञ्जयः.....

५.३. धनञ्जयस्य तीर्थयात्रा।

तस्मान्निर्याय सकौण्डिन्यो गच्छन्नमुष्मात् पौरन्दर्याशया पूर्वाम्भोधिमुपेत्यास्य पश्चिमया वेलया दक्षिणाभिमुखो गच्छन्नयं तया दत्तं कटाक्षपाथेयं हृदयात्किञ्चित्किञ्चिदुद्धृत्य वयस्येन सहामुना अनुभवन् विस्मृतवर्त्म-दैर्घ्यो जाह्नवीमभ्येत्य तज्जलैः पूततनुर्भवन्नत्रस्थया कयापि नागकन्यकया नीयमानस्तया सह रममाण-स्तस्यास्सञ्जातपुत्रस्ततो[७] गत्वा पाण्ड्यविषयानभ्येत्य पाण्डीशं च तत्पुत्रीम[८] वाप्य ततो गत्वा राघवबाहुशक्तिलेश एष इति दर्शयन्तं तं सेतुं[९] प्रणम्य तत्तीर्थतस्तीर्थसेवां कृत्वा दक्षिणाम्भोधेरुत्तरतीरेण पश्चिमाभिमुखो गच्छन्नयं कुमारीतीर्थं[१०] प्रणम्य पश्चिमाम्भोधेः पूर्वतीरेण उत्तराभिमुखो गच्छन्नयं गतकल्पवत्सरं वीक्ष्य कौण्डिन्यमित्यवदत्।

कदा नु खलु कौण्डिन्य हरिप्रस्थपुरं गतः।
मातुश्च मोदिनोर्भ्रात्रोमूर्ध्ना एष्यामि पदाम्बुजम्।।
कुमारावश्विनौ पुत्रौ तरुणौ रूपसम्मतौ।
प्राप्स्यामि परमां भ्रातः कदा नु पदनिर्वृतिम्।।
अथाद्यतनादह्नो मासेऽत्र गतवत्यपि।
मत्कृते कृतसङ्केतो भविता वत्सरो हि सः।।
प्रतीक्ष्यमाणया तं च मां तस्मिन् गते तदा।

> I have come to see you all living happily with your wife.
>
> There is a reason – Cupid, as you know, is very strong. It is my wish that you should not behave like Sunda and Upasunda[4] in your relation to Draupadī. You are wise. Hear from me of an arrangement that you have to follow.
>
> Let Draupadī stay each year with one of you in the respective order of your age. During that period none else should approach her. Any one who violates this rule will have to go on a pilgrimage, as an act of atonement, for a full year.

In accordance with this order fixed by Nārada, Draupadī joined the elder brother Yudhiṣṭhira in the first year.

5. ii. Dhanañjaya Breaks the Agreement

When there was one month left to complete the full term of that year, one day a Brahmin of perfect practice of Vedic rites, came to Dhanañjaya crying in distress 'Ha! Ha! My cows are stolen by rogues.' Feeling pity on the poor Brahmin Dhanañjaya searched for his bow and arrow and realized to his shock that they were kept in the residence of Yudhiṣṭhira where he was living with Pāñcālī. He thought:

My bow is there in the abode of the king where he is in the company of Pāñcālī. What shall I do now? Take it from there or not? How can I be inactive when the thieves take away the wealth of a noble soul? Shall I, breaking the vow, enter his abode?

> The great sage has prescribed the mode of atonement too. Hence I will not be blamed as going astray. Yes. I shall take the bow immediately, the thieves have already gone a long way raiding the cows.

Thus having resolved, he dashed like an arrow shot from the bow into the house where the king was living with Draupadī, came out in the same way with the weapon, killed the enemies, retrieved the cows and returned.

Dharmaputra ruled a part of the country allotted to Pāṇḍavas. Ādiparva C. 26-27, for the visit of Nārada, Ādiparva C. 207.

4 The demon Nikumbha had two sons – Sunda and Upasunda. The two brothers obtained a boon from Brahmā that none other than they themselves will be able to kill the two. They became arrogant and created all kinds of troubles to the Gods. The Gods, then, sent the damsel Tilottamā. Both the brothers were infatuated by her beauty. They quarrelled and at last killed one another (Ādiparva Ch. 21. Nārada). Nārada refers to this story to convince them that the five brothers will quarrel over Draupadī unless some arrangements are made in their relation to her. There is an interesting text सुन्दोपसुन्दोपाख्यानप्रबन्धः which tells this story. The actors use it for their narration.

मद्दर्शनाय तिष्ठन्त्या बाह्योद्याने सहालिभिः।।
सप्रेम वीक्ष्यमाणोऽहं तत्र गच्छन् कदा तया।
मदीयां तां चतुश्शालां प्रविश्य स्थितवान् यदा।।
तदा सुधाभिपूर्णेन हेमकुम्भनिभेन माम्।
आलिङ्ग्योरजयुग्मेन वह्नि तद्विरहोद्भवम्।।
निर्वापयन्त्या प्रेयस्या प्रेम्णा दृष्ट्याभिवीक्षितः।
शर्म तद्वीक्षणोद्भूतं प्रयास्यामि कदा सखे।।[११]

इति तद्गुणगणानेव वदन् गच्छन्नयं परिणतशुचौ काले प्रभासाख्यं तीर्थं सवयस्यः प्राप।

तत्र घर्मांशुसन्तप्तं वारि स्नात्वा सुरान् पितॄन्।
तर्पयित्वा सकौण्डिन्यः स्निग्धच्छाये स्थितः क्वचित्।।
धनुर्बाणौ च निक्षिप्य द्रौपदीगतमानसः।
तत्प्रवृत्तिप्रशंसीनि वचांसि स्थितवान् वदन्।।
चक्रवाकयुगं रात्रिमधिगच्छेत् सखे सुखम्।
काल्ये स्वसङ्गमोद्देशं कालं गन्तुं न चोत्पतेत्।।

५.४. सुभद्राया अनुरागः

इत्यादि तत्सङ्गमोत्सुकः प्रलपन्नयं तद्विरहवह्निना दन्दह्यमानस्तत्र स्थितः सन्नयं सहसा गदनामानं कञ्चित् वृष्णिवीरमपश्यत्।[१२]

अथेति तं दृष्ट्वा कुतः सम्प्रतीति पृष्टेन गदेनाहं द्वारवत्या निर्यायेतस्ततः सञ्चरन् भानुकिरणसन्तप्ततनुः तत्तापशान्त्यर्थमत्र प्राप्तवानस्मीति तेन प्रोक्तोऽयं धनञ्जयः 'कस्यां धुरि प्रवृत्तमानौ तौ साम्प्रतं सीरारिपाणी अपि कुशलिनौ कच्चित्' इति पृष्टेन तेन स च सादरमित्यवादि –

अद्य तावपि तत्रस्थौ सुखिनौ सीरिचक्रिणौ।
कुतश्चित्कारणाच्चित्तं नानयोश्शर्म गच्छति।।
एकं च कार्यमुद्दिश्य तावन्योन्यं धिया मिथः।
पार्थ सम्प्रति वर्तेते, न जनैर्ज्ञायते हि तत्।।

इति तेन प्रोक्तोऽयं तत्कारणमपृच्छदिति तेन प्रोक्तोऽयं भूय इत्यवदत्। तर्हि श्रूयतां हेतुर्निगदतोस्य मया।

रहस्यमिदमन्यैश्च क्वचिन्न ज्ञायतां जनैः।
त्वयि वाच्यमिदं पार्थ धीरत्वान्मित्रभावतः।।
त्वत्तोन्यत्र न गच्छेत्तदिति तत्प्रवदाम्यहम्।
अस्ति कन्या सुभद्राख्या चार्वङ्गी च स्वसा तयोः।।
वयो बाल्यात्परं यान्ती वरयोग्याद्य सा भवेत्।
तथैनामेकदा वीक्ष्य प्रोद्यद्वक्षोजकुड्मलाम्।।

Dhanañjaya prostarted at the lotus-feet of his brother and came out with his permission to go on a pilgrimage. Much inflicted Draupadī prayed with her winning eyes 'oh! Dear, don't leave'. Her passionate look, still and starring, was streaming with love. His eyes reciprocated 'words of the great have to be obeyed.' Her longing glances he took as the Provender[5], tied it tight in the casket of his heart and started for pilgrimage.

Pāñcālī then sent for Kauṇḍinya, the jovinal companion to Dhanañjaya. She requested:

> 'Oh! Respected Brahmin, be of help to my lord on his way. Follow him all the time and see that he does not meet with any difficulty. He has to be saved from any frustration on the way.

Instructed thus Kauṇḍinya accompanied him on the way.[6]

5. iii. The Year-long Pilgrimage

Moving in the direction of God Indra they reached the eastern sea. From there proceeded to the south through the western coast. Refreshed of and on by the provender provided by Draupadī, he knew no fatigue of travelling long distance. Then they came to the bank of Ganges, sanctified by the cool water, Dhanañjaya plunged deep in to the river. A servent maid took him to the nether world. Enjoying amorous sports, she was gratified with a son.[7]

Then they went to the King of Pāṇḍya. Dhanañjaya wooed his daughter.[8] Going further they reached the southern ocean. He bowed before the bridge which looked like a relic of the colossal valour of the arms of Rāghava.[9] Moving west through the

---

5 For a similar idea see *Kirātārjunīya* III, 37.

अकृत्रिमः प्रेमरसाभिरामं रामार्पितं दृष्टिविलोभिदृष्टिम्।
मनः प्रसादाञ्जलिना निकामम् जग्राह पाथेयमिवेन्द्रसूनुः।।

Dhanañjaya, the son of Indra, accepted by folded palm in the shape of placidity of mind, as provender that attractive look cast by Draupadī – look which was also beautiful owing to natural affection. Mallinātha comments that the provender provided for by an affectionate lady is conducive to one's good.... : रमार्पितपाथेयं पथि क्षेमाय भवतीत्यागमः।

6 Here Pāñcālī is deputing Kauṇḍinya to follow Dhanañjaya in order to save him from deviations from the right path. In many other versions it is Dhanañjaya who asks Kauṇḍinya to follow him.

7 Ulūpī is the daughter of the Nāga King Kauravya. Irāvan, the son born to her assists the Pāṇḍavas in their war against Kauravas. *Mba.*, Ādiparva, 121.

8 The Pāṇḍya princess was Citrāṅgadā. The son born to Dhanañjaya in her was named Babhruvāhana.

9 The bridge constructed by Rāma to cross the ocean to reach Laṅkā.

वक्षः पाण्डुरतां लज्जां प्रयान्तीमित्यचिन्तयत्।
अन्या स्वसुरुरोजाभ्यां प्रयान्त्या यौवनं वयः।।
रचितव्या मया गात्रिकातिमनोहरा।
अन्योन्यविजयाशास्या भवेद्वक्षोजयोर्द्वयोः।।
तन्नाम द्योतयन्ती सा नानावर्णैर्विचित्रिता।
रचितव्या मया सेयमिति निश्चित्य माधवः।।
निर्माय गात्रिकां तस्यै प्रायच्छत्।
तैर्दर्शयन्ती नामास्याशु तोषं निमित्ततः।।
पार्थवर्णविराजन्तीं तां सा बध्नात्युरोजयोः।
प्रेम्णेव तेऽद्य नामाश्रितैर्वर्णमनोहरैः।।[१३]
स्तनांशुके भवन्त्यस्मिन् सामुना माधवे हिते।
पार्थस्य नाम्नारूढा भवेदेव प्रीतिर्गरीयसी।।
रथप्रेरण इत्येषस्तच्छिक्षां तामशिक्षयत्।
सापि स्वोरजतो नास्या वियोगं क्षमते क्षणम्।।
गात्रिकाया मनोज्ञाया तान्तवर्णतया तथा।
तस्यास्तद्वर्णसाङ्कर्यं पश्यन्ती सस्मितेन सा।।
द्योतयद्दशनामेयं प्रेम तस्मिन् करोत्यदः।।
अथ सीरी सुभद्रां तां दातुं राज्ञेऽहिकेतवे।
साधु कल्पितवान्सर्वैस्सह सम्मन्त्र्य गाधधीः।।

इत्यावेद्यतां तस्मै भूयस्तदनुज्ञातस्सोऽपायात् इति तं गदनिगदितं तत्सौन्दर्यद्योतकं वचः श्रृण्वन्नयं धनञ्जयः श्रवणमात्रेणैव मन्मथस्याद्येन पद्मारव्येन शरेण विद्धहृदयो भूत्वा तद्दर्शनोत्सुको भवन् नयनप्रीति-दशाहेतोः ततः ततः तद्वचनमार्गप्रकारेण मयि भगवत्पक्षपाततामप्यज्ञात्वा किमिति स्मरन्नास्ते। स तदानीमेव तदयं भूयस्सीरिणा सुयोधनाय दातुं कल्पितमित्युक्त्वा सहसा गतवति तस्मिन् किमनेनोक्तमिति ध्याय-न्नाकुलीकृतचित्तो भवन् स सर्वथास्मात् गन्तव्यमिति निश्चित्य –

५.६. अर्जुनस्य द्वारकाभिगमनम्।

उद्धृतशरासनो भूत्वा कौण्डिन्यद्वितीयो नदीतीरमारुह्य तीरादुत्तराभिमुखो गच्छन् पुरतस्तत्र मार्गद्वयं दृष्ट्वा तत्रास्थायेत्यस्मरत्।

वर्त्मना यदि गच्छामि दक्षिणेनामुना।
हरिप्रस्थं पुरं प्राप्तः पूर्णाब्दे भवितास्म्यहम्।।
यदि गच्छामि वामेन वर्त्मना सतपोभृता।
प्राप्तो द्वारवतीं भूयां कृष्णेन सम्प्रवर्तिनीम्।।

northern side of the ocean they bowed before the holy shrine of Kumārī[10] proceeded further northward through the eastern bank of western sea.

The year had almost come to an end. Dhanañjaya told his friend:

> Dear Kauṇḍinya, when on reaching Hariprastha will I have the pleasure of prostrating before the lotus-feet of my mother and also of my brothers, overjoyed on my return?
>
> When these feet will attain the supreme bliss caused by the touch of the young and handsome twins of Aśvins?
>
> The year meant for me starts at the end of one month from this day. Pāñcālī will be waiting with her maids in the outer garden eager to greet me. When oh my dear! can I run taking her up in my arm into the inner apartment? When will she extinguish the burning fire in my heart, caused by her separation, pressing hard both her breasts against my heart – the heavy breasts that resemble two big golden jars quite full with nectar.
>
> Dear friend tell me, being looked by her passionately, when will I have the pleasure of enjoying the bliss of her love long glances?[11]

Praising her beauty and recollecting her effeminate qualities, they reached Prabhāsatīrtha.

The sun had gone high above by that time. They took bath in the water heated by the rays of sun, paid their oblations to the God and forefathers. Dhanañjaya placed his bow and arrow on the ground; took rest in the cool shade of a tree. Deeply involved as he was in the thought of Draupadī Dhanañjaya went on talking all in praise of her conduct. He lamented:

> The Cakravāka couple, spend the night calmly
> only to reach the time of reunion at day-break,
> Alas! the time has not yet come for me.

5. iv. Subhadrā's Love for Dhanañjaya

In the meanwhile a person by name Gada[12] belonging to the clan of Vṛṣṇis reached there; he spoke about the purpose of his visit:

10 Kanyākumārī.

11 This is the summary of the verse अम्बास्तन्य... (I, 1) of the drama.

12 Gada is the son of Vasudeva in Rohini. He was closely associated to the Pāṇḍavas on many occasions.

इति विमृशन्नयं पुष्पेषुविशिखैः प्रेर्यमाणो बलात् वामेन वर्त्मना प्रतिष्ठमानस्सविदूषकेणेति प्रोच्यमानो – मन्ये द्रौपद्या वितीर्णं पाथेयमद्यतनेन दिवसेन नष्टमिति। भो श्रूयतां मम गीः –

वामो भुवनमार्गेण यात्राद्य भवतः क्वचित्।
तृष्णया दक्षिणालापो यात्रायां नात्र गद्यते।।
पाथेयहीनस्य तवाद्य यात्रा प्रवर्तते यदिति
सक्षुधोऽस्य कान्तोपभोग भबा...भामतवंशहेताः।।
यात्रायां मन्तव्या प्रवृत्तिमिति बुद्धिना सालोकेति।
सन्दृश्य मे लोकैरपहास्या यात्रयाद्य भवामीति।।
दक्षिणेतरमार्गस्थो भवेत्तद्दक्षिणोत्तरः।
अनया यात्रयैव स्वा वामा वामा भवेत्तव।।[१४]
अलं यदासीत् पायेथं वितीर्णं कृष्णया तव।
तन्मा सन्त्यज तादृक् ते कुतश्चित् भविता न हि।।
वाममार्गेण गच्छन्तं नरं नानुसरेत् सुहृत्।
अपि चाबद्ध्य रोद्धव्यस्तेनेति सहसा स तम्।।

इति सान्यापदेशया गिरा प्रोच्यमानोऽपि गच्छन्तमेव दृष्ट्वा भूयोप्ययमित्यस्मरत्। अहो मां बलात्कृत्य गच्छति यत् ततोप्यहमेतत् पृष्ठानुगामी भूत्वा यथावसरमसाध्यमेतदिति प्रबोधयामि इति मत्वा पृष्ठेऽनुगम्यमानेन विदूषकेणायं तत्र स्मरेण वार्यमाणशर... प्रवेशायाक्षमस्सन् स्मरशराकलितहृदयः सः द्वारवतीधिया सुमुनिसेवाछलेन प्रभासतीर्थसेविना मुनिवृन्दानामभ्याशमभ्यागमत्। तत्रस्थोऽयं भगवत्सम्मतेरनभिज्ञत्वं तत्र तपोभृत्सेवाकारित्वं लोकान् भावयन् स द्वित्रिदिनोनं मासमत्र वसन्नित्यस्मरत्।

निवसमानमयं लोकं किन्नु मामत्र वक्ष्यति।
मुनिवेश्मनि वासोऽयं प्रमादं बहुलं भवेत्।।
ततो गत्वा विविक्तेऽस्मात् कौण्डिन्येन विना क्वचित्।
स्थित्वा संस्मृत्य गोविन्दं विज्ञाय तत्वगतिस्ततः।।
बहुकृत्वा कथं तेन गात्रिकावर्णवर्णनम्।
क्रियते स्म तदास्थेन ज्ञायते नान्यकारणम्।।
तस्मादधुनैवाद्य कौण्डिन्येन विना मया।
गन्तव्यो हि तपोयोग्यं प्रदेशं क्षमिणा क्वचित्।।

इति निश्चित्य तस्मात् श्रुतिमुनिवृन्दान्निर्गत्य गजाभ्याशस्थेन वर्त्मना[१५] तरणिकरनिकरसन्तप्तपांसुना गच्छन्नयं कपिलदृढस्युपैलवधौम्यवात्स्यायनाख्यैर्मुनिभिराहूतः प्रत्युद्गम्यमानस्तैः कृतसपर्यस्सधनञ्जयो द्वारकाभिमुखो गच्छन् स भगवत्स्मृत्यै योग्यं प्रदेशमन्विष्यन् प्रातिष्ठत। य गच्छति कोप्यस्मिन् वृद्धतापसस्तस्मान्निर्गत्य माध्यन्दिनस्नानार्थं शनैश्शनैः स्खलितपदो गच्छन्नयं सहसा कञ्चिदतिथिमुनिवृन्दं प्राप्य काले निर्गच्छन्तं दृष्ट्वेत्यस्मरत्।

> I am coming from Dvārakā, roaming about reached here. Fatigued by the burning sun, I am here to get some rest.

Dhanañjaya asked him about the welfare of Balarāma and Śrīkṛṣṇa. He replied with great respect.

> Both of them are at Dvārakā now. It seems that something has clouded their minds. Both hold different views regarding a particular issue. Nobody knows the matter of their concern.

Being pointedly asked, Gada continued:

> Hear me oh Dhanañjaya. This is strictly confidential. Nobody knows it. I may reveal it to you out of friendship, since you are a man of fortitude. It should not be divulged to any one else.
>
> Balarāma and Śrīkṛṣṇa have a sister, young and beautiful Subhadrā by name. The girl has crossed her adolescence and has attained the age of matrimony.
>
> One day seeing the blush on her face and budding of her breasts Kṛṣṇa thought – she has attained youth. I will make a beautiful bodice to cover her bosom so that the two breasts shall vie with each other for success. He made a beautiful *gātrikā* in which was stitched the different names of Pārtha in attractive colours.[13]
>
> Subhadrā showed a special fascination for this dress. Never did she allow it to be separated from her bosom. When faded, the colours got mixed up. She smiled – all the ten names love one another so much that they want to be one with him.

Balabhadra had planned to give her in marriage to Suyodhana, his disciple.

After the conversation, Gada took leave with his permission. Merely by hearing of the beauty of Subhadrā, Dhanañjaya was attracted towards her. Padma, the first arrow of Cupid had its first shot on him. Agitated in his mind he became anxious to meet Subhadrā. But the elder brother is in favour of Suyodhana. Much distressed, Dhanañjaya was at a loss to determine the future course.

---

13 The ten names of Dhanañjaya are: Dhanañjaya, Phalguna, Jiṣṇu, Kirīṭi, Śvetavāhana, Bibhatsu, Vijaya, Kṛṣṇa, Savyasāci and Dhanañjaya.

अये, कश्चिदतिथिः किन्नु कालो प्राप्तोऽयम्? तदकृतसपर्यो गच्छति किम्? 'यद्वेश्मातिथिः काले तत्पूजां सत्क्रियां मुदा नो चेत् शप्तोऽमरैस्स भवेदि'ति ब्रूते हि सा श्रुतिः। तस्मादकृतसपर्यस्य तस्य पूजार्थमस्मत्पुत्रशिष्यभूतानुपमुनीनाहूय प्रेषयामि। इति निश्चित्य तानाहूय प्रोक्तैस्तैः कृतसपर्योयमित्युक्तः स कृतकृत्यो भूत्वा प्रस्तुते कर्मणि गतोऽभूत्।

अथेति गच्छन्नयं ललाटन्तपेन पूष्णा दन्दह्यमानेन गच्छन्नेवमित्यस्मरत्

मदभीष्टप्रदं देवं चोपगम्य हरिं क्वचित्।
भक्तानुकम्पिनं स्थित्वा ध्यात्वा तस्मात् व्रजामि ताम्।।

इति संस्मृत्य रैवतके गिरौ तत्समाधिक्षमं देशमन्विष्य कञ्चित् प्रदेशं प्राप्य अयं तत्क्षम इति निश्चित्येत्यस्मरत्।

अपगतजने शुभ्रच्छाये शुभद्रुमसञ्चये।
शुभजलयुते शून्यागारे शुचिस्थलरञ्जिते।।
विरहितसखो देशे विहीनखेदोध्वगः।
सपदि निवसन् कृष्णध्यानं धिया विदधेऽधुना।।

इति स्मृत्वा निश्चित्य तद्ध्यानाय तत्रासीनोऽयं भगवति चित्तं नेतुं यत्नं कुर्वते मन्मथशरशकलितहृदयत्वाद क्षमः सन् नात्माहमित्यगर्हयत्।

अहो कष्टमहोकष्टं कृष्णप्राणसखस्सखा।
धर्मानुजश्शक्रसुतो धीरम्मन्योऽस्मि केवलम्।।
यन्मदीयम्मनो तु....... शक्तो मत्सखो।
हरौ ततः केवललोला ....।।

इति मत्वा भूयोप्याशयं भगवति नेतुं यत्नं कुर्वन्नयं स्मरशरदहनदन्दह्यमानचित्तत्वादक्षमोऽयं सनिर्वेद प्रोत्थाय गृहीतशरशरासनपाणिः[१६] किमिदं कृत इति वर्तत इति सचिन्तं क्वाप्यतिष्ठत्।

5. v. Dhanañjaya Goes to Dvārakā

He took the bow and started with Kauṇḍinya. Moving north from the riverbed they saw two routes. Dhanañjaya thought:

> If I go through the right path I can reach home at the end of the term of atonement. On the other hand, if I move to the left, I will reach Dvārakā, the abode of Śrīkṛṣṇa.

Prompted by the arrows of cupid he deviated to the left.[14]
Vidūṣaka wanted to dissuade him. He exclaimed that by now, the provender provided by Draupadī has been exhausted.

> Dear friend, hear me – 'This path does not suit you. Do you suffer from hunger for want of food? Don't make yourself a laughing stalk for others.'
>
> By choosing a way deviating from the right path you have become unkind to your wife. By the journey to the left your beloved will become hostile to you. Will not the provender given to you by Pāñcālī suffice to sustain this one month?
>
> It is not proper on the part of a true friend to follow one who has chosen the wrong path. He has to be prevented by all means.

These words allegorically uttered had no effect on Dhanañjaya. Vidūṣaka pondered over this – 'He proceeds ignoring my words. Any how, I will follow him so that I can dissuade him at the proper time.

Dhanañjaya, his heart agitated by the love for Subhadrā, reached a grove for penance under the pretext of serving the ascetics. They stayed there for nearly one month. Dhanañjaya thought:

> The stay in this hermitage is not proper. I will go to some lonely place, contemplate on Govinda and know the details regarding the *gātrikā*. Hence I should leave Kauṇḍinya behind and find out a place suitable for meditation.

The route, passing by the side of the elephant-grove[15], was burning with hot sun. He proceeded through it. On the way he was honoured by Sage Kapila, Dṛḍhasyu, Pylava, Dhaumya and Vātsyāyana. Further on the way an old hermit moving slowly

---

14 Note the pun in the two words: Dakṣiṇa means right and kind to one's wife. Vāma means left, beloved, hostile etc.

15 Refers to the story narrated in the Viṣkambha.

for his mid-day bath saw him. The sage thought 'a guest has arrived. He has to be received with due hospitality. A guest should not go unattended. I will call my sons and disciples.' The sages then informed him that they had already extended due hospitality to the guest.

Dhanañjaya proceeded to Dvārakā. Inflamed by the heat of the sun he thought:

> I will meditate on Lord Kṛṣṇa who is worshipped by the Yogins. He is kind to his devotees and is capable of fulfilling my desire.

He found out a spot in the Raivataka Mountain suitable for blissful contemplation.

> This is an ideal place for meditation; all around there are auspicious trees providing cool shade and pure water. I am alone, relieved of my fatigue. Even Kauṇḍinya is not here to disturb me.

He sat there; tried to reflect on the Lord. He could not concentrate his mind as it was shattered by the arrows of cupid. He blamed himself.

> Fie upon me! Kṛṣṇa is dear to me as the very breath of my life; I am the brother of the great Dharmaputra and the son of Indra. Yet my mind is so fickle! In vain I fancy myself as brave!

His repeated attempts to remain absorbed in meditation, were futile. Kāma, the God of love was burning his heart. Depressed, he took his bow and arrow[16] and pondered over the cause of his anguish.

(Here ends the narration intended to relate the past to the present.)

16 Refers to the stage direction in the beginning.

VI
The Hero in Action

(ततः प्रविशति धनुर्बाणपाणिर्धनञ्जयः)

धनञ्जयः (सचिन्तं निःश्वस्य) अहोनुखल्वतीतेऽपि कथञ्चित् तीर्थयात्रानियमयापयितव्ये संवत्सरे ।[1]

---

1 The dramatic text begins only here. The first Act is given in three subsequent chapters – Entry of the Hero, Entry of the Jester and the Entry of the Heroine. The original dramatic text is shown in Devanāgarī script and its translation to English in italics. The Dhvani in the text emanates from the dialogue of the characters. Hence, it is given along with the running mater. Text of *VV* in Sanskrit is given in full at the end of each chapter.

The *Vyaṅgyavyākhyā* commentary has the following components:

i. **Prāveśikam**: It gives details of the entry of the characters. The actor in the costume of the character comes to the stage; stands behind the curtain. Then he looks steadily to the flames of the three wicked lamp. Then the curtain is removed. These and other details regarding the entry of the character are included in the Prāveśika.

ii. **The Sthāyibhāva**: Details regarding the mental disposition of the character at various stages are explained in the commentary. Sthāyibhāva here does not strictly mean the eight/nine permanent sentiments like *rati*. All the mental conditions come under this category. Temporary moods/ situations are also embraced by this term.

iii. **Dhvani:** It is the most important point of deliberation in *VV*. The term is used in a wider sense and embraces all that are not included in the primary meaning like kāku, vakrokti, dhvani, anyāpadeśa and allegory. There will be only primary meaning for some verses. *VV* notes that केवलार्थोऽयं ग्रन्थः। At times the character will use स्पष्टोक्ति।
Dhvani is the inner consciousness of the character which he is reluctant to share with others. He gives expression to this through movements of his eyes. Dhvani arises from the situation. On many occasions the suggested sense is intelligible only to the prekṣakas – connoisseurs.. In some cases they may appear far-fetched.

iv. **Prayogamārga**: *VV* gives the details of presentation on all occasions. The general instruction is that the primary meaning has to be presented in the ordinary way through four-fold acting for the benefit of the common audience, nānāloka. The suggested sense has to be communicated through the movement of the eyes to the prekṣaka.

v. **Narration**: Kulaśekhara's new technique of Pūrvasambandha gives ample opportunity for actors for narrations. Acting alone comes to the help of the actor. A major part of *VV* is devoted to narration.

vi. **Commentaries**: As in other commentaries *VV* also interpretes the textual portion, explains meanings and quote authorities to prove its point. It enters on elaborate discussions to justify the action of the character. The discussion on the appropriateness of fickleness of mind in a *dhīrodātta* like Dhanañjaya in the second Act can be cited as an example.

(Dhanañjaya enters holding bow and arrow)[2]

Dhanañjaya: (Sighing thoughtfully) Ah! Even though the year-long pilgrimage has already come to an end-

Vyaṅgyavyākhyā

Prāveśikam

Pitiable indeed are my deeds! I am at a loss to carry out my obligations.

Brave as I am I have seen all the beautiful objects with a mind dettached, heard all that are melodious. Yet, my mind becomes fickle.[3]

(Controls the mind and takes a long breath. Condemning his own behaviour he continues)

अहो ! Ah! How did this change come to my mind?

The alluring sidelong glances of Pāñcālī held me back when I was leaving Indraprastha. She prevented me from leaving her with words drenched in the nectar of love.

Lord! most beloved! dear one! the very life and breath of me! Please don't go, don't go.

She looked longingly as though praying with her eyes-

Don't leave me. Don't forget our enchanting mutual love when you come across other women, on your way.

When I insisted on leaving, she looked me in rancour.

Alas! What she feared has come true.

I had pledged an ascetic life during the period of pilgrimage. Yet, when I reached the Ganges, I married the daughter of the serpent king; later I enjoyed the company of the daughter of the Pāṇḍya King. Travellers who pass through different places will tell these stories among themselves and they will one day fall in the ears of Pāñcālī. She will think that what she had

---

We give, in this text the suggested sense in brief, which the actor presents through eyes as ordained by the commentator under the instructions of the dramatist. Only a hint is given regarding the inner meaning in the translation. Details are available in *VV*. This format is adopted for the benefit of the actors as also for easy understanding of the readers.

2 Translated into English by Professors NP Unni and Bruce M Sullivan.

3 Fluctuation is the mental condition of the hero at the time of entry. This is explained in the long soliloquy that follows. He condemns the fickleness of his mind, yet he is unable to control it. This continues till he meets the heroine.

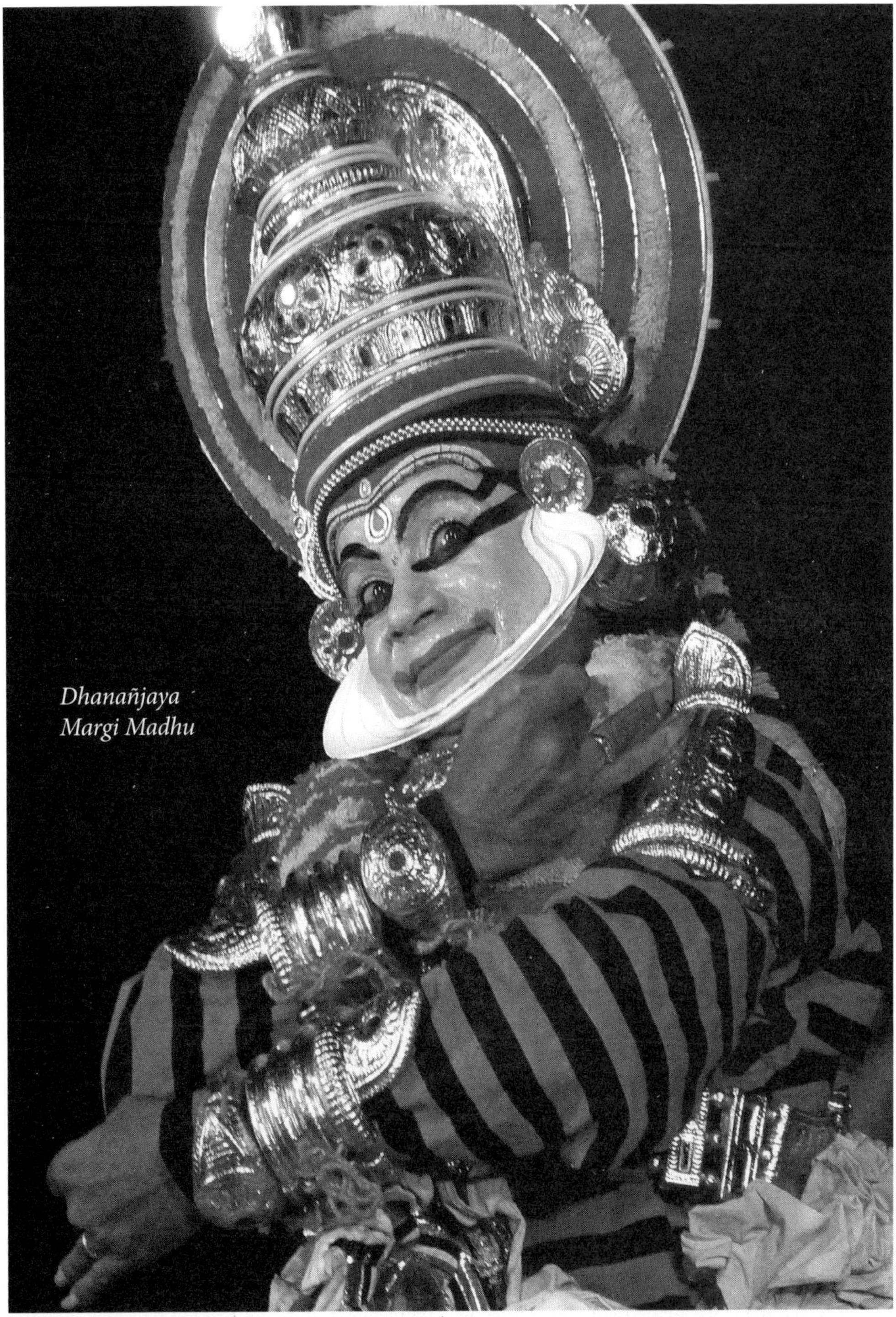

Dhanañjaya
Margi Madhu

feared has come true. In order to avoid any suspicion, I used to narrate to my friend Kauṇḍinya, in spite of his scolding me, sweet things about Pāñcālī.

Dear friend! when will I see the moonlike face of Pāñcālī?

How lovingly will she receive me when I enter the city at the end of the pilgrimage?

Somehow I completed the period of pilgrimage and reached Prabhāsatīrtha. Then having heard of Subhadrā, I became disinterested to return to Indraprastha.

The two years reserved for the two elder brothers to live with Pāñcālī are exhausted. This year, with the first month passed, is my turn to live with her.

My friend does not like my affair with Subhadrā and is reluctant to follow me to Dvārakā. It will be difficult if he returns to Indraprastha and reveals all these things to Pāñcālī.

अम्बास्तन्यमहाभिषेकमुपरि प्रेमाश्रुपातं गुरो-
रार्यस्यापि वृकोदरस्य चरणाश्लेषं यमाश्लेषणम्।
कृष्णायाश्च कटाक्षवीक्षणसुखं नासादयं, प्रापितः
पुष्पेषोर्विशिखैर्मुकुन्दसहजासन्मार्गपुष्पस्पृहाम्।। ७।।

I could not be moistened by my mother's breast-milk;
nor enjoy a loving elder brother's rain of tears;
could not touch the feet of Vṛkodara; nor enjoy the embrace of the twins,
nor experience the pleasure of Draupadī's loving glances;
instead, compelled by Kāma's flowery arrows,
I long to search for the rare flower that is the sister of Mukunda.(7)

Vyaṅgyavyākhyā

Though the period of pilgrimage is over I did not obtain these things. Moreover I have been tormented by the arrows of Cupid. Subhadrā is as unattainable as a flower in the sky.[4] Her elder brother has promised to give her to Suyodhana.

4 सन्मार्ग is svarga. Subhadrā is compared to a beautiful flower in the garden of heaven. But there is a twist in the meaning in *VV.* Sky-flower is something which is non-existing. The former denotes rarity and the latter impossibility. Śivarāma, the commentator, does not seem to be happy with the interpretation of *VV.*

The only way left to me, therefore, is to go back to Pāñcālī who is eagerly waiting for me. There is a predicament even there.

(Actor transforms himself to Pāñcālī)

As Pāñcālī:Dhanañjaya travelled a lot under the guise of pilgrimage searching for women to marry. Though he wandered everywhere he could get none and disappointed he has come back to me.

(transforming to the role of Dhanañjaya)

As Dhanañjaya:It will be difficult if Pāñcālī thinks in this way. Even then, I can pacify her falling on her feet with sweet words. But I am terribly struck by the arrows of cupid. I cannot return without getting Subhadrā. Even if I am able, somehow, to obtain Subhadrā with the help of Lord Kṛṣṇa, the response of Pāñcālī poses a greater problem.

(Actor transforms to Pāñcālī)[5]

As Pāñcālī:Dhanañjaya's pilgrimage is some how justified. In the svayamvara by a rare act of heroism he struck the arrows on the eyes of the bird amidst the rolling machine. I put the garland on his neck. He won me defeating all the heroes including Karṇa and Suyodhana. When we reached home, by the words of mother, I became destined to be shared equally by all the five brothers. After that sage Nārada prescribed the term of one year for each one. While, thus, I was living with the elder brother, Dhanañjaya, to help the Brahmin deprived of his cows, entered our room to take the bow and arrows and himself broke the terms of the agreement. Then he started for the year-long pilgrimage. I presume that pilgrimage is only a pretext and his journey actually is in search of women who will exclusively, be his own. Hence he was attracted by Subhadrā. I shall, here after, be indifferent towards him.

(transforming to Dhanañjaya)

Dhanañjaya:If Pāñcālī interprets things in this way and becomes indifferent towards me, again there is a problem.

I can, in no way, hurt her feelings because she is created for me.

When I had completed my studies in archery under Droṇācārya, I approached him and conveyed my desire to pay dakṣiṇā to him. Ācārya told me:

5 Kulaśekhara introduces here the technique of transformation of roles in Sanskrit drama.

Pārtha, if you are capable, go and bring king Drupada as dakṣiṇā for me.

I went, defeated and brought Drupada tied by arrows and offered him at the feet of my preceptor as dakṣiṇā. Later, I released the king by force. Hurt and humiliated, the king went to a Brahmin Yaja and narrated the whole thing to him. He stayed in the āśrama for many years. Yaja asked him the purpose of his prolonged stay. King said:

Give me a strong son who can exterminate Droṇa and a daughter exquisite in qualities to give to Dhanañjaya. Thus prayed, the sage granted him Dhṛṣṭadyumna and Draupadī.

The king became fond of his daughter. It grew up constantly. Hence I cannot think of humiliating Pāñcālī who is born for me.

Therefore, if I marry Subhadrā or not henceforth I will have no peace of mind. My mind is perplexed. It is oscillating between Pāñcālī and Subhadrā as though in a swing. What can I do?

Strong-minded as I am I will strive hard to achieve the object of my desire. I will take all efforts to get Subhadrā.[6]

(पुनर्विचिन्त्य सानन्दम्) अथवावञ्चित एवाहममुना कुसुमधन्वना। कुतः

व्यालोलहारमुरसा तरसा समेत्य
लक्ष्मीकुचाङ्कितमुरः परिपीडयानि।
श्च्योतन्मधूनि सुहृदश्च सखे! किरीटि-
न्नित्यक्षरणि शृणवानि जनार्दनस्य।। ८।।

(Thinking again with pleasure) But I have not been cheated by one who wields the bow of flowers (ie, Kāma). For,

I had the rare previlege
of being embraced firmly by Janārdana,
whose garlanded chest is blessed by the embrace of Lakṣmī,
and hearing the sweet words: 'O my firend, Kirīṭin!' (8)

6 The mental condition of the character from here upto the meeting of heroine is this – 'my mind will not be satisfied till I get Subhadrā'. The actor should communicate this fluctuation of his mind through eyes to the Prekṣakas.

Vyaṅgyavyākhyā

I am not duped by cupid. I observe the vital air gushing out of the left nasal cavity and entering the right cavity. I feel horripilation in the right half of my body. This, no doubt, is a promising good omen. The Lord has prompted cupid to send his arrows towards me. Hence Subhadrā whom I considered unattainable as a sky flower has become obtainable to me. Therefore I will try to win her.

> May I embrace the breasts of Subhadrā.[7]
> Definitely I will embrace her
> Oh! Lord! Let me embrace her.
> Please inform me whether I will get her or not.

(समन्तादवलोक्य) अहो महानुभावता महितमहिम्नां तपोधनानाम्। इह हि [8]

> शिखिनि शलभो ज्वालाचक्रैर्न विक्रियते पतन्
> पिबति बहुशः शार्दूलीनां स्तनं मृगशाबकः।
> स्पृशति कलभः सैंहीं दंष्ट्रां मृणालधिया मुहु-
> र्नयति नकुलं निद्रातन्द्रीं लिहन्नहिपोतकः।। ९।।

अये सर्वैरेव सस्त्रीबालैर्मुनिभिर्माद्ध्यन्दिनसवनस्नानाय प्रभासतीर्थं प्रति प्रचलितैः शून्यीकृतोऽयमाश्रमा भोगः। सखा च मे कौण्डिन्यः कौसीद्यादद्याप्यध्वनि मन्दायते। तदधुना निकषा तपोवनमवस्थितस्यास्य वटविटपिनः प्रच्छाये प्रतीक्षिष्ये वयस्यागमनम्। (प्रवेशं नाटयति)
(Looking around) How wonderful is the greatness of penance. Here,

> *Butterflies hovering over the fires are not burned;*
> *young deer often drink the breast milk of a tigress;*
> *elephant calves often smite a lion's fangs, mistaking them for lotus stalks,*
> *and a young serpent licks a lazy mongoose slowly to sleep. (9)*

All the hermits, women, and children have gone to Prabhāsatīrtha for the mid-day bath, leaving the hermitage empty. My friend Kauṇḍinya is too tired to keep pace

---

7 The first half of the verse denotes the imagined pleasure of enjoyment of Subhadrā. Second half is a prayer to Lord Kṛṣṇa. The chest of Kṛṣṇa blessed by the embrace of Lakṣmī is taken to be Dhanañjaya's own experience of embracing of Subhadrā. The लोट् is used in the sense of question and affirmation. Will I embrace? Definitely I will. Again it is used in the sense of prayer. Oh! Lord, let me embrace her.

8 This verse is elaborated on stage at present. The behaviour of animals and their life in harmony is presented in all its details. The acting extending to nearly an hour is done through eyes alone. This is the most exciting experience in Kūṭiyāṭṭaṃ. Surprisingly, *VV* is silent on this point. The absence of dhvani can be cited as the reason for the omission. Or the elaborations of discriptive verses might be improvisations of actors at a later stage.

with me on the way; hence I shall wait for his arrival, resting under the shade of this fig tree. (Enters)

Vyaṅgyavyākhyā

This place is deserted and hence suitable for meditation. I will contemplate the Lord and wait for him. My friend is late since he is not sympathetic to me in this matter.[9] To the people around I will pretend as though I am waiting for Kauṇḍinya.[10]

(नेपथ्ये)

भो भो भअवन्तो महेसिणो भिक्खं देथ भिक्खं देथ। (भो भो भगवन्तो महर्षयः! भिक्षां दत्त भिक्षां दत्त) धनञ्जयः (कर्णं दत्त्वा) अये कौण्डिन्यस्येवायं भिक्षायाचनस्वनः।

(Behind the curtain)

Oh! Oh! Mendicants, give away alms! Give away alms!
Dhanañjaya : (Listening) Ah, the sound of Kauṇḍinya begging.

Vyaṅgyavyākhyā

These words disturb my absorption in meditating the Lord. Is it a bad omen?
No. What I hear are auspicious words like bhagavān, maharṣayaḥ etc. They indicate good fortune.

Moreover the feminine gender in Bhikṣā suggests Subhadrā. The Lord, by the word Bhagavān seems to give a subtle suggestion to me to disguise as a mendicant while going to Dvārakā to achieve Subhadrā.[11]

व्यङ्ग्यव्याख्या

अथैवं धनञ्जयभूमिकालङ्कृततनुर्भरतवरो धनुर्बाणपाणिस्सचिन्तं यावत् तिष्ठेदिति तिष्ठन्[12] निजपारवश्यादितिकर्तव्यतामौढ्यं व्रजन्निति स्मरेत्[13] – धीरोदात्तत्वात् श्रोतव्यं यत् श्रुतं प्रायः द्रष्टव्यं यत् तदीक्षितम्।

9 The primary meaning of कौसीद्य is क्षुधित (hungry) and inner meaning is कार्यवामित (indifference). Kauṇḍinya is delaying as he is hungry. Suggested sense is that he is against my love for Subhadrā and hence he is delaying.

10 वयस्य is Kauṇḍinya in the general sense. Śrīkṛṣṇa also is his friend. The suggested sense is that I will wait for Kṛṣṇa and pretend to be waiting for Kauṇḍinya.

11 This suggested sense can be communicated either by the eyes or through symbolic gestures by single hand.

12 Here it is the praveśika – mode of presentation of the entry of the character.

13 स्मरेत्, अस्मरत्, अचिन्तयत् etc. are phrases used by Kulaśekhara to denote the process of विचाराभिनयः। The recollection and story line are similar to that of retrospection. But in the former, the actor was a narrator like the purānic sūta. Stress was on the incidents unfolded; here the stress is to his inner feelings. The character keeps his self.

तथाभूतेन हि मया गम्यते चित्तचापलम्। हन्त! कष्टतरा मे प्रवृत्तिरिति स्मरन् कथञ्चित् चित्तं स्थिरीकृत्या-त्मानमेवंभूतमिति मत्वा भूयोप्यात्मानं गर्हयन् स्वस्मिन् निन्दायां दीर्घनिश्वासं कुर्वन् कस्मादहमेवम्भूतस्संवृत्त इति मत्वा भूयः 'अहो' इति वदेत्। अहो इति विवेके। तत्प्रकारं दर्शयति अहो इति।
अहं पुरोदरान्निर्गच्छन् अनया प्रेयस्या पाञ्चाल्या मामनुव्रजन्त्या दीयमानया कटाक्षशृङ्खलया बद्धहृदयः पुर्येवाकृष्यमाणोऽपि कथञ्चित् शरीरादसव इव प्रतिष्ठमाने मयि सा भूयोऽपि सादरं निष्यन्दमानप्रेम्णा दृशा तदानीमिति वदन्तीवातिष्ठत्।

नाथ! प्रियतम! प्रेय! प्राणनाथाद्य वल्लभ!
कान्त! कारुण्यचित्तेश! मा याहीति मुहुर्मुहुः।।

इति वदन्तीव तिष्ठन्त्यां तस्यामेव भूयो गच्छति मयि सा भूयोऽपि दृशेत्यवदत्। तीर्थयात्रापदेशात् त्वं काञ्चित् कन्यकां प्रियसङ्गहितां प्रयास्यस्यस्मादास्तां रतिरावयोः। तद्गच्छेति दृशा वदन्तीव तिष्ठन्ती भूयः तस्यामवतिष्ठन्त्यामपि गच्छति मयि सरोषं मां पश्यन्त्यन्तःपुरं गतवतीति यत् तदिदानीं तथा संवृत्तम्। कुतः-

तपस्विधर्ममवलम्ब्य संवत्सरं तीर्थसेवी भवामीति प्रतिज्ञातवान्। तथा प्रतिज्ञातवता ततो गतवता सवयस्येनादौ भागीरथीं प्राप्तवता काचिन्नागकन्यकावापि। अथ ततो गच्छता तीर्थानि चरता द्वितीयां पाण्ड्यपतेस्सुतामपि यत् तदिदं नानादेशं गच्छद्भ्यः पान्थेभ्यः इन्द्रप्रस्थपुरवर्तिना महापथेन पर्यट द्भ्यः परस्परं नानाकथाप्रसङ्गे मदुदन्तमेवम्भूतमिति कथयद्भ्यो मदुदन्तं श्रुत्वा द्रौपद्या प्रेयस्या मया चिन्तितपूर्वमिति विमृशेत्।[14] किञ्च मयाथाकस्मात् गच्छता सदासखायं कौण्डिन्यं तत्प्रवृत्तिमेव कथयता तेनाधिक्षिप्यमाणेनापि मया तदेति सोऽवादि – सखे!

शरत्पूर्ण तुषारांशुछविराजन्मुखश्रियम्।
द्रौपदीं प्रेयसीं द्रक्ष्ये निवृत्तसमयः कदा।।
कदा नु उन्निद्रपद्माक्षी नीलकुञ्चितमूर्धजा।
पुरनिविशमानं मां सखे प्रत्युद्गमिष्यति।।

इत्यादि तत्कथामृतसुधाधारामविच्छिन्नं पायं पायं तीर्थानि चरतो मम समयवत्सरे कथञ्चिदतिक्रामति प्रभासतीर्थं प्राप्तवतः केनापि श्रावितसुभद्रोदन्तस्यातः परं यात्रा सुखप्रदा न स्यात्। कुतः –

आर्ययोर्यमकभ्रात्रोरतीता वत्सरद्वयी।[15]
मदीयेऽद्यतनेऽब्देऽपि मासमात्रमभूद्गतम्।।

अपि च

मया सह चरन्नेषः नानुगच्छेत् सुखेन माम्।
द्रौपद्यां दृढभक्तायां भक्तो ह्यच्छलमानसः।।
रुध्यमानोऽप्यहं तेन बलादागतवानिह।
सोऽद्य गत्वाथ पाञ्चालीं मदुदन्तं वदेन्न किम्।।

---

14 The thoughts here are of Draupadī, hence the direction विमृशेत्।

15 यमकयोः भ्रात्रोः आर्ययोः धर्मपुत्रभीमसेनयोः वत्सरद्वयी अतीता इति पूर्वार्धस्य अन्वयः।

इत्येदत्सर्वं विमृशन्नयं दुःखस्थचित्तत्वात् सान्तस्तापं अहो इति वदन् तिष्ठेत्। एवं नायकस्य दोलायितमनस्कत्वं द्योतयितुं 'कुत' इति शब्दः तत्र क्षिप्तवानयं कविरिति विज्ञेयम्। तस्मादहमेतादृशः संवृत्तः इत्यर्थः।

अथैवं **अहो** इति वदन् तिष्ठन्नयं एवं स्मरेत्। तथा तत्कथालापैः कथञ्चिदाश्रयमाण एषोऽहं कथञ्चित् तद्वत्सरेऽतीतेऽपि एतानि नासादयमिति सम्बन्धः। अपि च **पुष्पेषोर्विशिखैर्मुकुन्द-सहजासन्मार्गपुष्पस्पृहां** प्रापितश्च। सन्मार्गपुष्पस्पृहामिति – सन्मार्गं खम्। तज्जं पुष्पं खपुष्पम्। तदुत्पन्नां स्पृहामित्यर्थः। अविद्यमाने वस्तुनि असाध्यपुष्पस्पृहामित्यर्थः। असाध्यायां सुभद्रायां स्पृहां शुद्धां प्रापितः सुयोधनाय दातुं तत्प्रदानकर्त्रा सीरिणा कल्पिता सा अस्मदसाध्या हि। तस्यां स्पृहा खपुष्पस्पृहैव।

तर्हि अन्यविरक्तो भूत्वा सत्वरमस्मद्वरप्राप्तिकृतदीक्षां पाञ्चालीमेव गच्छेयं ननु। अत्रापि दोषः स्यात्। कुतः। तत्रेति तया स्मर्तव्यम्।[16]

असौ तीर्थयात्राव्यपदेशेनास्माद्यदानिर्गतवान् तदा प्रभृति इतरपरिग्रहाकांक्षी सञ्चरिष्णुः। तत्कृतपरिश्रमोऽपि कर्माभावात् तदप्राप्तौ दैवमेव प्रमाणं पुरुषपरिश्रमे इति मत्वापि अफलीभूतमनोरथो अस्मिन्नेव साम्प्रतं सम्प्राप्तवानिति। एवं स्मरन्त्या पाञ्चाल्या मन्तव्यो भवेयम्। तस्मादत्र हि दोषः स्यात्।[17]

तथापि पादप्रणामादिशपथैः उत्तमस्त्रीत्वात् विश्वासिता सा भवेदिति तत्परीक्षितुमपि शक्यते। इमामदृष्ट्वैव मास्मादन्यत्र पदं गन्तुं मां पुष्पेषुरेष रुणद्धि। तत्कीदृशी मे यात्रा। एवं स्मरन् तिष्ठन्नयमिति विमृशेत्।

अथवा कृष्णप्रसादात् येनकेनाप्युपायान्तरेण सा साध्या यदि तत्रापि दोषः। कुतः? तयेति स्मार्यम्।[18] अहो अस्य तीर्थयात्रा सहेतुका मन्ये। पुरास्मदीये स्वयंवरेऽनन्यसाध्यं परिभ्रमणयन्त्रं जित्वा मत्प्रक्षिप्तमालोऽयं तत्र प्राप्तान् कर्णसुयोधनादीनपि राज्ञो विजित्य प्रसह्य मां कुलालवेश्म प्रापितवति तस्मिन् गुरुवचनगौरवं[19] समर्थयता मुनिवचने[20] नाहं तैः पञ्चभिः समं परिग्रहीता भवामीति यत् ततोऽहम् इतरपरिग्रहाकांक्षी आसीदिति किञ्च ततोऽन्येन मुनिना कृतसङ्केतां दशां प्रापितास्मि। ततः कृतसङ्केतायां यथाक्रमं राज्ञानुभुज्यमानायामपि क्षत्रधर्मतश्चापमाहृत्य सत्राणं कृत्वा भिन्नमर्यादोऽहमिति तीर्थयात्राभिमुखो गच्छामीति निर्गच्छन्तं मामार्येण तया च गृहीतपाणिः निरुद्धोऽस्मीति यत् ततोऽहं मद्वशगामिनीं काञ्चित् कन्यां परिग्राह्य यथेष्टं सुखीभवामीति मत्वैष सम्प्रति तथा सम्प्राप्त इति मन्यमानया तया मयि औदासीन्यमाचरितव्यं हि। तथा कृतमिति चेत् तत्रापि दोषः। कुतः?

पुरा गृहीतधनुर्वेदेन गुरुदक्षिणां कर्तुकामेन मया गुर्वन्तिकं सम्प्राप्य गुरुदक्षिणां दातुकामोऽयमिति विज्ञापितेऽयं द्रोणाचार्य[21] इति मामवदत्

यदि पार्थ समर्थोऽसि कुरुषे यदि दक्षिणाम्।
पाञ्चालाधिपमाबध्य द्रुपदं प्रापयाशु माम्।।

---

16 यथा सा पाञ्चाली स्मरति तथा तेन नटेन स्मर्तव्यम्, नार्जुनेन।

17 चिन्तेयमर्जुनस्य।

18 तथा पाञ्चाल्या, धनञ्जयभूमिकां स्वीकृतवता नटेन पाञ्चालीति आत्मानं विभाव्य नटनीयम्।

19 Kuntī directed all the five sons to share the Bhikṣā.

20 Refers to the arrangements made by Nārada for their living with Draupadī.

21 Actor transforms to Droṇācārya. Droṇa and Drupada were classmates. Later when Drupada became king, he insulted Droṇa. Thenceforth he was waiting for an opportunity for revenge.

इत्युक्तेन मयापि जिताखिलनरेशं ज्यायाबध्यबाहुं मद्गुर्वन्तिकं प्रापय्य गुरुदक्षिणेन मया बलात् स मोचितोऽभूत्। ततस्तस्मात् मुक्तोऽयं व्रीलया.. निरीक्षितस्वजनमुखः स्वपुरं गत्वा तेनैव पथैव गत्वा याजाख्यं द्विजवरं प्राप्य कथितनिजवृत्तान्तः तस्मिन्नेव वसन् बहुवत्सरान् नीत्वासीनोऽयं किमर्थमिहस्थः निवससीति मुनिना पृष्टेन तेनेत्युक्तम्[22]

> द्रोणहन्ता बली पुत्रो दीयतां भवता मम।
> प्रदातुमर्जुनायैका कन्या वाप्रतिमा भुवि।।
> इति प्रलपते तस्मै यजमाने मुनीश्वरः।
> पुत्रं पुत्रीं च मे दातुं स च यद्दत्तवान् पुरा।।

ततस्तदानीमेव तेनास्मदर्थं जनितायां तस्यां बद्धस्नेहोऽभवत्। अन्वहं वर्धमानप्रेम चाभवम्। कदाचिदपि नापमन्तव्या नाम। तस्मात् करग्रहे तदभावे चोभयत्राप्यद्यप्रभृति तत्कृत्यता मे न स्यात् हि इत्यादि दीपाग्रे तिष्ठन् अभिनयेन दृग्भ्यां सह प्रेक्षकान् ससुखयेत्।[23]

> एतावानस्य श्लोकस्य सम्बन्धः; प्रयोगमार्गश्च।।

अथ नायकस्यातः परं स्थायिभावो दृश्यते।[24] अस्मात्प्रभृत्यानायिकादर्शनादस्याः प्राप्तौ च मन्मनस्सौख्यं न स्यादिति दृशोर्दर्शयता नायकेन प्रयोगः क्रियताम्। अथैवमुभयथा न मे सौख्यमिति दृशोर्दर्शयंस्तिष्ठन्नयं डोलायितमनस्कतयेतिकर्तव्यतामजानंस्तिष्ठेत्।

तथा तिष्ठन्नपि धीरोदात्तत्वात् तत्कालौचित्यमिति स्मरेत्। कुतः सर्वथाहमेतत्प्राप्तेरेतादृशः संवृत्तः। अतस्तत्र प्रवर्तितव्यम्।

> कृतयत्नो भवेद्विद्वान् सत्कर्मणि विशेषतः।
> अभ्यर्थयन् सदा देवं साधयेत् तस्य तच्च तत्।।

इत्यस्ति गुरुवचनम्। अतस्तस्यां यत्नकारी। एवं सविमर्शं तिष्ठतोऽस्य वामाद् घोणरन्ध्रात् दक्षिणे रन्ध्रे सङ्क्रान्तोऽभूदन्तर्वर्ती देवः।[25]

पुनर्विभाव्य। अथ स्वनासाद् दक्षिणरन्ध्रं गच्छन्तं देवं दृष्ट्वा तद्विभावयेत्। एतदर्थं पुनर्विभाव्येति पदं तत्र क्षिप्तवान् स कविः। ततस्तथाभूतं देवं प्रतिपालयन् यदा तिष्ठति तदानीमेव स्वदेहांशं दक्षिणार्धं रोमात् निरगात्। तथाभूतं स्वदेहार्धं दृष्ट्वा अस्मत्कार्यसिद्धिर्भवितेति नितरामानन्ददर्शनात् तदर्थमतःपरं ग्रन्थं सानन्दमुत्तरग्रन्थं वदति।

---

22 Actor transforms to Drupada. He becomes grateful to Arjuna because he did not allow his preceptor to inflict more insults on him.

23 The mode of presentation prescribed is four-fold acting. Verbal rendering is confined to textual parts. For independent narration bodily movements are primarily used. Eyes communicate the suggested sense.

24 The mental condition is that of fluctuation till he meets the heroine in the latter part of the Act.

25 This is an auspicious omen not found in the dramatic text.

सानन्दम्। अथवा इत्यादि। अथैवं तिष्ठन्। सानन्दं विमृशति। **अथवा** कुसुमधन्वना अवञ्चित एवास्मि। **कथमि**ति। कथं ज्ञायते इति चेत् अमुना श्वासानुकूल्येन अथवा प्रत्युत अन्यथा कल्पितवानस्मि। दैवप्रेरितेन कुसुमधन्वना प्रापितोऽस्मीति मन्यमानोऽहं स एव साध्व्यायां तस्यामेव स्पृहां प्राप्तोस्मीत्यमुना श्वासानुकूल्येन भावितवानस्मि इति भावः। तस्मात् तत्प्राप्तेरहं प्रवर्तितव्य इति निश्चित्य स्वानुभवार्थमागामिनः कार्यस्यावस्थां स्वया धिया विमृशन् स्थाणुवदास्थाय चित्तं स्वमुत्तरश्लोकेन रमयति। तत्र पूर्वार्धेन सुभद्रालिङ्गनं मम भवेदिति विमृशति। अपरार्धेन भगवदागमनं चेत्युत्तरश्लोकं विवक्षुस्तिष्ठन् इति स्मरेत्।

इतस्ततः सञ्चरद्भिर्यतिभिः स्थाणुवत्तिष्ठन्नहं नापहास्ये किम्? तस्मादयं भगवद्दर्शनाय भगवदागमनं प्रतिपालयामीति मुनीन् विभावयामीति निश्चित्य तत्समर्थयितुं श्लोकस्य पूर्वार्धं ध्वनियुक्तं वदति **व्यालोलहारमि**ति।

तत्र ध्वनिर्दृश्यते – अहं तरसा लक्ष्मीकुचाङ्कितमुरः उरसा परिपीडयानि इति सम्बन्धः। लक्ष्मीकुचाङ्कितमिति – लक्ष्म्या श्रिया शोभया युक्ताभ्यां अङ्कितं मुद्रितं तथाभूतं सुभद्रायाः उरः मदीयेनोरसा परिपीडयानि। कथमिति चेत्, व्यालोलहारं निर्दयमाश्लिष्य परिपीडयानि। तत्र लोडादौ सम्प्रश्ने; पुनः सम्प्रधारणं गाढाश्लेषं करोम्येवेत्यर्थः। भूयः प्रार्थने च, हे भगवन् तस्या उरः परिपीडयानि, तद्भर्ता भवेयमिति भावः। एवं तदभ्यर्थनं कृत्वा भूयो भगवद्दर्शनं भगवन्तं प्रार्थयति। हे भगवन् अत्र पुण्यस्थले क्वापि स्थित्वा भगवद्ध्यानपरे मयि सत्वरमभ्येत्य 'सखे किरीटिन्' इति त्वन्मुखोदरान्निस्सरन्त्यक्षराणि शृणवानि। तत्र लोट् प्रश्नप्रार्थनयोः। त्वन्मुखात् यानि निस्सरन्ति तानि अक्षराणि नाशशून्यानि शृणवानि तस्मादत्राभ्येत्य सुभद्राप्राप्तिः कर्तव्या न वेति मां विज्ञापयेत्यर्थः इति ध्वनिं दृशोर्विभावयन् बाह्यार्थेन नानालोकान् सुखयेत्। एवमस्य प्रयोगमार्गः इति।[26]

अत्र श्लोके वक्ष्यमाणदैवानुकूल्यं तव भवतीति द्योतयन्तीं निश्वासप्रवृत्तिं यदा दृष्टवान् तदा तद्धतयाकरसंस्कारं कृतः समन्तादवलोक्य अथैवं नयनप्रीतिदशातः तद्दर्शनेच्छुरपि नायकभेदात् स्वयमेव तत्कालोचितं ज्ञात्वा स च इति स्मरेत्। अत्र भगवद्ध्यानक्षमं प्रदेशमन्विष्य दृष्ट्वा तत्रास्थाय भगवद्ध्यानं कृत्वा तमत्र प्रापय्य तेन सह निरूप्यमिति निश्चित्य तद्ध्यानक्षमं प्रदेशमन्वेष्टुं समन्तादवलोकितवान्। एतदर्थं तस्यावलोकनम्। एवं पश्यन् कञ्चित्प्रदेशं अद्भुतं दृष्ट्वा सर्गान्योन्यस्यावैरिणां प्राणिनां साङ्कर्यं तद्ध्यानक्षमोऽयं तद्देश इति निश्चित्य भूयः एवं स्मरेत्।

सद्वृक्षविततच्छाये नीरवे गतमक्षिके।
सतीर्थे शीतले देशे स्थित्वा योगं समाश्रयेत्।।

इत्यस्ति योगशास्त्रे। योगक्षमो देशः प्रदर्शितः। ततः तथाभूतत्वादेष योगक्षम इति निश्चित्य तिष्ठेत्। पुनर्विलोक्य अथायमेवं तिष्ठन् अमुष्य शान्ततां पश्यन् अत्र कोऽपि नास्ति किमिति परिच्छेत्तुं पुनरपि विलोकितवान्। एवं विलोक्य शून्यीकृतोऽयमाश्रमभाग इति मत्वोत्तरग्रन्थेन तत्समर्थयति तत्कथमिति चेत्

26 Suggested sense is communicated through eyes to the elite and the outer sense by normal acting to the ordinary people. That is the mode of presentation followed through out.

शून्ये मनोहरे देशे क्षुद्रजन्तुविवर्जिते।
पूते कुहरसंयुक्ते योगी योगं समाचरेत्।।

इतीमं श्लोकार्थं विमर्शयन् शून्यीकृतोऽयं देशः अतोऽस्मिन् स्थित्वा तद्ध्यानपरो भवामीति निश्चित्य पश्यन्नयं स्वनर्मसचिवमप्यदृष्ट्वा चेति स्मरेत्। अत्र लताकुञ्जकुहरे गजोपेतो कश्चिद्वा क्वचिद्वासीने मयि ध्यानपरे मत्प्रवृत्तिं न पश्येत् किं तस्माद् ध्वनियुक्तेन वचनेन स्वनर्मसचिवं कौण्डिन्यं प्रतिपालयन्नेष तिष्ठतीति तान् विभावयेयमिति निश्चित्य तथोत्तरग्रन्थेन समर्थयति **सख**यित्यादिना। कौसीद्यात् इति ध्वनितेऽर्थे मनाक् पूर्वमेतं यस्स इति ध्वनिः।

कुसीदशब्द एषोऽत्र क्षुधिते जामितान्विते।
निश्वास्ये वृत्तिहीने च वर्तते कार्यवामिनि।।

ध्वनौ कार्यवामित्वादित्यर्थः। अन्यत्र क्षुधितत्वादिति। इति निश्चित्य तिष्ठन्निति स्मरेत्। अहमिदानीमत्र वृक्षच्छायायां स्थित्वा स्ववयस्यं कौण्डिन्यं प्रतिपालयत्ययमिति युवमुनीन् विश्वासयामीति निश्चित्येति स्मरेत्। तस्मात् तदागमनात् प्रागेव अस्मिन्नासीनोऽहं कौण्डिन्यच्छलेन प्रतीक्षिष्ये। वयस्यागमनं यावदहमत्र स्थित्वा वयस्यशब्देन कौण्डिन्यं विभावयन्नात्मना कृष्णं ध्यात्वा तद्ध्यानार्थं निमीलितचक्षुः तिष्ठन् सादं विभावयन्नत्र तिष्ठेदिति भगवति चित्तं प्रापयन् तिष्ठेत्। (नेपथ्ये भो भ अवंतो महेषिणो भिखिं देथ)

धनञ्जयः (कर्णं दत्वा) **अये** इति। अथ धनञ्जय इति स्मरेत्। अये इति विवेके। तत्प्रकारं दर्शयति अये मयि भगवति चित्तं नीयमाने तत्प्रतिवचनेन प्रतिहतमासीदिति यत् तदसाध्यं वा साध्यं वेदमिति कथं निर्धार्यते। तद्वचनगत्या विमृशामि इति निश्चित्य तद्वचनगतिं विमृशति **भो भगवन्तो महर्षिणः भिक्षां दिशतु** इत्यनेनोक्तम्। अनेन तद्ध्यानविहतिरभूत्। कुत इति चेत् पश्य

कार्यारम्भे स्मरेद् देही मनसेष्टं स्वदैवतम्।
यायादवहितं तच्चेत् ततः सिद्ध्येदमुष्य हि।।

इत्यस्ति गौरवं वचः। तद्दर्शनादसाध्यमित्यूह्यम्। किञ्च

शुभेन शुभया वाचा कर्मणा येन केनचित्।
क्रियते ध्यानविघ्नञ्चेत् तत्ततोऽन्यत्र सिध्यति।।

इति चास्ति। मय्यस्मिन् भगवति मनो नीयमाने कौण्डिन्येन भिक्षामहर्षिशब्दाभ्यां मन्मनोविहतिः क्रियत इति यत् तदस्मादन्यत्र ध्यानपरे मयि साध्यमिदमित्यूह्यम्। तत्र गत्वा स्थितवति मयि तद्दर्शनाप्तिर्भवेदि त्यूह्यम्। किञ्च भिक्षाभगवच्छब्दाभ्यां भिक्षेति स्त्रीलिङ्गनिर्देशात्[27] भगवन्त इति सम्बोधनाच्च तस्या दर्शनं प्राप्तिश्च स्यादित्यूह्यम्। पुनरपि स्मरन् – किञ्च सम्प्रति मे प्रतिभाति विप्रवाक्यं जनार्दन इति

27 The word bhikṣā is highly significant in the context of suggestive signification. Kulaśekhara uses the metaphor of alms later in the text as Kumārībhikṣā. The meaning is plain here. Vidūṣaka highlights the signification of the feminine gender more than once. Draupadī herself was being refered to as bhikṣā earlier.
Bhikṣā prayed by Vidūṣaka, suggesting Subhadrā has become the key-notion in this context.

तत् भगवच्छब्देन भवान् सन्यासवेषधारी भूत्वा तद्ध्यानपरो भवेदिति दैवेन दर्शितमित्यूह्यम्। तद् भगवद्ध्यानपरे मयि भगवानत्राभ्येत्य मम तत्प्राप्तेरुपायं दर्शयिष्यतीति सूचितम्। मे तच्छब्देनेत्येतावानयेति शब्दस्यार्थः। एवं द्योतयितुं सः कविः भगवद्भिक्षाशब्दौ विदूषकान्निरगमयत् इत्यादि सर्वं **अं य भ अवन्तो** इत्यादिना ग्रन्थेन निश्चिन्वानः तत्र तिष्ठेदिति इममर्थं दृग्भ्यां वा पाणिनैकेन वा प्रेक्षकान् बोधयित्वा अन्येन नानालोकान् सुखयेत्। इत्येतावतो ग्रन्थस्य प्रयोगमार्गः।।

VII
Entry of the Jester

(ततः प्रविशति श्रमालसो विदूषको भिक्षापात्रहस्तः)

(A tired Vidūṣaka enters holding a begging bowl)

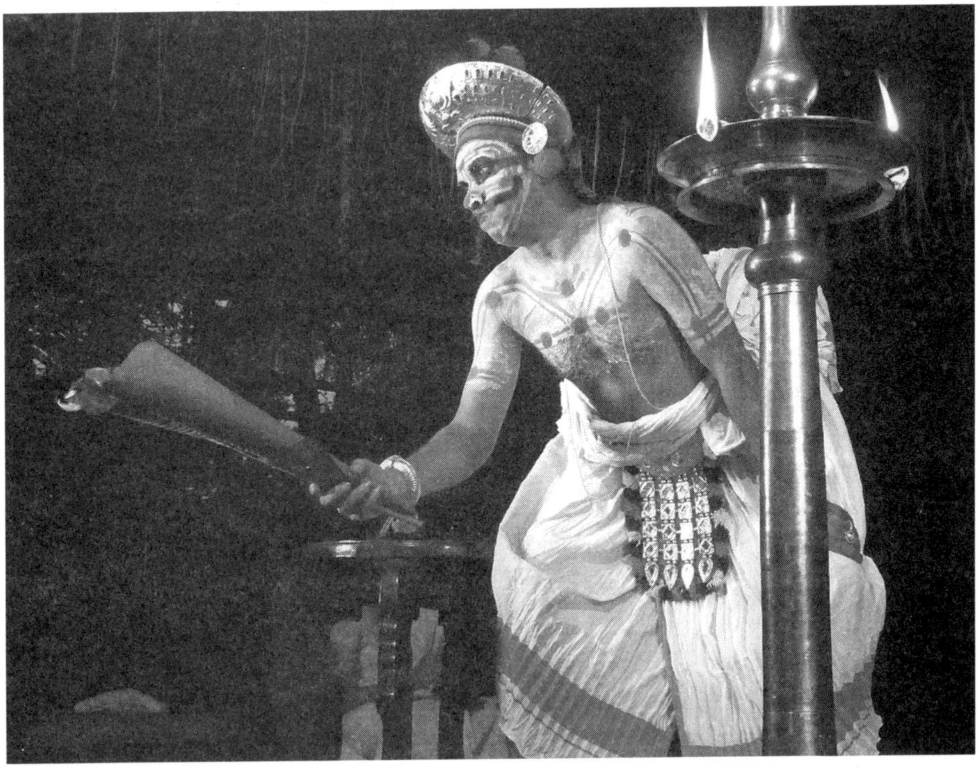

Vidūṣaka (Bho Bho Bhayavanto), Margi Madhu Chakyar

Vyaṅgyavyākhyā

Pūrvasambandha

Vidūṣaka is a pious Brahmin who has undergone all the sixteen ceremonies prescribed for true Brahmins. He comes from a distant village[1] to Hastinapura and befriended the Pāṇḍavas, especially Dhanañjaya and lived in the palace. He was fond of Draupadī who treated him lavishly with sweet dishes. One day he saw his friend Dhanañjaya going out of the city for a pilgrimage. Pāñcālī, thinking that a warrior should be accompanied by a Brahmin who can prevent him from going astray[2], encouraged Kauṇḍinya to accompany Dhanañjaya. They travelled through holy places. At the end of the year, they were eager to return to Indraprastha. Meanwhile Gada came and informed Dhanañjaya about the qualities of Subhadrā. Hearing this, he became fascinated by love towards Subhadrā. Then, instead of moving to Indraprastha, he started to Dvārakā.

> I was worried. I understood that the provender provided by Pāñcālī is exhausted. How can one move about without food? In spite of my strong objection, he moved towards Dvārakā and reached the hermitages near Prabhāsatīrtha. I followed him reluctantly with the intention of dissuading him from his infatuation towards Subhadrā.
>
> He stayed with the sages for about one month. One day, after finishing the daily rituals, he was deeply immersed in some thought. I understood that he is frustrated and is thinking to leave the hermitage. Throwing away the sumptuous meal at hand, he goes begging. He is courting the life of ascetics wandering here and there disregarding his beloved who is the real fortune of his household. I followed him determined to dissuade him from his infatuations.

---

1 Epic characters like Dhanañjaya have a past history to narrate in their Pūrvasambandha. But Vidūṣaka does not have anything like that. Hence the actor has to invent a history for him. Here the commentator simply says that he came from a village to the capital. Depending on this cue of native village the actors created a past for the jester. Accordingly he belonged to a village of illiterates, Anadhītimaṅgala. The Villagers could not follow the prescriptions for attaining the four Puruṣārthas of *dharma*, *artha*, *kāma* and *mokṣa*. So they found out parodies for Puruṣārthas. This artificial antecedents attributed to the Vidūṣaka shifts from the textual context to the local atmosphere of a true Kerala village. See chapter 19, V.

2 She sends Kauṇḍinya deliberately as a precaution to keep Dhanañjaya away from the company of other women.

No sage is seen around, this is a lonely place. I will tell him directly, in clear words, to give up his unfounded fascination for the object which he is not going to attain.

You boast Indra to be your protector, but put on your foot carefully like a silkworm lest you shall reach the fate of birds shot down.

Remember the popular saying – Don't apply sandal paste to the feet first hearing the cloud's first thunder. Rainy season is the time for union. Don't be in a hurry. You have only heard of Subhadrā, nothing more.

If some one overhears my words, it will undermine his stature as a brave warrior. Hence, I will convey my intention through suggestive words. I will tell him that he is now begging for the impossible. This, I will convey by a device. I will pretend as begging alms from the sages.

भो भो भगवन्तो महर्षयः ! भिक्षां दत्त भिक्षां दत्त !
Oh! mendicants give away alms.[3]

Vyaṅgyavyākhyā

O! Lord Kṛṣṇa! If, by unavoidable fate, Dhanañjaya somehow attains Subhadrā, please do it in such a way that she lives in harmony with Pāñcālī.

Oh! Respected sages! confer your blessings on Subhadrā.

Where has he gone alone, leaving me. Oh! he is immersed in meditation. The word bhikṣā uttered by me, seems to have disturbed the mind of Dhanañjaya. I will tell him in disguise, that he is dreaming the impossible.

This journey, prompted by Gada, forgetting Draupadī is through the bye-ways hot with the rays of sun. It, will definitely make you sad. You will become the object of the anger of Suyodhana to whom Balabhadra has promised to give her in marriage. You will be shattered by the rays of the burning sun. Please keep away from this path.

(Dhanañjaya, though understood the implied sense, remains unmoved.)

---

3 Kauṇḍinya is quite satirical in his narration here. His intention is to ridicule Dhanañjaya. The emptiness of the hermitage according to him suggests the futility of all his efforts to find out other women exclusively devoted to him.
तपोवनं – तपसे वनम्। Primary meaning of वनं is कानन (forest). Suggested sense is आश्रय (dependent).

He fully relies on Lord Kṛṣṇa for the accomplishment of his love. But Kṛṣṇa keeps no fondness for him. It is evident from the Lord's inaction in this matter. He has not yet appeared before Dhanañjaya in spite of his continuous meditation.

Alas! my friend now is in the pitiable position of Triśaṅku. He has left Pāñcālī, but did not reach Subhadrā.

The greatness of cupid! My friend is unmoved by my words. I will some how continue to dissuade him.

अहो शून्यानि सर्वाण्युटजाभ्यन्तराणि।
Oh! The whole of the hermitage seems to be deserted.[4]

Vyaṅgyavyākhyā

All the hermitage seem to be deserted. You started under the pretext of pilgrimage in search of other women who will, exclusively be devoted to you since Pāñcālī's devotion was divided among the five brothers.

You reached the banks of the sacred Ganges which removes the sin of all the beings.

How pity it was! There you enjoyed the company of a nāga-girl emitting poison. She does not deserve to be approached by noble men for cohabitation. Yet you did it. By ill-fate she was devoid of children. Immediately on getting a son she kicked you out! After that you approached king Pāṇḍya and without shame, begged for his daughter of inferior birth, not suitable for a person like you. Reluctantly he gave her for enjoyment for a short while. After two three days you desired to run away with her. But the Pāṇḍya King who was afraid of the wrath of Pāñcālī, did not permit it. Humiliated you left the Pāṇḍyas. Now you go to Dvārakā to get Subhadrā. She also will be out of your reach.

Hence your entry to the many homes seeking women, proved futile. All the houses seemed deserted for you.

अहो अधन्यस्य ममोदरभागधेयस्य प्रभावः, यो नित्यसन्निहिततपोधनमपि तपोवनं शून्यं करोति। अथवा ममैवेष दोषः, येन तत्र युधिष्ठिरमन्दिरे चतुर्विधमाहारजातमष्टाशीतिसहस्राणां स्नातकानां मध्ये निष्कपात्रेष्वनुपभुज्यैतस्य सव्यसाचिनस्तीर्थयात्राकामुकस्य पृष्ठत आहिण्ड्यते।

4 The external meaning is Vidūṣaka's misfortune. What is suggested is the misfortune of Dhanañjaya. He communicates it through eyes.

What a pity! Such is the state of my poor stomach, that this hermitage is empty though usually it is full of hermits. Perhaps it is my own fault. He who used to enjoy the four-course meals supplied by Yājñasenī in golden vessels in the company of 88,000 young Brahmins in Yudhiṣṭhira's house is now roaming about behind the left-handed archer who has set out on a pilgrimage.

Vyaṅgyavyākhyā

For both of us Dhanañjaya and me, this has become a difficult situation. Whether he gets Subhadrā or not, in both ways I will have to suffer. Pāñcālī will be angry with me.

You too miss your fortunes! Though Pāñcālī resides with Yudhiṣṭhira and is shared by other brothers she is particularly attached to you. You miss the sexual feast accompanied by the four kinds of dishes of kissing, embracing, sweet words and infatuation offered by Pāñcālī.[5]

अत्र पुनस्तपोवन आहारस्य कथापि नासाद्यते। तद् जलाशयमन्विष्य पिपासामात्रस्यापि तावत् परिहारं करिष्यामि। एष समुद्रप्रमाणो जलराशिर्दृश्यते। अत्र गत्वा यावन्मनोरथं पानीयं पास्यामि।

And here in this hermitage there is no question of getting any food. Hence I shall search for a pond to quench my thirst. (Turning around and looking ahead) Here I see enough water for an ocean. I'll go there and drink as much as I like. (Approaches in haste)

Vyaṅgyavyākhyā

The Lord did not appear, in spite of your meditation, to say that Subhadrā will be given to you. Your attaining Subhadrā is like my getting water from mirage to quench my thirst.

धनञ्जयः कष्टमसौ मृगतृष्णिकया समाकृष्यते तपस्वी। तदेनं निवारयामि। सखे! कौण्डिन्य! मा मा व्यर्थपरिश्रमो भूः। इतस्तावदागम्यताम्।

Dhanañjaya: *What a pity! This naive fellow is being attracted by a mirage. So I shall stop him. O friend, Kauṇḍinya! Don't waste your time. Please come over here.*

Vyaṅgyavyākhyā

Kauṇḍinya thinks that Subhadrā is unattainable like a mirage. Poor fellow does not know the powers of my friend Kṛṣṇa.

5 The four-fold dishes of the feast of Pāñcālī are kissing, embracing, sweet words and the infatuation caused by sexual union.

विदूषकः (विलोक्य) कहं वअस्सो मं णिवारेदि। (ससंरम्भम्) भो पत्थ! तित्थपिसळल! कीस अहं तिण्हादाहदट्ठाए जीहाए तिहाअमत्तसेसं एदस्सिं जळासए अप्पायअंतो तुए णिवारिदो। (कथं वयस्यो मां निवारयति! भोः पार्थ! तीर्थपिशाच! कस्मादहं तृष्णादाहदग्ध जिह्वाया स्त्रिभागशेषमस्मिन् जलाशये आप्यcraft्यायंस्त्वरया निवारितः।)

Vidūṣaka : (Looking) What! It is my friend who stops me. (Hastily) O Pārtha! Pilgrimage addict! Why do you prevent me from plunging at least attraction of my thirst-scorched tongue into the waters of this lake?

Vyaṅgyavyākhyā

You were eager to return to Pāñcālī. Only one third of the route remains to reach Indraprastha. Then you heard of Subhadrā. You rely on the Lord and became addicted to Tīrtha.

धनञ्जयः मूर्ख! नैष जलराशिः। पश्य

ज्वलदवनिभिरातपावलेपैरतिजडनेत्रमरीचिरंशुभर्तुः।
उपचितबहलप्रतापशक्तीनुदकमयानभिमन्यसे मरीचीन्।। १०।।

Dhanañjaya : You fool! This is not a lake. See,

Here the earth is parched by the sun's hot rays so that the eye cannot see, thus one misperceives a mirage. (10)

Vyaṅgyavyākhyā

You wrongly take that the mind of God is unsteady. It is not your fault that you do not know the greatness of the Lord. You are, by ignorance unable to understand him.

विदूषकः (संप्रधार्य) एव्वं एदं। भो ण एसा केवलं मिअतिण्हिआ, अज्जप्पहुदि बह्मणतिण्हिआ वि संवुत्ता। किं एदिणा। तुवं दाव मारुइसोदरोपेसळजङ्घाबळो तिच उरेहि पदक्खेवेहि अहिमदं देसं पाविदुं पारेसि। अहं पुण दुब्बणपादसञ्चारो णिञ्चबुभुक्खिओ जोळणजाळुग्गारिहि तरणिइरणेहि दूमिओ तत्तपंसुपडले मग्गे भूळदाविसेसो विअ इदोतदो ळुढन्तो कहं कहं वि आअदो। ता पुणो वि जलासअं अण्णोसामि।

Vidūṣaka : (Realising) Yes! It is so.

Vyaṅgyavyākhyā

My friend is confident that he will win Subhadrā by the blessing of Lord Kṛṣṇa.

For great men, the authority is their own inner consciousness. So this object of desire is attainable by the grace of God. Hence I will also help my friend to fulfil his desire. I will convey my consent to him.

भो नैषा केवलं मृगतृष्णिका, अद्य प्रभृति ब्राह्मणतृष्णिकापि संवृत्ता।[6]
This is not only a deer-deceiver but hereafter it may be called Brahmin-deceiver too.

Vyaṅgyavyākhyā

> Oh! my friend. You believe that the Lord will give you Subhadrā. So hereafter she is attainable to you. No more she is a mirage. Till now she was a mṛgatṛṣṇa. Here after she has become a Brāhmaṇatṛṣṇikā too – an object this Brahmin wishes to attain for his friend. Hence forth I will help you.

किमेतेन ! त्वं तावन्मारुतिसोदरः पेशलजङ्घाबलस्त्रिचतुरैः पदक्षेपैरभिमतं देशं प्राप्तुं पारयसि।
Away with it! You can reach your destination by moving a few steps forward, since as the brother of Māruti you have strong muscles.

Vyaṅgyavyākhyā

> You contemplate the Lord by hymns consisting of three or four syllables and enter into the mind of Kṛṣṇa.[7]

(He looks to the face of Dhanañjaya and concludes that Dhanañjaya is pleased)[8]

Dhanañjaya: I am unable to concentrate here as there are sages all around.

Vidūṣaka: Move to a deserted place with three or four steps away and meditate the Lord. He will appear and bless you.

Dhanañjaya: Dear friend be favourable to me hereafter.

Vidūṣaka: If I favour him or discourage him – my position in both ways is tricky. If I encourage him Pāñcālī will be angry with me. She will no more treat me with sweet dishes. If on the contrary, I oppose him it will be against his wishes.
Any how from now onwards I will be favourable to Dhanañjaya.
Some how I will console Pāñcālī later.

अहं पुनः दुर्बलपादसञ्चारो नित्यबुभुक्षितो ज्वलनज्वालोद्गारिभिस्तरणिकिरणैस्तप्तपांसुपटले मार्गे भूलताविशेष इवेतस्ततो लुठन् कथं कथमप्यागतः।
But I have only weak legs and, always hungry, totter about these dusty roads parched by the sun's hot rays like a vine dangling back and forth, though I have somehow reached here.

---

6 Brāhmaṇatṛṣṇikā, covetable to a Brahmin, is a new coinage on the analogy of mṛgatṛṣṇikā.

7 अभिमत denotes Kṛṣṇa and देश means mind. You reach the mind of the Lord. Meditate upon the Lord.

8 Vidūṣaka's Prayogamārga when he knows that Dhanañjaya is pleased is this: Moves around the stage murmuring something with eyes fixed on the Prekṣakas.

Vyaṅgyavyākhyā

I will be burned by the rays of anger of Pāñcālī.[9] On behalf of the excessive love[10] towards you I have become timid and fickle towards Pāñcālī.

तत् पुनरपि जलाशयमन्विष्यामि।
So I'll search again for a lake.

Vyaṅgyavyākhyā

Is there any other way I can go?

(परिक्रामन्नूर्ध्वमवलोक्य) भो वअस्स! पेक्ख पेक्ख! अच्छेरं अच्छेरं। एसो को वि अआलजलधरो अक्कन्दन्तीं कं पि अपुव्वं अइरप्पहं उच्छङ्गे करिअ धावेइ। (एवमेतत्।)

भो वयस्य। पश्य पश्य। आश्चर्यमाश्चर्यम्। एष कोऽप्यकालजलधर आक्रन्दन्तीं कामप्यपूर्वामचिर प्रभामुत्सङ्गे कृत्वा धावति।

(Moving about and looking upwards) O friend! Look – what a wonderful sight! Here an untimely cloud takes away by force a streak of lightning which seems to cry out.

Vyaṅgyavyākhyā

You come and save this girl who is crying helplessly.

धनञ्जयः किं नु खल्वयमुद्दिश्य प्रलपित माणवकः। भवतु पश्यामस्तावत्। (परिक्रम्योच्चैर्दत्तदृष्टिः) सखे! नायं तडित्वानम्बुधरः। अयं हि धूमप्रकरधूम्रः प्रमथः कामपि कन्यकां प्रसह्याकर्षति। (सक्रोधम्) आः दुरात्मन्! अतिनृशंस! तिष्ठ तिष्ठ।

आक्रन्दन्तीमनाथामिव मम मिषतः कन्यकां कृष्यमाणां
मुक्त्वैनां याहि नो चेदुदयगिरिशिरोवर्ष्मणः कृष्णधाम्नः।
आग्नेयास्त्रास्यनिर्यद्बहलशिखिशिखाश्रेणिनिर्दग्धमूर्तेः
सोऽहं सद्यो विदध्यां तवसितभसितापाण्डरां भूतधात्रीम्।। ११।।

(शरं सन्धत्ते)

विदूषकः (सविस्मयम्) भो वअस्स! अच्छेरं अच्छेरं। एदस्स दिव्वसरस्स पुङ्खेण सन्दट्ठमत्ताअं मोवीअं तिउरदाहवेळाअं विअ तिहुवणं पळित्तं। मोक्खे उण स च्चलो अट्ठिअस्स सरोआसणस्स वि पाणसंसअ त्ति तक्केमि। ता पडिसंहर एवं। एसो उण पमहाहमो तं कण्णअंफुरन्ति मोत्तूण तुरिअतुरिअं पळाअदि! (भो वयस्य! आश्चर्यमाश्चर्यम्। एतस्य दिव्यशरस्य पुङ्खेन सन्दष्टमात्रायां मौर्व्यां त्रिपुरदाहवेलायामिव त्रिभुवनं प्रदीप्तम्। मोक्षे पुनः सत्यलोकस्थितस्य सरोजासनस्यापि प्राणसंशयइति तर्कयामि। तत् प्रतिसंहरैतम्। एष पुनः प्रमथाधमस्तां कन्यकां स्फुरन्तीं मुक्त्वा त्वरितत्वरितं पलायते।)

---

9 Inner meaning of तरणि is harem (अवरोध) and of किरण is anger (क्रोध). Anger of Pāñcālī is suggested.

10 पांसुशब्देन स्नेहो ध्वन्यते; द्वयोरपि मार्दवं गुणः।

धनञ्जयः बाढम्। (प्रतिसंहरति)

(नेपथ्ये)

रक्खह मं रक्खह मं। (रक्षत मां रक्षत माम्)

धनञ्जयः (ससम्भ्रमम्) अहो अत्याहितम्। सैषा प्रमथकरमुक्ता प्रायशश्छिन्नपातं पतति। तदवलम्बे तावदेनाम्। (प्रसारितकरस्तिष्ठति)

Dhanañjaya: What does this young, naive Brahmin mean by his nonsense? All right, I shall see for myself. (Moving about and looking intently upwards) O friend! This is not cloud and lightning. It is a dark demon taking away a maiden by force! (Angrily) O wicked one! O merciless miscreant! Stop! Stop!

Do you dare in my presence to carry off this maiden
who wails helplessly? Leave her alone,
lest I burn your mountainous body with my fiery arrows, then
sprinkle the earth with your white ashes. (11)

(Fixes the arrow to the bow)

Vidūṣaka : (With surprise) O friend! What a wonder! As soon as this divine arrow is fixed to the bowstring, the three worlds blazed forth like the fire of Tripura's destruction. Even Lord Brahmā sitting on a lotus in his heaven must have feared for his life. So withdraw it. The demon is retreating in haste, leaving behind that brilliant maiden.

Dhanañjaya : All right. (Withdraws)

(Behind the curtain)

Protect me! Protect me!

Dhanañjaya : (Anxiously) Oh, what a pity! This lady released from the demon's grip will fall and be crushed. So I shall support her.

(He stands with outstretched palms)

व्यङ्ग्यव्याख्या

ततः प्रविशति श्रमालसो विदूषकः।

विदूषकः – भो भो इति। अथ स कविर्नायकप्रवृत्तिरेवम्भूता निर्माय कौण्डिन्याख्यं कञ्चिद् द्विजवरं तं नर्मसचिवं कृत्वा तत्र निर्गमयितुमुपक्रामतेति यत् ततो मयापि तत्प्रावेशिकप्रयोगमार्गौ प्रदर्श्येते।

अथ विदूषक इति सकलवेदशास्त्रवेत्ता कश्चिद् द्विजो[11] यथाविध्यनुष्ठितषोडशक्रियः स्वदेशात् हस्तिनपुरं प्राप्तः तत्र यथेष्टवस्तु यथाकालमनुभुञ्जानः पाण्डवेषु स्निग्धोऽपि विशेषात् अर्जुने पक्षपाती भूत्वा नियमेन द्रौपदीमेवानुवर्तमानः तस्याः पिण्डोदनं मोदकपूर्वकदलीफलानि इष्टवस्तूनि यथाकाममादायानुभुज्य निवसन्नयं सहसा पुरान्निर्गच्छन्तं स्वाभिमतं धनञ्जयं दृष्ट्वा तेन सह गच्छामीति अवधार्य प्रतिष्ठासुः तदा द्रौपद्या तेन सह प्रयातुं द्विजहीनस्य क्षत्रियस्य क्वचिदपि चित्तपरिभ्रमता भवेत् तत्परिहारार्थं वा पथि तदस्खलनाय वेति तया प्रेर्यमाणोऽयं ततो निर्गत्य तेन सह तीर्थानि चरन् इतरेतरद्रौपदीकथाकथनं कुर्वन् कथञ्चित् परिपूर्णे तद्वत्सरे प्राप्ते प्रभासतीर्थे तज्जलपरिपूतदेहः सन् अमुष्मिन् क्वचित् स्थित्वा यक्षेण द्रौपदीकथासुधापानपर्याप्तमनसं धनञ्जयमभिमुखीकृत्यासीनोऽयं सहसा तमपि वृष्णिवीरं दृष्ट्वा ततः सम्प्रतीति पृष्टकुशलप्रश्नस्तं सम्मान्यासीनोऽयं तन्मुखान्निर्गच्छत्सुभद्रावृत्तान्तं सौत्सुक्यं श्रृण्वन्नयं धनञ्जयं तच्छ्रवणमात्रेण स्मरेण बाध्यमानं दृष्ट्वा तद्गतचित्तोऽयं किं भवेदिति स्मरन् तपा...दे तत्तीरमुत्प्लुत्य तस्मादुत्तराभिमुखं गच्छन्तं अनुगच्छन् मार्गद्वयं दृष्ट्वावमृश्य तयोर्वामेन वर्त्मना गच्छन्तं दृष्ट्वा इत्यवदत्' भोः कीदृशीयं ते यात्रा तेन यात्रा स्यात् तदस्यां वृत्तिः स्मर्तव्या। मन्ये तया वितीर्णं पाथेयमद्यतनेन दिनेन साकं नष्टमिति। पाथेयहीनस्य नरस्य अभिमताप्तिः कुतः स्यात्। तस्मात् मैवं भवेदिति प्रोच्यमानमपि गच्छन्तमेव दृष्ट्वा तदनुसरन्नेष प्रभासतीर्थपरिसरे निवसतां मुनिवृन्दानामाश्रममुद्दिश्य गच्छन्तं तं दृष्ट्वा किमिदमिति स्मरन् इत्यवदत्।

इन्द्रगोप इवैष त्वं यात्रायां चरणं न्यसेत्।[12]
नोचेदित्थं व्रजस्तस्यां सूरिणां पक्षिणां दशाम्।।
वार्ध्वनिश्रवणेनेव पादेनोपानहं हरेत्।
इति लोकवचो जानन् ततस्तत्कथां त्यज।।

इति प्रोच्यमानमपि मुनीनामुटजानि प्रविशन्तं दृष्ट्वा तेन सह प्रविश्य तत्र निवसता तेन सह मासमात्रमवसदिति तत्र निवसन्नयं कस्मिंश्चिदह्नि सत्वरमनुष्ठितनित्यक्रियो भूत्वा मध्याह्नेऽभियास्य स्वयमेव तस्मान्निर्गत्य किमपि विमृशन्तमिव गच्छन्तं दृष्ट्वेत्यस्मरत्

सुस्थिरादाश्रमाद् गन्तुमाश्रयान्तरमाश्रमम्।
यतते चलचित्तोऽयं सोऽम्बावस्थां व्रजेदिमाम्।।
तया वितीर्णपाथेयं नाशयित्वा गृहान्तरम्।
भिक्षावृत्यानयाभ्येत्य यात्रां पुष्णाति किन्वयम्।।

---

11 The role of jester is inflated later. See the Chapter on Post-Kulaśekhara reconstructions.

12 Vidūṣaka tries to dissuade Dhanañjaya cleverly using words with double meaning. Indragopa is one protected by Indra; Dhanañjaya is the son of Indra. Indragopa is also the tender earth worm (ñāññūl in Malayalam) He also uses a popular saying – Don't start to decorate your body applying sandal paste just by hearing the thunder of the cloud. When cloud appears lovers feel happy. But it is very early to start decorating to receive the lover. The idea is that you do not know anything about Subhadrā. Who is she? Where from does she come? Which is her family? Is she attainable? Don't start to meet her without knowing her details simply relying the words of Gada.

भिक्षुकोऽयं भवेन्मन्ये कालतो विचरन्महीम्।
गर्हयन्नात्मनः कान्तां गृहलक्ष्मीं न किं बलात्।।

तथाप्यहमेनमनुगच्छन्नसाध्यवस्तुनि स्पृहां मा कृथा इति वदन्ननुगच्छामीति निश्चित्यानुगच्छन्नित्यस्मरत्। अहमिदानीं श्रिततपस्विजनेन पथा चरन्तमिममसाध्यवस्तुनि स्पृहां मा कृथाः इति स्पष्टोक्त्या[13] वदेयम् यदि तस्य लाघवं सर्वजनश्रुतिगम्यं भवेत्। तस्मात् व्यपदेशेनेव रुद्धामि न साध्यं तवेदं कर्मेति तमपश्यन्नपि विज्ञापयामीति भूय एवं स्मरेत् – तदिति कर्तव्यं भवान् भिक्षायाचनार्थी सम्प्रति गच्छतीति वक्तव्यम्। तच्च व्यपदेशेन वाच्यमिति स्मरन् भूय इत्यस्मरत्। किमन्तरीकरणेन व्यवहरन्नेवं रुद्धामीति स्मरन् अयमिति निश्चितवान्। मयेदानीं तपस्विजनोऽत्रत्याकर्तव्या। तत्कथङ्कारमिति चेत् यथा कृष्णया च पूर्ववच्चतुर्विधैराहारजातैरुपेता भिक्षा मह्यं तस्मै च दीयमाना भवेत् पुनः कृष्णेन स्वसा च तथाभूता सा कर्तव्या। अपि च येनकेनाप्युपाययुक्तेन व्यपदेशेन यत्नेन शक्यं यदि तत्प्रवृत्तेरयं निवर्तितव्यः। तत्तपस्विनः उद्दिश्य भिक्षा क्रियतामिति निश्चित्य तपस्विनोऽन्तरेण भिक्षाया वचनं कृतवान्। अहं भृशं क्षुधित इति विभावयन्नाह – भो भ अवन्तो महेसिणो भिंखि देथ इति।

भो भगवन्तो महर्षयः भिक्षां दिशन्तु। तत्र ध्वनिर्निर्दिश्यते। अत्रादावमुना कृष्णो याच्यते। हे भगवन् कृष्ण महर्षे त्रिकालज्ञ भवितव्यतया सुभद्रानेन गृह्यते यदि द्रौपद्या सह वर्तमानायाः यात्रायाः विरोधः यथा मा स्यात् तथा घटयत। असाध्यं यदि तथाभ्येत्येतद् विज्ञापय। तत्र बहुवचननिर्देशो भागवद्गौरवात्। एवं प्रार्थनां कृत्वा भूयस्तपस्विनोऽपि प्रार्थयति। हे भगवन्तः भिक्षां दिशन्त्विति। अतः परमावयोर्दिनयात्रा पूर्ववद् भवेदिति ध्वनिना प्रार्थयति। किञ्च भिक्षेति स्त्रीलिङ्गनिर्देशात् सुभद्रा चानुगृह्यतामिति द्योतयन्नाह – अपि च भूयस्स भिक्षाशब्दे वाच्यमाने लोकानात्मानं क्षुधित इति विभावयितुं श्रमालसो भवेत्। एतदर्थं स कविः तं श्रमालसन्निर्गमयति। एवं श्रमालसो भूत्वा सक्षीणं सप्रवणं तत्र क्वचिदतिष्ठत्। एवं पूर्वसम्बन्धः।

यथानिर्दिष्टमेव व्यपनीय यवनिकां दीपपुरः सविवेकमीषदुद्गतदृष्टिः मुहूर्तं तिष्ठेत्।[14] एवं तिष्ठन्निति विमृशेत्। क्वनु खलु मया हीनेन वयस्येन गतवता भवितव्यमिति स्मरन् विलोक्य एवं तिष्ठन्नेव तमन्वेष्टुं विलोकितवान्। एवं विलोक्य तं दृष्ट्वा च इति स्मरेत्। स्मरणप्रकारमुत्तरग्रन्थेन दर्शयति अहो इति। अहो अयं भगवद्ध्यानाभिमुखः सन् अस्मद्भिक्षाशब्दाकर्णनेन इतस्ततो मनो भ्रमयति। तन्मन्ये कृच्छ्रसाध्यमस्य मनोरथमिति। तस्मादसाध्यं तवेदं कर्मेति कैश्चिद् ध्वनियुक्तैः श्लोकैरेनमस्मात् विरतो भवेति द्योतयन् वदामीति निश्चित्य कांश्चित् श्लोकान् वदेत्।

यात्रैषा द्रौपदीहाया दुःखकृद् गददापथा
भानुतप्तेन चरतो ममापि तव किं भवेत्।
गास्तु भानुभुवः क्रूराः न सहे नरपाण्ड्यपि
विपदं धार्त्रराष्ट्रस्य निर्यान्ति त्वय्यतः परम्।।

---

13 Spaṣṭokti is direct speech; vyapadeśokti is suggestive one.

14 This in the praveśika of vidūṣaka. The direction to remove the curtain at this time gives room for confusion. Does it mean that the Pūrvasambandha was presented from behind the curtain?

प्रदाय सहजां लक्ष्मीं सुधीरामश्रमेण नः।
याति तीव्रकरस्मार्यो यो न सोऽनेन गण्यते।।
नियतीभिर्हरेर्गोभिरयं नीलाम्बराश्रयात्।
सेव्यमानो भवेत् हन्त परं तापात् कृशो भवेत्।।
इति गोप्रचयैस्सोष्णैर्नाम नागध्वजश्रमात्।
तं त्वां परिवदन्त्येष ततोस्माद् विरतो भव।।
अपि चोपेत्य सौभद्रं पयोवाहं बृहत्तरम्।
काङ्क्षन्मनोभुवः पीडास्तत्तापात् कार्श्यमेष्यति।।

इत्युभयार्थैः श्लोकैः[15] अनुशास्य तदनुशासनं श्रृण्वतोऽप्यस्य विषण्णतां दृष्ट्वा धिया स्वयमेवेत्यस्मरत्

भूजयात्तसुखः सन् य श्रीरनन्तरजा हरेः।
गम्येति यत्नी तद्भ्रष्टः प्राप्तः त्रैशङ्कवीं दशाम्।।[16]

इति स्वयमेव स्मृत्वा भूयस्तं श्रावयितुमाह -

प्रेम कृष्णे भवत्यस्मिन् यत्ते स्यान्नष्टमद्य तत्।
फल्गुनाशान्त्यजामुष्मादिह नायातवान् स यत्।।

इति भावयन्नत्र निर्विकारं दृष्ट्वा विमृश्य सशिरःकम्पं तमेव पश्यंस्तिष्ठेत्। पुनरप्यहो इत्याश्चर्ये वदेत्।

अहो आश्चर्यम् – पुष्पेषोर्माहात्म्यम्। एवं विधानि वचांसि श्रावयन्ति तानि न श्रृणोति। यत् एवं यदि तवात्रत्यानि कर्माण्यसाध्यानीति तं विज्ञापयामीति निश्चित्य तज्ज्ञापयितुं सध्वनिना उत्तरग्रन्थेनाह। **अहो सुंज्ञाणि उडजं भंतराणि** इति। तत्प्रकारं दर्शयति। अहो आश्चर्यं ते भाग्यराहित्यम्।[17] कुतः? तीर्थसेवाव्यपदेशेन गच्छतस्तेऽद्य उटजाभ्यन्तराणि सर्वाणि शून्यान्यभवन्। अहो आश्चर्यम्। इयं कृष्णा ममेच्छानुसारिणी न स्यादिति मत्वा चेतरोद्वाहं कर्तुं तीर्थसेवाच्छलेन गच्छन्नादौ गाङ्गे सकलपापवारिणि वारिणि पुण्यक्षेत्रेऽपि तत्रस्थां काञ्चिन्नागकन्यकां विषमुद्वमद्भिर्निश्वासैः कैश्चिदप्यगम्यामपि तां रन्तुं प्रापितवानसि। ततः सन्ततिविच्छेदात् भवितव्यतया जातपुत्रा यदासीत् तदैव भवन्तं बहिष्कृतवती ततस्तया निर्गमितः त्वं तीर्थार्थीति भावयंस्ततोऽपि गत्वा पाण्ड्यविषयानभ्येत्य तत्पतिं दृष्टवानसि। तं दृष्ट्वा तत्रस्थः सन् सहसा तत्सुतां काञ्चित् कन्यकां म्लेच्छजातिजातामपि तां च तं याचितवानसि। ततः सोऽपि त्वद्याचनावैमुख्यं तत्प्रदानं चासहमानः क्षणानुभवार्थमेव तुभ्यं तां दत्तवानभूत्। अथ तां परिगृह्य तया सह रममाणे द्वित्राण्यहांसि व्यतीतया सह तस्मान्निर्जगमिषौ त्वयि तत्पित्रा द्रौपद्यां शङ्कमानेन सा रुद्धाभूत्। अथ

15 Here also the words have different meanings. The author includes such meanings also under dhvani.

16 Refers to the story of Triśaṅku who is either on earth or in heaven. Kālidāsa also used this incident in Śakuntalā

17 The tone of vidūṣaka is unusually biting to his friend. His interpretation as to why the houses are deserted is interesting. Dhanañjaya went everywhere in search of women, but he was rejected by all. There was no sign of welcome from anywhere. Hence vidūṣaka says that the houses are deserted-closed as far as Dhanañjaya is concerned.

ततो दुर्मना निर्गत्य तदन्वेषणाय तीर्थच्छलेनेमं देशं प्राप्तवानसि। अथेतोऽपि द्वारकाभिमुखो गन्तुमभिलषसि। तत्रस्था सा सुभद्रापि तव वश्या न स्यात्। तां सुयोधनाय सीरी दातुं कल्पितवान्। यत्तस्मात् शून्यान्युटजाभ्यन्तराणीति तव यस्याः कस्याश्चित् परिग्रहाय वेश्मानुवेश्मप्रवेशकर्माणि यान्यभवन् तानि शून्यानि भवन्तीति ध्वनिः। इति ध्वनियुक्तया वाचा तं विज्ञाप्य तिष्ठन्नयं तवेयमसाध्येति भूयोऽपि साधयति। कृच्छ्रसाध्येयमिति मन्वानोऽपि भूतकरविसृष्टायास्सुभद्रायाः आदर्शनात् कृच्छ्रसाध्येयमिति जानन्नपि तवेयमसाध्येति समर्थयन् प्रयोगं कुर्यात् इति विदूषकस्यासुभद्रादर्शनात् स्थायिभावः।[18] निश्वस्य इति ब्रुवन्नयं निजवचनश्रवणे निर्विकारं तिष्ठन्तं तं दृष्ट्वा तस्य तद्गतचित्ततया स्थैर्यं ज्ञात्वा इति स्मरेत्। कृच्छ्रसाध्यामप्येनां येनकेनाप्यनवाप्य न शक्रप्रस्थं पुरं गच्छतीति तद्गतचित्ततया मन्तव्यमिति स्मरन्नेतत्कार्यस्य दुरन्ततया निश्वसितवान्। एतदर्थं निश्वस्येति शब्दस्तत्र प्रक्षिप्तः। एवं निश्वस्य भूयस्तत्र कर्मणो दुरन्तत्वं तस्य तादृश्या दुरवस्थाया प्राप्तिं च स्मरन् सविवेकमुत्तरग्रन्थमाह अहो इति। तद्विवेकप्रकारं दर्शयति। अहो इत्यत्र विवेकेन। एवं ध्वन्यर्थेन तद्विज्ञापयद्वचो याथातथ्यं न श्रृणोत्ययमिति यत् ततो मन्येऽस्य चित्तं तस्यां बद्धमिति। अहो अस्य मम च सुखान्तरायो भविता। तत्प्राप्तावप्राप्तौ च कष्ट मुभयथास्मै मह्यं च। पाञ्चाली क्रुद्धा स्यात्। स्मृत्वा तदेव समर्थयितुं उत्तरग्रन्थमाह अ ज्ञं सेत्यादि ग्रन्थादारभ्य आहारं स कहारिण आसदिजे इ इति यतो ग्रन्थादनेन ग्रन्थेन समुद्दिश्य वदन्नयमिति लोकान् विभावयन् ध्वनिना अर्जुनमुद्दिश्य वदति अहो इति। आश्चर्यं तव उदरभागधेयस्याधन्यतायाः प्रभावः। तदेव हीनतायाः प्रभाव इति दर्शयन्नाह

गार्हस्थ्यस्य गृहस्थोऽयं...चरत्कर्मान्वहं वसन्
दाराश्रितमनास्स स्यात् सुखीह च परत्र च।।

इति श्रुतिस्मृतिप्रसिद्धिः। तथापि भगवद्वचनोत्फुल्लगगनकुसुमे त्वय्यभीष्टां कृष्णां विहाय स्पृहां करोषि इति यत् प्रभावो महानिति मन्ये। अहो एतत्प्रवृत्ते त्वयि द्रौपद्यां कोप एव शिष्यते। कुत इति चेत् पश्य-जो- इत्यादि। यः नित्यसन्निहिततपोधनं तपोवनं शून्यं करोति इति सम्बन्धः। तत्र ध्वनिर्दृश्यते। अनेन ग्रन्थेन तस्य दैवराहित्यं ध्वनिना विवृणोति। बाह्येन स्वस्य च। यस्तपोवनमपि तपस्विशून्यं करोति। तपोवनमिति। तपसोपवनं वनमाश्रयः।

आश्रये कानने वारि मूकेऽन्धे च तपस्यपि।
उन्मत्ते च जडे बाले वनशब्दः प्रवर्तते।।

अत्र ध्वनावाश्रये अन्यत्र कानने इत्यनेकार्थः। तपोवनं तपसामाश्रयीभूतम्। भगवन्तं जगदवनाय कृष्णम् इति प्रख्यातं तपोवनं तपसामाश्रयं तदपि प्रभावात् शून्यं करोति। सर्वदा तदभिमतं तमपीदानीं यस्त्वया शून्यं करोति। **नित्यसन्निहिततपोधनानामि**ति। किञ्च नित्यसमवच्छिन्नं यस्मिन् सन्निधत्ते तपोधनाः स तथोक्तः। तथाभूतं भगवन्तं विशेषात् तदभीष्टप्रदमिति ममापि त्वकार्ये तमपि विमुखं करोति। तथाभूतं तमपि एतावन्तं कालमत्रागमने शून्यं करोतीति यत् ततोऽहं प्रभावो महानिति मन्ये। किञ्च सर्वजनहृदयज्ञोऽयं विशेषात्

18 Vidūṣaka thinks that Subhadrā is not attainable to Dhanañjaya. He is in a serious predicament. If Arjuna gets Subhadrā, Draupadī will be angry with him for not avoiding it. If Dhanañjaya does not get her, his friend will be in great distress.

त्वयि तथाभूतः सन्नपि तद्ध्यानपरत्वं न श्रितवान् यत् ततोऽसाध्यं तन्मनोगतमिति विज्ञेयमिति ध्वनिना तवेयमसाध्येति पूर्वग्रन्थेन समर्थयन्तमेव पश्यन् मुहूर्तं तिष्ठेत्। एवं तिष्ठन्नयं ध्वनिना विज्ञाप्यमानमर्थं श्रृण्वन्नपि अश्रृण्वन्निव तिष्ठन्तं तं दृष्ट्वा भूयोऽपि ध्वनिना इत्युत्तरग्रन्थं वदति **अहम्** इत्यादि। अथेति स्ववचनेनाभिमुख्यं दृष्ट्वा भूयोऽपि सध्वनिनोत्तरग्रन्थेन तमधिक्षिपति। अथवा हेतुप्रश्ने प्रमेयव्यत्यासे कात्स्न्र्ये चाथवाशब्दः। अत्र बाह्ये प्रमेयव्यत्यासे अन्तरे पुनः कात्स्न्र्ये प्रकारेण मैवं दोष इति। अत्र एवशब्देन तवेति ध्वन्यते। तत्र ममेति पदे प्रोच्यमाने तवेति दृशोर्विभावयन् वदेत्। अथवा कात्स्न्र्यप्रकारेण सर्वप्रकारेणायं दोषः तवैव। तस्याः प्राप्तावप्राप्तौ चेति तं प्रोच्य ध्वनियुक्तेनोत्तरग्रन्थेन तं विवृणोति येनेत्यादिना। येन त्वया एतत्सङ्केतनात् प्राक् युधिष्ठिरमन्दिरे इति भर्तृभूतयुधिष्ठिरशरीरे वर्तमानेऽपि अष्टाशीति सहस्राणां ब्राह्मणानामिति पञ्चानां पाण्डवानां भर्तृभूतानामपि मध्येभूते त्वयि त्वद्विषये तया वितीर्णमाहारजातं कीदृग्भूतमाहारजातमितिचेत् याज्ञसेनीकरकमलसंसर्गसुभगमिति। याज्ञसेनी अस्य प्रदानायाहं यज्ञसेनेन मत्पित्रा जनिता साहमेषेति मन्वाना या भर्तृषु त्वयि विशेषात् बद्धप्रेमा वर्तते तस्याः याज्ञसेन्याः करकमलसंसर्गमित्यर्थः। कस्याः करकमलसंसर्गसुभगमिति तस्याः गाढाश्लेषे सप्रेम स्पृश त्करकमलसंसर्गसुभगमित्यर्थः। तथा सुभगमाहारजातं तादृग्भूतया तया वितीर्यमाणं चतुर्विधमाहारजातं उपभोगरतमाहारजातं रतजातं तत् यथेष्टमनुभुञ्जानेन येन त्वया तत्र पुरे समुषितम्। चतुर्विधमिति

रतेरङ्गानि चत्वारि ज्ञेयानि रसविज्जनैः।
चुम्बनं निर्भयाश्लेषं चापलं चित्तमोहनम्।।

एभिर्युक्तमाहारजातं शर्मेत्यर्थः। तथाभूतं तथानुभवता ततः परित्यज्येदानीं तस्य पृष्ठतः भिक्षा याच्यते। एतस्येत्यादिग्रन्थेन अर्जुनमन्तरेण भगवानुच्यते, एतस्य कृष्णस्य पृष्ठतः पृष्ठं बलमाश्रित्य तं तां भिक्षां याचतेति सम्बन्धः। **तीर्थयात्राकामुकस्ये**ति

गुरौ जले च तीर्थे च शुचिचित्ते तपस्यपि।
कृतौ सर्पिषि वेश्यायां तीर्थशब्दः प्रवर्तते।।

अत्र गुरौ। गुरुविनियुक्ते कर्मणि निष्णातस्यानुगच्छतः शुचिमानसस्य सव्यसाचिनः निर्दयमानसः एवं भूतस्य भगवतः कृष्णनामधेयस्य विष्णोः पृष्ठबलं मे स्यादिति मत्वानेन त्वया तस्मात् सा दातव्येति इतस्ततः परिभ्रमता अधुना भिक्षा याच्यत इति यत् तत् कष्टतरं भवेत्। कुतः यथापेक्षमनुभवक्षमं वस्तु विहाय तत्प्रसादात् गगनकुसुममपि साध्यमिति मत्वा तमिदानीं भिक्षा याच्यते तत् कष्टतरम्। पञ्चस्वपि पतिषु सत्सु त्वद्गतचित्तां त्वदिच्छानुसारिणीं तां परित्यज्यास्मदरये सुयोधनाय प्रदातुं सीरिणा तदुदकपूर्वकर्त्रा कृतशपथां सुभद्रां गगनकुसुमसदृशां बलभद्रवचनानुसारिणः कृष्णस्य प्रसादात् साध्येयमिति मत्वा तथाभूतां तां प्राप्तुं यत्नमाचरतेदानीं भिक्षा याच्यते? **भिक्षेति** इयमसाध्या चेदत्रोपेत्य तवेयमसाध्येति मां ब्रूहीति कुतः प्राप्तत्रिशङ्कुदशः कान्दिशीको भूत्वा तन्मात्रमेव भगवन्तं प्रार्थयंस्तिष्ठसीति ध्वन्यर्थः। इत्यमुना ध्वन्यर्थेनासाध्या सेति विज्ञाप्य तत्र तमेव पश्यन्मुहूर्तं तिष्ठेत्। एवमितःपूर्वं ग्रन्थस्य ध्वन्यर्थः।

अथेति तेन श्राव्यमाणध्वन्यर्थं श्रुत्वा धनञ्जयोऽपि अध्वश्रमजनितसन्तापोऽस्मीति विभावयंस्तिष्ठेत्। अथ विदूषकस्तथाभूतः तं दृष्ट्वा इति स्मरेत् **अहो** अयं शाखाचंक्रमणं कृतवान्। तथापि सोऽत्रागतस्य

नास्य साध्येयमिति वचनं ब्रवीति इति ध्वनियुक्तया वाचा निवेदयामीति निश्चित्य भूयः उत्तरग्रन्थेन सध्वनिना तन्निवेदयति **अंथ उण** इत्यादिना। अत्र पुनस्तपोवने आहारस्य कथापि नासादयिष्यति। अत्र तपोवने तपः आश्रये भगवति कृष्णे आहारकथापि न भविष्यति। अयं भगवानत्रोपेत्य सा तेन दातव्येति कथनमात्रमपि न करोति। इति तं विज्ञाप्य तत्र किमयं करोति इति परिच्छेत्तुं तमेव पश्यंस्तिष्ठेत्। अथैवं विज्ञापितो धनञ्जयः तच्छृण्वन्नयं मार्गतापसन्तप्तोऽस्मि यत् तत्पदमपि चलितुं न शक्नोम्यहमिति भावयन्नत्र तदुक्तवत् निर्विकारः तिष्ठेत्। अथैवं विदूषकः स्ववचसि निर्विकारं दृष्ट्वैनमितिस्मरेत्। अहो कष्टतरेयमस्य दशा। कुत कृष्णो नात्रेष्यति तेनैव कार्यसिद्धिर्न स्यादिति विज्ञेयमिति विज्ञापितोऽप्ययं तत्कार्याभिनिविष्टमानसो भूत्वा भूरिद्विजदशां प्रपन्न इति – कर्तव्यतामजानंस्तिष्ठतीति यत्ततोऽहं तृणपूलपाणिर्मासाध्यवस्तुनि स्पृहां कुर्यादिति दूरतस्तिष्ठन्नपि क्रियया विज्ञापयामीति निश्चित्य भूयोऽपीति स्मरेत्। कीदृशीं क्रियां दर्शयन् बाहौ तृणपूलं गृहीत्वा क्रियया कथङ्कारमिमं रुद्धामीति स्मरन् मुहूर्तं तिष्ठेत्। एवं तिष्ठन्निति कल्पितवान् केवलं अविद्यमानं वस्तुविभावनयाविद्यमानया मृगतृष्णिकया तुल्या ते सुभद्राप्राप्तिरिति तमस्मच्चेष्ट या प्रबोधयामीत्युत्तरत्रग्रन्थेन निश्चिनोति **ता** इति। तस्मात् किमन्तरेण व्यवहरन् प्रबोधयामीति। अस्तु अहं पिपासामत्त इति यत् ततो मया पानीयं पेयमिति विबोधयन् मृगतृष्णिकास्वासु पानीयभ्रान्तिसम्पा दयन्ननया तुल्या तवेयं प्रवृत्तिरिति दर्शयन् इतस्ततस्तद्धेतोः परिभ्रमन् प्रबोधयामीति निश्चित्योत्तरग्रन्थेन वदति **जला स अं अणे सि अ** इत्यादि। जला स अं इति। अत्र जलाशयशब्देनार्जुनमन्तरेण वदति। जला स अं इति जलाशयम्। अर्जुनमन्विष्यानुप्राप्य पिपासामत्तस्य सुभद्राभोक्तुमिच्छया इति प्रतिवचनं करिष्ये इति ध्वनिः इत्यमुनाध्वन्यर्थेनैनमनुगच्छामीति निश्चित्योत्तरग्रन्थेन तथा समर्थयति। पुरतोऽवलोक्य अथेति निश्चित्यात्मानं पिपासुरिति लोकान् विभावयन् वारिपानाभावे शुष्यत्कण्ठनालान्तर्वर्त्मत्वादुच्चैस्तरां साद्यस्मि। तत्क्वनु खल्वयं मे जलराशिरिति वदन् जलराशिं वीक्ष्यतेऽयमिति लोकान् विभावयितुं पुरतो विलोकितवान्। एवं विलोक्य तदानीं तथाभूतं धनञ्जयं वीक्ष्येति स्मरेत्। कुतः अहमिदानीं मृगतृष्णिकासू त्पन्नपानीयभ्रान्तिरिति विभावयन् लोकानिमं वयस्यं ध्वनियुक्तया गिरा वदन्नुद्वेजयामीति निश्चित्योत्तरग्रन्थेन तथा समर्थयति। **एसो समुं दपमाणो जलरासी दिस इ** इति।

पूर्वं समुद्रप्रमाणमेष धनञ्जयः इदानीं जलराशिर्दृश्यते, पूर्वं द्रौपदीस्वयंवरे सर्वे क्षत्रियाः सकर्णसुयोधनाः जेतुमिममैकमत्यमुपेत्य यत्नं कृतवन्तः तदानीं निश्चलं तिष्ठता तेनामुनैकेन जितास्ते धैर्यादगाधत्वाच्च समुद्रप्रमाणमेष धनञ्जय इति ब्रुवन्त एव गच्छन्ति स्म सोऽयमिदानीं सुयोधनाय दातुं कल्पितां सुभद्रां प्राप्तुं यत्नं कृत्वा द्रौपदीस्वयंवरे यदाहृतं जयन्तमिदानीं सुयोधनाय शत्रवे ददातीति यत् फल्गुनस्य मृगतृष्णिकासमा सुभद्राप्राप्तिरिति च विज्ञापयन् पुनरनेनैव ग्रन्थेन अहो एष जलराशिः इति ध्वन्यर्थेन तस्य जलं विवृणोति। अत्र जलराशिशब्देन जल इत्येवोच्यते। अन्यस्मै प्रदानाय कल्पितां सुभद्रां यायुरयं एवं संवृत्तः तस्माद् दृश्यमानपारेऽयमस्य जलपरम्परा। कुतः यत्तीव्रकरादुद्यन्तं तापं स्मरतोपि गच्छतोऽस्यैवमेतेन दन्दह्यमानग्रीवानालान्तःप्रदेशस्य पुरे वाप्यन्तस्थकृष्णाप्रीतिप्रेमशब्दानाप्तिश्रितसन्तोषस्य कष्टमीदृश्यवस्थाभूत्। तथापीदानीं **एं थगदु अ** इत्यादिना।

तथाप्यद्याधुना सौभद्रस्य करस्य सदा मित्रस्य प्राप्तितस्सजलाशयं स्मरंस्तदुपान्तस्थोऽपि तत्रत्य-बलगौरवादक्षमस्सन्नेतं निन्दनीयं जलं ततो मित्रजलकरसन्तप्तं तदपेयमपीति तन्निकामं पाययिष्यामित्युक्त्वा – ध्वनिना पुनरात्मानमन्तरेण वदन्नयं इति लोकान् विभावयन् त्वत्सुभद्राप्राप्तिर्मे मृगतृष्णिकासु पानीयप्राप्त्या

तुल्येति तं बोधयितुं पानीयव्यपदेशेन इतस्ततस्त्वरं तत्पुरः सत्वरमुत्सर्पति मृगतृष्णिकासु पानीयभ्रान्त्या परिभ्रमतीति यत् ततोऽनेन तुल्यम् ते प्रवृत्तिरिति ध्वनिः।

धनञ्जयः अथ धनञ्जयो यतिशब्दनविमृशंस्तिष्ठन्नयमिति द्वयं विमृश्य गौरवादेकं निश्चिनेति। कुतः भगवद्ध्यानपरेण मया भगवति नीयमानं चित्तं सखिप्रतिवचनेन विमुखीकृतमिति यत् ततो असाध्यमिति विज्ञेयम्। आहोस्विदमुना वचनेनैवान्यथा च भगवन्त इति त्वन्मुखान्निर्गतं भगवच्छब्दो मङ्गलवाचकः तथाभूतत्वात्। किञ्च अमुना श्वासानुकूल्येन च तस्मात् साध्यासाध्यविवेके साध्यत्वे कर्मवल्ली च इति भगवच्छब्दत्वात् साध्यमित्येवोह्यम्। तस्मात् कालान्तरेण भगवान्मया दृष्टः स्यात्। भगवति दृष्टे किमसाध्यं नाम। अपि च भगवति नीयमानं चित्तं भगवच्छब्देन हि पराङ्मुखीकृतम्। तच्छब्दगौरवात् तदात्रैवायं साक्षात्करिष्यति यदा मस्करिवेषधारी भवितास्मि इतिस्मरन्नमुष्य भगवतस्साक्षात्करणं भविष्यतीत्युपपत्तिभिर्निश्चित्य तिष्ठन्नयं धनञ्जयस्तथाभूतं तं पश्येत्। एवं तमेव पश्यन्नयं निश्चलस्तत्र दीपपुरस्तिष्ठन् सस्मितमिति स्मरेत्।

अहो एष मामन्तरेण परिभ्रमतीत्युत्तरग्रन्थेन विवृणोति ध्वनियुक्तेन। कष्टमसौ मृगतृष्णिकया समाकृष्यते इत्यसौ सुभद्रा अनया मृगतृष्णिकया समा इत्यनेनाकृष्यते कष्टमाश्चर्यम्। दवदहनशिखाभिः परितो दह्यमानात् वनान्तरात् वारिचयमन्वेष्टुं पिपासवो निष्पत्य तस्मादपवृक्षच्छाये भूप्रदेशे पानीयार्थं सञ्चरन्तस्तदानीमातपा वलेपात् ज्वलन्त्या भुवो निर्गच्छन्तमातपोष्माणं अविद्यमानमपि स्यन्दमानं जलौघमिव मन्यमानास्तत्पानार्थं यथा सञ्चरन्ति तथा त्वमपि सुभद्रापरिणयनकर्मशून्यपरिणाममन्विच्छसीत्यनेनाकृष्यते विभाव्यते। कष्टं हन्त अयं तपस्वी अयमनभिज्ञो मत्सखस्य भगवत कृष्णनाम्नो मनोवृत्तीनां प्राकृतत्वात्तदयं रोद्धव्य इति स्मरन्नात्मना निस्चित्योत्तरग्रन्थेन तथा करोति **सखे कौण्डिन्ये**त्यादिना। सखे त्वया क्रियमाणमिदं साम्प्रतमसाम्प्रतमित्युक्त्वा पुनरिति स्मरेत्। अयं मयेदानीमिति बोद्धव्यः खलु कौण्डिन्यः आप्तमित्रे भगवते मम कथमकथनीयं प्राप्तं नेच्छामि केवलं मम पराक्रमतः भगवत एवेति दृशोर्विभावयन् भूय उत्तरग्रन्थेन तत्समर्थयति **ममे**त्यादिना इति ग्रन्थमुक्त्वा तदागमनं प्रतिपालयंस्तिष्ठेत्।

विदूषकः – सरोषं। अथ विदूषकस्त्वयैषा न लभ्येति विज्ञापनार्थं मृगतृष्णिकासु सजलभ्रान्तिरितस्ततः परिभ्रमन्निति वदेत्। अद्येदानीं शैवलकेशाढ्यां कल्लोलभ्रूविराजितां परिस्फुरच्छफरनेत्रां नीलोत्पल-प्रचलद्भृङ्गतारां परिलसद्विजावलिं प्रोत्फुल्लकमलवदनां विराजन्मुक्ताहारां प्रोद्यदम्भोजकुलकुचां सदाश्रयकर्मसु भद्रां तां प्राप्य तृडार्तिरपनेतव्येति मत्वायं यत्र यत्र यदा यदा हन्त तां प्राप्तुं यत्नकार्यभवन्नयनसुखदां तस्मात् तस्मात् तदा तदा दूरदूरमपगच्छन्तीयं भवेत् तदास्मादियमप्यननुभोग्या नाम इत्युच्चैर्वदन्नितस्ततः परिभ्रमन्नयं सखे कौण्डिन्येत्यावर्जनपूर्वां तदीयां वाचं श्रुत्वेति स्मरेत्। अहो असौ क्रियमाणां प्रवृत्तिं दृष्ट्वा अनेन सा त्वया ग्राह्येत्युक्तमिति जानन्नपि स्वसमीपं मां प्रापयोपपत्तिभिरेषा मया लभ्येति मां बोधयितुं अनुवर्तनपूर्वया गिरा मामाहूतवान्। तथाप्यहमपि पानीयं मां चान्तरेण व्यवहरन् किमिन्द्रप्रस्थप्रवेशाभिमुखं तावकं चित्तं रुणत्सीत्येनं पृच्छेयम्। तत्कथङ्कारं? पुनः स्मृत्वा अस्तु एवं क्रियताम्। अहं रोषीभूत्वा किमर्थं जलराहित्यात् तृषादन्दह्यमानं मां वारिपानाय गच्छन्तं रुणत्सीति वदेयमिति निश्चित्य तत् समर्थयितुं सरोषमुत्तरग्रन्थेन तथा समर्थयति **कहमि**त्यादिना।

तत्र ध्वनिर्दृश्यते – कथं वयस्यो मां निवारयति इति केन हेतुना तवैषा न साध्येति विभावयन्तमनन्यज्ञेयं मां रुणत्सि तत्र का उपपत्तिः किञ्चानुपपत्तिर्विद्यत इति उत्तरग्रन्थेन साधयितुं ससंरम्भमाह – अथ विदूषक स्ससंरम्भमात्मानमुद्दिश्य व्यवहरन्निव तच्चित्तमन्तरेण वदति **भो पंथ** इत्यादिना। भो पार्थ, तत्र ध्वनिर्दृश्यते

– भो पार्थ यदेन्द्रप्रस्थप्रवेशान्निर्गतवानसि तदा प्रभृति द्रौपदीवीक्षणालापनाश्लेषजाः प्रवृत्तिरेव कथयन् सखे कति हताः सम्प्रति तीर्थयात्रानियमिता दिवसाः। कदानु तान् द्रक्ष्यामीति प्रलपंस्त्वं परिपूर्णकल्पं संवत्सरं प्राप्य प्रभासं च तस्मादिन्द्रप्रस्थप्रवेशाय त्रिभागावशिष्टं मार्गमेवाप्रापयन्नत्र मुहूर्तं स्थीयतामिति निर्बन्धितः त्वं त्वरमाणोऽपि मदपेक्षया तत्र स्थितवानसि। एवं पाञ्चालीं दिदृक्षुरत्र स्थितस्सन्नसि यदा गदगदितां तां कथां श्रुतवानसि तदा तच्छ्रवणेनैव भगवन्तं जलाशयं दृष्टवानसि।

तिंथ विसंउ इति। तच्छ्रवणेनैव जलाशयत्वात् त्वां तीर्थविशल्य इति मन्ये। तीर्थोपाधेरेतस्मिन् भवति जलाशये सति त्रिभागमात्रावशेषमिन्द्रप्रस्थमात्मानमप्रापयन् जलाशयोऽस्मीति साम्प्रतं दर्शयसि। कुत इति चेत् पश्य तच्छ्रवणमात्रेणैव तृष्णादग्धया जिह्वया अधुना त्वया निवारितोऽस्मीति यत् तत् तीर्थसेवेत्युपाधि मवलम्ब्यान्यां भार्यां प्राप्तुं यतस इति निश्चितवानस्मि इति ध्वनिना सा ह्यसाध्येति तं विज्ञाप्य भूयस्तदुत्तरं किमयं वक्ष्यतीति ज्ञातुं तच्छुश्रूषुस्तमेव पश्यन्नत्र तिष्ठेत्। एवमस्य ग्रन्थस्य ध्वनिप्रयोगमार्गः। 'रसनायां च चित्ते च जिह्वाशब्द प्रवर्तते' इत्यनेकार्थः। मृगतृष्णिका समैषा तव न साध्येत्यर्थः।

धनञ्जयः – अथ धनञ्जयस्तमाहूयागच्छेति तमुक्त्वा तत्र किमनेनोच्यत इति ज्ञातुं तमेव पश्यंस्तिष्ठन्नयं तदानीं तेन तवासाध्यायां सुभद्रायां तद्वचनश्रवणमात्रेणैव जलाशये त्वयि वर्तमाने तद्गतेन सा मां निवारितवानसीति ध्वनिना सा तवासाध्या तदर्थं त्वं जलाशयः संवृत्त इति ज्ञापितं तद्वचः श्रुत्वा तदेति स्मरेत्।

कुतः अहो तीर्थव्यपदेशेन गच्छंस्त्वमितरजायापरिग्रहाकाङ्क्षी वर्तमानस्त्वमस्यां जलराशिःसंवृत्त इत्यनेनोक्तं यत् तस्मादिति वाच्यं 'भो मत्सामर्थ्येनास्यां यतते चेदहं जलाशयो भवेयम्। तथा न भवत्सामर्थ्येनैषा साध्या भवेदिति मन्वानोऽहमेतादृशस्संवृत्तः' इत्यनेन ध्वनियुक्तया वाचा विज्ञापयामीति निश्चित्योत्तरग्रन्थेन नाहं जलराशिरिति समर्थयति। **मूर्खे**त्यादिना। मूर्ख इति पदे प्रोच्यमाने मूर्खशब्दस्यान्वयार्थं यस्सतामपि चेतांसीत्यनेन दर्शयेत्। भूयोऽपि तस्य पदस्यैवं त्वादृतेन जनेन ज्ञायते भगवन्मतिविगतिरिति विज्ञाप्योत्तरग्रन्थेन भूयोऽपि तथा समर्थयति **नैष जलराशिरि**ति। तत्र ध्वनिर्दृश्यते। पूर्वं जलाशयोऽसि संवृत्त इति यत्तेनोक्तं तदुत्तरग्रन्थेनान्यथाकरोति नैष जलराशिरित्यादिना। एष जनो न जलराशि एषोऽहं जलीभूतः किञ्च अविदितभगवन्मतिगतिस्त्वमतिजलनेत्रमरीचिश्च इति तं विज्ञाप्येति स्मरेत्। अहमिदानीं त्वं कृष्णं यथाभूतं न जानासीह तस्य गतिमति चेति मृगतृष्णिकावर्णनच्छलेन ध्वनिना तमनन्यविज्ञेयं विज्ञापयामीति आत्मना निश्चित्योत्तरश्लोकेन तथा विज्ञापयति भूयोऽपि मूर्खेति सम्बुद्ध्याह – पश्य! इत्युक्त्वा तस्य स्वरूपं न जानासीत्युत्तरश्लोकेन समर्थयति **ज्वलदवनिभिरि**त्यादिना। तत्र ध्वनिः। त्वमंशुभर्तुः मरीचीनुदकमयानभिमन्यसे इति सम्बन्धात् त्वमंशुभर्तुर्जगद्भर्तुः मरीचि मनोगतीरुदकमयानभिमन्यसे अस्थिरान्।[19]

असौ जगतिरश्मौ च मानसे गगने बुधौ।
मौक्तिकेप्यथमन्तेस्मिन्नंशुशब्दः प्रवर्तते।।
रश्मौ चैव मनोवृत्तौ मरीचिरिह वर्तते।

19 अंशुभर्तुः – कृष्णस्य, मरीचिः – मनोगतिः, उदकमयान् – अस्थिरान्। You think that Kṛṣṇa is not firm in his love to his devotees; he is not fickle. He will somehow fulfill my desire.

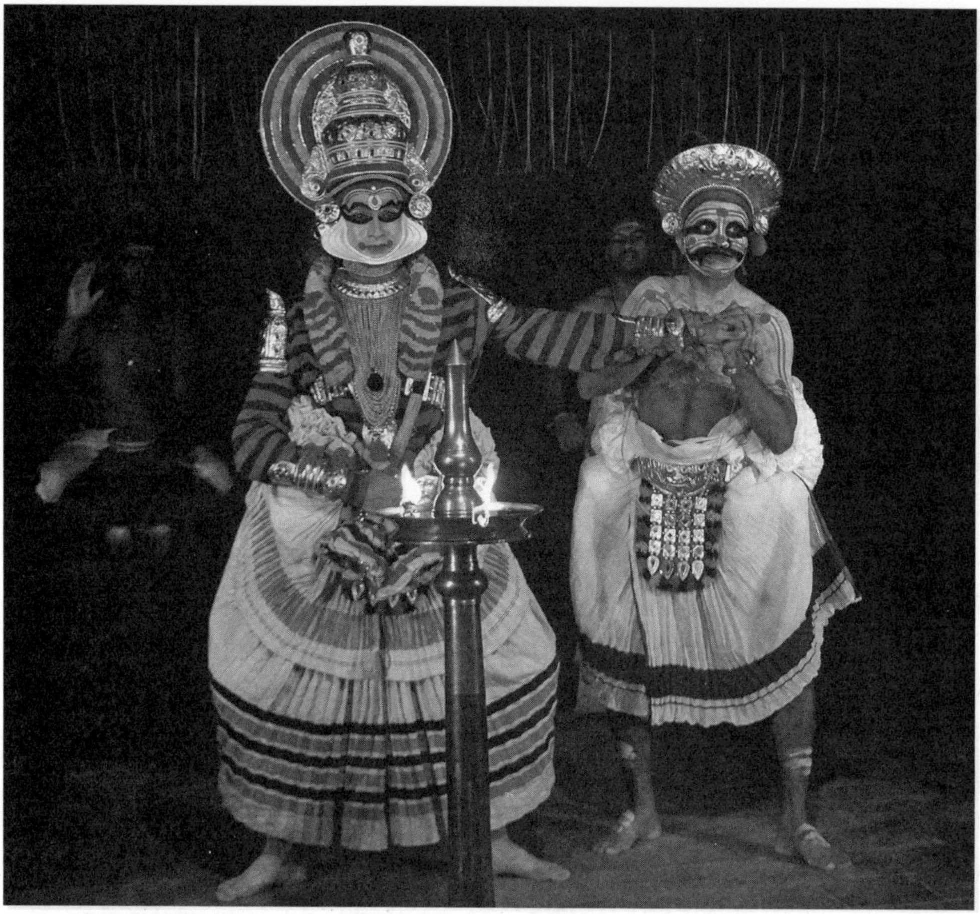

Arjuna and Vidūṣaka, Margi Madhu Chakyar and Sooraj Nambiar

जगद्भर्तुः कृष्णस्य मनोवृत्तिरित्यर्थः। कृष्णस्य मनोवृत्तेर्याथातथ्यं न विदितवानसीति यत् तत्र तव दोषो न स्यात्। कुतः आतपावलेपैरिति जलनेत्रमरीचिरसि आतपावलेपैरज्ञानावलेपैरिति जलनेत्रमरीचिरसि जलप्रवृत्तिरसीति यत् ततस्ते दोषो न स्यात्।

वस्त्रे पाशे च नयने चित्तेऽहंसेजगत्प्रभौ।
वर्तते नेत्रशब्दोऽयं कर्णधारे च भास्वति।।
आतपाख्यस्य शब्दस्य स्थितिरेषु प्रवर्तते।
अज्ञाने सप्रभायां च क्रोधे तापे परश्च धे।। इत्यनेकार्थः।

ज्वलदवनिभिः ज्वलद्गात्रैः अज्ञानावलेपैरित्यर्थः। अवनेः स्वरूपं देहः तस्मादवन्या देह उच्यते कृष्णसामर्थ्येन सा मम वश्या भवितेति मन्वानोऽहमेतत्कर्मणि कुर्वद्यत्नो भवामि विगतश्रमः तत्प्रवृत्तेयाथा

तथ्यमजानता हि त्वया हि श्रमो गन्तव्यः इत्यस्मिन् श्लोके ध्वनिना तं विज्ञाप्य भूयस्तदुत्तरं श्रोतुं तमेव पश्यंस्तिष्ठेत्। एवमस्य प्रयोगमार्गः।

विदूषकः सावधानं निर्वर्ण्य – अथ तदानीं भगवत्प्रसादान्मद्वशगामिनी भवेदियमिति ध्वनिना विज्ञापितोऽयं विदूषक इति स्मरेत्। अहो तत्प्राप्तेरुपायं भगवान् स्वयमेव दर्शयतीत्यनेनोक्तं तत्तथा भवेत् कुतः

कार्ये सन्देहवत्यन्तर्यदवस्फुरन् सताम्।
तद्धि प्रमाणमिति हि ब्रुवते मुनयोऽमलाः।।[20]

इत्यस्ति वसिष्ठेन दाशरथये प्रोक्तः। तत् तथा स्यादिति तस्यां कर्म सावधानं निर्वर्णितवानित्येनाममुष्मै भगवान् सर्वप्रकारेण मह्यं दास्यतीत्यनेनोक्तमिति सावधानं यथार्थं दृष्टवानित्यर्थः। इत्येतदर्थं **सावधानं निर्वर्ण्ये**त्येतत्पदं तत्र क्षिप्तवान् स कविः। अथ विदूषकस्तदानीं भगवत्प्रसादसाध्या भवेदिति निश्चित्येति स्मरेत्। तस्मादहमद्यप्रभृति तत्प्रवृत्त्यनुसारी भूत्वा द्रौपदिहेतोः कथञ्चित्कर्तव्यम्। यदि सुभद्राप्राप्तौ यतमानोऽयं तस्मान्निर्वर्तितव्यः। अथवा भवितव्यतयायं तत्परिणयनकारी भवेच्चेदेतत्प्रवृत्त्यनुसारी भूत्वामुना सह गच्छेयम्। तस्मादादौ श्रितसन्देहोऽहमिदानीं नष्टसन्देह इति तद्ध्वनिना विज्ञापयामीति निश्चित्योत्तरग्रन्थेन तथा समर्थयति **भो ण एसा** इत्यादिना भो इत्यादौ विवेके। अथ दीपाग्रे प्रेक्षकमुखे दीयमानदृष्टिस्तिष्ठन्नयं सविवेकं भो इति तदेतीति वदन् भूयोऽपि भो इति वदेत्। भो तर्हि परमियमनासाद्या न स्यात्। अस्याः परिणयने भगवानेव प्रमाणमिति निश्चितवानसि। तर्हि परं केवलमासाद्यैव स्यात् सेति मन्ये तस्मादियं मृगतृष्णिकातुल्या न स्यात् केवलमासाद्यैव स्यादित्यर्थः। तस्मादद्य प्रभृति ब्राह्मणतृष्णिका संवृत्ता इति भगवदनुग्रहेण साध्येयमिति विज्ञापितेन मयापि तेन तस्यां यत्नः कर्तव्य इति तस्यां तृषा कृता ब्राह्मणतृष्णिका च संवृत्ता इति विदूषकोऽद्यप्रभृति तत्प्राप्तौ तृष्णावानस्मीति विज्ञाप्य भूयस्तं भगवन्तं द्राक् क्वचित् स्थित्वा मनसा प्राप्नुहीत्युत्तरग्रन्थेन समर्थयति **अल ए दिणा** इत्यादिना। अलमेतेनेति तस्मात् तां प्रति सेयमासाद्येति मया प्रोच्यमानेन वचसा अलमित्युक्त्वा भूयस्तत्कार्यसिध्यर्थमुपायः कीदृगिति स्मरेत् इत्ययमिदानीं मया वक्तव्यः। त्वयेदानीं तत्प्राप्तिमभिलषता संश्रितमुनिजनतोऽस्मात्प्रदेशादन्यत्र गत्वा क्वापि विविक्तस्थले स्थितिं कुर्वता भगवदुपासना कर्तव्येति। इति विदूषकं स्मृत्वा मनसा निश्चित्योत्तरग्रन्थेन सध्वनिना तथा वदति, **तुवं दावे**त्यादिना। त्वं तावदभिमतं देशं प्रापयसीति सम्बन्धः। अत्राभिमतशब्देन कृष्ण उच्यते देशशब्देन चित्तं च। त्वदभिमतं कृष्णं देशं चित्तं प्रापयितुमिच्छसि। तस्मात् त्रिचतुरैः पदक्षेपैः प्रापयैनं चित्तम्। तत्र द्विकर्मापेक्षया णिजन्तं पदं तत्र प्रक्षिप्तवान् स कविः। त्रिचतुरैरिति त्रिभिः पदक्षेपैर्वा चतुर्भिः पदक्षेपैः वाक्याक्षरिमन्त्रक्षेपैर्ध्यानैर्वा चतुरक्षरिमन्त्रक्षेपैर्ध्यानैः वा ध्यात्वा तमभिमतं कृष्णं देशं चित्तं प्रापय।

अक्षरे प्रपदे राज्ये गोष्ठे वेदस्य खण्डने।
वर्तते पदशब्दोऽयं कुले नाममहोत्सवे।। इत्यनेकार्थः।
मानसे च प्रदेशे च देशशब्दः प्रवर्तते।

---

20 सतां हि सन्देहपदेषु वस्तुषु।
प्रमाणमन्तःकरणप्रवृत्तयः।। Abhijñānaśākuntala, Act I

तस्मान्मन्त्रध्यानादिभिः कृष्णं त्वच्चित्तं प्रापयेति मयोक्तमिति तं विज्ञाप्य तत्रास्य सौमुख्यमस्तिवा नवेति परिच्छेत्तुं तन्मुख एव पश्यन् दीपपुरस्तिष्ठेदिति तिष्ठति धनञ्जयस्तस्मिन् विज्ञाप्यमानमर्थं श्रृण्वन् समस्तः प्रवदन्तं तं श्रितप्रसादया दृष्ट्या पश्यन् सुप्रसन्नमुखो भूत्वा तमिति विज्ञापयेत्।

सखे अस्य देशस्य मुनिजनबाहुल्यात् तद्ध्यानं कर्तुं अक्षमोऽस्मीति तं विज्ञापयंस्तिष्ठेत्। अथैवं विज्ञापयति तस्मिन् स विदूषक इति स्मरेत्। भो अत्र भवते इदानीमिति प्रवर्तितव्यम्। अस्मात्किमिति दूरस्थं विविक्तस्थलं प्राप्य तत्रस्थो भूत्वा तद्ध्यानं विधेहीति वाच्योऽयमर्थमिति निश्चित्य तेनैव ग्रन्थेन तं तथा वदति, **त्रिचतुरैरि**त्यादिनेव। त्रिचतुरैः पदक्षेपैर्गत्वा विगतमुनिप्रदेशंप्राप्य तद्ध्यानपरे त्वयि भगवान् कृष्णः स्वयमेवात्राभ्येत्य स्वाभिमतं सुभद्रापरिणयनं कारयति हि इति विज्ञाप्य तद्ध्यानकार्याधिकार्यसीति समर्थयति **मारुतिसोदर** इति ग्रन्थेन। पेशलजङ्घाजवः निर्मलमानसश्च तदस्माद् गत्वा तद्ध्यानपरो भवेति विज्ञाप्य तिष्ठेत् तन्मुखं पश्यन्नेव। अथेति तेन विज्ञाप्यमानोऽयं धनञ्जयस्तथा दीपाग्रे तिष्ठन्नेतद् वचश्रृण्वन्नमुष्य स्वप्रवृत्त्यनुकूलतां वचसि दृष्ट्वा तन्मुखे प्रसादः पिशुनयन्त्या दृष्ट्या वीक्ष्य तं सम्मान्य त्वं सखेऽद्यप्रभृति मत्प्रवृत्त्यनुकूलो भवेति तया विभावयेत्। एवं दीपमुखस्तिष्ठन्नेतन्मुखे पश्यन्नयं विदूषकस्तवास्य प्रसादः स्यादिति गिरार्धमर्धं व्यवहरन् स्मितपूर्वया प्रेक्षकान् सुखयित्वा रङ्गतले प्रेक्षकमुखेषु पश्यन्नेव चरेत्।[21] एवं चरन्नयमित्येवमर्धमर्धं वदेत्। मयेदानीमवस्थोभयत्रापि दुरन्ता स्यात्। एतद्वचनकारी भूत्वास्य प्रवृत्तौ प्रयते यदि द्रौपदी हन्ताद्य प्रभृति स्वबाहुभ्यां पृथुकापूपमोदकेक्षुरसमध्वादीनि स्वादुवस्तूनि मम ददती भक्षयन्तां भवतेति पूर्ववन्न दास्यति हि, किञ्च मधुरोपदंशमिलितोदनपिण्डं चापि। अस्यानुकूलो भवेयमिति चेत् तत्र श्रुतिस्मृतिविरोधो विद्यत इत्युभयत्र दोषः। तथाप्येतदनुगामी भूत्वा चरन् सा दिष्टवशादेतद्भार्या भविष्यति चेत् तदानीं तथा पाञ्चाल्याः कोपो मा स्यात् तथाप्यपहरन्नमुष्यामप्रियो भविष्यामि। तस्मादद्य प्रभृति अस्यानुकूलो भूत्वा द्रौपद्यां वर्तमानं याथातथ्यं विज्ञापयेयमिति मनसा निश्चित्**याहं पुन** इत्यादि ग्रन्थेन द्रौपदींप्रति स्वावस्थामितः पूर्वं याथार्थ्यं विज्ञाप्यातः परं तवानुकूलो भवामिति समर्थयति **अहं पुनरि**ति। अहं पुनः ज्वलनज्वालोद्गारिभिः तरणिकिरणै तत्र मार्गे परिलुठन् कथमप्यागत इति सम्बन्धः।

भो विस्मृततरणिकिरणस्य गच्छतस्तव पृष्ठानुगामी अहं तरणिकिरणैर्भ्रामितः परितप्तः। इह तरणिशब्देनावरोधमुच्यते। किरणशब्देन क्रोधं च।

> भवेत् तरणिशब्दोऽयं चण्डांशौ मानसे सुते।
> सर्वज्ञे ब्रह्मणि द्रोण्यां अवरोधे तपस्विषु।।

इत्यनेकार्थः। अत्र तरणिशब्दो ध्वनौ अवरोधे अन्यत्र रवौ।

> क्रोधकररत्नहेमत्विडध्रिपाः......
> प्रतापोशनि वह्निस्ते भवन्ति किरणाश्रिताः।

ध्वनौ क्रोधेऽन्यत्र रश्मौ। भो अहं विस्मरदितरकार्यं गच्छन्तं भवन्तं दृष्ट्वा भवन्तमनुसर्तुमक्षमोऽपि कौण्डिन्य भवता प्रमादादवस्थायुक्ते जगति रक्ष्यो मे नाथ इति पाञ्चाल्या प्रेषितोऽहं यत् ततस्तत्र

21 This direction is to the actor regarding his movements. What follows is like a soliloquy of vidūṣaka.

पाञ्चालीविषये लुठन्तो लुठन् इतस्ततश्चेतसा किं कर्तव्यमिति मार्गे परिभ्रमन्तमनुसरन् भृशं तरणिकिरणैः कृष्णाख्यावरोधक्रोधैः ज्वलनोद्गारिभिः ज्वलनोद्गमद्भिः सुभद्राप्राप्तावप्राप्तावपि तथाभूतैरवरोधक्रोधैर्बाध्यमानौ भविष्याव इति मन्वानोऽहं तत्र तद्विषये भृशं परितप्तोऽहमितः पूर्वमभवम्। कस्तत्र हेतुरिति चेत् तत्रावरोधपांसुपटले, पांसुशब्देन स्नेहो ध्वन्यते पांसोः स्नेहस्य च द्वयोरपि मार्दवं गुणः तथाभूतत्वात् पांसुशब्देन स्नेह उच्यते। पूर्वमतीष्टायां कृष्णायां त्वन्निमित्तं भवति पांसुपटले स्नेहराशौ सति दुर्बलपादसञ्चारो दुर्बलमनस्सञ्चारः दुर्बलमनःप्रसारो नित्यबुभुक्षितो ब्राह्मणत्वान्नित्यचलचित्तस्संवृत्तोऽस्मि। 'पादशब्दोऽङ्घ्रिचेतसो'रित्यमरसिंहः। तथा संवृत्तोऽपि सोऽहमतःपरस्मिन् कार्ये भवतस्थैर्यादस्मात् किमपि दूरं गत्वा जलाशयमन्वेषयामीति निश्चितवानधुनास्मि। अतिजलमरीचिरसीत्युक्तोऽपि अहमतःपरमेनां घटयितुं जलाशयोपेतमपि भवन्तमन्वेषयामि। एवं ध्वन्यर्थेनास्मात्पूर्वं स्वावस्थामतः पश्चाच्चतामिति ज्ञाप्यते। तस्मादन्यत्र गन्तुं प्रसादोऽस्ति वा नवेति परिच्छेत्तुं तन्मुख एव पश्यंस्तिष्ठेत्। तत्र जलाशयमिति शब्दः क्रियाविशेषणम्। तथा विज्ञाप्यमानां विदूषकगिरं श्रृण्वन्नयं धनञ्जयो यथाभूतमात्मावस्थां श्रुत्वा जिगमिषुमिमं वीक्ष्य सस्मितं तथा कुर्वति दिशा प्रेरयंस्तिष्ठेत्। एवं तिष्ठति विदूषकः किमपि किमपि चार्धमर्धं ध्वनिद्योतकं वाचो व्यवहरन् प्रेक्षकान् सुखयंस्तस्मादन्यत्र गन्तुं परिक्रामति। एवं परिक्रामन् कथंकारमेतद्भविष्यतीत्युद्गतदृष्टिर्विमृशेत्। एवं विमृशन् गच्छन्नयं भूयोऽधोदृष्टिर्विमृशेत्। एवं विमृशन् सहसा मेघावृतत्वमिव भानोरवनिं नष्टतापां वीक्ष्य किमिदमिति स्मरन् एतद् वेदितुं ऊर्ध्वमवलोकितवानित्यूर्ध्वं पश्यन् विवेकार्थं **भो** इत्युत्तरग्रन्थं वदेत्। भो किमेतत् पुनरपि तमेवमपश्यन् भो मन्ये काञ्चिदबलां बलादुद्धृत्य कश्चित् स्वदेहकार्ष्ण्यकार्कश्यनिर्जितमन्दरगिरिराधावतीति स्मरन्। भूय आश्चर्यमिति उत्तरं वदति कीदृग्भूतमिदमवस्थान्तरं भवितव्यता भवतीह नृणामविवेकिनामपि विवेकधियां किमये न कां पिकगिरां च दशामियमेव देहिषु हि तत्प्रभूता तस्मादेतदवस्थान्तरं कीदृग्भूतमिति निरूपणीयं वयस्येन सह सत्वरमेतद् वयस्यायायं तिरोधत्ते पुरो निवेदितव्यम्। तस्मात् कथङ्कारं निवेदयामि।

श्रृण्वतां व्रतिनामेषामीषद्ध्वनियुता गिरा
एतद् विज्ञापयाम्यस्मै प्रायः प्रहसनोत्तरम्।

इत्यात्मना निश्चित्योत्तरग्रन्थेन तथा विज्ञापयति **भो व अस्ये**त्यादिना। कोऽपि काचिदुत्सङ्गे कृत्वा धावति इत्यन्वयः। कोऽपि अकालजलधरः काञ्चिदचिरप्रभां इति काञ्चित् स्त्रियमचिरप्रभां भङ्गुरायुषं कृत्वा धावति – अकालजलधर इति। जलधरःगगनचारी प्रमथः अकाले मध्याह्ने कश्चित्प्रमथः कामपि स्त्रियं भङ्गुरायुषं कृत्वा अकाले मध्याह्ने अयमाधावति

भूतानां च पिशाचानां नगानां यक्षरक्षसाम्।
कालस्सञ्चरितुं धात्रा मध्यरात्रं प्रकल्पितम्।।

इत्यस्ति शास्त्रे परमेश्वरेण दर्शितम्। तदर्थमकालेत्युक्तवानस्मि। तस्मादनाथामिवाक्रन्दन्ती स्वां निजं नीयमानमेनामिह सत्वरमभ्येत्य परित्राहीति ध्वनिना यथार्थं विज्ञाप्य बाह्यार्थं प्रहसनोत्तरं कथयेत्। एवमितस्ततस्ससम्भ्रममुत्पतत्परिभ्रमेत्। एवमस्य प्रयोगमार्गः।

अथ भगवदनुग्रहात्किमसाध्यमिति तस्मै विज्ञाप्य तिष्ठन्नयं धनञ्जयस्तदानीं भगवद् स्मृत्या तद्दर्शने किमसाध्यं नामेति प्रोच्य स्वयमनादृत्य गच्छन्तं दृष्ट्वेति स्मरेत्। अहो मामत्र स्थापयित्वा गतोऽभूत् माणवकः। तस्मात् किन्नु खलूद्दिश्य अस्माद् गच्छामि भगवत्स्मृत्यै स्थानमिदं न शस्तमिति चेत् तेन प्रोक्तं कर्तव्यं हि स्यात्। तस्माद् तत्र गन्तुमुपायं न पश्यामि तत् कथङ्कारं गच्छामीति सविवेकं तत्र तिष्ठन्नयं तेन साश्चर्यमुच्यमानां वाणीं सहसा श्रृणुयात्। एवं श्रृण्वन्निति स्मरेत्। हन्तेदानीमयमस्माद् गत्वा तस्य प्रलापोक्तेर्याथातथ्यं इच्छतीति विभावयन् वच्मीत्यात्मनो निश्चित्य तत्साधयितुमुत्तरग्रन्थेन समर्थयति, **किन्नु खलु** इत्यादिना। अयं धनञ्जयस्तदानीमेव सन्ध्येयं तत्र तिष्ठन् किन्नु खल्वयमित्यादि ग्रन्थं सविवेकं वदति परिक्रामति तदर्थं तत्पदं तत्र प्रक्षिप्तवान्। एवं परिक्रम्य तत्समीपं समभ्येत्य स्वयमप्यूर्ध्वं विलोकितवान्। अथैवं पश्यन्नूर्ध्वमिति स्मरेत्। कोनु खल्वयं नभसा प्रतिष्ठसे। मन्येऽस्य गगनचारित्वात् कश्चित्प्रमथ इति। किमनेन नीयते एषा किं काचिदबला तामेव सावधानं पश्यन्नियं काचित् स्त्री वा कन्यका वा पश्यन्नियं कन्यका नाम। पश्य

अच्छिन्नमलकजालं श्रवसि क्षिप्तवञ्चुले।
कण्ठोऽमाङ्गलिकोऽस्यायं मन्येऽतः कन्यकेति ताम्।।

इति निश्चित्योत्तरग्रन्थेन तथा तस्मै तां विज्ञापयति **सखे** इत्यादिना इति विज्ञाप्य भूय इति स्मरेत्।

नारक्षिष्यदिमां बालां प्रमथाङ्कात् भयप्रदात्।
रक्ष्ये रक्षणशीलोऽयं स्थातव्यश्चापवानिह।।

स्मरन्नरुणायमानदृग्धनुरादाय सहसा क्रोधाविष्टहृदयो भूत्वा सक्रोधं सधैर्यं सक्षात्रं तस्यां सानुकम्पमुत्तरग्रन्थेन तस्मै क्रुध्यति **आः दुरात्मन्नि**त्यादिना। इत्युत्क्रान्तं हत्वा तां रक्षितुं शरं सन्धत्ते।

विदूषकः अथैवं कुर्वन्तं तिष्ठन्तं तं पश्यन्नयं विदूषकः तथेति स्मरेत्। इदानीं सुभद्रार्थं यतमानस्यास्य प्रशंसामुपपादयन्तीभिर्गीभिर्व्याहृत्य तस्यां गतचित्तमेतदीयममुष्मिन्नरौ तन्निन्दाकृतिक्षत्रियत्वात् प्रक्षेप्तव्यं न किं सर्वथाहं तत्र प्रवर्तितव्य इति निश्चित्योत्तरग्रन्थेन तत्प्रशंसां करोति। तदर्थं केवलबाह्यार्थोऽयं ग्रन्थः।[22]

अथ धनञ्जयस्तथाभूतं दृष्ट्वा शरं प्रतिसंहरेत्।

(नेपथ्ये) रक्ष हा रक्ष।

अथैवं तिष्ठन्नयं धनञ्जयस्सहसोर्ध्वभागाद् रक्षेति कञ्चित् स्त्रीविलापरवं श्रृण्वन्नितस्ततः परिभ्रमन्निति स्मरेत्। अहो मयैषा छिन्नपातं निपतति पुरा रक्षितव्यैषेति निश्चित्योत्तरग्रन्थेन तथा समर्थयंस्तदवलम्बनाय प्रसारितकरस्तिष्ठेत्।

22 There in no inner-meaning in the words that follows. Bāhyārtha stands in contrast with Dhvanyartha.

VIII

The Heroine on Stage

(ततः प्रविशति पतन्ती कन्यका)

(A maiden is seen falling down)

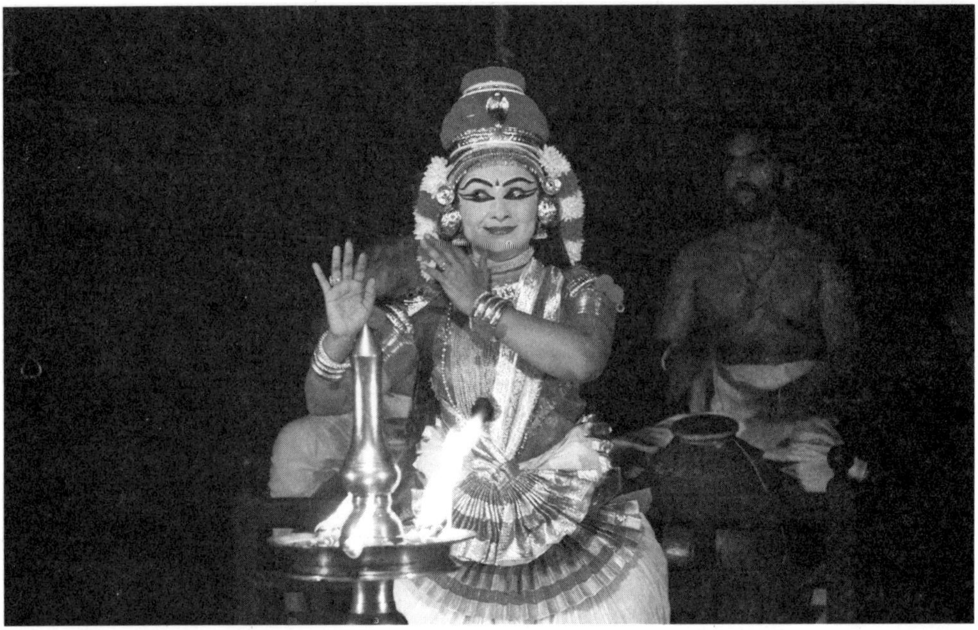

Dr. Indu G as Subhadrā

Vyaṅgyavyākhyā

Prāveśika

Subhadrā, sister of Lord Kṛṣṇa, reading the ten names of Dhanañjaya stitched in the bodice and hearing constantly stories about his adventures from elders, fell deeply in love with him. She was longing to have some how, a look at him. One day, while she was sitting alone on the terrace of her house immersed in the thoughts of Dhanañjaya, a demon Alambusa forcibly carried her on the instruction of Balabhadra who wanted to distance her mind from Dhanañjaya and to give her in marriage to Duryodhana. She saw an exalted youth standing below near Prabhāsatīrtha and cried aloud for help. Suddenly, being released by the demon she fell on his hands. Terribly upset and trembling with fear she looked upon her saviour who excelled cupid in appearance.[1]

कन्यका (ससाध्वसं सकम्पं च धनञ्जयं तिर्यक् पश्यन्ती स्वगतम्) को णुखु एसो महाणुभाओ तेल्लोक्कदुल्लहरूवादिसओ मं अमुकम्पेदि। (को नु खल्वेष महानुभावस्त्रैलोक्यदुर्लभ रूपातिशयो मामनुकम्पते)

Maiden (Looking at Dhanañjaya with embarrassment and shaking with fear; to herself) This great man, whose good looks are unequalled in all three worlds – who is he to take pity on me?

धनञ्जय (सस्पृहं सरोमविक्रियं च स्वगतम्)

Dhana (With anxiety, hair bristling; to himself)

Vyaṅgyavyākhyā

Draupadī was my first love; then I heard of Subhadrā; now I see this beautiful girl. I am attracted to all the three.

How this fickleness to the mind of Dhanañjaya who is the brother of King Dharmaputra, son of the wind-god Bhīma and the twins Nakula and Sahadeva?

How Dhanañjaya, the brave has fallen to fluctuations!

Leave Draupadī. Subhadrā described by Gada and this maiden before me – are they one and the same?

Who knows the mind of Lord Kṛṣṇa?

Let both Kṛṣṇa my benefactor and Kāma the embodiment of love, be my close associates.

चलकुवलयधाम्नोरञ्जनस्निग्धमक्ष्णो-
भयचलधृतियुग्मं केयमालोलयन्ती।
मुखपरिमललोभाद् भृङ्गदत्तानुयात्रा
शिथिलयति सुभद्रामुद्रितं मानसं मे।। १२।।[2]

---

1 This is the Praveśika and the transient mood of the heroine. She is excited by the sight and touch of the youth. She feels guilty of herself as she is already in love with Dhanañjaya. This is the conflict caused in her mind.

2 This verse is performed in an elaborate manner in Kūṭiyāṭṭam today. Actors take the word अञ्जनस्निग्ध to present the decoration of a woman (Kōppaṇiyikkal). All the make-up is done, orna-

This woman's eyes, beautiful as a pair of blue lotuses,
adorned with black collyrium, agitated from fear,
the fragrance of her face attracting a flight of bees
Who is she to unfasten my heart from Subhadrā? (12)

Vyaṅgyavyākhyā

These words come out involuntarily as though prompted by my inner conscience. What does this outburst means?

Does it mean that the pair of beautiful eyes unlocks my mind sealed out by Subhadrā?

Or do the eyes of Subhadrā unfasten the mind sealed by Draupadī?

Who is this maiden? Is she Subhadrā?

I cannot reveal to Kauṇḍinya before ascertaining the truth. Therefore I will convey him in ordinary words.

कन्यका (दीर्घं निःश्वस्य स्वगतम्) अहो अदिविसमसीळदा वम्महस्स, जं भूदअरविमद्दकादरं अण्णगआणुराअं च इमं पि जणं उद्दिसिअ पहरन्तो बन्धइत्तणं आरोवेदुं आढत्तो। (अहो अतिविषमशीलता मन्मथस्य, यद् भूतकरविमर्दकातरमन्यगतानुरागं चेममपि जनमुद्दिश्य प्रहरन् बन्धकीत्वमारोपयितुमारब्धः)

Maiden (Sighing deeply, to herself) Strange is the nature of the God of Love, who afflicts me though I am already shaken by a demon's touch, and emotionally attached to someone else. Is he trying to reduce me to the status of a harlot?

Vyaṅgyavyākhyā

I had only Dhanañjaya in my mind. He was with in me while playing, eating, bathing, praying and everywhere. Now this handsome youth attracts me. This is unbecoming of a chaste woman born in the lineage of Vṛṣṇis. Why this fickleness to my mind?

धनञ्जयः (सवितर्कं स्वगतम्) (Surmising, to himself)

Vyaṅgyavyākhyā

My mind locked tightly by Pāñcālī is now opened by Subhadrā. Now this maiden fallen from the sky. Will she be of divine origin? Otherwise how does she fly in the air?

---

ments are put on. Yet something is lacking. Then the maid finds out that collyrium is not applied to the eyes. She does it and completes the process of decoration.

As *VV* is silent on this kind of elaboration, it has to be presumed that actors added it later.

No. The feet of divine ladies when they come down the earth will not touch the soil, the flowers they wear will fade, their body will sweat and become pale. These are not true in her case. Hence she is not a celestial being. Then how she moved through the sky?

The Lord, always compassionate to his devotees, heard my prayer and has shown her to me. My mind is attracted towards her. I did not experience such a feeling either in the company of the Nāga girl or with the princess of Pāṇḍya.

I have no evidence to prove that she is Subhadrā revealed to me by the Lord.

But I confirm on the strength of my inner consciousness that this maiden is none other than Subhadrā.

But, then, the brazier described by Gada is not seen on her breasts. What is the reason for that?

क्षिप्तक्षौमो प्रकम्पादुरसिजकलशावुच्छ्वसत्पत्रभङ्गौ
मीलन्नीलाम्बुजश्रीरनतिमुकुलितो मुग्धपातः कटाक्षः।
रोहद्रोमाञ्चभाजः श्रमजलकणिकाभ्युद्गतिर्गण्डसीम्नो-
र्भीत्या किं वा कियत्यामपि मदनदशायाममुष्याः प्रवेशात्।। १३।।
Silk slips from her fear-shaken breasts, their cosmetics cracking;
timid, sidelong glances vie in beauty with closing blue lotuses,
her body's hair stand up, and her neck perspires.
Is this due to fear or to the stimulation of love? (13)

Vyaṅgyavyākhyā

The bodice might have fallen down when she was carried away by the demon. It will be somewhere here on the ground.

How rare and enchanting is her beauty! Does she love me or not? Her eyes, half-closed, indicate her love. Sweating, horripilation, all show that she is passionately in love with me.

Vidūṣ This fellow has fallen in love with this woman too. He thinks that she is in love with him. Hence he looks at her and enjoys her beauty. I will take him to Indraprastha.

Maiden When will I be gratified enjoying, in nights, incessantly this cupid-incarnate? Oh! My eyes! Drink passionately the nectar in the form of youthful body until you are satisfied.

कन्यका को णु खु मं पुणो वि कड्ढेइ। (निष्क्रान्ता) (को नु खलु मां पुनरपि कर्षति)

Maiden *Who is that pulls at me again! (Exit)*

विदूषकः (ससम्भ्रमम्) अविहा, एसा का वि जिक्खिणी णो भक्खेदुं अदंसणं उवगदा। अहो मम भग्गदोसो, जं भूदसंभमेण अन्तरिअबुभुक्खापिवासस्स अण्णारिसो पाणंससओ उवणदो। ता पलाअहा। (अविहा, एषा कापि यक्षिणी नौ भक्षयितुमदर्शनमुपगता। अहो मम भाग्यदोषः, यद् भूतसम्भ्रमेणान्तरितबुभुक्षापिपासस्यान्यादृशः प्राणसंशय उपनतः। तत् पलायावहे)

(With anxiety) She is some nymph, remains concealed in order to devour us. How unfortunate I am! I had forgotten hunger and thirst due to the demon but now, afraid of death. So let's get away!

धनञ्जयः (स्वगतम्) हन्त क्षणभङ्गुराणि भाग्यविलसितानि, यदनयोर्नयनयोरपर्यवसित एव विधिना स माच्छिन्नोऽयममृतपानोत्सवः।

(To himself) Alas! Good fortune is short-lived; before these eyes could be satiated by drinking nectar, fate has taken her away.

Vyaṅgyavyākhyā

When will I get an opportunity to embrace her? My friend is testing me. I will reveal to him a bit of my love towards her by telling that she is not a celestial woman.

(प्रकाशम्) मूर्ख ! न सा दिव्यकन्यका। तस्याः खलु

घर्माम्भः कणिका कपोलतलयोरालुप्तपत्रक्रिया
नेत्रेन्दीवरयोः प्रतिक्षणकृतप्रस्पन्दिते पक्ष्मणी।

(Aloud) Fool! She is not a divine nymph. For,

Sweat on her cheeks has washed off some of their make-up;
her lotus-like eyes have constantly trembling lashes;

Vyaṅgyavyākhyā

Friend! Her responses show that she loves me.

पादौ स्पृष्टभुवौ स्थलाम्बुरुहयोः प्राप्तौ प्रतिस्पर्धितां
her feet touching the earth are like lotuses on the ground,

Vyaṅgyavyākhyā

The imprints of lotus-feet indicate that she will be married to a man born of higher order.

म्लायन्ति स्म शनैर्मिलन्मधुकरा धम्मिल्लमालागुणाः।। १४।।
her hair's bee-infested garlands are slightly wilted. (14)

Vyaṅgyavyākhyā

The garlands show that she will be married within the seven day circle.

She is a human being. And we are in love with each other.

Vidūṣaka: My friend has spoken quite convincingly. No doubt they love each other.

Is she Subhadrā herself? I will test him again.

विदूषकः भो पंण्डिदग्गेसर ! कहं पुण माणुसीए तिस्से तिरक्खरणीसंभवो। (भो पण्डिताग्रेसर ! कथं पुनर्मानुष्यास्तस्यास्तिरस्करणीसम्भवः)

O foremost among the learned, how did that human damsel vanish?

धनञ्जयः वयस्य ! तत्राप्येष एव मे तर्कः।

Friend, I too have the same doubt.

Vyaṅgyavyākhyā

How did she disappear? God alone can give an answer. Yes. I will meditate the Lord.

(Stands some time in a meditative mood.
Then, as though he got the answer tells the Prekṣakas)

The Lord tells me:

'Oh! Dear Pārtha! The girl who fell from the sky and exchanged loving glances, is none other than Subhadrā.

I showed my younger sister to you and caused her disappearance before your eyes.

Do you not know that Kṛṣṇa will offer himself to his devotees – he be a sage or a savage. Why do you worry?

Your doubts, if any, will be cleared when you see the gātrikā that Gada had described to you.'

Hence, I will search for the bodice.

Now, I have to reach Dvārakā. If I go in my real attire it will raise many doubts. The intoxicated retinue of Balabhadra who are close friends of Duryodhana will ask themselves – Why Dhanañjaya has come to Kṛṣṇa's house leaving Pāñcālī in the year allotted for him? People around will say 'Yes. We too have heard that he had a secret discussion with Gada in Prabhāsatīrtha.

If Gada met him in the last month he might have told him about Subhadrā's proposed marriage to Duryodhana. Therefore, Dhanañjaya has come here to seek secretly the hand of Subhadrā to Kṛṣṇa who is his close friend.

Oh! Kṛṣṇa give me your sister. Both of us will live happily.

Nothing is impossible to you who is the overlord of all the three worlds.

Kṛṣṇa will tell him:

Away with these words of praise. My elder brother has resolved to give her in marriage to Suyodhana. This is a mutual agreement. Authority in such matters rests with the elder brother.

When they hear these words they would in joy, clap their thighs – 'right right.' Should I forcefully carry away Subhadrā entering the city in the night as a thief? Then the gate-keepers will create obstructions. I will not get her if I go undisguised. Hence I will disguise myself as a mendicant and invoke the Lord. The great Ātreya has prescribed that ascetics should live together for three maṇḍalas starting from the full-moon in the month of Āṣāḍha. I will accordingly become an ascetic. Then people will not ask me as to why you are wandering here. I can walk freely without causing doubt to anyone. The only difficulty is that ascetics by nature have renounced worldly pleasures, especially those related to women.

My friend Kauṇḍinya, using words with implied meaning, will ridicule me.

However, there is no other option for me to achieve the object of my desire.

Now, how will I give an answer to his questions? I will select words which can be interpreted in both ways.

अन्तर्हितेन केनाप्यन्तर्धानमुपनीतया भवितव्यम्।
Somebody who remained unseen must have dragged her away.

Vyaṅgyavyākhyā

She has been taken away by Garuḍa.[3]

विदूषकः जइ एव्वं, रक्खिदो अहं देव्वेण। (सकरुणम्) सा उण तवस्सिणी पुणो वि तेण च्चिअ भूदेणणीदत्ति तक्केमि। (यद्येवं रक्षितोऽहं दैवेन। सा पुनस्तपस्विनी पुनरपि तेनैव भूतेन नीतेति तर्कयामि।)
If so, I have been saved by fate. (Sorrowfully) I think the poor girl must have been snatched away again by that demon.

Vyaṅgyavyākhyā

You speak me in words that can be interpreted in many ways. I also will resort to the same technique.
We[4] have then been blessed by the Lord.

3 केन by whom? Suggested sense – by Garuḍa. ध्वनौ ताक्ष्ये। Refer the commentary for different meanings of कः।

4 The verbal rendering is अहं (I), but enacts through eyes आवां (we). Both of us are saved.

धनञ्जयः सखे! मा मैवम्। न खलु मद्भुजपरिघसकाशवर्तिनीं तां भूयस्तर्कयिष्यन्ति परिपन्थिनः। तन्मन्ये बान्धवैरपवाहितेति।

Not likely, my friend. No enemy could again snatch away somebody who is under the protection of my mighty arms. So I think that her own relatives must have taken her away.

विदूषकः भो अदिपण्डिदेण वि कदाइ असंबद्धं मन्तिदव्वं होइ। जइ सा माणुसी, कहं पुण तिस्से बन्धवा अत्ताणं तं च अदंसणं णेदुं इस्सरा होन्ति। (भो अतिपण्डितेनापि कदाचिद् असंबद्धं मन्त्रयितव्यं भवति। यदि सा मानुषी, कथं पुनस्तस्या बान्धवा आत्मानं तां चादर्शनं नेतुमीश्वरा भवन्ति।)

Sir, even a very learned person may say something improbable. If she is human how could her relatives snatch her away while remaining unseen, and make her invisible too?

धनञ्जयः मूर्ख! गरुत्मद्वाहनबाहुविहितक्षेमक्षितिमण्डलवर्तिनीनां प्रजानामापदि सम्बन्धिन्यो देवताः।

Fool! For those who are protected by the mighty hands of the Lord whose vehicle is Garuḍa, divine intervention occurs in dangerous situations.

विदूषकः भो एदस्सिं विवादे तुह मए दिण्णो जणो। अण्णं किं पि रहस्सं पुच्छिस्सं। तदाणिं तिस्से पहासूईहि णिरवसेसं दुक्खअं मे अक्खिजुअलं। तदे मए ण सा दिट्ठा। केरिसो तत्तहोदीए रुवादिसओ। (भोः एतस्मिन् विवादे तव मया दत्तो जयः। अन्यत् किमपि रहस्यं प्रक्ष्यामि। तदानीं तस्याः प्रभासूचिभिर्निरवशेषं दुःक्षतं मेऽक्षियुगलम्। ततो मया न सा दृष्टा। कीदृशस्तत्र भवत्या रूपातिशयः।)

I concede victory to you in this argument. Let me ask you something confidential. At that time my eyes were dazzled by her brilliance and so I did not see her properly. What about her extraordinary beauty?

Vyaṅgyavyākhyā

He is very much disturbed by the thought of Subhadrā. I will ask him directly without resorting to any kind of suggestion

This place is deserted. The situation is also not suitable for pretentious words of suggestions.[5]

I will ask him in clear words.

धनञ्जयः (निःश्वस्य) सखे! मन्ये ममापि वाचस्तद्रूपातिशयवर्णनास्वपर्याप्तनैपुणाः। एतावत् तु कथयामि-

सौन्दर्यं सुकुमारता मधुरता कान्तिर्मनोहारिता
श्रीमत्ता महिमेति सर्गविभवान् निश्शेषनारीगुणान्।

---

5 केवलार्थोयं ग्रन्थः, व्यङ्ग्यं विना रूपवर्णनं करोति – There are instances in the dramatic text which do not bear suggested sense. But such verses have Malayalam parodies added later. See the next chapter.

एतस्यामुपयुज्य दुर्विधतया दीनः परामात्मभूः
स्रष्टुं वाच्छति चेत् करोतु पुनरप्यत्रैव भिक्षाटनम्।। १५।।

(Sighing) Friend, I think my words are not capable of describing her extreme beauty. This much I shall tell you -

Exhausting in her creation all the feminine qualities of charm, delicacy, sweetness, lustre, grace, majesty, and dignity,
Brahmā has put himself into a predicament: if he wants to create another lady, he will have to borrow them from her! (15)

विदूषकः (सविषादं स्वगतम्) सव्वहा सिविणे वि मम णत्थि इन्दप्पत्थप्पवेसो, जेण जदाकदाइ दिट्ठं वा सुदं वा इत्थिअं कामेदुं एसो पवुत्तो। इत्थिआमई दुवारवई त्ति सुणीअदि। तं पविट्ठो ण आणामि केरिसे उम्मादे पडिस्सदि त्ति। तो एव्वं उवालम्भिस्सं। (सर्वथा स्वप्नेपि मम नास्तीन्द्रप्रस्थप्रवेशः, येन, यदाकदाचिद् दृष्टां वा श्रुतां वा स्त्रियं कामयितुमेष प्रवृत्तः। स्त्रीमयी द्वारवतीति श्रूयते। तां प्रविष्टो न जानामि कीदृश उन्मादे पतिष्यतीति। तदेवमुपालप्स्ये।)

(Sorrowfully, to himself) There is absolutely no chance for me to enter the city of Indraprastha even in a dream, since this fellow has begun to love any damsel he sees or even hears about. The city of Dvāravatī is said to be full of women. I don't know into what sort of a confusing situation he is likely to fall, so I'll chastise him like this.

Vyaṅgyavyākhyā

He is in an excited mood while describing her. The journey to Indraprastha will take place only after marrying her. I fear that he will forget Pāñcālī for ever.

Nobody is here to overhear us. I will ask him straight away whether his love towards Pāñcālī is lost altogether.

(प्रकाशम्) भो वअस्स! किञ्चि मए पुच्छिदो किं अकुविदो कहेदि अत्तभवं। (भो वयस्य! किञ्चिन्मया पृष्टः किमकुपितः कथयत्यत्रभवान्।)

(Aloud) Friend! If I ask you something will you answer without getting angry with me?

धनञ्जयः ननु प्रभवति भवानस्मदनुबन्धेषु व्यापारेषु। विस्रब्धं पृच्छ्यताम्।
Of course, you are free to share knowledge relating to my own activities. You may ask without any restraint.

विदूषकः तत्तहोदीए पञ्चालीए वुत्तन्तो पाहेअसङ्गहो विअ मग्गे उवभुञ्जिअ खअं णीदो। पुणो को वि सुभद्दासद्दो तुमं विहुरेदुं आढत्तो। सो वि इमाए आआसइत्थिआए उवमद्दिओ। कुदो दे उवणदा अपुव्वा इअं लोलदा। (तत्र भवत्याः पाञ्चाल्या वृत्तान्तः पाथेयसङ्ग्रह इव मार्गे उपभुज्यक्षयं नीतः। पुनः कोऽपि सुभद्राशब्दस्त्वां विधुरयितुमारब्धः। सोऽप्यनयाकाशस्त्रियोपमर्दितः। कुतस्ते उपनतापूर्वेयं लोलता।)

The story of Draupadī has already been exhausted, like food consumed on the way. Then some word like 'Subhadrā' has started to give you uneasiness. Now that has been subdued by this 'lady from the sky'. Why this fickleness, which is quite unnatural to you?

धनञ्जयः सखे! अपरमार्थवेदिना भवतैवमभिहितं, यतो मम हृदयमशक्यमन्याभिः पार्षतीकटाक्ष-शृङ्खलासङ्घटितं विघटयितुम्। अन्ययोः पुनः कन्यकयोरस्मच्चेतोवृत्तेर्याथातथ्यं कथयामि।

एकस्याः किमपि वपुः श्रुतेन नाम्ना
सङ्कल्पैर्लिखितममुत्र चित्तभित्तौ।
अन्यस्याश्चरितफले दृशौ शरीरे
प्रेयस्योः पृथुलदृशोरियं दशा मे।। १६।।
(सचिन्तस्तिष्ठति)

Friend, You say this since you do not know the truth. No one could separate my heart from the bonds of the sidelong glances of Draupadī. I shall tell you about my feelings in relation to the other two damsels.

Imagination pictures one in my heart, though I've only heard her name
As for the other, my eyes are fortunate to have seen her form.
This really is my situation
in the case of the two beautiful women. (16)
(Remains thoughtfully)

विदूषकः भो वअस्स! एदं कहेहि। अहो ण किञ्चि एदेण सुदं। किं पसुत्तो अत्तभवं, जेण मए पुच्छिअमाणं ण सुणीअदि। (भो वयस्य! एतत् कथय। अहो न किञ्चिदेतेन श्रुतम्। किं प्रसुप्तोऽत्र भवान्, येन मया पृच्छ्यमानं न श्रूयते।)

O friend! Tell this ! Strange, he has not heard me. Are you asleep since you have not heard my words?

धनञ्जयः सत्यं, व्याक्षिप्तं मे मनः। (आत्मानं निर्दिश्य) सखे! सम्प्रत्यपि पश्य –

श्रमजलभिन्नं गात्रं रोहद्रोमाञ्चकञ्चुकच्छन्नम्।
तस्याः खलु मे पाणी नमयत इव ते स्तनश्रोण्यौ।। १७।।

(पुनर्विचिन्त्य) किं पुनः पूर्वं प्रष्टुमुपक्रान्तमत्रभवता।

Yes, my mind has been carried away. (pointing to himself) Friend, see even now,

My body is sweating and my hairs are bristling.
Even now her breasts and hips seem to press down my hands. (17)

(Thinking again) What was it that you wanted to ask me?

विदूषकः तं मए विसुमरिअं। अआळन्तरक्खमा एदस्स पज्ञत्ति जाणन्तो वि तुवं तदाणिं असुणिअ एह्णिं पुण पृच्छन्तो जळनिहिदाए अक्खराइ कालन्तरे वाइदुं उव क्कमसि। (तन्मया विस्मृतं। अकालान्तरक्षमैतस्य प्रज्ञेति जानन्नपि त्वं तदानीमश्रुत्वेदानीं पुनः पृच्छन् जललिखितन्यक्षराणि कालान्तरे वाचयितुमुपक्रमसे।)

I have forgotten. You know very well that my mind is incapable of recalling something later; now you are trying to read letters written on water.

धनञ्जयः अलमेभिरसत्प्रलापैः। तत्सङ्गमोपाय एव तावच्चिन्त्यताम्।

Enough of this nonsense. Think about how I might be united with her.

विदूषकः (स्वगतम्) एदस्स आआसवासस्स ण अवसरं दइस्सं। एव्वं दाव भणिस्सं। (प्रकाशम्) भो वअस्स! ण दाव सा किण्णामहेआ, केरिसगोत्ता, कुदो आअदा, कहिं वा गदति जाणीअदि। केवलं अदिट्ठमूळेण भमेण पय्याउळो होसि। का णाम एत्थ उवाअचिन्ता। (एतस्याकाशवासस्य नावसरं दास्यामि। एवं तावद् भणिष्यामि। भो वयस्य। न तावत् सा किन्नामधेया, कीदृशगोत्रा, कुत आगता, क्व वा गतेति ज्ञायते। केवलमदृष्टमूलेन भ्रमेण पर्याकुलो भवसि। का नामात्रोपायचिन्ता।)

(To himself) I shall not give his imagination a chance. So I shall tell him this. (Aloud) O friend, it is not known what her name is, from what kind of family or from where she came, or where she has gone. You are worried needlessly. Why?

धनञ्जयः सखे! सत्यमीदृशमेवैतत्। अमुष्याः प्राप्तौ दैवमेव प्रमाणम्। तदधुना वासुभद्रभगिनीप्राप्तये पुरीमिमामनुप्रविशावः।

Friend, that's true. Only fate bring about union with her. Now we shall enter this city in order to achieve union with the sister of Vāsubhadra.

विदूषकः भो वअस्स! तहिं पविट्ठोहिं अह्मेहिं सा वि सुभद्दा कहं आसादिज्जइ। किं पुण पच्चक्खं एव्व गदुअ कुमारीभिक्खं याचह्य, आदु अद्धरत्ते अद्धूणा होदूण चोरह्य। (भो वयस्य! तत्र प्रविष्टैरस्माभिः सापि सुभद्रा कथमासाद्यते। किं पुनः प्रत्यक्षमेव गत्वा कुमारीभिक्षां याचावहे अथवार्धरात्रे चोरौ भूत्वा चोरयावः।)

O friend, once we enter there, how are we going to obtain, Subhadrā? Shall we go straight in the open and beg for the damsel? Or shall we steal her during the night?

धनञ्जयः (सस्मितम्) अतिकृपणोऽयमत्रभवता दर्शितो मार्गः। अहं पुनः सुहृदो वासुदेवादवाप्तानुमतिः प्रमथ्य वृष्णीन् प्रसह्य प्रेयसीं हरिष्यामि। तन्मस्करिवेषधारी तु कालं प्रतीक्षिष्ये। भवता च वर्णिव्यञ्जनेन कर्मण्यस्मिन्नवहितेन भवितव्यम्।

(Smilingly) The way you suggest is terribly vulgar. I shall obtain the permission of my friend Vāsudeva and abduct my beloved by force after thrashing the Vṛṣṇis. So I shall wait for a suitable time, assuming the attire

of a mendicant. You too should assume the role of a Brahmacārin and remain vigilant to achieve our aim.

विदूषकः (स्वगतम्) सव्वहा समरपरिणामो अअं आरम्भो संवुत्तो। (प्रकाशम्) भो वअस्स! सव्वंकसा एसा णीदी, जं एत्ति अमत्तो अह्माअं संबन्धिवग्गो, एदं पि जादवअळं सअं एव्व सत्तुणो सुयोधणस्स देसि त्ति तक्केमि। (सर्वथा समरपरिणामोऽयमारम्भः संवृत्तः। भो वयस्य! सर्वङ्कषैषा नीतिः, यदेतावन्मात्रोऽस्माकं सम्बन्धिवर्गः, एतदपि यादवकुलं स्वयमेव शत्रवे सुयोधनाय ददासीति तर्कयामि।)

(To himself) This effort is sure to result in a conflict. (Aloud) O friend, this ruse in all-embracing. The clan of our relatives is limited in number. It seems that you are going to give the Yādavas to your enemy Suyodhana.

धनञ्जयः मदधीनसकलजन्मफले सति चराचरगुरावपरे सङ्गच्छन्तां सात्त्वताः सुयोधनेन।

When the supreme Lord of the movable and immovable is on my side, let all the Sāttvatas join the side of Suyodhana.

विदूषकः जं होइ तं होदु। सव्वहा तुमं अणुसरेदुं एसो ह्यि बद्धपरिअरो। जाव अस्समं गदु अ अह्माअं वेसोवअरणाणि आणइस्सं। (परिक्रामति) (यद् भवति तद् भवतु। सर्वथा त्वामनुसर्तुमेषोऽस्मि बद्धपरिकरः। यावदाश्रमं गत्वावयोर्वेषोपकरणान्यानेष्यामि।)

Vidūṣaka: As you like. Of course, I am at your service. I shall go to the hermitage and bring back the necessary items for our change of form. (*Walks about*)

धनञ्जयः (विचिन्त्य) कष्टं भोः कष्टम् –

भ्राता धर्मसुतस्य भीमसहजो भीष्मस्य नप्ता स्वयं
बीभत्सुर्यमयोर्गुरुः सुरपतेः सूनुः सखा शार्ङ्गिणः।
भूत्वायं मम किङ्करः प्रणयिनीहेतोः पृथानन्दनः
प्रव्रज्यां प्रतिपन्न इत्युपगतो मन्ये स्मरः स्मेरताम्।। १८।।

(Thoughtfully) What a pity it is!

I think that the God of love would smile to know that the son of Pṛthā has become his servant,
assuming the form of a mendicant for the sake of his beloved,
despite being the brother of Dharmasuta and Bhīma,
nephew of Bhīṣma, elder brother of Nakula and Sahadeva,
son of the Lord of the Gods, and the dear friend of Śārṅgin. (18)

विदूषकः (सभयं परावृत्य) भो वअस्स! परित्ताआहि परित्ताआहि। एसो को वि अपुव्वो महाणाओ भो अमज्झगएणसमुम्मिसन्तमहामणिमरीइजाळेण फणवित्थारेण अदिभीसणो में भस्सीकादुं पवुत्तो। (भो वयस्य! परित्रायस्व परित्रायस्व। एष कोऽप्यपूर्वो महानागो भोगमध्यगतेन समुन्मिषन्महामणिमरीचिजालेन फणविस्तारेणातिभीषणो मां भस्मीकर्तुं प्रवृत्तः)

(Returning with fear) O friend! Protect me! Protect me! Here is an extraordinarily long snake with jewels on its hood, fiercely blazing and it's trying to burn me to ashes!

धनञ्जयः को नु खल्वेनं व्यामोहयि। (उपसृत्य पश्यन्) मूर्ख! मा भैषीः। काचिदियं प्रवरमणिप्रत्युप्त मध्यमण्डला जाम्बूनदमयी गात्रिका। मन्ये तस्या एवं कन्यकायाः प्रमथप्रक्षोभे प्रच्युतयानया भवितव्यम्। (सादरमादाय हृदये निक्षिपन्) अयि प्रक्षीणपुण्यसञ्चये!

ध्रुवमनुभववार्त्ता विद्धि नातः परं ते
कुचसरसिजयोर्यत् कुङ्कुमाकल्पधाम्नोः।
अयमयमवकाशो मण्डले यौवनेन
क्षणसुलभमहिम्नोर्गात्रिके! नात्र तस्याः।। १९।।

Who is it that deceives him? (Approaching and watching closely) Fool! Don't be afraid. It is golden bodice studded with costly jewels in its centre. I think it belongs to the same woman from whom it must have slipped off during the alteration with the demon. (Taking it with care and putting it on his breast) O unfortunate one, whose merit has diminished!

O bodice! Hereafter you have no chance to adorn
that lady's lotus breasts that increase in size
moment by moment due to her youth,
and which are anointed with saffron. (19)

विदूषकः (सावधानं निरूप्य) अदिभीरुएण विमए एत्थ को वि उवलक्खिओ विसेसो। सिप्पनरेसु एसा अक्खरपन्ती दीसइ। (अतिभीरुणापि मयात्र कोऽप्युपलक्षितो विशेषः। शिल्पान्तरेष्वे षाक्षरपङ्क्तिर्दृश्यते।)

(Looking carefully) Though I am easily scared, I noticed some peculiarity in it. In between the artistic stitches I see some letters.

धनञ्जयः (निरूप्य सहर्षम्) अये मदीयानि दशनामधेयान्यत्रोत्कीर्णानि। सोऽयमुभय-प्रार्थनारमदीयो मदनव्यापारः। कदाचिदमुष्यापि स्त्रीरत्नस्येदमेव द्वारकापुरमाकरः स्यात्। तदुभयप्राप्तये प्रयतिष्यावहे। स्वीक्रियतामियं गात्रिका। (विदूषकस्य हस्ते समर्पयति)

(Looking carefully and with joy) Oh, my ten names are stitched to it! So this affair of love is mutual and as such relishable. Perhaps this jewel of a girl is from the city of Dvārakā itself. Hence I shall try to obtain both of the women. Take this bodice. (Hands it over to the Vidūṣaka)

विदूषकः एव्वं होदु। (ऊर्ध्वमवलोक्य) भो वअस्स! पेक्ख पेक्ख। एसो दुल्लङ्घणभोमग्गलङ्घण-दुब्बलपादसञ्चारो अहं पिपासिओं लवणजलहिजलं उवसप्पइ भअवं सहस्सरस्सी। (एवं भवतु। भो वयस्य, पश्य पश्य। एष दुर्लङ्घननभोमार्गलङ्घनदुर्बलपादसञ्चारोऽहमिव पिपासितो लवणजलधिजलमुपसर्पति भगवान् सहस्ररश्मिः।)

All right. (Looking up) O friend, look here! Look here! The thousand-rayed Sungod is slowly approaching the salty ocean, like me walking about on feeble legs, eager to quench my thirst.

धनञ्जयः (विलोक्य) अये अस्तमितो भगवानंशुमाली। तथाहि –

अपरगिरिनिषण्णं वासरं वासरश्री-
रभिमतमभिसर्तुं प्राणनाथं प्रदोषे।
स्वतनुमतनुरागा संवृणोतीव साक्षा-
दसितजलदनीलेनान्धकारांशकेन।। २० ।।[6]

(Looking) O, the Sun god has set. Thus,

The day's lustre wears clothing as dark as the rain cloud
to conceal her deep anguish of love, and prepares to go
to the side of her lover the day at the western horizon. (20)

Vyaṅgyavyākhyā

Subhadrā is eager to meet her lord who is waiting in the Raivataka mountain.

तदाश्रमं प्रविश्य प्रस्तुतसिद्धये व्याप्रियावहे।

(इति निष्क्रान्तौ)

Let us enter the hermitage and engage ourselves to the fulfillment of our mission.

(Both exit)

Here ends the First Act

व्यङ्ग्यव्याख्या

ततः प्रविशति पतन्ती कन्यका। पूर्वोक्तमेव पठति।

(धनञ्जयः गगनान्निपतन्तीं तां भूमाववतारयति कन्याम्।)

अथ सुभद्रानामधेया काचित् वृष्णिकन्या वासुभद्रभगिनी स्वगात्रिकायां पार्थस्य दशनामानि दर्शयन्ती कृष्णलिखितान्यक्षराणि नित्यमेव पठन्ती तद्गतचित्ता कृष्णेन पितृभ्यां पार्थप्रतापद्योतकाः कथाः काश्चित् तां श्रावयितुं कथ्यमानानि वचांसि श्रृण्वन्ती पार्थदर्शनलोलुपा तमेव चिन्तयन्ती कन्यात्वाददिवदन्ती कामाद्यश रावसरीकुर्वच्चित्ता सहृदयवेदनं चरन्ती कस्मिंश्चिदह्नि स्वाभिमताभ्यां सखीभ्यां विरहिता बाह्यालिन्दस्थाने स्थिता गात्रिकाश्रितानि तन्नामाक्षराणि स्वयमेवानुभवन्ती तद्दर्शनलोलुपा तद्दर्शनोपायमविदन्ती सा केनचित् तदानीमेव वासुभद्रं विशङ्कमानेन सीरिणा मम भगिनीं सुभद्रां वासुभद्रमनोरथामस्माद् बलादुद्धृत्य दुर्योधनाय महाराजाय प्रयच्छेत्यादिष्टेनालम्बुसनाम्ना प्रमथेन दुर्योधनसखेन तत्रस्थेयं बलाद्धृता वियता नीयमाना पुरात् किमपि दूरं गच्छन्ती प्रभासोपकण्ठमाक्रोशन्ती ससाध्वसं सहसा भूतलगतं कमपि महानुभावं पश्यन्ती सकरुणं रक्ष रक्षेति प्रवदन्ती नीयमाना सा सहसा तत्करात् विमुक्ता भूमिं प्रापिता तदग्रे

6 This last stanza allegorically hints at the disguise of Dhanañjaya as an ascetic and Subhadrā's wait for him.

तिष्ठन्त्यासीत्। एवं तिष्ठन्ती सा देहजितमन्मथं पश्यन्नपि तद्भयात् साध्वसकम्पं आत्मगतमित्युत्तरग्रन्थेन विमृशति। इति ग्रन्थं वदन्ती भवत्प्रेम्णा तमेवं पश्यन्ती तिष्ठेत्।

एवमस्याः प्रावेशिकस्तत्कालभावश्च।

अथैवं पश्यन्ती सा तद्दर्शनलोलुपापि तमभिमुखं वीक्षितुमक्षमा सभयं सप्रेमचलत्तारं यदा तिष्ठेत् तदा शरेण मन्मथेन कुशेशयेन विद्धहृदयाभूत्। ततः प्रभृत्येषोऽस्याः स्थायिभावः। हन्तास्मिन्महानुभावे तस्मिन्नपि धनञ्जये च वर्धते प्रेम ममेति यत् ततोऽहं भिन्नचारित्रा स्यां इति मन्यमानोत्तरोत्तराधिकसन्तापैषा स्यात् इत्यस्य स्थायिभावः। सा तथा तिष्ठन्नुभयचलद्धृतितारे सप्रेम विलोलयन्ती सावधानं पश्यन्ती तिष्ठेत्।

उदयत्पुलकात्तगण्डयुग्मा
प्रभवत्स्वेदकणाभिरामवक्त्रा।
श्लथयत्कबरीभरात्तश्रृङ्गा
सहज प्रेमयुता च गात्रिकेयम्।।
उरसा श्रितलज्जमात्तकम्पं
गलयत्प्रेमभरं विलोलतारम्।
चलदुत्पलकान्तिनीलभासा
नयनेनैनमसौ विलोकयन्ती।।
द्रुपदात्मजया कटाक्षपातैः
दृढमाबद्ध्य समुद्रितं मनोऽस्य।
अपि यद् गुरुदृक्त्रिभागजेन
श्लथयन्ती निजवीक्षणेन तिष्ठेत्।।[7]

इति तं पश्यन्ती दृशा तस्य रूपामृतमनुभवन्ती तस्मै तथा तिष्ठते।
धनञ्जयः – अथैवं तया वीक्षमाणोऽयं धनञ्जयस्सरोमविक्रियं सस्पृहमात्मगतमिति स्मरेत्।

भार्यासीत् प्राक् द्रौपदी यस्य मेऽन्या
भद्रा भूयस्संश्रुतेयं च दृष्टा।
तस्यां तस्यामप्यमुष्यां च जात-
प्रेमा तस्यैवामुनास्मीह लोलः।।
चेष्टां कामं कामिनां लौल्यभाजां
भूभृत्सूनोर्याम्यवायव्ययोर्यः।
भ्राता धन्वी शक्रपुत्रोऽर्जुनोऽयं
कष्टं कष्टं तादृशश्शन्तनोति।।[8]

---

7 This is the description of the heroine on her entry. Such descriptions were, later on, developed into alamaśloka where in every character is described in this way.

8 This reveals the inner conflict of Dhanañjaya.

स्मरन्, आस्तां द्रौपदी –

गदस्य या मया वक्त्रात् श्रुता दृष्टेह या तयोः।
ऐक्यं न कुर्यात् कृष्णोऽयं दुर्विज्ञेया हि तद्गतिः।।

इति स्मरंस्तिष्ठेत्। पूर्वगदवचनश्रवणमात्रेणैव तस्य हृदयं श्रृङ्गाररसवल्लीबीजावापनायाकरो जातः। ततस्तु गम्यागम्यविचारणे निमित्तानुकूल्येन तत्संस्कारं कृतवान्। एवं संस्कारं कृत्वा तं बीजावापनक्षमं विधाय बीजमन्विच्छन् यमातिष्ठेत्। तदा स्मरेण तां पुरतो निधाय तत्कमलेन शरादिना दग्धमासीत्। अथैवं तद्दग्धहृदयोऽयं यदाभूत्, तदातच्छरदशाविकृतिभूतरोमाञ्चमस्याभूत् तदर्थं स कविस्सरोमाञ्चमिति क्रियाविशेषणपदं तत्र प्रक्षिप्तवान्। तथाभूतत्वात् सस्पृहं तामवलोकयति। एवं तद्बीजमन्विच्छं सद्क्षेत्रोचितं बीजं विलोक्य तदानीमेव तद्बीजं तस्मिन्नुप्तवान्। एवं कृतबीजवापनस्यास्य स्थायिभावस्मरदशायाः क्रमौन्नत्यमिति ज्ञायताम्। अथैवं सरोमाञ्चं सस्पृहं तामवलोक्य तिष्ठन्नयं धनञ्जय इति स्मरेत्। एषा सा चैका स्याच्चेद् धातृभूतोऽयं भगवान् श्रृङ्गाररसप्रदो मारश्च द्वौ मे बन्धू स्यातामिति स्मरन् तिष्ठेत्। इतः पूर्वं साध्या वा नवा उभयत्रापि शर्म न लक्ष्यत इति स्थायिभावः। अतः परमेषा सा चैका भूत्वा भवितव्यतया मां प्राप्स्यति यदि तदा प्रभृति कथङ्कारं द्रौपदीमुपगतकोपां विहायेमां तदा योजयिष्यामि इत्यापुरप्रवेशाद् दृशो दर्शयेदित्युक्ते स्थायिभावे वर्तमाने दृशोरेतच्च विभावयन्नयं नयनप्रीतौ तद्दर्शनलब्ध-रोमाञ्चविक्रियस्सन्नयं केयमिति स्मरंस्तिष्ठेत्।[9] एवं तामेव पश्यतस्तस्याबुद्धिपूर्वकं चित्तात् कश्चित् श्लोकः प्रोत्पतेत्, **चलकुवलयधाम्नोरि**ति। अथैवं धनञ्जयभूमिकालङ्कृततनुर्भरतवरस्तादृशं स्थायिभावं दृशोर्विभावयं-स्तिष्ठन्नयमबुद्धिपूर्वकमिति स्ववक्त्रादिमं श्लोकं निर्गमयेदिति निर्गमय्य आत्मगतं स्मरेत्। कोऽयमबुद्धिपूर्वकं मम मानसादुद्भूतः श्लोकमार्गः। मम अन्तःकरणप्रवृत्तिभिः प्रेर्यमाण इव। अहो कथङ्कारमस्य योजना।

चलकुवलयधाम्नोरक्ष्णोः युग्ममालोलयन्तीयं का; एवमस्य पूर्वार्धं योज्यम्। अपरार्धे च चतुर्थे पादे योजना द्रष्टुं पटीयसी मे बुद्धिः शिथिलयति। सुभद्रामुद्रितं मानसं मे इत्यत्र कथङ्कारमस्य योजना।[10]

अक्ष्णोर्युग्ममालोलयन्तीयं सुभद्रामुद्रितं मे मानसं शिथिलयतीति वा अन्वयः, अथवा अक्षियुगमालोल-यन्तीयं सुभद्राद्रौपदीकटाक्षपाशैर्मुद्रितं मानसं शिथिलयतीति वा। एतद् याथातथ्यमनिश्चितोऽस्मि। अपि च भो केयं कुत आयाता इति पृच्छते कौण्डिन्याय किं वक्तव्यमियं सुभद्रेति वान्येति वानिर्धार्यास्मै जातु न वक्तव्यैषा। कुतः –

प्राकृतान् वा स्त्रियः किञ्चिदनिर्धार्य वदन्नेतत्।
अपि चेत् न तथास्यात् चेत् तौ तन्वातेऽस्य लाघवम्।।

तस्यां – द्रौपद्याम्, तस्यां – सुभद्रायाम्, अमुष्यां – अस्यां कन्यकायाम्। भूभृत्सूनुः – धर्मपुत्रः, यमौ – नकुलसहदेवौ। वायव्यः – भीमः, एतेषां भ्राता, शक्रस्य – इन्द्रस्य पुत्रश्च।।

9 Somehow he concluded that Subhadrā and this maiden are identical; then his embarrassment is as to how he can pacify Draupadī. Pleasure to the eyes – nayanaprīti- is the sprout of his love towards Subhadrā.

10 The verse came out abruptly from his unconscious mind. He had not conceived the sense as is done in usual practice. Hence these doubts.

इति चिन्तयाचार्येण दर्शितम्। सर्वथा अनिर्धार्य न वक्तव्यम्। तत्किं करिष्ये। अस्तु,

यावन्निर्धार्यं ते बुध्या स्मरता चोपपत्तिभिः।
तावत्साधारणैर्वाक्यैः कौण्डिन्यः प्रोच्यतां मया।।

इत्यात्मगतं स्मृत्वा तदवधातुमुपपत्तिं स्मरेत्। कन्या दीर्धं निश्वस्यात्मगतम्। अथ सा सुभद्रा तद्गतप्रेमेति स्मरेत्। अहो! अहमितः पूर्वमेवं हि क्रीडाकाले भोजने स्नानकाले, स्वापे, देवाराधने सर्वदा मां बाणैर्मारो बाध्यमानोऽर्जुनो यत् सोऽयं कष्टं बाधते पुरुषेऽस्मिन् देवश्चाहं वृष्णिवंशेऽमले जाता साध्वी यत्तदेषा न योग्या, वेश्येवास्त्रैः पुंसु नूनं प्रहर्तुं तेन स्मरेण किं अद्य इति स्मरन्ती भूयोऽप्युत्तरग्रन्थेन सदीर्घनिश्वासमात्मगतिं तदेव समर्थयति। अहो यदि **विसमसि इदा महंस** इत्यादिनेति। समर्पयन्ती तं पश्यन्तीति तिष्ठेत्।

धन. – सवितर्कमात्मगतम्। अथ धनञ्जयस्तमुपपत्तिभिरात्मगतमिति वितर्कयेत्। तया मुद्रितं मे मानसमियं सुभद्रा शिथिलयति इत्यस्य योजनेति मन्ये। कुतः तत्रोपपत्तिः सम्भवेत्। पश्य यदेषा नभसोऽपतत् ततो नभो जाता कापि दिव्यकन्यकेत्यूह्यम्। तत्रानुपपत्तिर्न स्यात्।

खेचराणां च दिव्यानां न सन्त्येतानि पार्थिव।
भूस्पर्शम्लानपुष्पत्वं स्विन्नत्वं गौरवं तनोः।।

इति मत्पितामहेन पुराणे दर्शितम्। तद्वचःप्रामाण्यादेषा नभश्चारिणी न स्यादित्यूह्यम्। तर्हि नभसा कथङ्कारं गतेति चेत् तत्रेति सम्भवितव्यम्।

कृष्ण मे दर्शय त्वं तां याचितेनेति सामुना।
दर्शितात्र भवेदेषा मह्यं भक्तानुकम्पिना।।
अस्यां सुदृशि कन्यायामेव मग्नमनो मम।
पश्य नान्यत्र कुत्रापि सुतयोर्नागपाण्ड्ययोः।।
कान्न सम्प्रापयेत् जन्तून् विधाताभिमुखो यदि।
सम्पदं विमुखश्चेद्वा विपदं ते अपारगे।।

तस्माद् भगवन्मनोऽनुगामिनी सुभद्रा स्यादपीयं अस्याः परमार्थनिर्णये प्रमाणं न स्यादित्युपपत्तिभिः स्मरन्नयं शनैश्शनैरन्तःकरणप्रामाण्यादियं सुभद्रेति निश्चिन्वानोऽसौ भूय इति स्मरेत्।

वर्णश्रीर्वर्णिता पूर्वं गदेन गदता मम।
गात्रिकाया तु सा चाद्य स्तनयोर्नात्र दृश्यते।।

सा दृष्टा चेत् तत्सौन्दर्यादियं सुभद्रेति दृढीकर्तुं शक्यम्। किमर्थमस्या स्तनक्षौमविहीनता भवतीति स्मरन्नयं तद्धेतुमुत्तरश्लोकस्य प्रथमपादेनात्मगतं निश्चिनोति – क्षिप्तक्षौमावित्यादिना। अस्याः प्रमथेन नीयमानायाः स्तनक्षौमं भयकम्पात् परिभ्रष्टमासीत्। तेनात्र भूतले पतितेन क्वापि भवितव्यम्। एवं स्मृत्वा भूयस्तामेव पश्यन्निति स्मरेत्। अहो अजातपूर्वमेतादृशं रूपामृतम्। किमियं मयि रागिणी वा नवेति ज्ञातव्यम्। एवं संस्मृत्य मदनाशया स्वस्मिन्नियं रागिणीति मीलन्नीलाम्बुजश्रीरित्यादिभिस्त्रिभिः पदै निश्चिनोति। तमेव पश्यन्नहो एतादृश्यस्या दशा। कुतः? तस्याः कटाक्षः अनतिमुकुलितः रोहद्रोमाञ्चभाजः गण्डसीम्नो

श्रमजलकणिकाभ्युद्गतिः। भीत्या किमस्यास्तनुरेवम्भूता इति स्मरन्नयं भीत्या नेत्युपपत्तिभिर्निश्चिनोति किं मह्यं तिष्ठमाना या दृष्टिरस्या भीतौ वर्तमाना यदि सचकितमुद्वर्तिततारा भयाद् विषण्णतां यान्ती शुचा छिन्नपातं निर्गमयेदश्रुधारा; तादृशी नास्या वर्तते दृष्टिः। अत्र प्रत्युत एष दृष्टेः कटाक्षः कस्मिंश्चित्प्रेयसि मनो भवतीव विभाति; कुतः मीलन्नीलाम्बुजश्रीः अनतिमुकुलितः मुग्धपातस्तथाभूतः कटाक्षः इति यावत्। अस्याः कटाक्षः आकेकराख्यः इति विज्ञेयम्।

अन्तिकं प्रेयसि प्राप्ते श्रितनानाजने यया
नीयमानात्र सप्रेम दृष्टिराकेकरा हि सा।।

तथाभूतेन कटाक्षेण पश्यन्तीति यत्तदर्थं भीत्या न मदनदशायामस्या वीक्षणमिति मन्ये। किञ्च श्रमजलक णिकाभ्युद्गतिर्गण्डसीम्नोरेव वर्तते यत्। मदर्थमेव मदनदशायामिति मन्तव्यम् –

सदृशं वयः कुलशरीरगुणैः
पुरुषं यदैक्षत सुदृक् कथितम्।
कमलेन तां शरवरेण तदा
प्रहरत्यरज्वलसदृशं मदनः।।
कमलं शरौघमपि या दधती
हृदि सोत्तमा निजकपोलयुगे।
धरते श्रमाम्बुजितमुक्तमसौ
पुलगोद्गमं च मदनातुरता च।। इत्यस्ति कामशास्त्रप्रसिद्धिः।

एतस्माद् गण्डोद्यत्स्विन्नकणिकया प्ररोहत्पुलकयानया मदनदशायां वर्तमानया भवितव्यम् भीतौ न इत्यात्मगतम्। सवितर्कं तिष्ठन्नयमुद्वृष्टिरप्यन्तरान्तरा तामपि पश्यन् भूय उद्वृष्टिरिति स्मरेत्। मामुद्दिश्यान्यमुद्दिश्य वास्या स्मरविकृतिः पुनस्तामेव पश्यन् मां पश्यन्त्या अस्या देहप्ररोहद्रोमाञ्चं धत्ते यत्ततो मन्निमित्तमस्या मदनविकृतिरित्यूह्यम्। अपि च यदेषान्तरान्तराकेकरदृष्ट्या मां पश्यन्तीति यत्ततो मय्यनुरागिणीयमिति मन्तव्यम्। अथैवं तामेव पश्यन् तिष्ठेत्। रोहद्रोमाञ्चभाज इति शतृसमासत्वात् स्वविषयमस्याः मदनविकृतिरिति अभिप्रायः। अर्धमुकुलितं प्रान्ते विकसत्स्निग्धनिश्चलं प्रतिदृक्पतने लज्जां वितन्वन् प्रोल्लसद् भ्रमन्नेत्रसुखप्रदं यूनां तदत्राकेकरम्।

विदू. – तथाभूतया दृष्ट्या वीक्षत इत्यर्थः। एवमस्य प्रयोगमार्गः। स्वविषयमस्याः प्रेम इति मन्यमानेन तेन पूर्वमुक्तं तं बीजं सिक्तमेवम्। नयनप्रीतौ पश्यन्नेनां बलादुद्धृत्य परमिन्द्रप्रस्थं गच्छेयम् किमिति स्मरंस्तिष्ठेत्। कन्या अथ तमेव तथा पश्यन्ती तिष्ठन्तीति स्मरेत्।

कदा नु प्रेयसानेन रममाणानन्यविद्।
देहनिर्जितकामेन सह सुप्स्ये निशास्वहम्।।

इति स्मरन्ती प्रेम्णा तमेव यियासुरिति स्मरेत्। अयि नेत्रे एतद्देहसुधां यथाभिलाषं पिबतामिति स्मरन्ती तिष्ठन्ती केनाप्युद्गम्यमाना पुनरुत्तरग्रन्थेन वदती सहसाप्यदर्शनं गता।

इति निष्क्रान्ता।

विदू. – ससम्भ्रमम्। अथ विदूषकः क्रोधात् बाणं सन्धाय तिष्ठन्तं दृष्ट्वा हसन्नेव तमेव पश्यंस्तिष्ठेत्। अथ कन्यका तद्भीत्या विमुच्य गतवन्तं प्रमथं च दृष्ट्वाश्चर्यं अयं विषादमार्जवं च मुखे दृशोर्विभावयंस्तिष्ठेत्। अथ तस्माद्विमुक्तां निपतन्तीं दृष्ट्वा अविहा इति ससम्भ्रममुच्चैर्वदन् दयालुत्वं दृशोर्विभावयन् एषा भूमौ निपतति पुरा बाहाववतरयेति दृग्भ्यां प्रेरयंस्तिष्ठेत्।[11] तदनन्तरमेव बाहुभ्यां भुवं कन्यामवतारयन्तं दृष्ट्वा धनञ्जयमुपरि पश्यन्नप्यन्तरान्तरा तां च पश्यन् प्रतापद्योतकानि वचांसि वदंस्तिष्ठेत्। अथ तदानीं तत्र तस्मै तिष्ठमानां कन्यां च दृष्ट्वा तां च तं च परस्परं वीक्षमाणः सशिरःकम्पमीषदुद्दृष्टि विमृशंस्तिष्ठेत्। ततोऽन्योन्यं सप्रेम परस्परं वीक्षमाणौ दृष्ट्वेति स्मरेत्। एषा कापि कन्यकेत्यनेन पूर्वमुक्तं तत् तथ्यं नाम। अहो अनया रूपश्रिया जीयन्ते अन्यास्त्रियः। कैषा नु इयं सुभद्रा वा इतरा वा। यदेषा अमुष्य पुरतो निर्विशङ्कं तिष्ठति यदयमेनां दृशौ आबध्य स्थापितवानिति मन्ये। अहो अस्य चित्तममुष्यां दृग्भ्यां सगमनम्। अहो अस्य रागो अमुष्यां कियानिति न जानामि। अस्तु पृष्ट्वा ज्ञेयम्। तत्कथङ्कारमिति स्मरन्नयं सहसा तां तिरोधानं गतवतीं दृष्ट्वेति स्मरेत्। हन्तेदानीमिति प्रष्टव्यम्।[12] इयं कापि गगनचारिणी देवतेति मन्ये। यदावयोः पश्यतोरेवादर्शनं गता। तदितोऽन्यत्र गच्छाव इत्ययं वाच्यो भवेदित्युक्तोऽयमस्यां बद्धप्रेमा चेदेषा दिव्या नेति समर्थयन्नत्रैव तिष्ठति नो चेत् सदा गमिष्यतीति स्मृत्वा निश्चित्य तच्चोद्योतनार्थं सहसा ससम्भ्रमं कृतवान्। एवं तस्यां रागः कियानिति परिच्छेत्तुं **मे से**त्यादिना समर्थयति।

धन. – आत्मगतम्। अथ धनञ्जयस्तामेवाविच्छिन्नदृष्टिपातं पश्यन्निति स्मरेत्। अहं पद्मपलाशाक्षी-मुद्गच्छत्कुचकुड्मलामंसविक्षिप्तविहारामुद्यत्स्विन्नकणाननामुद्गच्छत्पुलकामेनां स्तोकनम्रां सुमध्यमां बालां कान्तं गाढमालिङ्ग्य वक्षसा 'निर्वाप्यमानो वह्निं शठत्वं नात्र दर्शय' इति नेत्रत्रिभागस्थैर्वीक्षणैर भिवीक्ष्य मां वदन्तीमिव तिष्ठन्तीं स्पृशाम्यद्योरसा नु किमिति स्मरन्नयं सचक्षुषोः पश्यतोरेवादर्शनं गतां तां दृष्ट्वात्मगतमिति वदति **हन्ते**त्यादिना। एवं तस्यामात्मगतं प्रलप्य भूयः धीरोदात्तत्वादिति स्मरेत्।[13] अहो असौ मां परिच्छेत्तुं वा तामिमां याथातथ्यं ज्ञातुं वायं मामिति पृच्छति स्म। तस्मादहमस्या जन्मनो याथातथ्यज्ञानात् प्राक् साधारणैः पदैरेव तस्यामेनं वदेयम्। भूयस्तस्यां मम मनोवृत्तिं परिच्छेत्तुं सा यक्षिणी दिव्यकन्यकेति यदनेनोक्तं तदर्थं सा दिव्यकन्यका नेति समर्थयन् ममास्यां मनोगतिं मय्यस्याः प्रेम विज्ञापयामीत्यात्मना निश्चित्य प्रकाशमुत्तरग्रन्थेन तथा समर्थयति **मूर्ख न सा दिव्यकन्यके**त्यादिना।

तस्याः खलु घर्माम्भकणिकेत्यादि। अथैव मूर्खेति वदन्नयं तस्य मुखे पश्यन्नुत्तरश्लोकेन विज्ञापयति तत्प्रकारो दृश्यते। अथ तेनेति पृष्टो धनञ्जयः **घर्माम्भः कणिका** इति श्लोकेन तस्या दिव्यत्वं नेति समर्थयन् पूर्वार्धेन तस्याः स्वस्मिन् प्रेम स्यादिति समर्थयति – सखे यदावयोः पुरतस्तिष्ठन्त्यास्तस्याः मां पश्यन्त्याः कपोलतलयोरुद्गच्छन्ती घर्माम्भः कणिकेति ततो मय्यस्याः प्रेम वर्तते न वेति कामशास्त्रेण सिद्धं स्यात्। किञ्च यन्मयि स्वमुखं पश्यति मन्मुखे प्रेम्णा वीक्षितुमक्षमत्वान्नेत्रेन्दीवरयोः प्रतिक्षणप्रस्यन्दिते। तेन च मयि प्रेम स्यादिति मन्तव्यम्। अथैवम्भूतायां मन्मनसो यियासुत्वं तस्यां कथं न स्यात्।

---

11 Vidūṣaka through his eyes requests him to hold the falling woman in his hands. In Kūṭiyāṭṭam today this scene in presented humorously by the jester. See the details in the next chapter in the relevant context.

12 Vidūṣaka asks this intentionally to know whether Dhanañjaya has fallen in love with her. If he answers that the maiden is not of celestial origin, it can be concluded that he is in love with her.

13 Dhanañjaya understands the trick of his friend and becomes cautious in his answer.

एवं पूर्वार्धेनान्योन्यमावयोः प्रेम स्यादिति विज्ञाप्य भूयो परार्धे पूर्वपादेन तस्या स्ववशादुन्नते वंशे जातं कमपि भर्तारमेष्यतीति समर्थयति **पादौ स्पृष्टभुवौ**। सखे भूयो नु दृष्टवानसि किं भुवि स्पृष्टपादं तिष्ठन्त्यास्तस्याः पादपद्मत्योरुभयोः पादतलरेखालिखितौ द्वौ पद्मावद्यापि दृश्यमानौ राजतः, ताविदानीमपि स्थलाम्बुरुहयोः स्पर्धितां प्राप्तौ ताभ्यां स्वजन्मनो वंशादधिके वंशे जातं कमपि भर्तारमेष्यतीयमिति मन्तव्यम्। हि कुतः –

रेखा पद्माकृतिः स्याच्चेत् वामाया वामपक्ष्मले।
पतिं स्वजातितुल्यं सा द्वयोश्चेदधिकं व्रजेत्।।

इति सामुद्रिकप्रसिद्धिः। तदर्थमिति विज्ञेयमिति तं विज्ञाप्य चतुर्थपादेन सप्तमण्डलादर्वागस्या विवाहाप्तिः स्यादिति च ज्ञेयम्। कुतः –

पश्य कलभैरिवाविवाहात् पत्रस्रग्भिर्नृपात्मजाम्।
अविच्छिन्नमलङ्कुर्यात् दिनं मण्डलसप्तकम्।।
एभिस्तन्मण्डलात्पूर्वं क्वचिन्नालङ्क्रियेत सा।
दर्शितं मुनिनेति प्राक् शास्त्रं श्रुत्यनुसारितम्।।

तदर्थं सप्तमण्डलतोऽर्वाग्विवाहाप्तिः स्यात् अस्या इति निश्चितवानस्मीत्यादि सर्वं दिव्यत्वं नास्या स्यादिति समर्थयता श्लोकेन विज्ञाप्य भूयस्सहसा कथङ्कारमदर्शनं गतेयमिति विमृशंस्तिष्ठेत्। एवं तावदस्मिन्नर्थमभिनयेनापि प्रेक्षकान् सुखयेत्।[14] एवमस्या प्रयोगमार्गः।

विदू. – अथ तेनोपपत्तिभिश्चित्रैरिति विज्ञापितोऽयं विदूषक इति स्मरेत्। सशिरकम्पम्। अहो सोपपत्तिकमनेन प्रोक्तुमखिलं हि तस्मादेतयोरन्योन्यं प्रेम स्यादिति मन्तव्यम्। अपीयं सुभद्रेतरा वा। अस्तु कालेन ज्ञातव्यं तत्। तस्मादिदानीमस्य मतिपारवश्यम् तस्या याथातथ्यं च ज्ञातुं दिव्या नेयमिति मां विज्ञाप्य भूयः किमपि तर्कयन्नुत्पतिष्यन्तमिमं कथं मानुषीति साधितायास्तस्यास्तिरस्करणीसम्भव इति पृच्छामीति निश्चित्य तं सम्मान्योत्तरग्रन्थेन तथा पृच्छति **भो पण्डिताग्रेसरे**त्यादिना।

धन – अथ धनञ्जयः कथङ्कारमेषाऽदर्शनं गतेति विमृशंस्तिष्ठन्नयमिति स्मरेत्। अहो कथङ्कारमस्यास्तिरस्करणीसम्भवः सा सुभद्रा वान्यावा मन्ये। तत्परिज्ञाने भगवानेव प्रमाणमिति इत्यात्मना मन्यमानो भगवन्तमेव स्मरन् मुहूर्तं तिष्ठेदिति स्मरन्नयं कैश्चित् पद्यैरिति बोध्य एवास्मि इति प्रेक्षकांस्तच्छ्लोकान् बोधयेत्।[15]

पतिता त्वया पार्थ प्राग् या दृष्टात्र कन्यका
सप्रेमत्वेक्षमाणा सा सुभद्रेत्यवगम्यताम्।
प्रकाशितेन केनापि दर्शयित्वा कनीयसीं
अन्तर्धानं पश्यतस्ते प्रापितास्तर्हि तेन सा।।

---

14 The instruction here is to communicate the hidden meaning through abhinaya also. Normally suggested sense is expressed by the movements of eyes. It seems that here the author permits hand gestures also. Otherwise the api become meaningless.

15 This instance of the character reciting non-textual verse is strange. Normally character uses textual passages of the dramatist only. The verses enacted here are not by the dramatist. The practice in later period in Naṅṅyārkūttu is that verses are recited by others, not by the character. But that is in recapitulation.

आत्मानमपि दद्यात्सः स्वभक्ताय जनाय हि।
मुनयेश्वपचायापि कृष्णस्त्वं केन खिद्यसे।।
भूयश्चेतसि सन्देहि प्रत्ययो भविता तव।
गात्रिकायां तु दृष्टायां वर्णिता प्राक् गदेन या।।

इत्यन्तःकरणैः प्रबोध्य एवाहं तदप्रमादमेषान्वेष्टव्या गात्रिका। तस्माद् कस्तदन्वेषणक्षमयोग्यः प्रदेशः। यदयं प्रमथो वायव्यदिशात्रायातः। ततः दिगस्याः अन्वेष्टव्या। किञ्च तस्यास्तयानुरूपस्थया भवितव्यम्। ततः मम भुवि पुरस्तिष्ठन्त्या मां निरीक्ष्य गतत्रपं क्षणमनुगुरुवर्धिष्णुत्वादिमौ सुतनोः स्तनौ दृढीभूते निजांशुकबन्धनात् तदेतदन्वेषणे दुश्चिन्तयापतिततम्। तच्चिन्तितव्या काचिदवस्था द्वारकामेव प्रापिता। सा कथङ्कारं मया गृह्यत इति किमेवम्भूतेन मया द्वारवतीमधिवसन्नस्मत्सखः कृष्णो नानावृष्णिलोकं समक्षं गम्यः। अत्रापि दोषो विद्यते। मय्येवम्भूते द्वारकां गतवति पृथुकृतवर्मादीनां वृष्णीनां सुयोधनमित्राणां मदिरापानघूर्णितदृशां बलाश्रयिणां चर्वितनागवल्लीदलानां[16] विस्मृतात्मनां सायाह्ने श्रिताश्वत्थचैत्यानां मन्दानिलभाजां परवार्तारतानामितरेतरं मामन्तरेणेति परिहासस्सम्भवितव्यः कथमिति चेदर्जुनोऽत्र किलायातो वर्तते कृष्णवेशमन्यस्ति किं वदन्त्यत्र तया मे गम्यते श्रुतिः इति कोऽपि इति वाच्यो अन्यस्त्वजाननृतगीरिति स्वाब्दे सति स पाञ्चाल्या रमेत किं न फल्गुनः?

वाच्योऽन्यैरिति वक्तव्यं श्रुतोऽस्माभिरपीति सः।
गदेन सम्मन्त्र्य प्रभासे स्थितवान् किल।।
वदत्सु कृतवर्मेषु वदेदिति नु यादवान्।
श्रृणुतेदं वचो यूयं यादवास्सत्यमेव तत्।।
अतीतान् मासतो वाक् चेदपश्यत्स गदोऽर्जुनम्।
श्रुता तेन प्रवृत्तिर्नः सुभद्रामन्तरेण सा।।
तदर्थमिह सम्प्राप्तः किरीटी कृष्णबान्धवः।
कृष्णं रहसि मित्रत्वात् याचते माधवीमिति।।
'दातव्या ते स्वसा मे किं पूर्वसम्बन्धिने त्वया।
आवां लभेत शर्मैषा प्रार्थना सफला यदि।।
पुरीयं त्वदधीनेति वच्मि यत्तद् विडम्बनम्।
त्रैलोक्यं च जगन्नाथ तवेछातः प्रवर्तते'।।
तस्मिन् वदति गोविन्दमिति तं स वदत्यथ।
'तिष्ठ पार्थ तवानेन प्रशंसावचना कुतः।।
प्रदातुं कल्पितार्येण राज्ञे नागध्वजाय सा।
शपथश्च कृतान्योन्यमार्येणाहिध्वजेन च।।
ईदृशं कर्मणामार्य कर्तैवाहं न जातुचित्'।

16 This is a native practice where people sit under the banyayan tree chewing beetles and engaging in chatting, leisurely in the evenings.

एवमेव वदेत् तं स भ्रातृस्नेहाद् गुरुत्वतः।।
वचो मामन्तरेणेति ब्रुवाणे कृतवर्मणि।
कम्पयन्तं प्रणीयोरौ स्थित्वा पादं तु दक्षिणम्।।
अन्ये युगनिभैर्दोर्भिर्घ्नन्तस्स्वोरुस्थलानि ते।
तथ्यं तथ्यमनेनोक्तमित्यत्रोच्चैर्हसन्त्यमी।।
अपि चेतदमीभिस्तैरुध्यते कर्म मामकम्।
तत्समक्षं पुरीं प्राप्य तां याचेताञ्जनार्दनम्।।
सीरीयं च भविष्यन्मे पश्य प्रत्यक्षतः पुरीम्।
गत्वा प्राप्य सुभद्रायाः कथन्नामोत्सवैस्समम्।।
तस्मात्पुरीं गत्वाशु हरेयं माधवीमहम्।
अथवा चोरवद्रात्रौ हरेयं किम्पुरादिमाम्।।
भवेद् दोषो हि दोषायां बहु द्वारायता पुरी।
द्वारपालैर्विनिद्रैश्च रक्ष्यते ...मनेन तं।।
यदि वेषान्तरछन्नो नागमिष्यं पुरीमिमाम्।
कन्यां कमलपत्राक्षीमायास्यन्नामतः ध्रुवम्।।
इदानीं किं यतिर्भूत्वा स्मरार्तोऽपि यथामनः।
मत्सखं वासुदेवं तं स्मरेयं भक्तवत्सलम्।।
सर्वथा स्मार्य एवासौ तत्र दोषो न विद्यते।
बाधते नहि दोषोऽयं कुर्वाणं देहिनं गुणात्।।
स्यातां तत्र गुणावेतौ दोषश्चैको हि विद्यते।
मयि सर्वजनैर्वन्द्ये मस्करीवेषधारिणि।।
आषाढमासि पूर्णेन्दोस्तिथेरारभ्य सन्मनाः।
मण्डलत्रयमेकत्र निवसेन्मस्करी सुखम्।।
इति प्राक्कल्पितोऽनेन भर्तात्रेयेण धीमता।
इहान्त्याश्रयिणामेषामाचारे देहिनां सताम्।।
आषाढाख्यो हि मासोऽयं भविष्यत्यचिरादिव।
तस्मिन्वसेयमेकत्र सन्यासी स्यामहं यदि।।
किमत्र भवतः कार्यं स्थीयतेऽत्रैव किं त्वया।
पृच्छन्ति नेति लोका मां मयि सन्यासिनि स्थिते।।
चातुर्मास्यापदेशेन स्थित्वा ध्येयो गिरावपि।
अगच्छता मयान्यत्र भगवान्मण्डलत्रयम्।।
इति कश्चिद्गुणोऽन्योन्यं मयि सन्यासितां गते।
सुप्तवेश्यापुरी सेयं मया सन्यासवेषिणा।।
सन्नहं मस्करीवेषी स्वां पुरीं मधुविद्विषा।

प्रत्यक्षमेव लोकानां गामितो भवितास्मि तम्।।
दोषोऽत्र मे महानेको यतिवेषेण सम्भवेत्।
यतिस्सर्वविमुक्तात्मा प्रत्युत स्त्रीपरिग्रहः।।
वयस्यो मम कौण्डिन्यो व्यपदेशतया गिरा।[17]
कथयेद्विहसन् सर्वान् नोचेद्द्वारकौकसः।।
तथाप्युपायस्सन्यासः कर्मसिध्यै भवेन्मम।
तद्भवेयं हि सन्यासी भवेत् सिद्धिर्हि तेन मे।।

इति तत्प्राप्तेरुपायस्सन्यास इति निश्चिन्वानस्तिष्ठन्नयं तदानीं मनुष्याः कथं तिरस्करणीसम्भव इत्यनेन पृष्टं तद् वक्तुं कीदृशी मे वचनपद्धति या त्वयेह दृष्टा सैव सुभद्रेति ज्ञेया सा ते भगवता दर्शिता तेनैवान्तर्धानं नीता चेति मेऽन्तकरणतो यदुदेति तस्या हि प्रामाण्यं न स्यात्। कुतः?

औत्सुक्यं चेतसो यस्य यत्रोद्वेलं शरीरिणाम्।
उदेति तत्र तस्मात् यत्तस्य न स्यात् प्रमाणता।।

इति स्मृतिप्रसिद्धिः। एतस्मादन्तःकरणप्रत्ययस्य प्रामाण्यं न स्यात् तस्मात् कथङ्कारमेतदीयस्य प्रश्नस्य प्रतिवचनं प्रदद्याम्। अस्तु द्विधा योजनां विभावयन्त्या वचनपद्धत्यास्य प्रश्नोत्तरं वदेयमिति स्मरंस्तिष्ठन्नयं भूयोऽपि तेनानर्थक्यं पूर्ववत् वाच्यमानोऽयं तमेव पश्यंस्तिष्ठेत्। स्मरन्नेव तदुत्तरग्रन्थेन वदति **तत्राप्येष एव मे तर्क** इति उक्त्वा भूयोऽपि प्रस्तुतमेव पूर्ववत् स्मरन्निव तिष्ठेत्।[18] अथैवं तिष्ठन्नयं द्विधा योजनां विभावयन्त्या तया तदुत्तरं वाच्यमिति निश्चित्य तन्मुखे पश्येदिति पश्यन्नयं भो श्रूयतामिति विभावयन् तिष्ठेत्; इति तिष्ठति तस्मिन् विदूषकोऽपि वद वदेति दृष्ट्या विभावयंस्तिष्ठेत्। अथैवं तेन प्रेरितोऽयं धनञ्जयस्तदुत्तरं द्विधार्थं विभावयतोत्तरग्रन्थेन तं वदति अन्तर्हितेन केनापीत्यादिना।
तत्र केनापीति पदस्य गरुत्मतान्तर्धानं नीतया भवितव्यमिति विभावितम्।

मूर्ध्नि पद्मासने वारि परब्रह्मणि तेजसि।
तार्क्ष्ये राशिनि पद्मे च कशब्दः खे च वर्तते।। इत्यनेकार्थः।

तत्र ध्वनौ तार्क्ष्ये। अथायमेवं तं विज्ञाप्य भूयसा गात्रिका क्व वर्तते इयं सुभद्रा भवेदिति स्मरंस्तिष्ठेत्।

विदू. – अथ विदूषकस्तथैवमुभयार्थप्रतिपादितवचः श्रृण्वन्निति स्मरेत्। अहो अस्य नैपुण्यं तत्कथङ्कारमयमस्मिन् कर्मणि मयोच्यो भवेत्। अस्तु तर्हि देवभूतेन कृष्णनाम्ना भगवता त्वय्यनुग्रहः कृत इति ध्वनियुक्तया वाचा तमिमं विज्ञापयेयमित्यात्मना निश्चित्योत्तरग्रन्थेन तथा तथा विज्ञापयति।

ज एवं रंखितोहं देवेणेति। एवं यदि यथा अनेकयोजनां प्रतिपादयन्त्या गिरा मामपि विधाय त्वयोक्तं, तथाहमपि भवन्तं ब्रवीमि, यद्येवम्, एवमस्मिन् कर्मणि भगवदनुग्रहकारी संवृत्तो भगवान् यदि तर्हि रक्षितोऽहं दैवेन

17 Vyapadeśa also stands for dhvani

18 The situation in truly dramatic. Dhanañjaya tries to recollect words with double meaning and Vidūṣaka prompting for speedy utterance. What he said means that she was taken away by somebody (kenāpi): it also means that Garuḍa did it as the word kaḥ also signifies bird.

तर्हि तेन रक्षितौ भवेव। तत्र रक्षितोऽहं शब्दे प्रोच्यमान आवामिति दृशोर्विभावयन् ब्रूयादिति तं विज्ञाप्य भूयोऽप्यन्य विवेकनैशित्यस्य तद्गतचित्ततया शैथिल्यं भवेत् किमिति परिच्छेत्तुमुत्तरग्रन्थं सकरुणमाह **सा उण** इत्यादि।

धन. – अथ धनञ्जयस्तया सुभद्रया भवितव्यमिति मन्वानोऽयं तद्रूपं तस्य वर्णितुं वाक्यगर्भं दधानोऽपि तेनापृष्टः कथं वदामीति स्मरन् प्रस्पन्दमानाधरोष्ठो भूत्वापीति स्मरेत्। अस्य वात्स्यायनसूत्रार्थं दर्शयतो भगवदाचार्यस्य श्लोकस्य माहात्म्यम् –

कामेनास्त्रैः स्त्रीयुवानोपयोधैः
संविश्लिष्टौ बद्धमानौ स्वमित्रम्।
आप्तौ वक्तुं तत्कथां तौ भवेतां
वाग्गर्भत्वात् स्पन्दमानाधरोष्ठौ।।

इत्यस्य सूत्रार्थस्य माहात्म्यादस्मै तद्वर्णनं क्रियतामिति मन्मनसा प्रेर्यमाणोऽपि तदुदन्तं यावदेष न पृच्छति तावत् वर्णनमस्मै न करोमीत्यात्मना निश्चित्य भूयोऽपीति स्मरेत्। अहो अस्या याथातथ्यं ज्ञातुं तेनैव भूतेनैव नीतेयमिति तर्कयामीत्यनेन कथ्यते तदहमस्या याथातथ्यमनिश्चित्येव न वदेयमेनम्। तथापि यत्किञ्चित् वाच्यमस्मै एतस्मादात्मप्रशंसातिनिन्द्यापि वचन एतदीये सैवोपायः। तस्मात् सात्मप्रशंसया वाचा सा तेन न नीतेति समर्थयित्वा भूयः कथङ्कारमन्तर्धानं नीतेति प्रश्नस्यैतदीयस्य तद् बान्धवैरियं नीतेत्युत्तरं ब्रूयामित्यात्मना निश्चित्योत्तरग्रन्थेन तथा समर्थयति। **सखे मद्भुजपरिघवर्तिनीमि**त्यादिना।

विदू. – अथेति प्रोक्तो विदूषक इति स्मरेत्। यदयमात्मप्रशंसापुरस्सरया वाचा मां विज्ञाप्य भूयात्तद्-बान्धवैरित्यादिग्रन्थमनिश्चित्यैव न वदामीव साधारण्या वाचा मां विज्ञापितवान्। ततोऽहं पूर्ववन्मति-नैशित्यमस्यास्ति वा न वेति परिच्छेत्तुमिति पृच्छामि कथं तद्बान्धवैरिति त्वयोच्यते स्म। सा मानुषीति पूर्वं निर्धारितं तस्मात्तद्बान्धवा अपि मानुषा भवेयुः। किं तेषां किमदर्शनं कर्तुं सामर्थ्यं भवेदित्यस्मिन् मया पृष्टे सत्यमेतत् गतचित्ततया मनश्शैथिल्यमभ्येत्य शिथिलितमनस्कत्वादस्योत्तरं कथङ्कारं वदेदिति विज्ञातव्यमिति निश्चित्योत्तरग्रन्थेन तथा पृच्छति **विहस्य भो पडिदेही** इत्यादिना।

धन. – अथेति तेन पृष्टोऽयं धनञ्जय इति स्मरेत्। अहो सदृशमनेन पृष्टम्। एतत् प्रश्नस्योत्तरं वक्तुमेतद्गतचित्ततया वाच्यमर्थं विधाय तद् यथामनश्शक्ति ब्रूयामिति मत्वा किमपि विस्पष्टमपि तिरोधायोत्तरग्रन्थेन तथा वदति **गरुत्मवाहने**त्यादिना। इति तं विज्ञाप्य भूयोऽपि तद्गतचित्ततया तद्वर्णनं कर्तुकामोऽपि तेनापृष्टत्वात् वक्तुमशक्तस्तिष्ठन्नयं वाग्गर्भाधानोत्तरं विवक्षुः कम्पयन् अधरोष्ठौ तिष्ठेत्।

विदू. – एवमुक्तोऽयं विदूषक इति स्मरेत्। अस्य तद्गतचित्ततया परवशीकृतोऽयमात्मा उत्तरोत्तरं चित्तलाघवं भविता अत्र दोषो न स्यात्। 'श्रृङ्गारस्य गुणो ह्येष' इति श्लोकमाहात्म्यात्। किञ्च एतद्वर्णनाभिमुख-चित्तोऽयमस्यारम्भ इति मे प्रतिभाति। तस्मात् पूर्वध्वनियुक्तया वाचा व्यवहृत्यालम्। तस्मात् एतदनुसारी भूत्वा तद्वर्णनं कारयितुं कीदृशी तस्यानुरूपशोभेति पृच्छामीति पृष्टोऽत्रोद्भविष्यति प्रीतिरस्य चेत् तत्र मुखप्रसादः स्यादिति स्मृत्वा भूय **एदं सी विवद** इत्युत्तरग्रन्थेन प्रागुद्भूतां वाक्सरणीं विहाय **अं णं कि पी**त्यादिना केवलग्रन्थेन स्पष्टमेव पृच्छति। अत्र स्पष्टोक्तिं वक्तुमयं प्रदेशोऽपि सदृशःदूरीकृततपोजनत्वादस्य चित्तलाघवाद् व्यङ्ग्यस्य गौरवं न विद्यत इति निश्चित्य स्पष्टमेव वदति।[19]

---

19 Direct speech in easier; suggestive is difficult to comprehend.

धन – निश्चित्य; अथ धनञ्जयस्तद्वर्णनाभिमुखः सन्नेतद्बद्धचित्ततया विस्मृतव्यम्। व्यङ्ग्योक्तिर्भूत्वा तन्मुखे सप्रसादं पश्यन् एतद्वर्णनारम्भे तद्रूपचिन्तया कमपि श्वासं कृतवान्। एवं निश्चित्य व्यङ्ग्यं विना तद्रूपवर्णनं करोति **सौन्दर्यमि**त्यादि श्लोकेन।

अथैवं तद्रूपवर्णनं यदा प्रारब्धवान् तदाप्रभृति नयनप्रीत्या चित्तासङ्गं प्राप्तवान् तत्प्राप्तिहेतोर्जृम्भणाङ्गेण ते प्राप्यान्तरान्तरा जृम्भमाणपरस्सन् प्रयोगं कुर्यात्। यदा तद्रूपवर्णनमनेन क्रियते तदैव पूर्वं सिक्तं बीजमङ्कुरितुं बृंहितम्। अथैवं धनञ्जयस्तामेव स्मरन् जृम्भमाणस्तिष्ठेत्।[20]

विदू – अथ विदूषकस्तद्वर्णने सन्तुष्टोऽयमिति यत् ततोऽस्याः प्राप्तेरनन्तरमेवेन्द्रप्रस्थप्रवेशो भवितेत्यूह्यम्। किञ्च कृष्णायामौदासीन्यमनस्केनामुना भवितव्यमिति स्मरन् सविषादम् भूयोऽपीति स्मरेत्। अहो द्वारवती स्त्रीमयि च कष्टमेतस्याः प्राप्तावप्राप्तौ वा आवयोश्शर्म तत ऊर्ध्वं न स्यादित्यूह्यम्। तस्मादपगतजनेऽस्मिन् प्रदेशे वर्तमानेन मया पाञ्चाल्यां नष्टप्रेमा भूत्वा इतरोद्वाहनपरोऽसीति स्पष्टोक्त्यैव पृष्टव्योऽयमिति निश्चित्योत्तरग्रन्थेन तथा पृच्छति। **भो व अ स्स तत्त हो दि ए** इत्यादिना।

धन. – अथ धनञ्जयस्तदानीं तेन प्रोच्यमानं गिरं तथा श्रृण्वन्नयं सलज्जमिति स्मरेत्। अहो पाञ्चाल्यां विरागित्वमनेन समर्थ्यते तस्यादावेवाङ्कुछेदः कर्तव्यः। भूयस्त्वं श्रुतायां द्रष्टायां बद्धरागोऽसीति च, पुनः कुतस्ते अदृष्टपूर्वा लोलता जातेति च अनेन प्रोक्तम्। कुत इति कुत्रत्याःस्त्रियः सम्भूतेत्यनेन पृष्टं तस्मादादावेव पाञ्चाल्यां बद्धरागोऽस्मीति समर्थयन् भूयस्तयोरैक्यमुपपत्तिं दृष्ट्वा सम्भावितव्यमित्यूह्यमिति विज्ञापितव्यमिति स्मरन् भूय इति विमृशेत्। अत्रेदानीं स्मरशरशकलितचित्तत्वाद् ध्वनिना वक्तुं न प्रभुरस्मि तथापि तयोरैक्यं भवेदिति व्यपदेशेन विज्ञापयेयमिति निश्चित्योत्तरग्रन्थेनादौ पाञ्चाली बहुमान्या उत्तरग्रन्थेनानयोः पुनरित्यादिना तयोर्दशाविज्ञापनच्छलेनैक्यं समर्थयति **एकस्या** इत्यादिश्लोकेन।

गदतछ्रुतेन नाम्ना एतस्या वपुस्सङ्कल्पेन यादृशं मम चित्तभित्तौ लिखितमन्यस्यास्या दृष्ट्या वपुस्तादृशमेव। अनयोरेवं दशा तयोरनयोश्शरीर एवं दशाप्रकारः तयोशशरीरस्यैकप्रकारत्वमस्तीव प्रतिभाति।[21]

> दशाप्रकारोऽवस्थायां काले वार्ता तथाम्बरे।
> मेदस्यायुषि तेष्वेषा दशाशब्दः प्रवर्तते।।

अत्र प्रकारे इति तयोरैक्यमस्तीव मे प्रतिभाति इत्यनेन श्लोकेन समर्थयित्वा तदानीं तत्समर्थनतस्तद्गतचित्तो भूत्वानन्यवित् सचिन्तं तिष्ठेत्।

विदू – अथैवं तिष्ठन्तं धनञ्जयं दृष्ट्वा सखे इति स्मरेत् अहो तयोरैक्यमस्तीत्यूह्यमित्यनेन प्रोक्तमिव मे प्रतिभाति यदयमिदानीं तद्गतचित्तत्वादनन्यवित्सचिन्तं तिष्ठति तस्मादस्य तद्गतचिन्तादार्ढ्यं परिच्छेत्तुं प्रष्टव्येयमिति निश्चित्योत्तरग्रन्थेन पृच्छति **भो व अ से**त्यादि।

एवं पृष्ट्वा सखे सत्यं व्याक्षिप्तमित्यादि तद्वचनं केवलार्थीभूतमेव श्रुत्वा तद्गतचित्तोऽयमिति निश्चित्य तस्माद् केवलार्थं वचनमेव मयापि वक्तव्यमिति मया तं मम एव तमित्यादि ग्रन्थं तथा वदति। एवमियतो ग्रन्थास्य प्रयोगमार्गः। अतः परं केवलार्थोऽयं ग्रन्थः। आगात्रिकादर्शनात् चित्तासङ्गे प्रयोगः। अतः

20 The first two arthaprakṛtis – bīja and bindu. The latter is suggested by bṛmhitam.

21 The form before my eyes is identical to the one imaginatively painted in the canvas of my mind hearing the words of Gada.

परमागात्रिका-लिखिताक्षरदर्शनात् सङ्कल्पावस्थायां यदाक्षरदर्शनात् तयोरैक्यं निर्णीतं तदपूर्वमङ्कुरितं बृंहितं बीजमङ्कुरति।[22]

अत्र गात्रिकायां लिखिताक्षरपङ्क्तिर्यदा दृश्यते तदैवं स्मरेत्। अहो पूर्वं गात्रिकायां वर्णं बहुकृत्वानेन वर्णितं यत् तद्वर्णनाक्षरसाङ्कर्यमनेन प्रोक्तमिति तत्र निश्चित्य सामुना मयि अनुरागिणीति च निश्चित्य भूय इति स्मरेत्। अहो सा वैषा वैका भवेत्। तथापीमं तयोरैक्यं अनुक्त्वास्याः प्राप्तौ दैवं कृष्ण एव प्रमाणमित्युक्त्वा त**दधुने**त्यादि ग्रन्थेन पुरी प्रवेष्टव्येति निश्चित्य मस्करीवेषधारी भवितुं निश्चित्य तत्प्राप्तये पुरीं प्रविवित्सुः कृष्णानुमत्यै कालं प्रतीक्षमाणो द्विगुणितमदनावस्थोऽपि सहसा विदूषकेन दर्शितां परसन्ध्यां दृष्ट्वा तस्यावस्थां किमपि व्यङ्ग्येन विदूषक**मपरगिरिनिषण्णमि**त्यादि श्लोकेन विज्ञापयति। तत्र मदनसन्तापशिथिलितमनस्कोऽपि तदेकतया किमपि स्वास्थ्यमभ्येत्य विज्ञापयति **अपरनिषण्णमि**त्यादिना।

तत्र प्रयोगमार्गं दर्शयति वासरश्रीः अपरगिरिनिषण्णं प्राणसक्तुमिव। वासरश्रीः सुभद्रा। अपरगिरिनिषण्णमपरसमुद्रतीरस्थे रैवतके निषण्णं स्थितं प्राणनाथं मामभिसर्तुमिति ध्वन्यर्थः।[23] अतनुरागात् रागबाहुल्यहेतोः एवं ध्वन्यर्थेन सतः प्रेक्षकान् बोधयित्वा बाह्यार्थेन नानालोकान् सुखयेत्। एवं सन्ध्यावर्णनछलेन तदीयामवस्थां कन्दलीदर्शयित्वा भूयस्तत्सिद्धये भगवन्तं स्मर्तुमाश्रमाय गन्तव्यमिति निश्चित्योत्तरग्रन्थेन तत् साधयति। **तदाश्रमाये**ति ग्रन्थेन विज्ञाप्य प्रेक्षकान् प्रणमन् भक्तिपूर्वं सवयस्यो गतवानभूत् स देहश्रीः।

एवं निष्क्रान्तौ।

प्रथमोऽङ्कः।

22 Until seeing the *gātrika* the mental condition of the hero is that of attraction towards her; till the names stitched are recognized it is of hope and the sprout has grown when the identity is established.

23 The Act ends with the expression of the hero's hope to meet his love who will be waiting for him. The outer meaning is the description of the evening. For Vidūṣaka the sun is thirsty like him, and goes to sea to drink water.

IX
Traditional Acting Manual (Āṭṭaprakāram)

Given below is the stage script of the first Act *Subhadrādhanañjaya* kept by the actors. It shows many changes from the acting pattern of *Vyaṅgyavyākhyā*. The most important among them is the inflation of the role of Vidūṣaka and introduction of Malayalam language on the Sanskrit stage. Kulaśekhara did not allow his Vidūṣaka to use regional language on Sanskrit stage. Use of Malayalam is a post-Kulaśekhara development. The single act by these additions takes eleven days for completion[1]. The acting manuals came to be prepared between 13-14 centuries of Common era.

First Day

The Cākyār after his bath comes to the Kūttampalam. He gives a pair of dress to the Nambyār and the Naṅṅyār, prays obeisance seeking permission to conduct the Kūṭiyāṭṭam without any obstruction and sets about attiring himself. The Nambyār does the make-up for the Cākyār. After the lamp is lighted in the stage, the Mizāvu is sounded, Goṣṭhi is played. He performs the Araṅṅutaḷi and purifies the stage.[2]

---

1 During Kulasekhara's time this Act took one day for its performance.

2 Bharata describes Pūrvaraṅga in chapter V of *Nāṭyaśāstra*.
Nineteen items are mentioned there. Kūṭiyāṭṭam follows *NŚ* with minor modifications. The important items of Pūrvaraṅga in Kūṭiyāṭṭam are -

i. The actor in the green room meditates and ties the red band round his head. Here starts the process of transformation of the individual to that of the character.

ii. The Nambyār who is the organizer spreads a cloth on the right side of the stage and keeps the cymbals on it. He lights the lamp. Then moves to the mizāvu, salutes it and sounds it.

iii. Naṅṅyār sits on the cloth spread and sings the akkitha verse in praise of Gaṇapati, Nandikeśvara, Sarasvatī and Śiva.
Nambiār recites a benedictory verse standing in the middle of the stage. See chapter 23 for the verses for SD. He sprinkles water and offers flowers after the recital.

iv. Mizāvu is sounded. Orchestra consists of Mizāvu, Iḍakka, Cymbals, Kuruṅkuzal and Śaṅkhu.

v. A half curtain is held on the stage. Character enters behind the curtain and takes some dance steps to the accompaniment of orchestra.
Pūrvaraṅga is to be performed prior to the dramatic performance.

(The curtain is held)

(ततः प्रविशति धनुर्बाणपाणिर्धनञ्जयः)

(Dhanañjaya enters holding bow and arrow)

धनञ्जय : (सचिन्तं निश्वस्य) अहो नु खल्वतीतेऽपि कथञ्चित् तीर्थयात्रानियमयापयितव्ये संवत्सरे, अम्बास्तन्यमहाभिषेकमुपरि ...... मुकुन्दसहजासन्मार्गपुष्पस्पृहाम्।। (७)

After the curtain is held, the Cākyār having put on the costume of Dhanañjaya, comes to the stage and after doing the ritual dances[3] behind the curtain, goes to the dressing room, ritually sprinkles water on his face, takes up a bow and arrow and comes to the stage. The curtain is removed, looks at the audience and after that keeps the bow and arrow on the floor describing with gestures the five parts of Subhadrā's form and gets hit by the arrows of Kāmadeva and becomes intensely love sick.[4]

अहो नु खलु.... Recites the line in Sanskrit, enacts the meaning of it.

अम्बास्तन्य... Reciting it performs the meaning of it in detail.

प्रापित... Performs the meaning of the whole verse. Then repeats the word Prāpitaḥ. Performs the nityakriyā and completes the performance for the day.

Second Day

Starts, looks at the audience, sits on the seat, salutes. After that salutes in the 'lotus gesture manner'. Technically throws the eyes, shows gestures. 'How are the state of affairs?'

Anukramaṃ[5]

Then long ago Dhanañjaya the scion of the lunar race having heard about the good qualities of Subhadrā from Gada;

how did he stay thinking about it? Before that,

how did Dhanañjaya reach the shores of Prabhāsa lake at the end of an year; Before that, how did he take purificatory baths at various holy waters and travel about; before that, how did he start for the pilgrimage with his friend Kauṇḍinya, having violated the code of agreement;

(shows gestures in this way and completes the narration)

---

3 Ritual dance as above

4 Śṛṅgāra is being enacted in this way. Hero pretends to be hit by the arrows of cupid; describes her in an erotic way from hair to feet. Unable to withstand the arrows of cupid he swoons completely surrendering to Kāma.

5 Pūrvasambandha of Kulaśekhara is developed into Nirvahaṇa in Kūṭiyāṭṭam. It has three parts – Anukrama – the story backwards, Saṅkṣepa – forward in brief and nirvahaṇa – recapitulation with details.

Saṅkṣepa

Then long ago, the Pāṇḍavas, the able members of the lunar race were staying happily in the city of Indraprastha. One day sage Nārada happened to come there and he ordered them that the brothers should cohabit with Pāñcālī in the order of their seniority. They followed that order and were living happily.

(showing gestures for it, completes the narration)

Nirvahaṇa

During that period one day Dhanañjaya performed his evening prayers, had his food, reached his bed room and slept soundly. At that time he heard somebody crying. What is being heard?

Oh sir, I am a Brahmin having only some cattle as my wealth. Robbers have come and are taking away all the cattle. Won't some one come and rescue me? Did I hear like that?

Then let me go to save the cattle and help the Brahmin.

(showing gestures, thinking)

Alas, my weapons are inside the bed room of my elder brother. If I go there and take them it will violate the agreement on timings. After hearing that the cows of the Brahmin are being robbed, it is not dharma, if I do not help. What am I to do? (thinking and deciding) Rescuing the cows of the Brahmin is good for me.

(Went to the bed room of the elder brother, checked if the door is open, went inside, saluted him took up his weapons, went over to the robbers and let off arrows; showing gestures accordingly.)

As Robbers: When they were taking away the cattle, were hit by arrows, got frightened, abandoned the cows and ran away.

As Dhana: (Saw it, felt pleased, looked around if there were any more fellows, saved the cows, went over to the Brahmin) Oh Brahmin! I have saved your cows and have brought them. Please accept them.

As Brahmin: May you get unlimited prosperity.

(Accepting that benediction as something prosperous Dhanañjaya returned)

Early morning, got up, did his morning ablutions and prayers, went over to Dharmaputra: Oh elder brother, yesterday night robbers carried away the cows which were the only assets of a Brahmin. Because of that, I came to you when you were with the wife. I took up my weapons and saved the cows. Because of that I have broken the rules of our agreed timings. Therefore I must go on pilgrimage. May I go for that.

(stands in a reverential pose)

As Dharmaputra: (heard what was said, thought about it) Oh Dhanañjaya, there is nothing wrong in seeing an elder brother in the company of his wife. Therefore you need not go.

(showing gestures fo it)

As Dhana: Oh elder brother, please don't say like that. Let me go.

(saluted and started, went over to Bhīma)

Oh elder brother, I have violated the agreement on timings. May I go for a pilgrimage?

As Bhīma: (thinking about it) Oh younger brother, this is the work of Duryodhana and his followers. Therefore you need not go.

(shows gestures)

As Dhana: Oh elder brother, don't say like that, I shall go.

(showing gestures, started, blessed Nakula and Sahadeva, went to the mother and paid obeisance)

Oh mother, as I have violated the stipulation on timings, I must travel about, for one year doing pilgrimage, may I go for that?

As Kuntī: (standing in the stance of a lady, heard it and felt sad) Oh God! May no harm befall my son. (prays like that)

As Dhana: I have been permitted half-heartedly. Let me go.

(saluting, went over to beloved Pāñcālī).

Oh my beloved, yesterday night I saved the cows of a Brahmin. I violated the rules regarding timings. I must travel about for a year on a pilgrimage. May I go for that.

As Pāñcālī : (standing in the pose of a heroine) May no harm befall on my husband. (pray like that)

Oh fie, things have come about like this.

Oh God, what am I to do? (thinking)

Oh husband, it is due to this self that all this trouble has happened. You don't look at this accursed woman. (thinking)

Oh please don't abandon me.

Oh fie! (showing gestures, again felt unhappy)

As Dhana: Oh beloved, live here happily. I shall spend one year like that and shall return quickly. Hence don't feel vexed.

As Pāñcālī: Oh husband, I feel very unhappy, I have none to depend on. Please return soon.

(looked at him with side glances)

As Dhana: Don't be unhappy. (showing gestures, seeing her side glances, took two or three steps backwards) How were the side glances?

अकृत्रिमप्रेमरसाभिरामं रामार्पितंदृष्टिविलोभिदृष्टम्।
मनप्रसादाञ्जलिना निकामं जग्राह पाथेयमिवेन्द्रसूनुः।।[6]

It was beautiful by the very natural love. Further they were very interesting to watch.

In this way Dhanañjaya considering the side glances bestowed by Pāñcālī as food for the journey, accepted it by the scoop of his mental grief. Then let me go now.

Oh friend Kauṇḍinya let us go on a pilgrimage.

(Showing gestures accordingly, holding the hand of Kauṇḍinya, walk in Kaḷapuṟattu steps[7], taking bath in various holy waters reached the holy place called Gaṅgādvāram.)

(Showing gestures for it, went and washed his feet, ritually sipped water, took a couple of dips in the water, showing gestures turned and sat down. When he looked saw a beautiful maiden standing.)

किमिदं साहसं भीरु कृतवत्यसि भामिनी
कस्यायं सुभगो देशः? का च त्वम्? कस्य चात्मजा?[8]

Oh young one, why are you standing like this? Oh beautiful one which is this place? In which family were you born? Who is your father and who is your mother? What does she say?

(Showing gestures, stopping the miḻāvu)
(acts this śloka, hearing it recited, as if the girl is acting)

ऐरावतकुले जातः कौरव्यो नाम पन्नगः।

6 In the recapitulation verses are used from different sources; not in the dramatic text. But actor will render only the verses of the author: Non-textual verses will be recited by the Naṅṅyār.

7 Mode of gait for heroic characters in Kutiyattam.

8 All these verses are from non-textual sources. Verses in Sanskrit composed by the actors or quoted from source books are called upaślokas. Malayalam verses parodies – are called pratiślokas. Stories are also used for elaboration.

तस्याहं दुहिता पार्थ उलूपी नाम पन्नगी।।

Oh noble sir, Oh Dhanañjaya, I was born in the family of Airāvata as the daughter of the famous Nāga Kauravya. I am a Nāga girl by name Ulūpī.

(again stop Miẕāvu by the elbow)

Have the verse recited, again acts in her role.

साहं त्वामभिषेकार्थमवतीर्णं सरिद्वराम्।
दृष्टवत्यस्मि कौन्तेय, कन्दर्पेणाभिपीडिता।।

Oh noble one, hearing about your various good qualities, from my childhood I wanted to see you. I saw you and was overcome with passion and did like this. Now please marry me without delay.
As Dhana: Did she say like that? (then hearing it)

ब्रह्मचर्यमिदं भद्रे मम द्वादशमासिकम्।
धर्मराजेन निर्दिष्टं नाहमस्मिस्वयंवशः।।[9]

Oh beautiful one, I heard what all you said. I am now under a vow of celibacy as per instructions from Dharmaputra. I must travel like this for one year. Therefore I cannot be amenable to you.

(After stopping the Miẕāvu with the elbow hears and acts this verse in her role.)

परित्राणं च कर्तव्यं आर्तानां पृथुलोचन।
कृत्वा मम परित्राणं तव धर्मो न च लुप्यते।।[10]

Oh noble one, it is only proper to save people who are in difficulty. By doing that, no fault will be attached to your Dharma. I am extremely love sick, please marry me quickly and save my life.

Having heard what was said like this, then saluting sage Nārada and the elder brother, he married her. He lived with her happily. At that time she became pregnant, she delivered a son. Seeing the face of the son he was pleased and gave him the name Irāvan.

Oh beautiful one, you live happily with the son, let me go. (showing gestures, turn around)

तत्र तीर्थाम्भसि स्नात्वा पार्थ पन्नगकन्यकाम्।
परिणीय सुतम् तस्यां इरावन्तमजीजनत्।।

9 Celibacy is not ordained for one year. Arjuna probably gives an excuse to avoid her.

10 Her argument is that as this is not the year allotted to Draupadī, there is nothing wrong in Arjuna accepting her. It would be uncharitable only if he does it violating the claims of Draupadī.

In this manner Dhanañjaya reached, took bath at the holy waters of Gaṅgā and begot a son by name Irāvan, in the damsel named Ulūpī.

Holding the hand of Kauṇḍinya and walking in Kalappuṟattu steps travelled, taking bath at various holy places. Travelling about in the holy places of the southern region, reached the Pāṇḍya kingdom. (show gestures for Pāṇḍyan king) sit on the seat, think, heard that Dhanañjaya was coming, welcomed and offered him a seat.

As Pāṇḍyan : Please listen, after getting married, it was a daughter that I got. There is a blessing of Lord Śiva, that a son born to her will be like my own son. Because of that please marry my daughter, please accept her hand and beget a son in her.

When he said like that Dhanañjaya hearing the Pāṇḍayan king saying like this, thought about it, married her and lived with her happily. She became pregnant.

In this manner Dhanañjaya reached the Pāṇḍyan kingdom, married the king's daughter Citrāṅgadā and gave her a son by name Babhruvāhana.

तत्र चित्रांगदां प्राप्य सुतां पाण्ड्यस्य पाण्डवः।
प्रददौ तनयं तस्यै सुभ्रुवे बभ्रुवाहनम्।।

Oh beautiful one, you must name the son you are going to deliver as Babhruvāhana.

(Making her happy, he started, turning round)

(Walk Kaḷappuṟattu steps, taking bath in various famous holy waters, at the end of the year reached Prabhāsatīrtha and took bath there and stayed there. Showing gestures for it, sitting on the seat completes the performance of the day.)

Third Day

(get attired, starts, sits on the seat)

(Think, saw, Gada coming, looked as to who was coming, understood, act as if he has come near)

What is it that you say? (Stopping Miḻāvu with the elbow hear and act.)

अस्ति द्वारवती नाम पारे पश्चिमसागरम्।
पुरुहूतपूरिभूतिपरिभूतिकरी पुरी।।[11]

---

11 Gada starts the story of Subhadrā with the description of Dvārakā. This is actually what Kalpalatikā does as part of her recapitulation in Naṅṅyārkūttu. The story line there develops in favor of Kṛṣṇa and come to Subhadrā in course of narration.

As Gada : In the middle of the western ocean there is a capital city by name Dvārakā. How is that kingdom? How is that capital city? It will put to shame even the city of Amarāvatī of Indra, the chief of God.

As Dhana: Did you say like that?

Sit again, hear (stop Miẕāvu with the elbow)

अस्ति प्रस्तुततारुण्या तत्रैवात्यन्तसुन्दरी।
भगिनी वासुभद्रस्य सुभद्रा नाम कन्यका।।[12]

As Gada : In that city there is a beautiful damsel by name Subhadrā, the sister of Śrīkṛṣṇa. How is that damsel? She is one who is attaining youth.

As Dhana: (Hearing it, thinking about it) Describes the Pañcāṅgam of Subhadrā. Get hit by Kāmadeva's arrows and become acutely love sick, faint, then wake up.

In this manner Kāmadeva with his arrows made me desirous of the flower in the sky by name Subhadrā who is the sister of Kṛṣṇa. Because of that, the greatness of Kāmadeva is wonderful.

(Showing gestures, turn around, stands in the stance of the start of the performance)[13]

Act the meaning of that and recite the verse: अम्बास्तन्य...

After the entire verse is recited, say, Prāpitaḥ. Then recite along with the Miẕāvu.

Repeat the recitation of the entire verse. Then think, get pleased.

अथवावञ्चित एवाहममुना कुसुमधन्वना। कुतः, व्यालोलहारमुरसा.......जनार्दनस्य।। (८)

अहो महानुभावता महितमहिम्नां तपोधनानाम्। इह हि, शिखिनि शलभो.......लिहन्नहिपोतकः।। (९)[14]

अये सर्वैरेव............ वयस्यागमनम्। (Here the actor describes, by gestures, the tree)

(नेपथ्ये)

भो भो भअवन्तो महर्सिणो भिक्थं देथ भिक्खं देथ।

धनञ्जयः (कर्णं दत्वा) अये कौण्डिन्यस्येवायं भिक्षायाचनस्वनः।

(When this much is over, turn round, go to the dressing room)

---

12 See the introduction of Dr. NP Unni for elaboration of this verse.

13 Here ends the recapitulation of Dhanañjaya. This closely follows the Pūrvasambandha as prescribed in *Vyaṅgyavyākhyā*. The difference is this : Pūrvasambandha was more or less like reporting. But here every point is expanded to create dramatic situations enabling the actor to present them on the stage. Dhanañjaya's affection towards Pāñcālī and eagerness to get back to her is live through out in Pūrvasambandha; in the Nirvahaṇa it is only formal. Dhanañjaya takes three days to complete his recapitulation.
Please note that the dramatic text here is given in Devanāgarī script. Those transliterated are additions.

14 In this verse the actor acts with his eyes and face, the falling of the flies into the fire and then flying away without getting hurt, the fawns drinking milk from the udder of female leopards, elephant calves pulling at the canine teeth of a lion from its mouth as if they be lotus stalks. Young cobras licking mongoose to sleep etc.

Fourth Day

(ततः प्रविशति श्रमालसो विदूषको भिक्षापात्रहस्तः)[15]

Vidūṣaka comes to the stage, stands behind the curtain, the curtain is removed, holds a vessel of folded leaves, enacts seeking alms. He performs the ritual steps. Stops the Mizāvu. Recites the verse.

ब्रह्मा येन कुलालवन्नियमितो ब्रह्माण्डभाण्डोदरे
विष्णुर्येन दशावतारगगने क्षिप्तो महासङ्कटे।
शम्भुर्येन कपालपाणिपुटके भिक्षाटनं सेवते
सूर्यो भ्राम्यति नित्यमेवगगने तस्मै नमः कर्मणे।।[16]

---

15 The first entrance of the Vidūṣaka can be on the same day or on the next day. The costume is the same as that of the Cākyār who does Prabandhakkūttu. The name of the Vidūṣaka is Kauṇḍinya. Vidūṣaka begins his recapitulation. This is interesting from several angles.

i. The Pūrvasambandha of Vidūṣaka in Vyaṅgyavyākhyā closely resembled that of Dhanañjaya. Vidūṣaka starts from Nārada's visit and passes through the incidents that led to pilgrimage and his accompanying Dhanañjaya. He was following the story line along with the hero. Vidūṣaka did not have a separate past of his own in *VV*.

ii. The Nirvahaṇa here presents an entirely different picture. Vidūṣaka creates a past for him. He belongs to a village of illiterates. They have different values of life. His villagers chose him to serve the king. It was thus he became the friend of Dhanañjaya.
It is interesting to bear in mind that he creates a purely Kerala atmosphere to trace the past life quite suitable to the language he speaks: Malayalam. The point to be noted here is the blend of the *NŚ* tradition of Dhanañjaya with the indigenous tradition of a poor Malayālī Brahmin.

iii. This stage also marks a compromise between two streams. The innovation of Kulaśekhara were popular only in the central and southern parts of Kerala. His capital Mahodayapuram, the present Koṭuṅṅallūr is in this region.
The Brahmin village of the extreme North did not approve Kulaśekhara. His plays were forbidden in Taḷipparampu Peruntṛkkōvil. This temple became the centre for the later developments. The district among the Payyannūr, Periñcellūr and Īśānamaṅgalaṃ villages reflected on the stage as solving the dispute (Vātutīrkkal) in the Nirvahaṇa of Vidūṣaka. Īśānamaṅgalam is the much discussed Anadhītimaṅgalam; Mekkāntala is the custodian (Ūrūlar) of Śiva temple west (Mēkku) of Perantṛkkōvil and Kīzkkāntala is the Ūrālar of the temple east of it. The dispute of the two is solved by interpreting a verse both in the sense of Viṣṇu and of Śiva. The Iṇṭiṇṭināykkarappan ridiculed in the narration of aśana is the leader of Periñcellūr Grāmattoṭṭaṃ village.
All that we know now as the Nirvahaṇa of Vidūṣaka – Vātutīrkkal, the four parallel Puruṣārthas – were the contribution of northern stream. This was added to the frame of Kulaśekhara in the twelfth and thirteenth centuries. Thus at this stage we get a much inflated form of Kūṭiyāṭṭaṃ. For details, please refer to the article of Kurumāttūr Nārāyaṇan Nampūtiri in the journal *Sāṃskārikakēraḷaṃ* (VII – 3/1993) of the Cultural Department of Govt. of Kerala.

16 When the recitation of the verse as an example to show that the whole world is under the control of Karma is over he mentions the stories of the ten incarnations of the Lord and the story of the son of Ōṭṭakkāzayan Mūss, who jumped into the well. After that starting from the story of his spending

I have come to wander about in this forest suffering thirst and hunger, it is all the fault of Karma, nothing else. Going to the hermitage of the sages, let me beg for some food.

भो भो भअवन्तो महोसिणो ! भिक्खं देथ भिक्खं देथ। (पारितो विलोक्य)

(Perform Cārī steps and close the performance for the day)

Fifth Day[17]

Putting end to the disputes (Vātutīrkkal)

There is a small village called Anadhītimaṅgalam, so called because all the people there are illiterates. The village has two leaders Mēkkāntala and Kīẕkāntala. They indulge in quarrels very often. Kauṇḍinya interfers and solves their disputes by interpreting the verse *yena dhvasta manobhavena* to the satisfaction of both in favour of Viṣṇu and Śiva. The people of the village decide to lead a good life choosing values for their life: vinodam, vañcanam, aśanam and rājaseva.

Sixth Day

Description of sexual enjoyment and cheating (vinodam, vañcanam)

To attain these two goals they go on choosing women. The qualities of good and bad women are discussed in detail. At last they decided to approach a particular woman in the village. Prostitute is like a holy river union with whom is a dip in holy water. Bath in holy river remove all the sins. This is the philosophy behind the narration. After the enjoyment they returned cheating her.[18]

Seventh Day

Eating (Aśanam)

The villagers decide to have a grand feast. All the arrangements are discussed in detail. The Vidūṣaka identifies four kinds of hosts (Sarasavirasan, Virasasarasan,

---

his time with Cakki, the maid in his house, in the dehusking shed, his starting to serve the king at the instance of other Brahmins and coming to Dharmaputra and when talking with him must recite the verses required for it.

17 The four parallel values of life for Brahmins are enunciated by Vidūṣaka in the following verse:

bhūmidēvarkkūṭṭu tān dharmamatrē
bhūpālan tan sēva tānarthamūlaṃ
vārastrīyil saṅgamēkunnu kāmaṃ
vārastrītan vañcanaṃ mokhahētu.

For the Brahmins the goal of righteous life (dharma) is eating; financial gain (artha); is through service to royality; amorous life (kāma) is through the union with prostitutes and the final emancipation (mokṣa) is attained by cheating them.

18 These parts are not elaborated nowadays since they contain many vulgar descriptions.

Virasavirasan, Sarasasarasan) and advises to accept the hospitality only of the last one. Gluttony is exaggerated to the maximum.

Eighth Day

Serving the King (Rājasēva)

The villagers choose the poor Brahmin to serve the king. He comes to court of Dharmaputra. The king offers a cordial reception and engages him to the company of his brother Dhanañjaya. Thus Kauṇḍinya became the friend of Dhanañjaya. Having narrated his previous life the Vidūṣaka now connects it to the context and starts in search of Dhanañjaya who had gone ahead to Dvārakā.[19]

Ninth Day

(The First Day of Kūṭiyāṭṭam)

Performance of the drama in the regular order.

भो भो भगवन्तो महर्षयः! भिक्षां दत्त भिक्षां दत्त!

daivādhīnamaśēṣaminnumanasā cinticcu bhūmībhujāṃ
sēvāduḥkhamiḷaccukoṇṭu sukhamē vāẓunna sādhukkaḷē/
strībhōgādiviraktipūṇṭu vipinē vāẓuṃ mahātmākkaḷe
bhō bhō bhikṣa tarēṇamē munikaḷe pāraṃ valaññēnaham//

Oh holy people, thinking in your mind that everything in this world is under the control of the Lord and living happily without the regret of having to serve someone, having got over the desire for sex, oh great men who live in this forest, oh sages, give me some food. I am very much wearied wandering about.

अहो शून्यानि सर्वाण्युटजाभ्यन्तराणि।

ellā nāḷuṃ tāpasanmār vasikkuṃ
cellērunnorāśramaṃ śūnyamāvān/
colliṭāminnenṭe māṟṟittamenno-
nnallātonnuṃ mūlamillentu ceyvū//

On all days the sages live here, this is their famous hermitage, why are they empty, I will say it is only my bad luck, nothing else is the cause. What else to say?

अहो अधन्यस्य..........अहिण्ड्यते।

eṇpatteṭṭu sahasramantaṇanmārōṭukūṭi sukhaṃ
munpil cērnnuṭanūṭṭukeṭṭililiṭaṃ vaccaññirunnādarāl

---

19 The recapitulations of both the characters are over. The text of the drama begins on the next day. For these eight days the performance was solo. Hereafter it is multi-charactered.

tumpappūvinu kampamēkina naṟuñcōṟuṃ puḷiśśēriyuṃ
vampiccōramṛtāmaṭaprathamanuṃ kūṭṭi bhujiccēnaham.

Going ahead of some eighty eight thousand Brahmins to the dining hall and sitting there, with rice that is more white than Tumpa flowers, and with Puḷiśśēri, a type of cuisine and then with the famous nectar like Aṭaprathaman, a type of pudding, there I used to eat.[20]

ōrttālen bhāgyadōṣaṃ śivaśiva sukhamē bhakṣaṇaṃ talkṣaṇaṃ ñān
ūrddhvaṃ kṛtvā puṟappeṭṭiha dharaṇitalē maṇṭi maṇṭi kitaccuṃ
tīrthānte muṅṅi muṅṅi paladiśinaṭamāṭunna pārthanṭe pimpē
pārttālāścaryamallō paẕutiluẕaṟuvān nammuṭe karmadōṣaṃ.

Oh Lord! it is my ill luck. For the moment discarding that food I started to this part of the world, walking and walking gasping for breath, taking bath at every holy waters, following Dhanañjaya who goes about to various places. It is all a wonder, getting caught up in this verse, it is all the fault of my Karma.

अत्र पुनस्तपोवन आहारस्य कथापि नासाद्यते।[२१]
तद् जलाशयमन्विष्य..........जलराशिर्दृश्यते।

uḷḷaṃ taṇuppatinu samprati daivayōgāl
veḷḷaṅkuṭippatinenikkorupāyametti
kaḷḷaṃvinā kaṭalinōṭetiriṭṭu nikkuṃ
veḷḷaṃ niṟaññōru taṭākamitagrabhāgē.

By gods grace now, to cool my inside, I have got an opportunity to drink water, to be honest, it can compete with the sea, a lake in front full of water.

अत्र गत्वा यावन्मनोरथं पानीयं पास्यामि।

धनञ्जयः कष्टमसौ मृगतृष्णिकया[22].......इतस्तावदागन्यताम्।

(Three different Bhāvas have to be acted here)

विदूषकः कथं वयस्यो मां निवारयति।...... आप्यायंस्त्वरया निवारितः।

tīrthasnānēna pāpōlkaramakhilamakaṟṟunna kauntēya dhīman
ēṟṟaṃ paidāhapīḍāmanavadhi viḷaviccīṭu majjāṭharāgnau
kāṭṭīṭunnāvil mūnnoẕuki jalacaye mūkkumannērammettī-
ṭṭentītaṇṇīr vilakkunnitu balavaẕiyallentāṇu vairamūlaṃ.

---

20 The gluttony of Vidūṣaka is famous. *VV* also gives evidence to this nature of the jester.

21 The suggested sense in this part of Vyaṅgyavyākhyā is completely omitted here.

22 Mṛgatṛṣṇikā has only the ordinary meaning of mirage; suggestive sense of *VV* is missing here.

Oh wise Dhanañjaya who is getting all his sins removed by taking bath in holy waters, I am extremely thirsty. The fire inside me is burning up. The time has come to immerse my burning tongue in the expanse of water. Why are you preventing me in this manner from the water. What is the reason for this enmity.

veḷḷaṃ kuṭi virōthikkānuḷḷa mārgaṃ tuṭaṅṅolā
ullakālamanarthaṅṅaḷuṇṭāmante ca pātakaṃ.

Don't prevent me from getting even water. This sin will create trouble for you in your future life.

पानीयं प्राणिनां प्राण विश्वमेव च तन्मयम्।
अतो वैद्यजनेनापि न क्वचिद्वारि वार्यते।।

Water is the life of all beings, the whole universe is full of water. Even physicians do not forbid the drinking of water.[23]

धनञ्जयः मूर्ख! नैष जलराशिः! पश्य, ज्वलदवनिभि..................मरीचीन्।। (१०)

विदूषकः एवमेतत्। भो नैषा केवलं मृगतृष्णिका, अद्य प्रभृति ब्राह्मणतृष्णिकापि संवृत्ता।

mṛgatṛṣṇikayenna pērupaṇṭē
mṛgatṛṣṇākaraṇēna kāraṇēna
dvijatṛṣṇikayennu pēridānīṃ
dvijanākuṃ mama tṛṣṇikāprabhāvāl.

Mirage was called Mṛgatṛṣṇa because it produces desire for water among the deer. Because it has produced a desire in this Brahmin it should hereafter be called Brahmin Tṛṣṇā.

किमेतेन! त्वं तावन्मारुतिसोदरः ....लुठन् कथं कथाप्यागतः।

collēṟuṃ bhīmasenananujaniha bhavānuddhatan maṇṭimaṇṭi
collēntuṃ dikkilēṭṭanoru taṭavu bhavānilla villāḷivīra
vallāte cūṭubhūmipoṭiyiluṭaniẕaññuḷla ñāññuḷupōle
collāvonnalla vallanti mama dame hanta kuntīkumāra

You here is the younger brother of the famous Bhīmasena. Oh great archer, there is no trouble for you to go walking and walking to anywhere you want. Like the earth worm that is dragging itself along powdery earth that is too hot, oh son of Kuntī, you can't find fault with my walking somehow.[24]

---

23 Here the vidūṣaka finds out an opportunity to criticize the physician. The vaidyaninda is a pet theme of the jester.

24 These ideas are from Vyaṅgyavyākhyā.

तत् पुनरपि जलाशयमन्विष्यामि। (Walking around and looking up)
भो वयस्य। पश्य पश्य।............धावति।

taṭiyanatāyoru mēghaṃ
taṭitāṅganaye piṭiccu vaṭivōṭe
maṭiyiliruttikkoṇṭatha
maṭikūṭātaṅṅuyarnnupōkunnu.

You fat demon, get away. Your evil desires won't work with me, giving blows with the stick this Kauṇḍinya will smash your body into powder.

धनञ्जयः किं नु खल्वयमुद्दिश्य.......प्रसह्याकर्षति। (सक्रोधम्) आः, दुरात्मन्! अतिनृशंस! तिष्ठ तिष्ठ।

pōṭā bhūtattaṭiyā kūṭānanpoṭu
ninṭe durmōhaṃ
taṭikoṇṭaṭikoṇṭuṭane tava
taṭipoṭiyākkumēṣa kauṇḍinyan[25]

You fat demon, get away. Your evil desires won't work with me, giving blows with the stick this Kauṇḍinya will smash your body into powder.

parattikkoṇṭuṃ paẕamālakoṇṭuṃ
kuranṭikoṇṭuṃ punaranṭikoṇṭuṃ
aṭiccuninmēni takarppanippōḷ
karuttanāyuḷḷoru bhūsuran ñān.

I am a strong Brahmin, I shall smash your body with Paratti, cotton and old garland, with my plank – for sitting and with nuts and Aṇṭi. I shall smash your body giving blows.

ōtikkōnāṇu puṇāñcikaḷuṭe
vaṭivāmaccanāṇammayāṇu
ñānikkanṭabhyasiccīṭina
maṟuporuḷāṇakṣarattāṇidānīṃ

Oath on my Vedic teacher, oath on the beauty of my sacred thread, on my mother, on my father, on all the training I had on the other meaning, you scum of the nether world, without killing you I shall not take back one step from here.

kanyāratnaṃ kavarnnīṭina kapaṭavaṭō
bhūtalōkādhamā ñān
ninnekkollāte kanṭaṅṅōrupadaṃ
iha ninnaṅṅu vāṅunnatilla.

---

25 The jester creates very humorous situations here. He is least bothered about the dramatic effect of the scene or of the anxiety of the spectators who wait to see what happens next.

Oh! Cheat who steals the gem of a girl! Wretched of all worlds! I will not move a step further without killing you.

धनञ्जयः आक्रन्दन्तीमनाथामिव ....भूतधात्रीम्। (११) (शरं सन्धत्ते)

विदूषकः (सविस्मयम्) भो वयस्य! आश्चर्यमाश्चर्यम्।.....पलायते।

āgneyāstraṃ kaṇṭupēṭiccu bhūtaṃ
kanyāratnaṃ kaiveṭiññāśu maṇṭi
kauṇḍinyan ñān tōẕarum kūṭinērttāl
kālan pōlum kālkal vannaṅṅu viẕuṃ.

The demon got frightened on seeing the fire arrow
If I Kauṇḍinya and the friend oppose.
Even the God of death will come here and fall at our feet.

धनञ्जयः अहो अत्याहितम्।.......तावदेनाम्। (प्रसारितकरस्तिष्ठति – stands spreading his hands)

(ततः प्रविशति पतन्ती कन्यका)

कन्यका (ससम्भ्रमम्) रक्खह मं रक्खह मं। (रक्षत मां रक्षत माम्)

Vidū *allā kuyilpēṭayuṭe kuyaṟṟō*
nallōru viṇāravamō na jānē
allallariññēnoru kōmaḷāṅgyāḥ
allalkkorālambanamāṃ karaccil

Oh, is it the cooing of the Koil bird, is it the sound from a Viṇā, I do not know, No, No, I know it is the crying of a beautiful girl who is much distressed.

atra viẕukilasmākaṃ
tōẕarkkāṇyatra viẕukil
madhyē viẕukilakkanyāṃ
pappāti vibhajikkaṇaṃ.

If it falls here, it is for me, it is for the friend if it falls there, if it falls in the middle, the girl should be divided into two halves.

(Dhanañjaya catches her immediately with his hands and keeps her on the ground)

The performance of the first day's Kūṭiyāṭṭam is over

Tenth Day
(Second day of Kūṭiyāṭṭam)

कन्यका (ससाध्वसं सकम्पं च धनञ्जयं तिर्यक् पश्यन्ती स्वगतम्) को णुखु.....अणुकम्पेदि।

धनञ्जयः (सस्पृहं सरोमाविक्रियं च स्वगतम्) चलकुवलय..............मानसं मे।। (१२)

कन्यका (दीर्घं निश्वस्य स्वगतम्) अहो अदिविसमसीळदा......अरोवेदुं आढत्तो।
धनञ्जयः (सवितर्कं स्वगतम्) क्षिप्तक्षौमो....................मदनदशायममुष्याप्रवेशात्।। (१३)
कन्यका को णु शु मं पुणो वि कड्ढेइ। (निष्क्रान्ता)

Vidū *timirabharameṭuttiṭṭēkamēṇāṅkabimbaṃ-*
malakaḷatinu tā̲ze raṇṭitākāśagāmi
tadanu kariśirassuṃ tatkaraṃ raṇṭumellā-
moru kanakalatāyāṃ keṭṭiyōrindrajālaṃ.

Going up into the sky, after that a dark head with two hands, it is a magic performed by a golden creeper holding up a mass of darkness is the idol of a moon below that are two hills,

चित्रं चित्रं क्षितितलगता स्थायिनी कापि विद्यु-
त्तस्याश्चाग्रे तिमिरभरभृत् पार्वणं चन्द्रबिम्बम्।
तस्मिन् बिम्बे कुवलययुगं विद्रुतस्तत् समीपे
तस्याधस्थात् कनककलशौ नैव किञ्चित् ततोधः।।

Wonderful! Wonderful indeed! Lightning stationed on earth! On the top of it a moon surrounded by a mass of dark hair, in the moon there are two blue lotuses, a red pearl below; two heavy golden pots beneath and nothing is visible there under.

cūṇṭāṇi mēlāyiramānakkāṭṭāṃ
śailaṃ mi̲zuṅṅāmavi̲zāmuḍūni
aṃbhōdhi tīikkanalākkiṭāṃ tī-
yambhōdhiyākkāṃ mama pārtu kāṇkil.[26]

I shall show a thousand elephants on the tip of my finger, I shall swallow a hill, shall cause a shower of stars, I shall set on fire the sea, and shall make the fire a sheet of water, just look and see.

विदूषकः (ससम्भ्रमम्) अविहा..........पलायावहे।
ivaḷoru yakṣippeṇṇō
śiva śiva namme piṭiccu bhakṣippān
iviṭe ma̲rattutiriccāḷa-
vikalamōṭi namikka nāṃ tō̲za.

Is she an evil goddess, oh my lord, who has come to eat me up here, let us turn round and ran away, let us go my friend.

---

26 These are exaggerated statements. Perhaps it refers to some magicians of that time who befooled the people by spurious means.

bhūtabhayēna viśappuṃ dāhavumellāṃ
maṟannirikkumpōḷ
jātamorāpattaparaṃ, hā hā mama
bhāgyadōṣamahō.

When I have forgotten my thirst and hunger due to the fear of the demon, another calamity has fallen, oh, it is my ill luck.

खर्वाटो दिवसेश्वरस्य किरणैस्सन्तापितो मस्तके
वाञ्छम् देशमनातपं विधिवशात्तालस्य मूलं गतः।
तत्रस्थस्सतु तत्फलैर्निपतितैर्भिन्नं समस्तं शिरः
यत्रायन्ति हि मन्दभाग्यविभवाः तत्रैव यान्त्यापदः।।

A bald headed man heated by the rays of the sun took shelter under a tala tree to cool down to his head. Alas! Fruits from the tree fell on his head scattering the skull. Calamities follow unlucky persons wherever they go.

इष्टे भुजगविनष्टे पित्रादीनां च रोगवार्तायाः।
गृहदाहेपि च जाते त्वरैव कार्या शिशौ च जलपातिते।।

Quick action is warranted when somebody close to you is bitten by serpent, when the news of parents falling ill reaches you, when the home is burning and when a child has fallen in water.

शनैस्कन्धा, शनैः पन्थाशनैःपर्वतमारुहेत्।
शनैर्वित्तं च विद्या च पञ्चैतानि शनैश्शनैः।।

The following five can be attained slowly: getting on the shoulder, walking the way, climbing the mountain, amassing wealth and acquiring knowledge.[27]

धनञ्जयः (स्वगतम्) हन्त क्षणभङ्गुराणि......दिव्यकन्यका।
Vidū काकस्य कति दन्ता स्युः मेषस्याण्डं कियत्पलम्।
गर्दभे कति रोमाणि एते मूर्खविचारणा।।

The fools always think on these thinks: How many teeth a crow has? How weighty are the testicles of a goat? How much hair a donkey has?

खादन्न गच्छामि हसन् न जल्पं
दत्तं न शोचामि कृतं स्मरामि।
द्वयोः तृतीयो न भवामि राजन्
कस्मात् भवान् मूर्ख इति ब्रवीति।।

---

27 An example of didactic teaching.

Oh king! Why do you call me a fool? I do not walk eating, laughing or murmuring; nor do I repent on what is given away; I do always acknowledge the good things done to me; nor do I overhear when two persons are talking.

धनञ्जयः तस्या खलु – घर्माम्भः कणिका.................धम्मिल्लमालागुणाः।। (१४)

विदूषकः भो पण्डिताग्रेसर! कथं पुनर्मनुष्यास्तस्यास्तिरस्करणीसम्भवः।

manuṣyappeṇṇu tānennāl
maṟaññatiha cērumō
aṟivuḷḷa bhavānippōḷ
paṟaññatucitaṃ varā.

If she belongs to the human race, tell me, how could she disappear? You are a learned man. Answer to this question.

धनञ्जयः वयस्य! तत्राप्येष एव मे तर्कः। अन्तर्हितेन केनाप्यन्तर्धनमुपनीतया भवितव्यम्।

विदूषकः यद्येवं रक्षितोऽहं दैवेन। सा पुनस्तपस्विनी पुनरपि तेनैव भूतेन नीतेति तर्कयामि।

ivvaṇṇamennālumahaṃ tu manyē
bhūyōpi nītā pramathādhipēna
daivēna tanne parirakṣitōhaṃ
sūkṣiccu nilkkēṇaminibhavānuṃ.

This is my thinking – she was again taken away by the demon. If she is protected by heaven it is better that you be careful here after.

धनञ्जयः सखे! मा मैवम्।.............बान्धवैरपवाहितेति।

विदूषकः भो अतिपण्डितोनापि........नेतुमीश्वरा भवन्ति।

vidvajjanattinumabaddhamōrkkiluṇṭā-
middikkiluḷḷa narajātiyilaṅṅoruttan
tānuṃ maṟaññu taruṇīmaṇimauliyēyuṃ
tānē maṟaccatha gamippatinīśanāmō?

Even learned men can commit blunders at times. Will a person be capable of taking away by himself a woman hiding behind or below?

धनञ्जयः मूर्ख!........सम्बन्धियो देवताः।

विदूषकः भो एतस्मिन् विवादे.......रूपातिशयः।

annēraṃ tatprabhāsūcikaḷuṭanuṭanē vannu mē kaṇṇu raṇṭuṃ
nannāyi kūṭṭippoṭiccu kuruṭanavaḷe ñānoṭṭumē kaṇṭatilla
unnidran tōzarālinnavaḷadhikataraṃ sannidhau dṛṣṭayāyi
nannāyi collēṇamennōṭavaḷuṭeyakhilaṃ rūpaśōbhāprakāraṃ.

At that time I could not see her properly as the radiance of her beauty pierced both my eyes. You could see her well. Tell me eloquently all about her exquisite beauty.

धनञ्जयः (निःश्वस्य) सखे! मन्ये ममापि...........एतावत् तु कथयामि।

(Tenth day performance is over)

Eleventh Day

Third day of Kūṭiyāṭṭam

धनञ्जयः सौन्दर्यं सुकुमारता.......... ....भिक्षाटनम्।। (१५)

Vidū *vānāṟṟaṃ kavarnāṟṟamīṟa poṭiyuṃ bhāvaṃ kaṭuṅkrūramāṃ*
vākkuṃ nōkkumitādi sargavibhavān niśśēṣa cakkīguṇān
ētasyāmupayujya padmajanahō śakyanna cakyantaraṃ
sṛṣṭippānatuvēṇameṅkiliha vannellāmirannīṭaṇaṃ.[28]

Smelly mouth, smelly armpits and the mood that shows out is very cruel. The words, and the look and the creative materials and all the qualities of Cakki, having used all of them, thc lotus seated creator, if he wants to create some one like Cakki, he will have to come here and beg.

सर्वथा स्वप्नेपि................कथयत्यत्रभवान्।

indraprasthapurē gamippatinini kālaṃ namukkillahō
indrasyātmajanēṣa kaṇṭavaḷeyuṃ kēḷkkuṃ naṭāṅgīmapi
kāmippāniha kōppukūṭṭi vaḷare peṇṇuḷḷa kaṇṇanpure
kāmīcennu karēṟiyāl kalaśalennallātē collāvatō

I won't have an occasion to go to the city of Indraprastha. This son of Indra, Dhanañjaya, is getting ready to love all the beautiful girls he sees or hears about. He is ready to love her in the city of Kṛṣṇa where there are plenty of girls. If the lover goes there, can there be anything other than quarrel.

धनञ्जयः ननु प्रभवति भवानस्मदनुबन्धेषु। विस्रब्धं पृच्छ्यताम्।

विदूषकः तत्र भवत्याः पाञ्चाल्याः........लोलता।

drupadanandini tannuṭe vibhramaṃ
sapadi hanta vaẕikkaṟiyāyitō[29]
vaẕiyil ninnu bhujiccataśēṣavuṃ
vakayilākkiyatentiha tōẕarē.

---

28 Vidūṣaka has created a meta-world of his. Such verses of parody are common in the words of vidūṣaka. At times it goes to the extent of being repulsive.

29 Vaẕikkari is a colloquial expression for patheyam.

The beauty and charm of the daughter of Drupada, Pāñcālī, was food for the travel. It was all eaten up on the way. What happened to the stock you had once?

subhadrayennuḷḷoru śabdamātraṃ
subhadramāyi kēṭṭurukunnu cittaṃ
atikramiccāḷuṭenambarāntāl
paticca peṇṇennu namukku pakṣaṃ.

The moment the sound of Subhadrā is heard, the mind melts on hearing it. From the sky some one trespassed. My opinion is that it is the one that fell down.

धनञ्जयः सखे! अपरमार्थवेदिना......कथयामि। एकस्या.......दशा मे।। (१६) (सचिन्तस्तिष्ठति)
विदूषकः भो वयस्य!.............न श्रूयते।

uṟakkamō hē mama tōẓarē ñān
paṟaññatonnuṃ bala kēṭṭatillyē
maṟaññu cittaṃ tava hanta kaṣṭaṃ
kuṟaññu dhairyaṃ kuruvīranippōḷ.

Are you asleep my friend, did you hear anything that I said your mind has disappeared, oh! Fie, the Kuru hero's bravery is reduced.

uṟakkaṃ pōmallō muḷakeẓutiyāl kaṇṇinuṭanē
taraykkuṃ kōl mūkkil puṟakilatha nuḷḷīṭukilumāṃ
ghaṭippikkāṃ karṇṇe ceṟiyoru ciraṭṭappoḷi tathā
veṟuttīṭuṃ kūrkkaṃ nikaṭabhuvi kēṭṭīṭukilumāṃ.

If you apply pepper to your eyes sleep will disappear, you can insert a stick in the nose or you can punch the back your ear can be got bitten by a Ciraṭṭappoli or you can hear the hated snores near by.

māraśaraṅṅaḷinālē pūritamāyō bhavānṭe cevi raṇṭuṃ
kāraṇamentiha tōẓā dhīranāyi badhiranāyatentu bhavān?

Are your two ears filled up with the arrows of Kāma, oh friend why you are being deaf?

धनञ्जयः सत्यं व्यक्षिप्तं मे मनः..... श्रमजलभिन्नं.......स्तनश्रोण्यौ।। (१७) प्रष्टुमुपक्रान्तमत्रभवता।
विदूषकः तन्मया विस्मृतम्।..........वाचयितुमुपक्रमसे।

appōḷ nirūpiccu paṟaññatellāṃ
ippōḷ namukkokke maṟannupōyi
nakhēna veḷḷattil varaccavaṇṇaṃ
sukhēna kālāntaravācyamāmō?

What I thought about and told you, all that I have forgotten now, oh friend, like the writings on water, it has become words sent long ago.

धनञ्जयः अलमेभिरसत्प्रलापैः। तत्सङ्गमोपाय एव तावच्चिन्त्यताम्।

विदूषकः (स्वगतम्) एतस्याकाशवासस्य.......... का नामात्रोपायचिन्ता।

pērentennumaṟiññatilla kulamētennuṃ grahiccīla nāṃ
āracchan punarammayāriha kutōvannū kutō vā gatā
nērallinnane vannu cāṭiya cila strīrūpa mōrttālahō
pāraṃ mānasatāpamentinu vṛthā cintunnaten tōẕarē

We don't know the name, we did not gather the family name who the father, who the mother, where did she come from, where did she go. Thinking about such female forms which come jumping over here why torment your mind, why are you doing this unnecessarily.

धनञ्जयः सखे ! सत्यमीदृशामेवैतत्........पुरीमिमामनुप्रविशावः।

विदूषकः भो वयस्य ! तत्र........भूत्वा चोरयावः।

aviṭeccennu subhadrāmirakkayō vēṇṭu dīnabhāvēna
rātriyoḷiccu kaṭannatha kaṭṭuṃ koṇṭiṅṅu pōrayō vēṇṭu
vēṭṭuṃ koṇṭu gamippān mōhiccoru tōẕar cennu mōṣṭiccāl
veṭṭaṃ koṇṭu kiṭappān saṅgataṃ varumennenikku tōnnunnu.

Going there are you to beg Subhadrā in a plaintive mood, are you going there stealthily at night, steal and bring over, is the friend wishes to marry and go, if he goes and steals, I don't think you would be able to come out during day time anymore.[30]

धनञ्जयः (सस्मितम्) अतिकृतणो............भवितव्यम्।

विदूषकः (स्वगतम्) सर्वथा.......तर्कयामि।

enikkitoṭṭuṃ sukhamilleṭō sakhē
tanikku tānpōnna yadukkaḷokkavē
tanikku śatrukkaḷatāy varuṃ vidhau
janikkumāpattukaḷ mēlkku mēlahō.

I don't think this is all right my friend. All the Yādavas will become your enemies and more and more calamities will come up. The Yadus who are to be your allies in war will turn to be enemies.

paṭaykku bandhukkaḷatāṃ yadukkaḷē
piṭiccu duryōdhanādikaḷkkahō

30 The idea is taken from Vyaṅgyavyākhyā.

koṭuppatinnō tuniyunnu tōzarē
kaṭuppamikkarmamaśēṣa dūṣaṇaṃ.[31]

Catching them all, are you trying to give them to Duryodhana. This terrible work is full of faults.

धनञ्जयः मदधीनकलजन्मफले सति चराचरगुरावपरे सङ्गच्छन्तां सात्त्वताः सुयोधनेन।

विदूषकः यद् भवति तद्भवतु।........गत्वावयोर्वेषोपकरणान्यानेष्यामि।

koḷḷāmentinnu cētaṃ tava manamakhilaṃ sammataṃ manmathan-
vannuḷḷaṃkuttikkalakki pala taruṇikaḷe taḷḷiyaṅṅuḷḷilākki
kaḷḷasannyāsiyākkānabhimatamavanennākilō śiṣyanāyi
bhaḷḷinnokkunna vēṣōcitasakalapadārthaṅṅaḷuṃ saṃharikkāṃ.

All right what is the loss, your entire mind is fully agreeable. Kāmadeva came and troubled your mind and has let in a number of damsels into it. If it be your desire to make your self into a false Sannyāsi then I shall collect all the costumes required, suited to the impudence.

धनञ्जयः (विचिन्त्य) कष्टं भोः कष्टम्, भ्राता धर्मसुतस्य...........स्मरः स्मरेताम्।। (१८)

विदूषकः भो वयस्य! परित्रायस्व............भस्मीकर्तुं प्रमृत्तः।

rakṣikka rakṣikka piriñña namme
bhakṣikkumennallitu bhasmamākkuṃ
akṣikku munpil phaṇavuṃ virutti
kukṣikku teṇṭunnoru pāmpitallō.

Save me, save me, if we separate it won't eat it will burn us to ashes. In fact it has spread its hood, it is a snake that searches for food.

phaṇamennuḷḷatu maddhyē
maṇigaṇa ghṛṇijālamatibhīmaṃ
nālu vaśattuṃ kālukaḷ nālu-
ṇṭīpāmpinennatāścaryaṃ

The hood is in the center, the rays from its gems are terrible but that there are legs on the four sides, is indeed a wonder.

धनञ्जयः को नु खल्वेनं ....प्रक्षीणपुण्यसञ्चये। ध्रुवमनुभववार्त्त..........नात्र तस्याः।। (१९)

Vidū *mañcāṭiprāyamāyī kulirmula miniyānninnale paṅkajattil*
moṭṭōṭoṭṭoṭṭu sāmyaṃ taruṇikulamaṇe svarṇakumbhābhamadya
nāḷē kumbhīndra kumbhattōṭu paṭaporutuṃ maṟṟannāḷ kunnuvelluṃ
nālānnāḷ nākalōkakkaḷariyil virutuṅkāṭṭi mēppōṭṭucāṭuṃ.

---

31 Vidūṣaka crosses over, unusually, to political thoughts. Actually *VV* has put these words into his mouth.

The day before the cool breasts are the size of a seed, yesterday it has the size of a lotus bud, today its size, in the gem of a damsel is that of a golden pot, tomorrow it will vie with the bulge on the hand of the elephant, the day after it will compete with a hill on the fourth day, it will jump up to perform feat in the gymnasium of heaven.

विदूषकः अतिभीरुणापि..........शिल्पान्तरेष्वेषक्षरपङ्क्तिर्दृश्यते।

pēṭiyuḷḷa puruṣan tathāpi ñān
mōṭiyuḷḷoru mulappaṭāntarē
gūḍhamakṣaramihāvalōkayē
mūḍhanāṃ mama vadikka durghaṭaṃ.

Though, frightened and idiot, I see secret letters, in the brassier, please tell me what it is.

धनञ्जयः (निरूप्य सहर्षम्) अये ....गात्रिका।(विदूषकस्य हस्ते समर्पयति)

विदूषकः *vēśyappeṇmaṇiyāḷuṭe*
viyarpin saurabhyamennu tōẕarkku
kavanāṟi tuṇiyenniha
mamapakṣaṃ gātrikē varika

For the sweat of this courtesan, the friend feels there is fragrance, oh bodice, my opinion is that this is a cloth of girl that smells like armpits.

भो वयस्य, पश्य पश्य............सहस्ररश्मिः।

periya vaẕinaṭannaṅṅambarē dāhamōhāl
paravaśata muẕuttiṭṭennapōle dinēśan
avikalajalapānattinnekkaṇakke-
jjalanidhāne cenniṟaṅṅunnu mandaṃ.

Wandering a long way in the sky, out of thirst, the sun becoming exhausted like me, wanting to drink pure water, is slowly getting down into the water.[32]

धनञ्जयः (विलोक्य) अये अस्तमितो भगवानंशुमाली। तथाहि –
अपरगिरिनिषण्णं.....................नीलेनान्धकारांशुकेन।। (२०)

kākkakkūṭṭaṃ karaññu kalitakaḷakaḷaṃ kānanāntaṃ niṟaññu
kōkadvandaṃ piriññu kumudakuvalaya śrēṇiyellāṃ viriññu
tārājālaṃ parannu taruṇa taruṇimārvīṭutōṟuṃ niṟaññu
mārāṭōpaṃ kalarnnu manataḷirakamē mā nanīnaṃ taḷarnnu.

32 Vidūṣaka sees his own image in the setting sun. Arjuna sees sun as a lover who is eager to embrace his beloved. Sunset makes him more optimistic.

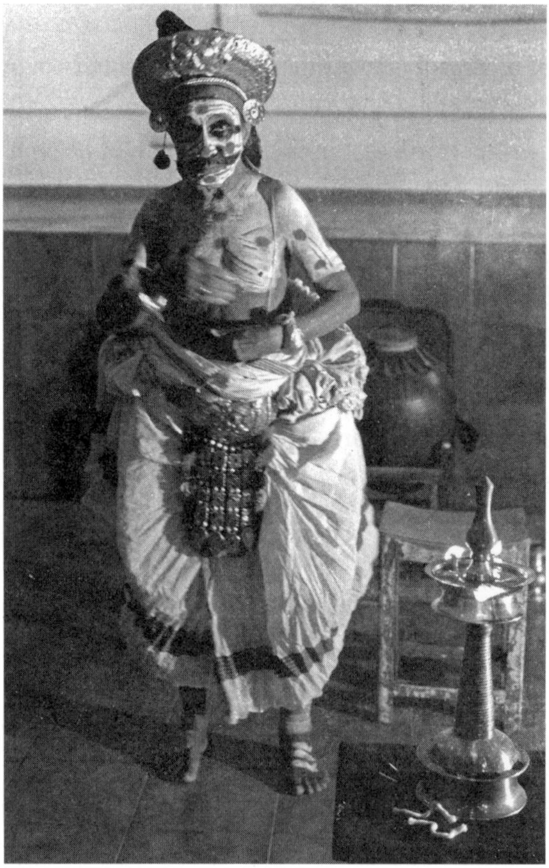

The stage-manuals inflated the role of Vidūṣaka by the introduction of Malayalam language. He recites his textual portion first in Prākr̥t, then in Sanskrit followed by translation into Malayalam. The jester also elaborates with the help of non-textual Sanskrit verses, parodies in Malayalam and with his own interpretations. He also translates Sanskrit texts of other characters. He, thus, became the fourth-estate with his wit and criticism in an otherwise closed society. This is one of the main reasons for the survival of Sanskrit theatre in Kerala.

Muzhikulam Kochukuttan Chakyar as Vidūṣaka

---

tālppūṭṭayanti takarāḥ kaṟikoytaśēṣāḥ
minnāminuṅṅanivahaśca ninuṅṅayanti
maṇṭanti pāntanivahāḥ paṭibandhabhītyā
kākāḥ karaññu maramēṟiyuṟaṅṅanti.

The crow's caw, the forest is filled with the chattering of birds, the Koka pair separate, the water-lillies have all bloomed, the stars have spread, the young men and women have assembled in the house, love overcomes them, the mind of the young woman becomes exhausted, locks are locked after the food is eaten, the fireflies are glowing, travellers walk on being afraid of the gates closing, the crows caw and climb the trees to sleep.

तदाश्रमं प्रविश्य प्रस्तुतसिद्धये व्याप्रियावहे। (इति निष्क्रान्तौ।)

X
Performance Text for Contemporary Stage

This is a new version of the traditional Āṭṭaprakāra abridged to suit the taste of the modern audience. Duration is brought down from 11 days to 8. Elaboration on Puruṣārthas is avoided. Ślokas are retained but some parodies are omitted. Editing is done to concentrate on the development of plot and for the realization of Rasa.

The play was presented to the students and faculty from The Hebrew University of Jerusalem in September 2011. The response of Prof. David Shulman, the renowned Indologist who led the team is both interesting and instructive. Given below are the extracts of his response expressed in 'The Hindu', dated 23.09.2011.

> "The Fourth Annual Kūṭiyāṭṭam Festival presented by Nepathya in Muzhikkulam offered the first act of Kulasekhara's *Subhadrādhanañjayam* (8 nights). The festival began with a splendid Naṅṅyārkūttu by Dr. Indu G. of Akrūragamanam. As is always the case at Nepathya, the acting, miẕāvu drumming, and all other aspects of the performance were at the highest level, and the result was an aesthetic experience that was overpowering, sometimes leaving us in tears. What distinguishes these performances from most others is the fact that the entire work is presented, each night contributing something indispensable to the whole. One cannot even begin to understand the meaning of these complex works by seeing only a two or three hour excerpt from them, as one often does today. They require the attentiveness of a spectator who allows the work to enter deeply into his or her awareness and who slowly becomes sensitized to its natural rhythm and meaning.
>
> Already on the first night, when Arjuna enters (enacted by Margi Madhu Chakyar, an actor of genius and international acclaim), we see the intricacies of his mental world. He sings the famous verse *ambāstanyam*, expressing his disappointment that his long exile from his brothers, wife, and mother is not yet over, and thinking about 'what might have been' if only he could have met them. The *nirvahaṇa* on night 2 explains, from Arjuna's viewpoint, how he arrived at this point of time. On night 3 he enters the ashram outside Dvārakā and shows us- moving only his eyes

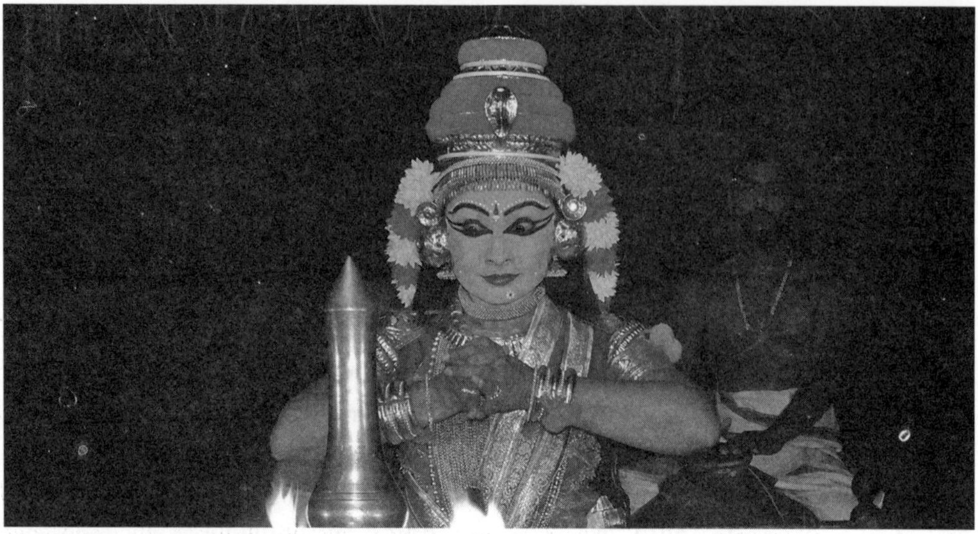

Nannyarkuttu by Dr. Indu G. of Akrūragamanam

for the most part – the wonders of this gentle place, where moths that fall into the fire are not burned and the fawn drinks milk from the breasts of the tigress. (this is the well-known verse *śikhiniśalabha*, one of the high points in all of Kūṭiyāṭṭam). I knew as I watched Margi Madhu perform the verse with his eyes that I was seeing a masterpiece at the edge of what is humanly possible, and I was grateful that I had been given the gift of eyes of my own to see it.

The fourth night, and throughout the remaining half of the composition, the Vidūṣaka enters – the good friend and ironic companion of Arjuna and, in a sense, the other half of the Nāyaka's own character. The Vidaṣaka pokes fun, in fast-paced Malayalam, at the romantic phantasies that have until now constituted the play's main theme. This pairing of hero and clown added immense depth to the characters, with command performances by Margi Sajeev Narayana Chakyar and Sooraj Nambiar, among others. Perhaps the culmination of the entire action came with the extended enactment on Night 7 of Brahmā's creation of Subhadrā, upon whom he lavished all female qualities – beauty, delicacy, sweetness, and so on, leaving nothing over, holding nothing back; so now every time Brahmā wants to produce another woman, he has to go begging to Subhadrā. This verse, like so many moments in Kūṭiyāṭṭam, also shows us the Kūṭiyāṭṭam actor at work, modeling and shaping a creative performance at a level of surpassing perfection.

This great play, together with the equally rich and compelling *Toraṇayuddham*, thrilled us and changed us – the delegation of Sanskrit and Malayalam students from the Hebrew University of Jerusalem – as only great art can do."

Day -1, Arjuna's Puṟappāṭu

(Arjuna enters. Salutes the audience and completes the preliminaries)

He thinks. 'How does Kṛṣṇa's sister Subhadrā look like'?
(Here he describes Subhadrā from head to foot. His erotic feelings increase gradually. Later the cool breeze and the cupid's arrow enhance his passion and he falls down unconscious. Gets up. The acting continues.)

'The pilgrimage of one year is over. The comforts which should be enjoyed have not been there yet. How can it be so?

(Recites the śloka 'Ambāstanyam.', the 'mudrās' are shown and acting is continued in the prose order.)

'I'll go and salute my mother.'
Kuntī laments: 'Why hasn't Arjuna come back after pilgrimage?' Suddenly she sees him. When he bows she anoints him with breast- milk. It would be happy so. But I don't have this comfort.
'The tear-drop of big brother Dharmaputra will fall on my head.'

(Acts as if Dharmaputra is waiting and the tears of joy is falling on his head.)
Similarly I don't experience the comfort of embracing brother Bhīma. Nakula and Sahadeva would come running to me with great joy.
I couldn't even enjoy the bliss that I might have at the loving glances of Pāñcālī when she sees me after a long period.

(Here the actor transforms as brother, mother and Pāñcālī.)
The rest of the śloka is shown entirely with the 'mudrās'. The performance of the day ends with the customary dance known as nityakriyā.

Day – 2, Arjuna's Nirvahaṇa

Anukrama – How this situation? How did the noble member of Somavamśa, Arjuna contemplate about Subhadrā's virtues? Before that after a year, how did Arjuna reach Prabhāsatīrtha? Before that how did Arjuna travel around bathing in different sacred waters? Before that how did Arjuna after breaking the agreement travel for pilgrimage with his friend Kauṇḍinya?

Saṅkṣepa – Long back Pāṇḍavas were living happily in Indrapastha. One day the sage Śri Nārada made the Pāṇḍavas promise that they would enjoy Pīñcālī one year each in the order of their seniority. The Pāṇḍavas kept that promise.

Nirvahaṇa – At that time one day Arjuna after his evening prayers and meal came to his sleeping chamber and fell asleep. Then, on hearing a cry, 'What do I hear'?

Oh! I am Godhana, the Brahmin. My cows are being stolen by thieves. Somebody come and helps me' was heard.

The Brahmin's cows have to be saved. The weapons are in the brother's sleeping chamber. If one went there the promise could be broken. If one did not act after hearing about the Brahmin's cows that will be against Dharma. Alas! What will I do? Saving the Brahmin's cows will be my honour.

Deciding thus Arjuna enters his brother's chamber, picks up the weapons, approaches the thieves and shoots arrows at them making them abandon the cows in fear and flee. Looking around if there were more of the thieves, Arjuna herded the cows and approached the Brahmin. 'Oh! Brahmin, I have saved your cows accept them'. The Brahmin was overjoyed and blessed Arjuna saying, 'May you be blessed with prosperity'.

Receiving this blessing Arjuna goes back to the capital and upon dawn after ablutions, goes to Dharmaputra and pays obeisance saying, 'Oh, brother when Godhana's cows were robbed, I entered your chamber to pick up weapons to save them, and hence I have broken the agreement for that I have to go for pilgrimage for a year. May I leave?'

When this was said Dharmaputra says, 'O Arjuna, there is nothing wrong if a younger brother saw an elder brother together with his wife. You do not have to leave'. Arjuna says, 'Oh, do not say so. Let me go'. Becoming Bhīma, says, 'Oh Arjuna, this is the deed of the wicked Duryodhana and others, you do not go'. Arjuna says, 'Oh brother do not say so' and taking permission from them and blessing Nakula and Sahadeva and approaching his mother, paying his obeisance says, 'Oh, mother, my promise has been broken. I have to travel around for a year bathing in sacred waters. May I leave?' Becoming Kuntī, prays 'Oh God, save my little one from dangers. 'Then Arjuna approaches Pāñcālī and announces the same. Pāñcālī sadly remarks 'Oh, husband! You have come to this fate because of me. Do not desert me thinking that I am wicked'. Arjuna says, 'Oh, beloved do not be sad. Live happily here. I will return soon after a year. Pāñcālī looks deeply at him and says, 'Oh husband, I am, very sad. I have no other refuge. Return soon'. Arjuna accepts her gaze as his vaẕikkari (sustenance for the journey) and starts out. How was this gaze? Beautiful with pure love. Not only has that it created awe for the eyes. (Śloka)

Arjuna with Kauṇḍinya in hand travels to various sacred waters and carries ablutions. While bathing at Gaṅgā, he spots a beautiful woman there and asks, 'Oh why this daring act? Oh, beautiful lady, what is this place? Which family do you belong to? Who is your father? Mother? I wish to know these. (Śloka)

What is being said? (Śloka)

Oh! Great one! I am Ulūpī, the daughter of the great serpent Kauravya of Airāvatakula (Śloka). I have heard praises of you since childhood and desired to meet you and knowing that you are here has come to meet you. Accept me'. Arjuna gestures whether this was said and speaks to her.

'Oh beauty, what you spoke is true. I am observing the vow of celibacy as directed by Dharmarāja. I have to travel this way for a year with sacred oblations. I cannot accept you now'. (Śloka)

At this time hearing what she says gestures? 'What is your saying? (Śloka) 'Oh, great one you should save people in grief. No harm will come upon you due to that: I am in a state of heightened desire, accept me. Save my life', was this what was said?

Arjuna marries her and while living happily with her she gets pregnant and gives birth to a son. At that time Arjuna, pleased at seeing his son's face names him Irāvan saying 'Oh, beautiful, live here happily with our son, I have to go', and starts out from Gaṅgā (Śloka) and with Kauṇḍinya in hand travels to different sacred waters and reaches the Pāṇḍya Kingdom.

At that time the Pāṇḍya king hearing of Arjuna's arrival welcomes him with joy and provides him a seat and says, 'Oh, Arjuna I have only a daughter in marriage. I have a boon from Śiva that my daughter's son would be a son to me. Marry my daughter and bear her a son and bless me. Arjuna lives happily with her after marrying her, when she gets pregnant, he says to her, 'Oh beautiful lady, name your son Babhruvāhanan' and making her happy thus started. Thus he reached Pāṇḍya kingdom, married Citrāṅgada the daughter of the Pāṇḍya king and gave her a son (Śloka).

Thus after traveling to different sacred waters for a year he reaches Prabhāsatīrtha.

Day – 3, Iḷakiyāṭṭam

Actor enters as Arjuna, sits and thinks. Enter Gada. Arjuna listens to Gada's words. (Śloka) In the western ocean there is a kingdom called Dvārakā. How is it like? It is magnificent and beautiful than the palace of Lord Indra.

Śloka continues – There is a beautiful girl named Subhadrā at Dvārakā. How does she look like? 'She is as fresh as a budding flower'.

Hearing about Subhadrā, Arjuna started imagining her from hair to the whole body and is excited of love and lust. He enacts and connects the act to thought by reciting the sloka 'Kāma, the God of love has succeeded in kindling my passion towards Subhadrā, sister of Kṛṣṇa. Arjuna reaches Dvārakā 'Has Kāmadeva cheated me? No, it is not possible – he has favoured me, but how? I am going to Kṛṣṇa – keeping close to his heart – I want to embrace him. Krishna's chest bears the symbol of Lakshmidevi's breasts. When, he calls me dear friend Arjuna how does it sound? It's like the flow of sweet honey. And who is Kṛṣṇa. He is my closest friend.
Arjuna goes round the stage watching the hermitage and is surprised.

> 'The greatness of penance cannot be imagined. Oh! The butterfly falling into the fire is not hurt – it is flying out. The deer cub is drinking milk from the mother tiger. Elephant cub plays with the teeth of lion-thinking that it is the lotus stem. The little snake is licking mongoose to sleep.

(Details are initially expressed with eyes and later with mudrās in a chronological order in detail).

(Śloka) 'Despite being the born enemies, these animals are living in harmony' and that is the greatness and power of meditation. These sages are so great! They have gone to river to have their bathe. The place looks deserted. The lazy friend Kauṇḍinya hasn't reached yet. Let me wait under the great banyan tree'. (Sits below the tree. Enacts listening to the sound of Kauṇḍinya's begging.)

Day – 4, Entry of the Vidūṣaka

Vidūṣaka enters begging alms in leaves strewn together. Bowing to the Karma, he says. I bow before the karma. As a reply to the doubt whether karma has such greatness to be bowed before; he says that even the Trinities are subjected to the dictates of karma. First he describes the case of Lord Brahmā. Brahmā and potter are alike. Both are engaged in creation. The lord creates everything using pañcabhūta (earth, water, fire, air and space).The potter too creates with the same things. The only difference is that the creation of Brahmā is burned after use, whereas the creation of a potter is burned before use. The creation goes on at every time. At no time rest is taken. Why does it happen so? It is his karma.

As a reply to the remark that Lord Viṣṇu may not be like that, the Vidūṣaka says that Viṣṇu too is subjected to karma. His duty is to sustain the world. He is born and he dies for it. Once Hayagrīva stole the Vedas from the face of Brahmā and hid in the sea. It made the Brāhmins forget their mantras. Here the Vidūṣaka describes the situation where the Brāhmins forgot the mantras and when they approached their teacher he also doesn't remember it. It was at this juncture that Viṣṇu incarnated as a fish and killing the demon retrieved the Vedas. At the time of churning the milky ocean, he incarnated as a turtle in order to lift the mountain Manthara which was used for churning. How much he suffered in taking the different incarnations!

Take the case of Śiva, the lord of destruction. Smearing ashes on the whole body, wearing the skin of trees, having a long knot of hair, he lives on alms. It is all because of his karma. The sun always rotates in the sky, rising and setting again and again. Karma is the reason.

Look at our ōṭṭakkaẕiyan mūs. He remarried after having no issue from his first marriage. Then too, he was childless. Again he married. But it was of no use. He did many a good deed and prayer and as a result at last one of his wives became pregnant. She gave birth to a girl. Again he performed good deeds with a hope of getting a male child. The next conception was also a girl child. Thus he had a lot of daughters. At last he got a boy in his old age. But when he was playing with children, he died of falling in well. It was his karma!

Why should I say about other people? Take my case. I was living at my home comfortably. Cakki was our maid servant. It was at this time that I was sent to the king by the whole villagers to serve him for the welfare of the village. This made me too happy. I had hoped earlier to be a courtier at the sight of courtiers riding on the horseback. Without a second thought I set out to be a courtier not knowing who to be served. Hearing people praising Dharmaputra, I came to him. Here he enacts blessing Dharmaputra. He reveals the poverty of his home interestingly. There was no study of Vedas for the last four generations and the leaves of muriṅṅa usurped the share of rice in his meal. He makes Dharmaputra happy and thus gets a sumptuous meal from there. While leading such an easy life, after a few days, I was sent to get acquainted with his brothers. Thus I reached Arjuna, my friend. I lived with him. There was an additional drink of milk besides the feast. Then there came the bearded monk, Nārada who made rules for sharing Pāñcālī. Thus when Pāñcālī was with the Dharmaputra I had to sleep with the servants. It took away all comforts of my sleep. I spent sleepless nights at the sight of light. But my friend needed light to sleep. Thus I spent the nights putting out and lighting lamps. It was in the morning when he went out that I had a sound sleep.

Even after the sun rays touched my buttocks I slept turning here and there. One day I slept at another place. On the day, my friend had to break his pledge for a

Brāhmin entering the inner chamber of Dharmaputra. As an act of atonement he set out for a pilgrimage with me. During the pilgrimage he began to sway because of lust. He was fascinated by a serpent maid when he took a dip at the mouth of the river Gaṅgā. As he was infatuated by the maid, I began to be starved. At last we reached the Prabhāsatīrtha. There a man called Gada told him about a girl and so, my friend went in search of her. Though I ran with him, I could not get at. I came here in search of alms in order to maintain my life breath. I hoped that a bearded man, a bearded woman or a bearded child would have been here. But nobody is to be seen here. Please give alms!

Here in the hermitage there is nobody. I am unfortunate. The ill-luck of my stomach! How does the place full of monks emptied so soon! Or else it was my fault. I had to leave behind the sumptuous food served by Pāñcālī at Indraprastha in golden plates, sitting among 88000 Brāhmins. I followed this Arjuna for a pilgrimage. How unfortunate I am! Nobody here even speaks about food. Let me see whether there is any chance for getting drinking water. There sees a large lake. I will drink from there.

Day – 5, Arjuna and Vidūṣaka

Arjuna enters, describes in detail the height, branches, trunk, leaves, blossoms, flowers, fruits, and the roots branching out from the top to bottom of the banyan tree. He approaches the shadow of the tree. He notices Vidūṣaka passing by and thinks: 'He is attracted to a mirage. I must stop him'.

He calls Vidūṣaka 'Friend.' Hearing this Vidūṣaka wonders if it is the sound of water or if the frogs are refreshing their old acquaintance with him. Many years ago during his Vedic study days while he was staying at Peruntṛkkovil he had pierced and split the eyes of the frogs. The Vidūṣaka wonders if the frogs from that place who are married to the frogs in this area are reminding him of his action. Arjuna calls him again and Vidūṣaka feels that it is a human voice and that if it is his friend then he will be called by his name. At that moment itself, Arjuna calls him 'Kauṇḍinya'. He goes near Arjunan and tells him that he was expecting him for a long time. Vidūṣaka tells Arjunan that he will drink some water and come back. Arjunan blocks him. Vidūṣaka refuses to be stopped. Arjuna gets angry. Vidūṣaka tells him that he has not 'cut off the tree in his ancestral house', meaning that he has the means to live life in his own terms. He starts to proceed but Arjuna gestures him not to go. Vidūṣaka asks Arjuna why he is preventing him from proceeding to drink water. Even cruel physicians do not forbid a person's need for water. Vidūṣaka ridicules physicians. Physicians are worse than the God of death. Yama only takes life; but physicians take both life and money. Vidūṣaka acts out how difficult it is to get a doctor and how they prescribe horrible, bitter tasting medicines and harsh diet rules. As soon as the physician exits with money, Yama comes and exits with the patient's life. Even such cruel physicians will not prevent from having water.

The water one drinks after having searched and yearned for it a very long time is the real nectar. The nectar produced by gods is nothing compared to such water. Vidūṣaka complains that when he is so thirsty and going to drink water, his friend is stopping him. At that time Arjunan tells him: 'Hey you fool. That is not water. It is a mirage, an illusion, caused by the sun's rays. 'Vidūṣaka then says it is a mirage fooling Brahmins and so should be renamed like that. He tells Arjuna that as Arjuna is the brother of the strong Bhīmasena, he can walk fast but his own legs are weak and he needs food and water at regular intervals. Vidūṣaka wonders what he should do to get water and when he looks at the sky, he notices an astonishing sight. The dark sky seems to be carrying on its lap a streak of lightening. Arjuna inspects carefully and realizes that it is a demon and a maiden. The demon seems to have forcefully taken away the maiden and she is crying in distress. He enters into a quarrel with the demon. Arjuna threatens that if he does not release the maiden he will strike him with a powerful weapon that will turn him into ashes. Vidūṣaka explains this in local dialect and he also threatens the monster in a humorous way. Arjuna sounds the Āgneyāstra upon which, Vidūṣaka comments the three worlds shuddered. Vidūṣaka tells Arjuna that if he really shoots the weapon then even Lord Brahmā in heaven will feel terrified. The demon hearing the sound of the arrow string flees and escapes, throwing down the maiden down to earth.

Behind the stage, a cry is heard 'Help help.' Arjuna holds both his hands together so as to catch and rescue the maiden who is falling down. Vidūṣaka tells Arjuna that if the maiden falls on place specified by him, then the maiden belongs to him. Thereafter, Subhadrā enters the sage, terrified. Arjuna and the girl look at each other and are struck by the arrows of cupid.

Day – 6, Love – lorn Arjuna and Subhadrā

Subhadrā enacts the 'Pañcāṅgaṃ' (seeing the crown, face, eyes, chest and feet of Arjuna) and faints love struck. She gets up and is immersed in various thoughts. Who is this gentleman who saved me? How could he do it? From my child hood days I have grown up with a craving for Arjuna. Once my friends, seeing despair on my face tried to engage me in some fun activities.(Here Subhadrā enacts the 'Panthaṭi', playing the instruments etc). Disinterested in all these I retired to my room and was engaged in his thoughts when the demon appeared and dragged me by my hair. On hearing my cries, this man geared up and appeared with bow and arrow in his hand. Seeing him the frightened demon left me and fled. Who is this man who saved my life? I have not come across a handsome man like him any where in all the three worlds.

Arjuna also sees Subhadrā and is lost in thoughts – Who is she? Where is her home? Who are her parents? She is no common woman to attract me. Subhadrā, through Gada's description has won over my heart and sealed it off for another woman. She had with the strings of her virtues bound me. But this lady through the eyes had entered into my heart. Who is she? Her eyes shivering with fear resembles the petals of the blue lotus flowers dangling in the light breeze.

(Here Arjuna enacts the maids dressing up Subhadrā-doing her hair- decorating with flowers- adorning her with ornaments- at the end they feel some thing is lacking-then realizes that kājal has not been applied to her eyes – applies añjanaṃ also)

The fragrance of her face attracts many a bees to her. Who is this enchanting lady?

Arjuna continues with the 'keśādipādavarṇana.

Vidūṣaka enters while Arjuna is languishing in her thoughts. Vidūṣaka narrates the flash backs and describes the lady. He feels that it is a wonderful sight like magic. He describes the magical feats like- visualizing many elephants at the finger tip engulfing a whole mountain- make the stars disappear etc. (At this point of time Subhadrā disappears). Vidūṣaka thinks that she is a Yakṣī who had disappeared to overwhelm them. Here he goes to describe the things that need to be done on priority. Arjuna is upset that the beautiful lady has been lost and calls Vidūṣaka 'fool'.

Vidūṣaka 'I have not done anything to be fool -like laughing while talking, have food while walking etc. and still why do you call me a fool?'

Arjuna She is not a divine lady because there is sweat on her cheeks, the pathikeetu on her breasts have faded, she blinks, her feet touches the ground and the jasmine flowers on her hair have faded.

Vidūṣaka Then how did she disappear?

Arjuna That is what even I wonder..

Vidūṣaka Thank god. That demon night have snatched her.

Arjuna No. Not even the enemies would dare to touch her who has been rescued by me.

Vidūṣaka Even the wise can speak blunders. How can a human being then disappear?

Arjuna Fool, The devas themselves protect the people when Lord Kṛṣṇa Rules over the world.

Vidūṣaka You win my friend. But tell me about that lady whom I was not able to see properly.

Day – 7, Patantī

(He describes the exhilarating beauty of the heroine from tip to toe in detail the thick locks of hair, the crescent-shaped forehead, eye brows that are perfectly curved like Kāmadeva's bows, the beautiful eyes, neck, full round breasts ankles and feet, and at the end gets struck with Cupid's arrows and faints. On waking up, acts as if replying to Kauṇḍinya.)

Words fail to describe her beauty. Even Lord Bhrahmā, the Creator, himself will have to go to her and beg. What for? That is, if he wants to create yet another beauty of this kind. You know, why I said 'if he wants to Create'? Because, by creating this lady, Bhrahmā must be resting fulfilled and content. But he cannot continue to stay idle like that. Is he not the Lord who is responsible for all creations? But then, is it sufficient enough to beg once? No, not enough! 'Please give me the alms of all those ethereal qualities, please give me the alms of all those ethereal qualities,' like these he has to keep on begging till he receives them. He is deprived of the materials for future creations by expending them all on this women. It is because he had used all the qualities that are required for the creation of beauty and exhausted thoroughly. What are these qualities of a noble woman? Beauty, loveliness, sweetness, charm, cuteness, grace, elegance and dignity: etc. He should beg for each of these. This much is what I can tell of her beauty.'

(Here the act of creation by Bhrahmā is enacted in detail.)

(Vidūṣaka enters)

Arjuna hails Vidūṣaka: 'Oh! My friend!' Vidūṣaka answers Arjuna's call, imitating maid servants. He interprets Arjuna's words and sloka in Malayalam. He essays a nonsensical anecdote making fun of people indulging in loose talks. Recites parodies entirely opposite in meaning to the depiction of heroine's beauty by Arjuna. He describes the beauty of 'Cakki,' parallel to that of the heroine. He says, that he can never, even in his wildest of dreams, reach Indraprastha. His friend is terribly hooked up to the ladies around and, that, since Arjuna is proceeding to Dvārakā, can't say anything of what can happen there, a place full of beautiful girls.

Anyway, he decides to offer some advice to Arjuna. He asks Arjuna to answer his questions without getting irritated. Arjuna agrees.

Vidūṣaka 'The story of Panchali was over like a parcel of morsel. Then it was the name Subhadrā that made you upset. And now, a girl from the sky makes you distraught. How come that your mind is so wobbly?'

Arjuna 'Hi, You are saying all these without knowing the real truth. Nobody can move my mind. I am fettered by that tender, affectionate glances of Pāñcālī. I was only painting the other one's picture on the walls of my mind when I heard her name. Now my eyes too are enriched by the sight of this girl. I do have an interest in both of them.'

Arjuna stands still as if in meditation. Vidūṣaka tries to awaken Arjuna doubting that he must have fallen asleep. Thinking that Arjuna is dead he cries out that he is also going to die and bids farewell to all the food articles. Arjuna wakes up and tells 'my mind is lost! Hey, here, look my friend!'

Day – 8, Conclusion

Arjuna Oh! friend, my body is drenched with sweat and quivering. My hands Feel lowered holding her breasts and hip'. What were you telling me?

Vidūṣaka Oh! I forgot that. You know I am brainless.. It disappeared like what was written in water.

Arjuna Do not bluff. Tell me a way to get her.

Vidūṣaka How can that happen – Dear friend we do not know her name or Family. How can we search for such a person?

Arjuna That's right. Only God can help us. So let's strive to win Subhadrā.

Vidūṣaka We should either beg or steal her.

Arjuna That's not fair' with the help of Kṛṣṇa, I will defeat the Yādavas and make her mine. Till the time comes I will wait in the disguise of an ascetic. You can assist me as my disciple.

Vidūṣaka This will only lead to conflict. Your endeavor will only make the Yadavas who are our sole aids now join with our enemies, the Kauravas.

Arjuna I do not mind that. As long as the Almighty Kṛṣṇa is with us, let anyone go with the enemies.

Vidūṣaka Let it be so. I shall go and get the costumes of hermits.

(Exit Vidūṣaka. Arjuna is engrossed in his thoughts)

'Cupid will have a good laugh by making me an ascetic to get one women'.

Vidūṣaka (On mistaking Subhadrās 'gātrika' for a snake enters screaming. Arjuna consoles him that it is her gātrika which might have fallen down when the demon carried her away.)

Arjuna embraces the gātrika – O gatirika, you are unlucky to have fallen down from her breasts.'

Vidūṣaka Finds some letters printed on the Gātrika which happens to be the ten names of Arjuna. They realize that she is also from Dvārakā.

Arjuna gives the gatrika to Vidūṣaka telling that they would try to get both the ladies. He describes the difficulties in marrying twice.

They see the Sun moving towards the Ocean in search of water.

(First Act ends with a description of sunset)*

---

* Here we have three specimens of the presentation of the same Act in three distant ages – the first in 9th century under the guidance of the author himself, the second after five centuries in 15c when acting manuals were prepared by the actors themselves and the last on contemporary stage distanced from the former by five centuries. Comparison of these performances is instructive for the students of theatre.

a. **Vyaṅgyavyākhyā - 9-11 c**
   i. Performance follow the language of the dramatic text, i.e., Sanskrit/Prākṛt.
   ii. Pūrvasambandha is introduced where the acting is devoid of verbal rendering.
   iii. The characters in retrospective narration gives their past as detailed in the source text (Mahābhārata) or in the dramatic text.
   iv. Multiple impersonation along with imaginative acting is introduced in a slight way.
   v. Mono-acting gets predominance over acting by multiple characters.
   vi. Prime concern of the artist is the satisfaction of the elite and hence importance is given to communication of suggestive sense through ocular movements.
   vii. The play is performed in a secular space ie, play-house attached to the palace, one Act per day.

b. **Traditional Acting Manual - 14-15 c**
   i. Along with the languages in the dramatic text, Malayalam is also used on the stage through vidūṣaka. The play is shifted from the Sanskritic locale to the indigenous Kerala atmosphere.
   ii. Pūrvasambandha is modified as nirvahaṇa and anukrama and saṅkṣepa are added.
   iii. Vidūṣaka creates a new past for himself. The fusion of Mahodayapuram and Cellūr traditions are quite visible on stage.
   iv. Elaboration on descriptive lines has improved. Two verses – śikhiniśalabha and calakuvalaya are chosen for special acting. Pakarnnāṭṭam and manodharmābhinaya have developed fully.
   v. Significant additions are:
      i. interpretation in Malayalam of Sanskrit/Prākṛt dialogues of other characters by the jester,
      ii. quoting of suitable upaślokas (sub-verses) in Sanskrit from other sources by vidūṣaka,
      iii. use of counter verses (pratiślokas),
      iv. parodies in Malayalam and
      v. sub-stories to explain the situation. The role of Vidūṣaka is inflated disproportionately.
   vi. The nānāloka has gained prominence in the audience. Presentation of suggested meaning has completely vanished.
   vii. Performance has become confined to the temple premises and rituals are added. The one day performance takes 11 days for completion.

c. Performance on Contemporary Stage - 21 c

i. An overall editing is done on the traditional manual. Vidūṣaka's role is curtailed. Duration is brought down to 8 from 11 days. This performance is aesthetically more delightful.

ii. Venue of performance is brought back to public space.

iii. Actors drawn from different strata of society are exposed to the principles of theatre.

iv. There is less of ritual in performance. The aim of the presentation is to please the audience.

XI
The Interlude Recapitulation of Kalpalatikā

(ततः प्रविशति चेटी)

चेटी आणत्तह्मि भट्टिदारिआए सुभद्दाए – हञ्जे कप्पलदिए! तस्सिं भूदसम्मद्दे पभसतित्थपरिसरे पब्भट्ठा मे गत्तिआ। तं गवेसिअ आणेहि। अण्णं च, जेण अहं भूदहत्थादो मोआविदा, सो वि महाणुभाओ ळो अणाणन्दअरो तहिं सण्णिहिदो ण वेत्ति संपहारिअ आ अच्छत्ति। सुइरं च मए अण्णोसिअं। ण सा गत्तिआ, ण सो पुरिसो दिट्ठो। किं णु हु भट्टिदारिआए कहइस्सं। (विचिन्त्य) कुमारधणञ्जअस्स णामङ्किदत्ति गत्तिआअं से बहुमाणो। अण्णो वि अण्णोसिऽज्जइ पुरुसत्ति किं विअ एदं। अण्णं च, मए कुदो तस्सिं पमहवुत्तन्ते परमत्थो जाणिदव्वो। (नेपथ्याभिमुखमवलोक्य) एसो अय्यविणअपालिदो इदो एव्व आअच्छइ। एव्वं दाव पुच्छिस्सं। (आज्ञप्तास्मि भर्तृदारिकया सुभद्रया सखि! कल्पलतिके! तस्मिन् भूतसम्मर्दे प्रभासतीर्थपरिसरे प्रभ्रष्टा मम गात्रिका। तां गवेषयित्वानय। अन्यच्च, येनाहं भूतहस्तान्मोचिता, सोऽपि महानुभावो लोचनानन्दकरस्तत्र सन्निहितो नवेति सम्प्रधार्यागच्छ इति। सुचिरं च मयान्वेषितम्। न सा गात्रिका न स पुरुषो दृष्टः। किं नु खलु भर्तृदारिकायै कथयिष्यामि। कुमारधनञ्जयस्य नामाङ्किकतेति गात्रिकायामस्या बहुमानः। अन्योप्यन्विष्यते पुरुष इति किमिवैतत्। अन्यच्च, मया कुतस्तस्मिन् प्रमथवृत्तान्ते परमार्थो ज्ञातव्यः। एष आर्यविनयपालित इव एवागच्छति। एनं तावत् प्रक्ष्यामि।)

मिश्रविष्कम्भकः

(A maid enters)

Maid I have been ordered by my Lady Subhadrā: 'Friend, Kalpalatikā! Somewhere near Prabhāsatīrtha I lost my bodice during the fight with the demon. Search for it and bring it. Also, carefully find out before to return whether that handsome and noble man who saved me from the hands of the demon is still around.' And I have searched a long time. I found neither that bodice nor that person. What shall I report back to my Lady? She has a special liking for that bodice since it contains the names of Dhanañjaya stitched to it. Why is another person also being searched for? And from whom shall I learn the truth of the demon episode? Ah, here comes the honourable Vinayapālita. I shall ask him.

व्यङ्ग्यव्याख्या

ततः प्रविशति चेटी। अथ सुभद्राज्ञप्ता कापि कल्पलतिकाख्या चेटी प्रभासतीर्थपरिसरं प्राप्य तत्र गात्रिकया सह महानुभावः पुरमन्विष्य द्वयमप्यदृष्ट्वा तस्मात् सविवेकमायान्ती भूयः पुरपरिसरे बहिः क्वचित्प्रदेशे सविवेकमीषदूर्ध्वदृष्टिरतिष्ठत्।

एवं पूर्वसम्बन्धः।

अथैवं चेटीभूमिकालङ्कृततनुस्स्वयं चेटीभूत्वा यथा निर्दिष्टमेवं त्रिवर्त्युज्ज्वलितस्य दीपस्य पुरो यवनिकाच्छन्नदेहो यावत् तिष्ठेत् तावद् व्यपनयेत् यवनिकाम्। अथ व्यपनीतयवनिका सा तथैव मुहूर्तं तिष्ठेत्। एवं तिष्ठन्ती सेति स्मरेदित्याज्ञप्तास्मि भर्तृदारिकया। **हज्जे** एतस्मिन् भूतसम्मर्द्दे प्रभ्रष्टा मे गात्रिका। एतस्मिन् भूतसम्मर्द्द इत्यनया प्रोक्तमि... च्छब्देन प्रसिद्धमिव विज्ञाप्याप्यज्ञातपूर्वां मां न्ययुङ्क्तेति यत् तत्तस्मादस्याश्चित्तपारवश्यादित्यूह्यम्। कीदृग्भूतोऽयं भूतसम्मर्द्दः सेयमत्र कथं तस्मात्प्रत्यानीता। किञ्च येनाहं मोचिता सोऽपि **एतस्सिं संणि हि दो णवे**ति न चान्वेष्टव्य इत्यनयोक्तं तदस्मिन् कार्ये तदन्वेषणं विधेयमिव मे प्रतिभाति। तस्मात्तस्मिन्नपि संसक्तचित्तया तया भवितव्यम्। हन्त एवं गात्रिकालिखितदशनाम्नि धनञ्जये देहविजितमन्मथे निजशक्तिसहायविजितसकलक्षेत्रबद्धमूलोऽस्याः रागः इदानीमस्मिन्नपि तथेत्यूह्यम्।

किमिति वैतद् भवेत्। अस्मिन्नपि बद्धप्रेम्णा तया भवितव्यमित्यादि सर्वं दृग्भ्यां समपात्रत्वात् सह पाणिनैकेन अतो विज्ञापयन्ती तिष्ठेत्। एवं तिष्ठन्ती सा भूयोऽपीति स्मरेत्। अयमस्या भूतस्सम्मर्द्दः कथमासीत् को नु खलु भगवद्बाहुपालिताया अस्या भूतसम्मर्द्दस्य हेतुः। स कुतो मया ज्ञातो भवेत् मया तु औदासीन्यमुदन्ते नाचरितव्यमितरास्वपि चेटीषु वर्तमानासु वेश्मनि सा प्रणीय मामेव ब्रूते स्मेदं हि। मह्यं ज्ञापयन्त्याः तस्याः विज्ञापनप्रकारः **हज्जे** इत्यादि ग्रन्थेन दर्शयति। **हं जे तं गंवे सि अ आणेदि** इत्यनयोक्तं हज्जे इति मामाहूय भूयोऽवनतमुखी भूत्वा वक्तुं किमपि वाक्यगर्भं दधानां तन्निर्गमयितुमक्षमत्वात् प्रस्फुरिताधरा वसनाञ्चलं पदाङ्गुष्ठेन भुवमालिखन्ती विश्वस्तां मां किं वाच्यं न स्यादिति मया प्रेर्यमाणा सा तथाभूयः कथञ्चिदित्युक्तवती **अं णं च** इति। अन्यच्चेत्यादि ग्रन्थेन यस्तयोक्तः सोऽपि न दृष्टो भवेत् स क्व वर्तत इति ज्ञातुं उक्तिसदृशं प्रवर्तितव्यम्। स च भूतसम्मर्द्दहेतुश्च तावुभौ कस्य मुखाद् ज्ञेयौ भवेतामिति स्मरन्ती तिष्ठन्ती पुरतोऽवलोकितवती। एवं पश्यन्तीयं सह कमप्यायान्तं दृष्ट्वेति स्मरेत्। **को नु खल्वेष** इत एवाभिवर्तते पुनः सावधानं पश्यन्ती अये सोऽयमार्यो विनयपालकः। तस्मादिमं पृष्ट्वा मदभीप्सितममुतो ज्ञातव्यं किं सर्वथा एनमवाप्य प्रमथवृत्तान्तः प्रष्टव्येति मत्वा निश्चित्य सा तमुपसर्पति।

Vyaṅgyavyākhyā

Pūrvasambandha

As instructed by Subhadrā her servant maid Kalpalatikā went in search of her bodice lost in the struggle with the demon and the handsome youth who saved her from the demon. Having failed in her mission she stands despondently with eyes raised upwards.

Prāveśika

Remove the curtain when the actress dressed in the costume of the maid stands before the three-wicked lamp. She stands still for a moment.

She recollects:

My mistress has ordered me to search her bodice lost in the fight with the demon. She seems to be much distressed. What kind of fight did she have with the demon? How was she brought back? Which demon dares taking her who is well protected by the Lord?

She also asks me to know the details of the attractive youth who saved her. It seems that she is fascinated by his heroism. How is it possible? She is already in love with Dhanañjaya whose ten names are stitched to the gātrikā she wears.

She has bestowed much confidence on me. Hence she entrusted this confidential mission with me, though there are many other maidens around her. So I will be helpful to her in this matter.

When I encouraged her to reveal her mind to me as I am her trusted maid, she looked down bashfully drawing on the floor with her toe. Her lips throbbed to tell me to search that handsome youth also.

From whom can I know the truth?

XII
Vyaṅgyavyākhyā in Practice (Naṅṅyārkūttu)

This interlude which seems to be trivial from a general point of view is significant in the study of Vyaṅgyavyākhyā since it paved the way for the emergence of an important offshoot of Kūṭiyāṭṭam, popularly known, now, as Naṅṅyārkūttu which survives as a true representative of the mode of performance envisioned by Kulaśekhara, unaffected by the changes in society[1].

Subhadrā sent Kalpalatikā to enquire the whereabouts of the handsome youth who saved her from the demon. On her way she recollects the past incidents. She thinks of her mistress Subhadrā and her brother Lord Kṛṣṇa. This provides her an opportunity to narrate the story of Śrīkṛṣṇa. She starts her thoughts from the formation of the city of Mathura, explains many exploits of Kṛṣṇa and ends up with the description of his sister Subhadrā who was darling to the eyes of all in the city. Then she relates the story of the textual incidents of the demon snatching Subhadrā away and loss of her gātrika. Thus the maid under the pretext of recapitulation unfolds the Kṛṣṇalīlā in a beautiful way.

This elaboration of the recapitulation is not seen in the present manuscript of VV[2]. It is added later, most probably under the instructions of Kulaśekhara himself.

The introductory part of Subadrādhanañjaya gives a clue for this assumption. Sutradharā who has just returned from a pilgrimage discusses the details of presentation of the play. His assistant reminds him that the troupe is incomplete since Sutradharā's consort, who has to take the lead role is not present. Sutradharā pacifies him telling that the performance can be made successful with the cooperation of a

1 The word naṅṅai means a respectable lady. Ār is added as a mark of respect. When Kūṭiyāṭṭam moved to temple premises and acting became hereditary the term naṅṅyār came to denote, exclusively, the female partners in Kūṭiyāṭṭam. The kūttu enacted by nannyar is Naṅṅyārkūttu. Girls from all sections of society now learn and practice Naṅṅyārkūttu.

2 The present writer earlier held the view that Kulaśekhara had no role in the evolution of Naṅṅyārkūttu as Vyaṅgyavyākhyā was silent on it. The statement in the prologue and its possible biographical references were brought to my notice only later. The earlier view now stands modified.

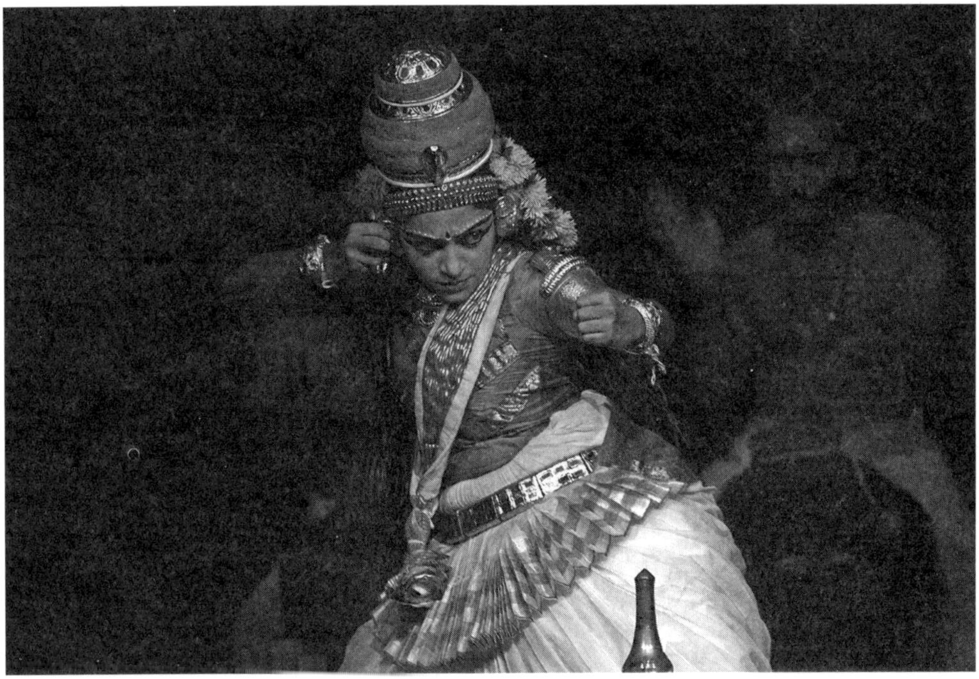

Nannyarkuttu, Kapila Venu

gifted girl belonging to the lineage of actors whose marriage with him is objected to by all relatives except one of her brothers.

Śivarāma, the commentator explains this as a clever dramatic device to introduce the play to the audience[3]. Can we read anything more in this case? The statement as

3 She is referred to as Bharatakulaprasūta. Bharata means actor. There were troupes of actors who inherited the tradition. Boys and girls born in these families were given training in various disciplines related to performance. The present girl is skilled in recitation, singing and other arts ie. all that are needed to make her an accomplished artiste. Śivarāma sees no biographical reference in the words of Sutradhara. He interprets it only as a dramatic device – see his commentary on this part - अत्रत्या काचित् कन्यकास्त्येव। तस्याःप्रयोगपाटवं न चेत् किं फलम् अत्राह – गीतसङ्गीतादिषु। आदिशब्देन तदुपयोगिन्यो नैपथ्यशिल्पादिकला गृहीताः। कलाकौशलेषु कौशलप्रयोज्यासु कलास्वित्यर्थः। अद्वितीया प्रथमा।तस्या अभिरुचिर्न चेत् कलाकौशलेन किं फलम् अत्राह – मयि निबद्धभावा मयि सानुरागा। निबद्धशब्देन भावस्याचलनीयत्वं प्रकाशितम्। तथापि दातृसापेक्षः कन्यालाभः, अत्राह – विनैकमित्यादि। एकं केवलं प्रधानं च भ्रातरं वर्जयित्वा अपरैर्बान्धवैः भ्रातृप्रभृतिभिः। अनभिमतपरिणयना अनङ्गीकृतमत्कर्तृकपरिग्रहा। अत्रानभिमतपरिणयनत्वं साध्यविरुद्धम्। अतोऽन्यैर-नभिमतपरिणयनापि प्रधानेन भ्रात्राङ्गीकृतपरिग्रहेति वक्तव्यम्। अतोऽन्यनिरोधेऽपि प्रधानेन निर्वाहः। तेन भ्रात्रा मह्यं दित्सितेति विधेयम्। तेन तयैवेत्यवधारणम्। भरतकुलप्रसूता नटोत्तमकुलोत्पन्ना। अभिजन्मसम्पन्नतया ग्राह्येत्यर्थः। प्रस्तुतमर्थं परिषन्नियोगनुष्ठानरूपं साधयामीत्यर्थः। परिग्रहोपायं स्फुटयति – स्निग्धामित्यादिना। स्निग्धता मुग्धताच भरतसोदर्येति च बलात्कारेणाप्यपहारनिमित्तम्। अत्र दृष्टान्तत्वेन सूच्यार्थं स्फुटयति – धनञ्जयो वासुदेवस्य सोदर्यां दशार्हान् जित्वा यथापहृतवान्। इति विपरिणामेन सम्बन्धः। अत्र स्निग्धामित्यादि योज्यम्। अत्र 'सूचयेद्वस्तुबीजं वा मुखं

such is not fully correct thematically. All the relatives of Subhadrā are not against the marriage of Subhadrā to Arjuna. The objection is only for Balarāma, that too due to his weakness towards his disciple, Duryodhana. Secondly, there is a strong popular belief that Kulaśekhara had married an actress, which seems quite possible considering his aesthetic sense. If it is so the statement of Sūtradhāra contains an autobiographical reference to the dramatist.

The play might have been presented well with the said girl in the lead role and naturally she might have made an excellent performance to the appreciation of all. King married her with the support or otherwise of all her relatives. Thereafter, she became an active participant in the theatrical activities of the king[4]. Naturally, to provide her an opportunity to exhibit her histrionic talents king added the Kṛṣṇa story to the recapitulation of Kalpalatikā. Recapitulation he had given in brief: it was expanded. He took the Kṛṣṇa story because just after this the chamberlain elaborates the role of Kṛṣṇa in achieving her union with Arjuna. Giving the details of his earlier life through the words of the maid will make the description by Kañcuki more relevant and also natural. Moreover, being an ardent devotee of Kṛṣṇa this satisfied the poet's own sentiments. The audience will only appreciate the narrations of Kṛṣṇa story as it was common during festive occasions[5]. Thus we have to believe that the aesthetic genius of Kulaśekhara embraced Naṅṅyārkūttu as well.

The text followed now for the presentations of Naṅṅyārkūttu is the Srīkṛṣṇacaritam[6]. It contains 217 Ślokas in different meters. It starts with the description of the city

---

पात्रमथापि वा' इत्युक्तत्वात् तीर्थयात्राप्रसङ्गादित्यनेन नायकस्य तीर्थयात्रानिर्वहणं सूचितं, सुभद्राधनञ्जयमिति प्रतिपाद्यप्रतिपादकयोरभेदोपचारेण मत्वर्थीयोपश्लेषेण वा नाटकनामकथनेन नायकस्वरूपमपि प्रकाशितं, दूरस्थितेत्यादिना इन्द्रप्रस्थाद् दूरस्थितिः, आत्यन्यनुरक्तायाः सुभद्राया लिप्सा, वासुदेवानुमतिः बलभद्रादीनां विमतिरित्यादिः दृष्टान्तरूपेण परिग्रहप्रकारश्चोक्तः। एवं सूच्यसूचनानन्तरं तयोर्निष्क्रान्तिः।।

4 There are epigraphic evidences to show that stories taken from Bhāgavata / Harivamśa were enacted on festive occasions. Donations were made in AD 1027 for the performance by a Naṅṅyār of Kāḷiyaṅkam in Thiruvalla Temple.

5 *Śrīkṛṣṇacaritam Naṅṅyārkūttu* – P.K. Narayanan Nambiar, Kerala Kalamandalam, Cheruthuruthy, 1984.

6 Dr. Heike Mosser has made a brilliant study of Naṅṅyārkūttu. (Ein Teilaspekt des Sanskrit Theatre Komplexes Kutiyattam 2008 Harrassowitz Verlag. Wiesbaden.) She has painstakingly found out the different sources of Śrīkṛṣṇacaritam as given below.

Vers 48	Visnupurana 5.5.7 bzw. Brahmapurana 184.7
Vers 49	Visnupurana 5.5.9 bzw. Brahmapurana 184.9
Vers 50	Visnupurana 5.5.10 bzw. Brahmapurana 184.10
Vers 89	Rama Panivada: Kamsavaho 4.20 [Prakrit]
Vers 101	Bhasa: Balacaritam Akt 4, Vers 12
Vers 112	Rama Panivada: Kamsavaho 4.32 [Prakrit]

of Madhura. All the important incidents in the early life of Śrīkṛṣṇa are described. A complete performance of the text requires many days. Normally a particular incident like Pūtanāmokṣa, Kamsavadha etc which extends to one hour is selected for presentation.

Manuals are available for the performance of Naṅṅyārkūttu. Specimens are given below to show the nature of the manuals.

12. i. Kramadīpikā (Stage Manual)

Pur̲appāṭinnu cēṭikku aṇivu patantiyeppole kur̲ikumpaḷakkuru iṅṅane. Uttarīyam vēṇṭa. Mar̲ayil mutal naṭa – suhaddāye, ennu colli. Cer̲iyokkam iti ādikriyā. Śrīkṛṣṇacaritam nerccakku eṅkil nityakriyā okkave āṭi. Nirvahaṇa pāṭikka – astīty ādi karuṇāvihe o – ityantam – pinne pīṭhattinmēl irunnu bhūtahastattil ninnu rakṣicca puruṣanṭēyuṃ arjunanṭēyuṃ kēśādipādaṃ āṭi mōhicccuṇarnnāl – hañje, ityādi sampahāriya āccha. Ennu vare ārttanil irunnātiyāl – pinne pīṭham nīkki ninnu cetīpañcamattil colli ādiye colli āṭuka. Kinnu khu bhattidārie kahaissam – ennucolli colliyuntinatanı kūttu mutikkuka – tamiḷum colluka – muṭiyakkittayum koṭṭikkuka tēvare kaṇṭu dakṣiṇayuṃ vāṅṅuka. paṇam 32 (muppattiyārinṭe) pāṭunna naṅṅyārkku

---

Vers 113 Rama Panivada: Kamsavaho 4.33 [prakrit]
Vers 123 Jayadeva: Gitagovinda 7.1
Vers 124 Kalidasa : Sakuntalam Akt3, Vers 3
Vers 125 Jayadeva: Gitagovinda 8.1
Vers 127 Amaruka: Gitagovinda 28
Vers 128 Jayadeva: Gitagovinda 9.1
Vers 130 Jayadeva: Gitagovinda 9.10
Vers 131 Jayadeva: Gitagovinda 10.1
Vers 132 Jalhana: Suktimuktavali 57.11
Vers 183 Bhagavadapurana 10.43.17 bzw.
Gargasamhita 7.36-37
Vers 205 Dhananjaya-Nirvahanam Vers 9 (Akt 1 SD)
Vers 206 Subhadra-Nirvahanam Vers 5 (Akt 5 SD)
Vers 207 Subhadra -Nirvahanam Vers 6 (Akt 5 SD)
Vers 208 Subhadra -Nirvahanam Vers 7 (Akt 5 SD)
Vers 209 Subhadra -Nirvahanam Vers 8 (Akt 5 SD)
Vers 210 Subhadra -Nirvahanam Vers 9 (Akt 5 SD)
Vers 211 Subhadra -Nirvahanam Vers 10 (Akt 5 SD)
Vers 214 SD Akt 1, Vers 11
Vers 215 Subhadra -Nirvahanam Vers 11 (Akt 5 SD) [prakrit]

The kramadīpikā and āṭṭaprakāram given in here are quoted from the above text.

Also refer to her research paper on 'The Changing Role of Female Performers in the Nannyar-Kuttu Tradition of Kerala' in *Between Fame and Shame in Drama und Theater in Sudasien*, series 9.

raṇṭu paṇam. nampyārkum raṇṭu paṇam. Uṭuppānum maṭṭum kōṭi. araṅṅu aṇiyukayum veṇam. Iṅṅine nerca. Allenkil tiriññu grantham colliyāl matiyākum.

This shows that naṅṅyārkūttu by this time had two methods of presentation. One is as a religious sacrament. The believers sponsored this as an offering to the deity for specific prayers like begetting children etc. The other mode of presentation was aesthetic performance meant for connoisseurs. We also understand that the practice of using the local language (Tamil) was prevalent in naṅṅyārkūttu also. The major share of the remuneration (32 paṇam) went to the actress. The share of the reciting naṅṅyār and the coordinating percussionist Nambyār was a meagre two paṇam each.

12. ii. Āṭṭaprakāram (Acting Manual)

Raṅgasajjīkaraṇānantaraṃ nambyār mizāvoccappeṭuttiyāl subhadrayuṭe ceṭiyāya Kalpalatika pravēśiccu mizāviṅkal abhivādyam ceytu tiriññu viḷakkinnu nere ninnu sabhānirīkṣaṇavuṃ kamalaparivarttanattil toḷukaḷum kazinnnāl pīṭhaṃ nīkkiyiṭṭirunnu abhivādyam, sabhā-nirīkṣaṇam, kamalaparivarttanattil toṭuka iva kaziññāl anukramam āṭunnu.

At the time of Kulaśekhara incidents depicted in the purāṇas related to the early life of Śrīkṛṣṇa were enacted with the help of verses selected from different sources. Lack of a proper performance text did not create any problem for the artistes because verses are not enacted, as such, on stage. Acting alone is done on stage, verses are recited by the Naṅṅyār sitting nearby at the end of the acting as is the practice in recapitulations.

Śrīkṛṣṇacaritam available to us now is a compilation of such verse from different sources[7]. The text attained its present form in the 16th – 17th centuries[8].

Among the classical forms of Kerala, it was Kūṭiyāṭṭam which extended equal treatment both to men and women[9]. There are several stories popular among the people that extol the histrionic talents of female participants in performances. Kulaśekhara encouraged women on stage. But later on, due to several reasons the role of women were relegated to back-stage.

---

7 Dr. M. Vijaykumar after a careful analysis of the contents of the verses of Śrīkṛṣṇacaritam has concluded that the source of the author was neither Harivamśa nor Bhāgavatapurāṇa, but the Nārāyaṇīya of Melputtūr (17.c).

- Annual Journal of Indological Studies -2011, Calicut University.

8 In other classical forms like Kṛṣṇanaṭṭam and Kathakaḷi women's roles are taken by men. Kūṭiyāṭṭam is the only exception. Here too women were sidelined when the technique of Pakarnnāṭṭam was evolved. Women got their rightful place only in modern times.

9 Natāṅkuśa – A Critique on Dramaturgy, VI -2

The anonymous author of Naṭāṅkuśa (15.c) has criticized this tendency[10]. When theatre moved to the temple premises it became part of ritual. The socio-economic changes in the society in the latter half of the last century became favorable for the revitalization of women's role. The empowerment of women in various fields of society brought actresses to the centre-stage in Kūṭiyāṭṭam. Lost roles in the play were retrieved. Naṅṅyārkūttu resurrected from oblivion with vigor and beauty. Now it is the most sought-after piece among the classical forms in Kerala and we have many women performers who excel in international standards.

The most important reason for the attraction of Naṅṅyārkūttu is the charm inherent in it. Its frame is fair and presentation strictly disciplined. Concentration on rasa does not receive top priority in the training of an actor in Kūṭiyāṭṭam. His attention is diverted to many other angles. Naṅṅyārkūttu has no such distractions. The enjoyment of aesthetic experience is at its zenith in Naṅṅyārkūttu.

12. iii. Navarasa

Take for example the myriad forms of acting in Kamsavadha[11].

Kamsa finds out that Kṛṣṇa, destined to be his destroyer, lives in Ambāṭi. He deputes the Yādava leader Akrūra to bring Balarāma and Kṛṣṇa to Mathura. Reaching the city of Mathura, Kṛṣṇa kills Kuvalayāpida, the elephant and also the wrestlers in Kamsa's court. These deaths evoke a mixed reaction in the spectators. Subsequently Kṛṣṇa rushes up to Kamsa, fights with him and kills him.

> [Looking at Kṛṣṇa, different persons react in different ways according to his or her character and state, thus giving rise to different emotions and sentiments. The performer here delineates in detail the Navarasa.]

Raudrarasa

At that time, one of the wrestlers of Kamsa, seeing Kṛṣṇa, said to the others:

> Look, this is the man who is the great enemy of our master Kamsa; he is the villain living at Ampāṭi. Haven't we heard of him?

---

10 *mallānāṃ aśanirnṛṇāṃ naravaraḥ strīṇāṃ smaro mūrtimān*
gopānāṃ svajano satāṃ kṣitibhṛtāṃ śāstā svapitrośśiśuḥ/
mṛtyur bhojapateḥ virāṭaviduṣaṃ tattvaṃ paraṃ yogināṃ
vṛṣṇīnāṃ paradevateti vidito raṅgaṃ gataḥ sāgrajaḥ//
This sloka is included as 83rd in Śrīkṛṣṇacaritam.
It is seen in Bhāgavatapurāṇa X.43.17; and also in Gargasamhitā 7.36-37.

11 Navarasas in Mahābhārata in the beginning of Vyaṅgyavyākhyā for the second Act.

Then (peering at the body of Kṛṣṇa) he adds:

His body is as hard as diamond. But we can, with our mighty fists, beat him into pulp and kill him. He shows his anger and determination by rubbing his hands.

Adbhuta

Next some others seeing Kṛṣṇa coming, stare at him and say :

How amazing! We can never see another man having such confidence and faith in himself. Is he a prince? (Gazing at him) No, he is only a cowherd! Yet, how wonderful!

Śṛṅgāra

Some women gazing at Kṛṣṇa say.

Who can be this man who has such a beautiful body? Is he one of the Aśvinīdevas?' (Thinking). 'No, he cannot be because the two Aśvinadevas always go together; they are never separated. Then who is he? He must be Kāmadeva himself who was supposed to have been burnt to ashes by Śiva with his third eye. No, that story is wrong; Kāmadeva is not dead; here he stands before us as Kṛṣṇa.

Hāsya

Next, the Gopas, (looking at Kṛṣṇa is an amusing way) say:

Look here, look here, see what is happening. The people of Mathura are gazing at Kṛṣṇa with wide open eyes. This Kṛṣṇa is only a man like us. Do you feel anything else? I don't see any cause for wonder .

Vīra

Then the wicked kings: So we have seen Kṛṣṇa, this is the boy living at Ambāṭi, of whom we have heard as the boy who is born to kill Kamsa.

(Peering at Kṛṣṇa) His mind is full of pride and arrogance. What is his arrogance? He thinks that all the kings in the world must obey him. If they do not do so he has the strength to kill them. This arrogance seems to have filled his body. Therefore let us get ready to fight with him. (On seconds thoughts) : Oh, shameful. It is not proper for us to go to fight with this insignificant boy. Why? Because we are great kings and if we become angry and go to fight, even Devendra will not stand against us. So how can we go to war with this insignificant boy? (Thinking) Hey, servants, go at once, make Kṛṣṇa a captive and bring him here. We shall play tricks with him as we do with a monkey.

Karuṇa

At that time Vasudeva and Devakī are shown as waiting anxiously for the arrival of Kṛṣṇa. Enacting the part of Devakī, 'I see Kṛṣṇa coming'.
Owing to excessive love for her son milk flows out of her breasts.

(Thinking). Alas ! after giving delivery to him, this is the first time that I am seeing him. So I am very happy. But my sorrows also increase. Why? He is young boy. He is not at all competent to face Kamsa's boxers in a fight. So I pray to God that no danger should come to him.

Bhayānaka

As Kamsa: sees somebody coming through a window on the seventh floor of the palace.

What was the news? Kṛṣṇa came and has killed my elephant, Kuvalayāpiḍa ? Is that the news? (Thinking, slightly frightened) Alas! My boxers cannot kill Kṛṣṇa? Is it possible? No it cannot be true. Why? If glow-worms can shine in the full glare of sunlight, then Kṛṣṇa's might will shine before that of my boxers

(at this moment he sees Kṛṣṇa coming) This man is not a Gopāla; he is the Antaka (Yama) himself who takes always the life of all. Surely he is coming to take away my life.

Bībhatsa

Some people do not know the strength of Kṛṣṇa because they notice a contradiction – the contradiction between his soft body and his real strength.

There is no pleasure in seeing the fight between Kṛṣṇa with a soft and light body and the *mallas* with hardened bodies and iron muscles. It is unfair. Who was it who designed a fight between these two unequals? Fie, we do not want to see such a fight. Let us go from here.

Śānta

Next yogis react thus : Is Kṛṣṇa whom we, the yogis, consider the cidānandasvarūpa Bhagavān who is beyond the reach of man's sense and minds? On account of our past

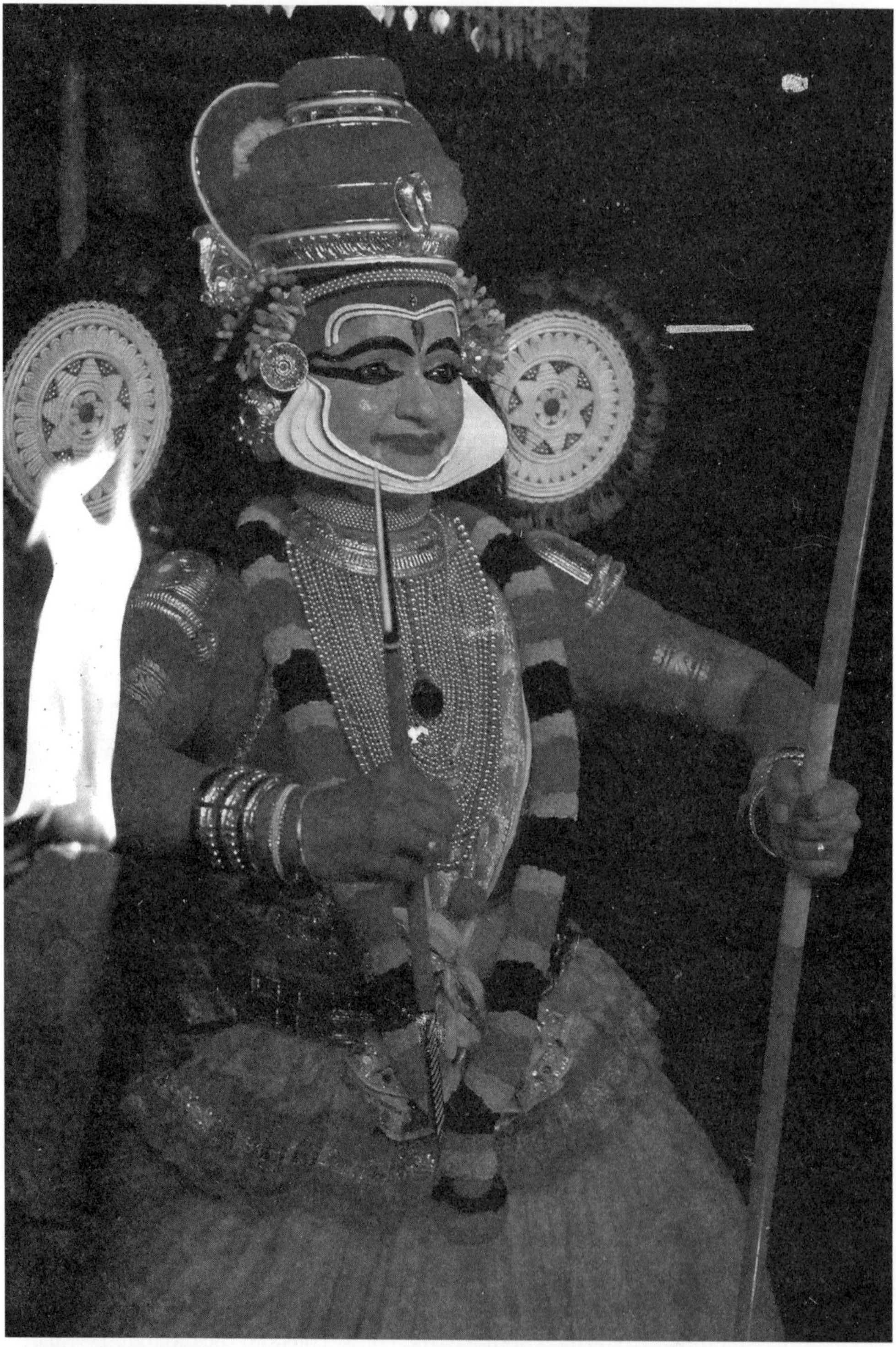

Usha Nangyar as Kathyayani in the fifth Act of Subhadrādhanañjaya

virtuous actions we have been granted a vision of this supreme God. So let us take advantage of this opportunity to get the ultimate fulfillment of our lives.

> Deciding so, they sit, withdrawing their minds from all external objects, and go into meditation.
> Next Vṛṣṇis react thus: This Kṛṣṇa is Śrīnārāyaṇa himself, our family-deity. There is no doubt about it. (They stand in a pose of reverence).

All classes of people in the assembly including the mallas, respond in their own way to the arrival of Kṛṣṇa. We can compare this with Kulaśekhara's description of the nine rasas in Mahābhārata12. There is no doubt that this scene was designed by Kulaśekhara himself or by a genius of his caliber.

Naṅṅyārkūttu preserved the pristine purity of elaboration in the Vyaṅgyavyākhyā tradition and unlike her counterpart on stage she does not deviate from her sweet prakṛta. It is only in the lips of Naṅṅyār that various prakṛts still live.

12. iv. Devīmāhātmyam

A recent addition to this genre, related to SD is Devīmāhātmyam, enjoined to the entry of Kātyāyanī in the fifth Act, which was presented by Usha Nangyar.

Devīmāhātmyam is added here as the recapitulation of Kātyāyanī. The first day is devoted to the entry of Kātyāyanī and the customary nityakriyā.The killing of Madhu and Kaiṭabha, Mahiṣāsuravadham, Dhūmrākṣavadham, Raktabījavadham and death of Sumbha and Nisumbha are described in the next eight days. At the end, these are connected to the story telling that even I who have done such heroic acts, am filled with fear to approach Dhanañjaya in this condition.

The verses are mostly selected from different purāṇas. Dr. K.V. Vasudevan who is closely associated with this production is of opinion that those pieces that cannot trace a link to the dramatic context do not deserve to be classified under the classical Naṅṅyārkūttu. According to him Devīmāhātmyam is connected to Kātyāyanīpraveśa of the drama like the Śrīkṛṣṇacaritam to Kalpalatikāpraveśa.

There are many innovative productions from other sources also which have attracted serious attention of the connoisseurs.

XIII

Entry of Chamberlain (Interlude Continued)

(ततः प्रविशति काञ्चुकीयः)

काञ्चुकीयः आदिष्टोऽस्मि देवेन देवकीनन्दनेन, यथा – विनयपालित ! विविक्ते किल रैवतकप्रस्थवर्तिनि काञ्चनोद्याने कश्चिदागन्तुको भवान् परमहंसः सन्निधत्ते। सोऽयमार्येण साकं सङ्कर्षणेन साक्षात्करणीयो मया। तत् सज्जीक्रियतां रथ इति। मया च तदार्यदारुकाय निवेदितम्। जरावक्तव्यचरणतया पुनरियमतिविडम्बना संवृत्ता। कुतः,

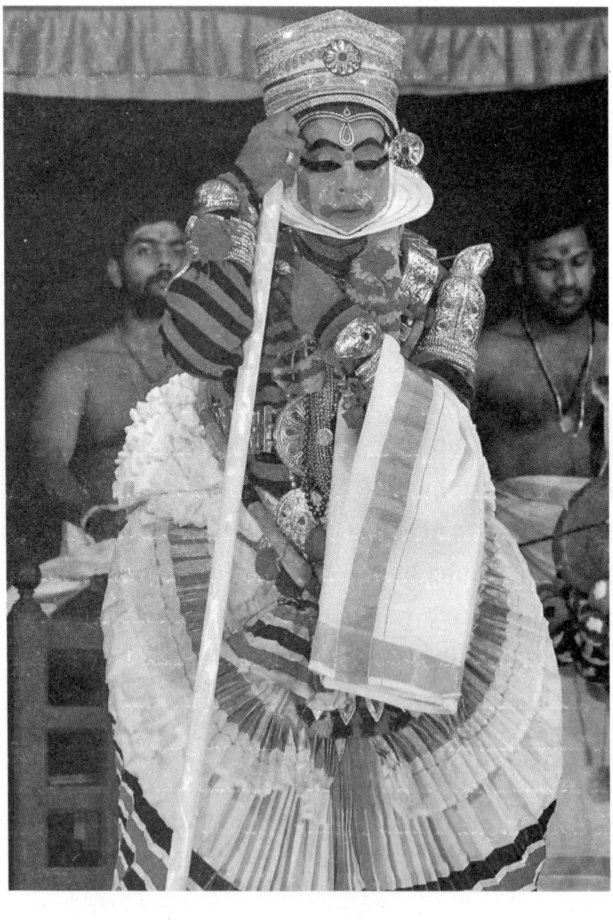

पातं जलत्वेन समाचरन्ती सदेति हासास्पदतामवाप्ता।
मूर्तिः परामेत्य पुराणतां मे कथं न वाच्या परतन्त्रवृत्तिः।। १।।

चेटी (उपसृत्य) अय्य! कुदो मं अणवेक्खिअ गच्छसि। (आर्य, कुतो मामनवेक्ष्य गच्छसि)

काञ्चुकीयः (सावधानं निर्वर्ण्य) कच्चित् कल्पलतिका भवती।

चेटी अय्य! तह। अय्यादो किञ्चि जाणिदुं इच्छामि। को तस्सिं पमहवुत्तन्ते परमत्थो। (आर्य! तथा। अर्यात् किञ्चिद् ज्ञातुमिच्छामि। कस्तस्मिन् प्रमथवृत्तान्ते परमार्थः।)

काञ्चुकीयः वत्से! अतीतायां खलु रजन्यामाननारविन्दवर्तिनीमाकस्मिकीं स्मितचन्द्रिकामवलोक्य निमित्तपरीप्सया देव्या सत्यभामया पर्याप्तपर्यनुयुक्तस्य भगवतः श्रीमुखाम्भोजादेतावदवगत मस्माभिः, यथा – बलभद्रानुमतिलेशोपलम्भाद् भर्तृदारिकायां सुभद्रायां सञ्जाताभिलाषस्य सुयोधनस्यादेशात् परिवर्तितरूपेण रक्षसालम्बुसेन सा विहायसा नीता भगवत्सङ्कल्पवेदिना गरुत्मता पुनः कुमारीपुरं प्रत्यानीतेति।

चेटी जीवाविदह्मि पदत्तिणाहेण। गच्छदु अय्यो। जाव अहं पि भट्टिदारिआए सआसं गमिस्सं। (जीवितास्मि पवित्रनाथेन। गच्छत्वार्यः। यावदहमपि भर्तृदारिकायाः सकाशं गमिष्यामि।)

(निष्क्रान्तौ)

(An old chamberlain enters)

Chamber *I have been ordered by my Lord, the son of Devakī (Vāsudeva), thus: 'Oh Vinayapālita! In that goldengarden on the slops of Mount Raivataka a great sage who is a visitor, the noble Saṅkarṣaṇa, is camping, and I want to see him. Hence prepare the chariot' I have conveyed this to the respected Dāruka. Because my old age hampers my feet, I have been delayed. For,*

Stricken by old age
and frequently falling,
my body is ridiculous.
Dependence on others is always regretable. (1)

Maid *(Approaching) Sir, where are you going without noticing me?*

Chamber *(Looking carefully) Are not you Kalpalatikā?*

Maid *Yes sir, it is so. I would like to know something from you. What is the truth regarding the demon episode?*

Chamber *Child! During the previous night the Lord just smiled casually and Satyabhāmā, his consort, wanted to know the reason for it. Pressed by her, he told her the fact which was thus known to us. 'Having obtained the tacit approval of Balabhadra, Suyodhana, who had nourished a desire for Subhadrā, told the demon Alambusa to change his form and abduct her and fly off, but Garuḍa knowing the intention of the Lord, interfered and rescued her and restored her to her quarters.'*

Maid *Oh! I have been saved by the Lord of the birds. Sir, you may go ahead. I shall also report to the side of my Lady.*

(*Both exit*)

End of the Interlude

व्यङ्ग्यव्याख्या

ततः प्रविशति काञ्चुकीयः।

अथ कश्चित् परिणतवया भगवत्पक्षपाती तदिङ्गितज्ञस्तद्वक्रोक्तिज्ञो काञ्चुकीयः कस्मिंश्चित् प्रभाते किमपि कार्यान्तरमुद्दिश्य भगवता नियुक्तः। अयं पुरतो निर्गत्य गच्छन् भगवतो वचनप्रकारगौरवं अतीतायां रात्रौ सत्यभामया नर्मप्रोच्यमानस्य श्रीमुखेन्दोर्न्निस्सृतामाकस्मिकीं स्मितचन्द्रिकां (दृष्टवान्) तद्धेतुं चाजानन्नपि स्मृत्वा ज्ञेयमिति गत्वा सचिन्तं निरूपणाय क्वचित्प्रदेशं (कश्चित्पथि) प्रत्यतिष्ठत्। एवं काञ्चुकीय-भूमिकालङ्कृततनुर्भरतवरोऽयं वयःपरिणतत्वात्पदमपि गन्तुमक्षमोऽहमिति विभावयन् सचिन्तं यवनिकाच्छन्न-तनुर्यावत् तिष्ठेत् तावत् यवनिका व्यपनीयताम्।

यथानिर्दिष्टमेवमेवं सचिन्तं तिष्ठन्नयमिति विमृशेत्। विमर्शनप्रकारं ग्रन्थे दर्शयति। **आदिष्टोऽस्मि देवेन देवकीनन्दनेने**ति। सचिन्तं तिष्ठन् वचनप्रकारगौरवं श्रूयता भगवता यथाहमाज्ञप्तः तद्वचनप्रकारगौरवेण प्रोक्तमर्थं परिणतेन वयसा परवशचित्तत्वात् स्मर्तुमक्षमोऽपीदं नास्मादपसर्पामि। तत् स्मर्तुमाधारद्वयी भगवता मे दर्शिता परमहंसशब्दो हासश्च। तौ कथमिति चेत् पश्य –

सतीनां रक्षणे यत्नो द्वारि तिष्ठन् दिवानिशम्।
कष्टवृत्तिर्विनिद्राऽस्मि जातं कञ्चुकिधर्मतः।।
निशायामप्यतीतायां तदाश्रृणवमेतयोः।
दशां काश्चिदपश्यं च भगवत्सत्यभामयोः।।
न्यङ्कुचर्मासृतामृद्वां शय्यामधिशयानयोः।
बद्धप्रेम्णोस्तदन्योन्यनर्मालापस्तयोरभूत्।।
दीपरत्नप्रभाज्वालविद्योतितमुखेन्दुना।
तया तेनोच्यमानेन प्रापिताप्यन्यचित्तता।।
चिन्ता कास्येति तन्वङ्ग्या वीक्ष्यमाणे मुखेन्दुतः।
सहसाकस्मिकी तस्मान्निस्सृता स्मितचन्द्रिका।।
सेयमाकस्मिकी जाता दहत्युच्चैर्मनो मम।
अपि श्रितागसी नाथ त्वद्बद्धहृदया सती।।
श्रोतुमिच्छामि तन्मूलं वक्तव्यं यदि ते मयि।
इत्युच्यमाने भगवान् बहुकृत्वास्तया तदा।।

Vyaṅgyavyākhyā

Then enters the Chamberlain

One morning Lord Kṛṣṇa assigned an important errand to the old Chamberlain who was always inclined to him and knew his heart and suggestive modes. Coming out he recalled the instruction and thought of its seriousness. He also recollected his Lord's irresistible smile last night while chatting with Satyabhāmā in their chamber. He stood at a lonely place on his way pondering over the reasons.

Thus the actor in the attire of Chamberlain stands behind the curtain pretending to be unable to move a step further due to old age. The curtain is removed then.

Standing as directed he internalises the thoughts and enacts like this:

I have been ordered by my Lord, the son of Devakī (Vāsudeva), thus: ' Oh! Vinayapālita! A great sage, Paramahamsa is camping in the golden garden on the slopes of mount Raivataka. I want to see him with the noble Saṅkarṣaṇa. Hence prepare the chariot!'

Memory fails me due to the advanced age. Hence I am unable to recollect all that has been said. Yet, I am aware of the significance of the situation. Lord has given two clues to remind me the seriousness of the matter – his smile and the use of the word Paramahamsa.

The duty of a Chamberlain, holding for a hard living, has rendered me sleepless being stationed day and night in front of the harem to ensure the safety of women inside.

In the previous night, while on duty, I heard and observed something going on between the Lord and his beloved in their chamber.

Deep in love, sharing the bed spread by beautiful skin of antelope they were engaged in delightful talks.

While the Lord was talking, his moon-face shining in the radiance of jewels, he slowly slipped into some other thoughts.

Satyabhāmā looked on, then a bright moonlike smile flashed on his face.

> Oh! Lord!
>
> This unexpected change burns my heart. Have I, deeply devoted to you, gone wrong somewhere?
>
> I want to know the cause of your smile. Tell me if it can be revealed.
>
> Repeatedly asked, the Lord still in a pensive mood, did not satisfy her. Instead he pretended sleeping and prompted her too to sleep.

बलान्निद्रावशं प्राप्ता तथैव प्रेरिता हि सा।
रहसि प्रियया सार्धमासीनस्य स्मितोद्गतिः।।
यदि स्याच्चेदिदं भद्रे स्त्रीणां सङ्कोपकारणम्।
इति जाने प्रियतमे शीतांशुसदृशानने।।
उपज्ञा निर्गता स्यान्मे निर्यान्ती ज्ञायते स्म सा।
भूत्वेत्यस्यां लघुमनाश्शपथीकृत्य वाक्पटुः।।
आलिङ्गाय तदीयाय शनैरुद्युक्तवान् प्रभुः।
तत्र सा रोषताम्राक्षी प्रणयाहतमानसा।।
तदिच्छन्त्यप्यनिच्छन्ती वाक्यमेवं तमब्रवीत्।
वक्रचेतः कथं भर्तः त्वद्बद्धहृदयां सतीम्।।
मां चानृतं वदेर्यत्वं तन्मे दहति मानसम्।
अमुनानुनयेनालं समर्थोऽन्यत्र हि स्वयम्।।
पुंसां वटूनामीदृश्यामवस्थायामयं नयः।
स्निग्धेन विदधत् ताः रतिं लघुधियः स्त्रियः।।
चापलं स्यात्समोहायास्तेन हासो न सम्भवेत्।
इति ब्रुवन्ती तं दृष्ट्वा निरुत्तरगिरं प्रियम्।।
अतिप्रवृद्धकोपा सा पुनस्तीव्रं वचोऽब्रवीत्।
वैराग्यनिर्दयैतावत् तव जातं मयीदृशम्।।
न जाने हन्त कस्याश्चित् प्रेम स्यात् पुंसि नेदृशम्।
शरणं त्वमितःपूर्वं सर्वावस्थासु मे शठ।।
शरणं स्यादितः पश्चादुद्बन्धनविषाग्नयः।
इति ब्रुवति सा वक्तुं नाशकद्गद्गदान्विता।।
नखेनाश्रुकणान्मन्दं क्षिपत्यक्ष्णोस्ततोदगात्।
ध्यानमूकं स्वनिश्वासैर्मार्जयन् दशनच्छदम्।।
उद्वमद्वह्निभिस्तस्याः प्रेर्यमाण इवोदगात्।
शय्यायां स्वयमासीनः प्रियां नीत्वाङ्कमात्मनः।।
परिष्वज्यावदश्चैनां नखेनाश्रु क्षिपन् दृशोः।
मा प्रेयसि कृथाश्शोकं मयि जीवति मानिनि।।
कर्माणि सन्ति धीराणां न वाच्यानीति नावदम्।
बुधा धीरतमेति त्वां वदन्ति मुनयोऽपि यत्।।
ततस्त्वां नावदं हेतुं स्मितस्य लघुमद्य ते।
किं चार्ये भवितव्यं ते निन्दारुग्भ्यां कदाचन।।
तेनाहं त्वयि सम्भूतं भवेदशिवदं प्रिये।
इति ब्रुवति सा पत्नी व्यस्पष्टमवदत्प्रियम्।।

He replied at last:

> Oh! My beloved, lovely-moon faced, if the man in the company of his love laughs without reason, I know, it is sufficient reason for the woman to get angry.
>
> Something that I know, if revealed, will cease to exist.

Telling this, in a light vein, he moved to embrace her.
Being carried away by love she was longing to be embraced. Yet, pretending to be otherwise she told him with her eyes red in anger.

> Oh! Crooked man, you tell a lie to me who is devoted to you. This burns my heart.
>
> Fie with your efforts to console me. Fickle-men always behave like this.
>
> Righteous women, light hearted as they are, respond to love. Those infatuated become victims of unsteadiness. This is not a matter for laughter.

The Lord did not utter a word in reply. This made her more angry. She chided him with harsh words:

> Oh! You show the cruelty of your mind by not responding to my love.
>
> You have cheated me. No woman ever have had loved a man so profoundly.
>
> Oh! Deceptive lover! Till now you were my shelter. Now, I have to resort either to hanging, jumping on fire or consuming poison.

She could not continue as her words were choked in her throat.
The Lord moving close removed the teardrops from her eyes by the tip of his nails and gently wiped up her lips with his warm breath. Then he sat on the bed and put her on his lap. Embracing her, he said these words as though prompted by the emission of fire from her heart.

> Oh! Beloved, you are easily provoked. Don't be distressed when I am alive. There are things that need not be revealed always. The wise and brave bear it. Hence I did not tell you the reason for the silly smile. This need not cause ire in you. Nor it be a reason for distrust on me.

In a vague and subdued tone, she replied:

> Those who have mutual love should share the secrets; let it be good or bad.

The Lord gently touched her beautiful hand and said with a smile.

रहस्यं सदसद् वाच्यं स्निग्धे जने हि यत्।
इत्युक्तः प्रियया देवः स्मरन्नवददित्यमुम्।।
अन्यचित्त इव श्लक्ष्णं तद्बाहुं परिमृश्य च।
शुचं मा दयिते यायाः शोचनीयासि न क्वचित्।।
मयि त्वद्बद्धहृदये जीवतीन्दुसमानने।
आर्यं कदाचिदेकान्ते किल प्राप्तस्सुयोधनः।।
ययाचे भगिनीं कान्ते सुभद्रां बलिनं वरम्।
आर्यः किलावदच्चैनं शिष्यस्नेहतया जनम्।।
अत्रत्या जानतो राजन् अन्तरायोऽस्य जायते।
गत्वा त्वया विमृश्यास्मादुपायान्तरतः प्रभो।।
कस्माच्चिद् भगिनी नेया मदीया मदनुज्ञया।
इत्युक्तस्स ययौ वेगादसुरं प्रापयत्पुरम्।।
अलम्बुसं फल्गुनारिं सम्मान्येत्यवदत्किल।
त्वयाधुनाऽसुरश्रेष्ठ गन्तव्या द्वारकापुरी।।
बलस्वसा सुभद्रा सा द्राक्समानीयतामिह।
इत्युक्तोलम्बुसोऽप्येनमवदत् प्रीणिताशयम्।।
राजन्ननामयां कान्तां हरिष्ये नात्र संशयः।
वसुदेवसुतां दीनां वृष्णीनां पश्यतामपि।।
प्रोद्धृत्य पुरतः कन्यां प्रापयामि नभस्तलम्।
अनपायन्नरेशैतां दास्ये हृत्वा पुरात्तव।।
भवतात्र मनःखेदो न कार्यमार्य जीवति।
तां न दास्यति चेत् तुभ्यं असुरेशो ह्यलम्बुसः।।
जीवेत् क्षणं न भूयोऽसाविति विज्ञायतां विभो।
इत्युक्तोऽहिध्वजः प्रीतो वदति स्मेति तं पुनः।।
पथि स्यात्ते शिवं रौद्रात् सङ्गमोऽपि प्रियो हि तत्।
इत्युक्तेनासुरेणाशु प्राप्यात्रोद्धृत्य तां बलात्।।
कुर्वता भयदं रूपमनीयत विहायसा।
तेनास्यां नीयमानायां गरुत्मान् प्रेरितो मया।।
तदग्रे मा प्रयाहीति रुरोध प्रमथं बलात्।
तेन रुद्धोऽथ तां वेगादपहाय भियान्वितः।।
अपयात् तदपायात्स क्षुद्रकारी विहायसा।
तेन तद्विजयेनैषा प्रापिता शर्म पत्रिणा।।
अनीयत पुरं त्राता सुभद्रा सा विना भिया।
तस्य तत्र प्रवृत्तिं च प्रतिज्ञां च भियं तथा।।

> Don't be annoyed, dear moon-faced! I am deeply devoted to you...
>
> Once king Suyodhana met my respected brother Balarāma and prayed to give our sister Subhadrā to him in marriage.

Balarāma, affectionate as he was to his disciple, told him:

> Oh! King, people here will raise objection if they know this. You find out alternate means to take away my sister from here. You have my permission.

Immediately Duryodhana reached the city of demons and met Alambusa, the foe of Dhanañjaya. He told the demon.

> Oh! Lord of demons! You should hurry up to Dvārakā.
>
> Subhadrā, sister of Balabhadra is there. Bring her immediately.

Alambusa was pleased very much.

> Oh! King! I shall carry the sister of Vāsudeva without any hindrance from Dvārakā ignoring the might of the Vṛṣṇis. I will lift her up, take through air and present her to you. You need not worry over this when I am here. This demon-god if fails to deliver her to you as promised, shall not live for a single moment.

Pleased, the serpent-flagged Duryodhana said:

> Let the journey be auspicious. Union with women after using force is also dear to me.

Soon the demon reached Dvārakā. He transformed himself to his frightful form and forcibly carried away Subhadrā through the air.

At that time I sent Garuḍa. He stood in front of the demon obstructing his onward march. Frightened, the demon threw her away and flew in fear.

Thus Subhadrā was saved and brought back to Dvārakā without fear by the bird with wild wings.

Dear Satyabhāmā, this is the story. The deeds of Alambusa, his promise and fear all came to my mind while lying here.

This was the cause for the smile.

Satyabhāmā laughed, her anger melted away. Pleasing her the Lord spent the night.

The Lord told her that the reason for his smile was the act of Alambusa and Suyodhana. But I feel that he suggested something more to me who was present

शयानोऽहं स्मरन्नद्य प्रिये हसितवान् बलात्।
इति प्रसादयन् देवीं सत्यभामां शुचिस्मिताम्।
गतक्रोधां विधायान्तमनयत् तां निशीथिनीम्।।

तस्मात् स्मितोद्गतेर्हेतुः अलम्बुससुयोधनयोः प्रेमदर्शनमिति तस्यै विज्ञापयता भगवता तत्रस्थाय मह्यं कस्यचिद्रहस्यमवस्थान्तरं विज्ञापितमिति मन्ये। कुत? सुयोधनोदन्तं तस्यैव विज्ञापयता भगवता दृशोरन्यत् किमपि स्मर्यत इति तदीयाकारेण मह्यं नावदत्। तत्र किमनेनोक्तमिति स्मर्तुमाधार-द्वय्यामेकोऽयमाधारः तद्विज्ञापनच्छलेनान्यदवस्थान्तरं मह्यं न विज्ञापितमिति स्मरन् काञ्चुकीयः मुहूर्तद्वयं तत्र तिष्ठेत्। एवं तिष्ठन्नयं तद्वचनप्रकारगौरवं विमृशेत्। विमर्शनप्रकारगौरवं दर्शयति। एवं तेनोक्तम् –

तेन तद्विजयेनैषा प्रापिता शर्म पत्रिणा।
त्राता सानीयत पुरं सुभद्रात्र विना भिया।।

' तत्र विनाशब्देन पक्षी प्रोच्यत इत्यूह्यम्। विना पक्षिणा गरुत्मता अभिया रहितभिया। तेन रहितभिया गरुत्मता पुरमनीयतेति चोक्तं भवतीति मे हृदि प्रतीयते। स्मरन् तर्हि किमर्थं तदा सा भगवता भार्या प्रेयसी सा तथाभूतया गिरा विज्ञापिता? तत्रानेन हेतुना भवितव्यम्। ननान्दुरुन्नतिं न न विज्ञापनीयमिति मन्वानेन भगवता तथा प्रोक्तमिव प्रतिभातीत्येको मद्विवेकायाधारोऽयं हासः।

भूयोऽन्यः परमहंसशब्दश्चेति स्मरन्नयं काञ्चुकीयस्त्वेवं निर्दिश्य भगवतो वचनप्रकारगौरवं विमृशेत्। एवं भगवताहं समादिष्टः विविक्ते रैवतकप्रस्थवर्तिनि काञ्चनोद्याने कश्चिदागन्तुकः परमहंसः किल सन्निधत्ते तत्राप्यनुपपत्त्या भवितव्यम्। कुतः, योगं कुर्वद्भिर्भगवद्भिः काञ्चनोद्यानं नाघिषीयते, किञ्च भगवद्भिस्सर्वैः प्रभासतीर्थपरिसरमपि गन्तव्यम्। तस्माद् तथाभूतैर्भगवद्भिः काञ्चनोद्यानस्थैः भवितव्यम्। किञ्च पूर्वं कदाचित् कस्यामपि दशायां किमप्यवस्थान्तरमुद्दिश्य प्रलपत्सु वृष्णिषु सदुःखं स्थितेषु भगवन्तमेकान्तस्थं दृष्टवानस्मि। तदानीमन्तर्भूतं दृष्ट्वा अहमभ्येत्य रहसि रचितप्राञ्जलिरित्यवदम्।

दासस्य मे मनो ब्रूते भगवन् भक्तवत्सलः।
प्रष्टव्यो हि त्वया देवो दशेयं कीदृशीत्यदः।।

इति पृष्टो भगवानपि स्वमुखेन्दोर्निर्गमयन्त्या स्मितचन्द्रिकया मां प्रसादयन्नाश्रित प्रसादाभ्यां दृग्भ्यां स्वसमीपं रहसि मां प्रापय्य तदानीमित्यवदत्

रहस्यं हि त्वया श्राव्यं मत्तो विनयपालित।
त्वत्तोऽन्यस्मिन् जने क्वापि नास्यां मे निस्सरेदिदम्।।
दग्धव्या पाण्डवा नात्र मयि जीवति शत्रुभिः।
जिष्णुः परमहंसोऽयं कौन्तेयेषु विशेषतः।।

एवं पुरा भगवता अर्जुनः परमहंस इत्युक्तः। तदिदानीमपि परमहंस इति वचनात् काञ्चनोद्यानस्थेन तेनार्जुनेन भवितव्यम्। भूयोऽपि भगव-न्नियोगवचनमेव स्मरन् परमहंसः किल सन्निधत्ते परमहंसोऽर्जुनः। परमयं शब्दोऽत्रैव शब्दे वर्तते। तस्मात्परमहंसशब्देनार्जुनः तत्र सन्निधत्त इत्यनेन मह्यं विज्ञापित इति ज्ञेयम्।

there. His eyes revealed to me more than what he said. The basis for this assumption is his intentional gesture towards me.

Thinking so the Chamberlain pauses for few moments. He thinks over the suggestive import of the words used by the Lord:

The Lord told like this

> *tena tadvijayenaiṣa prāpitā śarma patriṇā/*
> *tratāta sāniyata puram subhadrātra vinā bhiyā//*

Then told 'Vijayena'

The words mean something more to me.

The arrows of Dhanañjaya saved Subhadrā from the demon. Vijaya denotes Dhanañjaya and Patri the arrows. Vih here means the bird Garuḍa; Abhiyā fearless. The suggested sense is that Dhanañjaya saved Subhadrā by his arrows from the demon.

Garuḍa took her without fear to Dvārakā.

Why did the Lord then conceal the matter related to Dhanañjaya from his beloved? This may be the reason. Kṛṣṇa might have thought that the news of good fortune of the sister-in-law need not be conveyed to her now.

The smile thus provides the clue to distinguish the guest of the day.

The other thing that is significant is the use of the particular word Paramahamsa in the context. The Lord has instructed me like this:

> A great sage who is a Paramahamsa is camping in the golden valley on the slops of Raivataka mountain.

There is a contradiction in it. Ascetics do not go to the golden mountain for meditation. They normally reside around the Prabhāsatīrtha. Hence this ascetic is different from the ordinary ascetics.

Moreover, I remember an incident occurred long ago. Ere long, the Vṛṣṇis were afflicted by a calamity. All of them were wailing aloud. I then saw the Lord alone at a distance. I approached him, with folded hands prayed him confidentially.

> O! Lord affectionate to the devotees, the mind of this servant prompts to ask you the reason for this pitiable condition.

किञ्च आर्येण साकं साक्षात्करणीयः स मयेति च विज्ञापितः। तेन वः काञ्चनोद्यानवर्तिनं भगवद्विग्रहिणं तं गुरुभूतेन सङ्कर्षणेन प्रापयिष्यन्निमां परमयं देवः इति मन्ये। तस्माद् ऋजुधिया शुद्धमानसेन यथार्थज्ञेन सङ्कर्षणेन काञ्चनोद्यानादत्र प्रापितेन किमपि वस्तु सहोदर्याः उरोजांशुकालिखितविजयनामायं देवः साधयिष्यति। नूनं स्मरन् तदर्थमाबद्धरथं दारुकमिह प्रापयेति मां नियुक्तवानसौ देवः। तस्मादनुष्ठित-तच्छासनोऽस्मि यत् तत् साम्प्रतमिति स्मरन्नयं काञ्चुकीयः किमपि भगवता मह्यमनुक्तं नासीदिति समर्थयिष्यन् भूय इति स्मरेत्। एवं स्मरन्तं मां पश्यद्भिः किमनेन स्मर्यत इति कैश्चिन्न विमृश्येरन् किं यदि केचित् तैरन्योन्यमुच्यमानानि वाक्यानि श्रोतुं द्रष्टुं वा तद्वयोधिकत्वादभ्रणी मे श्रोत्रचक्षुषी तस्मादयमेतावन्तं कालं स्ववयाधिक्यात् पदमपि चलितुमक्षमस्सन्नयं सचिन्तं तिष्ठतीति लोकान् विभावयन्तीं काञ्चित् श्लोकसरणीं मन्मुखान्निर्गमयानीति निश्चित्य तथा समर्थयन्तं कञ्चिदुत्तरश्लोकं वदन् देवेन किमपि भगवता मह्यमनुक्तं नासीदिति भूयोऽपि श्लोकान्वयविशेषेण दृढीकरोति **जटावक्तृचरणते**त्यादिग्रन्थेन। उत्तरश्लोकेन च तत्प्रयोगमार्गं दर्शयति – जटावक्तृचरणतया पुनः यतिविडम्बना संवृत्ता। जटावक्तृचरण इति भगवानुच्यते। तत्कथमिति चेत् तत्र जटाशब्देन परिणत उच्यते। वक्तव्यशब्देन स्तोतव्य इति च। चरणशब्दः पूज्यवाचकः। परिणतजनेन विद्यावृद्धेन जनेन स्तोतव्या चरणौ यस्य तथोक्तः तस्य भावश्चरणता परिणतजनस्तोतव्यचरणभावेन पुनर्यतिविडम्बना संवृत्ता। तत्र चरणशब्दः पूज्यवाचक एव, परिणतजन-स्तोतव्यभावेनेत्यर्थः। तस्मात्तथाभूतेन तेन परमहंस इति प्रोक्तत्वात् यति-विडम्बना संवृत्ता तेन स यतिरिति विडम्ब्यते परिहास्यते, तस्मादयमर्जुनो यतिवेषधारी भूत्वा किं वस्तूद्दिश्यात्मानं भगवता पुरं प्रापयिष्यन्नत्रास्त इत्यूह्यम्।

पदप्रचारसन्धौ च सन्यासिनि गतौ तथा।
यतिशब्दो भवेदत्र प्रवृत्तौ च सुरद्विषि।।

ध्वनौ सन्यासिनि अन्यत्रगतौ तस्मात्परिणतजनस्तोतव्यभावेन भगवता यस्य सिद्धान्तविरोधिनीवेषप्राप्तिं प्राप्तवन्तं तं दृष्ट्वा तेन हसितमिति विमृशन्नेवोत्तरश्लोकेन तथा निश्चिनोति। तत्प्रवृत्तिः कथं मे न वाच्यासीत् कुत इति, तत्कथमिति चेत् –

पातञ्जलत्वेन समाचरन्ती सदेति हासास्पदतामवाप्ता।
मूर्तिः परामेत्य पुराणतां मे कथं न वाच्या परतन्त्रवृत्तिः।।

इति तत्प्रवृत्तिः प्रायेण मे तेन न नोक्तासीदिति समर्थयत्यनेन श्लोकेन। कथं तेनोक्तासीदिति चेत् परं पुराणतामेत्य समाचरन्ती तन्मूर्तिः दृश्यमाना सहसा मया हासास्पदतामवाप्तेति तेनोक्तमित्यूह्यम्। परां पुराणतामिति परा-मुत्कृष्टां पुराणपुरुषताम्। पुराणशब्देन परः पुमान् विष्णुरुच्यते, तस्य भावः पुराणता सोऽहमिति तस्य भावः प्राप्तवतः सन्यासिजनस्यानुरूपरूपश्रियमेत्य जडत्वेन पातं समाचरन्ती तस्य मूर्तिः तथाभूता सहसा मया दृष्टा हासास्पद-तामवाप्तेति तेन भगवता मह्यं विज्ञापितोऽयमर्जुन इति मन्ये। तस्मात् तथाभूता या मूर्तिरिति कथं तेन मे न वाच्यासीत्, अनुक्ता नासीदित्यर्थः।

परतन्त्रवृत्तिः तथाभूतोऽयं धनञ्जयः द्रौपदीतन्त्रवृत्तिरित्यर्थः। द्रौपद्यां मग्नस्य तस्य हृदयेन भगवता स्मर्यमाणेकार्ये पदं क्रियेत। किमित्यस्मिन् श्लोके केनापि योजनाप्रकारभेदेन भगवत्सिद्धान्तविरोधिनीं

Blessing me with his bright smile, he called me near with his pleasing look and told me:

> Dear Vinayapālita, hear these secret words from me. I will not reveal this to anyone else. The Pāṇḍavas are not to be burned as long as I am alive, especially Dhanañjaya, the Paramahamsa.

The Lord then had qualified Dhanañjaya as Paramahamsa. Now also the ascetic coming to the golden valley is designated as Paramahamsa. Hence, the ascetic is none other than Dhanañjaya.

He recollects the words: Paramahamsa kila sannidhatte/ Paramahamsa is Dhanañjaya. Thus the Lord has instructed me that the ascetic is Dhanañjaya himself.

The Lord has instructed me that the Paramahamsa has to be greeted along with his elder brother Balabhadra. The Lord intends that Balabhadra himself should invite and bring the one in the guise of the ascetic to Dvārakā. Balabhadra is straightforward. Kṛṣṇa wants to achieve something through him. It is for this purpose that the Lord had asked me to bring the chariot ready with Dāruka, the charioteer.

I have only obeyed the orders of the Lord. There is nothing the Lord has not revealed to me.

What the people will think seeing me like this. In order to mislead them I pretend inability to move due to old age. I am unable to see and hear due to the defective eyes and ears. This I have to communicate to them.

jarāvaktavya caraṇatayā punaḥ yativiḍambanā saṃvṛttā/

This much delay was caused by inability of my legs due to old age.

This is the meaning common to all.

This has another meaning:

Jarāvaktavyacaraṇa denotes Lord Kṛṣṇa. Jarā – old, vaktau – being praised, caraṇa – signified reverence. One who is praised and honoured by the learned. Yativiḍambanā relates to Dhanañjaya designated by the Lord as Paramahamsa.

The word Yati is used in the following senses:

Pause in prosody, sage, journey, activity and god. The suggested sense here is that the Lord praised by the learned smiled ridiculing the ascetic garb of Dhanañjaya that this is against the principles and also of his valor.

sticken by old age

निजचेष्टां प्राप्तवानयमर्जुन इति यत् तस्मात् परतन्त्रवृत्तित्वं मे स्यादिति तेन दर्शितेन किमिति मन्वानोऽयं कञ्चुकीयस्तेनैव श्लोकेन भगवत्सिद्धान्तो यथा न स्यादिति समर्थयति। पातञ्जलत्वेनेत्यादि श्लोकेनैव पुनरस्य श्लोकस्यार्थं भगवति समर्पयति। तत्समर्पणप्रकारं तेनैव श्लोकेन दर्शयति – कुतः परां पुराणतामेत्य समाचरन्ति वा मूर्तिः साम्प्रतं पातञ्जलत्वेनेतिहासास्पदतामवाप्ता। तया परतन्त्रवृत्तिः कथं मे न वाच्य इति सम्बन्धः। परां पुराणतामिति पूर्वं तपःक्षयात् जगति लयं गतवति भूयस्तत्स्रष्टुमप्रभुत्वादनन्ताङ्गीभूते वटपत्रे शयानो निद्राच्छलेन परब्रह्मोपासनां कृत्वा प्राभवमुपेत्यादौ स्वयं विराड्भूत्वा चतुर्दशभुवनस्य चरणं यो भवति विराडित्युक्तोऽयं पुमान् कीदृग्भूत इति चेत् स ईदृग्भूत इति इतिहासैरुच्यते –

यस्य द्यौर्जायते शीर्षं यस्य श्रोत्रो जगद्दिशः।
यस्य नेत्रे पुष्पवन्ते यस्य नाभ्यां वियद् भवेत्।।
यस्याङ्घ्रितो भवेद् भूमिः यस्य चित्तात्तु चन्द्रमाः।
विप्रभूपविशश्शूद्रो मुखबाहूरुपादतः।।
यस्याभवत् किं बहुना समस्तं तन्मयं जगत्।
शिरोऽक्षिबाहुपादानां सहस्रं येन धार्यते।।
स विष्णुरिति विख्यातस्तेनैव भुवनेष्विह।
इति श्रुतं मया देवादितिहासानि सादरम्।।
वचयन्त्यै सदुद्देव्यै वदतोर्थांस्तदुद्भवान्।।

तस्मात् परं पुराणतामेत्य जगति रक्षितुं समाचरन्ती या मूर्तिः पातञ्जलत्वेनेति हासास्पदतामवाप्ता।

पातञ्जलत्वेनेति। पातञ्जलं श्रीमद्भाष्यं पातञ्जलत्वं तद्भावः। श्रीमद्भाष्यभावेन कृतसंस्कारैः पदैर्गद्यपद्यैरिति हासास्पदतामवाप्तेति हासास्पदमिति हासानामास्पदं प्रमेयपुरुषत्वमवाप्तायां सा मूर्तिः स्वसिद्धान्त-विरोधिनीं रूपश्रियं प्राप्तवन्तमर्जुनं स्वसिद्धान्तेन घटयेत्। किमत्राश्चर्यं चतुर्दश-भुवनवासिनो जनान् स्वस्मृत्यनुरूपं वर्तयेदिति यत् ततः तस्मात् तया मूर्त्या परतन्त्रवृत्तिः कथं मे न वाच्या। तस्मात् तेन पुनर्यतिविडम्बनैव संवृत्ता। यतिरिति तेन विडम्बनं कृतम्। परतन्त्रवृत्तिरिति प्रवृत्तिप्रकार उच्यते। अयमर्जुनस्तस्य प्रवृत्तिरीदृग्भूता एवं भगवता निजवचनप्रकारभेदेनायमर्जुनो यतिवेषधारी रैवतके वर्तत इति मे कथं नानुक्तमासीत्। अथैवं काञ्चुकीयस्तदा भगवद्वचनप्रकारेणायमर्जुन इति निश्चित्य भगवतो-ऽनुष्ठितनियोगोऽहमिति विज्ञापितुं तस्मात् गन्तुमुद्युक्तो भवेत्। अथैवं कञ्चुकिभूमिकालङ्कृतनुर्भरतवरः सावधानमेवं दर्शितमर्थं प्रेक्षकान् बोधयित्वा बाह्यार्थेन नानालोकान् सुखये-दित्यस्य प्रयोगमार्गः।

चेटी उपसृत्य। एवं तस्माद्गन्तुमुद्युक्तं चेटी सम्प्राप्य पृष्टप्रमथवृत्तान्तेन कञ्चुकिना अतीतायां रात्रौ भगवत्सत्यभामयोः परस्परसञ्जातावस्थां प्रमथवृत्तिं गरुत्मत्प्रवृत्तिं च तस्यै विज्ञाप्य समासेन स च सा च तन्नियोगमनुष्ठातुं तस्माद् गतवन्तौ स्याताम्।

पुनः काञ्चुकीयस्य यतिविडम्बनां परतन्त्रवृत्तिरित्युभाभ्यां पदाभ्यामयमर्जुनोऽतः परं यतिवेषधारी भूत्वा प्रविशतीति च कविना नासूचकस्य प्रवेशनकाल इति लक्षणो दर्शितः।

एवं मिश्रविष्कम्भस्य प्रयोगमार्गः।

and falling frequently

my body has become ridiculous

dependence is regrettable.

This is the meaning associated to the Chamberlain. But this has a suggested sense. The Lord has suggestively communicated this meaning to me.

paraṃ purāṇatāmetya samācarantī
tānmūrti hāsāspadaṃ avāpta

Dhanañjaya in the disguise of ascetic is referred to here. His appearance in the attire of an ascetic is a cause of ridicule to all. Paratantravṛtti also has to be attributed to him since he is dependent on Pāñcālī. Thus the Lord has conveyed to me that the ascetic coming to golden valley is Dhanañjaya and that his disguise has caused smile in him.

According to this interpretation Dhanañjaya is represented as having done something that the Lord does not like. Now a further interpretation is attempted. Here the word *sadetihāsāspadata* is taken as sadā *itihāsāspadata*. Thus this becomes an invocation of the cosmic form of God where the sky is the head, the quarters the ears, eyes the flowers etc. Interpreted like this the verse is an eulogy to the cosmic form praised in the Itihāsas.

According to another interpretation, Pātañjala is taken to mean the *Mahābhāṣya*.

By all means, the Lord has suggested that Dhanañjaya is the ascetic. He has revealed everything to me.

The chamberlain having concluded that the ascetic is Dhanañjaya goes to inform the Lord that he has carried out his instructions.

Thus the actor in the role of Kāñcukīya carefully communicates the subtle meaning to the Prekṣaka. He should please the Nānāloka by the outer meaning. This is the mode of presentation.

XIV
Kāñcukīyam

An Innovative Reconstruction[1]

Interlude (viṣkambha) is a device used by poets to inform the audience what has occurred between the intervals of the acts and what is likely to happen in future. Middle or low level characters are employed for this, the first is viṣkambha and other is praveśaka. If a low character is also included viṣkambha becomes miśra.

1 The present writer took up the study Vyaṅgyavyākhyā seriously in the nineties of the last century when he published in 1993 the critique of dramaturgy- Naṭāṅkuśa. It criticizes the aberrations brought to the sacred Sanskrit stage by the actors. To understand the text well, I had to concentrate on Kulaśekhara and his contributions. The study convinced me that Kulaśekara had a great vision of theatre which, unfortunately, his successors grossly misunderstood.

During this time a group of theatre enthusiasts started at Tripunithura the International Centre for Kūṭiyāṭṭam for the promotion of the ancient art form. Our attempts thereafter were to preserve the tradition of Vyaṅgyavyākhyā keeping the aberrations out. In all its deliberations, the Centre highlighted the vitality of that tradition. Quite unexpectedly, we got a chance to demonstrate our resolve.

The Centre submitted a project to the Ministry of Tourism and Culture for production of a new play in Kūṭiyāṭṭam. The Project was to present the role of the chamberlain in the second act of *Subhadrādhanañjayam* according to the description of *Vyaṅgyavyākhyā*. In the interlude the chamberlain, enters and informs that Lord Kṛṣṇa has ordered him to prepare the chariot for him and his brother Balarāma to go the Raivataka Mountain to receive an ascetic. The interpretative genius of Kulaśekhara develops this terse ordinary sentence of the dramatic text to a whole drama giving ample scope for the actor to exhibit his histrionic talents. As there is only one character on the stage this has to be accomplished by solo-acting. This also serves to illustrate the potential of Indian narrative techniques.

The ministry accepted the project and we started the work.

Through a series of deliberations with leading artistes, consultation with scholars, periodic workshop and seminar we were able to frame a broad outline. We had to work on three things-

i. The dramatic text of Kulaśekhara

ii. His stage script given in *Vyaṅgyavyākhyā.*

iii. Preparation of a performance text based on the above.

We had to live up to our resolve to keep ourselves away from the alleged aberrations of the post – Kulaśekhra period.

Margi Madhu dared to take up the challenge on our request. After year-long preparations he reconstructed an *Āṭṭaprakāram* and trained himself for presentation. This stage – script is given here as the performance manual for Kāñcukīyam.

The second act of *Subhadrādhanañjaya* starts with a miśraviṣkambha. Kalpalatikā and the chamberlain are the characters here. Kalpalatikā enters searching the bodice of Subhadrā lost during the fight with the demon. Then the chamberlain enters.

This normally insignificant text of the drama is developed in *Vyaṅgyavyākhyā* to a full performance.

After the mizāvu has been sounded and the *gohosti* has been completed, the araṅṅutaḷi śloka is recited.

रहसि हसितभासा भामया यो निशायां
वदसि परमहंसो यो यतिं वेत्स्युपायम्।
स्मरसि तदखिलं तं व्यञ्जयन् काञ्चुकीयं
भणसि सदसि सा त्वं माधवोऽव्यात् सदा वः।।[2]

The curtain is held up on the stage to the accompaniment of the mizāvu and Kañcuki (Vinayapālita) will then come on to the stage and pay obeisance before the mizāvu and walk in staggering circular steps behind the curtain. He will then turn away from the mizāvu and face the lighted lamp in the front. The curtain will then be removed and the tired looking chamberlain makes his appearance[3]. Displaying the mannerisms of a feeble old man he makes a staggering circular movement and pauses to think.

I have come here upon Lord Śrīkṛṣṇa's orders. How is this? (Elaboration follows) expressing this through a mudrā the he stops the beat of the mizāvu and enters into speech.

Vākyam: Ādiṣṭosmi devena devakīnadanena yathā- Vinayapālita! Vivikte kila raivataka-prasthāvartinī kanchandoyane kaschidāgantuko bhagavān paramahmsa sannidhatta (ceṭīpañcamam)

This will be enacted as follows:

Enactment : Lord Kṛṣṇa called me to his side and said, Oh, Vinayapālita, a Paramahamsa is seated in a deserted spot on the golden garden near the Valley of the Raivathaka mountain.

---

2 This introductory verse was composed by Dr. E.N. Narayanan, Asst. Professor of Sanskrit, S.B College Changanachery.

3 Kañcuki in costume is like the *aṇiññāṭunna sūtradhāran* (with *pazukka* facial make up and normal costumes of Kūṭiyāṭṭam) and differs only in the *headger* which is like that of the 'ney techa sūtradhāran' (with ghee used for facial make up). An uttarīyam (upper cloth) would be worn across the forearm and a staff should be carried in the hand.

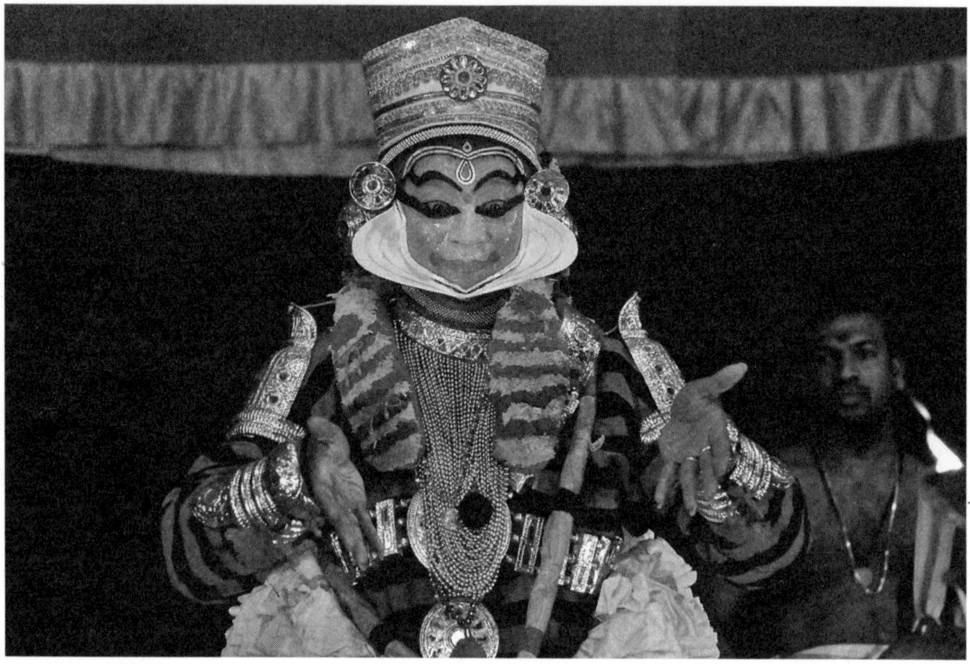

Margi Madhu in Kāñcukīyam

The beat of the mizāvu is stopped and the *vākyam* is repeated.

Vākyam: *soyamāryeṇa sākam saṅkarṣaṇena sākṣātkaraṇīyo mayā. tat sajjīkriyatāṃ ratha iti.*

Enactment: so prepare the chariot four the journey

The beat of the mizāvu is stopped and the vākyam repeated. Vinyapālitha thinks:

> There is some hidden meaning in Lord's words. Though I am too old and feeble to find out what, I am not giving up the effort. I base myself on two sources. One, the smile on the Lord's face and second, the use of the term Paramahamsa. How did I get to know of the Lord's smile?

As I stood guard before the ladies chamber, I happened to overhear a conversation between the Lord and his consort Satyabhāmā. How was this? (elaboration)

The Lord after his evening prayers and meal arrived at Satyabhāmā's sleeping chamber and was resting there.

> After showing these *mudrās*, Kañcuki sits on the stool and transforms himself to Lord Kṛṣṇa. The Lord gave a mysterious smile.
>
> Kañcuki now shows the relevant mudrā and becomes Satyabhāmā.

Satyabhāmā lies in the Lord's embrace and feigns anger at the Lord's smile. 'Oh, my beloved. Your smile pains my heart. It is not befitting you to ridicule me when you alone are the sole support to me. Why are you hurting me so?
Kañcuki transforms himself to the Lord:

> Oh my beloved, the fate of those women who depend solely on me is sad. How is this? (elaboration)
>
> A union with the beloved which is so pleasurable for all leaves me sleepy. This is the reason for my smile.
>
> The Lord embraces Satyabhāmā while she disengages from his arms.

As Satya — My Lord, why do you lie to me so? Stop these painful words. You are adept in lying. All men are skilled in such ways. Women who take it for love are stupid.

(The Lord smiles on.)

As Satya — You callous and dispassionate one, you were never like this before. Alas! No women ever loved a man like I have loved you. If you do not open up the truth, fire or poison will decide my destiny.

(Satyabhāmā continues sobbing)

As the Lord — The Lord takes Satybhāmā on his lap, wipes her tears and says,

> 'Oh, beautiful one, you should not be saddened while I am alive, I remain silent because the brave are not entitled to speak of bad deeds. You know that even the noble sages refer to you as brave. I was only engaging in light conversation with you. It has caused deep pain within you and made you to accuse me.

As Satyabhā — My Lord secrets whether good or bad have to be shared with the one you love.

As the Lord — The Lord holds Satyabhāmā's arm. My beautiful one, don't be sad. I will tell you the truth. One day Duryodhana came here secretly.

As Duryo — Duryodhana pays respects to Balabhadra and seeks the hand of his sister in marriage.

As Balabha — (with fondness towards his disciple) Oh, Duryodhana this matter will invite opposition from those here. So take Subhadrā away stealthily with my permission.

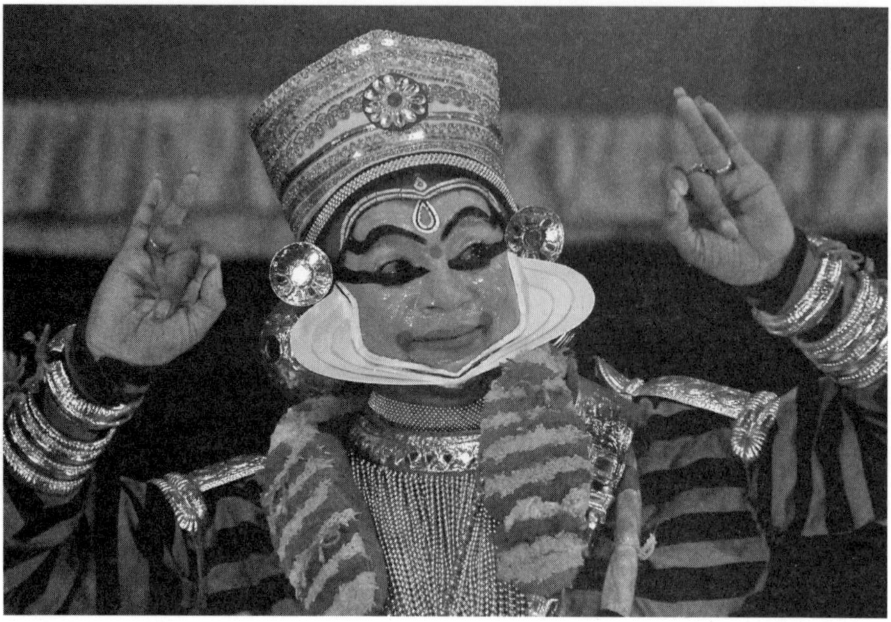

As Duryo Duryodhana bows and returns to Hastinapura calls upon the Asura Alambuṣa who is Arjuna's enemy and tells him. Alampoosa, you should go to Dvārakāpuri and bring Subhadrā back with you.

As Alamb Oh, king, I will proceed to Dvārakā and before the watching Vṛṣṇis, will grab her with force and bring her across the skies to you. If not, I will not live another moment. I swear!

As Duryo May you succeed . May your journey be auspicious. Love by force is dear to me.

As Alamb May I take leave. Bows and turns and magically assumed a horrible form, goes to Dvārakā and looks around. Spots Subhadrā in the seventh floor seated in a melancholy mood. Alampoosa grabs her violently and carries her away.

As Lord Kṛṣṇa : At this point I called Garuḍa to my side and sent him to deal with Alambusa.

As Garuḍa As you wish my Lord. Garuḍa prepares for flight and meets Alambusa in the midst of his flight.

As Alamb Alambusa is terrified at the sight of Garuḍa, Drops Subhadrā and flees.

The beat of the mizāvu is stopped and the śloka follows.

tena tadvijayenaiṣā prāpitā śarma patriṇā
ānīyata puram trātā subhadrā sā vinā bhiyā (indalam)

After the śloka is recited only the *mudrās* without the *śloka* follows. This is followed by the *anvayam* of the *śloka* : *patriṇā tena tadvijayena yeṣa śarma prāpitā*

Subhadrā became safe due to victory of Garuḍa over Alambuṣa. Not only that

Anvayam follows: *trātā sā subhadrā bhiyā vinā puram ānīyata.*

Subhadrā thus saved was brought to Dvārakā. Thus Garuḍa brought her after saving her from Alambusa.

As the Lord I smiled thinking of Alambuṣa's oath and his flight in fear of Garuḍa. Saying this the Lord consoled Sathyabhāmā and embraced her.

As Kañcuki However I recognize a hidden meaning in the Lord's words. What is that? (elaboration)

Śloka follows in ceṭīpañcamam

Anvayam *tena tadvijyena patriṇā yeṣa śarma prāpitā*
She became saved due to the arrows of Vijaya (Arjuna)
How is that (elaboration)

Arjuna on his way back from holy ablutions and proceeding towards Dvārakā spots Alambuṣa carrying away Subhadrā. Arjuna prepares to fight and stringed his bow with the *āgneyāstra*. Alambuṣa fled in fear. Arjuna received her in his arms. Thus Arjuna saved Subhadrā.

Anvayam continues: Trata sa Subhadrā abhiya vinā puram aniyata

The Subhadrā saved by the fearless bird was brought to Dvārakā. Garuḍa brought back Subhadrā, who was saved by Arjuna, to Dvārakā.

Therefore the Lord meant secretly that it was Arjuna who saved Subhadrā. I think he must not have wanted his sister's good fortune to reach his wife's ears.

The other reason is the reference to the term *Paramahamsa*. The Lord told me that a *Paramahamsa sannyāsi* had arrived at the golden garden of the Valley of Raivataka Mountains. But, ascetics would only dwell near *prabhāsatīrtham*. So I am sure that this has a hidden meaning. The Lord has referred to Arjuna as Paramahamsa to me before. How was this (elaboration)

One day I found the Lord in a saddened state at the time when the Yādavas were also feeling miserable. I walked up to him and after paying due respects asked him,

Oh Lord, my mind tells me that I should ask you why you are so sad now.

The Lord smiled at me and beckoning me to a corner told me secretly.

Oh, Vinayapālita, I will tell you a secret. No one should know of this. The Pāṇḍavas are not to meet their death while I am alive, especially, the Paramahamsa Arjuna, Kuntī's son.

The Lord had told me thus long back. Hence the ascetic who has arrived here must surely be Arjuna. Not only that, Lord said that he would visit the ascetic along with his brother. So the Lord will bring Arjuna and get some purpose fulfilled along with his straight forward brother. The Lord has commanded me to get the chariot ready for this purpose.

The mizāvu is stopped and speech follows.

Vākyam: *mayā ca tadāryadārukāya niveditam*
Enactment: I have informed Dāruka of the Lord's order and have returned.

Mizāvu is stopped and vākyam repeated.

Thus there is nothing that the Lord does not tell me. No one who sees me should suspect what I am thinking about. So I will tell them thus.

Stops mizāvu
Vākyam: *jarāvaktavya caraṇatayā punaryativiḍambanā samvṛttā.*
(ceṭīpañcamam)

My feet tremble as I walk out of old age

Mizāvu is stopped and vākyam repeated. How is this? (elaboration) Śloka follows:

pāṭam jaḷatvena samācarantī
sadeti hāsāspadatām avāptā
mūrtiparāmetya purātanam me
kathaṃ na vācyā paratantravṛttiḥ. (cēṭīpañcamam)

Mudrā repeated without śloka

Anvayam *me mūrtiḥ paratantravṛtti iti katham na vācyā*?

How would I say that body is not under some one's control?

How is my body?

Anvayam: *parām pūraṇatām etya jaḷatvena pātaṃ samācarantī*

People will laugh at me as I will stagger and fall when I try to walk as my feet are feeble with old age. How will I say then that my body is not under the control of others?

The reason for the Lord's smile is also this, what is this ? (elaboration)

Vākyam *jarāvaktavya caraṇatayā punaryativiḍambanā samvṛttā (indalam)*

Enactment Arjuna held in great respect by all has now donned the sannyāsi's robes in disguise. The Lord told me that this has become reason for his smile. How is this (elaboration)

Anvayam *mūrtiḥ sadā me hāsāspadatām avāptā iti katham na vacyā*?

How will I not say that his form has not been the reason for my smile every time? What is this? (Elaboration)

Anvayam continues:

jaḷatvena pātam samācarantī

His sannyāsi form born out of his petty and unfitting ways has become the reason for my smile. Arjuna is not to be belittled.

Anvayam *paratantravṛttiḥ*

He is submissive to Pāñcālī. Such a person's trifling acts cause laughter.

The Lord told me this indirectly.

(Thinking that nobody around should know this;
Kañcuki feigns weakness and staggers away.)

14. i. Production Note by Margi Madhu

I have conceptualized four *Āṭṭaprakārams* and had given stage presentations to three of them in my artistic career. Among these Kāñcukīyam[4] is the latest one. This was a very different experience, differing greatly from the Kūṭiyāṭṭam style of composing manuals for Bhāsa's *Karṇabhāram* and Macbeth, which I did earlier. For these two, the texts were the plays themselves and *Āṭṭaprakāras* were to be composed and then performed. The case with *Vyangyavyākhyā* was different. Usually Sanskrit plays are the basis for stage performances. The ancient playwright Kulaśekhara had himself composed a stage manual for his play. But this manual is not explicit enough to be accepted as an *Āṭṭaprakāram.* It only

4 Margi Madhu, the internationally acclaimed Kūṭiyāṭṭam artist, dared take up the challenge of putting Kulaśekhara on stage. After year-long work he prepared the performance manual and trained himself for presentation. This short production note contains the difficulties he encountered while applying the concepts of Kulaśekhara to actual practice.

provides certain tools for the actor to interpret the play. So an *Āṭṭaprakāram* had to be composed based on *Vyangyavyākhyā* and then performed. The author of Dhanañjayam conceived an *Āṭṭaprakāram* upon which I reconstruct another *Āṭṭaprakāram.* This would mean that the performance evolves out of two *Āṭṭaprakārams* that emerged in two distant ages.

In the first round of discussions, Dr. K.G. Paulose elaborated on the content of Kañcuki's entry in *Vyangyavyākhyā*. I felt that the first part contains lot of potential for Bhāvābhinaya.

Though I have heard a lot about *Vyangyavyākhyā*, I had no knowledge of the existence of a system for its performance. It was a challenge to express in Kūṭiyāṭṭam what a playwright conceived ten centuries ago. Since it was *abhinaya* oriented I felt it would be easy considering my experience as a performer. Even then how would I convey the double meanings *(śleṣam)* and the scholarly interpretation into the techniques of Kūṭiyāṭṭam? Even if this were made possible how would it communicate? This remained a big problem.

Further, I thought of how I would transform this into the techniques of Kūṭiyāṭṭam. The first problem I encountered was this. The conversation between Satyabhāmā and Kṛṣṇa has been composed by Kulaśekhara in a style similar to that of *nirvahaṇa*. This is the story telling of the past. The actor becomes a narrator here. There is no *vācika* here. After the *abhinaya,* the Naṅṅyāramma recites that *śloka*. If that tradition is followed *ślokas* like *tena tatvijayena* that expressed meaning through *śleṣa* will lose their *abhinaya* potential. Only if the abhinaya is differentiated and recited can the theatrical interest of the *śloka* be maintained. Only if this is maintained we can claim success for Kulaśekhara's scheme of acting. So it is clear that the technique of *nirvahaṇa* cannot be accepted fully. Now, if the traditional style of reciting the *śloka* and acting is followed, the rule is that the character cannot use the *śloka* or *vākyam* not present in the play. Here the *ślokas* of *Vyangyavyākhyā* are not from the dramatic text. Hence I had to encounter two difficulties in presentation.

i. If it is a *nirvahaṇa* the *śloka* has to be recited by a Naṅṅyāramma. This will take away the possibility of *śleṣābhinaya*.
ii. If it is the Character, the *ślokas* or *vākyas* not present in the play cannot be used. Here, all the *ślokas* are from outside the play.

This means that it is not possible to prepare *Vyaṅgyavyākhyā* for performance without breaking the traditional rules of Kūṭiyāṭṭam. The decision to

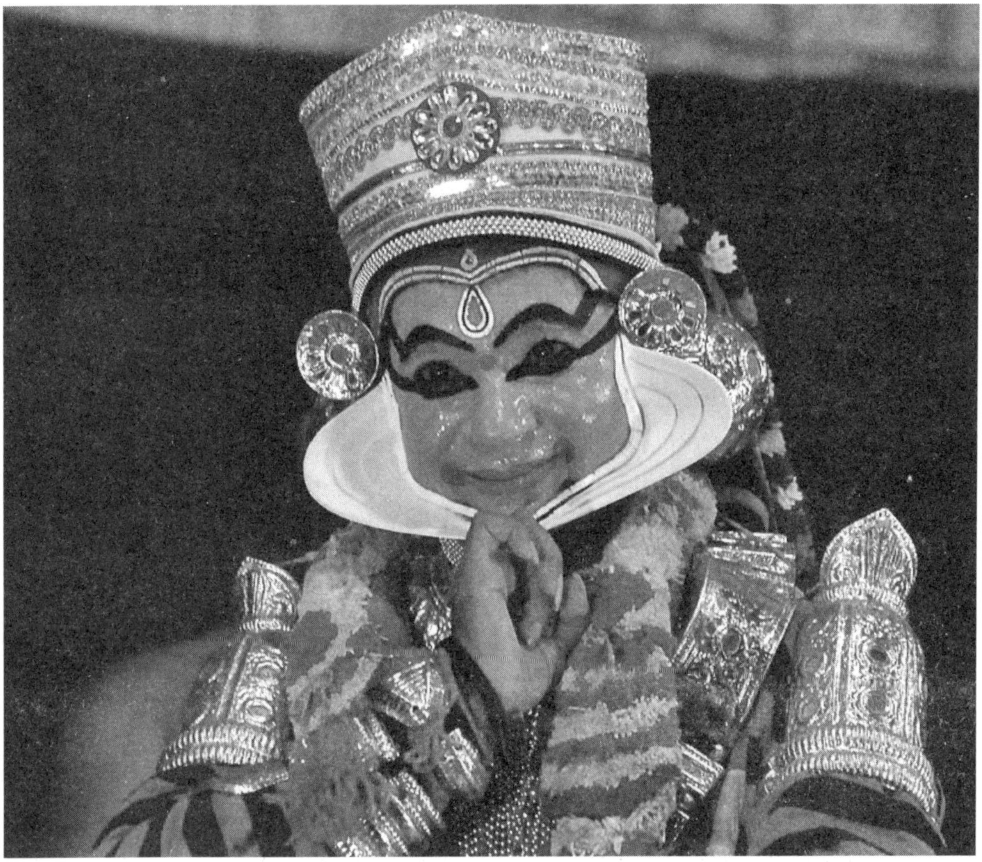

break these two rules was another important phase of conceptualizing the *Āṭṭaprakāram*.

More than forty *ślokas* have been included in the conversation between Satyabhāmā and Kṛṣṇa. It has been included as the interpretation or elaboration of Kañcuki's thoughts in the play. Only, that the interpretation became through the *śloka*. Hence it was not intended that these were for the elaborate acting of each *śloka* as is done in Kūṭiyāṭṭam today. So, it was decided that only the *śloka 'tena tadvijayena...* was taken up for acting and other ślokas expressed through *abhinaya* only. These ślokas without potential for *pakarnnāṭṭam* were enclosed within the narrative mode of the *Āṭṭaprakāram* and the Sathyabhāmā-Kṛṣṇa conversation was developed into the pakarnnāṭṭam form. When this is done, slight differences were felt from the existing style of pakarnnāṭṭam. In Kūṭiyāṭṭam, pakarnnāṭṭam generally present the events happening at a particular period of time; here, when *ślokas* were structured for pakarnnāṭṭam, different events and personal exchanges of different time became evident in different layers. The conversation between Kṛṣṇa and Satyabhāmā contained in it the conversations held between Balabhadra, Duryodhana and Alambuṣa and again the conversation between Garuḍa and Kṛṣṇa. These signify four events happening at four places and periods that reveal themselves like in parting the petals of a flower. Earlier only a few *ślokas* were meant to be developed into pakarnnāṭṭam. These layers became apparent in the process of writing the *Āṭṭaprakāram*. Since such a structure was new to Kūṭiyāṭṭam, there was an anxiety about how much it can communicate. However, this crisis was overcome without much difficulty in the course of training and on the occasion of performance.

Only the performance of the first half is over when pakarnnāṭṭam was concluded. Breaking the rules and utilizing pakarnnāṭṭam to the maximum was not a big problem compared to the second phase of the conceptualization. There was at least the confidence from the past experience for performing the pakarnnāṭṭam*s*. The story of the second half is different. Firstly, the possibilities within the communicative difference between the *prekṣaka* and *nānāloka* as conceived by Kulaśekhara, was present in the second half. So, it was with lot of anxiety that I went into the second half. The Kāñcukīya elaborates two reasons to suggest that the ascetic who has arrived is Arjuna. First reason was Kṛṣṇa's smile. It was presented in the first part. The Second reason is the use of the term Paramahamsa. Kulaśekhara has not provided any vākyas or *ślokas* for expressing the term Paramahamsa through *abhinaya*. However, there is an indication in Kulaśekhara of Kṛṣṇa having said long back that the Pāṇḍavas were not to be burned while he was alive. Here there is a possibility of a pakarnnāṭṭam describing the episode of burning the *arakkillam* in Mahābhārata. I have not explored this possibility. It could be used for performances extending to more than a day. The time limit in the performance does not allow for performing two important segments on the same day. So, only the meaning is expressed through mudrās.

At this stage of conceptualization, what created great anxiety was the *śloka 'patam jalatvena samācaranti'* – Kulaśekhara suggests many meanings. How to express it through *abhinaya?* Firstly, I thought of expressing it through *vācika*. There is lot of possibilities in this. What becomes a potentiality in *vācikam* becomes a limitation in *abhinaya*. This is because of the differences in language. Only a literary reading is possible here. Even now it cannot be claimed that this was fully overcome. All the different meanings ascribed by Kulaśekhara is not accepted, only two were accepted to get an idea of Kulaśekhara's mode of acting – the one related to Kṛṣṇa and the other to Kañcuki.

This portion amply justified Kulaśekhara's analysis of the audience into different layers of prekṣaka and *nānāloka*. The difference in *anvayam* has been expressed through differing *mudrās* and differing *rāgas* (Indalam for Kṛṣṇa and ceṭīpañcamam for Kañcuki). This is the first time that the same śloka relates in full to denote two characters in Kūṭiyāṭṭam.

All said, if this part has to be appreciated in full, the spectator should have good knowledge of *mudrās, rāgas* etc. He should also be a scholar in Sanskrit. In Kulasekhara's terms, one should be a *prekṣaka*. However this is a limitation as far as a performance is concerned. This limitation could have been overcome, if it was done through *vācika*. Since I took Kulaśekhara's *abhinayaprakāra* as a challenge, I decided to express the whole part through *abhinaya*.

14. ii. The possibilities Verbal Rendering.

On first reading of Vyaṅgyavyākhyā (Kañcuki's entry) itself, the possibilities for words more than that of *abhinaya*, came to light. This might be because the later Cākyārs used Kulaśekhara's interpretations for interpreting *prabandhas*. In the presentation of Subhadrāharaṇaprabandha, the conversation between Kṛṣṇa and Satyabhāmā is described more or less in the same manner. The Vyaṅgyavyākhyā must have inspired Melputtūr in his composition of the śloka *'Govinda Sathyabhama...* It became closer to Vyaṅgyavyākhyā with the explanations of Cākyārs.

The experience of performing and including this *prabandham* must have brought the possibility of verbal rendering to my notice. The literary and linguistic excellence of the second part can be revealed only through *vācikābhinaya*. Thus if expression is fully through *vākku*, it will create an entirely new experience. I would like to experiment this in the second phase.

The experiment will not be complete even then. I conceive of a third phase bringing together the possibility of *abhinaya* of the first half and the possibility of the *vākku* in the second half together into one performance as the final stage of this experiment. This does not limit itself to the alternate use of *vākku* and *abhinaya*. A costume suited for both and a style mingling both has to be designed. That is, this performance is only the first phase in my conceptualization.

I do not look at this as an isolated experiment. If the investigation started only from Kāñcukīyam it would never have ended. I could bring the concepts

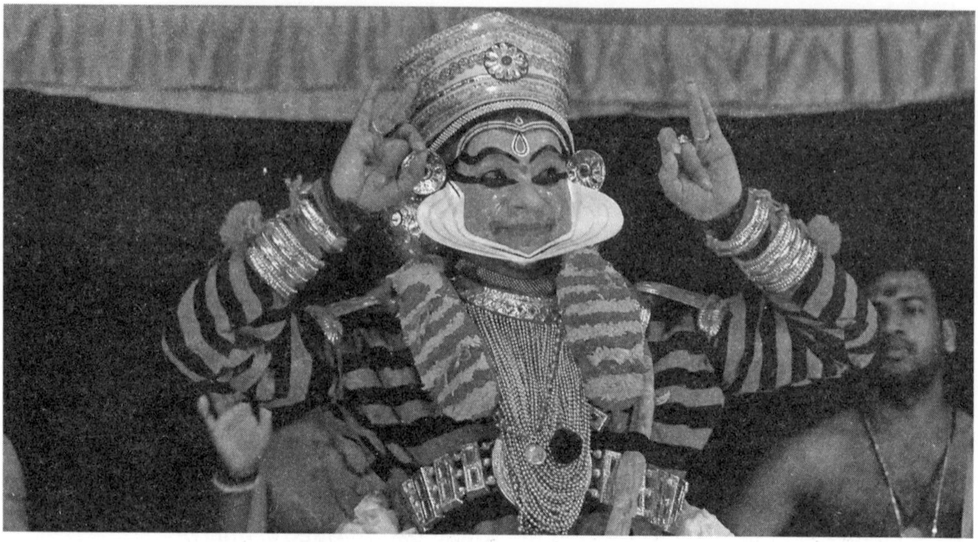

regarding *Āṭṭaprakāram* and its performance into reality only through the constant training and performance of nirvahanas and the *pakarnnāṭṭams* which transformed those techniques into my body and soul. If an idea enter into the soul a well trained actor can proceed without much difficulty. That is why I suggested that though the *pakarnnāṭṭam* was exciting it was not as difficult as the performance of the second part.[5]

5 Kāñcukīyam was first presented before an invited audience on 24.01.2003 at Tripunithura. This preview was followed by a discussion on various aspects of the play. Many eminent theatre persons including the actors participated in the deliberations. The core of the discussion centered round the following points:

Varma	I am not a scholar or a performer. Yet I enjoyed the play. Now what is the special significance attached to this presentation?
Paulose	One cannot easily define the special significance. The performance is based on *Vyaṅgyavyākhyā*. The message of *Vyaṅgyavyākhyā* is – 'there are many dramas hidden in a drama. Kāñcukīya is one of the many' Secondly, this illustrates the basic tenants of Kūṭiyāṭṭam- additional functions assigned to the actor as narrator and interpreter, the method of narration and above all the power of internalizing emotions. The powerful energy that permeates from the actor is fully utilized here. So the significance of it is that it introduces *Vyaṅgyavyākhyā* in practice.
Chandradasan	I have not gone through *Vyaṅgyavyākhyā* as my encounters were with the modern theatre. This presentation proved the potential of Kūṭiyāṭṭam as also of the actor in Madhu. This provides many spaces for the actor. The first part is actor – based. Possibilities for the expression here are boundless. But the second part is crowded with

If the complete performance involving *nirvahaṇas* is not adopted at least in the training stage of Kūṭiyāṭṭam, we would end up with a generation that would have difficulty in radiating the energy of Kūṭiyāṭṭam into the new experiments staying back with isolated enactments. Or, they would take time with such experiments and will need more hard work. Therefore, what I have to say to the Kūṭiyāṭṭam world in the light of this experience is that the *nirvahaṇas* which carry the energy and aesthetics of Kūṭiyāṭṭam have to be retained at any cost.

---

	linguistic intricacies. I fear how far the present audience will receive it, especially when rendered in Sanskrit.
Margi Madhu	Action-oriented pieces are easy to comprehend. Not so the *śleṣa* – based narrations. I have used different ragas to distinguish them.
Chandradasan	I doubt whether the narrative form fits in the rigid Kūṭiyāṭṭam frame.
Margi Madhu	It is for the audience to decide. From our experience the audience of Kūṭiyāṭṭam does not have any difficulty in understanding this complexity.
Achyuthan	Can we avoid such portions?
Margi Madhu	No, it is not correct. That narrative tradition has to be preserved. Institutions like this Centre should educate the audience and elevate them to the level to appreciate the subtleties in such performances.
Chandradasan	Can you attempt this part in Kūttu also?
Margi Madhu	I am doing it.
Mini	The lines in this second part are repeated several times.
Margi Madhu	That is needed to bring out the different meanings.
Indu	There is another point. Usually verses outside the dramatic texts are recited by Naṅṅyārs. Here the verse *vinā bhiya*, found not in the text is rendered by the actor.
Paulose	In such cases there is no harm in becoming unconventional. I think that this distinction was not there at the time of *Vyaṅgyavyākhyā*. Pūrvasambandha is different from nirvahaṇa. Anyhow here it has to be done by the actor himself to bring out the difference in meanings.
Achyuthan	Is it time for us to search for another drama hidden in *Vyaṅgyavyākhyā*?
Sarala	Before that the text of *Vyaṅgyavyākhyā* has to be thoroughly corrected and edited. The text as now is a mass of errors. The manuscript is so loose that you can read anything from it.
Chandradasan	That is the greatness of *Vyaṅgyavyākhyā*!
Varma	The author himself gave the interpretation in *Vyaṅgyavyākhyā*. He could very well have included this in his drama. Why the author did not do it?
Paulose	Then there will be no theatre. Text is a seed. Theatre develops it to a tree. *Vyaṅgyavyākhyā* illustrates how to get the tree from the seed. The silence of a poet in his drama is eloquent. We have to interpret it. *Vyaṅgyavyākhyā* gives the key; the highways and byways, we have to find out.

It was an inspiring experience of re-living Kulaśekhara after ten centuries. Kāñcukīyam is successfully presented on Kūṭiyāṭṭam stages. *Improvisations of Ancient Theatre* Published by The International Centre for Kutiyattam is a documentation of this exciting experience.

XV
Hero in the Disguise of a Mendicant

ACT II

(ततः प्रविशति यतिवेषधरो धनञ्जयः)

(Dhanañjaya enters disguised as a mendicant)

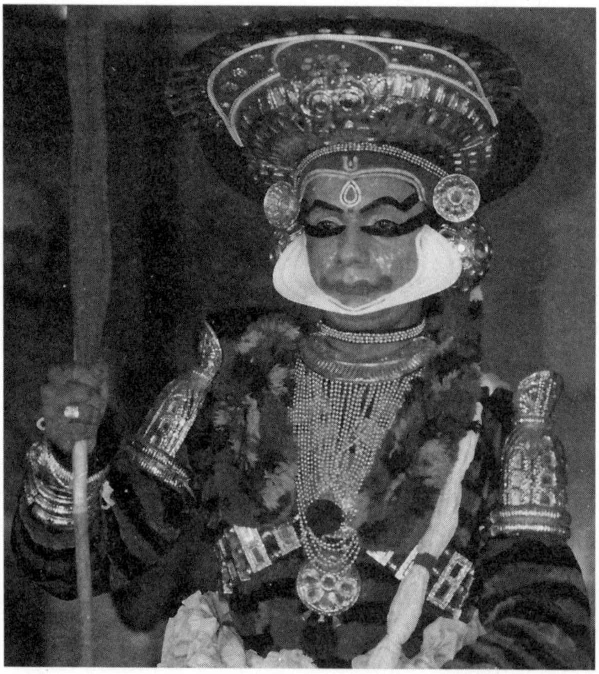

Dhanañjaya disguised as a mendicant

Sajeev Narayana Chakyar

Prāveśika and Pūrvasambandha

धनञ्जयः (दीर्घं निःश्वस्य) (Sighing deeply)

Vyaṅgyavyākhyā

Dhanañjaya disguised himself as a mendicant to attain Subhadrā thought within himself: I will contemplate on my friend Kṛṣṇa without my mind deviating to anything else. I will get necessary advice from him who will reach here.

He searched for a suitable place for meditation and found out the beautiful golden garden in the Raivataka mountain which is only at a distance of the throw of an arrow from Dvārakā. The garden, alluring all around was suitable for young men to engage in amorous sports. Dhanañjaya found it difficult to concentrate his mind on the Lord. When he forcefully drew his mind and five senses to the Lord, the Aśoka[1] arrows of Cupid instigated by the Lord, fell constantly on him. Thus tormented, Dhanañjaya tried his best to focus his affection on Lord, but was perpetually disturbed.

Cupid then sent the arrow of cūta to Dhanañjaya. It induced great heat in his mind. Then again cupid struck him strongly with the arrows of mallikā. Stupified he could no more bear the sounds of cuckoo and the enchanting atmosphere of the garden. Raising his eyes in distress he stands fixing the eyes at the wicks of the lamp. Remove the curtain when the actor in the costume of Dhanañjaya disguised as a mendicant stands before the lamp.

Cupid leads my mind again to her. I do not know what to do now.

Having decided his course of action he sends a deep sigh of relief.

अयि भोः शूर्पकशासिन्! अवितथमाहुरागमविदः, यत् परनिबर्हणपराणामपरिहरणीया दुःखपरम्परेति। तथा हि मम,

अतिलङ्घयसि लज्जां धैर्यबन्धं धुनासि
प्रथयसि परितापं प्रश्रयं प्रक्षिणोषि।
अविरतिभिरमीभिः कर्मभिः क्षीयमाणः
स्वयमपि परिपीडामात्मनस्त्वं तनोषि।। २।।

---

1 The five arrows of cupid are Aravinda (lotus), Aśoka, Cūta (mango sprouts) Navamālikā (Jasmine) and Nīlolpala (blue lotus)

अरविन्दमशोकं च चूतं च नवमालिकाम्।
नीलोत्पलं च पञ्चैते पञ्चबाणस्य सायकाः।।

Their functions are, given below:
Aravinda induces Unmāda, Aśoka Tāpa, Cūta Śoṣaṇa, Navamālikā Stambhana and Nīlolpala causes Mohālasya.

उन्मादस्तापनश्च शोषणस्तम्भनस्तथा।
सम्मोहनं च कामस्य पञ्च बाणाः प्रकीर्तिताः।।

O subduer of Śūrpaka (Kāma), it is truly said by those proficient in ancient lore that oppressors of others cannot avoid a series of miseries. Thus in my case,
You reduce my shyness, shatter my fortitude, increase my misery, and do away with my humility.
Doing all these almost regularly, you too slip in the view of others and become miserable. (2)

Vyaṅgyavyākhyā

Dhanañjaya now becomes so conquered by cupid that he has already lost his strength.

Will depiction of such love-lorn pathetic condition adversely affect the heroic nature of Dhanañjaya?[2]

No. Vātsyāyana prescribes that one who has done his duty (कृतकृत्यः) has the right to indulge in sexual pleasures. Dhanañjaya is a person so gratified.

Kings who always worry over the enemies will have no peace of mind. But those who have put the burden on their ministers can relax without fear. In such a mood he seeks the pleasure of the enjoyment of kāma.

Dhanañjaya is fully satisfied. His enemies, the Kauravas, are struck with panic by his strength. The two elder and two younger brothers are capable of protecting the country. Dharmaputra has ascended the throne. By his patience and diplomacy he has endeared himself to all. Thus having defeated the enemies, everything was accomplished for the welfare of the people, Dhanañjaya now can indulge in amorous pleasures.

Moreover, the omniscient Vyāsa, son of sage Parāśara, who divided the Vedas into four created the ocean of Mahābhārata to instruct all, including

2 The commentator here enters upon an elaborate discussion on the propriety of strong characters being depicted in weak situations. He has two authorities to defend him – Vātsyāyana and Vyāsa.
Vātsyāyana prescribes that heroic characters who have accomplished their objects can indulge in erotic activities. This involvement will not do harm to their strong nature.
Sage Vyāsa has described the love of Dhanañjaya towards Subhadrā. Hence portraying Dhanañjaya with a shattered mind inflicted by the arrows of cupid does not belittle his heroic character.
It seems that under the pretext of defending the characterisation of the hero, king Kulaśekhara is providing the actors a golden opportunity to present all the nine Rasas on the stage. This is a unique situation where the actor can exhibit all his histrionic talents.
Kulaśekhara follows the Kashmir tradition of accepting nine Rasas including Śānta on the stage. Dhanañjaya, the author of Daśarūpaka who excludes Śānta on stage was unknown to the royal dramatist.

women and the low-born, the principles of dharma and to enable them to distinguish the right from the wrong. He has delineated in a delightful manner all the nine rasas in Mahābhārata.

Karuṇa (Pathos) is seen in the lamentation of women who lost their husbands in war.

In the gruesome act of killing the sleeping sons of the Pāṇḍavas, the sage has depicted the disgusting sentiment of Bībhatsa.

Raudrarasa horrifying to the wicked, is described in the killing of Duśśāsana by Bhīma. Vīrarasa, heroic, is shown in the battle to retrieve the cows carried away by the Kauravas. Hāsya is seen in the scene where the God encourages Dhanañjaya to break the bow in the svayamvara of Draupadī in the city of Yajñasena. Śāntarasa is depicted in the epic where Dharmaputra in the scene of dice-game watches dispassionately the disrobing of his wife Draupadī by Duśśāsana.

The sage has portrayed Śṛṅgāra where Dhanañjaya disguised as an ascetic carries, by force, Subhadrā to marry her.

Vedavyāsa, inseparable constituent of the omnipotent, has described Dhanañjaya in a love-lorn condition. Following him Kulaśekhara overlord of the land of Kerala, who has consumed the nectar of Bharata, has also depicted Dhanañjaya in a state tormented by the arrows of cupid. As the sage who is the authority in this matter, has done it himself, depiction of love-lorn conditions, does not diminish to the heroic stature of Dhanañjaya. Dhanañjaya, standing still, thinks.

(विचिन्त्य) अप्राप्तसुभद्रासङ्गमे मयि सोऽयमुचितस्ते व्यापारः। अन्तरेण पुनरन्यामन्याय्यमाचरसि। कुतः

मया किं सा नोढा प्रमथकरदत्ता प्रियतमा
तया किं नाश्लिष्टो रतिरपि न जाता मनसि मे।
दुनोषि त्वं कस्मादनृणमपि तस्यां जनमिमं
स कौण्डिन्यः साक्षी मम भवति तस्मिन् व्यतिकरे।। ३।।

(Thinking) Your efforts are only proper since I could not yet attain union with Subhadrā. But what you do in the case of another woman is just unworthy of you. For,

Did I not receive that beloved lady who fell from the hands of the demon?
Did I not then have her embrace? Did not love grow in my heart then?
So why do you blame me when I am not under any obligation to her in this matter (of love),

and Kauṇḍinya is a witness to that episode? (3)

(पुनर्विचिन्त्य) किन्नु खलु प्रस्तुते कर्मणि व्याप्रियमाणं मामनुमंस्यते वयस्यो वासुदेवः।

(Thinking again) Wouldn't Vāsudeva approve of my actions in this affair?

Vyaṅgyavyākhyā

It is not proper for me to give away my life. At one time we led a blissful life in Indraprastha in the company of Kṛṣṇa with mother, Draupadī and others. Kṛṣṇa stayed with us for sometime. Later, when he started to leave for Dvārakā I could not bear the pangs of his separation. While my heart was thus burning my friend looking at my despondent face consoled me: 'Dear Dhanañjaya! do not be worried. If you encounter any difficulty, I will be there to solve it.'

With the usual smile, he left for Dvārakā. I do not know why that Mādhava is not coming to help me. Oh! Lord come soon. I have none to depend on other than you. With the smiling face, come and console me; who is afflicted by the arrows of cupid. Please let my ear hear the sound of your chariot approaching. If you want to see me alive, please be with me without further delay.

When Dhanañjaya praised the Lord in this way, he felt relieved of his pain. Then he stood still concentrating his mind and senses on Kṛṣṇa.

Thus the actor disguised as ascetic, sits there in meditation. Then he pretends as hearing the sound of a chariot approaching.

(आकर्ण्य) अये कुतोऽसौ स्यन्दनध्वनिः। (पुरतो विलोक्य सानन्दम्) एतौ सङ्कर्षणवासुदेवौ स्यन्दनादवतरतः। (पुनर्वासुदेवमवलोक्य सरोमाञ्चम्) कथमहमेनमपरिरभमाणस्तिष्ठामि।

(Listening) Oh, from where do I hear the sound of that chariot? (Looking ahead, with pleasure) Here Saṅkarṣaṇa and Vāsudeva get down from the chariot. (Looking at Vāsudeva, with hairs bristling) How can I remain here without having embraced him?

(ततः प्रविशतः सङ्कर्षणवासुदेवौ)

सङ्कर्षणः – वासुभद्र! इमौ स्वः प्राप्तौ काञ्चनोद्यानम्। अहो रामणीयकमस्य। इह हि-

सान्द्रैः कृतान्यलिकुलानि हिरण्मयानि
हेमप्रसूनमकरन्दरजोवितानैः।
आनीयते परिणतोऽपि महीरुहाणां
छायाभिराभिरतिशैशवमातपोऽयम्।। ४।।

(Saṅkarṣaṇa and Vāsudeva enter)

Vāsubhadra, we have reached this golden garden.

How attractive it is. Here, covered with
golden pollen and honey, the bees seem to be gold.
The golden trees' thick foliage reduces the heat greatly. (4)

Vyaṅgyavyākhyā

Pūrvasambandha

(Kṛṣṇa)[3]

In the age of Kali, Lord resting on the serpent king took birth, by name Vāsudeva and lived in the city of Mathura to protect the world. After exterminating Jarāsandha, Śiśupāla etc. constructed a city in the western coast and lived there. One day after observing the morning rites he reached mother's residence to pay homage to her. Suddenly, his sister Subhadrā came to his notice. He thought -

Ha! This is time for giving her in marriage. She is twelve years now and has come of youthful age. Before attaining puberty she has to be given in marriage to a youth who excels her in learning, beauty and lineage. To whom shall she be given?

It is through her son my reputation on earth has to be sustained. Hence I will give her to the son of my father's sister[4] who is adventurous, heroic and skilled in all branches of knowledge and archery alike.

But there is a flaw in him. He is already married to Draupadī and she is very much affectionate to him.

But there are two things favorable to us in this matter; one is that she is wedded to all the five brothers. Dhanañjaya after winning her in the svayamvara came with brothers to his mother and said – Oh! Mother. We have brought today's bhikṣā. Mother said – share it jointly by all the five. Thus Pāñcālī became wife to all the five brothers. Hence he need spend only one-fifth of the time for her. The other thing favorable is this – sage Nārada has made an arrangement for the five brothers to live with Pāñcālī. Accordingly, she is approachable for one only in an year. Dhanañjaya thus, is free for the other four years. Hence I can give my sister to Dhanañjaya. This small defect can be ignored like avoiding supper when bitten by a non-poisonous snake.

But Draupadī will definitely get angry with Dhanañjaya, Kuntī and me. I can solve it some how. Subhadrā wearing the costume of a milk-maid will approach

3 Balabhadra is simple and straightforward. Hence there is neither suggested sense nor crookedness in his words. But both are employed in the words of the Lord.

4 Kuntī, mother of Dhanañjaya is the sister of Kṛṣṇa's father.

Draupadī for her blessing. Draupadī will be told that she wears this dress fearing her wrath. Pāñcālī, out of her eagerness to see Dhanañjaya, will pardon her and accept their marriage. When the couple enter the city everything will end happily.

Once decided to give the daughter in marriage, parents should inform her the qualities of her would be husband. Then her mind will be struck on him with love. So how can I tell this to her? I will encourage mother to tell her about the adventures and heroic nature of Dhanañjaya.

Thus, mother began to narrate her, occasionally, the stories of Dhanañjaya and his qualities to be a good husband. A few weeks passed by. I understood that she is eager to hear more about him. Then I made a gātrikā where in the ten names of Dhanañjaya were stitched in attractive colours and decorated her breasts with it.

There is a problem giving her to Dhanañjaya. Respected elder brother has resolved to give her in marriage to his disciple Duryodhana. Dhanañjaya's entry to Dvārakā has to be through brother. Dhanañjaya stays in the nearby mountain disguised as an ascetic. Then I can provide facilities for Subhadrā and Dhanañjaya to meet together. Deceiving brother and others in the clan, I will somehow, give Subhadrā to my friend. When Dhanañjaya carries her stealthily, brother, proud as he is, will fight with Dhanañjaya. When the Vṛṣṇis start fighting with all kinds of deadly weapons, none in his senses, will dare to drive the chariot of Dhanañjaya. Subhadrā should then, be of help to Dhanañjaya by driving the chariot. I can pacify and please my brother some how prostrating at his feet with fine words. After that the couple, blessed, shall enter the city with due jewels and other paraphernalia. Hence from today onwards I will teach her to drive a chariot.

Thus Kṛṣṇa taught his sister the art of driving chariot. A few days passed by. One day Kṛṣṇa heard from travellers the details about the pilgrimage of Pārtha. Kṛṣṇa thought:

> I shall give my sister during the occasion of this pilgrimage. When Dhanañjaya reaches Prabhāsa in course of his journey I will send the eloquent Gada and love-inflaming Kāma to Dhanañjaya to bring him here.

How will I show to the handsome Dhanañjaya my beautiful sister who is in the budding stage of her youth.

After a few days Lord Kṛṣṇa realised that Dhanañjaya has reached Prabhāsa. He called Gada secretly and told –

> Dear Gada! go to Prabhāsa immediately and tell Dhanañjaya, without being noticed by others, about my sister Subhadrā.

Then he told Kāmadeva -

> Dhanañjaya immersed in the thought of Draupadī is moving to Indraprastha. Please obstruct him and make an opportunity for him to meet my sister.

After arranging these, Kṛṣṇa engaged Garuḍa to take back Subhadrā from the clutches of the demon. Then Kṛṣṇa came to understand that Dhanañjaya, inflicted by the arrows of cupid, is meditating him.

As my friend is contemplating on me I should go and pacify him. If his marriage to Subhadrā is further delayed he will go to Draupadī, who is waiting for him. I shall give the hand of my sister to Dhanañjaya in the month of Caitra after the winter. I will not allow Pārtha to go to Indraprastha without marrying Subhadrā.

Kṛṣṇa encouraged Kāma to send the arrows again and again. Dhanañjaya, though tried to concentrate his mind on the Lord, could not do so as his mind targeted by Kāma, was shattered. Suddenly he rises up from his seat, then moves around and utters words condemning his own actions: During night he wanders as a mad man in and around the Raivataka mountain.

Realising this pitiable condition of his friend, the Lord smiled. Satyabhāma asked the reason for the untimely laughter. Somehow, by indirect words, he pacified her and won her confidence.[5] In the morning he ordered the chamberlain to make the chariot ready. Completing his morning rites he got into the chariot with Saṅkarṣaṇa and went to the Raivataka mountain. Kṛṣṇa saw Dhanañjaya disguised as an ascetic. He got down from the chariot with his brother and stood there for some time.

The actor in the attire of Kṛṣṇa, transforms to be Kṛṣṇa, and stands still before the lamp, for a while.

वासुभद्रः (आत्मगतम्) नूनमनिच्छतोऽपिच्छद्मान्यसत्ये कर्मण्यवतारयन्त्यतिगुरूणि मित्रकार्याणि। तथा हि,

वेषं दोषानुषङ्गक्षयविशदधियामाश्रयन् मुक्तिभाजां
पार्थः प्रध्वस्तधैर्ये मनसि कृतपदां माधवीं ध्यायतीति।
प्रोद्भिन्नस्य स्मितस्य प्रभवमुपचितप्रेमविक्षिप्तशङ्कां
पृच्छन्तीं सत्यभामामकरमयथाभूतवस्तूपलम्भाम्।। ५।।

(To himself) Though not willing to be untruthful, often the serious affairs of friends force one to resort to falsehood. Thus,

5 Refer to the Miśraviṣkambha of this Act.

Knowing well that Pārtha, having lost his fortitude, is meditating upon Mādhavī assuming the form of a mendicant whose goal ought to be liberation,

I happened to smile involuntarily and Satyabhāmā, after much deliberation, dared to ask the reason behind it, so I misrepresented the fact to her. (5)

Vyaṅgyavyākhyā

One should not speak lie, especially to elders. I can speak the truth, but I have to achieve the union of Dhanañjaya and Subhadrā.

Hence I will convey my elder brother in words mixed with truth and untruth. I will introduce Dhanañjaya as 'Bhagavān'. It is not untrue as he has reached the final stage of smaradaśa.

(प्रकाशम्) आर्य! अयं स भगवानन्त्यमाश्रममनुगृह्णानो हैममध्यास्ते शिलातलम्। उपसर्पावस्तावदेनम्।
(Aloud) Sir, here is that holy saint passing the last of the four stages of human life, occupying a golden rock. Let us approach him.

Vyaṅgyavyākhyā

Here, see the Bhagavān who has reached the last stage of Āśrama.[6]

(Aside)

We used to embrace one another when we meet. But now, I am not able to do that. No harm. Earlier he has prayed me the embrace of Subhadrā only.

Afflicted by the arrows of cupid he may forget the observances of an ascetic. What to do? Yes. I shall do like this -

Oh! Kāma I had ordered to send the arrows to Dhanañjaya. Withdraw them. All the pain caused by your arrows also may disappear from Dhanañjaya. On seeing me he will get back to his heroic stature.

Kāma need not come near to him till he sees Subhadrā. Thinking this, moves....

व्यङ्ग्यव्याख्या

ततः प्रविशति तीर्थवेषधारी धनञ्जयः।

---

6 Āśrama means Dharma and Kāmadaśa. Latter is the suggested sense. He has attained the last stage of Madanāvasthā.

धन – दीर्घं निश्वस्य। तत्र दीर्घनिश्वासनिस्सृतिः कस्मिन् वर्तते सङ्कल्पावस्थाद्योतकं इति विज्ञेयम्। तत्किमर्थमशोकाख्यैश्शरैर्बाध्यमानस्य दशासङ्कल्पं हि तादृशतो अतिमात्रमारूढमदनदशोऽयं तदानीं तत्कथमिति चेत् पश्य! धनञ्जयोयमथ मस्करीभूत्वा तत्र गिरौ वर्तमानोऽयं तत्प्राप्तेरुपायार्थमित्यस्मरत्।

मत्सखोऽद्य मया देव स्मर्तव्योऽनन्यचेतसा।
निजस्मृत्यात्र सम्प्राप्तादुपायो लभ्यतेऽमुतः।।

एवं निश्चित्य तत्र तिष्ठन्नयं तद्ध्यानाय क्षमं प्रदेशमन्विच्छन् किमप्याश्रमचिह्नीभूतस्थं दृष्ट्वा तत्र गत्वा ध्येयो अयमिति निश्चित्य द्वारकापुर्या प्राकारतः शरत्पातमात्रे पुरः पूर्वभागे रैवतकप्रस्थवर्तिनं कञ्चित् काञ्चनोद्यानमभ्येत्य तत्र स्थित्वा मनो भगवति निनीषुरयं धनञ्जयस्तदानीं रसविदां गोष्ठीं कुर्वतां यूनां क्रीडार्थं रचितामतिमनोहरां विचित्ररूपां दृष्टिप्रसादप्रियां तपोनर्हामुद्यानश्रियं वीक्ष्यमाणत्वाद् भगवति नीयमानं चित्तं स्वामेव गच्छदिदं भगवति नेतुमक्षमो भवन्नासीनोऽयं बलात् कथं चित्तं तस्मिन्निन्द्रियाणि मनषट्काणि निनीषुर्यदासीत् तदेव भगवता प्रेर्यमाणेन तत्पुत्रीभूतेन स्मरेणाशोकाख्यान् बाणान् पुङ्खानुपुङ्खं प्रहरता तामेव तद्गमितम्। अथायं भूयोऽपि सशिरःकण्डूभगवन्तमेव कथञ्चिदनयत्। अथ भूयोऽयं स्मरोऽपि तत्रानयतोऽर्जुनस्येन्द्रियपञ्चकचित्तं तस्यामेव बलादकुरुत। अथायं अर्जुनोऽपि तच्छरैर्बाध्यमानत्वाद् ध्यातुमक्षमोऽप्यन्तरान्तरा भगवद्ध्यानं कुर्वंस्तद्बाधया सनिर्वेदमास्त।

अथ स्मरोऽपि भूयः तथासीनमर्जुनं भूयः चूताख्यैश्शरैः प्राहरत्। अथायमर्जुनो भगवति नीयमानं चित्तं बलात् स्वमेव प्राप्तं दृष्ट्वा पारवश्याद् अस्त्वित्युक्त्वा सङ्कल्पेन तामेव स्मरन्नयं चूताख्यैश्शरैर्बाध्यमानत्वाद् तदानीं सङ्कल्पावस्थातो क्षोभजनविरक्तिदायामवस्थायां न्यस्तचित्तो भूत्वा कम्पमानशरीरत्वात् तद्ध्यानाक्षमस्तत्रास्त। अथैवमासीनस्तत्रस्थोऽयं तं स्मरः सत्वरं मल्लिकाख्यैश्शरैराकर्णमाकृष्याविच्छिन्नधारं प्राहरत्। अथ तेन तैर्बाध्यमानोऽयं स्रक्चन्दनाद्युपभोगवस्तुनि विरक्तो भूत्वा पिकभृङ्गेभ्यः प्राक्गतारव-मालाश्रृण्वन्नसहमानस्मरवेदनो भवन्नुत्तरं वर्धिष्णुं मदनदशामवाप्य तदसहिष्णुतया नष्टत्रपतामवाप्यातिमनोहरे कुण्ठिततरणि हृष्यत्कूजत्पिकभृङ्गे तस्मिन्नुद्याने स्थातुमप्यशक्तो भूत्वा तस्मादुद्विष्टिः किं करोमीति स्मरन्निति कर्तव्यतामौढ्यं प्राप्य सचकितं सविवेकं विदूषकेण विना दीपशिखे द्वाभ्यामेव दृग्भ्यां पश्यन्नयं सादयुक्तोऽपि कन्दलितानुभावो भूत्वा तत्रातिष्ठत्।[7]

अथ धनञ्जयभूमिकां विहाय मस्करीभूमिकालङ्कृततनुर्भरतवरो यथानिर्दिष्टमेवं यवनिकाच्छन्नदेहो भूत्वा त्रिवर्त्युज्ज्वलितस्य दीपस्य पुरतो यावत् तिष्ठेत् तावत् यवनिका व्यपनीयताम्।

इत्यपयवनिको भूत्वा यथानिर्दिष्टमेव मुहूर्तं तिष्ठेत्। एवं तिष्ठन्नयमिति स्मरेत्। भगवत्स्मृतिमात्रेणैवात्र प्राप्तवता तेन सह निरूप्य साध्यं मदीयं कार्यमिति मत्वा तद्ध्यानं कुर्वतो मे चित्तमयं मन्मथः तस्यामेवायोजयत्। तस्मात्किं तत्र कार्यमिति न जाने इति स्मरन् मुहूर्तद्वयं तिष्ठेत्। एवं तिष्ठन्नयमिति स्मरेत्। अहो यदहं स्मरेण बाध्ये, तस्मादधुना समया वाच्यो भवेदिति निश्चित्य दुरन्तायाः स्वदशायाः प्रतिक्रियामेव कर्तुं यदा निश्चितवान् तदा सहसा सदीर्घनिश्वासमकरोत्। एवं तदानीन्तनस्य निश्वासस्यायं हेतुः 'दुर्गं कार्यं यदत्येतुं प्राप्योपायं स्मरन् यदा कुर्वतेति कृतधीः पुमान्' इत्यस्ति गुरुवचनम्।

7 The mental condition of the character is analyzed till now. Instruction in the next line is to the actor who takes the role of the character.

तथायं धनञ्जयोऽपि शूर्पकराशीमयेति वाच्य इति यदा निश्चितवान् तदा तस्य श्वासोद्गतिः तदर्थमत्र निस्सृता।[8]

एवं पूर्वसम्बन्धः प्रावेशिकश्च।

अथायमतःपरं भगवदलब्धिहेतोः कामपीडया च चित्तपरवशतया वा भगवद्दर्शनगिरा वक्तुमप्रभुः यथोक्तार्थोऽयं श्लोकः। एवं तिष्ठन्नयं शूर्पशासिनमिति व्यवहृत्य मदनदशामूर्च्छाहेतोर्विस्मृतपूर्वरागो भूत्वा प्रमथकरोन्मोचितां तामन्यामिति समर्थयन् मन्मथमुत्तरश्लोकेन वहति। मया किं सा नोढा इत्यादिना।

तथाभूतास्य मदनदशेति दर्शयितुं स कविस्तथाभूतं कञ्चित् श्लोकं तत्र प्रक्षिप्तवान्। ननु च अत्र क्षणं क्षणं वर्धिष्णुं मदनदशां प्राप्य मदनदशां गच्छतोऽस्य धीरोदात्तस्य नायकस्य बाधा न स्यात्। तत्र दोषो न विद्यते। कुत इति चेत् – पश्य 'कृतकृत्यस्य कामेऽधिकार' इति वात्स्यायनसूत्रम्। ततो अस्य बाधा न स्यात्। किमस्य कृतकृत्यतेति चेत् पश्य –

चिन्तितव्यं सदा सर्वैरेवमामरणान्नृपैः।
कथं मया निराक्रोशं सदसद्वितताविनिः।।
सा मित्रा साब्धिमर्यादा सचोराश्रितदुर्जुना।
सतस्संरक्षतानित्यमसतो निघ्नतादयम्।।
यथेदं मिलितं क्षारैः वयः क्षारं विना विना।
गृह्यतेऽहं स नाम्नात्र तद्वत्सा रक्ष्यते कथम्।।
इति संस्मरतां राज्ञां दुर्लभा कृतकृत्यता।
प्रक्षिप्तानां च केषाञ्चित् स्वधुरं सचिवे पटौ।।

क्वचिज्जातु भवेदेषा नृपाणां जितविद्विषाम्।

तदा स्मररसं भोक्तुं यतते हि नरेश्वरः।
उपक्रोशो मामुना मे स्यादित्ययं स स्मरन् सदा।।
सैवं महीक्षितामेषा रक्षणे भुवि वर्तते।
सचिवे न्यस्तभाराणां तद्भारभरणक्षमे।।
जिष्णोश्चास्य विशेषेण वर्तते कृतकृत्यता।
पित्र्यं वितीर्णं तैरेव धार्तराष्ट्रैर्भियैव तत्।
ज्यायांसौ च कनीयांसौ भवन्त्यवनिरक्षणे।।
क्षमा वीर्यनयोपेता युधिष्ठिरमतानुगा।
युधिष्ठिरोऽभिषिक्तोऽभूत् स च रञ्जितसज्जनः।।
सर्वज्ञोऽयं दीर्घदर्शी सदृशज्ञो महामतिः।
अयं धनञ्जयश्चापि श्रितराजगुणोऽभवत्।।

---

8 A detailed description is given regarding the mental disposition of Dhanañjaya at this time. Dramatist has suggested this in his instruction- dīrgham niśvasya. The explanation hitherto gives the mode of theatrical application of the niśvāsa.

सुखित्वात् कृतकृत्यस्य यद् भवत्यधुना बली।
सुखी तस्मादयं वीरो जितवैरिजितावनिः।।
दशामारोहति स्मारीं वेगाद् वेगाद् क्षणं क्षणम्।

अपि च

श्रीपराशरजातेन मुनिनाखिलवेदिना।
चतुर्धा व्यस्तवेदेन सङ्क्रान्तहरितेजसा।।
वेदानामागमानां च स्मृतेरप्यतिदुर्लभान्।
अर्थानपि तथापारान् धर्माधर्मान् विशेषतः।।
अल्पायुषोऽल्पमनसः द्विजभूपविशः कलौ।
सम्प्रदर्शयितुं तस्माद् पृथक् श्रावयितुं तथा।।
स्त्रियश्शूद्रानमूनर्थान् रचितो भारतार्णवः।
स सुहृत्सम्मितत्वेन रचितेऽस्मिन् महामुनिः।।
प्रदिदृक्षयिषिष्यंस्तान् रसान्नव पृथक् पृथक्।
रणान्ते प्रलपद्भिस्तैः स्त्रीगणैः करुणो रसः।।
तत्र सुप्तवधस्तेन द्रौणिना कुर्वता तथा।
बीभत्सरसमेतस्मिन् निन्द्यं वीरैर्नृपोत्तमैः।।
दुश्शासनवधं तत्र कुर्वता वायुसूनुना।
वीराख्यं रौद्रनामानं रसं चासद्भयप्रदम्।।
मात्स्ये पुरे धार्तराष्ट्रैर्ह्रियमाणे च गोधने।
युद्धं चिकीर्षता तत्र मात्स्यजेनाद्भुताह्वयम्।।
नगरे यज्ञसेनस्य यत्र छेदाय कार्मुकम्।
अमुनोद्धरता हास्याज्जिष्णुना विष्णुरूपिणा।।
दुश्शासनेन दुर्वार्यां कृष्यमाणां दिगम्बराम्।
सभायामक्षवत्यां च निजभार्यां च पुष्पिताम्।।
पश्यता धर्मपुत्रेण निष्कम्प्यं शान्तनामकम्।
अथ अत्र सुभद्राया विवाहं काङ्क्षतामुना।।
बलादाहरता कन्या जिष्णुना यतिरूपिणा।
रसश्शृङ्गारनामानं स मुनिस्सम्प्रदर्शयत्।।

एवं हरेरंशीभूतेन श्रीवेदव्यासनाम्ना महामुनिना धनञ्जयं तथाभूतमिति दर्शितत्वात्; कुलशेखरनाम्ना केरलविषयाधिपेन बहुकृत्वः पीतभारतसुधेन धनञ्जयो अनुक्षणवर्धमानमदनदशो दर्शितः। प्रमाणीभूतेन मुनिना तथा तं दर्शितत्वादस्यामुना नायकबाधा न स्यादिति विज्ञेयम्।

अथैवं दीपपुरस्तिष्ठन्नयं धनञ्जय इति स्मरेत्; अहोऽसाम्प्रतं मया प्राणान् परित्यक्तुम्। कुतः

पुरा शतमुखप्रस्थे पुरेऽस्मासु यथासुखम्।

कुन्त्या भगवता सार्धं याज्ञसेन्या सुहृज्जनैः।।
निवसत्सु निराक्रोशन्नाकतुल्ये निरामयम्।
स्वपुरं गन्तुमुद्युक्तः तदाभून्मधुसूदनः।।
तथाभूतं हरिं पश्यन्नहं कमललोचनम्।
वेदनामगमंस्तीव्रां तद्वियोगमनुस्मरन्।।
स्ववियोगाग्निदन्दह्यमानमानस एष माम्।
ईक्षमीक्षं विषण्णास्यमित्यवोचत्सखा हरिः।।
सखे धनञ्जयैष त्वमशुचं प्राप्नुहि श्रमी।
दशान्तरेण केनापि विपदं यदि यास्यसि।।
तदाहमेत्य तस्याम्बा जवादुक्त्वा ...सौ।
इति प्रोच्य प्रहसन्नात्मा स ययौ द्वारकां प्रति।।
ततोऽयं किं करोतीति न जाने हन्त माधवम्।
भगवन् क्षणमेहि मदीयमिदं हृदयम्।।
हृदयङ्गमकान्ततनो शरणम्।
मम नापरमङ्गहरे त्वदृते।।
त्वदृते यदतोऽत्र दयां कुरुताम्।
स्वजनैस्सह माधव कैश्चिदिमम्।।
स्मितचन्द्रिकया सुखयन्नधुना।
जनमार्तमनङ्गशरैर्निशितै-
स्त्वमिहेत्य चकारय तं विपदः।।
अवतारय मे श्रुतिवर्त्म विभो
त्वदधिश्रितस्य च रथस्य रवम्।
इह मां स जीवयितुमिच्छति चेत्
स्वतनुं व्रजाद् दर्शयाद्य मम।।

एवं धीरोदात्तत्वात् भगवन्तं स्तुत्वा तत्स्तुतेः किञ्चित्प्रशमितमदनजवह्निर्भूत्वा कथञ्चित्पुनरपि स्वकीयं चित्तं चेन्द्रियपञ्चकं अन्तर्मुखं कृत्वा भगवद्ध्यानपरोऽनन्यविन्मुहूर्तद्वयमात्रमत्र स्थितवान्।

एवं मस्करीभूमिकालङ्कृततनुरयं भरतवरोऽपि भगवत्यर्पिताशयस्तत्रासीनो भवेत्। एवमासीनो यदा भवेत् तत् तनुर्यवनिकयाच्छाद्यताम्।[9] एवं भगवत्यर्पिताशयस्तत्रासीनो धनञ्जयो भवन् भरतवरस्सहसा रथध्वनिं श्रृण्वन्निव दर्शयेत्।

कर्णं दत्त्वा **अथे**त्यादि ग्रन्थं वदति। एवं स्यन्दनध्वनिं श्रुत्वा भगवतो निर्वर्तितमना भूत्वा पुरतो विलोकयेत्। एवं विलोक्य सानन्दम्, 'भूयोऽव्ययं' इति वदति पुनर्दामोदरं पश्यन्नाह **सरोमाञ्चम्**।

9 This direction to cover with the curtain seems to be strange. At the entry of the hero curtain was held as usual. Now when he sits on contemplation again curtain is held. If the character is fully covered the audience will not see his responsive acting when he hears the sound of the approaching chariot.

कथमहमित्यादिग्रन्थमुक्त्वा स सङ्कर्षणात् तदागमनादात्मानं सीरिणं यतिरिति विभावयितुमुपासनापर इवासीनो भवेत्।

ततः प्रविशतः सङ्कर्षणवासुदेवौ।

अत्र सङ्कर्षणो बुद्धेः ऋजुतया वक्रोक्तिं वक्तुं ज्ञातुं न प्रभुः। ततोऽस्य ग्रन्थे श्लोके वा वक्रोक्तिध्वनी तेन कविना न प्रयुक्तौ, भगवदुक्तौ द्वावपि विद्येते। तस्मात्तदुक्तौ वक्रोक्तिध्वनी दृश्येते।

वासु – अथानन्तशय्याशायी श्रीपतिः कलौ प्राप्ते भूभारहरणहेतोर्वृष्णिकुले पुरः पुमान् वासुदेवनामा प्रादुर्भूय मधुराख्यां पुरीमधिवसन् जरासन्धविग्रहे तदनुगामिनो महासुरान् निहत्य बहुकृत्वस्तेन विग्रहं कुर्वन् प्रायेण जरासन्धशिशुपालमुक्तासुरान् निघ्नन्नेष पूस्तं रोद्धुमक्षमेति मत्वा पारे पश्चिमसमुद्रद्वारकेति कञ्चित्पुरं निर्माय तस्यां वसन्नयं कस्मिंश्चिदहनि अनुष्ठितनित्यक्रियो भूत्वा स्वमातृवन्दनं कर्तुं मातृभवनमभ्येत्य तद्वन्दनं कृत्वा तत्र तिष्ठन्नयं सहसा तत्रस्थां सुभद्रां निजसोदरीं वीक्ष्येत्यस्मरत्।[10]

हन्त मम स्वसुः प्रदेयकालस्सम्प्राप्तः। कुतः,

पाण्डुत्वं कोष्णतामेति कन्यकायाः कुचद्वयम्।
दृशं लज्जां तनुं कान्तिं प्राप्ता या द्वादशीं समाम्।।
प्रदेयैव तदा पित्रा जन्मरूपाधिकाय सा।
यूने च विदुषे तेन प्रागेवमृतुकालतः।।

इति श्रुतिस्मृतिप्रसिद्धिः। इति तद्विधिं स्मरन्नयं प्रदानकालवयःप्रयान्तीं स्वसारं दृष्ट्वेत्यस्मरत्।

कस्मै स्वसा प्रदेया मे संश्रियद्वीर्यसम्पदे।
जितमन्मथरूपाय यूने सत्राय मानिने।।

किञ्च,

अस्यां मच्चरितश्रोत्रा स्वसुः पुत्रेण मे यशः।
सम्प्रापयिषितव्यस्तत् सदन्वयभुवा भुवि।।[11]
तस्मादेतत्सदृशोऽद्य भुवि पौरवो वासविः।
अयं पराक्रमी वीरो रूपेणाप्रतिमो बली।।
मानी पितृष्वसुः पुनश्शस्त्रास्त्रकोविदः।
तस्मै देया स्वसेयं मे मुखश्रीनिर्जितेन्दवे।।
उत्फुल्ला लोलनीलाक्षी तत्र दोषोऽपि विद्यते।
कृतोद्वाहो नरश्रेष्ठो द्रौपद्यास्स च वल्लभ।।

---

10 The entry is of Saṅkarṣaṇa and Vāsudeva. But the former has no role actually. Hence he does have neither recapitulation nor particular mental disposition.

11 The girl has to be married before she attains the stage of puberty ie. at the age of 12 – prāpta ya dvādaśim samam. Kṛṣṇa's interest in this case is that the son born on his sister will inherit his qualities and he will bring fame to him. This shows that the matrilineal system of inheritance followed at that time. Kerala had accepted matriarchy.

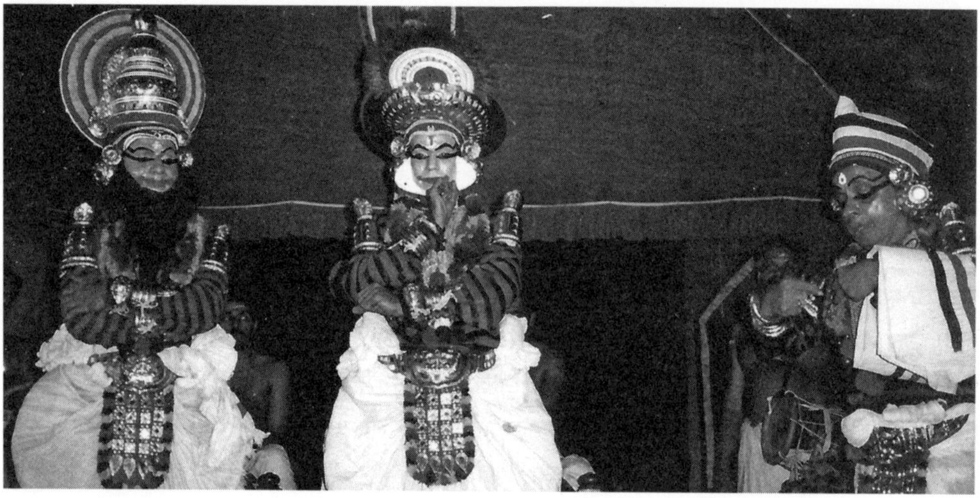

Sajeev Narayana Chakyar (Bālabhadra), Margi Madhu (Śrīkṛṣṇa), Muzhikulam Kochukuttan Chakyar (Kañcukī)

तदीया प्राणनाथेयं तत्र किं शरणं स्मरन्।
भवितव्यतया तत्र गुणद्वयमजायत।।
तद्दुःखापनयार्थं मे सख्युर्जिष्णोरपि स्वसुः।
कुलालभवने पूर्वं यातोऽयं कृष्णया सह।।
जनन्यद्यतनी भिक्षा प्राप्तैषेत्युक्तया तया।
मात्रोक्तोऽयं सुत प्राप्ता युष्माभिर्भुज्यतामियम्।।
विभज्येत्युच्यमानास्तैः पाण्डवैः पञ्चभिस्समम्।
गृहीतपाणिस्सम्भूता यदेषा द्रौपदी पुरा।।
तस्मात् तु पञ्चमो भागो वर्ज्योब्दस्तेन नेतरे।
चत्वारोऽन्येन यस्सार्धं भोज्यास्ते श्वेतसप्तिना।।
एष कश्चिद्गुणोऽयं स्यात् भवितव्यतया मम।
अन्योयं हि गुणोऽयं यो भूयो भूयान् विशिष्यते।।
गुणाम्भोजतनूजेन सङ्केतो यः कृतः पुरा।
तदर्थं स च तन्वङ्ग्या प्राप्यो नाब्देषु कृष्णया।।
तस्मादस्मै प्रदातव्या भगिनी माधवी मया।
लघुस्तत्रेतरो दोषो न गण्योऽगण्य एव सः।।
निर्विषेणाहिना दष्टो मर्त्यस्सन्ध्यागमे यदि।
भोजने तस्य रात्रौ धीः पदं न विदधीत किम्।।[12]

---

12 This is a popular saying in Kerala. One bitten by a poison-less serpent will only loose his supper.

स्वस्रे पार्थाय मह्यं च क्रुद्ध्येद्धि द्रुपदात्मजा।
विदधीत पदं नास्यां यथा रुद्धविवेकिनीम्।।
कार्यस्तद्वदुपायोऽस्मै दत्तायां सह ब्रुम्यथ।
प्राप्स्यन्तौ द्रौपदी यावदिन्द्रप्रस्थाभिधं पुरम्।।
येन केनाप्युपायेन मोहयिष्यामि ताविमौ।
अथ मोहितयोस्तत्र दम्पत्योर्विशतोः पुरम्।।
दशेयं भाविता सा स्यात् पाञ्चाली फल्गुनप्रिया।
त्वद्भयात् धृतगोपालीवेषेयं माधवस्वसा।।[13]
नमितुं त्वान्तरा यान्ती कष्टां गतवती दशाम्।
तद्वात्सल्याच्च तेनाथस्सोऽपि तद्वदभूत् किल।।
इति श्रावितत्तद्वृत्ता भर्तृदर्शनलोलुपा।।
दुःखेन महताविष्टा नूनं शुचमुपेष्यति।
कोपोऽयं प्रेयसि स्त्रीणामभूत् प्राप्तेतराङ्गने।।
अन्यथा नावगच्छेत् स यदा मोहं न यात्यसौ।
इति वात्स्यायनस्योक्तेः प्रभावादपकोपया।।
द्रौपद्या भवितव्यं हि मया सम्भूतदुःखया।
मदर्चनाय वत्सेयं धृतगोपालिका तनुः।।
आयान्ती ह्यन्तरा कष्टां दशां भगवतीति यत्।
तत्कथङ्कारमधुना जीवितं ध्रियते मया।।
वेदोक्तिमन्यथा कृत्वा सदस्य ... वह्निसाक्षिणीम्।
भगिन्याः पत्युरप्येषां काङ्क्षन्ती जीवनं तदा।।
मुमूर्षुश्चेत्सरेदित्थं तौ वीक्ष्य च पुनर्म्रिये।
इति निश्चित्य सा तत्र प्रत्युदेष्यति दुःखिनी।।
भावितौ च तदापेतौ ...गुरुधर्म मत्सुतौ।
उपेष्यतश्च तौ द्रष्टुं दुःखिनौ वेदनान्वितौ।।
तस्यां तयोरथायान्त्यां जीवयिष्यामि तावद...।
येन केनापि तौ ते च दृष्ट्वा यास्यन्ति शर्म च।।
तौ ते सभाजयिष्यन्तः स्वपुरं दम्पती तदा।
मदाहितजनप्रीतिः प्रापयिष्यन्ति ते पुनः।।

It will do no harm to him. In the present case, Arjuna's earlier marriage to Draupadī is not of much consequence since Arjuna's share is limited to one year in five years. Hence Subhadrā can be given to Arjuna. The Malayalam saying reads like this 'nīrkōli kaṭiccāl attāẕaṃ muṭaṅṅuṃ.'

13 In order to pacify Draupadī, Subhadrā enters their city disguised as a cow-herdess. This is described in Act V.

इति स्मरन्नयमागामिनी दशेति भवेदिति निश्चित्य भूयोऽपि तद्विषयमित्यस्मरत्।

दातुं यस्मै सुतां कन्यां पिता निश्चितवान् धिया।
गुणानमुष्य रूपादीन् ज्ञापयेत् कन्यकां तदा।।

इति श्रुतिस्मृतिप्रसिद्धिः। तत्कथमिति चेत् ,

यस्मै दातुं विनिर्दिष्टं जनकेनात्मजां स्वयम्।
तत्र सप्रेम तच्चित्तं बद्धं स्याद् दैवचोदितम्।।

इति श्रुतेरुक्तिः। किञ्च तत्स्रष्टा कल्पितश्च। तस्मात् कथङ्कारमेनं सकलगुणोपेतं तथाभूतं तां श्रावयामीति स्मरन्निति निश्चितवान्।

तस्मान्मात्रन्तिकं प्राप्य प्रापयात्र सहोदरीम्।
यद्दिक्षु दिक्षु कौलीनं तन्मात्रे ज्ञाप्यतां मया।।
तत्प्रस्तावेऽर्जुनं वीरं श्रावयेयं कदाचन।
मातरं स सुभद्रां च यान्तं क्षत्रेपि तान् गुणान्।।

इति निश्चित्यान्वहं मातरं सुभद्रामर्जुनस्य पत्युचितान् गुणान् ज्ञापयन् कतिचित् वाराननयत्। अथ कस्मिश्चिदह्नि तच्चरितश्रवणोत्सुकेऽयमिति विज्ञायेत्यस्मरत्।

रचयिष्याम्यहं तस्यै गात्रिकां बन्धुरद्युतिम्।
तस्यामर्जुननामानि वर्णैस्सन्दर्शयामि ताम्।।

इति स्मरन् निश्चित्य तथाभूतया गात्रिकया तस्याः कुचयुगमलङ्कारयति स्म। भूयोऽपीत्यस्मरत्।

अस्त्यनर्थो महानत्र प्रदानेऽस्यास्तु जिष्णवे।
आर्यस्सुयोधनायैनां दातुकामो हि सर्वदा।।
तस्मादेतत्पुरं जिष्णुं विजने यतिवेषिणम्।
निवसन्तं गिरौ क्वापि नयिष्याम्यत्र सीरिणा।।
अत्र सम्प्रति तं जिष्णुं दर्शयेयं सहोदरीम्।
अन्योन्यं दर्शयिष्यामि घटयिष्यामि तौ बलात्।।
आर्यप्रभृति वृष्णीन्द्रान् येनकेनापि वञ्चयन्।
सख्ये सम्बन्धयोग्याय च प्रदास्याम्यर्जुनाय ताम्।।
अपहृत्य बलादेनां जिष्णौ गच्छति मानिनीं।
आर्यो न क्षमते मानी हली योद्धुं प्रयास्यति।।
अथार्यप्रमुखास्सर्वे यादवाः युद्धदुर्मदाः।
शस्त्रैरस्त्रैरथैकस्मिन् प्रहरिष्यन्ति तेऽर्जुने।।
कुर्वतस्तैस्तदा युद्धमर्जुनस्य तदा रणे।

करिष्यति न सारथ्यं कोऽप्यत्र गतविज्वरः।।
अनया तत्र सारथ्यं कर्तव्यं तत्र गच्छतः।
फल्गुनस्याप्रमेयस्य युद्धशौण्डस्य मानिनः।।[14]
पुनः प्रसादयाम्यार्यमेनमाशु रजस्विनाम्।
वचनैरनुनीयैनं पादप्रणमनादिभिः।।
आर्ये शमितकोपेऽस्मिन्नहं तेनैव सान्त्वयन्।
हरणं प्रापयिष्यामि रत्नमिश्रं सहोदरीम्।।
तस्मादद्यप्रभृत्यैनां रथशिक्षामितःश्रमम्।
शिक्षयिष्यामि तां कन्यामिति निश्चितवानसौ।।

एवं निश्चित्य स्वसारं रथप्रेरणपटीयसीम् कारयन् कतिचित् दिनानि नीत्वा तत्रासीनोऽयं पान्थमुखतोऽर्जुनस्य तीर्थयात्रोदन्तमश्रृणोत्।

अथ श्रुत्वा स भगवान् तीर्थयात्रां महामतेः।
फल्गुनस्य तदा देवः कृष्णः इत्यस्मरत् धिया।।
अमुष्य तीर्थयात्रायामेव देयापि सा स्वसा।
कुर्वाणस्तीर्थयात्रां तां प्रभासमपि चेष्यति।।
प्रभासं फल्गुने प्राप्ते प्रेरितव्यौ मया तदा।
स्मरो युवजनाकाङ्क्षी वाग्मी स गद एव तौ।।

इति स्मृत्वा स्थितोऽयं कृष्ण इत्यस्मरत्।

कथं सर्वगुणोपेतां जिष्णवे चारुदर्शनाम्।
स्वसारं दर्शयिष्यामि सुरूपाय महात्मने।।
बाल्यात्परं वयो यान्तीं कन्यकां कमलेक्षणाम्।
प्रोद्यत्कुचसरोजाभ्यां विराजद्वक्षसं स्वयम्।।

इति स्मरन्तं तं भगवन्तं केषुचित् दिनेष्वतीतेषु काप्यन्तःकरणप्रवृत्तिरर्जुनस्तीर्थसेवार्थं प्रभासतीर्थं प्राप्तवानिति विज्ञापितवती। एवं विज्ञापितोऽयं भगवानर्जुनं प्रति गदकामौ प्रेषितव्याविति स्मृत्वा प्रथमं गदं रहस्यानीयतामिति अवदत्।

गद! गत्वाधुना क्षिप्रं प्रभासस्थं किरीटिनम्।
आवेदय स्वसारं नोऽनन्यविज्ञेयमद्य ताम्।।

भूयः स्मरञ्चेत्यवदत् ,

14 Subhadrā has to run the chariot when she elopes with Arjuna. It is a strange coincidence that the brother also becomes Arjuna's charioteer later in the Kurukṣetra war.

त्वं यियासुं हरिप्रस्थं द्रौपदीगतमानसम्।
अपि रुद्ध्वा स्वसारं मे स्मर सन्दर्शयार्जुनम्।।

एवं तौ नियुज्य कथङ्कारमेनामेनं दर्शयिष्यामीति स्मरन्नयं कृष्णस्स्वसृप्रदाने सुयोधनसीरिणोश्शपथमवगम्य तदर्थमलम्बुसप्रवृत्तिं च ज्ञात्वायमवसरः सहभूपार्थयोः परस्परदर्शनायेति निश्चित्य तद्दर्शनानन्तरं तां पुरं नेतुं पत्रीशमपि नियुज्य स्थितोऽयं सहसा गदवेदितसुभद्रावृत्तान्तं स्मरेण बाध्यमानत्वात् चित्तपारवश्यं यान्तं तत्प्राप्त्युपायार्थमात्मानं ध्यातुमक्षमं दृष्ट्वा भूय इत्यस्मरत् ,

स्मर्यमाणोऽमुना सख्या फल्गुनेन विशेषतः।
तस्माद् गम्यः पुरोऽस्याहमप्ययातमनोरथः।।
अस्याः परिणये कालो दवीयान् मासतोऽमुतः।
त्वरमाणस्स च द्रष्टुं कृष्णां विरहिणीं भवेत्।।
अतीते शैशिरे काले मधावप्यागमिष्यति।
सकाले मत्स्वसुः पाणिं पार्थेन ग्राहयिष्यति।।
तथापि तं हरिप्रस्थमेनामग्राह्यन्नहम्।
न जिष्णुं प्रापयिष्यामि पीडयित्वा मनोभुवम्।।

इति निश्चित्य भूयो भूयस्तं प्रहर्तुं प्रेरयन्नास्ते स्म। एवममर्जुनं बलात्स्वां पुरं स्मरेणानीयमानं तद्गतप्रेमाणं तत्प्राप्तेरुपायो भगवतो लभ्य इति मत्वा भगवन्तं स्मर्तुमक्षमास्थाय तद्ध्यानं कुर्वन्तमपि तन्नियुक्तेन स्मरेण पुङ्खानुपुङ्खं प्रह्रियमाणं तं तत्प्रहरणप्रशकलीकृतचित्तत्वात् ध्यानं कर्तुमक्षमोऽपि भूयो भूयो भगवति चित्तं निनीषुस्तदक्षमत्वात् ततो डोलायिततामेत्य क्षणमासीनं सहसोत्तिष्ठन्तं पुनः किमपि गच्छन्तं पुनः स्वमप्यात्मानं गर्हयन्तं कस्याञ्चिद् निशायां रैवतके गिरौ स्वयमेवोन्मत्तवदाचरन्तं एवम्भूतां दुरवस्थां गच्छन्तं तं दृष्ट्वा हसितवानभूत्।[15] सत्यभामया सह शयानोऽयं भगवान् निशायां हसन्तं प्रेक्ष्य तद्धेतुं पृच्छन्तीं सत्यभामां सङ्क्रान्तशाखान्तरेण वचसा कथञ्चित् विश्वस्तहृदयां तां विधाय काल्ये प्रोत्थाय कञ्चुकिनमाहूय तदानयनार्थं रथं प्रापयेति तं नियुज्यानुष्ठितपूर्वाह्निकक्रियो भूत्वा तेनानीतेन रथेन सङ्कर्षणेन सार्धमागच्छन् यतिवेषिणं धनञ्जयं दृष्ट्वा रथादवतीर्य सङ्कर्षणेन सार्धं कमपि प्रदेशमतिष्ठत्।

एवं पूर्वसम्बन्धः।

अथैवमपनीतयवनिकोऽयं कृष्णभूमिकालङ्कृततनुर्भरतवरः स्वयं कृष्णो भूत्वा दीपाग्रे सप्रसन्नं मुहूर्तं तिष्ठेत्। एवं तिष्ठन्नयं भगवान् आत्मगतं मित्रकार्यगौरवं समर्थयन् सङ्कर्षणेन सार्धं गच्छतः फल्गुनं तथाभूतं दृष्ट्वेति स्मरेत्। अहो उभयथा मे दुरवस्था न न स्यात्।[16]

नानृतं जातु वक्तव्यं विशेषेण गुरूनपि।
अथवा तथ्यवादी स्यां यदि कर्म न मे भवेत्।।

15 This incident was elaborated in the interlude.

16 Śrī Kṛṣṇa is in a predicament. He should speak only the truth, especially to his elder brother. Then how to introduce Arjuna to him? His identity cannot be revealed at this stage, also he cannot tell his brother a lie. He has to speak in words of 'satyānṛta' – true and false!

तस्मात्सत्यान्मिश्रैर्वाक्यैरार्याय फल्गुनः।
मया विज्ञापितव्योऽयं भगवानेष इत्यसौ।।
भगवानिति वाच्योऽयं तदन्वर्थं श्रयन् यतः।
किञ्च स्मरदशामन्त्यां प्राप्नोत्ययमिति छलात्।।

तस्मादर्जुनस्सत्यानृतेर्मयार्याय विज्ञापितव्य इति निश्चित्य उत्तरग्रन्थेन विज्ञापयति **आर्ये**त्यादिना। तत्प्रकारं दर्शयति **अयं स भगवानन्त्यमाश्रममनुगृह्णानो हैममध्यास्ते शिलातलमि**ति। हैमं शिलातलमध्यास्त इति विज्ञाप्यमानेऽस्य वेषविरुद्धेयं चेष्टा किमिति भावेन विज्ञापयन् ग्रन्थं वदेत्। अत्राश्रमशब्दस्सत्यानृतवाचकः,

आचाराधारधर्मेषु प्रतिवेश्मनि च व्रते।
ख्यातो ह्याश्रमशब्दोऽयमासु कामदशास्वपि।।

इति भावेन विज्ञापितोऽयं सङ्कर्षणस्तदा मैव रेरेति सरोषं तमेव पश्यंस्तिष्ठेत्। एवं तेन वीक्ष्यमाणोऽयं सान्तर्मोदम् त्वदवेक्षयैवं तर्हीति विभावयन्नुपसर्पाव इति विज्ञाप्य गच्छन्निति स्मरेत्। हन्तेतः पूर्वमावयोः परस्परदर्शनेनावामुद्वेलस्नेहचपलावपरिरम्भमाणौ कदाचिदपि मनस्विनावतिष्ठाव। इदानीं कथमतथा-भूतस्तिष्ठेयम्। स्मृत्वा तथा मया स्थातव्यम्। पूर्वं लक्ष्मीकुचाङ्कितमुरःपरिपीडयानीति सुभद्रापरिरम्भणमेष प्रार्थितवानिति यत्।[17] ततस्तस्मादपरिरम्भणे प्रार्थनावैमुख्यभाग् न भवामि इति स्मृत्वा सङ्कर्षणेन सार्धमुपसर्पन् भूयोऽपीति स्मरेत्; हन्तार्येण साकं मयि गतवति फल्गुनस्मरदशामूर्छितः श्रितरान्यासवेषः सन् आवां विस्मृतपूर्वापरश्चपलतामेत्यापहास्यौ भवेव। तत्र किं शरणम्। (स्मृत्वा) अस्तु एवं करिष्ये।

पूर्वं बाध्यतामेष त्वयेति प्रेषितो मया।
सवाच्योऽद्याधुना मा प्रहरेत् फल्गुनं प्रति।।
मारज्याचापतो वेगा ज्जिष्णोः शिथिलय क्षणात्।
अस्त्रजा वेदना या स्यात् तस्मात्तामाहरेत्ययम्।।
भूयो मद्दर्शनादेनं प्रापयिष्यामि वीरताम्।
आदर्शनात् सुभद्राया भूयः पश्यतु तं स्मरः।।

इति स्मृत्वा गच्छन्नयं..............[18]

17 Normally when Kṛṣṇa meets Arjuna both the friends used to embrace each other. Now it is not possible because Balabhadra is watching. Kṛṣṇa justifies the action – Arjuna had prayed only for the attainment of Subhadrā, not for meeting him. Recall the suggested sense of 'Lakṣmīkucāṅkitamura'. etc.

18 Vyaṅgyavyākhyā abruptly ends here. The author might definitely have written more, but it is lost to us.

XVI
Recapitulation of Subhadrā in Act V
(New Production)

It has to be presumed that all the Acts of SD were presented on stage earlier, since we get introductory verses for all the five Acts.[1] But for a long time the first Act alone remains in the repertory of the actors. Recently, the second Act also was performed.

Two important productions of the fifth Act are made recently. The first is the entry of Kātyāyanī by Usha Nangyar. The other is the recapitulation of Subhadrā. Both are developed from the context of ततः प्रविशति द्रौपदीवेषधारिणी कात्यायनी गोपालिकावेषधारिणी

1 Araṅṅutaḷiśloka for each Act of Subhadrādhanañjaya is given below:

Act I
कृत्वा प्रदक्षिणमशेषवसुन्धराया-
स्तीर्थावगाहपरिशुद्धमतिप्रभासे।
श्रुत्वा मुकुन्दसहजा मुदिताभिलाषः
पायात्स वः पृथुलकीर्तिभुजः किरीटी।।

Act II
तीर्थस्नानप्रथितमहिमा यस्सुभद्रां प्रणेतुं
पर्याप्तश्रीः परमथ परिव्राजकव्याजवेषः।
यो वा गोपीनयनकुमुदव्रातचन्द्रस्य बन्धुः
सोऽयं युष्मान् शतमुखसुतः पातु गाण्डीवधन्वा।।

Act III
मदनधनञ्जयबद्धो धनञ्जयो माधवीलतागेहे।
तिष्ठन् मुररिपुसहजां ध्यायन् वः पातु यतिवेषः।।

Act IV
रे रे पाण्डव दुष्टयोगिवपुषा भद्रामिमां मायया
धृत्वा धृष्टतरं क्वयासि कुमतेत्याबद्धरोषोद्धतान्।
ज्याघोषेण यदून् विनय्य समितिं रामादिकांस्त्रासयन्
पायाद् कृष्णसहोदरीरथगतः सोऽयं सुरेन्द्रात्मजः।।

Act V
तीर्थस्नाननिराधिरद्भुतयतिर्भूत्वा मुकुन्दानुजा-
मादायाथ विजित्य यादवकुलं गत्वा पुरं चात्मनः।
साक्षात्कृत्य गुरुं वृकोदरयुतः कात्यायिनीलालितः
कृष्णालोकननिर्वृतोऽस्तु भवतां भूत्यै सुरेन्द्रात्मजः।।

सुभद्रा च in the fifth Act. The former is developed as Devīmāhātmyam Naṅṅyārkūttu, the details of which were given in the chapter XII. Dr. Diane Daugherty commissioned the performance of the second, i.e. Subhadrā's entry and nirvahaṇa in 2001 with a grant from the American Institute of Indian Studies.

> 'We decided that there would be five performance: one devoted to Subhadrā's entry (puṟappāṭu) and four to nirvahaṇa. Using copies of the 1989 Āṭṭaprakāram (manual) that I had presented to them, both Usha Nangyar and Margi Sathi began the preparation process by writing their own Āṭṭaprakārams. Usha's acting of śloka X in Subhadrā's nirvahaṇa-First Day- is an example of the license an artist may take in departing from the received Āṭṭaprakāram. This śloka also appears in the manual for Naṅṅyārkūttu -
>
> Hearing of Arjuna's valor and good qualities, etc,
> Subhadrā, the sister of Kṛṣṇa, became lovesick
> With her heart placed in him
> Put on a bodice inscribed with his ten names
> and placed it on her breasts.
>
> The manual for Subhadrā's nirvahaṇa offers this guidance for showing the meaning:
>
> At that time, hearing about the valor, beauty and other qualities of Arjuna, Subhadrā became lovesick. She got the ten names of Arjuna painted on her brassiere and wore it on her chest.
>
> In the manual Usha wrote, Kṛṣṇa orders a breast cloth with the ten names of Arjuna embroidered on it and sends it to his sister, just as does in the manual for Naṅṅyārkūttu. L.S. Rajagopalan asked Usha why she deviated from the manual that she received from me: Why couldn't you do it the way this fellow has it? Usha did not answer. But, she did not really have to; for Kūṭiyāṭṭam grants mature artists liberties.
>
> Both Usha Nangyar and Margi Sathi performed Subhadrā's nirvahaṇa the third day and the fourth day. The similarities and differences between the two interpretations of the same source material by two artists who have the form's gesture vocabulary equally at their command were fascinating.'[2]

---

2 Subhadrā Redux – Reinstating Female Kūṭiyāṭṭam by Diane Daugherty in 'Between Fame and Shame Performing Women – Women Performers in India.' Pages 153 to 167.

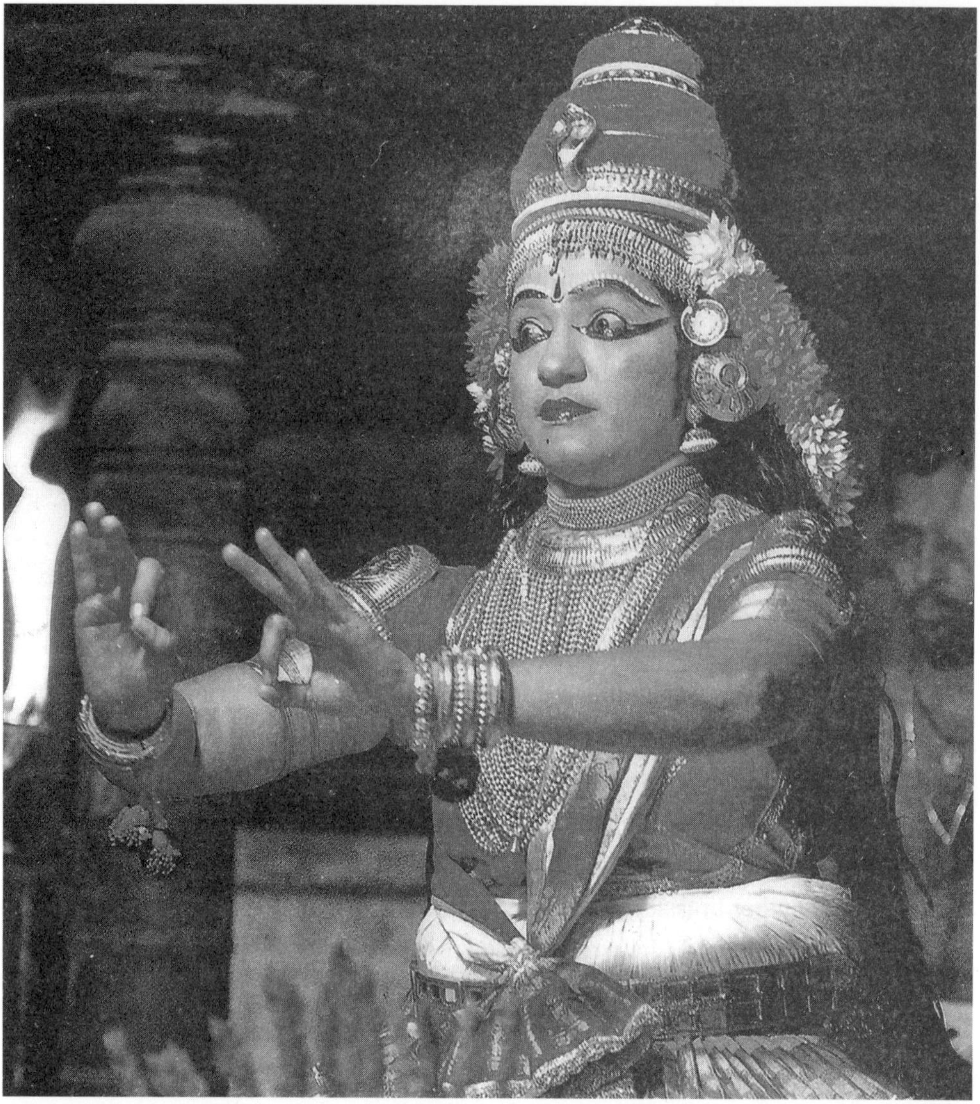

Recapitulation of Subhadrā in Act V, Usha Nangyar

The text of the performance is given below:

Araṅṅutaḷiśloka

तीर्थस्नाननिराधिरद्भुतयतिर्भूत्वा मुकुन्दानुजा-
मादायाथ विजित्य यादवकुलं गत्वा पुरञ्चात्मनः।
साक्षात्कृत्य गुरुं वृकोदरयुतः कात्यायनीलालितः
कृष्णालोकननिर्वृतोऽस्तु भवतां भूत्यै सुरेन्द्रात्मजः।।

अस्ति प्रशस्तविभवा क्षितिकल्पवल्ली
रत्नप्रसूनकलिकेव समुल्लसन्ती।
पुण्या पुरी जलधिवीचिपरीयमाणा
या द्वारकेति विदिता भुवनेषु कीर्त्या।। १

हरिश्च हेमांगदघृष्ट-
मन्दरोगिरिश्च रत्नोपलघट्टिताम्बुदः।
तटाद्रिसंभिन्नजलश्च सागरो
बभूव यस्यां त्रितयं विभूषणम्।। २

त्वष्टुः सदाभ्यासगृहीतशिल्प-
विज्ञानसम्पत्प्रसरस्य सीमा।
अदृश्यतादर्शतलामलेषु
छायेव या स्वज्जलधिर्ज्जलेषु।। ३

मध्ये समुद्रं ककुभः पिशंगी
या कुर्वती काञ्चनशोणभासा।
तुरंगकान्तामुखहव्यवाहा-
ज्वालेव भित्वा जलमुल्ललास।। ४

सुमुहूर्ते तु नक्षत्रे
सकलैर्यादवेश्वरैः।
तस्मिन् प्रवेशनं चक्रे
चक्रपाणिः समंगलम्।। ५

तामध्यास्त पुरीं कृष्णः
सर्वयादवनन्दनैः।
अभिप्रेतजनाकीर्णां
सोमः खमिव भासयन्।। ६

मुररिपुसहजा तस्यां
समजनि कन्या तथा सुभद्रेति।
सकलजननयनकुवलय-
निबोधन चारुचन्द्रलेखेव।। ७

सुरतरुमञ्जरिकेव
प्ररूढनवयौवना मनोज्ञांगी।
कल्पलतिकया च सख्या
बाला षड्पदिकया च साकं ववृधे।। ८

अनुपमगुणरूपां यौव्वनारम्भजृम्भां
निरतिशयमनोज्ञां तां सुभद्रां निरीक्ष्य।
निरचिनुत स कृष्णो जिष्णवे सम्प्रदातुं
निखिलनरपतीनामग्रगण्याय तस्मै।। ९

श्रुत्वार्जुनस्य गुणरूपपराक्रमादीन्
मारातुरा मुररिपोस्सहजा सुभद्रा।
तस्मिन्निविष्टहृदया दशनामधन्यां
तां गात्रिकां स्तनतटे सदयं ननाह।। १०

को एत्थ कोमळयुवापि महाणुहावो
तेळ्ळोक्कदुळ्ळह मणोहर रूपसोहो।
मं पीडियुं पमह हत्थगयं णहादो
पाळ्ळेयि वीरपुरुसो करुणाविहेयो।। ११

अहो विसमसीळोसौ
मदनो वन्धकीमिव।
प्रहरत्यन्यसक्तां मां
दूषयत्येव मानसम्।। १२

सा फल्गुने बद्धमनोभवापि
भूतात् परित्रातरि पूरुषाग्र्ये।
विशेषसञ्जातमनोभवार्ता
समादिदेशात्मसखीं कदाचित्।। १३

प्रमथेन यदा नीता
प्रभासे पतिता तदा।
दशनामाङ्कितां जिष्णो-
स्तां गवेषय गात्रिकाम्।।१४

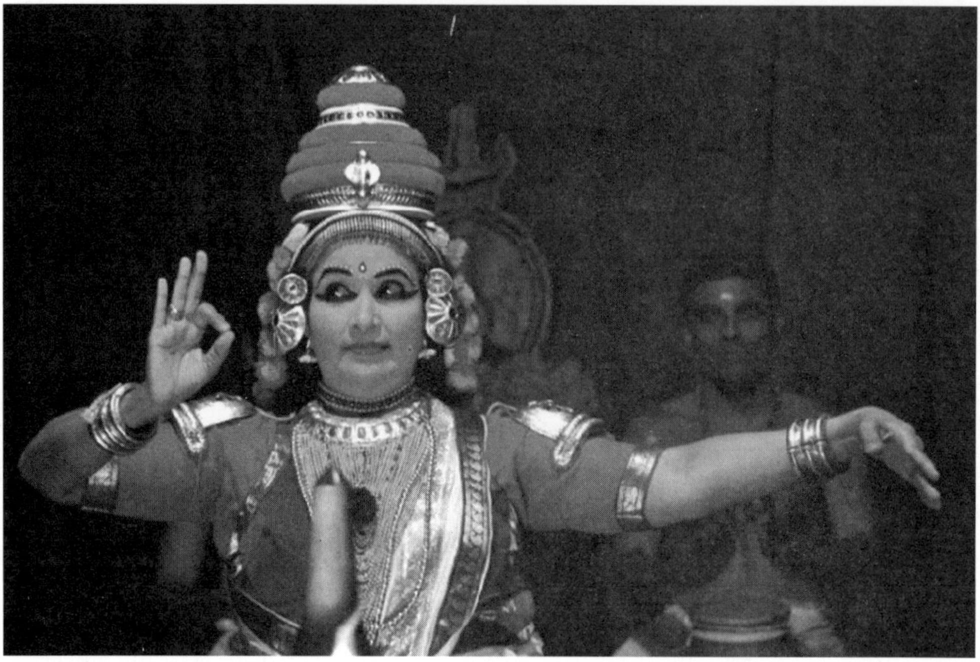

Margi Sathi

भूतकरपरिभ्रष्टा
निपतन्ती येन रक्षिता कृपया।
जननयनानन्दकरः
तत्र गतो वा न वेति जानीयाः।। १५

इति तामादिश्य सखीं
सख्या षट्पदिकया च साकं विजने।
निजनामधेयधन्यं
लतागृहं सा ययौ तन्वी।। १६

पार्थानुरागबद्धं
मम हृदयं पुनरन्यमभिलषतीति
कथमिवाहमधुना
लज्जाहीना वदिष्यामि।। १७

प्रमथग्रहसम्भूता भीतिरद्यापि मां सखि।
न मुञ्चति ततो हेतो नित्यमस्वस्थता मम।। १८

शक्या षट्पदिका न ते छलयितुं
पाण्ड्यत्वमङ्गे परं
वैमुख्यं रमणीयवस्तुषु विना
कान्तिक्षयं क्षामता।
भीत्या किं भवतीदमात्मसदृशी-
भूत्वाधुनाभाजनं
दुःखांशस्य न खल्वतः परमहं
सन्धारयिष्याम्यसून्।। १९

आळि, मा साहसं कार्षी-
रेतच्छुत्वा त्वमेव माम्।
परित्यक्ष्यसि तस्मात्त्वं
शृणु तावद्वचो मम।। २०

जन्मनः प्रभृतिकर्णगोचरं
सांगतैर्विजयविक्रमैर्हृतम्।

अन्यसक्तमपि कुर्वता मनो
मन्मथेन हतकेन दूषितम्।। २१

नह्येष परमो हंसः
मन्ये मदनो गृहीतयतिवेषः।
आयाति पीडितां मां
भूयोपि व्यथयितुं दयाहीनः।। २२

वल्लभत्रयमिष्टं मे कुलस्त्रीणां न तत्क्षमम्।
अस्मिन् जन्मनि तस्मान्मे नैषाशीः सम्भविष्यति।।

आगच्छ, कल्पलतिके
षट्पदिके त्वमपि तावत्।
भगवतो भिक्षां क्षिप्रं
सम्पादयितुं गच्छामो भवनमार्यशासतः।। २४

कन्यकानां शचीदेवी
परमं किल दैवतम्।
तां पूजयित्वाभरणं
प्रधानं ब्राह्मणेर्पय।। २५

अभीष्टवरलाभार्थमागत्य निजमन्दिरात्।
तामपूजयदिन्द्राणीमिन्द्रानुजसहोदरी।। २६

कस्मादात्मैक्यभाजं मा-
मपहायैवमापदि।
अपास्तकरुणाः प्राणाः
यूयं गन्तुं व्यवस्यथ।। २७

किं मन्यद्ध्वे भवत्या सह बहुपुरुषप्रेष्ठया नो वसामो
पापीयस्येति पृच्छाम्यहमिह तु महेन्द्रात्मजे तत्र तावत्।
मत्सक्तेर्वान्यता का भवतरियस्नेह एषोभ्यर्थनीयो
युष्माभिः प्रेमयद्योगिनि न खलु तत्रोत्तरं तत्प्रयातु।।
यावदुपागतवत्यौ सख्यौ
मच्छन्दोर्वहति मा तनुत तावत्।

बहुपुरुषोत्सुकं
ममात्मनां मे बलादपास्यामि।। २९

शङ्कित एव स्थाने
पतितास्मि समागते इमे सखौ।
मन्दायाः मम मरण-
व्यवसायो हन्त विघ्नितो विधिना।। ३०

सख्यौ हन्त भवत्यौ
सम्प्राप्ते किं कुतश्चिदप्यधुना।
पृच्छत उच्चैरस्मत्
कुशलं यस्माद्युवां अपूर्वमिव।। ३१

दुर्लभार्थान्तरौत्सुक्योपहतस्वान्तसम्पदः।
सख्यौ कथयत यावत् किं ममोपनतं सुखम्।। ३२

किमेतेनायान्तं यतिवृषभमुच्चैरविनया-
दधोगत्यां क्षिप्त्वा विधु विमलमस्मत्कुलमिदम्।
कदाचिच्चाप्येवं न खलु हतधीरस्मि मलिनीभूता
करिष्ये दुःखाब्धौ निरवधि निलीयेत्र हि ततः।। ३३

सुष्ठ्वेतद् व्यपदेशेन
सन्त्यज्या तावदेकिका।
गत्वा विज्ञापयाम्बाया
आज्ञापयसि मां तु यत्।। ३४

हन्त सा खलु निर्याता
पुनरस्मादिमामपि।
विसृजामि कथङ्कारं
भवत्वेवमुपायतः।। ३५

कौस्तुभसोदरभूतै-
रमृतमयैरस्ति मौक्तिकैर्घटितः।
सन्तापहरो हारः
सखि, गत्वा समानय त्वरितम्।। ३६

प्रयाते ते सख्यौ स्थलमपि च निर्मानुषमिदं
तदीदृश्यां तावन्मनसिजदशायां निपतिता।
न डोलायिष्येहं त्वरितमतिमुक्ताख्यलतया
समुद्बन्ध्य त्यक्ष्याम्यतिकृपणमात्मानमनया।। ३७

हा हा मातर्जनक वसुदेवार्य हा सीरपाणे
हा मय्युच्चैरविरतकृतस्नेहवात्सल्यशौरे।
हा नन्दात्मन्, पितरयि यशोदाम्बे सैषास्म्यनाथा
पञ्चत्वं याम्यहमिह भवद्दर्शनानन्दहीना।। ३८

हा श्वेतवाहन मनोरथवर
जन्मान्तरेष्वनन्यपदा।
तव परिचरणैकव्यापारै-
र्वेयमस्मि भूयासम्।। ३९

वल्लीपाशैरलमलमदः पीडयित्वा मनोज्ञं
ग्रीवानालं तव तनुतरं चण्डि गाढोपगूढम्।
कर्तुं वाञ्छन्ननुदिनमिदं बाहुपाशो, मदीय-
स्तत्रासक्तं न खलु सहते कर्कशं कालपाशम्।।

भगवन्नयमञ्जलिस्तवायं
समयस्यास्य न दूषणं विधेहि।
मम वा पुरुषत्रयाभिलाषं
परिहारेपि मर्तीं न दूषये।। ४१

सार्धं प्रेम्णा स्तनसरसिजेयत्गते प्रोद्गतेन
त्वत्संस्पर्शात् पुलकितवपुर्यः प्रभासोपकण्ठे।
प्रव्रज्यां प्रणयमकरोद्यश्च सम्प्राप्त एते
तानेवामूनसितनयने तानपि त्रीनवेहि।। ४२

हृदयदयितास्त्वेकीभूता धनञ्जय एव चेत्
विधिरभिमुखीभूतो हर्षः शुचोधिकपीडिता।
अकरवमिदं हर्तुं यत्नं महद्धि शुचाकुला
हर्षजनिता पीडा प्राणान् क्षणेन हरिष्यति।। ४३

जानन् नो दुर्दशामेता-
मभ्येत्य जनको मम।
भ्रातरं वासुदेवं ते
सुत्रामात्वं वरिष्यति।। ४४

सहसुरवनिताभिर्लोकपालैर्मुनीन्द्रैः
अवतरति मरुत्वानम्बरादेषदेवः।
कतिपयपरिवारः कान्तिमानम्बुदश्री-
रयमयमभियातो वासवं वासुदेवः।। ४५

सुरवनिताभिः सुतरां
विभूषिता माधवीलताभवने।
मधुसूदनस्य भगिनी
परिणीता फल्गुनेन सा गूढम्।। ४६

अथ निजपुरयानायोद्यतं कान्तमेषा
रथगतमनुयान्ती साधु सख्यासमेता।
तुरगनिवहतोत्रग्राहिणी मन्दमन्दं
रथमतिमृदुलापि प्रेरयामास साध्वी।। ४७

विपृथुरयमुपयातः प्रस्थिता वृष्णियोधाः
प्रणयिनि, परिखेदं मा कृथाश्चोदयाश्वान्।
अनतिजवमिदं तेनाक्षिणोति श्रमार्ता
श्रमजलकणमुक्ता मुक्तमूलं कपोलम्।। ४८

आर्यपुत्रमुखलग्नलोचना
सावधानमतिरत्र याम्यहम्।
वासुभद्रगुरुशिक्षयापरं
प्रग्रहग्रहणसङ्गतौ करौ।। ४९

अङ्घ्रिक्षेपैरजस्रं धरणि धरभृतः
कम्पयन् भूतधात्रीं
निर्यन्नेत्रानलार्चिः कपिशितभुवनः
कामपालः क्षणेन।

आधावत्येष भीमभ्रुकुटि विषमितः
स्विन्नवक्त्रः समस्तं
क्रुद्धः संहर्तुकामःस्वयमिव भगवान्
धूर्जटिर्धूतसीरः।। ५०

अन्तर्भवद्रिपुसुयोधन सख्यबन्ध-
प्रेंघोलिता प्रणयिना मधुसूदनेन।
मच्छस्त्रकृत्त बलभद्रगलाभिधान-
ग्रन्थिच्छिदाच्छिदुरदुःस्थितिरस्तु मैत्री।। ५१

आजन्मनस्त्वद्गतबद्धचित्ता
त्वामेव नित्यानुगतार्यपुत्र।
कुलक्षयस्याद्यमियं निमित्तं
यथा न शोच्या क्रियतां तथैव।। ५२

लक्ष्यः क्षेपः खुराणां न वियति न भुवि
व्यायताग्रनमंघ्री-
नश्वा, नावक्षिपन्ति क्षपितविचलिता
नाप्यमूनुत्क्षिपन्ति।

यावत् सम्पर्कमेता विदधति पतितै-
श्चाक्षुषैर्नः कराग्रैः-
स्तावत् दूरापयाता न खलु तरुलता-
बुद्धिमुत्पादयन्ति।। ५३

कान्तोपेता पुरमधिगता पाण्डवप्रस्थमस्मिन्
बाह्योद्याने स्थितवति सखीं द्वारकां यापयित्वा।
मानार्थं सा द्रुपददुहितुर्भावमाच्छाद्य गूढं
दुर्गां द्रष्टुं भवनमगमत् गोपिकावेषरम्या।। ५४

देवीं दृष्ट्वा निर्गतालम्बुसेन
व्याजादेषा नीयमाना क्षणेन।
देव्या तस्माद्रक्षिता सानुयाता[3]
कान्तं द्रष्टुं द्रौपदीरूपिणीं ताम्।। ५५

3 *Abhinetri* by Usha Nangyar, Keli, Bombay, 2004.

XVII
Subhadrādhanañjayam Acts II to V

द्वितीयोऽङ्कः।

(ततः प्रविशति चेटी)

चेटी आणत्तह्मि भट्टिदारिआए सुभद्दाए – हञ्जे कप्पलदिए! तस्सिं भूदसम्मद्दे पभसतित्थपरिसरे पब्भट्ठा मे गत्तिआ। तं गवेसिअ आणेहि। अण्णं च, जेण अहं भूदहत्थादो मोआविदा, सो वि महाणुभाओ ळो अणाणन्दअरो तहिं सण्णिहिदो ण वेत्ति संपहारिअ आ अच्छत्ति। सुइरं च मए अण्णोसिअं। ण सा गत्तिआ, ण सो पुरिसो दिट्ठो। किं णु हु भट्टिदारिआए कहइस्सं। (विचिन्त्य) कुमारधणञ्जअस्स णामङ्किदत्ति गत्तिआअं से बहुमाणो। अण्णो वि अण्णोसिऽज्जइ पुरुसत्ति किं विअ एदं। अण्णं च, मए कुदो तस्सिं पमहवुत्तन्ते परमत्थो जाणिदव्वो। (नेपथ्याभिमुखमवलोक्य) एसो अय्यविण-अपालिदो इदो एव्व आअच्छइ। एव्वं दाव पुच्छिरसं। (आज्ञप्तास्मि भर्तृदारिकया सुभद्रया सखि! कल्पलतिके! तस्मिन् भूतसम्मर्दे प्रभासतीर्थपरिसरे प्रभ्रष्टा मम गात्रिका। तां गवेषयित्वानय। अन्यच्च, येनाहं भूतहस्तान्मोचिता, सोऽपि महानुभावो लोचनानन्दकरस्तत्र सन्निहितो नवेति सम्प्रधार्यागच्छ इति। सुचिरं च मयान्वेषितम्। न सा गात्रिका न स पुरुषो दृष्टः। किं नु खलु भर्तृदारिकीयै कथयिष्यामि। कुमारधनञ्जयस्य नामाङ्कितेति गात्रिकायामस्या बहुमानः। अन्योप्यन्विष्यते पुरुष इति किमिवैतत्। अन्यच्च, मया कुतस्तस्मिन् प्रमथवृत्तान्ते परमार्थो ज्ञातव्यः। एष आर्यविनयपालित इव एवागच्छति। एवं तावत् प्रक्ष्यामि।) (ततः प्रविशति काञ्चुकीयः)

काञ्चु आदिष्टोऽस्मि देवेन देवकीनन्दनेन, यथा-विनयपालित! विविक्ते किल रैवतकप्रस्थवर्तिनि काञ्चनोद्याने कश्चिदागन्तुको भवान् परमहंसः सन्निधत्ते। सोऽयमार्येण साकं सङ्कर्षणेन साक्षात्करणीयो मया। तत् सज्जीक्रियतां रथ इति। मया च तदार्यदारुकाय निवेदितम्। जरावक्तव्यचरणतया पुनरियत्यतिविलम्बना संवृत्ता। कुतः –

पातं जलत्वेन समाचरन्ती सदेति हासास्पदतामवाप्ता।
मूर्तिः परामेत्य पुराणतां मे कथं न वाच्या परतन्त्रवृत्तिः।। १।।

चेटी (उपसृत्य) अय्य! कुदो मं अणवेक्खिअ गच्छसि। (आर्य, कुतो मामनवेक्ष्य गच्छसि)

काञ्चु (सावधानं निर्वर्ण्य) कच्चित् कल्पलतिका भवती।

चेटी अय्य! तह। अय्यादो किञ्चि जाणिदुं इच्छामि। को तस्सिं पमहवुत्तन्ते परमत्थो। (आर्य! तथा। अर्यात् किञ्चिद् ज्ञातुमिच्छामि। कस्तस्मिन् प्रमथवृत्तान्ते परमार्थः।)

काञ्चु वत्से! अतीतायां खलु रजन्यामाननारविन्दवर्तिनीमाकस्मिकीं स्मित-चन्द्रिकामवलोक्य निमित्तपरीप्सया देव्या सत्यभामया पर्याप्तपर्यनुयुक्तस्य भगवतः श्रीमुखाम्भोजादेतावदवगत-मस्माभिः, यथा – बलभद्रानुमतिलेशोपलम्भाद् भर्तृदारिकायां सुभद्रायां सञ्जाताभिलाषस्य सुयोधनस्यादेशात् परिवर्तितरूपेण रक्षसालम्बुसेन सा विहायसा नीता भगवत्सङ्कल्पवेदिना गरुत्मता पुनः कुमारीपुरं प्रत्यानीतेति।

चेटी जीवाविदह्मि पदत्तिणाहेण। गच्छदु अय्यो। जाव अहं पि भट्टिदारिआए सआसं गमिस्सं। (जीवितास्मि पवित्रनाथेन। गच्छत्वार्यः। यावदहमपि भर्तृदारिकायाः सकाशं गमिष्यामि।) (निष्क्रान्तौ)

मिश्रविष्कम्भकः

(ततः प्रविशति यतिवेषधरो धनञ्जयः)

धन (दीर्घं निःश्वस्य) अयि भोः शूर्पकशासिन्! अवितथमाहुरागमविदः, यत् परनिबर्हणपराणामप रिहरणीया दुःखपरम्परेति। तथा हि मम –

अतिलङ्घयसि लज्जां धैर्यबन्धं धुनासि
प्रथयसि परितापं प्रश्रयं प्रक्षिणोषि।
अविरतिभिरमीभिः कर्मभिः क्षीयमाणः
स्वयमपि परिपीडामात्मनस्त्वं तनोषि।। २।।

(विचिन्त्य) अप्राप्तसुभद्रासङ्गमे मयि सोऽयमुचितस्ते व्यापारः। अन्तरेण पुनरन्यामन्याय्यमाचरसि। कुतः,

मया किं सा नोढा प्रमथकरदत्ता प्रियतमा
तया किं नाश्लिष्टो रतिरपि न जाता मनसि मे।
दुनोषि त्वं कस्मादनृणमपि तस्यां जनमिमं
स कौण्डिन्यः साक्षी मम भवति तस्मिन् व्यतिकरे।। ३।।

(पुनर्विचिन्त्य) किन्नु खलु प्रस्तुते कर्मणि व्याप्रियमाणं मामनुमंस्यते वयस्यो वासुदेवः। (आकर्ण्य) अये कुतोऽसौ स्यन्दनध्वनिः। (पुरतो विलोक्य सानन्दम्) एतौ सङ्कर्षणवासुदेवौ स्यन्दनादवतरतः। (पुनर्वासुदेव-मवलोक्य सरोमाञ्चम्) कथमहमेनमपरिरभमाणस्तिष्ठामि।

(ततः प्रविशतः सङ्कर्षणवासुदेवौ)

सङ्क वासुभद्र! इमौ स्वः प्राप्तौ काञ्चनोद्यानम्। अहो रामणीयकमस्य। इह हि-

सान्द्रैः कृतान्यलिकुलानि हिरण्मयानि
हेमप्रसूनमकरन्दरजोवितानैः।
आनीयते परिणतोऽपि महीरुहाणां
छायाभिराभिरतिशैशवमातपोऽयम्।। ४।।

वासु (आत्मगतम्) नूनमनिच्छतोऽपिच्छद्मान्यसत्ये कर्मण्यवतारयन्त्यति-गुरूणि मित्रकार्याणि। तथा हि –

वेषं दोषानुषङ्गक्षयविशदधियामाश्रयन् मुक्तिभाजां
पार्थः प्रध्वस्तधैर्ये मनसि कृतपदां माधवीं ध्यायतीति।
प्रोद्भिन्नस्य स्मितस्य प्रभवमुपचितप्रेमविक्षिप्तशङ्कां
पृच्छन्तीं सत्यभामामकरमयथाभूतवस्तूपलम्भाम्।। ५।।

(प्रकाशम्) आर्य! अयं स भगवानन्त्यमाश्रममनुगृह्णानो हैममध्यास्ते शिलातलम्। उपसर्पावस्तावदेनम्।।[1]

(उभावुपसृत्य प्रणामं कुरुतः)

धन स्वस्तिमन्तौ भूयास्तामिहभवन्तौ।

सङ्क उभौ परमनुगृहीतौ स्वः। अपि च भगवन्!

आत्मानं विविनक्षि निह्नुततमोग्रन्थिं प्रकृत्याः परं
कच्चित् कच्चिदुदासते तव धियः कर्मच्छिदः कर्मसु।
अप्यत्येषि गुणानविप्लवकथाभिज्ञां प्रपन्नश्च किं
क्लेशच्छेदपटीयसीमसि दशां द्वन्द्वप्रतिद्वन्द्विनीम्।। ६।।

धन प्रयतेतराममुष्मै श्रेयसे। सिद्धिस्तु पुनरस्य, हृषीकेशस्य कटाक्षपातापेक्षिणी।

वासु न खल्वन्यापेक्षिणी भगवतः सिद्धिः। तथा हि –

यस्याः कृते यतिधुरामवलम्बमानो
    योगं दधासि नचिरादपुनर्निवृत्तिम्।
क्लेशं जहत् सहभुवं मधुरां मतिर्मे
    प्राप्नोषि निर्वृतिमचिन्त्यरसां सुभद्राम्।। ७।।

धन (सहर्षं स्वगतम्) दिष्ट्या दत्तैवामुना मम माधवी। (प्रकाशम्) पुष्करेक्षण! अहममुष्माद् युष्मदनुग्रहात् प्राप्तामेव तां मन्ये।

वासु (अपवार्य) आर्य! क्वनु विविक्तो योगसिद्धये वस्तव्यमिह भगवद्भिः।

सङ्क वासुभद्र! किं नामान्यदतिविविक्तात् कन्यापुरादस्याभिमत-सिद्धयेऽनुरूपम्। (परितो विलोक्य) कोऽत्र भोः।

काञ्चु (प्रविश्य) विजयेतां देवौ। अयमस्मि।

सङ्क विनयपालित! इमं भगवन्तं पुरोधाय कुमारीपुरमुपगतेन भवता वक्तव्या सा माधवी 'अस्य भगवतो विविक्ताभिलाषिणो निजकरपरिवर्धितमाधवीमनोहरं माधवीलतागृहं ध्यानस्थानीकृत्य यथाभिमतमेनं शुश्रूषस्वे'ति। (वासुदेवमवलोक्य) वासुभद्र! किं वा भवान् मन्यते।

वासु नन्वार्य एव प्रमाणमीदृशेषु कर्मसु।

---

1 VV is available only upto this portion.

काञ्चु यथा देवावाज्ञापयतः।

सङ्क भगवन्! पादपांसुभिः पवित्रीक्रियतां कन्यापुरम्। आवामपि निजप्रयोजनाय प्रचलावः। (निष्क्रान्तौ)

काञ्चु (सप्रणामम्) भगवन्नित इतः।

धन बाढम्। (उभौ शैलादवतरणं नाटयतः)

धन (सचिन्तं निःश्वस्य स्वगतम्) अहोतु खलु सत्यमाह लोकः 'साधीयसां वचसां कामदुघाः शक्तय' इति। तथा हि –

भ्रमदलिकुललोलापाङ्गमङ्गं मृगाक्ष्याः
स्तनविनमितमङ्गस्पर्शमप्रत्यनीकम्।
मनसि गिरमुदारां गन्धमघ्रातपूर्वं
जनयति हि सुभद्राशब्दचिन्तामणिर्मे।। ८।। (ध्यायन् परिक्रामति)

काञ्चु (सप्रणामम्) भगवन्नग्रतस्ते कुमारीपुरोपान्तवर्ति प्रमदवनम्। मुहूर्तमत्र विश्रम्यताम्। यावदहमपि चित्रकूटप्रासादगतायै भर्तृदारिकायै सुभद्रायै भगवदागमनं निवेदयामि। (अवलोक्य विचिन्त्य स्वगतम्) अहोतुखल्ववधानशून्योऽयमस्य दृष्टिपातः। मन्ये महात्मनाम् एतादृशानामात्मनि जाग्रतां बहिरिन्द्रियाणि निद्रान्ति। (प्रकाशं भगवन्निति पूर्वोक्तमेव पठति)

धन (श्रुत्वा) एवमस्तु।

काञ्चु अनुगृहीतोऽस्मि। (निष्क्रान्तः)

धन (प्रमदवनप्रवेशं रूपयित्वा परितोऽवलोकयन्) अहोतुखलु रमणीयोऽयमस्य शिशिरात्ययस्य शैशवातिवर्तिनो यौवनोपक्रमः। कुतः –

विश्लिष्यद्दलमालया प्रविरलैः पृथ्वीरुहामासवै-
रन्तर्बद्धकलङ्कया कलिकया प्रस्तूयते मञ्जरी।
गायन्तो गलरागमङ्कुररसैश्चूतस्य चञ्चुक्षते-
श्च्योतद्भिः शिशिरोपरोधशिथिलं पुष्णाति पुंस्कोकिलाः।। ९।।

(स्मृत्वा) क्षणादक्षिणी मे पाययत्येव निजरूपसुधारसं सुभद्रा। यत् पुनरपरमर्थान्तरं, यदि तदप्यस्यां पुरि समासादयेयम्, अहमस्मि पुरस्सरः पुण्यकृताम्।

(नेपथ्ये) हला छप्पदिए! छप्पदिए! (सखि! षट्पदिके! षट्पदिके!)

धनञ्जयः (कर्णं दत्त्वा) अस्मिन् माधवीलतागृहे तन्त्रीस्त्रनसंवादी कलमधुरो ध्वनिः श्रूयते। उपसृत्योपलक्षयामि। (उपसृत्य स्थितः) (ततः प्रविशति कामयमानावस्था सुभद्रा चेटी च)

सुभद्रा हला छप्पदिए! छप्पदिए! (सखि! षट्पदिके! षट्पदिके!)

चेटी भट्टिदारिए! पुव्वं पि अहं सद्दाविदह्मि, ण किञ्चि भणिअ पुणो वि सद्दावीए। किं विअ एदं। (भर्तृदारिके! पूर्वमप्यहं शब्दापितास्मि न किञ्चित् भणित्वा पुनरपि शब्दाप्ये। किमिवैतत्।)

सुभद्रा हला! किं मए सद्दाविदासि। (सखि! किं मया शब्दापितास्मि।)

चेटी (आत्मगतम्) को विअ एसो संमोहो भट्टिदारिआए। तदो भूद सम्भसादो आरहिअ

अण्णादिसी विअ एसा। पुच्छिस्संणं। (प्रकाशम्) आम, सद्दाविदह्मि। किं पुण वत्तुकामासि। (कइवैष सम्मोहो भर्तृदारिकायाः। ततो भूतसंभ्रमादारभ्यान्यादृशीवेषा। प्रक्ष्याम्येनाम्। आम, शब्दावितास्मि। किं पुनर्वक्तुकामासि।)

सुभद्रा हला! सुमरिअ कहइस्सं। (ध्यायति) (सखि, स्मृत्वा कथयिष्यामि।)

धनञ्जयः कथमन्योन्यान्वयशून्यान्यस्या वचांसि। नूनमनया मन्मथशर-शरव्यतामुपगतया भवितव्यम्। भवतु तावदेनां निर्वर्ण्ये निर्णेष्यामि। (लतावलयान्तरेणावलोक्य सहर्षं सरोमोद्गमं च) अये स एवाय-मनिर्णीताकरो मणिः, यदुपलम्भे वयमनाशंसवः संवृत्ताः। (विचिन्त्य) दुर्विभाव्या दैवगतयः। कुतः,

प्रत्यासीदत् पथि कमलिनीं मानसाय प्रयात-
स्तत्रापश्यत् पुनरितपयः पूरदूरावगाढाम्।
भ्रान्त्वा मोहान्न तदुपगतो मानसं राजहंस-
स्तामेवाम्भोविगमसुभगामेष भूयोऽभ्युपैति।। १०।।

चेटी भट्टिदारिए! किं सुमरिअं। (भर्तृदारिके! किं स्मृतम्।)

सुभद्रा (सनिर्वेदं स्वगतम्) पत्थगआणुराअं मम हिअअं अण्णहिं पि पुरुसे ओदरइत्ति सहीणं पि कहं आचक्खी अदि। ता एव्वं कहइस्सं। (प्रकाशम्) हला! पमहबन्दिग्गहणसंभूदा भीदी अज्ज वि मं ण मुञ्चदि। तण्णिमित्ता एसा अस्सत्थदा। (पार्थगतानुरागं मम हृदयमन्यस्मिन्नपि पुरुषेऽवतरतीति सखीनामपि कथमाख्यायते। तदेवं कथयिष्यामि सखि, प्रमथवन्दिग्रहणसम्भूता भीतिरद्यापि मां न मुञ्चति। तन्निमित्तेषास्वस्थता।)

चेटी भट्टिदारिए! ण सक्का छप्पदिआ एव्वं वञ्चेदुं। एदं दाव भणाहि, रम्मेसु विमुहदा, अङ्गेसु पण्डुहावो, अपरिहीयमाणसोहा, परिक्खी-णदत्ति एदं पि किं भीदीए होइ। किं एदिणा। एत्तिअं कालं तुह हिअअणिव्विसेसा भविअ अज्ज एदस्स दुःखसंविभाअस्स अभाअणं अहं इदो वरं ण जीविअसुहाणि अणुभविस्सं। (उत्तिष्ठति) (भर्तृदारिके, न शक्या षट्पदिकैवं वञ्चयितुम्। एतत् तावद् भण। रम्येषु विमुखता, अङ्गेषु पाण्डुभावः, अपरिहीयमाणशोभा, परिक्षीणितेत्येतदपि किं भीत्या भवति। किमेतेन। एतावन्तं कालं तव हृदयनिर्विशेषा भूत्वाद्यैतस्य दुःखसंविभागस्या-भाजनमहमितः परं न जीवितसुखान्यनुभविष्यामि।)

धनञ्जयः (सप्रत्याशम्) सत्यमाह षट्पदिका। अत्रान्तरे किन्नु खलु प्रतिवचनमस्याः।

सुभद्रा (ससंभ्रमं तस्या हस्तमवलम्ब्य सास्रगद्गदम्) हला! मा साहसं करेहि। एदं सुणिअ तुमं एव्व मं परिच्चइस्ससि। ता सुणाहि एदं। (सखि! मा साहसं कुरु! एतच्छ्रुत्वा त्वमेव मां परित्यक्ष्यति। तच्छृणुष्वैतत्।)

चेटी अणुगहिदह्मि। (तया सहोपविशति) (अनुगृहीतास्मि।)

धनञ्जयः (सवितर्कम्) किन्नु खल्वेतत् परिणंस्यति।

सुभद्रा हला! जम्मदप्पहुदि कण्णगोहरगदेहि पत्थपरक्कमेहि असाहारण-परिग्गहिअं में हिअअं अण्णरस वि साहारणं करन्तेण मअणहदएण पण्णइत्थिआणं पदविं आरोविअह्मि। (सखि,

जन्मतः प्रभृति कर्णगोचरगतैः पार्थपराक्रमैरसाधारणपरिगृहीतं मे हृदयमन्यस्यापि साधारणं कुर्वता मदनहतकेन पण्यस्त्रीणां पदवीमारोपितास्मि।)

धन (सोद्वेगम्) धिग् धिग्, विरुद्धशीले!

निष्यन्दमानविनयैरतिसौम्यकान्तैः
प्रख्यापयद्भिरभिजातिममीभिरङ्गैः।
चारित्रलक्षणजुषः प्रतिपूरुषं ते
चेतश्चलच्चलयति प्रसभं मनो मे।। ११।।

अलमनया स्वकुलकलङ्कभूतया। तदमुतः स्थानादन्यत्र प्रतीक्षिष्ये सुभद्रान्वेषिणं कञ्चुकिनम्। (प्रस्थातुमिच्छति)

चेटी (सकौतुकम्) भट्टिदारिए! को णु खु सो पुरुसो। (भर्तृदारिके! को नु खलु स पुरुषः।)

सुभद्रा जेण अहं भूदहत्थादो परिरक्खिदह्मि। (येनाहं भूतहस्तात् परिरक्षितास्मि।)

धन (सहर्षम्) दिष्ट्या सोऽयमेव किलैको जनः पुरुषद्वयभ्रमहेतुरस्याः। मम खलु –

इमौ कर्णौ कर्णौ श्रुतिसुखनिविष्टेदृशगिरा-
वमू दृष्टी दृष्टी सपदि परिपीताकृतिसुधे।
अमून्यङ्गान्यङ्गान्यवशमपतद् येषु गगना-
दिदं चित्तं चित्तं वहति यदिमां वामनयनाम्।। १२।।

(विचिन्त्य) यदवशिष्टमिदानीमस्याः प्रभवसमागमोपायौ चिन्तनीयावित्यत्र कृत्ये सहायः स कौण्डिन्यश्चिरयति।

(नेपथ्ये) अब्बह्मण्णं अब्बह्मण्णं। (अब्रह्मण्यम् अब्रह्मण्यम्।)

धन (कर्णं दत्त्वा) कौण्डिन्यः फूत्कुरुते। किन्नु खल्वस्य व्यसनमापतितम्।

सुभद्रा (ससम्भ्रमम्) को णु खु ब्रह्मणं पीडेइ। (को नु खलु ब्राह्मणं पीडयति।)

चेटी (विलोक्य) भट्टिदारिए! एसा कप्पलदिआ उत्तरीयवासपीडिअगलं णवबद्धं विअ वणवाणरं इदो तदो ओलम्बन्तं अणिच्छन्तं कं पि बह्मणं आकण्ढअन्ती इदो एव्व आअच्छइ। (भर्तृदारिके! एषा कल्पलतिकोत्तरीयवासः पीडितगलं नवबद्धमिव वनवानरमितस्ततोऽवलम्बमानमनिच्छन्तं कमपि ब्राह्मणमाकर्षन्तीत एवागच्छति।)

(ततः प्रविशति यथानिर्दिष्टो विदूषकश्चेटी च)

विदू अब्बह्मण्णं अब्बह्मण्णं। (अब्रह्मण्यम् अब्रह्मण्यम्।)

चेटी एहि दुट्ठबह्मण! (बलादाकर्षति) (एहि, दुष्टब्राह्मण!)

धन हन्त पतितोऽयमीदृश्यामापदि वयस्यः। किमत्र प्रतिविधेयम्। अथवा धर्मोपरोधभयादियमेव साध्वी परिपालयिष्यति।

सुभद्रा (सरोषं) हला! कीस सव्वदसाअं पुअणीआणं बह्म णाणं सरीरोवरोहं करेसि। (सखि! कस्मात् सर्वदशायां पूजनीयानां ब्राह्मणानां शरीरोपरोधं करोषि।)

कल्प पसीददु पसीददु भट्टिदारिआ। इक्कणो ए सो, ण बह्मणो। (प्रसीदतु प्रसीदतु भर्तृदारिका। चोर एषः, न ब्राह्मणः।)

सुभद्रा हला! किं णेण चोरिअं। (सखि! किमनेन चोरितम्।)

कल्प भट्टिदारिए! इदं णेण चोरिअं। (तस्य कर्पटादादाय गात्रिकां दर्शयति) (भर्तृदारिके! इदमनेन चोरितम्।)

विदू (आत्मगतम्) अहो विहिणो पहावो, जो अहं कुम्भीलोत्ति सद्दमत्तं सुणिअ भएण मरणसंसए वत्तामि, सो एव्व दाणिं अहं कुंभीलो णाम संवुत्तो। (प्रत्यक्षं कृपणम्) भो दि अदि बह्मण्णसीले! मम वि वअणं सुणिअ पच्चा अक्खीणि में अवहरिअव्वाणि। (अहो विधेः प्रभावः, योऽहं कुम्भील इति शब्दमात्रं श्रुत्वा भयेन मरणसंशये वर्ते, स एवेदानीमहं कुम्भीलो नाम संवृत्तः। भवति अतिब्रह्मण्यशीले! ममापि वचनं श्रुत्वा पश्चादक्षिणी मेऽपहर्तव्ये।)

सुभद्रा (सस्मितम्) ब्रह्मण! अच्छउ अक्खिवत्ता। कहेहि जहवुत्तं। (ब्राह्मण! आस्तामक्षिवार्ता। कथय यथावृत्तम्।)

विदू (सहर्षम्) भोदि! वअणं विणा कहं कहइस्सं। (भवति, वचनं विना कथं कथयिष्यामि।)

सुभद्रा कहं वअणं विणत्ति। (कथं वचनं विनेति।)

विदू मुहसिरावेहवज्जेण वि एदाए दिढवद्धगलस्स मे कहं वअणणिग्गमो। (मुखसिरोवेधवज्रेणैतया दृढबद्धगलस्य मे कथं वचननिर्गमः।)

सुभद्रा (सस्मितम्) बह्मण! किं अबद्धादो गळादो णिग्गदाणि एदाणि अक्खराणि। (कल्पलतिकामवलोक्य) हला! मुञ्चणं। (ब्राह्मण! किमबद्धाद् गलाद् निर्गतान्येतान्यक्षराणि। सखि! मुञ्चैनम्।)

कल्प जं भट्ठिदारिआ आणवेदि। (मुञ्चति) (यद् भर्तृदारिकाज्ञापयति।)

धन (सहर्षम्) दिष्ट्या मुक्तः कौण्डिन्यः। अहो रूपानुरूपमस्याश्चेष्टितम्।

षट्पदि (जनान्तिकम्) कप्पलदिए! एदेण ब्रह्मणेण एक्को ळाभो उवणओ, जं पञ्चसरपरिपीडिआ एसा एदस्स असंबद्धप्पलावेहि किञ्चि रसन्तरे ओदिण्णा। (कल्पलतिके। एतेन ब्राह्मणेनैको लाभ उपनतः। यत् पञ्चशरपरिपीडितैषा एतस्यासम्बद्धप्रलापैः किञ्चिद् रसान्तरेऽवतीर्णा।)

कल्प सुट्ठु तुए अवहारिअं। (सुष्ठु त्वयावधारितम्।)

विदू (कण्ठं संवादयन्) सुणादु अत्तहोदी। अहं तित्थजत्ताकामुअस्स कस्स वि परमहंसस्स जो असम्भारवाहओ बढुओ। सो अहं हिज्जो पहासतित्थणिअडतवेवणे भिक्खं अडन्तो समावुत्तिअ एदं देक्खिअ गोह्णिअ आदोह्मि। अज्ज उण एदस्सिं णअरे तं भअवन्तं अण्णेसअन्तो एदाए हत्थे पडिदोह्मि। अदो वरं अत्तहोदी एव्व पमाणं। (श्रृणोत्वत्रभवति। अहं तीर्थयात्राकामुकस्य कस्यापि परमहंसस्य योगसम्भारवाहको वटुकः। सोऽहं ह्यः प्रभासतीर्थनिकटतपोवने भिक्षामट न् समावृत्यैतद् दृष्ट्वा गृहीत्वागतोऽस्मि। अध्य पुनरेतस्मिन् नगरे तं भगवन्तमन्विष्यन् एतस्या हस्ते पतितोऽस्मि। अतः परमत्रभवत्येव प्रमाणम्।)

सुभद्रा जुज्जइ। (विदूषकमपवार्य) कप्पलदिए! जाणिदो गत्तिआए आगमो। सो दाणिं कहिं। (युज्यते। कल्पलतिके! ज्ञातो गात्रिकाया आगमः। स इदानीं कः।)

कल्प भट्टिदारिए! दाणिं मए ण सो दिट्ठो। (भर्तृदारिके, इदानीं मया न स दृष्टः।)

सुभद्रा (स्वगतम्) कहिं णु खु सो गओ भवे। (क्व नु खलु स गतो भवेत्।)

धन कथं स इति।

षट्पदि भट्टिदारिए! को अण्णेसिओ पुरुसो। (भर्तृदारिके! कोऽन्विष्टः पुरुषः।)

सुभद्रा (निःश्वस्य) जेण अहं भूदहत्थादो परिरक्खिदा। (येनाहं भूतहस्तात् परिरक्षिता।)

धन (सप्रमोदम्) क्षणादहं दुःखगर्ते पतितोत्तीर्णः।

काञ्चु (प्रविश्य) भर्तृदारिके सुभद्रे! आहतुस्त्वां भ्रातरौ सङ्कर्षणवासुदेवौ।

धन (सप्रमोदं सपुलकोद्गमं च) भगवन्! विधे! इयन्तं कालमपकुर्वन्नपि मम –

तां प्रियां प्रमथपाणिपीडितां
पीवरस्तननिबद्धवेपथुम्।
मुक्तमत्सरमिमां च माधवी-
मेकयन्नुपगतोऽसि बन्धुताम्।। १३।।

विदू (स्वगतम्) दिट्ठिआ एसा सुहद्दा। थाणे खु वअस्सस्स अहिणिबेसो। (दिष्ट्यैषा सुभद्रा। स्थाने खलु वयस्यस्याभिनिवेशः।)

सुभद्रा (सबहुमानम्) अय्य! किं अय्येहि आणत्तं। (आर्य! किमार्याभ्यामाज्ञप्तम्।)

काञ्चु भर्तृदारिके! एवमिव।

सुभद्रा (सबहुमानम्) कहिं पुण दे भअवन्तो। (क्व पुनस्ते भगवन्तः।)

काञ्चु एष प्रवेशयामि। (परिक्रामति)

धन असौ मामन्वेष्टुमायाति। तद् यथास्थाने तिष्ठामि।

सुभद्रा हळा छप्पदिए! तुवारेहि एदाणं पूओवअरणाणि। (सखि! षट्पदिके! त्वरयेतेषां पूजोपकरणानि।)

षट्पदि जं भट्टिदारिआ आणवेदि। (निष्क्रम्य प्रविश्य) भच्चिदारिए! किदं जहाणत्तं। (यद् भर्तृदारिकाज्ञापयति! भर्तृदारिके। कृतं यथाज्ञप्तम्।)

काञ्चु (उपसृत्य सप्रणामम्) भगवन्! एषा माधवी माधवीलतागृहमध्यास्ते। सा भगवद्दृष्टिपातेन पावनीक्रियताम्।

धन बाढम्। प्रथमः कल्पः। आदिश्यतां मार्गः।

काञ्चु भगवन्नित इतः। (परिक्रम्योपसर्पति)

सुभद्रा (ससंभ्रममुत्तिष्ठन्ती स्वगतम्) अम्मो ण एसो परमहंसो। मण्णे मणसिओ परिगहिअवेसन्तरो मं पीडेदुं उवट्ठिओ। अण्णं च दिट्ठमत्तेण एव्व परवसीकिदाणि मे अङ्गाणि। कहं एदस्स उवआरं पडिवड्डिस्सं। (साध्वसकम्पिताभ्यांकराभ्यामञ्जलिं बध्नाति) (सगद्गदम्) भअवं! वन्दामि। (अम्मो नैष परमहंसः मन्ये मनसिजः मां पीडयितुमुपस्थितः। अन्यच्च दृष्टमात्रेणेव परवशीकृतानि मेऽङ्गानि। कथमेतस्योपचारं प्रतिपत्स्ये। भगवन्! वन्दे।)

धन भद्रे! अभिमतभर्तृभागिनी भूयाः।

सुभद्रा (दीर्घं निःश्वस्य स्वगतम्) मम दाव मन्दभाआए वल्लहत्तअं अहिमदं। न कुलइत्थिआणं एसो समुदाआरो। ता एदस्सिं जम्मे ण संभावणीआ एसा आसी। (ममतावद् मन्दभागाया वल्लभत्रयमभिमतम्। न कुलस्त्रीणामेष समुदाचारः। तदेतस्मिन् जन्मनि न सम्भावनीयैषाशीः।)

काञ्चु भर्तृदारिके! अनुष्ठितं शासनं देवयोर्विज्ञापयामि।

सुभद्रा अय्य! एव्वं। (आर्य! एवम्।) (काञ्चुकीयो निष्क्रान्तः)

विदू (सहर्षं स्वगतम्) दिट्ठिआ अवमुच्चुमुहादो कहं वि परिब्भट्ठेण मए दिट्ठो वअस्सो। तक्केमि इदो वरं करग अं अविग्घेण वरिससदीवणं। (दिष्ट्यापमृत्युमुखात् कथमपि परिभ्रष्टेन मया दृष्टो वयस्यः। तर्कयामीतः परं करगतमविघ्नेन वर्षशतजीवनम्।)

षट्पदि (जनान्तिकम्) हला कप्पलदिए! देक्ख जदिसमअविरोहीणि एदस्स चेट्ठिदाइ। (सखि। कल्पलतिके। पश्य यतिसमय-विरोधीन्येतस्य चेष्टितानि।)

कल्प सुट्ठु तुए अवहारिअं। एदाए भट्टिदारिआए एदस्स दंसणेण विउणिओ विअ पञ्चसरपरक्कमो। (सुष्ठु त्वयावधारितम्। एतस्या भर्तृदारिकाया एतस्य दर्शनेन द्विगुणित एव पञ्चशरपराक्रमः।)

सुभद्रा भअवं! सणाहीकिज्जउ एदं आसणं। (भगवन्! सनाथीक्रियता-मिदमासनम्।)

धन बाढम्। (उपविशति)

षट्पदि भट्टिदारिए! संपादिज्जउ एदाणं पूआ। (भर्तृदारिके! सम्पाद्यतामेतेषां पूजा।)

धन (स्वगतम्) अहोतुखल्वकालज्ञा षट्पदिका, यदिमां मनोभवातङ्ककातरामीदृशे कर्मणि नियुङ्क्ते।

सुभद्रा (स्वगतम्) किं करोमि मन्दभाइणी। (प्रत्यक्षम्) हळा! उबणेहि पादोदअं। (किं करोमि मन्दभागिनी। सखि। उपनय पादोदकम्।)

षट्पदि एदं। (उपनयति) (एतत्।)

(सुभद्रा साध्वसकम्पिताभ्यां कराभ्यां कथञ्चित् पादप्रक्षालनं करोति।)

धन (सरोमाञ्चं स्वगतम्)

मम हि रागमिमावतिकोमलावरुणयोस्तलयोरतिपेशलम्।
चरणयोर्निहितौ करपल्लवौ मनसि चित्तममुत्र निषिञ्चतः।। १४।।

सुभद्रा हला! उवणैहि अग्घं। (सखि! उपनयार्घ्यम्।)

षट्पदि एदं। (उपनयति) (एतत्।)

कल्प (विलोक्य) अहो पमादो भट्टिदारिआए। एदं पब्भट्ठं अग्घभाअणं। (अहो प्रमादो भर्तृदारिकायाः। एतत् प्रभ्रष्टमर्घ्यभाजनम्।)

धन अलमिदानीमतिकोमलान्यङ्गान्यायासे निक्षिप्य। पुरस्कृतोऽस्मि। स्वैरमास्तामत्रभवती।

सुभद्रा (अलज्जं स्वगतम्) अस्मो तुलिअह्मि एदेहि। (अम्मो तिलता-स्म्येताभ्याम्।)

विदू एसो वि चोरो एदाणं भअवदाणं सिस्सदाए किं वि पूअणिणो। (एषोऽपि चोर एतेषां भगवतां शिष्यतया किमपि पूजनीयः।)

सुभद्रा (स्वगतम्) अम्मो एदस्स एसो, अणवरुद्धोदाणि। (प्रत्यक्षं कल्पलतिकामुद्दिश्य) हळा! इमं वि पूएहि। (अम्मो एतस्यैषः। अनपराद्ध इदानीम्। सखि, इममपि पूजय।)

विदू जइ किदो ववसाओ, इमाए सग्गरुक्खिआए हत्थे मं णिक्खेवं करेहि। (यदि कृतो व्यवसायः अस्या स्वर्गवृक्षिकाया हस्ते मां निक्षेपं कुरु।)

कल्प (सस्मितं) णामहेअपण्डिद! जदा एदाणं भअवन्दाणं सिस्सोत्ति जाणिदोसि, तदप्पहुदि किदक्खेमं दे सरीरं। (नामधेयपण्डित! यदैतेषां भगवतां शिष्य इति ज्ञातोऽसि, तदाप्रभृति कृतक्षेमं ते शरीरम्।)

विदू जीवाविदोह्मि। अदिसुहिआ होदु अत्तहोदि। (जीवितोऽस्मि। अतिसुखिता भवत्वत्र भवती।)

सुभद्रा (स्वगतम्) अम्मो एदस्स पुरदो खणं वि ण ट्ठादुं पारेमि। ता एव्वं करिस्सं। (प्रत्यक्षम्) हलां छप्पदिए! एहि कप्पलदिए! एहि। एदाणं भअवन्दाणं भिक्खं संपादेह्म। (सप्रणामं परावृत्यावलोकयन्ती सह सखीभ्यां निष्क्रान्ता) (अम्मो एतस्य पुरतः क्षणमपि न स्थातुं पारयामि। तदेवं करिष्यामि। सखि षट्पदिके! एहि! कल्पलतिके! एहि। एतेषां भगवतां बिक्षां सम्पादयामः।)

विदू भो केण दाणिं मूढेण पाडच्चरो भण्डाआररक्खाहिआरं लंभिओ। (भोः केनेदानीं मूढेन पाटच्चरो भाण्डागाररक्षाधिकारे लम्भितः।)

धन (सस्मितम्) स्वयं सङ्कर्षणवासुदेवाभ्याम्।

विदू कहं पुण तुए उवक्कन्तं। (कथं पुनस्त्वयोपक्रान्तम्।)

धन एवमिव।

विदू जुज्जइ। चिट्ठदु एदं। तत्तहोदी सुहद्दा तुह णीदीए अणुदिणं दिट्ठिगोअरे पडिआ। अण्णा अण आ आसइत्थिआ किं आआस-इत्थिआ एव्व संवुत्ता। (युज्यते। तिष्ठत्वेतत्। तत्रभवती सुभद्रा। तव नीत्यानुदिनं दृष्टिगोचरे पतिता। अन्यथ पुनराकाशस्त्री किमाकाशस्त्र्येव संवृत्ता।)

धन सखे! मा मैवम्। इयमेव सुभद्रा तेन प्रमथेन प्रमथ्य नीता।

विदू (विहस्य) सा दाव दाणिं सुहद्दा संवुत्ता, तदाह जण्णसेणी भवे। (सा तावदिदानीं सुभद्रा संवृत्ता, कदाचिद् याज्ञसेनी भवेत्।)

धन वयस्य! अदायपि द्विधाभूतैव मे प्राणेश्वरी। कुतः –

तिष्ठति सततं हृदये
बद्धा प्रेमप्रबन्धपाशेन।
स्तनभरविनमन्मध्या
चलति च दयिता पुरस्तान्मे।। १५।।

विदू (ऊर्ध्वमवलोक्य) भो वअस्स। चिट्ठदु एदं। उट्ठेहि उट्ठेहि। एसो भअवो पहाअरो णहोमज्झं आरूढो। ता ह्मणं करेह्य। (भो वयस्य। तिष्ठत्वेतत्। उत्तिष्ठोत्तिष्ठ। एष भगवान् प्रभाकरो नभोमध्यमारूढः। तत् स्नानं कुर्वः।)

धन बाढम्। (उत्थाय परिक्रामन्नग्रतो विलोक्य) अहो जलविहङ्गमानपि जडयति मध्यन्दिननिदाघावलेपः। तथा ह्यस्यां –

वाप्यामाप्यायितास्यः कमलमधुजलैर्जालपादो विषीद-
न्नार्द्रीकृत्योपयुङ्क्ते रविकिरणपरिक्लिष्टमिष्टं मृणालम्।
वीजन् विक्षेपवत्या सुखयति दयितां वामया चक्रवाक-
श्छत्रीकृत्य प्रयच्छन् प्रणयपरवशो दक्षिणां पक्षपालीम्।। १६।।

तदावामपि प्रकृतं प्रतिपद्यावहे।

(निष्क्रान्तौ)

तृतीयोऽङ्कः।

चेटी (ततः प्रविशति चेटी) आणत्तह्मि भट्टिणीपादेहि – हला गोवद्धणिए! एसु दिअसेसु अदिक्खामगत्तलट्ठी दूसहसन्दावदूमिआ अणहिणंदिआहारावच्छा मे सुहद्दा दीसइ। कण्ण आणं किल देवदा इन्दाणी। तं पूआविअ णिआहरणाणं पहाणभूदं एक्कं भूसणं संपण्णा अ बह्मणा अ दावेहित्ति। मए वि सव्वं भट्टिदारिआए णिवेदिअं। ताए वि सव्वं करिअ कञ्चुई अस्य हत्थेबह्मणणिमित्तं हारो पेसिदो। ता अणुट्ठिअणिओअं अत्ताणं भट्टि णीपादाणं णिवेदइस्सं। (परिक्रामति) (आज्ञप्तास्मि भट्टिनीपादैः सखि गोवर्धनिके! एषु दिवसेष्वतिक्षामगात्रयष्टिः दुस्सहसन्तापदूनानभिनन्दिताहारा वत्सा में सुभद्रा दृश्यते। कन्यकानां किल देवतेन्द्राणि। तां पूजयित्वा निजाभरणानां प्रधानभूतमेकं भूषणं सम्पन्नाय ब्राह्मणाय दापयेति। मयापि सर्वं भर्तृदारिकायै निवेदितम्। तयापि सर्वं कृत्वा काञ्चुकीयस्य हस्ते ब्राह्मणनिमित्तं हारः प्रेषितः। तदनुष्ठितनियोगमात्मानं भट्टिनीपादानां निवेदयिष्यामि।)

द्वितीया (ततः प्रविशति द्वितीया चेटी) आणत्तह्मि देवीए रुव्विणीए। जह-हञ्जे ळव ङ्गिए। आणत्तह्मि अहं सस्सुपादेहि 'अज्ज उक्खमा पुत्ती मे मुभद्दा तेसं भअवन्दाणं भिक्खं संपादेदुं। ताए भारं तुवं ओलम्बेहि'त्ति। ता तुवं गदुअ सुहद्दाए कहेहि मा अत्ताणं आआसेहि। अज्जप्पहुदि तुए कादव्वं तेसं अहं करिस्सं त्ति। ता कहिंणुखु भट्टिदारिआ। (अग्रतो विलोक्य) एसा गकोवद्भणिआ कण्णाउरादो णिक्कमदि। एदं पुच्छिस्सं। (उपसृत्य) सहि! कहिं भट्टिदारिआ वट्टइ। (आज्ञप्तास्मि देव्या रुक्मिण्या। यथा – सखि! लवङ्गिके! आज्ञप्तास्म्यहंश्वश्रुपादैः 'अद्याक्षमा पुत्री में सुभद्रा तेषां भगवतां भिक्षां सम्पादयितुम्। तस्या भारं त्वमवलम्बस्वेति। तत् त्वं गत्वा सुभद्रायै कथय मात्मानमायासय। अद्यप्रभृति त्वया कर्तव्यं तेषामहं करिष्यामीति। तत् क्वनु खलु भर्तृदारिका। एषा गोवर्धनिका कन्यापुरान्निष्क्रामति। एतां प्रक्ष्यामि। सखि! क्व भर्तृदारिका वर्तते।)

प्रथमा अम्मो लवङ्गिआ। सहि! कञ्चणकमलवापिआतीरगए सहआरलदामण्डवे चिट्ठइ। (अम्मो लवङ्गिका सखि! काञ्चन कमलवापिकातीरगते सहकारलतामण्डपे तिष्ठति।)

द्वितीया (सर्वतो विलोक्य) चिट्ठदु इदं। अण्णं किं वि रहस्सं पुच्छिस्सं। कीस एदं अवहदसोहं कण्णाउरं दीसइ। केण वा एक्कहत्थपल्लत्थकवोलमूलाहिं इदोतदो णिसण्णाहिं विसण्णाहिं वि अ दोहिंदोहिं महिलाहिं किं वि मन्तीअदि। (तिष्ठत्वेतत् अन्यत् किमपि रहस्यं प्रक्ष्यामि।

कस्मादेतदुपहतशोभं कन्यापुरं दृश्यते। केन वैकहस्तकपोल-मूलाभ्यामितस्ततो निषण्णाभ्यां विषण्णाभ्यामिव द्वाभ्यां महिलाभ्यां किमपि मन्त्र्यते।)

प्रथमा सहि! तुए वि सुदा भट्टिदारिआए अस्सत्थदा। कीस एदाणं विसादकारणं पुच्छसि। (सखि! त्वयापि श्रुता भर्तृदारिकाया अस्वस्थता कस्मादेतासां विषादकारणं पृच्छसि।)

द्वितीया सहि! तुवं दाव उव्वेलरस मअराअरस्स तरङ्गावलेवं हत्थेण णिवारेसि। तं भअवन्तं भट्टिदारिअं च उद्दिसिअ उट्ठिअं कोलीणं सव्वंस्स णअरजणस्स मुहे सुणाहि। (सखि! त्वं तावदुद्वेलस्य मकारकरस्य तरङ्गावलेपं हस्तेन निवारयसि। तं भगवन्तं भर्तृदारिकां चोद्दिश्योत्थितं कौलीनं सर्वस्य नगरजनस्य मुखे श्रृणु।)

प्रथमा णिम्मूला हि पावआणं पलावा होन्ति। (निर्मूला हि पापकानां प्रलापा भवन्ति।)

द्वितीया एदं विअच्चाहिदं विअ मे मडिहादि, जंसव्वो एव्व जादवसमूहो मासमत्तणिव्वत्तणीअस्स छणस्स किदे अन्तरदीवं गदो। इदाणीं इत्थिआमत्तसारं णअरं। एसो वि वेसन्तरप्पडिच्छण्णो देवउमारो महप्पहावो मक्खरी। ण आणामि किं होदित्ति। (एतदप्यत्याहितमिव मे प्रतिभाति, यत् सर्व एव यादवसमूहो मासमात्रनिर्वर्तनीयस्य क्षणस्य कृते अन्तरद्वीपं गतः। इदानीं स्त्रीमात्रसारं नगरम्। एषोऽपि वेषान्तरप्रतिच्छन्नो देवकुमारो महाप्रभावो मस्करी। न जानामि किं भवतीति।)

प्रथमा उज्जुए! का णाम इअं कहा देवपादभुअरक्खिअस्स णअरस्स। अव्वं एदिणा। तुम अत्तणो णिओअं अणुचिट्ठ। अहं पि भट्टिणीपादाणं सआसं गमिस्सं। (ऋजुके! का नामेयं कथा देवपादभुजरक्षितस्य नगरस्य। अलमेतेन। त्वमात्मनो नियोगमनुतिष्ठ। अहमपि भट्टिनीपादानां सकाशं गमिष्यामि।) (निष्क्रान्ते)

प्रवेशकः।

(ततः प्रविशत्यारूढमदनावस्थो धनञ्जयः)

धन – (दीर्घं निश्वस्य) अयि भोः कुसुमधन्वन्! अपहतहृदयलक्षे मयि मा नीनशः कुसुमशरान्। अविमृश्यकारिणश्च ते मुधाधनुर्धरम्मन्यस्य किञ्चिदुपदिशामि। पश्य –

नेत्रे कर्णान्तयात्राव्यसनिनि कुटिले कुन्तलीमञ्जरीणां
जाले मालेयपङ्कप्रणयिनि कुचयोर्मण्डले पाण्डुबिम्बे।
फुल्लाम्भोजभ्रमाद्वा भ्रमदलिकुलयोःपादयोरङ्गजन्म-
न्नङ्गे त्वं पक्ष्मलाक्ष्याः पुलकिनि मनसः क्वापि मार्गस्व मार्गम्।। १।।

(विचिन्त्य) कष्टं बत प्रेयसीरूपामृतपानविच्छेदविपुलीकृतमहिम्नो वासरस्यास्य यापनसाधनं तत्पयोधरभारपीडनसुभगा गात्रिका, सखा च मे कौण्डिन्य इति द्वयमपि दुर्लभदर्शनमभूत्।

(ततः प्रविशति गात्रिकाहस्तः प्रहृष्टो विदूषकः)

विदू (सविस्मयम्) भो दुवारवदीदो अपरा ण का वि णअरी ब्रह्मणदुब्भिक्खत्ति तक्केमि, जहिं अहं णाम ईरिसस्स महादाणस्स पत्तं होमि। अण्णं च सक्कुणोमि दाव ओट्ठपरिप्फन्दमत्तेण चेडीओ

वञ्चेदुं। अणुदिणं ह्णाणं करन्तो अवस्सं मरिस्सं। एदस्स किं करिस्सं। भोदु, दिट्ठं। पित्तरो आहिभूदो अहं त्ति सव्वजणसमक्खं उग्घोसइस्सं। जाव इमाए गत्तिआए सुभद्दाणुराअपरवसं वअस्सं समासासइस्सं। (परिक्रम्यावलोक्य) एसो वअस्सो माहवीळदामण्डवे माहविं एव्व चिन्तअन्तो उक्किण्णा विअ पडिमा चिट्ठइ। जाव उवसप्पिस्सं णं। (उपसृत्य) जेदु भवं। (भो द्वारवत्या अफरा न कापि नगरी ब्राह्मणादुर्भिक्षेति तर्कयामि, यस्यामहं नामेदृशस्य महादानस्य पात्रं भवामि। अन्यच्च शक्नोमि तावदोष्ठपरिस्पन्दमात्रेण चेटीर्वञ्चयितुम्। अनुदिनं स्नानं कुर्वन्नवश्यं मरिष्यामि। एतस्य किं करिष्यामि। भवतु, दृष्टम्। पित्तरोगाभिभूतोऽहमिति सर्वजनसमक्षमुद्घोषयिष्यामि। यावदनया गात्रिकया सुभद्रानुरागपशं वयस्यं समाश्वासयिष्यामि। एष वयस्यो माधवीलतामण्डपे माधवीमेव चिन्तयन्नुत्कीर्णेव प्रतिमा तिष्ठति। यावदुपसर्पिष्याम्येनम्। जयतु भवान्।)

धन (दीर्घं निःश्वस्य) अहो दुस्सहो मे सन्तापः। किममुष्मात् प्रदेशात् प्रदेशान्तरं शीतलमाश्रयिष्ये। (विचिन्त्य) अथवायमेव श्रेयान्। अत्र हि –

मन्दप्रेङ्खितपल्लवाः स्मरसखैर्मन्दागमैर्मारुतै-
बिभ्राणा मधुवाहिनीर्मधुकरीझङ्कारिणीर्मञ्जरीः।
प्रच्छायप्रतिबद्धशैत्यविभवाः पीडां दधत्योऽपि मे
मन्ये किञ्चिदिमा भवन्ति धृतये तन्नामधन्या लताः।। २।।

विदू अहो ण किञ्चि एदेण सुदं। एव्वं दाव भणिस्सं। भोवअस्स! मारसरेहि तुज्झ कण्णपुडाइ परिपूरिदाइत्ति तक्केमि, जेण बहिरो संवुत्तो। (अहो न किञ्चिदेतेन श्रुतम् एवं तावद् भणिष्यामि। भो वयस्य। मारशरैस्तव कर्णपुटे परिपूरिते इति तर्कयामि, ये बधिरः संवृत्तः।)

धन (विलोक्य) अये वयस्यः कौण्डिन्यः। सखे! किमर्थं विलम्बितोऽसि।

विदू (गात्रिकां दर्शयित्वा) एदं में विलम्बणकारणं। (एतन्मे विलम्बनकारणम्)

धन (सानन्दम्) सखे! कुत इयं समासादिता।

विदू तुमं अन्तरेण मणुस्सा मं पि बह्मणोत्ति पडिवज्जन्ति, जेण अज्ज प्पभादे एव्व तत्तहोदीए सुहद्दाए अणेण एक्को वुड्ढकञ्चुई ओ मह पादयप्पक्खालणं कादूण पडिगेह्ण एदं हारं त्ति मं लम्भिअ गओ। अहं पुण एदस्स अन्धदाविलासो एस भूसणविवज्जासोत्ति चिन्तिअ, होदु, एदाए वअस्सं विणोइस्सं त्ति धेत्तूण आअदो। (त्वामन्तरेण मनुष्या मामपि ब्राह्मण इति प्रतिपद्यन्ते, येनाद्य प्रभात एव तत्र भवत्याः सुभद्राया वचनेनैको वृद्धकाञ्चुकीयो मम पादप्रक्षालनं कृत्वा प्रतिगृह्णैतं हरिमिति मां लम्भयित्वा गतः। अहं पुनरेतस्यान्धताविलास एष भूषणविपर्यास इति चिन्तयित्वा, भवतु, एतया वयस्यं विनोदयिष्यामीति गृहीत्वागतः।)

धन (सहर्षम्) सखे! महत् खलु मित्रकृत्यमनुष्ठितम्। (आदाय हृदये निक्षिपन् सरोमाञ्चम्)

अधुना हृदयममुष्याः स्पर्शामृतवारिपूरसंसिक्तम्।
मनसिजहुतवहदग्धं पुनरिव पश्य प्ररूढं मे।। ३।।

विदू (सविषादम्) भो वअस्स! को णु खु अमाए दुरवत्थाए परिणामो। (भो वयस्य! को नु खल्वस्या दुरवस्थायाः परिणामः।)

धन सखे! नाहमपि जाने। पश्य –

भवति नियतिपाशो नेत्रयोः षट्पदाली
निशिनिशि निशिताग्राः सूचयश्चन्द्रपादाः।
विषहुतवहपातं मालयो मातरिश्वा
मम वपुषि विधत्ते वेत्ति शेषं मनो भूः।। ४।।

विदू भो! चिट्ठदु दाव अणङ्गो। जो तदा पढमदसणे पइट्ठमाणाए तत्तहोदीए सुहद्दए तइ णिक्खित्तो, सो च्चिअ अवङ्गप्पआवई ताए तुमं घटइस्सिदित्ति तक्केमि। (भोः तिष्ठतु तावदनङ्गः यस्तदा प्रथमदर्शने प्रतिष्ठमानया तत्र भवत्या सुभद्रया त्वयि निक्षिप्तः, स एवापाङ्गप्रापतिस्तया त्वां घटयिष्यतीति तर्कयामि।)

धन सत्यमाह भवान्। ममाप्येष एव तर्कः। तथाहि –

याच्ञा प्रेम्णा प्रतीच्छ प्रणयमिति मम त्वं प्रियोऽसीति रागः
सङ्केतस्त्वां प्रपत्स्ये पुनरिति पुरतस्ते स्थितास्मीति लज्जा।
किं भूयोऽपि प्रलापैर्धृतिमुषि ललितभ्रूलतालास्यधन्ये
मन्ये नासीन्न किञ्चिद् विजितकुवलये तत्र नेत्रत्रिभागे।। ५।।

विदू जइ एरिसो से अणुराओ, कीस अदिमत्तं अत्ताणं आआसेसि। ता उभयाणुराअसुहअं सङ्गमकालं पडिक्खन्तो सेरं चिट्ठ। (यदीदृशोऽस्या अनुरागः, कस्मादतिमात्रमायासयति। तदुभयरागानुसुभगं सङ्गमकालं प्रतीक्षमाणः स्वैरं तिष्ठ।)

धन सखे! नाहं न प्रतीक्षिष्ये कालम्। मां पुनरयं बलवदुपरुन्धानो न प्रतीक्षते कामः।

विदू भो वअस्स! का णाम इअं अहीरदा। जस्स दे जण्णसेणीसअंवरसमसंखोभिदाणं खत्तिआणं णं एक्को वि अपरसमूहो आसी, तस्स किल दे एदेहि अदिसुअमारेहि मणसि अपरक्कमेहि विहुरं होइ हिअअं। (भो वयस्य, का नामेयमधीरता। यस्य ते याज्ञसेनीस्वयंवरसमयसंक्षोभित ानां क्षत्रियाणां नैकोऽप्यपराङ्मुख आसीत् तस्य किल ते एतैरतिसुकुमारैर्मनसिजपराक्रमैर्विधुरं भवति हृदयम्।)

धन (विचिन्त्य) सखे! सत्यमश्रद्धेयमेवैतत्। कुतः –

भवति धनुरमूर्तेर्यस्य सङ्कल्पयोने-
र्मधुकरमयमौर्व्यः पेलवाः पुष्पमालाः।
परभृतपरिवारौ यस्य मासावमात्यौ
स किल मयि विधत्ते साहसानीदृशानि।। ६।।

विदू जइ एव्वं, एस पिण्डिअत्थो – पञ्चसरो कुसुमआवो मअरकेदुत्ति एदेहि अदिसुउमारेहि णिरत्थएहि अक्खरोहि केवलं तह्मारिसा कामुआ उग्धोसान्ति। परमत्थदो उण सुण्णपय्याओ कामसद्दो त्ति।

(यद्येवम् एष पिण्डितार्थः पञ्चशरः कुसुमचापो मकरकेतुरित्येतैरति-सुकुमारैरर्थकैरक्षरैः केवलं त्वादृशाः कामुका उद्घोषन्ति। परमार्थतः पुनः शून्यपर्यायः कामशब्द इति।)

धन सखे! नासौ परिहासावसरः, यदियन्तं कालमालम्बनमतिविधुरस्यास्य हृदयस्य, यत् प्रतिदिनं सा दृश्यत इति, तदपि विधिरपहृत्य सङ्क्रमयति स्म मदाराधनाधिकारं तत्रभवत्यां वैदर्भ्याम्। तद्दर्शनदुर्ललितं गलितबन्धनमधुना पततीव मे हृदयम्।

विदू भो! कीस विसीदसि। एदेसु सुरभिससअविअसिदेसु पादवेसु दिट्ंठिह विणोदेहि। (भोः कस्माद् विषीदषि। क्षतेषु सुरभिसमयविकसितेषु पादपेषु दृष्टिं विनोदय।)

धन सखे! अतिदुष्करमुपन्यस्तम्। कुतः,

चकितचकितं चन्द्रालोकाद् भयादपवर्तिते
विकचकमलात् प्रत्यानीते हतात् कमलाकरात्।
मधुकरविषक्षोभाक्लिष्टे वसन्तमहीरुहां
कथमिव सखे! कुर्वीयाता दृशो कुसुमे पदम्।। ७।।

तदलमतिदुस्सहदर्शनैः पदार्थैः। प्रियतमानिरीक्षणोपाय एव तावच्चिन्त्यताम्।

विदू भो वअस्स! सा वि तादिसं पदेसंतरं उव अदत्ति मए सुदं, जहिं पवणस्स विणस्थि पसरों। ता छिंदी अदु एको पक्खो। अण्णं पुण कं पि उवा अं में पण्णाचक्खू दक्खइ। जइ सद्धा,तं सुणाहि। (भो वयस्य! सापि तादृशं प्रदेशान्तमुपगतेति मया श्रुतं यस्मिन् पवनस्यापिनास्ति प्रसरः। तत् च्छिद्यतामेष पक्षः। अन्यं पुनः कमप्युपायं न प्रज्ञाचक्षुः पश्यति। यदि श्रद्धा, तं श्रृणु।)

धन (सप्रत्याशम्) सखे! कथ्यताम्।

विदू अत्थि किल सग्गसारं दामोदरेण अवहुणिअ महीदं आणीदो कामप्पदो रुक्खविसेसो। तं पत्थिअ ए क्कं सुहद्दं याचह्म। (अस्ति किल स्वर्गसारं दामोदरेणापहृत्य मह्यमानीतः कामप्रदो वृक्षविशेषः। तं प्रार्थ्यैकां सुभद्रां याचावहे।)

धन मूर्ख! किं नाम तादृशं कन्यारत्नं सोऽपि पारिजातः प्रसूते। तत् किमेभिर्नर्मप्रलापैः। दुर्निवारनिर्गमा इवामी प्राणाः।

विदू (ससम्भ्रमम्) मा खु मा खु अमङ्गलं भणिअ। संठावेहि अत्ताणं। (माखलु मा खल्वमङ्गलं भणित्वा। संस्थापयात्मानम्।)

धन सखे! सोऽयमशक्यारम्भस्ते नियोगः। कुतः –

मलयशिखरजातैर्मारुतैर्दूरशुष्कं
हिमकरकरजालैः पीडयद्भिः प्रपिष्टम्।
कथय मदनबाणैर्नो गवाक्षीकृतायाः
कथमिव मम तन्वा निष्पतेत् प्राणचूर्णम्।। ८।।

विदू (सविषादमात्मगतम्)पच्चिमं अवत्थं पडिवज्जिदुका मो विअ एसो फलविद। अण्णं च एरिसो एदस्स संमो हो, जं अदिक्कंदं पि सज्झं ण पडिवज्जइ। किं मए कादव्वं। (विचिन्त्य) एव्वं दाव भणिस्सं। (प्रकाशम्) भो! कीस अआरणे अत्ताणं आआसेसि, जं वासुदेवेण सुभद्दा दिण्णत्ति सअं एव्व कहोसि। सा वि साणुराआ तइ त्ति जाणासि एव्व। अप्पच्चणीअं च दे बाहुवलं पच्चेसि। को विअ एसो सम्मोहो। ता मा सन्तप्प। इदाणीं पुण कञ्चणकमलवापिआतीरगणं सह आरलदामण्डवं गच्छह्म। तत्थ गअस्स दे मिणाललदिआतरङ्गाणिलादिहिं सुहअरो सिसिरोवआरो। ता ताहिं एव गच्छह्म। (पश्चिमामवस्थां प्रतिपत्तुकाम इवैष प्रलपति। अन्यच्चेदृश एतस्य सम्मोहः, यदतिक्रान्तामपि सन्ध्यां वप्रतिपद्यते। किं मया कर्तव्यम्। एवं तावद् भणिष्यामि। भोः कस्मादकारण आत्मानमायासयसि, यद् वासुदेवेन सुभद्रा दत्तेति स्वयमेव कथयसि। सपि सानुरागा त्वयीति जानास्येव। अप्रत्यनीकं च ते बाहुबलं प्रत्येषि। क इवैष सम्मोहः। तद् मा सन्तप। इदानीं पुनः काञ्चनकमलवाणिकानीरगतं सहकारलतामण्डपं गच्छावः। तत्र गतस्य ते मृणाललतिकातरङ्गानिलादिभिः सुखकरः शिशिरोपचारः। तत् तत्रैव गच्छावः।)

धन (निःश्वस्य) यद् भवते रोचते। (विदूषांसावलम्बी खेदालसं परिक्रामति)

(ततः प्रविशति दुस्सहमदनातङ्का सुभद्रा)

सुभद्रा (सबाष्पम्) पाणा! कीस मं परिच्चय्य गच्छह। (प्राणाः! कस्मान्मां परित्यज्य गच्छथ।)

विदू (कर्णं दत्त्वा) एदस्सिं सहआरलदामण्डवे किस्से वि इत्थिआए विहुरोह आलावो सुणीअदि। ता ओवारिअस्सरीराओ पेक्खह्म का एस त्ति। (एथस्मिन् सहकारलतामण्डपे कस्या अपि स्त्रिया विधुर आलापः श्रूयते। तदपवारितशरीरौ पश्यावः कैषेति।)

धन सखे! एवं कुर्मः। (तथा कृत्वा पश्यन्) सखे! पश्य पश्य –

श्रमजलजटिलकपोलं बाष्पाम्बुप्रकरसिक्तनेत्रान्तम्।
विधुरं मम खलु हृदयं दीर्घश्वसितं तदेवेदम्।। ९।।

विदू दिट्ठिआ अबुद्धिपुरुवा वि मे णीदी एदस्सिंदसा अं वि पाणसंसआदो तुमं ओवाहेदि, बुद्धिपुरुवा उण सङ्गमं वि कदाइ संपादेदि त्ति तक्केमि। (दिष्ट्याबुद्धिपूर्वापि मे नीतिरेतस्यां दशायामपि प्राणसंशयात् त्वामपवाहयति, बुद्धिपूर्वा पुनः सङ्गममपि कदाचित् सम्पादयतीति तर्कयामि।)

सुभद्रा किं मण्णह, ण तुए भिण्णचारित्ताए सह वसामो त्ति। का णाम तेल्लोक्केक्कधणुद्धरे महिन्दतणए महिन्दाणुअमित्ते रुत्वविहसिअवम्महे अज्जुणे अणुराअस्स वअणीअदा। भूदहत्थादो तुह्माणं परिरक्खए तस्सिं महाणुहावे तुह्मोहि ण दूसणीओ सिणेहो। जो उण अजोग्गे आअन्तुए पव्वजिदे दिढबद्धमूलो अप्पडिआरो अहिलासो, तहिं अणुत्तरह्मि। तण्णिमित्तं जहेट्ठं गच्छह। (किं मन्यध्वे, नत्वया भिन्नचारित्रया सह वसाम इति। का नाम त्रैलोक्यैकधनुर्धरे महेन्द्रतनये महेन्द्रानुजमित्रे रूपविहसितमन्मथेऽर्जुनेऽनुरागस्य वचनीयता। भूतहस्ताद् युष्माकं परिरक्षके

तस्मिन् महानुभावे युष्माभिर्न दूषणीयः स्नेहः। यः पुनरयोग्ये आगन्तुके प्रव्रजिते दृढबद्ध-मूलोऽप्रतीकारोऽभिलाषः, तत्रानुत्तरास्मि। तन्निमित्तं यन्थेष्टं गच्छता।)

धन (सहर्षं सरोमोद्‌गमं च) अहोतुखल्वतिरमणीयोऽयमस्मद्‌भागधेयानां परिपाकः। अमुना पुरनेतानि स्नेहमयान्यक्षरामृतानि श्रावयता कन्दर्पेण प्रमृष्टानि पूर्वकृतान्यागांसि। (पुनः सस्पृहमवलोकयन्) अयि मुग्धे!

अस्यामुल्लसदूर्मिभङ्‌गकलिकाक्लृप्तप्रभेदः प्रिये!
वाप्यामेष परिस्फुरत्प्रतितनुः सूतिः सुधानामिव।
सङ्‌क्रान्तस्तव मानसाम्भसि मुहुः सङ्‌कल्पवीचीचयै-
र्मूर्छद्‌भिर्बहुधा भिदामुपगतः सोऽयं सुजन्मा जनः।। १०।।

विदू एसा दाव तुमं एक्कं एव्व तिहा करिअ कामेदुं पवुत्ता। तुए वि किदं एव्व परिणअणं। अदो वरंपुण जइ मत्तो एक्कं उवदेसं सुणिअ पवुत्तेसि, तदो णिरुवद्दवो दे कामो। (एषा तावत्त्वामेकमेव त्रिधा कृत्वा कामयितुं प्रवृत्ता। त्वयापि कृतमेव परिणयनम्। अतः परं पुनर्यदि मत्त एकमुपदेशं श्रुत्वा प्रवर्तसे, ततो निरुपद्रवस्ते कामः।)

धन (सस्मितम्) सखे! उपदिश्यतां तावत्।

विदू जइ एसा पआसं इन्दप्पत्थं णीअदि, तदो सो धम्मपिसाओ सा अ वुड्ढा तुह बाहुवलणिज्जिदाणं तत्तहोदीअं दोवदीअं विअ एदाअं वि दारविभाअं करेन्ति। तुवं पुण जेट्‌ठरस जणणीए अ सासणं अणणुचिट्‌ठिअ ण चिट्‌ठसि। एव्वं च अदिसङ्‌कडे पडिस्ससि। ता जह .... णेहि णं। (यद्येषा प्रकाशमिन्द्रप्रस्थं नीयते, तदा स धर्मपिशाचःसा च वृद्धा तव बाहुबलनिर्जितायां तत्र भवत्या द्रौपद्यामिवैतस्यामपि दारविभागं कुरुतः। त्वं पुनर्ज्येष्ठस्य जनन्याश्च शासनमननुष्ठाय न तिष्ठसि। एवं चातिसङ्‌कटे पतिष्यसि। तद्यथा न कोऽपीमां न पश्यति, तथैकस्यां मञ्जूषिकायां निक्षिप्यात्मनो नाममुद्रां दत्वा नयैनाम्।)

धन वैधेय! गुरूनप्यधिक्षिपसि।

सुभद्रा (सबाष्पगद्‌गदम्) जाव सहीओ आअच्छिअ मम मरण ववसाअविग्धं उप्पादेन्ति, ताव एदं बहुपुरुसाभिलासपां सुलं पावसरीरं परिच्चइस्सं। (प्रस्थातुमिच्छति) (यावत् सख्यावागत्य मम मरणव्यवसायविघ्नमुत्पादयतः, तावदेतद् बहुपुरुषाभिलाषपांसुलं पापशरीरं परित्यक्ष्यामि।)

धन का नामात्र प्रतिपत्तिः।

(ततः प्रविशतश्चेट्यौ)

चेट्यौ (उपसृत्य सप्रणामम्) अवि सुहं भट्‌टिदारिआए। (अपि सुखं भर्तृदारिकायाः।)

सुभद्रा (स्वगतम्) हद्धि सङ्‌किद एव्व ठाणे पडिदह्मि। (प्रत्यक्षम्) सहीओ! किं अज्ज तुह्मे आअ, जेण अपुव्वं विअ से मुहवुत्तन्तं पुच्छह। (हा धिक् शङ्‌कित एवं स्थाने पतितास्मि। सख्यौ! किमद्य युवामागते, येनापूर्वमिव मे सुखवृत्तान्तं पृच्छथः)

विदू भो! पडिवत्तिमूढाणं अह्माणं बुभुक्खिआणं विअ पाअसं उवट्‌ठिदाओ चेडीओ। (भोः प्रतिपत्तिमूढानामस्माकं बुभुक्षितानामिव पायसमुपस्थिते चेट्यौ।)

धन (सानन्दम्) सखे! सत्यमाभ्यां कृच्छ्रादुत्तारितौ स्वः।

कल्प पसीददु पसीददु भट्टिदारिआ। उवणदं भट्टिदारिआए सुहं अवहारिअ अह्मेहि किं सुहं त्ति पुच्छिदं। (प्रसीदतु प्रसीदतु भर्तृदारिका। उपनतं भर्तृदारिकायाः सुखमवधार्याभ्यां किं सुखमिकि पृष्टम्।)

सुभद्रा किं मे उवणदं सुहं। (किं मे उपनतं सुखम्।)

षट्पदि भट्टिदारिए! दाणिं तुह पादमूलं उवसप्पिदुं आअच्छन्तीहि अह्मेहि तहिं माहवीलदामण्डवे भट्टिदा रिअं अन्तरेण तेसं भअवन्दाणं तस्स गत्ति आचोरस्स अ वम्महामअविसुणं आलावं सुणिअ दूसहाए एदेसं दसाए अदिलहुई भट्टिदारिआए कामपीडत्ति चिन्चिअं। (भर्तृदारिके! इदानीं तव पादमूलमुपगच्छन्तीभ्यामावाभ्यां तत्र माधवीलतामण्डपे भर्तृदारिकामन्तरेण तेषां भगवतां तस्य गात्रिकाचोरस्य च मन्मथामयपिशुनमालापं श्रुत्वा दुस्सहाया एतेषां दशाया अतिलध्वी भर्तृदारिकायाः कामपीडेति चिन्तितम्।)

विदू (स्मृत्वा) जो गत्तिआचोर त्ति एदिगा उग्धादेण सुमरिअं। तहिं माहवीलदामण्डले विसुमरिअं गत्तिअं गोह्णिअ आगमिस्सं। (निष्क्रान्तः) (भो गात्रिकाचोर इत्येतेनोद्घातेन स्मृतम्। तत्र माधवीलतामण्डपे विस्मृतां गात्रिकां गृहीत्वागमिष्यामि।)

सुभद्रा (सावज्ञम्) किं एदिणा। ण दाव अहं तं भअवन्तं हेट्ठदोगईअं णिक्खिविअ अत्तणो वा ससङ्कणिम्मलं कुलं कलङ्कइस्सं। आमरणं पुण एदस्सिं दुक्खण्णवे णिमज्जन्तीचिट्ठामि। चिट्ठदु एदं। किं त्ति तुह्मेहि पुणो विलम्बिअं। (किमेतेन। न तावदहं तं भगवन्तमधोगत्यां निक्षिप्यात्मनो वा शशाङ्कनिर्मलं कुलं कलङ्कयिष्यामि। आमरणं पुनरेतस्मिन् दुःखार्णवे निमज्जन्ती तिष्ठामि। तिष्ठत्वेतत्। किमिति युवाभ्यां पुनर्विलम्बितम्।)

धन सबहुमानम्) अयि प्रेयसि! त्वया खल्वलङ्कतमिदं यादवकुलम्। अपि च –

रागप्रपञ्चपिशुनानि तथा न नाम
पूर्वं त्वया प्रणयपेशलमीरितानि।
निर्वेदयन्ति रमयन्ति यथेदृशानि
चारित्ररूषितपदानि वचांसि चेतः।। ११।।

षट्पदि ताव अ भट्टिणीपादेहि आआरिअ आणत्तह्म। बाल्लिआ मम वअणेण वत्तव्वा वच्छा मे सुभद्दा। जइ तुमं अज्ज देहवुत्तिं ण करेसि, पुण अहं वि सरीरजत्तं ण करिस्सामि त्ति। (तावच्च भट्टिनीपादैराहूयाज्ञप्ते स्वः। बालिका मम वचनेन वक्तव्या वत्सा मे सुभद्रा। यदि त्वमद्य देहवृत्तिं न करोषि, पुनरहमपि शरीरयात्रां न करिष्यामीति।)

सुभद्रा (स्वगतम्) सुट्ठु दाव एदं संवुत्तं। एदेण एव्व ववदेसेण एक्का णिग्गमणीआ। (प्रत्यक्षम्) हला छप्पदिए! गदुअ बिण्णवेहि, जह अम्बा आणवेदि त्ति। (सुष्ठु तावदेत्तत् संवृत्तम्। एतेनैव व्यवपदेशेनैका निर्गमनीया। सखि षट्पदिके। गत्वा विज्ञापय यथाम्बाज्ञापयतीति।)

षट्पदि अमुग्गहिदह्मि। (निष्क्रान्ता) (अनुगृहीतास्मि।)

सुभद्रा (स्वगतम्) एसा दाव कहं णिव्वासइदव्वा। होदु, एव्वं दाव भणिस्सं। (प्रत्यक्षम्) हला कप्पलदिए! अदिदूसहो मम सन्दावो। अत्थि कोत्थुहसोदरेहि मोत्तिएहि अमुअमएहि घडिओ सव्वसन्दावहरो त्ति किदणामहे ओ हारो। तं गह्णिअ आअच्छ। (एषा तावत् कथं निर्वासयितव्या। भवतु, एवं तावद् भणिष्यमि। सखि कल्पलतिके! अतिदुस्सहो मम सन्तापः। अस्ति कौस्तुभसोदरैर्मौक्तिकैरमृतमयैर्घटितः सर्वसन्तापहर इति नामधेयो हारः। तं गृहीत्वागच्छ।)

कल्प कहं एआइर्णी भट्टिदारिअं उज्झिअ गमिस्सं। (कथमेकाकिनीं भर्तृदारिकामुझित्वा गमिष्यामि।)

सुभद्रा (सरोषम्) किं तुवं मं जीवन्तिं णेच्छसि। (किं त्वं मां जीवन्तिं नेच्छसि।)

कल्प का गई। जं भट्टिदारिआ आणवेदि। (अनिच्छन्ती निष्क्रान्ता)। (का गतिः। यद् भर्तृदारिकाज्ञापयति।)

धन अये निर्जनीकृतोऽयं लतामण्डपः, आरब्धं मन्ये मरणायानया। भवतु। दृढपरिकबन्धस्तदवहितीस्तिष्ठामि।

सुभद्रा (समन्तादवलोक्य) दिट्टिआ णिम्माणुसो अअं पदेसो। ण इदो वरं कामुम्मादे वन्धइत्तणेडोलाइस्सं। ता एदस्स वालसहआरस्स साहावलम्बिदाए अदिमुत्तलदाए जहासमीहिदं करिस्सं। (लतामादाय बाष्पं मुञ्चन्ती) हा अम्ब! हा ताद! हा अय्य बलभद्द! हा मइ णिच्चबद्धजीविअसुह वासुभद्द! हा अम्ब जसोदे! हा ताद णन्दगोव! एसा अहं अणाहा विअ तुह्माणं दसणसुहस्स अच्चन्दागोअरं पच्चिमं दसं पडिवज्जामि। हा अज्जुण! मणोरहदइअ! जम्मान्तरे वि अणण्णसाहारणाणुराआ तुज्झा पादसूस्सूआ भवेअं। (कण्ठे पाशमर्पयति) (दिष्ट्या निर्मानुषोऽयं प्रदेशः। नेतः परं कामोन्मादे बन्धकीत्वे दोलायिष्ये। तदेतस्य बालसहकारस्य शाखावलम्बितयातिमुक्तलताया यथा समीहितं करिष्यामि। हा अम्ब! हा तात! हा आर्य बलभद्र! हा अम्ब यशोदे! हा तात नन्दगोप! एषाहमनाथेव युष्माकं दर्शनसुखस्यात्यन्तगोचरां पश्चिमां दशां प्रतिपद्ये। आ अर्जुन! मनोरथदयित! जन्मान्तरेऽप्यनन्यसाधारणानुरागा तव पादशुश्रूषिका भवेयम्।)

धनञ्जयः (ससम्भ्रममुपसृत्य लतापाशमाक्षिपन्)

वल्लीपाशैरलमलमदः पीडयित्वा मनोज्ञं
ग्रीवानालं तवतनुतरं चण्डि! गाढोपगूढम्।
कर्तुं वाच्छन्ननुदिनमयं बाहुपाशो मदीय-
स्तत्रासक्तं न खलु सहते कर्कशं कालपाशम्।। १२।।

सुभद्रा (सरोषम्) को मम पणअभंगं करोदि। (पुनर्विलोक्य) भअव एसो दे अञ्जली। मा दाव इमिणा समअविरो हिणा वावारेण अत्तणो मुत्तिपहं दूसेहि। मम वि तिपुरुसपणअपापप्पडिआरं परलोअगइं ण पण्डिबन्धेहि। (को मम प्रणयभङ्गं करोति। भगवन्। एष तेऽञ्जलिः मा तावदमुना समयविरोधिना व्यापारेणात्मनो मुक्तिपथं दूषय। ममापि त्रिपुरुषप्रणयपापप्रतीकारं परलोकगतिं न प्रतिबधान।)

धनञ्जयः अयि मुग्धे! अलमेभिरसन्मूलैः सङ्कल्पविकल्पैः।

सार्धं प्रेम्णा स्तनसरसिजे प्रोद्गते यद्गतेन
त्वत्संस्पर्शात् पुलकितवपुर्यः प्रभासोपकण्ठे।
प्रव्रज्यायां प्रणयमकरोद् यश्च सम्प्राप्तये ते
मामेवामूनसितनयने! तानपि त्रीनवेहि।। १३।।

सुभद्रा (सप्रमोदं स्वगतम्) अम्मो एदे मम हिअआवहारिणो दइओ धणञ्जओ एव्व संवुत्तो। (हर्षकम्पिताङ्गी) हद्धि, सो आदो विउणं असज्झवेदणा मे पीदी। सो ए दाव पाणाणं परिच्चाए महन्तो पआसो किदो। एह्निं पुण सअं एव्व णिग्गच्छन्ति विअ मे पाणा। (कथञ्चिदात्मानं धारयन्ती तिष्ठति) (अम्मो एते मम हृदयापहारिणो दयितो धनञ्जय एव संवृत्तः। हा धिक् शोकाद् द्विगुणमसह्यवेदना मे प्रीतिः। शोके तावत् प्राणानां परित्यागे महान् प्रयासः कृतः। इदानीं पुनः स्वयमेव निर्गच्छन्तीव मे प्राणाः।)

कल्प (प्रविश्य हारहस्ता, लतापाशमवलोक्य सविषादम्) किण्णु खु भट्टिदारिआए ववसिदं। (सबाष्पं पादयोः पतति) (किन्नु खलु भर्तृदारिकया व्यवसितम्।)

सुभद्रा (ससम्भ्रममुत्थाप्य) सहि! मा विसादं करेहि। (कर्णे) एव्वं विअ। (सखि, मा विषादं कुरु एवमिव।)

कल्प विट्ठिआ जीवाविदह्मि भट्टिदारिआए। इमं दाव हारं विणा अण्णो को वि सव्वसन्दावहरो संवुत्तो। (पार्तमवलोक्य) जेदु कुमारो। (प्रणामं करोति) (दिष्ट्या जीवितास्मि भर्तृदारिकया। अमुं तावद् हारं विनान्यः कोऽपि सर्वसन्तापहरः संवृत्तः। जयतु कुमारः।)

धन प्रिये! मया किलायमनन्यजन्मा क्षत्रसमुचितेन गान्धर्वेण परिणयमार्गेण तव पाणिमग्राहयन् न विरमति। तदस्य परिपूर्यतामभिलाषः।

(सुभद्रा सस्पृहं धनञ्जयमवलोक्य दीर्घं निःश्वस्य बाष्पं मुञ्चन्ती तिष्ठति)

धन (सवितर्कं स्वगतम्) ध्रुवमियं विना वासुदेवानुमतिमपारयन्ती मत्प्रार्थनां परिपूरयितुमीदृशं वैधुर्यमवलम्बते। तदेवं तावत्। (प्रत्यक्षम्) प्रिये! मा स्म विषीदः।

जानन् नो दुर्दशामेतामभ्येत्य जनको मम।
भ्रातरं वासुभद्रं ते सुत्रामा त्वां वरिष्यति।। १४।।

सुभद्रा (जनान्तिकम्) सहि! दाणिं सङ्कडादो उत्तारिदह्मि। (सखि! इदातीं सङ्कटादुत्तारितास्मि।)

(माधवीधनञ्जयौ माधवमहेन्द्रौ ध्यायतः)

विदू (सर्वतो विलोक्य) भो पेक्खपेक्ख। एदे रक्खसा पि सा आ अ आआसादो ओदरन्ति। एदे उड्डी अन्तो पापाद भूमीअ णिपडन्ति। ता तुरिअं खेमअरं पदेसं गच्छह्म। (भो पश्य पश्य एते राक्षसाः पिशाचाश्च आकाशादवतरन्ति। एत उड्डीयमानाः प्रासादभूम्यां निपतन्ति। तत् त्वरितं क्षेमकरं प्रदेशं गच्छावः।)

सुभद्रा (सभयम्) हद्धि, किण्णुखु एदं। (हा धिक्! किन्नु खल्वेतत्।)

धन भीरू ! मा भैषीः। स एष कौण्डिन्यस्य सम्मोहः। मन्ये स्मृतमात्रोपनतस्य पितुर्मे पाकशासनस्य समवतारपिशुनोऽयं दिव्यजनपरिच्छदः।

(नेपथ्ये)

सह सुरवनिताभिर्लोकपालैर्मुनीन्द्रै-
रवतरति मरुत्वानम्बरादेष देवः।

धन (आकर्ण्य) केनेदमावेदितम्।

देवदूतः (प्रविश्य, सह सुरेत्यादि पूर्ववत् पठित्वा अन्यतो विलोक्य)

कतिपयपरिवारः कान्तिमानम्बुदश्री-
रयमयमभियातो वासवं वासुदेवः।। १५।।

अपि च माधवीलतागृहे सम्भृतविविधवैवाहिकोपकरणो होतुं सन्नह्यति भगवान् काश्यपः। इमां च माधवीं मङ्गलस्नानपुरस्सरमाकल्पविधानं कल्पयितुमाहूतवती जननी ते पौलोमी। त्वया च पितरं प्रणम्य प्रस्तूयतां परिणयनविधिः।

धन यदाज्ञापयन्ति गुरवः।

देवदूतः इतइतो भवति। (सपरिवारया सुभद्रया सह निष्क्रान्तः)

विदू भो वअस्स ! किं एदं। (भो वयस्य ! किमेतत्।)

धन (सस्मितम्) एवमिव।

विदू (सानन्दम्) जइ एव्वं, मम वि वरव अस्सस्स मण्डणेण होदव्वं। ता पडिग्गहगहीदाए इमाए गत्तिआए अत्ताणं मण्डइस्सं। (गात्रिकां कण्ठे समर्पयति) (यद्येवं ममापि वयवस्यस्य मण्डनेन भवितव्यम्। तत् प्रतिग्रहगृहीतयानया गात्रिकयात्मानं पण्डयिष्यामि।)

धन वेत्सितरामाभरणविनियोगस्थानानि। (नेपथ्ये)

अत्रभवत्याः सुभद्रायाः –

माणिक्योन्मिषितां बधान जघने त्वं मेनके ! मेखलां
केशान् मिश्रय मिश्रकेशि ! कुटिलान् मन्दारमालागुणैः।
रम्भे ! लम्भय पत्रभङ्गरचनामस्याः कपोलस्थली-
मुर्वीमुर्वशि ! कल्पय स्तनतटीमामुक्तमुक्तावलीम्।।

विदू भो ववसिदं बहूमण्डणं। तुवरदुतुवरदु अत्तभवं। (भो व्यवसितं वधूमण्डनम्।त्वरतां त्वरतामत्र भवान्।)

धन बाढम्।

(इति निष्क्रान्तौ)

चतुर्थोऽङ्कः।

(ततः प्रविशति षट्पदिका)

षट्पदि अणुट्ठिअणिओणं अत्ताणं भट्ठिदारिआए णिवेदइस्सं। (परिक्रम्यावलोक्य) एसा गोवद्धणिआ तुरिअतुरिअं आअच्छइ। किण्णुखु एदं। (अनुष्ठितनियोगमात्मानं भर्तृदारिकायै निवेदयिष्यामि। एषा गोवर्धनिका त्वरित्वरितमागच्छति। किन्नु खल्वेतत्।)

गोवर्ध (ततः प्रविशति गोवर्धनिका, विलोक्य) अम्मो छप्पदिआ। छप्पदिए! कुदो उण तुवं. (अम्मो षट्पदिका! षट्पदिके। कुतः पुनस्त्वम्।)

षट्पदि हला! अत्थि भट्टिदारिआए अणुट्ठिओ सन्दणव्वदअं णाम वदविसेसो। तस्स पारणणिमित्तं सो ङ्गमिअं रहं आणेहि त्ति रण्णो उग्गसेणस्स सारहिं सन्दिसिअ आअदह्मि। सो वि तह रहं उवकप्पिअ उवग दो भट्टिदारिआए समीवं। तुवं उण कहिं पत्थिआ। (सखि! अस्ति भर्तृदारिकायानुष्ठितः स्यन्दनव्रतकं नाम व्रतविशेषः। तस्य पारणनिमित्तं साङ्ग्रमिकं रथमानयेति राज्ञ उग्रसेनन्य सारथिं सन्दिश्यागतास्मि। सोऽपि तथा रथमुपकल्प्योपगतो भर्तृदारिकायाः समीपम्। त्वं पुनः क्व प्रस्थिता।)

गोवर्ध आणत्तह्मि भट्टिणीपादेहि, जह 'तुमं गदुअबहिणिआए जसोदाए कहेहि जो तुह धीदाए सुभद्दाए अस्सत्थदाणिमित्तं तुए अवआइदो गिरिजण्णो, सो अज्ज एव्व तिस्से अणुऊले णक्खत्ते सह गोवालेहि आरहीअदु'त्ति। तण्णिमित्तं तुरिअं गच्छीअदि। तहवि तुमं एत्तिअमत्तं पुच्छिदुं इच्छामि। (आज्ञप्तास्मि भट्टिनीपादैः, यथा त्वं गत्वा भगिन्यै यशोदायै कथय यस्तव धीतायाः सुभद्राया अस्वस्थतानिमित्तं त्वयोपयाचितो गिरियज्ञः, सोऽद्यैव तस्या अनुकूले नक्षत्रे सह गोपालैरारभ्यतामि'ति। तन्निमित्तं त्वरितं गम्यते। तथापि त्वामियन्मात्रं प्रष्ठुमिच्छामि।)

षट्पदि कामं पुच्छीअदु। (कामं पृच्छयताम्।)

गोवर्ध एदं वि णाम किं कहेहि सुदपुरुवं दिट्ठपुरुवं वा, जं पव्वजिदेहि परिणअणं किज्जइत्ति। (एतदपि नाम किं कथय श्रुतपूर्वं दृष्टपूर्वं वा यत् प्रव्रजितैः परिणयनं क्रियत इति।)

षट्पदि हला! एत्थ कण्णाउरे चिरपरिइदा वि णिच्चप्पसुत्ता विअ तुमं। ण दाव एव्वं एदं। सो जइवेसन्तरप्पडिच्छण्णो कुरुउलप्पदीवो कुमारधणञ्जओ। देवपादोहि पुण बलभद्दुद्धवप्पमुहं दासालुहचक्कं वञ्चिअ अप्पआसं एव्व तस्स दिण्णा भट्टिदारिआ। (सखि! अत्र कुरुकुलप्रदीपः कुमारधनञ्जयः। देवपादैः पुनर्बलभद्रोद्धवप्रमुखं दाशार्हचक्रं वञ्चयित्वाप्रकाशमेव तस्मै दत्ता भर्तृदारिका।)

गोवर्ध (सप्रमोदम्) जइ एव्वं, ठाणे मं उवालंभसि। दिट्ठिआ जइच्छएव्व पदुमाअरं पविट्ठा कलहंसिआ। (यद्येवं स्थाने मामुपालभसे। दिष्ट्या यदृच्छयैव पद्माकरं प्रविष्टा कलहंसिका।)

षट्पदि तुमं पुण अत्तणो णिओअं अणुचिट्ठ। अहं पि भट्टिदारिआए सआसं गमिस्सं। (निष्क्रान्ता) (त्वं पुनरात्मनो नियोगमनुतिष्ठ। अहमपि भर्तृदारिकायाः सकाशं गमिष्यामि।)

गोवर्ध (परिक्राम्यावलोक्य) एसो तादस्स अन्दगोवस्स परिजणो इसहओ इदो एव्व आअच्छइ। (एष तातस्य नन्दगोपस्य परिजन ऋषभक इत एवागच्छति।)

(ततः प्रविशति गोपालकः)

गोपा भो भो गोलक्खआगोलक्खआ! आणवइ तुह्मे शामी अन्दगोए 'इमे गोशमूहे हलिअतिणप्पवे अपेशलं पदेश शङ्कमिअ एत्थ किल गिलिजण्णाणुभवणत्थं लेवदअप्पत्थं आअच्छह त्ति।' (भो भो गोरक्षका गोरक्षका। आज्ञापयति युष्मानु स्वामी नन्दगोपः 'इमं गोसमूहं हरिततृणप्रवेकपेशलं प्रदेशं सङ्गमय्यात्र किल गिरियज्ञानुभवनार्थं रैवतकप्रस्थमागच्छते'ति।)

गोवर्ध इसहअ! कहिं संपदं जसोदज्जुआ चिट्ठइ। (ऋषभक! कस्मिन् साम्प्रतं यशोदाज्जुका तिष्ठति।)

गोपा कहं गोवद्धणिआ। गोपद्धणिए! एशा शह शामिणा णन्दगोएण आलद्धगिलिजण्णा लेवदअशाणुगए कञ्जणुज्जाणेवट्टइ। (कथं गोवर्धनिका। गोवर्धनिके! एषा सह स्वामिना नन्दगोपेनारब्धगिरियज्ञा रैवतकसानुगते काञ्चनोद्याने वर्तते।)

गोवर्ध अम्मो आरद्धो पुव्वं एव्व एदेहि पव्वजण्णो। तह वि णिदेसमत्तं अणुचिट्ठामि। (निष्क्रान्ता) (अम्मो आरब्धः पूर्वमेतैः पर्वतयज्ञः। तथापि निदेशमात्रमनुतिष्ठामि।)

गोपा (विलोक्य) एशे एशे महिशए भीद भीदं शव्वदो दिण्णदिट्ठी तुलिअतुलिअं आहावइ। किण्णुहु एदं। (एष एष महिषको बीतभीतं सर्वतो दत्तदृष्टिस्त्वरितत्वरितमाधावति। किन्नु खल्वेतत्।)

(ततः प्रविशति यथानिर्दिष्टो द्वितीयो गोपालकः)

गोपा (सभयम्) अले अले इशहअ! का एशा अशं भमदा, जं अवलाविअ चिट्ठसि। (धावति) (अरे अरे ऋषभक! कैषासम्भ्रमता, यदपलाय्य तिष्ठसि।)

प्रथमः (बलान्निगृह्य) अले! कुदो दे शंभमे। (अरे! कुतस्ते सम्भ्रमः।)

द्वितीयः अले! किं ण पेक्खशि, एशे एशे के वि लोशघडिअभिउडिदुप्पेक्खललाडे कोशादो अशिं कड्ढेइ। अवले धणुम्मि मोव्विं आलोवेइ। अण्णे शन्दणं आलुहए। एक्के शलधीदो शलं उक्खिवइ। इदले शण्णाहं आमुञ्चइ। किं बहुणा, एसा दुवालवई मइलामअमत्त विअमहिला इदोतदो घोलइ। (अरे किं न पश्यसि, एष एष कोऽपि रोषघटितभ्रुकुटिदुषप्रेक्षललाटः कोशादसिं कर्षति। अपरो धनुषि मौर्वीमारोपयति। अन्यः स्यन्दनमारोहति। एकः शरधितः शरमुत्क्षिपति। इतरः सन्नाहमामुञ्चति। किं बहुना, एषा द्वारवती मदिरामदमत्तेल महिलेतस्ततो घूर्णते।)

(नेपथ्ये कलकलानन्तरम्)

भो भो मधुमथनभुजवनप्रच्छायोपसेवननिरस्तसमस्तपरिभवधर्मावलेपलेशाः। कथंकथमीदृशमिदमादिन्यक्कारावतारमुपेक्षन्ते भवन्तः। अपि च –

गृह्णीध्वं प्रहरध्वमस्यत शरानारोहत स्यन्दना-
नाददध्वं विपृथुश्रवः प्रभृतयो वीर्याणि वृष्ण्यन्धकाः।
कोऽप्येष स्मरवैरिशौरिशिखिनो निस्तेजयन्नोजसा
भद्रां स्यन्दनवर्तिनीमपहरन्नस्मान् विधत्ते स्त्रियः।। १।।

प्रथमः (विलोक्य ससम्भ्रमम्) अले अले! एशे एशे महापुलिशे कलकलिअकम्मुए पिट्ठप्पडिट्ठाविअतूणीले आमुक्कशण्णाहे णामिणीए शुहदाए शअंगहिअअश्शलश्शी गच्छइ। अण्णं च एदश्श जाघोशश्शवणमत्तेण एव्व पलम्मुले आशी कुकुलवलशमूले। (अरे अरे एष एष महापुरुषः

करकलितकार्मुकः पृष्ठप्रतिष्ठापिततूणिर आमुक्तसन्नाहः स्वामिन्या सुभद्रया स्वयं ग्रहीताश्वरश्मिर्गच्छति। अन्यच्चैतस्य ज्याघोषश्रवणमात्रेणैव पराङ्मुख आसीत्। कुकुरबलसमूहः।)

द्वितीयः (विलोक्य सहासम्) अले ! कीश एशे शंलम्भं कलीअदि। एशे खु वाशुदेवे शहजं अवहलदि। (अरे कस्मादेष संरम्भः क्रियते। एष खलु वासुदेवः सहजामपहरति।) (नेपथ्ये) भो भोः पुरन्दरावरजपुररक्षणदीक्षाधिकारबद्धकक्षाः! कलितकतिपयास्त्रोपशीलनजनितदुःश्लाघाः! कदर्थितजगत्रयाः! कुकुरवृष्ण्यन्धप्रमुखप्रवीराः! नखलु नखलु पलायन्तां भवन्तः। अपि च,

पार्थं तीर्थोपलब्धस्फुरितशिखिशिखाप्रोज्ज्वलच्छस्त्रजालं
ज्यानिष्पेषप्ररूढप्रचितघनकिणश्यामपीनप्रकोष्ठम्।
प्रोन्मथ्यैनां हरन्तं सपदि सहभुवं सीरपाणेः सुभद्रां
शक्ताश्चेत् सत्वरंमां परनृपपृतनाघस्मरं वारयन्तु।। २।।

प्रथमः अले ! ण एशे वाशुदेवे। वाशुदेवशदिशलूवे पत्थे। ण हु एदश्श शलमुहादो कश्श वि मोक्खो। (अरे नैष वासुदेवः। वासुदेवसदृशरूपः पार्थः। न खल्वमुष्य शरमुखात् कस्यापि मोक्षः।)

द्वितीयः अले! के अण एशे अवले लहच्छङ्गगए केदुलट्ठिं ओलम्बते अतिविलूवे वाणले विअ भीद भीदं इदोतदो पलोअअन् चिट्ठइ। एशा वि किण्णामहे आ शामिणीए शमीवे चामलहत्था दीसइ। (अरे कः पुनरेषोऽपरः रथोत्सङ्गगतः केतुयष्टिमवलम्बमानोऽतिविरूपो वानर इव भीतभीतमितस्ततः प्रलोकयंस्तिष्ठति। एषापि किन्नामधेया स्वामिन्याः समीपे चामरहस्ता दृश्यते।)

प्रथमः (सावधानं विलोक्य) अले! एदेण एदश्श वअश्शेण केणवि बह्मणेण होदव्वं। एशा उण मए दिट्ठपुलुवा छप्पदिआ णाम तिश्शे शही। (अरे एतेनैतस्य वयस्येन केनापि ब्राह्मणेन भवितव्यम्। एषा पुनर्मया दृष्टपूर्वा षट्पदिका नाम तस्याः सखी।)

द्वितीयः अले! अच्छलिअं अच्छलिअं। एदश्शिं णअले एदश्श शलेहिं अणालीढे णहु अङ्गुलमत्ते वि पदेशे। (अरे आश्चर्यमाश्चर्यम्। एतस्मिन् नगर एतस्य शरैरनालीढो न खल्वङ्गुलमात्रोपि प्रदेशः।)

प्रथमः अले! अज्जुणश्श ण एदं अच्छलिअं। (पुनर्विलोक्य) अले! एशे अदिक्कन्दे गोवुलदुआलं। एदे विपुहुप्पमुहा दासालुहवीला शशंलम्भं अणुहावन्ति। ता महन्तेण शमलेण होदव्वं। अविअ अहके पुव्वं पि पत्थपलक्क मदंसणे पवड्ढिअकुदूहले। ता एहि एदश्श लेवदअश्श शूललोअलिहिअं शिहलदलं आलुहिअ वुलोअइश्शामो। (अरे ! अर्जुनस्य नैतदाश्चर्यम्। अरे एषोऽतिक्रान्तो गोपुरद्वारम्। एते विपृथुप्रमुखा दाशार्हवीराः ससंरम्भमनुधावन्ति। तन्महता समरेण भवितव्यम्। अपि चाहं पूर्वमपि पार्थपराक्रमदर्शने प्रवर्धितकुतूहलः। तदेह्येतस्य रैवतकस्य सूर्यलोकलिखितं शिखरतलमारुह्य विलोकयिष्यावः।)

(उभौ परिक्रम्य शिखरारोहणं नाटयतः)

प्रथमः अले! अहके दाव एदं शिहलदलं आलूढे। तुवं पुण वल्लीओ ओलम्बन्ते पए पए पडिक्खिलशि। अदि विह्मए एशे, जं इशहआदो महिशए दुब्बले शंवुत्ते। (अरे अहं तावद् एतच्छिखरमारूढः। त्वं पुनर्वल्लीरवलम्बमानः पदे पदे प्रतिस्खलसि। अतिविस्मय एषः यद् ऋषभकाद् महिषको दुर्बलः संवृत्तः।)

द्वितीयः (कथमप्यारुह्यावलोक्य) अले! पेक्खपेक्ख, अणुशलन्त शत्तुबलं पेक्खिअ धणञ्जएण पडिणिवत्तिए लहे। अण्णं च अच्छलिअ पेक्ख। एदश्श शलहेहिं विअ शलशमूहेहिं विद लिअधअकुहकङ्कडशिलत्तच्छत्तप्पमुहेहिं पडन्तेहिं णललहतुल असिन्धुलाणं ण एक्के वि विदलिए। तहवि पलम्मुहा जादवजोहा। एशे विपुहू शअं उवशप्पिअ शेब्बशुग्गीवमेहपुल्लवला-हअतुलङ्गमवलेहिं घडिअंदेवश्श शन्दणलदणं विश्शाणिअ किदपडिलम्भणे शन्धिं कलिअ पडिणिवुत्ते। (अरे पश्य पश्य, अनुसरत् शत्रुबलं प्रेक्ष्य धनञ्जयेन प्रतिनिवर्तितो रथः। अन्यच्च आश्चर्यं पश्य। एतस्य शलभैरिव शरसमूहैर्विदलितध्वजकुथकङ्कटशिरस्त्रच्छत्रप्रमुखैः पत द्भिर्नररथतुरगसिन्धुराणां नैकोऽपि विदलितः। तथापि पराङ्मुखा यादवयोधाः। एष विपृथुः स्वयमुपसृत्य शैब्यसुग्रीवमेघपुष्पवलाहकतुरङ्गमवरैर्घटितं देवस्य स्यन्दनरत्नं विश्रारण्य कृतपरिरम्भणः सन्धिं कृत्वा प्रतिनिवृत्तः।)

प्रथमः अले! अदिकादले एशे, जं शत्तुणो भीदीए शलणं उवगदे। (अरे अतिकातर एषः, यत् शत्रोर्भीत्या शरणमुपगतः।)

(नेपथ्ये)

अलममुना परिमितावकाशव्यापिना कनककठिनकोणाभिघातसमुद्भूतेन दुन्दुभिध्वानेन। तथाह्यामुष्य फल्गुनस्य –

विनष्टमददिग्गजश्रवणरन्ध्रविस्फोटनी
जगत्रयभयं मुहुर्विदधती धनुष्टङ्कृतिः।
प्रबोधयति सात्त्वतान् प्रथमसूकरोग्रानन-
प्रवान्तगुरुबृंहितप्रतिरवप्रतिस्पर्धिनी।। ३।।

द्वितीयः अले अले! के एशे पलवदि। (अरेऽरे क एष प्रलपति।)

प्रथमः (विलोक्य) अले! एशे शभापाले भेलिं ताले दुकामे घोशेदि। किं इमिणा। इमं वुत्तन्तं ण न्दगोवश्शणिवेदइश्शामो। (अरे एष सभापालो भेरीं ताडयितुकामो घोषयति। एतं वृत्तान्तं नन्दगोपस्य निवेदयिष्यावः।) (निष्क्रान्तौ)

प्रवेशकः

(ततः प्रविशति सभापालः)

सभा (अलममुनेत्यादि पठित्वा) अथवाविकल्पितमनुष्ठेयानि राजशासनानि। ताडयामि तावद् भेरीम्। (तथा करोति)

(ततः प्रविशति सुभद्रया वाह्यमानरथो धनञ्जयो विदूषकश्चेटी च)

धन (सुभद्रामवलोक्य) अयि प्रेयसि!

विपृथुरयमपेतः प्रस्थिता वृष्णियोधाः
प्रणयिनि! परिखेदं मा कृथाश्चोदयाश्वान्।
अनतिजवमिदं ते नः क्षिणोति श्रमार्तं
श्रमजलकणमुक्तामुक्तमूलं कपोलम्।। ४।।

सुभद्रा (आत्मगतम्) अय्यउत्तमुहलग्गलो अणवावाराए मम हिअअं अण्णहिं ण देहइ अवहाणं। केवलं आउणो वासुभद्दस्स सिक्खाविसेसो पग्गहेंसु पवत्तेदि हत्थे। (प्रत्यक्षम्) जं अय्यउत्तो आणवेदि। (मन्दं वाहयति रथम्) (आर्यपुत्रमुखलग्नलोचनव्यापाराया मम हृदयमन्यत्र न ददात्यवधानम्। केवलं भ्रातुर्वासुभद्रस्य शिक्षाविशेषः प्रग्रहेषु प्रवर्तयति हस्तौ। यदार्यपुत्र आज्ञापयति।)

विदू (जनान्तिकम्) भो वअस्स! ण दाव एक्को वि दे कामरसाणुभवो अकलहोपदंसओ। पुडसं दाव पञ्चाली देवासुरसमं सङ्गामं पवत्तिअ पाविदा। एमाए पुण वासुदेवेण दिण्णाए कुदो कलहप्पसङ्गोत्ति मए चिन्तिदं एत्थ उण तदो विउणो खेहो संवुत्तो। सव्वहा ण मे अवमुच्चुमुहादो मोक्खो। (भो वयस्य! न तावदेकोऽपि ते कामरसानुभवोऽकलहोपदंशकः। प्रथमं तावत् पाञ्चालीं देवासुरसमं सङ्ग्रामं प्रवर्त्य प्रपिता। अनया पुनर्वासुदेवेन दत्तया कुतः कलहप्रसङ्ग इति मया चिन्तितम्। अत्र पुनस्ततोऽपि द्विगुणः क्षोभः संवृत्तः। सर्वथा न मे अपमृत्युमुखान्मोक्षः।)

सुभद्रा हला! अदिदिढबद्धा गत्तिआ पीडेइ मे पयोहर जुअलं। ता सिडिलेहि दाव णं। (सखि! अतिदृढबद्धा गात्रिका पीडयति मे पयोधरयुगलम्। तच्छिथिलय तावदेनाम्।)

षट्पदि (सस्मितम्) भट्टिदारिए! तदाणं परिणअणमङ्गलमण्डणपत्थावे सुसण्णिहिदेसु दिव्वभूसणेसु कुमारणामहे अङ्किदत्ति अय्यकोण्डिण्णस्स हत्थादो घेत्तूण जा पुढमं आमुक्का, ताए एव्व इदाणिं इमाए कुदो दे मच्छरो। (परिणयनमङ्गलमण्डनप्रस्तावे सुसन्निहितेषु दिव्यभूषणेषु कुमारनाधेयाङ्किकतेत्यार्यकौण्डिन्यस्य हस्ताद् गृहीत्वा या प्रथममामुक्ता, तस्यामेवेदानीं कुतस्ते मत्सरः।)

सुभद्रा (सासूयम्) चिट्ठदु एसा मुहरा। अय्य! तुमं एदं अवणेहि। (तिष्ठत्वेषा मुखरा। आर्य! त्वमेतामपनय।)

विदू तह। (गात्रिकामपनयति) (तथा।) (नेपथ्ये)

अयमयमक्रूरानिरुद्धचारुदेष्णनिशठविडूरथसाम्बसारणसात्यकप्रसेनप्रद्युम्नप्रमुखप्रवीरनायकपुरस्सरः परस्परसङ्घट्टनप्रपिष्टपट्टमकुटकटककवचकेयूरधूलीमेदुरीकृतमेदिनीपरागपटलपाण्डरदिक्चक्रवालः ससंरम्भमहमहमिकया सत्वरमाधावति सात्त्वतसमूहः।

सभा (ससम्भ्रमं नेपथ्याभिमुखमवलोक्य) अये, किमसौ समरसंरम्भपिनद्धवर्मणा कृतवर्मणानुगम्यमानः कृतान्तः। नहि नहि

अङ्घ्रिक्षेपैरजस्रं धरणिधरभृतां कम्पयन् भूतधात्रीं
निर्यन्नेत्रानलार्चिः कपिशितभुवनः कामपालः क्षणेन।
आधावत्येष भीमभ्रुकुटिविषमितस्विन्नवक्त्र समस्तं
क्रुद्धः संहर्तुकामः स्वयमिव भगवान् धूर्जटिर्धूतसीरः।। ५।।

धन (आकर्ण्य सक्रोधम्) कथं कथं कामपालो मामनुबध्नाति। अयि प्रेयसि! सन्ततपीतहालाक्षीबभावविक्लवं हलिनं ते भ्रातरं प्रति निवर्तय रथम्। अपि च,

अन्तर्भवद्रिपुसुयोधनसख्यबन्ध-
प्रेङ्खोलिता प्रणयिना मधुसूदनेन।
मच्छस्त्रकृत्तबलभद्रगलाभिधान-
ग्रन्थिच्छिदाच्छिदुरदुःस्थितिरस्तु मैत्री।। ६।।

(धनुर्विष्फारयति)

सुभद्रा (सबाष्पगद्गदम्) अय्यउत्त! सेसवादो आरहिअ तुह चलणकमलगणं में अणुराणं अवेक्खिअ जह अहं कुलविणासकारिणित्ति ण लोअपरिवादाणं भाअणं होमि, तह विहेहि। (पादयोः पतति) (आर्यपुत्र शैशवादारभ्य तव चरणकमलगतं मे अनुरागमवेक्ष्य यथाहं कुलविनाशकारिणीति न लोकपरिवादानां भाजनं भवामि, तथा विधेहि।)

धनञ्जयः (ससम्भ्रममुत्थाप्य) प्रिये! मा स्म विषीदः। अमी हि त्वन्नेत्रकुवलविगलिता गलदायुषो गदाधराग्रजस्य शरणमासन्नाश्रुबिन्दवः। यदि पुनरस्मद्रथमनुबध्नीयुर्वृष्णयस्तदा त्वद्बाष्पजलैरप्यप्रतिधेयवेगा मद्विशिखमुखशिखिनः। तदधुना यथाभिमतं वाह्यतां रथः।

विदू भोदि! जाव एसो पुणो वि जस्स कस्स वि आगमणमत्तं सुणिअ जाओसेण णो कण्णं फोडेइ, ताव तुरिअं वाहेहि रहं। (भवति, यावदेष पुनरपि यस्य कस्याप्यागमनमात्रं श्रुत्वा ज्याघोषेण नः कर्णं स्फुटयति, तावत् त्वरितं वाहय रथम्।)

सुभद्रा अणुग्गहिगदह्मि अय्यउत्तेण। (रथं वाहयति) (अनुगृहीतास्मि आर्यपुत्रेण।)

धन (सविस्मयम्) सुन्दरि! अप्रतर्क्योऽयं तव सारथ्यशिक्षातिशयः। कुतः –

लक्ष्यः क्षेपः खुराणां न वियति न भुवि व्यायतान् नूनमङ्घ्री-
नश्वा नावक्षिपन्ति क्षपितविचलिता नाप्यमूनुत्क्षिपन्ति।
यावत् सम्पर्कमेता विदधति पतितैश्चाक्षुषैर्नः कराग्रै-
स्तावद् दूरापयाता न खलु तरुलता बुद्धिमुत्पादयन्ति।। ७।।

(निष्क्रान्तः सपरिवारो धनञ्जयः) (नेपथ्ये)

आः दुरात्मन्! पाण्डुकुलपांसन! परमहंसवेषघटितमत्सोदर्यापहरणप्रकटितवीर्यविपर्यास! सव्यसाचिन्! क्वक्व प्रयासि।

सभा (सत्रासम्) असौ समरसंरम्भपिनद्धवर्मणा कृतवर्मणानुगम्यमानः कृतान्त इव क्रुद्धो हलायुधः। अहोतुखल्वमुष्य-क्रोधानलदीप्तेन मुहुर्मुहुः परिवर्तमानेन नेत्रयुगलेन परिवर्तित इव सकलो जीवलोकः।
(ततः प्रविशत्यपटाक्षेपेण कृतवर्मणानुगम्यमानो यथानिर्दिष्टः क्रुद्धो हलायुधः)

हला (आः दुरात्मन्नित्यादि पूर्वोक्तमेव पठित्वा)

पातालं चेद् व्रजेस्त्वं तदपि निरिशतैः पूर्णयन् चूर्णयेयं
गीर्वाणैकः प्रयायाः सपदि हलमुखाकृष्टमूर्ध्वाण्डखण्डम्।
कृत्वा निष्पेषयेयं बहुतरकथया किञ्च यत्र क्वचित् त्वा
जीवन्तं नैव मृष्यत्यरिरुधिरवसापिच्छिलं लाङ्गलाग्रम्।। ८।।

कृत (सोद्वेगम्) अहो दुरवबोधः खलु विधेः प्रक्रमः। कुतः,

पातारौ बलभद्रकंसमथनौ सेयं पुरी द्वारका
प्रोत्सिक्ताः पृथुबाहुनिर्जितजगच्छक्रा वयं वृष्णयः।
तां भद्रामहरत् स पाण्डुतनयः कष्टं मृगः प्रस्थितो
भित्त्वा दिग्गजकुम्भमण्डलतटीमाच्छिद्य मुक्तावलीम्।। ९।।

सभा (सभयम्) पार्थकृतपरिभवपरिवर्धितकोपानलवपुः पुरा सोऽयं संहरति भुवनत्रयम्। तावदहमिममुदन्तं देवाय देवकीनन्दनाय निवेदयिष्ये। (निष्क्रान्तः)

हला (सावज्ञम्) कृतवर्मन्! किमेकेन फल्गुनहतकेन।

पञ्चानां पाण्डवानां प्रतिभयमुसलोद्घातनिर्घातपात-
क्षुण्णक्ष्लक्ष्णास्थिचूर्णान् हलमुखदलितान् विग्रहाण् विग्रहे मे।
पायंपायं प्रभूतं विगलितमसृजां पूरमाकण्ठपूरं
खादन्तु क्षीणकुक्षिस्तनहनुतनवः प्रीतिमत्यः पिशाच्यः।। १०।।

कृत देव! सैषा सप्तसमुद्रीं धरित्रीं क्रोडीकर्तुकामा कौरवादीनामतिगरीयसी लक्ष्मी, यया प्रेरिता पाण्डुतनया मित्रमिहभवन्तं शात्रवयन्ति।

हला तेऽपि तावदासतामवज्ञातसकलक्षत्रमण्डलाः कौरवपशवः, यत्पितृव्यतनयाः पाण्डुदायादाः। अपि च मत्क्रोधहुतभुजि रिपुजीवितलिहि देदीप्यमाने –

क्षिप्तभ्रश्यच्छिरस्त्रैर्दृढविहितकचाकृष्टिभिर्मुषटिबन्धैः-
र्निष्पिष्टोरः कवाटस्फुरितशिखिरशिखास्रेणिशोणैः शरीरैः।
दुर्वारे द्वन्द्वयुद्धे भियमतिशयिनीमादधानाः परेषा-
मद्यारभ्य प्रवीराः समरभुवि कुतः कौरवाः सञ्चरन्ति।। ११।।

(सावष्टम्भम्) अथवा तिष्ठन्तु तावदस्मद्भुजबलपराक्रमविस्फूर्जथोरपर्याप्तवीर्यप्रसराः पृथ्वीवलयनिलयास्तपस्विनः पृथ्वीपतयः।

दृप्तद्विष्टद्बहललोहितपुरशार-
सीराग्रकोटिपरिघट्टिथसन्धिबन्धः।
सत्यावधिः ससुरदैत्यगणः सकृन्मे
लोकः स एष सहतां मुसलाभिघातम्।। १२।।

कृत देव! अलमिदानीमात्मानममर्षाय दत्त्वा, दैवदत्तायुषा दूरमन्तरमपयातेन पाण्डवपशुना भवितव्यम्। तद् देवेन शाङ्र्गधन्वना सह सम्प्रधार्य प्राप्तमत्र प्रतिविधास्यामहे।

(ततः प्रविशति प्रहृष्टो वासुदेवः सात्यकिश्च)

वासु (सानन्दम्) सात्यके! निजशास्त्रशल्यशिखिभिरभस्मीकुर्वन्नन्धकानादाय माधवीमपयातः किल धनञ्जयः। अपि च –

ज्योत्स्नां चन्द्रमसा द्युतिं दिनकृता हव्याहुतिं वह्निना
जीमूतेन शतह्रदां सुरभिणा मासेन पुष्पश्रियम्।
यः कान्तिं कमलाकरेण घटयामास ध्रुवं वेधसो
वार्ष्णेयीं बलभित्सुतेन घटयन्नस्मादभिन्नोऽस्म्यहम्।। १३।।

सात्य साम्प्रतमाह देवः। अस्थाने पुनरत्रभवानाविग्नो हलायुधः। कुतः,

कौन्तेयं शशधरवंशमौलिरत्नं
प्राणेभ्यः प्रियतरमात्मजं मघोनः।
प्राप्तायां स्वसरि वरं प्रमोदकाले
सम्मोहः किमयममुष्य सीरपाणेः।। १४।।

तद् देवेन देवः प्रशान्तकोपः करणीयो रौहिणेयः।

हला कृतवर्मन्! मावं वादीः। तमतिदूरान्तरगतमपि दुरात्मानमेषा सीरकोटिरनासाद्य न निवर्तते। तदनुबध्नामि तावदेनम्। (उद्धतं परिक्रामति)

वासु (उपसृत्य प्रणामं कुर्वन्) प्रसीदत्वार्यः। आर्य! कोऽयमात्मीयेष्वनुचितः कक्ष्याबन्धः। प्रति संह्रियतामयमतिवेलतीव्रः कोपवह्निः।

हला (विलोक्य) वासुभद्र! कथमात्मीयेष्विति –

कुर्वन् कौरुकुचीं वृत्तिमातिष्ठन्नन्त्यमाश्रमम्।
अपहर्ता सुभद्रायाः क्व वयं क्व धनञ्जयः।। १५।।

वासु कस्यायमपराधः। नन्वार्य एव तावत् तं मस्करिवेषप्रतिच्छन्नं कुमारीपुरे विनिवेश्य साम्प्रतं कस्मै क्रुध्यति।

हला वासुभद्र! परवञ्चनापटीयसां पापीयसामशक्यावबोधानि खलु दुश्चेष्टितानि। अत एव विस्रब्धवञ्चयिता वध्यः। उपेक्षतां च भवानाकस्मिकपक्षपातपरवशः पापिनः पाण्डुतनयान्। अपि च,

अस्मच्छस्त्रकठोरपातपदवीवान्तास्रपूरच्छटा-
नैपथ्यान् करवालकृत्तशिरसः पार्थानपार्थायुधान्।
प्रेक्षन्तां पिशिताशिनः प्रियतमाकण्ठप्रसक्तैर्भुजै-
रारब्धारभटीनविक्षतघटाबन्धाः कबन्धान् रणे।। १६।।

सात्य देव! देवस्यास्य सम्भाव्यता भ्रातुस्तव कंसशत्रोरनुनयः। अनुपलक्षितफलश्च लघुक्रियतामय मतिदुर्भरसंरम्भातिभारः।

कृत (सक्रोधम्) सात्यके! अतिक्लीबमभिहितं भवता। अपूर्वपरिभवबद्धमूलः समुचितस्थानवर्ती केन खलु मनस्विना मधुकुलसम्भवेन निवारणीयोऽस्य कोपानुबन्धः। अपि च स पाण्डुतनयः-

अविदितभयमार्गं मार्गणैः शात्रवाणां
प्रविजयि मधुसैन्यं मन्यमानस्तृणाय।
कलितकतिपयास्त्रप्राप्तमिथ्याभिमानः
पशुरयनुपेक्ष्यो मूर्ध्नि नः क्षिप्तपादः।। १७।।

सात्य (सक्रोधम्) आः दुरात्मन्नयं तावदरिष्वप्रतिहतपराक्रमः कुप्यतु किरीटिने कामं कामपालः। भवादृशाः पुनर्जन्मनः प्रभृत्यपरिचितवीरवीथयः भुवनैकधनुर्धरं धर्मानुजन्मानमस्मदाचार्यमधि-क्षिपन्तीत्यहो बलीयाननात्मज्ञानामवलेपः। अपि च –

प्रलम्बनरकद्विषौ सपदि सन्निधत्तो न चेद्
गुरोर्मम धनञ्जयादधिगतोऽयमस्त्रांशकः।
तमित्थमतिनिन्दतः शितकठोरघोराननः
प्रवक्ति नृपशोस्तव प्रतिवचः करोम्यत्र किम्।। १८।।

कृत (सक्रोधम्) रे रे वृष्णिकुलकीट!

यतः प्राप्तास्त्रांशः परुषमवलिप्तः प्रलपसि
प्रमध्याजौ तस्य प्रबलमवलेपं छलमुनेः।
प्रलापैरत्रालं गगनतलनीलच्छविरिदं
निकृत्तं नाकृत्वा विरमति ममासिस्तव शिरः।। १९।।

वासु (सक्रोधावुभौ पश्यन्) को नाम युवयोरन्तरेण पार्थमयमाकालिकः कलहप्रसङ्गः। तज्जोषमासातां भवन्तौ।

(सात्यकिकृतवर्माणौ प्रयत्नस्तम्भितरुषौ तृष्णीं तिष्ठतः)

वासु आर्य! अलमुत्तरोत्तरकथाभिः। पितुर्नः स्वस्रीयतां पृथायाः पुत्रतां मित्रतां च मम समाकलय्य सुरपतिसूनावपनीतामर्षसन्तमसेन साम्प्रतमनुग्रहणीयोऽहमार्येण।

हला (करेण करं पिबन्) कष्टं भोः कष्टं –

परिक्षतं परिभवपत्रिणा मन-
स्तदक्षमं क्षमयितुमक्षमा वयम्।
अकर्तुमप्यनुनयगर्भिणीर्गिरो
न शक्नमस्तव धिगहो हता हताः।। २०।।

(कथमपि क्रोधं प्रतिस्तम्भयन् निष्क्रान्तः कृतवर्मा च)

सात्य देव! उपशमित इवेदानीमन्तःक्षोभार्णवबडवानलायमानो रौहिणेयः कोपपावकः।

वासु सात्यके! एवमेतत्। त्वं तावदितो गत्वा मद्वचनादार्यकोपोपशममिममवबोध्य प्रशान्तप्रक्षोभं सम्भृतविविधहरणद्रविणोपकरणमन्धकचक्रमापाद्य शौवस्तिकाय प्रयाणाय सन्नाहय। वयमपि –

प्रणयगुरुभिरार्यस्यानुकूलैर्वचोभि-
र्मनसि गलितशेषं रोषमुन्मूलयन्तः।
सह मुदितमनोभिस्तस्य वृष्णिप्रवीरै-
र्ध्रुवमभिमतयामः खाण्डवप्रस्थयात्राम्।। २१।।

सात्य यदाज्ञापयति देवः।

(इति निष्क्रान्तौ)

पञ्चमोऽङ्कः

(ततः प्रविशति प्रतिहारकः)

प्रति – भो भोः पौरमहत्तराः ! पुरुहूततनयस्य पुण्डरीकाक्षसहजासमेतस्य पुण्डरीकाक्षस्य चागमनमहोत्सवलाभादानन्दपरवशीकृतात्मनो महाराजयुधिष्ठिरस्य शासनात् कुरुत पुरीमिमामद्योद्यावोत्तराम्। तथाहि –

कार्या पिष्टातकौघैः पिहितरविकरैर्धूसरा वासरश्री-
र्धूपैर्धूम्रीक्रियन्तां बहलपरिमलैर्दूरमाशामुखानि।
उच्चैस्तुच्छीकुरुध्वं ध्वजपटपटलैः पावनंमार्गमेताः
पूर्यन्तां पुष्पपूरैर्मधुकरशबलैः सर्वतो राजवीथ्यः।। १।।

(ततः प्रविशति चेटी)

चेटी आणत्तह्मि देवीए जण्णसेणीए, जह – णन्दिणिए ! तुवं दाव गदुअ णाहस्स मे इन्दप्पत्थप्पवेससमअं जा णाहि। अण्णं च सुदं मए 'सवत्तीमच्छरावणअणत्थं पडिवण्णगोवालिआवेसेण मं अहिगमिस्सदि बहिणिआ सुहद्द'त्ति। सुदमत्तेण च्चिअ मे पीदी समुप्पण्णा। तिस्से सो वेसपडिग्गहो सोहइ ण व त्ति जाणिअ आअच्छ त्ति। कहिंणुखु सो कुमारधणञ्जओ, सा अ भट्टिदारिआ वट्टइ। (अग्रतो विलोक्य) एसो अय्यपडिहारओ दुवारे चिट्ठइ। पुच्छिस्सं णं। (उपसृत्य) अय्य ! को अज्ज अपुव्वो राअउलवुत्तन्तो। (आज्ञाप्तास्मि देव्या याज्ञसेन्या, यथा – नन्दिनिके ! त्वं तावद् गत्वा नाथस्य मे इन्द्रप्रस्थप्रवेशसमयं जानीहि। अन्यच्च श्रुतं मया सपत्नीमत्सरपनयनार्थं प्रतिपन्नगोपलिकावेषेण मामभिगमिष्यति भगिनी सुभद्रेति। श्रुतमात्रेणैव मे प्रीतिः समुत्पन्ना। तस्याः स वेषप्रतिग्रहः शोभते नवेति ज्ञात्वागच्छेति। क्वनु खलु स कुमारधनञ्जयः, सा च भर्तृदारिका वर्तते। एष आर्यप्रतिहारको द्वारे तिष्ठति। प्रक्ष्याम्येनम्। आर्य ! कोऽद्यापूर्वो राजकुलवृत्तान्तः।)

प्रति अये, नन्दिनिकागता। नन्दिनिके ! कुमारधनञ्जयो नगरबाह्योद्याने मुहूर्तं प्रतीक्ष्य क्षपयति कालम्। भर्तृदारिका पुनः सुभद्रा परिगृहीतगोपालिकावेषा ज्यायसीं पाञ्चालराजतनयां प्रणन्तुं प्रतिष्ठमाना प्रविष्टा किलान्तरा नमस्कर्तुमेकानङ्गाया भगवत्या मन्दिरम्। देवश्च पुनर्दामोदरः सम्भृतविविधहरणद्रविणं सङ्कर्षणसनाथं संकलसात्त्वतसमूहमितो गव्यूतिमात्रे सन्निवेश्यागतः साम्प्रतमजातशत्रोर्मन्दिरमध्यास्ते। एषोऽत्र वृत्तान्तः। तदहं प्रारब्धमिममुत्सवं देवाय निवेदयिष्ये। त्वमपि स्वाधिकारमनुतिष्ठ।

चेटी गच्छदु अय्यो। अहं पि दुग्गामन्दिरं एव्व गच्छामि। (गच्छत्वार्यः अहमपि दुर्गामन्दिरमेव गच्छामि।) (निष्क्रान्तौ)

मिश्रविष्कम्भकः

(ततः प्रविशति धनञ्जयो विदूषकश्च)

धन (सानन्दम्) अहोतुखल्वारभ्य तीर्थयात्रादिवसादागता क्लेशपरम्परा सेयमनेकानन्दप्रसविनी संवृत्ता। कुतः,

चेतोभूरकरोन्मिलत्कुचतटीं मद्वक्षसा माधवीं
प्रत्यासीदति यज्ञसेनदुहितुर्गाढोपगूढोत्सवः।
अङ्गं मे सहजैरवाप्स्यति चिरादाश्लेषम्
(निमित्तं सूचयन् सविषादम्) अत्रान्तरे
ब्रूते कष्टमदक्षिणः किमपि मे प्रस्पन्दमानो भुजः।। २।।

विदू – (स्वगतम्) जाणिदं मए एदस्स वामभुअपरिप्फन्दस्स फलं, जं मए सन्दणस्सदपरवसेण मग्गे अवहत्थिआ गत्तिआ। तं एदं अत्थहाणिं अणिमित्तं सूएदि। (प्रत्यक्षम्) भो वअस्स! मा विसादं करेहि। किं ण तुए सुदो वाउणा आ आसेण अ आरद्धं सरीरं त्ति लो आअदिआणं सिद्धन्तो। ता केण णिवारीअदि सरीरे वाउप रिप्फन्दो। (ज्ञातं मयैतस्य वामभुजपरिस्पन्दस्य फलं, यद् मया स्यन्दनस्यदपरवशेन मार्गे अपहस्तिता गात्रिका। तामेतामर्थहानिमनिमित्तं सूचयति। भोवयस्य! मा विषादं कुरु। किं न त्वया श्रुतो वायुनाकाशेन चारब्धं शरीरमिति लोकायतिकानां सिद्धान्तः। तत् केन निवार्यते शरीरे वायुपरिस्पन्दः।)

(ततः प्रविशति गात्रिकाहस्तो दीर्घाध्वगः)

दीर्घा (सशूत्कारम्) अहो णिप्फलो में अद्धगमणपरिस्ससो संवुत्तो, जं अदिक्कन्दे वि संवच्छरे अच्छो धणञ्जअहो ण आअच्छइ। ता सिग्घं गदुअ तस्स पवुत्तिं जाणिअ आअच्छ त्ति महाराअजुहिट्ठिरेण आणत्तेण मए पण्डअजणपदे मलअसिहरे कुमारीतित्थे केरलेसु सज्झपव्वदपब्भाए गोअण्णे अण्णेसु अण्णवतीरतित्थत्थाणेसु अण्णेसिअ अकिदत्थेण मए पविट्ठा दुवारवई। तहिं पि अदक्खिअ अहं णिग्गदो। तहिं एव्व मए सुदं इन्दप्पत्थे कुमारधणञ्जओ दट्ठव्वो आसि त्ति। सुदं च मए णअर वाहिरुज्जाणे वत्तदि कुमारो त्ति। ता उवपप्पिस्सं णं। (परिक्रम्योपसृत्य) इदं तं उज्जाणं। जाव पविसामि। (प्रविश्य) जेदु कुमारो। (अहो निष्फलो मे अध्वगमनपरिश्रमः संवृत्तः यदतिक्रान्तेऽपि संवत्सरे वत्सो धनञ्जयो नागच्छति। तच्छीघ्रं गत्वा तस्य प्रवृत्तिं ज्ञात्वागच्छेति महाराजयुधिष्ठिरेणाज्ञप्तेन मया पाण्ड्यजनपदे मलयशिखरे कुमारितीर्थे केरलेषु सह्यपर्वतप्राग्भागे गोकर्णे अन्येष्वर्णवतीर-तीर्थस्थानेषु अन्विष्याकृतार्थेन मया प्रविष्टा द्वारवती। तत्राप्यदृष्ट्वाहं निर्गतः। तत्रैव मया श्रुतम् इन्द्रप्रस्थे कुमारधनञ्जयो द्रष्टव्य आसीदिति। श्रुतं च मया नगरबाह्योद्याने वर्तते कुमार इति। तद् उपसर्पिष्याम्येनम्। इदं तदुद्यानम्। यावत् प्रविशामि। जयतु कुमारः।)

धन (विलोक्य) ननु त्वमार्यस्य जङ्घाकारिको वातजवः। किमादाय शासनमागतोऽसि।

दीर्घा (सप्रणामम्) कुमार! महाराअसासणेण कुमारं अण्णेसिदुं महीमण्डलं परिब्भमन्तेण कुमारणामहेअङ्किदं गत्तिअं मग्गे दक्खिअ एदं कुमारकेरअं ति चिन्तअन्तेण मए एसा आणीदा। (विदूषकस्य हस्ते समर्पयति) (कुमार! महाराजशासनेन कुमारमन्वेष्टुं महीमण्डलं परिभ्रमता कुमारनामधेयाङ्कितां गात्रिकां मार्गे दृष्ट्वा एषा कुमारसम्बन्धिनीति चिन्तयता मयैषानीता।)

धन सखे! कथमपविध्य गात्रिकामियन्तं कालमनाकुलोऽभूः।

विदू तत्तहोदीअं तुए कोवो कादव्वो, जिस्से तुरअवाहणजवेण इअं परिब्भट्ठा। (तत्र भवत्यां त्वया कोपः कर्तव्यः यस्यास्तुरगवाहनजवेनेयं परिभ्रष्टा।) (नेपथ्ये कलकलानन्तरम्)

> कष्टं हा करवालखण्डिततनुं कंसद्विषः सोदरीं
> बीभत्सोः सहचारिणीं प्रतिभयः सङ्गृह्य दोर्भ्यामयम्।
> खादंखादमगात् खरांशुपदवीं कश्चित् त्रियामाचरः
> किं कुर्मः क्षितिगोचरा वयमियं कात्यायनी निर्घृणा।। ३।।

धन (सविषादमाकर्णयन्) है प्रिये! (इति मूर्छितः पतति)

विदू (सास्रगद्गदम्) हा किदन्तहदअ! एदस्स महिन्दणन्दणस्स भुवणेक्कधणुद्धरस्स वासुहद्दमित्तस्स धम्माणुअस्स अप्पडिआरं विणिवादं दंसअन्तो अज्ज तुवं इस्सरो सं वुत्तो। (विचिन्त्य) अहो मे णूडदा, जं एदं अणस्सासअन्तो परिदेविउं पवुत्तो। भो वउस्स! समस्ससिहिसमस्ससिहि। (हा कृतान्तहतक! एतस्य महेन्द्रनन्दनस्य भुवनैकधनुर्धरस्य वासुभद्रमित्रस्य धर्मानुजस्याप्रतीकारं विनिपातं दर्शयन् अद्य त्वमीश्वरः संवृत्तः। अहो मे मूढता, यदेतमनाश्वासयन् परिदेवयितुं प्रवृत्तः भो वयस्य। समाश्वसिहि समाश्वसिहि।)

दीर्घा अहो अच्चाहिदं। ण एसो दाणिं पि पडिबुद्धो। हा देव्व! कुमारस्स ईरिसं दसं दंसेदुं तुए अहं एत्थ अज्ज आणीदो। (अहो अत्याहितम्। नैष इदानीमपि प्रतिबुद्धः। हा दैवः कुमारष्येदृशीं दशां दर्शयितुं त्वयाहमत्राद्यानीतः।)

विदू हा कहं ण एसो दाणिं पि सण्णं पडिवज्जइ। हा वअस्स! आहण्डलेण वि अहण्डणीयपरक्कमादो जादवसेण्णसमुद्दादो बलक्कारेण अवहरिअ दाणिं रक्खसगोप्फदे णिमज्जन्तिं माहविं कहं उवेक्खसि। भो वादजव! कहं तुमं अम्बाए कुन्तीए भादूणं जण्णसेणीए अ एदस्स एदं दसं अणिवेदिअ चिट्ठसि। हा अम्ब कुन्ति! दक्खदक्खं दे पिअतणअस्स अज्जुणस्स अपुव्वं आआरलङ्घणं, जं चिरकालादो आसादिअ अकिदपादवन्दणो एव्वपरलोअजत्तं पडिवज्जइ। (हा कथं नैष इदानीमपि संज्ञां प्रतिपद्यते। हा वयस्य आखण्डलेनाप्यखण्डनीयपराक्रमाद् यादवसैन्यसमुद्राद् बलात्कारेणापहृत्येदानीं राक्षसगोष्पदे निमज्जन्तीं माधवीं कथमुपेक्षसे। भो वातजव! कथं त्वमम्बायाः कुन्त्याः भ्रातॄणां याज्ञसेन्याश्चेतस्येतां दशामनिवेद्य तिष्ठसि। हा अम्ब कुन्ति! पश्य पश्य ते प्रियतनयस्यार्जुनस्यापूर्वमाचारलङ्घनं यच्चिरकालादासाद्याकृतपादवन्दन एवं परलोकयात्रां प्रतिपद्यते।)

दीर्घा सुट्ठु अय्यो भणादि। कदाइ सोदराणं सण्णिहाणादो एदस्स पडिबोधो भवे। हा अहं एत्तिएण कालेण उवगदो एदस्स दुज्जादस्स णिवेदओ संवुत्तो। (रुदन् निष्क्रान्तः) (सुष्ठु आर्यो भणति। कदाचित् सोदराणां सन्निधानादेतस्य प्रतिबोधो भवत्। हा अहमेतावता कालेनोपगत एतस्य दुर्जानस्य निवेदकः संवृत्तः।)

विदू किं दाणिं मए उवक्कन्दं, जं परलोअजत्ताहिमुहं अणणुगच्छन्तो चिट्ठामि। अहव एसा दाव गत्तिआ तिस्से अङ्गसंसग्गसुहआ एदस्स बहुसो सन्दावहारिणीदिट्ठा। ता कदाइ मोहं वि अवणेइ। परिक्खिअ इदं पच्छा मे पाणा परिच्चाइदव्वा। (गात्रिकां तस्योरसि

ददासि) (किमिदानीं मयोपक्रान्तं, यत् परलोकयात्राभिमुखमननुगच्छन् तिष्ठामि। अथवैषा तावद् गात्रिका तस्या अङ्गसंसर्गसुभगाएतस्य बहुशः सन्तापहारिणी दृष्टा। तत् कदाचिद् मोहमप्यपनयति। परीक्ष्यैतत् पश्चान्मे प्राणाः परित्यक्तव्याः।)

धन (सहसा समाश्वस्य सहर्षमालिङ्गन्) अयि सुन्दरि! कथं प्रतिनिवृत्तासि। (पुनर्विलोक्य सविषादम्) कथमियं गात्रिका। (सबाष्पम्) अयि गात्रिके! किमिति तामेकाकिनीं प्राणेश्वरीं गच्छन्तीमनुगच्छन्तं मां रुणत्सि। (ऊर्ध्वमवलोक्याश्रूणि मुञ्चन् बद्धाञ्जलिः)

पुरमुपगतां तात! प्रेम्णा पुरन्दर! माधवी
मम सहचरीमुत्सङ्गे त्वं निधाय वधूं तव।
व्यपगतशुचं शच्या तावद् विधेहि सहाम्बया
विघटिततनुर्यावत् प्राणैरुपैमि तवान्तिकम्।। ४।।

विदू (सहर्षं स्वगतम्) दिट्ठिआ मम भाअहेअसेसेण एसो पडिबुद्धो। ता जह ण पुणे वि मोहं पडिवज्जइ, तह उवक्कमिस्सं। (प्रत्यक्षम्) भो वअस्स! कोदे ववसाओ, जं तुह बाहुबलाअत्तसव्वपुरुसत्थं जेट्ठं दे जुहिट्ठिरं जणणिं अण्णं च भादुवग्गं अणवेक्खिअ जीविअणिरवेक्खं उव क्कमसि। (दिष्ट्या मम भागधेयशेषेणैव प्रतिबुद्धः यद्यथा न पुनरपि मोहं प्रतिपद्ये, तथो प्रक्रमिष्ये। भो वयस्य! कस्ते व्यवसायः, यत् तव बाहुबलायत्तसर्वपुरुषार्थं ज्येष्ठं ते युधिष्ठिरं जननीमन्त्रं च भ्रातृवर्गमनपेक्ष्य जीवितनिरपेक्षमुपक्रमसे।)

धन वयस्य! परित्यक्तजीवलोकसुखस्य जनस्य का ना बन्धुष्वपेक्षा। (सकरुणम्) मातः! कुन्तिभोजतनये! अद्यप्रभृत्यर्जुनगतमपत्यवात्सल्यमन्येषु चतुर्षु पुत्रेषु संविभजस्व। अपिच –

लक्ष्मीर्धर्मसुते सुयोधनकरादाच्छिद्य न स्थापिता
न क्षोणी चतुरर्णवोर्मिरशना तस्यैकपत्नी कृता।
मूर्धानो धरणीभृतां नगमितास्तत्पादपीठस्थलीं
कुक्षावम्ब! पृथे! वृथैव विजयः कृच्छ्रादुपोढस्त्वया।। ५।।

विदू भो इदं दाव कहेहि। उभअलोअसुहप्पच्चूहो अप्पपरिच्चाओ त्ति एदं पि किं तुह मए आचिक्खीअदि। (भो इदं तावत् कथय। उभयलोकसुखप्रत्यूह आत्मपरित्याग इत्येतदपि किं तव मया आख्यायते।)

धन सखे! सत्यमेवैतत्। न पुनरमी मया परित्यज्यन्ते प्राणाः। तथाहि –

गत्वा पदानि कतिचित् परिवर्तितास्यं
क्षिप्तस्तया हृदि ममाद्य कटाक्षपाशः।
आबध्य तेन सुदृढं परिकृष्यमाणाः
प्राणाः सखे! परवशाः खलु निष्पतन्ति।। ६।।

विदू (स्वगतम्) ण दाव एसो बन्धु जणसिणेहेण वा अण्णेण वा केण वि संपदं परिदिं णेदव्वो भवे। ण अण एआरिसा रिपुजणतिरक्खारक्खमिणो होन्ति। ता एदस्स मणम्मि मणा संरम्भं

ओदरइस्सं। (प्रत्यक्षम्) भो वअस्स! ण खु एत्थ तेल्लोक्के सोअपारवस्सादो अलङ्घणीओ अण्णो अत्थि भावो, जेण परवसीकिदो तुमं वि णाम दइआपाणावहारपरुसस्स पावरक्खसस्स पडिआरं अणाअरन्तो परिदेविउ पउत्तो। (न तावदेष बन्धुजनस्नेहेन वान्येन वा केनापि साम्प्रतं प्रकृतिं नेतव्यो भवेत्। न पुनरेतादृशा रिपुजनतिरस्कारक्षमिणो भवन्ति। तदेतस्य मनसि मनाक् संरभमवतारयिष्यामि। भो वयस्य, न खल्व त्रैलोक्ये शोक – पारवश्यादलङ् घनीयोऽन्योस्ति भावः, येन परवशीकृतस्त्वमपि नाम दयिता प्राणापहारपरुषस्य पापराक्षसस्य प्रतिकारमनाचरन् परिदेवयितुं प्रवृत्तः।)

धन (ससम्भ्रममुत्तिष्ठन्) आः, किं नाम कृतागस्स्वरिष्वप्रतिकुर्वन्नास्ते धनञ्जयः। (ऊर्ध्वमवलोक्य) भो भोः पिशिताशानापशद! मत्प्राणवल्लभाप्राणापहारिन्! क्व गत्वा मद्बाणपातं परिहरसि।

> यमः शरणमस्तु चेत् तव नृशंस! दिव्याशुगैः
> पुरत्रयमिव क्षणात् पुररिपुः स्फुरत्पावकैः।
> प्ररुष्टभुजगेश्वरप्रतिमचापटङ्कारिभि-
> स्त्वया सह न किं यमं यमपुरं च मथ्नाम्यहम्।। ७।।

अथवा मत्प्राणनाथां सोदर्यामात्मनः शरणागतां राक्षसादरक्षन्ती चण्डिका मम दास्यति। धनुर्धनुः। (ततः प्रविशति द्रौपदीवेषधारिणी कात्यायनी गोपालिकावेषधारिणी सुभद्रा च)।[2]

कात्या अहोनुखल्वचिन्तनीयोऽयमर्जुनस्य प्रभावः, यदमुष्य संरम्भो ममापि प्रक्षोभयति हृदयं, यद्भयादहं गृहीतयाज्ञसेनीरूपा प्राप्तवती।

सुभद्रा (भयं रूपयन्ती) अम्मो, एदं भअवदिं मम बहिणि अं कच्चाअणि बणुगच्छन्तीए अय्यडत्तसमीवं उवसप्पन्तीए मम पुरदो विअ सो दुट्ठकुणवासणो। (अम्मो एतां भगवतीं मम भगिनिकां कात्यायनीमनुगच्छन्त्या आर्यपुत्रसमीपमुपगच्छन्त्या मम पुरत इव स दुष्टकुणपाशनः।)

कात्या (उपसृत्य) जेदु णाहो। णाह! उवसंहरीअदु एसो संरम्भो। एसा दे सहअरी भअवदीए एआणङ्गाए अक्खदसरीरा म हत्थे दिण्ण। पडिच्छणं। (जयतु नाथः नाथ! उपसंह्रियतामेष संरम्भः। एषा ते सहचरी भगवत्या एकानङ्गयाक्षतशरीरा मम हस्ते दत्ता। प्रतीच्छैनाम्।)

सुभद्रा जेदु अय्यउत्तो। (जयत्वार्यपुत्रः।)

धन (सहर्षं सविस्मयं च स्वगतम्) यदिनाम सत्यमेवैषा माधवी, ममैव मन्ये चरितफलं जन्म। किन्तु दयितया द्रौपद्या अस्यां प्रत्यानीतायां का नामात्र प्रतिपत्तिः। (पर्याकुलस्तिष्ठति)

विदू (जनान्तिकम्) भो! पच्चक्खं एव्व तुज्झ पाणवल्लहाओ देवीओ दक्खिअ कहं पडिवत्तिमूढो विअ चिट्ठसि। (भो प्रत्यक्षमेव तव प्राणवल्लभे देव्यौ दृष्ट्वा कथं प्रतिपत्तिमूढ इव तिष्ठसि।)

धन सखे! सत्यमेवैषा याज्ञसेनी, इयं च सुभद्रैव। तथाप्यहमसुलभत्वादीदृशानां भागधेयानां न श्रद्दधे।

---

2 This is the context of the entry of Katyayani which has been recently developed as *Devimahatmyam* Nannyarkuttu. The recapitulation of Subhadra also is drawn from this context. See Chapters XII and XXIII.

विदू भो! मा खु अइन्तिदोवणदं अब्भुदअं अणिमित्तेण सन्देहेण विणासेहि। (भो मा खल्वचिन्तोपनतमभ्युदयमनिमित्तेन सन्देहेन विनाशय।)

सुभद्रा – (सरोषं स्वगतम्) कीस दाणिं अय्यउत्तो कहं पि कालहत्थादो परिब्भट्ठाअं अदिट्ठपुरुवाअं विअइत्थिआअंमइ उदासीणो विअचिट्ठइ। (कस्मादिदानीमार्यपुत्रः कथमपि कालहस्तात् परिभ्रष्टायामदृष्टपूर्वायामिव स्त्रियां मयि उदासीन इव तिष्ठति।)

विदू (सुभद्रामवलोक्य जनान्तिकम्) भो वअस्स! एसा दाव तत्तहोदी सुहद्दा भङ्गुरेण भूविक्खेवेण आअंमेण दिट्ठिपादेण अंतग्गअं अमरिसं पिसुणेइ। तुवं पुण णट्ठसन्देहो वि कीस चिरदिट्ठाअं पाञ्चाली अं इमाअं च अन्तअपुरादो आअदाअं विअ उदासीणो विअ चिट्ठसि। (भो वयस्य एषा तावत् तत्रभवती सुभद्रा भङ्गुरेण भ्रूविक्षेपेणायामेन दृष्टिपातेनान्तर्गतममर्षं पिशुनयति। त्वं पुनर्नष्टसन्देहोऽपि कस्माच्चिरदृष्टायां पाञ्चाल्यामस्यां चान्तकपुरागतायामिवोदासीन इव तिष्ठति।)

धन सत्यमपगतः सन्देहः। तथापि –

नास्यामाश्वासवाचः सपदि शिथिलतप्राणसन्देहवृत्तौ
वर्तन्ते रुद्धमार्गाः स्वसरि मधुरिपोर्द्रौपदीसन्निधानात्।
शक्येते वक्षसा मे न च कुचकलशौ मण्डलीकर्तुमेतौ
पाञ्चाल्या विप्रवासव्यसनपरिगतौ माधवीसन्निधानात्।। ८।।

(प्रत्यक्षम्) प्रिये! पाञ्चालि! परमनुगृहीतोऽहं भगवत्या कात्यायन्या, ययात्वमहं च प्राणदानादस्या अमुष्माद् व्यसनार्णवादुत्तारितौ स्वः।

सुभद्रा (स्वगतम्) दिट्ठिआ ण मइ उदासीणदाए एरिसो अय्यउत्तो। एदं भअवइं सच्चं एव्व अय्यां दोवहं उप्पेक्खिअ दक्खिणदाए तुह्णीओ संवुत्तो। मए उण एदं भअवइं एव्व चिन्तअन्तीए कुविदं। जइ णामजोग्गे अय्यउत्तो बहुमाणसङ्कडे पडिओ। जइ एदं पडि कुप्पिस्सं, अवस्सं अदिलहूई होमि। (दिष्ट्या न मय्युदासीनतयेदृश आर्यपुत्रः। एतां भगवतीं सत्यमेवार्यां द्रौपदीमुत्प्रेक्ष्य दक्षिणतया तूष्णीकः संवृत्तः। मया पुनरेतां भगवतीमेव चिन्तयन्त्या कुपितम्। यदिनाम योग्ये आर्यपुत्रो बहुमानसङ्कटे पतितः। यद्येतं प्रति कोपयिष्यामि, अवश्यमतिलघ्वी भवामि।)

द्रौपदी (ततः प्रविशति सबाष्पा द्रौपदी चेटी च) हला णन्दिणिए! ताअं वासुभद्दभहिणि आअं मम चित्ताराहणत्थं पडिवण्णगोवालिअवेसाअं पच्चिमं दसं पडिवण्णअं ण खणं पि जीविअं धारइस्सं। जइ धरइ संपदं णाहो, तं दट्ठूण किदत्था मरिस्सं। ता आदेसेहि णअरवाहिरुज्जाणस्स मग्गं। (सखि नन्दिनिके! तस्यां वासुभद्रभगिन्यां मम चित्ताराधनार्थं प्रतिपन्नगोपालिकावेषायां पश्चिमां दशां प्रपन्नायां न क्षणमपि जीवितं धारयिष्यामि यदि धरति साम्प्रतं नाथः, तं दृष्ट्वा कृतार्था मरिष्यामि। तदादेशय नगरबाह्योद्यानस्य मार्गम्।)

चेटी (सास्रगद्गदम्) भट्टिणि! ण दाव अहं णन्दिणिआ, जा एस्स मरणपरिणामस्स दुक्खस्स एक्कं कालणं संवुत्ता। एदुएदु भट्टिणी। (भट्टिनि न तावदहं नन्दिनिका, या एतस्य मरणपरिणामस्य एकं कारणं संवृत्ता। एत्वेतु भट्टिनी।) (शोकालसं परिक्रामतः)

चेटी (अग्रतो विलोक्य सहर्षम्) भट्टिणि! मा मा सन्तप्प। एसा भट्टिदारिआ माहवी कुमारस्स समीवे चिट्ठइ। (भट्टिनि! मा मा सन्तप एषा भर्तृदारिका माधवी कुमारस्य समीपे तिष्ठति।)

द्रौपदी (दृष्ट्वा सहर्षं सविस्मयं च) हला! किण्णुखु सच्चं एव्व एदं भवे। (सखि! किन्नुखलु सत्यमेवैतत् भवेत्।)

चेटी (पुनर्विलोक्य सविस्मयम्) अम्मो, अवरं अच्छरिअं। कहं एत्थ गच्छन्ती भट्टिणी कुमारस्स समीवे लक्खी अदि। किं विअ एदं। (अम्मो अपरं आचर्यम्। कथमत्र गच्छन्ती भट्टिनी कुमारस्य समीपे लक्ष्यते। किमिवैतत्।)

द्रौपदी हं भअवं। (परवशा तिष्ठति) (हं भगवन्।)

चेटी भट्टिणि! मा भाआहि। अं कुमारो चिट्ठइ। अव सप्पिअ जाणह्म। (भट्टिनि! मा बिभीहि। ननु कुमारस्तिष्ठति। उपसर्प्य जानीवः।)

द्रौपदी हला, सच्चं एदं। तह वि परवत्थं अआणन्ती पय्याउला होमि। (शङ्किता समुपसर्पति) (सखि! सत्यमेतत्। तथापि परमार्थमजानती पर्याकुला भवामि।)

सुभद्रा (स्वगतम्) अम्मो, परिवत्तिअरूवाए भअवदीए सरिसरूवा का वि इत्थिआ आअच्छइ। तक्केमि अय्या जण्णसेणि त्ति। जइ दाव अवआरं पडिवज्जिस्सं, एदाए भअवदीए रहस्सभेदो भवे। ता कालं पडिक्खिस्सं। (अम्मो परिवर्तितरूपाया भगवत्याः सदृशरूपा कापि स्त्री आगच्छति। तर्कयाम्यार्या याज्ञसेनीति। यदि तावद् उपचारं प्रतिपत्स्ये, एतस्या भगवत्या रहस्यभेदो भवेत्। तत् कालं प्रतीक्षिष्ये।)

विदू (विलोक्य सभयम्) भो वअस्स! परित्ताआहिपरित्ताआहि। रक्खसमअं इदं उज्जाणं संवुत्तं। किं ण पेक्खसि पडिदिसं आअच्छन्तीओ पञ्चालीओं। अवस्सं माआए इमाए होदव्वं। (भो वयस्य! परित्रायस्व, परित्रायस्व, राक्षसमयमिदमुद्यानं संवृत्तम्। किं न पश्यति प्रतिदिशमागच्छन्तीः पाञ्चालीः। अवश्यं माययानया भवितव्यम्।)

धन सखे! मा भैषीः। ननु सम्प्रधार्य निर्णेष्यावः।

कात्या (स्वगतम्) अये, विफलयन्ती मम रूपपरिवृत्तिमागता पाञ्चाली।

द्रौपदी जेदु णाहो। (जयतु नाथः।)

चेटी जेदु कमारो। (जयतु कुमारः।)

विदू भो! किं तुए संपहारिअं का एत्थ परमत्थादोव्वइत्ति। (किं त्वया सम्प्रधारितं कात्र परमार्था द्रौपदीति।)

धन (सवितर्कम्) सखे! द्वितीयामिमां द्रौपदीं मयि प्रेमगर्भं पतन् पिशुनयति परमार्थां दृष्टिपातः। प्रथमया च पुनरौदासीन्यमाचरन्त्या मायाविन्या भवितव्यम्। तदियमनुशासनीया। (सक्रोधम्) अनार्ये। का त्वमेवमनार्यमाचरसि।

कात्या (द्रौपदीवेषमपनयन्ती) वत्स!

किरीटिन्! मा स्म कुप्यस्त्वं सहजां मे कनीयसीम्।
आर्याहमागता दातुमेनां ते सहचारिणीम्।। ९।।

(सर्वे सम्भ्रमं नाटयन्ति)

विदू भो! मम दाणिं संसओ इअं पि पाए त्ति। (भो! मम इदानीं संशयः इयमपि मायेति।)

धन (सप्रमोदम्) सखे! मैवं वादीः। ब्रुवते मे रोमाङ्कुरदन्तुरितानि परमार्थां भगवतीममून्यङ्गानि। (सवयस्यः प्रणमन् बद्धाञ्जलिः)

अङ्घ्रिभ्यामम्ब! पीठीकृतमहिषशिरोमण्डलाभ्याममूभ्या-
मष्टाभ्यः श्लिष्टमौर्वीवलयझणझणानिक्वणेभ्यो भुजेभ्यः।
कोटीरेभ्यश्च प्रश्चात्कृतकलमशिखाविभ्रमेभ्यो नमस्ते
मूर्छन्मुग्धेन्दुलेखाकुटिलतनुगलच्छन्द्रिकाशेखरेभ्यः।। १०।।

अपिच मया यदज्ञानादयुक्तमभिहितं तदम्बया क्षन्तव्यम्। (पादयोः पतति)

कात्या (तमुत्थाप्य) वत्स! धनञ्जय! मा पर्याकुलो भूः। अपिच –

भद्रः, सौभद्रस्ते भूयात् तनयः समस्त्वया धनुषि।
आशां जय विजय! त्वं जहि सुरपरिपन्थिनः सर्वान्।। ११।।

धन अनुगृहीतोऽस्मि।

द्रौपदी भअवइ! वन्दामि। (पादयोः पतति) (भगवति! वन्दे।)

कात्या (उत्थाप्य) भद्रे! पाञ्चीलि! पञ्चभ्यस्ते पतिभ्यः पञ्च तनयानप्रतिरथानवाप्नुहि। अपिच यदपायशङ्कया त्वया व्यवसितमत्याहितं, सेयं ते भगिनी प्रतिगृह्यताम्। (सुभद्रां दर्शयति)

द्रौपदी अणुग्गहिदह्मि। (अनुगृहीतास्मि।)

सुभद्रा (स्वगतम्) हद्धि, मण्णिमित्तं किदो अय्याए मरणववसाओ। (प्रकाशम्) अय्ये! वन्दामि। (हा धिक् मन्निमित्तं कृत आर्यया मरणव्यवसायः। आर्ये! वन्दे।)

द्रौपदी भत्तुणो दे अविरहिआ होहि। एहि, आलिङ्गेहि मं। (आलिङ्गति) (भर्तुस्ते अविरहिता भव। एहि, आलिङ्ग माम्।)

सुभद्रा (स्वगतम्) इअं में सिणेहेण अम्बा देवइ। (इयं मे स्नेहेनाम्बा देवकी।)

धन (सप्रणामम्) भवगति! अमुष्य नो व्यसननिपातस्य याथातथ्यमवगन्तुमिच्छामि।

कात्या वत्स! श्रूयताम्। पुरा खलु दुर्योधनः परिणेतुमिच्छन्निमां माधवीं वासुभद्रभयाद् गूढमलम्बुसेन रक्षसा भूतरूपधरेण समाजीहरत्। तदा त्वयैव परित्राता।

धन (स्मृत्वा) एवमेतत्। ततस्ततः।

कात्या अद्यापि पुनस्तेनैव दुरात्मना तस्यैव नियोगात् प्रदर्शितमायाकलेबरेण नीयमाना मया परिरक्षिता।

धन परमनुगृहीतोऽस्मि।

कात्या (विचिन्त्य) वत्स! आर्यो वासुभद्रः सह धर्ममरुत्तनयाभ्यां भवन्तमभ्येति। तदहं साधयामि। (निष्क्रान्ता)

धन (पाञ्चालीमवलोक्य) देवि! तव खलु सौहृद्येन माधव्याः प्रत्यानीताः प्राणाः।

द्रौपदी णाह! मा खु एव्वं। मम भगसेसेण एसा आणीदा। (स्मृत्वा) णाह! इदाणिं एव्व किल जादवा आ अच्छन्ति, तेसं सम्माणणत्थं मए गन्तव्वं। (नाथ! माखल्वेवं, मम भाग्यशेषेणैषानीता। नाथ इदानीमेव किल यादवा आगच्छन्ति, तेषां सम्माननार्थं मया गन्तव्यम्।)

धन देवि! अनुरूपमभिहितम्। गम्यतां तावत्। अहमप्यनुपदमागत एव।

(द्रौपदी प्रणम्य निष्क्रान्ता चेट्या सह)

विदू दिट्ठिआ अवअदग्गाहा दाणिं सेरगोट्ठीवाहिणी। सेरं अवगाहीअदु अत्तभवं। भो सव्वआलदुल्ललिओ दे सिणेहो, जं पुव्वं एदाए विवत्तिं सुणिअ मुच्छाए पाणसंसए पडिओ, दिट्ठाणं पुण एदाअं आणन्दपरवसो चिट्ठसि। (दिष्ट्यापगतग्राहेदानीं स्वैरगोष्ठीवाहिनी। स्वैरमवगाहतामत्रभवान्। भो! सर्वकालदुर्ललितस्ते स्नेहः, यत्पूर्वमेतस्यया विपत्तिं श्रुत्वा मूर्च्छया प्राणसंशये पतितः, दृष्टायां पुनरेतस्यामानन्दपरवशस्तिष्ठति।)

सुभद्रा (स्वगतम्) हं, अधण्णाए मम किदे मुच्छिदो अय्यउत्तो। (हम्! अधन्याया मम कृते मूर्छित आर्यपुत्रः।)

धन प्रिये! इदानीमस्मद्वक्षसः पूर्यतामभिलाषः। (आलिङ्गति)

विदू भोदि! किं णिरवसेसं रक्खसेण भक्खिदा छप्पदिआ, जेण एआसिसे पमोदआले वि अ आअदा। (भवति, किं निरवशेषं राक्षसेन भक्षिता षट्पदिका येनैतादृशे प्रमोदकालेऽपि नागता।)

सुभद्रा मुक्ख! मा अकल्लाणं भणाहि। सा खु तवस्सिणी अवराओ सहीओ आणेदुं जादवसिविरं पत्थिआ। (मूर्ख! माकल्याणं भण। सा खलु तपस्विनी अपराः सखीरानेतुं यादवशिबिरं प्रस्थिता।)

विदू भो वअस्स! एसा दाव गत्तिआणो भण्डाआरं पवेसीअदु। अहव अत्तहोदीए थणसिहरं आरो वीअदु। मए दाव असुरक्खो एसो भारो। (भो वयस्य एषा तावद् गात्रिका नो भण्डारं प्रवेश्यताम्। अथवात्रभवत्याः स्तनशिखरमारोप्यताम्। मया तावदसुरक्ष एष भारः।)

धन सखे! सम्यगनुप्रबोधितोऽस्मि। सोऽहमस्या मत्प्राणदायिन्याः प्रत्युपकरोमि। (गात्रिकां तस्याः स्तनयोर्बध्नाति)

(ततः प्रविशति वासुदेवो युधिष्ठिरो भीमश्च)

वासु (सानन्दम्)

रत्नालङ्कारमिश्रं हरणमुपहृतं पादपद्मौ पृथायाः
प्राप्तौ मूर्ध्ना प्रयातं सकलमफलतां कर्म दुर्योधनस्य।
निःशेषामृष्टरोषः सह मधुनिवहैरागतः सीरपाणि-
र्धर्मः साक्षात्कृतोऽसाविहसह सहजैः साम्प्रतं निर्वृतोऽस्मि।। १२।।

युधि (सहर्षं) देव! वयं तावद् भवत्पादाधीनसकलपुरुषार्थसिद्धयो निर्वृताः, यतो जङ्घाकारिक वचनजनितशोकान्धीकृतचेतसां नस्तत्त्वं प्रकाशयता भगवता साधु सम्पादितम्। अपिच –

स्थित्युत्पत्तिप्रलयविधयो यद्वशे प्राणभाजां
जागर्त्येतद् भुवनमखिलं जागरूके च यस्मिन्।

स त्वं देव! त्रिभुवनगुरुः शर्मणे यस्य सज्जः
सोऽहं जातः खलु परिवृढः सोऽहेव त्रिलोक्याम्।। १३।।

भीम (स्मृत्वा सावज्ञम्) आर्य! ममापिनाम मह्यमनर्थापगमो नातितरां रोचते। कुतः,

भ्रातुर्मे दयितामम्बुसबुसः पापीयसा प्रेरितः
प्रध्वंसाय सुयोधनेन हरतु क्षुद्रक्रियो राक्षसः।
नारक्षिष्यदिमां यदि स्वभगिनीं कात्यायनी कर्कशौ
कण्डूलावकरिष्यतामरिकुलं निःशेषमस्मद्भुजौ।। १४।।

(सर्वे परिक्रामन्ति)

वासु इदं तदुद्यानम्। प्रविशामस्तावत्। (प्रवेशं नाटयन्ति)

धन (विलोक्य) अये, अयमार्याभ्यामागतश्चक्रपाणिः।

(उपसृत्य युधिष्ठिरवृकोदरौ प्रणम्य वासुदेवमालिङ्गति, सुभद्राप्यागत्य क्रमेण तान् प्रणमति)

सर्वे वत्से! अविधवा चिरमेधस्व।

विदू भो! जह तुह्मे। (भो! यथा यूयम्।)

युधि वत्स! धनञ्जयः! अपिनाम विप्रवासक्लेशमलीमसः समतिक्रान्तस्तव संवत्सरावधिस्तीर्थयात्राव्यतिकरः। सोऽयममुना सकललोकगुरुणा सङ्कर्षणानुजन्मना सम्बन्धहेतुरिति नः कल्याणकरः संवृत्तः।

भीम वत्स! बीभत्सो! प्रत्यासीदति पुरप्रवेशाय मुहूर्तः। प्रतीक्षते च देवेनामुना प्रत्यानीतं सङ्कर्षणसनाथं सकलसात्त्वतचक्रं त्वदागमनम्। तत् त्वर्यतां पुरप्रवेशाय।

धन (सपरितोषम्) आर्यौ! कथमिवामुना त्रैलोक्यनाथेन मैत्रीस्वयङ्ग्राहानुगृहीतस्य मम नाभिमुखीभवन्ति सर्वा सम्पदः।

वासु सखे! धनञ्जयः! किं ते भूयः प्रियमुपहरामि।

धनञ्जयः कात्यायन्या निशिचरकरादाहृतेयं सुभद्रा
दाता त्वं नस्त्रिभुवनगुरुः श्रेयसामागतोऽसि।
मूर्ध्ना स्पृष्टा मुदितमनसोरार्ययोरङ्घ्रिपद्मा
विद्मः पद्मादयित! न पुनः प्रार्थनीयान् पदार्थान्।। १५।।

तथाप्येतावदस्तु। (भरतवाक्यम्)

मेघाः कुर्वन्तु पृथ्वीं प्रतिनवकलमश्यामकेदारबन्धा-
माधीनासां प्रजानामपहरतु भवान् नित्यमानन्दबन्धुः।
प्रध्वस्तध्वान्तवृत्तेर्जलधरपटलश्रीमुषश्चक्रपाणे-
र्मैत्रीपात्रीभवेयं तव जनितजगच्चक्र! जन्मान्तरेऽपि।। १६।।

(इति निष्क्रान्ताः सर्वे)

समाप्तमिदं सुभद्राधनञ्जयं नाम नाटकम्।

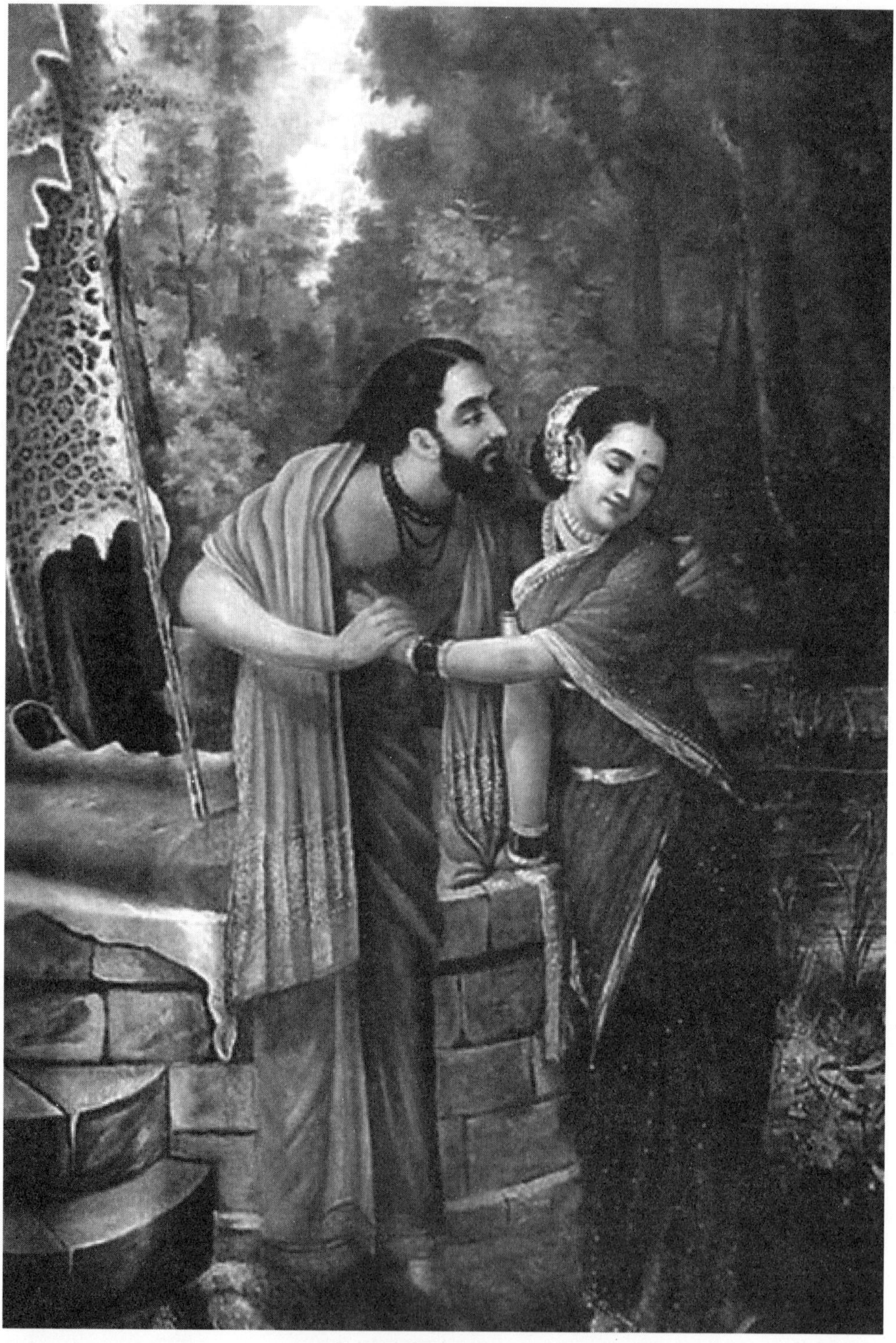

Subhadrā and Arjuna as painted by Raja Ravivarma. Arjuna is disguised as ascetic (Act 2)

Vyaṅgyavyākhyā

II

Saṃvaraṇadhvani

अथ संवरणध्वनिरारभ्यते

अथाहं केरलभूभृत्कृतेऽस्मिन् नाटके स्थायीभावं प्रयोगमार्गं च तत्सहृदयः प्रदर्शयामि। कथमिति चेत्,

भूभृत् स्वयं भूमिकया निरेत्य
निजामलङ्कृत्य तनुर्मनस्वी।
यं दर्शयित्वेति विनिश्चितात्मा
प्रयोगमार्गं प्रदर्शयामीमम्।।

तेन मया महीसुरेणापि तत्सहृदयेन पिष्टपेषणं क्रियते।

तथापि महत्कवेरभिप्रायं ज्ञातुमेतत्कृतं मया।
तत्प्रदर्शितमार्गेण विच्छिन्नस्योपदेष्टरि।।

नाटकनायकलक्षणं सर्वं दशरूपके द्रष्टव्यम्। अत्र तन्मात्रमेव दर्शयामि। अत्रादौ संवरणनाम्नि नाटके विदूषकस्य स्थायीभावप्रयोगमार्गौ दृश्येते।।

Here starts Saṃvaraṇadhvani

Then, I will present the mental state and mode of presentation in this drama composed by the Kerala king Kulaśekhara who shares the same sensibility. How is it?

> The King, determined as he was, put on the costumes
> and ornaments of different characters and showed the
> mode of their acting. I do present the same here.

I, a great Brahmin repeats this out of affection towards the king.

> Moreover, I do this as demonstrated to make the ideas of
> the great dramatist known to the actors who are cut off
> from the tradition of preceptors.

They are advised to learn the types of dramas and the nature of heroes from Dasarūpaka (in Nāṭyaśāstra). I confine myself only to that which is shown by the dramatist. Now, to start with, I will explain the mental condition and mode of acting of Vidūṣaka in the play named Saṃvaraṇa.

XVIII
Tapatīsaṃvaraṇam Dramatic Text Act I

प्रथमोऽङ्कः

(नान्द्यन्ते ततः प्रविशति सूत्रधारः)

सूत्रधारः लक्ष्मीर्धर्मजलच्छलेन सुधया दन्तच्छदच्छद्मना
सौदर्येण च कौस्तुभेन शकलेनेन्दोर्ललाटात्मना।
पाणिस्पर्शविधावमीभिरुचितैर्नीतेव दातुं विभो-
रालम्ब्याङ्गमधोक्षजस्य भवतां कामप्रसूः कल्पताम्।।१।।

(विचिन्त्य) अलं प्रविस्तरेण। अधुनातनमभ्युदयप्रमोदातिभारमात्मकुटुम्बिन्यै संविभजामि (परिक्रम्य नेपथ्याभिमुखमवलोक्य) आर्ये! इतस्तावत्।

नटी (प्रविश्य) अय्य! इअह्मि। (आर्य! इयमस्मि।)

सूत्र आर्ये। अद्याहमार्यमिश्रैराज्ञप्तः यथा – भवता तावद् अपूर्वेऽस्मिन्नादिराजकथासनाथे तपतीसंवरणनाम्नि नाटके नवरसानि प्रयोगामृतान्तराणि वयं पाययितव्या इति।

नटी अय्य! सुद्दअकालिदासहरिसदण्डिप्पमुहाणं महाकईणं अण्णदमस्य कस्स कविणो इदं णिबन्धणं, अण अय्यामिस्साणं एत्तिअं कोदुअं बड्ढोवेइं। (आर्य! शूद्रककालिदासहर्षदण्डि-प्रमुखाणां महाकवीनामन्यतमस्य कस्य कवेरिदं निबन्धनं, येनार्यमिश्राणामेतावत्कौतुकं वर्धयति।)

सूत्र आर्ये! मा मैवम्। यस्यपरमहंसपादपङ्केरुहपांसुपचलपवित्रीकृतमुकुटतटस्य वसुधाविबुधधना-यान्धकारमिहिरायमाणकरकमलस्य मुखकमलादगलद् आश्चर्यमञ्जरीकथामधुद्रवः। अपि च,

उत्तुङ्गघोणमुरुकन्धरमुन्नतांस-
मंसावलम्बिमणिकर्णिककर्णपाशम्।
आजानुलम्बिभुजमञ्जितकाञ्चनाभ-
मायामि यस्य वपुरार्तिहरं प्रजानाम्।। २।।

तस्य राज्ञः केरलकुलचूडामणेर्महोदयपुरपरमेश्वरस्य श्रीकुलशेखरवर्मणः कृतिरियमधुना प्रयोग-विषयमवतरति।

नटी अय्य! अणवच्चस्स अवच्चुप्पत्तिणिबन्धणेण तुज्झ परणयणन्तरब्भुदएण जणिदो प्रमोदो इमिणा अय्यमिस्ससासणेण विउणिओ। (आर्य! अनपत्यस्यापत्योत्पत्तिनिबन्धनेन तव परिणयनान्तराभ्युदयेन जनितः प्रमोदोऽनेनार्यमिश्रशासनेन द्विगुणितः।)

सूत्र आर्ये! तत् प्रस्तूयतां सङ्गीतकम्।

नटी (खेदमभिनीय) अय्य! एत्तिणं कालंणिअमकिलेसिअसरीरा तणअदुरासाए ण पारेमि अत्तणो अहिआरं कादुं। (आर्य! एतावन्तं कालं नियमक्लेशितशरीरा तनयदुराशया न पारयाम्यात्मनोऽधिकारं कर्तुम्।)

सूत्र (नेपथ्याभिमुखमवलोक्य) अये अयं मम शिष्यः शिवदासो विदूषकभूमिकामादायते। एवाभिवर्तते। श्रान्ता च त्वम्। अमपि शिष्यगुणसङ्क्रान्तमात्मप्रयोगप्रतिबिम्बं द्रष्टुं कुतूहली। तदावां प्रेक्षकौ भवावः। अपि च,

तनयसमुद्भवहेतोरमुतो नियमान्निवर्ततासि मया।
संवरणेन यथेयं साल्वसुता सार्वभौमेन।। ३।।

(इति निष्क्रान्तौ)

स्थापना।

(ततः प्रविशति विह्वलाङ्गो विदूषकः)

विदू (अङ्गानि संवाहयन् शूत्कृत्य) अज्ज खु अहं पच्चूसे एव्व 'देविं सल्लराअपुत्तिं पुत्तीआदो णिअमादो णिवत्तिअ सिविणसवणत्थं सिग्धं आअच्छ'त्ति वअस्सेणं कञ्चुइमुहेण णिउत्तो अस्सआणेण गदुअ अणुट्ठिअणिओओ अहं आअच्छंतो राअवीहीअं तेण दुव्विणीदेतुरएण पल्लत्थोह्मि। देण अविहेआणि मे गत्ताणि। तह वि वअस्सरस पस्सं उवसप्पिअं घेत्तिस्सम्। (नीचिकया परिक्रामन् पुरतो विलोक्य) अहो मम प्पहावो, जं सव्वो एव्व हत्थिणपरवत्थव्वो जणो अस्सो पारासरिओ त्ति अप्फुडं आलवंतो हस-णिरोहदुप्पेक्खमुहो हसिदुं अहसिदुं अ अपारअन्तो पज्जाउलो होइ। (नेपतथ्याभिमुखमवलोक्य) एसो वअस्सो परिसमाविअपडिकम्मविहाणो इदो एव्व आअच्छदि। ता कीस अत्ताणं खेदइस्सं। एत्थ एव्व च्चिाट्ठिस्सं। (स्थितः) (अद्य खलु अहं प्रत्यूष एव 'देवीं साल्वराजपुत्रीं पुत्रीयान्नियमान्निवर्त्य स्वप्नश्रवणार्थं शीघ्रमागच्छे'ति वयस्येन कञ्चुकिमुखेन नियुक्तोऽश्वयानेन गत्वानुष्ठितनियोगोऽहमागच्छन् रजवीथ्यां तेन दुर्विनीततुरगेण पर्यस्तोऽस्मि। तेनाविधेयानि मे गात्राणि तथापि वयस्यस्य पार्श्वमुपसर्पितुं ग्रहिष्यामि। अहो मम प्रभावो यत्सर्वं एव हस्तिनपुरवास्तव्यो जनः अश्वः पाराशर्य इत्यस्फुटमालपन् हासनिरोधदुष्प्रेक्षमुखो हसितुमहतिसुं चापारयन् पर्याकुला भवति। एव वयस्यः परिसमापितप्रतिकर्मविधान इत एवागच्छति। तत् किमर्थमात्मानं खेदयिष्यामि। अत्रैव स्थास्यामि।।)

(ततः प्रविशति सान्तस्तापः सपरिवारो राजा)

राजा (सविमर्शम्) अहोनुखलु अपत्याभिधानस्य पदार्थान्तरस्य महिमा। कुतः,

ACT ONE[1]

(At the end of the benediction, the Stage Manager enters)

Stage Manager: May Lakṣmī, with nectar in the form of her sweat, the co-born Kaustubha jewel as her lips and the crescent moon disguised as her forehead, being guided to the side of Adhokṣaja (Viṣṇu) the omnipotent, to be given away in marriage, be the source to fulfill your desires. (1)

(Reflecting) Enough of prolixity. I shall share with my consort this great happiness due to my good fortune. (Walking about and looking to the side of the curtain) Madam, come here please!

Actress (Entering) Sir, here I am.

SM Madam! Today I have been ordered by the distinguished audience that : "You should treat us with the nectar of the nine sentiments as depicted in the new drama named Tapatīsamvaraṇam representing the story of the ancient king."

Actr Sir, who among the great poets like Śūdraka, Kālidāsa, Harṣa and Daṇḍin, is the composer of this piece since the respectable audience evince this much interest?

SM Madam, say not so! Whose crown is purified by the dust shed by the lotus feet of the great sages; whose lotus hands emulate the sun in dissipating the darkness of poverty from the Brahmin supplicants and from whose lotus face the sweet story of Āścaryamañjarī flowed out; and further,

Whose tall golden figure with an elevated nose, a thick neck, lofty shoulders, decorated earlobes touching the shoulders and hands stretching down to the knee, banished the afflictions of his subjects. (2)

It is the composition of that great king Kulaśekharavarman, the lord of Mahodayapura and the crest-jewel of the Kerala race that is going to be staged presently.

Actr Sir, childless as you are, the pleasure you derive from your re-marriage to beget an issue has indeed been doubled by this mandate from the noble audience.

SM Madam, you start the music.

Actr (Showing the sorrow) Sir! Having exhausted my limbs for so long by vows in the vain hope of begetting a son, I am unable to perform my task.

SM (Looking towards the curtain) Ah! Here comes my pupil Śivadāsa dressed in the costume of the jester. And you are really tired. For myself I am, just interested in seeing the image of my performance reflected by him. So let

1 Translated into English by Professors NP Unni and Bruce M Sullivan

प्रियतनयवियोगे पुत्रिणां खेदवृत्ते-
र्विगणयितुमियत्तां कः पुमानुत्सहेत।
प्रसवगुणवियुक्तां मन्यमानस्य देवी-
मपि मम हृदि तापो जृम्भते दुर्निवारः।। ४।।

मया हि प्रातरेव स्वप्नप्रतिष्ठापनप्रयोजनायाहूतः प्रियवयस्यः पाराशर्यो नाद्याप्यायातः। (समन्तादवलोक्य) अये अनुन्मिषितबालातपोऽयं दिवसावतारः। तथा हि –

शालीनां परिपच्यमानकणिशश्रेणीशिखापाटलै-
रप्रौढैरतिमात्रमर्कमहसामग्रैरनालीढया।
सङ्कोचादधिपश्चिमाशमपरिध्वस्तावकाशं दृशा-
मद्यापि स्थितमम्बुराशिलहरीतन्व्या तमोमात्रया।।

(पुरतो विलोक्य)अये असौ वयस्यः पाराशर्यः किमप्युद्विग्न इव तिष्ठति। तत् को नु खल्वस्यायासहेतुः।

विदू (उपसृत्य कथमपि दक्षिणं पाणिमुन्नमयन्) जेदु भवं। (जयतु भवान्।)

राजा सखे! कथमयथापुरस्तवायमवयवव्यापारः।

विदू पसादादिसओ। (प्रसादातिशयः।)

राजा कोऽभिप्रायः।

विदू (सहासम्) अणक्खरं अणाआरसूइदं पि अत्थं उप्पेक्खिअ भणन्तो तुमं एह्णिं अक्खरलक्खिअं आआरसूइदं पि एदं जाणिदुं अकुसलो होहि। ता कहिं दे गअं पण्डिच्चं। (अनक्षरमनाकार सूचितमप्यर्थमुत्प्रेक्ष्यभणन् त्वमिदानीमक्षरलक्षितमाकारसूचितमप्येतद् ज्ञातुमकुशलो भवसि। तत् क्व ते गतं पाण्डित्यम्।)

राजा ननु भवादृशामम्भोधिगम्भीरचेतसामतिदुरवबोधाश्चित्तवृत्तयः प्रस्पष्टमभिधीयताम्।

विदू जइ एव्वं कहइस्सं। अहं आरूढहयो गदुअ णिवत्तिअ देविं णियमादो आअच्छन्तो राजवीहीअं तेण दुट्ठतुरएण कंदुअक्कलिं मए कीलन्तेण कहिं पि पक्खित्तो ह्मि। तदो चिन्तिअं च मए। अज्ज आसणस्स अत्थिरदाए अस्सारोहणेण गअणगमणस्स अद्धमेत्तं सिक्खिअं, ता देवासुरविमद्द-परिइदम्बरगमणस्स वअस्सस्स सआसादो सअलं सिक्खिस्सं त्ति। ता अवदिसदु मे वअस्सो। (यद्येवं कथयिष्यामि। अहमारूढहयो गत्वा निवर्त्य देवीं नियमादागच्छन् राजवीथ्यां तेन दुष्टतुरगेण कन्दुकक्रीडं मया क्रीडता क्वापि प्रक्षिप्तोऽस्मि। ततश्चिन्तितं च मया। अद्यासनस्यास्थिरतयाश्वा-रोहणेन गगनगमनस्यार्द्धमात्रं शिक्षितम्। तद् देवासुरविमर्दपरि-चिताम्बरगमनस्य वयस्यस्य सकाशात् सकलं शिक्षिष्य इति। तदुपदिशतु मे वयस्यः।)

राजा मूर्ख! अस्या क्रियायामकिञ्चित्करा मादृशामुपदेशाः पश्य –

पवनविजयमार्गा मन्त्रसिद्धिप्रकारा
मुनिवरवचनं वा देवतानां प्रसादाः।

us be spectators. Further, I have just persuaded you to desist from your penance for begetting a son, as did King Samvaraṇa with the daughter of King Sālva. (3)

(Both exit)

End of the prologue

(The Vidūṣaka enters trembling all over)

Vidū (Rubbing his limbs and mourning) Commanded by my friend through a chamberlain to persuade the Sālva princess, the queen, to desist from her penance to beget a son and to rush back to hear about the dream, I set out on horseback early in the morning and, after performing the errand, was returning through the main avenue when that devil of a horse threw me down. Hence my body is not quite in shape; but still I must try to reach the side of my friend. (Walking hunch-backed and looking in front) Ho! Wonderful is my prowess! For, all the citizens of Hastinapura murmured the words 'horse' and 'Pārāśarya' and, unablc to smile or not to smile, made their faces horrible. (Looking towards the curtain) Here comes my friend having put on his usual ornaments, so why should I trouble myself? I shall remain right here. (He stands) (The king enters looking worried, with attendants following)

King (Reflecting) What a great fortune it is to have a son! For,

Whoever will be able to reckon the grief of a father who just lost his dear son? As for myself, the knowledge that my queen is barren breaks my heart with unbearable grief. (4)

My dear friend Pārāśarya, whom I have summoned with a view to inform him of my dream, is yet to arrive. (Looking around) Ah! It is only daybreak and the morning light has not yet radiated. Thus:

The speck of darkness like the thin waves of the ocean lingers even now on the western horizon, untouched by the tender rays of the sun which bear semblance to shoots of ripe paddy. (5)

(Looking in front) Ah! There stands my friend Pārāśarya as though he is a little grieved. What can be his trouble?

Vidū (Approaching and raising his right hand with difficulty) Hail your majesty!

King Friend, how is it that your body behaves unnaturally?

Vidū On account of your majesty's favour!

उपचयिभिरुदर्कस्वादुभिः पुण्यपूरै-
रपगतदुरितौघानम्बरे वर्तयन्ति।। ६।।

अल्लं एदिणा। अणुप्फुल्लं दे वदणकमलं सन्दावगब्भं पिसुणे इहिअअं। को एत्थ हेदू। (अलमेतेन। अनुत्फुल्लं ते वदनकमलं सन्तापगर्भं पिशुनयति हृदयम्। कोऽत्र हेतुः।)

राजा सखे! सम्यगुपलक्षितम्। अतीतायां खलु रात्रौ स्वप्ने सूर्योपस्थानमातन्वतः –

आराद् दृष्टं चलदलपुटैर्दीर्घिकापद्मिनीना-
मर्द्धोन्मीलन्मुकुलनयनैः प्रस्फुरद्भृङ्गतारैः।
तुच्छीकुर्वत् तुहिनकणिकाजालकं मे पुरस्ता-
दाविर्भूतं किरणनिकरैरम्बरादर्कबिम्बम्।। ७।।

विदू तदो तदो। (ततस्ततः।)

राजा ततस्तत्माद् भक्तिभारावर्जितमौलिं प्रणमन्तमन्तरेण मामासीदतिगम्भीरा भारती।

विदू केसि। (कीदृशी।)

राजा 'वत्स! संवरण!

दयितां तव तन्वङ्गीं साल्वराजसुतामिमाम्।
अवेहि प्रसवापेतां शरच्चूतलतामिव' ।। ८।।

इति। अनन्तरमन्तरधत्त च भगवान्। अहं च प्राभातिकमङ्गलगीतिभिः प्रतिबोधितोऽस्मि।

विदू सेत्थि होदु। मा भवं सन्दप्पदु। (स्वस्ति भवतु। मा भवान् सन्तप्यताम्।)

राजा कथमहमधर्मणो नानुशये।

विदू (विहस्य) अहो तुह अणेअपसण्डिरअणपरिपूरिअभण्डाआरसहस्सस्स वि रिणसन्दावो त्ति अच्छरिअं। (अहो तवानेकप्रशस्तरत्नपरिपूरितभाण्डागारसहस्रस्यापि ऋणसन्ताप इत्याश्चर्यम्।)

राजा मूर्ख! नाहं भवदभिमतमृणमधिकृत्य ब्रवीमि। अन्यदिदमपत्याभिधानमृणमुद्वहामि पितृणाम्।

विदू मए वि एदं अण्णोण्णं विवदंताणं तक्किआणं मुहादो सुदपुरुवं एव्व। अत्तभवं पुण सुय्यवअणस्स तप्पज्जत्थं अजाणन्तो अतिमेत्तं संतप्पदि। एसो तस्स अभिप्पाओ। इअं देवी अणवच्चा। अण्णं परिणेहि। सा दे तणअं जणइस्सदि त्ति। (मयाप्येतदन्योन्यं विवदमानानां तार्किकाणां मुखात् श्रुतपूर्वमेव। अत्रभवान् पुनः सूर्यवचनस्य तात्पर्यार्थमजानन् अतिमात्रं सन्तप्यते। एष तस्याभिप्रायः 'इयं देव्यनपत्या। अन्यां परिणय। सा ते तनयं जनयिष्यति' इति।)

राजा सखे! सम्भाव्यत एवैतत्। न पुनरहं देवीगुणगणनिगलितां चित्तवृत्तिमन्यतः क्षेप्तुमलम्। तदधुना निर्वर्तितनियमां तत्रभवतीं द्रक्ष्यावः।

विदू एदु एदु भवं। (एत्वेतु भवान्।) (उभौ परिक्रामतः)

राजा (निमित्तं सूचयन्) सखे!

वामेतरमिदमधुना स्फुरति मदीयं विलोचनं केन।
न सुतसमुद्भवलाभादपरः प्रीतिप्रसङ्गो मे।। ९।।

King What do you mean?

Vidū (Derisively) You who are able to find out things unspoken and unexpressed now fail to notice what has been spoken and expressed. What has become of your learning?

King It is impossible to guess the thoughts of profound fellows like you. Please, make it clear.

Vidū If that is so, let me explain. After persuading her majesty to desist from her penance, I was returning on horseback through the main road when that devil of a horse kicked me around like a ball and threw me down. Then this thought occurred to me. Today I have learned half the art of flying, since I was riding a horse without being seated. Henceforth I shall learn it fully from my friend who has gained much experience in traversing the sky by his regular participation in the conflicts between the gods and demons. Please, instruct me, Oh my dear friend!

King Fool. The instructions of people like me are of no use in this business. You see,

> That traversing the sky is accomplished by controlling the air, by working spells, By the favour bestowed by Gods, or by increasing merits that dispel the sins. (6)

Vidū Enough of that. The gloom of your lotus face indicates the grief concealed by your heart. Why is it so?

King Friend, you have guessed it right. During the previous night I was worshipping the sun in my dream, when

> There appeared from the sky the orb of the sun before me, drying up the dew drops, and observed by the lotuses of the lake, opening their petals, and releasing the bees entrapped. (7)

Vidū And then?

King I bowed my head in reverence before it, from which a deep voice addressed me.

Vidū To what effect?

King Oh Samvaraṇa, my dear son,

> Know that your beautiful and beloved wife, the tender daughter of the Sālva king, is as barren as the mango twigs of the autumnal season.(8)

And then the lord disappeared. For myself, I was aroused by the morning songs of the bards.

विदू अदिट्ठपुरुवाए देवीए पदविं अण्णेसन्तस्स किं ण होइ सुणिमित्तं। (अदृष्टपूर्वाया देव्याः पदवीमन्विष्यतः किं न भवति सुनिमित्तम्।)

राजा किमदृष्टपूर्वेति।

विदू एत्तिअं कालं णिअमन्तरिददंसण त्ति मए भणिदं। (अग्रतो विलोक्य) पेक्खदु पेक्खदु भवं, एसा भअवई भाईरही दीसइ। (एतावन्तं कालं नियमान्तरितदर्शनेति मया भाणितम्। पश्यतु पश्यतु भवान्, एषा भगवती भागीरथी दृश्यते।)

राजा (साञ्जलिबन्धम्)

भगवति! पुनतीभ्यस्तावकीभ्यस्त्रिलोकीं
प्रणतिमुपगतोऽहं स्वर्गनिश्रेणिकाभ्यः।
मदकलकलहंसश्रेणीपारिप्लवाभ्यः
शशिकरविशदाभ्यो वीचिकामालिकाभ्यः।। १०।।

विदू (पुरतो निर्दिश्य) एसो गुहघरपरिसरारामे। पविसदु भवं। (ए, गुहगृहपरिसरारामः। प्रविशतु भवान्।)

राजा (प्रवेशं नाटयन् विलोक्य) सखे! अतिसुभगोऽयमुद्यानाभोगः। इह हि –

आरामलक्ष्मीचरणच्युतानां
बिभ्रत्यमी विभ्रमयावकानाम्।
शोभां शुकालीढफलावलीनां
बीजोत्करा दाडिमवल्लरीणाम्।। ११।। (उभौ परिक्रामतः)

विदू (सभयं परावृत्त्य) भो पला अह्म। अग्गदो महन्तो संपहारो वट्ठइ। (भो पलायावहे। अग्रतो महान् सम्प्रहारो वर्तते।)

राजा कोऽयमकाण्डे सम्भ्रमः।

विदू एआरिसं पाणसंसअं मोत्तूण को अण्णो संभमस्स अवआसो होइ। (एतादृशं प्राणसंशयं मुक्त्वा कोऽन्यः सम्भ्रमस्यावकाशो भवति।)

राजा कस्ते प्राणसंशयस्य हेतुः।

विदू (अङ्गुल्या निर्दिश्य) एदर्स्मि मरगअसिलादले लोहिदपूरो दीसइ। (एतस्मिन् मरकतशिलातले लोहितपूरो दृश्यते।)

राजा (निपुणं निरूप्य सस्मितम्) सखे! सत्यं प्रवृत्त एव सम्प्रहारः कस्याश्चिद् दिव्ययुवतेः –

लाक्षाविषदिग्धाभ्यां हृदि मन्येऽहं पदाब्जबाणाभ्याम्।
विद्धः स्मरेण शेते मरतकमणिरेष कीर्णकरः।। १२।।

विदू केण उण वअस्सो जाणइ दिव्वकण्णाए पदविण्णासो ण माणुसीए त्ति। (केन पुनर्वयस्यो जानाति दिव्यकन्यायाः पदविन्यासो न मानुष्या इति।)

राजा पश्यतु भवान् अम्बरावतरणसमयसङ्क्रान्तं पिण्डीतरुपलाशेषु पिण्डालक्तकरसम्।

Vidū May it be well with you. Your majesty need not worry.

King Indebted as I am, how could I escape worrying?

Vidū (Laughing) It is strange that you worry yourself as though indebted, despite your thousand coffers filled with famous gems!

King Fool! I am not talking about the debt of which you think! I bear a different kind of debt in the form of offspring for the ancestors.

Vidū I have heard of that from the debating dialecticians. But your majesty fails to understand the purport of the words of the Sun God and is much distressed. What he means is this: "This queen is barren. Marry another. She will bear you a son."

King Friend, this is quite likely. But I am unable to shift elsewhere my heart held fast by the noble qualities of my wife. Now we should meet her majesty, who has desisted from her penance.

Vidū This way, your majesty. (Both walk about)

King (Showing that he noticed some omen) Friend!

> Here throbs my eye, the one other than the left! To what effect? To me,
> there is nothing more pleasant than the birth of a son. (9)

Vidū When you are in search of a queen who is still unseen what would not be a good omen?

King Why do you say, "still unseen?"

Vidū I was saying that she shut herself away during the period of penance. (Looking in front) Behold your majesty! Here we see the venerable Bhāgīrathī.

King (With folded hands)

> Oh Goddess! I bow before your waves, pure as the beams of the moon,
> floated upon by the intoxicated swans; purifying the three worlds and
> forming the stairway to heaven.

Vidū (Pointing in front) Here is the garden in the precincts of the temple dedicated to Guha. May your majesty enter.

King (Gesticulating entrance and observing) The appearance of the garden is extremely beautiful. Here....

> The seeds of the Dāḍima fruits strewn all over by the parrots that settle
> on them bear close resemblance to the footprints of the ṣylvan goddess
> tinged by juice of lac.(11)

(Both walk around)

विदू जुज्जइ एदं। (पुनर्निरूप्य) एदस्स पदजुअलंतरस्स को वक्खाण विसेसो। अहवा एत्तिअमेत्तं अहं एव्व संपहारिअ वक्खाणइस्सं। (ध्याननिमीलितचक्षुस्तिष्ठति) (युज्यत एतद्। एतस्य पदयपगलान्तरस्य को व्याख्यानविशेषः। अथवैतावन्मात्रमहमेव सम्प्रधार्य व्याख्यास्यामि।)

(ततः प्रविशति देवी सपरिवारा)

देवी हल्ला! उप्पलिए! एत्तिअं कालं तणअसंभवकोदुआदिसएण अय्यउत्तविरहुक्कण्ठाविलुलिअं पि हिअअं अप्फुडिअं आसि। अज्ज उण णिवत्तिअणिअमाए दूसहवेदणं एदं मुहुत्तअं पि मं णाणुमण्णइ विलम्बिदुं। ता तुरिअं तस्स दंसणूसवं अणुभविस्सं। (सखि! उत्पलिके! इयन्तं कालं तनयसम्भवकौतुकातिशयेनार्यपुत्रविरहोत्कण्ठविलुलितमपि हृदयमस्फुटितमासीत्। अद्य पुनर्निवर्त्तितनियमाया दुस्सहवेदनमेतन्मुहूर्तमपि मां नानुमन्यते विलम्बितुम्। तत् त्वरितं तस्य दर्शनोत्सवमनुभविष्यामि।)

चेटी भट्टिणि! पावुसणिरोहमुक्का सरअचंदचंदिआ कहं अणासादिअ कुमुदाअरं चिट्ठइ। ता एदु एदु भट्टिणी। (भट्टिनि! प्रावृण्णिरोधमुक्ता शरच्छन्द्रचन्द्रिका कथमनासाद्य कुमुदाकरं तिष्ठति। तद् एतु एतु भट्टिनी।) (परिक्रमतः)

विदू भो ण केवलं णिमीलन्ताणं अक्खिणं एव्व, चित्तस्स वि महन्तो अन्धआरो संवुत्तो। ता तुमं एव्व वक्खाणेहि। (भो न केवलं निमीलतोरक्ष्णोरेव, चित्तस्यापि महानन्धकारः संवृत्तः। तत् त्वमेव व्याचक्ष्व।)

राजा किमत्र दुरवबोधम्। आभ्यामपि तद्वयस्यायाः कस्याश्चित् पदाभ्यां भवितव्यम्।

विदू एदं पि जुज्जइ। (ऊर्ध्वमवलोक्य) अविह अंबरादो एदं पिसिअखण्डं णिवडइ। तक्केमि सग्गे महन्तो देवासुरसङ्गामो वट्टदि त्ति। (इदमपि युज्यते। अविह अम्बरादेतत् पिशितखण्डं निपतति। तर्कयामि स्वर्गे महान् देवासुरसङ्ग्रामो वर्तत इति।)

चेटी (कर्णं दत्वा) भट्टिणि! अग्गदो अय्यपारासरिअस्स विअ आलावो सुणीअदि। तक्केमि महाराएण एत्थ सण्णिहिदेण होदव्वं ति। (भट्टिनि! अग्रत आर्यपाराशर्यस्येवालापः श्रूयते। तर्कयामि महाराजेनात्र सन्निहितेन भवितव्यमिति।)

देवी हला! जइ एव्वं मुहुत्तअं लदावलअन्तरिदाओ भविअ तेसं अण्णोण्णसेरालावं सुणह्म। (सखि! यद्येवं मुहूर्तकं लतावलयान्तरिते भूत्वा तयोरन्योन्यस्वैरालापं शृणुवः।) (तथा कुरुतः)

राजा (पुनर्निरूप्य) न खल्वियं पिशितपेशी। मन्ये मन्दारपल्लवापीडकल्पितः कस्याश्चित् –

क्रमैः कैश्चिन्मृदुमणिदलैर्गण्डसंसर्गलाभा-
द्धन्यैः स्वेदप्रकरसुभगैश्चित्रितैः पत्रभङ्गैः।
सोऽयं शुभ्रैः शबलिततनुः षट्पदक्षोभलग्नैः
सान्द्रामोदैरलकसुमनोरेणुभिः कर्णपूरः।। १३।।

देवी हला! एसो मन्दारकण्णउरवुत्तन्तो अदिमेत्तं मं संकावेदि। (सखि! एष मन्दारकर्णपूरवृत्तान्तो-ऽतिमात्रं मां शङ्कयति।

Vidū (Retreating with fright) Sir, we must run away. A fierce fight is raging ahead.

King Why this sudden fright?

Vidū What else is there but fear for one's life?

King Why do you think that your life is in danger?

Vidū (Pointing his finger) See, there is blood in this emerald seat!

King (Observing with care and smiling) Friend! It is true that a fight has taken place.

Some celestial damsel's Darts of lotus feet tinged with the poison of lac juice have pierced the heart of this emerald stone and there it lies with hands stretching out. (12)

Vidū How do you know that it is the footprint of a celestial damsel and not that of a human one?

King Look at the clots of lac juice on the foliage of Aśoka and Palāśa trees smeared (by the feet) in the act of descending from the sky.

Vidū It agrees. (Observing again) What explanation is possible for this other pair of feet? But I shall offer an explanation after thinking a while. (Stands meditating with closed eyes; the Queen enters followed by her retinue)

Queen Friend, Utpalikā! Till now my heart, though uneasy at the separation of my lord, did not break owing to the eagerness for begetting a son. But now that I have stopped my penance, it hurts greatly, unable to wait even a moment. So I shall have the delight of seeing him soon.

Maid Your majesty, how could the beams of the autumnal moon freed from the rain clouds abstain from reaching the lotuses? This way, my lady! (Both walk about)

Vidū Darkness pervades not only my closed eyes, but also my mind, so please explain it yourself.

King What is there incomprehensible? This pair of feet must belong to her companion.

Vidū That also is consistent. (Looking upwards) Help! Here falls a piece of flesh from the sky! I guess that a terrible fight is raging in heaven between the gods and demons.

Maid (Hearing) Your majesty! Ahead the voice of the honourable Pārāśarya can be heard. I guess that his majesty must be present here.

Queen Friend, if so, we shall conceal ourselves behind the creeper for a moment and listen to their unrestrained conversation. (They act accordingly)

King (Scrutinising again) This is not flesh. I think that this, belonging to some damsel and made of tender mandāra twigs:

चेटी भट्टिणि! एत्तिएण ण णिण्णओ। अवहिदाओ सुणह्य। (भट्टिनि! एतावता न निर्णयः। अवहिते शृणुवः।)

विदू भो मम खलु सिद्धन्तो उदअलिहिअं विअ अक्खरं सुण्णपरिणामं होदि। (कर्णपूरमादाय) किस्से अअं कण्णउरो त्ति एदं पि किं जाणिदुं पारेसि। (भोः मम खलु सिद्धान्त उदकलिखितमिवाक्षरं शून्यपरिणामं भवति। कस्या अयं कर्णपूर इत्येतदपि किं ज्ञातुं पारयसि।)

राजा (अङ्गुल्या निर्दिशन्) यस्या इयं पदपद्धतिः, मन्ये तदीयामेवावतंसकभुवमसावलङ्कृतवानिति।

विदू को एत्थ हेदू। (कोऽत्र हेतुः।)

राजा यतः पदवतंसकयोरालक्ष्यन्ते घर्मसलिलबिन्दवः।

देवी हला! पअकहा वि एत्थ आपडिआ। (सखि! पदकथाप्यत्रापतिता।)

चेटी भट्टिणि! कि वा एदिणा। (भट्टिनि! किं वैतेन।)

विदू भो समाणे वि समीरपहगमणपरिस्समे कहं अक्काए च्चिअ समजलं उब्भिण्णं। (भोः समानेऽपि समीरपथगमनपरिश्रमे कथमेकस्या एव श्रमजलमुद्भिन्नम्।)

राजा न खलु मार्गश्रमजनितैरेभिर्भवितव्यम्। श्लाघ्यजन्मानं कञ्चिद् युवानम् –

अपाङ्गपातैरनुरागगर्भैरावल्गितभ्रूलमापिबन्त्याः।
रोमाञ्चसम्भेदसखेषु सोऽयमङ्गेष्वनङ्गप्रथमावतारः।। १४।।

विदू भो अप्पण्णो वि अहं एत्थ किं पि उप्पेक्खिदुं इच्छामि। तुमं एव्व तिस्से अपङ्गसरस्स लक्खो। को अण्णो एत्थ माणुसलोए दिव्वकण्णआजणप्पत्थणीओ। (भो अल्पज्ञोऽप्यहमत्र किमप्युत्प्रेक्षितुमिच्छामि। त्वमेव तस्या अपाङ्गशरस्य लक्ष्यः। कोऽन्योऽत्र मानुषलोके दिव्यकन्यकाजनप्रार्थनीयः।)

देवी हला! किं सुदो माणवअस्स उवण्णासो। (सखि! किं श्रुतो माणवकस्योपन्यासः।)

चेटी आम सुदो। को उण एदिणा महाराअस्स अवराहो। (आम श्रुतः। कः पुनरेतेन महाराजस्यापराधः।)

देवी का वा मनेतेदि सो अवरज्झो त्ति। (का वा मन्त्रयते सोऽपराद्ध इति।)

विदू (सावधानं कर्णपूरमवलोक्य) भो वअस्स! अच्छेरं अच्छेरं। एत्थ किं पि सत्थं आलिहिदं। (भो वयस्य! आश्चर्यमाश्चर्यम्। अत्र किमपि शास्त्रमालिखितम्।)

राजा (सस्मितम्) तर्हि वाच्यतां शास्त्रम्।

विदू (वाचयति) किकुचासविमेसुतिदिपुआ। कहं पि वाइदाइ अक्खराइ। अत्थं पुण जाणिदुं अकुमलह्मि। ता कहेतु अत्तभवं। (कथमपि वाचितान्यक्षराणि। अर्थं पुनर्ज्ञातुमकुशलोऽस्मि। तत् कथयत्वत्रभवान्।)

राजा (सविमर्शम्) शङ्के मदनसन्देशपराया गाथायाः पदाद्यक्षराण्येतानीति।

विदू पच्चेमि भवदो मदिकोसलं, जइ णहेहि लिहिअ तं पूरेसि। (प्रत्येमि भवतो मतिकौशलं, यदि नखैर्लिखित्वा तां पूरयसि।) (राजा कर्णपूरमादाय तथा कृत्वा ददाति)

> Is an ear ornament fortunate on account of its touch with her cheeks, decorated with tiny drops of her sweat and marks of pigments from her forehead, variegated in colour from pollen scattered by bees that hover about flowers adorning her locks. (13)

Queen Friend, this talk about the ear ornament of Mandāra gives me much apprehension.

Maid My lady, this is not enough to decide;let us listen with attention.

Vidū Friend, my theory is as futile as letters scribbled on water. Can you make out whose ear ornament it could be?

King (Pointing his finger) I think that this ornament adorned that girl whose footprints are seen here.

Vidū What reason can there be?

King Since the drops of sweat are to be seen in both the footprints and the ear ornament.

Queen Friend, the incidence of footprints also is here.

Maid My lady! What of that?

Vidū Friend, since the effort of travelling through the air is common to both, why is one maiden alone sweating?

King This cannot be due to travelling.

> Some youth of worthy existence was seen by her with lovely glances through the corner of her eyes, and thus for the first time she felt the thrill of love. (14)

Vidū Friend, though I am not very learned I would like to suggest something: you alone are the target for the dart of her glance. Who else is there in this world of humans to be sought after by a celestial damsel?

Queen Friend! Have you heard the suggestion of this silly Brahmin?

Maid Yes, I have heard. What fault is there with his majesty?

Queen Who says that he is at fault?

Vidū (Looking carefully at the ear ornament) Oh friend! Strange! Marvelous! Some note is scribbled on it.

King (Smiling) Then read that note!

Vidū (Reads) kikucāsavimesutidipuā. I have somehow deciphered the letters, but I am unable to understand the meaning. Be pleased to tell me, your majesty!

King (Pondering) I think that these are the initial letters of a lyric conveying a message of love.

विदू (पुनर्वाचयति)

किं कुणइ चादअवहू सन्दसिणेहा वि मेहपअरम्भि।
सुहिआ तिस्से दिट्ठी पुण्णा आणन्दबाहेण।। १५।।
(किं करोति चातकवधूः सान्द्रस्नेहापि मेघप्रवरे।
सुखिता तस्या दृष्टिः पूर्णानन्दबाष्पेण।।)

भो आखु विअ तुवं। सो खु अप्पं पि छिद्दं अदिमेत्तं वित्थारेदि। तुए कि पञ्चसेहि अक्खरेहि महन्तो गन्थसन्दब्भो रइओ। अलं एदिणा, अण्णं किं पि रहस्सं पुच्छिस्सं। पददंसणादो आरहिअ अण्णादिसो विअ दे आआरो। अत्थि वा वम्महस्स वि एत्थ अवसरो। (भो आखुरिव त्वम्। स खल्वल्पमपि च्छिद्रमतिमात्रं विस्तारयति। त्वयापि पञ्चषैरक्षरैर्महान् ग्रन्थसन्दर्भो रचितः। उक्तमेतेन, अन्यत् किमपि रहस्यं प्रक्ष्यामि। पददर्शनादारभ्यान्यादृश इव ते आकारः। अस्ति वा मन्मथस्याप्यत्रावसरः।)

देवी हला! मम वि एसो संसओ। (सखि! ममाप्येष संशयः।)

चेटी भट्ठिणो उत्तरं सुणिअ णिण्णअं करहा। (भट्टिनि! भर्तुरुत्तरं श्रुत्वा निर्णयं कुर्वः।)

राजा (आत्मगतम्) अहो नु खलु मदीयामवस्थामनुकरोति माणवकस्य वचनम्। तथा हि अनालक्षितलक्षा कापि रणरणिका स्पृशतीव मदीयं चेतः। (प्रकाशम्) सखे! अलमन्यथा सम्भाव्य। आक्षिप्तोऽस्मि केवलं विस्मयेन।

चेटी भट्टिणि! किं सुदं। (भट्टिनि! किं श्रुतम्।)

देवी उज्जुआ खुतुवं। ण एआरिसा महीरहिअआ हिअअं पआसेन्ति। (ऋज्वी खलु त्वम्। नैतादृशा गभीरहृदया हृदयं प्रकाशयन्ति।)

विदू (गन्धग्रहणमभिनीय) जह दिक्खणाए दिसाए बहलामोदमंसलो मारुओ वाहइ, तह तक्केमि तहिं तेण दिव्वजणेण होदव्वं त्ति। ता दक्खिस्सं णं। (यथा दक्षिणस्या दिशो बहुलामोदमांसलो मारुतो वाति, तथा तर्कयामि तत्र तेन दिव्यजनेन भवितव्यमिति। तद् द्रक्ष्याम्यनम्।)

राजा मूर्ख! प्रभावान्तर्हितमूर्तिः कथमन्विष्य दृश्यते दिव्यजनः।

विदू असम्भाविअतिरक्खरणीओ वि कदाइ चिट्ठिदि त्ति मए सुदपुरुवं एव्व। ता धेत्तिस्सं। (परिक्रम्यावलोक्य च साटोपम्) मुक्खेण एव्व मए दिट्ठे सो दिव्वजणो विवेअरासिणा तुए वि दट्ठव्वो आसी। ता सिग्धं एहि। (असम्भाविततिरस्करणीकोऽपि कदाचित् तिष्ठतीति मया श्रुतपूर्वमेव। तद्ग्रहिष्यामि। मूर्खेणैव मया दृष्टः स दिव्यजनो विवेकराशिना त्वयापि द्रष्टव्य आसीत्। तच्छीघ्रमेहि।) (रजानामाकर्षति)

राजा (भ्रमपरिणामेनानेन भवितव्यम्) भवतु पश्यामस्तावत् (उपसृत्य दृष्ट्वा सविलक्षं जनान्तिकम्) कथमियं देवी संवृत्ता। सखे! सोऽयमीदृशो भवच्चापलपरिणामः।

विदू बुभुक्खातिमिरेण अन्धिकृदा मे दिट्ठी, येण देवीं दिव्यजणो त्ति सम्भावेमि। (बुभुक्षातिमिरेणान्धीकृता मे दृष्टिः, येन देवीं दिव्यजन इति सम्भावयामि।)

देवी पारासरिअ! अलं सङ्काए। णाहं सा, जिस्से सोकण्णऊरो, तं पादजुअलं वा। (पाराशर्य! अलं शङ्कया। नाहं सा, यस्याः स कर्णपूरः तत् पादयुगलं वा।)

Vidū If you can complete the lyric writing with your nails I shall believe in your intelligence. (The king takes the ornament, does accordingly and gives it to him)

Vidū (Reads again)

> What can a female Cātaka do if she is enamoured of the great cloud? She
> just feels ecstasy, her eyes filling with tears of joy (15)

Oh, you are like a mouse! For he could make a small hole big, while you have transformed five or six letters into a great composition. Enough of that! I would like to ask you about the secret. Your disposition has changed since seeing the footprint. Is it possible that love has found an opening?

Queen Friend, I too have the same doubt.

Maid My lady, we shall ascertain it from his majesty's answer.

King (To himself) Strange that the words of the Brahmin reveal my disposition. For, my mind is tormented by an uneasiness towards something unknown. (Aloud) Friend, don't speculate wildly. I am just surprised.

Maid My lady, did you hear?

Queen You are simple. Deep men like him will never reveal their minds.

Vidū (Gesticulating that he smells something) Since a fragrant wind is blowing from the southern direction, I am presuming that the celestial maiden must be there. I shall see her.

King Fool! How can you find a celestial concealed by her divine powers?

Vidū I have heard that they are not always concealed. I shall find out. (Walking about and observing with pride) Though an idiot, I have seen her, and you the intelligent one must also see her. Please come quickly! (Pulls the King)

King This must be a mistake. All right, we shall see. (Going near and seeing; aside with embarrassment) What! This is really the Queen. Friend, this is how your rashness boomerangs!

Vidū Hunger has darkened my eyes so that I mistook her majesty for the celestial.

Queen Pārāśarya! Don't be mistaken. I am not that damsel to whom belongs the ear ornament or the footprints.

विदू (जनान्तिकम्) भो वअस्स! सव्वं एव्व सुदंतत्तहोदीए। तक्केमिं हिज्जो आरहिअ एत्थ चिट्ठदि त्ति। (भो वयस्य! सर्वमेव श्रुतं तत्रभवत्या। तर्कयामि ह्य आरभ्यात्र तिष्ठतीति।)

राजा (प्रकाशम्) देवि! कथमस्थाने कुपितासि। अद्भुतरसोऽयमत्रापराध्यति।

देवी कुविद त्ति भं महाराओ एव्व मन्तेदि। (कुपितेति मां महाराज एव मन्त्रयते।)

राजा प्रिये! मा मैवम् ,

अकुटिलविषमाभ्याँ भ्रूलताभ्यामिदानी-
मुपहितकुचकम्पैरश्रुसंरोधयत्नैः।
प्रणयकुपितगर्भैर्मुग्धहासैर्मदीयं
चकितयसि मुधैव त्वं चकोराक्षि! चेतः।। १६।।

चेटी परीदद पसीददु भट्टिणी। अणवरद्धो एव्व एत्थ भट्टा। (प्रसीदतु प्रसीदतु भट्टिनी। अनपराद्ध एवात्र भर्ता।)

देवी हला! एव्वं एदं। अहं खु णियमकिलेसिअसरीरा अणीसह्मि उत्तरोत्तरकहाअं। ता अत्तणो आवासं गमिस्सं। (सखि! एवमेतत्। अहं खलु नियमक्लेशितशरीरा अनीशास्म्युत्तरोत्तर कथायाम्। तद् आत्मन आवासं गमिष्यामि।) (निष्क्रान्ता देवी सपरिवारा)

राजा कथं गतैव देवी।

प्रथमः आरूढोऽयमवलग्नमम्बरस्यांशुमाली। तथा हि –

अभिलषति न भृङ्गी पौष्पमुद्वेलतप्तं
मधु मधुपसपीतिप्राप्तपीयूषभावम्।
अपि तु तरणितापात् सङ्कुचद्भिः स्वगात्रै-
रधिसहचरपक्षच्छायमालीयतेऽसौ।। १७।।

द्वितीयः न चरति मृगतृष्णावञ्चितः कृष्णसारः
शिशिरमपि तृषार्तः सारसं सत्यतोयम्।
द्युमणिकिरणजालैर्नूनमत्यर्थतप्तं
परिमृशति न पौष्पं कार्मुकं पुष्पकेतुः।। १८।।

विदू जीवाविदह्मि वेदलिएहिं। तुवरदु तुवरदु वअस्सो ह्णाणत्थं। अण्णं च कल्लम्मि मिअआवावारो। तत्थ अडवीअं दुल्लहं संपण्णं असणं। ता इट्ठपुट्ठं अह्णिदव्वं। (जीवितास्मि वैतालिकाभ्याम्।)

राजा न केवलं भवदभिमतसिद्धिरेव। देवी चानुनेतव्या। तदभ्यन्तरमेव प्रविशावः। (इति निष्क्रान्ताः सर्वे)

इति प्रथमोऽङ्कः।

Vidū (Aside) Friend, her majesty has overheard everything. I presume that she must have been here since yesterday.

King (Aloud) My lady! You are angry without any reason. Here a sense of curiosity alone is to be blamed.

Queen It is your majesty who says I am angry.

King Beloved! No, not so

Oh red-eyed one! Your frowning eye-brows, efforts to control the tears, heaving of breasts, and innocent smile concealing the anger of love are enough to trouble my heart! (16)

Maid May your ladyship be pleased. His majesty is not at all to be blamed.

Queen Friend, it is true. Fatigued on account of my penance, I am unable to prolong this conversation. I shall retire to my chamber. (The queen retires followed by her maid)

King Ah! Her majesty has gone! (Bards behind the curtain)

First The sun has reached the middle of the sky. And thus,

The female bee does not long for the honey of flowers, for it is now hot, though drinking with her beloved had made it sweet as nectar. Instead, with her limbs withered by the heat of the sun she huddles under the wings of her consort. (17)

Sec Deceived by the mirage, the spotted deer, despite its great thirst does not drink even the real and cool water from the lake. The God of love does not touch his bow of flowers since the rays of the sun have made it hot. (18)

Vidū The bards have saved my life. Rush my dear friend for your bath! Remember the hunt tomorrow morning! Tasty food is hard to get in the forest. Therefore, we must eat well.

King Fulfillment of your desire alone is not enough. Her majesty also is to be pacified. So we shall enter he inner apartments. (Exit all)

End of Act One

व्यङ्ग्यव्याख्या

(ततः प्रविशति विदूषकः अङ्गानि संवाहयन् शूत्कृत्य)[1]

अथ विदूषकस्तां मालिनीनामधेयां संवरणभार्यां स्वसुताराहित्यखिन्नमनस्कां तन्नियोगात् काल्ये एवोत्थाया-सम्पूर्णकालावधेः पुत्रीयान्नियमादानीय पुरं प्रापय्य वयस्येन सङ्केतितं प्रदेशं गच्छन् पथि जाह्नवीतीरे तत्सिद्धान्तज्ञानाद् खिन्नमानसो भूत्वा मध्यपात्रतया खिन्नमनसां सोढुमक्षमः किमपि विवेकदृष्टि-स्तदज्ञानात् शरीरसादेनाङ्गसंवाहनादिचेष्टां कुर्वन् सशूत्कारं पथि कमपि प्रदेशं सविवेकं व्यतिष्ठेत्।

अथ सचकितं साङ्गसंवाहनं अदृष्टदृष्टिस्सविवेकं त्रिवर्त्युज्वलितस्य दीपस्य पुरस्तद्वत् प्राङ्मुहूर्तं तिष्ठेत्। एवं तिष्ठन्नयमेवं विमृशेत्। कुतः तस्मादहं वयस्येनाहूतः? कीदृग्विधः स्वप्नमार्गः। किमर्थमसम्पूर्णकालावधेः नियमान्निर्वर्त्य देवी पुरं प्रापितेत्यादिसर्वमपि जानन् मध्यमपात्रतया विह्वलाङ्गस्सन्नयमन्तर्वेदनया शूत्कारसंवाहनादि चेष्टां कुर्वन् प्रेक्षकेभ्य स्तिष्ठमानस्सचोद्गती तारे कुर्वन् शनैः शनैस्सविवेकं विमृश्य सशिरः कम्पं सुप्रसन्नमुखो भूत्वोत्तरश्लोकार्थं प्रेक्षकांस्ताराभ्यामेव बोधयेत्। कुतः –

स्वपत्न्यां श्रितवैराग्यो यद्भयस्यात्सकुण्ठधीः।
ततो पुत्रोऽपि हृदि तत् गोपयत्यात्मनापि माम्।।

इतीमं श्लोकार्थं दृग्भ्यामेवं दर्शयित्वा सविवेकं मुहूर्तं तिष्ठन् सशिरःकम्पं मनसेति निश्चित्य तत उत्तरग्रन्थार्थं मनसेति स्मरेदिति। मां कञ्चुक्यवदत् – देवीं साल्वराजपुत्रीं पुत्रीयान्नियमान्निर्वर्त्य स्वप्नश्रवणार्थं शीघ्रमागच्छेति इत्येतद्वचनात् स्वप्नदर्शनमस्या नियमवैराग्यहेतुरित्यूह्यम्। सर्वप्रकारेणास्यां विरागीति मन्तव्यमित्यादि स्वसिद्धान्तं सर्वं दृशोरेव दर्शयित्वा बाह्यार्थः कथ्यताम्। नायकस्य पत्नीवैराग्यमस्मिन् ग्रन्थे गोप्यम्। स्वप्नस्यामिथ्यात्वं दृशि दर्शयता विदूषकेणातःपरं तत् तेनैव प्रकाशयितुं यत्नः क्रियते।

एवं विदूषकस्यातः परं स्थायीभावः।

(ततः प्रविशति सान्तस्तापः सपरिवारो राजा।)

ततः स राजा संवरणोऽनभिमतां स्वभार्यां मालिनीनामधेयामपास्य सकुण्ठचेता भूत्वा सवेदनं निवसन्नपि निजहृद्गतं सर्वदा गोपयन्नयं कस्यामपि निशायां जघन्ये शोकमपि स्वप्नं दृष्ट्वा किमिदमिति स्मरन्नयं वन्दिभिर्बोधितस्सहसा शय्याया उत्थाय स्ववयस्यं वक्तुं कञ्चुकिनमाहूय तं सम्मान्य विदूषकं ब्रूहीति 'देवी पुरं नीयताम्। नीत्वा पुनः स्वप्नश्रवणार्थं शीघ्रमागच्छेति विदूषकं वदे'ति तं प्रेषयित्वा भूयो यथापूर्वं निर्गन्तुकामस्सतथा त्व... यथापुरं निजनिर्गमनं दृष्ट्वा निर्गच्छन्तं परिवारजनं दृष्ट्वा गोप्यवचनं कथङ्कारं विदूषकाय विज्ञापयामीति स्मृत्वा तदुपायमविन्दन् सान्तस्तापं तेन जनेन सार्धं पुरतो निर्गतवान्। अथेति निर्गत्य तं जनेन साकं गच्छेत्। सान्तस्तापं विदूषकं प्रतिपाल्य क्वचित्प्रदेशे समतिष्ठत्।

एवं पूर्वसम्बन्धः।

---

1 Dramatic characters are categorised into three – uttama, madhyama and adhama. Vidūṣaka though a Brahmin, comes under the middle type. Movements of the first category are refined and sophisticated. Vidūṣaka need not adhere to those restraints. Moreover, he has to cause laughter by his actions. This explains his over-acting on stage.

एवं संवरणभूमिकालङ्कृततनुरयं भरतवरः सान्तस्तापं सविवेकं किञ्चिदुद्दृष्टिर्यावत्तिष्ठेत् तावत् त्रिवर्त्युज्ज्वलितस्य दीपस्याग्रादुपाङ्गीभूता यवनिका व्यपनीयताम्। अथैवं व्यपनीतयवनिकः प्रविष्टो राजा किञ्चिदूद्दृष्टिरपि दीपशिखे पश्यन्नयं शनैश्शनैः उद्दृष्टिरेवं स्मरेत्। कुतः – आहूताय मया पाराशर्याय स्वप्नावस्था वाच्या वाऽवाच्या ननु। उभयत्रापि देषो विद्यते। कुतः –

अवाच्यं यदि तत्कार्यं न ज्ञात्वागामि सिद्ध्यति।
वाच्या चेत्स स्मरेदित्थं मां तु पत्नीविरागिणम्।। इति। अपि च,
एकं पुमांसं विश्वास्य स्वकर्मानेन साधयेत्।
नैव वाक्पतिरप्येष कर्म कर्तुं स्वयं प्रभुः।।

इति वचनात्। तर्हि वाच्या ननु, अयमत्रापि दोषः।

सतीह लोके यैवं स्यात् भाजनं भर्तृचेतसः।
तस्याः कथञ्चित्सद्यत्नैस्तन्तु रागिरसीति गीः।।

अनया च। अपि च पत्न्यां ममौदासीन्यमिति नियमितमपि याथातथ्यं विदितवानेषः अपि च स्वप्नश्रवणार्थं सत्वरमायाहीति मया नियुक्तेन कञ्चुकिना विज्ञापितश्च। तस्मात् सर्वप्रकारेण स्वप्नः प्रकाशयितव्यः। एवं चेत् तन्मनोवृत्तिं याथातथ्यं ज्ञात्वा शनैश्शनैः विज्ञापयामि इत्यादि सर्वं विवेकभाजो दृष्ट्योः प्रेक्षकान् भावेनैवं बोधयंस्त्रिवर्युज्ज्वलितस्य दीपस्य पुरस्तिष्ठेत्।

यावत्प्रेक्षकमुखं मुदा तु विकसति तावत् भावेनैव प्रयोक्त्रा प्रयोक्तव्यः। कथं भावेनैवेति चेत्,[2]

नृत्तस्याङ्गीह भावः स्यादङ्गान्यस्यापि तानि षट्।
दीपौज्वल्यं लयैक्यं च भूमिकासौष्ठवं ततः।।
रागप्रयोगनैपुण्यं प्रयोक्त्राकृतिभद्रता।
गातुर्ज्ञेयानि तान्येवं प्रयोक्त्रा प्रेक्षकैरपि।।
ऐक्यमङ्गाङ्गिनो कृत्वा भावैस्तु रमयेत् स तम्।
अन्यानभिनयेनेमान् नानालोकान् विनोदयेत्।।

के पुनः प्रेक्षका इति चेत्।

अष्टौ दश च विद्यास्तान्नाट्यवेदो यथाविधि।
स्मरशास्त्रं च यैर्ज्ञातं तान् विदुः प्रेक्षकान् बुधाः।।

तथाभूता हि प्रयोक्तारः। तेषामाधिक्यं प्रयोक्तृत्वम्। एवं प्रेक्षकप्रयोक्तृसम्बन्धः। अथैवं भावेनैव दृशोर्दर्शयित्वा तिष्ठन्नयं सर्वथा वक्तव्यमिति निश्चित्य तदागमनमन्वेष्टुं तिर्यगवलोकितवान्। एवं शनैः शनैः तिर्यक् पश्यन् स्वपरिवारजनं दृष्ट्वा अहो इत्यात्मना स्मृतवान्।

2 The word bhāva has multiple significance in Sanskrit aesthetics. Kulaśekhara gives a new interpretation to this concept. This is the key-word in the aesthetic theory of the royal dramatist. See Part I for details.

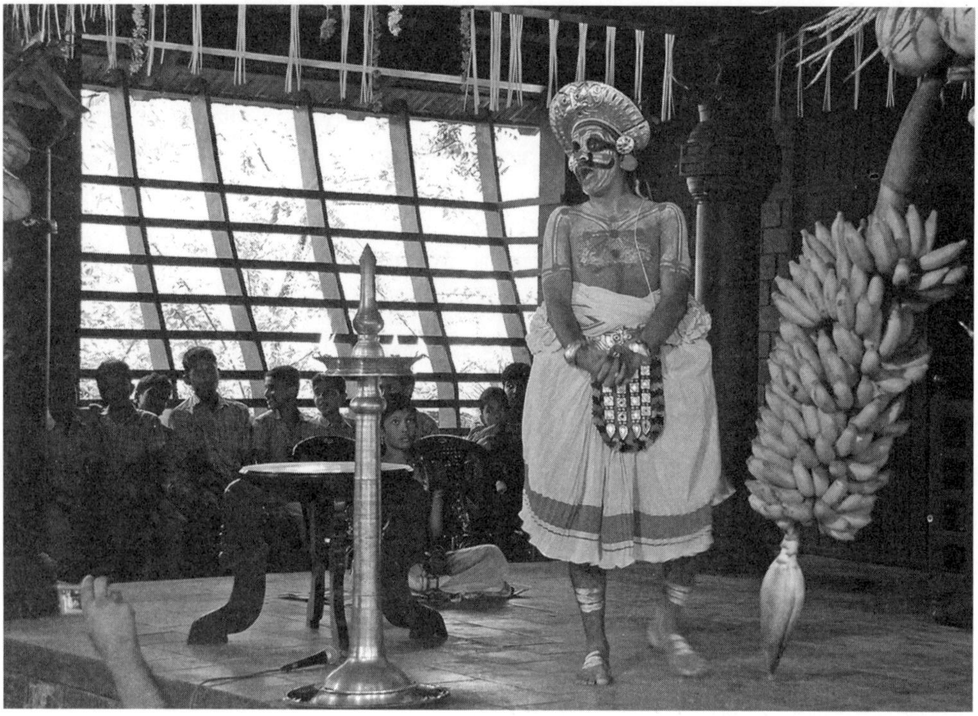

अहो इत्यत्रादौ विवेके। अहो मम मनःखेदचिन्तेऽमुना परिवारजनेन ज्ञायेतेति किं मदाकारादिभिश्चेष्टाभिः तस्मात् तत्कथमाछादयामीति सुमुहूर्तं सविवेकमास्थाय भूय इति कल्पितवान्। अस्तु मन्मनःखेदचिन्ते पुत्राहित्ये समर्थयन् पुत्राहित्यात् खिन्नमानसोऽयमिति मदनुगामिनो जनान् प्रबोधयामि। तर्हि पुत्राभावान्निर्दुःखोयमिति चेत्; मा मैवम्। किन्तु भगवता विवस्वता दर्शितेन स्वप्नेनान्यस्यां पुत्रसम्पत् भविष्यतीति निश्चित्य पुत्रवियोगजं दुःखं नष्टम्। एतेन तद्घटयितुं पुत्राभावे दुःखं समर्थयन्नहो इति प्रकाशं वक्तुं प्रारब्धवान्।।

अतःपूर्वमेवं प्रयोगमार्गः।

अतः परं स्वदारे वैराग्याच्छादनमन्यस्याः कस्याश्चित्कन्यकायाः पाणिग्रहणमन्विच्छन् काङ्क्षन् वक्ष्यतीति स्थायीभावः। इमं स्थायीभावं दृशोर्विभावयन् विदूषकं वदेत्। अस्मादारभ्य आनायिकादर्शनात् ध्वनिलक्षणम्।[3] पुनः तृतीयाङ्कपरिसमाप्तेश्च। विदूषकदर्शनादारभ्य आपादतलदर्शनात् तावदन्योन्यं ध्वनिना विज्ञाप्यमानमर्थं जानन् तावप्यजानन्तौ इव प्रातिकूल्येन वचसा विश्वासमेष्यतः। तस्माद् आनुकूल्येन ध्वनिना पुरस्सरं विज्ञापयति। एवं प्रयोगमार्गः।

अहो अपत्याभिधानस्येत्यादिग्रन्थो वर्ण्यताम्। तस्मिन् ध्वनिर्दृश्यते। प्रियतनयवियोग इत्यादौ। अहो इत्याश्चर्ये। अहो अनिष्टभार्याप्राप्तौ पुंसः खेदवृत्तेरियत्तां विगणयितुमिति कः उत्सहेत। अहो

3 This justifies the contention that *VV* for TS is complete in three Acts. The author does not find any justification to extend it further as there is no dhvani thereafter.

प्रसवगुणवियुक्तां प्रसवगुणः सौभाग्यगुणः तेन वियुक्तां मन्यमानस्य स्मरतो मम हृदि परितापः दुर्निवारः जृम्भते इति ध्वनिः। अहो इति। अहो सत्यमेव सद्वचनम्। कुतः –

सूनौ भ्रातरि जायायां यो द्वेषो वर्तते नृणाम्।
वियोगेऽस्मिन् मृते नश्येत् तयोरन्योन्यजातुचित्।।

इत्यादि सर्वं नासिकारोपिततर्जनिस्तिष्ठन् दृशोरेवं विभाव्य बाह्यार्थमभिनयेन नानालोकान् विभावयेत्।
एवमस्य प्रयोगमार्गः।

समन्तादवलोक्य। अथ राजा स्वाभिप्रायमपि कैश्चिदपि न ज्ञायते। किमपि परिच्छेत्तुं समन्तादवलोकितवान्। भूयस्तदीक्षणाच्छादनार्थं चोत्तरकार्यगौरवसमर्थनार्थं च कविस्वभावाच्च उत्तरश्लोको वर्ण्यते उत्तरकार्यमिति। स्वप्नप्राधान्यं समर्थयन्नित्यर्थः। अये अनुन्मिषितबालातपोयं दिवसावतार इति। अथ राजा स्वप्रेक्षणं कालमानं ज्ञातुं विलोकितवानस्मीति परिजनप्रबोधं विभावयन्नात्ममनोरथं स्वानुभवार्थदिवसवर्णनच्छलेनो भयकालो ध्वनिना वर्ण्यते। अये इत्याश्चर्ये। साश्चर्यं स्वप्नदर्शनात् प्रभृति मे हृदये अनुन्मिषितबालातप इति। अनुन्मिषितमव्यक्तं किमपि किमपि मे प्रतिभातीति ध्वनिः।

शालीनामिति। अथ राजा सान्तर्मोदं नासिकापुटाग्रैः अनालीढयापि तमोमात्रयापि पश्चिमांशं स्थितम् भगवता दर्शिता स्वप्नादर्कमहो वद प्रधृष्या काचित्कन्यका मया लभ्यत इव मे प्रतिभाति। अपि च तद्गात्राणामग्रैः प्रवृत्तिभिरनालीढया अस्पृष्टयापि तमोमात्रया तगोभूतया पूर्वगदृभ्यां अधिपश्चिमांशमय्यवसन्नाशा प्राप्तेति ध्वनिः। इति पश्यन्नर्थं दृशोरेव विभाव्य बाह्यार्थेन नानालोकान् विनोदयेत्। अथ राजा तदैवमुदयवर्णनं कृत्वा तिष्ठन्नयं विदूषकं पुरतो विलोकितवान्।

तदा विदूषकोपि देवीं पुरं नीत्वा स्वाकारादि चेष्टाभिस्तमनुशास्तुं तिष्ठेत्। अथ राजा विदूषकं सोद्वेगं दृष्ट्वा चेति स्मरेत्। कानुखल्वित्यादिना। अस्यायासहेतुर्विमृशति। अयं मत्कार्यप्रातिकूल्यं निजचेष्टया दर्शयति। तस्मादेनमपि वञ्चयामि। किमत्र हि दोषः –

एकं पुमांसं स्वमित्रं कार्येनाच्छादयेत् सुधीः।
आच्छादयेच्चेत् तन्नास्य सिद्ध्यतीति गुरोर्वचः।।
यदि गोप्यं न तदवाच्यं आप्ताय सुहृदर्पितम्।
मिथ्योत्किंचि.. स...द्य वदन्नन्यत् किमप्यमुम्।।
यत्नं तेन समं कुर्वन् साधयेदिति वाक् गुरोः।।

इति तच्छरीरविकृतिं दृष्ट्वा तत् हृदयं जानन्नपि उभयोर्मतं निरूप्यौशनसेन साधयितुं प्रारब्धवानिति दृशोः प्रेक्षकान् दर्शयित्वा भूय इमं श्लोकं स्मरेत्। कुतः,

गोप्यं साध्यं वञ्चयित्वा मित्रं मधुरया गिरा।
आवर्ज्यान्यत् वदेत् तस्मै स्वाकारं सन्नियम्य च।।

इत्यमुना तमावर्जितुकामस्तिष्ठेत्।

विदू. – कथमपि दक्षिणं पाणिमुन्नमयन् स्वाभिप्रायं विज्ञापयितुं चिह्नेन 'त्वमपमार्गगामी मा भूः' इत्युक्तवान्। एतदर्थं पाणेरुन्नमनमिति चेष्टया तं निरुध्य भूय एवं वदति च – जेदु भव इति। सन्मार्गगामिना मनसा

स्वधर्मं विमृश्य स एवम्भूत इत्यवधाय भूयश्चातुर्वर्णान् स्वं स्वं धर्मं प्रापय्य शत्रून् विजित्य करानादाय तथार्जितानि द्रव्यजालानि ब्राह्मणेभ्यो दत्वा तैर्यज्ञादिकर्म कारयित्वा भूयस्तेन देवान् सन्तोषयित्वा ततस्तैर्वर्षयित्वा भूयस्तेन लोकान् पोषयित्वा सुखमित्यनुदिनं तान् परिपाह्य यथाविध्यै हितसुखमनुभूय तेनैव सर्वस्मादुपरिवर्ता भूपाः।[4]

यथाविधि प्रजास्सर्वाः पातिर्यस्तु नरेश्वरः।
सचेद् सुखमश्नाति भूयोऽनन्त्यं व्रजेत् सुखम्।।

इति श्रुतिस्मृतिसिद्धमाचारमनुस्मृत्य 'तद्वचनानुगामी भूया' इति ध्वनिरित्यादि सर्वं दृशो राज्ञे दर्शयित्वा गोप्यं साध्यं वञ्चयित्वेति श्लोकार्थेन तमनुस्मृत्य भूयस्तदानुकूल्यं ज्ञात्वा तं विश्वास्य भूयस्तेन सहोत्तरकार्यप्रयत्नं कृत्वा तत्साधेयमिति निश्चितवानस्मि। उत्तरकार्यप्रवृत्तिं तस्मादिदानीं औशनसेन तमनुनयामीति निश्चित्य तमनुसर्तुं दीपपुरं तिष्ठन्नयं सप्रवणं सस्नेहं तस्याभिमुख्यं कर्तुकामस्तिष्ठन्नुत्तरग्रन्थं वदति। **कथमयमयथापुर** इत्यादि ग्रन्थेनानुसरति – अनुसरणप्रकारमाह । सखे इत्यस्मिन् पदे वाच्यमाने सखिशब्दस्यान्वयार्थं दृग्भ्यां दर्शयेत्। अयथापुर इत्यादि 'पूर्ववन्न तवाकारचेष्टा मत्कार्याभिमुखो भव' इति ध्वनितः तन्मनोगतं सत्यं वदेति दर्शयित्वा दीपपुरस्सधैर्यं तिष्ठेत्।

विदू. – अथ विदूषकस्तद्दर्शितं जानन्नपि अजानन्निव तिष्ठन् स्वस्मिन् तदविश्वासतां दृग्भ्यां विभावयन्नुत्तरग्रन्थमाह – **पसादाधिसओ** इति मयि ते प्रसादराहित्यमिति ध्वनिः।

राजा दीपपुरस्तिष्ठन् तद्ध्वन्यर्थं जानन्यप्यजानन्निव विभावयन् छन्दसा मन्मनोगतं क्वचिन्निर्गतं स्यान्न किमिति तं परिच्छेत्तुमाह 'कोऽभिप्राय' इति।

विदू – अथ विदूषकस्तत्स्मरणं ज्ञात्वाप्यजानन्निव विभावयन् दर्शितध्वनिनोत्तरग्रन्थेन विज्ञापयति – **अणखर**मित्यादिना अणखर क्षणनश्वरं अफलसिद्धिदं स्वप्नमुत्प्रेक्ष्यं मां वक्तुं प्रारब्धवानसि। एद्धि। प्रत्युत अक्षरलक्षितमिति अक्षरलक्षितं कथञ्चित् सद्यत्नैरिति बृहस्पतिना दर्शितं नाशशून्यं वचनमास्वाद्य मां वदंस्त्वं **आ आरक्ष** उदमिति तदा मया एवम्भूया इत्याकारेण सूचितमपि पुनरपि त्वं पूर्वप्रस्तुते कर्मण्येव प्रवर्तसे यदि कुत्र गतं ते पाण्डित्यमिति ध्वनिः।

राजा – अथ राजा तेन तथोक्तं ज्ञात्वाप्यजानन्निव तिष्ठन् भवच्छब्देन तत्प्रशंसां कृत्वा तन्मनोगतं प्रकारयितुमाह – प्रस्पष्टमिति।

विदू – अथ विदूषकस्तेन तथोक्तं याथातथ्यं विदित्वा किमप्युद्दृष्टिस्तिष्ठन् कथङ्कारमेनं वदतामिति मनसा स्मरन् व्यङ्ग्येनैव एनं मदीयामवस्थां विज्ञापयामीति मनसा निश्चित्य दीपपुरस्तिष्ठन्नयं सस्मितं नायकमुखे पश्यन्नुत्तरग्रन्थमाह – जइ एव्वं इति। मया ध्वनिना विज्ञापितं न जानामीति विभावयन्तं भवन्तं ईषद्विगलितेन मदभिप्रायेणातः परं प्रबोधयामीति दृशा तं बोधयित्वा भूयः **कहइस्सं** इत्युक्तवान्। कथयिष्य इति पदे प्रोच्यमाने त्वामतःपरं लज्जयामीति वदंस्तिष्ठेत्। एवंस्तिष्ठन्नायकमुखे पश्यन्नुत्तरग्रन्थमाह – **अहं आरूढह्यो** इत्यादिना। असम्पूर्णकालावधेः पुत्रीयान्नियमात् किमर्थं देवी देवेन पुरं प्रापितेति हयवत्संचरिष्णुमनोधिरूह्य सम्प्राप्यागच्छन्नहं **रा अ विहि अं** राजवीथ्यां राजनयमार्गे निष्णातस्य

4 This description is historically important. The state policy of Cera empire promoted Brāhmaṇical hierarchy on all walks of life. It became stratified by 10th c. C.E.

तव मनोवृत्तेरपरिज्ञानात् दुष्टतुरगेण नयविमुखिना मनसा त्वत्सिद्धान्तं स्मरता कन्दुकक्रीडं कुर्वता कन्दुकक्रीडायमानेन मनसा स्मृत्वा तस्मिन्नपि त्वत्सिद्धान्ते मया पतितं तत् किमपि ज्ञातम्। **चीन्ति अ चम ए** इति। अद्य गगनगमनस्य वृथा प्रयत्नस्य तव आसनस्यास्थिरतया त्वत्पत्न्यां मनसो स्थैर्यादिति त्वत्सिद्धान्तस्यार्धमात्रं शिक्षितं मय्युत्पन्नमर्धमात्रमिति। किमिति चेत् त्वं पत्नीविरागीति मया चिन्तितं कल्पितम्। अतः परं कीदृशी तव मनोगतिरिति अपि विदन्नहं त्वसिद्धान्तस्यैकदेशं ज्ञात्वा सकलं ज्ञातुं त्वां पृष्ट्वा ज्ञातव्यमिति मत्वा गतवानस्मि। **उवदि स दु** इति तस्माद् ब्रूयादिति ध्वनिः। इमं ध्वन्यर्थं दृग्भ्यां विज्ञापयन् बाह्यं केवलहास्यार्थं वदन् नायकमुखे पश्यन् दीपपुरस्तिष्ठेत्।

राजा – अथ राजा तद्दर्शितध्वन्यर्थं ज्ञात्वा पत्नीविषयामुदासिकामिति प्रच्छादितमपि तद्वत्ज्ञातवानयं तस्माद् अयमहमपि ध्वनिनैव गोप्यव्यवहारस्य विप्रस्य तव चलचित्तत्वादनधिकारित्वं विद्यते त्वयीति विभावयन् प्रबोधयामीत्यात्मगतं मत्वा तदनुसार्युत्तरग्रन्थमाह – तन्मुखे पश्यन् **मूर्ख** इति पदं वदन्नयं अनधिकारित्वम्। किमपि दृशा विभावयन् वदेत्। **अस्यामि**त्यादि। अस्यां क्रियायामिति – अस्यां साल्वराजपुत्र्यां वर्तमानायां क्रियायां अकिञ्चित्करो यादृशमुपदेशः किमपि वक्तुं न शक्या मदीया दशा।

पवनविजयेत्यादि। एतैरपहतदुरितौघान् नॄन् अम्बरे वर्तयन्तीति सम्बन्धः। मुनिवरवचनं येऽवगच्छन्ति मुनिवरवचनं बार्हस्पत्यनयं येऽवगच्छन्ति पवनविजयमार्गाः शुद्धिविजयमार्गाः मन्त्रसिद्धप्रकाराः रहस्सु वक्तुं योग्याः तथाभूता मुनिवरवचनं अथवा देवतानां प्रसादा वा। देवतानां पञ्चदेवतानां प्रसादः। यैः प्राप्ताः निसर्गतो कुटिलधिगो निश्चलचित्ता ये इति बृहस्पतिप्रोक्तुर्नयैर्वा देवताप्रसादैर्वा अपगतदुरितौघान् निश्चलचित्तान् गोप्यव्यवहारे निष्कलङ्कान् जातुचिदप्यप्रकाशितगोप्यान् बुद्धिमतो नरान् सन्तोऽम्बरे वर्तयन्ति।

मन्त्रे वा गोप्यसाध्येऽस्मिन् गगने च पयोनिधौ।
वर्ततेऽम्बरशब्दोयं वस्त्रे कार्पासिके तथा।। इत्यनेकार्थः।

अत्र मन्त्रेत्यादि सर्वं दृशोर्विभावयन् त्वमनर्ह इति समर्थयन् दीपपुरस्तिष्ठेत्। प्रेक्षकान् बोधयित्वा बाह्यार्थाभिनयेन नानालोकान् विनोदयित्वा तन्मुखे तद्भावं पश्यन् तत्रैव तिष्ठेत्।

विदू – अथ विदूषकस्त्वमनर्होसि इति समर्थयत् राजवचः श्रृण्वन् दीपपुरस्तिष्ठन् उन्मिषत्तारके नेत्रे कुर्वन् सधीरं विमृश्योद्गच्छतीतारे कुर्वन्नयमौशनसं स्मरेत्। ततः

दण्डेन साधयेत् साध्यं मनीषी नेतरैस्त्रिभिः।
कालापेक्षान्वितर्यस्माद् तस्माद्दण्डः प्रयोज्यताम्।।
दण्डश्चतुर्धा विज्ञेयो भावैः परुषया गिरा।
क्रियाभिस्तन्नरैः पुंसो दण्ड्यमानात् सुसिद्ध्यति।।

इत्यौशनसे विनिश्चित्य तथातिष्ठत्। अथ विदूषकः तस्मिन्नेवं तिष्ठति यदा तदेति स्मरेत्। अहो मत्प्रश्नानुकार्ययं तिष्ठति। तदिदानीमनेन दर्शितं मुखवैवर्ण्यमन्तरेण पृच्छामीति मत्वा स च तन्मुखे पश्यन् एवोत्तरग्रन्थेन पृच्छति। **अणुत्फुल्ले**त्यादिना। पृष्ट्वासत्यमेतद्वदेति दर्शयन् दीपपुरस्तन्मुखे पश्यंस्तिष्ठेत्।

राजा – अथ राजा तेन दर्शितं ज्ञात्वा चेति स्मरेत्। कुतः कथमिदानीं स्वप्नदर्शनविज्ञापनेऽस्य प्रत्ययं सम्पादयामीति विमृशन्नेवं स्मरेत्।

शत्रुं वाप्यथवा मित्रं उदासीनमथापि वा।
कार्यारम्भे त्वनुनये देवमाह बृहस्पतिः।।

इतीमं श्लोकार्थं स्मरन्ननुनेतुं प्रारभ्य सप्रवणं दीपपुरस्तिष्ठन्नुत्तरग्रन्थेन तमनुसरति **सखे** इत्यादिना। सखिशब्दे वाच्यमाने एवं दर्शयेत् – कुतः दीपपुरस्सप्रवणं तिष्ठन् सखे मया व्यवहृतमिदं अन्यथा मामन्यथाः अपि च –

आप्तस्ससुखदुःखेषु कार्यस्वस्मात् सततपरः।
स एव कार्यं सन्धत्ते स एव परमा गतिः।।

इत्यस्ति बृहस्पतिना दर्शितो नयः। तस्मादेनं सख इत्यनुनीय मद्वचनं करोमीति स्मृत्वा तन्मुखे सप्रवणं पश्यंस्तिष्ठन् सख इति तमाहूय सखिशब्दस्यान्वर्थं दृशा तं दर्शयंस्तिष्ठेत्।

कार्ये स सुखदुःखे यः कर्तुरस्माच्च तत्परः।
प्रवृत्या घटते कार्ये स सखेहोच्यते बुधैः।।

तस्माद् मद्वचनानुगामीति दृशा दर्शयन् सप्रवणं दीपपुरस्तिष्ठेत्। अथ तस्मिन्नेवं तिष्ठति विदूषकस्तमेवं पश्यन् सत्यमेव वदसि चेत् त्वत्प्रवृत्त्यनुसार्यस्मीति दृशा दर्शयंस्तिष्ठेत्।

अथ राजा तस्मिन्नेवं तिष्ठति 'सत्यमेव वदामी'ति तं दृशा दर्शयित्वा भूय उत्तरग्रन्थमाह – **अतीताया**मित्यादि। एवं तं विज्ञाप्य स्वप्नप्रकारो वर्ण्यते – **आराद्दृष्ट**मित्यादिना। अथ स्वप्नप्रकारं वक्तुमारभमाणोऽयं स्वमुखे तदीक्षणमन्विच्छन्नपातं दृष्ट्वा भूयोप्येवं स्मरेत्। भूयः कथङ्कारम् एनं स्वप्नप्रकारं बोधयामि। अयमुत्स्वप्नप्रकारवर्णने अनृतमस्ति वा नवेति परिच्छेत्तुमुन्मुख एव पश्यन्नयं तिष्ठति। तस्मात् स्वप्नप्रकारवर्णने स्वप्नप्रकारं व्यङ्ग्येन दर्शयामीति मत्वा तमेव पश्यन् सप्रवणमुत्तरग्रन्थेन स्वप्नं विज्ञापयति – आराद्दृष्टमिति श्लोकस्य प्रयोगमार्गो दृश्यते।

अथ राजा दीपपुरस्सप्रवणं दृग्भ्यां सखीशब्देन तमनुनीय ताभ्यामेवावस्थां विज्ञापयति। पद्मिनीनां दीर्घिका। उत्तमस्त्रीणां दीर्घिका शस्ता काचित् कन्यारत्नं मे अर्कबिम्बं क्षेत्राश्रयमारादिति वेगादाविर्भूतं प्राप्तं दृष्टुं तुच्छीकुर्वन् तुहिनकणिकाजालकमिति तुच्छीकुर्वन् न्यक्कुर्वन् तुहिनकणिकाजालकं पूर्वकलत्रं न्यक्कुर्वन् पूर्वकलत्रमर्धोन्मीलन-मुकुलनयनैः उत्तमस्त्रीवंशजातकन्यकाहेतोस्तथाभूता। अत्र प्रबन्धे तुहिनसंज्ञा पूर्वभार्यायां निर्दिष्टा इतीमं ध्वन्यर्थं दृग्भ्यामेव बोधयित्वा बाह्यार्थमभिनयेन नानालोकान् विनोदयेत्। एवमस्यप्रयोगमार्गः।

समीपे चण्डरश्मौ च कलत्रेपि प्लुके तथा।
कल्लोले च विहारे चाप्यर्कशब्दः प्रवर्तते।।[5]

अत्र ध्वनौ कलत्रे। अन्यस्मिन् भानौ।

5 The word अर्क has several meanings. Primary meaning here is Sun, suggested sense is wife. तुहिन is snow, here it denotes the queen.

अथ राजैवं विज्ञाप्य तत्कर्मणि तदाभिमुखमस्ति वा नवेति परिच्छेतुं तन्मुखे पश्यन् सप्रवणं दीपपुरस्तिष्ठेत्।

विदू – अथ विदूषकस्तेन दर्शितं ध्वन्यर्थं जानन्निव तिष्ठन्नयं स्वप्नस्य मिथ्यात्वं दृशोर्विभावयन् 'न स्यात् त्वद्वैराग्यहेतोः स्वप्नदर्शने भगवन्तं प्रमाणीकृत्य अन्यस्या परिणयनमिच्छन्नसी'ति विभावयन्नपि स्वप्नमार्गं श्रोतुं पृच्छति। **तदो** इति। एवं पृष्ट्वा दीपपुरस्तन्मुखे पश्यंस्तिष्ठेत्।

अथ राजा ज्ञातसिद्धान्तो उद्वाहचिकीर्षाहेतोरजानन्निव भावयन्नुत्तरग्रन्थेन विज्ञापयति ततोमामन्तरेणेत्यादिना। एवं विज्ञाप्य तन्मुखमेव पश्यंस्तिष्ठेत्।

अथ विदूषकः तन्मार्गं ज्ञातुं पूर्ववद्विभावयन् पृच्छति **केसी**ति। इति पृष्ट्वा तन्मुख एव पश्यंस्तिष्ठेत्।

राजा – अथ राजा उद्वाहचिकीर्षतां वक्तुं प्रारब्धोपि तद्भावरुद्धो वक्तुमशक्यस्तिष्ठन्नात्मगतमेवं स्मरेत्। कुतः अस्यामस्योदासीन्यमनस्कतया भगवद्वचनप्रामाण्यं समर्थयन्नस्या परिणयनमाकांक्षन्नयमिति यथायं स्मरेत्। कथं तथैनं विज्ञापयामि। अस्तु भार्यायां बद्धरागतां मम भगवदुक्तौ विभावयन् विज्ञापयामि इत्यात्मगतं निश्चित्य भगवदुक्तिप्रकारमुत्तरग्रन्थेन विज्ञापयति – **दयितां तव तन्वङ्गी**मित्यादिना। अथ भगवान् ममान्तिकमभ्येत्य मद्भक्तिहेतोरस्यां पुत्राहित्यखिन्नमानसस्य मम पुत्रसम्पदं वक्तुमारब्धे भगवति तदिङ्गितज्ञानान्मुखवैवर्ण्यमस्मदीयं दृष्ट्वा मामित्यब्रवीत् – **दयितां तव तन्वङ्गी**मिति श्लोकं विज्ञापितवान्। तवेमां दयितां तन्वङ्गीं प्रसवापेतामवेहि। दयितां तन्वङ्गीमित्युभयोः पदयोः वर्ण्यमानयोरेवं दृशा विभावयेत्। तवास्यां पुत्रसम्पन्न भवितेति विज्ञापनेन मन्मुखवैवर्ण्यं दृष्ट्वा मयि रुष्ट इवानन्तरमन्तरधत्त भगवान् इति श्लोके विज्ञाप्यमाने तन्मुखं पश्यन्निति श्रृण्वन्तं तं स्वप्नमिथ्यात्वं दृशोर्विभावयन्तं दृष्ट्वानन्तरमन्तरधत्तेत्युक्तवान् इत्यनन्तरमित्यमुना ग्रन्थेनान्या परिग्रहणविधये न केवलं वास्तवनिवेदनायैव भगवान् साक्षात्कृत इति तं विज्ञापयितुमनन्तरमित्युक्तवानिति इतीमं ध्वन्यर्थं दृग्भ्यामेवं विभावयंस्तन्मुखे पश्यन्नेव दीपपुरस्तिष्ठेत्। एवं तस्मिन् तिष्ठति विदूषकः स्वप्नस्य मिथ्यात्वं नेति दर्शयति। कैश्चित्प्रयत्नैरप्यन्यां पुत्रसम्पन्न प्राप्स्यतीति स्वप्नप्रामाण्यं समर्थयन् स्वप्नलक्षणं दृशा दर्शयंस्तिष्ठेत्।

रात्रौ त्रेधा विभक्तायां दृष्टः स्वप्नो वदेत् फलम्।
भूतस्य वस्तुनोऽग्रेंशे जघन्ये च भविष्यतः।।

एवं गौहं वचनं विदूषकाय दर्शयंस्तिष्ठेत्।

विदू – अथ विदूषकस्तङ्गोपनं मनसा ज्ञात्वापि एवं स्मरेत्। कुतः – अहो अस्य गोपनपाटवम्। तत् कथमस्य मनोगतं विगलयामि। स्मृत्वा, अस्तु। वानीरन्यायेनैनमनुस्मृत्य[6] तद्विगलयामीति निश्चित्य दीपपुरस्तन्मुख एव पश्यन्नुत्तरग्रन्थेन तमनुसर्तुमाह – **सोत्थि होदु मा संतंपदु** इति। स्वस्ति भवतु इति ग्रन्थे प्रोच्यमाने यत्त्वया प्रारभ्यते तस्या विघ्नपरिसमाप्तिः क्रियतामिति विभावयन् मा सन्तपत्वितिप्रोच्यमाने इतरोद्वाहनविधयेऽद्य प्रभृति यतयिष्ये इति दर्शयितुं प्रारब्धे सति।

---

6 वानीर is a plant that grows on the shores of river. In torrential flow it bows down the direction of the current and saves itself from being uprooted. वानीरन्यायः therefore means to move with the current without resisting. Vidūṣaka decides to be favorable to the King's desire.

राजा – अथ राजायमिति स्मरेत्। कुतः अयं मत्सिद्धान्तगामी भूत्वा मामनुस्मृत्य मन्मनोगतं स्वीकर्तुमभिलषति तत् ब्राह्मणाय करिष्ये। अस्य छन्दसतया गोप्यव्यवहारानधिकारिता दृश्यते। तस्मादेनमधिकारिणं विधाय शनैः शनैः शिथिलयितव्यः। तस्मादिदानीं अनेन प्रोच्यमानमार्गान्नाङ्कुरं विधास्येति आत्मगतं स्मृत्वा[7] निश्चित्य सरोषं तन्मुख एव पश्यन् तिष्ठेत्। एवं तिष्ठन्नेवोत्तरग्रन्थमाह **कथ**मिति। पृथक्कृत्य त्वया स्मृतम्। इदमहं कथमाचरामीति विभावयंस्तिष्ठेत्। अथ सरोषेण तेनेति वीक्षितो विदूषकः कुलविच्छित्तिम् इत्यैवाहमिति स्मरामीति दर्शयंस्तिष्ठेत्। तस्मिन्नेवं तिष्ठति राजधर्मण इति नानुशये इत्युक्तवान्। तत्परित्यागादधर्मणत्वं स्नेहं इति विभावयंस्तिष्ठेत्।

विदू – उच्चैर्विहस्य सोऽपीति स्मरेत्। अहो अयं मां वाचालैर्मूकीकरोति। तस्मादेनमपि यथामार्गं विज्ञाप्य लज्जायामीत्यात्मना निश्चित्य तन्मुख एव पश्यंस्तिष्ठेत्तवेयमभिमत्त दयिता नेति दर्शयन्नुत्तरग्रन्थमाह – ग्रन्थे प्रोच्यमाने 'तवेयमभिमता यदि सतीह लोके यैवंस्यादित्यादि बार्हस्पत्यं वचो मामित्यकुर्यां श्रुतेश्च विधिम्। अथवान्यथा चैतद् वयः प्रामाण्याद् पितृप्रसादपरे कर्मणि श्रोत्रियान् भूसुरान् कोशसञ्चयैः सन्तोषये'त्यादि सर्वं दृशोर्विभावयन् ग्रन्थमुक्त्वा भूयो बाह्यार्थः प्रहसनप्रधानं कथ्यताम्।

राजा – अथ राजा तेनैवं यथाभूतेन दर्शितेन तद्वचःप्रामाण्येन निर्जितस्सन्नपीति स्मरेत्। एवं जितोऽहं कतमेन मार्गेणैनं योजयामि। अस्तु। एवं विधास्ये। ध्वनिद्योतितमर्थम् अजानन्निव तिष्ठन् बाह्यार्थेन केवलं यदुक्तं तत्प्रमाणीकृत्य केवलमूकोऽसीति विभावयन् श्रुतिस्मृत्येनं दर्शयामीत्यात्मना निश्चित्य भूयस्तन्मुखे पश्यन् साक्षेपं सशिरः कम्पमुत्तरग्रन्थमाह **मूर्ख** इति। मूर्खेति सम्बुद्धौ प्रोच्यमानायां स्वपाण्डित्यं प्रकट यन्निमं श्रुतिस्मृत्यर्थं दृग्भ्यां पाणिना च प्रदर्शयेत्।

> जाते पुंसि यदा गर्भादृणयुक्तस्तदैव सः।
> देवैश्च पितृभिश्चैव भूसुरैरपि सद्गुणैः।।
> हविर्दाने सुराणां तत् पितॄणामपि तन्तुना।
> भूसुराणां तथातिथ्यैस्त्रयाणां तत् स नाशयेत्।।

इति श्रुतिस्मृतिसिद्धाचारः सक्रोधं दर्शयंस्तिष्ठेत्।

विदू – अथैवं प्रोक्तो विदूषक इति स्मरेत्।

> क्रुद्धाय स्वामिने कश्चिन्न तिष्ठेत् सुधीः पुमान्।
> तिष्ठेच्चेन्नैव विवादे देवमाचार्ययोर्मतम्।।

तस्मादत्र न विवादः कर्तव्यः। तस्मादयमतःपरमनुनेयः। अपि च,

> यत्पुंसो दृढचित्तस्य नयभाजो मनोगतम्।
> स्वधियाच्छाद्यमानं वा ज्ञेयं तच्चापि तत्सखैः।।
> तत्कार्यानुगुणो भूत्वा शनैरनुनयेद्यदि।
> जातु तद्वक्रता तस्मिन् गलितं तद् भवेद् ध्रुवम्।।

---

7 This is a kind of bribery to placate the Brahmin. There is a hint here to the social life of that period.

तस्मादेतत् प्रामाण्यात् तन्मार्गानुसारि अनुगच्छामीति आत्मना निश्चित्य तद्वशोः प्रेक्षकान् बोधयित्वा भूयस्तन्मार्गभाजो भूत्वा उत्तरग्रन्थेनानुसरति एवमित्यादिना।

राजा – अथ राजा तत्प्रेरणयार्द्रीकृतचित्तो विस्मृतनिजगोपनो भूत्वा सप्रवणं तिष्ठन् निजवसनाञ्चलं बाहुभ्यां परिमृजत्पदेन भुवमालिखन् नीचैस्तं पश्यन् सहसेति वदेत्। **सम्भाव्यत एवै**तदिति। इति प्रमादादुक्तः भूयः क्षणात् स्वप्रमादमज्ञायेति स्मरेत्। अहो प्रमादात्किं मयोक्तं, अहो निर्गतगोपनोस्मि संवृत्तः। तत् किं विधास्ये। अस्तु एतदप्यन्यथा योजयामीत्यात्मना निश्चित्य पूर्वं तिष्ठन्नुत्तरग्रन्थेनान्यथा योजयति **न पुनरि**त्यादिना। तदधुनेत्यादिना। पूर्वप्रमादात् तद्विरहजवह्निदग्धमात्मानं समर्थयंस्तद्दर्शनोत्सुक इति त्वरमाणो गन्तुमारब्धवान्।

विदू – अथ विदूषकस्तस्य प्रमादवैदग्ध्ये दृष्ट्वा स्वस्मिन्नमुष्याविश्वासतां चेति स्मरेत्। अहमिदानीमेवैनं देवीसकाशं नेतुमेव त्वरयामीत्यात्मना निश्चित्योत्तरग्रन्थेन त्वरयन्नाह **एदु**।

अथ राजा तेनैवं गन्तुं प्रेर्यमाणस्सान्तस्तापं सचकितं तिष्ठन्नपि तद्गोपने कृतयत्नस्सन् दृष्ट्वाग्रतो गच्छेति दर्शयंस्तिष्ठेत्। अथ विदूषकस्तत्प्रेरणया सस्मितं किमपि शनैश्शनैः वदन् अग्रतो गच्छेत्। राजा अपि सविमर्शं सान्तस्तापं सचकितं तत्पृष्ठतो गच्छेत्। एवमुभौ परिक्रामतः।

राजा – अथ राजा तथागच्छन्नेवैवं स्मरेत्। कीदृक् फलप्रदं मे स्वप्नदर्शनम्। अपि च स्वप्नदर्शनात् प्रभृति कस्यचित् सत्कन्यकायाः प्राप्तौ सङ्गि मदीयं चेतः। एवं स्मरतो गच्छतस्तस्य दक्षिणनेत्रं स्फुरति।[8] अथ तत्पृष्ठानुगामि राजा नेत्रस्पन्दनं सूच्यंस्तिष्ठेदिति स्मरेच्च। गय्येवं स्मरति किमर्थं मे दक्षिणनेत्रं स्फुरतीति इदमनुक्त्वा। विदूषकस्तिष्ठन्नेव स्वश्वासं प्रतिपालयन्नेवं स्मरेत्।

स्फुरति स्मरतः कार्यं पुंसो दक्षिणगेऽक्षिणि।
तद्गोणगामि दिवश्चेत् सद्यस्सिद्ध्यति तत्फलम्।।

तद्वामं वामं दृशः। एवं गौहं वचनं स्मरंस्तिष्ठेत्। तदग्रगामी विदूषकस्तच्चरणशब्दं अश्रुत्वा किमिदमिति स्मरन् व्यावृत्य तं वीक्षमाणस्तत्प्रवृत्तिं सहसा पश्यन्नप्यपश्यन्निव शनैर्निर्गच्छेत्। तदा राजापि तेन दृष्टं स्वनिमित्तप्रतिपालनमितीति ज्ञात्वेति स्मरेत्। अहो मन्निनिमित्तप्रतिपालनमनेन दृष्टं हि तत् किं करिष्ये, एतद्गोपनं न कर्तव्यं ततः।

दृष्टे कर्मणिराख्यापि तद्गोपयति यः पुमान्।
कार्यतन्त्रे च कस्मिंश्चित् विश्वसेत् तन्न तत्सखम्।।

अपि च

मयि क्रुद्धे न स क्रुद्धः परुषोक्तौ स सामगः।
अयं ..यं गुरोर्वेत्ति विश्वास्योतरशनैश्शनैः।।

तस्मादमुष्मिन् मन्मनोगतं शनैश्शनैः शिथिलयामीत्यात्मगतं निश्चित्यामुष्मिन् स्वापराधमपनेतुमुत्तरग्रन्थेन तमनुसर्तुं सप्रवणं तिष्ठन्नाह **सखे** इति। सखिशब्दे प्रोच्यमाने सखिशब्दस्यान्वर्थं दृग्भ्यां पाणिना च तस्य दर्शयेत्।

---

8 Throbbing the right eye, horripilation in the right part of the body etc., are good omens indicating fulfillment of desire. The author exploits them profusely in both the plays.

कार्ये स सुखदुःखे यः कर्तुमस्माच्च तत्परः।
प्रवृत्या घटयन् कार्यं स सखेहोच्यते बुधैः।।

इति दर्शयन्नुत्तरश्लोकेन पत्नीवैराग्यगोपनं दृढीकुर्वन् केवलं स्वनिमित्तप्रतिपालनहेतुमेव वास्तवं वदति – **वा मेतरमिदमधुने**त्यादिना। इति पूर्वार्द्धेन वास्तवं विज्ञाप्य ननु सुतसमुद्भव-लाभादित्यपरार्द्धेन शनैश्शनैरिति मन्यमानस्सदा अवैराग्यमन्याप्राप्तिश्रद्धां च गोपयन् विज्ञापयति अथ राजेति। पूर्वार्द्धेन विज्ञाप्यं परार्द्धभूतेन सुतसमुद्भवलाभादित्यादिग्रन्थे प्रोच्यमाने दृग्भ्यां पाणिनैकेन वेति दर्शयेत्। सखे दयितादर्शनोत्सुकस्त्वया सह गच्छन्नहम् अस्यामेव पत्न्यां मम पुत्रसम्पत् भूयादिति मन्यमानो यदा प्रतिष्ठते दैवं मद्दक्षिणनेत्रेण स्फुरितं यत् ततोऽस्यामेव पुत्रसम्पत् भविष्यतीति स्मृत्वा मम हृदि प्रीतिस्सम्प्रत्युत्फुल्ला। किमिति चेत् सुतसमुद्भवलाभादपरः प्रीतिप्रसङ्गो मे नेति यावदित्येवं विज्ञापने तस्मिन्ननेन राज्ञा चैवम्भूतेन केनचि-द्दर्शितेनार्थेन स्वाभिप्रायो हृद्गतो भावं विना शिथिलितः। अनया यात्रयैव पुत्रफलस्य कार्यस्य कारणं सम्भवितव्यमित्यूह्यमानेन नेत्रस्पन्दनेनेति। किमर्थमिदमितिचेत् शनैश्शनैस्तस्मिन् विश्वस्ते भूयः पूर्वमेवाहं मदभिप्रायं तुभ्यं विज्ञापितवानस्मीति वक्तुम्। अथैवं विदूषकाय विज्ञाप्य भूयस्तं गच्छगच्छेति दृग्भ्यां विभावयंस्तिष्ठेत्।

एवं प्रयोगमार्गः।

विदू – अथ विदूषकस्तथाभूतं तद्गोपनं दृष्ट्वा चेति स्मरेत्। अहो मां तन्मार्गानुसारिणमपि निजहृद्गतं भूयोप्येष गोपयति। यत् ततोऽस्य गूढप्रवृत्तिं केवलमलौकिकेन वचसा व्यवहृत्येषद्विगलितेन ततः प्रकाशयामित्यात्मना निश्चित्योत्तरग्रन्थेन तत प्रकाशयति **अदिट्ठपुरुवाए** इत्यादिना।

राजा – अथ राजा तेन तथोक्तां भारतीं श्रुत्वेति स्मरेत्। अहो कस्याश्चित् कन्यकाया अन्वेषणतत्परोऽयमिति मां विदितवानेषः। तस्मात् किमदृष्टपूर्वाया इति त्वयोच्यत इतीमं पृष्ट्वा भूयस्तदुत्तरमाकर्ण्य भूयस्तु गोप्यवस्तुशैथिल्यं शनैश्शनैः कुर्यामित्यात्मना निश्चित्य भूय उत्तरग्रन्थेन तत् पृच्छति किमित्यादिना।

विदू – अथ विदूषकस्तेनेति पृष्ट एवं स्मरेत्। अहोऽयमिदानीं मय्युत्पन्नविश्वासः संवृत्तः यदयमुत्पन्नप्रीतिमुखो पृच्छति। ततो जाने तस्मादहं तावत् तन्मार्गं नानुसरामि। यावदयं निजहृद्गतं स्वयमेवैकदेशं भावैर्वा गिरा वा वदिष्यति। तर्हि किमिदानीं करोषि इतस्ततः किमपि दृष्ट्या विभावयन् स्मृत्वा। अस्तु अहमिदानीमन्यत् किमप्युक्त्वा अनेन पृष्टस्य तस्योत्तरमन्यथा देव्यां कथञ्चित् समर्पयामि इत्यात्मना निश्चित्य भूय उत्तरग्रन्थेन तथा समर्थयति **ए ति अम** इत्यादिना।

अथ तदा राजा विदूषकस्यान्यथाकरणं पश्यन् समुखवैवर्ण्यं तिष्ठेत्। अथ तदा विदूषकोपि तं तथाभूतं दृष्ट्वा चेति स्मरेत्। मदुक्तौ न विश्वस्तोऽयं वर्तमानोदन्तान्तरं प्रापयामि। तत् केन किं नु स्मृत्वा, अस्तु। एनां भागीरथीं दर्शयन् प्रमेयप्रसङ्गं विस्मारयामि। तत् किमप्येनमनुक्त्वा गच्छन्नेव दर्शयामि इत्यात्मना निश्चित्य गच्छन्नेव तदर्थमग्रतो विलोक्य सविस्मयमुत्तरग्रन्थेन तां दर्शयति **भो पेखदु** इत्यादिना।

अथ राजा तमभिप्रायं ज्ञात्वेति स्मरेत्। अहो अयमुदन्तान्तरहेतोर्भागीरथी मां दर्शयति। तस्मादहमप्यधुना औदासीन्यमुपेत्य मत्कार्यसिद्धौ दर्शितामुनेयमिति मन्यमानस्तां प्रणमामि। अपि च

कार्यारम्भे नमेत् तां स्वां देवतामिष्टसिद्धये।
अविच्छिन्नं ततस्तत् स्याद् एवमाहुर्मनीषिणः।।

पूर्वपूर्वजेन तामिमां स्वकुलदेवतां कर्तुमेव पुरमत्र विरचितम्। तस्मात् प्रभृति मत्कुलदेवतेयं संवृत्ता। अथ राजा साञ्जलिबद्धमुत्तरश्लोकं वदन् भक्तिपूर्वं तिष्ठन्नेव दृशोरिति दर्शयेत्। कुतः 'भगवति पुनतीभ्य' इति श्लोकेन मदभिमतकार्याविच्छिन्नपरिसमाप्त्यै भवतीमहं प्रणमामि। अपि च, भगवति! अहं सोमवंशराजः त्वं भागीरथी। तस्मात् मदभिमतं त्वत्सम्बन्धमहितात् अहिमकराल्लभ्यम्। किञ्च अद्योषसः प्राक् स्वप्ने मया दृष्टेन भगवताङ्गवे हि प्रसवापेतामिति वदता नेत्राभ्यामचिरेण पुत्रहेतोरेष्यसीति दर्शितस्य पदार्थान्तरस्य प्राप्तिः कुत इति चिन्तयित्वा यदा मय्यमुष्मादागच्छति तदा दैवप्रेरित इव दक्षिणनेत्रकम्पः कुत इति यत् ततः सद्य एव तत्फलप्राप्तिः द्रष्टव्येति मत्वा तत्कार्यारम्भतश्च भवतो प्रणमामि। अपि च स्वप्नफलं सद्य एवानुभोक्तव्यमिति च। किञ्च अस्मात् प्रदेशात् पुरस्यान्तरालभूरतीव लघ्वी। तस्मात् त्वज्जलस्पर्शनपवित्री-कृतेऽस्मिन्नेव तीरे कार्तिकेयावाससमाहिते क्वचिदपि मदभिमतं सत्वरं प्रापयेति बद्धाञ्जलिर्भक्तिपूर्वं तिष्ठन् दृशोरिममर्थं विभावयन् भगवतीति श्लोकमुक्त्वा प्रार्थयन्नयं स्वदक्षिणदेहार्धं सरोमाञ्चं दृष्ट्वा भगवतीममुनाभिष्टूय भावैः प्रेक्षकान् सुखयित्वा पूर्ववत् तिष्ठेत्।

विदू – अथ विदूषकस्तमन्तश्चिन्तया परवशीकृतदेहं दृष्ट्वेति स्मरेत्। किन्नु खल्वस्य चिन्ता। सम्प्रत्युभयत्र चिन्तावकाशो विद्यते। देवीदर्शनाय गच्छाव इत्यतिगोप्यवस्तुप्रस्तावे मामुक्त्वा गच्छन्नयं तदभ्याशहेतोरभिमत-देवीदर्शनप्राप्तवेदनोऽमुना मन्दं मन्दं गच्छता भवितव्यम्। अथवा तस्मादमुष्यागमनवेलायां सुनिमित्तप्राप्तिहेतोः मन्मनोरथसिद्धिः। कुतः किं रसं भविष्यतीति चिन्तयतामुना च भवितव्यम्। अनयोः कस्मिन्नमुष्य चिन्तां स्मृत्वा, अस्तु, एवं करिष्ये, इदानीं मेऽत्र कार्तिकेयपरिसरोद्यानं नीत्वा तस्मिन्नस्मिन् सुखप्रविष्टे पृष्ट्वा ततस्सोऽयं वदिष्यतीत्यात्मना निश्चित्योत्तरग्रन्थेन तद्दर्शयित्वा तत्र नयति, **एसो गुह** इत्यादिना।

तदा राजा पूर्ववत् तिष्ठन्निति स्मरेत्। कुतः तस्मादस्मात् प्रभृति अप्रमादमन्वेष्टव्यमिति स्मरंस्तिष्ठन्नयं तेन कार्तिकेयावासमन्तरेण प्रोच्यमानां वाणीं श्रृण्वन् सहसा तत्र श्रिताभिरुचिरेवं स्मरेत्। अनेनोद्यानं नीतस्य मम मनोरथसिद्धिस्साध्या स्यान्नु तस्मादनेन सहोद्यानं प्रवेष्टव्यमिति निश्चित्यामुना सह गच्छति।

उभौ परिक्रामतः। अथोभयोर्गच्छतोः पृष्ठगामी राजेति स्मरेत्। मम तावदुद्यानप्रवेशे द्वौ गुणौ स्तः। तद्दर्शनमेतदन्वेषणं चेति। स्मरन्नेव गच्छेत्। (उभावुद्यानप्रवेशं रूपयतः)[9]

राजा – अथ राजा तस्मिन् प्रविष्टोऽयं तत्प्राप्त्यन्वेषणहेतोस्तिर्यक् पश्येत्। एवं तिर्यक् वीक्ष्यमाणोयं राजा सहसा तत्र मरतकमणितले काश्चित् पदपद्धतीर्दृष्टवान्। अथ ता एव सान्तर्मोदं सवञ्चनं वीक्षमाणः पुनरपि स्मरेत्। कुतः,

तांश्चैव श्रृणुयात् पश्येत् श्रावितं यच्च दर्शितम्।
श्रृण्वन् पश्यन् स्वयमपि क्षोणीभृदिति वाग्गुरोः।।

तस्मादनेन दर्शितमेव मया द्रष्टव्यम् इति निश्चित्य तन्मुखे पश्यन् तिष्ठेत्। अथ विदूषकोपि प्रविश्य तत्र तां दृष्ट्वापि अदृष्ट्वेवान्यत्र वृक्षोपरि तिर्यक्पश्यन्निममदृष्ट्वा तिष्ठेत्। अथ राजा तदा तथाभूतं

9 This direction रूपयतः indicates that the acting is stylised, नाट्यधर्मी। The other method is realistic – लोकधर्मी। Now, this play is presented in Kutiyattam upto this point, i.e. only the roles of king and jester are enacted on stage.

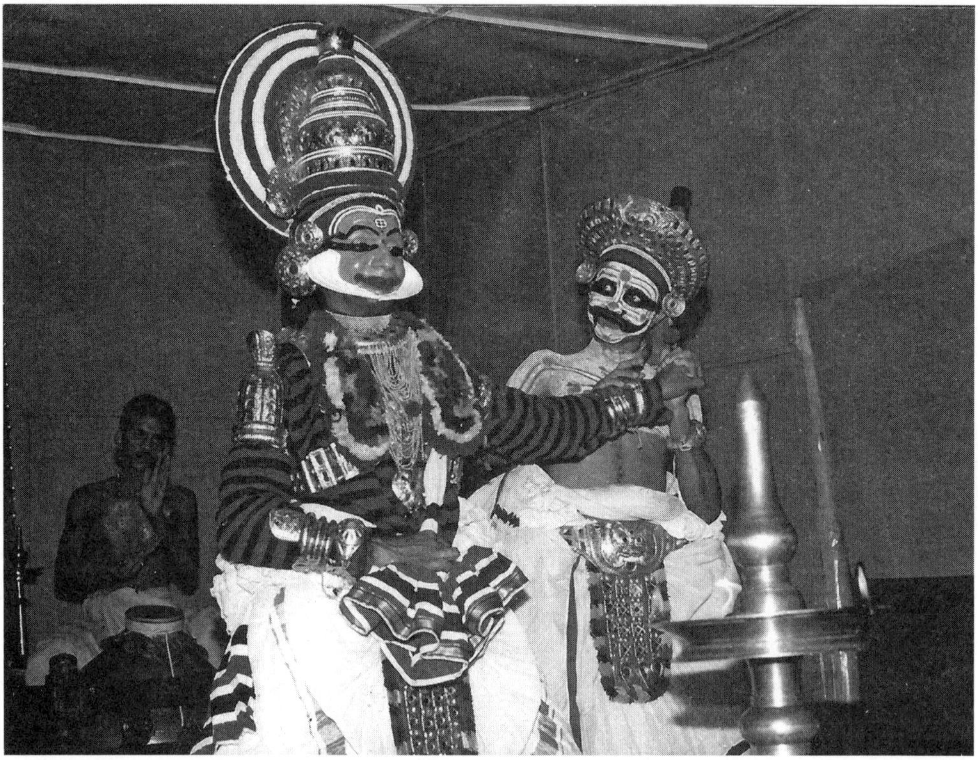

Sajeev Narayana Chakyar as Saṃvaraṇa and Margi Madhu as Vidūṣaka

दृष्ट्वेति स्मरेत्। मयि विस्रब्धोऽयमपि मन्मनोदोषतया भूयोपि गोपितवानस्मि। तदर्थमयं वैमुख्यं दर्शयति। तस्मादिमम् ऋजुभिर्वचोभिराभाष्य विश्वस्तोस्मीति विभावयन् परस्परस्वैरालापं कथयित्वा मन्मार्गानुसारिणमेनं करोमि।[10] अपि चायं द्विकृत्वः त्रिकृत्वेमं मार्गमनुसर्तुं दर्शितसौहार्दभावः संवृत्तः। तदानीं निन्दितः तस्मादतःपरं विज्ञातगुरुनयेनामुना सह स्वैरालापमाभाष्य शनै रमयामि। सम्प्रति कथं दर्शितवैमुख्येनामुना एताः प्रदर्शयामि। अस्तु इति क्रियते उद्यानश्रीवर्णनच्छेलनोद्यानस्थलेऽस्य दृष्टिं नीत्वा तांस्तेन दर्शयिष्यामि। किन्तु एताः स्त्रियो वा पुंसो वेत्यनिश्चित्योद्यानवर्णनं कर्तव्यमित्यात्मना निश्चित्य किमपि तत्समीपं गत्वा ता एव सवञ्चनं पश्यन्नुपपत्तिभिः तन्निर्णयं करोति। हन्त इमा लाक्षारुषिता यत् ततः स्त्रीणामेवेत्यूह्यम्। इमा स्त्रियो वा कन्यकाया वेति कथं ज्ञायते। एतत् कर्त्री मम नेत्रस्पन्दनफलं किन्नु स्वन्तं करिष्यति इति स्मरन् तद्गतचित्तया किञ्चित् श्रितचित्तलाघवो भूत्वा सखिशब्देन तमावर्जयति।

---

10 Speech has two styles ऋजु and वक्र। The former is plain and linear. The latter is its opposite. While describing the look of Brahmacārin in Kumārasambhava, Kālidāsa says – ऋजुनैव चक्षुषा। The look was factual, innocent and direct. Its opposite is वक्र - crooked, intentional and pretentious. These two modes had its distinct impact on poetics – स्वभावोक्ति is ऋजु and vakrokti is circuitous. Kulaśekhara had this distinction in mind when he designed spaṣṭokti and dhvani in theatre.

अत्र नायकबाधा न विद्यतेति श्रृङ्गारधर्मोऽयमपि सर्वविदं नरं शनैर्नयति लघुतामिति धर्मविदो विदुः। तदर्थचित्तलाघवो भूत्वा सखिशब्देन तमावर्जयति सखे इति।[11]

अथ राजा तामेव पश्यन् भूयस्तमुद्दिश्य पश्यन् सखे इति वदंस्तिष्ठेत्। तथाभूते तस्मिन् विदूषकोपि वैमुख्यं दर्शयन्नन्यत् किमपि विभावयंस्तिष्ठेत्। तथाहूयमानः शनैः तन्मुखे पश्यंस्तिष्ठेत्। अथ तेन वीक्षितो राजा सख इति वदन् सखिशब्दस्यान्वर्थं दर्शयन् मम विश्वस्तोऽसि तन्मत्सिद्धानुगामी भवेति दर्शयता तेनोद्यानश्रीर्वर्ण्यते उत्तरश्लोकेन **आरामलक्ष्मी**रित्यादिना।

अथ राजा सुप्रसन्नमुखो भूत्वा तन्मुखे पश्यन्नुद्यानदारुणि लाक्षादिग्धा निदर्शयन् भूयश्शिलातलमपि दर्शयन् उत्तरग्रन्थमाह। श्लोकस्य प्रयोगमार्गं दर्शयति। आरामलक्ष्मीचरणच्युतानां विभ्रमयावकानां वीजोत्करा दाडिमवल्लरीणां शोभां विभ्रति इत्येतदन्वयमन्तर्गतं कृत्वा बाह्यार्थेन उद्यानश्रीर्वर्ण्यते – आरामलक्ष्मीचरणच्युतानां विभ्रमयावकानामित्युभयोः पदयोर्वर्ण्यमानयोरेवं दृशोर्विभावयेत्। कदाचित् स्त्रिया रूषितलाक्षपादया न्यस्तचरणो मरतकमणिरिति विभावयता तेनोद्यानश्रीरिति वर्ण्यताम्। एतदन्वयार्थं यावकदाडिमयोः षष्ठी निर्दिष्टा। एवमस्य प्रयोगमार्गः।

अथ राजैवं तद्वर्णनं कृत्वा ससन्तोषं तमेव पश्यंस्तिष्ठेत्।

विदू – अथ विदूषकः तं तथाभूतं दृष्ट्वेति स्मरेत्। कुतः अहो अयमनपराद्धे मयि विश्वासं पिशुनयन्त्या दृशा मामनुनयति। पदपद्धतीः स्वस्य दर्शयितुं तत् कथङ्कारमेताः एनं दर्शयामि। स्मृत्वा। अहमस्मात् प्रभृत्येतत्सिद्धानुवर्ती भूत्वा शनैश्शनैः स्वैरालापस्य पात्रं भवामि। तथापीदानीं देवीदर्शनाय गच्छाव इत्युक्त्वायान्तमेनं पदपद्धतीदर्शनप्रस्तावं पिशुनयद्भिर्वचोभिर्देवीदर्शनार्थं गच्छाव इति प्रहसनप्रधानं त्वरयामि। तस्मादार्जवं तेनैव ज्ञातव्यमित्यात्मना निश्चित्योत्तरग्रन्थं तथा प्राह **भो पलाअह्म** इति। एवमस्मिन् ग्रन्थे प्रोच्यमाने तद्दर्शनाय गच्छाव इति दृशोर्विभावयंस्तिष्ठेत्।

राजा – अथ राजा तद्गतचित्ततया तेन दर्शितमजानंस्तिष्ठन्नुत्तरग्रन्थेन पृच्छति **कोयमकाण्ड** इत्यादिना।

विदू – अथ विदूषक इति स्मरेत्। कुतः अहो अहमतःपरमस्य तद्गतचित्ततया दार्ढ्यं परिच्छेत्तुमेवेति ध्वनिना तद्दर्शनायैव त्वरयामीति निश्चित्योत्तरग्रन्थेन त्वरयति। **एआरिस**मित्यादिना। इत्यादौ प्रोच्यमाने इति दर्शयेत्। एतादृशमिति। पूर्वं त्वरयति प्रोक्तं देवीगुणगणनिगलितचित्तोऽस्मीत्युक्तं त्वमिदानीं तद्दर्शनात् सन्दग्धांसुसन्नपि अस्यादर्शमुक्तान्यस्मिन् क्वचित् सम्भ्रमावकाशः कुत इति ध्वन्यर्थं दर्शयन् बाह्यार्थः कथ्यताम्। अथ राजा तस्मिन्नेवं कथयति तद् याथातथ्यमश्रृण्वन्नपि किमपि किमपि श्रृण्वन् ता एव पश्यन्निति स्मरति। एता हित्वा देवी सकाशं कथं गच्छेयम्। हन्त साध्वाचार्योक्तिः। कुतः

यो मनस्कः पुमान् नार्या रमतेऽनेन हेतुना।
तस्य सह्यमिदं तस्मात् क्रकचोत्कृन्तनं तनोः।।

इति स्मरः तद्दर्शनलोलुपः केवलं बाह्यार्थः। उत्तरग्रन्थेन प्रष्टुमारब्धः तन्मुखे पश्येत्।

---

11 Being a King, heroic in himself, the dramatist was careful that he should not be blamed of despicable character. Their love-lorn condition in no way denigrates their heroic nature. The heroic deeds to protect the ascetics is introduced for this purpose.
The author enters upon a detailed discussion on नायकबाधा in SD.

राजा – **कस्ते** इति ग्रन्थेन पृष्टस्तिष्ठेत्।

विदू – अथ विदूषकस्तथाभूतं दृष्ट्वा चेति स्मरेत्। अहो ध्वनिनोत्कम्पयेदं श्रुत्वा कस्ते इत्यनेन प्रोक्तम्। तस्मादस्मिन् ग्रन्थे ध्वन्यर्थमयं नान्यचित्ततया वेत्ति। अपि च अमुष्य चित्तमेतद्दर्शनकुतूहली तदेनमेव दर्शयामीत्यात्मगतं निश्चित्योत्तरग्रन्थेन दर्शयति अङ्गुल्या निर्दिश्य **एदस्सिं** इत्यादिना।

अथ राजा तेन दर्शितास्ताः पश्यन् विदूषकमुखेऽपि पश्यन्निति दर्शयेत्। ता अहं पूर्वं नापश्यमिति तस्य विभावयन् सान्तर्मोदमुपसृत्य ता एव पश्यन्निति स्मरेत्। हन्तैताश्चतस्रो नाम। तासां द्वे शस्ते। तयोर्वामायां राजमहिष्याः लक्ष्माणि भवेयुः –

यस्याः पादतले नामे तस्यैतद्वर्तते स्थितः।
मुक्तामालादर्पणादि सा राजमहिषी भवेत्।।

इति गुहप्रोक्तेन ज्योतिश्शास्त्रेण शरीरलक्ष्म दर्शितम्। तस्मादनया राजमहिष्या भवितव्यम्। तस्मादयं कन्यका वा महिषी वा। पुनस्ता एव पश्यन् इमे कन्यकाया स्याताम्। अन्ये स्त्रियः यद् गुहपरिसरे लाक्षारहितेन पदद्वयेन शनैश्चरन्ती गुहपूजां कृतवती ततोऽम्बरादवतीर्य गुहपूजां कर्तुं काचित् कन्यकारत्नमायात इत्यूह्यम्। अन्ये तद्वयस्या इति च। अपि च अथ सा कृतगुहपूजास्मिन् स्थित्वा पदद्वयं लिप्तलाक्षं विधाया स्मान्मरतकमणिशिलातलादुत्प्लुत्य सम्प्रत्येवाम्बरगमनमाचरितवती आवयोर्दर्शनादेवेति यथातथं निश्चित्य भूय इति स्मरेत्। अहमतःपरं मच्चेतोवक्रतामपहाय मन्मनोगतमस्मै विज्ञापयन् भविष्यामि इत्यात्मना निश्चित्य तद्विज्ञापयितुमुत्तरग्रन्थेनावर्जितुकामस्तिष्ठेत्। इतःपूर्वं स्थितगाम्भीर्येण ध्वनिवचसा गूढमानोरथयोः तयोर्दर्शितगूढोक्तिरसः। इतःपश्चात् श्रृङ्गाररसो दृश्यते तत् कथमिति चेत् – श्रृङ्गाररसमूर्तिमतीं वल्लीं कल्पयित्वा रसस्य क्रमतो वर्धिष्णुतां दर्शयति क्वचित्क्षेत्रे श्रृङ्गाररसवल्लीबीजस्य वापनं कृत्वा तत् सिक्त्वाङ्कुरयित्वा भूयः पल्लवयित्वा शनैर्नरा शोष्यतां कुसुमयित्वा फलयतीति स्थायीभावः तत्प्रकारं दर्शयति।[12] पूर्वं स्वप्नदर्शनं क्षेत्रं पुनर्नेत्रस्पन्दनमाकरसंस्कार इदानीं पदतलदर्शनेन बीजावापनं कृतम्। अतः परं शनैः क्रमौन्नत्यं द्रष्टव्यम्। अथ राजा पूर्ववत् तमेव तद्वचनगौरवं दृग्भ्यां पश्यन् समर्थयन्तीभ्याम् उत्तरग्रन्थेन तमावर्जयति **सखे** इति। सख इति पदे प्रोच्यमाने तदन्वर्थं दर्शयन्नुत्तरग्रन्थेन तद्वचनगौरवं समर्थयति सत्यमित्यादिना। सत्यं प्रवृत्त एव सम्प्रहार इति। तत्र सम्प्रहारशब्दे प्रोच्यमाने स्मरस्य मया सह सम्प्रहारः प्रवृत्त इति दृशोर्दर्शयेत्। तस्मिन्निति दर्शयति। विदूषकोपि तदनुकूलो भूत्वा तस्य मदनलतामङ्कुरयितुं वचसा प्रष्टुकामस्तिष्ठेत्।

अथ राजा सान्तर्मोदं नम्रतनुस्तिष्ठेन्नतन्मुख एव पश्यन्नुत्तरग्रन्थेन तं विवृणोति कस्याश्चित् दिव्ययुवतेः लाक्षाविषदिग्धाभ्यामित्यादि श्लोके ध्वनिना निजावस्थां विज्ञापयति। कस्याश्चित् दिव्ययुवतेः पदाब्जबाणाभ्यां स्मरेणायं मरतकमणिविद्धश्शेते इति सम्बन्धः। सखे अयं मरतकमणिः अहमेतद्दर्शनमात्रेणैव स्मरेणाब्जाख्येन बाणेन हृदि विद्धोऽस्मि। स्मरशराणां पञ्चानामाद्येन शरेण मे ध्वन्यर्थं दृशोरेव विभावयन् बाह्यार्थेन नानालोकान् विनोदयेत्। एवं दर्शयित्वा भूयस्तच्छरजावस्थावस्थित त्वान्नयनप्रीतौ ते पदपद्धती एव पश्यंस्तिष्ठेत्।

---

12 The metaphor of रसवल्ली is both poetic and theatrical. Actors can depict the development of rasa in a concrete way through the creeper. The image is repeated.

अरविन्दमशोकं च चूतञ्च नवमालती।
नीलोत्पलं च पञ्चैते पञ्चबाणस्य सायकाः।।[13]

एभिर्विद्धस्य पुंसो दशा दशधा ज्ञेयाः।

नयनप्रीतिः प्रथमं चित्तानन्दः ततोपि सङ्कल्पः।
भोजनविरुचिस्तनुता निद्रानाशस्त्रपानाशः।
उन्मादस्सा मूर्च्छा मृतिरेता स्मरदशा दशैव स्युः।।

इति कामशास्त्रे प्रसिद्धिरिति। तच्छराणामाद्येन शरेण विद्धत्वात् सज्जातया दशया सम्प्रेर्यमाणहृदयत्वान्नयनप्रीतौ प्राप्ताभिरतिस्ते एव पश्यंस्तिष्ठेत्। अस्मात्प्रभृत्याकर्णपूर दर्शनान्नयनप्रीतौ प्रयोक्तव्यम्।

अथ राजा तद्दर्शनादेवेमे कन्यकाया इति निश्चित्य विदूषकमुखे पश्यन् कन्यकाया इमे इति दृशोरेवं विभावयन् तिष्ठेत्।

अथ राजा तस्मिन्नेव दर्शयति दृशोस्तत्प्रत्ययार्थमिममर्थं दर्शयेत्। कुतः,

द्वादशाब्दादथारभ्य द्वात्रिंशत् वर्षतो वयः।
प्रयान्ती याङ्गना लोके युवतिस्सोच्यते बुधैः।।
देवानामापतिप्राप्तेः कुर्यात्पूजां यथाविधि।
आवैधव्यात् स्वभर्तॄणां परिचर्यां समाचरेत्।।
मन्त्रानामरणाज्जप्त्वा मोक्षदानायुराहरेत्।
एवं सतीनामाचारः कल्पितो मनुना पुरा।।

एतद्वचःप्रामाण्यात् गृहाराधनतत्परायाः कस्याश्चित् दिव्यकन्यकाया इति निश्चितवानस्मि इत्यादि सर्वं दृशोर्विभावयंस्तं विज्ञाप्य भूयो नयनप्रीतौ एते एव पश्यंस्तत्कर्त्री मम भार्यास्यादिति मनसा प्रार्थयन् साशस्तिष्ठेत्।

विदू – अथ विदूषकस्तथा युक्तिर्भिर्विज्ञाप्य तिष्ठन्तमेनं दृष्ट्वेति स्मरेत्। अहमतःपरमस्यानुकूलो भूत्वा तामन्तरेण पृच्छाम्यस्योहापोहपटुत्वं तन्मनस्कतां च विज्ञातुमिति निश्चित्योत्तरग्रन्थेन तथा पृच्छति **केण उण** इत्यादिना।

राजा – तत्करस्थिताशस्ते एष पश्यंस्तिष्ठेदिति तेन मया पृष्टः तदा मन्दं मन्दं पश्यन् तदानुकूल्यं दृष्ट्वेति स्मरेत्। कर्तव्यमिदानीं यदनेन पृष्ठं तस्योत्तरं तस्मादिमं सम्मानयन् वदामीति निश्चित्योत्तरग्रन्थेन तथा करोति, **पश्यतु भवानि**ति। भवच्छब्दे प्रोच्यमाने मामनुकूलो भूयादिति दृशोर्विभावयन् भूयः आह पश्यत्विति। अहं भवता पृष्टोऽस्मि 'कथं दिव्यकन्यकाया इति ज्ञातवानस्मी'ति तद्विज्ञापकानि चिह्नानि पश्यतु। वीक्षता तरुपलाशेष्विति पिण्डालक्तकदिग्धानि शाखाजालानीति विज्ञाप्य तत्प्रत्ययं सम्पादयंस्तिष्ठेत्। तस्मिन्नेवं तिष्ठति विदूषकत्तरुषु दृष्टिं नीत्वा सविस्मयमिव विभावयंस्तिष्ठेत्।

13 This is described in SD also.

अथ राजा तमेवं विज्ञाप्य भूयोपि तेनैव ग्रन्थेन विज्ञापयति तमेव पश्यन् पश्यतु भवानिति। एवं स्मरतु, एषा मद्वंशकरी चेत् किं न स्यादिति अपि च इयं चेत् कीदृशाशारतं मां घटयतीति च। दिव्यकन्यकापरिग्रहोपायः चिन्त्यतामिति इमं ध्वन्यर्थं विभावयन् भूयो नयनप्रीतौ ते एव पश्यंस्तिष्ठेत्। विदू – अथ तेनैवमुक्तो विदूषकस्तद्विधिं प्रतीति स्मरेत्। इयं तव वशङ्करी चेत् व्यज्यत इति ध्वनिः। अथेति विज्ञाप्य तस्मिन् तिष्ठति राजा मद्वंशतुल्यकुलजेयं किमिति च पश्यतु स्मरतु। स्मरत्विति च विभावयंस्तिष्ठेत्। अथैवं तेन दर्शितो विदूषकः पुनरपि तदर्थं निरूपितवान्। पुनरेवं स्मृत्वा भूयो युक्तिभिस्तस्या एकतुल्यतां स्मरेत्। इतरपदयुगलं दर्शयन्नुत्तरं वदामीत्यात्मना निश्चित्य ध्वनियुक्तेनोत्तरग्रन्थेन तत् समर्थयति **एदस्स पदजुअलंतरस्स** इत्यादिना।

अथ विदूषकः तमेव पश्यंस्तिष्ठेत्। एवं तिष्ठतानेन एदं सीमीत्यादिग्रन्थे प्रोच्यमाने एवं दर्शयेत्। एषा सवयस्या यत् ततः कः कथ्यते। इयं ममोचिता वा नवेति तत्र कः संशय इत्यर्थः। इति विज्ञाप्यमाने तस्मिन् स राजा तदश्रृण्वन्नेव तस्या जन्म च प्राप्तेरुपायश्च स्मरन् तिष्ठेत्। तदा विदूषकः कस्तथाभूतं दृष्ट्वा चेति स्मरेत्। अहोऽयं मयोक्तं तदनेन अन्यचित्ततया न श्रुतं भवेत्। तस्मात् तत्प्राप्तुमुपायमहमेव स्मृत्वा भूयस्तदुपायं विन्दन् वाऽविन्दन् वा पुनस्तस्या एतद्योग्यतां आचारशास्त्रेण दर्शयामीति निश्चित्य एत्ति अमेत्तमित्यादि ग्रन्थेनाहमेव स्मरामीति समर्थयन् तदर्थं निमीलितचक्षुस्तिष्ठेत्। राजापि तद्ध्यानैकपरतया तिष्ठेत्। एवमुभौ यदा निमीलितचक्षुषौ तिष्ठेतां तदा यवनिकयाच्छाद्यताम्।

एवमितःपूर्वं तयोः प्रयोगमार्गः।
ततस्तेन देवीप्रावेशिको दृश्यते।

(ततः प्रविशति सान्तश्चिन्तं सपरिवारा देवी।)

अथ देवी साल्वराजपुत्री विदूषकेण या पुरं नीता सा निजनियमप्रवृत्तिनिवृत्तिहेतोः अनभिज्ञा निजसखीभूतयोत्पलिकया निजभर्तुः प्रातरेव निर्गमनं विज्ञाप्यमानं श्रृण्वन्ती सान्तश्चिन्तया सह तद्व्यवसितं ज्ञातुं पुरान्निर्गत्य गच्छन्ती दुश्चिन्तया इतिकर्तव्यतामौढ्यं प्राप्य क्वचित्पथि तथा तया सहातिष्ठत्। एवं सान्तश्चिन्तं सधीरं सेर्ष्यं सविवेकं त्रिवर्त्युज्ज्वलितस्य दीपस्य पुरस्तद्भूमिकालङ्कृतनटी यावत् तिष्ठेत् तावत् यवनिका व्यपनीयताम्।

एवं तिष्ठन्ती सेति स्मरेत्। ततः किमर्थमसम्पूर्णकालावधेः पुत्रीयान्नियमात् आर्यपुत्रेणायासं प्रापितास्मि। अहो अस्य वचनस्य प्रभुता –

पिता रक्षति कौमारे भर्ता रक्षति यौवने।
पुत्रस्तु स्थविरे भावे न स्त्री स्वातन्त्र्यमर्हति।।

अपि च सतीह लोके यैवं स्यादित्यस्यापि तस्मात् सर्वप्रकारेणार्यपुत्रस्य मय्युदासीनता भवतीति मन्तव्यम्। किमर्थं मां पुरं प्रापय्यार्यपुत्रदर्शनाय सत्वरं गतवानयं पाराशर्यः। एतस्मात् यत्किमपि कार्यान्तरमन्तरेण व्यवहर्तुममुना कृतसङ्केतो भूत्वा तदर्थं त्वरितवानयम् इत्यूह्यम्। तस्मात्तत्सन्निधिमुपेत्य येनकेनाप्या च्छादिततनुर्भूत्वा तत्प्रवृत्तिं मयि चान्यस्मिन्वान्यस्यां वेति तयोः परस्परस्वैरालापात् तामीदृग्भूतामिति निश्चित्य भूयो यथोचितं करिष्ये इत्यादि दृशोर्विभावयन्ती प्रेक्षकान् बोधयित्वा भूयोऽप्येवं स्मरेत्। तत्र

गमनहेतुस्सख्यैको विज्ञातपूर्वायै मयोच्यते। स्मृत्वा अस्तु, सखि चिरात् तद्दर्शनात् वर्धितोत्कण्ठास्मि संवृत्ता। अपि च मदनोपि तद्दर्शनाय त्वरयतीव मामिति तस्यै विज्ञापयामि इति निश्चित्योत्तरग्रन्थेन तत् साधयति। **हल्ला अप्पलिए** इत्यादिना। हला इति शब्देन सा सखीति प्रोच्यते।

एवं तत्प्रयोगमार्गः। नायिकोत्तरोत्तराधिकसन्तापा भवेदिति तत् स्थायीभावः।

एवं तद्दर्शयित्वा भूयः पूर्वप्रविष्टयोः नायकविदूषकयोरतःपरं स्थायीभावप्रयोगमार्गौ दृश्येते।

विदू – अथैवं यवनिकान्तरितदेहौ पूर्ववत् तिष्ठन्तौ तौ व्यपगतयवनिकौ निमीलिताक्षौ समं मुहूर्तं दीपपुरस्तिष्ठेताम्। एवं तिष्ठतोस्तयोः पूर्वपूर्वं विदूषक इति स्मरेत्। – चक्षुष्युन्मील्य – भो! स्मरणप्रकारो दृश्यते। कुतः भो इत्यत्र भोशब्दः आदौ विवेके भोत्तस्यास्तत् योग्यता विद्यते। कुतः –

शुभे गोत्रे च या जाता साध्वी भूतिप्रदोभयोः।
सा द्वितीया क्वचिद्भूयान्नतत् बाधामुतो भवेत्।।

इति सुरासुराचार्ययोरेतल्लोकान्वये विवदतोर्मतमाद्यं स्मृत्वा तद्योग्येयमित्युत्तरपदेन निश्चित्य भूयस्तन्मुख एव पश्यंस्तिष्ठेत्।

तथाभूते विदूषके राजापि तच्चिन्तापरो भूत्वा विस्मृतेतरकार्यस्तिष्ठेत्। अथ विदूषकस्तथाभूतं तं दृष्ट्वेति स्मरेत्। इदानीमेनमाहूय श्रिताभिमुख्यं कृत्वा स्मृत्यर्थं दर्शयित्वा तव योग्येयमिति विज्ञापयामीति निश्चित्योत्तरग्रन्थं वदन् स्मृत्यर्थेन तद्योग्यतां समर्थयति। **भो** इत्यत्र सम्बुद्धौ।

अथ विदूषकः तं पश्यन् भो इति सम्बुद्ध्याहूतवान्। अथ राजा तद्गतचित्तो भूत्वा तिष्ठन्नयं तथाहूतश्चक्षुष्युन्मील्य चेति स्मरेत्। कथमिदानीमाचारशास्त्रोक्त्यास्या मद्योग्यतां प्रकाशयामीति स्मरन्निति निश्चितवान्। कथमिदानीं भवता मद्योग्यता दर्शितेति विभावयंस्तस्मै इति निश्चित्य तथा तिष्ठेत्। तथा विदूषकस्तथा तस्मिंस्तिष्ठमाने तेन दर्शितं ज्ञात्वेति स्मरेत्। अहमेनमिदानीं कबलितायाश्शास्त्रेण वयसास्यास्त्वद्योग्यतां पदान्तरेण द्रष्टव्येति आत्मगतं निश्चित्योत्तरग्रन्थेन तत् समर्थयति। भो एषा सवयस्या यत् ततः तत्र कः व्याख्यानावशेषः 'शुभे गोत्रे च जाते'त्यस्य श्लोकस्योभयोर्मतं दृशोर्विभावयन् आचारशास्त्रविशेष इति दर्शयित्वा भूयस्तदयोग्यताप्रामाण्यात् स्मृत्यर्थमिति दर्शयेत्। कुतः,

तादृश्याः कन्यकाया वै पाणिग्रहणमङ्गले।
न जातु कुर्यात् समं चित्तं दुर्विकल्पं सुधीः पुमान्।।

इत्यादि सर्वं दर्शयन् भूयस्तत्प्राप्त्युपायो मया न लब्ध इत्युत्तरग्रन्थेन समर्थयति। भोणकेवलमित्यादि ग्रन्थं वक्तुं प्रारब्धे तस्मिन्नथ तदा मध्ये राजा मद्योग्येयमिति निश्चिता सा चेदादौ तद्दर्शनोपायं निश्चिन्त्यतामिति दृशोर्विभावयंस्तिष्ठेत्।

अथ विदूषकस्तस्मिन्नेवं तिष्ठति भूयोपि पूर्वप्रस्तुतग्रन्थेनैवोभयस्यापि न मयोपायश्चिन्तित इति विज्ञापयति केवलं तद्दर्शनप्राप्त्युपायं स्मरतो मम परं निमीलितामक्ष्णां नान्धकारस्संवृत्तः; चेतसोपि। तस्मात्त्वमेव तदुपायं स्मृत्वा निश्चित्य मां ब्रूयाः इत्यनेन ध्वन्यर्थेन विज्ञाप्य तिष्ठेत्।

राजा – अथ राजा पूर्वमेवेतरपदयुगलं दृष्ट्वा तत् स्वयोग्यतां निश्चितवानपि भूयस्त्वाचारविधिं तेनैव वादयितुं तिष्ठन्नयं तन्मात्रकथनश्रवणात् भूय एवं स्मरेत्। अहमिदानीमाभ्यामितरपदपद्धतीभ्यां

तद्दर्शनप्राप्त्युपायो न विद्यत इति समर्थयामीत्यात्मना निश्चित्य भूय उत्तरग्रन्थेन तत्समर्थयति। तद्वयस्यायाः कस्याश्चित्पदाभ्यां भवितव्यमपि मद्योग्यतैव समर्थिता। आभ्यां किमिति तद्दर्शनप्राप्त्युपायदर्शनमाभ्यां दुरवबोधमिति ध्वनिना विदूषकं विज्ञाप्य भूयस्तद्दर्शनप्राप्त्युपायचिन्तां राजा स्वयमेवेति स्मरेत्। यया सवयस्यया न्यस्तमिदं पदयुगलं सेदानीं मां पश्यन्ती विटपिनि स्थित्वा मन्निमित्तं स्मरबाणलक्षणतां प्रयान्ती चेत् सा येनकेनापि मया दृष्टा भवेत्। तस्मादस्मिन् विटपिनि मया दृष्टिः नेयेत्यात्मना निश्चित्य भूय उद्दृष्टिर्विवेकभाक् तिष्ठेत्।

विदू – अथ विदूषकस्तेनैवं विज्ञापित तत्साध्वित्युत्तरग्रन्थेन समर्थयति। **एदं पि** इति। एतस्मिन् युज्यते इत्येषा विषयसप्तमीति विज्ञाप्य तन्मुखं दृष्ट्वा स्वयमप्युन्मुखो भूत्वा किमनेन स्मर्यत इति ज्ञातुकामस्तिष्ठेत्। अथ राजा उदृष्टिस्तिष्ठन्नयं भूयस्ते पदपद्धत्यौ पश्यन्नेवं स्मरेत्। कुतः 'या दृष्टा सेति विमृश्यताम्' इति वात्स्यायनसूत्रम्। तस्यार्थं स्मरेत् गम्यागम्येयं, किं गम्या चेत् रागिणिमयीयं; किं रागवती चेत् सैषा तत्प्राप्त्यै चिन्त्यतामुपायः। पुंसा रूपेण जन्मना भूयश्शीलेन वयसा नृभिः विमृश्य ज्ञायताम्। सा गम्येयं किं न वेति स्मरशास्त्रेऽङ्गनापरिग्रहे पुरुषविवेकपद्धत्या विमृश्यमानायां गम्येति निश्चितवानस्मि। कुतः,

यावत्सख्यं प्रकोष्ठं स्यात् तावत् सख्यं पदद्वयम्।
आयतं तच्चतुर्भागं मध्यं पत्तलयोद्वेयोः।
ईदृग्विधं पदतलं मदीयं साधु वर्तते।
सर्वाङ्गैः सुन्दरी सेयमिति विज्ञाप्यतां बुधैः।।

इति गुहप्रोक्तेण स्मरश्लक्ष्मशास्त्रेण अयं दृष्टम्।

दिव्याङ्गना सवयस्या च यत्। तेन जन्म च।... मय्यागमिष्यति यदा तदैवान्तरधत्तेति यत् ततश्शीलं च। कन्यका यत् ततस्तु वयश्च। तस्मात् गम्यागम्यविवेके स्त्रीलक्षणैर्गम्येयमिति मया निर्दिष्टा। अतः परं रागिणी न वेति द्रष्टव्या। तत् केन ज्ञायते?

रागिणी पुंसि या यस्मिन् वियुक्ते तस्य सा तया।
प्रयोक्तव्या बलाद्दूती गाढावस्थानिवेदिनी।।

इति रागिणीं विज्ञातुं जयमङ्गलोक्तचिह्नम्। पुनस्तरुमापादमस्तकं पश्यन्निव स्मरेत्।।

अस्य तरोर्मध्यप्रदेशादूर्ध्वमरूषितलाक्षाश्शाखा यत् ततस्तत्रस्थया माहात्म्यं प्रच्छन्नया तया भवितव्यम्। भूयोप्युदृष्टिर्भूत्वा पूर्वन्दर्शितस्वप्नं भानुमन्तं मनसेति प्रार्थयेत्। भगवन्! यदीयोयं पदपद्धतिः तां मयि अनुरागिणीं विधाय तत् येनकेनापि मे विज्ञापयेति स्मरन्नुदृष्टिरेव तिष्ठेत्। स्वप्नदर्शनं क्षेत्रं, दक्षिणनेत्र-स्पन्दनमाकरस्संस्कारः पददर्शनं बीजवापनं, गम्यागम्यविवेचनालवाल रचितं; गम्येति निश्चिततया धिया सिक्तं, रागिणी वा नवेति अज्ञानादुत्प्तं श्रृङ्गाररसवल्ली बीजमङ्कुरितं बृंहितमिति स्थायीभावः।

विदू – ऊर्ध्वं पश्यति। अथ विदूषकस्तेन दर्शितं सकलं बुध्यावधार्य तिष्ठन्नयं तन्मुखं दृष्ट्वेति स्मरेत्। किमर्थमस्योर्ध्वदर्शनम्। सशिरःकम्पं तयाप्यम्बरस्थया भवितव्यमिति स्मृत्वा स्वयमप्यूर्ध्वं पश्यति। तदा अम्बरात् किमप्यापतति। अथोर्ध्वं तिष्ठन्नयं विदूषकस्सहसाम्बरात् पतितं दृष्ट्वा चेति स्मरेत्।

अथ राजा तन्निमित्तं भानुं प्रार्थयंस्तिष्ठन्नेतं पतितं ज्ञातवानपि न ज्ञातवानस्मीति विभावयन् पूर्ववत् तिष्ठेत्। अथ विदूषकः तथाभूतं दृष्ट्वेति स्मरेत्। अहमतःपरमस्य बुद्धिविवेकनैशित्यं ज्ञातुं तस्यां रागं कियानिति च परिच्छेत्तुमस्यानुकूलो भूत्वा व्यङ्ग्यं विहाय तत्सहृदयो भूत्वा केवलहास्यरसेन तमिमं विज्ञापयामीति निश्चित्योत्तरग्रन्थेन तं दर्शयति **अविहा** इत्यादिना।

अतः परमाप्रथमाङ्गाद्ध्वनिना विज्ञापयन् प्रयोगः तयोः।

चेटी – अथ तद्दर्शनाय गच्छन्त्योस्तयोः अग्रगामिनी न्यायहेतोरुत्तरग्रन्थेन तां विज्ञापयति **अग्गदो** इत्यादिना।

देवी – अथ देवी गच्छन्ती तद्वचनश्रवणात् पूर्वशङ्कामुत्तरग्रन्थेन विवृणोति **जइ एव्व**मित्यादिना।

राजा – अथ राजा पतितं तं तेन दर्शितं दृष्ट्वा सुप्रसन्नमुखो भूत्वा तमेव पश्यन् भूयो विदूषकं च पश्यन् अस्य याथातथ्यमुत्तरग्रन्थेन विदूषकाय विज्ञापयति। सखे न खल्वयं पिशितपेशीति ब्रुवाणे तस्मिन् विदूषकस्साद्भुतं किमपि किमपि शनैर्व्यवहारं तव बुद्धेरुन्मेषाय सम्मानयन् तन्मुखे तस्मिंश्च दृष्टी नीयमानस्तर्हि कोऽयमिति मे ब्रूहीति विभावयंस्तिष्ठेत्।

अथ राजा तस्मिन्नेवं विभावयति, सुप्रसन्नमुखो भूत्वा तं च तं च पृथक् पश्यन् एवं तस्य विज्ञापयत्युत्तरग्रन्थेन। **मन्ये मन्दारपल्लवापीडकल्पित** इति ग्रन्थे प्रोच्यमाने विदूषकायेति विज्ञापयेत्। स्वस्तरुपलाशच्छदैर्विरचितत्वात् तस्या एव दिव्ययुवतेरयमित्यूह्यमिति विज्ञाप्य कस्याश्चिदिति कीदृग्गोत्रजा केयमिति न जाने इति ग्रन्थेन तं विज्ञाप्य भूयस्तमेव नयनप्रीतौ पश्यन्नमुष्मिन् कानिचिदक्षराणि दृष्ट्वा तद्व्यक्ततां सम्पादयितुं तद्वर्णनच्छलेन तैरक्षरैः कीदृशमर्थं एतत्कर्त्री बोधयतीति विमृशता अनेनोत्तरश्लोकेन वर्ण्यते – **कम्रैः कैश्चिद**ित्यादिना।

अथ राजा तस्मिन् नीयमानदृष्टिस्तिष्ठन् विदूषकमनुक्त्वा तानि दृष्टानीति भूयस्तमेव पश्यंस्तैरेव तत्सिद्धान्तव्यक्तिमविन्दन् तैरेव तत्सिद्धान्तं विमृशति। कम्रैः कैश्चिदिति शिलासम्पर्कात् दुर्निरीक्षैः मृदुमणिदलैः मृदुभूतैः मणिदलैः अक्षरदलैः। वज्रादिरत्नेक्षरे च मणिशब्दः प्रवर्तते। अत्र ध्वनावक्षरे। तथाभूतैरक्षरैः शबलितधनुः अज्ञाततत्सिद्धान्तोऽस्मीति भावः। अपि च अव्याकृतायां हेतुद्वयं स्वेदप्रकरनिकरैः अलकसुमनोरेणुभिश्च मच्चेतच्चित्तविकारदर्शिन्येतानीत्येव केवलं निश्चित्य भूयस्तद्ध्वन्यर्थेन प्रेक्षकान् सन्तोषयित्वा भूयो बाह्यार्थेन नानालोकानभिनयेन सुखयेत्। एभिश्शबलिततनुरयं कर्णपूरः इति बाह्यार्थस्य सम्बन्धः। एवं तदीयवर्णनां कृत्वा स्वनिमित्तमिति निश्चित्य द्वितीयावस्था चित्तानन्दं सम्प्राप्य विदूषकमुखे पश्यंस्तिष्ठेत्। एवं प्रयोगमार्गः।

अथ राजा तदक्षरपङ्क्तिर्दृष्ट्वा सा रागिणी स्वस्मिन्निति यदा निश्चितवान् तदैवाङ्कुरिता रसवल्ली। अङ्कुरितायामस्यामस्य चित्तानन्दस्समभवत्। तथाहि –

यद्गतं चित्तं स्यात् तच्चित्तं स्वेप्यजानतः।
अहं त्वद्गतचित्तेति ज्ञापितस्स तया यदा।।
तदा प्रभृति तच्चित्तं महानन्द एधते। इति वात्स्यायनोक्तम्।

'शर्मणे रसिनां नृणां' इत्यनेन विधिनातःपरमागाथां पूरणाच्चित्तानन्द एव प्रयोक्तव्यम्।

देवी – अथ सा लतान्तरितदेहा सख्यामादिष्टन्ती तस्य कर्णपूरदर्शनौत्सुक्यस्य तद्गतचित्ततां पिशुनयद्वचः श्रृण्वन्ती स्वभर्तुर्निजपक्षपातराहित्यं शङ्कमाना स्वमनोदुःखमुत्तरग्रन्थेन पिशुनयति। **हला एसो मन्दारकण्ण उर** इत्यादिना।

चेटी – अथ चेटी स्वन्यायादुत्तरग्रन्थेन शमयति। **एत्ति एण** इत्यादिना।

विदू – अथ विदूषकः कर्णपूरं व्यक्तीकर्तुमुत्तरग्रन्थेन पृच्छति **भो मम खलु** इत्यादिना।

राजा – अथ राजा तेन तदा पृष्टः सानन्दं तं तं च पश्यंस्तस्यामेवेति निखिन्वन् उत्तरग्रन्थं वदति यस्यायमिति। तस्या एवेति निश्चिततया धिया प्रक्षिप्तदोहला सा रसवल्ली।

विदू – अथ विदूषकस्तेन तथा विज्ञापितस्तन्मतिविवेकनैशित्यं परिच्छेत्तुमुत्तरग्रन्थेन पृच्छति **को एथ हेदू** इत्यादिना।

राजा – अथ राजा तेन तदा पृष्टः तच्चरितवर्णने मितमनोरथो उत्तरग्रन्थेन घर्मसलिलबिन्दुर्हेतुं विज्ञापयति। अत्र कथं तद्दर्शनसमय एव तत्पदतले प्राप्ताः स्वेदबिन्दव इति चेत् तत्सहेतुकमिति ज्ञेयम्।

यदैतामङ्कमारोप्य ज्ञापिता मुनयो गुणाः।
जगन्नेत्रेणाजमीढे तन्मनस्का तदैव सा।। इति ज्ञातव्यम्।

देवी – अथ देवी तद्वचश्शृण्वन्ती सान्यमनस्कोऽयमित्युत्तरग्रन्थेन समर्थयति। **हला पअकहा**वित्यादिना।

चेटी – अथ चेटी तनो दुःखं नियतुमुत्तरग्रन्थेन आह किंवेत्यादिना।

अथ विदूषकस्तस्याः पदतलस्थं स्वेदबिन्दुं दृष्ट्वायं मदनविकृतिं पिशुनयन्निति विज्ञापितवानपि राज्ञैवं वर्णयितुमुत्तरग्रन्थेन पृच्छति **कहं एक्काए** इत्यादिना।

राजा – सानन्दम्। अथ राजा तद्व्याचिकीर्षतां कर्तुकामस्सन्नप्यपृष्टवन्तं न ब्रूयादिति विधिना वक्तुमशक्तस्तिष्ठंस्तेन तथापृष्टं सप्रमोदं श्रमजलबिन्दुषु दृष्टिं नीत्वा भूयस्तन्मुखे पश्यन् विदूषकं दृग्भ्यामेवावर्ज्याभ्यामेव मदीयं रागिणी न नस्यात् इति दर्शयंस्तत्प्रामाण्यं कामशास्त्रेण समर्थयंस्तच्छास्त्रार्थं दृग्भ्यां पाणिना च विज्ञापयेत्।

दशासूक्तासु दशसु स्मरस्याशु प्रवर्तते।
आसप्तम्या दशायास्ताः विकृतिद्वन्द्वमादिभिः।।
एकैका जनयत्येतदेवमेवं यथाक्रमम्।
प्रोक्तमेवं रसविदे रतिशास्त्रेण साधुना।।
रोमाञ्चं स्वेदवार्याभ्यां जृम्भणं गोष्णते परा।
विविक्तशर्म चोच्छ्वासं चतुर्थ्युक्तं च वेपथुः।।
स्रक्चन्दनादौ वैराग्यसंस्कारेऽङ्गस्य पञ्चमी।
पिकभृङ्गरवे श्राव्ये वयौ षष्ठी विरागता।।
चन्द्रालोके जीवने या जनयत्यतिवेदना।।

एवं स्मरविकृतीनामादिदशाया विकृतिद्वन्द्वं प्राप्तैवेति दृशा तस्य दर्शयन् श्रृङ्गारवल्लीं पल्लवयन्नुत्तरग्रन्थेन तदेव दर्शयति – न खलु मार्गश्रमजनितैरेभिर्भवितव्यमिति विज्ञाप्य भूयः श्लाघ्यजन्मानं कञ्चिद् युवानमित्युक्त्वा भूयः स्वनिमित्तमस्या मदनपीडेति समर्थयन्नुत्तरश्लोकेन दर्शयति। **अपाङ्गपातै**रित्यादिना। अपाङ्गपातैरिति। अनुरागगर्भैरपाङ्गैः कञ्चिद् युवानमापिबन्त्या कस्याश्चिदङ्गेषु अनङ्गप्रथमावतारोऽयं स्वेदसलिलनिकरः। रोमाञ्चसम्भेदसखेष्विति पदे प्रोच्यमाने तच्छराद्यदशविकृतिद्वयं प्राप्तैषेति दृग्भ्यां

पाणिभ्यां च दर्शयेत्। एवं दृग्भ्यां बोधयित्वा पुनः स्वयं नायिका भूत्वा श्लोकाभिनयेन सुखयेत्। अस्मिन्नङ्केऽयं श्लोको वर्णनीयः।[14]

एवमुभयथा सुखयित्वा भूयस्सानन्दस्तिष्ठेत्। एवं प्रयोगमार्गः।

विदू – अथ विदूषकस्तथा दर्शयन्तं तं दृष्ट्वेति स्मरेत्। अहमिदानीं तद्विषयस्त्वमेवेति समर्थयन्नेनं प्रहर्षयामीति निश्चित्योत्तरग्रन्थेन तथा समर्थयति **भो अं पज्ञो वि अहं** इत्यादिना।

देवी – अथ देवी तद्विषयस्त्वमेवेति समर्थयति विदूषकगिरं श्रृण्वन्ती सा सरोषं सदुःखं सान्तस्तापमुत्तरग्रन्थेन विदूषकमधिक्षिपति **हला** इत्यादिना।

चेटी – अथ चेटी राजानमपराधवन्तं मन्वानाऽपि स्वन्यायहेतोस्सम्यगनपराद्ध इत्युत्तरग्रन्थेन समर्थयति आमसुदोति।

देवी – अथ देवी तद्वचस्तथा श्रृण्वन्ती सान्तरीर्ष्यमुत्तरग्रन्थं सरोषमाह का वा इति। एवं तद्वचनश्रवणा-दुत्तरोत्तराधिकरोषसन्तापं बहिस्तिष्टन्त्योस्तदुदन्तमन्तरेणेति कथयन्त्योस्तयोः राजा स्वमुद्दिश्य वा न वास्यचित्तविकार इति अवधारयितुं तदक्षरपङ्क्तिभिः कर्णपूर एव दृष्टीचारयंस्तिष्ठेत्।

अथ विदूषकस्तस्मिन् नीयमानदृष्टिराजानं दृष्ट्वेति स्मरेत्। अहो पञ्चषैरव्यक्ताक्षरैः तद्गतैरज्ञाततासिद्धान्तो भवन्नयमिदानीमेनं ग्रहीतुकामस्तिष्ठति। तस्मादहमिदानीमेतद्गतै-रक्षरैस्शास्त्रं किञ्चिदनुकुर्वन्नेनमुद्धृत्यामुना सन्तोषयामीति निश्चित्य भूयस्तस्मिन् सावधानं पश्येदिति तस्मिन् सावधानं पश्यन् साश्चर्यं तन्मुखे तस्मिंश्च मुहुर्मुहुः पश्यन्नयं उद्धर्तव्यः किमिति हृष्याविज्ञापितेन राज्ञा गृहाणेति प्रेरितोऽयं केवलं प्रहसनप्रधानं सविस्मयमुद्धृत्यैनं स्वकरतले निक्षिप्य सविस्मयं पश्यतश्शास्त्रमनुकुर्वन्नुत्त रग्रन्थेन तदक्षरपङ्क्ती राज्ञे दर्शयति। **भो वअस्स** इत्यादिना।

राजा तथा विज्ञापितस्सन्नयं मोदहेतोस्सस्मितमुत्तरग्रन्थमाह **तर्ही**त्यादि।

विदू – अथ विदूषकस्तं दीपपुरो दर्शयन् केवलं नानालोकविनोदार्थमेव यथाबुद्धि प्रहसनं कृत्वा तानि वाच्यन्ताम्। **किकुचा सविमेसु किदिपुआ**। एवं वाचयित्वा भूयस्तात्पर्यार्थजिज्ञासुरुत्तरग्रन्थेन पृच्छति कहंपीत्यादिना।

राजा – अथ राजा तेन दर्शिते तद्भुजगते तस्मिन् दृष्टिसावधानं नीत्वा भूयस्सचिन्तं तिष्ठन्नेतदक्षराणि गणयन् विमृश्य स्वधिया मदनसन्देशपरायाः गाथायाः आद्यक्षराण्येतानीति निश्चित्य ससन्तापं तन्मुख एव पश्यन्नादावुत्तरग्रन्थसमग्रेण तदक्षरशरीरेण विज्ञापयन्तमर्थं विज्ञापयन् भूयो ग्रन्थैकदेशेन स्वस्य तदयोग्यतां शङ्कमानस्तु भूयः स्वस्य तद्योग्यतां च निश्चिनुयात्। तत्प्रयोगमार्गो दृश्यते।

---

14 This part is significant from theatrical point of view.

i. The primary meaning is described.
ii. The emotional aspect is suggested.
iii. Actor transforms himself to the role of heroine and enacts as though he is the heroine. This is the first instance of multiple impersonation/transformation of role in dramatic performance. Kulaśekhara is indebted to dance where transformation of roles is a regular feature.
This technique known as Pakarnnāṭṭam exerted tremendous influence on the development of Sanskrit theatre. Bharata does not permit such multiple acting in his scheme.
iv. Kulaśekhara introduces another practice here. One śloka in an Act is selected for elaborate acting. All the others are presented in a routine manner. This enables the actor to concentrate on Pakarnnāttam.

अथ राजा ससन्तापं तन्मुख एव पश्यन्नुत्तरग्रन्थेन विज्ञापयति **शङ्के** इति। अथ राजा विदूषके ऊहे एतान्यक्षराणि दृष्ट्वेत्यूहे। भूयः किमप्युद्बृष्टिस्सविमर्शं तिष्ठन्नेव तदक्षराणि गणयन् बुद्ध्या विमृश्य तैरेवेदृग्भूतेति निश्चित्य तन्मुख एव पश्यन् विज्ञापयति, **मदनसन्देशपराया** इत्यादि ग्रन्थेन। तत्तात्पर्यार्थं विज्ञाप्य भूयस्ससन्तापं मुहूर्तं तिष्ठेत्। तस्मिन्नेव तिष्ठति विदूषकः तत् सर्वं साश्चर्यमवधार्य तिष्ठन् सहसा ससन्तापं नायकं दृष्ट्वा चेदृग्भूतमर्थं विज्ञापयन्तीयं तत्प्रयुक्ता गाथा यदि किमर्थं सन्तापी तिष्ठसीति विभावयंस्तिष्ठेत्। अथैवं राजा तस्मिन् विज्ञापयति सक्षीणं ससन्तापं सलज्जं स्वसन्तापहेतुं विज्ञापयति शङ्के इति। भूयोपि शङ्कापदस्यार्थमेव विवृणोति। ईदृक् तात्पर्यार्थं दर्शनीयम्। तत्प्रयुक्तां गाथां मन्यमानोऽहं तां वेश्येति मत्वा शङ्के गर्हे। कुतः तन्निमित्तं रागिणीन्यायं मयि स्मृतवति जितशुकतुण्डाग्रेण नखाग्रेणास्मिन् गाथाद्योतकानि अक्षराण्यालिख्य अस्मत्पुरतः प्रक्षिप्तवती यत् तेनैवं शङ्के गर्हे। किञ्च सतीकन्यकाचारमार्गं प्रकाशयतो भगवतो मनोरथप्रतिहितैर्वचोभिस्तन्मर्यादास्थितिः प्रागेव दर्शिता हि। कुतः,

एतानि कन्यामाकुर्यात् स्वां लिप्तकलभां तनुम्।
केशं सुगन्धपुष्पाढ्यं शुकतुण्डसमं नखम्।।
दशमाद्वत्सरादूर्ध्वं न नेत्रपथगां तनुम्।
मनुना कन्यकाभ्यः प्राक् आचार इति कल्पितः।।

एतद्वाममाचरन्तीमेनां शङ्के। अपि च उत्तमकन्यकयैतादृशा न भवितव्यम्। किञ्च गाथा अतीव लघीयः तस्मादनेन परपरामृष्टेन वनिताजनेन भवितव्यम्। पुनरपि स्मरन् किञ्च तत्रासक्तं मम मनो यत् ततोऽन्यथा च शङ्के ऊहे। तर्हि तथाभूता चेदलं दुर्विकल्पेनेति चेत् तत्राप्यन्यथा शङ्के। कुतः एवमुत्तमकन्यकानामवस्था। तथाभूतापि तां तथा न परस्य विज्ञापयति इति स्मरन् स राजा भूयोपीति स्मरेत्। कुतः तादृशां पश्यन्त्यां तद्वयस्ययास्मिन् गाथां पदाद्यक्षराण्यालिख्य तमिमं प्रक्षिप्तया भवितव्यम्। किन्नु अथैवं राजा चिह्नेन मद्वयस्यायाः लिखिदमिदमिति निश्चित्य तद् विदूषकाय विज्ञापयितुं तन्मुखे पश्यंस्तिष्ठेत्। सखे अहमिदानीं बुध्या शङ्के ऊहे। तत् करगते कर्णपूरे तरौ च दृष्टिं नयंस्तिष्ठेत्। सखे तत्कृता नेयं अक्षरपङ्क्तिरिति चिह्नैः पश्य। कुतः – यदीयमन्यत्पदयुगलं तया तद्वयस्यया स्त्रिया जितसूच्यग्रेण नखेन लिखितेयमक्षरततिः। तत्कथमिति चेत् पश्य। कर्णपूरे कीदृक् प्रमाणमक्षरपङ्क्तेर्लेखाविस्तारमितरपदयुगलात् गच्छन्त्या तद्वयस्यया तरावारुह्यमाणे तत् करेण गृहीते तरुप्रदेशे लिप्तलाक्षेण नखेनाङ्कितं तादृक् प्रमाणं दृश्यते हि। अपि च एतत्पदयुगलं गच्छन्त्यां मन्मनोरथजन्मभूम्या तयारुह्यमाणे तरौ तत्करेण गृहीते प्रदेशे केवलमपनखाग्रं करतलमेव दृश्यते। तस्मादियं कन्या अन्या श्यामा वनिता नामेत्यहं शङ्के ऊहे निश्चितवानस्मि। एवं शङ्कापदस्यार्थः[15]

15 शङ्के is used in different meanings -

i. शङ्के = ऊहे (guess) – I guess that these words are from one afflicted by love.

ii. शङ्के = गर्हे (blame) – These letters are scribbled by parrot-peak-like sharp nails. Hence she is not of good character. She deserves to be condemned.

iii. शङ्के = ऊहे (infer) – Her companion wrote it. I infer the heroine is of noble character.

Kulaśekhara is fond of giving multiple meanings to words.

इत्यादि सर्वं सविमर्शं सहर्षं विदूषकाय दृग्भ्यां पाणिना च विज्ञापयेत्। एवं विज्ञाप्य भूयो ग्रन्थमुक्त्वा नानालोकान् सुखयेत्। एवमेव प्रयोक्तृभिः प्रयोक्तव्यम्। नोचेन्नायकबाधा भवेत्। एवं प्रयोगमार्गः।

एवं विदूषकविज्ञापनच्छलेन प्रेक्षकान् सुखयित्वा चित्तानन्दे सहर्षं सधैर्यं दीपपुरस्तिष्ठेत्।

अथ विदूषकः तेनोपत्तिभिरिति दर्शितं दृष्ट्वा सविस्मयं सुप्रसन्नमुखो भूत्वा तरौ कर्णपूरे च दृष्टी चारयन्नुभयत्राप्येकनखाङ्कितं दृष्ट्वा सशिरःकम्पमवधार्योत्तरग्रन्थेन शक्यते चेत् त्वमपि नखेन पूरयेति भावः।

राजा – अथ राजा पूर्ववत् तिष्ठन्नयं तेन तथा विज्ञापितस्समोदं तस्मादादाय सावधानं विमृशन् यथार्थमेव गाथामापूर्य विदूषकाय ददाति। **कोकुण** इत्याद्यां गाथां वाचयित्वा चेति स्मरेत्। भो इति।

विदू – भो इत्यत्रादौ विवेके। भो यथार्थदर्शितमार्गं गाथां पूरयितवानेष इत्यात्मना निश्चित्य पुनरपीति स्मरेत्। कुतः इदानीमेतत्प्रशंसां करोमीति निश्चित्योत्तरग्रन्थेन तत्प्रशंसां करोति भो इत्यादिना। **भो** इत्यत्र सम्बुद्धौ। **आखुवि अ** इत्यादिना। अत्राखुना समीकरणमेतदर्थमाखुर्मूषिकपोत्रिणोरिति वैजयन्ती। अत्राखुरिति मूषिक उक्तः। आरकः सन्धिकारायां रात्रौ। छिद्रमर्थो योपि तत् प्रविश्य भूगर्भगतमदृश्यं वस्तु यत् तत् सर्वं स्वधुरा प्रकाशयित्वा प्रभाते तथातथं लोकान् दर्शयति। यथा तथा त्वमपीति तत्प्रशंसाप्रकारः। एवं विदूषकस्तत्प्रशंसां कृत्वा भूय एवं स्मरेत्। अस्य कतमेदानीं मदनदशा वर्तते। अस्तु इदानीं यथायथं पृच्छाम्येनमित्यात्मगतं स्मृत्वा चोत्तरग्रन्थेन पृच्छति। **अल एदिणे**त्यादिना।

देवी – अथ देवी तथा श्रृण्वन्ती तिष्ठन्ती सा चेति स्मरेत्। किमस्य मनःपारवश्यं गाथा कृतेति वा न वेति। अविदन्ती च तिष्ठन्ती स्थिता भूत्वा तत्प्रश्नं श्रुत्वा साकुलं सदुःखं सभयं सखिन्नमुत्तरग्रन्थमाह – **हलाममापी**त्यादिना।

चेटी – अथ चेटी तस्य तद्विषयधुरा साकुलापीति स्मरेत्। अयं शनैश्शनैस्तद्गतचित्तो भवेत्। अपि स्वामिनमनपराद्धं समर्थयामीत्यात्मना निश्चित्योत्तरग्रन्थेन समर्थयति। **भट्टिणो**ति सम्बुद्धौ प्रोच्यमानायामिति विभावयेत्। मा मिथ्यारोषिणी भूयाः। तदुत्तरं श्रुत्वा पुनर्यथोचितकारिण्यौ भवाव इति पाणिना दर्शयन्ती पुनस्तद्वचश्श्रोत्रुकामा तिष्ठेत्।

राजा – अथ राजा तदुक्तं तथा श्रृण्वन्नात्मगतमिति स्मरेत्। अहो मदीयां मदनावस्थां ज्ञातुमनुकरोति माणवकस्य वचनम्। एवमनुकरोति हि यदि तथा यदि याथार्थ्यं शनैश्शनैरेव वदामि। अत्रायं दोषः। कापि रणरणिका मदीयं चेतः स्पृशति हि। अनालक्षितलक्षा सा अनेनालक्षितलक्षेव विधायानालक्षितस्पन्देव विधायान्यथा योजयामीत्यात्मगतं निश्चित्य पुनः प्रकाशमुत्तरग्रन्थेन तदन्यथाकरोति **सखे** इत्यादिना।

अथ राज्ञः स्थायीभावो दृस्यते। यदा स्वनिमित्तमस्याः चित्तविकार इति गाथायाः निश्चितवान् तदा प्रभृति पल्लवितां श्रृङ्गाररसवल्लीमुद्गतग्रीवां विधास्यन् चित्तानन्ददशायास्सङ्कल्पदशामारूढवान्। अस्मादारभ्य ातपनवनप्रवेशात् सङ्कल्पाख्यावस्थेति स्थायीभावः। अतः परं सङ्कल्पावस्थायां प्रयोक्तव्यम्।

अथ राजेति तं विज्ञाप्य चेति स्मरेत्। मय्यनुरागवती सा मया दृश्येति तदङ्गप्रत्यङ्गप्रत्यक्षाभावात् यथाभूतं सङ्कल्पसमागमं कर्तुं अक्षमोपि पदतललक्षणयुक्तां काञ्चित्कन्यकां पुरतो निधाय सङ्कल्पसमागमोत्सवमनुभवन् प्राप्तसङ्कल्पसमागमावस्थस्सन्नयं तिष्ठेत्।[16]

16 The description of the heroine from head to toe, pretending to have struck by the arrows of cupid etc., are techniques adopted now in Kūṭiyāṭṭam to depict śṛṅgāra. It seems that those practices originated from this.

चेटी – अथ चेटी तद्वचश्शृण्वन्ती तिष्ठन्ती सा तथाभूतं स्वामिवचश्श्रुत्वोत्तरग्रन्थेन तदपराधमप्यपनयति भट्टिणि **सु दं ति** इत्यादिना। सम्प्रति त्यज्यतां भर्तरि तावककोप इति विज्ञापयन्ती तिष्ठेत्।

देवी – अथ सा देवी तद्वचस्तथा शृण्वन्ती सक्रोधमुत्तरग्रन्थमाह **अज्जुआ** इत्यादि। एवं सक्रोधं सेर्ष्यं सशिरःकम्पं तिष्ठेदिति तिष्ठन्त्यां तस्यां पुनर्नायकविदूषकौ समं दीपाग्रे तिष्ठेताम्।

तथा तिष्ठतोस्तयोर्विदूषकस्तं प्राप्तसङ्कल्पसमागमावस्थां दृष्ट्वेति स्मरेत्। अहो तद्दर्शनलालसोऽयं संवृत्तः। तस्मात् कथमियं संदृश्येत। अस्तु, एवं करोमि तावत्। अस्मात् गत्वान्वेष्टव्यः स दिव्यजनः।

यैश्च दिव्यजनो दृष्टः क्वचिच्चेत् स्वदृशौ ततः।
निवर्तयेन्मा मुहूर्तं सोऽननुज्ञो न यास्यसि।।

इति पुराणवचनं स्मरन्नेवं विचुनोमीति स्वोपक्रमे तस्याभिमुखमस्ति वा नवेति परिच्छेत्तुं गन्धग्रहण-मभिनीयोत्तरग्रन्थेन पृच्छति **जहदखिणा** इत्यादिना।

राजा – अथ तथा तिष्ठन् राजा तेन तथा पृष्टः तं सानन्दं पश्यन्नकर्मणि मूर्खेत्याहूय तद्दर्शनासाध्यता-मुत्तरग्रन्थेन समर्थयति – प्रभावात् तर्हि तन्मूर्तिरित्यादिना। तत्र कथंशब्दे प्रोच्यमाने दृशोरेवं दर्शयेत्। प्रभावान्तर्हितां देवतां प्रकाशयितुं त्वयि कश्चिन्मन्त्रो विद्यते नवेति किमिति दर्शयंस्तिष्ठेत्।

विदू – अथ विदूषकस्तदाभिमुख्यमस्तीति विज्ञाय दिव्यजनोपि कदाचित् दृश्यो भवेत् इत्युत्तरग्रन्थेन समर्थयति **असम्भावि** इत्यादिना। श्रुतपूर्वमिति पदे प्रोच्यमाने यैश्च दिव्यजन इत्यादि व्यासवचनं विभावयन् तदाभिमुख्यं दृष्ट्वा व्यासवचोविस्पष्टं वदन् तस्मात् गत्वा परिक्रमन्नग्रतो विलोक्य देवीं सद्वितीयांस्तन्नयनप्रीतिपाते लताभिस्तिरोधानमिच्छन्तीं सम्भ्रमयुक्तां तां पश्यन्निमिषदृष्टिरेव तां व्यासोक्तिं वदंस्तां परमात्मदिव्ययुवतिं मन्वानस्तं वयस्यमाटोपेनाहूतवान्।

पाणौ समुष्टावेकस्मिन् मध्यमेऽरितयान्वया।
तर्जन्या ताडनं यत्तु तदाटोपं विदुर्बुधाः।।
यद्वस्त्वन्विष्यते पुंसा क्षणात् तददर्शने।
दृश्यते चेत् तादृगन्यं तेन ज्ञेयं तदित्यदः।।

इत्यस्ति वसिष्ठोक्तिः। यथा सृजि सर्पभ्रान्तिः।[17] तथायं तस्मिन् जने कृतदिव्यजनभ्रान्तिरुत्तरग्रन्थेन विस्पष्टं विज्ञापयति। मूर्खेण एवमित्यादिना। सा तदानीं ससम्भ्रमं तिरोधानमुखीति तिष्ठेत्।

राजा – अथ राजा तस्या अदर्शनहेतोर्वर्धिष्णुं मदनावस्थामवाप्य तद्दर्शनोत्सुकं तिष्ठन्नयं सहसा तद्वचश्श्रुत्वा विस्मृतविवेकः तस्मात् गत्वा तत्रस्थां देवीं दृष्टवान्। अथ दृष्ट्वा तां सविलक्षं विदूषकं जनान्तिकं नीत्वोत्तरग्रन्थेन प्रलपति कथमित्यादिना।

अथैवं विलप्य तस्मै क्रुध्यन्नुत्तरग्रन्थेन तमधिक्षिपति। सखे सोऽयमीदृशो भवश्चापलपरिणाम इति ग्रन्थे वर्ण्यमाने एवं दृशोर्विभावयेत्। कुतः सखे एतादृशमहं भवन्तं विश्वसितुं अतिशङ्कितवानस्मीति

17 The erroneous cognition of serpent on a rope (garland) is a stock example used in logic. Believing her to be a divine lady is like this.

विभावयन्।[18] विदूषकमधिक्षिप्य भूयस्सप्रवणं नायिकासमीपमुपेत्यापधैर्यं तां पश्यन्नयमहमपराद्ध इति विभावयंस्तिष्ठेत्।

विदू – अथ विदूषकः स्वप्रमादात् विदितरहस्यां देवीं दृष्ट्वेति स्मरेत्। अहो मम प्रमादादेतादृशं संवृत्तं। किं करिष्ये, तावदस्तु। अहं छान्दसं प्रकटयन् वेतसवृत्यैनं अनुनीय यत्किञ्चिदव्यवहरन् दम्पतिपुरं नयामीति आत्मना निश्चित्योत्तरग्रन्थेन तथा करोति बुभुक्षातिमिरेत्यादिना।

देवी – अथ देवी तत्सर्वं दृष्ट्वा श्रुत्वा च श्रितकोपेति स्मरेत्। किं करिष्ये तावत्। अहमिदानीं कोपदहनदग्धायसाक्षिणा वा क्षुरजालानि पुङ्खानुपुङ्खं विमुच्य हृदयगतामेनामस्य हृदयं शिलासारमपि संविध्य हनिष्यामि। किन्नु तत्रापि दोषो विद्यते।

> यश्च वह्निं पुरस्कृत्य व्याधत्ते च करग्रहम्।
> कुर्वते विप्रियं तस्मै क्रुध्येत् साध्वी न जातुचित्।।

इत्येतद्वचनात्। तस्मान्मनुवचनमनुसरामि। कुतः –

> कोपो यस्मिन् प्रभौ जातः कर्तव्यस्तत्र नैव सः।
> किं कार्यमिति चेत् तेन क्षेप्तव्यस्सचिवेऽस्य स।।

तस्मादेनगाचरामीत्यात्मना निश्चित्योत्तरग्रन्थेन सक्रोधं पाराशर्यमन्तरेणाह **पारासरि अ** इत्यादिना। पाराशर्य इति सम्बुद्धौ प्रोच्यमानायां त्वं व्यासगोत्रजातो यत् ततोऽन्यथा शिखिशिखाभ्यामुपहितकच.. वीक्ष्यमाणोत्तरग्रन्थं वदन्तीति तिष्ठेत्। कथमत्र महाकविना देवी देवी तद्दर्शितेति चेत् तत्सहेतुकम्। कुतः राज्ञस्तद्दर्शनात् वर्धिष्णुं मदनावस्थां किञ्चित् शमयितुं कविना सा तस्य दर्शितेति।

विदू – (जनान्तिकम्) अथ विदूषकस्तथाभूतां दशां विलोक्येतिकर्तव्यतां विस्मरन्नुत्तरग्रन्थेन जनान्तिके तथा विज्ञापयति स एवेत्यादिना।

राजा – अथ राजा तद्वचश्रवणाभिरतिरिति स्मरेत्।

> अपराधवता पुंसा क्रोधसंश्रितचेतसः।
> तस्याः पदद्वये मूर्ध्नां प्रणामः क्रियतां भृशम्।।

इत्यस्ति जयमङ्गलायामाचार्योक्तिः।

तस्मादहमप्येनामनुनीय प्रसादयामीत्यात्मना निश्चित्य सप्रेमगर्भाभ्यां नेत्राभ्यां तमेव पश्यन्नुत्तरग्रन्थेन सप्रवणं तामनुनयति। **देवी कथमस्थान** इत्यादिना।

देवी – अथ देवी तस्य वैदग्ध्यं दृष्ट्वा द्विगुणितकोपोत्तरग्रन्थमाह **कुविदंति** इत्यादिना।

राजा – अथ राजा पुनरपि तां तथाभूतां दृष्ट्वेति स्मरेत्। अहमिदानीमेनामुत्तमनायिकां समर्थयन् गुणसङ्कीर्तनसाम्ना अनुनयामीति निश्चित्योत्तरश्लोकेन तामनुनयति – मा मैवं अविषमकुटिलाभ्यामित्यादिना। अतिक्रुद्धायाः उत्तमकन्यकायाः कुचकम्पचिह्नम्।

---

18 The suggestive import in this Act mainly depends on the hero's mistrust of his companion on his efforts to cover up the truth from him. This is not seen in the dramatic text and certain occasions seems to be far-fetched. Kulaśekhara justifies the mistrust citing Vidushaka's clumsy conduct on former occasion.

चेटी – अथ चेटी तं तथानुनयन्तं दृष्ट्वेति स्मरेत्। अहमिदानीं स्वामिप्रियहेतोरमुष्याः कोपं शमयामीत्यात्मना निश्चित्योत्तरग्रन्थेन तथा समर्थयति **पसीददु** इत्यादिना।

देवी – अथ देवी तस्यै च क्रुध्यन्ती भूय उत्तरग्रन्थेन त्वद्वचनस्य पात्रमस्मीति समर्थयन्ती सक्रोधं नायकं पश्यन्ती निष्क्रान्ता देवी चेटी च।

राजा – अथ राजा सक्रोधं गच्छन्तीं दृष्ट्वोद्दृष्टिरिति स्मरेत्। कुतः अहो इयं कुपिता। अन्याप्राप्तिहेतोरनभिज्ञोऽस्मि। कथमिदानीं करिष्ये इति स्मरन्नुत्तरग्रन्थेनोद्दृष्टिरिति स्मरेत्। **कथ**मिति कथं शब्दोऽत्रादौ प्रश्ने भवन् अंशुमालिन् कथं तद्दर्शनोपायो मम दृश्येत। कुत्र गता सा भवेत्। एवं तिष्ठति तस्मिन् वृक्षशाखावलम्बिन्यौ ते उभे वियतोद्गते स्याताम्। तयोर्गच्छन्त्योर्मेनका तरुशाखाकर्षमाणा तत्पर्णानि पातयन्ती साहमनया सह हिमवङ्गिरिं गन्तुं पश्चिमोत्तराभिमुखो गच्छामीति निवेदयन्तीव गताभूत्।

अथ राजा तद्दर्शनोपायं स्मरन् उद्दृष्टिस्तिष्ठन्नयं सहसा तरुशाखा केनाप्याकर्षमाणा इव पश्चिमोत्तराभिमुखं गच्छती दृष्ट्वेति स्मरेत्। कथमियं गतैव देवी। देवीति दिव्यजन उच्यते। कथमितिपदस्यैव कथं नु कृच्छ्रसाध्यं पुरुषं स्त्रीजनो वशीकरोति स्मरन् तदेवं हि जयमङ्गलायामाचार्येण दर्शित उपायः कुतः –

यया सा गाथया पुंसो रतिं स्त्री ज्ञापयत्यसौ।
तस्यामनन्यविज्ञेयस्सङ्केतश्चाक्षरक्रमैः।।

इति। इत्यस्योदाहरणमिव व्यासेन भगवता पुराणे कञ्चित् युवानमुद्दिश्य कयापि युवत्या प्राप्यमाणायां स्वदशां विज्ञापयितुं गाथायां तत्रैहीति सङ्केतः कृतो मया श्रुतवचनेनेति गाथायामुक्तवत्येपि दर्शितो महामुनिना।

कान्तभोगे कृती तूर्णं मत्कृते प्रणयं कुरु।
चेत स्मरेण भग्नं मे मृतास्म्यत्र न ते दया।।

इत्यनया गाथया स्वदशाशंसिन्या तयैव सङ्केतश्च कृत इति तद्वदनया कर्णपूरश्रितया गाथया न किं सङ्केतः कृत इति तस्मिन् गाथाक्षराणि गणयन् हन्त कृतसङ्केतोऽस्मि साम्प्रतमनया इत्यात्मना निश्चित्य विदूषकं विज्ञापयेत्।

अथ राजा सुप्रसन्नमुखो भूत्वा तं तद्दशां दृग्भ्यामेव विज्ञापयति। सखे कृतसङ्केतोऽस्त्यनेन दिव्यजनेनावस्था स्वा न केवलं मह्यं विज्ञापिता इति विज्ञापयति तस्मिन् विदूषकः कथं सङ्केतितोऽसि इति भावैः पृच्छंस्तिष्ठेत्।

इति तस्मिन् पृच्छति राजा व्यासवचनेन सङ्केतप्रकारं दर्शयेत्। 'कान्तभोगे कृती'ति गाथां विज्ञाप्य भूयः साल्वराजपुत्रीं गतां दृष्ट्वोत्तरग्रन्थेन तद्गमनमाक्षिपति। कथं गतैव देवीति साक्षेपं वदन् भूयस्तद्दर्शनोत्सुकश्रितसङ्कल्पावस्थस्तिष्ठेत्। एवं तिष्ठति तस्मिन् विदूषक इति स्मरेत्। 'अहो सकलवेदी महानयं वयस्यः। तस्मादस्यानुकूलो भूत्वास्य च्छायामनुसरामी'ति निश्चित्य तिष्ठेत्। एवं तिष्ठतोस्तयोर्नेपथ्ये वैतालिकानां काचित् वचनपद्धतिर्भवति।

आरूढोऽयमवलग्नमंबरस्यांशुमाली

अभिलषति न भृङ्गी पौष्पमुद्वेलतप्तं
मधु मधुपसपीतिप्राप्तपीयूषभावम्।

अपि तु तरणितापात् सङ्कुचद्भिस्स्वगात्रै-
रधिसहचरपक्षच्छायमालीयतेऽसौ।। इत्येकस्योक्तिः।

अमुना कालविज्ञापनच्छलेनातः परं देव्यवस्थां विज्ञाप्यते। अतः परं भृङ्गी साल्वराजपुत्री पौष्पं मधु भर्तारं नाभिलषति। स अतःपरं कथङ्कारं वर्तत इति चेत् तद् विवृणोत्यपरार्धेन। तरणितापात् कामतापात् सङ्कुचद्भिः स्वगात्रैः शान्तमनस्कतया नियमितशरीरा भूत्वा अधिसहचरपक्षच्छायं अधिगतसहचरवर्ती। स्नेहमिति क्रियाविशेषणम् तथाभूता आलीयते तथोपरता भविष्यति इति तदवस्था दर्शिता। एवमस्य ध्वनिः।

द्वितीयः

न चरति मृगतृष्णावञ्चितः कृष्णसारः
शिशिरमपि तृषार्तस्सारसं सत्यतोयम्।
द्युमणिकिरणजालैर्नूनमत्यर्थतप्तं
परिमृशति न पौष्पं कार्मुकं पुष्पकेतुः।।

अमुना श्लोकेनातःपरं नायकप्रवृत्तिर्दृश्यते। मृगतृष्णिकारूपेण भ्रमयन्त्या तया वञ्चितः कृष्णसारः राजा शिशिरं सत्यतोयं, शिशिर इति तद्रतिक्रियासक्तः पञ्चेन्द्रियद्रवीभूतचित्तं सत्यतोयं निर्व्याजस्नेहं पूर्वकलत्रं न चरति नास्वादति। तृषार्तोपि स्मरशरशकलचित्तोपि। एवं पूर्वार्धेन दर्शितातःपरं तदवस्था तथा परार्धेन तद्विषये मदनोपि निरस्तचाप इत्यर्थः। निसर्गानि तया तस्य वय आधिक्येन। एवं हि मदनप्रवृत्तिः।

विकसन्त्यत्र पुष्पाणि स्मरोऽन्विच्छन् स्मरत्यसौ।
सम्लानानि स चान्यानि मनसापि न पश्यति।।

विदू – अथ विदूषकः तन्मतिनैशित्यं स्मरन् साश्चर्यं तिष्ठन्नयं सहसा वैतालिकोक्तं श्रुत्वेति स्मरेत्। हन्तेदानीमाभ्यां जीवितोस्मीति स्मृत्वोत्तरग्रन्थेन तदेव समर्थयति, **जीवा विदह्मि** इत्यादिनेत्युक्त्वा राजानं पश्येत्। तदानीं राजा तदुक्तं श्रृण्वन्नपि इदमेवं स्मरेत्। अहमिदानीमागामिकार्यं प्रत्युद्योगमस्मै विज्ञाप्य भूयोऽमुना सह मत्कार्यं साधयामीति निश्चित्य तन्मुखे पश्येत्। एवं विज्ञापयेच्च। सखे अहमिदानीं केवलं भवद्वितीयो भूत्वा हिमवत्प्रस्थश्रितनानामृगगणत्वात् मृगयार्थमिति लोकान् बोधयन् अत्र गन्तुमुद्युक्तोऽस्मि। तद्गच्छाव इति पाणिना दृग्भ्यां च बोधयन्तं तं राजानं दृष्ट्वा विदूषकस्तथाभूत वचनकृतसङ्केतं हिमवत्पर्वतमिति मत्वा भूय उत्तराभिमुखी गच्छतीस्तनुरास्वाद्य दृष्ट्वेति स्मरेत्।

हिमवत्भूप्रदेशे क्वापि प्रदेशे क्वापि वसता दिव्यजनेन भवितव्यमिति मत्वा मृगयाव्यपदेशेन तत्र गन्तुमुद्युक्तोऽयम्। तथाप्यहमद्यभोजनछलेनानुशास्य देवीं वितीर्णभोजनामनुनेतुं पुरं प्रापय्य भूयोस्यां रात्रौ तमेनमनया सह विश्रमयित्वा भूयः काल्य एव मृगयाव्यपदेशेन गच्छन्तं तमेनमनुगच्छामीत्युत्तरकार्यं निश्चित्य चोत्तरग्रन्थेन तद्वयस्यं विज्ञापयति **वअस्स** इत्यादिना। इत्यादिग्रन्थमुक्त्वा तं पुरं नेतुमारब्धस्तिष्ठेत्।

अथ राजा तेनेति विज्ञापितः एव पुरं गन्तुं त्वरयन्तं विदूषकं दृष्ट्वेति स्मरेत्।अस्तु अहमद्यानेन सह पुरं गत्वा देवीं प्रसाद्य प्रभात एव स्वैरं जितमरुता हयेन दूरीकृतपरिवारो भूत्वा मृगयाव्यपदेशेन हिमवतः क्वचित्प्रदेशे स दिव्यजनोन्वेष्टव्यः इति निश्चित्य स्वाभिमताप्तिहेतोरेव पुरप्राप्तिरिति समर्थयन्नुत्तरग्रन्थमाह

न केवलमित्यादिना। देवी चानुनेतव्येत्यत्र चशब्देन स दिव्यजनोपीति विभावयन् ग्रन्थमुक्त्वा प्रेक्षकान् सुखयित्वा विदूषकश्रितभक्तिना मनसा पाणिभ्यां च प्रणम्य नमस्कृत्य प्रेक्षकै सद्भिराशीर्भिर्वाच्यमानः सङ्कल्पावस्थां दृशोर्दर्शयन् स राजा सवयस्योन्तःपुरं गतवान्।

एवं प्रथमोङ्कस्थायीभावः प्रयोगमार्गश्च दर्शितः।।

Vyaṅgyavyākhyā for Act I

(Entry of Vidūṣaka)

Vidūṣaka, on instructions received from the king through the chamberlain, persuaded queen Mālinī to break untimely, the observance of her vow for begetting progeny and brought her back to the city. Then he started to the banks of river Ganges to meet the king, unaware of his intentions. On the way, he stood worried immersed in thought.

Thus the actor in the role of vidūṣaka stands for a moment in front of the three wicked lamp. He reflects:

Why did the king send word for me?
What would the dream be about?

He raises the pupil of his eyes in contemplation. Slowly, with a pleased countenance, shaking his head in discernment, he converses with the connoisseurs through eyes:

The king has grown indifferent to his queen.
The dream seems to be the cause of his disinterest.
He hides this to himself, lo! even from me!

Vidūṣaka knows the fact; yet he wants this to be revealed by the king. Hence he pretends to be ignorant of these things. This is the mental condition of vidūṣaka.

The efforts of the king to conceal his aversion towards the queen constitute the mode of acting in this context.

Entry of the King

King Saṃvaraṇa leaving his queen who has become undesirable to him because of her barren state is burning inwardly; Yet he conceals his feeling from others. He had a dream in day-break. By the time he was recollecting the details of it, the royal bards awakened him. He called the chamberlain and ordered to bring his friend vidūṣaka immediately to discuss the details with him after sending the queen to the city.

The king then started from the city to meet his friend. His attendants, as usual, followed him. He was worried over their presence. How to communicate confidential matters when all are around. Confused, he stood waiting the arrival of vidūṣaka. This is how the past is related to the present.

The curtain be removed when the actor in the role of the king, deeply agitated, stands in front of the three-wicked lamp, his eyes raised in contemplation. Slowly he fixes his eyes on the lamp and thinks –

I have summoned Pārāśarya. Should the dream be revealed to him or not? Both are harmful. If I tell him he will know of my enstrangement towards the queen. That is not desirable. But, one has to take some person into confidence to get things done. Even the Lord of words is helpless to do everything by himself. Therefore I will tell everything to my friend.

Looked from a different angle, it may give rise to unpleasant situations. Mālinī is deeply devoted to me. If she gets a hint from him, of my enstrangement, it will hurt her. But I have already sent word to him about the dream. He is called specially for sharing the details of it. Hence it will not be proper to hide it from him at this stage. I will disclose only gradually my feelings after ascertaining his response.

King stands close to the lamp divulging the conflict in his mind through 'Bhāva' to the connoisseurs. He should continue to please them until their faces expand in ecstasy.

What is meant by bhāva?

> The principal feature of dance is bhāva.
> It has six attributes – brightness of lamp,
> harmony of bodily movements, elegant
> costume, dexterity of usage, attractive figure
> and music.
> The actor should please the spectators by
> bringing harmony between the principal
> and the subordinates and the common
> folk by four-fold acting.

Who are the spectators (prekṣaka)?

> Wisemen say that the connoisseurs are those
> who have mastery over the eighteen śāstras,
> besides Kāmaśāstra and Nāṭyaśāstra.

Accomplished actors are those who are capable of enthralling the spectators through 'bhāva'. How much higher, so much better. Spectators are erudite scholars. This is the ideal actor-audience relation.

The king looked around to see whether vidūṣaka has arrived. Seeing his aides all around he thought – Aho! My expressions are sure to convey the hidden sorrow to them. How to conceal it from them? Yes, I will pretend that my sadness is caused due to the absence of descendants. Actually the Sun god has assured me in the dream that I will get offspring. Yet I will mislead my attendants to believe that I am worried over that matter.

The mental disposition of the hero hereafter will be concealing the aversions towards his queen on the one hand and expressing in tense desire for another marriage. This conflict of mind is shown through eyes, to vidūṣaka in their conversation. There is dhvani in his words till he meets the heroine. It continues till the end of third Act.

Both the king and the vidūṣaka know this state of mind; Yet they pretend to be unaware till they see the foot-prints. Thereafter they freely interact positively.

King I grow more and more indifferent to my wife who failed to give an offspring to me.

From the time of the dream something strange reverberates in my heart. I hope that I will get a maiden in marriage to me.

King sees the vidūṣaka and ascertains by his explanations that he is negatively inclined to him in this matter.

I will interact in words deceiving him. Śāstras do not prohibit such behavior. Gaining stealthily the desired object deceiving a friend through sweet words is not against the canons of good conduct.

Vidu Don't go astray. This is the right path – uphold the hierarchy of the four varṇas; win over the enemies; collect taxes and hand them over to the Brāhmins for sacrifice to please the gods. Always protect your subjects. The king who safeguards his people properly enjoy unending pleasure. Follow strictly these instructions of the scriptures.

King Dear friend! Be favorable to me.

Vidu You do not trust me. Then how can I follow you. I presume that you have lost interest in your wife.

King You are fickle indeed. Secrets are to be guarded. Confidential matters do not deserve to be shared with people like you.

I will continue to be careful in concealing my mind

Hence he addresses the vidūṣaka as fool – mūrkha.

Vidu Of the four means, intelligent people resort to daṇḍa to achieve their object. Hence it is in the form of harsh words. I will use it.

King How can I gain his confidence to reveal the secret of the dream. Before starting anything serious one should ensure the support of friends, foes or others by tactful means. I will employ diplomatic means to win over him. Dear friend! A friend is one who shares joy and grief alike, who takes more interests in the friend's matter than that of his own and who tries by what ever means to obtain the object of desire of the friend. You are my good friend. Be favorable to me.

Vidu I will be favorable to you if what you say is true.

King (Narrates the details of the dream) I will tell the truth to you. I have come across a beautiful maiden in my dream, who by her birth belongs to a worthy lineage. (Looks to his eyes eager to know his response)

Vidu Though he understood, pretends otherwise and shows through eyes that the dream has no significance.

King (Started his words expressing desire for marriage, but withdraws seeing negative response from vidūṣaka) How to create faith in him? Yes. I will tell like this. The sun-god in the dream blesses me with progeny. The dream of day-break will come true; will never be false.

Vidu How cleverly does my friend hide his mind! Your efforts will be fruitful without any obstruction. Don't be sad. You will soon have another marriage.

King Good. My friend has turned positive. To please him I will ordain him eligible to receive cows, which privilege he does not enjoy now. I will slowly bring him to my side.

Stares at his face pretending anger as though disliking the idea of remarriage.

Vidu (I will cause him embarrassment) Scriptures does not prohibit another marriage for you. Even if they prohibit, you can earn the support of the learned Brahmins offering them enormous money. This is a matter pertaining to the accomplishment of the desire of ancestors. Another thing in your favour is that your age is running out.

King I have some how won over him. Any how I will pretend to be ignorant of the suggested sense. I will convince him by the authority of scriptures.

Every one born on earth bears debts to Gods, to forefathers and to the Brahmins. Offerings in sacrifice clear the debt to the Gods, offsprings clear the debts to forefathers and the rites of hospitality that to the Brahmins. One has to clear all the three debts.

Vidu My Lordship is furious. One should not stand before the master when he is in an angry mood; if so stands should not enter into altercation. Hence I will try to pacify my friend. Friends should know the inner feelings of a strong minded man. His evasive mind will become clear if approached in a tactful way. Therefore, I will follow him in all his endeavours.

King *The change in his approach melted the King's heart. For a moment, forgetting the need for confidentiality, he expressed his feelings – he rubbed with hands the tinge of his garments, wrote with his feet on the ground, looked down and blushed. The next moment he regained control and felt guilty on his exposure. Correcting himself he tells -*

I am burned by the separation from the queen. Let us hurry up to meet her.

Vidu *Understood the eagerness of the king to cover up. He felt slightly disturbed on the thought that the King has not yet taken him to full confidence. He leads the King to meet the queen. He walks in front with an enigmatic smile on his face and murmur in his lips.*

King *Walking through the way shown by the vidūṣaka, the King despondently recollects:*

How fruitful will the dream be? Ever since the dream my mind is anxious to join together with that maiden. (*his right eye throbs*) Why my right eye throbs?

Vidu Throbbing of right eye indicates that the desire in mind will be realised.

King (*Realising that vidūṣaka has understood the omen*) I need not hide it from him. If one conceals the words or action directly perceived, the friend will no longer rely on him. He is not angry even when I reacted hotly, he was soft in words when I used harsh words. Hence I will take him into confidence. He calls him in a soft tender voice – Oh! Dear Friend! While going to meet the queen my right eye throbbed indicating that I will get a son from the queen. I am overjoyed. What else is more joyful than getting a son!

Vidu (*Understands King's efforts still to cover up*) I will extract the truth from his mouth in different words.

King He informs me that I am searching for a maiden.

Vidu Now he has confidence in me. I will reveal only a part of my heart either by words or through expressions. I will now take deviation from this topic. (*He shows to the King the river Ganges*)

King He is deliberately leading me away from the topic. Yes. I will pretend ignorance of his intuitions. It is auspicious to bow devotionally before the deity when something new is started. This holy river has been brought by my ancestor down here to make his own family deity.

Oh! Ganges, I bow before you for the attainment of my object of desire. I belong to the lunar dynasty. You are the one brought down by Bhagīratha. My object of desire has to be got from the one closely related to you – the sun god! I had a dream before day break today. The sun god informed me that my wife is barren. While I was contemplating on the means of begetting progeny there was an auspicious throb in my right eye. I pray to you for the realisation of the dream.

While he prayed with folded hands he felt horripilation in the right half of his body.

Vidu (*Saw him disturbed*) Two causes can be ascribed for his distress – i. We have started to meet the Devī (queen); but the Devī in his mind may be the one whom he desires to marry. ii. He may perhaps be too much immersed in though and excited over the auspicious omen. Any how I will ascertain the fact after reaching Kārtikāvāsa.

King My object of desire may perhaps be attained in this garden. (*An emerald seat with foot-prints comes to his notice. He pretends not to have seen it*) King should not see or hear anything of his own; it should be brought to his notice by others. Still I conceal things from my friend. He has shown signs of agreement. Hereafter I will talk to him in direct words. It will please him. Under the pretext of describing this garden I will invite his attention to the foot-prints. These foot-prints – are they of men or women? As lac is applied in has to be presumed that they are of women. Then, of wedded or unwedded? Are these foot-prints of her who caused my eyes to throb?

King calls his friend in sweet voice. He pretends to be indifferent.

Somebody has made imprints with lac-dyed feet on this seat.

Vidu He shows his trust on me. I will also be relaxed. I will any how persuade him to meet the queen. Earlier you were anxious to meet the queen. Now your mind is somewhere else.

King There are four foot-prints of which two show the signs of queenship. The other two foot-prints without lac may be of the servant maid. Presumably the heroine, accompanied by her maid, was on her way to pay offerings to Lord Subrahmaṇya. After the homage she put her imprints here and flew over to the sky.

Here after I will inform vidūṣaka in plain words my inner-feelings.

Śṛṅgārarasa is developed hereafter. The creeper of śṛṅgāra the seeds of which were sworn, watered, blossomed and will flower to bear fruits. Dream is the field, throbbing of eyes preparation of the soil and the foot-prints the seeds. The seed is sown, now it will come up gradually.

Dear friend! Kāma strikes with the first of his arrows – the lotus. May I enjoy the delightful sight which pleases the eyes – nayanaprītiḥ.

Passionately looking at the foot-prints he concludes that the two lac-dyed prints are of a maiden.

Women are at their youthful age from twelve to thirty two years. She has to worship Gods till she gets a husband and thereafter has to serve him till his end. Then she leads her life muttering sacred verses which lead to final emancipation. This foot-prints are of divine damsel who came to offer homage to the Lord praying for a suitable husband. Let she be my wife.

Dear friend! Find out the means to obtain her.

Both stand closing their eyes in contemplation – the King indulged in her thought and his friend in finding out the ways and means to get her for the King.

(*They are covered by the curtain*)

The queen enters accompanied by her maid.

Queen Mālinī daughter of King Sālva, broke the observance of her penance on the direction of vidūṣaka and came back to the city. She did not know the reason for asking her to end the vow which she undertook hoping to get an offspring. She heard the announcement of her husband going out. She started, with an wounded heart, to meet him accompanied by her maid Ulpalikā.

Curtain be removed when the actress in the role of the queen thus stands indignant, impatient and sorrowful in front of the three-wicked lamp.

Queen Why did Āryaputra prevent me from completing my penance. How powerful is his authority! Father protects women in childhood, husband in her youth and son in the old age. Never does she deserve to be independent. I doubt that Āryaputra has lost love for me. Pārāśarya rushed to him after bringing me here. No doubt they have some secret to discuss. I will go to him and hiding myself, some how, will overhear their free talk. I will take my trusted maid Ulpalikā with me. I will impress upon her that cupid hastens me to meet the King.

She becomes more and more afflicted by grief. This is her mental condition.

The mode of acting of King and vidūṣaka.

Both stand behind the curtain, their eyes closed.

Vidu (*Opens his eyes and looks at the King*) I will call and inform him that, the virgin deserves to be married by him.

King (*Understands his suggestion*) Please think how we can meet her.

Vidu By closing the eyes darkness has entered not only to my eyes, but to my mind also. Hence you think and find out.

King The other two footprints are of the maid. They may be hiding somewhere here. I will send my eyes upto the trees.

Whether the maiden is eligible for marriage; if so does she love me; if she loves me how to meet her? Yes, she is fit to be married by me. She disappeared seeing us. It shows the nobility of her character. How to know of her love towards me? A loving girl will indicate her mind through her maid. Raising his eyes he prayed the sun-god! Oh! Bhagavan! Cause her to fall in love with me.

The thought about her eligibility became a trench around the roots to water the seed of śṛṅgāra-creeper sown earlier. It grows up by the confirmation followed by the anxiety to know of her love. This, in this context, is the mental condition of the hero.

Vidu (*Looks upward and sees something falling down*)

King (*Involved in meditating sun-god, King knew that something fell down. He pretends to have not known it. When vidūṣaka brought it to him he enjoys the pleasure of nayanaprītiḥ*)

She has sent her ear-rings as a token of her love towards me. The letters scribbled carry her message of love.

He enters to the second stage of ecstasy – cittānanda. The rasa seed sprouts. Both the queen and maid watch all these hiding behind. Queen becomes grief-sticken when she knows that the King loves another woman. The maid somehow tries to pacify her.

The sweat in the ear-rings shows that she has passed to the second stage of love-lorn condition; the first being horripilation.

The hero transforms himself to the heroine and enacts the imagined love-sick state of the heroine.

Vidu I will please him stating that he is the target of her love.

King *Reads the verse and realises that it is a message of love. Yet he is confused.*

Vidu Why he is not cheerful reading the message?

King The verse is scribbled by nails that surpass the sharpness of the peak of a parrot. Manu prohibits such nails to noble maiden. This raises doubts about her character. (*He is confused*) Yes, her maid might have written this with her nails. It is possible. No room for doubt.

Vidu You please complete the verse.

(*King completes the verse*)

I will congratulate him for this and extract from him the present stage of his love.

King He wants to read my mind. I will allow him only gradually.

The state of mind hereafter is that of imagination – manassaṅkalpaḥ. It continues till his entry into the forest – Tapanavana -in the second Act. King enjoys the pleasure of union with the woman whose foot-prints were imprinted on the stone. He describes, as imagined, her physical beauty.

Vidu He enjoys the company of the damsel. She has to be found out somehow.

(*They are confronted with the queen*)

Alas! All the secrets have been disclosed due to my fault. How to pacify the queen and lead her to the harem.

Queen I could finish him by torrential flow of sharp arrows emanating from my burning heart. But a woman whose wedding was consecrated in the presence of the holy fire should not do anything harmful to her husband. I will therefore follow my husband and divert my anger to his friend -

Oh! Pārāśarya! You bear the name and lineage of the great sage. Alas! Your action does not betray that greatness.

(*Goes with her companion*)

King Oh! Devī has disappeared (*Suggested sense of Devī is the damsel*) How can I meet her? Is there an indication of the place of meeting in the message?

(*Counting the letters he decides that she has hinted the place for meeting*)

Song of bards from behind.

First The queen hereafter does not cherish love for her husband. She will opt for penance and her body will be shrunk due to the austerities of stringent vows.

Second One who runs after the mirage does not enjoy the water at hand – his queen.

King Friend! I plan to go to the premises of Himālayas in search of the divine lady under the pretext of hunting. You also follow me.

XIX

Tapatīsaṃvaraṇam Dramatic Text Act II

अथ द्वितीयोऽङ्कः।

(ततः प्रविशति रम्भा मेनका च)

रम्भा सहि! महिन्दसासणन्तरवावुदा एत्तिअं कालं अणभिण्णह्मि एत्थगअस्स वुत्तन्तस्स। ता कहेहि, को दे मुहवेवण्णस्स हेदू। कहिं वा पिअसही तवदी। (सखि! महेन्द्रशासनान्तरव्यापृतैतावन्तं कालमनभिज्ञास्म्यत्रगतस्य वृत्तान्तस्य। तत् कथय, कस्ते मुखवैवर्ण्यस्य हेतुः। कुत्र वा प्रयिसखी तपती।)

मेन सहि! पुव्वं कदाइ पिअसहिं तवदिं उच्छङ्गे करिअ उपविट्ठेण को इमाए अणुरूवो वरो त्ति णारदमहेसिणा पय्यणुउत्तेण भअवदा भाणुमालिणा भणिअंको हि अज्ज तेल्लोक्के राएसिं संवरणं मोत्तूणा इमाए अणुरुवो अण्णो त्ति। (सखि! पूर्वं कदाचित् प्रियसखीं तपतीमुत्सङ्गे कृत्वोपविष्टेन कोऽस्या अनुरूपो वर इति नारदमहर्षिणा पर्यनुयुक्तेन भगवता भानुमालिना भणितं को ह्यद्य त्रैलोक्ये राजर्षिं संवरणं मुक्त्वास्या अनुरूपोऽन्य इति।)

रम्भा मए वि एव्वं सुदपुरुवं एव्व। तदो तदो। (मयाप्येवं श्रुतपूर्वमेव। ततस्ततः।)

मेन तदो आरहिंअ सा तग्गआहिलासा वि लज्जाए अप्पणासेन्ती वट्टमाणा एअदा मए सह तवणवणं पत्थिआ। अन्तरा तस्स राएसिणो राअहाणीं णाअपुरं हेट्ठदो दट्ठूणा ठिआ। (तत आरभ्य सा तद्गताभिलाषापि लज्जयाप्रकाशयन्ती वर्तमानैकदा मया सह तपनवनं प्रस्थिता। अन्तरा तस्य राजर्षे राजधानीं नागपुरम् अधो दृष्ट्वा स्थिता।)

रम्भा तदो तदो। (ततस्ततः।)

मेन तदो मए उण से भावं जाणिअ कहिदंसहि! परिस्सन्ता विअ लक्खीअसि। एदं खु भाईरहीतीरगअं कत्तिकेआंवासपरिसरुज्जाणं। एत्थ विस्समिअ गच्छाह्म त्ति। (ततो मया पुनरस्या भावं ज्ञात्वा कथितं – सखि! परिश्रान्तेव लक्ष्यसे। एतत् खलु भागीरथीतीरगतं कार्तिकेयावासपरिसरोद्यानम्। अत्र विश्रम्य गच्छाव इति।)

रम्भा (सस्मितम्) सेविअं तुए सहीहिअअं। तदो तदो। (सेवितं त्वया सखीहृदयम्। ततस्ततः।)

मेन तदो जाव हरिमणिसिलादले ओदरह्म, दोव तहिं एव्व सवअस्सो राएसी आअदो। (ततो यावद्धरिमणिशिलातलेऽवतरावः, तावत्तत्रैव सवयस्यो राजर्षिरागतः।)

रम्भा तदो तदो (ततस्ततः।)

मेन तदो तदाणिं अणङ्गबाणेहिं लज्जाए अ दूमिआ तस्स अग्गदो ठादुं असमत्था मए सह

तिरक्खरणीतिरोहिआ उप्पडिआ णहअलं। (ततस्तदानीमनङ्गबाणैर्लज्जया च दूना तस्याग्रतः स्थातुमसमर्था मया हि तिरस्करणीतिरोहितोत्पतिता नभस्तलम्।)

रम्भा तदो तदो। (ततस्ततः।)

मेन तदो अत्तणो पदवीअं सिणिद्धदिट्ठिं तं पेक्खिअ विउणिअमणोभवाअल्लआए ताए दसं ओलोइअ मए आचक्खिअं-सहि! दे कवोलमूलुल्लसिआणं से अकणिआमोत्तिआणं सोहं तिरक्खरइ कण्णेउरो त्ति। (तत आत्मनः पदव्यां स्निग्धदृष्टिं तं दृष्ट्वा द्विगुणित मनोभवायल्लकायास्तस्यादशामवलोक्य मयाख्यातं – सखि! ते कपोलमूलोल्लसितानां स्वेदकणिकामौक्तिकानां शोभां तिरस्करोति कर्णपूर इति।)

रम्भा तदो तदो। (ततस्ततः।)

मेन तदो तस्स राएसिणो रूवाणुरूवं बुद्धिकोसलं परिक्खिउं तिस्से अवत्थापत्थावणत्थं च सो कण्णेउरो आच्छिन्दिअंलिहिअ गाहापदज्जकक्खराइ पमादेण विअमए तस्स पुरदो पक्खित्तो। (ततस्तस्य राजर्षे रूपानुरूपं बुद्धिकौशलं परीक्षितुं तस्या अवस्थाप्रस्तावनार्थं च स कर्णपूर आच्छिद्य लिखित्वा गाथापदाद्यक्षराणि प्रमादेनेव मया तस्य पुरतः प्रक्षिप्तः।)

रम्भा चउरं आअरिअं। तदो तदो। (चतुरमाचरितम्। ततस्ततः।)

मेन तदो तं गाहं तेण पूरिअक्खरं सुणिअ रोसपरिप्फुरिआहरं ताए भणिदं – अविणीदे! कीस तुए अहं लहुईकिदत्ति। (ततस्तां गाथां तेन पूरिताक्षरां श्रुत्वा रोषपरिस्फुरिताधरं तया भणितम् – अविनीते! कस्मात् त्वयाहं लघूकृतेति।)

रम्भा तदो तदो। (ततस्ततः।)

मेन तदो तस्सिं अ पत्थावे सुणिअ सव्ववुत्तंत्तं कुविदं तस्स देविं दक्खिअ परिहसन्ताए मए भणिदं – सहि! सूएदि दे दिट्ठी इमाअं सवत्तीमच्छरं त्ति। (ततस्तस्मिश्च प्रस्तावे श्रुत्वा सर्ववृत्तान्तं कुपितां तस्य देवीं दृष्ट्वा परिहसन्त्या मया भणितं – सखि! सूचयति ते दृष्टि रस्यां सपत्नीमत्सरमिति।)

रम्भा तदो तदो। (ततस्ततः।)

मेन तदो कुविदा मं उत्तरीअं ओलम्बन्तिं अवहुणिअ पत्थिआ। (ततः कुपिता मामुत्तरीयमवलम्बमानामवधूय प्रस्थिता।)

रम्भा णिब्भिण्णं खु हिअअरहस्सं कोवावेइ कण्णआजणं। तदो तदो। (निर्भिन्नं खलु हृदयरहस्यं कोपयति कन्यकाजनम्। ततस्ततः।)

मेन तदप्पहुदि वअणाणं पि अगोअरं तिस्से अणङ्गातङ्कं णिसामअन्ती एआरिसह्मि संवुत्ता। अज्ज उण पच्चूसे एव्व मं पि अणालविअ तवणवणं गआ। सुदं च मए सो वि राएसी मिअआप्पसङ्गेण पत्तो तं उद्देसं त्ति। ता तहिं एव्व गदुअ पिअसहिं आसासेह्म। (तदाप्रभृति वचनानामप्यगोचरं तस्या अङ्गातङ्कं निशामयन्त्येतादृश्यस्मि संवृत्ता। अद्य पुनः प्रत्यूष एव मामप्यनालप्य तपनवनं गता। श्रुतं च मया सोऽपि राजर्षिर्मृगयाप्रसङ्गेन प्राप्तस्तमुद्देशमिति। तत् तत्रैव गत्वा प्रियसखीमाश्वासयावः।)

रम्भा एव्वं करह्म। (एवं कुर्वः।) (निष्क्रान्ते)

इति द्वितीयोऽङ्कः।

ACT TWO

(Enter Rambhā and Menakā)

Ram Friend, having been out till now on another errand of Mahendra, I am not aware of the happenings here. Please tell me why your face looks pale. And where is out dear friend Tapatī?

Mena Friend! Sometime back while the Sun God was sitting with out friend Tapatī on his lap, sage Nārada asked him who would be a suitable husband for her and the God replied, "Who else suitable for her in all the three world except king Samvaraṇa?"

Ram I have already heard of that. And then?

Mena Thereafter, she (Tapatī) pined for him though she concealed her emotions owing to her timidity. One day she set out for Tapana Forest in my company. On the way seeing Nāgapura, the capital of the king below, she stopped.

Ram And then?

Mena Then, knowing her mind, I told her "Friend, you seem to be tired. Here is the garden around the temple of Kārtikeya on the banks of Bhāgīrathī. We shall proceed after resting for a while.

Ram (Smiling) You have served her well according to her wish. And then?

Mena The moment we descended on an emerald seat the king arrived there along with his friend.

Ram And then?

Mena Then afflicted alike by shyness and darts of love, unable to stand his presence she rose to the sky along with me using the charm of concealment.

Ram And then?

Mena While she saw the King scrutinising her footprints with interest, her anxiety of love doubled and, knowing her mind, I said, "Friend, the earring detracts from the beauty of the drops of sweat lining your cheeks."

Ram And then?

Mena To test whether his intelligence accords with his form and to tell him of her feelings, I snatched her earring, scribbled the initial letters of a love lyric, and flung it before him, feigning carelessness.

Ram Your action was ingenious. And then?

प्रवेशकः।

(ततः प्रविशति हयावरूढो राजा)

राजा (सवितर्कम्) अहोतुखलु भयातिरेको नाम तपोवनसधर्मा सत्त्वानां शाश्वतमपि विरोधं शमयति। तथा हि प्रवृत्ते मम मृगयाव्यतिकरे –

क्रोडं क्रोडवधूरुपाश्रितवती शार्दूलिकानां भया-
निश्शङ्कं शरभावलीषु महिषाः संसर्गमातन्वते।
भ्राम्यद्दृष्टिरशिश्रियद् वृककुलं भीता कुरङ्गाङ्गना
मद्बाणैश्च कलुषीकृतः स्म कलभः सैहीं गुहां गाहते।। १।।

सोऽहमनेन मृगयाप्रसङ्गेनातिदवीयसीम् अम्बिकापितुरचलस्याधित्यकाभुवमानीतोऽस्मि। अन्यच्च। तस्मात् पदवतंसकदर्शनादारभ्य मां प्रति –

आदत्ते धनुरभिमार्ष्टि षट्पदज्यां
सन्धातुं प्रगुणयति प्रसूनबाणान्।
उत्कण्ठामरतिकरीं मनस्यलक्षा
माधन्ते मनसिशयोऽस्य केयमाशा।। २।।

अपि च गृहीतकर्णपूरः पाराशर्यस्तुरङ्गमजवेन दूरीकृतः। तत् केनेदानीमुत्कलिकां विनोदयामि।

(नेपथ्ये) अब्बह्मण्णं अब्बह्मण्णं। (अब्रह्मण्यमब्रह्मण्यम्।)

राजा (कर्णं दत्वा) अये पाराशर्यस्येव स्वरः। (ततः प्रविशति त्रस्तरूपो विदूषकः।)

विदू अब्बह्मण्णमब्बह्मण्णं (भयं निरूप्य) ईदिसे वि भअट्ठाणे दुग्गामनन्तेण वि अणहिट्ठिअजीहस्स रक्खासाहणं ब्रह्मसुत्तं अह्माणं दण्डअट्ठं चणट्ठं। (अब्रह्मण्यमब्रह्मण्यम्। ईदृशेऽपि भयस्थाने दुर्गामन्त्रेणाप्यनधिष्ठितजिह्वस्य रक्षासाधनं ब्रह्मसूत्रमस्माकं दण्डकाष्ठं च नष्टम्।)

राजा वयस्य! मा भैषीः। किमेतत्।

विदू (राजानमवलम्ब्य सबाष्पगद्गदम्) हा वयस्य! अवहिदोद्गमंरक्ख। (हा वयस्य! अवहितो मां रक्ष।)

राजा अतिमात्रमाविग्नोऽसि, किं ते भयकारणम्।

विदू (दिशो विलोक्य सहासम्) तुज्झ सण्णिहिमेत्तेण पणट्ठो मे सत्तुवग्गो। (तव सन्निधिमात्रेण प्रनष्टो मे शत्रुवर्गः।)

राजा कथं शत्रुवर्ग इति।

विदू मए खु एत्तिअं वेलं इन्दइदा विअ वाणरसेण्णपत्थिवेहि बहुपरक्कन्तं। (मया खल्वेतावतीं वेलामिन्द्रजितेव वानरसैन्यपार्थिवैर्बहूपक्रान्तम्।)

राजा (सस्मितम्) अभिज्ञोऽस्मि भवत्पराक्रमस्य। मन्ये स्वयूथ्यबुद्ध्या समागतैः पीडितोऽसि वानरैरिति। आस्तामेतत्। क्व वतंसकः।

विदू कहं वतंसओ त्ति अत्थलुद्धो अत्तभवं। अहं पुण णठ्ठसव्वस्सो कहं बि अत्ताणं धारेमि। मए खु तं कण्णेउरं राअसारं रक्खिदुकामेण दण्डअट्ठस्सो अग्गे ब्रह्मसुत्तेण उब्बन्धिअ

Mena Then hearing the King reading out the whole lyric, I was chided by her. "You immodest girl! Why do you make me look silly?"

Ram And then?

Mena Then pointing out to her Samvaraṇa's queen who became angry on hearing his words, I told her jokingly, "Friend, your looks betray jealously towards your co-wife."

Ram And then?

Mena Then she went away in a huff ignoring me as I was hanging onto her garments.

Ram A maiden feels huffy when the secret kept in her heart is exposed. And then?

Mena Then on listening to her words suggestive of her indescribable pangs of love, I have changed like this. And today, early in the morning, she has left for Tapana Forest without even telling me. I have heard that the King also has reached the same spot for a hunt. Let us go there and try to cheer her up.

Ram That we shall do.

End of the interlude

(The King enters riding a horse)

King (Surmisingly) It is strange that fear could be likened to a hermitage as it puts an end to natural enmity between creatures. Thus when my hunt is on,

Driven by fear the female boar clings to the bosom of the tigress; the buffaloes fearlessly mingle with the herds of Śarabhas; the female deer with tremulous glances takes shelter among wolves, and troubled by my arrows the elephant-calf enters a lion's den. (1)

In the course of the hunt, I have reached the distant highlands of mount Himavān, father of Ambikā. Further,

Ever since I saw the earring and the footprints, Kāma takes his bow against me, pulls the string of bees, sets straight the darts of flowers, and instills a vague uneasiness in my mind. What is he up to? (2)

Moreover, Pārāśarya who keeps the ornament is left far behind owing to the speed of my horse. How can I do away with my anxiety?

(Vidūṣaka behind the curtain) Help! Help!

King (Listening) Ah! It is like the voice of Pārāśarya. (The Vidūṣaka enters frightened)

आणिज्जन्तं मक्कटप्पडिरोहएहि आच्छिन्दिअं। (कथं वतंसक इत्यर्थलुब्धोऽत्रभवान्। अहं पुनर्नष्टसर्वस्वः कथमप्यात्मानं धारयामि। मया खलु तं कर्णपूरं रागसारं रक्षितुकामेन दण्ढकाष्ठस्याग्रे ब्रह्मसूत्रेणोद्बध्यानीयमानं मर्कटप्रतिरोधकैराच्छिन्नम्।)

राजा अहोतुखल्वतिप्रमादमाचेष्टितमत्र भवता।

विदू मा कुप्प। भो किं तेण दासीएपुत्तेण कण्णेउरेण, जण्णिमित्तं कुविदा देवी महन्तेण पआसेण पसादिआ। (मा कुप्य। भो किं तेन दास्याःपुत्रेण कर्णपूरेण, यन्निमित्तं कुपिता देवी महता प्रयासेन प्रसादिता।)

राजा अलमनेन। मम खल्वापदकथोद्धातमाविर्भूतामपि रणरणिकां भवज्जिह्वाचापलभयादप्रकाशित-वानस्मि। अतः तद्विनोदनक्षमं वनोद्देशमन्वेषयावहे।

विदू जह तुए मिआणं पदं अण्णेसिअदि, तह अहं पि तुह पदविं अण्णेसन्तो भिउणो णाम महोसिणो पबिट्ठो ह्मि अस्समपदं। तस्स मुहादो महदी कहा मए सुदा। तं पुण सअलं अवहारिअ कहिदुं अकुसला मे बुद्धी। तस्सिं सारभूदं कहेमि। इदो उत्तरदिसाअं कल्लाणवामणं णाम पुरुसोत्तमस्स अत्थि मन्दिरं। तहिं किल भअवन्तं आराहिअ देवेण तवणेण तेल्लोक्कप्पआसणसत्ती आसादिआ। तदप्पहुदिं तं रण्णक्खेतं तवणबणं त्ति संवुत्तं। तहिं एव्व किल भअवदो वामणस्स तिविक्कमत्थं विउम्भिन्तस्स करदलादो जं दाणसलिलं पडिअं, तं करदलोदअं त्ति सरसी संवुत्ता। ता तहिं एव्व गच्छह्म। (यथा त्वया मृगाणां पदमन्विष्यते, तथाहमपि तव पदवीमन्विष्यन् भृगोर्नाम महर्षेः प्रविष्टोऽस्म्याश्रमपदम्। तस्य मुखान्महती कथा मया श्रुता। तां पुनः सकलामवधार्य कथयितुमकुशला मे बुद्धिः। तस्यां सारभूतं कथयामि। इत उत्तरदिशायां कल्याणवामनं नाम पुरुषोत्तमस्यास्ति मन्दिरम्। तत्र किल भगवन्तमाराध्य देवेन तपनेन त्रैलोक्यप्रकाशनशक्तिरासादिता। तदा प्रभृति तद् अरण्यक्षेत्रं तपनवनमिति संवृत्तम्। तत्रैव किल भगवतो वामनस्य त्रिविक्रमार्थं विजृम्भितस्य करतलाद्दानसलिलं पतितं, तत् करतलोदकमिति सरसी संवृत्ता। तत्तत्रैव गच्छावः।)

राजा तर्हि वन्दनीयं चराचरगुरोः पादकमलम्। गच्छाग्रतः।

विदू एदु एदु भवं। (एत्वेदु भवान्।) (परिक्रामतः)

विदू भो वअस्स! सव्वकालरमणिज्जं एदं वणं पविट्ठस्स मे दिसामोहो विअ कालमोहो संवुत्तो। ता को कालो वट्टइ। (भो वयस्य! सर्वकालरमणीयमेतद्वनं प्रविष्टस्य मे दिङ्मोह इव कालमोहः संवृत्तः। तत् कः कालो वर्तते।)

राजा – (सावधानं समन्तादवलोक्य सविमर्शम्) शिशिरवसन्तयोरयमान्तरालिकः कालः।

अप्रत्यूहमहर्मुखार्कमहसामत्यर्थमम्भोरुहा-
मातङ्कार्पणदुर्बलं हिमजलं जातं जराजर्जरम्।
प्रत्यस्तप्रसवामपोह्य फलिनीं भृङ्गीकटाक्षः शनै-
रभ्यर्णप्रसवामशोकलतिकामभ्येतुमाकाङ्क्षति।। ३।।

Vidū Help! Help! (Showing fear) In this fearsome spot when my tongue fails to chant the hymns of Durgā, the sacred thread, my only means of protection, is lost along with the staff.

King Don't be afraid. What is it?

Vidū (Clinging to the King with tears and choking) Ah! My friend; be ready to protect me.

King You are worried too much. Why are you afraid?

Vidū (Looking around and smiling scornfully) Simply because of your presence my enemies have disappeared!

King What do you mean by 'enemies'?

Vidū So long I have been fighting like Indrajit with monkey kings!

King (Smiling) I am aware of your fighting qualities. I think that you have been put to trouble by monkeys who mistook you for one of them. Enough of that. Where is the earring?

Vidū How greedy you are for the earring! Losing all my possessions, I just managed to save my life. I was bringing the colourful earring, tied to the staff with my sacred thread to preserve it, when it was snatched away by the attacking monkeys.

King You have committed a big blunder.

Vidū Don't be angry. What use is that worthless earring, on account of which her majesty had to be pacified with great effort.

King Enough of that. For fear of your wagging tongue I was withholding from you my pangs of anxiety ever since seeing the footprints. So we shall search for a spot in the forest suitable for enjoyment.

Vidū While you were on the trails of beasts, following your tracks I entered the hermitage of a sage called Bhṛgu. From him I heard a great story. I am not intelligent enough to recount it in all its details – I shall just narrate the gist of it. A little to the north, there is a shrine dedicated to Puruṣottama known as Kalyāṇavāmana. It is said that the Sun God acquired his power to illuminate the three worlds by worshipping this God. The water which consecrated the gift given to Vāmana, who expanded to conquer the three worlds, flowed from his palms there to form Lake Karatalodaka. So let us go there.

King If it is so, the lotus feet of the Lord of the movable and immovable are to be saluted. You lead the way.

Vidū May your majesty come this way. (Both walk about)

विदू (विलोक्य सविस्मयम्) भो वअस्स ! पेक्ख पेक्ख। एदाओ अदिट्ठपुरुवाओ मन्दसमीरवेबिदङ्गीओ मोक्तिअमुउव्टसेदकणिआचिदाओ रदणसुमणोणअणेहिं ओलोकआन्ति विअ तुम मअणपरवसाओ हेममईओ वणलदाकण्णआओ। तक्केमि एदं तवणवणं ति। (भो वयस्य! पश्य पश्य। एता अदृष्टपूर्वा मन्दसमीरवेपिताङ्ग्यो मौक्तिकमुकुलस्वेदकणिकाचिता रत्नसुमनोनयनैरवलोकयन्तीव त्वां मदनपरवशा हेममय्यो वनलताकन्यकाः। तर्कयाम्येतत् तपनवनमिति।)

राजा सखे! सम्यगुपलक्षितम्। इयं हि –

आपाटलं किसलयाधरमर्पयन्ती
व्यावृण्वती मधुपझङ्कृतिसीत्कृतानि।
अभ्याशचूतमरविन्दकुचोपपीड-
मत्यायतं समुपगूहति कल्पवल्ली।। ४।।

विदू ही ही सिविणे वि अदिट्ठपुरुवाणि एआरिसाणि दक्खन्तस्स आसा मे आसी पुव्वप्पत्थुअं अम्बरगमणं पि कदाइ सम्भविस्सदि त्ति। (ही ही स्वप्नेऽप्यदृष्टपूर्वाण्येतादृशानि पश्यत आशा मे आसीत् पूर्वप्रस्तुतमम्बरगमनमपि कदाचित् सम्भविष्यतीति।)

राजा (स्पर्शमभिनीय) प्रत्यासन्नेन गोविन्दमन्दिरेण भवितव्यम्। तथा हि –

सम्मूर्च्छन्महिषाक्षधूपकलिकाधूम्राः पयोरेणुभिः
शुभ्राः कुङ्कुमकेसरारुणरुचः कर्पूरचूर्णस्पृशः।
आघ्राता मदमञ्जुलैरलिकुलैरस्माकमध्वक्लमं
लुम्पन्तः शिशिरा वनान्तमरुतो लिम्पन्ति नासापुटम्।। ५।।

(उभौ परिक्रामतः)

विदू भो सम्पत्तह्म देवमन्दिरं। ता पविसिअ पणमह्म। (भो सम्प्राप्ताः स्वो देवमन्दिरम्। तत्प्रविश्य प्रणमावः।)

राजा (प्रवेशं रूपयित्वा बद्धाञ्जलिः प्रणमन्)

धृताषाढं शश्वच्छुचि शबलकृष्णाजिनधरं
शिखाबद्धग्रन्थि क्रतुवरनुतिव्यापृतमुखम्।
दधद् ब्राह्मं सूत्रं कटितटलुठन्मौञ्जिरशनं
हसीयो वन्देऽहं वनजनयनं वामनवपुः।। ६।।

विदू भो! तुज्झ लिहिदक्खराए जीहाए वअणप्फुल्लेहि अच्चिदो देव्वो। अणक्खरविभवो अहं केवलकुसुमाणि आणीअ अच्चिस्सं। (निष्क्रान्ता) (भो तव लिखिताक्षरया जिह्वया वचनफुल्लैरर्चितो देवः। अनक्षरविभवोऽहं केवलकुसुमान्यानीयार्चिष्यामि।)

राजा अत्र तावदनिर्वाणमाणिक्यदीपमालादूरीकृतगर्भगृहान्धकारा जाम्बूनदाकल्पकल्पितादि व्याकृति-वेषविशेषा सुधासौरभसुभगसुरतरुसुमनः सम्पादितभक्तिसन्ताना सेयं सपर्या सूचयति दिव्यजनसम्पातम्।

Vidū Oh my friend! Having entered this ever attractive forest I have no idea either of the seasons or of the directions. What season is on?

King (Looking around with care and thoughtfully) I think it is the transition between the winter and the spring.

> The scarce drops of dew could no longer hinder the morning rays of the sun, or trouble the lotus. The bees abandon the Priyaṅgu creeper which has stopped to blossom, and slowly approach the Aśoka which is about to bloom. (3)

Vidū (Looking dismayed) Oh friend, behold! These golden damsels of wild creepers never seen elsewhere, love-lorn, trembling in the gentle breeze, sweating with the buds of pearl, are glancing at you with their eyes of gems.

King Friend, you have observed well. And this one,

> The creeper of the Kalpa plant embraces the neighboring tall mango tree, pressing with lotus breasts, giving lips of sprouts and producing inarticulate murmur of ecstasy by the humming of bees. (4)

Vidū Ah! Ah! Seeing such things never even dreamt before, I nurture the hope that one day it will be possible for me to travel through the sky, about which I have already spoken.

King (Gesticulating a smell) The temple of Govinda must be very near. For,

> The cool breeze blowing from the far ends of forest made gray by the pollen of Mahiṣākṣa, whitened by the tiny drops of water, reddened by the filaments of Kuṅkuma, carrying the powder of camphor and smelt by intoxicated bees, enters the nostrils, removing the fatigue of travel. (5)

(Both Walk about)

Vidū Sir, we have reached the temple. We shall enter and perform worship.

King (Gesticulating entrance and bowing with folded hands)

> I salute the tiny lotus-eyed form of Vāmana, pure, wearing the skin of a black spotted deer and with a tuft sprouting from his head, chanting sacrificial hymns, donning a sacred thread, a girdle of Muñja grass wrapped about the loins. (6)

Vidū Sir, you have worshipped the God offering blossoms of words by your eloquent tongue. Illiterate as I am, I shall fetch some flowers to offer in worship. (Exits)

(ततः प्रविशत्युपविष्टा कामयमानावस्था नायिका)

नायि (दीर्घं निश्वस्य) अहं खु मणोरहसिद्धिसम्पादणत्थं कहं वि सण्ठविअ अत्ताणं अणुट्ठिअमहुमहणपूजा आअदह्मि। ता सहीजणेण वि असङ्किण्णे एत्थ विवित्ते तेण जणेण सह अणिवारिअप्पसरेहि सङ्कप्पेहि सङ्गमिस्सं। (अहं खलु मनोरथसिद्धसम्पादनार्थं कथमपि संस्थाप्यात्मानमनुष्ठित-मधुमथनपूजागतास्मि। तत् सखीजनेनाप्यसङ्कीर्णेऽत्र विविक्ते तेन जनेन सह निवारितप्रसरैः सङ्कल्पैः सङ्गंस्ये।) (ध्यानस्तिमिता तिष्ठति, ततः प्रविशति रम्भा मेनका च)

रम्भा सहि! कहिं णु खु पिअसही तवदी। (सखि! क्व नु खलु प्रियसखी तपती।)

मेन करदलोदअतीरगए फलिहमण्डचे तिस्से हिअअं अहिरमदि। तहिं ताए होदव्वं। (करतलोदकतीरगते स्फटितमण्डपे तस्या हृदयमभिरमते। तत्र तया भवितव्यम्।)

रम्भा ता तहिं एव्व गच्छह्म। (तत् तत्रैव गच्छावः।)

मेन एसा किं षि चिन्तअन्ती अपरिप्फन्दं चिट्ठइ किं णु ख एदं। (एषा किमपि चिन्तयन्त्यपरिस्पन्दं तिष्ठति। किं नु खल्वेतत्।)

रम्भा अम्मो अपुव्वा इअं सहीए दसा। ता इह एव्व ठिदाओ एदाए ववसाअं जाणिअ पुणो अत्ताणं पआसह्म। (अम्मो अपूर्वेयं सख्या दशा। तदिहैव स्थिते एतस्या व्यवसायं ज्ञात्वा पुनरात्मानं प्रकाशयावः।) (भित्त्यन्तरिते स्थिते, प्रविश्यापटाक्षेपेण विदूषकः)

विदू भो वअस्स! अच्छेरमच्छेरं। दिट्ठो मए विह्मअणिज्जसण्णिवेसाए सरसीए तीरगओ घणपडलेहि घणीभूदो जलरासी। अण्णं च तस्सिं जले भअवदीए लच्छीए आइदी आलिहिदा। ता तुरिअं ओलोएदु अत्तभवं। (भो वयस्य! आश्चर्यमाश्चर्यम्। दृष्टो मया विस्मयनीयसन्निवेशायाः सरस्यास्तीरे घनपटलैर्घनीभूतो दलराशिः। अन्यच्च तस्मिन् जले भगवत्या लक्ष्म्या आकृतिरालिखिता। तत् त्वरितमवलोकयत्वत्रभवान्।)

राजा मूर्ख! निम्नोपसर्पीणि वारिणि, तेषां कथमूर्ध्वगमनं स्थिरीभावो वा। कथं वा तेष्वालेख्यानि लिख्यन्ते।

विदू करदलगए आमलए किं दुव्विवादेण। पच्चक्खप्पमाणेण एव्व अहं साहेमि (राजानमाकर्षति) (करतलगत आमलके किं दुर्विवादेन। प्रत्यक्षप्रमाणेनैवाहं साधयामि।)

राजा मन्ये भ्रमरपरिणामेनानेन भवितव्यम्। भवतु त्वदिच्छां पूरयामि। (उभौ परिक्रामतः)

विदू भो वयस्स! पेक्ख पेक्ख एसा सा सरसी, आदु अण्णं किं पि वत्थु। किं एत्थ वि अत्थि भमो। (भो वयस्य! पश्य पश्यैषा सा सरसी, उतान्यत् किमपि वस्तु। किमत्राप्यस्ति भ्रमः।)

राजा सत्यमेवैषा सरसी। इयमेव मन्ये भगवता भृगुणा निर्दिष्टा। पश्य –

माणिक्यभूतलगता मणिभङ्गतोया
कल्याणिनी करतलोदकनामधेया।
अद्यापि भाति सरसी सरसीरुहाक्ष-
हस्ताम्बुजन्मतलमध्यविवर्तिनीव।। ७।।

King The inextinguishable lamps of gem that remove the darkness from the sanctum sanctorum, the golden articles of celestial origin and the flowers of heavenly trees scattered around spreading fragrance of nectar – all these tokens of worship suggest the presence of celestials.

(The lovelorn heroine appears sitting)

Heroine (Heaving a deep sigh) Controlling myself with effort I have come here after worshipping Madhumathana with a view of obtaining my desire. In this secluded spot not even accompanied by my friends I shall unite myself with my lover in my unbridled fantasies. (Remaining meditating, Rambhā and Menakā enter)

Ram Friend, where can be our dear friend Tapatī?

Mena She is fond of the crystal seat on the banks of Lake Karatalodaka. She must be there.

Ram Then we shall go there.

Mena Here she remains motionless immersed in her thoughts. What could it be?

Ram Alas! It is rather unusual for her. Let us remain here and present ourselves later after knowing her mind. (They remain concealed behind the wall) (Vidūṣaka enters tossing aside the curtain)

Vidū Oh friend, strange! Marvelous! I have just witnessed a solid structure of water on the banks of an expansive lake. Moreover, there is a picture of Goddess Lakṣmī drawn on that water. Your majesty may please hurry to see it.

King Fool. Water flows downward; how can it flow upwards or become solid? How could one draw pictures on it?

Vidū What need is there for argument when it is evident as the fruit of Āmalaka in one's palm. I could prove it by means of perception. (Pulls at the King)

King I am sure it is a mistake. However, I shall defer to your wishes. (Both walk about)

Vidū Oh friend, see, here is the lake, or is it something else? Is there any misperception?

King True, it is a lake. I think that it is the one hinted at by the revered sage Bhṛgu. You see,

This lake of Karatalodaka spread on the ruby ground with pearl-grey water, possessing purifying qualities, still appears as whirling on the palms of the lotus-eyed God. (7)

विदू जइ एव्वं अण्णं किं पि भमं दंसेमि। (परिक्रम्याग्रतो निर्दिशन्) एसो सो जलसेलो। एदं आलेक्खं। एदं पि किं सच्चं। (यद्येवमन्यं कमपि भ्रमं दर्शयामि। एष स जलशैलः। एतदालेख्यम्। एतदपि किं सत्यम्।)

राजा वैधेय! सर्वमेतदवरमार्थम्। स्फाटिकोऽयं दिव्यजनगोष्ठीमण्डपः। इदं च स्वच्छस्फटिकभित्त्यनिवारित-दर्शनमात्मतेजः पटलावगुण्ठितं किमपि दिव्याङ्गनारत्नम्। (पुनः सस्पृहं सावधानं निर्वर्णयन्) अहोतुखल्वप्रतिष्ठा लावण्यातिशयान्तराणां, यदद्यतनेन वेधसा सृजता पदार्थान्तरमिदं पराजिताः पुरातनाः प्रजासृजः। कुतः –

अम्लानामहिमोपरोधकलुषामम्भोरुहाणां श्रियं
दीप्रां दीपशिखामकज्जलतमालेशामनुष्णार्चिषम्।
स्त्रीसर्गप्रथमाङ्कुराकृतिमिमामध्यक्षयन्नात्मनो
निष्पत्राकुरुते चिराय हृदयं मन्ये स पुष्पायुधः।। ८।।

विदू भो! जिससे तं पदजुअलं कण्णउरो अ, जइ इअं सा अ एक्का भवे, सुट्ठु संपज्जइ। (भोः यस्यास्तत् पदयुगलं कर्णपूरश्च, यदीयं सा चैका भवेत्, सुष्ठु सम्पद्यते।)

राजा को जानीते विधिविलसितानि। अप्रकाशं स्थित्वा स्वैरालापैरमुष्या एव निश्चिनुमः। (तथा कृत्वा स्थितौ)

नायि (सविषादम्) धिक्खु मं जाए अप्पच्छन्देण तं जणं अहिसरन्तीए कण्णआजणविरुद्धं आचरिअं। (धिक् खलु मां, ययात्मच्छन्देन तं जनमभिसरन्त्या कन्यकाजनविरुद्धमाचरितम्।)

(सख्यौ सत्रासमुरसि हस्तं दत्वा परस्परमवलोकयतः)

राजा (सनिर्वेदं परावृत्य) अहोतुखलु ममापि नाम परपरामृष्टे वनिताजने प्रवृत्ते मनश्चक्षुषी। सखे! साधयामस्तावत्।

विदू भो! एअदेसणिसमणेण पआवइणो वि ण सक्कं परमत्थं जाणिदुं। ण एसा आइदी णिन्दणिज्जं कम्म कादुं पारेइ। ता पुणो वि किंचि सुणिअ गच्छह्म। (भो! एकदेशनिशमनेन प्रजापतेरपि न शक्यं परमार्थं ज्ञातुम्। नैषाकृतिर्निन्दनीयं कर्म कर्तुं पारयति। तत् पुनरपि किञ्चित् श्रुत्वा गच्छावः।)

नायि (निश्वस्य प्रत्याकलय्य) कीस मए सङ्कप्पसङ्गमादो अत्ता अत्थाणो उवालद्धो। (कस्मान्मया सङ्कल्पसङ्गमादात्मा अस्थान उपालब्धः।)

सख्यौ (सहर्षं) ऊससिअह्म। (उच्छ्वसिते स्वः।)

विदू भो वअस्स! किं सुदं तुए। (भो वयस्य! किं श्रुतं त्वया।)

राजा (प्रतिनिवृत्य) न खल्वेतावता भवतः समाश्वासः। पश्य –

आरूढप्रणयेन यूनि मनसा क्लान्तां क्वचित् कामिनी-
मेनां मत्पुरतो निधाय किरतः पौष्यानमून् मार्गणान्।
पुष्पेषोर्यदि नाम शक्तिकलया मोहान्धकारस्पृशा
सम्भिद्येत सखे! ममापि हृदयं धैर्याय बद्धोऽञ्जलिः।। ९।।

Vidū If it is so, I shall show you yet another 'misperception'. (Walking about and pointing in front) There is that hill of water and there is that picture. Are they real?

King Fool. All this is not real. That is a crystal hall belonging to the celestial. And that one is a gem among the celestial maidens veiled by her own lustre and seen through the crystal wall without obstruction. (Again observing longingly) Strange! All other beauties of pre-eminence have lost their footing; the creator of the present day has surpassed his ancient predecessors by forming this rare object. Because,

> Seeing this beauty of lotus unfaded and undisturbed by the snow, this
> shining flame untouched by even a speck of soot and shedding cool rays;
> this perfect personification of feminine charm, I think Kāma will subject
> my heart to intense torture. (8)

Vidū Sir, it would be appropriate if this girl is the same one whom the earring and the footprints belong.

King Who knows the course of fate? We shall ascertain it from her own unrestrained words by remaining ourselves concealed. (They remain accordingly)

Heroine (With disgust) Shame on me who has behaved unbecoming of a maiden in going out to meet her man on her own initiative. (The maids look at each other placing their hands on their breast in apprehension)

King (Turning back in dejection) Shame on me for turning my mind and eyes towards a girl who obviously belongs to somebody else. Friend, we shall go our way.

Vidū Sir, even the Creator could not, by listening partly, find out truth. A person of such appearance could never do evil. So we shall listen a little more before we leave.

Heroine (Heaving a sigh and with restraint) Why should I blame myself on account of fancied relations?

Maids (With joy) We are relieved!

Vidū Friend, did you hear that?

King (Returning) You are not satisfied yet. See,

> If Kāma chooses to place before me this lovelorn maiden whose mind is
> smitten with love towards some other young man and to shower darts of
> flowers on me to pierce my heart with their delusive force, Oh friend, then
> I must pray for courage with folded hands. (9)

नायि सहि! मेणए!। (सखि! मेनके!)

मेन किं आलक्खिदह्मि इमाए। (किमालक्षितास्म्यनया।)

नायि कहिं मेणआ। (क्व मेनका।)

मेन सहि! सङ्कप्पो खु तवस्सिणीए मं सद्दावेइ। (सखि! सङ्कल्पः खलु तपस्विन्या मां शब्दापयति।)

रम्भा (सेर्ष्यम्) ईदिसे विमअणसंभमे इमाए अहं ण सुमरिआ। (ईदृशेऽपि मदनसम्भ्रमेऽनयाहं न स्मृता।)

मेन सहि! मा कुप्प। असण्णिहिदा तुवं एदस्सिं उदन्ते। अहं किंपि अब्भन्तरा, तदो एव्वं आलविअं। (सखि! मा कुप्य, असन्निहिता त्वमेतस्मिन् उदन्ते, अहं किमप्यभ्यन्तरा, तत एवमालपितम्।)

नायि हिअअ!कहिं वा हिअअं। (स्मृत्वा) आ तेण च्चिअ सुउमारेण मुसिअं। भअवं कुसुमाउह! तुंवं किं पि पहरिदुं आअदो सि। तुह सराणं लक्खभूदं मम हिअअं सअलभुवणेक्कणाहस्स हत्थे पडिअं। जइ समत्योसि तहिं एव्व गदुअ परक्कमेहि। (हृदय! कुत्र वा हृदयम्। आ तेनैव सुकुमारेण मुषितम्। भगवन् कुसुमायुध! त्वं किमपि प्रहर्तुमागतोऽसि। तव शराणां लक्ष्यभूतं मम हृदयं सकलभुवनैकनाथस्य हस्ते पतितम्। यदि समर्थोऽसि तत्रैव गत्वा पराक्रमस्व।)

राजा (सस्पृहं) यन्निमित्तोऽयमस्याश्चित्तविकारः स चेदत्र सन्निहितः, स्याज्जन्मिनां प्राग्रेसरः। कुतः,

आयासितानामशरीरबाणै-
र्नितम्बिनीनां परिदेवितानि।
आत्मार्थमाकर्णयतां हि यूनां
समागमो नाम सुखान्तरायः।। १०।।

विदू भो! अलं दुव्विकप्पेहिं। तुवं एव्व भुवणेक्कणाहसद्देण पडिचिदो त्ति तक्केमि। (भो अलं दुर्विकल्पैः। त्वमेव भुवनैकनाथशब्देन प्रतीष्ट इति तर्कयामि।)

नायि (सनिर्वेदम्) केत्तिअं वा अत्ताणं खेदइस्सं। सो मणोरहदइदो सइ हिअअकिदाहिवासो वि मं णाणुकम्पइ। जस्स भअवदो पसादेण अहं उप्पण्णा, एसो सो कल्लाणवामणो सण्णिहिदो अज्ज मए भत्तिपुरुचं आराहिदो वि मं णाणुगह्णइ। (कियद्वात्मानं खेदयिष्यामि। स मनोरथदयितः सदा हृदयकृताधिवासोऽपि मां नानुकम्पते। यस्य भगवतः प्रसादेनाहमुत्पन्ना, एष स कल्याणवामनः सन्निहितोऽद्य मया भक्तिपूर्वमाराधितोऽपि मां नानुगृह्णाति।)

राजा (छोटिकां दत्वा) तदपि देवस्य सपर्याविधानमस्या एव हस्तकौशलमभूत्।

नायि तस्सिं एव्व एदं दुक्खेक्कभाअणं सरीरहदअं उवहारं करिस्सं। (सबाष्पगद्गदम्) हा अणाहा अहं सहीए मेणआए रम्भाए अ पच्चिमालिङ्गणसुहं अणासादअन्ती विवज्जामि। (उत्तिष्ठति) (तस्मिन्नेवैतद् दुःखैकभाजनं शरीरहतकमुपहारं करिष्यामि। हा अनाथाहं सख्या मेनकाया रम्भायाश्च पश्चिमालिङ्गनसुखमनासादयन्ती विपद्ये।)

Heroine Oh friend, Menakā.

Mena Did she notice my presence?

Heroine Oh, where is Menakā?

Mena Friend. It is sheer fancy that makes that poor girl call for me.

Ram (With envy) She fails to remember me in this frenzy of love!

Mena Friend, Don't be angry. You have not been in this affair; whereas, I am somewhat involved and hence she calls for me.

Heroine Oh my heart! Or where is my heart? (Remembering) Ah yes! It was stolen by that handsome one. Oh God Kāma! Did you come to assail it? But my heart, the target of your arrows, has fallen into the hands of that lord of the worlds.

King (Longingly) If the one for whom she pines were present here he would be the foremost among living being. For,

> To those young men who happen to listen to the wailing of their beloved,
> troubled by the arrows of Kāma, actual union may become and impediment
> to bliss. (10)

Vidū Sir, away with your silly doubts. I presume that the words 'lord of the world' indicate you and you alone.

Heroine (With dejection) How long shall I worry myself? That beloved of my desires is not compassionate though he resides always within my heart. The God Kalyāṇavāmana present here, by whose favour I was born, though worshipped with devotions does not favour me now.

King (Snapping the thumb and fore-finger together) That arrangement for the worship of the God must have been made by the hands of this girl.

Heroine To him I shall make an offering of this worthless body, a repository of pain. (choking and with tears) Alas! Helpless, I die without even having the solace of the embrace of my friends Menakā and Rambhā. (Rises up)

राजा अहो अत्याहितम् (उपसर्पितुमिच्छति)

सख्यौ (ससंभ्रममुपसृत्य सास्त्रम्) सहि! सन्तं सन्तं पावं। पडिहदं आमङ्गलवअणं। अणेआणि कप्पन्तराणि अह्ने आलिङ्गन्ती होहि। (सखि! शान्तं शान्तं पापम्। प्रतिहतममङ्गलवचनम्। अनेकानि कल्पान्तराण्यावामालिङ्गन्ती भव।)

नायि अम्मो सहीओ। (लज्जां नाटयति) (अम्मो सख्यौ।)

राजा (सानन्दम्) सखे! अन्यगतहृदयामेनामाभ्यामेव सखीभ्यामभ्युपपादयता विधिना साधु सम्पादितम्।

विदू एदाणं सल्लावादो से अभिलासविसओ वि मण्णे फुडीहोइ। (एतांसां सल्लापादस्या अभिलाषविषयोऽपि मन्ये स्फुटीभवति।)

नायि (स्वगतम्) इदाणीं एदाहिं मम भादुणो वेवस्सदस्स दंसणं पडिसिद्धं होइ। पुणो वि अत्तणो पभाविस्सं। (इदानीमेताभ्यां मम भ्रातुर्वैवस्वतस्य दर्शनं प्रतिषिद्धं भवति। पुनरप्यात्मनः प्रभविष्यामि।)

सख्यौ सहि! कीस तुए पाअडइत्थिआणं ओलम्बिअ मग्गं अकालणेण अत्ता परिच्चतो। किं अह्मो पाणणिव्विसेसाओ तुज्झ मणोरहं पुरेदुं असमत्थाओ। को वा एत्थ जीवलोए दे जो व्वणरुवविब्भमप्पमुहाणं गुणाणं अविहेओ। (सखि! कस्मात् त्वया प्राकृतस्त्रीणामवलम्ब्य मार्गमकारणेनात्मा परित्यक्तः। किमावां प्राणनिर्विशेषे तव मनोरथं पूरयितुमसमर्थे। को वा जीवलोके ते यौवनरूपविभ्रमप्रमुखाणां गुणानामविधेयः।)

नायि (प्रकाशम्) अलं एदेहि वअणेहि मं पीडिअ। बलीओ ख हिअअसन्दावो। ओलम्बह मं। (अलमेतैर्वचनैर्मां पीडयित्वा। बलवान् खलु हृदयसन्तापः। अवलम्बेथां माम्।)

मेन (अवलम्बते)(स्पर्शं पयित्वा) हद्धि एदाए अङ्गसंसग्गादो अदिसुअरो हुदवहुच्छङ्गरूप्पवेसो। सहि! सरसीदो सरसीरुहपत्तं आणीय वीजेहि णं। (हा धिग् एतस्या अङ्गसंसर्गाद् अतिसुकरो हुतवहोत्सङ्गप्रवेशः। सखि! सरसीतिः सरसीरुहपत्रमानीय वीजेमाम्।)

रम्भा (तथा कृत्वा वीजयति)

मेन सहि! णालिणीपण्णससमीरप्पसरं रुन्धइ थणंसुअं। ता अवणेहि एदं। (सखि! नलिनीपर्णसमीरप्रसरं रुणद्धि स्तनांशुकम्। तदपनयैतद्।)

नायि अदिप्पआसो अअं पदेसो। ता को वि अं पेक्खे। लज्जेमि अत्ताणं पआसेदुं। (अतिप्रकाशोऽयं प्रदेशः। तत् कोऽपि मां पश्येत्। लज्जे आत्मानं प्रकाशयितुम्।)

मेन उम्मत्तिए! दक्ख अह्माणं मणोरहासिद्धिसम्पादइत्तअं संवरणं। (उन्मत्तिके! पश्यास्माकं मनोरथसिद्धिसम्पादयितृ संवरणम्।)

नायि (ससम्भ्रमं दिशो विलोक्य) कहिं कहिं अय्यउ। (क क्वार्यपुत्रः।)

(इत्यर्द्धोक्ते लज्जावनतमुखी तिष्ठति)

मेन (सस्मितम्) सहि! अलं अत्थाणे संभमेण। भित्तिभाअं उद्दिसिअ संवरणं ति मए भणिदं, णउण दे हिअअट्ठिअं पुरुवंसप्पदीवं राएसिं। (सखि! अलमस्थाने सम्भ्रमेण। भित्तिभावमुद्दिश्य संवरणमिति मया भणितं, न पुनस्ते हृदयस्थितं पुरुवंशप्रदीपं राजर्षिम्।)

King Alas! What a calamity! (Wants to go near)

Maids (Approaching hastily, with tears) Friend! Away with your inauspicious words. May you live long to embrace us for years to come.

Heroine Oh my friends! (Shows bashfulness)

King (Joyfully) Friend! Fate has done well in uniting her with these maids since she is in love with somebody else.

Heroine (To herself) Now these friends have prevented my meeting with my brother Vaivasvata. I shall try again.

Maids Who do you throw away your life in the manner of illiterate girls? Are we, as dear as your life, incompetent to fulfill your desire? In this world of mortals, who would not be attracted by your qualities of youth, beauty and charm?

Heroine (Aloud) Don't torment me by such words. Great is the pain in my heart. Both of you please support me.

Mena (Supports) (Feeling the sense of touch) What a pity! It is easier to jump into the lap of flames than touching her limbs. Friend, fetch some lotus leaves from the lake and fan her. (Rambhā does accordingly)

Mena Friend, your bodice obstructs the air circulated by the lotus leaves. Please remove it.

Heroine It is too open a place. Someone may see me. I am ashamed to reveal myself.

Mena Foolish girl! See this enclosure which suits your purpose.

Heroine (Looking in all directions with haste) Where? Where is my lord? (She stops her sentence abruptly and remains ashamed with her face cast down)

Mena (With a smile) Friend, your agitation is in vain. By 'Samvaraṇa' I meant the enclosure and not that royal personage, the light of the Puru clan, who dwells in your heart.

रम्भा सहि! अच्चारुढो से मअणुम्मादो मं विहत्थअन्तो वि थणाभिणिवेसो त्ति मम पीदिअरो संपुत्तो। (सखि! अत्यारूढोऽस्या मदनोन्मादो मां विहस्तयन्नपि स्थानाभिनिवेश इति मम प्रीतिकरः संवृत्तः।)

राजा (सम्प्रमोदम्) श्रुतानि श्रोतव्यानि। हृदय! निरर्गलमिदानीमस्मिन् जने प्रथय प्रणयप्रवृत्तिम्। अपि च,

तुहिनगिरितरुणामद्य पुष्पावतंसान्
मदन! मलयवाताः पल्लवान् प्रेङ्खयन्तु।
जनमिममभियोक्तुं भृङ्गकल्माषपुङ्खैः
कुरु कुसुमशरौघैः पूरिते पुष्पतूणी।। ११।।

विदू एसा देव्वेण उवणीदा दे तणअणामहेअस्स अग्गिणो अरणि त्ति समत्थेमि। (एषा दैवेनोपनीता ते तनयनामधेयस्याग्नेररणिरिति समर्थये।) (नेपथ्ये)

सवनमुपगतं तृतीयमह्नः क्षपयत तीर्थजलेन किल्बिषाणि।
त्वरयत करवीरपुष्पगन्धानहिमरुचेरुपनेतुमर्घ्यपूजाम्।। १२।।

सख्यौ (ससम्भ्रमम्) सहि! उट्ठेहि उट्ठेहि। अदिक्कमइ सुय्योपट्ठाण समओ। (सखि! उत्तिष्ठोत्तिष्ठ। अतिक्रामति सूर्योपस्थानसमयः।)

नायि (आत्मगतम्) कहं एरिसं अवत्थन्तरं तादस्स दंसेभि। कहं वा अण्गसरपीजसारेहिं अङ्गेहिं गन्तुं पारेमि। तह वि अलङ्घणीओ देवसमुदाआरो। (प्रकाशम्) सहीओ! एव्वं करह्म। (सह सभीख्यां निष्क्रान्ता) (कथमीदृशमवस्थान्तरं तातस्य दर्शयामि। कथं वानङ्गशरपीतसारैरङ्गैर्गन्तुं पारयामि।)

राजा हा कष्टम्। अन्तर्हितेयमस्मन्मनोरथभूमिः। केन खल्विदानीमशनिदारुणमुद्घोषितम्। अथवा अवसानमेवैतदस्मन्नयनभाग्यानाम्।

विदू एत्थ अदिणिअडे तवोवणे इसीहि उग्धोसिअं। (अत्रातिनिकटे तपोवने ऋषिभिरुद्घोषितम्।)

राजा (विलोक्य) सखे! अवसित एवायमरुणसारथेर्दिवसदीक्षाधिकारः। कुतः,

अरुणमणिनिकाशैरभ्रसोपानमार्गे-
रवतरति दिनश्रीरम्बरादम्बुराशिम्।
मधुपरिमलवाही मल्लिकामञ्जरीणां
विधुरयति नभस्वान् पद्मिनीचक्रवाकीम्।। १३।।

सखे! किमतःपरं करणीयम्।

विदू अब्भत्थिदो अहं रक्खसभीरुणा कुलवइणा, तुह वअस्सो एत्थ सण्णिहिदो कादव्वो त्ति। ता तहिं एव्व गच्छह्म। (अभ्यर्थितोऽहं राक्षसभीरुणा कुलपतिना, तव वयस्योऽत्र सन्निहितः कर्तव्य इति। तत् तत्रैव गच्छावः।)

राजा बाढम्। प्रथमः कल्पः। (इति निष्क्रान्ताः सर्वे)

Rambha Friend, though her intense pangs of love perturb me, still it is a matter of gratification that love is bestowed in a proper place.

King (With pleasure) I have heard what is worth hearing! Oh my heart, proclaim your affection to this girl without inhibition. Moreover,

Oh Kāma let the breeze from Malaya Mount now swing the flowering creepers of the snowy peak, and may you fill your quiver with flowery arrows feathered by dark bees to assail me. (11)

Vidū I suggest that she is the tinder brought by fate to kindle the fire of a son. (Voice behind the curtain)

The third part of the day is on. Wash away your sins with holy waters. Rush with Karavīra flowers and perfumes to offer oblations to the Sun. (12)

Maid (Excitedly) Friend, get up. The time to worship the Sun is passing.

Heroine (To herself) How can I show my present condition to my father? Or how can I move the limbs whose essence has been drained by the arrows of Kāma? Still, duties to a God are unavoidable. (Aloud) Friends, we shall do accordingly. (Goes along with her maids)

King: Alas! The haven of dreams has just disappeared. Who pronounced these words as terrific as lightning? Oh, the good luck of my eyes has come to an end.

Vidū: It is the sages of the neighbouring hermitage who made the announcement.

King: (Observing) Friend, the jurisdiction of the sun in administering the day is over. For,

The radiance of the day steps down the scarlet stairs of clouds into the ocean. The air still bearing the honey and fragrance of Mallikā blossoms bothers the Cakravāka birds of the lake. (13)

Friend, now what shall we do?

Vidū: The chief among the sages, for fear of demons, has asked me that "Your friend must be persuaded to be present here." So let us go there.

King: Certainly we should.

(All exit)

The End of Act Two

व्यङ्ग्यव्याख्या

द्वितीयाङ्कस्थायीभावः प्रयोगमार्गश्च दर्श्यते।

अथ स कविः प्रथमोऽङ्के समेनकाया नायिकायाः प्रवृत्तेर्वक्त्रीं मेनकां श्रोत्रीं रम्भां विधाय तत्प्रवृत्तिं ताभ्यां प्रकाशयितुं उपक्रमः। ततो मयाप्यत्रादौ तयोः स्थायीभावप्रयोगमार्गौ प्रदर्श्येते।

ततः प्रविशति रंभा मेनका च।

अथ मेनका कार्तिकेयावासे तदर्चनं कृतवत्या तपत्या सह तत्रतिष्ठन्ती सा सहसा सवयस्यं संवरणं तत्रागच्छन्तं दृष्ट्वा तया सहोत्प्लुत्य क्वचित् तरुशाखायामासीना राजर्षिं तत्प्रवृत्तिं च दृष्ट्वा स्मरशरलक्षतां गच्छन्त्या तपत्या सहोपगन्तुकामा सा मेनका कर्णपूरश्रितगाथविदितसङ्केतं राजानं विधाय गच्छन्ती तरुपर्णानि पातयन्ती कृष्टतरुशाखा तया सह तस्मात्तपनवनं यान्ती सा वियता तदृशामूर्च्छनां पश्यन्ती तपनवनं प्राप्य तत्रस्थस्य कल्याणवामनाख्यस्य देवस्य पूजां कृतवत्या तया सहास्मादुत्प्लुत्य भूयोपि नभसञ्चारिणी तपनलोकं प्राप्यताम्। रात्रिमध्युषिता प्रत्युषस्येव तपतीं विचिन्तयन्ती तां गतेति श्रुत्वा किमपि मामनुक्त्वा तत्र गतेयमिति स्मरन्ती श्रितसन्तापा भूत्वा तया तपनवनाभिमुखं गतया भवितव्यमिति स्मरन्ती तां दिदृक्षुरेव सत्वरं तस्मान्निर्गत्य प्रयान्ती सा मेनका सह रम्भया समागम्य तत्समागमहेतोः श्रितमुखवैवर्ण्या विस्मृतसमुदाचारा तत्पृष्टकुशलप्रश्ना भूयस्तया सह यान्ती दृष्टतन्मुखवैवर्ण्यया रम्भया किमेतदिति विचिन्तयन्त्या क्वचित् प्रदेशे स्थातव्यमावाभ्यामित्यर्थं प्रेरिता सा मेनका तत्प्रियहेतोस्तत् क्वचित् गच्छाव इत्युक्त्वा गच्छन्ती मेनका तदनुकूलभावा रम्भा च ते उभे प्रदेशे क्वचिदतिष्ठेताम्।

एवं पूर्वसम्बन्धः।

अथ तयोः प्रावेशिकस्तात्कालिकभावश्च दर्श्यते।

अथ तयोर्मेनका सान्तस्तापं समुखवैवर्ण्यं सचकितं सधैर्यं सविवेकं ईषदुद्दृष्टिर्यवनिकाच्छन्नदेहा तिष्ठेत्। अथ रम्भा सान्तश्चिन्तं सविवेकं यवनिकाच्छन्नदेहा तिष्ठेत्। यथानिर्दिष्टमेवमुभे यावत् तिष्ठेतां तावत् त्रिवर्त्युज्ज्वलित दीपाग्राद्यवनिका व्यपनीयताम्। एवं प्रावेशिकः।

एवं व्यपनीतयवनिकयोर्यथानिर्दिष्टं मुहूर्तं तिष्ठन्त्यो रम्भा तन्मुखवैवर्ण्यं यथावृत्तमजानन्ती डोलायितमनस्का भूत्वा साकुलं सविवेकं दृढं तन्मुखे पश्यन्ती तिष्ठन्तीति स्मरेत्। कुतः को नु खल्वस्या मुखवैवर्ण्यहेतुः। तस्मादियं सन्ततानुसञ्चारिण्या प्रियसख्या तपत्या विरहिता स्वयमेवायातवती। अहमिदानीमस्या मुखवैवर्ण्यहेतुं पृच्छामि। ततः पृच्छामि तावदिति निश्चित्य शनैस्तन्मुखे दृष्टीं नीत्वा ताराभ्यामेव सम्बुध्य तिष्ठेत्। अथेति तिष्ठन्त्यां स मेनका यथानिर्दिष्टं तिष्ठन्ती सहसा तद्दृष्टिसंबोधिता तदाभिमुख्यं कर्तुं किञ्चिन्नम्रतनुस्तिष्ठेत्। एवं तिष्ठन्ती सा किमपि पृष्टुकामेव त्वां पश्यामीति चेत् पश्य,

रचिते भराख्येन शास्त्रेस्मिन् मुनिना पुरा।
दर्शितो नृत्तमार्गोयं द्विधा वेदसमन्वितः।।
ताण्डवं त्विति विज्ञेयमेकं लास्यमथापरम्।
पुंसा यत् क्रियते नृत्तं ताण्डवं तद्विधुर्बुधाः।।
अङ्गना रङ्गमध्यस्था सकलेन्द्रियहारिणी।

सुखा सुन्दरा वाचा लास्यं सा यत् करोत्यदः।।
दीपाग्रे निष्कला भूत्वा सन्मुखे तद् दिदृक्षुणि।
ताभ्यां ग्रन्थार्थमुद्धृत्य ताराभ्यां तत् स विक्षिपेत्।।[1]

एवं पुरोत्तमस्त्रीपात्रप्रयोगमार्गो दर्शितः।

यत् स्त्रियालङ्कृतं गात्रं साधु चोपरिवाससा।
तत् सधैर्यं महाशोभमुत्तमं पात्रमुच्यते।।[2]

अथ सा रंभा उत्तरग्रन्थार्थं दृग्भ्यामेवादौ बोधयित्वा भूयस्सधैर्यं तिष्ठन्ती चाभिनयेन नानालोकान् सुखयेत्। अतःपरम् उत्तमस्त्रीपात्रप्रयोगमार्ग एवं द्रष्टव्यः।

मेनका – अथ मेनका पृष्टेति स्मरेत्। कुतः अहमिदानीमस्मत्प्रियसखीं यथावृत्तं वदामीति निश्चित्य सप्रवणं तन्मुखं पश्यन्ती सान्तस्तापं तदीयां पूर्वकथां तस्याः श्रावयितुमुपक्रमेणोत्तरग्रन्थेन **सहि पुंव कदाइ** इत्यादिना। इत्यादि ग्रन्थेन मेनका विवस्वदङ्कारूढायास्तपत्या भानुमुखात् संवरणगुणगणश्रवणादारभ्य तस्या वर्तमानां दशां रंभायै विज्ञापयति।

अत्रादौ प्रवेशके ग्रन्थे ध्वनिः न विद्यते। भूयोऽत्रानयोस्थायीभावप्रकारो दृश्यते।

मेनकाया अन्तस्तापोत्तरं रम्भा च उत्तरोत्तरग्रन्थं श्रृण्वन्ती चोत्तरोत्तराधिगततापं तिष्ठन्ती तज्जिज्ञासुः पृच्छेत्। एवं तयोस्थायीभावः। एवमागुहावासावतरणात्। तत्र तु **तदो जाव हरि अमणिसिलादले** इत्यस्मिन् ग्रन्थे ओदरिय इति ग्रन्थं वदन्तीति दर्शयेत् पाणिभ्याम्। कुतः अवतीर्य गुहपूजां कृत्वा यावल्लिप्तलासं पदयुगलं कृतवत्या तावत्सम्प्राप्त इति विज्ञापयेत्। अस्मात् प्रभृति रंभा सविस्मयं श्रृण्वन्तीति स्थायीभावो। अमुष्या मेनकायाः पूर्ववदेव। **सुद च म** इत्यत्र च शब्दे प्रोच्यमाने एवं पाणिभ्यां विज्ञापयेत्। कुतः गतेऽहसि मयि तपनवनं प्रति सर्वस्यायां गच्छन्त्यां अस्मत्स्थितिं राज्ञो विज्ञापनार्थं वृक्षशाखा आकृष्य गतवत्यस्मीति च शब्दस्यार्थः। ततस्तं दृष्ट्वा तच्चिह्नविच्छिन्नहृदयो भूत्वा स राजर्षिर्मृगयाछलेन गतवान् किल।

एवं प्रयोगमार्गः।

इत्यादि सर्वं मेनकोदन्तं श्रोतुकामायै रम्भायै विज्ञाप्य उभे तपतीदर्शनाय तपनवनाभिमुखे गतवत्यौ स्यातामिति प्रवेशकः।

---

1 Bharata's concern was nāṭya; nṛtta was added to it later on the advice of Śiva. It was one among the six auxiliaries that enhances the beauty of presentation. Kulaśekhara gives more importance to nṛtta. According to him it is an inherent part of performance. Thus he transformed the classical theatre of Kerala from nāṭyam to āṭṭam- drama to dance. Kūṭiyāṭṭam, Kṛṣṇanaṭṭam, Rāmanāṭṭam, Mohiniyaṭṭam etc., contain predominantly elements of dance.
Bharata included all dance forms under nṛtta. By the time of *Daśarūpaka* (11 c CE) nṛtta had two distinct forms as nṛtta and nṛtya, the former rhythmic and the latter emphasising on emotional expressions. Kulaśekhara denotes the latter, but uses the terminology of Bharata. This shows that he was not aware of the classification of *Daśarūpaka*. This is a strong point to place him before the 11th century.

2 *Naṭāṅkuśa* (15c) refers to women bare in upper parts of the body. उपरिवाससा is significant in this context.

अथ राज्ञः स्थायीभावः प्रावेशिकश्च दृश्यते।

ततः प्रविशति हयारूढो राजा सविमर्शः। अथ राजा कार्तिकेयावासाद्गत्वा पुरं सवयस्यं प्राप्य तां रजनिं कथञ्चिदन्तं प्रापय्य काल्य उत्थाय कथङ्कारं बहु योजनपथं हिमवत्वादेभिः परिवारजनैर्विना गमिष्यामीति स्मृत्वा भूय एवं कर्तव्यमिति निश्चित्य विदूषकमानीयतामित्यवदम्। सखे – सावधानं कर्णपूरं रक्षता त्वया सह मृगयाच्छलेन हयमारुह्य हयजवेन दूरीकृतपरिजनो भूत्वा हिमवत्पार्श्वं गमिष्याम इति इममुक्त्वा तथा कुर्वं इत्युक्तवता विदूषकेण सह तथा पुरान्निर्गत्य हयेन गत्वा हयजवेन दूरीकृतविदूषको भूत्वा सत्वरं हयवेगात् हिमवदधित्यकभुवं प्राप्याविच्छिन्नगत्या मृतवन्तं हयं दृष्ट्वा तमपहाय पद्भ्यां स्वयमेव चरन् भूयस्तत्रत्यया भुवो दिव्यत्वं मृगसाङ्कर्येण विज्ञायात्रस्थेन दिव्यजनेन भवितव्यमिति स्मरन् सा कुत्र वर्तत इति सविमर्शं क्वचिदतिष्ठत्।

एवं पूर्वसम्बन्धः।

एवं सकलवेदी भरतवरः संवरणालङ्कृततनुः स्वयं परवर्णो भूत्वा त्रिवर्त्युज्ज्वलितस्य दीपस्य पुरो यवनिकाच्छन्नदेहो यावत्तिष्ठेत् तावत् यवनिका व्यपनीयताम्।

एवं प्रावेशिकः।

एकनाडिकयात्येति यस्त्वन्तं षष्ठियोजनम्।
कर्त्रा सद्योद्यमानस्सन् स हयः प्रोच्यते बुधैः।।
तं हयं पाययेद्वारिव्यतीतः शतयोजनम्।
नो चेत् षण्णाडिकया तं अर्वाङ्वारयति श्रमः।।

इत्यश्वशास्त्रे अश्वरक्षणविधौ दर्शितः। तदभावान्मृत इति दर्शितः ज्ञेयः।

अथैवं प्रविष्टो राजा सविमर्शमुद्दृष्टिः सधीरं श्रितसङ्कल्पावस्थो मुहूर्तं तिष्ठेत्। इति तिष्ठन्नयमेवं विमृशति। कुतः अहं मृगयाप्रसङ्गादारूढहयो भूत्वा यत्रयत्रागच्छं तस्मात्तस्मात् मद्भीत्या सत्वरमुद्गच्छन्ति स्म मृगाः। अत्रान्योन्यवैरिमृगसाङ्कर्यात् संश्रितदिव्यजनया सम्भूततपस्विन्यानया हिमवद्भुवा भवितव्यम्। एवं विमृशन् नासिकापुटारोपिततर्जनीर्भूत्वा ससन्तोषं तिर्यक् पश्यन्नयं मृगसाङ्कर्यं दृष्ट्वा **अहो** इत्यात्मगतं विमृशेत्। शङ्के निसर्गवैरिणां मृगाणां साङ्कर्यादियं दिव्यभूरिति। तस्मादत्र सन्निहितेन दिव्यजनेन भवितव्यम्। किञ्च तपोवनमिदमिति च। एवं विमृश्य मृगसाङ्कर्यं दृष्ट्वा पूर्ववत्तिष्ठन्नहो इत्याश्चर्यं वदंस्तपोवनानां प्रभावाधिक्यं मृगसाङ्कर्येण दर्शयन् मद्धृदयङ्गमयात्र स्वया भवितमित्य**हो तु खल्वा**दि ग्रन्थेन समर्थयति।[3] अतःपरं यो यो ग्रन्थो राज्ञा वर्ण्यते तेन तेन तस्या दिव्ययुवतेः सान्निध्यमुत्तरोत्तराधिकं समर्थयंस्तं तं विवृणोतीति स्थायीभावः।

अथ राजैवं वर्णितक्रोडादिश्लोको भूत्वा स्वेप्सितप्रदेशावाप्तिहेतोः श्रितमनोरथस्सन्नयं तिर्यक् पश्यन्नत्र स्वपरिवारजनान् कानप्यदृष्ट्वा स्वोपायसौष्ठवमुत्तरग्रन्थेन समर्पयति **सोहमनेने**त्यादिना। सोऽहमनन्यविज्ञेयं साधुतामन्वेषयामि। सोहं गतोऽहन्यन्यारूढहयो भूत्वा गन्तव्यमिति प्रकल्प्यते। नागच्छन् दूरीकृतपरिवारजनस्संवृत्तः सोऽहमित्यर्थः। अनेनेत्यादि ग्रन्थेन तस्य प्रदेशस्य तदन्वेषणार्हत्वं निर्दिश्य शनैर्गच्छन्निमां विचिन्वन्नदृष्ट्वा तद्दर्शनात् सङ्कल्पसमागमं याथातथ्यमश्रमोपि तत्त्वदर्शनात्

3 Please note the similarity to शिखिनि शलभ in SD.

किमपि किमपि कुर्वन् स्मरशरशकलीकृतचित्तो भूत्वा वर्धिष्णुमुत्कलिकां सोढुमक्षमस्तिष्ठेत्। एवं तिष्ठन्नात्मान-मुद्दिश्यारभ्यमानाया मदनप्रवृत्तेस्सन्नाहोदयो न वसान इत्युत्तरग्रन्थेन च सव्यथं स्मरति।

अन्यच्च; इत्युक्त्वा प्रत्युत एव बुद्धिप्रापय्य तस्मादारभ्येति ग्रन्थेन स्मरधुरः क्रमोन्नत्यं समर्थयन्ना**दत्तेत्**यादिना तत्प्रवृत्तिं विवृणोति। किञ्च तस्मात् **पदवतंसकादारभ्ये**ति ग्रन्थप्रक्षेपात् कवेरेतावानभिप्रायः – केवलं मृगयार्थमेवायं गत इति मत्वाऽनुपदिष्टगुरुणा पूर्वापरमपश्यता केनचित् भरतकुलजातेन प्रयोक्त्रा प्रयोगः क्रियते यदि तस्यापि पूर्वप्रस्तुतं स्थायीभावं विज्ञापयितुं च स कविः तस्मात् पदवतंसकदर्शनादारभ्येत्यादिग्रन्थं तत्र प्रक्षिप्तवान्।[4]

अथ राजेति स्वावस्थानवसानतां चिन्तयन् स्मरशरपरवशीकृतहृदयस्तिष्ठेत्। एवं मुहूर्तं तिष्ठन्निति-कर्तव्यतामूढतया तत्कार्यासाध्यतया च द्विगुणितस्मरातुरस्तिष्ठेत्। एवं तिष्ठन् स्वसङ्कल्पावस्थं सधैर्यं सान्तर्वेदनं तिष्ठन् किं मे शरणमिति विभावयेत्। एवं तिष्ठन्निति स्मरेत्। बुद्धिमत्तया धैर्यमात्रावलम्बी किमिदानीं मया सर्वत्रास्मिन् वनप्रदेशे सञ्चरता अद्वितीयेन स दिव्यजनोऽन्वेष्टव्यः अत्रापि दोषो विद्यते।

द्विजेन रहितो राजा चरेन्न जात्वपि क्वचित्।
चरेश्चेदन्तरायोऽस्य लोकवादश्च सम्भवेत्।।

एवमनुप्रयोक्तेन विधिनाहमेक एव सञ्चर्तुनालं; एवं स्मरन् मुहूर्तं तिष्ठेदिति तिष्ठन्नयं भूय एवं स्मरेत्। पाराशर्यद्वितीयेन मया सान्वेष्टव्येति निश्चित्य तत् तिर्यक् पश्येत्। एवं पश्यन्नयममुमदृष्ट्वेति स्मरेत्। क्व इदानीमस्मन्नर्मरक्षाकृत् सततानुगामी पाराशर्यो गतवानिति स्मरन् तद्दूरीकरणहेतुमुत्तरग्रन्थेन निश्चिनोति **गृहीतकर्णपूर** इत्यादिनेति निर्धार्य तां च तं च विदूषकं चालभमानो वर्धिष्णुमुत्कलिकामसहमानः तद्वचश्श्रवणे दत्तकर्णस्सधीरमहो तेनेदानीमुत्कलिकाविनोदयामीति ग्रन्थे प्रोच्यमाने तेन प्रयत्नेनेति विभावयन् सक्षीणं सान्तर्वेदनं समुखवैवर्ण्यं तद्वचश्श्रवणे दत्तकर्णस्तिष्ठेत्।

एवं तिष्ठति नेपथ्ये अंबह्मण्णमिति काचिद् वाग्भवति।

अथ राजा दीपाग्रे तां च तं च विदूषकं चालभमानः केनेदानीमुत्कलिकां विनोदयामीति स्मरन्नयं तद्वचनैकदेशं श्रुत्वा दृग्भ्यां ससम्भ्रमं विभावयन् कस्य नु वच श्रूयत इति दृढीकर्तुं दत्तकर्णस्तिष्ठेत्। एवं तिष्ठन्नयं राजा भूयोपि तद्वचश्शृण्वन्नुत्तरग्रन्थेन विदूषकस्येति निश्चिनोति **पाराशर्ये**त्यादिना। एवं निश्चिन्वानस्ससंभ्रमं सान्तर्वेदनं सलज्जं दृढपरिकरबन्धं तिष्ठेत्। एवं तिष्ठन्निति स्मरेत्। **अये** इति।[5]

अयेऽद्भुते विवेके च स्यात् वयस्यविषादयोः।।

अत्र प्रथमं विवेके। अये इति मनसो दृष्टिरिति स्मरेत्। कुतः? पूर्वं मया स्वप्नश्रवणार्थमाहूतेन तेन कार्यवैमुख्यमाचरितम्। तदानीं तमः स्वस्थचित्ततयानुनीय कथञ्चिन्मन्मार्गानुसारिणमकरवम्। स चेदानीं मत्कार्यवैमुख्यमाचरेच्चेत् तस्यां स्मरशरनुन्नचित्तत्वात् तमनुनेतुं न प्रभुरस्मि। तर्हि मत्कार्योदासीन्य-विषयोऽयमिति चेत् अत्रापि दोषो विद्यते। 'द्विजेन रहितो राजेत्यादिना'। तस्मादस्मिन् विमुखे ममाभिमतप्राप्तिर्नस्यात्।

---

4 This instruction to actor is important. Actors not well-trained under a Guru are not capable of understanding the subtleties of acting.

5 अये is used in the meanings of surprise and disinterest. Surprise in the King on knowing the whereabouts of his friend and disinterest in him towards the love-affair of the King.

अत्रास्य रोषस्सम्भाव्यः। यन्मया हयारोहणेनायं दूरीकृतः तस्मान्मामपि दूरीकर्तुमारूढहयो गतवानयमिति गत्वा किञ्चेति स्यात् तदनायि। वनोद्देशे जवजितवायुना हयेन दूरीकृतस्तत्र महारण्येन गच्छन् भ्रष्ट मार्गस्सन्नितस्ततः सञ्चरन् मन्मार्गणजालकलुषीकृतचित्तैः भयपरवशैः नानाजातिमृगगणैः छान्दसः पीडितो न किं स्यात्। पुनरपि दत्तकर्णस्सावधानं तिष्ठन् अये इति पुनः प्रकाशं वदेत्। अत्राय इति विषादे। अये पाराशर्यस्येव स्वरः सम्प्रत्ययं स्मरः पाराशर्यस्येवा श्रूयते वयस्यस्येव न। कुत? पराशरगोत्रजातेनाति-मेधाविना सकलशास्त्रविदानेनाल्पभाषणेन बहुविधमार्गं दर्शयता मत्कार्यानवाप्तिता दर्श्यते। कुतः किमेवं विमृशंस्तिष्ठन्नयं पाराशर्यं त्रस्तरूपं उद्विग्नचेतसमायान्तमपश्यत्।

एवं पश्यन्नयं तस्य त्रस्तरूपत्वात् कार्यानाभिमुख्यं दर्शयत्ययं पूर्वचिह्नेनेति मन्वानस्सोद्वेगं समनोदुःखं सचकितं सक्षीणं तमेव पश्यंस्तिष्ठेत्। कथं तथा तिष्ठतीति चेत्। अयं कश्चिन्नायकभेदः। कुतः?

यस्तु विश्वसितस्यास्य वैमुख्यात् सुहृदोऽक्षमः।
स्वं कार्यं साधितुं राजा स धीरोद्धतनायकः।।[6]

एवं धीरोद्धतेषु कस्यचिद्भेदः। एवम्भूतनायकं स कविस्संवरणेनास्मिन्प्रबन्धे दर्शयति। तदर्थं तं विदूषकप्रवेशकाले तथा तिष्ठन्तं व्यधात्।

अथैवं तिष्ठन्नयं राजा विदूषकस्यातिगच्छतोऽतित्रस्तरूपिणः **अं बह्म** आनमिति वदतस्तस्य तद्वचः श्रृण्वन्निति स्मरेत्। कुतः? अहो अब्रह्मण्यमब्रह्मण्यमिति वदन्नायाति, तत् तस्मान्मत्कार्यवैमुख्यं सत्वजातिभयं चानेन दर्शितम्। अब्राह्मण्यं मयि ब्राह्मणानर्हं कर्म कैश्चिज्जनैस्सम्पादितमित्यनेनोच्यत इत्यूह्यम्।

सकलवेद्यमन्त्रदातारं मां न मिथ्यावचो वदेत्। तस्मात् किन्ते भयं कस्मात्सञ्जातमितीमं पृष्ट्वा यथार्थवेदी भूयस्तद्धर्मप्राभृतं करिष्यामीति स्मृत्वेति निश्चित्य सक्रोधं ससंभ्रमं तत् श्रोतुकामः विस्मृतेतर कार्यस्तिष्ठेत्। किमर्थं विस्मृतेतरकार्य इति चेत् पश्य –

प्रायेण भूमिपास्सर्वे स्त्रीषु संसक्तचेतसः।
तत्र लज्जावमाना स्यात् नान्यत्रेदृशभूभृतः।।

इत्यस्ति नाट्यशास्त्रे नायकभेदो दर्शितः।

तदर्थं विस्मृतेतरकार्यान्तरं स्थापितवान्। नायकस्यानुक्षणं वर्धिष्णुं मदनदशां किञ्चिच्छमयितुं विदूषक प्रावेशिकस्सकविस्तथाकरोत्।

अथ राजा विदूषकागमनं प्रतिपालयंस्तथा दीपाग्रे तिष्ठेत्।

ततः प्रविशति त्रस्तरूपो विदूषकः।

अथ विदूषकः प्रत्युषस्येव राज्ञा प्रबोधितः स्वमन्दिरान्निर्गच्छन्नयं सावधानं कर्णपूरं संगृह्य 'मया सहागच्छे'ति तेनोक्तस्सः गृहीतकर्णपूरो गच्छन्नग्रगामिनमारूढहयं स्ववयस्यं दृष्ट्वा 'हन्त हतो वयस्य' इति वदन् ससम्भ्रमं कथमपि किमपि अनुष्ठितप्राह्णिकक्रियो भूत्वा तमनुगच्छन् जवजितमरुतहया गत्या दूरीकृतस्सन्नपि हयखुराङ्कितेन लम्बिताम्बरमध्ये भानुमानिति तदा क्षुत्तृड्भ्यां गन्तुमक्षमस्तत्र क्वचिद्वृक्षच्छायां स्थित्वा पिपासुस्तिर्यक् पश्यन् दयया छिन्नं दम्भस्तम्भं दृष्ट्वा तत्र क्वचित्कस्य

6 Treating Saṃvaraṇa as धीरोद्धत is strange; normally he is Dhīrodātta (धीरोदात्त).

चिन्मुनेराश्रमो वर्तत इति मत्वोत्थाय तमन्विष्यन् सहसा ज्याहूतिसुरभितवायुप्रणीतं धूपजालं जिघ्रंस्तदङ्कितेन पथा गत्वा तं प्राप्य तपस्विजनात् तमृषिं भृगुनामधेय इति विज्ञाय तं नमस्कृत्य प्रोक्तनिजप्रवृत्ति सत्कुर्वतस्तस्मात् कृतातिथ्यस्सशर्म तत्रासीनो भृगुणा हिमवति वर्तमानं तपनवनं तद्वनान्वर्थं तस्मात् किमपि दूरे उत्तरदेशे कल्याणवामनाख्यभगवन्मन्दिरं तत्सविधे करतलोदकाख्यसरश्च च शब्दोत्तरतीर गोष्ठीमण्डपं तां चैतानि विज्ञापयता तेन गच्छेत्यनुज्ञातः कृतकृत्यश्च तं प्रणम्य तस्मान्निर्गत्य पूर्वमेव यष्ट्यग्रे केनचित्कार्पासिकेन सूत्रेण बद्धं कर्णपूरं परिपाल्य श्रितकर्णपूराग्रं यष्टिमादाय गच्छन्नुद्गतयष्टिः भूयोपि तद्गततत्खुराङ्कितेन पथा गच्छन् महता पवनेन सक्रीडाप्रधानैश्चूतविटपस्थैः कैश्चिदपि वानरचयैः अपहृतकर्णपूरयष्टिरासीत्। सोऽपहृतकर्णपूरोऽयं प्रमादीभूत्वेत्यस्मरत्। कुतः,

न दातव्यो नृभिर्न्यासो लघुर्वाथमहानपि।
भूपाज्जात्वपि केभ्योपि धीमद्भिरपि वाग्गुरोः।।

अहो गुरुवचनस्य प्रामाण्यम्।

सर्वेभ्यो व्याहरेन्न्यासं कुर्यात् तद्व्ययमापदि
तन्न्यासता महत्यापन्मम जातेत्युदीरयत्।।
तं वक्तुमप्रभुं कुर्वन् तत्कर्तारं चाटूक्तिभिः।
श्रमी चानुभवेत्तेन सुखमेतन्मतं भृगोः।।

अथवौशानसः प्रयोक्तव्यो; ननु कुतः?
इति भार्गवं मतं स्मृत्वामुना तमनुसरामीति निश्चित्य त्वं न्यासतो महतीं विपदं प्राप्तवानस्मीति वयस्यं विज्ञापयंस्तूपयामीति निश्चित्य कथङ्कारमिति स्मरन्नीदृक् प्रकारमित्यस्मरत्। कुतः अद्य मिथ्योक्त्या न भ्रमयितव्यः। कुतः,

कदाचिन्नानृतं ब्रूयादृते पञ्चदशाः पुमान्।
तत्रापि नो न दातारमेवमाचार्ययोर्मतम्।।

तस्मात्सत्यानृतोक्त्यैव भ्रमयितव्यः। दैववशात् कार्पासिकेन सूत्रेण बद्धः कर्णपूरः कपिभिरपहृतः। तस्मात्सत्यानृतोक्तिः कर्तव्यः – कुतः,

परमात्मनि कार्पासे प्रपञ्चे चतुरानने।
वेदे च प्रणवे चैषु ब्रह्मशब्दः प्रवर्तते।।

इत्यनेकार्थोक्तिः। तस्मात् ब्रह्मसूत्रेण ब्राह्मणाश्रयेण सुदृढमाबद्ध्य सङ्गृहीत इति भ्रमयितव्यः, तत्र मिथ्यावादित्वं न स्यात्। किञ्च कपिभिरपहृतः। तत्र शत्रुभिरपहृत इति वाच्यम्। कुतः बलीमुखाच्छभल्लश्च हरिश्शत्रु कपिष्विमे। तस्मात्तु तथा वक्तव्यम्। तर्ह्युपवीत्यसीति मां स पृच्छति चेत् तत्रायं विधिर्दर्शयितव्यः। कुतः

उपवीते सदा विप्रो धारयेदविगलेन सः।
तावती स्वत्कृते दोष्णिश्चुत्येत्याचार उच्यते।।

इत्यमुना, तस्मात् ब्राह्मणश्रयेण ब्रह्मसूत्रेण मत्पात्रयष्ट्यग्रे त्वन्न्यासमिति मत्वा सुदृढं बध्वा गच्छन्नहं शत्रुभिः पीडित इति विज्ञापयामीति निश्चित्य त्रस्तरूपो भूत्वा मुक्तकण्ठं विलपन् निमीलितचक्षुश्शत्रुवर्गै-रतिपीडितोस्मीति राज्ञोऽभयं सम्पादयितुं वदंस्तत्सन्निधिं प्राप्यातिष्ठत्।

एवं भरतवरस्तद्भूमिकालङ्कृततनुर्यवनिकाच्छन्नदेहो भूत्वा यथानिर्दिष्टं यावत् तिष्ठेत् तावद्यवनिका व्यपनीयताम्। एवं पूर्वसम्बन्धः प्रावेशिकश्च। एवं व्यपनीतयवनिको दीपाग्रे पूर्वोक्तमेव पठन् यथानिर्दिष्टं तिष्ठेत्।

अथ राजा तथा स्वसन्निधिं प्राप्य तिष्ठन्तं तं दृष्ट्वा दीपाग्रे तिष्ठन् सगाम्भीर्यं ससम्भ्रमं सविषादं विषण्णतां दयालुत्वं दृशा विभावयंस्तद्वचनं श्रोतुकामस्तिष्ठेत्।

विदू – तदा तथाभूतो विदूषकः तं भ्रमयितुं पूर्वोक्तं ग्रन्थमुक्त्वा तदाकारादिचेष्टां ज्ञातुं किञ्चिदुन्मीलितदृष्टिस्तं विलोकयंस्तन्नयने दररक्ते दृष्ट्वेति स्मरेत्। अहो ईषदेवास्याक्षिरोषः संवृत्तः। तस्मात् मूर्खजनोचितेन वाग्जालेनास्य मनो विदार्य स्ववयस्यस्य मम पीडयास्यरोषं शत्रावज्जृंभयन्निमं क्रुद्धतरं कुर्व इति निश्चित्य त्वन्न्यासपरिग्रहादेवापद्गतसर्वस्वः शत्रुभिः पीडितोस्मीत्युत्तरग्रन्थेन समर्थयति **ईदिसे** इत्यादिना।

अथ विदूषकः तं भ्रमयन् स्वदशां विज्ञापयति ईदृशोपि भयस्थो न इत्येतावन्तं ग्रन्थमुक्त्वा सहसेति स्मरेत्। अहमिदानीं नयशास्त्रसूत्रविधिमार्गेणायं विज्ञाप्येति मत्वा भीत्या वक्तुमक्षमोस्मीति अयं भयनिमीलितचक्षुस्तत्सूत्रार्थमेवं स्मरेत्।

'गुर्वपाये चिन्त्यमाने किञ्चिन्यूने सुखं स्यात्' इति सूत्रविधानेन साधितुं शेषग्रन्थमाह **दुग्गामतेणवि** इत्यादिना। अपठितदुर्गामन्त्रमनन्यगतिं छान्दसमेकाकिनं ब्राह्मणं वनेन परिभ्रमन्तं दरिद्रं मां हित्वा गतिजितवायुं हयमारुह्य गच्छन्तं त्वां वीतशत्रुणा वनेनानुगच्छतो मम सर्वस्वं त्वन्निमित्तं नष्टम्। किञ्च कथमेकाकिनं द्विजं मां रक्षितुमप्रभुणा त्वयाब्धिमेखला भू रक्ष्येत इत्यादि वाक्शल्येन तं व्यथयन् सत्रासं सान्तर्वेदं सदुःखं कम्पितशरीरस्तिष्ठेत्।

राजा – अथ राजा पूर्ववत् तिष्ठन्तं तथाभूतं दृष्ट्वा तद्गिरमश्रृण्वन्निति स्मरेत्। अहो विततशत्रुणा वनेनागच्छन्नयं कैश्चिद् व्यपहृतसर्वस्वो भवेत्। अहो वचनीयतायाः पात्रं खलु मम राजत्वम्। कुतः

रक्षन् मित्राणि तैस्सार्धं शत्रुं जित्वा ततः करान्।
आहृत्यैभ्यः कृतावेते भूसुरान् योजयन् सतः।।
त्रिलोकीं निजयार्चिष्या यः पाति स महीपतिः।
योऽतथाभूत एषोऽत्र सजीवं मृतिमेत्यसौ।।

इति राजनयं विमृशन् स्वाधिकारं कुर्वन्निति स्मरेत्। अहमिदानीमनेन परुषवचोभिः पीड्यते; यदहं तस्मात् परुषवादीभूतमिमं नियम्य कीदृग्भूताच्छत्रोस्ते भयमिति याथातथ्यं तन्मुखादेव विदित्वा भूयस्तस्तत्प्रतीकारपरो भवामीत्यात्मना निश्चितवानस्मीति निश्चित्य तमनुनेतुं निमीलितचक्षुष्पादक्षम इति स्मरेत्। कुतः –

मूर्खान्मनीषी मा पश्येद्यदि पश्येत्तु मा वदेत्।
यदि ब्रूयात्तथा ब्रूयाद्भृगुणेति स्मृतं मतम्।।

इति स्मृत्वा निश्चित्य चोत्तरग्रन्थेन तत्सम्बोधनं करोति; मूर्खमूर्खेति वदंस्तदंसे गृहीत्वा पालयन् भूयोप्याह मूर्ख इति वदन् सरोषं तिष्ठेत्। तथोक्तो विदूषकोपि अर्धोन्मीलितदृष्टिस्तमेव पश्यन् सरोषं तिष्ठेत्। अथ

राजा तथाभूतेन तेन वीक्षमाणस्तं मूर्खशब्दस्यान्वर्थं दर्शयेत्।

यस्सतामपि चेतांसि व्यथयत्यपि भूसुरः।
परुषाभिर्वदनवाग्भिः स मूर्ख इति गम्यते।।

अपि च इति च दर्शयेत्; कुतः,

विद्यान्नदात्रोर्वागुग्रा प्रयोक्तव्या न जातुचित्।
तत्रावर्जनमात्राणां मोचनं पुरतो भवेत्।।

इति श्रुतिस्मृतिसिद्धाचारः त्वया दृष्टो भवेदिति मूर्खपदप्रोच्यमाने दर्शयंस्तिष्ठेत्। अथ तदा विदूषकोपि मूर्खेत्याहूतस्तत्सर्वं विदित्वाय मन्निमित्तं परवशीकृतचित्तस्सन्नपि तं नियम्य मूर्खेत्यभिहितवान्। तस्मादयं भयहेतोरेवं कृतवानस्मीति रोषं न्यस्य भयपरवशतां दर्शयामीति मत्वा तथा तिष्ठेत्।

अथ तदा राजा मूर्खेति वदंस्तिष्ठन्नेनं विशेषं दृष्ट्वेति स्मरेत्। अहो छान्दसः परं भयहेतोर्मम वादी संवृत्तः। तस्मादयं सूक्त्या रक्षितव्य इति निश्चित्योत्तरग्रन्थेन तथा करोति **मा भैषीः** इति।[7]

अथ राजा सक्षात्रं प्रथमं विधौ वदेत्। भूयः प्रार्थने। अथ विदूषकस्तदा तच्छ्रुण्वन् किञ्चिद्भीतमनो अर्धोन्मीलितदृष्टिस्तं पश्यंस्तिष्ठेत्।

अथ राजा तं तथाभूतं दृष्ट्वेति स्मरेत्। अस्य भयहेतुरिदानीं द्रष्टव्य इति मत्वा भूयस्तेनैव ग्रन्थेन प्रश्ने वदति मा भैषीरिति। एवं त्रिविधमस्य प्रयोगम्। अथैवं राजा तदेति स्मरेत्। अहमिदानीं पृच्छागीति मया चोत्तरग्रन्थेन पृच्छति **किमेतदि**ति।

विदू – राजानमवलम्ब्य। अथ विदूषकः किमेतदिति पृष्ठः स इति स्मरेत्। कथङ्कारमेनं तं परित्यागजाभ्यां दुःखक्रोधाभ्यामीड्यमानं विधाय विज्ञापयामि। अस्तु एवं करिष्ये भयाधिक्यं विभावयितुमालिङ्ग्य तं सबाष्पगद्गदं 'मां रक्षे'ति ब्रवीमीत्यात्मना निश्चित्य तदर्थमालिङ्ग्य सबाष्पगद्गदमुत्तरग्रन्थमाह **अवहिदो**त्यादि।

अथ तेनालिङ्ग्यमानो राजा सान्त्वेवंदं तज्जितासुरुत्तरग्रन्थमाह **अतिमात्र**मित्यादि।

विदू – अथैवं तेन पृष्टो विदूषकः इति स्मरेत्। अहमिदानीं कृत्रिमेण भयेन शमयितुं त्रासकम्पितसर्वाङ्गो भूत्वा शनैश्शनैर्दृष्ट्युन्मीलितदृशः पश्यन् गुणसंकीर्तनेन साम्नातमनुसरामीत्यात्मना निश्चित्य तथाकुर्वन्नुत्तरग्रन्थेन तथाकरोति। **तुज्ज सण्णिहित** इत्यादिना।

अथ राजा तत् श्रुत्वा तत्स्तुतिसंवर्धितभिया तत्परिभववर्धितक्रोधो भूत्वेति स्मरेत्। केषा द्विषा त्वं बाधित इत्यमुं पृच्छामीति मत्वा चोत्तरग्रन्थेन तं पृच्छति **कथं शत्रुवर्ग** इत्यादिना।

विदू – अथ विदूषकः तं क्रुद्धतरं दृष्ट्वेति स्मरेत्। अहो शत्रुवर्ग इति मद्वचनश्रवणमात्रेण एवास्य रोष उज्जृंभति। किमत्राश्चर्यम्। उपपन्नमेतत् –

स भूपो योऽजयत् शत्रून् यद्भूतस्तैर्नमस्कृतः।
यो ध्रुवं त्रिजगत्पतिः सार्वभौमस्स उच्यते।।

---

7 मा भैषीः – Do not fear (विधि); Please, need not fear (प्रार्थना) what causes fear (प्रश्ने). The *loṭ* verb is used in these three senses.

तस्मात् क्रुद्धतरमिमं कथङ्कारमपक्रुद्धं करोमि अस्तु; तावदेवं त्वदभिमताप्तेरुपायो मया भृगोर्लब्ध इति दृशोः प्रीतिं विभावयन् अङ्गैः त्रासं दर्शयन् प्रहसनप्रधानेन तद्भयहेतुं सत्यमुक्त्वास्य कोपं शमयामीत्यात्मना निश्चित्य उत्तरग्रन्थेन तथाभूत्वा विज्ञापयति। **एति अमि**त्यादिना।

राजा – अथ राजा तत्परिभवक्रोधं तिष्ठन्नयं तद्वचश्श्रुत्वा तमापादतलमस्तकं पश्यस्तद् दृशोर्विशेषान् वीक्ष्यमाणः एवं स्मरेत्। अये विरुद्धैतदीया चेष्टा, कुतः,

वयः खेदवदस्येदं वपुश्चालक्ष्यते तथा।
दृष्ट्योरमुष्य हृत्तुष्टिं कीदृगाशास्य वर्तते।।

न्यासीभूतः कर्णपूरः परित्यक्त इव प्रतीयते। तथापि मन्न्यासपरित्यागात् चित्तवेदनामस्य न पश्यामि। किञ्च दृशोस्सुचित्तसन्तुष्टिर्दृश्यते। तस्मादन्वेषणार्थं मां मृगयाच्छलेनायातवानस्ति। तद्दर्शनोपायसिद्धिरमुना लब्धेव मे प्रतिभाति। तस्मान्निन्दापुरस्सरयासौहार्द्दर्शिन्या वाचा एनं न्यक्करोमि। ततः श्रुत्वा तन्न्यक्करणजया क्रुधा वा प्रीत्या वा किं वदेदित्यात्मना निश्चित्य परिहासपूर्वमुत्तरग्रन्थमाह **अभिज्ञोऽस्मी**त्यादि। इत्यादिग्रन्थे प्रोच्यमाने विदूषकस्तं ज्ञात्वापि तन्निन्दामनाहत्यान्यत् किमपि स्मरन्निव तिष्ठेत्।

अथ राजा तथाभूते तस्मिन्निति स्मरेत्। किन्नु अस्य चित्तविकारं स्वनिन्दया, न दर्शने। मयैवमुक्तोपि स्वहृद्गतं न निर्गलति यत् तस्मादहं सरोषं 'अवतंसकमुद्धरे'ति वदन्निर्गलयामीत्यात्मना निश्चित्योत्तरग्रन्थेन तथा करोति **आस्तामेतदि**त्यादिना।

विदू – अथ विदूषकस्तद्बुद्धिवृद्धिं जानन्नपीति स्मरेत्। अहो मामधिक्षिप्य मन्मनोविगलयितुमस्यायमारंभः; तथाप्येतेन विधिनावैवं ब्रवीमि। कुतः –

तस्माद् पृष्टो न वदामि। तत् किं करिष्ये त्वन्न्यासपरिग्रहेण ब्राह्मणनिसर्गाभरणं ब्रह्मसूत्रमपि नष्टमिति दोषमारोपयन् वदामीत्यात्मना निश्चित्य सरोषमुत्तरग्रन्थमाह **कहं वतंस** ओ इत्यादिना।

राजा – अथ राजा तस्य वैषम्यं ज्ञात्वा भूयोपीति स्मरेत्। अहो अदृष्टोऽयं मया यत्तदर्थं तं विज्ञापयति। तथापि काल एव पृच्छामि। तस्मादिदानीं किं करिष्ये। अस्तु, एवं करिष्ये। भूयोपि क्रोधप्रसादे पिशुनयता वचसा व्यवहरन्नस्य चित्तशैथिल्यं करोमीत्यात्मना निश्चित्योत्तरग्रन्थमाह **अहो तु खल्वपि प्रमाद**मित्यादिना।

स्वकोपविषये पुंसि विद्यावत्स्वपि सत्स्वपि।
भवेदत्र भवच्छब्दक्षोणीभृत् सुतपस्विषु।।

इत्यनेकार्थः। अत्र कोपप्रशंसयोः।

विदू – अथ विदूषकः तं तथा जानन्नपि इति स्मरेत्। अहमिदानीं त्वदभिमताप्तेरुपायं लब्धवानस्मीति दृशोर्विभावयन् वचसि सरोषं कर्णपूरं न्यक्कुर्वन् वास्तवकीर्तनेन तमिमं भेद यामीत्यात्मना निश्चित्य उत्तरग्रन्थेन तथा करोति। **मा कुप्येत्या**दिना।

राजा – अथ राजा तेन तथोक्तं श्रुत्वेति स्मरेत्। अहो केनाप्ययं स्वमनोगतं न निर्गमयति। तस्मात्कथङ्कारमेनं मद्वशतां नयामीति स्मरन् मुहूर्तं तिष्ठेत्। भूय एवं तिष्ठन् संस्मृत्येति निश्चिनुयात्। कुतः त्वं न मे जातु विश्वास्यः तदर्थमहं भवन्तं रहस्यं कर्म वक्तुं पृष्टवान् भेदवचनैस्सम्भेद्य भूयस्तन्मनोगतं व्यङ्ग्येन

पृच्छामीत्यात्मना स्मृत्वा भूयोपि भेदमार्गः कीदृग्विध इति स्मरन् भवच्चापल्यात् किमपि न वाच्यमिति समर्थयामीति निश्चित्योत्तरग्रन्थेन अलमनेनेत्यस्मात् ग्रन्थादारभ्या**प्रकाशितवानस्मी**त्येतावतः पदात् तथा समर्थयति। भूयस्त**द्विनोदक्षम**मित्यस्मात् ग्रन्थादारभ्यानायिकादर्शनात् तयोश्चेतो वक्रतामपहायान्योन्यं दृग्भ्यां वा ताभ्यां सह पाणिनैकेन वा परस्परं व्याङ्ग्यार्थं विज्ञाप्य तेनैव प्रेक्षकान् सुखयन्तौ तौ बाह्यार्थमभिनयन्नाभ्यां नानालोकान् सुखयेताम्।[8]

एवं प्रयोगमार्गः।

अथैवं राज्ञामुना ग्रन्थेन भेद्यमानस्तिष्ठन्नयं विदूषकस्तदानीं 'न जात्वपृष्टो' दूतोपि स्वभर्तारं च मा वदेत् इत्येष विधिरेव मयानुष्ठीयते, तस्मात् प्रष्टव्योहं भवते'ति दृशोर्विभावयंस्तिष्ठेत्।

अथ राजा तथाविभाव्य तिष्ठन्तं तं दृष्ट्वा मद्वश्य इदानीमयमिति निश्चित्य सव्यङ्ग्येनोत्तरग्रन्थेन तं पृच्छति। **तद्विनोदक्षमं वनोद्देशमन्वेषयावहे** इति।

अस्मिन् ग्रन्थे ध्वनिर्दृश्यते।[9] तद्विनोदक्षममित्यत्र तच्छब्दस्यैवमर्थं तया सह विनोदनाय क्षमं शक्यं वनोद्देशं ज्ञातवानसीत्येष मे प्रतिभाति। तस्मादिमं मां तथाभूतं वनोद्देशं नयेति ध्वनिः। इतीमं ध्वन्यर्थं प्रेक्षकान् विज्ञाप्य बाह्यार्थेन नानाजनान् सुखयेत्। अथ राजैवं विज्ञाप्य भूयोपि पारवश्यात् पूर्ववत् सङ्कल्पावस्थायामेव तिष्ठेत्।

विदू – अथ विदूषकस्तेनैवं पृष्ट इति स्मरेत्। अहमिदानीं भृगोर्लब्धा स्थितिर्व्यङ्ग्येन विज्ञापयामीत्यात्मना निश्चित्योत्तरग्रन्थेन तया विज्ञापयति – **जह** इत्यादिना।

अयं ध्वनिरन्यापदेशाख्य यथा त्वया मृगाणां पदवीमन्विष्यते[10] – मृगाणामिति पदे प्रोच्यमाने पदे तदीयां पदवीं स्थितिं विचिन्वन्नागच्छन्नहं दैववशात् भृग्वाश्रमपदं प्रविष्टवानस्मि। तत्र तदा तेन सत्कृतस्तदग्र आसीनोऽहं 'किमप्यस्ति भवत्प्रसादलेशो ज्ञातुं भवन्मुखादिच्छामी'ति विभाव्य स्थितवानस्मि। तत्रासीनेन मया मद्भावमात्रविज्ञातमत्सिद्धान्तस्य तस्य सदिव्यचक्षुषो भगवतस्सत्यवादिनो मुखान्महतीकथा श्रुता। महतीति पदे प्रोच्यमाने 'सा दिव्यकन्यका तत्र दिव्यभूमिस्थेत्यवैहीति मां विज्ञापितवानिव मे प्रतिभाति'। विभाव्य किमपि किमप्यर्धमर्धमुक्त्वा तिष्ठेत्। एवं तिष्ठन्नयं भूयोपि विज्ञापयेत्। अथाहं तथा विज्ञापितस्तदानीं तज्जिज्ञासुस्तन्महत्वात् प्रष्टुमप्रभुरपि भावैः 'कस्यां दिशि सा दिव्यभूस्तत्परिज्ञानचिह्नं कीदृशं तत्र कस्तत्प्राप्तिहेतु'रित्यादि बहुविधं भावेनैव पृष्ट्वा नम्रतनुर्मद्बाहुना स्थगयन्नोष्ठपुटं तदग्रे स्थितवानस्मि। एवं स्थितवन्तं मां मत्पाटवात् बहुमान्य तत्परिज्ञानचिह्नं तत्प्राप्तिहेतुं च विज्ञापितुमन्याप देशेनानन्यविज्ञेयं बहुकथां कथितवान्। तत् तथा तां कथां सकलां वक्तुं विस्मृतकथामार्गो प्रभुरस्मीत्युक्त्वा वा भूयः किमप्यवदंस्तिष्ठेत्। एवं तिष्ठति तस्मिन् तच्छ्रवणेच्छुः राजा यत्प्रवणं तिष्ठन्नयं तं 'वद वदे'ति दृग्भ्यां सम्प्रेर्य तिष्ठेत्। तथा संप्रेर्यमाणो विदूषकः किञ्चिदुद्दृष्टिस्तिष्ठेत्। भूयो नायकमुखे पश्यन्नुत्तरग्रन्थेन तत् कथयति। **तस्यां सारभूमि**रित्यादिना तत्प्रकारं दर्शयति। अथ विदूषकस्तदा भूयोप्युत्तरग्रन्थेन तद्वचनं विज्ञापयति **इदो उत्तरा दिसा अमित्यादिना**। भो तथा वक्तुमप्रभुरस्मि। तथापि संक्षेपेण तात्पर्यार्थं कथयामि। भो श्रूयताम्।

---

8 Hither to hidden meaning was from the actor to the prekṣaka. Here it is also between the actors.

9 तद्विनोदक्षमं – तस्मात् विनोदक्षमं देशमादेशयेति बाह्यार्थः। तया सह विनोदाय क्षमं देशमिति व्यङ्ग्यार्थः।

10 मृगाणां पदवीमन्विष्यते इति वाच्यः। तदीयां पदवीमिति अन्यापदेशरूपो ध्वनिः।

अस्मादर्धयोजनमात्रदूरे उत्तरस्यां दिशि हिमवन्मूर्धजाभूद्दिव्या। अपि च तत्र काचिद्बहुरूपिणी पुरुषोत्तमप्रतिमा वर्तते च; तत्रस्थया भगवत्सपर्यातत्परया दिव्यकन्यकया भवितव्यम्।

कुमारं वाथ दुर्गां वा विष्णुं वा वटुरूपिणम्।

इत्येतद्वचनादित्यादि सर्वं मां बोधयितुमिव महर्षिणा कथोक्तेः तद्भावैर्मे प्रतिभातीति ग्रन्थे प्रोच्यमाने तेन व्यङ्ग्येन राज्ञे विज्ञापयन्नयं तया तत्रस्थया भवितव्यमिति पुनःपुनः दृग्भ्यां विभावयन्नहं तद्वचनप्रामाण्यात् तत्रैव गच्छाव इति दृग्भ्यां विभावयंस्तिष्ठेत्। अथ तदा राजापि तद्वचश्रवणात् तथ्यमिति स्मृत्वा निश्चित्य तत्र जिगमिषुस्सन्नपि तद्बहुमानार्थम् उत्तरग्रन्थमुक्त्वा सत्वरं सङ्कल्पावस्थस्तेन सह तत्र गच्छति। एवमुभौ तत्र गन्तुं प्रयतेते।

अथैवं नायकविदूषकभूमिकालङ्कृततनू तावुभौ तद्गमनं रूपयन्तौ रङ्गतल एव परिक्रामतः। अथ तत्र गच्छतोस्तयोः प्रथमं राज्ञो गमनप्रकारं दर्शयति।

अथाग्रप्रतिष्ठमानविदूषको राजा केवलं स्वमहिमावेदितमार्गस्तस्मादुत्तरया दिशा शनैर्गच्छन्नयं दृष्टिः मार्गोपात्तवर्तिनि वने चारयन् सन्निहितदिव्यजने प्रदेशे तत्परिज्ञानचिह्नं गच्छन्नेव विमृशेत्। कुतः,

यत्र दिव्यजनश्शन्नस्सन्निधत्ते शुभे गिरौ।
तत् स्त्रिया द्योतितं तत्र द्रष्टव्यं जितविद्युता।।

इत्यादि पुराणसिद्धं व्यासवचनं विमृशन्नेव गच्छन् कदाचित् तथाभूतं किमपि वनं प्रविष्टः तद्वनमिदमिति मनसा स्मृत्वात्र मुहूर्तस्तिष्ठन्नयं तिरोधानपटुतरदिव्यजनचिह्नानि किमपि किमपि पश्यन्नत्र वने क्वचित् प्रदेशे वर्तते स दिव्यजन इत्यूह्यमिति चिन्तयन् प्रत्यक्षं तद्विग्रहदर्शनाभावात् याथातथ्यं सङ्कल्पसमागमं कर्तुमपारयन्नपि पदतलदर्शनात् बन्धुराङ्गीयमिति मन्वानः किमपि किमपि डोलायितस्य मनसः स्थैर्यं कुर्वन् सङ्कल्पावस्थायां तद्दर्शनौत्सुक्यस्तिष्ठन्नयं नायकः स्वक्रियामिमामवस्थां प्रेक्षकान् बोधयन् तां रसवल्लीं दिव्यजनचिह्नेन चोद्गमयंस्तद्दर्शनौत्सुक्यस्तिष्ठेत्। एवं नायकगमनप्रकारं दर्शयित्वा स कविः पुनर्विदूषकस्यास्मात् परं ग्रन्थप्राप्तिकस्तद्ग्रन्थस्य पौष्कल्यं तद्गमनप्रकारेण आम्रेडयितुं तद्गमनप्रकारं पश्चात् दर्शयति।

अथ तपनवनाभिमुखमग्रे गच्छन् स विदूषकोपि वनप्रदेशे प्रणीतदिग्वक्रितास्याश्रुतपादसञ्चारशब्दः शनैर्न्यस्तपदो गच्छन्नयं सहसा तथाभूतं वनं दृष्ट्वा व्यासवचनप्रोक्तचिह्नं किमपि विवेकदृष्टिर्विमृशत्तत्रस्थाय पृष्ठतो विलोक्य राजानं तथाभूतं दृष्ट्वा सावधानं नायकमापादतलमस्तकं पश्यन् सशिरःकम्पमेवं स्मरेत्। एतद्वनं प्रविष्टमात्रस्य अस्यमनःपारवश्यं केन नु भवेत्? किन्तु वनप्रविष्टोऽयं कदाचित् दिव्यजनं दृष्ट्वा तस्मात् स्वदृष्ट्याकर्षणे तत्तिरोधानशङ्कया तद्गतदृष्टिः तिष्ठेत् अथवा स्वस्मिन्नङ्कुरितां रसवल्लीं तदङ्गसुधारसस्सिञ्चन् वर्धयति। किं आहोस्वित् सञ्चरितादितरवनचयादतिद्योतितमेतद्वनं निरीक्ष्यतोऽत्रस्थ इति मन्यमानस्तत्प्राप्य उपायचिन्ता चिन्त्यते किम्। अत किं माहात्म्यप्रच्छन्नस्य समीप-स्थावाप्तिगबिन्दन् समीपगतायाः प्रेयस्या अप्राप्यतया वर्धितामुत्कण्ठां सोढुमक्षमः परवशचित्तो भवेत्,

यः पश्यन् प्रेयसीमग्रे स्थितां केनापि वर्तते।
अप्राप्यमन्तरायेण स्मरस्तन्मोहयेत् भृशम्।।

इति वचनशक्त्या, किञ्च

कयापि दशया लभ्यां पुरोगां निजवल्लभाम्।
पश्यन् न वर्तते ऽत्यन्तं तन्नयेन्मोहमङ्गजः।

इत्यस्ति जयमङ्गलायां वचनम्।

तद्वचनशक्त्या तथा तिष्ठेत्। किं कीदृग्भूतो व्यामोहः। एनं एनं संस्पृशति तद् यावदेनं पृच्छामीति स्मृत्वा तमभ्युपेत्य तत्पार्श्वे तमेव पश्यंस्तिष्ठन्नयं तदेकाग्रचित्ततां परिच्छेत्तुं कण्ठमार्गमर्द्दनरवैः संस्कृत्य तिष्ठन्नयं तद्गौरवं अप्यश्रृण्वन्तं तं दृष्ट्वा वचसा तं प्रष्टुमुपक्रममाणस्सन्नयमुद्दृष्टिरेवं स्मरेत्। कथङ्कारमेनं पृच्छामि स्पष्टोक्त्या व्यङ्ग्येन वा? स्पष्टोक्तिर्ग्राह्या हि। किञ्च –

स्पष्टोक्त्या पृच्छमाना सा वाणी चेत् केनचित् श्रुता।
राज्ञोऽस्य लाघवं लोके विततं तत् भवेत् ध्रुवम्।।[11]

तद्व्यङ्ग्येन पृच्छामीति निश्चित्य स ध्वनिनोत्तरग्रन्थेन तदवस्थां पृच्छति। **भो वउ स्स** इत्यादि।

अथ विदूषकस्तं भो वयस्य इत्याहूय तथाहूतोपि तदश्रृण्वस्तिष्ठन्तं तं पश्यन्नेव मुहूर्तं तिष्ठेत्। एवं तिष्ठन्नयं विदूषकः भो इति पदे पुनरपि प्रोच्यमाने वचसा तमिति वदेत्। 'भो किमप्यस्ति मया विचार्यते तदयमभिमुखो भव' इति केन ग्रन्थेन बोध्यमानं तं पश्यंस्तिष्ठेत्।

अथ राजा सङ्कल्पसमागमं कुर्वन्नयं तिष्ठन्ननन्यविदमपि केनाहूयमानं वचश्शनैर्न श्रृण्वन्निश्चलाङ्गस्तिष्ठन्नयं चक्षुषी मन्दं मन्दमुन्मीलयन् तं वीक्ष्य सस्नेहं सप्रेमबहुमानं सधैर्यं भावैस्तं सम्भाव्य तिष्ठेत्। स चेदानीं मयाहूतस्तु मद्वचनाभिमुख्यं कुर्वंस्तिष्ठति तस्मादिदानीमस्मिन् वने क्वचिदपि स दिव्यजनोऽपि वसतीति ध्वनिगर्भया गिरा तं विज्ञापयामीति निश्चित्योत्तरग्रन्थेन तमाह **भो व अ स** इत्यनेन ग्रन्थेन।

अथ भरतवरोऽस्मिन् ग्रन्थे छिन्नध्वन्यर्थमदञ्चरन् राज्ञे विज्ञापयन् प्रयोगं कुर्वन् प्रेक्षकान् यथा सुखयेत्। कथम्भूतं मार्गमेवमिति स कविर्दर्शयति।

अथ स विदूषकः विज्ञापयति ध्वनिना 'सर्वकालावच्छिन्न दिव्यजनमेतद्वनमिति वनभासानुमेयं तस्मादेतद्वनं तपनवनमिति महर्षिणोक्तमित्यूह्यम्'। **एदं वण पविठस** इति तथापि एतद्वनं प्रविष्टस्य मे दिङ्मोहस्संवृत्तः। दिङ्मोह इति केवलश्रमस्संवृत्त इति चेत् तन्न सर्वकालावच्छिन्नदिव्यजनविततमेतद्वनम्। तथापि दिङ्मोहस्संवृत्तः तत् कथमिति चेत्। एतद्वनं सन्निहितदिव्यजनं भूयिष्ठमपि यथास्थानमुदित्य तपनस्य तीरस्यास्मात्प्रदेशात् उत्तरगोचरेति मे प्रतिभाति। सन्निहितदिव्यजनमेतद्वनमप्यमुष्मात् किमप्युत्तरदेशमपि वसन्नयं तवाभिमतो जन इति विवस्वत्तेजोऽनुगामिना प्राक्कालिकया किमपि मन्दं मन्दं मध्याह्नहेतोरव्यक्तं दृष्ट पूर्वेणेदानीं सायाह्नीभूतदीनदिवसान्तः पिहितदिनकरकरे वनप्रदेशेऽस्मिन् तेजो शशिनोत्तरप्रदेशान्निर्गच्छतामुना स जन उत्तरदेशस्थ इति मे प्रतिभाति इत्युक्तवानस्मि। एवं दिङ्मोहपदे ध्वनिः।

एवममुना स ध्वनिना ग्रन्थेन तत्स्थितिं राज्ञे विज्ञाप्य तन्मुख एव पश्यंस्तिष्ठेत्। अथ राज एवं तस्मिन् विज्ञापयति किमपि किमपि श्रृण्वन्नपि तद्गतिं तथा मन्वानस्समीपस्थायां तस्यानवाप्तिहेतोरुद्भूतया स्मरपरवशतया तिष्ठन्नपि स्वमतिगतिं तत्र नीयमानस्तिष्ठेत्।

---

11 स्पष्टोक्तिः stands for ऋजूक्तिः, वक्रोक्तिः for dhvani.

अथ विदूषकस्तथा विज्ञाप्य तिष्ठन्नमुं तथाभूतं दृष्ट्वेति स्मरेत्। अहो असौ तत्सान्निध्यात् स्मरशरपरवशीकृतचित्तो वा तत्प्राप्त्युपायचिन्ता चिन्तयन् वा तद्गतचित्ततया किमितिकर्तव्यतामौढ्यं सम्प्राप्य वा तिष्ठेत्। तन्मयेदानीमस्य निजमतिमोहो विज्ञापयितव्य इत्यात्मना निश्चित्य भूयस्तच्छेषग्रन्थेन तं विज्ञापयति भो वयस्येति। पुनरपि सम्बुद्ध्याह **दिसा मोहे वि अकालमोहो संवुत्तो** इति। एतद्वनंप्रविष्टेन मया तद्गतिरनुमिता यदा तदा प्रविष्टस्य तवापि कालमोहः संवृत्त इव मे प्रतिभाति। काल मो संवुत्तो वि अ कालमोहो मतिमोहः। तत्र वने मतिमोहसंवृत्त इव मे प्रतिभातीत्यर्थः।

'कालादिपरिमाणे च कालशब्दो मतो भवेत्' इत्यनेकार्थोक्तिः। तस्मादत्र मतिरुच्यते। तस्या मोहः कालमोह इति भावः।

अथ विदूषकस्तथा विज्ञापयन्ननन्यविदिव तिष्ठन्तं तं पश्यन् भूयोपीति स्मरेत्। अहो विज्ञापितमेतदपीदं निवारयन् तिष्ठति। तस्य मतिगतिं पृष्ट्वा सा ज्ञेयेति निश्चित्य तन्मतिगतिं ज्ञातुं तच्छेषग्रन्थेन पृच्छति। तत्राप्युच्चैराहूय बोधयित्वाह **को कालो वंट इ**; कः कालो वर्तते।

भुक्तपूर्वां मालिनीं त्यक्त्वा अदृष्टपूर्वायामन्यस्यां त्वन्मतिगतिर्वर्तते किं कालः कः वर्तते। कालं कीदृग्भूतं वर्तते, यन्मतिः कीदृग्भूतो वर्तत इति भावः। कस्य त्वन्मतिर्वर्तते इति ध्वनिनोच्यते इत्यादि सर्वं ध्वनिना विज्ञाप्य तद्वचनं श्रोतुकामस्तमेव पश्यंस्तिष्ठेत्। एवं संव आलरमणिज्ज इत्यादि प्रयोगमार्गः।

राजा – सावधानं समन्तादवलोक्य अथ राजा स्वानुकूलतया निजमतिगतिं व्यङ्ग्येन पृष्ट्वा तां जिज्ञासुस्तिष्ठन्तं दृष्ट्वेति स्मरेत्। एनं मन्मतिगतिं विज्ञापयन्ती वाणी केनापि कदाचित् किं न श्रुता भवेदिति मनसा विमृश्य सावधानं समन्तादवलोकितवान्। इत्थमवलोक्य न कमप्यदृष्ट्वापि भूयोपीति विमृशेत्। कुतः,

यदि गोप्यं लतावृक्षं वनैः पिहितभूमिषु।
प्रदेशेषु न वक्तव्यं श्रोतव्योक्ता भवेद्यदि।। इत्यस्ति बृहस्पतेरुक्तिः।

किञ्च यत् किञ्चित् वक्तुकामः तं सखायं गोप्यमिष्टतः क्षेत्रेष्वह्निपदे वदेत् तं तत् श्रोतव्यं नामुतो भवेत्। अयं सुरासुराचार्ययोर्विधिश्चेत्येतदस्मात् गोप्यव्यवहारस्य न पात्रं वनप्रदेशं तस्मादहमपि ध्वनिगर्भया वाचा एवमनुनीय मन्मतिर्गतं यथावृत्तं कथयामीत्यात्मना निश्चित्य तदावर्जनाय सप्रवणं तिष्ठन् पश्येत्। अथ तस्मिन्नेवं पश्यति, विदूषकः स्वदृष्ट्या वदेति प्रेरयंस्तिष्ठेत्।

अथैवं प्रेर्यमाणो राजा सधैर्यं नम्रतनुर्भूत्वा बाहुभ्यां वसनाञ्चलमवभृतं दक्षिणपादाङ्गुष्ठेन भुवमालिखन् गूढं ताराभ्यां सप्रेम पश्यन् उत्तरग्रन्थमाह शङ्के इति। इमां मन्मतिगतिं यथावृत्तं गन्तुं शङ्कनीयं भवन्तं शङ्के शङ्कया न प्रभुरस्येति दृशोर्विभावयन् पूर्ववत् तिष्ठेत्।

अथ तेनेत्यावर्ज्यमानो विदूषकस्तदा तद्बाहुं स्वबाहुना गृहीत्वा 'वदवदे'ति दृग्भ्यां प्रेरयंस्तिष्ठन् नाना जनांस्तत्कालोचितानि व्यवहरन् तिष्ठेत्। तदा राजा तदाभिमुख्यं दृष्ट्वा तद्विश्वस्य पुनरपि तमेव ग्रन्थमाह शङ्कि इति। पूर्वं कार्तिकेयावासे कर्णपूरमुद्दिश्य परस्परमावाभ्यां क्रियमाणं स्वैरालापं यथाश्रुतवती मालती लतान्तरितदेहा तथेदानीमपि मयोच्यमानो मन्मतिं न श्रृणोमि किं सा इतीव शङ्के वक्तुं अथेति निशितधिया तेनेति प्रबोधितो विदूषकस्तदानीं साधारणस्त्रीभिरेवमगम्यमेतद्वनं यत् तस्मात् त्वया यथेच्छं वक्तव्या सेति बोधयंस्तिष्ठेत्।

अथ तदा राजा तथाभूतं वास्तववादिनं स्ववयस्यं तद्विश्वस्तस्तद्गतोपीति स्मरेत्। अहं कथङ्कारमिदानीं मय्यकृत्रिमस्नेहवानपीममेनां विज्ञापयामि। अथ किं व्यङ्ग्येन, तत्र गौरवं; तस्मात् पूर्वप्रस्तुतेन तत्पृष्टेन कालशब्देन मयापि तदुत्तरं पिशुनयता वचसा मन्मतिगतिर्विज्ञापितव्येत्यात्मना निश्चित्योत्तरग्रन्थेन स्वमतिगतिं स ध्वनिना विज्ञापयति। अथ राजैवं निश्चित्य तन्मुखे पश्यंस्तिष्ठन्निति विज्ञापयेत्।

'भो वयस्य त्वन्मतिगतिं कथङ्कारमिदानीं वर्तत इति त्वया पृष्टम्। तामीदृशीति वक्तुमहमपि न शक्नोति। तथापि समासेन कथयामि। तस्मात् त्वन्मनीषयैव सावधानं ज्ञायताम्। पश्य प्रायेण दृशि सा वर्तते शिशिरवसन्तयोरयमन्तरालिकः कालः। अनाश्रयीभूतो मे मनोयत्नः यत् कथङ्कारमिति चेत् श्रूयताम्। पूर्वं मालिन्या ममाभिमुख्यं कर्तुं शिशिरीभूतेन तत्प्रयत्नेन कथञ्चित् किमपि किमपि रममाणं काञ्चित् यात्रां मनोऽयं मदीयमालम्बते स्म। तत्पुनर्यान्या मन्मनःपद्मस्य वसन्तीभूतास्मद्दर्शनपथे तिरोधानतत्परा तां प्राप्तुमक्षमं च। पूर्वं मालिनीमालम्ब्य यथा कथञ्चिद्वर्तमानं मन्मनो यत् तदिदानीं मालिन्या निर्मूलं प्राग्गम्यान्यस्या अदर्शनात् यथा सुखं प्रवेष्टुं तत्राक्षमं भूत्वा तयोरन्तरालेनाश्रयमितस्ततः परिभ्रमति। एवम्भूतः कालः; एवम्भूतो मे मनोयत्नः तथापि एवं वर्तते।'

यदिति कुरुते कथमिति चेत् श्रूयताम् –

अप्रत्यूहमहर्मुखार्कमहसामत्यर्थमम्भोरुहा-
मातङ्कार्पणदुर्बलं हिमजलं जातं जराजर्जरम्।
प्रत्यस्तप्रसवामपोह्य फलिनीं भृङ्गीकटाक्षः शनैः
अभ्यर्णप्रसवामशोकलतिकामभ्येतुमाकाङ्क्षति।।

इति। इत्यस्मिन् ध्वनिर्दृश्यते। तथापि हिमजलमम्भोरुहामस्मच्चेतोवृत्तीनामातङ्कार्पणदुर्बलं, आतङ्कार्पणाय दुर्बलं हिमजलं मालिन्याख्यं कलत्रं जातमभूत्। सखे हिमजलं मम कलत्रं हि जलं यथा पद्मं मुकुलयत् तथा मन्मनःपद्मं मुकुलयत्। यत् कलत्रं ममासीत् तदिदानीमन्यामुद्दिश्य त्वहं प्रवृत्तमानामस्मच्चेतः तत्प्रवृत्तीनामातङ्कार्पणदुर्बलं जातम्। आतङ्कं भयं भयार्पणाय अशक्तं जातमशक्तमासीत्। कस्माच्चेत् अत्यर्थं जराजर्ज्जरमेतत् तत्पदं हेतुगर्भं तद्धेतोरित्यर्थः। अथवा हिमजलवदासारभूतं वा जराजर्ज्जरमिति वार्धकावस्थाहेतोः जर्जरं शोणितहीनं च, तथा भूतत्वादस्मच्चेतः प्रवृत्तीनामातङ्कार्पणदुर्बलं जातं; किञ्च

स्वान्यूनवयसः पुंसा कन्याया गृह्यतां करः।
अतुल्यवयस्का या नान्यस्यात्तन्तुमिच्छता।।

अपि च

स्याद्वयोधिकया यो मा रमतेऽङ्गनया यया।
तस्य प्रज्ञां बलं कान्तिं तन्तुमायुश्च सा हरेत्।।

इति श्रुतिस्मृतिसिद्धं वचनम् ज्योतिश्शास्त्रे गुहेन दर्शितम्।

तस्माच्च जराजर्जरं पूर्वकलत्रं सन्तत्यर्थमत्यर्थं प्रवृत्तमानानामस्मच्चेतः प्रवृत्तीनामातङ्कार्पणदुर्बलं यन्मे कलत्रमासीत्। तामपोह्य भृङ्गीकटाक्षः अशोककलिकामभ्येतुमाकाङ्क्षति प्रत्यस्तप्रसवहेतुगर्भमभ्यर्ण-

प्रसवमित्येतच्च तां फलिनां इति मालिनीनामधेयां जायामपोह्य परित्यज्य भृङ्गीकटाक्षः मच्चेतःप्रयत्नः प्रत्यस्तप्रसवामिति निश्चित्य शिशिरावसानत्वात् तथाभूतामपोह्याशोककलिकां भविष्यत्पत्नीं अभ्येतुमाकाङ्क्षति। अभ्यर्णप्रसवामिति दर्शितस्वप्नस्य भगवतो भानोः प्रसादत्वादभ्यर्णप्रसवामिति निश्चित्य तथाभूतामशोककलिकामभ्येतुमाकाङ्क्षतीत्यस्मिन्ननेन ध्वन्यर्थेन प्रेक्षकान् सुखयित्वा भूयोऽपीति निजमतिं वृत्तिं यथावृत्तं विदूषकाय बोधयित्वा तिष्ठन्नयं बाह्यार्थेन नानाजनान् सुखयित्वा सङ्कल्पावस्थया निमीलिताक्षस्तिष्ठेत्। एवमस्य प्रयोगमार्गः।

विदू – पुरतो विलोक्य सविस्मयात् अथ विदूषकस्तेनैवं यथावृत्तं विज्ञापितां निजमतिगतिं श्रुत्वा तस्यां गतिं परिज्ञानेऽनुपायज्ञश्चकितमनास्सविवेकमुद्दृष्टि स्तिष्ठन्नयं तस्मात् किमपि दूरे उत्तरप्रदेशे जितविद्युत्तेजो दक्षिणाभिमुखं गच्छन् शनैरुत्तरोत्तराधिकं दृष्ट्वा स्वदृगुन्मीलनाशक्तस्सविस्मयं पुरतो विलोकितवान्। एतदर्थं **पुरतो विलोक्य** सविस्मयमिति प्रयुक्तवान् स कविः। अथैवं पुरतस्तस्य विस्मयं पश्यन् विदूषक इति विमृशेत्। तस्मादुत्तरप्रदेशे जितविद्युत्तेजोराशिर्लक्ष्यते। यत् तस्मादित उत्तरप्रदेशे तस्याः कार्तिकेयावासे दर्शितपदतलायास्ससख्याः दिव्ययुवतेरयं तेजोराशिरित्यूह्यम्। तस्मात्प्रदेशा-दुत्तरप्रदेशस्सवयस्येन मया गन्तव्यः खल्वित्यात्मगतं निश्चित्य राजानं पश्येत्। अथ तदा राजा सङ्कल्पावस्थावस्थितचित्तो अनन्यचित्तोऽनन्यवत् तिष्ठत्ययमिति यत् तस्मादहं लतावर्णनव्यपदेशेनोत्तरदेशोऽस्मात् गन्तव्य इत्येनमाहूय बोधयामीति निश्चित्योत्तरग्रन्थेन तं सम्बोधयति **भो व अ स** इति। एवं स्वसम्बोधनेनाप्यबोध्यमानं तं दृष्ट्वोत्तरग्रन्थमाह अच्छेरन्न इति। अथ राजा निश्चलाङ्गस्तिष्ठन्नाश्चर्यशब्दं श्रृण्वन् शनैर्दृष्ट्युन्मीलितं पश्यन् 'किमाश्चर्यमाश्चर्यमित्युक्तवानसी'ति विभावयंस्तिष्ठेत्। अथ विदूषकस्तदाभिमुखीभूतं दृष्ट्वेति स्मरेत्। इदानीं सा दिव्ययुवतिः सा तद्वयस्या च ते उभे अस्मादुत्तरदेशमधिवसत इति विज्ञाप्य भूय उत्तरग्रन्थेन तं वदति **ता प वि स दुदाव अ** भव इति।

तस्मात् पञ्चषानि पदानि गत्वा प्रविशतु इति विज्ञाप्य गन्तुकामस्तिष्ठेत्। प्राकृतशब्दस्य द्विवचनाभावात् बहुवचनं लतासु निर्दिश्यते, सा सखी च तत्रस्थेति भावः।[12]

अथ राजा तेन विज्ञापितस्तदेकदेशमनेन ज्ञातम्। सा तत्रस्थेति अवगन्तव्यमिति निश्चित्य तत्प्रवेष्टुं परिक्रामति। तथोभौ परिक्रामतः।

अथ राजा तद्वनं प्रविश्य तिर्यक्पश्यन्नुत्तरककुभः प्रनिस्सरन् तं तेजोराशिं जितविद्युतं निश्चलं दृष्ट्वेति स्मरेत्। कुतः कस्यचिद्दिव्ययुवतेः कमपि युवानं हृदयस्थं कृत्वा सङ्कल्पसमागममनुभवन्त्या वा तपःकुर्वन्त्या वाऽयं दृश्यमानः तेजोराशिः किञ्चिदुद्दृष्टिस्मरन् तपःकुर्वन्त्या नेति महद्गिरा दर्शितेन वचनेन निश्चितवानस्मि। कुतः,

तपसे कल्पिता धात्रा भूश्शस्ता प्राग्गिरेस्तटे।
ऐन्द्रीमुद्दिश्य वा याम्यामाशां वा स्यन्दते जलम्।।

---

12 वणलताकण्णआओ (वनलताकन्यकाः). Heroine and her maid are referred to here. It should have been in dual number. But plural is used as the Prākṛt has no dual number.

This remark is significant. It shows that vidūṣaka followed the dramatic text strictly and used only Prākṛt. He did not use even the Sanskrit version which was added later to the text.

No more proof is needed to confirm that vidūṣaka did not use Sanskrit or regional language at the time of Kulaśekhara.

इत्यगस्त्येन भगवता तपोयोग्यां भुवं पृच्छते सनत्कुमारायोपदिष्टा। किञ्च,

गोष्ठीं कर्तुं रसविदो पुंसे भूः कल्पिता पुरा।
वारुण्या सौम्यया यत्र वारि याति गिरेस्तटे।।
तत्र स्त्रीभिरपां पुंभिर्गोष्ठी सा क्रियतां सुखम्।
समागमो वा सङ्कल्पैरलब्धे पुंसि वा स्त्रियाम्।।
दक्षिणाभिमुखं याति वारि यत्र गिरेस्तटे।
केनाप्यजानता तत्र गोष्ठी सा क्रियते यदि।
स्वदेशोऽस्य मनः पुंसः तस्याश्च भ्रमता नयेत्।।

इत्यस्ति कामशास्त्रे वनक्रीडाविधावाचार्येण देशविभागः कृतः।

तस्मादयं प्रदेश उत्तराभिमुखं गच्छन् वारि धत्ते यतः तेनाहं काचिद्दिव्ययुवतिः संकल्पसमागमोत्सवमनुभवतीति निस्चितवानस्मि। तस्मादहमेनं गोष्ठीयोग्या भूस्सेति विज्ञाप्य भूयस्त्वयैकदेशमेव लज्जितमिति विज्ञापयामीति निश्चित्य पुनः विदूषकं पश्यन् गोष्ठी समा भूस्सेति तं विज्ञाप्य भूयस्त दुक्तेरेकदेशानुवादायोत्तरग्रन्थमाह – **सखे सम्यगुपलक्षितम्**; त्वया सम्यगुपलक्षितम्। एकदेशं लक्षितं दृष्टं; भूयस्तमेव पश्यन् मयोपलक्षितमेव यथार्थं तं न लक्षितमिति कथं ज्ञातवानसीति चेत् पश्य। यत्वया लताव्यपदेशेन काचित् युवतिस्ससखी तत्रोत्तरदेशे वर्तत इति यद् विज्ञापितं तदेकदेशमेव तथा भवति। सा सखीति यदुच्यते तत् तथा न तया विरहितेति ज्ञेयम्। तदर्थमुपलक्षितमित्युक्तवानस्मि। सा तत्र वर्तत इति यत्, तत् तथा स्यात्। स्वयमेव तत्र वर्तत इति ज्ञायत इति विज्ञापयंस्तिष्ठेत्।

विदू – अथ विदूषकस्तथा विज्ञाप्य तिष्ठन्तं तं वीक्ष्य 'तर्हि किमर्थं सा स्वयमेव तत्र वर्तते। किञ्च स्वयमेव तत्र वर्तमानायास्तस्याः प्रवृत्तिश्च केति मां विज्ञापये'ति दृशोर्विभावयंस्तिष्ठेत्। अथ राजा तथा तिष्ठन्तं तं वीक्ष्येति स्मरेत्। अहमिदानीमेत-ज्जिज्ञासवेऽमुष्मै लतावर्णनव्यवदेशेनैव तदीयां प्रवृत्तिं विज्ञापयामीत्यात्मना निश्चित्योत्तरग्रन्थेन तां विज्ञापयति। तद्विज्ञापनप्रकारं दर्शयति। सखे तर्हि श्रूयताम्। अत्र हि

आपाटलं किसलयाधरमर्पयन्ती
व्यावृण्वती मधुपझङ्कृतिसीत्कृतानि।
अभ्याशपूतमरविन्दकुचोपपीड-
मत्यायतं समुपगूहति कल्पवल्ली।।

इति। सखे अत्र काचित् कल्पवल्ली अभ्याशपूतमुपगूहति हि इति संबन्धः। अत्र काचित् कल्पवल्ली दिव्ययुवतिः अभ्याशे हृदये पूतं प्रेयांसं सङ्कल्पैस्सन्निधायाशेषं समागमं करोति, कुरुते।

आपाटलं किसलयाधरमर्पयन्ती
व्यावृण्वती मधुपझङ्कृतिसीत्कृतानि।

अरविन्दकुचोपपीडमिति। अरविन्दं मुकुलवत् प्रोद्गतस्य कुचयुगस्य पीडां विस्मरन्ती तत् क्रियाविशेषणम्। अत्यन्तमनोभीष्टं प्रेयांसमित्यर्थः। उपगूहति हि इति निश्चये। कथं निश्चिनुष इति चेत्। पश्य,

प्रेयस्यलब्धे सङ्कल्पैरनन्यस्त्रीजनोऽमुना।
समं रहति सङ्गम्य प्रणश्येत् तत्सुखैश्शुचम्।।

किञ्च

रहस्थश्चेतसा लब्धे प्रेयसि स्त्रीजनोऽन्वितम्।
रमयेत् प्रतिपत्या स्वनिवासे तत् शुचं हरेत्।।

अपि च

अनन्यानन्यवित् प्राप्य रहस्था तन्मनस्कताम्।
आत्मानं रमयेत् स्त्रीणां घटेयं योगिनामिव।।

इत्यस्ति वात्स्यायनसूत्रं दर्शयता भगवताचार्येण तदलाभे तच्छर्मणे प्रदर्शितमुपायः। तदर्थं हि इति निश्चये प्रयुक्तवानस्मि। तस्मात् काचित् दिव्ययुवतिः स्वयमेव भूत्वा तदभावे संकल्पसमागमोत्सवमनुभवन्तीति निश्चिनु। इत्यनेन श्लोकेन तत्प्रवृत्तिः तथा भूतां विज्ञाप्य तन्मुखे पश्यन्नेवं तिष्ठेत्।

अथ विदूषकस्तदा तस्मिन्नेवं विज्ञापयति तदलाभे प्रदर्शित उपाय इति विज्ञापितः तच्छब्देनैव काचित्कल्पवल्लीति कथं निश्चितवानसि। कल्पतरुर्न किमित्यन्यापदेशेन पृच्छंस्तिष्ठेत्। अथैवमन्तराले पृच्छति तस्मिन्नपि राजा तच्छ्रुत्वा तदानीं कोपि न काचिदेवेति उपपत्तिभिर्दर्शयेत्। सखे तर्हि पश्य –

यत् तेजः पुरुषाज्जातं महत्वेन तपोभृतः।
तत् तु किञ्चित्सुतीक्ष्णं स्यात् भानुभागभिवर्धितम्।।
वामायाश्चापि यज्जातं महत्वेन तपोभृतः।
तत् सशैत्यं सलावण्यं चन्द्रभागभिवर्धितम्।।

इत्यस्ति प्रजासर्गविधाने परमेष्ठिना विभक्तं पुराणे व्यासेन भगवता प्रदर्शितम्। अनेन लक्ष्मणा कान्तारे लतागुल्मवृक्षशाखोपशाखे पिहितदिनकरे सायाह्नीभूतदिनदशायां तत्तेजस्तादृक् पश्यन् कस्याश्चिदिति निश्चितवानस्मि। तर्हि कथं सङ्कल्पसमागममनुभवतीति ज्ञायते इति चेत्। पश्य –

यस्मात्तन्निस्सृतं तेजः पुंसो वापि स्त्रियोऽथवा।
तद्यदि स्थिरतामेति तत् तेजः स्थिरतां व्रजेत्।।

इत्यस्ति शिल्पशास्त्रे विश्वकर्मणा प्रोक्तम्। तत उपगूहतीत्युक्तवानस्मीति ध्वन्यर्थेन तत्प्रवृत्तिं विज्ञाप्य भूयः स्वयं भरतवरः सा लता भूत्वा बाह्यार्थमभिनयेन नानालोकान् सुखयेत्। एवमस्य प्रयोगमार्गः।[13]

किञ्च अनेन श्लोकेनास्याः प्रवेशकालावस्था तथाभूतेति कविना दर्शिता।

अथ विदूषकस्तेनैवं प्रदर्शितमेतत् यथाभूतमेवैतदिति विज्ञाय तत्परिहारज्ञानहेतोस्सहसा हीहीत्युत्तरग्रन्थेन सविस्मयं तं सम्मानयन् उत्तरग्रन्थमाह **अदिट्ठपुरुवाणी**त्यादि। अदृष्टपूर्वाणि तादृशीनि स्त्रीणां सङ्कल्पसमागमादि कर्माणि द्रक्ष्यमाणो ममाशा इदानीमित्यासीत्। तवेयं प्रवृत्तिर्न साध्येयमिति मन्यमानस्य मम सम्प्रत्याशान्यथासीत्।

13 Another instance of multiple impersonation. This time the actor transforms himself to a creeper.

साध्येयमिति। तस्मात् पूर्वप्रार्थितमम्बरगमनमपि कदाचित् संभवेदिति तर्कयामि। पूर्वप्रार्थितमिति पूर्वं मया त्वत्सिद्धान्तस्यैकदेशं ज्ञात्वा भूयोऽम्बरगमनमूर्ध्वगमनमुत्तरसिद्धान्तमजानता मया पृष्टं यत् तच्छनैर्वा त्वयोच्यमानं श्रुत्वा सा न साध्येति मन्यमानोहं सा प्राप्येति तर्कयामीति इमं ध्वन्यर्थं राज्ञे विज्ञापयंस्तिष्ठेत्।

राजा – स्पर्शमभिनीय; अथ राजा तत्प्राप्तेरुपायचिन्तां स्मरंस्तिष्ठन्नयं समहिषाक्षं सकुङ्कुमरेणुं सकर्पूरं सधूपं कमपि मन्दमारुतं सहसा प्राप्तवान्। तदा स्पर्शमभिनीय गन्धं जिघ्रन्नेवं स्मरेत्। हन्त वृक्षलतागुल्मनिचयैः पिहितस्य मत्पुरोवर्तिनः कस्यचित् देवस्य काञ्चित् सपर्यां परिसमाप्तां शंसति मे मन्दमारुतः।

सा तया दिव्ययुवत्या सम्पादिता किं न भवेत्? तत्पुरोदेशे गत्वा देवप्रणमनेन सर्वं विज्ञातव्यं इत्यात्मना निश्चित्य पुनर्विदूषकमुखे पश्यन्नुत्तरग्रन्थेन तं देवमन्दिरं विज्ञापयति प्रत्यासन्नेनेत्यादिना। विज्ञाप्य भूयः कयाचित् युक्त्या सम्पादितेयं सपर्येत्युत्तरश्लोकेन समर्थयति –

सम्मूर्च्छं महिषाक्षधूमकलिकाधूम्रः इत्यादिना इत्यस्य प्रयोगमार्गो दर्श्यते। किञ्चित् नम्रतनुस्तिष्ठेत्। सखे इति दृग्भ्यामेनं सम्बुद्ध्या विज्ञापयेत्।

अमी वनान्तमरुतो मनसा पुटं तथा लिम्पति हि इति संबन्धः; तथेति कथमिति चेत्। यथा मन्मनोसिद्धिर्भविष्यतीति भावः। तत् कथं ज्ञायत इति तदा पृच्छन्निव विभावयन्तं तिष्ठन्तं विदूषकं वीक्ष्येति विज्ञापयेत्। कुतः कयाचित् कन्यया कृतेयं सपर्येति त्वमवगच्छ कस्मादिति चेत् पश्य –

कन्यां पूजाविधौ पूजाकल्पितेति पुरा परम्।
प्रणामार्चनं भक्त्या धूपं दिव्यैः सगन्धिभिः।।
महिषाक्षप्रधानेन प्रारम्भे धूपयेत् सुरम्।
सत्कुङ्कुमप्रधानेन पूजाया मध्यमे परम्।।
सत्कर्पूरप्रधानेन जधन्ये मुख्यमुच्यते।
अच्छिन्नधूपं क्रियतां कन्याभिः पूजनं विभोः।।
इषुपातमात्रगन्धेन धूपेनैनं प्रधूपयेत्।
इति प्रोक्तं भगवता महेशेन महात्मना।।
पृच्छन्त्यै पूजनविधिं पार्वत्यै कन्यकां प्रति।

इत्येतन्निमित्तमेषा सपर्या तया कृता भवेदिति स्मृत्वा मन्मनोरथसिद्धिर्भविष्यतीति मयोक्तम्। किञ्च अमी अस्माकमध्वक्लमं लुम्पन्त इति कथमिति चेत् श्रृणु –

कार्येषु यत्नः क्रियतां जनैरुच्चैर्बुधैरपि।
यत्नजस्यात् समो नष्टः कार्यप्राप्तौ सुखं व्रजेत्।।

इत्यस्ति बृहस्पतेरुक्तिः। तन्निमित्तमध्वक्लमं लुम्पन्त इत्युक्तवानस्मीत्यवगच्छ, मरुत इति बहुवचननिर्देशात् किमुच्यत इति चेत् श्रूयताम्

'चित्ते वायौ च विबुधे मरुच्छब्दोत्र वर्तते।' इत्यनेकार्थोक्तिः।

मम चित्तमन्तर्वर्ती वायुर्लोलवायुश्च इमां स्त्रीनुद्दिश्य मरुत इत्यत्र बहुवचनेनोक्तवानस्मि। नासापुटं लुम्पन्तीति कथमुक्तवानिति चेत्। पश्य नासिकाग्रस्थं रन्ध्रयुग्मं नासापुटं तयोरेकं लिम्पति। 'एकं प्रधानं

पुंसः प्रधानं दक्षिणं ममान्तर्वायुश्च तन्नासापुटस्थः यस्य कैर्यस्मृतौ। यस्यां तन्नासिकापुटस्थो देवश्चेत् सद्यः सिध्यति तत्फलम्।' इत्यस्ति वचनम्। अनेन च भूयश्चित्तं चैवं वदति। अमी त्रयः एवं वदन्ति, तस्मात्तन्मनोरथसिद्धि भविष्यतीत्यात्मना निश्चित्यामी वनगतमरुतो मम नासापुटं लिम्पन्ति हि नूनम्। इति चोक्तवानस्मीत्यनेन प्रेक्षकान् सुखयित्वा भूयः पूजावर्णनमभिनयेन कृत्वा नानालोकान् विनोदयेत्।

एवमस्य प्रयोगमार्गः।

अथ राजेत्थं पुनः प्रेक्षकान् नानाश्च विनोदयित्वा सप्रवणं सधैर्यं सलज्जं सान्तर्मोदं विदूषकं पश्यन्नयं तत्र गन्तुं मां त्वरयेति विभावयंस्तिष्ठेत्। अथ तत्मिन्नेवं तिष्ठति विदूषकस्तेन दर्शितमखिलं तथ्यमिति विदित्वाग्रे गन्तुमुद्युक्तश्चरणशब्दं नियम्य शनैः प्रक्षिप्तपादस्तिर्यक् पश्यन्नयं कृकलासादि प्राणसञ्चारणे सावधानं पश्य। हास्यरसं द्योतयन् ध्वनिद्योतितमर्थं किमप्यर्धमर्धं प्रहसनप्रधानेन वदन्नग्रतो गच्छेत्। राजापि तत्पश्यन् व्यवहारं विना पृष्टतो गच्छेत्।

एवमुभौ परिक्रमतः।

अथाग्रगामी विदूषकश्चोत्तरोत्तराधिकसौरभ्यं धूपं वहता देवमन्दिरान्निस्सृतेन मरुतादिष्टेन वर्त्मना गच्छन्नयं दक्षिणनासिकापुटेन तद्गन्धं जिघ्रन् वर्त्मन्यास्थाय स चैतं श्लोकार्थं मनसा स्मृत्वा सावधानमग्रे पश्यन् किमपि देवमन्दिरं दिव्यवृक्षलताच्छन्नं तद्विवरेण कथञ्चिद्दृष्ट्वा नायकमुखे पश्यन्निमं श्लोकार्थं व्यक्तं प्रबोधयेत्। कुतः,

कार्यमुद्दिश्य यत् किञ्चिन्निर्गच्छन्तं गृहान्तरम्।
यमन्वेति शनैर्वायुः सद्य एव तदेति सः।।
प्रविशन्तं च यं वेश्म यत्किञ्चित्साधितुं नरम्।
प्रत्युद्याति चलन् वायुः तस्य तत् सिध्यति ध्रुवम्।।

इत्यस्ति ज्योतिश्शास्त्रे यात्राविधौ कार्यावाप्तिपरिज्ञानार्थं निमित्तमार्गः प्रदर्शितो भगवता सुब्रह्मण्येन।

तस्मादेतत् वृक्षच्छन्नं देवमन्दिरं प्रविशतोर्नौ कार्यसिद्धिर्संभविष्यतीव मे प्रतिभातीति पथि तिष्ठता विदूषकेण विज्ञापिते देवमन्दिरे राजा सावधानमग्रतः पश्यन् देवमन्दिरं दृष्ट्वा स्वक्षीणदेहार्धं सरोमाञ्चं दृष्ट्वा स्वश्वासप्रतिपालनं कुर्वन्नयं स्वरोमाञ्चं वयस्याय दर्शयन् सन्तोषसन्तापे दक्षिणापरनेत्रयोः पृथक् विभावयन्निदं कार्यसिद्धिशंसिनिमित्तलक्ष्मेति तं प्रबोधयेत्।[14] कुतः 'पुंसः प्रविशतो वेश्म कार्यार्थं दक्षिणाङ्गके। सम्भूतं यदि रोमाञ्चं' दृष्ट्वा स्वश्वासप्रतिपालनं कुर्वन्नयं स्वरोमाञ्चं वयस्याय दर्शयन् सन् तेनैवालग्नसिद्ध्यै,

तन्नासायास्तु रन्ध्रेण देवो निर्याति चेदयम्।
तद् वेश्मन्येव सद्यस्तत् तस्य कार्यं हि सिध्यति।।
दक्षिणाङ्गे सरोमाञ्चनासाभ्यां चेत्स वर्तते।
तस्मादन्यत्र सिद्धिस्यादिति पुंसः स्त्रियोन्यथा।।

इति गुहवचननिर्दिष्टलक्ष्मणेन उच्छ्वाससंप्रतिपालनं कुर्वता मया देवं नासिकायुगगतं दृष्ट्वास्माद्देवमन्दिरादन्यत्र साध्यमस्मत्कार्यमिति निश्चितवानस्मि। तथापि शीघ्रं प्रवेष्टव्यमेतदिति दृग्भ्यां प्रेरितो विदूषकं शनैर्स राजा

14 This is a very important direction to the actor. At the Zenith of his histrionic talents the actor expresses different emotions in both the eyes. This later came to be called एकलोचनम्। Perhaps a conveniently shortened form for एकैकस्मिन् लोचने भिन्नभावौ।

व्रजन् देवमन्दिरमुपेत्य बहिरेव तिष्ठन् प्रसादान्तस्सावधानं दृष्टी चारयन्नवसान्द्रीकृतसपर्यं गर्भगृहं विलोक्य पार्श्वस्थस्य नायकस्य मुखे पश्यन् त्वन्निमित्तपरिज्ञाननैशित्येन त्वं बहुमन्यमानोस्मीति दृग्भ्यां तत्प्रशंसां कृत्वा भूयोपि गर्भगृहे दृष्टीं नीत्वा सा सम्प्रत्येवं तत्पूजां कृत्वा निर्गतवतीति दृग्भ्यां संबोधयित्वापि भूयोपि तमिति विभावयन् यदा स्वदेहार्धं वामभागात् प्रविश्य दैवं तथाविधे हीति समर्थयन्नुत्तरग्रन्थमाह **भो सम्पतह्न देवमन्दिरं पविसि अपणमह्म** इति तद्ग्रन्थस्य प्रयोगमार्गं दर्शयति सम्पतं ह इति। संप्राप्ता स्म इति पदे प्रोच्यमाने दृष्टिभ्यामिति बोधयेत्। सात्र संप्राप्तेति द्रष्टव्यं पूजाचिह्नैः इत्येतदाच्छादनार्थं पुनरुत्तमपदे समर्पयति सात्र सम्प्राप्तेति भावः। इतीमं ध्वन्यर्थं दृष्टिभ्यां तद्बोधयन् देवग्रहोदरे स्वदृष्टी नयन्नन्तरान्तरा नायकमुखं पश्यन्नयं विदूषकः सविवेकं तिष्ठेत्।

अथ राजा तेन विज्ञापितं तत् तथ्यमेवेति मनसा विमृश्य तन्मुखे शनैः पश्यन् सधैर्यं तर्हि तथाकुर्वं इति दृष्टिभ्यां तं सम्प्रेर्य तिष्ठेत्। अथैवं प्रेर्यमाणो विदूषकस्स च तावुभौ तदा तत्प्रविशतः।

अथैवं प्रविष्टयोस्तत्रस्थं कल्याणवामनाख्यं देवं बलिवैरिणमापादतलमस्तकं तं च तत्पूजाविधानं च पश्यन् भक्तिपूर्वं मूर्ध्नि बद्धाञ्जलिस्तं प्रणमन् नत्वा कयापि दिव्यकन्यकया कृतसपर्येयमिति निश्चित्य भूयोपि विदूषकमित्थं बोधयेत्। कुतः –

कर्णवेधेन शस्ताब्दादारभ्यादशमाब्दतः।
गणेशस्यैव भूयोऽस्मादारभ्याद्वादशाब्दतः।।
कुमारस्यापि दुर्गाया विष्णोर्वा वटुरूपिणः।
पूजास्सत्कन्यकाः कुर्युन्मन्मथारेर्न जातुचित्।।
मनुनेति पुराचारः कन्यकानां प्रकल्पितः।
वरस्य गुणिनो लब्ध्यै यत्ते तज्जन्मता भवेत्।।

इत्यतस्सैवेयमत्रोपेत्य वटुरूपिणं चराचरगुरुमभ्यर्च्य सम्प्रत्येवास्मान्निर्गतवती सैवायमिति। कथं ज्ञायत इति चेत् या पूर्वं यादृग्विधाभिस्सुमनोभिः कार्तिकेयाराधनं कृतवती तादृग्विधाभिरेवैनमपि एतदर्थं सैवेयमिति निश्चितवानस्मीत्यादि सर्वं तं बोधयित्वा भक्तिपूर्वं बद्धाञ्जलिर्नम्रतनुस्तिष्ठन्नुत्तरश्लोकेन कन्यकापूजार्होऽयं देव इति समर्थयति **धृताषाढमि**त्यादिना। 'आषाढो दण्ड उच्यते' धृतदण्ड इत्यर्थः। इत्यनेन श्लोकेनैनं प्रणम्य मम सन्तत्यर्थं तदुद्वाहनं कारयेति तं प्रार्थयन् भगवते तिष्ठमानस्तदा स्वदेहार्धं सरोमाञ्चं दृष्ट्वा स्वश्वासप्रतिपालनं कुर्वाणो दक्षिणनासारन्ध्रप्रस्थमन्तर्देवं विज्ञायेति स्मरेत्।

योयमुद्दिश्य यत्किञ्चित् देवमिष्टं प्रवन्दते।
तदा सव्येतरे घोणे देवश्चेत् वर्तते तनौ।
वामायां यदि रोमाञ्चं तस्य तत् कृच्छ्रतो भवेत्।। इत्यस्ति गुरुवचनम्।

तथाप्यस्य देवस्य प्रणामेन तथाभूतस्य मम तत्कार्यं कृच्छ्रसाध्यमित्यूह्यम्। इति स्मरन् नायकस्तस्या दुर्लभत्वात् सङ्कल्पसमागमात् परां शरीरस्थितिकारणेऽन्नरसेऽपि विरक्तिदां स्मरदशामारुह्य तं देवं भक्तिपूर्वं प्रणमन् तिष्ठेत्। एवमेतावतः सङ्कल्पावस्था स्मरदशा।

अतः परमाद्वितीयाङ्कपरिसमाप्तेः भोजनविरक्तिता। एतस्मात् भोजनविरक्तितां दशामारभ्य तं देवं प्रणमंस्तिष्ठेत्। अथ विदूषको नायकं तथाभूतं दृष्ट्वा स्मरावस्थया यथाक्रममापीड्यमानं दृष्ट्वेति स्मरेत्। अहो अस्यानवाप्तावमङ्गलदमेतद्दशा कार्यं हीति स्मृत्वा खिन्नमना उद्दृष्टिर्भूत्वा सविवेकं दीपाग्रे तिष्ठन् पुनरपीति स्मरेत्। अहो सम्प्रति कीदृशी अस्य स्मरदशा इति विमृश्य तां ज्ञातुं तन्मुख एव पश्यंस्तिष्ठेत्। अथ तदा राजा तदा भक्तिपूर्वं तमेव प्रणमन्नयं शनैः कम्पितदेहस्तिष्ठेत्। अथ तथा तिष्ठन्तं तमापादतलमस्तकं पश्यन्निति विमृशेत्। अहो अयं कम्पितदेहो यत् तस्माश्चतुर्थीं दशां सम्प्राप्तोऽयमिति निश्चितवानस्मि। तस्मात्कथङ्कारमेनमेनां प्रापयामीति स्मरन्नयं देवमन्दिरोदरे तिर्यक् पश्यंस्तिष्ठेत्।

अथ तदा राजा तामपश्यन् पूर्वं दृष्टं तत्तेजोऽपि देवमन्दिरस्थाभिः रत्नप्रभाभिस्तिरोहितत्वात् तेजसः तत्परिज्ञानचिह्नमजानन् सा देवसपर्यां कृत्वास्मात् गतवतीति निश्चित्य तत्प्राप्तौ च्छिन्नाशेन मनसा हृद्यङ्कुरितां रसवल्लीं श्लथयन् कम्पिततनुः कम्पिताभ्यां दोर्भ्यां मूर्ध्नि कृताञ्जलिः भक्तिपूर्वं **धृताषाढमिति** श्लोकमेवं वदन् तिष्ठेत्।

अथ विदूषकस्तथाभूते तस्मिन् देवमन्दिरोदरात् दृष्टी निवर्त्य तं पश्यन्नमुष्य हृद्गतां शुचं याथातथ्यं विदित्वा सनिर्वेदं सविवेकं तस्मात् गत्वा तिर्यक्पर्यटन्नयं सहसा तस्मादुत्तरप्रदेशादागच्छत् तद्रक्तदीपप्रभाभिर पहृतत्वान्नष्टं तत् तेजो रत्नदीपदूरत्वात् किमपि किमप्युत्तराधिकं तत्तेज एव दृष्टवान्। अथ तद्दृष्ट्वेति स्मरेत्। अहो तदीयमेवेदं तेजोवर्ती दृष्ट्वा वयस्ययानन्यविदे निवेदयामि। तस्मादेनमविज्ञाप्य विज्ञाप्य वा तामन्वेष्टुं गच्छेयम्। स्मृत्वा; विज्ञापनाशक्यत इति स्मृत्वा निश्चित्य नायकं पुनरप्युपसृत्य सव्यङ्ग्येनोत्तरग्रन्थेन नायकं विज्ञापयति **भो तुज्झलि हिद रव र ए** इति। अथ विदूषकस्तथाभूतं तं पश्यन्नयं स्वस्य स्वस्य तदन्वेषणेऽस्य प्रसादोऽस्ति वा न वेति परिज्ञातुं पृच्छति – भो वयस्य केवलं पौरुषेणैव महिषा पुंसाखिलं कर्म साध्यमिति स्मरता तपनवनं प्रविशता तत्तेजोत्तरोत्तराधिकं दृष्ट्वास्मिन् देवमन्दिरे ममाभिमतप्राप्तिः स्यादिति निश्चितवतात्रागत्य देवं पश्यता तत्कृतां पूजां परिसमाप्तां च दृष्ट्वा तत्तेजच्छिन्नमप्यदृष्ट्वा सा गतवतीति निश्चित्य सम्प्रति तदैवमेव प्रमाणमिति निश्चित्य तव चेतोभित्तौ अक्षरं अशून्यं लिखितया चित्तात् कदाचिदप्यनिर्गतया जिह्वयेति जिह्वया पुरुषार्थरसीसाधनीभूतया भविष्यत्पत्न्या अनुत्फुल्लैरिति तया दीप्यमानैः कम्पितगात्रैर्यत्नेन त्वयेदानीं देवोऽर्चितः। पौरुषं विना दैवमेव प्रमाणमिति। एवमिदानीं समर्पितवानसि न तत्र दोषो विद्यते। तथाहि –

यत्नं कृतवता पुंसा कार्यसिद्धिमविन्दता।
तां तेन खिन्नचित्तेन दैवमापदि चिन्त्यते।।

इत्यस्ति दाशरथये वसिष्ठेन विज्ञापितमित्येतद् वचनशक्त्या दैवमेवाधुना श्रितवानसीदानीमहमपि **अण खरिविभवो** इत्यादि अणवखरविभवो इति। नष्टपौरुषोपि केवलं परं कुसुमानि कुसुमवन्नश्यन्ति जातानि पुरुषकाराणि प्राप्य प्रयत्नमतःपरमपि कृत्वा तामन्विष्य दृष्ट्वा भवन्तमर्पयामि। इतीमं ध्वन्यर्थं नायकं विज्ञाप्य गन्तुकामस्तिष्ठेत्। अथ नायकः तत् श्रृण्वन्निमं पश्यन् तर्हि यत्र क्वापि तामन्विष्य दृष्ट्वा मामावेदयेति दृष्टिभ्यां संप्रेर्य तिष्ठेत्। अथ तौ दृष्टिभ्यामेवं परस्परं पृथक् पृथक् बोधयन्तौ तिष्ठेताम्। अथ विदूषकः पुनरपि स्वं ग्रन्थमुक्त्वा तदन्वेषणाय दैवमन्दिरतो निर्गतवान्।

एवं कुसुमान्वेषणच्छलेन तदन्वेषणाय गतोऽभूत् स विदूषकः।

राजा – सावधानमवलोकयन्। अथ राजा तस्मिन् गते पूर्वं कार्तिकेयावासे यादृग्भूतानि कुसुमानि तयार्चितानि मया दृष्टानि तादृग्भूतानि किमेतानीति गर्भगृहे वीक्ष्य निश्चिनोमीत्यात्मना मत्वा तदर्थं गर्भगृहे सावधानमवलोकयन् उत्तरग्रन्थं व्यङ्ग्यं विनाह। तत्र व्यङ्ग्यं विना किमर्थमिति चेत्, अयं तस्य हेतुं तस्मिन् विदूषके गते केवलं स्वयमेव विमृशति, किमपि ब्रवीति।[15] एतदर्थं सकविर्यथार्थमेवेमं ग्रन्थं प्रयुक्तवान्, अपि च 'नासूचकस्य प्रवेशकाल इत्यस्ति नाटकलक्षणम्।' तदर्थं दिव्यजनसूचकेनातःपरं दिव्यजनप्रवेशो भविष्यतीति प्रदर्शितः।

अथ राजा सावधानं पश्यन्नयं कुसुमचिह्नैस्सेवेयमिति निश्चित्य तद्दर्शनात् भोजनवेलायामपि विरतो भूत्वा कम्पितसर्वाङ्गः किञ्चिदुद्दृष्टिर्यावत्तिष्ठेत् तावदयं नायकोपि यवनिकायाच्छाद्यताम्।

अथ नायिकायाः प्रवेशो दृश्यते।

ततः प्रविशत्युपविष्टा, कामयमानावस्था नायिका। नायिका दीर्घं निश्वस्य।

अथ तपती नामधेया काचित् सवितुः पुत्री कन्या पूर्वं कस्मिंश्चिदह्नि यथाविध्यनुष्ठितनित्यक्रिया प्राप्तद्वादशवर्षा तपनलोके स्वपितृभूतदिनकरप्रणमनाय तदन्तिकमवाप्ता सा सहसा तेन वरयोग्या दृष्टा कन्यापितृत्वं गर्हयतामुना सस्नेहमङ्कारोपिता। प्रोद्यत्कुचसरोजबिम्बकदलितपाण्डुरं सकोष्णं वक्षप्रदेशं यान्ती वीक्षमाणा तन्नयननिपातलज्जितनयनयुगला तदुत्सङ्गे सलज्जमुपविष्टासीत्। अथेत्युपविष्टां दुहितरं पश्यन्नयं भानुमानित्यस्मरत्। हन्त मम दुहितुः प्रदेयकालस्सम्प्राप्तः। तथाहि –

पाण्डुत्वं कोष्णतामेति कन्यायाः कुचयोर्युगम्।
दृशो लज्जां तनोः कान्तिं प्राप्ता या द्वादशीं समाम्।।
प्रदेयैव तदा पित्रा जन्मरूपाधिकाय सा।
यूने च विदुषे तेन प्रागेवमृतुकालतः।।

इति श्रुतिस्मृतिसिद्धिः। इति तद्विधिं स्मरन्नयं प्रदानकालविधिवयःप्रयान्तीं स्वदुहितरं दृष्ट्वा कस्मै प्रदास्यामीमामिति देवानुद्दिश्य विमृशन्नेतेषां तदयोग्यताया हेतुद्वयमपश्यत्। किमिति चेत् ,

प्रायेणेन्द्रादयो देवाः मन्मातृकुलजा हि ते।
तस्मादेभ्यो न देयेषा तत् कस्तद्योगतां व्रजेत्।।
पुनस्संबन्धयोग्यास्ते विश्वे देवादयः सुरा।[16]
कस्यचित् तेषु तद्दानं हेतुरन्यो रुणद्धि तत्।।

कस्मादिति चेत् पश्य,

लोकेषु प्राणिनस्सर्वे केवलं पाञ्चभौतिकाः।
ये केह स्वर्गिणस्तत्र ये वियन्मार्गचारिणः।।

---

15 Suggestion is avoided because King says this to himself; Vidūṣaka is not there to hear. Dhvani is used also to conceal matters from others.

16 Sambandha is a peculiar kind of marriage prevelent among the caste hierarchy of Kerala. This reference shows that the practice goes back to the Chera period. See also FN 9 of Ch. XXI

मरुत्तेजप्रधानास्ते सर्वे स्वच्छन्दचारिणः।
तत्रेयमपि मत्पुत्री वायुतेजः प्रधानिनी।
तेजसस्तेजसा योगे शर्म क्वापि न लभ्यते।।

इत्यनेन हेतुद्वयेनास्याः पतित्वे वियच्चारिणो योग्या न भवेयुः। तस्मात्त्रिषु लोकेषु वियच्चारिणो योग्या न भवेयुः तस्मात् स्वर्गीभिश्चालम्। अथ भूलोके मनुजेन्द्रस्मर्तव्याः।

तत्र मद्वंशजैर्भूपैर्विततं पृथिवीतलम्।
तेन योग्यास्ततस्तस्याः कृतं तेष्वपि चिन्तनाम्।।
हिमांशुवंशजा भूपाः रणनिर्भयचेतसः।
ते हि योग्याः पतित्वेस्याः तेष्वेतद्विमृशाम्यहम्।।

इति तत्रस्थेनापि भगवता दिव्यचक्षुषा तद्वंशजान् भूमिपान् विमृशता तस्मिन् काले वर्तमानः कोपि संवरणनामा अजमीढी राजर्षिरलक्ष्यत।

तं तु सर्वगुणोपेतं युवानं रणनिर्भयम्।
विद्यावन्तं कीर्तिमन्तमायुष्मन्तं स्वधर्मिणाम्।।
तस्य देया मया कन्या साम्प्रतं विदुषे नु किम्।
तत्प्रदाने तयोरुच्चैः दम्पत्योः शर्म लभ्यते।।
मानुषोऽयं नृपश्रेष्ठो देवस्त्रीर्दुहिता मम।
पृथिव्यम्बुप्रधानोयं मरुत्तेजोधिकैव सा।।
भूमि वारिप्रधानानां नृणां सार्धं शरीरिभिः।
मरुत्तेजप्रधानैस्तैः संयोगो शर्म लभ्यते।।
तेषामन्यैरपि तयोः संयोगेन न देवयोः।
निर्वृतिः परमा भूयाद् रतिकर्मणि सर्वदा।।
तत्र दोषो महान् भूयादयं राजा महीपतिः।
विस्मृतेतरकार्यः स्याद्रममाणस्तया सह।।

कुतः?

नरश्चेद्दिव्यया सार्धं रमते त्वन्यथापि वा।
विस्मृतेतरकार्यौ तौ स्यातां विश्लेषकातरौ।।

इत्यस्ति श्रुतेरुक्तिः।

तस्मादस्याः प्रदानेऽस्मै सादनावृष्टिजं भयम्।
तयोरन्योन्यसङ्गेन स स्याद् विस्मृतपालनः।।
वारिपृथ्वीप्रधानस्य मरुदग्निप्रधानया।
पुंसि स्त्रीचान्यथा चेद् वा संयोगे प्रेम बध्यते।।

इत्यस्ति श्रुतिस्मृतिसिद्धिः।

तस्मादस्मै प्रदानेऽस्याः सोऽयं विस्मृतपालनः।
भविता हि नृणामत्र दुर्भिक्षादि भयं भवेत्।।

तत् किं करिष्य इति विमृश्यता तेनेति स्मर्यते स्म। कुतः

तथाभूते जगत्येनां मत्प्रवृत्या कयाप्यहम्।
वियोजयामि भूयोऽसौ शनैः स्वस्था भविष्यति।।
तस्मादयं सुताया मे वरयोग्यो नृपो भवेत्।
तस्मादस्मै प्रदास्यामि तामेवं निश्चिनोम्यहम्।।

इति निश्चिन्वानो भगवान् भूयोपि तं प्रति विमृशत्। कुतः

कृतोद्वाहोपि राजेन्द्रः पत्नीयं सापि वर्तते।
भवितव्यतया सोऽस्यां रागी तु पुत्रोऽलब्धवान्।।
तस्मादद्यैवाहं स्वप्ने यथार्थं बोधयामि तम्।
यैः कैश्चित्सप्रयत्नैस्ते तन्तुर्नास्यां भवेदिति।।

इति निश्चित्य स्थितवतो भगवतो हृदि कापि चिन्ता समभवत्। कुतः?

यस्मै पुत्रीप्रदानं स पिता निश्चितवान् धिया।
तद्रूपादिगुणान् सर्वान् श्रावयेत् कन्यकास्तदा।।

तत् किमर्थमिति चेत्, पश्य,

यस्मै दातुं विनिर्दिष्टः जनकेनात्मजां स्वयम्।
तत्र सप्रेम तच्चित्तं बद्धं स्यात् दैवचोदितम्।।

इत्युभयश्लोकार्थः शारवाख्यायां श्रुतौ दर्शितः। किञ्च इति ब्रह्मणा पूर्वं प्रजासर्गविधौ कल्पितम्। एतस्मात् वचनतः कथङ्कारमेनं सर्वगुणोपेतमेनां सर्वगुणोपेतां श्रावयामीमि डोलायितमनस्कतया तपतीमङ्कमारोप्य स्थितवता तेन भगवता भानुमालिना तद्विज्ञापनप्रकारो यदा चिन्त्यते तदैवादृश्यत पुरः कर्पूरसदृशच्छविः वीणी स नारदस्तेन जरीविष्णुश्रिताशयः। तदा तौ यथार्हं पूजितेन नारदमहर्षिणा तच्चित्तज्ञेन कोऽस्यानुरूपो वर इति पर्युक्तेन भगवता भानुमालिना भणितम्। 'कोऽन्यस्त्रैलोक्ये संवरणं राजर्षिं मुक्त्वे'ति। अथेति तेन महर्षये वर्ण्यमानस्य संवरणस्य सामुद्रिकोक्तैर्गुणैरुपेतस्य तस्य गुणानखिलान् यदा तपती श्रुतवती तदा तद्धृदयं श्रृङ्गाररसवल्लीबीजवापनायाकरो जातम्। अथ सा तथा वर्ण्यमानं राजानं श्रुत्वा तदा प्रकृति तद्गतमनस्कापि लज्जयात्यन्तमभिमताया मेनकाया अपि निजहृद्गतं अप्रकाशयन्ती बुद्धिपूर्वकमितस्ततस्सञ्चरन्ती स मेनका तपतीमातृसन्निधिमुपेत्य तामवन्दत। तदा तन्माता तत्सखीं मेनकामाहूय समेनकां तपतीमित्यब्रवीत्। 'वत्से तपति! अद्यप्रभृति समेनका त्वं तपनवनं गत्वान्वहं तत्रस्थं वटुरूपिणमभीष्टप्रदं देवं प्रणमे'ति तामुक्त्वा भूयस्तु मेनकाकर्णमूले चेत्यब्रवीत्।

'अयि मेनके! त्वमग्निदेवत्ये नक्षत्रे षष्ठ्यां च शुक्रवारे हस्तिनपुरबाहोद्यानस्थं कार्तिकेयं चानया मम दुहित्रा पूजये'ति भानुचोदितया तज्जनन्या भूयोप्युच्यते स्म। कुतः,

अयि मेनके त्वं तपनवनं गन्तुमुक्ताभ्यां युवाभ्यां हस्तिनपुरोपवर्तिना वर्त्मना गन्तव्यमिति च तया समादिष्टे तपतीमेनके तस्मादह्नः प्रभृति तद्वदत्कुरुताम्। अथ मेनका तया सह नित्यमेवैवं गच्छन्ती वियता सा भूलोकगतप्रदेशान् सर्वान् पृथक् पृथक् तस्यै विज्ञापयन्ती यान्ती भूलोकपालस्य संवरणनाम्नो राजर्षेः पुरमेतदित्यन्वहं विशेषात् विज्ञापयन्ती सासीत्। अथैवं तपती नित्यमेव तया विज्ञाप्यमानभूलोकप्रदेशापि कस्मिंश्चिदह्नि तया विज्ञाप्यमानं हस्तिनपुरं दृष्ट्वा वर्धमानमन्मथपीडा किमपि किमपि मन्दं गच्छन्त्यासीत्। अथ तथाभूतां तपतीं दृष्ट्वा तां तदा मेनकेत्युक्तवती।

'अयि प्रियसखि! अम्बरगमनायासो मामतीव बाधते। अपि च अद्य षष्ठ्यां तिथौ भवत्या कार्तिकेयो विशेषतः पूजनीयः। तस्मादत्रावतार्य स्थातव्य'मिति इमामुक्त्वा ते उभे तदैवावतीर्य कुमारार्चनं कृत्वा यदा बहिरतिष्ठतां तदैव राजर्षिं सवयस्यमायान्तं उभे अपश्यताम्।

तदा मेनका तद्गुणवर्णनं कृतवती तदाकरसंस्कारः कृतः। तदा सा तपती तं पश्यन्ती तया सह प्रोद्गत्य माहात्म्यप्रच्छन्ना, नयनपात्रेण तदङ्गसुधां यदा पीतवती तदा बीजावापनं कृतम्। तस्मादारभ्य स्मरस्य आद्यशरस्य द्वे अवस्था संप्राप्ता। मेनकया कालातिपातो वर्तत इति प्रेर्यमाणा गन्तुमनिच्छन्त्यपि तस्मात् तपनवनं गत्वा तत्रस्थदेवमभ्यर्च्य तस्मिन्नहनि समानोन्मादा तपनलोकं गत्वा तत्सङ्कल्पेन कथञ्चित् तां निशामन्तं प्रापय्य प्रत्युषस्स्युत्थाय सङ्कल्पसमागमाय विविक्तप्रदेशमभिलषन्ती मेनकामप्यनुक्त्वा तपनवनं गत्वा तत्रस्थे करतलोदकाख्ये सरसि स्नात्वा कल्याणवामनपूजां कथञ्चित् कृत्वा भूयोपि मदनतापशान्त्यर्थं स्नात्वा स्फटिककृते गोष्ठीमण्डपे त्वनन्यजेन प्रविष्टा स्वयमेव स्थित्वा सङ्कल्पसमागमं कुर्वती निमीलितचक्षुरन्यज्ञा निश्चलाङ्गी भूत्वा तत्रोपविष्टवती। अथैवं यथानिर्दिष्टं सा यदोपविशन्ती तदा यवनिका व्यपनीयताम्।

एवं पूर्वसम्बन्धः प्रावेशिकः, तस्य मदनावस्थाप्राप्तिश्च दर्शिता।

अथ विविक्ते समुपविष्टा सा स्वप्नावस्थां स्वयमेव व्याहरन्ती चित्तं रमयन्ती मेनकाप्यवरुद्धैः सङ्कल्पैर्निजप्रेयांसं हृदयस्थं कृत्वा यथेष्टमनुभवितुमक्षिणी निमील्य स्थितवती। एवं निमीलतनेत्रा स्थित्वा तज्जनं सङ्कल्पेन यथेष्टं अनुभवन्ती स्वयमेवानन्यविदासीना भवति।

ततः प्रविशति रम्भामेनका च।

अथ तपनलोकात् भुवि नभसो अवतरन्त्यौ ते उभे रम्भामेनके हिमवद्गिरौ वर्तमानस्य कल्याणवामनमन्दिरस्य वायव्यां दिशि वर्तमानाया करतलोदकनाम्नः सरस्या इषुपातमात्रे पौरन्दर्यां दिशि क्वचित्प्रदेशे ते अवतीर्य तस्मिन्नतिष्ठताम्। एवं तिष्ठन्त्योस्तयोः रंभा अन्तस्तापं विभावयन्ती तत्र मेनका सुप्रसन्नतां विभावयन्ती ते उभे एवं यवनिकाच्छन्नतनू यावत् तिष्ठेतां तावत् यवनिका व्यपनीयताम्। एवमुभयोः प्रावेशिकः।

अथैवमपयवनिकयोस्तयोर्दीपाग्रे तिष्ठन्त्यो रंभेति स्मरेत् कुतः हन्त सख्यास्तपत्या स्नेहपाशो मुक्तो मेनकायां वर्तते इति स्मरन्ती सान्तस्तापमुत्तरोत्तरं वर्धयन्ती तिष्ठेत्।

अथ तयोर्मेनका तत्तापं यथाभूतं जानन्ती तद्रसात्किमपि सुप्रसन्नमुखा भूत्वान्तरान्तरा कदाचिदपाङ्गेन तां सस्मितं पश्यन्ती तद्रसमनुभवन्ती तिष्ठेत्। तादृग्भूतोयं प्रदेश इति कथं ज्ञायत इति चेत् तदवगम्यताम्।

गिरेर्हिमवतो मूर्ध्नि वर्ततेऽद्यापि भूपते।
बलीवैरी हरिस्तत्र लोकानुग्रहतत्परः।।
दिशि तस्य च वायव्यां सरकरतलोदकम्।
किञ्चिदस्ति पवित्रं तत् दर्शनादेव पापहृत्।।
तत्र स्थापयते पुत्रीं पूजयेनं तदा हरिम्।
तत्पूजां कुर्वता चाशु प्राणतुल्यं पतिं व्रजेत्।।

इत्यस्ति व्यासप्रोक्तपुराणे जैमिनिना विश्वजिते महीपतये विज्ञापितम्। तत्पश्यता मया यथाभूतोयं प्रदर्शितः।

अथ तथा तिष्ठन्ती रंभा तद्भावं किमपि न पश्यन्ती तिष्ठन्ती सन्तापात् दरश्रितकोपना भूत्वा सोद्वृष्टिरेवं स्मरेत्। कथङ्कारमेनां मन्मनोगतं विज्ञापयामि। ध्वनिगर्भैर्वचोभिरेषा विज्ञापितव्येत्यात्मना निश्चित्य उत्तरग्रन्थेन विज्ञापयति **क हि ण खु असही**त्यादिना। तत्र ध्वनिर्दृश्यते। सखि अत्र वने कः प्रदेशः कया वस्तव्य इति न जाने। कुतः सदा त्वया समं परस्परं स्वैरङ्कुर्वतीह वर्तते। यतः ततस्तवातिपरिचितोयं प्रदेशः। तस्मात् तं प्रदेशं प्रदर्शयेति विभावयन्ती सा तेन ग्रन्थेन तं पृच्छन्ती तन्मुखे पश्यन्ती तिष्ठेत्।

मेन – अथ मेनका ध्वनिगर्भं वचनं श्रुत्वेति अहमिदानीमियमिव ध्वनियुक्तेन वचसा विनोदयेयं यद्यस्या दर्शनं न सिध्यति। तस्मान्निर्विवादध्वनिरहितेन वचसा याथातथ्यमेव विज्ञापयन्ती तददर्शनस्य भारमपनयामीत्यात्मना निश्चित्योत्तरग्रन्थेन यथार्थमेव विज्ञापयति।

अथ ते करतलोदकतीरगतं स्फटिकमण्डपं प्राप्तुमुभे परिक्रामतः।

मेन – अग्रतो विलोक्य अथैवं गच्छन्त्योस्तयोः रंभा अग्रगामी स्फटिकमण्डपसविधं गच्छन्ती सा भित्या जितोद्योतया तथाभूतां तां दृष्ट्वा सा तथाभूतेति तदवस्थां विज्ञापयन्ती तदव्यवसाय याथातथ्यं ज्ञातुं तत्र भित्त्यन्तरिते स्थिते आस्ताम्।

ततः प्रविशत्यपटाक्षेपेण विदूषकः।

अथ विदूषकः तस्मात् देवमन्दिरात् पुष्पच्छलेन तामन्वेष्टुं निर्यायोत्तरोत्तरवर्धमानतत्तेजोनिवेदितमार्गः शनैर्वायव्यदिशा गच्छन् सावधानं पश्यन् कदाचित् पथि किञ्चित् सरो दृष्टवानित्यस्मरत्। एतत् भृगुणोक्तं करतलोदकाख्यं सरः, तस्मादत्र सावधानमन्वेष्टव्या सेति विमृश्य तत्तीरे पर्यटन्नयं तस्मात् प्रतीच्युत्तरभागे स्फटिकशिलानिर्मितं कमपि गोष्ठीमण्डपं तत्तेजपटलाव्यक्तदर्शनं दृष्ट्वा किमिदमिति सावधानं तमेव पश्यन् सहसा तद्भित्तौ कन्दलितच्छायां कामपि दिव्यकन्यकां निश्चलमासीनां दृष्ट्वा प्राङ्नायकेन या सङ्कल्पसमागममनुभवन्ती काचित् दिव्यकन्यका ज्ञापिता सेयमिति निश्चित्य भूयोपि स्फटिकत्वात् भित्या तामेव वीक्षमाणस्य भूयोपि पदयुगलं सावधानं पश्यन् दृष्टपूर्वेण तेन सैवेयमिति निश्चित्य तद्विषये तन्मदनदशेति पश्यन्नयं तेनास्या विवाहः कृत इति विमृशन् पुनस्तां तस्मै विज्ञापितुं तस्मात् प्रतिनिवृत्य तेनैवागच्छन् पथीत्यस्मरत्। कथङ्कारमेनामेनं विज्ञापयामि। कोऽत्र सन्देहः। ध्वनिगर्भया गिरा एनं विज्ञापयामीति निश्चित्य सहसा अपटाक्षेपेणापगतयवनिकः स तं नायकं प्राप्तवान्। अथ तं सम्प्राप्य कम्पितगात्रस्तिष्ठन्तं तं दृष्ट्वा तमाहूय प्रवृत्तिमुत्तरग्रन्थेन ध्वनिना विज्ञापयति सरसी ए तीरग ए घणपणेलेहि इत्यादि ग्रन्थेन प्रहसनं विज्ञापयन्नयं तदवस्थं तेनैव विज्ञापयति।

अत्र सरस्तीरे घनपटलैर्घनीभूतो जलराशिर्वर्तते। अत्र जलराशिः स्फटिकशिलाविरचितो गोष्ठीमण्डपो वर्तते। कीदृग्भूतस्स इति चेत् घनपटलैर्घनीभूतं तेजःपटलैरव्यक्तविग्रहः।[17]

उदके स्फटिके शुभ्रे जलशब्दोऽत्र वर्तते।

जलराशिनात्र स्फटिकमण्डप उक्तः। घनपटलैः तेजःपटलैः –

वर्तते घनशब्दोऽब्दे गुरुवस्तुनि तेजसि। इत्यनेकार्थः।

अत्र तेजसि ध्वनौ। तस्मात्तेजःपटलैः द्रष्टुमशक्यः कञ्चित् स्फटिकमण्डपो मया दृष्ट इति ध्वनिना विज्ञाप्य भूयस्सा तत्रस्थेति ध्वनिना विज्ञापयति। **अण्णंचे**ति। अन्यश्चेति भगवत्या लक्ष्म्या आकृतिश्च दृष्टेति। भगवत्या ऐश्वर्यादिगुणपरिपूर्णायाः लक्ष्म्याः त्वदभिमतायाः दिव्यकन्यकायाः आकृतिः तया स्पटिकभित्त्या कन्दलितच्छाया तथाभूता या दृष्टा इतीमं ध्वन्यर्थं विज्ञापयन् बाह्यार्थः प्रहसनेन कथ्यताम्।

अथ राजा तदप्राप्तिहेतोः कम्पितदेहस्तिष्ठन्नपि सधीरं त्रिवर्त्युज्ज्वलितस्य पुरः तिष्ठन्नयमपगतपटो भूत्वा सधैर्यं साङ्गकम्पमपि निश्चलो भूत्वा तिष्ठन्नयं विदूषकवचनं सहसा श्रुत्वा तद्वचनं श्रवणपुटमनन्यवित् प्रापयन् शनैर्स्सन्तोषं तमेव पश्यन् 'वदवदे'ति दृष्टिभ्यां प्रेरयंस्तिष्ठेत्। अथ तेनैवं प्रेर्यमाणो विदूषकस्ससन्तोषं सहासं स्वं सम्मन्यमानं पुनरपि ग्रन्थं तमेव तथा वदेत्।

अथ राजा तेनेत्युच्यमानं ग्रन्थं सावधानं श्रृण्वन्नपि मदनार्तिहेतोः कथञ्चित् तद्ध्वनिमित्थं इत्यवधार्य सस्नेहं सधैर्यं तमेव पश्यन् तदुक्तौ परिसमाप्तायां तत्र तिष्ठन्नेवं स्मरेत्। हन्त साऽत्रस्था मया दृष्टेत्यनेन विज्ञापितं तं तत्रैव गच्छामीति गन्तुकामोपीति स्मरेत्। अहो अस्य केवललौकिकवचनं श्रृण्वद्भिर्जनैरयमुन्मत्त इति ज्ञायते। तदस्याघटितवचनं प्रमाणीकृत्य प्रयेत यद्यहमपि तथा मन्तव्यः। तन्न गच्छेयं किं तथा चेत् प्रयत्नवैफल्यं भविता। तस्मादुन्मत्तवदघटितवचनकारिणस्ते वचनं न प्रमाणीकरोमीति नानाजनप्रत्ययार्थं व्यङ्ग्यरहितेन वचनेनैनमुक्त्वा मया तस्मिन् विज्ञाप्यमाने दृष्टिभ्यां बलान्मा तत्र नयेति विभावयन्नुत्तरग्रन्थं वदंस्तदर्थं दूषयंस्तिष्ठेत्।

अथ विदूषकस्तेनेति विज्ञापितस्तं बलात् यथा प्रहसनं तत्र नयेत्। राजापि तद्दर्शनलालसोपि बलात् तेनैवमाकृष्यमाणः ससन्तोषमविक्रोधं विभावयन्नुत्तरग्रन्थेनैनं परिहसन् वेगात् पृष्ठतो गच्छति।

एवमुभौ परिक्रामतः।

अथाग्रे गच्छन् विदूषकः करतलोदकाख्यां सरसीं प्रापय्य तत्तीरे तत्र स्नात्वा सङ्कल्पसमागमं कर्तुं गच्छन्त्यास्तस्या स्फटिकरचितं तत् तीरे सान्द्राः पदपद्धतीर्दर्शयितुं अङ्गुल्या निर्दिश्योत्तरग्रन्थेन सरसीदर्शनं विभावयन्नाह -

भो पेख न एसा क्ष एसा स इति पदे प्रोच्यमाने, या कार्तिकेयावासे दृष्टपूर्वा सैवेयमिति विभावयन् ग्रन्थं वदेत्। इति वदन्नयं भूयस्तद्वचः सरस्यां सङ्क्रमय्य लौकिकेन वचसा सरसीं दर्शयेत्।

अथ राजा तद्दर्शनौत्सुक्यः तेन समं गच्छन्नयं सहसा सरसीतीरं सम्प्राप्य तेन तद्दर्शितायाः पदपद्धतिर्दृष्ट्वा सरोमाञ्चं ससन्तोषं ता एव पश्यन्नुत्तरग्रन्थे तदीयैवेयमिति समर्थयति। **सखे सत्यमेवैषेति** तदीया, सत्यम्। एवं तदीयैवेति निश्चित्य भूयो लौकिकेन वचसा उत्तरश्लोकेन सरसीवर्णनच्छलेन तस्या वर्णनं करोति,

---

17 घनपटलैः घनीभूतः जलराशिः = Crystal hall frozen by the multitude luster. जलः = स्फटिकः, घनः = तेजः।

माणिक्यभूतलगता मणिभङ्गतोया
कल्याणिनी करतलोदकनामधेया।
अद्यापि भाति सरसी सरसीरुहाक्ष-
हस्ताम्बुजन्मतलमध्यविवर्तिनीव।।

इति। अथ राजा सरस्तीरमुपेत्य पदपद्धतीर्यत्र विराजति तेन पथा पश्यन्नयं तस्मात् किमपि दूरे स्फटि कमण्डपे आसीनां तां भीत्या कथञ्चित् पश्यन्नपि सरसीच्छलेन वर्णयन् विदूषकाय विज्ञापयति, सखे माणिक्यभूतलगता इयं अद्यापि सरसीरुहाक्षहस्ताम्बुजन्मतलमध्यविवर्तिनीव भाति इति सम्बन्धः। सरसीरुहायामङ्किते कस्यचित् सार्वभौमस्य हस्ताम्बुजन्मतलमध्ये विवर्तमानेव भाति।

द्यूते वज्रेरथस्तम्बे नेत्रे चेतसि कामिनि।
अक्षशब्दो भवत्यत्र मदे पानाच्च शीथुनः।। इत्यनेकार्थः।

अत्र सरसीरुहाभ्यामङ्कितः इत्यर्थः। कल्याणिनी, अवैधव्ययोग्या मणिभङ्गतोया मणिरितीन्द्रनीलशिला तद्भङ्गवत् राजद्रोमराजियुक्ता

रोमराजौ जले शीते तोयशब्दोऽत्रवर्तते।

अत्र रोमराजौ इतीममर्थं विभावयन् भूयस्सरसि कल्याणिनी या प्रतिदिनं तया सेव्यते इयं कल्याणिनीत्यर्थः।

'यत्र प्रियजनो दृष्टस्स च देशोपि वल्लभः' इति वचनसामर्थ्यात् तद्गतस्नेहो भूत्वा सररीवर्णनं कुर्वन्नयं तत्सान्निध्ये दर्शनादवाप्तिहेतोर्वर्धमानां मदनपीडां गच्छन् विस्मृतपूर्वापरो भूत्वा स्मरशरस्य द्वितीयस्य द्वितीयां विकृतिं गच्छन् विस्मृतसर्वकार्यस्तिष्ठेत्। तस्मात्तथा तिष्ठेदिति चेत् पश्य –

चतुर्थ्यवस्था विकृतिं द्वितीयां योऽगमत्पुमान्।
स सर्वज्ञो दृढात्मापि मनश्शैथिल्यं सो व्रजेत्।।
वक्रोक्तिं सोपि चाटूक्तिं ज्ञातुं वक्तुं च न प्रभुः।
विहाय स्वमनोधैर्यं लघुर्भूयात् स्मरातुरः।।

इत्यस्ति वात्स्यायनाचार्येण जयमङ्गलायामङ्गनानां पुरुषस्मरदशामूर्च्छनक्लमं विज्ञातुमस्या विकृतेश्चिह्नमेवम्भूतमिति दर्शितम्। तस्मादयं तथा तिष्ठेत्। अतःपरमस्यानायिकादर्शनादेवमेव प्रयोगः। अथ विदूषकस्तं मण्डपं तद्गतां तां च भित्या दृष्ट्वा तथा तिष्ठन्तं तं पश्यन्नयं तद्दशां विज्ञातुं पूर्ववन्मतिगाम्भीर्यमस्ति वा नवेति परिच्छेत्तुमुत्तरग्रन्थेन पृच्छति। **कि स अ संच्चमि**त्यादिना।

अथ राजा तथा तिष्ठन्नयं तेन यथादर्शितं मण्डपं दृष्ट्वा शिथिलितमनोधैर्यो भूत्वा तद्विज्ञापितं व्यङ्ग्यमजानन्नयं व्यङ्ग्यं विना तादृशप्रभावात् यथार्थमेवोत्तरग्रन्थमाह **वैधे-ये**त्यादि। इत्यादिग्रन्थमुक्त्वा तामेव पश्यन् केवलं लौकिकेन वचसा तद्वर्णनमेव करोति,

महता यः प्रयत्नेन प्रेयसी दृष्टवांश्चिरात्।
सकामिना श्रृणोदन्यं न पश्यति रञ्जति।।

इति जयमङ्गलाप्रसिद्धिः।

अतः परं द्वितीयाङ्केऽस्मिन्नामानुवर्णनात् श्लोकात् तद्वचनश्रवणात् भ्रान्तिज्ञाने व्यङ्ग्यकथितेन वचसास्य प्रयोगः।

संवरणध्वनिश्रवणात् स्वमुद्दिश्य वा नवेति लोलायितचित्तो भूत्वा तद्रसमेव दर्शयति। अतः परं व्यङ्ग्यं विना तयोरेव प्रयोगमार्गः।

अथ राजा तां दृष्ट्वा तद्वर्णनं कृत्वा भीत्या पश्यन्नस्या वचनं स्वमुद्दिश्य वा नवेति श्रोतुकामस्ससखस्तिष्ठेत्। एवं प्रयोगः। लौकिके वचने किं द्रष्टव्यम्।

नायिका – अथ नायिका तथा सङ्कल्पसमागमोत्सवमनुभवन्ती सा क्षणं स्वस्थाभवत्।

रतिं विदधती बाला सङ्कल्पैर्या यदा व्रजेत्।
पादहीनां चतुर्नाडीं स्वस्थात् क्षणं तदा।।

इति सा स्वस्था क्षणमासीत्।

यत्प्रेयस्सङ्गमोऽभीष्टं सङ्कल्पैः क्रियते यया।
तस्या गुह्यप्रदेशं स प्रापयेत्तादृशार्द्रताम्।

एवं स्वस्थभूता सा तपती दीर्घं निश्वस्य स्थितवती सा स्वयोनिं तादृग्भूतां ज्ञात्वा सोत्तरग्रन्थेनात्मानं गर्हयति **कहं एरिंस** इत्यादिना।

एवं नायिकाप्रयोगः।

अथ नायिका तापसकुमारप्रोक्तं वचनं श्रुत्वा ससंभ्रमं सखीभ्यां तत्रैवान्तरधत्त। यदा तदायं राजा संवरणस्वनावस्या वचनं श्रुत्वा संभ्रमं च दृष्ट्वा स चेति स्मरेत्। अये मामुद्दिश्यास्या मदनपीडेतीदानीं निश्चितवानस्मीति निश्चित्य ससन्तोषं तमिव पश्यंस्तदङ्गसुधां स्वदृष्टिभ्यां पायं पायमनुभूयस्तिष्ठन्नयं सहसा सखीभ्यां सह तिरोहितां दृष्ट्वा ससन्तापं सस्मरपीडां सदुःखं समनोव्यथमिति स्मरेत्। हन्त तया कुतूहलतया भवितव्यम्। अतः परमागमिष्यति सा वा नवा। आयास्यति चेत् कदानु वा आशु वा मन्दं वेति स्मरन्नयमेतत् सर्वमनिश्चिन्वानस्तद्वियोगावसरे मदनेन चूतनाम्ना शरेण पुङ्खानुपुङ्खं तं प्रहृत्य तेन बाध्यमानस्तनुतां दशां गच्छन्नयं तदीयामुत्कण्ठां सोढुमक्षमः उत्तरग्रन्थं वदति। **हा कष्टमन्तर्हित** इत्यादि।

अथ विदूषकः इति सान्तर्वेदं नायकं तद्वक्तारं गर्हयन्तं दृष्ट्वेति स्मरेत्। अहमिदानीमनन्यवेदिनमिममेतत् वचनकर्ता कश्चिन्महामुनिस्तस्मात् तत्र परुषवाच्यसि चेत् भवन्तं भस्मसात्कर्तुं प्रभुरयमिति तत्प्रशंसयास्य मदनपीडां किञ्चिच्छमयित्वा भूयस्सायन्तनं कर्म कारयितुमपरसन्ध्येषा प्राप्तेति विज्ञापयामीत्यात्मना निश्चित्य स चोत्तरग्रन्थमाह **एत्थ** इत्यादि। अथ तथाभूतोऽपि राजा विदूषकवचनेन तद्वचोऽमुनेति बुध्वा समुनिजनोऽयं प्रदेशमिति मत्वा सद्भावं स्वमुनिजनान् दर्शयितुं स्मरपीडां वर्तमानमपि हृदि नियम्य सन्ध्यां पश्यन्निति स्मरेत्। अहो महती मे वेदना। तस्मात्कथङ्कारमेनां ममावस्थामस्य विज्ञापयामि। मुनिभीत्या लौकिकेन वचसा न शक्यते। तस्मात् सन्ध्यावर्णनच्छलेन तां विज्ञापयामीति निश्चित्य सन्ध्यां पश्यन्नयं विदूषकं च पश्यन्नयमुत्तरग्रन्थेन स्वामवस्थां विज्ञापयति।[18]

---

18 King: My efforts for union with her have failed. She belongs to heaven. Mālini, like Cakravaki has to bear the pangs of separation.

सखे अवसन्न एवाय**मरुणसारथेर्दीक्षाविकार** इत्यमुना। सखे अरुणसारथेः मम दिवसदीक्षाधिकारः अस्मिन् दिवसे विवाहदीक्षाधिकारः अवसन्न एव विघ्नित एव। अद्य दिवा नेति निश्चितवानस्मि कस्मादिति चेत् – अरुणमणिनिकाशैरित्यादिश्लोकेन तपत्या मालिन्याश्चावस्थां विज्ञापयति। अथ राजा विदूषकाय विज्ञापयति। सखे इयं दिनश्रीरम्बरात् अम्बुराशिमवतरतीति संबन्धः। दिनश्रीर्दिव्ययुवतिः। अभ्रसोपानमार्गैः वचःपरंपराभिः अम्बुराशिं मामवतरति अभिलषति। अरुणमणिनिकाशैः सुन्दरस्फटिकनिकाशैः इयं दिव्ययुवतिः सुन्दरस्फटिकवन्निर्मलाभिरभ्रसोपानमार्गैः वचःपरम्पराभिः व्यवहरन्ती मामभिलषति इति यदा प्रकाशितवती तदैवनभस्वान् पद्मिनीं चक्रवाकां विधुरयति कष्टम्। किञ्च, एतन्निमित्तादेव चक्रवाकीं च मालिनीं च नवपरिमलवाही नवविघ्नवाही।

विघ्ने प्रसूनसौरभ्ये क्लीबे परिमलं हि तत्।

इत्यादि स्वकीयां तदीयावस्थां विज्ञाप्य भूयोपि विदूषकं पश्यन्नेव सखे तस्मात् किमतःपरं विपरीतं विधात्रा मया करणीयमिति सकरुणं सान्तर्वेदनं विदूषकं विज्ञाप्य भूयो लौकिकेन वचसा यथार्थमेव भानुमभिष्टूय समदनोन्मादं तिष्ठन्नयं तृतीयेन शरसञ्चयेन विद्धत्वात् भोजनाशनसंस्कारादिकर्मणि विरक्तो भूत्वा भूय इतिकर्तव्यतामूढस्तिष्ठेत् –

'वायौ दिनकरो व्योम्नि नभस्वांस्याद् विधातरि'। अनेकार्थः।

अथ विदूषकः तं तथा निर्विण्णं दृष्ट्वेति स्मरेत्। कथङ्कारमस्य मदनोन्मादं इदानीं किञ्चित् शमयामि। अस्तु अमुना सः मदनपीडाया निर्वर्तयामि। कुतः

इष्टानवाप्तिको बाणैर्बाध्यमानस्मरेण च।
भूपः खिन्नो न वश्यः स्यादन्यत्रारिपराभवे।।

किञ्च

सुजन्मा क्षत्रियो लोकान् स्वे स्वे कर्मणि योजयेत्।
विशेषात् यतिनं पायादृषीनाश्रमकाननान्।।

तस्मात् प्रार्थितपूर्वे भृगुणा रक्षोवधकर्मणि तमिममेतत् श्लोकार्थेन प्रेरयन्निमं तत्कर्मणि क्रुद्धतरं कृत्वा तद्वधममुना कारयित्वा पुनस्तत्प्रसादादेवास्य मनोरथसिद्धिर्भवेदित्यात्मना निश्चित्योत्तरग्रन्थेन तत् विज्ञापयति **अब्भत्थिदो** इत्यादिना। इत्यादिग्रन्थं वदन्निति वदेत्। भो सुजन्मनः क्षत्रियस्य सद्रक्षणं परमधर्म, पश्य – सुजन्मा क्षत्रियेत्यादिमनुवचनात् तस्मात्तद्रक्षणाय गच्छाव इति तं प्रेर्य तिष्ठेत्।

अथ राजा तथाभूतोपि तद्वचनं श्रुत्वा सुजन्मितया स्वधर्मोच्चारिपरिभवात् किञ्चिन्नियमित मदनोन्मादः सत्वरं रक्षोवधार्थं सवयस्यः संवरणः तस्मात् गतवानभूत्।।

निष्क्रान्तो; द्वितीयोऽङ्कः।।

Vyaṅgyavyākhyā of Act II

The dramatist has assigned Menakā the role of narrator of the incidents of the first Act and Rambhā that of the hearer. I will now show their mental conditions and mode of presentations.

Menakā followed Tapatī to the abode of Kārtikeya for worshipping the Lord. When they had completed their offerings, they notice King Saṃvaraṇa and vidūṣaka coming to that direction. They, hurriedly flew up and sat hiding on the branch of a tree observing them. Menakā notes that seeing the King, Tapatī is inflicted by the arrows of cupid. They put down her earrings along with a message indicating the place of meeting. Menakā shook the branch causing the leaves fall down. Then they went to Tapanavana.

In Tapanavana they worshipped the venerable Vāmana and returned to the abode of sun-god. Early morning Menakā came out thinking of Tapatī. To her surprise she was told that Tapatī has already left. She became sad wondering as to where she had gone without telling her. Presuming that she might have gone to Tapanavana she rushed in that direction. On the way she met Rambhā. In her panic she failed to exchange the customary greetings. Seeing her face pale and withdrawn Rambhā asked her the reason for her anxiety. She invited Menakā to take rest for a while. Accordingly both the friends stand relaxed.

Menakā indignant and remorseful stands behind the curtain which is slightly raised. Rambhā immersed in thought stands behind covered by the curtain. Curtain is removed when they are positioned as directed in front of the three-wicked lamp. Rambhā, her mind disturbed, fixes her eyes on Menakā.

Menakā Her face is pale and lifeless. What would the reason be? Tapatī whom she always accompany is missing.

She sends her eyes to Menakā addressing her through the pupil of her eyes. Menakā so called stands, bit bent to answer.

You are inquisitive to get something from me. See – Bharata has formulated in the ancient science of nāṭya endowed in the Vedas two styles of dance – violent (tāṇḍava) and the graceful (lāsya). Dance performed by men is tāṇḍava. The dance, rich in melody, beautifully presented by enchanting women is called lāsya.

She moves with elegant steps, behind the lamp to beholds the faces of connoisseurs and convey the meaning through the pupil of her eyes.

This is the mode of acting of noble women. The female character presented with grace and composure by women well-decorated in upper-garments, is hailed to be the best.

Rambhā indicates the meaning of the text through the movement of eyes to the prekṣakas and pleases the nānāloka by four-fold acting. Here after this is the mode of acting intended for noble female character.

I will inform my friend Rambhā all that have happened.

She narrates all the incidents beginning from Tapatī hearing of Saṃvaraṇa from her father sitting in his lap to the present state of her mind. There is no inner-meaning in this early part.

The mental state of both are shown – Menakā is disturbed by inner-conflict. Rambhā realises the events unfolded and grows anxious.

Interlude is over

King – *Enters seated on a horse deeply immersed in thought.*

Retrospection

Saṃvaraṇa returned from Kārtikavana; spent the night somehow and waking up early he thought of the means to reach the Himālayas alone, unaccompanied by royal retinue. He called vidūṣaka and told him – 'Dear friend, please keep safely the earrings. We will keep our attendants far behind by the high speed of our horses.' They started. On the way by over-speed he distanced himself from vidūṣaka. Due to the strain of continuous race, the horse fell dead in the foot hill. Riding on another horse he reached Tapanavana and began his search for the divine maiden.

Pūrvasambandha

The highly proficient actor in the costume of Saṃvaraṇa stands in front of the three-wicked lamp as directed. The curtain is removed.

The King, eyes raised in deep thought, stands for a moment in a state of imagination.

Where ever I go for hunting animals run to save their lives. Here, on the contrary, they are not frightened. Those animals who by nature are enemies, coexist here in harmony. This is dear to me. Great is the power of penance.

All that the King finds and describes here after will be favorable in his search for the damsel. He feels her presence nearby. He is continuously tormented by the arrows of Cupid.

I will search alone the damsel in this woodlands relying my own intelligent fortitude. The move can be interpreted as fallacious. King shall not move unaccompanied by the Brahmin. If he does so he will have to face obstacles.More over it will give room for unsavory scandals. Therefore it is good to seek the help of Pārāśarya (looks around). Where has my joker friend gone?

He grows more and more desolate over the absence of any clue about the damsel, the earrings or of his friend. Pale and fatigued he waits for the words of Pārāśarya.

Vid (*From behind*) Abrāhmaṇyam!

King My friend ever since he knew of the dream is indifferent towards me. I have, somehow, turned him sympathetic to my cause. I have to obtain my desire with his help.

Well-founded is his ire. I deliberately rode away from him. Wandering alone in the woods, he might, perhaps, have been brutally attacked by wild animals.

Aye! The sound seems to be of my friend. Born in the clan of Parāśara, master of all branches of knowledge, quiet in words and efficient in solving problems, my friend is competent in achieving my object of desire.

Why does he cry? He suggests, unequivocally, his fear of animals as also apathy towards me. He may be thinking that he is being depended to acts that do not match his stature. He will not tell a lie to me – his benefactor. Hence I will look into the cause of his fear.

Vidūṣaka enters frightened.

Awakened by the king I got up early in the morning, took up the ear-rings with care and after completing the morning rites, somehow, got out of the house. 'Come with me' -directed the King. I followed. When I found myself far behind by his meteoric speed I cried out in vain 'Ha! He is gone.' Tracing the prints of the hoof, I followed. When the sun raised over the sky I got down and sat under a tree exhausted by hunger and thirst. By external signs I guessed that I am close to a hermitage. The wind carried the smoke fragrant with sacrificial ghee. I moved in that direction and reached the hermitage of sage Bhṛgu. Paying obeisance to the sage I accepted the hospitality extended by the ascetics. Then I narrated all the incidents to the sage. After a patient hearing, he gracefully informed me the whereabouts of Tapanavana and of the Vāmana temple of its northern side. There is a lovely lake Karatalodaka and an alluring crystal-hall at a calls distance.

Coming out of the grove I moved with great strain. I held upright the stick to which the ear-rings were tied tightly. To my great misfortune, animals up from a mango-tree snatched away the stick and earrings. Alas! All that happened due to my negligence.

One should hand over any deposit, small or big, to anybody for keep and return basis. King, on no account should give even to the intelligent. Don't accept any pledge and spend it in diversity. I encounter this tribulation because I accepted the earrings from the King for safe custody. I am ashamed of its loss. I do suffer the humiliation.

To my friend I will confess that I committed a mistake. How shall I converse with him? Never shall I tell a lie to my patron. Yes. I will resort to a device of truth mixed with falsehood. I will tell him that the earring tied to my sacred thread has been stolen by enemies.

Vidūṣaka, his eyes closed stands before the King trembling with fear requesting to save him from enemies. Curtain is removed when the actor is in position as instructed.

King (Expresses dejection, sadness and pity.)

Vid His eyes are red in anger. I will disturb him with sweet-talks and ignite his anger.

You failed to protect your intimate friend. I became a victim of attack on your behalf. Enemies targeted me only because I was keeping your earrings. Did I not follow your foot-steps obediently. Yet you left me alone this poor Brahmin, in the forest. I lost everything. How would you, unable to save a poor friend, be competent to protect the sea-girdled earth from enemies?

King – (*with anguish*) In the thick woods some might have taken away all his belonging. Surely it is an affront to my authority! A King is duty-bound to defend his friends, win over the enemies and offer the fund collected as taxes to the Brahmins. He uses crude words against me. I will soothe his feelings and know more about the enemies . You do not fear.

Which enemy did attack you?

Vid Oh! He has grown more annoyed! The best way to cool down is to give a hint about the whereabouts of the damsel.

King His behaviour seems to be contrary to his words. Perhaps, the earrings might have been lost from his hands. But he is unmoved and seems to be cheerful. He might have found solutions to my problem. I will talk him in agreeable words.

Vid It seems that he desires to extract something from me. I hold to myself the secret regarding the options to meet your sweet-heart.

Here onwards until they meet the divine figure both converse freely the suggested meaning through eyes supported by single-hand gestures.

King Friend, find out a place where I can spend time with her. Lead me to that place.

Vid I will reveal the details given by sage Bhṛgu. In the top of Himālayas northward there is a temple dedicated to Vāmana. The divine lady offers homage to the Lord there. She is sure to be there now.

Both Exit

Vidūṣaka leads the King. King looks around for any sign to ascertain celestial presence. He knows that there will be flash brighter than the lightening where the celestial beings move. He is disappointed unable to see any trace. Disappointed he depicts her imagined likeness in his mind and enjoys the ecstasy of fabulous union with her.

Leading the King vidūṣaka too looks around for any indication for his presence. Mildly does he put his steps with care. He could read the mind of the King.

His mind seems to be fractured. What would the reason be? Delighted in the illusionary pleasure of union he is reluctant to withdraw his eyes as though for fear of her disappearance! Is he sprinkling the nectar of her beauty on the sprouts of rasa-creeper? Is he making out her presence in this surrounding? Does he brood over alternate means to meet her?

How to ask him – directly or indirectly. Plain words are not proper. If overheard it will discredit his fame. So let it be a query put indirectly -

Friend, this Tapanavana is blessed with divine presence. The one whom you search dwells in north. After setting foot, are you lost on illusions?

King Even thick forests are not fit for open discussions. Therefore I too will communicate through indirect means.

Looking down the King scrawled with right foot on the ground, held the tip of garment up in hands and sent sensuous gazes.

On an earlier occasion Mālinī overheard us. It is safe not to be plain-spoken.

Vid This area is not accessible to ordinary women.

King To be on the safer side I will converse in symbolic terms. My consort turns to be too feeble to fascinate my imagination. My heart now is set on another who can conceive an offspring for me.

Vid Ha! A flash of beam that outshines the lightening moves from north to south. In all likelihood it is the divine lady. Oh! Friend that maiden and her maid are here just a few steps north of us. Let us enter.

King The brightness may be of a woman in penance or in love? No. She is not performing penance. This place is not suitable for penance. It fits well for amorous sports. She may be in raptures on the imagined union with her lover.

Vid But she stands alone?

King The position I will make clear in the guise of depicting a creeper.

The wind is mildly perfumed. The offering is over. This homage was done by a divine woman. Scriptures prescribe different kinds of worship to women in distinct stages. Judged by those principles, this particular offering was made by a maiden of divine origin.

Both move in the direction of wind inhaling fragrance.

Vid This is the sacred abode of the deity.

King experiences horripilation in the right part of the body and vibration in nostrils. This he shows to his friend and tells him that they signal the fulfillment of his desire. He demonstrated in this right eye the exhilarating pleasure and on the left the deplorable dejection simultaneously.

Entering the temple they paid obeisance to the deity. They realised on closer observation that a divine maiden has just gone out after worship.

The flowers she offered resembled those found in the Kārtikeyāvāsa. The obvious inference is that the one whose foot prints were found and the one who worshipped here are one and the same.

King The King became tormented more by cupid. He lost interest even in food. He stood in devotion before the deity.

Vid He has lost all his hopes. He entrusts everything in God. It is good. But that alone will not do. One should get things done by own valor. Friend, I move searching her. We will win her over by our own strength.

King Friend, look high and low to find out her.

Vidūṣaka goes out. King stands still in deep contemplation. Curtain covers him.

Entry of the Heroine

One day, Tapatī, the daughter of sun-god approached her father after the routine morning rites and paid respects to him. He affectionately held her on his lap. He watched all over. The body shows signs of her attaining youthful age. Engrossed in thought he reflected,

It is time to give my daughter in marriage. She has reached the age of twelve. Her breasts are blossomed, eyes betray shyness. She has matured. A daughter has to be tied in wedlock with a well suited youth before she attains puberty. Who is most suited for her?

Gods like Indra belongs to my maternal line; related by blood; they are not acceptable. Second, the other devas of the world moving through air. Constitutionally they are predominant in air and fire; Tapatī is also of the same combination. Union of fire to fire will be unpleasant. None among the celestial, therefore, is worthy to be the husband of my daughter. The search has, therefore, to be expanded to the celebrities among human beings. Any king on earth are originated from my lineage, the Solar race. Search among them is of no use. The valiant kings belonging to lunar dynasty alone deserve to be considered.

Evoking his divine power he searched and a king by name Saṃvaraṇa caught his attention. A repository of excellent qualities, young, fierce in war, learned, renowned, endowed with longevity and upholder of dharma – Saṃvaraṇa is the one best qualified to hold the hands of my daughter. The couple will lead a pleasant life. He is human, my daughter divine;

predominant elements in him are earth and water, for my daughter it is air and fire. The union of these elements gives unending pleasure. Conjugal relation of divine and human is a source of supreme bliss.

But if the king, forgetting his royal responsibilities, indulges too much in love, it will be dangerous. Human-divine couple when united will forget everything else. He may perhaps forget his duty. Then poverty and fear will rule over the state. In such an eventuality they will have to be separated for a while. Anyhow, I firmly resolve to give Tapatī in marriage to King Saṃvaraṇa of the lunar race.

But Saṃvaraṇa already has a wife. He is not fortunate to get an offspring in his queen. Therefore appearing in dream I will inform him that efforts to get progeny in his queen is futile.

Father once decides the marriage, shall introduce to the daughter the exquisite qualities of the would be husband so as to stick her mind on him. Brahmā himself has prescribed this procedure. How to convey the magnificence of Saṃvaraṇa to my dear one. While the sun-god was thus pondering, all on a sudden, there appeared the camphor-white Nārada with his lute. King received him with due hospitality. Sun-god requested the sage to forecast the most-suited partner to his daughter. Nārada asked – 'Who else in three worlds other than King Saṃvaraṇa?' Tapatī heard of the excellent qualities of the king from Nārada. Her heart prepared itself to be the grass-land to accept the seeds of the creeper of love. Though her heart thence-forth became immersed in the king she was timid to reveal it even to her close associates.

One day Menakā came to the palace of her mother. She bowed before her. Mother advised Tapatī and Menakā thus – 'From today onwards go to Tapanavana and worship Lord Vāmana.' Turning to Menakā she whispered in her ears – 'Take Tapatī to worship Lord Kārtikeya in the outer-garden of Hastinapura on the Kartika day of the third lunar mansion. Take the route close to Hastinapura.' Thereafter they use to offer prayers as instructed. On their way Menakā used to explain the different localities under the domain of king Saṃvaraṇa. Once, watching the different places of Hastinapura Tapatī became struck by cupid. Seeing her condition Menakā said – 'I am tired of going through the air. Being the sixth day, we have special offerings to Kārtikeya today. Hence let us land here.' They descended, worshipped the Lord and took rest in the outer-garden. It was at that time that they saw King Saṃvaraṇa coming in their direction accompanied by vidūṣaka.

Menakā then described the greatness of the King to her. This prepared the field. Tapatī invisible by divine power, drunk the nectar of the handsome youth. This sowed the seed. The cupid sent his first arrow -lotus – towards her. As it was late Menakā persuaded her to leave the place which she did reluctantly. She went to Tapanavana worshipped the deity and mad in love somehow spent the night thinking of the hero. Early morning even without a word to Menakā she left in search of a suitable place to contemplate on him. She took her bath in the Karatalodaka lake, offered homage to Vāmana, dipped again herself in the water to quench the heat, entered the crystal-chamber and sat there motionless with closed eyes, her heart lost in thought.

Curtain is removed when the heroine is in position as instructed.

Rambhā and Menakā enter.

Emerging from the domain of sun-god, Rambhā and Menakā descended in a place at the distance of an arrow-shoot in the eastern side of Karatalodaka lake, situated north-west to Kalyāṇamandira in Himālaya. Rambhā is visibly perturbed, Menakā maintains a pleasant mood.
Curtain is removed when they are on stage as above.

Rambhā Alas! Tapatī's noose of love seems to be beyond the reach of her Menakā.
Though aware of Rambhā's feelings Menakā simply smiles and casts sidelong glances through the corner of her eyes indicates the auspicious nature of that place.
There in the top of the Himālayas reside Viṣṇu incarnated as Vāmana to bless the world. North-Western quarter of it is the holy lake Karatalodaka the mere sight of which removes all sins. Maidens who worship the Lord there attains partners who love them than their own selves.
Rambhā, eyes raised in contemplation -
How can I inform her my mind? Yes. I will choose words pregnant with suggestions.

Rambhā Friend, I do not know who lives and where? As you are familiar with this place show me that place.

Menakā I will speak in plain words.

Both starts to the crystal hall. They saw Tapatī. They remain concealed behind the wall.

(Vidūṣaka enters teasing out the curtain.)

Vidūṣaka who went in search of the divine maiden followed the flash of brightness to the north-west and reached the lake.

Vid This is the lake which the sage Bhṛgu has revealed to me. She will be some where around. Inside the hall something indistinct fell on his eyes. Soon amidst the luster he identified the divine lady sitting motionless. This is the one whom we were searching for.

He rushed to the hero to convey the glad news.

How to tell him. What doubt? Not in plain words; but through suggestions. 'In the banks of the lake there remains lot of water frozen by mass of clouds. I have seen some one indistinctly visible in the hallow of brightness embodied her. The form of Lakṣmī is also seen reflected in the crystal wall.'

King (*Encourages the jester to speak more*) He tells me that she is nearby. I will go and see her.

People hearing him, unaware of the suggestion, will take him to be a lunatic. If I prepared to take his incongruous words seriously, I will also be counted like that. But if I do not go there all these efforts will turn to be futile. I will, therefore, pretend that I do not rely on his words and encourage him by the movement of eyes to take me forcefully to her side.

Vid (*Under the pretext of showing the king the lake points by fingers to the row of soft foot-prints*) They are the same we saw earlier.

King Yes friend. Yes. Same footprints!

This auspicious maiden with sapphire-like blue line of hair is to be shined in the lotus-palm of monarch.

King became intensely love-sick. Mind shattered he forgets himself. He is unable to hear or use coaxing or crooked words.

This is the terrible condition of the hero till he meets the heroine. There is not much scope for dhvani here. The acting is suggestive when he hears सकलभुवनैकनाथ *out of confusion as to who is referred to by her. Utterance of the word 'Saṃvaraṇa' also arises confusion and provides scope for suggestion, though it is no more than a pun of words. No scope for further dhvani in second Act. What remains to be searched for in plain words!*

XX
Tapatīsaṃvaraṇam Dramatic Text Act III

अथ तृतीयोऽङ्कः।

(ततः प्रविशति होमसाधनहस्तस्तापसकुमारः)

ताप (सविस्मयम्) अहोतुखल्ववाङ्मनसगोचरमद्भुतानुभावस्य महाराजसंवरणस्य विक्रमविलसितम्। तथा ह्यनिर्देश्यैराधिभिरतिक्षामशरीरस्यापि तस्य –

निर्भिद्यन्तां त्रियामाचरबलपतयः पर्वताकारकायाः
कामं शाताग्रशल्यस्फुरदनलशिखाभासुरैर्भल्लजालैः।
आसीदाश्चर्यमेतद् यदुत शरमरुद्वेगविद्रावितास्ते
पर्यस्ताः क्वेति विद्मो न हि वयमधुनाप्याश्रमाद् बाह्यभूमौ।। १।।

आदिष्टोऽस्मि गुरुणा, यथा 'वत्स! कौण्डिन्य! संवरणशरपरामृष्टानां पिशिताशिनां परिग्रहास्तं प्रति प्रकाशं प्रहर्तुमक्षमा मन्ये मायाः प्रयुञ्जीरन्। अतस्तत्प्रशमनकराय कर्मणे कुशपूलीर्बिल्वसमिधः सितसरोरुहाणि च समुपाहरेति। उपयुक्तप्रयाहोमसाधनत्वादाश्रमोपशल्यानां दूरादानीतोऽयं भारः। अतः खल्वतिक्रान्तमहः। प्रक्रान्तः प्रदोषसमयः। (समन्तादवलोक्य) अहो पतित्रिणामप्यतिकृपणः संसारधर्मः। तथा ह्यमुष्मिन् सरसि,

अर्द्धाभ्युद्गतपत्रकं परिलुठत् पत्रेषु पङ्केरुहां
प्रायः पोतकजातकं कुररिकाः पक्षैः समूहन्त्यमूः।
अन्तः सुप्तमधुव्रतां शिशयिषुः शीतांशुसङ्कोचितां
भृङ्गी दत्तदलार्गलां कमलिनीं पर्येति पर्युत्सुका।। २।।

(परिक्रामन्नग्रतो विलोक्य) अये असौ राजर्षिः सवयस्यः संरम्भदूषितमुखश्रीरित एवाभिवर्तते। तन्नायमाशीर्वादावसरः। साधयामि तावदाश्रमपदम्। (निष्क्रान्तः)

विष्कम्भकः।

(ततः प्रविशति राजा विदूषकश्च)

राजा – (ससंरम्भम्) आ दुरात्मन्! अङ्गजन्मजनङ्गम!

मत्वा मामस्त्रजालक्षपितसुरगणप्रत्यनीकं तृणाय
श्लाधां मोघावसानामतनुमतनुतावर्मितस्त्वं तनोषि।

ACT THREE

(A young ascetic enters carrying sacrificial materials in his hands)

Asc (Astonished) Strange! Beyond the comprehension of speech and mind is the prowess of king Samvaraṇa. For, though he is afflicted by some unknown malady, his,

Brilliant arrows spitting fire from their sharp edges penetrated the mountain like forces of demons, though it is odd that we don't know the whereabouts of the demons driven from the hermitage by his raging missiles. (1)

I have been ordered by the preceptor thus: "Kauṇḍinya, my dear, I believe that the relatives of demons hurt by the arrows of Samvaraṇa may retaliate with deception since they could not fight him in the open. Bring Kuśa grass, Bilva sticks and white lotuses to perform some preventive rites." Since the materials from the neighbourhood have already been used up I am bringing this load from distant places. Therefore, the day is almost over and the evening is on. (Looking around) How miserable is the course of life even for birds. Thus in this lake,

The female ospreys clasp and cover with their feathers their young ones who hop about the lotus leaves; the female bee, anxious to share a bed with her lover, hovers about the lotus closed by cool moonbeams. (2)

(Walking about and looking in front) Oh! Here comes his majesty whose lovely face is marred by excitement, accompanied by his friend. So this is not the right time to greet him. I shall go to the hermitage. (Exit).

End of the interlude

(The King and the Vidūṣaka enter)

King (With excitement) Ah, miscreant! Outcaste of the lowest class! Oh Kāma!

Regarding me as straw who has driven away the enemies of the Gods by his arrows, you indulge in boasting that you have bodilessness as your armour, though it does no good. Are not my arrows powerful enough to seek out your strength, reduced by fire from the eye of Hara, yet enough to rob the fortitude of ascetics? (3)

कच्चिन्नालं त्वदीया हरनयनशिखिप्लोषसंक्षोभलब्धीः
कामं कन्दर्प ! शक्तीर्मुषितमुनिधृतीर्मार्गितुं मार्गणा मे।। ३।।

(पुनः प्रत्याकलय्य) हन्त धिङ्मामनवस्थितवचसम्। सकृदभ्यनुज्ञात-पराक्रमोऽयं मयि तपस्वी। तदनुनयामि तावदेनम्। भगवन् ! मृष्यतामयमपराधः। एतावत्तु भवन्तमभ्यर्थये –

अभिनवसहकारैः षट्पदालीढसारै-
रलमलमतिलोलैर्दक्षिणैर्मारुतैर्वा।
यदि कुवलयनीलैरद्य शक्नोषि तस्याः
प्रहर कुसुमधन्वन्नायताक्ष्याः कटाक्षैः।। ४।।

विदू (सनिर्वेदमात्मगतम्) अहो अच्चाहिदं। एस्सो असङ्गदाणि पलविदुं पवुत्तो। अहं खु एदरस अणङ्गामए दुव्वेज्जो विअ अवट्ठिएसु महावाहिसु उवक्कमं अआणन्तो अदिमत्तं सम्भमामि। उम्मूलिदो णेण णअरगमणवुत्तन्तो, जेण सअलं आणुअत्तं विसज्जिअं। एत्थ अडवीअं एआई अहं किं करिस्सं। होदु एव्वं दाव भणिस्सं। (प्रकाशम्) भो वअस्स ! अअहावुरो दे वअणवदिअरो कादरेइ मे हिअअं। ता धीरो होहि। (अहो अथ्याहितम्। एषोऽसङ्गतानि प्रलपितुं प्रवृत्त। अहं खल्वेतस्यानङ्गामये दुर्वैद्य इवोपस्थितेषु महाव्याधिषूपक्रममजानन् अतिमात्रं सम्भ्रमामि। उन्मूलितोऽनेन नगरगमनवृत्तान्तः, येन सकलमानुयात्रं विसर्जितम्। अत्राटव्यामेकाक्यहं किं करिष्यामि। भवत्वेवं तावद् भणिष्यामि। भो वयस्य ! अयथापुरस्ते वचनव्यतिकरः कातरयति मे हृदयम्। तद्धीरो भव।)

राजा (आत्मानं संस्तभ्य) सखे ! सत्यमाह भवान्। वचांसि नाम मनस्कारमूलानि। तस्मिन्निर्मूलमुन्मूलिते तया तनुमध्यया कथमनाकुलानि प्रवर्तेरन्।

विदू (सविपादम्) एव्वं गदे किं दाणिं मे सरणं। (एवं गते किमिदानी मे शरणम्।)

राजा (दीर्घं निश्वस्य) किमन्यत्। तदङ्गसंसर्गश्लाघनीयः स एव शुचिमणिमण्डपः शरणम्। आदिश्यातामुष्य पन्थाः।

विदू (सप्रत्याशम्) एदु एदु भवं। (एत्वेतु भवान्।) (उभौ परिक्रामतः)

विदू एस्स्ल पविसह्य। (एष सः। प्रविशावः।) (उभौ प्रवेशं नाटयतः)

राजा (सर्वतो दत्तदृष्टिः सविषादम्) अहो अस्थिरता वस्तुसम्पत्तीनाम्। पश्य –

विहीनं पार्वत्या भसितसितमङ्गं पशुपते-
र्विना भागीरथ्या तुहिनधवलं धूर्जटिगुरुम्।
श्रिया दुग्धाम्भोधिं विगतमिव च प्राणसमया
तया शून्यं मन्ये शुचिमणिगृहं शोच्यमधुना।। ५।।

विदू एसो ताए अहिट्ठिदपुरुवो दिव्वपरिमलुग्गारी तुह सहधम्मआरीहि फुल्लन्धएहि अहिलसिज्जन्तो अअं पदेसो। एत्थ उपविसिअ विणोदेहि अत्ताणं। (एष तयाधिष्ठितपूर्वो दिव्यपरिमलोद्गारी तव सहधर्मचारिभिः फुल्लन्धयैरभिलष्यमाणोऽयं प्रदेशः। अत्रोपविश्य विनोदयात्मानम्।)

(Thinking again) Alas! Shame on me for speaking incoherently. This silly fellow has already shown his prowess to me, so I shall now entreat him. Oh Sir, kindly excuse my indulgence. This much I pray for,

Enough of the Sahakāras whose sap had been sucked by the bees; enough of the gentle southern breeze too. If you could command, Oh Kāma, shoot me with the dark sidelong glances of the long-eyed beloved. (4)

Vidū (To himself with dejection) Alas! What a pity! He has begun to speak incoherently. I am really embarrassed at his lovelorn condition just as a quack salver is at a loss to treat an ailment. The very idea of returning to the city has been obliterated by him for he has already despatched his retinue. What can I do by myself in this forest? Yes, I shall address him thus. (Aloud) Oh friend, that your words do not conform to your disposition worries my hearts. Be steady.

King (Controlling himself) What you say is true. Words arise from judgement. That being rooted out by that slender-waisted one, how could they be consistent?

Vidū (With dejection) In this condition what recourse is there for me?

King (With a long sigh) What else is there than the crystal hall made memorable by the association with her body? Show the way towards it.

Vidū (Hopefully) May your majesty come this way. (Both walk about)

Vidū Here it is. Let us enter. (Both gesticulate entrance)

King (Looking around, with dejection) Alas! How evanescent is the glory of things. See,

This crystal hall, bereft of that beloved, looks jaded as the ash-smeared limbs of Śiva deprived of Pārvatī, as the snow-white mount without the river Bhāgīrathī, and as the milky ocean lacking the Goddess Śrī. (5)

Vidū Here is the spot which she had occupied earlier emitting a heavenly fragrance and sought by your companions who feed on the blossoms. Sit here and amuse yourself.

राजा सखे! मा भैवम्। अमीभिः खलु,

धन्यैर्मधुकरराजैर्गेयाभिरिह प्रियाभिरुचिताभिः।
भुक्त्वा भोगमभीष्टं विचरद्भिरहं न तुलनीयः।। ६।।

(उपविश्य दाहवेदनां भावयन्) मां प्रत्यहो विधेर्वैपरीत्यम्। स एवायमतिनिर्वाणकरत्वेन परिकल्पितो देशः सन्तापमतिदुस्सहं तनोति। सखे! न शक्नोम्यात्मानं धारयितुम्। तदमुष्मात् करतलोदकादानीय शिशिकवस्तूनि विरचय शयनीयम्।

विदू तह। (तथा कृत्वा) भो एत्थ सइदव्वम्। (तथा। भो अत्र शयितव्यम्।)

राजा (शयनं नाटयित्वा पार्श्वतो विलोकयन्) सखे! येन तस्याः शिशिरसमीरदानादुपकृतं, तेनैवामुना नलिनीपत्रेण वीजय माम्। (विदूषकः तथा करोति)

राजा (स्मृत्वा सनिःश्वासम्) अयि प्रेयसि! तदानीमनेन नलिनीपत्रेण वीज्यमानायां त्वयि चोदितयापि सख्या विलोचने मम विफलयितुमिच्छन्त्या त्वया नोत्तरीयमपनीतम्। तथापि मम,

पश्चात्कृतस्फटिकभित्तिनिरोधयत्नै-
रप्यावृते नयनरश्मिभिरंशुकेन।
प्रालेयपाण्डुकलधौतपयोरुहाभे
पर्युत्सुकैः पतितमेव पयोधरे ते।। ७।।

सखे! नलिनीपलाशपवनैः सन्धुक्षितः स्मरवह्निः। तद् विरम मुहूर्तम्।

विदू बाहं (विरमति) (बाढम्।)

(ततः प्रविशत्याम्बरयानेन नायिका मेनका च)

नायि (दीर्घं निश्वस्य) सहि! किं संपत्तह्म हत्थिणउरसमीवं। (सखि! किं सम्प्राप्ते स्वो हस्तिनपुरसमीपम्।)

मेन (सविषादमात्मगतम्) कदाणु खु पिअसहिं उवसन्तमअणुम्मादं दक्खिस्सं। (प्रकाशम्) सहि! किं तत्थ अह्माणं पओअणं। (कदानु खलु प्रियसखीमुपशान्तमदनोन्मादां द्रक्ष्यामि। सखि! किं तत्रास्माकं प्रयोजनम्।)

नायि (सविलक्षमात्मगतम्) हं किं मए मन्तिदं। सखि! रमणिज्जो खु कत्तिएआवासपरिसरारामो। (प्रकाशम्) (हं किं मया मन्त्रितम्। सखि! रमणीयः खलु कार्तिकेयावासपरिसरारामः।)

मेन सहि! अज्ज अण्णहि सो। (सखि! अद्यान्यस्मिन् सः।)

नायि कीस अम्बद्धं मन्तेसि। (कस्मादसम्बद्धं मन्त्रयसे।)

मेन (सस्मितम्) जणिज्जइ एव्व एदं कावा एत्थ असंबद्धं मन्तेदि त्ति। (ज्ञायत एवैतत् का वात्रासम्बद्धं मन्त्रयत इति।)

नायि उन्मत्तिए! किं सो जङ्गमो। (उन्मत्तिके! किं स जङ्गमः।)

मेन आम जङ्गमो। (आम जङ्गमः।)

नायि को दे अभिप्पाओ। (कस्तेऽभिप्रायः।)

मेन जो दे हिअअगओ। (यस्ते हृदयगतः।)

King Friend, don't say so!

With these blessed swarms of bees enjoying all desires moving freely
with their singing consorts I should not be compared. (6)

(Sitting down and gesticulating the sensation of burning) Strange is the hostility of fate to me. The same spot considered extremely blissful now emits morbid heat. Friend, I am unable to bear up. So prepare a bed for me, collecting cool materials from this lake of Karatalodaka.

Vidū Alright. (Doing accordingly) Sir, here you may lie down.

King (Showing the acts of lying down and looking around) Friend, fan me with this same lotus leaf which served her well with cool breeze.

(Vidūṣaka does accordingly)

King (Remembering and heaving a sigh) Oh my beloved! At that time when you were being fanned by your friend with this lotus leaf, despite her persuasion you did not remove your upper garments, thus rendering my eyes fruitless. Still,

The eager rays of my eyes, overcoming the obstruction of the crystal
walls, fell on your breasts, though covered by cloths, looking attractive as
a pair of golden lotuses whitened by dew drops. (7)

Friend, the fire of love has been kindled by the breeze of the lotus leaves. Please stop it for a moment.

Vidū Certainly. (Stops) (The heroine and Menakā enter passing through the sky)

Heroine (Heaving a deep sigh) Friend, have we reached the neighbourhood of Hastinapura?

Mena (To herself with dejection) When am I to see my dear friend free of her love mania? (Aloud) Friend, what is of interest there for us?

Heroine (To herself with embarrassment) Oh! What did I say? (Aloud) Friend, the garden surrounding the temple of Kārtikeya is attractive.

Mena Friend, today 'it' is somewhere else!

Heroine What nonsense are you talking?

Mena (With smiles) It is easily known who is speaking nonsense.

Heroine Mad woman! Is it mobile?

Mena Yes, it is mobile.

Heroine What do you mean?

Mena The one enshrined in your heart.

नायि को मे हिअअगओ। (को मे हृदयगतः।)

मेन (सस्मितम्) महाराअसंवरणो। (महाराजसंवरणः।)

नायि (सरोषम्) अण्णगअमणोरहं तं जणमुद्दिसिअ कीस मं विडम्बेसि। (अन्यगतमनोरथं तं जनमुद्दिश्य कस्माद् मां विडम्बयसि।)

मेन तुह हिअअं एव्व जाणइ अहं विडम्बेमि णवत्ति। (तव हृदयमेव जानात्यहं विडम्बयामि न वेति।)

नायि अलं परिहसिअ। को मग्गो भअवदो भिउणो अस्समपदस्स। (अलं परिहस्य। को मार्गो भगवतो भृगोराश्रमपदस्य।)

मेन णअहो अस्समं पत्थिआ। तहिं रम्भ पेसिअ तवणवणमुद्दिसिअ आअदह्म। (नावामाश्रमपदं प्रस्थिते। तत्र रम्भां प्रेष्य तपनवनमुद्दिश्यागते स्वः।)

नायि आ तवणवणं एत्थिदह्म। कहिं पुण तं। (आ तपनवनं प्रस्थिते स्व। क्व पुनस्तत्।)

मेन (अधो विलोक्य) एदं फलिहमण्डवस्स सिहरं दीसइ। ता ओदरह्म। (एतत् स्फटिकमण्डपस्य शिखरं दृश्यते। तदवतरावः।) (अवतरणं नाटयतः)

(ततः प्रविशति बद्धकर्णपूर्दण्डहस्ता रम्भा)

रम्भा अहं हि सहीहि णिउत्ता, जहभिउणो अस्समपदं गत्तूण अवहारेहि सो राएसी तत्थ सण्णिहिदो ण व त्ति। सो उण अज्ज पओसोवक्कमे एव्व तवणपणाहिमुहो वअस्सेण सह पत्थिओ। ता तवणवणं एव्व गदुअ सहीओ दक्खिस्सं। (परिक्रामति) (अहं हि सखीभ्यां नियुक्ता, यथा – भृगोराश्रमपदं गत्वावधारय स राजर्षिस्तत्र सन्निहितो न वेति। स पुनरद्य प्रदोशोपक्रम एव तपनवनाभिमुखो वयस्येन सह प्रस्थितः। तत् तपनवनमेव गत्वा सख्यौ द्रक्ष्यामि।

मेन (विलोक्य) सहि! एसा रम्भा बद्धकण्णेउरलट्ठिं घेत्तूण आअच्छइ। (सखि! एषा रम्भा बद्धकर्णपूरयष्टिं गृहीत्वागच्छति।)

रम्भा (उपसृत्य) सहि! सुहावेइ तुमं जोह्णादुऊलावउण्ठिओ अअं पओसो। (सखि! सुखयति त्वां ज्योत्स्नादुकूलावगुण्ठितोऽयं प्रदोषः।)

नायि (निश्वस्य) अलं मम सुहवुत्तन्तेण। कुदो इदं समासादिअं। (अलं मम सुखवृत्तान्तेन। कुत इदं समासादितम्।)

रम्भा तवोवणादो पडिणिवत्तन्तीए मम उवरि कुदो वि सहआरसाहग्गादो एदं पडिअं। अहं पुण किण्णुं हु एदं त्ति गेह्णिअ आअदह्मि। (तपोवनात् प्रतिनिवर्तमानाया ममोपरि कुतोऽपि सहकारशाखाग्रादेतत् पतितम्। अहं पुनः किन्नु खल्वेतदिति गृहीत्वागतास्मि।)

मेन (निर्वर्ण्य) सहि! एदाणि ताणि गाहक्खराणि। तदाणिं हत्थिणउरे अह्माणं करादो पब्भट्ठो वतंसओ। ता तक्केमि तस्स राअवयस्सस्स को वि पमादो एसो त्ति। (सखि! एतानि तानि गाथाक्षराणि। तदानीं हस्तिनपुरेऽस्माकं करात् प्रभ्रष्टोवतंसकः। तत् तर्कयामि तस्य राजवयस्यस्य कोऽपि प्रमाद एष इति।)

नायि (रम्भां विलोक्य) सहि! दाणिं कहिं सो बह्मणो। (सखि इदानीं क्व स ब्राह्मणः।)

रम्भा (सस्मितम्) एदस्सिं एव्व तवणवणे कहिं पि वटइ। (अस्मिन्नेव तपनवने क्वापि वर्तते।)

Heroine Who is the one enshrined in my heart?

Mena (Smiling) King Samvaraṇa.

Heroine (Angrily) Why do you vex me by mentioning that person who is committed to somebody else?

Mena Your heart itself knows whether I am vexing or not.

Heroine Enough of joking. Which is the way to the hermitage of the venerable sage Bhṛgu?

Mena We are not going to that hermitage. Having already despatched Rambhā there, we are going to Tapana forest.

Heroine Yes, we are going to Tapana forest. Where is that?

Mena (Looking down) Here we see the roof of the crystal hall. Let us descend.

(Both gesticulate descent)

(Rambhā enters holding in her hands a staff to which the earring is tied)

Rambha I have been asked by my friends thus: "Go to the hermitage of Bhṛgu and ascertain whether his majesty is present there or not." But this evening he has set out for Tapana forest with his friend. So I shall go there and meet my friends. (Walks about).

Mena (Observing) Friend, here comes Rambhā holding a staff to which the earring is tied.

Rambha (Approaching near) Friend, does the evening couched in the silken shroud of moonlight bring comfort to you?

Heroine (Sighing) Enough with my comforts. From where did you get that?

Rambha While I was returning from Tapana forest this fell on me from the branch of a mango tree. I just took it with me out of curiosity.

Mena (Observing) Friend, here are the syllables of that lyric. It is the same earring that slipped down from your hands in Hastinapura. I presume that it shows the negligence of the King's friend.

Heroine (Looking at Rambhā) Friend, where is that Brāhmin now?

Rambha (With smile) Somewhere in this Tapana forest.

नायि (खेदमभिनीय) सहि! अम्बरणमणाआसो मं अतिमत्तं पीडेइ। ता एदस्सिं फलिहमण्डवे विस्समह्म। (सखि! अम्बरगणनायासो मामतिमात्रं पीडयति। तदेतस्मिन् स्फटिकमण्डपे विश्राम्यामः।)

सख्यौ सहि! एव्वं करह्म। (सखि! एवं कुर्मः।) (प्रवेशं रूपयन्ति)

विदू (ससम्भ्रमम्) कहं पओसोवक्कमे एव्व पहादं। (कथं प्रदोशोपक्रम एव प्रभातम्।)

मेन (जनान्तिकम्) सहि! एसो सो राएसी बलिअं सन्दावं उव्वहन्तो सिसिरोवआरेहि उवअरिज्जन्तो सइदो चिट्ठइ। एसो उण बह्मणो तुह पआसीकिदमण्डवब्भन्तरेण पहाजालेण विप्पलद्धो पबादं त्ति विप्पलवदि। ता तिरक्खरणीबिज्जाए पडिच्छण्णओ दक्खह्म एदाणं वावारं। (सखि! एष स राजर्षिर्बलीयांसं सन्तापमुद्वहन् शिशिरोपचारैरुपचर्यमाणः शयितस्तिष्ठति। एष पुनर्ब्राह्मणस्तव प्रकाशीकृतमण्डपाभ्यन्तरेण प्रभाजालेन विप्रलब्धः प्रभातमिति विप्रलपति। तत् तिरस्करणीविद्यया प्रतिच्छन्ना द्रक्ष्याम एतयोर्व्यापारम्।) (तथा कृत्वा तिष्ठन्ति)

विदू (सविस्मयम्) भो वअस्स! पुणो विरत्ती आसी। एत्थ रम्मे पदेसे उदुसङ्करो विअ अहोरत्तसङ्करो संवुत्तो। को एत्थ हेदू। (भो वयस्य! पुनरपि रात्रिरासीत्। अत्र रम्ये प्रदेशे ऋतुसङ्कर इवाहोरात्रसङ्करः संवृत्तः। कोऽत्र हेतुः।)

राजा (सविमर्शम्) सखे! सन्निहितदिव्यजनेषु प्रदेशेषु किमसम्भावनीयं नाम। सखे! किमितिन वीजयसि।

विदू (सोद्वेगमात्मगतम्) खणे खणे वड्ढन्तो भाआवेइ मं एदस्स मअणुम्माओ। (प्रकाशम्) भो वअस्स! को दे सम्मोहो। णं तुए णिवारिदो। (क्षणे क्षणे वर्द्धमानो भावयति मामेतस्य मदनोन्मादः। भो वयस्य! कस्ते सम्मोहः। ननु त्वया निवारितः।)

राजा सखे! हृदयमत्रापराध्यति। अयि हृदय! भवतु तावदलभमानस्य तां मम सम्भ्रमः। त्वं तु –

चकितनयनं चुम्बस्यंसे निवर्तितमाननं
प्रतिनववधूं लज्जालोलां बलादुपगूहसि।
अनतिशिथिलं नीवीग्रन्थिं पुनः परिलोलयद्
विचरसि शनैः श्रोणीचक्रे कुतः परिखिद्यसे।। ८।।

नायि (सासूयमात्मगतम्) वम्मह! अहो दे अविवेओ, जं अप्पत्तिअं पि एदेण मम हिअअं अच्छिन्दिअ दिण्णं। चिरप्पत्थिअं पि एदस्स हिअअं मम अहिमुहं कादुं ण पारेसि। (प्रकाशम्) एसो दाव देवीविरहुक्कण्ठिओ परिदेविउं पवुत्तो। ता किं एत्थ अह्माणं पओअणं। (मन्मथ! अहो ते अविवेकः, यदप्रार्थितमप्येतेन मम हृदयमाच्छिन्द्य दत्तम्। चिरप्रार्थितमप्येतस्य हृदयं ममाभिमुखं कर्तुं न पारयसि। एष तावद् देवीविरहोत्कण्ठितः परिदेवितुं प्रवृत्तः। तत् किमत्रास्माकं प्रयोजनम्।)

मेन सहि! अहिणवा खु तुवं। ण एसो देवीविरहुक्कण्ठिओ। किं ण सुदो तुए णववहूसद्दो। (सखि! अभिनवा खलु त्वम्। नैष देवीवरहोत्कण्ठितः। किं न श्रुतस्त्वया नववधूशब्दः।)

नायि तह वि कं मम। (तथापि किं मम।)

Heroine (Gesticulating exhaustion) Friend, I am very tired because of the journey through the sky. Let us take rest in this crystal hall.

Maids Friend, be it so.

(They gesticulate entrance)

Vidū (Showing confusion) What! Day breaks soon after the nightfall!

Mena (Aside) Friend, here lies his majesty suffering anguish and attended to with cooling materials. And the Brahmin calls out that it is the sunrise, deceived by your effulgence illuminating the interior of the halls. So we shall watch their action using the charm of concealment.

(They remain accordingly)

Vidū (With surprise) Oh friend, once again it is night. In this beautiful spot day and night commingle and so too the seasons. Why is it so?

King (Surmising) Friend, there is nothing impossible in such places frequented by celestial. Friend, why don't you fan me?

Vidū (To himself with anxiety) That his pangs of love grow every moment frightens me. (Aloud) Oh my friend, you are perplexed. Did you not stop me?

King Friend, here my heart is at fault. Oh my heart! Let there be perplexity in me since I failed to get her. But,

> You kiss the face with tremulous eyes turned towards the shoulders; embrace perforce the young and timid bride, and roam about her broad hips untying the already loosened knot of her garment. So why this unnecessary agitation? (8)

Heroine (To herself) Oh Kāma, strange is your insolence in plucking my heart and giving it to him without being requested. Despite my persistent appeal you would not turn his heart to me. (Aloud) He is grieving due to the separation from his queen. So what business is there for us?

Mena Friend, you are inexperienced. This man is not anxious of his queen. Have you not heard the words 'young bride'?

Heroine Even if so, what is that to me?

रम्भा अदो खु संसओ। पुणो विसुणह्म। (अतः खलु संशयः। पुनरपि शृणुमः।)

विदू भो! एदे पदुमराअगवक्खन्तरप्पविट्ठा किं णावणअन्ति दे अणङ्गमोहं चन्दमोहा। (भो! एते पद्मरागगवाक्षान्तरप्रविष्टाः किं नापनयन्ति ते अनङ्गमोहं चन्द्रमयूखाः।)

राजा सखे! असम्भृतपुण्यसञ्चयानामतिप्रतीपाः पदार्थशक्तयः। पश्य –

अबहुलविनिपातादार्जिताभिः कलाभिः
कुशलि कुमुदबन्धोश्चन्द्रिकोद्गारि बिम्बम्।
अपि मनसि गुरोर्मे हारगौरैः कराग्रै-
रपिहितगुणदोषानर्पयत्यन्धकारान्।। ९।।

नायि (आत्मगतम्) मूढहिअअ! तुवं दाव अण्णाए णामहेअस्स असङ्किक्त्तणमत्तं ओलम्बिअ दुरासाए मरणकिदव्ववसाअं मं पडिबन्धेसि। (मूढहृदय! त्वं तावदन्यस्या नामधेयास्यासङ्कीर्तन-मात्रमवलम्ब्य दुराशया मरणकृतव्यवसायां मां प्रतिबध्नासि।)

राजा सखे! पश्य मदीयां दशां, यतःशयितुमपि न शक्नोमि।

विदू (सविषादम्) किण्णु हु मए मन्दभाएण कादव्वं। जो किञ्चि अस्सासहेदु त्ति सम्भाविओ, सो वि कण्णेउरो मम प्पमादेण मक्कडहत्थगओ आसि। (किन्नु खलु मया मन्दभाग्येन कर्तव्यम्। यः किञ्चिदाश्वासहेतुरिति सम्भावितः, सोऽपि कर्णपूरो मम प्रमादेन मर्कटहस्तगत आसीत्।)

मेन (साकूतम्) सहि! अविस्सम्भसीले! जइ तइ एसो उदासीणो, कहं तुह केरएण कण्णेउरेण से आसासो। (सखि! अविस्रम्भशीले! यदि त्वय्येष उदासीनः, कथं त्वदीयेन कर्णपूरेणास्याश्वासः।)

नायि किं तुए ण सुदं देविं अणुणअन्तस्स वअणं 'अब्भुअरसो एत्थ अवरज्झदि' त्ति। (किं त्वया न श्रुतं देवीमनुनयतो वचनम् 'अद्भुतरसोऽत्रापराध्यति' इति।)

मेन बालिआ खु तुवं। अणहिण्णा चउरचाडूणं। (बालिका खलु त्वम्। अनभिज्ञा चतुरचाटूनाम्।)

नायि होदु एदं। विवित्ते पिअवअस्सस्स 'अक्खित्तोह्मि केवलं विह्मएण, ण अण्णह' त्ति भणिअं। एदं पि किं चाडू। (भवत्वेतत्। विविक्ते प्रियवयस्यस्य 'आक्षिप्तोऽस्मि केवलं विस्मयेन, नान्यथे'ति भणितम्। एतदपि किं चाटुः।)

मेन अदिगम्भीरा हि पुरिसा अत्तणो अहिणवं चावलं सव्वदो रक्खन्ति। (अतिगम्भीरा हि पुरुषा आत्मनेऽभिनवं चापलं सर्वतो रक्षन्ति।)

रम्भा सहि! जाणिदो कण्णेउरस्स आगमो बह्मणादो। ता दीणस्स एदस्स एदं दइस्सं। (विदूषकस्य पुरतो निक्षिपति) (सखि! ज्ञातः कर्णपूरस्यागमो ब्राह्मणात्। तद् दीनस्यैतस्यैतं दास्यामि।)

विदू (विलोक्य सविस्मयम्) भो! सदण्डअट्ठस्स सब-ह्मसुत्तस्स कण्णेउरस्स कहं अतक्किओ आगमो। मण्णे भिदहि अन्तलिहिदाहि वाणरजादीहि पक्खित्तो त्ति। (भो! सदण्डकाष्ठस्य सब्रह्मसूत्रस्य कर्णपूरस्य कथमतर्कित आगमः। मन्ये भीतभिरन्तर्हिताभिर्वानरजातिभिः प्रक्षिप्त इति।)

रम्भा धस्स गामिल! वटुअ! तुमं एव्व वाणरो। (अपगच्छ ग्रामिल! वटुक! त्वमेव वानरः।)

राजा (सालसं दृष्टिमुन्मील्य पश्यन्) सखे! समर्पयैनं मम हृदये। (विदूषको दण्डकाष्ठादवमुच्यार्पयति)

मेन सहि! इदाणिं पच्चेहि। (सखि! इदानीं प्रत्येहि।)

Rambha That is why you are doubtful. Let us listen again.

Vidū Oh friend, is not the moonlight entering through the ruby windows enough to remove your affliction?

King Friend, to those without merit the qualities of things appeal contrary to their nature. See,

Though possessing pearl-white rays like sun, the orb of the moon, the friend of lotuses, even when fully bright, spreads only darkness in my mind, suppressing vices and virtues. (9)

Heroine (To herself) Oh foolish heart! You deflect me from my resolve to commit suicide, hoping against hope, just because another's name has not yet been mentioned.

King Friend, you see my plight; I am unable even to lie down.

Vidū (With dejection) What can be done by this unfortunate one! The earring conceived as providing some consolation is in the hands of apes owing to my negligence.

Mena (Meaningfully) Friend, Oh unbelieving one! If he is indifferent to you, how can he have consolation from your earring?

Heroine It may be so. But in private he told his best friend that "I am just surprised and not otherwise." Is that also flattery?

Mena Men of depth conceal their new-born vagaries from all.

Rambha Friend, it is known that the earring came from the Brahmin. So I shall give it back to the miserable fellow. (Throws it before the Vidūṣaka)

Vidū (Noticing with surprise) Ha! Here comes the earring with the sacred thread and staff. I presume that it was thrown by the frightened apes who remain concealed.

Rambha Go away you uncultured Brahmin. You alone are the ape!

King (Opening his eyes lazily and noticing) Friend, put it on my chest.

(Vidūṣaka places it accordingly untying it from the staff)

Mena Friend, now be convinced!

राजा (स्मृत्वा सावज्ञम्) आः कस्या अयं कर्णपूरः। अपनीयतां तावत्। (विदूषकोऽपनयति)

नायि (आत्मगतम्) हं णट्ठह्मि (प्रकाशम्) इदो वरं किं सोदव्वं। (हं नष्टस्म। इतः परं किं श्रोतव्यम्।)

मेन तक्केमि तुह केरओ ण होइ त्ति अवहत्थिओ कण्णेउरो। (तर्कयामि त्वदीयो न भवतीत्यपहस्तितः कर्णपूरः।)

नायि (सरोषम्) पुव्वं तुह एसो वतंसओ एदस्स अस्सासहेतु त्ति भणिअं। इदाणि तुह ण होइ त्ति परिच्चत्तो त्ति भणासि। अहो दो एदस्सि पक्खवादो। (प्रस्थातुमिच्छति) (पूर्वं तवैष वतंसक एतस्याश्वासहेतुरिति भणितम्। इदानीं तव न भवतीति परित्यक्त इति भणसि। अहो तवैतस्मिन् पक्षपातः।)

राजा **प्रिये तपति निर्दये।**

मेन अप्पावमाणिणि! णिवत्तेहि दाणिं। (आत्मावमानिनि! निवर्तस्वेदानीम्।)

नायि (सहर्षं प्रतिनिवृत्यात्मगतम्) हिअअ! दे गओ संसओ सुणाहि गअसंभमं।
(हृदय! ते गतः संशयः। शृणु गतसम्भ्रमम्।)

राजा **शुचमुपैमि चन्द्रातपे।**

नायि (सशोकम्) हदह्मि। **(हतास्मि।)**

राजा **रविसम्भवे।**

नायि (पुनः सप्रमोदम्) हिअअ! तुस्स। **(हृदय! तुष्य।)**

राजा **सत्यातपे यथैव कुमुदाकरो।**

नायि (पुनः सशोकम्) ण अरिदं खु पुण्णं मए।। १०।। **(न चरितं खलु पुण्यं मया।)**

राजा (दीर्घमुष्णं च निःश्वस्य सकृपणम्) दयिते! तव खलु सख्या समुच्चारिते संवरणध्वनावन्यार्थेऽपि सम्भ्रान्तदृशा त्वया –

चलितधृति तदानीमार्यपुत्रेति वाचः
कतिचिदमृतगर्भाण्यक्षराण्युक्तवत्या।
करकमलमिदानीं कान्तमङ्गे मदीये
कथमिव निदधत्या नाहमुज्जीवनीयः।। ११।।

नायि (सस्पृहं सरोमविक्रियं च स्वगतम्) अम्महे एसो एव्व किल जणो एदस्स कामुम्मादहेदू। (हर्षमुर्च्छिता पतति) (अहो एष एव किल जन एतस्य कामोन्मादहेतुः।)

मेन (सहर्षबाष्पगद्गदम्) सहि! मुच्छेहि मुच्छेहि। अणुमदं मए। (सखि! मूर्च्छ मूर्च्छ। अनुमतं मया।)

रम्भा (ससम्भ्रमम्) सहि! को दे सम्मोहो। पमोदणिमित्तं पि एसा मुच्छइ एव्व। ता समासासह्म णं। (सखि! कस्ते सम्मोहः प्रमोदनित्तिमप्येषा मूर्च्छत्येव। तत् समाश्वासयाव एनाम्।)

उभे (उपसृत्य) समस्ससदु समस्ससदु पिअसही। (समाश्वसितु समाश्वसितु प्रियसखी।)

(नायिका प्रत्यागत्य प्रेमविस्मृतनिमेषा राजानं पश्यन्ती तिष्ठति)

King (Remembering; with contempt) Ah! Whose earring is it? Take it away!

Heroine (To herself) Ah! I am lost. (Aloud) What more is to be heard?

Mena I presume that the earring was rejected believing that it is not yours.

Heroine (Angrily) Earlier it was said that "Your earring brings consolation to him". Now you say that it is "rejected believing that it is not yours". oh biased you are in his favour! (Wants to go away)

King "Oh my beloved! Tapatī – unmerciful!"

Mena OH, self-denying one, come back!

Heroine (Returning with delight) "oH heart! your doubts are gone; hear without agitation".

King "In the moonlight i am anguished."

Heroine (Sorrowfully) "i have lost".

King "progeny of the sun!"

Heroine (Again with pleasure) "o heart; be delighted".

King "i like a pond full of lotuses in sunshine".

Heroine (Again with sorrow) "I do not have enough merit".(10)

King (Heaving a deep sigh helplessly) Beloved, when your friend with dilated eyes uttered the sound 'Samvaraṇa' though having a different connotation -

> You spoke certain nectar-filled words such as 'Oh mu husband,' breaking
> your fortitude. Now how am I to be revived without the touch of your
> lotus hands on my limbs? (11)

Heroine (To herself, longingly and with horripilation) Oh! I am the root cause of his pangs of love! (Falls down in a swoon of ecstasy)

Mena (Choking with delight) Friend, may you swoon! I approve it!

Rambha (With excitement) Friend, you are confused. She is really unconscious though owing to delight. So let us cheer her up.

Both (Approaching near) Take heart, dear friend, take heart. (Recovering from the swoon, the heroine remains looking at the king with steady eyes)

राजा (अविस्पष्टाक्षरम्) सखे!

मुक्तमूलममी प्राणाः प्रायः कण्ठविलम्बिनः।
निर्गच्छन्ति पुरा सोऽयं सुदृष्टः क्रियतां जनः।। १२।।

विदू (ससम्भ्रमं सास्त्रगद्गदम्) हा हदो ह्मि। एव्वं मयि उवक्कन्तं विहिणा। (सत्वरमुपसृत्य राज्ञोऽङ्गानि परामृशति) (हा हतोऽस्मि। एवं मय्युपक्रान्तं विधिना।)

राजा हा प्रिये! (इत्यर्द्धोक्ते मूर्च्छया परामृष्टः)

विदू (सविषादम्) समस्ससदु समस्ससदु वअस्सो। (पुनर्विलोक्य सविषादम्) कहं गदो एव्व अन्तं वअस्सो। (सशिरस्ताडनम्) हा वअस्स! हा सअलहरामण्डलेक्कणाह! हा मइ अआरणबद्धसिणेह! कसि मं अणण्णसरणं सव्वआलसहअरं वालमित्तं दइअं परिच्चय्य गच्छसि। दिग्धाउं वंसअरं एत्तं लभत्ते होहि त्ति सिद्धदेसिआणं वअणंपि अलिअं णअ। (स्मृत्वा) अहव किं मम परिदेविएहि। भिउपडणेण अणुसरामि पिअवअरसं। (निष्क्रान्तः) (समाश्वसितु समाश्वसितु वयस्यः। कथं गत एवान्तं वयस्यः। हा वयस्य! हा सकलधरामण्डलैकनाथ! हा मय्यकारणबद्धस्नेह! कस्मान्मामनन्यशरणं सर्वकालसहचरं बालमित्रं दयितं परित्यज्य गच्छसि। दीर्घायुषं वंशकरं पुत्रं लभमानो भवेति सिद्धादेशिकानां वचनमप्यलीकं सञ्जातम्। अथ वा किं मम परिदेवितैः। भृगुपतनेनानुसरामि प्रियवयस्यम्।)

नायि (खेदनिस्सहं भूमौ पतन्ती) हा मं एव्व आलविअ कहं गदो अय्यउत्तो। अय्यउत्त! खणं मं पडिवालेहि। एसह्मि आअदा (मोहमुपगच्छति) (हा मामेवालप्य कथं गत आर्यपुत्रः। आर्यपुत्र! क्षणं मां प्रतिपालय। एषास्म्यागता।)

सख्यौ (ससम्भ्रममुत्सङ्गे कृत्वा) समस्सदु समस्सदु पिअ सही। (समाश्वसितु समाश्वसितु प्रियसखी।)

नायि (समाश्वस्य) सहीओ! मा च्छिवह मा च्छिवह मं पदिवहपावमलीमसं। अणुमण्णह परलोअगअं पि तं जणं अहिसरिदुं। (सख्यौ! मा स्पृशतं मां पतिवधपापमलीमसाम्। अनुमन्येथां परलोकगतमपि तं जनमभिसर्तुम्।)

रम्भा (विचिन्त्य) सहि! अहो अह्माणं मूढदा। तुह करकमलसंसग्गं पत्थिअ एसो महाराओ एरिसं दसं पडिवण्णो। ता एदस्स हिअए तुरिअं णिहेहि करकमलं। जइ एदं पि विहलं होइ, पच्छा सव्वाओ विवज्जह्म। (सखि! अहो अस्माकं मूढता। तव करकमलसंसर्गं प्रार्थ्य एष महाराज ईदृशीं दशां प्रतिपन्नः। तदेतस्य हृदये त्वरितंधेहि करकमलम्। यद्येतदपि विफलं भवति, पश्चात् सर्वा विपद्यामहे।)

(नायिका सत्वरमुत्तिष्ठन् तिरस्करणीमपनीय ससाध्वसकम्पं तस्योरसि करकमलमर्पयति)

राजा (सत्वरमुत्तिष्ठन् करमाक्षिपन्तीं नायिकां दृष्ट्वा)

अलमलमाक्षिप्यामुं पाणिं पाणौ निधत्स्व गलदमृतम्।
यो मामुज्जीवयितुं हरिणाक्षि! समर्पितो हृदये।। १३।।

King (Instinctively) Friend,

These vital airs of mine have left their moorings and hang in the throat. Try to make that person visible ere they escape. (12)

Vidū (Confused and choking with tears) Ha! I am lost. Fate has done this to me! (Approaching quickly he feels the limbs of the King)

King Ah! My beloved! – (In the middle of the sentence he swoons)

Vidū (With dejection) Take heart, my dear friend, take heart. (Looking again, with dejection) What! My friend has breathed his last! (Knocking at his head) Oh my friend, Oh lord of worlds! Oh sincere companion! Why do you go away leaving me helpless, your close associate from childhood days? The prophecy of sages that "You will have a son endowed with longevity to perpetuate your lineage" has proved false! Oh what use is there with my grieving? I shall follow my friend in death by jumping down from a cliff. (Exit)

Heroine (Falling down with unbearable grief) Alas! My beloved has expired calling out for me! Oh beloved; wait for a moment! Here I come with you! (Faints)

Maids (Placing her in their lap, in confusion) Take heart, dear friend, take heart.

Heroine (Recovering) Friends, don't touch this sinful woman who just killed her husband. Permit me to follow him in death.

Rambha (Meditating) Friend, we are stupid! The king has reached the present condition beseeching the touch of your hands. Put your hands on his breast immediately. If it proves futile all of us shall perish together. (The heroine trembling with excitement, moves quickly discarding her invisibility; she places her hands on his breast)

King (Getting up suddenly and noticing the heroine taking away her hands)

"Oh deer-eyed one! No! Don't remove your nectar-dripping palm from my breast where it was placed to bring me back to life." (13)

(ग्रहीतुमिच्छति)

मेन (राजानमुपसृत्य) महाराअ! अलं दाणिं तुवरिअ। इअं णा पिअसही तेल्लोक्कप्पदीवस्स भअवदो सुय्यस्स धीदा भअवदीए सावित्तीए अवरआ तवदीणामहेआ। तस्स वि किल महाराओ एव्व जामादुओ त्ति सङ्कप्पो। ता अब्भत्थिअ देवं गोह्ण एदाए पाणिं। एसो उण दे वअस्सो तुह अवत्थं दक्खिअ णिरासो भिउपडणं कादुं पत्थिओ। ता तुरिअं गत्तूण पच्चुज्जीवेहि णं। गच्छह्म पुणो दंसणाय। (महाराज! अलमिदानीं त्वरित्वा। इयमावयोः प्रियसखी त्रैलोक्यप्रदीपस्य भगवतः सूर्यस्य पुत्री भगवत्याः सावित्र्या अवरजा तपतीनामधेया। तस्यापि किल महाराज एव जामातेति सङ्कल्पः। तदभ्यर्थ्य देवं गृहाणैतस्याः पाणिम्। एष पुनस्ते वयस्यस्तवावस्थां दृष्ट्वा निराशो भृगुपतनं कर्तुं प्रस्थितः। तत् त्वरितं गत्वा प्रत्युज्जीवयैनम्। गच्छामः पुनर्दर्शनाय।

(सह सखीभ्यां निष्क्रान्ता नायिका)

राजा (ससम्भ्रमं मण्डपनिष्क्रमणं रूपयित्वा परिक्रामन्) क्वासौ क्वासौ।

विदू ह्णाणसंसुद्धो अहं जहसमीहिदं करिस्सं। (स्नानसंशुद्धोऽहं यथा समीहितं करिष्यामि।)

(शिखरारोहणं नाटयति)

राजा (सत्वरमुपसृत्य) न खलु न खलु साहसमनुष्ठेयम्। अयमहं प्राणिमि।

विदू (श्रुत्वा ससम्भ्रमम्) कहिं सि कहिं सि। बप्फंधा मे दिट्ठी। तेण तुमं ण पेक्खामि (राजानं परिष्वज्य मुक्तकण्ठं रुदित्वा) एदस्सिं एव्व जम्मे तुवं मए आलिङ्गिदव्वो आसी। (क्वासि क्वासि। बष्पान्धा मे दृष्टिः। तेन त्वां न पश्यामि। एतस्मिन्नेव जन्मनि त्वं मयालिङ्गितव्य आसीः।)

राजा सखे! अलमावेगेन। उत्तीर्णा वयममुतो व्यसनार्णवात्।

विदू कहं विअ। (कथमिव।)

राजा एवमिव।

विदू (सहर्षम्) भो दिट्ठिआ वड्ढसि। अदो वरं किंअह्माण आरम्भो। (भो दिष्ट्या वर्धसे। अतः परं क आवयोरारम्भः।)

राजा किमन्यत् –

आचाराम्यहमतः परं सखे! तामुपोढनियमः पुरस्क्रियाम्।
प्रीणितः प्रणतवत्सलो यया नांशुमानलमदातुमात्मजाम्।। १४।।

(इति निष्क्रान्तौ)

इति तृतीयोऽङ्कः।

(Wants to hold it)

(The heroine turns back in embarrassment and remains helpless looking at her friends)

Mena Oh King; don't be in a hurry. This is our friend, Tapatī, the younger sister of Goddess Sāvitrī and daughter of the Sun God – the light of the three worlds. He has resolved that you alone shall be his son-in-law. You may approach him for her hand in marriage. Your hapless friend has gone to hurl himself down a cliff after seeing your plight. Please hurry to save him! Now let us depart to meet again.

(The heroine exits along with her friends)

King (Gesticulating exit from the hall in confusion and walking about) Where, where is he?

(Entering)

Vidū Having purified myself with a bath I shall now carry out my resolve. (Gesticulates that he is climbing a summit)

King (Going near in haste) Don't act rashly. Here I breathe!

Vidū (Hearing; in confusion) Where, where are you? My eyes are blinded by tears, so I cannot see you. (Embracing the king and weeping aloud) In this birth itself I could embrace you again!

King Friend, don't get excited. We are saved from this ocean of grief.

Vidū How?

King Like this!

Vidū (With delight) Friend, luck is with you! Now what shall we do?

King What else,

Oh friend, hereafter, I shall perform penance according to prescribed rules. Pleased with this, the generous Sun God could not refrain from giving me his daughter. (14)

(Both exit)

The End of Act Three

व्यङ्ग्यव्याख्या।

एवं द्वितीयाङ्कस्थायीभावप्रयोगमार्गौ दर्शितौ। अथ स कविरेवं द्वितीयाङ्कावसानं नाटकं निर्माय भूयस्तृतीयाङ्कं निर्मातुं प्रारब्धवान्। अथ स कविस्तत्रादौ तत्संबन्धप्रकारं केनचित्तापसकुमारेणोच्यमानं बोधयति। तदर्थममुना स तापसकुमारः प्रावेशितः। तस्मादहमादौ तस्य प्रावेशिकं स्थायीभावं प्रयोगामार्गं च दर्शयामि।

ततः प्रविशति तापसकुमारः सविमर्शम्।

अथ कोपि तापसकुमारः स्वगुरुणेत्यादिष्टः यथा 'वत्स कौण्डिन्य पूर्वं कदाचिदत्र संप्राप्तं संवरणवयस्यं पाराशर्यं दृष्ट्वा मोहिनिकैरक्षश्शतैः पीड्यमाना वयं सावधानं तपः कर्तुमक्षमा वयमिति तद्वयस्यसंवरणं विज्ञापये'त्युक्तेन तेन विज्ञापितोयं राजर्षिः केनापि हेत्वन्तरेण शिथिलितमनस्कोपि तच्छ्रवणजनितकोपः तत्क्षणमेव निजशक्तिद्वितीयस्तत्पुत्रशतमशेषं निहतवान्। अथ तेनेति निहते स्वपुत्रशते राक्षसी प्रोच्यत्क्रोधरोषा 'युधि प्रहतं हन्तुमक्षमेदानीं तदविज्ञेयं मायाभिरेनं पीडयामी'ति कृतसङ्कल्पा तदुद्योगमाचरिष्यतीति मद्वचनेनैव गत्वा करतलोदकतीरे यत् किञ्चिदुद्दिश्य संचरन्तं संवरणं तदेतत् यथार्थं मद्वचनं विज्ञाप्य तमिमं त्वद्वशे प्रापय्य स्वस्थचित्तं विधायास्मै पुनरग्निदैवत्यं मन्त्रस्त्वयोपदिश्यतामित्युक्तश्च। 'भो राजर्षे तयोपदिष्टमेनं सावधानं चेतस्यवतार्य तद्ध्यानपरेऽनन्यचेतसि त्वयि मत्समीपे स्थितवति तन्मायाप्रयोगात् प्रागेव तत्प्रशमनकरैः कैश्चिद्धामैर्मायानिवारणं करोमी'ति विज्ञाप्य तथाभूते तस्मिन् भूयस्त्वयापि तथाक्रियतामित्यादिष्टो गुरुणा कोपि तापसकुमारः तन्नियोगमनुष्ठितुं तस्मान्निर्गत्य करतलोदकं प्राप्य तत्र सायन्तनकर्म समाप्य राजानमन्विष्य तस्य अलाभात् पिशिताशिवधक्रोधादनुक्रमद्विगुणितक्रोधं तत्र सञ्चरन्तमितस्ततः सवयस्यं तमितरकार्यं परिभ्रमचिन्तं दृष्ट्वा सविमर्शमत्रातिष्ठत्। एवं पूर्वसंबन्धः।

यस्मान्निर्दिष्टं त्रिवर्त्युज्वलितस्य दीपस्य पुरस्तद्भूमिकालङ्कृततनुर्भरतवरो यावत्तिष्ठेत् तावदपयवनिको भूत्वा यथानिर्दिष्टं मुहूर्तं तिष्ठेत्। एवं तिष्ठन्नयं सान्तर्विवेकमुद्वष्टिरेवं विमृशेत्। कुतः हन्तास्मद्गुरुविनियोगविफलता फलिता। अहो इत्यत्रविवेके। कुतः मन्त्रस्मृत्या पूतचेतास्मि तस्मिन् सावधानमग्निसन्निधौ स्थितवति बिल्वसमिदादिभिरेभिर्होमसाधनैस्तन्मायां शमयितुमाहुतिः क्रियतामित्यादेशः।

तमनन्यचित्तीकृत्य मन्त्रं नास्य बोधयितुं न शक्यते यत् तेन नियोगविफलता फलितेति निश्चितवानस्मि।

यश्च कार्यस्य संसिध्यै क्रियामारभ्यते यदा।
निर्विघ्नं तत् समाप्नोति यदि सिद्ध्यति तत्तदा।।
विघ्नो भवति चेत्तत्र वैफल्यं तत् प्रयास्यति।

इत्यस्ति तन्त्रशास्त्रे क्रियाप्रयोगविधौ दर्शितम्। एतस्माच्च; अहो कष्टमयं मायाभिर्बाध्यो भविता; पुनरपि तमेव पश्यन् अहो इति स्मरशरशकलीकृतहृदयोयं तनुतां प्राप्नोति यैः कैश्चित् शत्रुभिस्सह योद्धुमलम्। अहो इत्यस्यैव, अहो कस्मादहं खिन्नो भवामि –

तामसा राजसाश्चैव सात्विकास्त्रिविधा जनाः।
त्रीनुपायैस्त्रिभिः पुंसो बुद्धिमान् स्ववशं नयेत्।।

अहो

यावद्दण्डयतामाद्यः प्रशंसाभिर्रजस्विनः।
सात्विकान् सेवया मौनी त्रीनेभिः स्ववशं नयेत्।। इति गुरुवचनम्।

तस्मादेनं वास्तवभूतैर्गुणसङ्कीर्तनैः प्रशंसावचनैरनुनयामीत्यात्मना निश्चित्योत्तरग्रन्थेन तत्प्रशंसां करोति। **अहो अवाङ्मनसगोचर** इत्यादिना। अथ राजा तत्र किमपि दूरे तिष्ठन्नहो इति ग्रन्थं ब्रूते। एवं ब्रुवाणस्तिष्ठन्नयं तमेव पश्यन्नेनं तत्पराक्रमं श्रावयित्वा तमात्मनो वशीकर्तुमुत्तरग्रन्थेन तत्प्रशंसामेव करोति **अहो** इति। अत्राहोशब्दोद्भुते भूयस्तत्प्रशंसाप्रकारं विवृणोति। अनिर्देश्यैराधिभिरतिक्षामशरीरस्यापि तस्येतदवसानं ग्रन्थमुक्त्वा तमेव पश्यन्नमुत्र भूयो वैमुख्यं भूयोप्युद्बष्टिरिति विमृशेत्। कुतः अहो इति अत्राहोशब्दः सिंहावलोकन्यायेन शब्दोऽत्राध्याहर्तव्यः। अहो इति गुरुवचनमिथ्यात्वं भवेत्। अत्राहो इति विवेके विमृशन् न हि अनया मत्प्रमादतया भवितव्यम्। कुतः,

स्वस्थचित्तो यथास्थानं स्थितवान् स यदा जनः।
तदैवेभिप्रयोक्तव्यो गच्छेत्तद्वशतां क्षणात्।।
अन्यचित्ते जने क्वापि योजयेन्नतु चेदमी।
वैफल्यं यान्ति चण्डाले मूढे वाग्देवतामिव।। इति चास्ति गुरुवचनम्।

तस्मादहमेवोत्पथगामी। तस्मात् स्मरशरपरवशीकृतचित्तमिममुद्दिश्यैभिरलम्। तस्मादत्र तिष्ठन्नेवैनमाशीर्वादच्छलां गिरं प्रयोज्य निजं पराक्रममेनं रजस्विनं श्रावयित्वा तमभिमुखीकरोमि इत्यात्मना निश्चित्योत्तरश्लोकेन तथा करोति। **निर्भिद्यतामि**त्यादि। श्लोकेन तत्प्रशंसां प्रथयन्तं तमात्मानमनीक्षमाणं तं पश्यन् भूयोपीति विमृशति।

हन्त इत्यादिष्टोस्मि गुरुणा 'वत्स ! कौण्डिन्य ! संवरणशरपरामृष्टानां पिशिताशीनां जननी मायाप्रयोगैस्तद्बाधां करिष्यति। तस्मात् तन्मायाशान्त्यर्थमद्यैव श्रितराक्षसबलायामेनं मन्त्रैकतत्परं विधायाग्निसन्निधिस्थं कृत्वा जुहुयात्। तदस्य मनःपरवशतयाद्य कर्तव्यम्'। तदकुर्वते मह्यं कदाचित् गुरवः क्रुध्येयुः। तत् कथङ्कारं तदशक्यं तेभ्योपि विज्ञापयामि। सविमर्शम्। एतदस्यापरिसमाप्तेः क्रियाविशेषणमिति विमृशति,

असदस्यं गुरुं जातु नान्तेवासी वचो वदेत्।
वक्तव्यं यदि केनापि संज्ञया तद्वदेत् सुधीः।। इत्यस्ति गुरुवचनम्।

तदेतदीयामवस्थां प्रदोषवर्णनच्छलेन तं श्रावयिष्यामीत्यात्मना निश्चित्य उत्तरग्रन्थमाह अतः **खल्वि**त्यादि, समन्तादवलोक्य इति। कथङ्कारमेतदागामिकर्म भविष्यति दिव्येन चक्षुषागामि कर्म पश्यति। अहो अस्मादारभ्य संवरणः शरशकलीकृतहृदयो लज्जां विहाय स्मराय क्रुध्यति। भूयः तमेवानुनेष्यति। भूयः स्फटिकमण्डपं प्राप्स्यति। भूयो मोहमाप्स्यति पुनस्तत्र तपती ससखी तत्र गमिष्यति, तत्र तपती तद्दर्शनं करिष्यति। तत्र पुनस्स तद्वचनं श्रोष्यति; तत्र स मूर्च्छामेष्यति; तत्र सा तदङ्गस्पर्शं करिष्यति। तत्र स च तत्पाणिग्रहणं करिष्यति इति तत्सर्वं समन्तादवलोकितवान्। इति **समन्तादवलोक्ये**त्यस्य पदस्य ध्वनिरिति। सर्वं दृष्ट्वा तत् सर्वं गुरुजनं श्रावयितुं सन्ध्यावर्णनच्छलेन उत्तरश्लोकमाह सविमर्शम्।

अहो पतत्रिणामप्यतिकृपणस्संसारधर्ममिति। पतत्रिणां अन्तरिक्षचारिणां दिव्यस्त्रीणामप्यतिकृपण इति ध्वनिः। तथाह्यमुष्मिन् सरसीति पदस्य सरसस्तीरे पतत्रिणामपीति। अपिशब्देन महाराजसंवरणस्य चेत्यर्थः। तयोस्संवरणधर्मः सरसीतिपदस्य सरस्तीरे इत्यर्थः। गङ्गायां घोष इव।[1] अथ तदवस्थां व्यङ्ग्येन तं श्रावयत्यर्धाभ्युद्गतपत्रकं इत्यादिश्लोकेन। अर्धाभ्युद्गतपत्रकः आकण्ठादुद्गतप्राणः परिलुठत्पङ्केरुहां पत्रैर्विरचितेषु शयनीयेषु परिलुठन्तं पोतकजातकं अज्ञीभवन्तं संवरणं कुररिका विदूषकप्रवृत्तयः पक्षैस्समूहन्ति।

कुरर्यां च प्रवृत्तां च कुरर्येषात्र वर्तते।

अर्धाभ्युद्गतपत्रकमिति –

पर्णे सुषु च पक्षे च पत्रशब्दोपि चिह्नके।।

अत्र पत्रजीविते तत्प्रवृत्तयः पक्षैर्धारयन्ति। पक्षैस्सुखप्रदवचनैः प्रवृत्तिर्वीजनादि कर्म। एवंभूतैः कर्मभिस्तस्य प्राणान् धारयन्तीति पूर्वार्धे व्यङ्ग्यार्थः।

अन्तस्सुप्तमधुव्रता इत्यादि। अथ भृङ्गी च कमलिनां कमलयुक्तामिमामटवीं पर्येति परितो वर्तते। अन्तस्सुप्तमधुव्रतां, अन्तः गोष्ठीमण्डपान्तः सुप्तमधुव्रतां मण्डपस्यान्तःप्राप्तमोह संवरणामटवीं पर्येतीति संबन्धः। अथेति गोष्ठीमण्डपे प्राप्ते मोहं वर्तमाने संवरणे तदैव तस्मिन्नवतीर्णा तपती तं प्राप्तं कन्यकात्वादक्षमा तत्राटवीं पर्युत्सुका सञ्चरन्तीति ध्वनिः। दत्तदलार्गलां शिशयिषुः।

अथैवं ध्वन्यर्थं तत् श्रावयित्वा बाह्यार्थेन नानालोकान् सुखयन्नमुष्मिन्निति तिष्ठेत्। एवं तिष्ठत् स च सहसा आ इति तस्य क्रोधरवं श्रुत्वाग्रतो विलोकितवान्। अग्रतः पश्यन्नयं सवयस्यं राजर्षि संरम्भदूषितमुखश्रियं स्वं समीपमायान्तं दृष्ट्वा तं प्रतीति स्मरति। अये इति विवेके। नायकाशीर्वादावसरः साधयामस्तावदित्युक्त्वा तस्मान्निर्गतवानिति सकविर्मुनिप्रवेशमागामिप्रमेयं प्रकाशयित्वा भूयोपि राजप्रवृत्तिं दर्शयतीति विष्कम्भः समाप्तः।।

ततः प्रविशति राजा विदूषकश्च।

राजा – ससंरम्भम्। अथ राजा संवरणः स्ववयस्यवचनं श्रुत्वा सहसा तत्रस्थान् मौहिनिकेयान् केवलं निजशक्त्यैव निहत्य तेषु हतेषु कृतकृत्यो यत्कृतकृत्यस्य च तद्गतमन्मथचित्तस्तद्विहीनतया वर्धितामुत्कण्ठां सोढुमक्षमस्सन्नयं स्मरस्य चतुर्थैर्मल्लिकानामभिरस्त्रैर्बाध्यमानो नष्टत्रपो भूत्वा तत्सरसीतीरमागम्य तत्र तामप्यदृष्ट्वा गोष्ठीमण्डपेप्यदृष्ट्वा वर्धितोत्कण्ठ इतस्ततश्चरंस्तन्मण्डपात् भूयोपि सरस्तीरमुन्मत्तदशां गच्छन्नत्र सवयस्योतिष्ठत्।

अथेति त्रिवर्त्युज्वलितस्य दीपस्य पुरस्तिष्ठन्नितिकर्तव्यतामजानन् ससंरभमंगजमाह **आ दुरात्मन्नि**त्यादि।

अतः परं आनायिकादर्शनात् ध्वनिर्न दृश्यते।

राजा पुनः प्रत्याकलय्य इति। अथ राजा मत्तदशामाश्रितत्वात् अङ्गजन्मानमेव निर्भत्स्य भूयस्तमेवानुवर्तते। **हन्त धिङ्मामनवस्थितवचसमि**त्यादिभिर्वचनैः राजानं गर्हयन् सप्रवणं लज्जया तिष्ठन्नमुं वीक्षितुमक्षमस्सन्वसनाञ्चलं बाहुभ्यां अवमृत्लन् पादाङ्गुष्ठेन भुवं विलिखन् गूढं नम्रया दृशा कथमपि शनैः पश्यन्नुत्तरग्रन्थमाह **भगवन्नि**ति। तत्र भगवच्छब्दस्यार्थं दृशा दर्शयति। मृष्यतामयमपराधः। अयं विमुखीकृत इति तत्र तिष्ठन्नभिनीय स्वयमपि तत्राग्रतस्तिष्ठन् मृष्यतामित्युक्त्वा तं दृशोः पश्यन् हन्त नेत्रे रक्तेनायं रोषं

---

1 गङ्गायां घोषः is a stock example to show different layers of meaning. The hamlet is on the shore. Hence गङ्गायां by lakṣaṇa denotes तीर instead of प्रवाह। Similarly सरसि here denotes सरस्तीरे shore of lake.

सन्त्यजतीत्यभिनीय एक एव मयापराधः कृतः तन्मर्षय। अपि च यद्येतस्मिन्नागसि त्वामवधीः यत् द्वयोरुत त्रिष्वेषु वा शूर कदाचिन्नावधीस्तु मां इत्यस्ति श्रुतौ त्रिशोकस्सापराधोपि अग्निं कृत्वातोषयत्। ममायमपराध इति तमेवमनुनीय गूढं तमेव पश्यन् मुहूर्तं सप्रवणं तिष्ठेदिति तिष्ठन् स च तदाभिमुख्यं किमप्यस्तीत्यभिनीय सप्रसन्नं सप्रवणं सस्नेहं सलज्जं वीक्षमाणस्तिष्ठन् सक्षीणमुत्तरग्रन्थमाह एतावत्तु भवन्तमभ्यर्थये **अभिनवसकारैरि**ति। सहकाराख्यैश्शरैरलं; अतःपरमेवं मयि क्रियताम्। कथमिति चेत्; कुवलयनीलैः कटाक्षैः प्रहर; उत्पलाख्यैश्शरैः पञ्चमैः प्रहृत्य मां जहीति याचे। नो चेत् तामप्येवं प्रहृत्यान्योन्यं घटय इति च।

अथ स कविरतःपरं पञ्चमेन शरेण विद्धस्तद्दशां प्राप्नोतीति च तेन दर्शितः। तद्दशायाः आद्यामवस्थां प्राप्य तदवस्थश्चेष्ट्यताम्। तदवस्था मोहावस्था तस्मात् शयान एव शनैः श्लोकान् वदन् सर्वान् विनोदयेत्।[2] यदा शय्यायां शेते तदा प्रभृति नायिकाया आकरस्पर्शाज्जातु नोत्तिष्ठेत। शयानेनैव श्रितमोहेन प्रयोज्यताम्। एतत् सर्वमनेन श्लोकेन दर्शितम्। अतःपरमाशयनारोपणादुन्मादावस्था। अतः परं मूर्छावस्था। अतःपरं आनायिकाप्रवेशादभिनयेनैव विनोदयेत्। अर्थो ग्रन्थस्य प्रयोक्तृ एव। तस्मादेवं प्रयोगमार्गः स्थायीभावश्च। अतः परं नायिकाप्रवेशात् प्रभृति ध्वनिर्दृश्यते।

ततः प्रविशत्यम्बरयानेन नायिका मेनका च।

नायिका – दीर्घं निश्वस्य। अथ नायिका प्रदोषदशायाः प्रागेव मुनिकुमारबोधितदिनदशा संवरणध्वनावात्म प्रमोदना विश्वासनीयमपि रंभां निजहृदयङ्गमामपि मेनकामुभे च निजहृदयङ्गतं रहस्यं यथार्थमुक्त्वा तत्र स्थिता सा सहसा मुनिवचनकम्पितहृदया ताभ्यामेवं सह तस्मात् उद्गम्य तपनलोकं तरुवन्दनं किमपि कृत्वा निजजननीवन्दनं च जननीपुण्यादेव समपद्यत तस्मादद्यनिशायां तपनवने वस्तव्यमिति तया चादिष्ट या तस्मान्निर्गम्य मेनकया सह गच्छन्ती रंभां भृग्वाश्रमाय प्रेषयित्वा सन्ततं तद्गतचित्ताग्रप्रतिष्ठमाना मेनका वियता यान्ती उन्माददशां प्रयान्ती सन्तापात् कृतदीर्घश्वासा इतिकर्तव्यतामौढ्यं अश्रुदीर्घश्वासं तापादेव मेनकामित्यवदत् **सहि**।

मेनका – अथ तया सह वियता यान्ती पुरतो मेनका सहसा तस्या एवंभूतं वचनमश्रृणोत्। तत् श्रुत्वा सविषादमात्मना स्मृतवती

> रूपजन्मवयस्तुल्यं पुमांसं यदि कन्यका।
> दृष्ट्वा कामयते हृद्यं सम्प्रापयतु तं सखी।। इति वात्स्यायनप्रसिद्धिः।

तस्मात् भूलोकनाथं राजानं पतङ्गसुतां कथङ्कारं प्रापयामीत्येतदर्थं सविषाद-मात्मगतमुत्तरग्रन्थमाह **कदाणु** इत्यादि। इत्यात्मगतं मत्वा तस्याश्चोद्यस्योत्तरग्रन्थमाह प्रकाशम् **सहि किं तत्थे**त्यादि।

अतःपरं नायिकाहृदयगतरहस्यं तयैव विगलयितुं मेनकायाः प्रयत्नः।

नायि – सविलक्षमात्मगतम्। अथ नायिका स्वमुखात् विगलितां प्रमादेन हृदयस्मृतिं मेनकया ज्ञातां विज्ञाय सहसा सविलक्षं सलज्जमात्मगतं स्मरति। **ह किं म ए** इत्यादि ग्रन्थेनेति ग्रन्थं स्मरन्ती किञ्चिदुद्दृष्टिरेवं

---

2 Rasavallī is a beautiful and poetic metaphor the dramatist has shown to depict the development of various stages of śṛṅgāra. This helps the actor to imaginatively concretise the emotion by gestures. Another device used here is the arrows of cupid and its increasing effects on the mental condition, the last of which is fainting. Normally an actor is not permitted to lie down for long on the stage. Here it is done as he has reached the acute stage – mūrchā.

स्मरेत्। कुतः कथं मत्प्रमादोक्तिमन्यथाकरोति इति स्मरन्ती निश्चितवती। तत्र कार्तिकेयावासप्रशंसया तां विश्वासयामीति निश्चित्योत्तरग्रन्थमाह **रमणिज्जोखु** इत्यादि।

मेन – अथ मेनका तस्याः प्रमादवाचि वैदग्धोक्तिं श्रृण्वता मुहूर्तं तिष्ठन्तीति स्मरेत्। अहो अनया प्रमादोक्तै शाखाभेदः क्रियते। तस्मादहमपि कार्तिकेयावाससंवरणमिति समर्थयित्वा वदामीत्यात्मना निश्चित्योत्तरग्रन्थमाह **अण्ण हि सो** इति। तत्र तस्याः प्रमादवैदग्ध्ये च्छलेन संवरणं दृशोर्विभावयति तां लज्जयेत्।

नायि – **कि स** इत्यादि।

मेन – सस्मितम्। अथ मेनका तस्याः प्रमादवैदग्ध्ये दृष्ट्वा तन्मुखमेव पश्यन्ती स्मृतपूर्वमुत्तरोत्तरग्रन्थेन तस्या हृदयगतिर्निर्गमयति। तद्वर्जनेन चित्तसंभ्रममुपपादयन्ती वियता तया सह गच्छन्ती स्फटिकमण्डपप्रदेशं प्राप्तवती उभे अवतरणं नाटयतः। तत्रोभे स्फटिकमण्डपस्य उत्तरप्रदेशे अवतरतः।

ततः प्रविशति बद्धकर्णपूरदण्डहस्ता रंभा।

अथ रंभा मेनकानिर्बन्धविश्वस्ततपती 'तपनलोकात् त्वं भृग्वाश्रममवाप्य स च राजर्षि-स्तत्रस्थो न वेति विज्ञाय सत्वरं तपनवनमेवागच्छे'ति सखीनियुक्ता तस्मिन् प्रदेशे तं विचित्य तमदृष्ट्वा तस्मात् प्रदेशात् प्रतिनिवृत्तन्ती पथि सहकारशाखाग्रात् स्वदेहपतितं दण्डाग्रे निबद्धं कर्णपूरं सहसा तदीयमिदमिति मत्वा तमप्यादाय प्रदोषसमये सत्वरं गोष्ठीमण्डपाभिमुखं आयान्ती क्वचित्प्रदेशे मुहूर्तमतिष्ठत्। एवं दीपपुरस्तिष्ठन्ती सा रंभा किञ्चि

दुद्वष्टिरिति स्मरन्त्युत्तरग्रन्थमाह **अह**मित्यादि। इत्यादिग्रन्थमुक्त्वा सख्यौ द्रक्ष्यामीति तस्मात् तयोः समीपमुपसर्पति।

परिक्रामति। एतदर्थं परिक्रमणम्।

मेन – अग्रतो विलोक्य। अथ तयोर्मेनका तत्रस्था सा स च भृग्वाश्रमस्थो वाऽत्रस्थो वेति निश्चयमविन्दन्ती कथन्नु रंभा तन्मार्गणाय प्रेरिता नायास्यतीति डोलायितमनस्कस्तिष्ठन्ती पुरो विलोकितवती। अथेत्यालोक्य तां दृष्ट्वा समोदं तपतीमुखे पश्यन्ती सोत्तरग्रन्थमाह **स हि एसा** इत्यादि।

अथ रंभा तत्सन्निधिमायान्ती पुरतः पश्यन्ती ते उभे अपश्यत्। दृष्ट्वा पथि चेति विमृशेत्। कुतः कथमिदानीं तदुदन्तं कन्यकायै निवेदयामि। स्पष्टोक्त्या वा ध्वनिना वा। स्पष्टोक्तिर्ग्राह्या हि

ध्वनिसंयुक्तया वाचा किंस्वित् भावेन केवलम्।
परं भावेन वा शक्या ज्ञातुं सा कन्यका यतः।।[3]

---

3 Author gives four layers in acting.

स्पष्टोक्तिः - Plain words. Same as ऋजूक्तिः।

ध्वन्युक्तिः - Suggestive words/action.

केवलभावः - Bhāva in the mundane level.

परंभावः - Bhāva in the sublime level.

Plain words need no explanations. The other three levels are the contributions of Kulaśekhara to acting. Dhvani embraces all that are beyond the linear level – vakrokti, anyapadādeśa etc. Bhāva is the ensemble of dance coupled with netrābhinaya to express emotions.

Parambhāva transports it to supreme bliss.

Rambhā here uses suggestive words and convey the emotional complex through bhāva, ie, second and third levels of acting.

तस्मात् ध्वनियुक्तां गिरमुक्त्वा तदर्थं भावैर्विज्ञापयामीति निश्चित्य भूय एवं विमृशेत्। कुतः कथमेनां ध्वनिपूर्वां गिरं दर्शयामि। विमृश्येति निश्चितवती; कुतः,

अद्य संवरणमन्तरेण प्रदोषसंज्ञया तदुदन्तं विज्ञापयामीति मत्वा तदपि मदाकारचेष्टाभिस्स्वन्तं कर्मेति विज्ञापयन्ती ते उपसर्पामीत्यात्मगतं मत्वा सुप्रसन्नमुखी भूत्वा ते उपसर्पति। एवमुपसर्पन्त्यां रंभायां नायिका मेनकया दर्शितां रम्भां सकर्णपूरहस्तां पश्यन्ती सावेगं, सान्तस्तापं, सलज्जं, सविवेकं ससन्तोषमेवं बहुविधजातभावा किमपि स्मरन्ती दीपपुरस्तिष्ठेत्। तस्यामेवं स्मरन्त्यां मेनकापि तन्मुखे पश्यन्नेवं स्मरेत्। कुतः किमित्थमियमेनां दृष्ट्वा बहुविधभावा वर्तते। अस्तु काले ज्ञायते इति स्मरन्ती दीपपुरस्तिष्ठन्ती तन्मुखे पश्यन्ती तिष्ठेत्। एवं स्मरन्तीति तिष्ठन्ती नायिका किञ्चिदुद्दृष्टिरिति स्मरेत्। कुतः अहो यदेषा तल्लिखितगाथं कर्णपूरं लब्ध्वायाता। ततः कन्यकाभूताहं अविनीता नानालोकमुखगामिन्यभूत्। अपि च मन्दारुकल्पतरुप्रसूनैः विरचितोयं यत् ततः कस्याश्चित् दिव्याया इति ज्ञातव्यम्; सर्वथा नष्टास्मि। तामेव पश्यन्ती कथङ्कारमनया गृहीतोऽभूदयम्। एतत् कोपि तया देव्या कृतविग्रहेण मय्यौदासीन्यं प्राप्तवतानेन परित्यक्तः परिगृहीतः किमनया? अथवा मद्भाग्यलेशादेषा ब्राह्मणं दृष्ट्वा सवयस्यं तेन सह व्यवहृत्य कमपि समयं कृत्वा मद्विश्वासहेतोरेनमादायायान्ती किम्? सर्वथास्यामायातायामादावेवास्याः प्राप्तिं पृच्छामीत्यादि सर्वं स्वदृशोरेव विभावयन्ती प्रेक्षकान् बोधयन्ती दीपपुरस्तदागमनमेव पश्यन्ती तिष्ठेत्। अथोपसर्पन्ती रंभा ते संप्राप्य सान्तर्मोदं त्वदभिमतसिद्धिरद्य भविष्यतीति भावेनैव दर्शयन्ती तन्मुखं बहुविधजातभावं दृष्ट्वा स्वविज्ञापनविलम्बनेन तदुदन्तं विज्ञापयति **सहि सुहा वे** इत्यादिना।

तद्ग्रन्थप्रयोगमार्गं दर्शयति। अथ रंभा दीपाग्रस्था तपतीमिति वदेत्। कुतः सखि अद्यायं त्वां सुखयति इति सम्बन्धः। इत्ययं शब्दे प्रोच्यमाने दृक्ताराभ्यां संवरण इति विभावयन्ती सुप्रसन्नमुखा भूत्वा इति विज्ञापयन्ती भूय एवं वदेत्। **जोहणादुऊलावउण्ठिओ** इति।

चन्द्रिकायां विवाहार्थं कल्पितोप्यहते स्थिते।
ज्योत्स्नाशब्दो वर्ततेऽयं तत्र वस्तुचतुष्टये।। इत्यनेकार्थः।

ज्योत्स्नादुकूलमित्यत्र विवाहार्थं कल्पिताहतवस्त्रावकुण्ठितः केवलं विवाहमप्यद्यैव करिष्यामीति निश्चित्यायं गतवानित्यर्थः। इममर्थं दृशोरेव दर्शयन्ती तिष्ठन्ती तदा तद्दृष्टी सचकिते दृष्ट्वा त्वनधिकारिणीं मामेवं वदसीति रुष्टेयमिति मत्वा भूयः प्रदोषे सर्वं समर्थयन्ती ग्रन्थमुक्त्वा तत्सर्वं दृशोरेव प्रेक्षकान् बोधयित्वा बाह्यार्थमभिनयेन नानालोकान् विनोदयेत्। एवमस्य प्रयोगमार्गः।

नायि – अथ नायिका तद्दर्शितमजानन्ती कथङ्कारं तत्प्राप्तिरित्यविदन्ती सचकितं सलज्जं सान्तर्वेदनं तिष्ठन्ती तद्भयव्यपनयनार्थमुत्तरग्रन्थेन पृच्छति **अल**मित्यादिना।

अथ रंभा तदानीमेवं तं भयहेतुं जानन्ती तदा तद्भयव्यपनयनार्थमनुष्ठितया निजधुरा विज्ञापयति **तपोवणादो** इत्यादिना। सहकारशाखाग्रात् ममोपरि पतितमित्येतेन नानालोकमुखगामिनीति नेयं गाथेति दृशोर्दर्शयन्ती तिष्ठेत्।

नायि – एवं दृशोर्विभावयन्त्या रंभायां नायिकाया स्वाविनीतता न विततेति नष्टतद्भया भूयोपि संवरणगतचित्ता भूत्वा तेन ब्राह्मणेन सह कृतसमया किमियमिति चिन्तयन्ती तदज्ञानभावान्तर्वेदिना तां प्रष्टुकामेव तिष्ठेत्।

मेन – अथ मेनका तत्सर्वं विदन्ती तिष्ठन्ती सहसा भयं त्यक्त्वा किमपि वक्तुकामेव तिष्ठन्तीयमिति परिचयहेतोस्तद्भावे ज्ञात्वा भूय एवं विमृशेत्। कुतः? रम्भोक्त्या नष्टलोकापवादभया यदैषा जाता। तदैव किमपि वक्तुकामेव तिष्ठन्ती यत् तत् किमिति सविवेकं दीपपुरो मुहूर्तं तिष्ठेत्। एवं तिष्ठन्ती भूय इति कल्पितवती। कुतः अविज्ञातं पूर्वसंज्ञया रंभया संवरणमुद्दिश्य यद्दर्शितं तदियं तद्भयहेतोरनन्यचित्ततया न ज्ञातवती। इदानीं तद्भये नष्टे तद्गतिं प्रष्टुकामापि कन्यकात्वात् तत्प्रष्टुमशक्ता तिष्ठति रंभा व्यपगतपरिचयादन्या गतवती याथातथ्यं न ज्ञातवती। तदहं कथङ्कारमस्या मनोगतं प्रकाशयामीत्यात्मना स्मृत्वेति निश्चितवती। कुतः?

अस्तु अहमिदानीं कर्णपूरवर्णनच्छलेन तत्प्रस्तावे कृते तस्या हृद्गतं वचनगोचरं भवेदिति निश्चित्येतत् सर्वं दृग्भ्यामेव प्रेक्षकान् बोधयित्वा कर्णपूरं निर्वर्ण्योत्तरग्रन्थं वदति **सहि एदाणि दाणि** इत्यादि।

अथ नायिका मेनकायाः कर्णपूरवर्णने तत्प्रसङ्गं श्रुत्वा तद्दर्शनकुतूहलिनी तच्छ्रद्धया तत्सर्वं विस्मृत्य सहसोत्तरग्रन्थेन तं पृच्छति **सहि दाणी**त्यादि।

रंभा – सस्मितम्। अथ रंभा मेनकाया प्रेरणपाटवं तपत्यास्तज्जनपक्षपातश्च स्मरन्ती किञ्चित् हसितवती। अथैवं स्मयमाना तिष्ठन्ती किञ्चिदुद्दृष्टिरेवं विमृशेत्। कुतः यदेषा तद्दर्शनाभावाच्चकितमना वर्तते। तदेतत् विज्ञापनं व्यङ्ग्यं विना कार्यमित्यात्मना स्मृत्वा निश्चित्योत्तरग्रन्थेन विज्ञापयति **एदस्सिं** इत्यादिना।

नायि – अथ नायिकैवं श्रुततदुदन्ता तद्दर्शनोत्सुकेति स्मरेत्। कुतः? कथमिदानीमेवात्रावतीर्य तद्दर्शनोत्सवमनुभवामि। अथैवं स्मरन्ती तिष्ठन्ती सविवेकं किञ्चिदुद्दृष्टिरिति स्मृतवती। कुतः अहमम्बरगमनेन खिन्ना तत्रावतीर्य स्थातुमिच्छामीति सख्यौ विज्ञाप्य ताभ्यां सहात्रावतीर्य तद्दर्शनोत्स वमत्रानुभवामीति आत्मगतं मत्वा तत्प्रेक्षकान् बोधयित्वा भूयः खेदं विभावयन्त्युत्तरग्रन्थं वदति **सहि अम्बरगमणा आ स** इत्यादि।

सख्यौ – अथ ते तस्यास्सिद्धान्तसाधनपाटवं दृष्ट्वान्योन्यमवेक्ष्य किं कुर्वत इति दृष्ट्या, तयोर्मेनका तथाकुर्व इति दृष्ट्या विभावयन्त्युभे दृष्ट्यान्योन्यं कृतानुवादौ ते तदनुकूले भूत्वा चोत्तरग्रन्थेनैवं वदतः **एव्वं करह्म** इत्यादि। एवं अतःपूर्वं तासां प्रयोगमार्गः।

अथ तत्सर्वा अम्बरादवतीर्य तं दिदृक्षवः स्फटिकमन्दिरं प्रवेष्टुं गच्छन्तीनां तासां नायिकापथा यान्तीति स्मरेत्। कुतः,

अयमस्मिन् वने क्वचित् दृश्यते, किं दृष्टो यद्यस्य मदनोन्मादो वर्तते। किं वर्तते यदि तदप्राप्तिजवेदनादग्धायां मयि वान्यस्याम्। किमन्यस्यामेव भवितव्यम्? कुतः – मत्कर्णपूरदर्शनविग्रहया देव्या मर्मसङ्घट्टनैर्घटि तस्तद्वेदनया मृगयाच्छलेन निर्गत्यापेत्य स्थितवता भवितव्यम्। अपि च तद्विषयमदनार्तिः कर्तव्या। एवं दृशोरेव विभावयन्ती गच्छन्ती ताभ्यां सह नायिका स्फटिकमण्डपोपान्तमायाता।

अतःपरं नायिकाया स्थायीभावो अन्यस्यामभिलाष इति। एवं ताः प्रवेशं रूपयित्वा तिष्ठेयुः।

विदू – ससंभ्रमं – अथ विदूषकस्सवयस्येन तदन्वेषणार्थं स्फटिकमण्डपं प्रविष्टस्तत्राप्यदृष्टायां मन्मथपञ्चमशरैर्विद्धेन राज्ञा मूर्छां गच्छता, शिशिरवस्तुभिश्शय्यां रचयेति प्रोक्तः, स च शय्यां विधाय रचिता शय्येति विज्ञापितस्तस्मिन् शयानस्तद्वेदनां सोढुमक्षमो 'वीज मामि'ति तेन प्रोक्तस्सविदूषको

नलिनीपत्रेण वीजंस्तेन सहसा 'विरमे'ति रुद्धस्तंस्तथा श्रितवेदनं दृष्ट्वा ससंभ्रममेवं स्मरेत्। कुतः अहो कामशास्त्रस्यापि मिथ्यात्वं किं नु भवेत्। स्मृत्वा न युज्येत। कुतः

कमलनियोगात् भगवता वात्स्यायनेन स्रष्टेन कामशास्त्रेण निर्दिष्टा कल्पना क्वचिन्न विफला स्यात्। एवं तेन कल्प्यते; कुतः,

यस्यकस्यापि वा जन्तोर्वामायां यत्रकुत्रचित्।
प्रेम चेत् कृच्छ्रसाध्यायां स्वोचितायां प्रवर्तते।।
तां तेनार्वाङ्नवम्याश्च दशाया घटयेत् विधिः।
तत्र नो चेन्नवम्यां तु घटयेन्नात्र संशयः।।

इति। अपि च

यया प्रेम्णा नरो मूर्च्छां गतस्तस्मात् प्रभृत्यपि।
शेषतोऽर्वाक् तथाभूता सापि गच्छेत् स्वयं नरम्।।

इति च। अस्य भगवद्विधेः प्रामाण्यं विद्यते हि; तत्प्रामाण्यादन्योन्यघटितं भवेत्। तस्मात् शेषकाल प्रतिपालयितव्यः। शेषकालो दशोत्तराद्विशतनाडिका वर्तते। तत् कालपरिमाणे मूर्च्छिते नाचरन्ती चतुरा नाडिका नीताः। तदस्मिन् विधौ कालदैर्घ्यं वर्तते। कथमेनं कालमेनं नयामीति सान्तर्वेदनं सचकितं नायकमुखे पश्यन्नासीनः सहसा जितभानुमालिनीं प्रभां दृष्टवान्। अथ स्फटिकमण्डपं प्रविशन्तीं तां दृष्ट्वा ससंभ्रममिति स्मरेत्। कथं यज्जितभानुमालिनी प्रभा दृश्यते। ततस्तयेदानीमिहागतया भवितव्यम्।

आश्चर्यप्रश्नयोरेष कथंशब्दोऽत्र वर्तते।

आश्चर्य आश्चर्यं! वात्स्यायनभगवतो महिमा ततः प्रदोषेणोपक्रम एव प्रभातमिति यत्। ततः मूर्छनकालं प्रदोषस्तस्योपक्रम एव प्रभातम्। यदैष मूर्छां प्राप्तवान् तदैव सा स्वयमेवात्रायातवती। इमं ध्वन्यर्थं दृशोरेव सद्भ्यो दर्शयित्वा नायकमपि ब्रुवाणो बाह्यार्थः कथ्यताम्।

मेन – अथ स्फटिकमण्डपं प्रविशन्तीनां तासामग्रगामिनी मेनका सहसा तदुक्तिं श्रुत्वा तत्र तां स्थापयित्वा तिष्ठन्तीति स्मरेत्। कुतः श्रूयते किन्नु कस्यचिदुक्तिः। पुनर्विमृश्य कर्णं दत्वा तिष्ठति। श्रितजनेनामुना मण्डपेन भवितव्यम्। तत् कोयं मण्डपस्थ इति याथातथ्यमविदन्त्यास्सहसा वयं मा तेन दृष्टा भवेमेति स्मृत्वा ते उभे जनान्तिकं रहो देशं नीत्वा ताभ्यां ताराभ्यामेव दर्शयेत्। कुतः 'एषा कस्यचिदुक्तिः श्रूयते। तत् कर्ता को नु खल्वविदित्वा सहसा मा तत्र गच्छेमे'ति दर्शयन्ती तिष्ठेत्। तदा तस्यामेवं दर्शयन्त्यां तपती 'सोऽयं मत्प्रार्थनीयोऽन्यो वेति जिज्ञासु'स्त्रपया तत्प्रष्टुमशक्ता सप्रीति सान्तर्वेदनं सपारवश्यं तिष्ठेदिति तस्यां तिष्ठन्त्यां रंभा तदीयामवस्थां ज्ञात्वा मेनकायै दृग्भ्यामिति दर्शयेत्।

मेनकात्वन्तरितदेहा 'तज्जानीही'ति दर्शयन्ती तिष्ठन् इति दर्शयन्त्यास्तस्या'मस्तु करोमी'ति दर्शयन्ती तस्मात् गच्छन्ती 'शिञ्जितशब्दो मा भवेदि'ति मत्वा लघुपादचारिणी प्रयान्ती स्फटिकभित्तिनिर्वर्तिनीभिर्लताभिरन्तरितदेहा भूत्वा तद्गवाक्षेण सवञ्चनं वीक्षमाणा तौ दृष्ट्वा तयोर्नायकं पश्यन्ती सान्तर्मोदं सुप्रसन्नमुखी भूत्वा भूयस्तत्कामदशां कष्टतरं जानन्निति स्मरेत्। कुतः – शिशिरविरचिते तल्पे शयानो यत् ततः क्वचिदङ्गनाविषये मूर्च्छितेनामुना भवितव्यम्। तस्य हेतुस्तपतीत्यूह्यम्। कुतः यदवस्थो यदन्तः

तत्कथमस्य मूर्छां शिथिलयामि। किञ्चिदुद्दृष्टिस्स्मृत्वा। एवं करणीयम्। येनकेनाप्यस्याः प्राप्तिरमुष्मै विज्ञापयामि। तदेनमिमं देशं प्रापय्य गवाक्षान्तरेण नीयमानया प्रभाश्रेण्या तदागमनमस्मै विज्ञापयामीति निश्चित्य तत्सर्वं दृशोरेव सद्भ्यो दर्शयन्ती भूयस्ते सम्प्राप्य दृग्भ्यां 'तत्रागच्छे'ति दर्शयन्ती ताभ्यां सह तत्रागत्य गवाक्षान्तरेण तत्प्रभां नीत्वा तया मण्डपोदरं प्रकाशयन्ती तिष्ठेत्। एवं तासु तिष्ठन्तीषु विदूषकस्ससंभ्रमं तिर्यक् पश्यन् प्रकाशितमण्डपोदरं दृष्ट्वा सुप्रसन्नो भूत्वा किमपि स्मृत्वा 'सायाते'ति निश्चित्य नायकमुखे पश्यन्नासीनस्साऽयातेति दृष्ट्या विभावयंस्थितो भवेत्।

तिष्ठन्तीनां तासां मेनका तमेवं दर्शयन्ती तिष्ठन्ती चोत्तरग्रन्थेनेति विज्ञापयति **सहि एसो सा** इत्यादिना। इति तच्छब्दे प्रयोज्यमाने यः कार्तिकेयावासे दृष्टः स एष इति दृग्भ्यां विभावयन्ती प्रयोज्यताम्। **स इदो चिट्ठइ** इति 'ष्ठागतिनिवृत्ता'विति धातुः। प्राणानां गतिनिवृत्तिर्भवतीति सिद्धान्तः। एवं विज्ञापयन्ती मेनका तन्निमित्तमस्य मदनपीडेति दृशोर्विभावयन्ती तिष्ठेत्।

तस्यामेवं तिष्ठन्त्यां नायिका 'अपायदर्शी स्नेह' इति तद्वचनप्रभुतयान्यत् विषयं न किमस्यावस्थेयमित्यात्मना स्मरन्ती सचकिता तिष्ठेत्। अथ तां तत्प्रवृत्तिं ज्ञातुं तिरस्करिणीविद्यया प्रच्छन्ना भूत्वा तमेव पश्यन्त्यस्तिष्ठेयुः।

विदू – अथ विदूषकस्ससंभ्रमं सुप्रसन्नस्तिर्यक् पश्यन्नयं सप्रभुं मण्डपोदरं विप्रभं दृष्ट्वा सविस्मयमिति स्मरेत्। 'किमर्थमाविर्भवन्तीयं प्रभा सहसा नष्टा जाता। मन्ये या पूर्वमत्रस्था दृष्टा सा भूयोपि शिशिरोपचारं कर्तुं मण्डपमायान्तीदानीमस्मान् सहसा दृष्ट्वात्र क्वापि माहात्म्यप्रच्छन्ना भवेदि'त्यादि सर्वं दृशोरेवं विभावयन् नायकमुखे पश्यन्नयमेतदागमनं न विदितवानिति मत्वा तदागमनं विज्ञापयितुमुत्तरग्रन्थेनेति वदति। **भो व अस्स पुणो विरत्ति आसि**। तस्मिन्निति विज्ञापयति मूर्च्छितश्शयानस्सराजा तदानीं तद्विज्ञापनं शनैर्शृण्वन् कथञ्चिद्दृशावुन्मील्य तन्मुखे ससादं पश्यन् तद्वचनं सावधानं श्रृण्वन् शयीत।

अथ विदूषकः तथाभूतं दृष्ट्वा भूयस्तं दृशा संज्ञया विज्ञापयति। एस इत्यादिना। अत्र रम्ये प्रदेशे पूर्वं यस्यां स्थितवत्यां दृष्टानि ऋतुसाङ्कर्यादाश्चर्यवस्तूनि जातानि तद्वदिदानीमहोरात्रसङ्कर इवास्य प्रदेशस्य प्रकाशमन्धकारत्वं च। ते उभे क्षणं क्षणं जाते इति तद्ग्रन्थं संज्ञया विज्ञापयेत्। स्वस्य वचनमश्रृण्वन्निव शयानं नायकं दृष्ट्वा भूयस्तच्चित्तव्यवस्थां परिच्छेत्तुमुत्तरग्रन्थेन पृच्छति। **को एत्थ** इत्यादिना। इति तं पृच्छन् तन्मुखे पश्यन् स्थितो भवेत्।

नाय – सविमर्शं। अथ राजा मूर्च्छया क्षणं विस्मृतधीर्भवन्नुत्थातुमशक्तस्तेन पृष्टं विस्मयहेतुं शनैश्शृण्वन् सावधानं स्मरन् शयान एव कथञ्चिदुन्मीलितदृष्टिरेवं विमृशेत्। कुतः?

यदयमहोरात्रभ्रान्त्या मां पृच्छति ततोऽत्र सन्नया माहात्म्यप्रच्छन्नया दिव्ययुवत्या भवितव्यम्। तदर्थं प्राकाश्यान्धकारते। तस्मात् कोऽस्य हेतुरिति पृच्छन्तमिमं विज्ञापयामीत्यात्मगतं शयान एव मत्वा तस्य मुखे पश्यन्नुत्तरग्रन्थेन सविमर्शं दृग्भ्यामेव विज्ञापयति। **सखे सन्निहितदिव्यजनेष्वि**त्यादिना। सन्निहित दिव्यजनेष्विति पदे प्रोच्यमाने 'सात्रस्थे'ति दृग्भ्यामेव विज्ञापयन् तत्सान्निध्यात् गतागतमदनावस्थः शयान एव तं विज्ञाप्य भूय एवं विमृशेत्। 'यदैषात्रस्था मां पश्यन्ती तिष्ठति। ततोऽहं तन्मनोदयामापादयितुं मूर्च्छापरव शीकृतदेहोप्युत्तरोत्तरवचने मूर्च्छाधिक्यं दर्शयिष्यन् शये। ततस्तया स्वयमेवमुपगमिष्यन्त्या भवितव्यम्'। किन्नु इति तदागमनकारिणा सिच्यमानचित्तः क्षणं याथातथ्यं स्मरन् तदानीमेव सन्निहितायास्तस्याः अप्राप्तिहेतोर्मूर्च्छया विस्मृतपूर्वापरो भूत्वा निमीलितदृष्टिश्शयानस्तदुत्कण्ठां सोढुमक्षमो भूत्वा सचोत्तरग्रन्थेन वेदनाशान्त्यै तं वदति **सखे किमि**त्यादिना। इत्युक्त्वा भूयोपि युक्तवेदनो भूत्वा तल्पे तस्मिन्नेव शयानो भवेत्।

अथ विदूषकस्तद्वचनं श्रृण्वन् आसीनश्चित्तस्य वशतां विवशतां च दृष्ट्वात्मगतमिति स्मरेत्। कुतः 'अहो अनुक्षणं कष्टतरा अस्य स्मरदशे'ति स्मृत्वात्मगतमुत्तरग्रन्थमुक्त्वा भूय एवं स्मरेत्। कुतः? अहमिदानीं जयमङ्गलायां सत्पुरुषपद्धत्यामाचार्येण दर्शितमङ्गनोक्तिमिमं विज्ञाप्य तं सलज्जं कृत्वा पूर्वावस्थां च भूतं विज्ञापयामीत्यात्मगतमुक्त्वा भूय उत्तरग्रन्थेन तं बोधयति। **भो वअस्स** इत्यादिग्रन्थे उच्यमाने प्रबुद्धो राजा चोन्मीलितचक्षुस्ससादं तन्मुखे पश्यन् शयेत। विदूषकोपि राजानं तथाभूतं दृष्ट्वा तमिमं श्लोकार्थं विज्ञापयेत्। कुतः?

स्त्रियां संसक्तचित्तस्सन्नलाभे स्यात्त्वर्पितशुक्रः।
पुमान् गंभीरचित्तोऽयं मूर्च्छां याति न जातुचित्।।

इतीमं श्लोकार्थं दृग्भ्यामेवं विज्ञापयन् **णं तु ए** इत्यादि ग्रन्थमुक्त्वा भूयस्तन्मुखे पश्यन् किञ्चित् 'धीरो भवे'ति विभावयन्नासीनो भवेत्।

राजा – अथ राजा मदनपीडितहृदयः क्षणं क्षणं विस्मृतात्मापि बुद्ध्वा तन्मुखे पश्यंस्तेन दर्शितेन श्लोकार्थेन विज्ञापितस्सन् लज्जया धैर्यमुपेत्य स्वस्थचित्तो भूत्वा शयान एवेति स्मरेत्। कुतः 'अहो शिक्षितोऽहममुना। तथापि कम्पितगात्रत्वात् स्थातुं न शक्नोमि। तत् किं करिष्ये'। स्मृत्वा 'एवं करिष्ये पूर्वं मया रुद्ध एवायं विरमितः तत्कृते जातोऽयमपराद्धो हृदयमस्यामेवेति समर्थयन्नत्रस्थां तिरोहितामेनां मन्मनोवृत्तिस्त्वन्निमित्तं ईदृशीति तां श्रावयामी'ति स्मृत्वा शयान एव तत्सर्वं दृशोरेव सद्भ्यो विभावयन् भूयस्तामुत्तरग्रन्थेन श्रावयति **भवतु तावदि**त्यादिनेत्यनेन ग्रन्थेन हृदयापराद्धः सम्पाद्य भूय**श्चकितनयनमि**ति श्लोकेन स्वनयनप्रवृत्तिं तां विज्ञापयति।

अथ राजा शयान एव तं श्लोकार्थं दृग्भ्यामेव वर्णयित्वा तद्रसं प्रेक्षकान् पाययेत्। तत्राशक्तश्चेत् श्रितोपधानश्शयानः श्रितपारवश्येनैकेनैव पाणिना भावप्रधानमभिनीय प्रेक्षकान् सुखयेत्। शयान एव भूयः स्वयं नायिका भूत्वा रमयेत्। एवं इमं श्लोकं वर्णयित्वा भूयस्तच्चिन्तया द्विगुणितमूर्च्छश्शयेत।[4]

एवं प्रयोगमार्गः।

नायिका – अथ नायिका तथाभूतं परिदेवनं श्रृण्वन्ती सा अपायदशौ स्नेह इति वचनप्रभावात् देवीविरहतप्त-चित्तोऽयमिति निश्चित्य सावेगं सन्मुखवैवर्ण्यं सेर्ष्यं निर्विण्णा भूत्वात्मगतमनङ्गमाक्षिपन्ती भूय इति स्मरेत्। कुतः मयास्मादपगन्तव्यमित्यात्मगतं मत्वा भूयः प्रकाशमुत्तरग्रन्थेन सख्येवं वदति, **एसोदावे**त्यादि। अतःपरं तदुत्तरोत्तरवचनं श्रृण्वाना भ्रान्तिज्ञानेन डोलायितमनस्का भूत्वोत्तरोत्तरं स्मरदशामूर्च्छां कुर्वन्तीस्तिष्ठेत्। एवमस्या स्थायीभावः।

रंभा मेनका च अस्य मदनपीडाहेतुस्त्वमेवेत्युत्तरग्रन्थेन समर्थयन्त्यौ तिष्ठेताम्। एवमनयोः स्थायीभावः।

अथ विदूषकः स्वप्रेरणया मुहूर्तं तस्मात् भूयोपि तदागमनसंज्ञया विज्ञापयत्यप्यस्यानङ्गमोहमित्यात्म गतं मत्वा सशोकमिव विभावयन्नस्याङ्गसंवाहनं शनैः कुर्वन् सविषण्णमुत्तरग्रन्थं वदति। **भो व अस्स** इत्यादि। इत्याहूय तन्मुखे पश्यंश्शनैः संवाहयन्नासीनो भवेत्।

4 Another example for Pakarnnāṭṭam where the hero transforms himself to the heroine and enacts here role.

तस्मिन् संवाहयति राजा निमीलितचक्षुश्शयानः तेनाहूतश्शनैः ससमुन्मीलितचक्षुरुच्छ्वसन् तन्मुखे पश्यन् शयेत्। अथेति शयान विदूषकस्तदाभिमुख्यं दृष्ट्वा संज्ञयेति तदागमनमुत्तरग्रन्थेन विज्ञापयति **एदे** इत्यादिना। विज्ञापनप्रकारं दर्शयति – तया स्वयमेवायातवन्त्या गवाक्षान्तरेण निजप्राणनाथं त्वां दृष्टवत्या आगमनमत्रस्थाय तुभ्यं विज्ञापयितुमस्मिन् प्रवेशिकां चन्द्रमयूखास्तप्रभाराशयः तवानङ्गमोहं नापयन्ती किं। मदर्थमनया ते प्रवेशिकेति स्मृत्वा त्वया मोहो दातव्यो न किं? दातव्य एवेत्यर्थः। तर्हि तदानीमेव कथं ते नष्टा इति चेत् तदुपपद्येत। भूयः सखीजनेन त्वं कन्यका यतस्तवैषा दशा कष्टतरेति तर्जिता तदानीमेव लज्जया सा तिरोहिताभूत्। तस्मादद्यैव घटयति विधिरिति मत्वा मोहं व्यपनय' इति ध्वनिः। अस्मिन् ग्रन्थे प्रोच्यमाने ध्वन्यर्थमिमं दृशोरेव विज्ञापयन् बाह्यार्थः कथ्यताम्। चन्द्रमयूखा इत्यत्र चन्द्रसंज्ञा तस्याः लोकानन्दकरत्वादङ्गनांशत्वाच्चेन्दोस्त्रिया साम्यकरणं कृतम्।

अथ राजा तेन संज्ञया प्रोच्यमानं तदागमनं श्रृण्वानश्शयान एव तन्मुखे पश्यन् कम्पितगात्रस्सदीर्घं निश्वसन् ससाददृष्टिरेवं स्मरेत्। कुतः? साम्प्रतमहं संज्ञयैवैनं तदागमनेनैव कथं ममाभिमताप्तिस्यादिति तं विज्ञापयामीत्यात्मना स्मृत्वा तन्मुखं पश्यन्नुत्तरग्रन्थं संज्ञयैवं विज्ञापयति। **सखे असंभृतपुण्यसञ्चयानामति प्रतीपाः पादार्थशक्तयः**। श्लोकेन तद्विवृणोति। सखे पश्य – स्मरकुमुदबन्धोः बिम्बमन्धकारानर्पयतीति संबन्धः। कुमुदबन्धुश्चन्द्रः; चन्द्र इति कृतसंज्ञायास्तस्या बिम्बं अङ्गं मे मनसि अन्धकारानर्पयति। तत् कथङ्कारमिति चेत् पश्य। तत्प्रकारं श्रृणु, अबहुलविनिपातादार्जिताभिः कुशलीबहुलजवं अबहुलविनिपाता दपजवागमनात् आर्जिताभिः सम्पादिताभिः कलाभिः प्रभाभिः कुशलो हृद्य तदीयमङ्गम्। अपि च चन्द्रिकोद्गारी च दिव्यकन्यकारत्नं च। एवंभूताङ्गी क्षात्रायत्यस्मान् दृष्ट्वा। ततः अन्धकारानर्पयति – सनिरपेक्षमस्मात् गतवती स्यादिति यद्यत् ततः गुरोर्मे गरीयसो मे मनस्यपि। अपिशब्देनात्र प्रदेशे चेत्यर्थः। तस्यां गतायां गुरोर्ममापि अन्धकारः मोहः संवृत्तः। तस्मादसंभृतपुण्यसञ्चयानामतिप्रतीपाः पदार्थशक्तय इति मयोक्तः। तस्मादनया नाहं पतित्वे व्रियते इत्यूह्यमिति।

पश्य स्मर इत्यस्मिन् श्लोके शयान एव वर्ण्यमाने तमिमं ध्वन्यर्थं दृग्भ्यामेव याथातथ्यं विदूषकाय विज्ञापनच्छलेन प्रेक्षकान् बोधयित्वा बाह्यार्थमेकेनैव पाणिना सकम्पं सधीरमभिनीय नानालोकान् सुखयित्वा भूयः तत्स्मृत्या तदलाभाच्च द्विगुणितमनोभववेदनो निमीलितचक्षुस्सकम्पं ससादं शयेत। एवमस्य प्रयोगमार्गः।

बहुवाक् सुजवे चैव विकल्पपरपक्षके।
अयं बहुलशब्दो वर्तते कृष्णवर्णके।। इत्यनेकार्थः। अत्र जवपरपक्षयोः।

नायिका – अथ नायिका सोऽयमितराङ्गनासक्तचित्त इति निश्चित्य तेनोक्तं श्लोकमश्रृण्वाना तिष्ठन्ती समनःपारवश्यमुक्त्वा विस्मृतेतिकर्तव्या मूर्च्छाधिक्यादुत्तरग्रन्थेन हृदयं वदति। हि अ अ इत्यादिग्रन्थेनात्मगतं स्मरन्ती भूयो दीपपुरस्सचकितं तिष्ठेत्। तदा रंभा तत्पश्यन्ती तिष्ठन्ती यदा तदा सास्मादपयातेति दर्शयन्तं नायकं दृष्ट्वा मेनकामुखं पश्यन्ती नास्मान् साऽपयातेति विज्ञापयामीति मेनकां विज्ञापयन्ती तिष्ठेत्। तदा मेनकाप्यवसर एव विज्ञापनीयोऽयं तस्मान्मुहूर्तं तिष्ठेति दृग्भ्यां विभावयन्ती दीपपुरस्तिष्ठेत्। अथ राजा स्मरमूर्च्छास्वभावात् कदाचित् बुद्धवान्। तत् कथमिति चेत्

स्मरमूर्च्छामूर्च्छितस्य जन्तोस्तेस्युरनुक्षणम्।
हृत्कम्पवेदना मोहबोधविस्मृतयः श्रमः।।

इति। अथेति कामशास्त्रप्रभावतः सहसा प्रबुद्धो राजा शयान एवेति स्मरेत्। हन्त सास्मादपयाता न वेति परिच्छेत्तुमसम्मतोस्मि तत् किं करिष्ये। किमप्युद्वृष्टिस्मृत्वा। अस्तु एवं करिष्ये। मदनावस्थां विदूषक-विज्ञापनच्छलेन सदयं तां श्रावयामि। सा पुनरत्रस्था चेन्निजस्थितिं येनकेनाप्यस्मान् विज्ञापयतीत्यात्मना स्मृत्वा तत्सर्वं दृशोरेव सद्भ्यो विज्ञापयन् भूय उत्तरग्रन्थमाह – **सखे पश्ये**त्यादि ग्रन्थमुक्त्वा सदयं पूर्ववत् शयेत्।

विदू – अथ विदूषकः तस्याभिसन्धिं ज्ञात्वेति स्मरेत्। कुतः सात्र तिरोहिता भवति यदि तदर्थमेवैष म्रियत इति प्रलापपूर्वामुक्तिं सदयां श्रावयामीत्यात्मना मत्वा उत्तरग्रन्थेन तत् समर्थयति **किं णुहु** इत्यादिना। इति विज्ञाप्य तिर्यक् सावधानं पश्यन् दुःखी चासीनो भवेत्। अथ मेनका तच्छ्रुत्वा त्वमेव मदनपीडाहेतुरिति समर्थयन्ती चोत्तरग्रन्थेन तां दर्शयन्ती तिष्ठेत्।

नायि – अथ नायिका तयेति निर्दिष्टा यत्ततश्रितान्तर्मोदापि 'अपायदशायां स्नेह' इति वचनप्रभुतया 'नेति नेति' समर्थयन्ती सान्तर्मोदं सचकितं तद्वचनं दत्तकर्णा तिष्ठेत्।

अथ रंभा तत्सर्वं दृष्ट्वा श्रुत्वा चेति स्मरेत्। कुतः इदानीमहं कर्णपूरश्रितगाथादर्शनेन मदननीतकृता लोकमुखगतस्यान्न किमित्यस्या या शङ्का तामिदानीं व्यपनयामीत्यात्मना मत्वा भूय उत्तरग्रन्थेन तामप्यपनयति। **स हि जाणिदो कण्ण उरं स आगमो ब्राह्मणादो** इति तां दृग्भ्यां च विज्ञाप्य भूयो मेनकामुखे पश्यन्ती दृग्भ्यामिति पृच्छेत्। 'अयि मेनके इदानीं कर्णपूरापेक्षी ब्राह्मणोयं यत् ततो अस्मात् कर्णपूरप्रक्षेपादस्मद्गतिमनयोर्विज्ञापयितुमयमवसरः। किमित्यनया पृष्टया मेनका दृग्भ्यामयमेव काल इति दर्शिता रम्भा सस्मितं मेनकामुखे पश्यन्ती तदानुकूल्यं दृष्ट्वा तयोरग्रे तं प्रतिक्षिपेत्।

विदू – अथ विदूषकः तद्गतिज्ञापनपराङ्मुखत्वादस्वस्थो भूत्वासीनः किमपि किमपि संस्मरन्नयमिति लोकान् विभावयन् पुनर्नायकमुखे पश्यन्नासीनोऽयमग्रे सहसा पतितं कर्णपूरं दृष्ट्वा सविस्मयं तिर्यगवलोकितवान्। कस्तत्र विस्मयहेतुरिति चेत् हेतुर्दृश्यते। तदानीं तद्गतीनामनभिज्ञतया सा गता वा नवेति साकूतं चिन्तयति पातितो यत्तदर्थं सविस्मयं विलोकितवान्। अपि च यदा तदत्यन्तापेक्षाचित्तः स्थितवान्। तदैवेति यत् ततश्च। अपि च दिव्यजनादर्शनं स्थितिपाटवं स्मृत्वा च एतदर्थं सविस्मयं समन्तात् विलोकितवान्। एवं तिर्यक् पश्यन् भूयस्सवञ्चनं गवाक्षैः पश्यन्नेवं स्मरेत्। हन्त कथङ्कारं साम्प्रतमयमत्र निपतितम्। मन्ये अस्यान्वेषणत्वरा हस्तिनपुरमभ्येत्य तत्र विचित्यादृष्ट्वा पुनरत्रमहर्षेराश्रममभ्येत्य तत्राप्यदृष्ट्वाप्यस्मिन्नायान्ती पथि कपिभिः परित्यक्तं शयानमिमं दृष्ट्वा तदादायात्राभ्येत्य तमेनं दृष्ट्वात्र तिरोहिता भूत्वा तां पश्यन्ती मम प्रलापोक्तिमस्य स्मरपीडां च श्रुत्वा दृष्ट्वा च तच्छान्त्यै च स्वतिरोधानस्थितिविज्ञापनार्थं च नूनमत्र प्रक्षिप्तवती। तस्मादेतदमुष्मै विज्ञापयामीत्यात्मना स्मृत्वा पुनरुत्तरग्रन्थेन तं विज्ञापयति **भो सदण्ड अट्ठस्स** इत्यादिना। अथ **मण्णे** इत्यादि ग्रन्थे प्रोच्यमाने भिदा हि भीताभिः त्वं मरणशङ्कया भीताभिः वानरजातिभिः दिव्यजनजातिभिरन्तर्हिताभिः प्रक्षिप्तोयमिति मन्ये इति संबन्धः। वानरजातिभिरित्यत्र वा शब्दस्यैवेत्यर्थः।[5] 'वा शब्दः समुच्चयविकल्पनिर्णयेषु' इति भोजसूत्रेणोक्तम्। अत्र निर्णये। अन्तर्हिताभिरेवेत्यर्थः।। इतीमं ध्वन्यर्थं राज्ञे दृग्भ्यां विज्ञापयन् बाह्यार्थः कथ्यताम्।

---

5 This sūtra attributed to Bhoja (11c) is controversial while fixing the date of the texts.

रम्भा – अथ रम्भा तत्प्रक्षिप्य तावेव पश्यन्ती तिष्ठन्ती विदूषकप्रहसनवचनं श्रुत्वा तं बाह्यार्थमेव जानाना सशेषमुत्तरग्रन्थं वदति **धसगामिल** इत्यादि।

राजा – अथ राजा शयान एव मोहादिस्मृतधीरियं तेनाश्रावितं तदुदन्तं श्रुत्वा सहसा बुद्ध्वा सालसं दृष्टिमुन्मील्य तं पश्यन्निति स्मरेत्। कुतः – 'हन्तेयमस्मान्नापयाता तया प्रक्षिप्तोऽयमिति मन्ये। तस्मात् तद्दर्शनायेमं मद्वक्षं प्रापयेति विदूषकं प्रार्थयामी'त्यात्मना स्मृत्वा तमुत्तरग्रन्थेन प्रथयति – **सखे समर्पये**त्यादिना। अथ तेनैवमुक्तो विदूषकस्सत्वरमुत्थाय नीचैस्तिर्यक् पश्यन् सत्वरं कर्णपूरं तस्योरसि निक्षिपेत्। अथ मेनका तच्छ्रुत्वा तत्क्रियां दृष्ट्वा च नायिकामुखे पश्यन्ती 'त्वमेवास्या मदनपीडाहेतु'रिति दृग्भ्यां समर्थयन्ती चोत्तरग्रन्थमाह **सहि इदाणीमि**त्यादि।

राजा – अथ राजा शयान एवेति स्मरेत्। कुतः अस्य प्रक्षेपात् शमितशुक्रो भूत्वा शयाने मयि तस्या मत्प्राप्त्यै कोपि हेतुर्न विद्यते। तस्मादेनं मद्वक्षसोपनीय मुक्तकण्ठं 'प्रिये मां प्राप्नुहीति प्रलपामी'त्यात्मना मत्वा दृशोरेव विभावयन् विदूषकमुत्तरग्रन्थेन तद्विज्ञापयति – **कस्याय**मित्यादिना।

अथ नायिका तत्प्रक्षेपं पश्यन्ती तिष्ठन्ती सान्तर्मोदं भूयस्तदानीमेवापनीतं दृष्ट्वा 'स्वविषयं नास्य पीडेत्यात्मगतमुत्तरग्रन्थं वदति। **हं णट्ठह्मि** इत्यादि। इत्यात्मगतं स्मृत्वा जीवितनिराशा भूत्वा कथङ्कारमस्मदसून् परित्यजामीति स्मरन्ती भूय एवेति चिन्तयेत्। कुतः 'अहमिदानीमेते प्रसह्यास्माद् गत्वा येनकेनाप्यस्मदसून् परित्यजामी'त्यात्मना निश्चित्य तत्र स्थातुमप्यशक्ता मूर्च्छादशां गच्छन्ती सचकितं सकम्पं सान्तर्वेदनं सदुःखं तस्मात् प्रस्थातुमिच्छन्ती तिष्ठन्ती तदनुमता भूत्वा तस्मात् गन्तुमेव प्रकाशं ते वदति **इदो वरं** इत्यादि ग्रन्थमुक्त्वा जिगमिषुस्तत्र तिष्ठेत्।

अथ मेनका तां तथाभूतावस्थां पश्यन्ती सभयं सदुःखं सान्तर्वेदनं इति स्मरेत्। कुतः 'यदेषा मोहदशां प्राप्तवती तस्मादिमामन्त्यदशायाः प्रागेव येनकेनापि तमवसरे नीत्वापि जीवयितव्ये'त्यात्मना निश्चित्य तस्मात् प्रयातुमारभमाणा दृग्भ्यां 'त्वमेवास्य मदनपीडाहेतुरि'ति समर्थयन्ती वदति **तक्केमी**त्यादि।

नायि – अथ नायिका तत् श्रुत्वा प्रयान्ती सरोषमुत्तरग्रन्थमाह – पुव्वमित्यादि। इत्येवं नायिकामेनके अन्योन्यमपकर्षणाकर्षणे डोलायितदेहे 'त्वमेवेति त्वमेवेति' समर्थयन्ती मेनका 'मदर्थं नेति' नायिका च परस्परं दृग्भ्यां विभावयन्ती विस्मृततिरस्करिणीविद्ये तिष्ठेताम्।

अथ राजा शयान एव तद्दयोत्पादनाय मरणावस्थां विभावयंस्तत्प्राप्तिं प्रतिपाद्य तथा शयानस्सहसा काञ्चित्प्रभां विरलीकृतां दृष्ट्वेति स्मरेत्। 'हन्त यदेषापयाता। तदेनामाहूय प्रिय एवास्मीति प्रलापोक्तितान् ज्ञापयामी'ति निश्चित्य ससादं सकण्ठगद्गदं सकम्पं शयान एवेति प्रलपति- **प्रिये तपति निर्दये** इत्यादि। आदौ प्रिय इति प्रलपन् शयान एवेति तिर्यक् पश्यन्नेनामदृष्ट्वा निर्दयमित्यालपति। तपति इति 'चन्द्रातपोः त्वद्वियोगान्मां तपति। मां किं नागच्छेः' इति प्रलप्य भूयस्तन्म्रियमाण इव शयेत।

मेन – अथ नायिकाभ्रान्तिज्ञानमुत्पादयता कविना दर्शितां तपतीत्युक्तिं श्रुत्वात्मगतमिति स्मरेत्। कुतः – 'मामुद्दिश्यास्य पीडे'ति आत्मगतं स्मरन्ती तिष्ठन्ती सान्तर्मोदं सलज्जं सकम्पमुत्तरग्रन्थेन हृदयमात्मगतं वदति **हि अ अ** इत्यादि।

अथ राजामुं श्लोकं प्रलापोक्तिभिः प्रलपन् शयानश्चलत्प्रभं मण्डपाभ्यन्तरं दृष्ट्वा पुनरिति स्मरेत्। कुतः 'अहो चलत्प्रभोऽयं मण्डपोदरो यत् तत इति मन्ये। कुतः मत्प्रलापोक्तिः श्रुत्वा मद्दशां पश्यन्ती विस्मृततिरस्करिणीविद्यया चेतः ततस्सञ्चरन्त्या भवितव्यमिति तस्मादनया तद्विकृत्या सत्वरं

मामभ्यागच्छेदिति ऊह्यम्। तस्मादतःपरं कृत्रिममोहमभिपतन्नेव शये' इत्यात्मना मत्वा निश्चित्य पुनर्म्रियमाणस्य चिह्नानि दर्शयन् शयेत। अस्मिन् श्लोके तपतीति शब्दप्रोक्तं तन्नामाजानन्नेव प्रयुक्तवान्।[6]

अथ नायिका तदुक्तिं भूयः तथा श्रृण्वानेति स्मरेत्। 'कुतः अहो अस्यां मयि नास्य मदनपीडेत्यात्मना निश्चित्य स्थातुमप्यशक्ता सकम्पं सवेदनं सोत्कण्ठं सचित्तमोहं सशोकमात्मगतमुत्तरग्रन्थे वदति **सुण्णहि** इति।

अथ राजा म्रियमाणस्य चिह्नानि दर्शयति यत् ततः सदीर्घमुष्णं निश्वस्य सादतः सकृपणं शयान एवेति स्मरेत्। 'कुतः अहो स्वविषया नास्य मदनपीडेति मन्यमाना मामभ्येतुमक्षमैवेतस्ततश्चरन्ती तिष्ठेदित्यूह्यम्। तत्र तन्नाम्नाह्वानं कर्तुं न जाने। तावत् तत् किं करिष्ये। किमपि स्मृत्वा। एवं करोमि। त्वद्विषयेयमित्येनां विज्ञापयामीत्यात्मना स्मृत्वोत्तरग्रन्थेन तत् समर्थयन् पूर्वदशां श्रावयति **दयित** इत्यात्मना।

नायि – अथ नायिका वेदनया तत्र स्थातुमशक्ता प्रस्थातुमिच्छन्ती तया रुद्धा तिष्ठन्तीति निजप्रवृत्या मुद्रितां प्रलापोक्तिं सहसा श्रुत्वा सरोमाञ्चं सगद्‌गदं सकम्पं सहर्षमुत्तरग्रन्थेनानुभवति **अम्महे** इत्यादिना। इत्युक्ता भूयस्सा हर्षमूर्च्छया पतति। अथ ताभ्यामाश्वासिता नायिका प्रत्यागत्य प्रेमविस्मृतनिमेषा राजानं तिर्यक् पश्यन्ती तिष्ठेत्।

राजा – अथ राजा नकामप्यायान्तीं स्मृत्वा शयान एवेति स्मरेत्। 'कुतः अहो इदानीमपि नायाता। यतः ततोऽहमविस्पष्टाक्षरं निर्गच्छन् प्राणान् विभावयन् प्रलपामी'त्यात्मना निश्चित्य चोत्तरग्रन्थेन विदूषकविज्ञापनच्छलेन निजावस्थां श्रावयति **मुक्तमूल**मित्यादि।

विदू – अथ विदूषकस्तेन दर्शितामवस्थां दृष्ट्वेति स्मरेत्। कुतः 'आहो एवम्भूतामेतद्दशां पश्यन्ती चेत्। किमर्थमियं सत्वरमिमं नाभ्ये'ति। स्मृत्वा एवं करोमि। 'तावत् अयं मृत एवेति प्रदर्शयन्ती प्रलापोक्तिना ज्ञापयामी'त्यात्मना निश्चित्य सास्रगद्‌गदमुक्तकण्ठं प्रलपति। एवमित्यादिना इति प्रलप्य तदङ्गानि परामृशति।

राजा – अथ राजा तदवस्थादर्शनेनापि तस्यामानायान्त्यामिति स्मरेत्। 'अहो नास्या मद्विषया हि मदनपीडेति स्मरन्नयं जीवितनिराशो भूत्वा प्रेयसीं च समीपस्थामिति श्लोकप्रभाव उत्कण्ठया सन्तप्तमानसो भूत्वा 'अहं म्रिय' इति वदन्नेव मूर्च्छया परामृष्टः परं मृत इव शयेत।

विदू – अथ विदूषकः तदानीमपि तामनायान्तीं दृष्ट्वा तदवस्थां तथाभूता चेति स्मरेत्। कुतः 'अहमिदानीं तदागमनाय प्रलापपूर्वया गिरास्यावस्थां सकलावस्थाक्षत्रियगुणित्वं च तां ज्ञापयामीत्यात्मना निश्चित्य सविषादमुत्तरग्रन्थेन प्रलपति। **समंस्सदु** इत्याद्युक्त्वा तदागमनं तिर्यगवलोक्यादर्शहेतोश्शिरस्ताडनादि प्रहेलिकाप्रयोगं दर्शयंस्तदानीमप्यनायान्तीं दृष्ट्वेति स्मरेत्। कुतः 'अहो मे मूढता

अद्वितीयो यदा भर्ता तदा साध्वीमवाप्नुयात्।
अवितर्क्यं नवोढा चेदेवमाचार्ययोर्मतम्।।

एतद् वचनादहमस्मान्निर्गन्तव्यः। तस्मात् केनोपायेन निर्गच्छामि'। स्मृत्वा। 'एवं हि। अहमिदानीं भृगुपतनच्छलेना-स्मान्निर्गत्य पर्वतशिखरमारुह्य तत्रस्थो भूत्वा तत्प्रवृत्तिं वीक्षे' इत्यात्मना निश्चित्याह **हा वअस्स** इत्यादि ग्रन्थमुक्त्वा मुक्तकण्ठं किमपि किमपि प्रलपन् तत्प्राप्त्यवसरप्रदानाय भृगुपतनच्छलेना

---

6 King doesn't actually know the identity, whereabouts or the name of the heroine. So he uses the word Tapatī not as her name, but in the sense of heat. This is a clear poetic device.

स्मान्निर्गत्य सवञ्चनं तिर्यग्वनोपान्तं पश्यन् भूयः स्नानच्छलेन सरस्तीरेपि विचित्य तत्राप्यदृष्ट्वा भूयः पर्वतमारुह्य छन्नो भूत्वा तामेव दिदृक्षुरत्रासीनो भवेत्।

तदर्थं निष्क्रान्तः।

नायिका – अथ नायिका तन्मोहं तन्निर्गमनं च पश्यन्ती धृष्टतरं प्रयान्तुमक्षमा लज्जया चोत्कण्ठया च सकम्पं सगात्रपारवश्यं मूर्च्छया भूमौ पश्यन्तीत्युत्तरग्रन्थमाह **हा मं एवे**त्युक्त्वा मूर्च्छया पतिता भवेत्।

सख्यौ – अथ ते ससम्भ्रममाश्वास्यान्योन्यं अयमेवावसर इति दृग्भ्यां दर्शयन्त्यौ तिरस्करणीमपनीयताम्। सत्वरं नायकं पश्यन् प्रापय्य तत्करं नायकोरसि नयन्त्यौ तिष्ठेताम्।

अथ राजा तत्करसुधया सिच्यमानः सत्वरमुत्थाय तत्करं गृहीत्वा तिष्ठन्नयं करमाक्षिपन्तीं नायिकां दृष्ट्वा ससन्तोषं दीपपुरस्तिष्ठन्नुत्तरश्लोकेन केवलार्थं दर्शयेत्। **अलमल**मित्यादौ भूयसद्विज्ञापितं विदूषकमानीय विवाहार्थं विवस्वतानुज्ञातः सविदूषको भृग्वाश्रममेव नायको गतवान्। अथ नायिका सखीभिस्सार्धं तदलङ्करणाय निष्क्रान्ता भवेत्।

एवं तृतीयाङ्कपर्यन्तस्थायीभावप्रयोगमार्गौ दर्शितौ। अतःपरं ध्वनिर्नस्यात्। षष्ठाङ्के नायकस्य मेनकारूपधारिण्या नायिकाया दर्शने किमपि ध्वनिर्दृश्यते।[7]

इति निष्क्रान्तास्सर्वे ।

तृतीयोऽङ्कः।

Vyaṅgyavyākhyā of Act III

Entry of an young Ascetic

Sage Bhṛgu instructed one of his disciples – Kauṇḍinya, go to Pārāśarya and tell him this on my words – 'Heeding to our request your friend King Saṃvaraṇa though otherwise engaged, annihilated all these who obstructed our sacrifices. But outraged by the loss of her hundred sons Mohinī has started revenge against the King. Unable to defeat him in direct fight she is planning many magic traps. Yet the King not to be perturbed by her tricks. I will advice Agni hymns to empower you.'

> As instructed by Bhṛgu an young ascetic came to empower him. He could see only Pārāśarya, the king disturbed by something else was not available to him.

7 *VV* for *TS* ends here. Author did not proceed further because by his own words, there is no dhvani hereafter. The mode of presentation and moods of characters can be well understood from the descriptions hitherto made. Almost all important characters are introduced. So praveśika also is not necessary. The author has presented his innovative ideas in the first three Acts. So there is no need to extend the commentary to the other Acts.

Pūrvasambandha

(*The ascetic stands in front of lamp as instructed.*)

Ascetic Alas! The words of my preceptor could not be carried over. He has ordered me to carefully perform the sacrifice in fire to counter the magical whims of Mohinī. I am unable to advice the mantra to the King as he has lost concentration and control over his mind. Sacred rituals will bear fruit only when they are performed with utmost care. If the process is obstructed it becomes futile.

Ha! The King will become a victim of the illusionary devices of the *rakshasi*. King is now feeble to fight the enemies. It makes me sad. People by nature belong to three categories – tāmasa, rājasa and sātvika. The tāmasas have to be struck down forcibly, rājasas can be won over by good words and sātvikas brought to side by hospitality. I can try to win him by salutary words and manners.

My words fail to have any influence on him because his mind is immersed in something else. Good words fail to work absent-minded persons like the words of Sarasvatī on fool on an out caste. Enough of my attempts to bring him back to sanity.

How can I convince my Guru of this situation? Will he be furious to me for my failure to carry out his orders.

A disciple should not convey such things to his Guru directly. He can do it only suggestively. I will therefore do it under the disguise of describing sunset.

Ah! Reprehensible is the act even of divine maidens who move in the sky without sense of shame. She serves the one swooned by illusion inside the crystal hall.

He pleases the nānāloka by the description of the setting sun and prekṣaka through the hidden sense.

Interlude

King and Vidūṣaka enter

The King in response to the request of the ascetics conveyed through vidūṣaka killed all the rākṣasas obstructing the sacrifice. He was struck continuously by the fourth arrow – Mallikā, Jasmine of Kāmadeva. He lost the sense of shame and wandered through the shores of the lake. Unable to see her there, entered the crystal hall and not seeing her there too rushed madly to the shore again. Then he stood restless with his friend.

Both stand before the lamp as instructed.

There is no dhvani in this part till the King meets the heroine.

King Oh! Kāma enough with the arrows of mango-sprouts. Leave me away striking with the blue lotus; Or strike her too and unite us both.

The dramatist now describes that he is hit with the fifth arrow – blue lotus – of cupid. He passes over to the stage of fainting. He lies on and enacts his role lying down. He need not rise up until the soothing hands of the heroine touches him. The state of his mind is next to insanity followed by insensibility.

Heroine and Menakā descend from sky.

Tapatī revealed her inner feelings to her friends. The word Saṃvaraṇa kindles her anxiety as also puts her to shame. She became a poor victim for the arrows of cupid. Somehow she offered the rites and bowed before mother who directed her to spend the night in the Tapanavana. He sent Rambhā to the hermitage of Bhṛgu to collect the details regarding the King and his friend and started through the sky accompanied by Menakā. She was inflamed in the thought of the King.

Menakā If a maiden falls in love with a man suitable in age, beauty and line her friend is bound to take her his side. How take Tapatī to the King?

(*Menakā's effort now is to get the request from her.*)

Tapatī (*Feels ashamed that the secret escaped her. She tries to interpret it otherwise.*)

(*Rambhā enters. Seeing both together*)

Rambhā I will tell Tapatī about him. But how to convey – through plain words or through suggestion. Direct speech is low. Hence I will converse with her through suggestive words without bhāva and at times with exalted bhāva. She can decode the words as she has now grown up to a woman.

Let me talk her in suggestive words and communicate the inner meaning with bhāva.

Does this (shows 'Saṃvaraṇa' through eyes) evening shrouded in the silken moon-light (shows 'new dress for marriage') Please you?

(Your union with the King will take place without delay.)

Tapatī (*Sees the ear-rings*) How did it come her hand? Was it abandoned by the King when the queen picked up a quarrel on this matter? Or in my good fortune, did the King send it as a token of love to intimate the time of union?

The King is somewhere in this forest. He might have left the city to meet me under the pretext of hunting?

(*All the three reach the premises of the crystal chamber*)

Vidūṣaka laid down the King on a cool bed of leaves to extinguish the fire inside. He began to fan him with wet lotus leaves. The King unable to bear asked for repeated fanning. Vidūṣaka is perplexed. Suddenly he noticed the flash moving to the crystal hall. He felt her presence nearby.

Menakā hiding behind understood the intensity of the King's mental strain. Others also moved towards her to see the King, hiding behind the wall. The three remained invisible to others.

King The verse - चकितनयनम्।

Lying on the back the King should depict the idea of the verse through he movement of his eyes. If he is too feeble to do this effectively use a pillow to raise his head and enact through eyes supported by single-hand gestures. Then he should assume the role of the heroine and act appropriately.

Tapatī *Doubts whether the gestures portray the pangs of his separation from queen. She wants to go away from the place. She is confused unable to identify the target of his love.*

Rambhā (*Throws the ear-ring*)

Vid (*Seeing the ear-ring he is surprised.*)

King (*Receives the ear-ring. Becomes more distressed. Holds it tight to his heart.*)

Tapatī (*Realises the love of the King.*)

Vid (*Moves out leaving King alone to pave the way for union.*)

Rambhā, Menakā – This is the appropriate moment for her to approach the King.

(*They come out of invisibility*)

Seeing the King so close they put her hand at his heart. King, enlivened by the touch, rises up.

I HAVE SHOWN THE MODE OF PRESENTATION AND THE MENTAL CONDITION OF THE THREE ACTS. DHVANI HAS NO OPERATION HERE AFTER. THERE IS SOMEWHAT A SUGGESTION IN THE SIXTH ACT WHERE THE KING MEETS THE HEROINE IN THE FORM OF MENAKĀ.

XXI
Tapatīsaṃvaraṇam Acts IV to VI

चतुर्थोऽङ्कः

(ततः प्रविशति मणिचषकहस्ता चेटी)

चेटी आणत्तह्मि भट्टिदारिए 'हळा! सोअन्धिए! महुअराणुच्छिट्ठं कुसुमासअं आणेहि'त्ति। ता विइणिस्सं दाव अहं। (परिक्रम्य दृष्टिं व्यापारयन्ती) एदं खु एदाए कप्पळदाए हेमणळिणमुउळं अप्पाच्छिद्दग्गं दीसइ। एत्थ दुक्खरो महुअराणं पवेसो। ता एदं गेह्णिस्सं। (नाट्ये गृहीत्वा) अम्मो एदस्स महुपेसळदा। एत्तिएण च्चिअ एसो मणिचसओ पुण्णकप्पो आसी। (अन्यतो विलोक्य) एदं हि एदस्सिं मन्दारे कणअकण्णिआरकुसुमं विअसिअं पि चूदपळ्ळवेहि पिहिदमुहं चिट्ठइ। एदं पि तेहि अणुवज्जुत्तं। (आवर्जयति) (आज्ञप्तास्मि भर्तृदारिकया 'सखि! सौगन्धिके! मधुकरानुच्छिष्टं कुसुमासवमानये'ति। तद्विचेष्यामि तावदहम्। एतत् खल्वेतस्याः कल्पलताया हेमनलिनमुकुलमल्पच्छिद्राग्रं दृश्यते। एत्र दुष्करो मधुकराणां प्रवेशः। एदेतद् ग्रहीष्यामि। अम्मो एतस्य मधुपेशलता। एतावतैवैष मणिचषकः पूर्णकल्प आसीत्। एतद्येतास्मिन् मन्दारे कनककर्णिकारकुसुमं विकसितमपि चूतपल्लवैः पिहितमुखं तिष्ठति। एतदपि तैरनुपयुक्तम्।)

चेटी एदं तवणवणं। ओदरिस्सं दाव। (अवतरणं नाटयति) (पुरतो विलोक्य) अम्मो पिअसही सोअन्धिआ। सहि! सोअन्धिए! किं कज्जइ। (एतत् तपनवनम्। अवतरिष्यामि तावत्। अम्मो प्रियसखी सौगन्धिका। सखि! सौगन्धिके! किं क्रियते।)

प्रथमा (विलोक्य) अम्मो जम्बूणदिअ। सहि! रइपूअणत्थं कुसुमासवं गेह्णामि। कुदो उण तुवं। (अम्मो जम्बूनदिका। सखि! रतिपूजनार्थं कुसुमासव गृह्णामि। कुतः पुनस्त्वम्।)

द्वितीया सहि! जदा महाराओ देवं अद्दिसिअ तवस्सं कादुं पवुत्तो, तदा भट्टिदारिआए कुसळवुत्तन्तं णिवेदिउं बहिणिआए जमुणादेवीए सआसं पेसिदह्मि। (सखि! यदा महाराजो देवमुद्दिश्य तपस्यां कर्तुं प्रवृत्तः, तदा भर्तृदारिकया कुशलवृत्तान्तं निवेदयितुं भगिन्या यमुनादेव्याः सकाशं प्रेषितास्मि।)

प्रथमा तदो तदो। (ततस्ततः।)

द्वितीया तदो अत्थि बहिणिआए तवदीए अणुरूवो तेल्लोक्कमुल्लो हारो। तेण भूसिअ गङ्गा हरसेवणत्थं केलासं गआ। सा जदा आगामिस्सदि, तदा तं गेह्णिअ गच्छसि त्ति एत्तिअं कालं ताए ठाविदह्मि। अज्ज उण त गेह्णिअ आअदह्मि। ता कहेहि एत्थगअं वुत्तन्तं। (ततोऽस्ति भगिन्यास्तपत्या अनुरूपस्त्रैलोक्यमूल्यो हारः। तेन भूषयित्वा गङ्गा हरसेवनार्थं कैलासं

गता। सा यदागमिष्यति, तदा तं गृहीत्वा गच्छसीत्येतावन्तं कालं तया स्थापितास्मि। अद्य पुनस्तं गृहीत्वागतास्मि। तत् कथयात्रगतं वृत्तान्तम्।)

प्रथमा जइ एव्वं, सुणाहि। जदा महाराअं वारहवासरमत्तणिअमं अणुचिट्ठन्तं भअवो वसिट्ठो णिवत्तिअ णिअमादो भट्टिदारिणं अब्भत्थेदुं गओ भअवन्तं सुय्यं। (यद्येवं, श्रृणु। यदा महाराजं द्वादशवासरमात्रनियममनुतिष्ठन्तं भगवान् वसिष्ठो निवर्त्य नियमाद् भर्तृदारिकामभ्यर्थयितुं गतो भगवन्तं सूर्यम्।)

द्वितीया तदो तदो। (ततस्ततः।)

प्रथमा तदो देवेण अणुमदा भट्टिदारिआ महेसिणा महाराअस्स दिण्णा। अण्णं च भट्टिदारिआए सिविणे गब्भं लम्भिअ सत्तिहरप्पहावो कुमारो पसूदो विअ दिट्ठो। एसो एत्थगओ वुत्तन्तो। (मणिचषकं विलोक्य) पुरिदो मए महूहि मणिचसओ। ता भट्टिदारिआए सआसं गच्छह्म। (ततो देवेनानुमता भर्तृदारिका महर्षिणा महाराजाय दत्ता। अन्यच्च भर्तृदारिकया स्वप्ने गर्भं लब्ध्वा शकिधरप्रभावः कुमारः प्रसूत इव दृष्टः। एषोऽत्रगतो वृत्तान्तः पूरयितोमया मधुभिर्मणिचषकः। तद् भर्तृदारिकायाः सकाशं गच्छावः।) (निष्क्रान्ते)

प्रवेशकः।

(ततः प्रविशतिललितवेषो राजा विदूषकश्च)

राजा **(स्मृत्वा सानन्दम्)** अहो दुरवबोधरसान्तरो मदनव्यापारः। तथाह्य –

अप्रत्यस्तकरावलेपमनतिव्याक्षिप्तनीवीग्रहं
प्रक्षीणप्रतिषेधजल्पितमपि प्राप्य प्रियाया रतम्।
लज्जालौल्यनिरुद्धरागलसितं नात्यर्थमाकाङ्क्षति
व्यावृत्तं रतिदुःखशीलललितं विस्मर्तुमस्मन्मनः।।१।।

विदू जइ एव्वं, कामरसो भोअणरसो वि एक्का जादी। भोअणरसो वि सुहलद्धो तह पीदिं ण उप्पादेदि, जह दुःखलद्धो। किं एदिणा। दप्पणं विअ दे दिट्ठिं पमज्जिदूण दक्ख मे ललिअबह्मवच्चससोहग्गं रुवं। एदं खु कुदो वि सन्दाणरुक्खादो पडिग्गहगहीदं तवणीयबह्मसुत्तं। अण्णदो लद्धं हेमदण्डअट्ठं। एत्तिअं कालं वाणरदूसिअजण्णोपवीदेण मए माणसेण बह्मसुत्तेण णिव्वत्तिदाणि णिच्चकम्माणि। अज्जप्पहुदि मुक्खेण एव्व अणुट्ठाणं करेमि। (राज्ञो मुखमालोक्य) भोअन्धआरे मए णत्तिदं। अत्तभवं पुण अण्णं चिन्तेदि। अण्णं मए पलविदं। किं विअ एदं। (यद्येवं, कामरसो भोजनरसोऽप्येका जातिः। भोजनरसोऽपि मुखलब्धस्तथा प्रीतिं नोत्पादयति, यथादुःखलब्धः। किमेतेन। दर्पणमिव ते दृष्टिं प्रमृज्य पश्य मे ललितब्रह्मवर्चससौभाग्यं रूपम्। एतत् खलु कुतोऽपि सन्तावृक्षात् प्रतिग्रहगृहीतं तपनीयब्रह्मसूत्रम्। अन्यतो लब्धं हेमदण्डकाष्ठम्। एतावन्तं कालं वानरदूषितयज्ञोपवीतेन मया मानसेन ब्रह्मसूत्रेण निर्वर्तितानि नित्यकर्माणि। अद्यप्रभृति मुख्येनैवानुष्ठानं करोमि। भो अन्धकारे मया नर्तितम्। अत्रभवान् पुनरन्यच्चिन्तयति। अन्यन्मया प्रलपितम्। किमिवैतत्।)

राजा – सम्यगाह भवान्। न केवलं तव सख्या विप्रयोगविधुरं हृदयमेव। कुतः –

वक्षः कुचकलशाभ्यां चक्षुर्वपुषा ममास्यमधरेण।
नैतत् क्षणमपि तस्याः क्षमते विश्लेषवैक्लब्यम्।। २।।

विदू (विहस्य) परिणअणादो पुव्वं सङ्गमो सङ्गमो त्ति परिदेविअं। अज्ज उण विरहो विरहो त्ति अक्कन्दसि। ता अदिदुस्सहो दे संसारो। (कर्णं दत्वा) भो मा सन्तप्प। एदेण णेउरसद्देण कमलिणी विअ कलहंसरवेण पच्चासण्णा सूइज्जइ तत्तहेदी। (परिणयनात् पूर्वं सङ्गमः सङ्गम इति परिदेवितम्। अद्य पुनर्विरहो विरह इत्याक्रन्दितम्। तदतिदुस्सहस्ते संसारः। भो मा सन्तप। एते नूपुरशब्देन कमलिनीव कलहंसरवेण प्रत्यासन्ना सूच्यते तत्रभवती।)

(ततः प्रविशति नायिका मेनका च विभवतः सपरिवारा)

नायि सहि! अदिदुक्खरं खु मए किदं, ज पडिकम्मप्पसङ्गेण अय्यउत्तं अपेक्खन्तीए मए जुअसहस्सं विअ णीदो कालो। आकप्पविहाणंपि सुट्ठु ण परिणिट्ठिअं। तह वि तुवरइ मे हिअअं अय्यउत्तदंसणुस्सवस्स। ता काहिं अय्यउत्तो। (सखि! अतिदुष्करं खलु मया कृतं, यत् प्रतिकर्मप्रसङ्गेनार्यपुत्रमपश्यन्त्या मया युगसहस्रमिव नीतः कालः। आकल्पविधानमपि सुष्ठु नपरिनिष्ठितम्। तथापि त्वरते मे हृदयमार्यपुत्रदर्शनोत्सवस्य। तत् क्वार्यपुत्रः।)

मेन एसो करदलोदअतीरगए मन्दारनदामण्डवे वअस्सेण सह एदं एव्व दिसं ओलोअअन्तो चिट्ठइ। ता एदु एदु पिअसही। (एष करतलोदकतीरगते मन्दारलतामण्डपे वयस्येन सहैतामेव दिशमवलोकयंस्तिष्ठति। तदेत्वेतु प्रियसखी।)

(परिक्रामतः)

राजा (नायिकामवलोक्य) सखे!

बिम्बाधरेण सुतरामरुणेन सैषा
क्षौमस्य कल्पकभुवः किरणैर्हरिद्भिः।
आताम्रकोमलकरा समुपैति देवी
प्रेमानुयातपितृसङ्ग्रहसङ्गतेव।। ३।।

नायि (उपसृत्य) जेदु अय्यउत्तो। (जयत्वार्यपुत्रः।)
मेन जेदु महाराओ। (जयतु महाराजः।)
राजा (सादरमुत्तिष्ठन्)

सर्वाङ्गीणेन तन्वङ्गि! स्तनस्पर्शामृतेन मे।
निर्वापयन्ती गात्राणां परिपूरय लालसम्।। ४।।

(परिष्वज्योपविशन्) सखि! मेनके! सनाथीक्रियतामासनम्।

मेन जं महाराओ आणवेदि। (यन्महाराज आज्ञापयति।) (सर्वे उपविशन्ति)
राजा (मेनकां विलोक्य) किंकृतमसन्निधानमद्य सख्या मे रम्भायाः।

मेन महाराअ! केण वि कज्जन्तरेण भअवदीए सावित्तीए सआसं पत्थिआ। (महाराज! केनापि कार्यान्तरेण भगवत्याः सावित्र्याः सकाशं प्रस्थिता।)

विदू (नायिकामवलोक्य ससम्भ्रमम्) भो! वअस्स! किं चिकिच्छआ वि आणुजत्तेण एव्व सह गआ। (भो वयस्य! किं चिकित्सका अप्यानुयात्रेणैव सह गताः।)

राजा किमिदानीं चिकित्सकैः प्रयोजनम्।

विदू तत्तहोदीए पण्डुरोओ समुप्पण्णो। एदस्स जुत्तिं पि कहेमि। पुव्वं कामोपद्दव त्ति सक्कं भणिदुं। अज्ज उण तुए सङ्गदाए कहं अणिमित्तं आपण्डुरं गत्तं होइ। (तत्रभवत्याः पाण्डुरोगः समुत्पन्नः। एतस्य युक्तिमपि कथयामि। पूर्वं कामोपद्रव इति शक्यं भणितुम्। अद्य पुनस्त्वया सङ्गतायाः कथमनिमित्तमापाण्डुरं गात्रं भवति।)

राजा कोऽन्यः परिज्ञाता व्याधिविशेषाणाम्। मुर्ख! हारप्रभा भवन्तं व्यामोहयति।

विदू (निरूप्य) जुज्जइ। (पुनर्मेनकां विलोक्य) भोदि! माणुसचावलादो विउणं बह्मणचावलं तुभं पुच्छइ। कुदो एदस्स विह्मअणिज्जस्स हारस्स आगमो। (युज्यते। भवति! मानुषचापलाद् द्विगुणं ब्राह्मणचापलं त्वां पृच्छति। कुत एतस्य विस्मयनीयस्य हारस्यागमः।)

मेन अत्थि पञ्चजण्णसम्भूदेहि मोत्तिएहि रइओ भणवदा तिविक्कमेण अत्तचरणसम्भूदाए गङ्गाए दिण्णो हारो। सो एसो तिस्से सहीए कालिन्दीए बहिणिआए पेसिदो। (अस्ति पाञ्चजन्यसम्भूतैर्मौक्तिकै रचितो भगवता त्रिविक्रमेणात्मचरणसमुद्भूतायै गङ्गायै दत्तो हारः। स एष तस्याः सख्या कालिन्द्या भगिन्यै प्रेषितः।)

राजा अयि सवितृसम्भवे! सोऽयमतिचिरादात्मोचितां भुवमवतीर्णः। अपि च –

कुचसरसिजबन्धोरस्य हारस्य गौराः
परभृतपरिपाटीपक्षतिश्यामलेऽस्मिन्।
नभसि परिपतन्तो भान्ति पूराः कराणां
स्वसुरिव तव सख्याः स्रोतसामम्बुराशौ।। ५।।

(नेपथ्ये)

सकुसुममधुगन्धधूपदीपाद्युपकरणान्युचितानि सम्भृतानि।
अयमिह रतिपूजनाय देव्यै समय इति त्वरितं निवेदनीयम्।। ६।।

नायि हं।

राजा सखि! मेनके! किमेतदुपक्रान्तम्।

मेन सुणादु महाराओ। महाराअसङ्गमादो पुव्वं एदाए भअवदीए रदिदेवीए उवआचिदं – जदा अय्यउत्तेण सङ्गमिस्सं, तदा महुआराणुच्छिट्ठेहि कुसुमासवेहि अग्धं दे दइस्सं त्ति। एसो अत्थो सङ्गमसुहेण एत्तिणं कालं विसुमरिदो सहीए। तण्णिमित्तो खु अअं आरम्भो। (श्रृणोतु महाराजः। महाराजसङ्गमात् पूर्वमेतया भगवत्यै रतिदेव्यै उपयाचितं यदार्यपुत्रेणाहं सङ्गस्ये, मधुकरानुच्छिष्टैः कुसुमासवैरर्ध्यं ते दास्यामीति। एषोऽर्थः सङ्गमसुखेनैतावन्तं कालं विस्मृतः सख्या। तन्निमित्तः खल्वयमारम्भः।)

राजा (नायिकामुखमवलोक्य सस्मितम्) अतिलितोऽयमाराधनकमः। इदं पुनर्विपरीतं वर्तते।

सम्प्राप्तुं रतिरसिताक्षि! कामदायाः
सा कामं वरमुपयाचतां भवत्याः।
नामुष्याः पशुपतिलुप्तभर्तृकायाः
सम्प्राप्यं तव दयिते! समर्थयामि।। ७।।

नायि अय्यउत्तमुहे एव्व किदवसदीणि चाडुवअणाणि। (आर्यपुत्रमुख एव कृतवसतीनि चाटुवचनानि।)

मेन एत्तिएण वि कालक्खेवेण सङ्किदं णो हिअअं। ता अणुमण्णेदु महाराओ। (एतावतापि कालक्षेपेण शङ्कितं नो हृदयम्। तदनुमन्यतां महाराजः।)

राजा प्रिये! यद्येवं निर्वर्त्यतां तव सखीप्रणयः।

विदू जइ एव्वं ववसिदं, जदा सोत्थिवाअणकालो भविस्सदि तदा सम्पण्णो बह्मणो सुमरिदव्वो। (यद्येवं व्यवसितं, यदा स्वस्तिवाचनकालो भविष्यति, तदा सम्पन्नो ब्राह्मणः स्मर्तव्यः।)

मेन मुक्ख! किं तव एदिणा। (मूर्ख! किं तवानेन।)

(राज्ञो मुखात् कथमपि दृष्टिमाक्षिपन्ती सख्या सह सपरिवारा निष्क्रान्ता नायिका)

राजा वयस्य! केनेदानीं विनोदेन सहचरीविप्रवासमलीमसं कालं यापयामि।

विदू (सनिर्वेदम्) को एत्थ णिम्माणुसे जिण्णाडवीमज्झे विणोदो। एत्तिअमत्तं एत्थ सारं। जइ रक्खसीणं फुल्लीणं च मुहे अपडिअ सञ्चरिदुं पारिज्जइ, तदो सक्कं सन्दाणरुक्खादो भिक्खं अडिदुं। (कोऽत्र निर्मानुषे जीर्णाटवीमध्ये विनोदः। एतावन्मात्रमत्र सारम्। यदि राक्षसीनां फुल्लीनां च मुखे अपतित्वा सञ्चरितुं पार्यते, ततः शक्यं सन्तानवृक्षाद् भिक्षामटितुम्।)

(ततः प्रविशति भीषणवेषा राक्षसी)

राक्ष (सरोषम्)

अहके लोशपलित्ता माआदण्डेहि तिक्खमोक्खेहि।
शंवलणश्श शलीलं भज्जिश्शं शलिलकुम्भं वा।। ८।।

अज्ज शंवलणशलशदमुशिदजीविअशअन्धाहिं शअललक्खशीहिं शाणुणअं अब्भत्थिदह्मि 'शाहि! मोहिणिए! तुज्झ माआबलेण इशिशलणं लाआवशदं शंवलणं कहं वि गेह्णिअ शमुद्दमज्झे पक्खिऊण मालेहि' त्ति। शा वि अहं तेण वावादि अपुत्तशदा विउणिअलोशा शहीणं णिओअं कादुं ववशिदह्मि।ता अण्णेशिश्शं दाव। (परिक्राम्यावलोक्य) एशे एशे केण वि बह्मणेण शह शन्दाणलदामण्डवे चिट्ठइ (विदूषकमवलोक्य सृक्किणी परिलिहन्ती) एदं बह्मणं खाइदुकामाए कुलुकुलाअन्ती विअ मे दन्ता, शवदि लालाशलिलं। किन्तु एदश्श महाणुभावश्श शमक्खं शुमलिदु पि ण शक्कं, किं पुण खाइदुं। ता एव्वं दाव कलिश्शं। (अतिरमणीयरूपा भूत्वा राजानमुपसर्पति)

(अहं रोषप्रदीप्ता मायादण्डैस्तीक्ष्णमोक्षैः।

संवरणस्य शरीरं भङ्क्ष्यामि सलिलकुम्भमिव।।

अद्य संवरणशरशतमुषितजीवितसगन्धामिः सकलराक्षसीभिः।। सानुनयमभ्यर्थितास्मि – 'सखि! मोहिनिके! तव मायाबलेन ऋषिशरणं राजापशदं संवरणंकथमपि गृहीत्वा समुद्रमध्ये प्रक्षिप्य मारय' इति। साप्यहं तेन व्यापादितपुत्रशता द्विगुणितरोषा सखीनां नियोगं कर्तुं व्यवसितास्मि। तदन्वेषिष्यामि तावत्। एष एष केनापि ब्राह्मणेन सह सन्तानलतामण्डपे तिष्ठति। एतं ब्राह्मणं खादितुकामायाः कुरुकुरायन्तीव मे दन्ताः, स्रवति लालासलिलम्। किन्त्वेतस्य महानुभावस्य समक्षं स्मर्तुमपि न शक्यं, किं पुनः खादितुम्। तदेवं तावत् करिष्यामि।)

राजा (विलोक्य सविस्मयम्) सखे! पश्य पश्य –

पृथुनितम्बपयोधरलोचनं तरलकेशचयं तनुमध्यमम्।
अनघमस्त्रमनङ्गधनुर्भृतः किमपि वस्तु कुतः समुपागतम्।। ९।।

विदू एदस्सिं रण्णे पडिच्छण्णं णिस्सरन्ति वञ्चणसीलाओ इत्थिआओ। ण आणामि किं होदि त्ति। (एतस्मिन्नरण्ये प्रतिच्छन्नं निस्सरन्ति वञ्चनशीलाः स्त्रियः। न जानामि किं भवतीति।

राक्ष (श्रुत्वा सविषादं सकम्पं च) कहं वञ्चणसील त्ति। लक्खिदह्मि इमिणा। भश्शीदूदे मे मणोलहे। (कथं वञ्चनशीला इति। लक्षितास्म्यनेन। भस्मीभूतोमे मनोरथः।)

राजा मैवं वादीः। न सर्वा नार्यो विप्रलम्भशीलाः।

राक्ष (सहर्षम्) दिट्ठिआ ण मं उद्दिसिअ एशे भणादि। (उपसृत्य) जेदु महाराओ। (दिष्ट्या न मामुद्दिश्यैष भणति। जयतु महाराजः।)

राजा स्वागतमत्रभवत्यै। कात्वम्। किञ्चागमनप्रयोजनम्।

राक्ष सुणादु महाराओ। अत्थि गन्धव्वराअस्स चित्तरहस्स धीदा गअ णमाला णाम रूवेण अप्पडिमा कण्णआ। अहं तिस्से वअस्सिआ सुमणावई णाम। सा महाराअस्स अणेअदेवासुरसङ्गाम-विजइणो गुणेहि अक्खित्तहिअआ मए सह महाराअं दक्खिउं हत्थिणउरं गआ। (श्रृणोतु महाराजः। अस्ति। गन्धर्वराजस्य चित्ररथस्य पुत्री गगनमाला नाम रूपेणाप्रतिमा कन्यका। अहं तस्या वयस्या सुमनावती नाम। सा महाराजस्यानेकदेवासुरसङ्ग्रामविजयिनो गुणैराक्षिप्तहृदया मया सह महाराजं द्रष्टुं हस्तिनपुरं गता।)

राजा ततस्ततः।

राक्ष तदो कत्तिएआवासपरिसरुज्जाणगअं अत्तणो पदजुअलं सकामलहं कण्णऊरं च दक्खन्तस्स महाराअस्स दिट्ठिराअं ओलोइअ किञ्चि अस्सासिअहिअआ पिदुपराहीणदाए अत्तणो णअरं पत्थिआ। (ततः कार्तिकेयावासपरिसरोद्यानगतमात्मनः पदयुगलं सकामलेखं कर्णपूरं च पश्यतो महाराजस्य दृष्टिरागमवलोक्य किञ्चिदाश्वासितहृदया पितृपराधीनतयात्मनो नगरं प्रस्थिता।)

राजा (जनान्तिकम्) सखे! पदवतंसकयोरीदृशः परिणामः।

विदू जज्जइ। एव्वं एदं। अण्णं च एसो णिरतिसओ गन्धो घाणगोअरं सम्पत्तो। ता तक्केमि अण्णाओ दिव्वकण्णआओ तुमं कामेदुं आअच्छन्ति त्ति। (युज्यते। एवमेतत्। अन्यच्चैष निरतिशयो गन्धो घ्राणगोचरं सम्प्राप्तः। तत् तर्कयाम्यन्या दिव्यकन्यकास्त्वां कामयितुमागच्छन्तीति।

राजा ततस्ततः।

राक्ष तदो अज्ज तुज्झसङ्गमणिबन्धणं किञ्चि अपेक्खन्ती भिउपडणाअ उच्चलिआ, मए कहं वि आशाजणणेहि वअणेहि णिवारिआ। जइ महाराओ सङ्गमाणुग्गहं ण करेदि, अवस्सं सा विवज्जइ। णाहं सहीमरणं दक्खिउं पारेमि। ता पडमं महाराअस्स पुरदो अत्ताणं वावादइस्सं। (ततोऽद्य तव सङ्गमनिबन्धनं किञ्चिदपश्यन्ती भृगुपतनायोच्चलिता। मया कथमप्याशाजननैर्वचनैर्निवारिता। यदि महाराजः सङ्गमानुग्रहं न करोति, अवश्यं सा विपद्यते। नाहं सखीमरणं द्रष्टुं पारयामि। तत् प्रथमं महाराजस्य पुरत आत्मानं व्यापादयिष्यामि।)

विदू (अपवार्य) भो वअस्स! अपुव्वो खु एदाए दोच्चोवक्कमो। बलक्कालेण किल कागो उप्पादइदव्वो। (भो वयस्य! अपूर्वः खल्वेतस्या दौत्योपक्रमः। बलात्कारेण किल काम उत्पादयितव्यः।)

राजा (आत्मगतम्) अस्तु तावन्मम मनागप्यनौत्सुक्यजननममुष्या वचनम्। तथाप्येवमिदानीमेनां यापयामि। (प्रकाशम्) भद्रे! केषामनभिमतानि सचेतसामेतादृशानि स्वयमुपनतानि स्त्रीरत्नानि। किं बहुना, स्थिता वयमत्रभवत्या वचसि।

राक्ष (सहर्षम्) जीवाविदह्मि महाराअस्स पसादेण। ता अज्ज पओसे सवअस्सेण महाराएण एत्थ सण्णिहिदेण एव्व होदव्वं। मं पि विमाणं गेह्णिअ आअदं एव्व मण्णह। (निष्क्रान्ता) (जीवितास्मि महाराजस्य प्रसादेन। तदद्य प्रदोषे सवयस्येन महाराजेनात्र सन्निहितेनैव भवितव्यम्। मामपि विमानं गृहीत्वागतामेव मन्यस्व।)

विदू भो वअस्स! किं तुए ववसिदं। (भो वयस्य किं त्वया व्यवसितम्।)

राजा अनभिज्ञो भवानस्मच्चित्तवृत्तीनाम्। किं वा तपतीगुणनिगलितां चित्तवृत्तिमन्यत्र चलयितुमलम्। साहसोपक्रमभीरुणा मयैतदुपन्यस्तम्। इदं पुनस्तदङ्गसम्पर्काभिमानदुर्ललितम् अन्यनारीगण्डोपश्लेषोपहतमपहस्तय कर्णपूरम्।

विदू (विहस्य) अहो राअउलसेवआणं परिवाओ, जं एत्तिअं कालं भुअन्तरोवलालिअस्स एदस्स कण्णेउरस्स खणेण अतक्किओ विणिवादो संवुत्तो। (कर्णपूरं क्षिप्त्वा) भो वअस्स! अच्छेरं अच्छेरं। एसो कण्णेउरो अम्बरेण णिइण्णो, ण उण पुहुवीअं पडिओ। (अहो राजकुलसेवकानां परिवादः, यदेतावत्तं कालं भुजान्तरोपलालितस्यैतस्य कर्णपूरस्य क्षणेनातर्कितो विनिपातः संवृत्तः। भो वयस्य! आश्चल्यमाश्चर्यम्। एष कर्णपूरोऽम्बरेण निगीर्णः, न पुनः पृथिव्यां पतितः।) (नेपथ्ये)

याभिः कल्पितमभ्युपैति नृपतिः सङ्केतमाकस्मिकं
दुःखोदर्कमनात्मनीनमपृथुश्रोणीजनप्रापकम्।
दग्धास्ता भृगुकर्मभिः शुभतरैर्मायाः प्रपन्ना निजं
देहं मोहिनिका प्रयाति विफलीभूतक्रिया राक्षसी।। १०।।

राजा (सहर्षम्) सखे! तस्यां सविमानायामुपस्थितायां को नु खलु प्रत्याख्यानप्रकार इति पर्याकुलोऽहममुना सकलमेतन्मायाजालमुपपादयता विधिना साधु सङ्कटादुत्तारितोऽस्मि।

विदू अहं पि रक्खसीए दाढाकुढारादो देव्वेण रक्खिदोह्मि। (अहमपि राक्षस्या दंष्ट्राकुठाराद् दैवेन रक्षितोऽस्मि।)

(प्रविश्यापटाक्षेपेण कर्णपूरहस्ता)

मेन तुवरदु तुवरदु महाराओ। (त्वरतां त्वरतां महाराजः।)

राजा (ससम्भ्रमम्) किमिति किमिति।

मेन जदा सा णिसाअरी तिस्से भिउपडणवुत्तन्तं कहेदुं पवुत्ता, तदा मए रह आअदा सही महाराअस्स सङ्केदवअणं सुणिअ कुविदा पलिथआ। मए उण कहन्तं पडिक्खन्तीए ठिदाए जाणिदो परमत्थो। ता सिग्धं गदुअ अणुणेदु महाराओ। (यदा सा निशाचरी तस्या भृगुपतनवृत्तान्तं कथयितुं प्रवृत्ता, तदा मया सहागता सखी महाराजस्य सङ्केतवचनं श्रुत्वा कुपिता प्रस्थिता। मया पुनः कथान्तं प्रतीक्षमाणया स्थितया ज्ञातः परमार्थः। तत् शीघ्रं गत्वानुनयतु महाराजः।)

राजा (सविषादम्) क्वासौ क्वासौ।

मेन (विलोक्य) एसा सही कल्लाणवामणधरं पविसइ। अवसप्प णं। (एषा सखी कल्याणवामनगृहं प्रविशति। उपसर्पैनाम्।)

(सर्वे ससम्भ्रमं परिक्रामन्ति)

नायि (प्रविश्य, सप्रणामम्) भअवं पदुमावल्लब! पुव्वं कामग्गिपलिज्जन्तं भअवदा पच्चज्जीविअं मे सरीरं। अज्ज उण अय्यउत्तपरिभवाणलदाहेण विवज्जन्त एदं अणुमण्णेहि। (भगवन् पद्मावल्लभ! पूर्वं कामाग्निप्रदीप्यमानं भगवता प्रयुज्जीवितं मे शरीरम्। अद्य पुनरार्यपुत्र-परिभवानलदाहेन विपद्यमानमेतदनुमन्यस्व।)

राजा (ससम्भ्रममुपसृत्य) प्रेयसि! किं किं, परिभवानल इति।

(नायिका सभ्रूभङ्गं परावृत्य प्रस्थातुमिच्छति)

राजा (अंशुकान्ते गृह्णन्)

मम भवतु न तत्त्वतः क्षमस्ते
प्रणयगतीरवगन्तुमन्तरात्मा।
असदृशमवमानमात्मनि त्वं
कथमिव मुग्धमृगाक्षि! सन्तनोषि।। ११।।

मेन सहि! अलं कोवेण। (कर्णे) एव्वं विअ। (सखि! अलं कोपेन। एवमिव।)

नायि हद्धि उत्थाणे कदत्थिदो अय्यउत्तो। (राजाभिमुखी) जेदु अय्य उत्तो। (हा धिग् अस्थाने कदर्थित आर्यपुत्रः। जयत्वार्यपुत्रः।)

राजा (सहर्षं परिष्वज्य) अयि! अस्थानकुपिते! तव तावदेतादृशा अलीकव्यलीका एव सम्भवेयुरमुष्मिन् दासजने कोपहेतवः।

मेन भो राअवयस्य! एसो दे आआसणिइण्णो वतंसओ। गेह्ण णं। (भो राजवयस्य! एष ते आकाशनिगीर्णोवतंसकः। गृहाणैनम्।)

विदू (सभयम्) ण दाव मे खेमअरो रक्खसीणं कण्णऊरो। ण गोह्णिस्सं। (न तावन्मे क्षेमकरो राक्षसीनां कर्णपूरः। न ग्रहिष्यामि।)

राजा (नायिकामपवार्य) सखि! मेनके! किमस्मान्मर्ण्युद्धट्टयसि।

मेन महाराअ! अलं सङ्‌काए। एदाए च्चिअ एसो कण्णऊरो तं पदजुअलं च। (महाराज! अलं शङ्‌कया। एतस्या एवैष कर्णपूरस्तत् पदयुगलं च।)

राजा (सपरिदोषम्) दिष्ट्या चिरादद्य हृदयनिखातं संशयशल्यमुद्धृतं भवत्या। सखे! सोऽयमकोपान्तरायः प्रियापरिष्वङ्‌गः। स्वीक्रियताम्।

विदू एव्वं होदु (गृहीत्वा परितो विलोकम्) भो! अकामुआणं अह्माणं अणदिक्कमणीओ सञ्झोवासणसमओ। (एवं भवतु। भो अकामुकानामस्माकमनतिक्रमणीयाः सन्ध्योपासनसमयः।)

राजा (समन्तादवलोक्य) सखे! सम्यगनुप्रबोधितोऽस्मि। प्रिये!
प्रविश त्वमभ्यन्तरम्। वयमपि –

अखिलभुवनयोनेरभ्युदीर्णत्रिवेदीं
तनुमपतमयन्तीमम्बुजन्मासनस्य
अहरुपगमरात्रिप्रक्रमावर्तनीयां
वरतनु! सहजं ते सायमाराधयामः।। १२।। (इति निष्क्रान्ताः सर्वे)

अथ पञ्चमोऽङ्‌कः।

(ततः प्रविशति बद्धकर्णपूरदण्डहस्तस्त्रस्तरूपो विदूषकः)

विदू (दीर्घं निश्वस्य) मुसिदो ह्मि भो मुसिदो ह्मि। इह तवणवणे आदिइरं कालं विहरिअ चिट्ठन्तो वअस्सो देवी परिजणो अ सिविणलद्धो विअ णिही अज्ज पच्चूस एव्व पवुद्धेण मए ण दिट्ठा। अण्णेसिअ च सव्वं तवणवणं। अण्णं च मिणसउन्तवज्जं सव्वं अवहरिअ गच्छन्तीए अदीदाए रत्तीए अहं तवणवणं च अवसेसिअं त्ति अच्छेरं। (सवितर्कम्) जदि तत्तहोदीए सह तवणलोअं गदो भवे, तदो मं अणवबोहिअ अवस्सं वअस्सो ण गच्छइ। अहवा माआदक्खेहि रक्खसीजणेहि कहिं पि वञ्चिअणीदो भवे। एदं पि णत्थि। भिउणो कम्मप्पहावेण एत्थ पदेसे माआओ ण प्पभवन्ति। जइ पच्चक्खं एव्वं परक्कमन्ति, तदो वअस्सस्स प्पहावो एव्व पडिबन्धेदि। ता अलं दुव्विकप्पेहिं। तवणवणादो णिक्कमिअ विउणिस्सं। (परिक्रम्य परितो विलोकयन्) अहो एदस्स वणगहणुद्देसस्स पडिभअदा। एसा केसरिणहकुलिसणिब्भिण्णकुम्भस्स सहअरस्स रसिआणुसारप्पहाविआ सवरपरिकप्पिअगत्तपडिआ करिणी करुणं विक्कोसइ। (अन्यतो विलोक्य) एदं पण अच्छभल्लोवहुत्तपिट्ठभाआए कुरङ्‌गवहूए उग्गिण्णजीहं मुहं णिच्चलुप्फुल्लाए दिट्ठीए अज्ज वि भअं सूएदि। क्रूरसत्तवावादिअदुब्बलमिअकलेबरदुस्सञ्चरो दुस्समपीडिअस्स जणपदस्स दसं अणुसरेदि एसो पदेसो। किं बहुणा, मम दिट्ठी वि भअविहुरा एत्थ परिब्भमिदुं ण पारोदि, किं पुण चलणा। पागेव्व णअररच्छाअं पि असहाओ गन्तुं भाआमि, किं पुण एत्थ महाडवीअं। ण उण सहाआणं सम्भवो। ता किं मे सरणं। का मे गई। (भयकम्पितो

दण्डकाष्ठमवलम्ब्य स्थितः) (मुषितोऽस्मि भोः मुषितोऽस्मि। इह तपनवने अतिचिरं कालं विहृत्य तिष्ठन् वयस्यो देवी परिजनश्च स्वप्नलब्ध इव निधिरद्य प्रत्यूष एव प्रबुद्धेन मया न दृष्टाः। अन्विष्टं च सर्वं तपनवनम्। अन्यच्च मृगशकुन्तवर्जं सर्वमपहृत्य गच्छन्त्या अथीतया रात्र्याहं तपनवनं चावशेषितम् इत्याश्चर्यम्। यदि तत्रभवत्या सह तपनलोकं गतो भवेत्, ततो मामनवबोध्यावश्यं वयस्यो न गच्छति। अथवा मायादक्षै राक्षसीजनैः कथमपि वञ्चयित्वा नीतो भवेत्। एतदपि नास्ति। भृगोः कर्मप्रभावेणात्र प्रदेशे माया न प्रभवन्ति। यदि प्रत्यक्षमेव पराक्रमन्ते, ततो वयस्यस्य प्रभाव एव प्रतिबध्नाति। तदलं दुर्विकल्पैः। तपनवनान्निष्क्रम्य विचेष्यामि। अहो एतस्य वनगहनोद्देशस्य प्रतिभयता। एषा केसरिनखकुलिशनिर्भिण्णकुम्भस्य सहचरस्य रसितानुसारप्रधाविता शबरपरिकल्पितगर्तपतिता करिणी करुणं विक्रोशति। एतत् पुनरच्छभल्लोपभुक्तपृष्ठभागायाः कुरङ्गवध्वा उद्गीर्णजिह्वं मुखं निश्चलोत्फुल्लया दृष्ट्याद्यापि भयं सूचयति। क्रूरसत्त्वव्यापादिदुर्बलमृगकलेबरदुस्सञ्चरो दुःषमपीडितस्य जनपदस्य दशामनुसरत्येष प्रदेशः। किं बहुना, मम दृष्टिरपि भयविधुरात्र परिभ्रमितुं न पारयति, किं पुनश्चरणौ प्रागेण नगररथ्यायामप्यसहायो गन्तुं बिभेमि, किं पुनरत्र महाटव्याम्। न पुनः सहायानां सम्भवः। तत् किं मे शरणम्। का मे गतिः।)

(ततः प्रविशत्यमात्यः)

अमा (सवितर्कम्) अहो जघन्य एवायं जघन्यो वर्गः, येन समाकृष्टः प्रकृष्टमहिमा सोऽयमपि देवो निसर्गविनयसमुद्भवशेमुषीप्रशमितप्रजोपद्रवः परित्यज्य स्वराज्यमियन्तं कालमिमां महाटवीमधिवसति। तदपि पुनश्चिरतरपरिवर्जितपर्जन्यम्। तथा हि –

आन्त्रव्रातविभीषणं बधिरितं घोरैः शिवावाशितै-
दूरीभूतपृथग्जनं नरशिरःश्रेणीभिरध्यासितम्।
राज्ञः संवरणस्य राज्यमधुना वेतालपालीवृतं
कालीकायभयङ्करं समभवत् कङ्कालमालाकुलम्।। १।।

श्रुतं च मया तपनवनाभिधानं देवारण्यमभिमतदेवीसमेतस्य देवस्य विहारभूमिरिति। तदन्वि(ष्ये? ष्यामि) तपनवनम् (परिक्रामन् पुरतो विलोक्य) अयो असौ वयस्यः पाराशर्यो देवस्य बहिश्चराः प्राणाः केनाप्याविष्ट इव तिष्ठति। तदमुष्मादुपलभे स्वामिवृत्तान्तम् (उपसृत्य) सखे! पाराशर्य! अपि कुशलं तव।

विदू (ससम्भ्रममवलोक्य) अये अमच्चो अय्यवसुमित्तो काएसा अदिट्ठपओहरा विट्ठी (सहर्षं परिष्वज्य) कहं अरसण्णिहिदराअं रज्जं परित्तजिअ तुवं पि आअदो। णं पुव्ववेरिणो वलाविलित्ता दासीए वुत्ता अणुपेक्खिदव्वा पञ्चाला। (सखे! कथममात्य आर्यवसुमित्रः। कैषादृष्टपयोधरा वृष्टिः कथमसन्निहितराजं राज्यं परित्यज्य त्वमप्यागतः ननु पूर्ववैरिणो बलावलिप्ता दास्याः पुत्रा अनुपेक्षितव्याः पाञ्चालाः।)

अमा आसतामतिक्षुद्रपराक्रमाः केवलं पाञ्चालाः। अधुना पुनरतिभयङ्करो दुर्भिक्षोपद्रवः पीडयति तं जनपदम्। तथा हि,

उद्युक्ता वागुराद्यैरहरहरुचितैर्मत्स्यबन्धप्रकारै-
मर्त्या निर्मत्स्यगङ्गाह्रदगतशफरीशेषमग्नावशिष्टाः।
आशन्नारूढकण्ठैरपचिततनवः प्रायशः प्राणशेषैः
सङ्गध्यद्दध्नचञ्चुव्रजकुटिलशिरः कर्मकर्मान्तभूमिः।। २।।

तदेतदतिदारुणं व्यसनमापतितमसन्निधानादस्मत्स्वामिन इति। तत् केनचिदुपायेन तं नागाह्वयं पुरं प्रापयितुं प्राप्तोऽस्मि। तदधुना क्व भवितव्यं देवेन।

विदू (सनिःश्वासम्) कहेमि मन्दभाओ। एत्तिअं कालं तत्तहोदीए तवणतणूजाए सह विहरिअ गदाअं खणादाअं पसुत्तं मं उज्झिअं वअस्सो सो दिव्वजणसत्था अ गन्धव्वणअरं विअ अदंसणं गओ। तदा अहं अण्णे-सन्तो सअलं कन्दारं वालमिअभीदीए इह ट्ठिदो तुए दिट्ठो। एदं सव्वं मम अधण्णदाए परिणामो। (कथयामि मन्दभाग्यः। इयन्तं कालं तत्रभवत्या तपनतनूजया सह विहृत्य गतायां क्षणदायां प्रसुप्तं मामुज्झित्वा वयस्यः स दिव्यजनसार्थश्च गन्धर्वनगरमिवादर्शनं गतः। ततोऽहमन्विष्यन् सकलं कान्तारं व्यालमृगभीत्येह स्थितस्त्वया दृष्टः। एतत्सर्वं ममाधन्यतायाः परिणामः।)

अमा मा मैवम्। मयि परिवादानारोपयितुकामस्य देवस्यायं मात्सर्योपक्रमः। कुतः

यं प्रायेण प्रथयितुमलं शाठ्यमन्तःपुराणां
यं कुर्वन्ति व्यसनसुहृदो राजपुत्रापराधाः।
राज्ञो यश्च स्वयमपनयात् सम्प्रवृत्तः किलायं
सर्वो दोषः सचिवमनसां धूसरिम्णो विपाकः।। ३।।

(विचिन्त्य) स्वामी नियतमपहाय भवन्तं तत्रभवत्या सार्द्धं नापयाति। शङ्के कुतश्चित् कारणादन्तर्हितां देवीमन्वेष्टुम् अटवीमटता देवेन भवितव्यम्। तद् यावदावां देवमन्वेषावहे।

विदू (स्वगतम्) अहो णिक्करुणा तत्तहोदी, जं तणअणामहेअस्स फलस्स पुप्फं विअ दंसिअ गआ। (प्रकाशम्) एव्वं होदु। (अहो निष्करुणा तत्रभवती, यत् तनयनामधेयस्य फलस्य पुष्पमिव दर्शयित्वा गता। एवं भवतु।)

(उभौ परिक्रामतः)

विदू (अग्रतो विलोक्य) एत्थ सिअदिले पदेसे केण वि वणअरेण गएण होदव्वं। एसा हि पदपन्ती दीसइ। (अत्र सिकतिले प्रदेशे केनापि वनचरेण गतेन भवितव्यम्। एषा हि पदपङ्क्तिकृद्दर्शयते।)

अमा (सावधानं निरूप्य सहर्षम्) अहो चिरादवाप्तजन्मफले मम चक्षुषी। देवस्य पदसरोरुहयोरेवेदं प्रतिबिम्बम्। पश्य –

एषा सा कलशी सरोरुहमिदं केतुः स एवाङ्कुशः
सोऽयं छत्रमिदं तुरङ्गमकरौ तौ शङ्खचक्राविमौ।
कस्यान्यस्य भवेयुरङ्घ्रियुगले राजन्यचूडामणे-
र्देवात् संवरणादृते समवतः सप्तार्णवां मेदिनीम्।। ४।।

(नेपथ्ये)

आः दुरात्मन्नचलाधम! अतिचिरान्विष्टोऽपि न मे प्राणेश्वरीं प्रकाशयसि। विश्वविजयसमनन्तर-विरमदैक्ष्वाक-क्षोणीधरकार्मुकोद्वहनकर्मकर! कच्चिदनभिज्ञो भवान् अद्यापि। जनितबहुजन्य पौरवराजन्यचापचक्रपराक्रमाणाम्। भवतु तावदधुनैव बोधयिष्यति संवरणः।

विदू (कर्णं दत्त्वा) दिट्ठिआ वअस्सस्स एव्व जलहरगम्भीरो सरो सुणी अदि। (दिष्ट्या वयस्यस्यैव जलधरगम्भीरः स्वरः श्रूयते।)

अमा (विलोक्य) अये अयं स्वामी सोन्माद इव हिमाचलापहृतां देवीं मन्यमानस्तमभिक्रुध्यन्नित एवाभिवर्तते। तन्नायमवसरः प्रकाशयितुमात्मानम्। तदवसरे समुपसर्पावः।

विदू- एव्वं होदु। (एवं भवतु।) (गुल्मान्तरितौ स्थितौ)

(ततः प्रविशति सोन्मादो राजा)

राजा (सोद्वेगम् आः दुरात्मन्नचलाधमेति पूर्वोक्तमेव पठित्वा)

प्रयाहि दुहितुः सुतं शरणमद्य शर्वात्मजं
पुरत्रयहरं हरं स्वयमुपेहि जामातरम्।
तथाप्यसुरवाहिनीरुधिरपूरगण्डूषण-
प्रमोदभरदुर्मदैर्मम शरैर्न मोमुच्यसे।। ५।।

धनुर्धनुः।

विदू (पतित्वा सभयम्) अविह केण वि पक्खित्तो ह्मि। (अविध! केनापि प्रक्षिप्तोऽस्मि।)

अमा (सविस्मयम्) अहोतुखल्वतिशयितशक्रप्रभावेवं देवस्य प्रभुशक्तिः यदयमपि नाम वर्षाचलो गौरीगुरुरस्योन्मादकोपकलुषीकृतः कम्पते। (विदूषकमुत्थापयति)

राजा (विचिन्त्य) हन्त धिङ् मामकृतवेदिनामग्रेसरम्। येन तदा तया मां सङ्गमयता गतकल्पा अपि प्रत्यानीताः प्राणाः, स किल मम बाणानां लक्षभूमिः तदन्यतो विचिनोमि। (अन्यतो विलोक्य) भगवन्! सङ्कल्पयोने!

अंसस्थेन भ्रमसि हिमवत्कानने कामिनीनां
चिल्लीवल्लीचलनतुलनश्लाघिना कार्मुकेण।
किं नेत्राभ्यां चकितहरिणीनेत्रमापीतमाभ्या-
मासीदम्मद्दयितमलसापाङ्गमर्थान्तरं ते।। ६।।

हहह अन्मत्तोऽहं तनुमन्तमिवैनं व्यपदिशामि। तदन्यतो विचिनोमि। (परिक्रम्य सहर्षम्) अये! समुल्लिङ्गितस्तस्या मार्गः, कुतश्चित् कारणात् कुपिताया विहाय मां प्रस्थितायाः –

नेत्रान्तवान्तान्यधिचन्द्रकान्तं
क्लान्तेरमुत्र क्षणमासितायाः।
देव्या वियोगातुरचित्तवृत्ते-
रास्राण्यमून्यञ्जनकर्बुराणि।। ७।।

(पुनर्विभाव्य) नैष चन्द्रकान्तः न चैतान्यश्रुजलजालानि। अमी हि विकच्थलपुण्डरीकनिषण्णाः षट्चरणगणाः। तदन्यतो विचिनोमि। अथवा किमनयान्विष्टया, यया मुहूर्तमपि विरहमसह मानमवयन्त्यापि मम हृदयं क्वापि प्रतिष्ठमानया समवलम्बितस्तूष्णीम्भावः (पुनर्विचिन्त्य) यद्वा नापराद्धं तया पतिदेवतया। इयमेव हि बन्धकी वसुन्धरा सपत्नीमात्सर्यात् तपस्विनीं तां ग्रस्तवती। उपलक्षितपूर्वा चेयममुष्याः शैली। तथा हि –

दशरथतनयस्य पश्यतः प्रियदयितामपहृत्य मैथिलीम्।
नृपसदसि यया तिरोदधे किमिव तया पुनरत्र दुष्करम्।। ८।।

(स्मृत्वा) अथवा भूपालसहस्रभुक्तमुक्तायाः कुतोऽस्याः कुलटायास्तस्यां पतिव्रतायां सप्तनीमात्सर्यावकाशः। तन्नेयं मन्ये पृथिवी प्राणवल्लभां मुषितवती। तदन्यतो विचिनोमि। (परिक्रम्य पुरतो विलोक्य सानन्दम्) अये! अयं देव्या मन्दारवतंसकः। सखे! पाराशर्य! कथमयं प्रमादिना त्वया भूयोऽपि परित्यक्तः। (आदातुमिच्छति)

अमा सखे! अयमवसरस्तव देवमुपसर्पितुम्। अहमपि केनाप्युपायेन शिथिलीकृत्य किञ्चिदस्योन्मादं पश्चाद् दर्शयिष्याम्यात्मानम्।

(निष्क्रान्तः)

विदू एव्वं होदु। (सत्वरमुपसृत्य) भो वअस्स! एसो कण्णऊरो। एसो अहं मन्दभाओ। अदं पुण पदुमराअभूमीए मरीइजालं वअस्सं मोहेदि। (एवं भवतु। भो वयस्य! एष कर्णपूरः। एषोऽहं मन्दभाग्यः। एतत् पुनः पद्मरागभूम्यां मरीचिजालं वयस्यं मोहयति।)

राजा अये! वयस्यः पाराशर्यः। सखे! प्रयच्छैनम्। (विदूषकः कर्णपूरं ददाति)

राजा (कर्णपूरमादाय हृदये निक्षिपन् सरोमाञ्चम्) अयि प्रियापरिग्रहसुभग! वतंसक!

अपि कुशलि कपोलं पाण्डुनेत्रप्रभाग्नैः
शबलितमलियूथश्यामलैः पक्ष्मलाक्ष्याः।
पुलकसुहृदि मन्ये यत्र संश्लेषसौख्य-
प्रतिहतिषु दलानामभ्यसूयापरोऽभूः।। ९।।

सखे! तदङ्गसङ्गमोत्सवदुर्ललितेनामुना किञ्चिद् विरलीकृतो मोहान्धकारः। तते केन पुनरधुना तदन्वयश्लाधिना वस्त्वन्तरेण संस्तम्भयाम्यात्मानम्।

विदू भो वअस्स! अम्बरआरिणीए तिस्से परिग्गहो माणुसमत्तेहि अह्मेनि कहं आसादिज्जइ। (भो वयस्य! अम्बरचारिण्यास्तस्याः परिग्रहो मानुषमात्रैरस्माभिः कथमासाद्यते।)

राजा (ऊर्ध्वमवलोक्य सानन्दम्) अये! विस्मृतोऽयमियतीं वेलां सुखसमासादनीयः समाश्वासः, अयं हि भगवान् भानुमाली तस्या जनयिता। भगवन्! पद्मिनीवल्लभ!

तस्यास्ते दुहितुरविप्लुतानुरागात्
संसर्गात् सुभगतरैः करैरमीभिः।
अङ्गानाममृतरसान्तराण्यमीषा-

मासीञ्चन्नमृतकरोऽसि नोष्णरश्मिः।। १०।।

हा कष्टमकालजलदः पापीयानंशुमालिनं तिरोधत्ते। भो भोः सौदामनीवल्लभ!

लास्यारम्भप्रविततशिखानपर्यन्तं कलापान्
केकापूरप्रचितकुहरां कन्धरां द्राधयन्तम्।
त्वं प्रेक्षस्व प्रणयविवशः प्रेमवन्तं मयूरं
मा भूर्मेघ! क्षणमपि रवेर्मण्डलस्योपरोधी।। ११।।

(नेपथ्ये) राजन् ऋक्षनन्दन!

विदूरस्थे नाथे पृथुमहसि पञ्चालपशुभि-
स्त्वयि व्याप्तं राज्यं तव सकलमत्यर्थकलुषैः
अतस्तूर्णं गत्वा कुरु निजपुरीमस्तविपदं
पुनस्ते भूयासुर्मनसि निहिताः कामगतयः।। १२।।

राजा (अमर्षपरिवर्तिताक्षमाकर्णयन्) किं किं पञ्चालापशदैः परामृष्टमस्मद्राज्यम्।

क्षणं मम रणाङ्गणे परिणिधेहि पञ्चालकान्
कृतान्त! यदि शक्नुयाः सरथपतिसप्तिद्विगान्।
क्षुरप्रमुखकुट्टितस्फुटितसन्धिबन्धान् क्षणाद्
यमक्षयकृत स्थितीन् परमरीन् निरीक्षस्व तान्।। १३।।

विदू (स्वगतम्) साहु ले वसुमित्त! साहु। अमच्चभावाणुरूवं तुए उवक्कन्तं। दिट्ठिआ एसो परिवत्तिदो कामुम्मादादो रोसङ्कुसेण। जाव अहं पि किञ्चि सन्धुक्खेमि कोवाणलं। (प्रकाशम्) भो तेहिं दासीएवुत्तेहिं पञ्चालेहिं पुव्वं पि तुज्झ बाहुजुणलेण अणुभाविअभअरसेहिं अज्ज वि अप्पविणासाअ एदं आढत्तं। (साधु रे वसुमित्र! साधु, अमात्यभावानुरूपं त्वयोपक्रान्तम्। दिषट्यैव परिवर्तितः कामोन्मादाद् रोषाङ्कुशेन। यावदहमपि किञ्चित् संधुक्षे कोपानलम्। भो! तैः दास्याः पुत्रैः पूर्वमपि तव बाहुयुगलेनानुभावितभयरसैरद्याप्यात्मविनाशायैतदारब्धम्।)

राजा (सविमर्शम्) सखे! किन्नु खल्वसन्निहितस्तत्रभवान् वसुमित्रः, येनैतदेवमापतितम्।

अमा (प्रविश्य) विजयतां देवः।

राजा (विलोक्य) अये अमात्यो वसुमित्रः प्राप्तः (परिष्वज्य) सखे! अप्रकाशितशरीरा वागभिहितवती कृतं जनपदोपरोधं शत्रुभिः। भवन्मतिबलनिरुद्धप्रसराणां तेषां कुतोऽयमद्य प्रसङ्गः।

अमा देव! सत्यमशङ्कनीयपराक्रमाः केवलं पञ्चालाः। किन्तु बहुशो भवद्बाहुबलनिर्जितैः सकलराजन्यचक्रैः सम्भूयैते समुल्लङ्घ्य मम मतिबलं प्रतीक्षन्ते देवस्य पराक्रमम्। तदनतिविलम्बितं तेषामभिलाषं पूरयतु स्वामी।

विदू भो! किं तुए सह वाहणं आणुअत्तं आणीदं, जेण तुरिअं गच्छीअदि। (भो किं त्वया सह वाहनमानुयात्रमानीतं, येन त्वरितं गम्यते।)

अमा बाढम्, आनीतम्, अपि तु क्वचिदितः क्रोशमात्रे सन्निवेश्य देवसमन्वेषणार्थमहमेकाकी प्राप्तः।

राजा किमानुयात्रेण। न खल्वयमखिलराजन्यप्राणामिषगृध्नुर्मम दक्षिणभुजः क्षणते कालक्षेपम्। तदालोच्यतामस्माकमम्बरगमनोपायः।

(ततः प्रविशत्यम्बरयायिना रथेन सारथिः)

सार आदिष्टोऽहमरुणसारथिना भगवता। यथा 'हयसेन! मम जामातुरसन्निधानादम्बुगर्भा अपि तज्जनपदे वर्षितुमक्षमा नाड्यः। तेन स दुःक्षामपीडितः समुत्सन्नप्रायो वर्तते। संवरणोऽपि तपतीसङ्गमसुखविस्मृतकृत्यः हैमावतानि स्वर्गोपवनसमानि वनानि समुत्सृज्य न प्रयातुं वाञ्छति। तेन च कञ्चित् कालं विघटनीयमेतन्मिथुनम्। सा च पतिदेवता न जाग्रती श्रृणोति कथामपि विप्रवासस्य। तन्निद्रायमाणे भर्तरि स्वपतिं तपतीं सपरिजनां प्रापय सावित्रीसकाशमि'ति। ततश्चाहं,

राज्ञः प्रियां पृथुपयोधरभारगुर्वी-
माक्षिप्य तां सहचरादिव चक्रवाकीम्।
आज्ञाबलाद दिनपतेरतिनीचवृत्ति-
रासं प्रवृद्धतमसां प्रथमः प्रदोषः।। १४।।

द्वितीयः पुनरयमादेशो देवस्य 'यदसौ संवरणः स्वराष्ट्रगमनाय सचिवेन सञ्चोदितस्त्वरित-गमनोपायमजानानस्तिष्ठति। तदमुना स्यन्दनेन पूरणीयस्तस्याभिलाष' इति। तद् यावदवतरामि (अवतरणं नाटयन्नधो विलोक्य) अहोतु खलु क्रमादमुष्मिन्नवतरति स्यन्दने,

किं तोये प्लवते पलाशवितितिर्नैव द्रुमेषु द्रुमा-
स्तास्वेवाप्सु न भूधरेषु गिरयः सिन्धौ न पृथ्वीतले।
पृथ्वी सिन्धुनिचोलकुक्षिकुहरादुत्कृष्यते चक्षुषे-
त्युत्खातप्रतिरोपिता मम भवन्त्येता मनोवृत्तयः।। १५।।

विदू (ऊर्ध्वमवलोक्य) भोवअस्स! एसो दे सोसुरो णो हिअअसन्दावं अवणोदुं ओदरइ त्ति तक्केमि। (भो वयस्य! एष ते श्वशुरो नो हृदयसन्तापमपनेतुमवतरतीति तर्कयामि।)

राजा अयं हि प्रभापटलदुर्विभाव्याभोगः कोऽपि दिव्यः स्यन्दनः।

अमा सदा खलु स्वामिनश्चित्तानुवर्तिन्यो देवताः।

सार (नीचैर्दत्तदृष्टिः) अये अयं महाराजः संवरणः शैलराजकानने स्थितः। यद्यहममुष्मै भूतार्थं प्रकाशयेयम्, असौ पृच्छेदप्यात्मदयितोदन्तं, ततश्चापतेयुः सङ्कटानि। तदेवं कथयामि। (अवतीर्योपसृत्य) विजयतां मध्यमलोकपालः। अहमसकृदसुरविजयसाहाय्य-सम्प्रीणितस्य भगवतः सङ्क्रन्दनस्य शासनादम्बरपथेन हस्तिनपुरमायुष्मन्तं नेतुमागतोऽस्मि। तदारोहत्वायुष्मान्।

राजा (सप्रमोदम्) अनुगृहीतोऽस्मि भगवता शतक्रतुना। (सर्वे रथारोहणं नाटयन्ति)

अमा भो सेनापते! सिंहघोष! अपरिबाधमानीयतामानुयात्रम्। किं ब्रवीषि तथा क्रियत इति।

सार आयुष्मन्! किं मुच्यन्तामभीशवः।

राजा बाढम्। प्रथमः कल्पः। (सारथिस्तथा करोति)

विदू भो वअस्स! पुव्वप्पत्थिअं अम्बरगमणं आसि त्ति पीदी समुप्पण्णा। रहवेअघुण्णिदक्खो छिण्णपादं पडिस्सं ति भअं मे उप्पण्णं। ता दिढं तुमं ओलम्बिअ चिट्ठिस्सं। (राजानमवलम्बते) (भो वयस्य! पूर्वप्रार्थितमम्बरगमनमासीदिति प्रीतिः समुत्पन्ना। रथवेगघूर्णिताक्षश्छिन्नपातं पतिष्यामीति भयं मे उत्पन्नम्। तद् दृढं त्वामवलम्ब्य स्थास्यामि।)

राजा (रथवेगं निरूप्य) अहोतुखल्वप्रतर्क्यक्रमोऽयमतिस्यदः स्यन्दनस्य। कुतः –

कालः पातेष्वमीषां खुरपुटयुगयोर्मेघपृष्ठे हयाना-
मेकस्यैव क्षणस्य प्रथमचरमयोः पूर्वपाश्चात्यभागौ।
वेगस्तब्धा इवामूः कनकवलयवद् व्याप्तपर्यन्तरेखं
नेमीरावर्तमानाः पिशुनयति तडिच्चक्रमाक्रान्तिलग्नम्।। १६।।

(इति निष्क्रान्ताः सर्वे)

अथ षष्ठोऽङ्कः।

(ततः प्रविशति वृद्धकाञ्चुकीयः)

काञ्चु (सविमर्शम्) अहो महानुभावता महाराजसंवरणस्य, यदमुष्य रथहयहेषितसमकालीनो घनाघनानां हुङ्कारः, पादपद्मपरागैः समं भुविपतिताः पयोवृष्टयः। अमुना प्रमोदातिभारेणाम्रेडितमङ्गानामपाटवम्। कुतः,

कुर्वन् नैकविधां गतिं प्रकटयन्नुद्भ्रान्ततारे दृशौ
चिन्ताग्लानिविषादविभ्रममुखान् भावान् समुद्भावयन्।
ऊरू सन्नमयन् मुहुर्विचलयन् वक्षो वलीकञ्चुकं
सोऽयं नर्तकवत् प्रनर्तयति मां वार्धक्यविस्फूर्जथुः।। १।।

आदिष्टश्चाहं देवेन यथा 'विनियत्रात! तूर्णं गत्वा प्रावृषेण्याहरतिवाहनक्षमः कार्तिकेयावासपरिसरोद्यानगतः सज्जीक्रियतां गङ्गालोकप्रासाद' इति। अनुष्ठितश्च मया नियोगः। महाराजोऽपि तमारूढवान्। अतो नियोगान्तरमनुतिष्ठामि। (निष्क्रान्तः)

विष्कम्भकः।

(ततः प्रविशति राजा विदूषकश्च)

राजा अहो! निसर्गनिष्णातमतिभिरपि दुरवबोधाः सचिवानां मनोवृत्तयः। तथा ह्यार्यवसुमित्रस्य-

यत् पञ्चालपराक्रमात् परिभवो दैवच्छलाद् व्याहतः
सम्मोहादपवाहितोऽस्मि यदहं यद्वा पुरं प्रापितः।
सज्जानां घनसम्पदामिह भुवि प्रायः पयो मेदुरा-
ण्यूधांसि द्रुतमेव दोग्धुमखिलं सोऽयं किल प्रक्रमः।। २।।

विदू भो अप्पज्जो सो अमच्चो, जेण तुवं सअलभुवणेक्कणाहो मेहदोहणत्थं वच्छो सम्पादिओ। भो अप्रज्ञः सोऽमात्यः, येन त्वं सकलभुवनैकनाथो मेघदोहनार्थं वत्सः सम्पादितः।)

राजा अलं परिहासेन। पञ्चालकोपस्तम्भितप्रसरो वियोगहुतवहो विशृङ्खलमधुना विजृम्भितुं प्रक्रमते। प्रवृत्तश्चायं विरहिणामतिभयङ्करः कालः। पश्य –

> निश्शेषं वनमल्लिकासुमनसां शेषः समुच्छिद्यते
> वृन्तेभ्यः पथिकोपरोधपरुषैः पौरस्त्यवातैरयम्।
> प्रांशूकृत्य पिबन्त्यमा सहचरैः कण्ठप्रणालीरिमा-
> श्चातक्यो हिमशर्कराशकलिनीमारम्भधारावलिम्।। ३।।

तत् किमिदानीं मे शरणम्। (ततः प्रविशति मेनकारूपधारिणी नायिका)

नायि (सविमर्शं दीर्घं निःश्वस्य) अहं हि सहीरूवेण अय्यउत्तं दक्खिअ अस्सासेमि त्ति सहीओ विञ्चिअ आअदह्मि। एत्तिएण वि तादसासणंण लङ्घिअं होइ। ता अय्यउत्तदंसणूसवं अणुभविस्सं। (परिक्रम्याधाविऽलोकयन्ती सानन्दम्) एसो सो वअस्सेण सह पासादग्गभूमीअं णिसण्णो। ता ओदरिस्सं दाव। (अवतरणं नाटयति) (अहं हि सखीरूपेणार्यपुत्रं दृष्ट्वाश्वसिमीति सख्यौ वञ्चयित्वागतास्मि। इयतापि तातशासनं न लङ्घितं भवति। तदार्यपुत्रदर्शनोत्सवमनुभविष्यामि। एष स वयस्येन सह प्रासादाग्रभूम्यां निषण्णः। तदवतरिष्यामि तावत्।)

विदू (विलोक्य) एसा तत्तहोदी तवदी सम्पत्ता। (एषा तत्रभवती तपती सम्प्राप्ता।)

राजा क्वासौ क्वासौ।

नायि (सविषादम्) हंजाणिदह्मि। (हं ज्ञातास्मि।)

विदू दक्ख एसा मेणआरूवेण सम्पत्ता। (पश्यैषा मेनकारूपेण सम्प्राप्ता।)

नायि (सविषादम्) अवस्सं जाणिदह्मि। सव्वहा अबलज्झह्मि तादस्स। (अवश्यं ज्ञातास्मि। सर्वथा अपराद्धास्मि तातस्य।)

राजा (विलोक्य) अये सखी मेनका सम्प्राप्ता। सखे! कथमेनां मे प्रियां व्यपदिशसि।

विदू एसा तिस्से सरीरहूदत्ति एव्वं मए भणिदं। (एषा तस्याः शरीरभूतेत्येवं मया भणितम्।)

नायि दिट्ठिआ दाणिं समस्ससिदह्मि। (उपसृत्य) जेदु महाराओ। (दिष्ट्येदानीं समाश्वसितास्मि। जयतु महाराजः।)

राजा स्वागतं सख्यौ। (गाढमाश्लिष्य स्पर्शं रूपयन्नात्मगतम्)

> आश्लेषेष्विव देव्याः कण्टकितेयं मुधा तुनः कस्मात्।
> अस्यां तस्याः स्पर्शः शङ्के संश्लेषसङ्क्रान्तः।। ४।।

(प्रकाशम्) सखि मेनके! अपि कुशलमस्मदसूनाम्।

नायि महाराअ! सम्पदं कुसलं। (महाराज! साम्प्रतं कुशलम्।)

राजा कथं साम्प्रतमिति।

नायि सुणादु माहाराओ। तदा तुए सह तवणवणे पसुत्ता सा सावित्तीए सआसे पबुद्धा। तदो तुमं अदक्खिअ मुच्छिदं समस्मासिअ सावत्तीए भणिअं 'वच्छे! मा सन्तप्प। तुइ गाढाणुराअस्स भत्तुणो असण्णिहाणादो अणाविट्ठीपीडिणो आसी जणपदो त्ति तादणिउत्तेण सारहिणा आणीदासि। तेण च्चिअदे भत्ता विरहुम्मादपरवसो णअरं पाविदो। ण किल तादणिओअं विणा अत्ता दंसइदव्व'त्ति। (श्रृणोतु महाराजः। तदा त्वया सह तपनवने प्रसुप्ता सा सावित्र्याः सकाशे प्रबुद्धा। ततस्त्वामदृष्ट्वा मूर्छितां तां समाश्वास्य सावित्र्या भणितं 'वत्से! मा सन्तप्यस्व। त्वयि गाढानुरागस्य भर्तुरसन्निधानादनावृष्टिपीडित आसीज्जनपद इति तातनियुक्तेन सारथिनानीतासि। तेनैव ते भर्ता विरहोन्मादपरवशो नगरं प्रापितः। न किल तातनियोगं विनात्मा दर्शयितव्य' इति।)

राजा सखे! सोऽपि सवितृसारथिः संवृत्तः; ततस्ततः।

नायि तदो तिस्से वुत्तन्तं विओअजणिअं च दुक्खं णिवेदिउं आअच्छन्तीए मए विट्ठी उवलक्खिआ। तदो देवो वि अणुजाणिदि त्ति सम्पदं कुसलं ति मए भणिअं। (ततस्तस्या वृत्तान्तं वियोगजनितं च दुःखं निवेदयितुमागच्छन्त्या मया वृष्टिरुपलक्षिता। ततो देवोऽप्यनुजानातीति साम्प्रतं कुशलमिति मया भणितम्।)

विदू भो! जाणिदा देवीमोसआ कुम्भीला। (भो ज्ञाता देवीमोषकाः कुम्भीराः।)

राजा (निश्वस्य) इदानींनष्टः सन्देहः। सखि! गेनके! अहं क्षणमपि तां विना स्थातुमुत्सहे। तदभ्युपगमय्य देवमानीयतां तव सखी।

नायि (राजानं सस्पृहमवलोकयन्ती) महाराअ! तुह दंसणसुहं कञ्चिक्कालं अणुभविअ गमिस्सं। (महाराज! तव दर्शनसुखं कञ्चित् कालमनुभूय गमिष्यामि।)

राजा (सवितर्कमात्मगतम्)

दूत्योचितं प्रियजने प्रतिवेदनीयं
कामं सखीप्रणयपेशलमस्तु वाक्यम्।
विष्यन्दमानरतिरागरसप्रवाह-
मालोकितं पुनरलक्षितपूर्वमस्याः।। ५।।

(प्रकाशम्) अलं स्वैरासिकासुखेन। मम पर्युत्सुकं मनस्त्वरयति भवतीं गमनाय।

नायि (जलधरध्वनिं श्रुत्वा प्रस्तुतं विस्मरन्ती) हं भीदह्मि। अय्यउत्त! गाढं मं आलिङ्गेहि। (हं भीतास्मि। आर्यपुत्र! गाढं मामालिङ्ग।)

राजा (सक्रोधम्) आः पापे! किमनार्यमाचरसि। नायमभिमतदयितागुणनिगलितहृदयो जनस्तथा मन्तव्यः, यथा त्वं तर्कयसि।

नायि (सरोषम्) जुत्तं एदं। तुमं अणुरूवाए देवीए सङ्गच्छिअ सेरं विहरेहि। अहं पुण अत्थाणबद्धसिणेहा अत्तणो अणुरूवं करिस्सं। (निष्क्रान्ता) (युक्तमेतत्। त्वमनुरूपया देव्या सङ्गम्य स्वैरं विहरस्व। अहं पुनरस्थानबद्धस्नेहा आत्मनोऽनुरूपं करिष्यामि।)

विदू भो वअस्स! किं एसा रक्खसी। सा खु मेणआ सिविणे वि ण एव्वं कुणइ। (भो वयस्य! किमेषा राक्षसी। सा खलु मेनका स्वप्नेऽपि नैवं करोति।)

राजा ईदृश एव स्त्रीस्वभावः। पश्य –

> नैवाभिजात्यं न गुरून् न बन्धून्
> नातिप्ररूढं गणयन्ति सख्यम्।
> शक्यं च रोद्धुं ध्रुवमङ्गनाना-
> मिच्छानुसारीणि न मानसानि।। ६।।

सा तु तपस्विनी स्वच्छहृदया पुंश्चलीमेनामज्ञानात् प्रहितवती। विनोदनत्वेनाभिमता सेयमीदृशी संवृत्ता। तदानीयतां कर्णपूरः।

विदू एव्वंहोदु। (एवं भवतु।) (निष्क्रान्तः)

(ततः प्रविशति रम्भारूपधारिणी राक्षसी)

राक्ष पुव्वं भिउणो कम्मप्पभावेण हिमगिलिकाणणे दुक्खला मे माआ एदश्श कुलक्खअं कलिश्शं। (उपसृत्य राज्ञः पादयोश्छिन्नपातं पतित्वा रोदिति) (पूर्वं भृगोः कर्मप्रभावेन हिमगिरिकानने दुष्करा मे माया एतस्यराजापशदस्य वशे आशीत्। तदिदानीमेवैतस्य कुलक्षयं करिष्यामि।)

राजा (ससम्भ्रममुत्थाप्य) सखि! किमेवं मामाकुलयसि। आवेद्यतां विषादहेतुः।

राक्ष (सबाष्पगद्गदम्) पिअसही मे तवदी तादणिरोहदुक्खरसङ्गमा तुह विरहाणलं असहन्ती। अत्ताणं, अदो वरं ण पारेमि भणिदुं। अहं पि अत्ताणं वावादइस्सं। (निष्क्रान्ता) (प्रियसखी मे तपती तातनिरोधदुष्करसङ्गमा तव विरहानलमसहमानात्मानम्, अतः परं न पारयामि भणितुम्। अहमप्यात्मानं व्यापादयिष्यामि।)

राजा हा प्रिये! (इति मूर्च्छितः पतति। चिरात् प्रत्यागत्य) हा दिवसकरोत्सङ्गलालिते! जनमिममाज्ञाकरमपहाय क्व प्रयासि।

भगवन्! वैवस्वत!

> कलत्रतां मे मिहिरात्मजात्वमचिन्तयित्वा सहजन्मतां ते।
> आमृष्टमायुर्भवता मृगाक्ष्या मन्ये ततो मानसमायसं ते।। ७।।

कथमहमसुलोलुप इव केवलमश्रूणि मुञ्चामि। तदधुना प्रायोपवेशनाय प्रक्रमिष्ये। (प्रासादादवतरणं नाटयित्वा परिक्रामन्) अमुना शुचिमणिबद्धसोपानेन तीर्थेनावतीर्य जाह्नवीमाप्लुततनुरारभे प्रस्तुतम्। (स्नानं नाटयति)

कथमहमसुलोलुप इव केवलमश्रूणि मुञ्चामि। तदधुना प्रायोपवेशनाय प्रक्रमिष्ये (प्रासादादवतरणं नाटयित्वा परिक्रामन्) अमुना शुचिमणिबद्धसोपानेन तीर्थेनावतीर्य जाह्नवीमाप्लुततनुरारभे प्रस्तुतम्। (स्नानं नाटयति)

(ततः प्रविशति गङ्गाजलैरुह्यमाना नायिका)

नायि सहि! मन्दाइणि! उवरदं अय्यउत्तं सोदूण इह विवज्जिदुकामाए कीस मम कण्ठादो भारो तुए अवणीदो। तातुरिअं पाणेहि विहडिअ उवरदेण अय्यउत्तेण मं मेलावेहि। (सखि मन्दाकिनि! उपरतमार्यपुत्रं श्रुत्वेह विपत्तुकामायाःकस्मान्मम कण्ठाद् भारस्त्वयापनीतः। तत् त्वरितं प्रैणैर्विघटय्योपरतेनार्यपुत्रेण मां मेलय।)

राजा (शब्दानुसारेण विलोकयन्)

कालुष्यभाजं कमलाभिरामां परिस्फुरन्मीनविलोलनेत्राम्।
कां नु स्त्रियं जह्नुसुता वहन्ती वहत्यसावात्मसमानरूपाम्।। ८।।

अलं वितर्केण। एषा मुञ्चति पुराप्राणान्। अवलम्बे तावदेनाम् (सत्वरमवलम्बते)

नायि (सरोषम्) को मं हत्थप्फरिसेण दूसेदि। (को मां हस्तस्पर्शेन दूषयति।)

राजा (निरूप्य) कथमियं देवी संवृत्ता। भगवति! जाह्नवि! सोऽयमतिप्रसादो, यदहमेवं प्रस्थितानपि प्रत्यर्पयन्त्या प्राणान् प्राणितोऽस्मि। प्रिये! मा शङ्केथाः। सोऽहमेव पातकिनामग्रेसरः संवरणः, यद्वियोगान्मरणं व्यवसितवती।

नायि हं अय्यउत्तो। जेदु अय्यउत्तो। (सप्रमोदं गाढं परिष्वज्य) अय्य उत्त। किं सिविणो आदु परमत्थो। (हं आर्यपुत्रः। जयत्वार्यपुत्रः। आर्यपुत्रः!किं स्वप्न आहोस्वित् परमार्थः।)

राजा अहमप्यत्र सन्दिहे। तदुत्तीर्य तीरं विचारयावः।

नायि (कम्पं रूपयन्ती) अय्यउत्त! वेवन्ति मे गत्ताणि। ता दिढं मं ओलम्बिअ गच्छ। (आर्यपुत्र! वेपन्ते मे गात्राणि। तद् दृढं मामवलम्ब्य गच्छ।) (राजा तथा कुर्वन् परिक्रामति)

(नेपथ्ये)

सहि! मेणए! महाराअं सहिं च विणा ण खणं पि सरीरं अव्वहामि। ता मम कण्ठे पासं अप्पेहि। (सखि! मेनके! महाराजं सखीं च विना न क्षणमपि शरीरमुद्वहामि। तन्मम कण्ठे पाशमर्पय।)

नायि हं। (पुनरपि नेपथ्ये)

सहि! रम्भे! तुज्झ वि मरणं मं सन्दावेइ। अहं एव्व पुव्वं विवज्जिस्सं। (सखि! रम्भे! तवापि मरणं मां सन्तापयति। अहमेवपूर्वं विपत्स्ये।)

नायि हद्धि सहीओ विवज्जन्ति। तुवरदु तुवरदु अय्यउत्तो। (हा धिक् सख्यौ विपद्येते। त्वरतां त्वरतामार्यपुत्रः।)

राजा (ससम्भ्रममुपसर्पन्) मा साहसं कुरुतमत्रभवत्यौ। एतावावां धियावहे। (निष्क्रम्य ताभ्यां सह प्रविश्य) प्रिये! एते ते कुशलिन्यौ सख्यौ।

नायि सहीओ! दिढं मं परिस्सज्जह। (सख्यौ! दृढं मां परिष्वजेथाम्।)

(सबाष्पमन्योन्यं परिष्वजन्ते)

राजा तदिदानीं भवत्याः पद्धतिमुद्रिते ह्यमुष्मिन् मरतकशिलातले मुहूर्तं विश्रम्य गमिष्यामः।

नायि जं अय्यउत्तो आणवेदि। (यदार्यपुत्र आज्ञापयति।)

(सर्वे उपविशन्ति)

राजा प्रिये! कथमिह भागीरथ्यां तव देहोत्सर्गप्रसङ्गः।

नायि सुणादु अय्यउत्तो। अहं सहीए मेणआए रुवेण अवट्ठिदा राअन्धदाए विसुमरिअ पत्थुदं आलिङ्गिदुकामा ओहीरिदा अय्यउत्तेण। (श्रृणोत्वार्यपुत्रः। अहं सख्या मेनकाया रूपेणोपस्थिता रागान्धतया विस्मृत्य प्रस्तुतमालिङ्गितुकामावधीरितार्यपुत्रेण।)

मेन (सलज्जं सरोषं च) णं तुए मं लहूकरन्तीए सहिप्पणयानुरुवं किदं। (ननु त्वया मां लघूकुर्वत्या सखीप्रणयानुरूपं कृतम्।)

राजा (सशिरःकम्पम्) एवमिदम्। ततस्ततः।

नायि तदो किदमरणववसाआए पुणो वि सुमरिअसहीरुवाए गरुएण अणुदावेण पडिणिवत्तन्तीए मम इमाए रम्भाए बप्फपुण्णमुहीए अय्यउत्तस्स अछ्चाहिदं आलविअ मरणाअ उलक्कन्तं। मए वि एव्वं किदं। (ततः कृतमरणव्यवसायायाः पुनरपि स्मृतसखीरुपाया गुरुकेणानुतापेन प्रतिनिवर्तमानाया ममानया रम्भया बाष्पपूर्णमुख्यार्यपुत्रस्यात्याहितमालप्य मरणायोपक्रान्तम्। मयाप्येवं कृतम्।)

रम्भा (सविषादम्) का रम्भा णाम। (का रम्भा नाम।)

नायि तुमं एव्व। (त्वमेव।)

रम्भा हं। एत्थ असण्णिहिदाए मए एव्वं किदं। (हं। अत्रासन्निहितया मयैव कृतम्।)

राजा कथमसन्निहितासि। यया त्वयैव मम देव्याममङ्गलवचनमभिहितम्।

रम्भा (सत्रासं उरसि हस्तं दत्वा) हद्धि किं एदं। (मेनकां वीक्षते) (हा धिक् किमेतत्।)

मेन महाराअ! ण एदं जुज्जइ। दुवे वि अह्मे अज्ज पिअशहिं अण्णेसिउं आअच्छन्तीओ अन्तरा परुण्णाए आअच्छन्तीए जम्बूणदिआए मुहादो सहीए विवत्तिं महाराअस्स पाओपवेसणं च सुणिअ इह विवज्जन्तीओ महाराएण परित्तादह्म। (महाराज! नैतद् युज्यते। द्वे अप्यावामद्य प्रियसखीमन्वेष्टुमागच्छन्त्यौ अन्तरा प्ररुदिताया आगच्छन्त्या जम्बूनद्या मुखान् सख्या विपत्तिं महाराजस्य प्रायोपवेशनं च श्रुत्वेह विपद्यमाने महाराजेन परित्राते स्वः।)

नायि (ससाध्वम्) अह्मो अय्यउत्तेण वि उवक्कन्तं एव्वं साहसं। ण उण एत्त जम्बूणदिआ आअदा। किं एदं। (अहो आर्यपुत्रेणाप्युपक्रान्तमेवं साहसम्। न पुनरत्र जम्बूनदिकागता। किमेतत्।)

राजा (सविमर्शम्)

इयमपि मोहिनिकायास्तस्या मन्ये मृगाक्षि! मायेति।
तपनवनेऽपि ययाहं राक्षस्या मोहितः पूर्वम्।। ९।।

नायि (स्मृत्वा सशोकम्) एत्तिणं वेलं अत्ताणं पआसन्तीए मूढाए मए लङ्घिदो गुरुणिओओ। ता विसज्जेदु मं अय्यउत्तो। (इयतीं वेलामात्मानं प्रकाशयन्त्या मूढया मया लङ्घितो गुरुनियोगः। तद् विसर्जयतु मामार्यपुत्रः।)

राजा कोऽयमकाण्डेऽशनिः। (विषण्णस्तिष्ठति)

सख्या मा खु मा खु विसीदह। आणीदो अह्मेहि भअवदो आदेसो 'अज्जप्पहुदि सहअरेण अविरहिआ होदु तवदि'त्ति। अण्णं च एदाणि अविप्पवासअणामाणि वासोजुअलाणि पेसिदाणि। ता वसह एदाणि। (मा खलु मा खलु विषीदतम्। आनीत आवाभ्यां भगवत आदेशः 'अद्य प्रभृति

सहचरेणाविरहिता भवतु तपती' इति। अन्यच्चैते अविप्रवासकनामनी वासोयुगले प्रेषिते। तद् वसाथामेते।) (उभौ तथा कुरुतः)

नायि (सहर्षम्) जीवाविदह्मि तादस्स पसादेण। (जीवितास्मि तातस्य प्रसादेन।)

राजा (सानन्दम्) भवत्योर्वागमृतेन निर्वृतौ स्व।

मेन (स्मृत्वा सभयम्) सहि! रम्भे! जम्बूणदिआरूवेण रक्खसी गुरूणं पि किं पि करेदि। ता गदुअ णिवेदिअ परमत्थं आअच्छह्म। (सखि! रम्भे! जम्बूनदिकारूपेण राक्षसी गुरूणामपि किमपि करोति। तद् गत्वा निवेद्य परमार्थमागच्छावः।)

(निष्क्रान्ते)

भो ओरक्कह ओसक्कह एद दावग्गिपडिज्जन्तं अञ्चणसेलसिहरं अम्बरादो णिवडइ। (भो अपसर्पत अपसर्पत। एतद् दावाग्निप्रदीप्यमानमञ्जशैलशिखरमम्बरान्निपतति।)

नायि (सभयम्) अय्यउत्त! परित्ताआहि परित्ताआहि। (आर्यपुत्र! परित्रायस्व परित्रायस्व।) (राजानमवलम्बते)

राजा भीरू! मा भैषीः। ध्रुवमनेन पाराशर्यस्य भ्रमेण भवितव्यम्।

विदू (प्रविश्य कर्णपूर्हस्तः सम्भ्रान्तो विदूषकः, पुनस्तदेव पठति)

(ततः प्रविशति शरपञ्जरनिरुद्धा पतन्ती राक्षसी)

राक्ष (राजानमवलोक्य) लक्खदु मं महालाए लक्खदु। (रक्षतु मां महाराजो रक्षतु।) (राज्ञः पादयोः पतति)

विदू पढमं एदाए सव्वभक्खाए मुहादो रक्खदु मं वअस्सो, पच्चा ण। (राज्ञः पश्चादात्मानं व्यवदधाति) (प्रथममेतस्याः सर्वभक्षाया मुखाद्रक्षतु मां वयस्यः, पश्चादेनाम्।)

नायि अय्यउत्त! वेवन्ति मे गत्ताणि। तुरिअं विसज्जीअदु एसा रक्खसी। (आर्यपुत्र! वेपन्ते मे गात्राणि। त्वरितं विसृज्यतामेषा राक्षसी।)

राजा प्रिये! अलं भयेन। नन्वहमस्मि। (राक्षसीमवलोक्य) कासि। कुतस्ते व्यसनम्।

राक्ष (आत्मगतम्) शच्चप्पिए एशे। ता शच्चं एव्व भणिअ अत्ताणं मुञ्चावइश्शं। (प्रकाशम्) शुणादु महालाए। अहं मोहिणिआ णाम लक्खशी तुए वावादिअपुत्तशदा सहिं इशिप्पभावपडिहदकम्मा अज्ज एत्थ आअच्छिअ लम्भाए जम्बूणदिआए अ रूवेण शआणिं शशहीअणं तुमं किदमलणववशाअं कलिअ शूललोअं गच्छन्ती अन्तला तुह तणअं विशिट्ठेण शह आअच्छन्तं खाइदुकामा णिलुद्धम्बलगमणशत्तीहिं शलेहिं तेण एव्वं कालिदह्मि। ता मलिशेदु एदं महालाए। (सत्यप्रिय एषः। तत् सत्यमेव भणित्वात्मानं मोचयिष्यामि। श्रृणोतु महाराजः। अहं मोहिनिका नाम राक्षसी त्वया व्यापादितपुत्रशता तस्मिन् ऋषिप्रभावप्रतिहतकर्माद्यात्रागत्य रम्भाया जम्बूनदिकायाश्च रूपेण सजानीं ससखीजनं त्वां कृतमरणव्यवसायं कृत्वा सूर्यलोकं गच्छन्ती अन्तरा तव तनयं वसिष्ठेन सहागच्छन्तं खादितुकामा निरुद्धाम्बरगमनशक्तिभिः शरैस्तेनैवं कारितास्मि। तन्मर्षयत्वेतन्महाराजः।)

विदू (ससम्भ्रमं जनान्तिकम्) भो वअस्स! किं अज्ज एदाए किदं। (भो वयस्य! किमद्यैतया कृतम्।)

राजा (कर्णे) एवमिव।

विदू अहो अच्चाहिदं। (राक्षसीमवलोक्य) हदासे! एत्तिअं उवआरं करन्तीं तुमं अरक्खिअ कहं चिट्ठह्म। (अहो अत्याहितम्। हताशे! इयन्तमुपकारं कुर्वतीं त्वामरक्षित्वा कथं तिष्ठामः।)

नायि (आत्मगतम्) कहं अणवच्चाए मम तणओ। अहव बहुपरिग्गहो अय्यउत्तो। (कथमनपत्याया मम तनयः। अथवा बहुपरिग्रह आर्यपुत्रः।)

राजा (सस्मितम्) सकलमेतदुपपन्नम्। कः पुनर्मम तनयप्रसङ्गः।

(ततः प्रविशति वसिष्ठश्चापहस्तः कुमारश्च)

वसि अहं तावत् ,

क्षीराम्भोधौ प्रथमपुरुषं ब्रह्मलोके विरिञ्चं
कैलासाद्रौ विषमनयनं नाकपृष्ठे महेन्द्रम्।
कृत्वा साक्षादथ च मिहिरं तस्य दौहित्रमेनं
दातुं पित्रोः पुरमुपगतः पौरवीयामिदानीम्।। १०।।

कुमा (सकौतुकम्)

पूर्वं निर्जेतुर्दानवीयां च सेना-
मासीन्नैवं सा पुष्पवृष्ट्या सुरूणाम्।
प्रीतिं गात्राणामद्ययामावहेयुः
पित्रोः पादानां पांसवो मामकानाम्।। ११।।

(उभौ परिक्रामतः)

विदू (स्मृत्वा) रक्खीसीसम्भमेण एत्तिअ वेळं विसुमरिदो एसो कण्णेउरो। (राक्षसीम्भ्रमेणेयतीं वेलां विस्मृत एष कर्णपूरः।)

राजा (सस्मितम्) अनवसरे दर्शितः कर्णपूरः। अथवायमेव वावसरः अयं हि –

सुरभिः सुकुमारो मे कण्टकयन् गात्रयष्टिमाश्लेषात्।
भूयोऽप्यात्मसमस्ते वतंसको यातु कर्णान्तम्।। १२।। (कर्णपूरमर्पयति)

राक्ष महाळाअ! विशज्जीअदु एशा ळक्खशी। (महाराज! विसृज्यतामेषा राक्षसी।)

राजा अपेहि तावत्। (अस्त्रबन्धं मुञ्चति।)

राक्ष चिळं जीवह (निष्क्रान्ता) (चिरं जीवतम्।)

वसि (अधो विलोक्य) वत्स! एतौ ते पितरे तिष्ठतः। तदेह्यवतरावः। (अवतरणं नाटयतः)

राजा (विलोक्य) अये गुरवः सम्प्राप्ताः। (उपसृत्य) भगवान्! अभिवादये।

नायि भअवं वन्दामि। (भगवन्! वन्दे।)

वसि (उभाववलोक्य)

परिवृद्धरसानुकूलभावं गुणवत् प्रोज्ज्वलसन्धि सम्प्रहर्षम्।
ललितं ललिताङ्गमङ्गभाजां तपतीसंवरणं तनोतु दीर्घम्।। १३।

वत्स! वन्दस्व पितरौ

कुमा (सप्रणामम्)

> मूर्ध्ना नम्रेण ताम्राणि पादपङ्केरुहाणि वाम्।
> तापत्यो वन्दते पित्रोरेष सांवरणिः कुरुः।। १४।।

राजा (सस्पृहमवलोक्य सरोमाञ्च) वत्स! योऽसि कोऽसि चक्रवर्ती भूयाः।

नायि (सानन्दम्) वच्छ! सिणोहो तुमं जाणइ, ण उणा अहं। दिग्घाऊ होहि। (वत्स! स्नेहस्त्वां जानाति, न पुनरहम्। दीर्घायुर्भव।)

विदू णत्थि मे सन्देहो। दप्पणे णिकखित्तो विअथुह्माणं एसो पडिबिम्बो। (नास्ति मे सन्देहः। दर्पणे निक्षिप्त इव युवयोरेष प्रतिबिम्बः।)

वसि अलं विचिकित्सया। श्रूयतामस्योदन्तः।

राजा (सादरम्) अवहितोऽस्मि।

वसि पुरैषा तपनवने गर्भभरणानन्तरमात्मप्रभावादात्मजजमिमं प्रसूतवती।

राजा ततस्ततः।

वसि ततः सुरैरवध्यानामसुराणां निग्रहार्थमस्य तेजोबलशरीरवर्धनैरभौमैराहारैः पोषणार्थं चानधिगतपुत्रविरहवेदनयोरेव युवयोः सूर्यशासनात् प्रसवसमय एव विमोह्यैनां रम्भया गूढमेव सावित्रीसकाशं नीतः। तदेवानया स्वप्नदर्शनमिवानुभूतम्।

राजा ततस्ततः।

वसि ततः कतिपयदिनजनितदेहमहिमानममुमसुरविजयार्थे प्रार्थितं सुत्राम्णा 'कुरु सुरकार्यमि'ति समादिदेशा मातामहः। तत्वायं कुरुरभवत्।

राजा ततस्ततः।

वसि अवसितसुरकार्यमिममद्यात्मसमीपे वर्तमानं मया सह प्रहितवानहिमभानुः।

राजा (सबाष्पगद्गदम्) एहि वत्स! (परिष्वज्य मूर्ध्न्युपाघ्रायाङ्कमारोपयति)

नायि अय्यउत्त अहो दे अत्तम्भरिदा। (तस्योत्सङ्गाद् बलादाकृष्यालिङ्गन्ती स्तन्यमिश्रैरानन्दाश्रुभिरभिषिञ्चति) (आर्यपुत्र! अहो ते आत्मम्भरिता।)

राजा (विदूषकं दर्शयित्वा) वत्स! वन्दस्व पितरम्। (कुमारस्तथाकरोति।)

विदू (हर्षकम्पिताभ्यां कराभ्यामालिङ्ग्य) वच्छ! सोत्थि होदु। (विलोक्याकाशे) उप्पळिए! कीस तुवं आअदा। किं भणासि देवीए सळ्ळराअपुत्तीए पुत्तसङ्गदं महराअं सम्भावेदुं पेसिदत्ति। एसो कुमारो पणमिदुं आअच्छइ। गच्छ दणिं तुवं। (वत्स! स्वस्ति भवतु। उत्पलिके! कस्मात् त्वमागता। किं भणसि देव्या साल्वराजपुत्र्या पुत्रसङ्गतं महराजं सम्भावयितुं प्रेषितेति। एष कुमारः प्रणन्तुमागच्छति। गच्छेदानीं त्वम्।)

वसि किं ते भूयः प्रियमुपहरामि।

राजा
> मिहिरदुहिता किं नानीता परेतपतेः पुरा-
> दिह भगवता किं वा दत्तो न वंशकरः सुतः।

मम शतमखो राज्ये वृष्टीरभीष्टाविधायिनी-
रपि न कृतवान् भूयः प्रार्थ्यं न वेद्मि फलान्तरम्।। १५।।

तथाप्येतावदाशंसामहे (भरतवाक्यम्)

अन्योन्यं जगतामपाकविरसा मूर्छन्तु मैत्रीरसाः
सङ्गृह्णन्तु गुणान् कवेः कृतधियां मात्सर्यवन्ध्या धियः।
विश्लिष्यद्द्विषयानुषङ्गकलुषीभावा घनश्यामले
भक्तिर्मे परिपच्यतामहरहः श्रेयस्करी श्रीधरे।। १६।।

(इति निष्क्रान्ता सर्वे)

समाप्तमिदं तपतीसंवरणं नाम नाटकम्।

Tapatīsaṃvaraṇam was as much popular as Subhadrādhanañjayam on Kerala stage. We get a reference to the performance of this play in Uṇṇunīlisandeśam of 14th century. Introductory verses are available for all the six Acts. The expertise of the Naṅṅyār to float over the water in the fifth scene has almost become proverbial. Unfortunately the play is not performed in full nowadays. Only the first Act, that too, the role of king and vidūṣaka is performed on the Kūṭiyāṭṭam stage at present. The Araṅṅutali verses for the six Acts are given below:

Act I

मेनकासेवितारम्भा पाराशर्याहिता मतिः।
तपतीतपनो भूत्यै राजा संवरणोऽस्तु वः।।

Act II

लाक्षाविषाक्तदिननाथसुतापदाब्ज-
बाणाहतार्तहृदयो मृगयां विहाय।
कल्याणवामनहरिं मनसा स्तुवन् वः
पायान्नृपः कुमुदबन्धुकुलाधिनाथः।।

Act III

आलोकनात्प्रभृति पद्म पदाब्जयोस्ता-
मालक्ष्य सद्गुणनिधेः कुसुमायुधार्तिम्।
राज्ञो निधाय सहसोरसि पाणिपद्मं
या जीवयद्दिनकरात्मसुतावताद्वः।।

Act IV

आराध्यवासरपतिं तपतीसमेतं
पाराशरेण सह मेनकया विहर्तुम्।
शृङ्गारवेषविभवस्सुचिरं विभूत्यै
मन्दारमण्डपगतोऽस्तु महीपतिर्वः।।

Act V

... तां सचिववाचमथात्मराज्य-
दुर्भिक्षतापपिशुनां तपतीवियोगात्।
...तशोकपरिमोहमपोह्य गच्छन्
तत् स्वधर्मनिरतो नृपतिः श्रिये वः।।

Act VI

यत्पादाब्जरजोभिराशुपतिता राज्ये पयोवृष्ट्यो
यद्भाग्येन सुरक्षिता सुरनदीतोयं सतांभस्वतः।
यत्पुत्रेण कुलक्षयं विदधती ....यै राक्षसी
सोऽयं पुत्रकलत्रबन्धुसहितो राजा चिरं पातु वः।।

Part III
Epilogue

XXII
Post-Kulaśekhara Reconstructions

(10th-14th Centuries of CE)

Kulaśekhara's innovative experiments, especially of imaginative acting and multiple impersonations reinvigorated the theatre in a big way. Talented actors could find out royal sanction to overcome the limitations imposed by the text. Post-Vyaṅgyavyākhyā developments can be studied in two distinct phases – the first two centuries that followed immediately (10-12 century) including the period of the composition of *VV* and the second, the two centuries 13th-14th (of CE) that followed.

22. i. 10th-12th centuries of CE

Vyaṅgyavyākhyā abruptly ends with the entry of Saṅkarṣaṇa and Kṛṣṇa. The king might have prescribed the principle of acting for the remaining parts also which is unfortunately lost to us. Anyhow, he might have seen it performed fully. One can only guess as to how the remaining portions were performed. Sivarāma, the 14th century commentator gives us valuable information regarding the presentation of the scene where the two brothers meet Arjuna disguised as an ascetic[1]. His description closely follows the Vyaṅgyavyākhyā mode of presentation.

---

1 Śivarāma's commentary on the verse 7 in Act II:

अमुष्मै श्रेयस इति। अत्र प्रश्नशेषतया वाच्यार्थघटनम्। व्यङ्ग्यतया वासुदेवं प्रति स्वसाध्यप्रार्थनम्। अमुष्मै भवत्प्रश्नोत्तरसमष्टिरूपाय। श्रेयसे प्रशस्यतमाय साध्यायेति वाच्यम्। अमुष्मै आवयोर्बुद्ध्युपारूढाय श्रेयसे धर्मपत्नीलाभाय। प्रयतेतरां दिवानिशमेवं वेषपरिग्रहादिरूपं प्रयत्नं करोमीति वासुदेवं प्रति व्यङ्ग्यम्। तत्र सर्वत्र न हस्ताभिनयः नयनविकारादिभिरेव प्रकाशनम्। सिद्धिस्तु कैवल्यरूपा फलोदयः। अमुष्येति श्रेयोविशेषणम्। हृषीकेशविशेषणत्वे व्यङ्ग्यमतिप्रकाशं भवेत्। यद्यपि कृष्णस्य हृषीकेशत्वमेव, तथापि मानुषाविर्भावानुगुणमेव वक्तव्यम् ईश्वरकटाक्षानुसारिणी न पौरुषसाध्येति। व्यङ्ग्ये तु किमनुमंस्यते वयस्यो वासुदेव इति विकल्पमपोहितुं मया प्रश्नः क्रियते भवन्मतमविज्ञाय। तद् अनन्यशरणे मयि कारुण्येनेदं साध्यतामिति प्रकाश्यते।।

एवं तदभिप्रायं ज्ञात्वा साधारण्येन भगवत उत्तरं – न खल्वन्यापोक्षिणीत्यादि। अत्राप्यन्यशब्देन विशेषगोपनं कृतम्। अन्यथा मदपेक्षिणीति वक्तव्यम्। यस्या इत्यादि। त्वं तां निर्वृतिं नचिरात् प्राप्नोषि निर्वृतिं मुक्तिम्। नचिरात् क्षणात् अनेनैव चरमदेहेन। यस्याः कृते यां निर्वृतिंनिमित्तीकृत्य। यतिधुरां निवृत्तिधर्मम् अवलम्बमानः। योगं 'संयोगो योग इत्युक्तो जीवात्मपरमात्मनोः' इति लक्षितं समाधिं धारयसि। क्लेशं जहदिति प्राप्तिसमकालोचितं फलमाह। क्लेशम् अविद्यादिकम्। सहभुवं द्वैतपरिग्रहानुबद्धम्। मधुरां हृद्याम्। यद्यपि मधुरशब्दो रसविशेषवाची, तथापि 'मधुरं वपुः', 'मधुरा दृष्टिः' 'मधुरं चरितम्' इत्यादिषु हृद्यत्वं लक्ष्यते। अचिन्त्यरसाम् अनिरूपणीय-परमानन्दात्मकस्वरूपवतीम्। अत एव हृद्यत्वमिति भेदः। सुभद्रां परमकल्याणरूपिणीम्। अतः परं किं कल्याणम्। एव-म्भूतां निर्वृतिं नचिरात्

The expansion of the retrospective narration of Kalpalatikā, as we have seen earlier, was done under royal guidance. The performance of this at the time was not done based on any text. Attractive episodes suitable to the occasion were chosen either from Harivaṃśa or Bhāgavatapurāṇa and were presented using the original verses or from those composed by the actors. The acting techniques were the same described in Vyaṅgyavyākhyā. Perhaps, the mudrās might not have been as expressive as they are today. Soon, the actors prepared a guide for hand-gestures – Hastalakṣaṇadīpikā- which is still used in Kūṭiyāṭṭam, Kathakaḷi and Mohiniyaṭṭam.[2]

Naṭāṅkuśa refers to the absence of Draupadī in the fifth Act. We have reference to the entry of Kātyāyanī and the detailed recapitulation of Subhadrā in Act V. There are descriptive verses for the entry in all the five Acts. All these go to prove that the play was presented in full. Acting manuals to these parts are available only in fragments. These performance texts might have been documented in the life-time of the author or in the immediate years that followed. All the Acts of TS were presented on stage. We get introductory verses for them. Moreover the floating scene in the last Act where Tapatī floats over the waters of Ganges was a challenging favourite item for actors.

Some of the lost texts of that period are reconstructed in recent times. Usha Nannyar retrieved effectively the entry of Kātyāyanī and the recapitulations of Subhadrā recently. This was a historic occasion for the resurrection of *VV* tradition.[3]

The success of *VV* mode of acting is believed to have inspired the actors and they would have attempted to apply this method to other pieces as well. Mattavilāsa and Bhagavadjjuka were the most attractive one act plays popular at that time. The plays now ascribed to Bhāsa, appeared on Kerala stage during this period. It is surprising that Kulaśekhara does not include Bhāsa in the list of dramatists in the introduction

---

प्राप्नोषीति मे मतिः इति वाच्यार्थः। व्यङ्ग्यस्तु – यस्याः कृते यतिधुरां विरुद्धमपि यतिवेषं साध्यनिर्बन्धेनावलम्बमानो योगं सङ्गमं तदुपायं वा दधासि आकाङ्क्षसि। क्लेशं लिप्सानिर्बन्धकृतं व्यसनं त्यजत्। सहभुवं सोदरीम्। मधुरां हृद्यतया भवच्चित्तवर्तिनीम्। अचिन्त्यरसाम् अचिन्त्यत्वद्विषयानुरागम्। अनेन परस्परानुरागकृतं प्राप्तियोग्यत्वं प्रकाश्यते। सुभद्रानामधेयां मे सोदरीं नचिरात् प्राप्स्यसीति मे मतिः। मतिरेवात्रानुसर्तव्या। दास्याम्येवेत्यर्थः। निर्वृतिं निर्व्यूढवरणां, पूर्वमेव त्वां मनसा वृतवतीमित्यर्थः। अथवा मतिर्मेनिर्वृतिं युवयोः सङ्घटनात् प्राप्नोतीति विपरिणामेन योज्यम्। अत्र व्यङ्ग्यस्य न हस्ताभिनयः, स्मितदृष्टिपातभ्रूविलासादिभिरेव प्रकाशनं युक्तम्।। ७।।

2 Hastalakṣaṇadīpikā (Light on the definitions on hand gestures) a small treatise with in 120 slokas describes 24 basic mudras and their various uses for different occasions. This might have been, originally designed by an actor around 12-13 centuries of CE for the use of Kūṭiyāṭṭam. Its application was further extended to Kathakaḷi, Mohiniyaṭṭam etc.

See for details the brilliant doctoral dissertation of Maya Tangeberg Grichin 'The Technique of Gesture Language' A Theory of Practice.

3 Entry of Kātyāyanī in the 5th Act of SD was reconstructed and presented by Usha Naṅṅyār as a wonderful piece. Āṭṭaprakāram for this was available only in fragments. See Abhinetri for details.

of TS. This supports the view that Bhāsa plays became popular on Kerala stage in the Post-Kulaśekhara period. The first play the actors put their hand on was *Mantrāṅka*, the 3rd Act of *Pratijñāyaugandharāyaṇa*. The influence of Mattavilāsa on it deserves to be studied further. The Mahābhārata plays ascribed to Bhāsa came in handy for the actors to experiment the new method.

Talented among the actors might themselves have been tempted to make new compositions for presentation in the novel way. Nīlakantha's Kalyāṇasaugandhika is a telling example. It remains the best play modelled on Vyaṅgyavyākhyā. Most important contribution of this period, of course, is *Āścaryacūḍāmaṇī*, the best *Rāmāyaṇa* play produced in Kerala.[4]

The salient features of this period were:

i. Performances strictly followed the model of VV
ii. The method of expansion of meaning was accepted.

---

4 Śaktibhadra is traditionally placed in the 8th century on two grounds-

i. The sūtradhāra in his introduction speaks of the rarity of Sanskrit plays in the South and hence it is the first play from Kerala.
ii. The legends that describe reading of the text before the great Śaṅkarācārya by the poet himself. Both these do not stand to scientific scrutiny.

A close look at the remarks of the Sūtradhāra will reveal that the introduction was added when the play was presented somewhere in the North. The people in the North were, naturally unaware of the theatrical activities in Kerala and hence the introduction of it to the distant audience. This does not help us to ascertain that Āścaryacūḍāmaṇi is the first play from the South. We have already the Mattavilāsa of 7th century for example. Reliable documentary evidences are required to validate the legendary accounts relating Śaṅkarācārya to the author..

The earliest reference to Āścaryacūḍāmaṇī, available to us, is in Naṭāṅkuśa (15th c.) The author refers to Śaktibhadra with great respect. He has also taken one act of the play for detailed discussion. Kulaśekhara would not have missed to make a reference to the poet had he been prior to him. Hence Āścaryacūḍāmaṇī has to be placed after Kulaśekhara. The nature of the text also supports this view. Kerala stage, in the Cera period was especially favorable to Mahābhārata. Rāmāyaṇa plays were not the characteristic of that period. It was in Kalyāṇasaugandhika that we get a harmonious blend of the two epics. Āścaryacūḍāmaṇī followed it.

Śaktibhadra seems to have been fascinated by the appellation of Āścarya in the prose work of Kulaśekhara (Āścaryamañjarī) to name his own work after it. The cūḍāmaṇī actually, has only a minor role in the development of the plot. The many transformations of the roles, especially of Kātyāyanī and Draupadī in SD and Tapatī, Rambhā and Menakā in the last Act of TS, might have kindled the imagination of Śaktibhadra to design the Māyāsītāṅka with a series of illusionary transformations. The very nature of the play makes it suitable for presentation in the post Vyaṅgyavyākhyā period. Hence it would be safe to assign Śaktibhadra to the 12th century until we get convincing evidences to take him prior to Kulaśekhara. Āścaryacūḍāmaṇī is t illustration of *VV*. Kulaśekhara, Śaktibhadra and the author of Natankuśa inherit the same Mahodayapuram tradition.

iii. The techniques of retrospective narration and imaginative acting were followed.
iv. Presentation of suggested sense through the movements of eyes remained confined to the two dramas of SD and TS.
v. Actors/Scholars prepared performance manuals for new plays limiting the presentations to three / four days.[5]
vi. The manuals were in Sanskrit and performance followed the principles of Nāṭyaśāstra with the innovations made by Vyaṅgyavyākhyā.
vii. Languages of the dramatic text i.e. Sanskrit / Prākṛts alone were permitted on stage.

22. ii. 13th-14th centuries of CE

The post-Kulaśekhara period witnessed tremendous changes in the social and cultural life of Kerala. The central administration of Ceras collapsed and Mahodayapuram lost it royal patronage. Small principalities emerged under warring chieftains. Brahmins, hitherto confined to intellectual activities, became patrons of the new chieftains claiming their share in power and administration.[6] The *agamic* practices began to assert their superiority over unorthodox faiths like Buddhism, Jainism and Lokāyata.[7] The period also witnessed the emergence of local languages.

Dialects dominated by Tamil became popular.[8] The local language entered the Sanskrit stage during this period. Nambiar, sūtradhāra and coordinator of the dramatic troupe, began the practice of introducing the contents prior to the performance in local language. This is known as Mārdaṅgikatamil or Nambyārtamil

5 Stage manuals were prepared for other plays on the model of Vyaṅgyavyākhyā. They were in Sanskrit. The first of its kind was the one for *Mantrāṅka*. It was called *Kriyākrama* – process of action. A similar script was prepared for *Bhagavadajjuka*. The performance according to this extended only for three days. *Mattavilāsa* also had a stage manual where in performance was limited to three days. The acting manuals at this stage were written in Sanskrit.

6 The political uncertainty due to the breakdown of the centralized administration of the Ceras was exploited by the local feudatories to assert their power.

7 The presentation of *Bhagavadajjuka* illustrates this stage. The simple farce was overloaded with extraneous descriptions extending the performance to 35 days. The poor disciple gives high-sounding sermons on the excellence of *agamic* thought and condemns unkindly all the unorthodox systems. Dr. K.K. Raja has edited this part in a separate monograph under the title *Nāstikaninda*. Interestingly, this gives valuable information regarding the atheistic belief deep rooted in Kerala society at that time. See for details, *Bhagavadajjuka in Kṭiyāṭṭam* by K.G. Paulose.

8 The language used in the narrations of Bhagaadhajjuka is mostly Sanskrit. The local dialect seen there is a proto-type of Malayalam.

where Tamil stands for local language. These narrations attracted the nānālokās more to the performance. The intermingling of Brahmins with others through 'grand alliance'[9] had enhanced the status of nānālokās in public life. The local language used by Nambiar was not the Sanskritised Maṇipravāḷa.[10] It was a prototype of it as

9 The marital relations of the emerging Brahmin group of Nambudiris are interesting. Only the eldest son is allowed to marry, a clever device invented to avoid sharing of the newly accumulated landed property. Others can have relation – Sambandha, with the women of lower strata of society.

'The successful domination by the Nambudiri community of medieval society and polity was the outcome of a grand alliance between the Nambudiris and the ruling groups. The ancient Ksatriya dynasties of Kerala like the Ceras and Mūṣikas were originally Aboriginals of the Saṅgham age upon whom the Brahmins conferred Kṣatriya status. Various other dynasties or svarupams of the post-Cera period, like the Perupaṭappu, Puṟanāṭ or Kottayam, Pūññār, Pantalam, Parappanat and Veṭṭam, also must have belonged to this category. None of them, except the Mūṣikas, preserves any tradition of having migrated from the north in the manner of the Brahmins themselves, and even the Mūṣikas are usually associated with the Konkan and mentioned as the relatives of Ceṭis and Kalingas (Narayanan 1973a) Therefore it would appear that the Brahmins of Kerala has 'aryanised' them, giving them Sanskrit names and Sanskritic culture. By the post-Cera period at least all these ksatriya ruling families had adopted the matrilineal form of succession (marumakkattāyam; Kunjan Pillai 1970, pp 292-323). Their women were usually married to Nambudiri Brahmins, with the result that all the rulers in Kerala were sons of Brahmins. This was also true of the Sāmanta and Nayar kings, chieftains, and landlords...'

'Another aspect of the Grand Alliance was the promotion of temple arts and culture by means of Nambudiri patronage. A large number of temple servants belonging to the Vāriyar, Potuvāḷ, Piṣāroṭi, Cākyār, and Nambyār subcastes acquired proficiency in Sanskrit language and literature and in Sanskritc studies through Brahmin contacts. Among Vāriyars and Piṣāroṭis we find an early tradition of studies in grammar, poetics, logic, medicine, astronomy, and literature. The Cākyārs made use of itihāsas, purāṇas, and later Sanskrit works for their Kūṭiyāṭṭam and kūttu performances.

Thus the Grand Alliance that the Nambudiris formed with the Kṣatriyas, Sāmantas, and Nāyars on the one hand, and with the Vāriyars, Potuvāḷs, Piṣāroṭis and such like on the other, was responsible for their socio-political domination and their success in promoting their traditions. It played a historic role in the formation of the essential character and distinctive feature of the culture of Kerala that gradually emerged in the middle ages. It may be noted that the legitimisation, at an unspecified date, of the loose form of unorthodox conjugal relationship called Sambandham, which brought the Brahmins and upper-class non Brahmins into a new plane of social, economic and political partnership, was the critical choice that set Kerala Brahmins apart from Brahmins elsewhere in the country and set Kerala society on a new course through the Grand Alliance.'

A History of Nambudiri community of Kerala, MGS Narayanan and Kesavan Veluthat in AGNI Vol II pp 256-278.

In this connection it is interesting to note that the word 'Sambandha' is used in *VV* to denote marital relation. See FN in Act II, TS.

10 *Līlātilakam*, the 14th century text on Maṇipravāḷa (intermixture of Sanskrit and Malayalam) does not allow the status of Maṇipravāḷa to the language used by Nambyār – Nambiartamil. It prohibits it because though Sanskrit and Malayalam words are mixed in the narration of Nambyār, the case endings used are not that of Sanskrit and hence it can be treated only as a dialect of Tamil.

seen in Rāmacaritam, Bhāṣākauṭalīyam, Rāmāyaṇasaṅkṣepam, Dūtavākyam etc. Anyhow, the narrations, at this stage, were not permitted to be part of the performance. It was only a preface for better understanding for the ordinary folk. The use of local language enhanced the popularity of Sanskrit theatre. This prompted those struggling to ascend to power to use theatre as a tool to stabilize their position – they wanted to acquire political and moral authority over the masses.

To educate the masses politically, the new masters used Vasantaka, minister to Udayana in *Pratijñāyaugandharāyaṇa*. He was transformed to a storyteller.[11] The incidents depicted in the classical Sanskrit play were fully localized. This was the beginning of the process of localization of the national tradition of *NŚ*. They further chose the beautiful farce *Bhagavadajjuka* to preach the authority of *agamic* thought over others. The poor disciple Śāṇḍilya was chosen to be the preacher. The local language used by both the minister and the disciple was distinct from the ordinary Malayalam; the former used an artificial one and the latter more of Sanskritised dialect. The new masters were unable to find suitable characters in other plays for this kind of enculturation.

22. iii. Brahmakṣatra

One word – *Brahmakṣatra*, encapsulates the effects of three centuries of Cera rule in Kerala. Cera kings owed their existence to the Brahmins. The spiritual overlords made the society believe that Paraśurāma created the land of Kerala and donated it to them as *Brahmakṣatra* (land where Brahmins played the role of Kṣatriyas) with the right to rule and protect the land they so got. There was a council – *Nālutali* consisting of four Brahmins who controlled the administration. They put the king on the throne and upon their bidding he continued to be on throne.[12]

This new social formation had far-reaching consequences in the history of Kerala. An agrarian society headed by the Brāhmaṇas centred around the temple mutilated the existing social order.

नन्विह मार्दंगिकैर्न्नाट्येऽन्यत्र वा 'तमिळ्' इति कथाकथ्यते, तत्रास्ति भाषासंस्कृतयोर्योगः दोषराहित्यात् श्लेषाद्यनुप्रासादि गुणालङ्कार योगाच्च। न तु तत्र मणिप्रवाळ व्यवहारः उच्यते। तत्र संस्कृतं नास्ति विभक्त्यन्तं। अपि तु प्रातिपदिकमात्रमेव। विभक्तिभागे भाषासंस्पर्श एव भवति। अतो न तत्कथनं मणिप्रवाळव्यवहारविषयतामालंबते। तद्व्यवहारस्य विभक्त्यन्त संस्कृतयोगो विषयः. विभक्तिभागे भाषासंयुक्त संस्कृतं भाषाभूयमापद्यते, भाषात्वप्रतीतेः उद्रेकात्। अत एव 'तमिळि'ति व्यपदेशः। एवं अभिमन्युवधादौ भाषाप्रबन्धे कथाकथनरूपे मणिप्रवाळव्यवहारभावस्य हेतुरयमवसातव्यः।

11 The general belief is that Vidūṣaka brought Malayalam to Sanskrit stage. The fact is that his language was a natural succession of that of the disguised minister, the illiterate disciple and of the learned Nambyār. This occurred in the 13-14 centuries of Common Era.

12 Kesavan Veluthat, *The Early Medeival in South India*, Oxford University Press, 2009.

The temple functioned as the centre of economic life of the country. The governing body of the temple was very powerful. The Bhaṭṭas and Cattirar constituted an influential group of scholarly Brahmin professors and students attached to the temple. Rituals were performed by the Brahmin priests. The non-Brahmin categories attached to the temple were Ambalavāsis like Potuvāḷ, Vāriyar etc. There were drummers, dancers and musicians drawn from non-Brahmins attached to the temple. Dancing maids were also there. Naṅṅa as a courtesan was a source of pleasures for land lords. Male dancers Cākyārs performed Kūttu. The Pulayar and Cerumar who worked on the soil constituted the base of the society. They were a servile group and were exchanged as goods along with land.[13]

22. iv. Cellūr

Cellūr near Taḷippaṟambu, in the North of Kerala, was a Brahmaṇical colony with strong Vedic culture with the tradition of sacrifice from the 2nd BC. It cherished the Paraśurāma legend and continued to be a strong settlement under the Ceras. Most of Kerala Brahmins still hold fond ancestral memories of Cellūr.[14]

Interestingly the two Kulaśekhara dramas were prohibited in Cellūr. Actually they were not staged north of Korappuẕa River i.e. the territory of Kolattunāṭu who were not friendly with the Ceras. The reason given by traditional scholars is that it was not staged first in the Taḷippaṟambu temple according to the convention followed in Kerala. A visibly enraged Kulaśekhara is said to have instructed his actors to abandon their profession by leaving their costumes in a banyan tree in front of the Tiravañcikkulam Temple when their art cease to have any takers.

22. v. Fusion of Cellūr-Cera Traditions

Kulaśekhara ruled over Kerala with his capital at Kodungalloor. Those belonging to the Northern part did not accept his authority. So his plays were not permitted to be performed further north to Korappuzha river (in the present Calicut district). In the North there was strong Brahmin settlement around Taliparambu from early days. They boast of their inheritance from Paraśurāma. The Brahmanic settlement there was centered around the Peruntṛkkovil Temple. The Anadhītimaṅgalam attributed to be the native place of Vidūṣaka belongs to this area and the local temple authorities

13 *The Kerala Temple,* Rajan Gurukkal.

14 Kesavan Veluthat, *Brahmin Settlements in Kerala – Historical Studies*, Calicut University, Sandhya Publications, 1978.

were fighting each other. The basic reason for the enmity can be the Śaiva-Vaiṣṇava feuds of those days. Anyhow, the Vidūṣaka solves it by interpreting a verse to praise Viṣṇu and Śiva alike. This northern narrative sūta tradition merged with the Vyaṅgyavyākhyā tradition of the central part two-three centuries after Kulaśekhara. Thus the sūta narrative tradition came to be imposed upon Vidūṣaka. It is interesting to note that Vidūṣakastobha in the beginning symbolically represents a long journey, the descending of the sūta from heaven or from Naimiṣāraṇya down to the earth. It represents the fusion of the epic narrative tradition of sūta with that of the abhinaya tradition of Vyaṅgyavyākhyā – a conglomeration of Vākku with Nokku.

Vidūṣaka now acquired an ancestral story like the epic characters. Hence his nirvahaṇa hereafter starts with Vātutīrkkal in the Taliparambu temple and progress through the four parallel goals of life. These additions were made to the Sanskrit stage during 13-14 centuries. This cultural atmosphere is seen reflected in literature also. This is the period of *Vaiśikatantra, Uṇṇicchirutevicaritam, Uṇṇiyaccicaritam* etc. The author of the latter was Dāmodaraccākyār (14c). He designates himself as belonging to the clan of Bharata-Bharatagotriyaḥ. He has also written a Sanskrit Mahākāvya – *Śivavilāsam*. The vinodam and vañcana portions of Vidūṣaka's Puruṣārtha narration are inspired by these literary works.

The Cellūr tradition, unlike the Mahodayapuram tradition of Kulaśekhara, puts its stress on *vākku*. It is the narrative tradition of the *sūtas*. The belief in Kerala that the Brahmins who came from the North brought along with them the *sūtas* becomes meaningful if we accept this argument.

Kūṭiyāṭṭam emerged in the 12-14 centuries as a conglomeration of three streams – *Nāṭyaśāstra* tradition as improved by Kulaśekhara, indegenous folk practices and the epic tradition of *sūta* from Cellūr.

22. vi. Revolt from the adherents of Kulaśekhara

Kerala has a deep-rooted heritage of *Nāṭyaśāstra*. Naturally deviations from the sacred tradition irritated the Puritans. Their ire took the form of a critical work *Naṭāṅkuśa*-hook on actors. Kūṭiyāṭṭam when it evolved became a blend of classical, epic and indigenous traditions. It is no longer the traditional Sanskrit theatre of Bharata, instead is an autonomous art form drawing strength from all the three streams. The realisation of this complex situation is the pre-requisite for a sympathetic understanding of the content of the text. The conflict is not between the actor and the author, but between two deep-rooted traditions. The causes are not personal but theoretical and theatrical.

These are the two streams:

> The actors inherit an ancient tradition. Their practices are governed by the injections contained in it. It is not proper for any one to cast doubts on it. VI. 7. This is the stand of the actors. Acting is Kuladharma to them. Elder actors – nāṭyācāryas – are their preceptors. The stage manuals prepared by them are transmitted from generation to generation. As the author of *Naṭāṅkuśa* repeatedly refers to them as Ācāryas let us call, for the sake of convenience, this tradition as Ācāryamata.

The position of their antagonists is this-

> The drama also springs from a tradition. The actor should respect that tradition, which no doubt, is anterior to his own tradition. As sage Bharata is their source, let us call it Munimata.
>
> The conflict in *Naṭāṅkuśa* is thus between Munimata and Ācāryamata. The problem was there in Kulaśekhara. He cleverly managed by accommodating both the *prekṣaka* and the *nānāloka* in his scheme of performance. His successors failed to emulate his example. There were reasons too:

1. The *prekṣakas* were erudite scholars, but all of them were not endowed with a theatrical bend of mind. Many took drama as a literary piece. The basic dictum they forgot – A drama is not to be read, but to be seen upon a stage.

   The commentators of Sanskrit dramas generally ignored Kūṭiyāṭṭam. Even Śivarāma who respectfully refers to the *dhvani* manuals did not think it worth to incorporate the *dhvani* in his commentaries. Pūrṇasarasvati, though influenced by the inner meaning of Kūṭiyāṭṭam does not betray any appreciation for their stage presentations. Thus the most learned kept themselves 'unpolluted' by the stage practices.
2. The actors were also responsible for the alienation of the elite. They deviated from the path of Kulaśekhara. In their eagerness to pull the crowd with the help of the newly acquired medium of local language, they showed scant respect to the drama or the dramatist; the aberrations at times crossed the limits of decency and decorum in public life, not to speak of propriety. The security provided by the authorities might have made some of them arrogant.
3. An interesting phenomenon is that the protagonists of Munimata who were also the beneficiaries of these social changes did not challenge the digressions, though more serious in content, which suited their interests. The distortion of stories like *Mattavilāsa* and *Bhagavadajjuka*, has to be

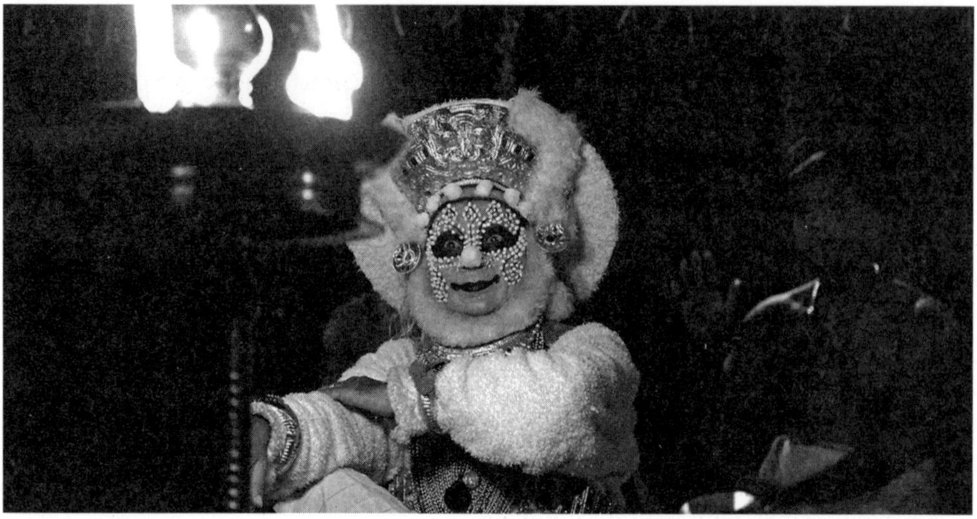

Margi Madhu as Hanumān in Aṅguliaṅka (Sixth Act of Āścaryacūḍāmaṇi)

understood in this background. They compromised to the anti Buddhist stance of the priestly class which converted the former to an offering to beget children and loaded latter with Vedāntic philosophy.

4. We have reasons to believe that the practice of staging Sanskrit drama as such, unaffected by the aberrations, was still in vogue; the reference to Śakuntala in *Naṭāṅkuśa* has to be read in this light. The author of *Śākuntalacarcā* criticises the ritual dance in the prologue as seen by him.

The emergence of new art forms like *Rāmanāṭṭam*, the stiff resistance from the traditional actors and the influence of Bhakti movement wherein Rāma plays reigned supreme left the secular plays only with two options – either submit for distortion surrendering the self or face extinction. *Mattavilāsa* chose the first; *Śākuntala* the latter.

It was thus as the representative of a vanishing tradition that the author of *Naṭāṅkuśa* waged his war. He might perhaps have been aware that he is destined to loose; Yet it did not deter him from upholding his tradition. A closer analysis of *Naṭāṅkuśa* will reveal that the criticism of the anonymous author was directed against the newly added epic and folk elements. He thought that these practices vilified the sacred *nāṭya* tradition. What should the actors do then?[15]

15 K.G. Paulose, *Naṭāṅkuśa* - A critique on Dramaturgy (Chapter 7), Govt. Sanskrit College, Tripunithura, in the Ravivarma Samskrta Granthavali, 1993. The English translation of the text was published in the SNA Journal, Kūṭiyāṭṭam special issue, 1995. Naṭāṅkuśa is translated to Hindi by Dr. Radha

'Listen. The performance should strictly adhere to the precepts of Bharata. Keep out the interruption to the story. Remove the things unconnected. Stop your elaboration. Close the eyes to the unwanted. Away with the sky-flower like intermixture. Reject the regional tongue. Discard the reluctance to present the characters. Let every thing be as it is.

Hanumān enters with the ring in hand – this is the direction of the poet. Present Hanumān with suitable make-up. On entering the stage he looks around, sees Laṅkā. Then pronounces his words – *samprati hi*. Then continue the text with '*mainākam*'. Don't interfere with '*kriyā*' or narration of the past. Similarly in all other occasions, enact freely the meaning of the verse; should never leave the posture of Hanumān. Follow this method through out. Enact the meaning of the text as freely and vividly as you can. Always keep the self of the assumed character. This is the essence of acting.

One follows the principles of *nāṭya* if things are presented in this way.'[16]

Vallabha Tripathi and is being serialised in Nāṭyṃ: A quarterly journal of theatre and aesthetics, Department of Sanskrit, Sagar Viswavidyalaya, Sagar, Madhya Pradesh.

16 The History of Sanskrit stage in Kerala can be studied under the following heads:

i. Pre- Kulaśekhara period (till 9th century CE)
In his introduction to SD Kulaśekhara refers to Śākuntala's popularity. He also refers to the playwrights before him. The Sanskrit plays of the North including Nāgānanda, were popular on Kerala stage. Mattavilāsa was the first drama from the South. Mamandur inscription refers to Bhagavadajjuka along with that. Plays, perhaps by lesser talents, were composed and used to be enacted on special occasions following the Natyasastra tradition.

ii. Kulaśekhara period (9th – 12th century CE)
Expansions of meaning, imaginative acting, multiple impersonations are the salient features of this period. SD, TS, plays ascribed to Bhāsa, Kalyāṇasaugandhikam, Āścaryacūḍāmaṇī are some of the brilliant improvisations on the stage. The medium was Sanskrit and conventions of Nāṭyaśāstra with the innovations of the royal dramatist, were followed. Naṅṅyārkūttu, represents the dynamism of the performance culture of this age.

iii. Post-Kulaśekhara period, fusion of Chera-Chellur traditions (13th-14th century CE)
Introduction of Malayalam, inflation of the role of Vidūṣaka and influence of indigenous practices mark this period. Spectacular items like niṇam, hanging / floating scenes etc., are the innovative practices added to the stage. Āṭṭaprakārams and Kramadīpikās came to be written in Malayalam. By the end of this period Kūṭiyāṭṭam became part of temple ritual where it continued till the 20th century.

iv. Age of renaissance (20th century CE)
Breakdown of the societal structure that supported Kūṭiyāṭṭam compelled the actors to create a public space for their art form.
Recognition of Unesco as the intangible heritage of humanity made it part of world theatre movement.

XXIII
From the Secular to the Sacred

As we have seen the innovative techniques of *VV* laid the foundation for classical theatre as a continuum at the same time a progression of the national tradition of Bharata. The emerging stage drew its strength from the classical epic and indigenous traditions and emerged as an autonomous form by 13-14 centuries. The political, social and economic changes in the fabric of Kerala society transformed the Sanskrit drama to a temple art. The space of performance was also shifted to theatre halls attached to the temples.

23. 1. Popular narratives

Sanskrit drama and poetry drew their themes from three sources- Rāmāyaṇa, Mahābhārata, and Bṛhatkathā. The latter was the source of many popular stories. Bhāsa took the story of Udayana from these tales. *Avimāraka* also draws its plot from popular sources. Many dramatists took inspiration from popular sources. The Bhakti movement in the early centuries of second millennia, perhaps out of a sense of insecurity born from foreign aggressions, shifted the attention from the profane to devotional themes. In this flow the theatre in Kerala moved from its open space to temple premises. Popular themes were ignored to concentrate on devotion .

But, the vidūṣaka preserved popular stories in his narrations. He drew his themes from Bṛhatkathā, Kathāsaritsāgara, Perumkathai etc. In the context of the recapitulation of Udayana, his mother's desire to bathe in a pool of blood and its consequences are narrated as described in Kathasaritsagara. The stories of 'husband and his two jealous wives', 'the hot fruits', 'the fools and Śiva's bull' and 'the parrot enticing the queen' are narrated interestingly by the vidūṣaka. The most attracting among these is perhaps the Brahmin's pregnant wife and the washer man's donkey, intended to ridicule the judicial system that followed rules in letter, forgetting the spirit. A seventeenth century poet Rāmapāṇivāda has described some of them in his mahākāvya.

23. ii. The Prākṛt Languages

We saw that Kulaśekhara's vidūṣaka spoke only the textual prākṛt; He did not even render it in Sanskrit. In course of time the prākṛt of North became unintelligible to the Kerala audience, forcing the vidūṣaka to give the Sanskrit cchāyā of the prākṛt text. Gradually the number of nānālokas increased and vidūṣaka added translation in local language with his own interpretations in his inimitable style. Thus the Kūṭiyāṭṭam vidūṣaka speaks three tongues – the original prākṛt, its Sanskrit version and Malayalam translation. The naṅṅyār, however stuck to the prākṛt assigned to her by the dramatist.

The sweet and melodious prākṛts (prakṛtimadhurāḥ prīkṛtagiraḥ) now lives only on the Kūṭiyāṭṭam stage. Kūṭiyāṭṭam preserved not only the classical mode of acting but also the narrative tradition and the sweetness of prākṛt.

23. iii. The Name Kūṭiyāṭṭam

The nomenclature in Kūṭiyāṭṭam indicates the localization of national theatre. Nāṭya is Sanskrit; āṭṭam is regional. Many scholars have tried to give fanciful derivations to this word. Kūttu is the common word used to denote all kinds of dance and drama in the ancient Tamiẕakam. *Cilappatikāram* gives vivid descriptions of various Kūttu used to be performed at that time. This word was used in its wide connotation when Malayalam got separated. Now it is confined to solo performances like Naṅṅyārkūttu and Prabandhakkūttu.

The innovations of Kulaśekhara favoured solo performance in retrospective narrations. This became the characteristic of Kūṭiyāṭṭam where it was described as nirvahaṇa – recapitulation. In SD for example the drama part is only the last three days. The first eight days are devoted for recapitulation – the first three days for Arjuna and the next five days for vidūṣaka. On the eighth day the characters join together- *kūṭi* (joined) *āṭuka* (acting). This is the meaning of Kūṭiyāṭṭam. Kūttu is the solo performance (*Oṟṟayāṭṭam*) and Kūṭiyāṭṭam is acting by multiple characters.

23. iv. The Cākyār

Cākyār is the traditional actor of Kūṭiyāṭṭam. Only those belonging to this community were permitted to perform Kūṭiyāṭṭam when it was confined to the temples.

The exact meaning or derivation of the term is not ascertained. There are references to Cākyārs in the Saṅgham literature and in many later inscriptions. The Ardhanārīśvara dance of the Paravūr Cākyār described in *Cilappatikāram* is famous. Those who performed dance/drama were known as Cākyārs. They were popular in all

Tamiẕakam i.e., Cola, Pāṇḍya and Cera countries. They became extinct in other places but were patronised in Kerala. In the post-Cera period when stratification of society in Kerala became rigid on caste line they were admitted to the intermediary classes. Acting became their kuladharma when theatre moved to the temple. Actors in Kerala prior to this amalgamation were generally referred to as Bharatas. Damodaraccākyār (14 *c.*) author of *Śivavilāsam* claims himself to be *Bharatagotriya* – one belonging to the clan of Bharata. Sūtas who came from the North also might have joined the Cākyārs at a later period. Children born on adultery might also have joined the group and hence the popular saying – *ottil ninnu* (from Vedic study) *kūttilēkku* (to acting).

23. v. The Naṅṅyār

Naṅṅa in Dravidian means lady. It was used to denote women who were respected in the society. During the Cera period we get references to them in many inscriptions. They are mostly attached to the temples and inherit the tradition of Mādhavī and *Maṇimekhalai* of the Saṅgham literature.

> The temple dancing maid or courtesan is referred to in the records as naṅṅa, tevaṭicci and kūttacci. In the south Indian temple records they are referred to as tevaraṭiśi. The earliest available epigraphic mention of a naṅṅa in Kerala is found in the Cokkur record where a record of the fifteenth year (AD 898) of Kota Ravi refers to the courtesans of that temple. An inscription from Neḍumpuṟam Taḷi of the seventeenth year of the same king refers to the remunerations of the naṅṅaimār of the temple and classifies them into uttama, madhyama and adhama. A different record of the same temple of AD 960 mentions a certain Mēṟāḷippuṟattu Cankara Naṅṅacci. Yet another record of the eighteenth year (AD 996) of Bhāskara Ravi referred to a certain Ciritara Naṅṅacci with the high sounding title Tribhuvanamahādevī, which was commonly used by South Indian queens of the time. It appears that this naṅṅacci could be a royal lady. The Ciṟṟariyil Naṅṅāyār of Cokkur inscription and Ciritara Naṅṅacci of the Neḍumpuṟam Taḷi record figure as donors to the concerned temples. So it is evident that in some of the temples courtesans were of high birth and material status. In addition to the epigraphic evidences there are a few sculptural representations of the period depicting dancing girls. Two panels from Tṛkkulaśekharapuram, a tenth century temple at Tiruvañcikkuḷam, depict catura and ghūrṇita postures described in *Nāṭyaśāstra*. A twelfth century panel from Trivikramamaṅgalam near Trivandrum exhibits dancing girls in arthamataḷḷi pose and musicians

> playing mṛdaṅgam. These dancing maids were the sacred courtesans of the temple who had submitted their sex for religious merit. It might be consecrated status and religious merit that prompted them to submit themselves to the deity as sacred courtesans. Certain South Indian temples had hundreds of devadāsis commensurate to their fabulous wealth and prosperity that bears no comparison with the situation of Kerala temples.
>
> The role of naṅṅa as a temple maid was essentially to attract the rich to the temple. The naṅṅa was performing the recreational function for the temple society and it was open to all who entered the temple. The naṅṅa as a courtesan was a source of pleasure for big merchants and land lords in a more restricted sense and therefore in a concealed sphere. The dancing girl as a source of libidinal gratification could have attracted the landed aristocracy as well as the moneyed trading class and indirectly caused the flow of wealth from them to the temple.[1]

When Sanskrit plays come to be performed there emerged another group of performing women. Members of the performing group of Sanskrit dramas were related to one another by family. The Sūtradhāra will be the coordinator and in many occasions the main character and his wife will be the heroine. All the others will either be brothers/ sisters or close relatives. The family was known as that of Bharatas – *bharatakula*. The women here were not dancers, but actresses and they along with the Sūtradhāra were responsible for maintaining the dramatic troupe. They were not attached to the temples and performed the Sanskrit plays in a secular space. The actors in the court of Kulaśekhara and the *Bharatakulaprasūtā kanyakā* represent this group of secular theatre. Nambyār was the manager of the troupe and he had to supervise all the works related to the performance. The story of the Nambyār-Cākyār quarrel in the evolution of Tuḷḷal has to be read in this background.

The reference to the Naṅṅyār performing *Kāḷiyaṅkaṃ* in the Tiruvalla inscription gain importance here. She was not a part of the temple administration. She came from another village on invitation accompanied by Nambyār. The Nambyār can either be her father/brother/close relative. There is no harm in speculating that she belongs to be one of the disciples of the new set of actresses whom the spouse-turned actress of Kulaśekhara trained. This is the beginning of a new era of actresses. These actresses of classical theatre will have to be distinguished from the temple dancers of the inscription.

1 *The Kerala Temple*, Rajan Gurukkal, pp. 54-56.

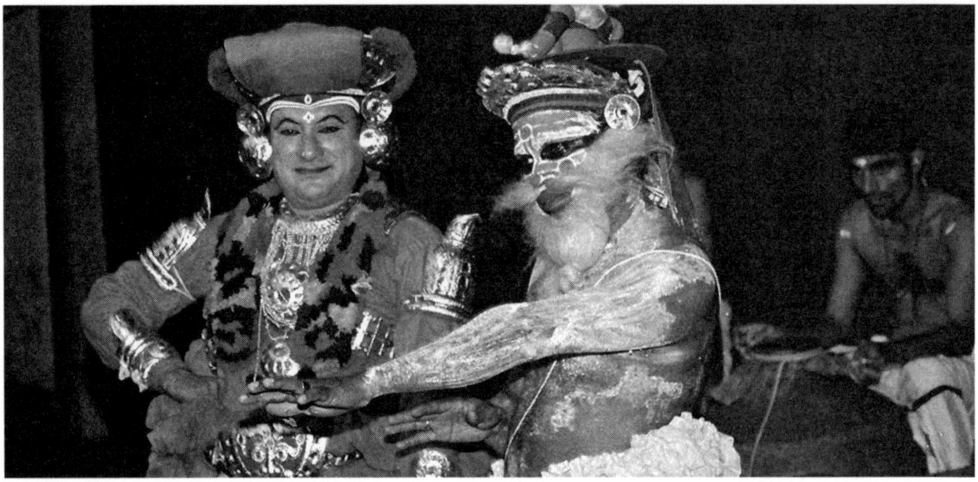

Bhagavadajjukam, Kalamandalam Sivan Nambuthiri (Hermit) and Kalamandalam Rama Chakyar (desciple) as coreographed by Painkulam Rama Chakyar

This bharatakula consisting of actors, actresses and managers of classical Sanskrit performances became attached to the temples when the Sanskrit stage was shifted to temples. Then they were assigned separate functions like other temple servants in the caste hierarchy. The status of Cākyār was elevated next to that of temple priest. This might have occurred in 14-15 centuries.

23. vi. Tolan?

It is generally believed that all that is extraneous to the Sanskrit tradition in Kūṭiyāṭṭam were added by Tolan who was the court-poet of Kulaśekhara. The tradition is so strong that there is not a single study related to Kūṭiyāṭṭam which does not repeat the story.

In the court of Kulaśekhara there might have been a gifted poet, whose name we do not know, along with Vāsudeva, Parameśvara, Śaṅkaranārāyaṇa and others. He might have been the other extreme of the Yamaka poet in simplicity and lucidity as is revealed by the two beautiful ślokas available to us of *Mahodayapureśacaritam* which he is supposed to have composed. Going through these verses one can generously justify his contempt for alliterations. Also he was mischievous and daring to criticise his own patron. By all these the genius deserves our respectful adoration. However it is not right to associate him with Kūṭiyāṭṭam and put on his shoulders the heavy responsibility of imposing the epic and folk-streams on a classical form. It is against history and contradicts our aesthetic sensibility.

Many writes that Kulaśekhara reformed Kūṭiyāṭṭam. The simple fact is that Kūṭiyāttam is a phenomenon that emerged at least two centuries after Kulaśekhara. *VV* is the application of *dhvani* to the performance of Sanskrit plays on stage.

All the inscriptions available to us from Cera period is in Tamil written in Vaṭṭeẕuttu. Malayalam language or its script had not evolved at that time. The first prose-work available to us belong to 13-14 centuries of CE. The most interesting thing is that there is not a single reference to Tola anywhere to substantiate his association either with the king or with Kūṭiyāttam. The 15th century author of *Naṭāṅkuśa* respectfully refers to Kulaśekhara; but does not mention Tola. More over he holds the actors responsible for all that he calls aberration.

When there is such a powerful document regarding the source of indigenous practices, parodies and extraneous explanations it is futile to put all the blame on an imaginary character. There is every reason to believe that Tolan is an invention of the actors to defend themselves from the virulent attack on them by the author of *Naṭāṅkuśa*. The evolution of Kūṭiyāṭṭam can historically be established without the intervention of Tolan.

23. vii. Period of Renaissance

20th century was a century of liberation for the nation as also for its performance traditions. The artists breathed fresh air. As in every other field a process of secularization and democratization took place in theatre. This led to the renaissance in the field of performing arts.

Kūṭiyāṭṭam was exclusively a temple phenomenon for the five centuries from the 15th. It came to public space in the second half of the 20th century. Opening a department of Kūṭiyāṭṭam for institutional studies in Kalamandalam in 1965 followed by a seminar next year participating renowned scholars was the beginning of the new awakening in the field. A ritual is not for spectators; but theatre owes the audience for its survival. All the restructuring of this period emphasised on the aesthetics of theatre.

The restructuring of Bhagavadajjukam by Painkulam Rama Cakyar who brought Kūṭiyāṭṭam to the public stage marked the process of revitalisation of the modern age.[2] The second notable effort was the presentation of *Āścaryacūḍāmaṇī* by Margi.[3]

---

2 The most salient feature of renaissance is a kind of systematic restructuring of the confused state of affairs. This is true with classical art forms also. The Kalluvaẕicciṭṭa was the beginning of modernity in Kathakaḷi. In Kūṭiyāṭṭam also ancient form were restructured with an eye on its aesthetics. This is the significance of remodeling, curtailing the 35 day performance of *Bhagavadajjuka* to a single night.

3 Margi Thiruvananthapuram under the guidance of Sri. K. Appukkuttan Nair presented the entire text of *Āścaryacūḍāmaṇī* in 105 nights during 1991-1995. This is perhaps the greatest event in

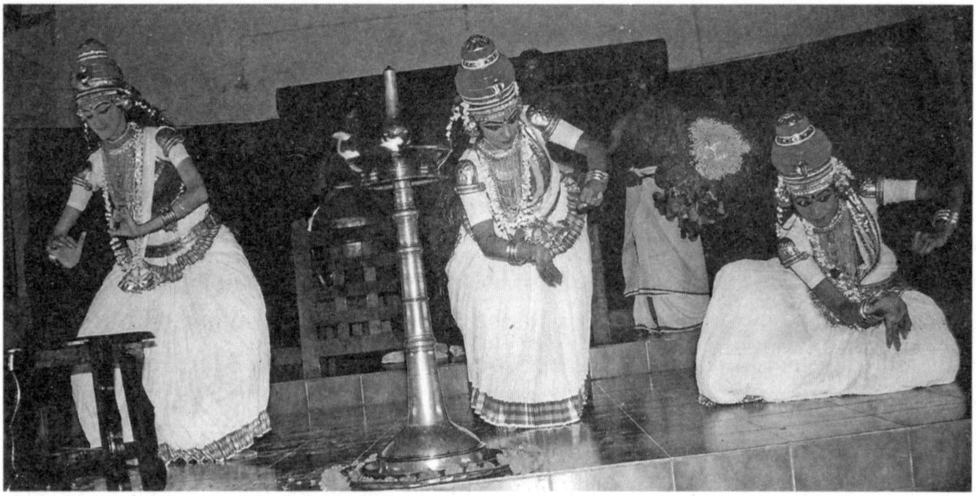

Anasūyā (Saritha), Śakuntalā (Kapila), Priyaṁvadā (Aparna)

The third was the presentation of *Śākuntala* in 2002.[4] All the three focussed on the delineation of emotions providing at the same time ample opportunities for actors to exhibit their histrionic talents.

Another important event of the century was the discovery of Bhāsa plays which resuscitated both the classical and contemporary performance of Sanskrit dramas.

Kūṭiyāṭṭam in modern period. The performance fully justifies the canons of *VV*.

4 The presentation of *Śākuntala* makes the beginning of a new sensibility with regard to the appreciation of Kūṭiyāṭṭam – the one comparable with the resurrection of *Naḷacarita* on the Kathakaḷi stage some years ago.

This performance, perhaps for the first time, gives life to frozen emotions. Kūṭiyāṭṭam usually freezes and later shatters the emotions which drama surcharges. Therefore, emotions appear in Kūṭiyāṭṭam as depersonalized. The emotion of love comes as a mechanical and ritualistic portrayal of *kāmaśara* and *pañcāṅga*. This performance gives them a personal touch and keeps the psychic distance required for a classical work.

A rigid classical framework for flexible structure is the challenge that this performance poses for the director. There is a destructive break and a positive incorporation. It seems that the multi-charactered sequences of the play requires a bit more pruning to attain complete harmony with the new medium. The general allegation against Kūṭiyāṭṭam is that it kills drama. Any experiment has therefore to be vigilant against a counter attack that Kūṭiyāṭṭam is turned into drama. My reading, is that this performance has succeeded in maintaining the balance between the *nāṭyam* and *āṭṭam*.

The dawn of 2002 became memorable in the history of Kūṭiyāṭṭam due to the presence of *Śākuntala* on our stage.

XXIV
Discovery of Bhāsa

The most remarkable event in the history of theatre in recent times was the discovery of Bhāsa's plays in the first decades of the 20th century. For the actors of Kerala there was nothing new in this discovery because they were in their repertoire for many centuries. Theatre outside realised the potential of Bhāsa by this discovery. They were shocked to know that he is different. They identified Bhāsa as the voice of dissent in Indian theatre. Its impact was not confined to Kerala or to Kūṭiyāṭṭam. Eminent directors from different parts of India and abroad read Bhāsa in a new light and made innumerable productions in different languages.[1]

In the second half of the century Kūṭiyāṭṭam, the only surviving relic of Sanskrit theatre came to the attention of the activists of world theatre. By the end of the century Kūṭiyāṭṭam, hailed by admirers as the mother of acting, was internationally recognised as the intangible heritage of humanity. In short, the discovery of Bhāsa plays had its impact on the theatrical activities all over the world.

The controversy regarding the authorship of thirteen Trivandrum plays which the learned editor Sri. T. Ganapati Sastri ascribed to Bhāsa still continues. Many scholars vehemently oppose the theory of common authorship.[2] Some of the antagonists of common authorship preferred to call Bhāsanāṭakacakra as *Keralanāṭakacakra* or

1 The first contemporary production seems to be of *Svapnavāsavadatta* in English by Santa Gandhi in 1964. Radha Vallabha Tripathi, Balraj Pandit, MK Raina, Zaheer Babbar, Prabhat Kumar Bhattacharya, Habib Tanvir, Srinivasa Rath, Kumar Thiyam and many others directed Bhāsa plays. The most outstanding among them is Kavalam Narayana Panikkar. P. Gangadharan, Chandradas and Ramesh Varma have made several productions recently.

2 See for details:

i. *Bhāsa's Works – A Criticism* by A. Krishna Pisharody, translated from *Rasikaratnam*, Vol. I, Nos. 2 & 3 of 1923.

ii. *The so called Bhāsa plays attributed to Bhāsa* by Herman Tieken, Leiden, 1993.

iii. *Text and Performance in Sanskrit Drama*, Hermen Tieken, Theatre Intercontinental.

iv. *Manuscripts and Performance Traditions of the So-called 'Trivandrum Plays' ascribed to Bhāsa*, Bulletin D'Etudes Indiennes, No. 17-18, 1999-2000.

v. *A Version of Dūtavākya and Their Sources*, Anna Aurelia Esposito, Bulletin D'Etudes Indiennes, No. 17-18, 1999-2000.

Cākyārnāṭakacakra. We do not enter into this controversy; instead accept all the plays as of Bhāsa until proved otherwise. Of the thirteen plays, theme of the four – *Pratijñā, Svapna, Avimāraka* and *Cārudatta* are drawn from popular sources. *Pratimā* and *Abhiṣeka* are based on Rāmāyaṇa and *Bālacarita* is derived from Bhāgavata. The other six plays are from different contexts of Mahābhārata. Bhāsa is at his best in Mahābhārata plays. The present writer believes that Bhāsa wrote those dramas at a mature age when he realized what he owes to posterity as a playwright.

24. i. Emotion / Reason

Dramatic theory lays emphasis on the emotional aspect in performance. It is pity and fear for the Hellenic world and eight basic sentiments for India. Too much concentration of emotions led the later Sanskrit plays, with few exceptions, to the depiction of various aspects of love, disregarding other serious avenues of life. Detached from the masses, many Sanskrit plays became narrations of frictions and conflicts inside the harem. The real life beyond the four walls of royal court, the hardship of people and their activities and expectations became conspicuous by their absence in the later Sanskrit performances.[3]

Bhāsa, is perhaps, the only dramatist who quarrelled with this tradition. According to him there are serious predicaments in human life than the hide and seek of young girls with the mischievous cupid. In his early days he also followed the same path. Imprints of his radical thought were visible even there. But when he took up Mahābhārata plays he became philosophic and prophetic. He realised that as a dramatist, he owes a vision to humanity. Life is full of predicaments. Existence is the most important question. War is most disastrous to life. Young widows who have lost their husbands, orphaned children and aged parents who have lost their young sons-all present problems which are not easy to solve. Bhāsa took theatre as a medium to share his anxiety with his fellow men in these points. Theatre, he thought, should enter the head through the heart.

According to the chronology of events *Madhyama* and *Pañcarātra* occurred while Pāṇḍavas lived in the forest, *Dūtavākya* just before the fateful war, *Dūtaghaṭotkaca* on the 13th, *Karṇabhāra* on the 17th and *Ūrubhaṅga* on the 18th day of the war.

All except *Pañcarātra* are one act plays. *Dūtavākya* where Lord Kṛṣṇa goes to Duryodhana's court as an emissary of peace follows the traditional way of presentation. It preaches peace against war. Each of the other five plays raises serious questions to

3 The Rasa theory laid stress on the philosophical depth as is evident from Ānandavardhana's treatment of Mahābhārata in the last part of *Dhvanyāloka*. Unfortunately, those who ranked śṛṅgāra as rasarāja failed to grasp this elevated level.

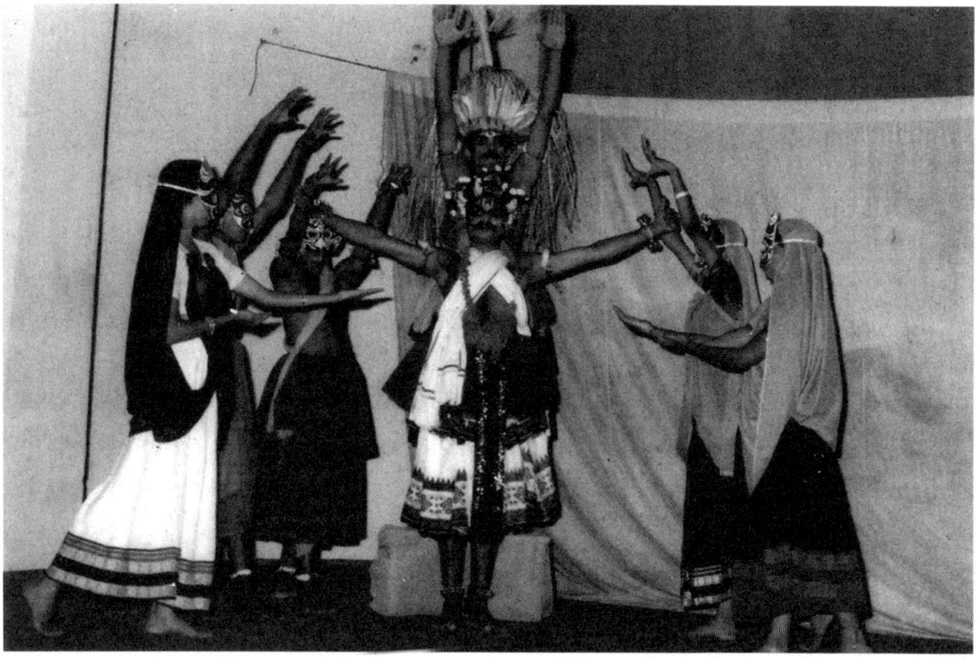

Karṇābharam directed by P Gangadharan

the audience. Situation in *Madhyama, Dūtaghaṭotkaca* and *Pañcarātra* are not from the epic. Bhāsa invented them retaining the characters and context of the epic.

24. ii. Concern for Subalterns

The present world order is built on the ruins of the original inhabitants of the land. Migrants annihilated red Indians and erected their empire over thier bodies.[4] Australian aborigines were wiped out to establish a new world.[5] Subalterns every where had to suffer. The heroes of Kurukṣetra really are the aborigines of India. According to some statistics 361 aboriginal classes fought the war. They belonged to different parts of India. The Śūraseni Ādivāsis and their Kāmboja counter parts were experts in duals, Ambas were experts in mace, Kirātas used poisoned arrows and the northern aborigines fought with stones. Anthropologists have identified 38 groups of ādivāsis who joind the Pāṇḍava camp and 59 with the Kaurava. The rest might, perhaps, have disappeared or merged with other clans. The Aboriginals fought with vigor, many fell dead and others returned to their native lands. The royal bards sang

4 For details : A People' History of United States of America -1980.

5 *Dūrakkāẓcakaḷ*, K. G. Paulose, 2010.

for the heroes of the cities, but the sincerity and heroism of the ādivāsis were neither acknowledged nor appreciated. Instead, they were condemned.[6]

Bhāsa always sympathized with the marginal groups. He thought that the behaviour of the city dwellers is not justified. To tell them the truth he wrote two dramas – the first to sing about the sincerity of their love and the second about their heroism. Hiḍimbā is Bhīma's first wife. She loved him blindly, he too felt at home in her presence. But Kuntī realised that she will lose her son if too much indulgence is permitted with Hiḍimbā. They were separated. Hiḍimbā waited for an opportunity to meet her husband and present the first born to his father. Bhāsa created a situation and wrote *Madhyamavyāyoga* where the reunion of the family is achieved. Along with that Bhāsa gives very clear hints at the miserable plight of the middle-born. Father opts for the eldest, mother for the youngest; the middle one is always left out by all. Bhīma had several instances of this neglect in his life.

The same Ghaṭotkaca is the hero of another play. He is sent as a messenger, reminding the messengership of the Lord earlier, on the 13th day of the gruesome murder of Abhimanyu. One wonders over the propriety of selecting a rākṣasa as the messenger. No messenger is sent in the epic in this context. Bhāsa does it deliberately.[7] He wants to tell the whole world that the rākṣasas who are counted as barbarians are more refined than those who live in cities. The love and respect the rākṣasa bestows on Dhṛtarāṣṭra and his dignified behaviour stand in the contrast with the arrogance of Duryodhana. When provoked, Ghaṭotkaca tells the whole court that those in the forest are more cultured than the citizens.[8] It seems that Bhāsa wrote this

---

6 When Abhimanyu was killed the entire Pāṇḍava camp wept and swore to revenge. Contrast to this the reaction when Ghaṭotkaca fell. There had a subdued joy. Lord openly says in Ghaṭotkacaparvādhyāya: 'If Karṇa had not slain the demon, then it would have been my duty to slay Ghaṭotkaca. It was to please you that I did not kill him before. This rākṣasa was a hater of Brahmins and violator of sacrifices and sinner. Therefore he has to be slain.'
There is no evidence for the grave charges of *Brahmaniṣedhi* and *Yajñadveṣi* leveled against him.

7 There is a veiled revenge. Ghaṭotkaca carries the message of the much mourned death of Abhimanyu who is his younger brother. If inheritance is decided, as Kuntī insists, through paternity, Ghaṭotkaca has every right to do it. The Lord is averse to this in his case. Bhāsa entrusts the job to him which the Lord himself did earlier!

8 You are indeed much crueler than the rākṣasas:

Rākṣasas don't burn sleeping brothers in a house of lac,
Nor do rākṣasas even touch the brother's wife on the head,
Rākṣasas can't think of killing a son on battlefield,
Though of ugly forms and ferocious, still not devoid of shame.

Śloka 47, translated by Dr. K.P.A. Menon.

play to declare to the civilized world that the foresters whom the citizens consider to be savages are more cultured.

The conflict between citizens and ādivāsis is a pet theme for Bhāsa. In *Abhiṣeka* he introduces a long conversation between the dying Bāli and killing Śrīrāma. Rāma becomes pale unable to answer the monkey. Śrīrāma echoes the arrogance of an oppressor which the brave Bāli does not accept. Bhāsa is the only dramatist who dares to challenge Śrīrāma in defense of a monkey.

24. iii. Safety of Silence[9]

Silence of the intelligentsia in crucial moments brings great calamities to a nation. Pāñcālī while she was disrobed before the elders requested to save her honour. None came forward. Bhīṣma looked down. Had Droṇa, Bhīṣma and other elders objected to Duryodhana would not have dared to humiliate Pāñcālī. Similarly these great men had several occasions to prevail upon Kauravas to avoid a war. But they did not. Kurukṣetra disaster would have been averted had they intervened effectively. Dhṛtarāṣṭra is blind by birth. Gāndhārī by willingly accepting blindness was absolving herself of her responsibility to bring up the children. Bhīṣma was great grandfather to all, similarly Droṇa was preceptor. Their silence cost the nation its future. Bhāsa by arranging an effective intervention of Bhīṣma and Droṇa prevents the Kurukṣetra war in *Pañcarātra*. At the end of a sacrifice Duryodhana generously offers Dakṣiṇā to all. Droṇa asks as Dakṣiṇā peace by sharing the country with Pāṇḍavas. Duryodhana grants it. Śakuni puts a condition that Pāṇḍavas should not be discovered in five nights. At the end of the play Pāṇḍavas come out of exile. Duryodhana gives them half of the country. Everything ends happily.

Bhāsa knows that Mahābhārata is incomplete without the war, yet he finds out a solution to the feud.

24. iv. Dharma Becomes Bhāra (burden)

Dharma has been defined by different authorities in their own way. The ultimate nature of it is still vague. Vyāsa does not give a direct answer. Bhāsa saw before his eyes several instances where virtue fails and wickedness wins. Karṇa is the best

9 This expression is borrowed from Dr. Howard Zinn, the famous historian who inspired civil rights movement in the US.

I wanted my students to leave my classes not just better informed but more prepared to relinquish the safety of silence, more prepared to speak up to act against injustice wherever they saw it. This of course was recipe of trouble.

example. Bhīṣṇa is unkind to Karṇa. His identity as Sūtaputra overshadows his real status of Sūryaputra. *Avimāraka* is also confronted with the same problem. His caṇḍāla position stands in the way of his achieving the beloved. The lower birth deprived Karṇa many of his chances. But what brings his life to a tragic end is his strict adherence to the principles of virtue. Pāṇḍavas commit frauds in the war front. They win by violating the rules prescribed for warriors. They can easily discard Dharma and can resort to any evil act. But Karṇa could not. His moral sense stands on the way. Dharma turns out to be burden for him.

He would have withdrawn his promise to give away the armour and earrings when he realized the deceit behind it. But he stood on his words. Violating the promise given in secret to his mother he could have killed the four Pāṇḍavas. He did not. The tragedy is that Arjuna did not grant him time even to lift the wheels of his chariot. The victory for the Pāṇḍavas was a divine gift for the violations of dhārmic principles. The defeat of Karṇa for sticking to his Dharma is more dignified than the victory of his deceitful foes.

Bhāsa asks the crucial question as to how one would adhere to Dharma if it becomes a burden on his onward journey.

24. v. Death as a Preceptor

Yakṣa asks Dharmaputra to name the greatest wonder in the world.

He replies – Every day creatures die,
yet the rest live as if immortal.

Death marks its strong presence in three dramas – *Bālivadha, Karṇabhāra* and *Ūrubhaṅga*.

Karṇa sees death before his eyes. But he is not terrified. Bāli also welcomes his fate. Heaven waits for them above.

In the last play *Ūrubhaṅga*, which by any standard is the strongest of Bhāsa plays, death is the principal character. It transforms Duryodhana to a noble being and elevates him to the abode of gods. Bhāsa has two images to bring out the present state of Duryodhana.[10] He is like Vāsuki floating over the milky ocean after its churning. The hood is crashed. Gods and demons got what they wished for. Now Vāsuki lay helpless, nobody wants him. Vāsuki was a tool and became useless when the objective is achieved. Duryodhana, also, is a tool. Victory or defeat does not disturb

10 *Śami* is traditionally believed to be a sacred tree which hides fire inside.

him. He repents. His misdeeds haunt him. Repentance purifies him. He advises his son not to follow him, but to love the Pāṇḍavas.

The second powerful metaphor that Bhāsa presents is that of an innocent child crawling on its legs. Like the child Duryodhana thinks of his mother. He wishes to be born again. Then he will lead a better life. Death has taught him many things. He leaves the earthly abode to join his brothers in heaven.

Bhāsa shares his sympathy with the marginalised section in his two subaltern plays, searches for an alternative in Pañcarātra and laments over the ill-fate of Dharma in *Karṇabhāra*. Bhāsa tells us that death is most amazing; it teaches us what life is.

24. vi. Jvalanamitra (friend of fire)

Bhāsa is different from other dramatists. He chose not to walk through the high way, instead wandered through the forests, streets and bye-ways. He distanced himself from the royal courts. Bhāsa restructured the epic world. All those who were worshipped as heroes were ignored, the anti-heroes were honoured. Rāvaṇa, Duryodhana, Karṇa and Bāli occupied the centre-stage in Bhāsa's theatre. Even Kaikeyī is exonerated. Duśśalā shares the same seat with Uttarā. Traditionalists could not easily digest these radical thoughts. When the stratification of social structure became more rigid, Bhāsa unfit to be accommodated, fell into oblivion. But the Kerala actors continued to carry this śami[11] tree being blissfully ignorant of the fire inside. Vākpatirāja, author of Gauḍavaho rightly designated Bhāsa as the companion of fire.[12]

11 Kerala actors performed Bhāsa plays on Kūṭiyāṭṭam stage and preserved the dramas. But they were concerned more with the external techniques than the content. The fire concealed did never burn their hearts.

12 *New Problems in Bhāsa Plays,* Dr. N.P. Unni, 1978, p.18.

XXV
Living Traditions of Vyaṅgyavyākhyā

It was rare and daring that a dramatist prepares the stage-script himself along with his dramatic text. The stage-script inspired generations of actors to design their own performances. This new-found freedom stimulated their talents. The results were generation of the innumerable new productions and choreographies. The richness of the Āṭṭaprakārams and Kramadīpikās in the repertory of the Kerala actors is simply amazing. The former are instructions to the actors where as the latter gives details of everything required for a production. These new creations are the direct result of Vyaṅgyavyākhyā. The years that followed became the most dynamic in the history of Kerala theatre. Vyaṅgyavyākhyā instilled vigor and vitality in the actors paving the way for the emergence of different forms of Performance.

The message of Vyaṅgyavyākhyā, in a word is, liberation – liberation of the actors from the rigidity of dramatic format and also from the author's text. Bharata had prescribed strict rules for the development of the plot and the delineation of *rasa* which he considered the very end of every performance. *Nāṭyaśāstra* thus prescribed a grammar for performance. Imaginative acting and multiple impersonations upset the apple cart. The avasthās, arthaprakṛtis and sandhis were of no use since the actors limited their performance to fragments of the story. *Rasa* also suffered because the interest of the actor was centered on elaborative narrations. In an exciting moment when Arjuna is exhilarated by the beauty of the descending damsel, the actor leaves him there and goes on to describe the dressing of a woman and finds out as a great thing that she had not applied collyrium to her eyes! Actor flies in the air in imagination. If *Nāṭyaśāstra* is the *Aṣṭādhyāyī* of theatre; Vyaṅgyavyākhyā is the Magnacarta of the actor!

The impact of Vyaṅgyavyākhyā can be studied under two heads – historical and contemporary.

25. i. In a Historical Perspective

Vyaṅgyavyākhyā became the fountain-head of all the later developments in classical theatre of Kerala. Kulaśekhara prescribed the peculiar mode of acting to Sanskrit plays. Soon it paved the way for the emergence of an autonomous art form universally acclaimed as Kūṭiyāṭṭam. Naṅṅyārkūttu, Prabandhakkūttu, Pāṭhakam and Tuḷḷal are allied to and derived from Kūṭiyāṭṭam. Kūṭiyāṭṭam exerted the greatest influence on Kathakaḷi. Kerala now is known as the land of Kathakaḷi.[1]

Mohiniyaṭṭam is indebted to Kūṭiyāṭṭam for elaboration, imaginative acting and above all the codex of scientific gestures. Thus the influence of Vyaṅgyavyākhyā on Kerala theatre in general and on the evolution of individual art forms in particular needs no elucidation.

Vyaṅgyavyākhyā exerts deeper impact on contemporary theatre; the potential to create sub texts from the dramatic texts, as illustrated in the production of Kāñcukīyam, is the most important contribution of Kulaśekhara. It made texts irrelevant and elevated the role of directors; the traditional Sūtradhāra was only a coordinator. Here he is the Prajāpati.[2] Author composes the text; director creates theatre out of it.

---

1 All the four Kerala Classical Art forms – *Kūṭiyāṭṭam, Kṛṣṇanāṭṭam, Rāmanāṭṭam (Kathakaḷi)* and *Mohiniyāṭṭam* – inherit a common tradition in Kerala. *Kṛṣṇanāṭṭam* is more or less confined to the temples. *Mohiniyāṭṭam* is the lāsya dance of women. *Kūṭiyaṭṭam* and *Kathakaḷi* are inter-related. They differ mainly on the following points:

Texts for *Kūṭiyāṭṭam* are Sanskrit dramas but for *Kathakaḷi* they are stories composed in Malayalam. There is no verbal rendering in *Kathakaḷi.*

Hand gestures in both are similar. In *Kūṭiyāṭṭam* hands cannot be extended beyond shoulders. *Kathakaḷi* does not impose such limitations. *Kūṭiyāṭṭam* employs *mudrās* for the minute propositions. Acting in *Kathakaḷi* is more *padārtha*, but in Kūṭiyāṭṭam it is mainly *vākyārtha*. Heels in *Kūṭiyāṭṭam* are kept closer facing each other. In the other they rest on the ground in their natural ways.

Kūṭiyāṭṭam has six types of acting:

Colliyāṭṭam gestures along with verbal rendering.
Kēṭṭāṭal Acting the meaning hearing the words of others.
Patiññāṭṭam Acting meaning followed by recital by Naṅṅyār.
Iḷakiyāṭṭam Contrary to the above. Heroic characters in anger enacts this way.
Anvayiccāṭṭam Words enacted in their prose order.
Irunnāṭṭam Acting while sitting on a stool.

Kathakaḷi has three kinds of acting : *Colliyāṭṭam, Iḷakiyāṭṭam, Tanṭeṭāṭṭam*

Tanṭēṭāṭṭam is for beard characters like Hanumān, Bāli etc.

Rasābhinaya is important in Kūṭiyāṭṭam, Kathakaḷi gives equal importance to Abhinaya, music and dance. Kūṭiyāṭṭam does not have *Tiranōṭṭam* as in *Kathakaḷi. Pacca, Katti, Tāṭi* are almost similar. There are minor changes in the costume of other characters. All female characters have the same costume in both.

Kūṭiyāṭṭam produces a kind of internal contemplation where as Kathakaḷi an exciting exhilaration.

2 May Nārāyaṇa, refuge of the three worlds protect us.

He who is keen to help the gods with devices diverse
Of the world's eternal drama, he's the stage manager,
He alone is the plot and theme, prologue and epilogue.

Bhāsa's Sūtradhāra in *Dūtaghaṭotkaca.*

The other principle relevant to the contemporary stage is that of the suggestive import in performance. Kulaśekhara vehemently advocated it; but his enthusiastic followers simply ignored it after his time.

There are three reasons for their rejection:

i. Kulaśekhara presented dhvani in his works. He had specially incorporated words with double meaning to bring out suggestion. This technique, the actors could not extend to the works of other authors who had composed them without the concept of dhvani in their mind.

ii. In his own works they did not continue the practice later because to express the hidden meaning through the movement of eyes alone is a difficult task and requires several years of strenuous training.

iii. By the introduction of Malayalam language and prominence given to the role of Vidūṣaka the presence of nānāloka among the audience became considerably large. The Prekṣakas of Kulaśekhara for whom he presented the hidden meaning ceased to have influence over the crowd assembled to laugh and applause the jester. The nature of the composition of the audience was not favorable for serious acting. More over talented among the actors diverted their attention to vākku from nokku.[3]

25. ii. Contemporary Relevance

But the actors, taking the cue from the royal dramatist would have developed their sub-texts to interpret the silence of the author in crucial moments. Some such 'golden silences' which would have inspired the actors for creating sub-texts, are shown below:

i. In *Ūrubhaṅga*, Balarāma hearing of the atrocity inflicted on his disciple Duryodhana jumps to the stage in rage. He swears to revenge all those who are responsible for the heinous act. This is a moment of action and

---

As Bhāsa himself has compared Sūtradhāra to the Lord Almighty, there is no meaning in leveling a charge that it encourages the 'tyranny of the director' in theatre.

'Directors have acquired greater importance over the years with the elaboration of the stage craft. In the new theatre, various conventional elements of stage craft have become secondary and their character and function have changed. The directors role has also changed.'

– *Theatre of Roots : Encounter with Tradition*, Suresh Awasthi, TDR (1988) vol 33, no . 4, pp 48-69

3 Vākku (word) represents the verbal acting and Nokku (look) the other two – āṅgika and sātvika. When the clown introduced narrations in Malayalam the masses turned to words. The subtle acting through eyes was appreciated only by a few. Naturally, actors began to concentrate on verbal acting to please the audience. This explains the popularity of Vidūṣaka as also of Prabandhakkūttu.

anxiety. But, alas, in the next moment, when he hears that his own brother is responsible, Bhāsa freezes him without even a comment!

The actor could have penetrated into the loud silence of Bhāsa and tell the audience of the fraudulent sense of morality exhibited by those whom the society considers with high esteem. Bhāsa actually anticipates an actor to expose the bubble. But our actors missed it![4]

ii. In *Āścaryacūḍāmaṇī*, Rāma went after the golden deer only to return empty-handed. Even a child knows that a deer in gold does not exist. But the great Rāma did not know this! Why our actors failed to share the eloquent smile of Śaktibhadra with the audience?[5]

iii. In *Karṇabhāra*, Bhāsa presents Karṇa in a gloomy mood. The dramatist prefaces the story with a significant metaphor of the fading brilliance of the sun covered by the clouds! Think of interpreting the predicament of Karṇa caught between two warring parents or the agony of a son due to the follies of parents![6]

---

4 Baladeva — Do you mean to say that Bhīmasena should survive after having played this trick on you in the combat?
Duryodhana — Do you hold that I have been tricked by Bhīmasena?
Baladeva — Who else has brought you to this plight?
Duryodhana — Listen to me !

By whom were robbed Indra's
divine flowers and his honour,
Who sleeps merrily for thousand
divine years in the sea,
By that Hari, so fond of battle
and dear to the worlds
By him was I given to death,
entering Bhīma's mace. *Ūrubhaṅgam*, Śloka 35.

5 Rāma - (In great sorrow) we have been duped. Where is the golden deer and where this ground? With no such care Rāma of steady wits cared for his wife's words' – I care not for such mocking words of the world. If one's own intellect is not depraved, how can calamities overtake him? *Āścaryacūḍāmaṇī*, Act 3, 42.

6 Soldier – Ah! Here comes out of his house the king of Aṅga clad in martial attire along with Śalya. But it is strange. How can one account for this unwarranted anxiety in the heart of one of the proven valor, always the leader in the festival of war?

Fierce in his prowess and foremost in battle and valor,
This wise one still seems to proceed in anxiety to war.
Karṇa in this state appears like the splendid summer sun.
Of innate brightness, yet enveloped in masses of clouds.

Karṇabhāra, Śloka 4.

These and hundred others were the missing opportunities. I have often wondered that the Kerala actors who preserved for us the great plays of Bhāsa failed to imbibe the fire hidden in Bhāsa. He was a different dramatist. Traditional actors celebrated him often ignoring his voice of dissent. But contemporary directors could discover him. Ganapati Sastri found out the 'Cākyārnāṭakacakra', but the directors rediscovered the potential of these plays in interpreting contemporary life. Discovery of Bhāsa plays in the first decades of the century and of the earliest performance tradition of Kūṭiyāṭṭam in the second half attracted the attention of theatre activists all over the world to the repertory of Sanskrit.[7]

Entry of Bhāsa to the world Theatre and the reintroduction of Kālidāsa to the Kūṭiyāṭṭam format are the two important historic events of our time. Renowned directors adapted Sanskrit plays to interpret the contemporary situations.[8] It was this enthusiasm

---

(All the translations are by Dr. K.P.A. Menon I.A.S from his *Complete Plays of Bhāsa* and *Āścaryacūḍāmaṇī* by Nag Publishers)

7 Given Venu's assertion of the centrality of the Vidūṣaka to Kūṭiyāṭṭam, his landmark 2002 production of Kālidāsa's Śākuntala – a play long excluded from the Kūṭiyāṭṭam repertoire comes as something of a shock. Venu, who was recently honored with the 2006 Kerala Sangeet Natak Akademi Award (the state's most prestigious recognition for excellence in the arts) for his contribution to Kūṭiyāṭṭam's current revival, describes his Śākuntala as a 'present-day Kūṭiyāṭṭam' which, in many ways, it is. Nonetheless, two of his major directorial choices seem to echo an anonymous 15th century text called the Natāṅkuśa, which severally criticizes the Kūṭiyāṭṭam approach to staging Sanskrit plays. Firstly, Venu's Śākuntala shifts the emphasis of the performance from the Vidūṣaka to the hero a choice with obvious and substantial consequences for the Kūṭiyāṭṭam stage. Pushing the Vidūṣaka to the margins of the performance leaves little room for satirizing either the hero or the audience (beyond what the text itself provides) The Natāṅkuśa, which presents itself as a defense of classical dramaturgy, faults the Kūṭiyāṭṭam Vidūṣaka for his use of Malayalam; as Raja explains – the sanction of local language found in the Nāṭyaśāstra is a suggestion to the poet, not to the producer or the actor'. By curtailing the Vidūṣaka's scope for vernacular improvisation, and thus his ability to connect the world of the stage and the world of the audience, Venu appears to be 'classicizing' Kūṭiyāṭṭam in two ways simultaneously: by privileging the play text over the performative practices of the Kūṭiyāṭṭam tradition, and by moving that tradition closer to the letter, though not the spirit, of the Nāṭyaśāstra.
Present-day Kutiyattam, G. Venu's Radical and Reactionary Sanskrit Theatre. By Christian Du Comb in TDR: The drama review 51:3 (T195)2007.

8 Nemi Chandra Jain in his paper presented on the occasion of the celebration of the 75th year of the discovery of Bhāsa plays gives elaborate details of the contemporary productions of Bhāsa plays. The list given below is taken from that paper. It may be noted that dramas of Kālidāsa, Bodhāyana, Mahendravikrama, Śūdraka and others also were performed during this period. Many Sanskrit dramas were produced in foreign countries also. All these go to prove that Sanskrit theatre became more dynamic during the last century than, perhaps in its heydays.
Svapnavāsavadatta (Hindi) – Song and Drama Division, govt. of India, New Delhi, Directed by B.V. Gupta, 1956.

Svapnavāsavadatta (English) – The Institute of advanced studies in Theatre Arts, New York, directed by Mrinalini Sarabhai. Madhyamavyāyoga (Hindi) – National School of Drama, New Delhi, directed by Shanta Gandhi. 1964.

Madhyamavyāyoga (Sanskrit) – Harinam Pradayini Sabha, Varanasi; Dūtaghaṭotkaca (Sanskrit) – Harinam Pradayini Sabha, Varanasi, 1968.

Svapnavāsavadatta (English) – Asian studies Centre, University of Hawai, Honolulu (USA), directed by Shanta Gandhi.

Madhyamavyāyoga (Sanskrit) – Natya Parishad, Sanskrit Department Sagar University, Sagar (M.P) Directed by Radha Vallabh Tripathi, 1974.

Dūtavākya (Hindi) – little Theatre Group, New Delhi, directed by Balraj Pandit. 1976.

Ūrubhaṅga (Hindi)- Rangashivir, Bhopal, directed by M.K. Raina, 1976.

Avimāraka (Hindi) – Rangaprabhat, Ujjain, directed by M.K. Raina,1977.

Svapnavāsavadatta (Hindi, under the title Rāja Ka Sapna) Agredoot, New Delhi, directed by Nadira Zaheer Babbar, 1978.

Pratimā (Sanskrit) – M.P. Natak Lok Kala Academy, Ujjain, directed by Prabhat Kumar Bhattacharya, 1978.

Madhyamavyāyoga (Sanskrit) – Thiruvarang, Trivandram, directed by Kavalam Narayana Panikkar, 1978.

Pañcarātra, Dūtavākya, Ūrubhaṅga (Chaatisparhi, all three under the title Duryodhana) – Naya Theatre, New Delhi, directed by Habib Tanvir, 1979.

Bālacarita (Hindi) – M.P. Natak Lok Kala Academy, Ujjain directed by Ravi Sharma, 1979.

Ūrubhaṅga (Sanskrit and Hindi) – Kalidas Academy, Ujjain, directed by Shanta Gandhi, 1979.

Dūtavākya (Sanskrit) – Kalidas Academy, Ujjain, directed by Kavalam Narayana Panikkar, 1980.

Karṇabhāra (Sanskrit) – alodyan, Bombay, directed by Shanta Gandhi, 1980.

Svapnavāsavadatta (Hindi) – M.P. Natak Lok Kala Academy, Ujjain, directed by M.K. Raina, 1980.

Madhyamavyāyoga (Hindi) – M.P. Natak Lok Kala Academy, Ujjain, directed by M.K. Raina, 1980.

Karṇabhāra (Hindi) – M.P.Natak Lok Kala Academy, Ujjain, directed by M.P. Raina, 1980.

Dūtaghaṭotkaca (Hindi) – M.P. Natak Lok Kala Academy, Ujjain, directed by M.K. Raina, 1980.

Dūtavākya (Sanskrit) – M.P. Natak Lok Kala Academy, Ujjain, directed by Shrinivas Rath, 1980.

Ūrubhaṅga (Hindi) – M.P. Natak Lok Kala Academy, Ujjain, directed by Raj Kumud, 1980.

Karṇabhāra (Sanskrit) – Kalidas Academy, Ujjain directed by Dhirendra Kumar, 1981.

Ūrubhaṅga (Manipuri) – Choorus Repertory Theatre, Imphal, directed by Rattan Kumar Thuyam, 1981.

Svapnavāsavadatta (Malavi, titled Sapna Mein Pani) – Kalidas Academi, Ujjain, directed by Shrinivas Reth/Sanjeev Dexit, 1981.

Ūrubhaṅga (Hindi) – National School of Drama, New Delhi directed by Kavalam Narayana Panikkar, 1983.

Karṇabhāra (Sanskrit) – Sopanam, Trivandrum, directed by Kavalam Narayana Panikkar, 1984.

Dūtavākya (Sanskrit) – Abhinaya Bharati, Varanasi, directed by Rajendra Upadyaya, 1985.

Svapnavāsavadatta (Hindi titled Raja Ka Sapna) Theatre Circle, New Delhi, directed by Ramesh Nanchanda, 1985.

Pratimā (Sanskrit, together with Uttar Rama Charit, titled Pratimottara)- M.P. Natak Lok Kala Academy, Ujjain directed by Prabhat Kumar Bhattacharya, 1985.

that Kulaśekhara anticipated ten centuries ago. The anonymous author of *Naṭāṅkuśa*, after five centuries, advocated the same thing – the classicizing of Kūṭiyāṭṭam.

25. iii. Classicization of Theatre

How can Kūṭiyāṭṭam be classicized?

1. The claim of Kūṭiyāṭṭam for classicism rests in its inherent strength for solo-performance with its myriad forms of multiple impersonations and

---

Karṇabhāra (Hindi) M.P. Natak Lok Kala Academy Ujjain directed by Prabhat Kumar Bhattacharya, 1986.

Karṇabhāra (Sanskrit) Abhinaya Bharathi, Varanasi, directed by Rajendra Upadhyaya, 1986.

Ūrubhaṅga (Sanskrit) University of Wisconsin, Madison, USA, irected by Kavalam Narayana Panikkar, Philip B. Zarilli, 1986.

Madhyama (Sanskrit ne Production) Sopanam, Trivandrum directed by Kavalam Narayana Panikkar, 1987.

Avimāraka, Hindi – M.K. Raina, 1977.

Bālacarita, Hindi – Ravi Sharma, 1979.

Dūtaghaṭotkaca, Sanskrit – Harinam, 1968, Hindi – M.K. Raina, 1980.

Dūtavākya, Hindi – Belraj Pandit, 1976, Chhattisgarhi – Habib Tanvir, 1979,

Sanskrit – Kavalam Narayana Panikkar, 1980, Sanskrit – Shrinivas Rath, 1980

Sanskrit – Rajendra Upadhyaya, 1985

Karṇabhāra, Sanskrit – Shanta Gandhi, 1980, Hindi – M.K. Raina, 1980

Sanskrit – Dhirendra Kumar, 1981,

Sanskrit – K.N. Panikkar, 1984,

Sanskrit – Rajendra Upadhyaya,1986, Hindi – Prabhat Kumar Bhattacharya, 1986.

Kavalam Narayana Panikkar, Madhyamavyāyoga (Sanskrit), 1978.

Dūtavākya (Sanskrit), 1978, Ūrubhaṅga (Hindi) ,1983, Karṇabhāra (Sanskrit), 1984

Ūrubhaṅga (Sanskrit), 1985, Madhyamavyāyoga (Sanskrit), 1987

Raina. M.K, *Ūrubhaṅga* (Hindi), 1976, Avimāraka (Hindi), 1977, Svapnavāsavadatta (Hindi), 1980, *Madhyamavyāyoga* (Hindi), 1980

Dūtaghaṭotkaca (Hindi), 1980, Karṇabhāra (Hindi), 1980

Raj Kumud, *Ūrubhaṅga* (Hindi), 1980

Rath, Shrinivas, *Dūtavākya* (Sanskrit), 1980, Svapnavāsavadatta (Malavi), 1981

Sarabhai, Mrinalini, Svapnavāsavadatta (English), 1964.

Sharma, Ravi, *Bālacarita* (Hindi), 1979.

Tanvir, Habib, *Pañcarātra, Dūtavākya, Ūrubhaṅga* (Chhattisgarhi-all together titled Duryodhana), 1979.

Thiyam, Ratan Kumar, *Ūrubhaṅga* (Manipuri), 1981.

Tripathi, Radhavallabh, *Madhyamavyāyoga* (Sanskrit), 1974-75.

Upadhyaya, Rajendra, *Dūtavākya* (Sanskrit), 1985, Karṇabhāra (Sanskrit), 1986.

'Meanwhile a momentous development of immense significance for the revival of Sanskrit theatre had taken place in the country. The Kalidasa Festival at Ujjain .... was reorganized in 1974 to seek active corporation of serious theatre people from all part of the country. In many cases prominent directors were invited to produce a Sanskrit play in the original or in any modern Indian language at Ujjain or with their own troupe and bring it to the annual Kālidāsa Festival.'

- Contemporary Productions of Bhāsa Plays by Nemi Chandra Jain in Bhasa Sopanam, Trivandram, 1994.

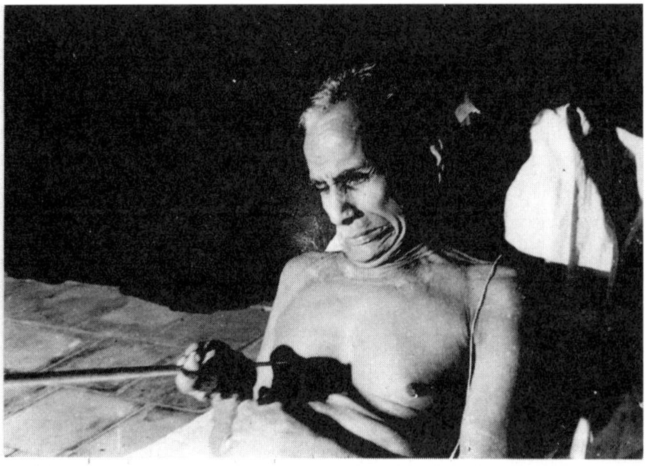

Rasavayu – Ammannoor rehearsing the death of Bali

imaginative acting. It is the essence and distinctive feature of the art form. Hence new actors should concentrate on nirvahaṇa which is the touch-stone of one's histrionic talents.

2. Attention of artists need not be on completion of a play; instead they can elaborate in all its subtleties in a given piece. *Śikhiniśalabham, Himakara* etc. can be chosen for single day and *Aśokavanikāṅkam, Toraṇayuddham* etc. for week-long performances.
3. The wit, humour and criticism of vidūṣaka has to be continued, but role has to be restricted to suit the dramatic situations.
4. The sūta narratives were added to theatre in a particular historical context. That significance exists no more. Hence the sūta narratives have to be de linked from theatre and performed as an independent form of Puruṣārthakkūttu.
5. Talented actors can take up the challenge of retrieving Kulaśekhara mode of presentation of suggested sense through movement of eyes at least in selected scenes.
6. Actors can take as models the contemporary reconstructions of *Bhagavadajjuka, Āścaryacūḍāmaṇī* and *Abhijñānaśākuntala* for new choreographies.
7. Kūṭiyāṭṭam now breaths in the open space. *Classifying* should not be mistaken for return to the past. Every action in this field should be aimed at minimizing the distance of theatre from the civil society. This has to be achieved without compromising to the principles of aesthetics.

XXVI
Sanskrit Plays on Contemporary Stage

Bhāsa's plays rejuvenated the Sanskrit theatre. They also brought back the relevance of Vyaṅgyavyākhyā on contemporary stage.

VV liberated the actor from the text. Bhāsa plays proclaimed the sovereignty of the director. New directors interpreted the plays in new ways. Sources of dhvani in *VV,* in most cases were the words and their different meanings. The royal dramatist had a comprehensive vision when he dealt with the Rasas in Mahābhārata under different situations. Yet it is difficult to say whether he envisioned a *Prabandhadhvani* as Ānandavardhana did while he assigned śānta to be the prominent rasa in Mahābhārata.

Contemporary directors on the other hand grasped the vision of Kulaśekhara and began to present Bhāsa's play with contemporary relevance. This was the immediate effect of the discovery of Bhāsa plays. Naturally the process was extended to other authors. Contemporary theatre has realised that the best way to present the predicaments of modern society is to put it through a classical Sanskrit drama.

26. i. Indianness of Indian theatre

The Indianness of Indian theatre is a matter of concern. The discussion on a national theatre was alive even in the colonial days. The debate continued more vehemently after independence. Several attempts were made to define Indian identity in theatre. In 1958 Forty distinguished scholars, educationists, journalists, and theatre-persons who were members of a steering committee for establishing a national drama institute, met for a seminar in Delhi. Adya Rangacharya summed up the discussions in the observation:

i. We ought to study Sanskrit drama.
ii. We ought to make experiments with their performances.
iii. We ought to gather from the Sanskrit drama anything which may help the proper evolution of modern drama.[1]

1 Vasudha Dalmia, 2006, *Poetics; Plays and Performances*, Oxford University press, p. 170.

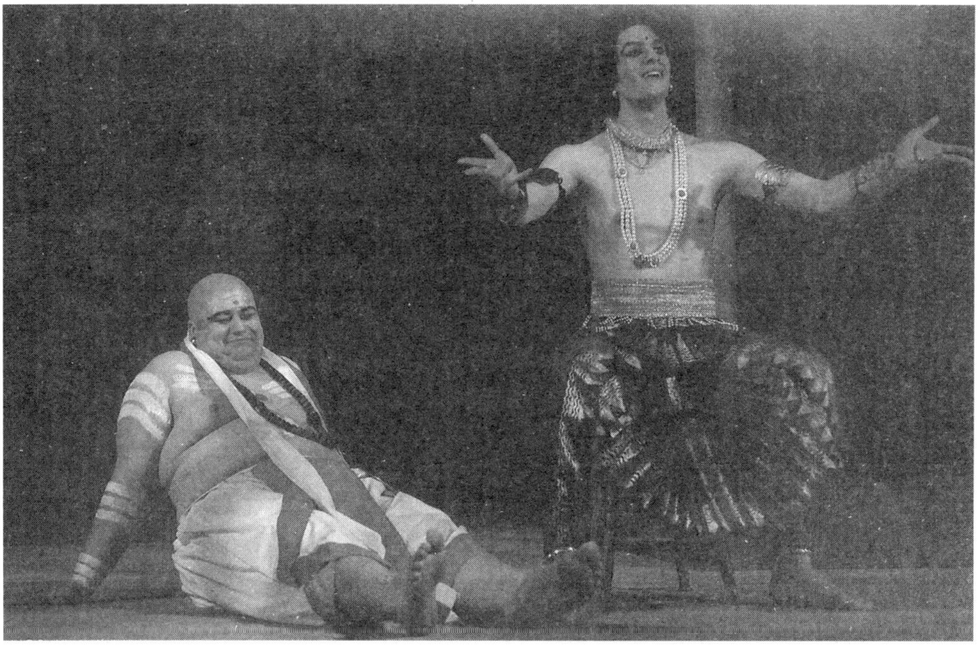

Vidūṣaka and King in Śākuntala, presented in US, directed by Kottakkal Sasidharan (right)

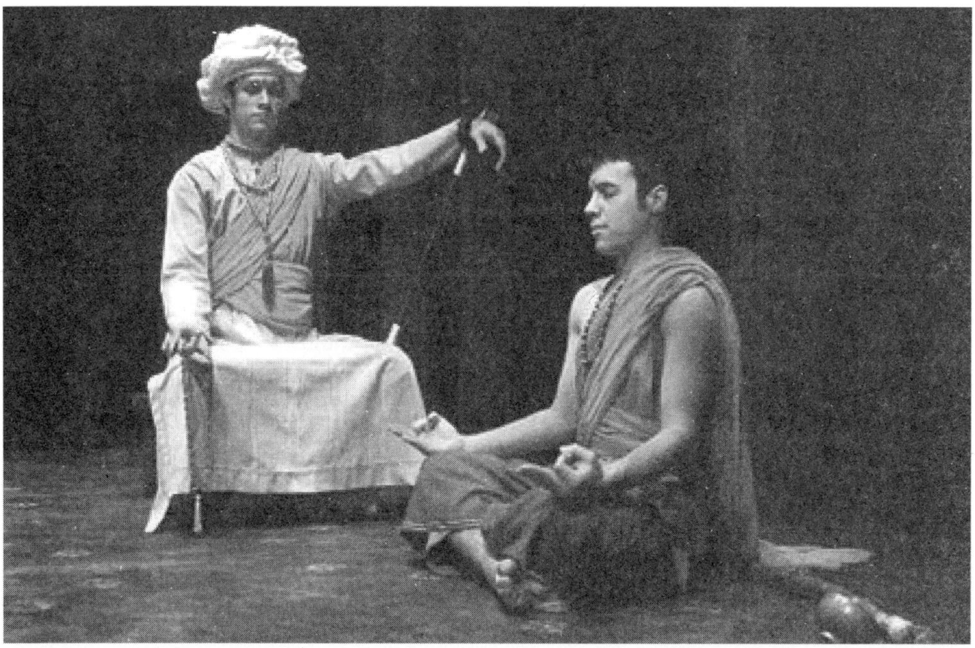

Hermit and disciple, Bhagavadajjuka directed by Kunju Vasudevan in Butler University, US

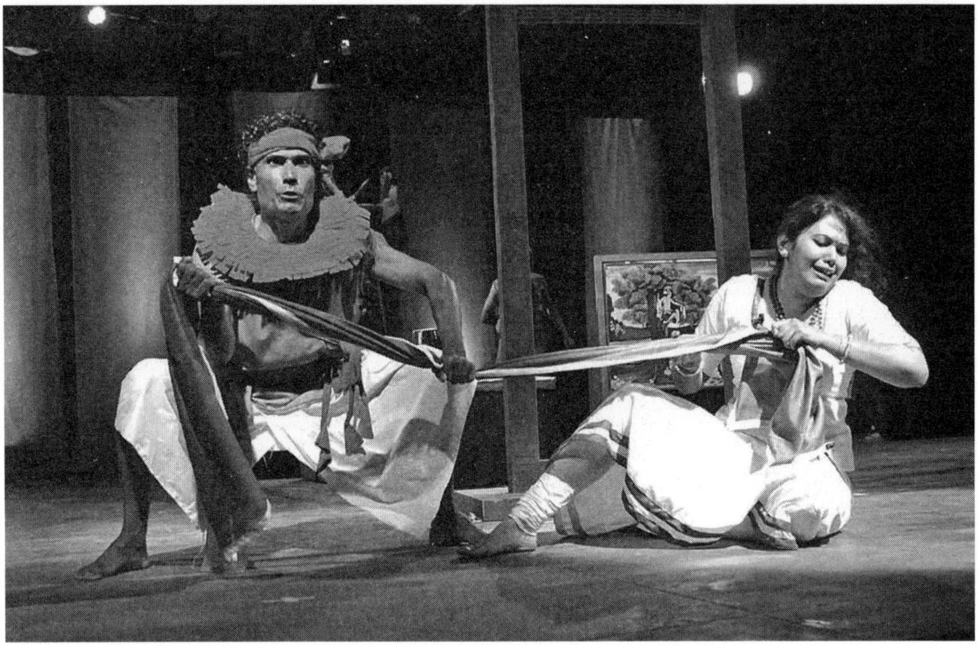

Sukanyā presents the inner conflicts of Draupadī (Malayalam), directed by Chandradasan. Selvaraj as Duḥśāsana

The Theatrical practices in India is not a monolith of classical tradition. There are several cultures and traditions in this plural society. The most dynamic among them is the folk traditions which are more spontaneous and energetic. By the sixties a new view gained dominance in the cultural circles of New Delhi. It argued that the folk forms were off shoots of classical Sanskrit tradition.

> 'When after the tenth century the classical Sanskrit language splintered into vernacular and took root in the form of regional languages. The Sanskrit drama petrified for many centuries was replaced by the growing folk-theatre. Old legends, purāṇic tales, mythological lore, philosophy and stories of Sanskrit plays were popularised by the present folk theatre. In this way the tradition flowed not from the folk to the classical, but from the classical to the folk. The folk theatre inherits many of the classical conventions'.[2]

Any how an awareness slowly grew up among theatre activists that the need of the hour is a synthesis of classical and indigenous traditions in performance. Realisation

2 *Ibid.*, p. 173.

of contemporary theatre as a classical – indigenous continuum inspired the new play writes and directors. This was visible in the productions of Badal Sarkar, Girish Karnad, Vijaya Tendulkar, Kavalam Narayana Panikkar, Habib Tanvir etc. Though they inherited different indigenous cultures there was something unifying in their productions. It was the classical Sanskrit tradition.

In our search for the new idiom in theatre the productions of Kavalam Naṛayana Panikkar deserves special mention. He stands in the forefront among modern directors. Kavalam is a poet, dramatist, director and musician. His mind always resonates the rhythm of rural life. His Sopanam Theatre troupe has hither-to produced 40 dramas in Sanskrit, Malayalam and Hindi. All his Malayalam productions are interpretations of rural myths/beliefs. He has drawn his sources from indigenous and classical traditions. His theatre is an ensemble of dance, stylised movements, acting and vocalisation. Concentrating on Padārthābhinaya he creates eloquently suggestive visual imageries on the stage. We concentrate on his productions for three reasons:

i. He has made the maximum productions of Sanskrit dramas in our time.[3]
ii. All his productions are illustrations of the classical-folk continuum, and
iii. His productions make use of the *VV* concept of multiple interpretations.

26. ii. Karṇabhāra

Karṇabhāra which he produced in 1984 is one of his many popular dramas. Bhāsa portrays in *Karṇabhāra* the downfall of the mighty epic hero Karṇa, projecting the inner conflict that develops in him when he enters Kurukṣetra to wage a crucial battle with the Pāṇḍavas. Karṇa looks back at his past at this late hour of trail and experience intense agony and remorse that shakes him to the very foundation of his

---

3 Panikkar's search for the roots and expressive possibilities of Indian theatrical traditions has taken him to the earliest sources; the Sanskrit dramas themselves. Kavalam Panikkar has been a major factor in the revival of pan-Indian interest in and understanding of the rich *theatrical* potential of Sanskrit classics by producing them in Sanskrit, but not as tired spoken dramas making using of outmoded and totally unsympathatic colonial/British Shakespearean-based modes of production. Rather, he has revived the Sanskrit dramas in modern productions by drawing on the extent regional performance traditions he knows so well: in particular Kerala's Kūṭiyāṭṭam, Kathakaḷi, Mohiniyaṭṭam and many lesser known pre-theatrical forms such as Theyyam (ritual performance), Paṭayaṇi (folk dance), and Kaḷarippayaṭṭu (martial art)., Phillip B. Zarrilli, Introduction to *Karimkutty and the Lone Tusker*, Seagull Books, Calcutta, 1992, p. viii.
The important productions of Sanskrit plays by Kavalam are the following:
Bhagavadajjukam (1976), Madhyamavyāyogam (1979), Śākuntalam (1982), Vikramorvaśīyam (1982), Karṇabhāram (1984), Ūrubhaṅgam (1987), Svapnavāsavadatta (1993), Dūtavākyam (1996), Pratimānāṭakam (1999), Cārudattam (2004), Mālavikāgnimitra (2006), Kaliveṣam (2012).

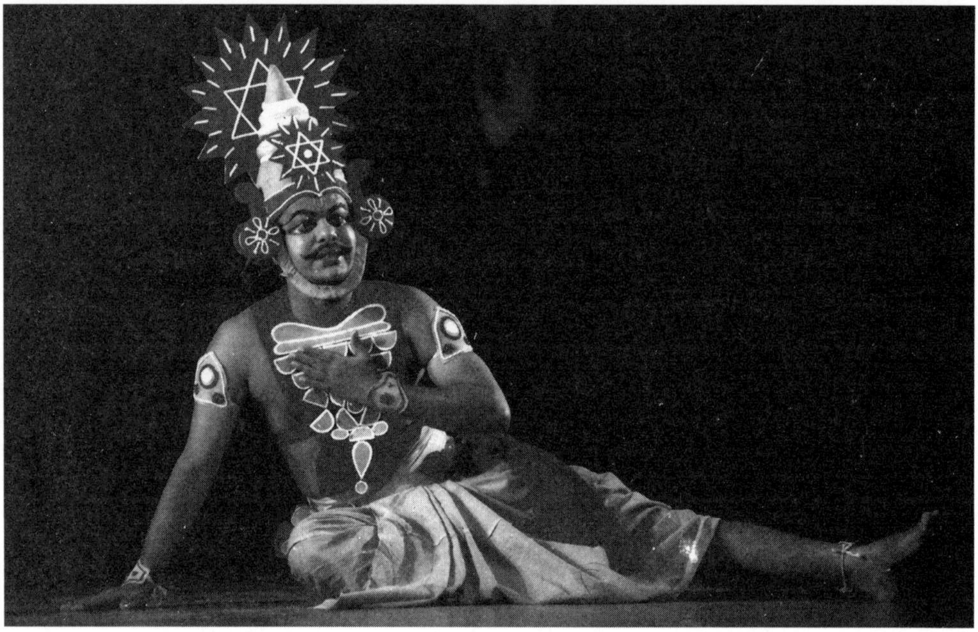

Gireesh as Karṇa, directed by Kavalam Narayana Panikkar

being. Right at the center of the battlefield he fights another battle within himself which assumes different dimensions.

A man endowed with supreme qualities made out of the best elements of nature failing for no fault of his own. Yet this does not make him a tragic character. He fights with conviction to the last knowing fully well that he is destined to loose. Kavalam presents his vision of Karṇa in his directorial note. 'When you probe into the reason you may have to land the primordial sources of a cosmic microcosm which involves an interruption of the very elements which constitute the inner and the outer being of the individual which readily has to respond to inevitable dictates that come from above. Here two major components of ingredients of nature can be located, one owning zealously and the other disowning strongly the poor man who is ultimately the victim of a universal conspiracy of the celestial. Sūrya the father of Karṇa and Indra the father of Arjuna represent the basic sources of the conflict, a phenomenon of universal dimension, reflecting and reacting on a single individual, whose destiny is put to a rigorous test, the consequences of which could not be borne by the fragile mortal frame of the man. The eternal interaction of the element of nature is continuously resulting in the downfall of man – an endless story in which the indomitable will of man struggles for ultimate liberation.'

Bhāsa in his inimitable style encapsulates the life of Karṇa in three incidents scattered in this epic- Kuntī's revelation of mother hood, the futile learning and the loss of divine defense with which he was born. The whole play, in a sense, is a retrospective narration. Karṇa talks to himself. This is Vicārābhinaya in terms of *VV.* Kavalam transforms the inner self of Karṇa to concrete visual images. Even Śalyarāja is one such externalisation. The three incidents, though different in details, have a common thread – the thought process of a disturbed mind. That process is presented on stage though a series of vocal, gestural and corporal visual signs.

Another point relevant to this study is the director's interpretation of the life of the hero. One cannot believe that Vyāsa did justice to Karṇa. In his eagerness to justify others, he humiliated him on several occasion which Karṇa did not deserve. Kavalam penetrates into the mind of his hero and finds out that he was a victim of a universal conspiracy of the celestial. When the Brahmin begs the kavaca the director presents Indra behind and makes it clear to the audience that he is the father of Arjuna in disguise anxious to save his son. The love and care of the disciple to his guru is evident in the Paraśurāma incident. Karṇa is an ideal disciple; ironically Paraśurāma is not the model of a preceptor. Kuntī vails, but there is an element of selfishness in her new fondness towards the eldest son. The common factor in all the three incidents is cheating. Mother cheats her son, guru his disciple and the God the foe of his son. Paraśurāma can raise a feeble justification that he was cheated. There too the blame does not fall on the student. The insect was a case of external intervention. However, Karṇa was at the receiving end in all these cases. None helped him nor understood his nobility. This interpretation instills new life to Karṇa. One leaves the hall believing that honor lies not in victory; defeat to is great, perhaps more rewarding.

26. iii. Ūrubhaṅga

Ūrubhaṅga is, perhaps, the best drama in Sanskrit. All the dramas play with life. This is but an encounter with death. How will it be when one sees death face to face? Duryodhana falls down in the battle field at Samantapañcaka, both his thighs fatally broken. He sees the chariot descending to take his life away. In a quick flash, he goes back in memory to the life he led. Many of his actions are repentable. He remembers the parental love he received, but not returned. He longs for another birth to lead a better life.

Duryodhana is an embodiment of all that is evil in the epic. But is it all? Incidentally, there is a temple dedicated to Duryodhana in Kerala where he is worshipped. Bhāsa

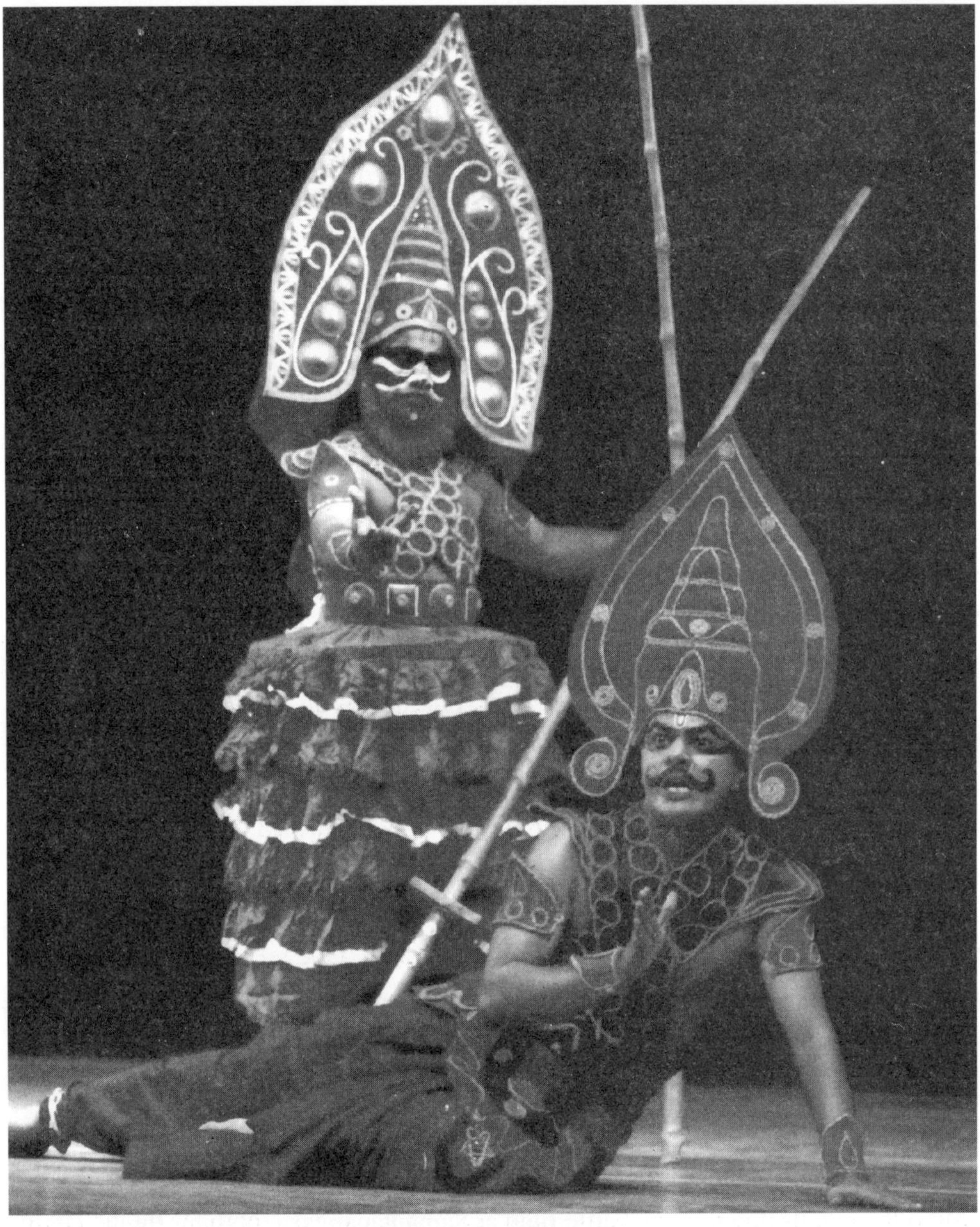

Ūrubhaṅga directed by Kavalam Narayana Panicker

presented him as an ideal king in one of his dramas-the Pañcarātra. His mother calls him only as Suyodhana-one who fights well. The ill-fight, here also, was not from his part. It was from the part of his adversary. So, who actually is the Kuru hero? Kavalam raises this question. He finds out the answer. The Kaurava king as may thank is not one. He is two – Duryodhana and Suyodhana, mutually contradictory. Yet complementary. See the note of the Director.

'In this production, it is attempted to recreate, the fury and tragedy by creating two Duryodhanas. One, the warmonger and the other his Theyyam, which we may call Suyodhana, suggesting the good qualities in him which spring out from at the ultimate moment his thighs are fatally broken by Bhīmasena. Of the two-fold aspect of the hero, the mundane one is the mortal existence of the Duryodhana struggling under the pangs of death. The other is his spirit, which unveils a supernatural dimension and is projected as his theyyam. Theyyam literally means daivam or godhead. It can be his death itself. It is the spirit half-released from the wounded Duryodhana, on its way towards *mokṣa* or salvation; his own conscience advocating all his virtues.'

But how to present a split person on stage? There he made use of the folk tradition of Malabar. Theyyam (Daivam-Deva) literary means God. The soul of dead ancestor become Theyyams. They new incarnation. Theyyam is folk legends represents the good spirit, divine nature in the mortals. The broken body is Duryodhana, his goodness raises from it as in the form of Theyyam. There are no better instances to show the use of indigenous myths and traditions to explain a classical drama.

This production is also unique with use of the technique of Pakarnnāṭṭam. This is normally used when one character transform to another character. There it is used not for a person, but for an idea-the innate goodness in the character and it is given a physical, though supernatural form. The split character is externalized in two concrete forms, transformation here touches a trans-dramatic level.

26. iv. Mālavikāgnimitra

Mālavikāgnimitra is the first among the three drams of Kālidāsa. We can see the sparks of genius even in the maiden play. He speaks of his concept of theatre as a visual sacrifice in this drama. In the first Act of it we get abundant reference to the *NŚ* tradition. The quarrel of the two nāṭyācāryas gives the poet an opportunity to express his notion on theatre. The description of the dance of Mālavikā presents the them prevailing practices of *NŚ* before our eyes. The play is more attractive as it deals with a highly romantic theme of love between the king and a prince in the harem whom the queen keeps away from his sight.

Mālavikāgnimitra is not the best play of Kālidāsa; but this is the best production of a lesser play. The plot has been reduced from five acts to two. Action centres round a single metaphor – Aśoka. How the *Tapanīyāśoka* becomes *Kusumitāśoka*? See the note of the director.

TRANSFORMING A METAPHOR TO THEATRE

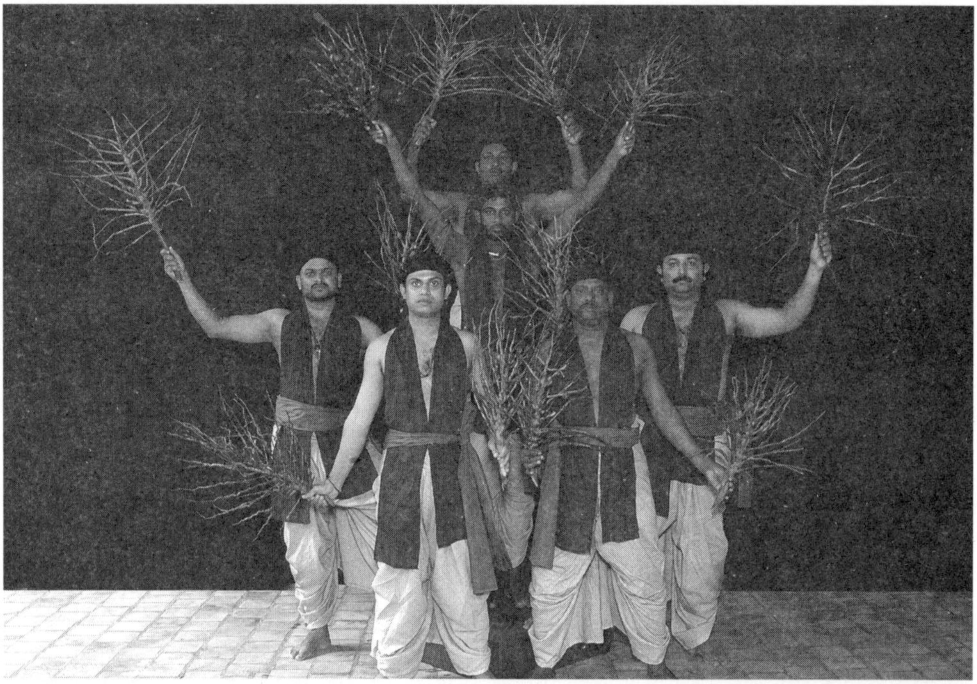

▲ *tapanīyāśoka* ▼ *kusumitāśoka*

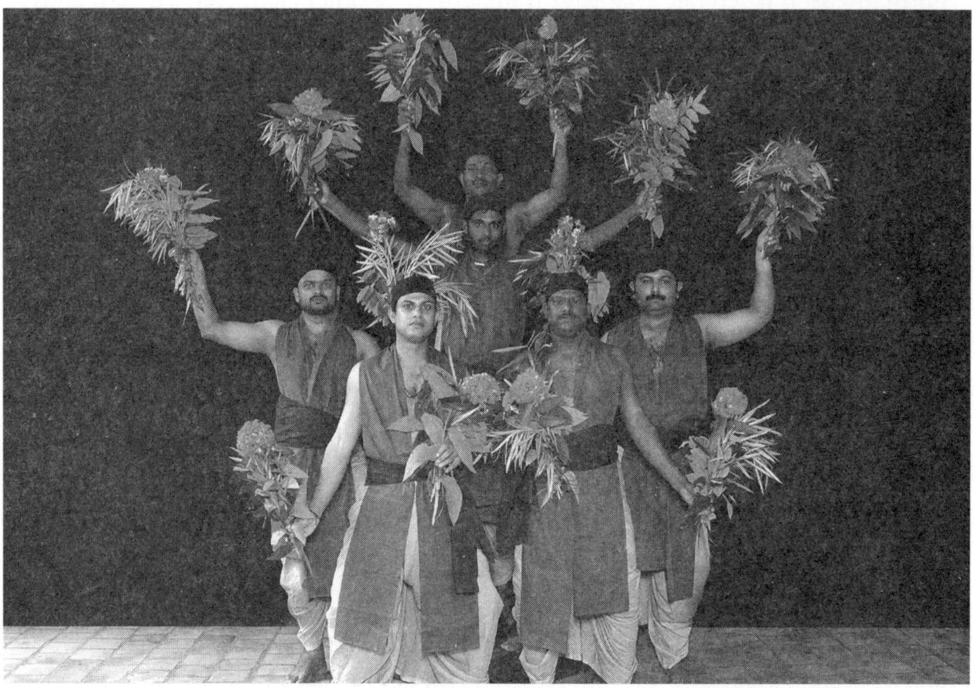

Directed by Kavalam Narayana Panikkar, Sopanam, Thiruvananthapuram

'*Mālavikāgnimitra* is widely acknowledged and accepted as a romantic play having Śṛṅgāra as its main rasa. However, this production is reinterpreted as combination of śṛṅgāra, karuṇa, vīra and hāsya rasas, which are woven around the *Aśokavṛkṣa*. Aśoka is not only a reference tree to establish the chastity of Mālavikā, but also a symbol of the aspirations of the country. Aśoka becomes śoka when it does not blossom within the natural cycle and hence becomes the main cause of the sorrow – *śoka* for the whole society. All incidents and characters of the play are supportive of *aśoka*.

That is why the *Aśoka* plays a significant role in this production and is depicted as a living character, instead of being just a tree.

King Agnimitra, friend of fire, is a source of strength and energy to lead the country men. Mālavikā is the daughter of the soil, Malav Pradesh, who is instrumental to give shape to human expectations and feelings. The myth of *Aśoka* tree is established by Mālavikā, supported by Agnimitra and Kauśiki.'

Vidūṣaka has a great significance in this production. He is not merely a friend of the king to create some lighter moments for the audiences, but more than that he is *Prajñācakṣuḥ* who could foresee the events and help his friend Agnimitra to find out the right solutions of the problems faced by his subjects. He speaks the local language. This is an accordance with the tradition of Kūṭiyāṭṭam.

Another interpretation is with regard to the character of Agnimitra. In the text he is Dhīralalita; here he is a Dhīrodātta who controls all the situations and keeps a balance between all the force of society. This change in brought out through the intervention of vidūṣaka who is a powerful character in the play. Following the practice of Kūṭiyāṭṭam, the speaks in the local language and excites the audience through his wit and humour. The production proves that Kālidāsa's plays have enormous contemporary value in our society.

These productions illustrate the never ending possibilities of interpretative sub texts postulated in *VV.* Karṇabhāram gives a new interpretation to the life of the hero, Ūrubhaṅga the dreadful death and Mālavikāgnimitra, a beautiful metaphor. These and similar other interpretations endear the classics to the present-world.

26. v. Dalit Reading of Bhāsa

Re-reading classics is social contexts is an important intellectual exercise for those endowed with a new consciousness. Indian society decided the identity of an individual not on merits but on birth. The rigidity of a class-ridden society deprived for crores of people what the really deserved. This was not a problem in the past.

Conflict arose when the constitution of India declared n 1950 that all equal. The conflict. The trauma that followed cannot be described in words.

We have an example here, how a contemporary director took theatre to the situation. The Lokadharmī Theatre have made several production during the past three decades. Its dynamic director Prof. Chandradasan took up the ancient text of Karṇabhāra to fight the cause of these who are marginalized in society due to their low birth listen his words.

'When I was about to do this play in the early nineties, the most important and hottest Indian debate was about the caste system that prevailed here. The Dalit consciousness was on the uphill route at that time. People were fighting vehemently on the road both supporting and protesting against the implementation of Mandal Commission Report. I saw youths burning themselves in protest and also vigorously fighting for it. India became more communal and the forces of caste/religion tried their best to be in the Indian mainstream.

I read this play in this very disturbed political and social context. And I could not resist this deep-rooted social cataclysm which was happening around me to be kept out this production. Thus this happened to be one production that has direct relation and relevance to the current and contemporary situation. As many people later said and wrote this was a Dalit reading of the classic text by Bhāsa.

For me the whole play is the answer to the question of the soldier who doubts about the reasons, of the anguish of Karṇa when he has to be heroic and throbbing with life. He is the one hero who was eagerly waiting for his chance to be in war but when the time was ripe, he appears to be sad and depressed. Why? The play analyses the various answers.

And I felt that the key answer lies in one of his first monologues – Who am I? Am I the son of Sūta or Rādhā? Or that of Sūrya and Kuntī?

The difference is big and basically it delves into the social status of the character. And he had faced instances of humiliation in the original story of Mahābhārata itself for not being in the high clan of the *Kṣatriya*. So he questions his own position in the battlefield being a non-*Kṣatriya*.

Thus thematically the play became a re-reading of the ancient text in the light of the social history and the contemporary realities. The play and the acting pattern are designed to suit to this interpretation.'

The methods used in the play to bring out the effect is also novel. Karṇa is in a state of contemplation and self-understanding. He is aware that he is the victim of a social structure and all those who pretend to be praising and adulating are really

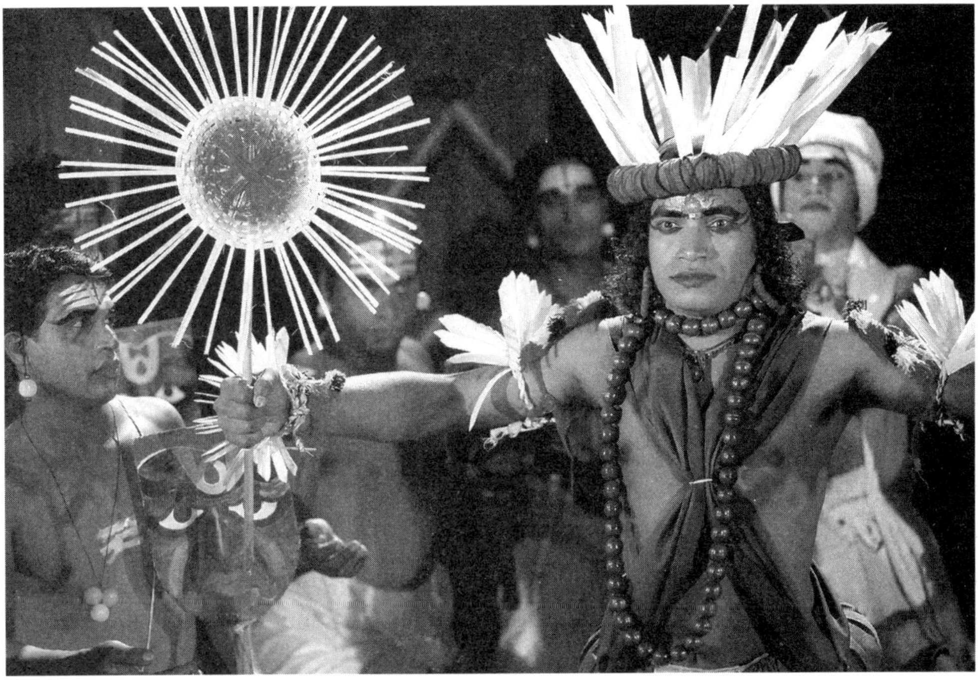

Karṇa directed by Chandradas, Lokadharmi, Tripunithura

planning for his finale downfall. But he cannot question and directly confront his fate nor foes, since he is a victim of a set of moral value systems, a sort of education on a value system – about absolute truth, dharma, offering to Brahmins, heroic death in war, *mokṣa* and rebirths etc – on which the caste and class structure is built upon. He is actually a prisoner of this set of value system which he reflects again and again.

The design of the play and the acting pattern also has been conceived as confronting dialectical components in conflict to each other. A group of Brahmins are always positioned on stage watching, plotting, rejoicing and calculating their strategies and mode of actions. All the other characters emerge from this group, do their role to defeat Karṇa and goes back to watch the anguish and agonies of protagonist.

Theatrically this production joins for the search for developing a visual language based on Indian performance tradition. In acting, physicalisation, movement and choreography, scenic setting, costuming, music etc., the link to the Indian theatre tradition is visible. Many forms – classical and folk – are used as the support material and springboard to develop this production.

The movement pattern and costuming of these characters resemble the classical forms like *Kathakaḷi* and *Kūṭiyāṭṭam*, while that of Karṇa is more primitive and tribal. The music and lighting pattern also are in synchronization with this dialect. This dialectical contrast is extended to the way lights is hued and the music is constructed.

About the modern techniques used Prof. Chandradasan says: 'Externally it looks a much stylised production but internally I have used Stanislavski, and his method-acting techniques to evolve the character of Karṇa. The actor externally does stylised language rendering, singing and movements, but the actor is contemplating to his own personal self and personal experience to bring in the warmth and passion to this epic character. The emotional memory is called upon in rehearsals and also while performing. Thus this play became an experiment to use Stanislavskian approach to a very stylized production. The very stylized and rhythmic movements and the text going into bordering poetry and verses was not a problem to the actor to use emotion memory quite successfully. This makes this production highly emotional and charged with energy unlike the many stylised productions that lack an emotional content and rely for aesthetics and craft. It is the emotional memory and personal experience that also help the actor to reach the state of possession and trance at the moment when he tears off the *kavaca* and *kuṇḍala* to be given to Indra disguised as a Brahmin. The tool of realism transformed into the vehicle of transformation typical to Indian rituals and rites is a successful idiom, I used in this play.'

I have tried to imbibe and relate the five elements – fire, water, air, space and earth – in this play, to lift it from the levels of mundane and the ordinary consciousness into deeper levels of human existence.

Karṇa is the son of Sun God and the vital energy in him is the continuation of a burning flame in him. Thus the image of a burning sun is the key motif in the play. Karṇa holds the effigy that is a representation of sun, to which he relates on different moments in the play. Towards the end he burns it as part of sacrifice and drops it to the *guruti/ niṇam* . And then proceeds into a sort of trance so that he can tear the *kavaca* and *kuṇḍala* that is fixed to his body as a shield and the celestial remaining given to him by his father, the Sun God. His emotional ups and downs are likened as to a burning flame. Whenever he rises to the crescendo the Brahmins who were watching and controlling him with invisible cords intervene and he is made to succumb to his ground reality. His flame like existence is visualized and constructed physically by the acting pattern of the character. His dialogue delivery is modulated such that certain lines he sneaks create opposite meaning than the dictionary meaning of the same word. Thus the meaning is inverted without changing the lines or the words. The words become the emotional responses of the character to the state of his mind. In this context the sonority of the language written by Bhāsa is reinstated with a contemporary sensibility to the current society and theatre and is in tune with re-reading of the epics from the margins as the pivotal centre.

The warm welcome Karṇabhāra received from show that public today earnestly expect theatre to take up more social responsibilities.

26. vi. The Aesthetics of Dhvani

Ānandavardhana propheticaly declares, at the end of *Dhvanyāloka* the aesthetics of dhvani in literature:

> दृष्टपूर्वा अपि ह्यर्थाः काव्ये रसपरिग्रहात्।
> सर्वे नवा इवाभान्ति मधुमास इव द्रुमाः।। IV-4
>
> Even familiar things look fresh by
> the application of dhvani
> like the trees in the spring season.

This is the aesthetics of *dhvani* in theatre too. As we have seen *VV* applied this to the stage. But as Śivarāma succinctly points out the author of *VV* employed the beautiful suggested sense (cārutarorthaḥ) to words and sentences (pade vākye). He did not envisioned a prabandhadhvani – the interpretative significance of a total text. Modern theatre has extended the signification to new horizons.[4]

---

4 Contemporary theatre of Kerala has made many memorable productions of Sanskrit plays during the past two decades. Important among them are enlisted below:
Bhagavadajjukam, Mattavilāsam and Karṇabhāram (all the three by Prof. P. Gangadharan); Mattavilāsam and Karṇabhāram (Chandradasan); Pañcarātram, Madhyamavyāyogam, Mayasitankam (Ramesh Varma); Mudrārākṣasam (Jose Chiramel) and Veṇīsamhāram (Narippatta Raju). School of Drama, University of Calicut has produced the following plays: Pañcarātram (B.V. Karanth), Dūtaghaṭotkacam (Vayala Vasudevan Pillai), Madhyamavyāyogam (Narippatta Raju), Abhijñānaśākuntalam (Narippatta Narayanan Namboodiri), Abhiṣeka-nāṭakam (Ramesh Varma), Karṇabhāram (Shibu S. Kottaram), Ūrubhaṅgam (Martin C.) and Svapnavāsavadatta (Venkitaramana Ithala).

XXVII
Reinventing Bharata

Indian theatre has rightly be compared to a banyan tree:

'Indian theatre tradition seems to resemble the banyan tree; its branches stretch in all directions, casting vast shadows, its roots go very deep, and from time to time new roots are sent down from the far flung branches, seeking a fresh mandate, as it were, from the earth, the source of life. At times the new roots take over all the functions of the old roots, and thus from generation to generation the theatre tradition has grown. The roots, of course, are not everything. The leaves, the flowers, the fruits are all important. The roots without the stem will wilt and whither away, even as the stem and the branches cannot and will not last without the roots. Grafting on to the old roots or stems is sometimes resorted to; but the exotic leaves or flower will drop after a brief while.'

(Dr. K. Ayyappa Panikkar in his introduction to *The Right to Rule and Domain of the Sun*, Seagull, Calcutta)

The roots as we have seen, is the indigenous folk tradition with Sanskrit in its epicenter. Kūṭiyāṭṭam well illustrates the synthesis of the regional with the classical. Vidūṣaka draws his wit and criticism from the surroundings. The *niṇam*, hanging, floating etc., are from local practices. Kūṭiyāṭṭam thus symbolises the inter-cultural and intra-cultural discourses in theatre.

We can say, without exaggeration, that the period we living is the golden era of Sanskrit theatre. Bhāsa, Kālidāsa, Viśākhadatta, Śūdraka, Kulaśekhara and Śaktibhadra re-live in our memories. Vāsavadattā, Udayana, Śakuntalā and Subhadrā are household names. Sanskrit dramas or its adaptations are played in different parts of the country and abroad. The Samskṛtaraṅga at Chennai Sopānam in Kerala, Kālidāsasamāroh in Ujjain, the annual Sanskrit theatre festivals conducted by the Rashtriya Sanskrit Sansthan, etc., provide ample opportunities for the production and performance of Sanskrit plays. There is an added demand for Sanskrit dramas abroad. Performance studies in foreign Universities, recently take more interest in the classical tradition of India. Śākuntala, Mṛcchakaṭika etc., are performed in these centres. Sanskrit theatre, never before, had been fortunate to receive such global attention.

Kerala inherits a rich tradition of Sanskrit tradition from the time of the Ceras. She has produced at least two dramatists who can share the first row – Kulaśekhara and Śaktibhadra. Dhvani born in Kashmir immediately reverberated in the minds of the connoisseurs of the South. The land of Kerala preserved the acting methods of Bharata in Kūṭiyāṭṭam and the plays of Bhāsa in practice. Kerala theatre tadition is also intertwined with Sanskrit. Classical plays are frequently performed on Kerala stage. Renowned directors of contemporary stage have interpreted Sanskrit plays afresh and made powerful productions which were well-received.

There are three distinct modes today for the performance of Sanskrit plays. The most common and popular way is to present the play on a proscenium stage in a realistic manner with the accompaniment of music, percussion, costumes and dance. This is how Sanskrit dramas are presented in festivals and anniversaries of educational institutions. The language will either be Sanskrit or regional adoptions. *Bhagavadajjuka, Mattavilāsa, Śākuntala, Karṇabhāra* etc., are successfully performed in this way and the audience, mostly urban, appreciate them with long applause. This mode of presentation is popular in the West also. A production of this type requires instant rehearsals for four or five months and a group of committed amateurs. Presentation in the stylized mode by well trained actors is another way. Kūṭiyāṭṭam is the best example. Audience mostly hail from the elite sections of the society. This is the traditional way of presentation. Actors can present this only after prolonged training. Hence it will not be possible in an amateurish attempt. The third method of the presentation is on contemporary stage. Modern directors choose classical plays as a tool to interpret the contemporary life. Apart from the props and techniques it is the possibility inherent in the plays for different interpretations that attracts them to classical dramas. Let us, for the sake of convenience, concentrate on the last two modes of presentation.

We started this discussion with the criticism of the anonymous author of *Naṭāṅkuśa*. The two names he refers to with respect are that of Kulaśekhara and Śaktibhadra. And what he criticizes is the deviations made by the actors from the *Nāṭyaśāstra* tradition. A close examination of his views will show that he is against the so called aberrations crept into the body of acting in the period from 13th century. If we listen to his words we have to weed out the extraneous descriptions and improper elaborations. This is the way to restore the purity and strength of the classical theatre. But one cannot accept the views of Naṭāṅkuśa in total. For example, he is not in favor of multiple impersonations as it is against the canons of *Nāṭyaśāstra*. He could have magnanimously accepted it as an improvisation on Bharata which forms the essence of Kūṭiyāṭṭam and without which Kūṭiyāṭṭam will not be what it is. Pakarnnāṭṭam elevates Kūṭiyāṭṭam to transcendental levels of aesthetic enjoyment. The criticism against the use of local language also has limitations. Introduction of Malayalam linked Sanskrit theatre to contemporary life. The survival of Bharata's theatre owes much to the wit, humour and sarcastic comments of the clown.

The aesthetics of Vyaṅgyavyākhyā mode of presentation mainly rest on two pillars – scope for imaginative acting to the practitioners and unending possibilities of interpretations to the directors. The renaissance movement in the field of Kūṭiyāṭṭam in the 20th century put stress mainly on the redaction of acting manuals. Painkulam Ramachakyar condensed *Bhagavadajjuka* limiting the performance to 2 from the 35 nights of the old generation. All that he felt thematically extraneous were weeded out and new portions aesthetically enchanting, were added. The greatest achievement of renaissance was the restoration of Naṅṅyārkūttu and the presentation of *Āścaryacūḍāmaṇī* extending to 105 days in 1991-94. Presentation of Kālidāsa's Śākuntalam in the Kūṭiyāṭṭam format in 2001 was another historic event. The savants who worked behind these productions were led by the aesthetics of Vyaṅgyavyākhyā. What they ignored in the Vyaṅgyavyākhyā tradition was its potential to create sub-texts. The modern directors took up this challenge. They gave wider dimensions to the concept of Dhvani of Kulaśekhara. Kulaśekhara's concept of dhvani always did not rise to the sublime level of *Prabandhadhvani* as that of Ānandavardhana whose discussion of *śāntarasa* in Mahābhārata takes the epic as a whole. Modern directors concentrate on this total effect. Productions of Kavalam Narayana Panikkar and other contemporary directors translate the concept of *dhvani* in theatre into reality. Painkulam Rama Chakyar and Kavalam Narayana Panikkar complement each other in the realization of the theatrical concepts of Kulaśekhara. Their journey searching the roots is to Bharata through Kulaśekhara.

THE END

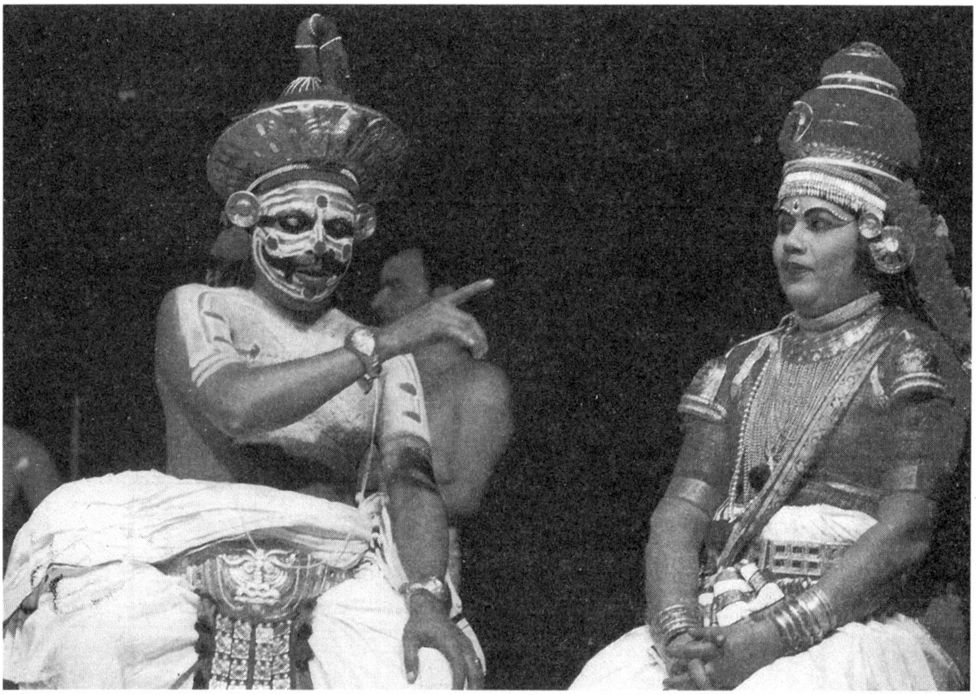

▲ *Kūtiyāṭṭam*

▼ *Kṛṣṇanaṭṭam*

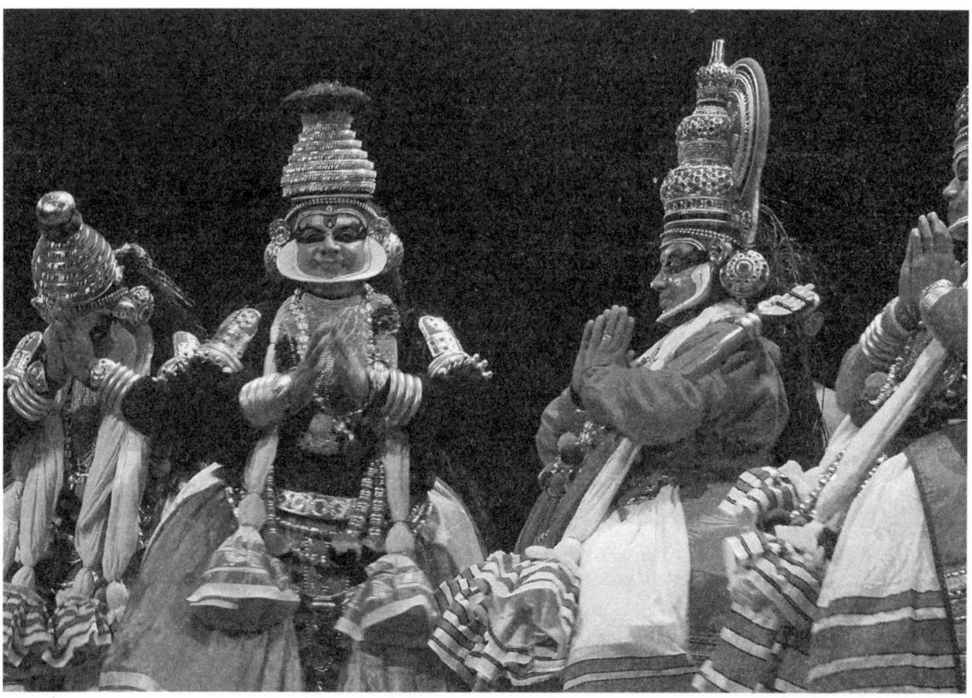

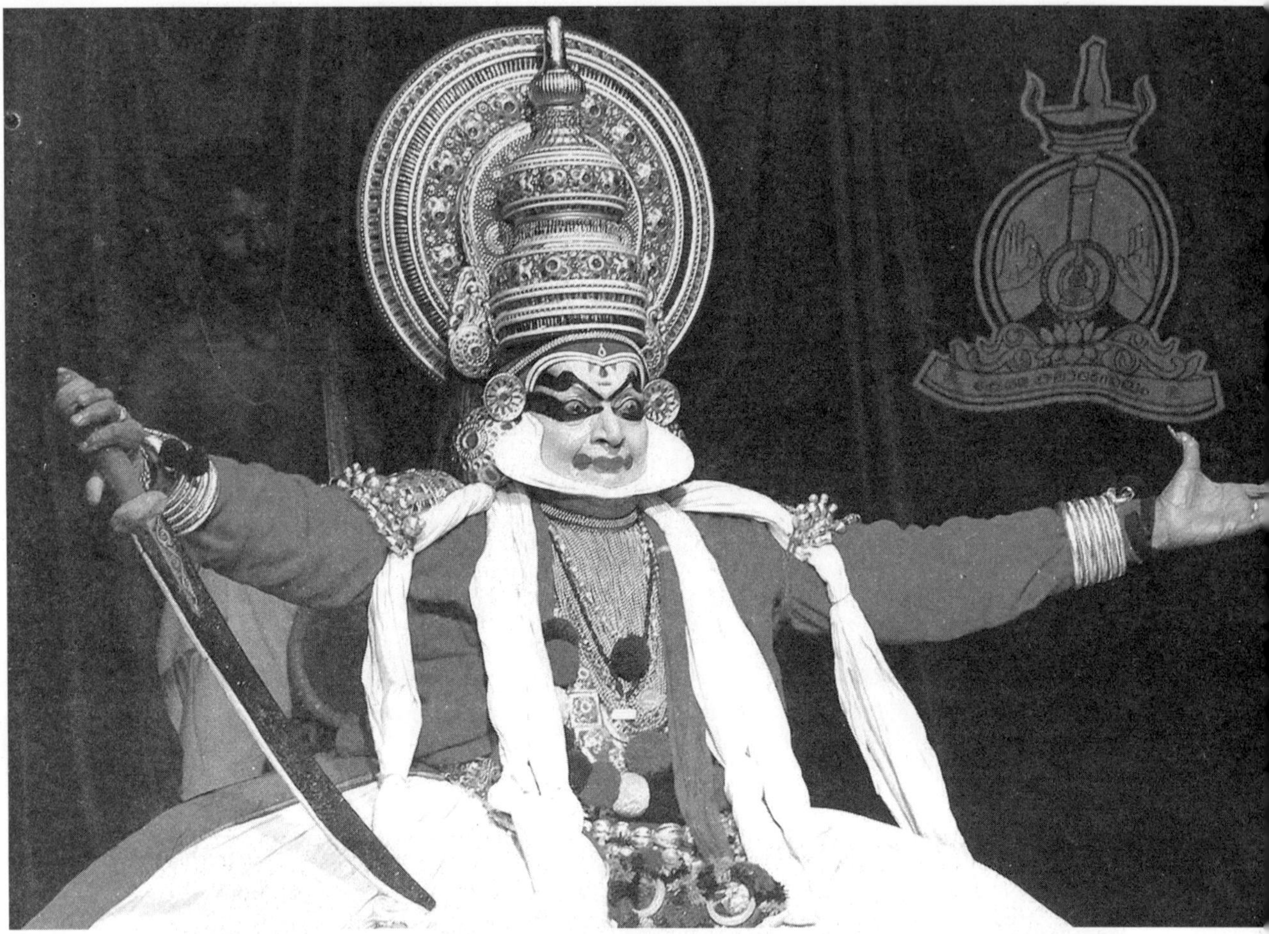

Kathakali, Kalamandalam Gopi

The aesthetics of all the classical art-forms of Kerala, Kūtiyāṭṭam (12th c.), Kṛṣṇanaṭṭam (15th c.), Rāmanāṭṭam - Kathakali (17th c.) and Mohiniyaṭṭam were formulated on the principles of Vyaṅgyavyākhyā.

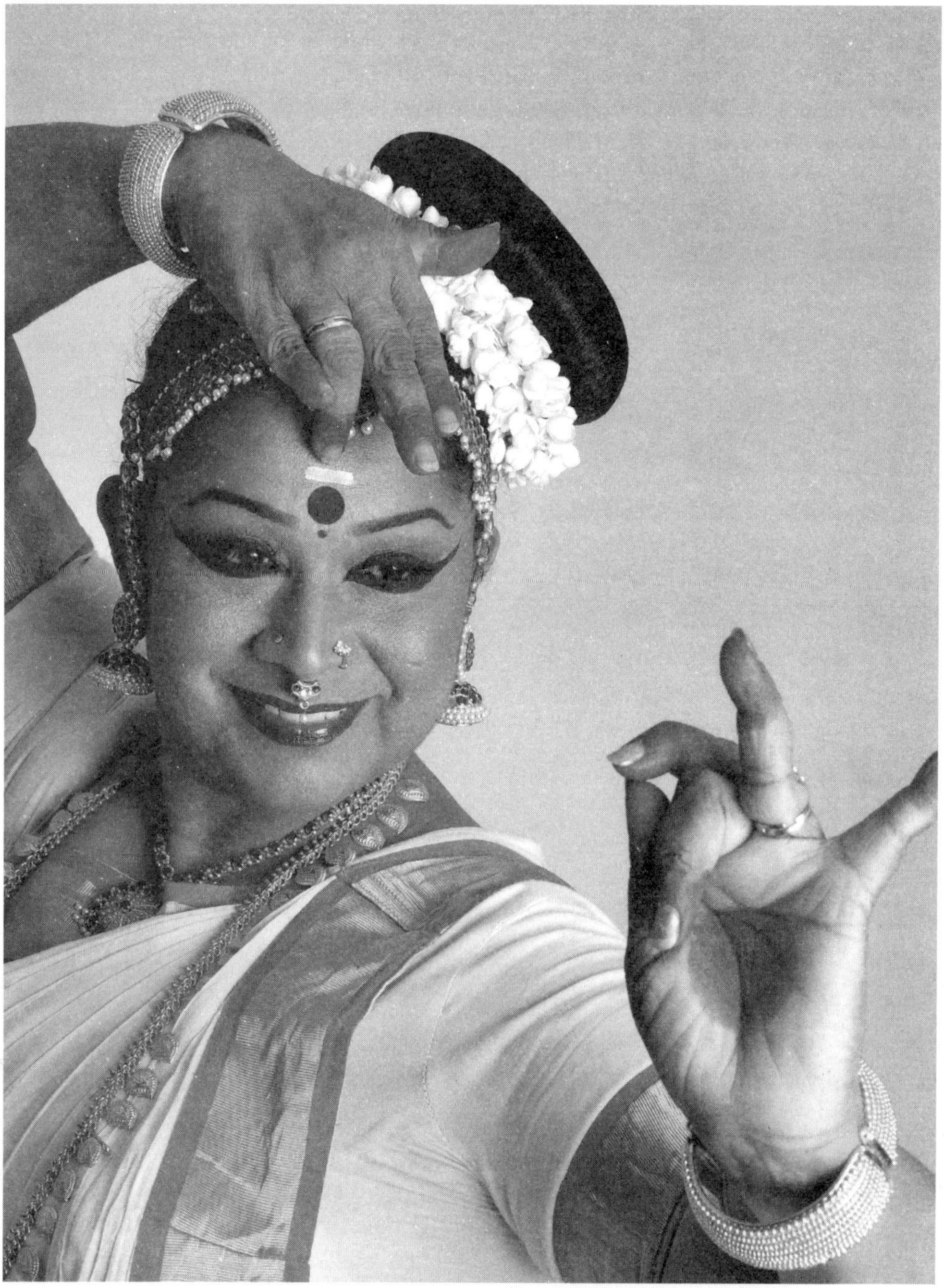

Mohiniyaṭṭam, Kalamandalam Kshemavathi

Kūtiyāṭṭam was introduced in Kerala Kalamandalam in 1965. The traditional nāṭyamantapa was constructed in 1976. Introduction of institutional studies and space for public performance rejuvenated Kūtiyāṭṭam. The ancient art-form thus became part of world-theatre movement and came to be recognized as the intangible heritage of humanity.

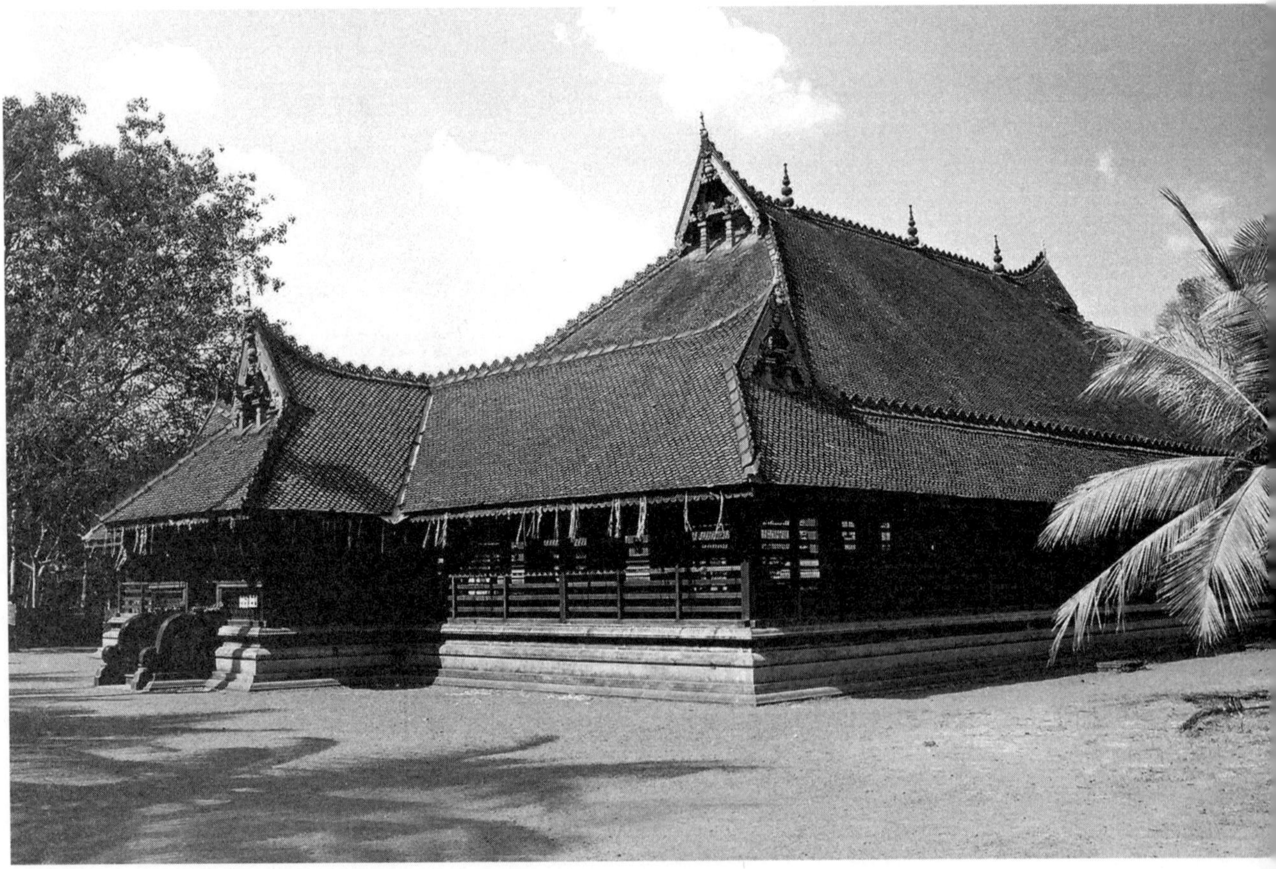

Public space for performance, Kerala Kalamandalam

Bibliography

Aparna Bhargava Dharwadker — 2008, *Theatres of Independence*, Oxford India Paper Backs.

Ayyappa Paniker K — 2003, *Indian Narratology*, Indira Gandhi National Centre for Arts, New Delhi.

1998, Book review, *Natankusa; Acritique on Dramaturgy*, RVSG.

1995, *Nangyarkoothu*, India International Quarterly. NewDelhi.

Barucha, Rustom — 1983, *Rehersals of Revolution: The Political Theatre of Bangal*, University of Hawaii Press, Honolulu.

Baumer RM, R Brandon — 1993, Producing Sanskrit Plays in the Tradition of Kutiyattam.

Bharata Iyer K — 1995, *The Kerala Stage*, Oriental Books Reprint Corporation, New Delhi.

Brown, John Russell — 1999, *New Sites for Shakespeare*, London/NewYork.

Bruce Sullivan M — 1997, *Temple Rites and Temple Servant*, International Journal of Hindu Studies.

Buckner, Heidrun — 2007, *New Light on Bhasa*, Monika Novakowska.

Byrski Maria Christopher — 1974, *Concept of Ancient Indian Theatre*. Munshiram Manoharlal Publishers, New Delhi.

Byrski Maria Christopher — 1995, *Natya and Yajna*, Tripunithura Govt. Sanskrit College Ravivarma Samskrta Granthavali 28.

Colin Counsell and LaurieWolf — 2001, Ed. *Performance Analysis*, Routledge, London.

Daugherty Diane — 1996, *The Nangyar Female Ritual Specialist of Kerala*, 13/1, ATJ.

1989-90, *Nangyar Kuttu from the Temple to the Concert Stage*.

2000, *Women's Role in Kutiyattam Diane*. ATJ 17/1, Distributed by New Bharatiya Book Corporation, New Delhi.

Eeva Anttila — 2003, *A Dream Journey to the Unkown*, Theatre Academy, Helsinki.

Enros, Pragna Thakkar — 1979, *A Reconstruction of the Style of Producing Plays in the Indian Theatre*, University of Toronto.

Eva Szili — 1997, *Hastalakshanadipika*, Paris.

Farley Richmond P — 1994, *Bhasa's Text Stage Directions and Performance*, Discussions on Farley Richmond's paper, Bhasasopanam, Trivandrum

1990, *Kutiyattam*, 87-117, University of Hawai Press, Honolulu.

1995, *Nangyar Kuttu,* 12/1, AT.

Gargi, Balwant — 1962, *Theatre in India*, New York Theatre Arts Books.

Geetha NK — 2012, *Kridaniyakam - Myriad Aspects of Comedy in Sanskrit Drama*, Chinmaya International Foundation, Sodh Samsthan, Veliyanad, Kerala.

Govardhan Panchal — 1972, *The Curtain in Classical Sanskrit Drama.*

Bharata's Stage in Action, 34, SNAJ.

Guru Rao Bapat — 1998, *Semiotic of Yakshagana*, Regional Resource Centre for Folk Performing Arts, MGM College Campus, Udupi.

Heidrun Bruckner — 2008, *The Changing Role of Women in the Nangyarkuttu Tradition of Kerala*, Drama and Theatre in Sudasien, Wiesbaden.

Heike Moser — 2000, *Manthrankam - The Third Act of Pratijnayaugandharayanam in Kutiyattam*, 17/18, BEI.

Iravati — 2003, *Performing Artistes in Ancient India*, DK Print World, New Delhi.

Janaki SS — 1995, *Sanskrit Drama in Theory and Practice*, Rashtriya Sanskrit Samstan, New Delhi.

Kanak Rele — 1992, *Mohini Attam: The Lyrical Dance*, Nalanda Dance Research Centre, Mumbai.

Kapila Vatsyayan — 1968, *Classical Indian Dances in Literature and the Arts*, Sangeetha Nataka Akademi, New Delhi.

Karnad, Girish — 1989, 'In Search of a New Theatre' in *Contemporary Indian Tradition*, Ed. Carla M Bordea, Washington, DC.

Krishna Pisharoti A — 1925, *Bhasa's Works*, Journal, Sree Cithira Tirunal Library and Reading Room.

Krishnan Nambootiripad PC — 1967, *Thesis on Kutiyattam*, Madras University.

Kulasekharavarman — 1987, *Subhadradhananjayam*, T Ganapati Sastri, Trivandrum Sanskrit Series, 13.

1987, *Tapatisamvaranam*, Trivandram Sanskrit Sries.

Kunjunni Raja — 1998, *Kutiyattam Resuscitation Attempts,* Kunjunni Raja, Madras Dr. SS Janaki Felicitation Volume,

1975, *Sanskrit Drama on the Stage*, Journal of the Madras University.

Manimadhavacakyar — 1996, *Natyakalpadrumam*, Kerala Kalamandalam, Cheruturutti.

Narayana Pisaroti KP — 1986, *Pratimanataka-Kramadipika*, Keli-168.

1971, *Attaprakarams and Kramadipika*, Keli 28.

1970, *Kutiyattam*, Subhadradhananjayam Natakam, Thrissur.

1976, *Thapatisamvaranam Kutiyattam*, Thrissur.

1967, *Ascaryacudamani*, Kerala Sangita Nataka Akademi.

Narayana Panikkar, Kavalam — 1997, *Deseeparamparyathil Kutiyattathinte Prasakti*, Keli 53.

1989, *The Right to Rule and the Domain of the Sun*, Seagull Books, Culcutta.

Karimkutty and the Lone Tusker, Seagull Books, Culcutta.

1977, *Thouryatrikam on the Traditional Theatre of Kerala*, Kerala Sangeetha Nataka Akademi, Thrissur.

Narayana Bhattatiri, Melputhur — 1998, *Prabandhamanjari*, Ed; NP Unni, Rastriya Samskrita Samsthanam, Delhi.

Narayanan MV — 2006, *Over Ritualisation of Performance: Western Discourses on Kutiyattam*, TDR 9/2.

2005, *From Exclusivity to Exposure,* CC 11.

Narayanan Nampyar PK — 1980, *Mantrankam*, Kerala Sahitya Akademi, Thrissur.

1984, *Nangnyarkuttu*, Attaprakaram, Kramadipika

2005, *Mizhavu: Nampiarute Kramadipika,* Killikurussimangalam Padmasree Mani Madhava Chakyar Smaraka Gurukulam.

1984, *Sreekrishnacaritam Nangyaramma kuttu*, National Book Stall, Kottayam.

Narayanan MGS — 1996, *Perumals of Kerala*, University of Kerala, Trivandrum.

Nirmala Paniker — 1992, *Nangiar Koothu*, Iringalakuda Natanakairali.

Patrice Pavis, Tr. Loren Kruger — 1992, *Theatre at the Crossroads of Culture*, Routledge, London.

Paulose KG — 1993, *Natankusa*, Tripunithura Sanskrit College, Ravivarma Samskrta Granthavali.

2000, Bhima in Search of Celestial Flower, Bharatiya Book Corporation, New Delhi.

2001, *Kutiyattam - Abhinayathinte Thutarcayum Valarchayum,* International Centre for Kutiyattam, Tripunithura.

1993, *Natankusa: A Critique on Dramaturgy*, Sanskrit College, Tripunithura.

1998, *Natya: How did it Become Attam.*

2003, *Improvisation of Ancient Theatre*, International Centre for Kutiyattam, Tripunithura.

1998, *Introduction to Kutiyattam - The Living Tradition of Ancient Theatre*, Sree Sankaracharya University of Sanskrit.

	2006, *Kutiyattam Theatre - The Earliest Living Tradition*, Bharatiya Book Corporation, New Delhi.
	1997, *Kutiyattathinte Caritram*, Keli, 55; 24-42.
	1992, *Kutiyattavum Anubandhakalakalum*, Bhs 16/3, 13-18. Sanskrit.
	1998, *Buddhism and Sanskrit Theatre*, Souvenir, South Indian History Congress, SSUS Kalady.
	1993, *Kulasekharanum Kutiyattavum*, Sl September 38-40
	1991, *Kutiyattam: A Historical Study*, Ravivarma Samskrita Granthavali.
Pfaff, Walter	1997, *The Ant and the Stone, Learning Kutiyattam.*
Raghavan Pillai K	1977, Abhijanasakuntalacarca, Sanskrit Series, Trivandrum, 195.
Raghavan V	1967, *Sanskrit Drama*, Madras.
	1993, *Sanskrit Drama: Its Aesthetics and Production*, Madras.
	1934, *Theatre of Hindus*, Kerala Theatre.
	1941, *The Ancient Indian Theatre*, Annamalai Cettiar Commemmoration Volume
	1932, *Theatre of Hindus*, Kerala Theatre.
Raghava Variyar, Rajan Gurukkal	1992, *Keralacaritam*, Vallathol Vidyapeetam, Sukapuram.
Rajagopal LS	1997, *Women's Role in Kutiyattam*, Kuppuswami Sastri Research Institute, Chennai.
	2000, *Kutiyattam Preliminaries and Performance*, Kuppuswami Sastri Research Institute, Chennai.
	2003, Rustom Barucha, *Kutiyattam*, The Oxford Encyclopaedia of Theatre and Performance.
	1991, *Angika and Satvika Abhinayas in Kutiyattam*, SRA 9.
Rajan Gurukkal PM	1992, *The Kerala Temple and the Early Medieval Agrarian System,* Vallathol Vidyapeedam, Sukapuram.
Rajendran C	1993, *Kutiyattam: The Sanskrit Theatre with a Regional Idiom*, MG University, Haritam, Kottayam.
Rama Pisharoti K	1932, *Kerala Theatre Theatre of Hindus*. Calcutta.
	1934, *Kerala Theatre*, JAU 3/2 .
	1941, *The Ancient Theatre*, Annamalai Chettiar Commemoration Volume, Annamalai.
	1932, Kerala theatre, JAU 1/1.
Rama Varma KT	1981, Ammannur Caccuccakyar, Vallathol Vidyapeedam, Sukapuram.

Renu Ramnath 2004, *Performing Kalidasa*, The Hindu 20.05.2004.

Rustom Barucha 1990, *Theatre and the World*, Routledge, London and New York.

Schechner, Richard 1985, *Ramlila of Ram Nagar,* The Drama Review 21/03: 51-82.

Sircar, Badal 1978, *The Third Theatre*, Culcutta: Badal Sircar.

Sowle, John Steven 1982, *The Traditions Training and Performance of Kutiyattam*, Sanskrit Drama in South India, University of California, Berkeley.

Sreedevi KP 2008, *Akhyayika Padhathi of Ramapanivada*, Calicut University, Series 31.

Sudha Gopalakrishnan 2011, *Kutiyattam - The Heritage Theatre of India*, Niyogi Books, New Delhi.

Sumatikutty PK 1990, *Nampiar Tamil*, Oriental Research Institute and Manuscript Library, University of Kerala, Thiruvananthapuram.

Swaminathan. CR
Sudha Gopalakrishnan 1997, *Krishnagiti*, Kalamula Sastra Series, New Delhi.

NP Unni, BM Sullivan 2001, *The Wedding of Arjuna and Subhadra: The Kutiyattam Drama*, Nag Publishers, New Delhi.

Tieken, Rodopi 1993, *The Text and Performance in Sanskrit Drama*, Amsterdam.

Tieken, Hermann 1993, *The So-called Trivandrum Plays Attributed to Bhasa*, WZKS 37, Tripunuthura.

Ullur S Paramesvara Iyer *Dutavakyam Gadyam*, Kerala Sahitya Akademi, Thrissur.

Unni NP 1978, *Bhasa Plays on Kerala Stage - New Problems in Bhasa Plays,* College Book House, Trivandrum.

Unni NP, Bruce Sullivan M 1996, *Tapati Samvaranam: A Kutiyattam Drama by Kulasekhara Varman*, ATJ 13.

1977, *Sanskrit Dramas of Kulasekhara: A Study*, Trivandrum.

1995, *The Sun God's Daughter and King Samvarana*, Nag Publishers, New Delhi.

1987, *Tapatisamvaranam Vivaranasametam*, Nag Publishers, New Delhi.

Unni NP 1998, *Natyasastra Text with Introduction,* English translation and indices in four volumes. Nag Publishers, New Delhi.

Vasudha Dalmia 2006, *Poetics Plays and Performances*, Oxford University Press, New Delhi.

Venu G 1995, *Kutiyattam and Nangyarkuttu: Techniques and Conventions*, Kutiyattam Mahotsavam, New Delhi.

2002, *Into the World of Kutiyattam with the Legendary Ammannur Madhava Chakyar Memories*, Natanakairali, Irinjalakuda. Documentation of Kutiyattam Series 3.

2005, *Kathakali, Kutiyattam and Other Prforming Arts: Fifty Years of Theatrical Exploration*, Natanakairali, Irinjalakuda.

Venugopal P — 2010, *Ascaryacudamani Attaprakaram*, Margi, Thiruvananthapuram.

Vijayan K — 1990, *A New Perspective on Vyangyavyakhya and Natankusa: Facets of Sanskrit Literature*, Aatira Publications, Trivandrum. 34-42.

Yarrow, Ralph — 2001, *Theatre of Origin Theatre of Freedom*, Indian Theatre.

Zarrilli Phillip B — 1984, *The Kathakali Complex: Actor Performance and Structure* Abhinav Publications, New Delhi.

2000, *Kathakali Dance Drama Where Gods and Demons Come to Play,* Routldge, London, New York.

2006, *Kutiyattam Sanskrit Theatre of India*, Routledge, London, New York.

Word Index

A

B

C

D

E

G

H

N

P

Q

R

S

T

U

V

Y

Z